The Bigfoot Filmography

The Bigfoot Filmography

Fictional and Documentary
Appearances
in Film and Television

DAVID COLEMAN

Foreword by Loren Coleman

McFarland & Company, Inc., Publishers
Jefferson, North Carolina, and London

LIBRARY OF CONGRESS CATALOGUING-IN-PUBLICATION DATA

Coleman, David.
The Bigfoot filmography : fictional and documentary appearances
in film and television / David Coleman ;
foreword by Loren Coleman.
p.   cm.
Includes index.

ISBN 978-0-7864-4828-9
softcover : acid free paper ∞

1. Sasquatch in motion pictures.   2. Yeti in motion pictures.
3. Sasquatch on television.   4. Yeti on television.
5. Motion pictures — Catalogs.   6. Television programs — Catalogs.
I. Title.
PN1995.9.S245C65 2012   001.944 — dc23   2011046295

British Library cataloguing data are available

On the cover: Poster art for the 1976 film *The Mysterious Monsters*

Manufactured in the United States of America

*McFarland & Company, Inc., Publishers
Box 611, Jefferson, North Carolina 28640
www.mcfarlandpub.com*

Contents

Acknowledgments vi

Foreword by Loren Coleman 1

Introduction 5

Part I: Ciné du Sasquatch as a Genre Convention 11

Part II: Bigfoot, Sasquatch, and Yeti
Films and Television Programs 39

Part III: Interviews with Bigfoot Filmmakers 319

Index 333

Acknowledgments

No amount of mere thanks by way of simple acknowledgment can ever really repay the enormously kind supporters who have made this volume possible. While the author's name adorns the title page, the frank reality is that no reference guide of this scope would be possible without the prior, selfless donations and contributions by truly innumerable individuals and organizations in the cinema and cryptozoology worlds. Nevertheless, I am greatly in debt to each of the following individuals and groups in particular, without any one of whom the sum of this book would definitely be diminished as a whole.

Thanks to Loren Coleman (no relation), who not only encouraged me when I sought his opinion on the concept of a Sasquatch cinema tome, but later contributed the superb foreword. He also provided research notes and the interview with Michael Worth from the mandatory *Cryptomundo* website, to which he contributes, and other valuable research materials from the cryptozoology museum he curates. Phil Raza supplied an enormous number of hard-to-find Bigfoot movies and TV shows I could not otherwise locate — some after years of research — which ultimately enabled a more in-depth overview. Craig Woolheater also provided much early encouragement and valuable introductions to various experts and professionals in the Bigfoot research field, and remains an ongoing source of support.

Much appreciation is also due to the interviewed filmmakers who took time to reflect on their various Bigfoot-directed efforts — Ryan Schifrin, Kevin Tenney, Adam Muto, Michael Worth, and Timothy Skousen — and offer a firsthand perspective of the more practical realities of filmmaking (as opposed to the often academic assessments such critiques as this are guilty of unevenly applying). It is easy to review a movie in the comfort of one's own home, courtesy of DVD, with unlimited time and little or no pressures, and write a critique; it is quite another task to assemble a creative team of diverse individuals week after week on an often changing set and concoct an entertaining film. All Bigfoot film fans owe these filmmakers (and many others who toil in the genre) thanks for working in an *oeuvre* that is considered in some elite circles to be only slightly less in bad taste than wrestling movies. It is hoped that future filmmakers attempting to cinematically hike the treacherous backwoods of Ciné du Sasquatch pay respect to the manner in which the interviewed filmmakers attempted to broaden the very genre they were firmly ensconced within as creative thinkers; comprehension of their shared experiences truly offers the possibility of the next groundbreaking film in a body of work in sore need of constant refinement.

There were many, many others who made behind-the-scenes and photo contributions. But a few names among the many are: James Van Hise; Pat Moriarity; Theresa Schifrin; Alecia Ashby; Justin Martin; Lloyd Kaufman; Sharon Lee; Mike White; Gary Kent; Shawn C. Phillips; Bill Dale Marcinko; Ed Naha; John Buechler; and Justin Meeks. For all of you who are not listed and deservedly should have been, this line must suffice in lieu of my aberrant inability to recall such information (despite the fact I can remember the credits to an obscure movie I have never even seen!).

My family is the real reason this book exists. For the countless months that the ever-elastic deadline of this obsessive reference guide expanded with the newest addition and threatened to drive me further around the bend of no return, my loved ones were there to pick me up, dust me off, and set me back at the computer. For all the times I wanted to quit because I could literally no longer see the forest for the trees, despite the unobstructed view of the cedars outside my home, I am beholden to my lovely wife and loving children, because they not only planted the seed for the book, but they nurtured the writer through many difficult times to enable its completion. For all of these people I have listed, I give thanks.

Foreword by Loren Coleman

"We shall pick up an existence by its frogs. Wise men have tried other ways. They have tried to understand our state of being, by grasping at its stars, or its arts, or its economics. But, if there is an underlying oneness of all things, it does not matter where we begin, whether with stars, or laws of supply and demand, or frogs, or Napoleon Bonaparte. One measures a circle, beginning anywhere." — Charles Fort

"There is not wanting a feast of broad, joyous humor, in this stranger phantasmagoria, where pit and stage, and man and animal, and earth and air, are jumbled in confusion worse confounded." — Thomas Caryle

We Shall Pick Up an Existence by Its Hairy Hominoid Films

Films illuminate, educate, illustrate and inspire. Motion pictures that deal with hominology (the study of unknown and yet-to-be verified higher species of hairy, upright primates, a sub-field of cryptozoology — which itself is the study of hidden animals that remain to be accepted as valid and zoologically-classified) also have the same objectives, goals, results, benefits and outcomes as cinema in general.

Some Bigfoot films stomp across the cinema landscape to no noticeable impact. Some Yeti movies haunt us long after we watch them. They may be documentaries, docudramas, narrative fictions, art experimentations or science fiction/fantasy explorations. They impact different people dissimilarly, with all the complexities that make human beings react diversely to the same stimulation.

As the 1960s were dawning, I, for example, was inspired to go into a new groundbreaking field, which, intriguingly, during the Victorian era was called "romantic zoology." To be exact, I became interested in cryptozoology fifty years ago — thanks to a single film.

On a Friday night, and then again on a Saturday morning, late in March of 1960, I watched a televised movie called *Half Human* about the search for Abominable Snowmen in some mountains in Asia. Little did I know it would change my life.

I went to school that following Monday long, long ago after seeing this one movie on my local Decatur, Illinois, television station over that special weekend. I was full of questions and curiosity about these misunderstood and curiously undiscovered creatures. I had been interested in animals since I could remember, having kept a backyard zoo, read books around the clock about the expeditions of people like Roy Chapman Andrews and Raymond Ditmars and, as well as having led my brothers on treks into the wilds of nearby woods and creeks. I knew what I wanted to be when I grew up. My career path as a 12-year-old was, I thought, zeroed in on becoming a naturalist.

But this movie *Half Human* made me curious. Despite having read volumes upon volumes about natural history, wildlife and biology, I asked myself, "Why have I not heard of the 'Abominable Snowmen' in any of these texts?"

I decided to go to school with a mission to find out more. I began by asking several different teachers at my school, "What is this business about the Abominable Snowmen?" I was given regular answers like, "Don't waste your time on that," "They don't exist," "Get back to reading your studies," and "They aren't worth your time."

Needless to say, I decided to do my own research. I read everything I could about Abominable Snowmen and learned they were also called "Yetis." I stumbled across a couple of friendly reference librarians at the Decatur Public Library who helped me learn bibliographical skills for digging out sources. I soon had files and clipping collections on Yetis, Loch Ness Monsters, Bigfoot and the whole world of cryptozoology, which was "hidden" from most students back then.

Before I knew it, during my next school year a teacher named Mr. Walton gave me primary materials on the 1960 search for the Abominable Snowmen by Sir Edmund Hillary. Having already discovered Bernard Heuvelmans' *On the Track of Unknown Animals* (1958), I located at that same public library a remarkable book, Ivan T. Sanderson's *Abominable Snowmen: Legend Come to Life* (1961).

I soon bought my own copy of Sanderson's book from the money I was earning from my paper route job. Then I systematically purchased every publication I could find that was listed in Sanderson's bibliography.

I began corresponding with Heuvelmans and Sanderson; within two years I had 400 other correspondents from around the world. I was also doing fieldwork with wildlife biologists throughout the Midwest, investigating reports with them of black panther sightings and interviewing eyewitnesses who had seen Bigfoot, other ape-like creatures, mystery cats and giant snakes.

I decided to attend a university in the midst of an area known for its sightings and folklore about reddish, unknown anthropoids: Southern Illinois University. There I majored in anthropology and minored in zoology during my undergraduate years, due directly to my interest in cryptozoology. I wrote my first article in 1969 and the first of over thirty books in 1975. Years later, and for two decades running, I would find myself teaching a university documentary film course, screening a mix of documentaries, docudramas and "based on a true story" fiction films for my students. One third of my class discussions would be on cryptozoology in films.

One movie, it had turned out, had opened a whole world for me to explore and assisted in deciding the plan my life would take. So, back to this little film that had so captivated me.

Half Human was directed by Ishiro Honda (best known for the original *Godzilla*), who (I would later learn) had previously been a documentary filmmaker. That background certainly gave *Half Human* a gritty, documentary feel that definitely appealed to me.

First released in Japan as *Jujin Yokiotoko* ("Abominable Snowman") in August of 1955, it was later released in the USA as *Half Human* in December 1958. In the American version, new footage was added starring John Carradine as an anthropologist named Dr. John Rayburn (I, of course, did not know any of this in 1960 when I first saw it on TV).

Peter H. Brothers has compiled more information on this film in his recent book *Mushroom Clouds and Mushroom Men: The Fantastic Cinema of Ishiro Honda* (Bloomington, Indiana: AuthorHouse, 2009). Brothers writes that the film echoes some of the themes "...found in *King Kong*, such as that of the primitive creature doomed by its coming contact with civilization."

Brothers further details that

> An attempt was made to make the Snowman look as authentic as possible by utilizing eyewitness accounts of the animal, as well as research information on the prehistoric Pithecanthropus and the mythical [*sic*] "Peking Man." The first sketches of the Snowman were begun in late 1954, with the clay prototype design not approved until nearly six months later. The original designs for the Snowman were as a ten-foot-high monster with a savage face, evil eyes and sharp, craggily [*sic*] teeth; a truly terrifying apparition. Possibly at Honda's request, however, the monster's appearance was toned-down to that of a more benevolent-looking beast with distinctively warm features, aided by [the designer and costume wearer Toshinori] Oohasi's own gentle eyes.
>
> The costume was an unqualified triumph, even more so when one considers the limited materials and resources available at the time. To this day, it is the best depiction of a "Yeti" ever seen on film, but perhaps Oohasi's greatest accomplishment was in the design of the Snowman's face, which had to be flexible and lifelike....
>
> Honda's documentary-style manner of filmmaking is in evidence as he focuses on both the travails of the human participants as well as the Snowman's habits and natural surroundings....
>
> Honda evokes sympathy for the "monsters" while at the same time evoking dread of the vast majority of the film's

human characters. Toward the end of the film we hope the Snowman will never be found to simply be left alone in peace, but Honda dictates that any contact with man bodes ill for nature (even if the Snowman were to survive, it would most likely be as part of a circus act with his son).... Indeed, the Abominable Snowman proves to be anything but abominable; it is compassionate, intelligent and even resourceful....

> The film is unquestionably the finest ever done on the subject of a Yeti, far surpassing contemporary efforts such as *The Snow Creature* (1954), *Man Beast* (1956) and *The Abominable Snowman of the Himalayas* (1957).

Peter Brothers notes in his book that Toho has not released *Jujin Yokiotoko* in the original Japanese, supposedly due to violent scenes in which the expedition members are shown beating the film's fictional aboriginal peoples. The movie's tribe was allegedly based on the Ainu and the Buraku, who still suffer from discrimination in modern-day Japan. In comparison, the Americanized, edited *Half Human* has been available routinely on video and DVDs.

Brothers ends his treatment of Honda's film with this:

> It is hoped that Toho will one day come to its collective and corporate senses and release *Abominable Snowman* on video. Grand and grim, *Abominable Snowman* was Honda's most uncompromising film and an unforgettable triumph which should be seen by the worldwide audience it so richly deserves.

I am biased and acknowledge I share Brothers' opinion of this film. Because of how important this movie is to me, I understand the psychological basis of why this film is my all-time choice for the best hominology film. But different viewers might think the Hammer classic *The Abominable Snowman of the Himalayas* or others are better entries in this genre. We all come to the screening room with our own set of personal preferences, needless to say.

Luckily, you now are reading Dave Coleman's book that contains scores of others' favorite choices. Coleman (who is not my relative, but must be a clansman at some point in our mutual ancestry) steers a wonderful course through the phantasmagoria of Bigfoot films, some of which may even be worthy of your viewing.

In my journeys around and about for five decades chronicling my discoveries in thousands of articles and blogs, I would often interview Bigfooters and Sasquatch seekers and ask them what first sparked their interest in this field. It rapidly became crystal clear that many people got into this field due to films, the wonderfully beautiful Bigfoot, Yeti and hairy bipedal monster movies that entertained and engaged them.

A few people who were young in the 1950s were wedded to cryptozoology by Yeti flicks, but most today in the field have grown up with Bigfoot movies. Indeed, there is an entire maturing generation of Bigfoot fans, as well as highly visible investigators who appear to have been hooked on cryptozoology and Sasquatch studies by viewing one specific film of the 1970s—*The Legend of Boggy Creek*. You can digest what Dave Coleman has to say in these pages about this docudrama, but what I want to point out is the widespread impact this drive-in movie has had on people. The movie created a whole new generation of dedicated Bigfoot hunters. Young people between the ages of 10 and 13 who were first attracted to Bigfoot research in the 1970s speak of *The Legend of Boggy Creek* as the source of their passion about the subject.

In his 1988 book *Big Footnotes*, author Daniel Perez wrote: "My personal interest in monsters was first ignited at about the tender age of 10 by the movie *The Legend of Boggy Creek*. This was the trigger which lead to casual to casually serious to serious full-fledged involvement in this subject matter."

Maryland *Bigfoot Digest* author Mark Opsasnick notes this movie inspired his interest in Bigfoot at the age of 11. Ditto for cryptozoology artist Bill Rebsamen, who told me, "I was about 10 years old when I saw it. I went immediately to the library the next day and checked out all the books I could find on Bigfoot after seeing the movie."

Chester Moore, Jr., Texan outdoors journalist and author of *Bigfoot South* (2002), writes: "Seeing *The Legend of Boggy Creek* lit my interest in the Bigfoot phenomenon into a full-blown passion. While the Pacific Northwest seemed a world away to me, Arkansas did not...the impact it had on me as a youngster was immense."

Many people in various organized Texas Bigfoot research groups, including Robert Dominguez, Tim Clay, Rick Hayes and Jerry Hestand, told me that they had seen the movie in their youth, and it had been what brought them into the field. Texas Bigfoot conference organizer and *Cryptomundo* founder Craig Woolheater said, "It sealed the deal for me."

The Legend of Boggy Creek was also the entry point for crypto-fiction author Lee Murphy and for Chad Austin, cryptozoology fan and president of Interactive Pilot, Inc. Eric Altman, head of the Pennsylvania Bigfoot Society, credits *The Legend of Boggy Creek* for spawning his research involvement.

Sociological studies have been conducted demonstrating that children between the ages of 10 and 13 may be influenced for the rest of their lives by once-in-a-lifetime dramatic events, such as the assassination of JFK, the shooting of the students at Kent State or the collapsing of the Twin Towers on 9/11. It is certain, too, that significant films can have their own life-changing impact, whether it is a film like *Nanook of the North, Roger and Me, The Thin Blue Line,* or *Half Human* and *The Legend of Boggy Creek*. (Not surprisingly, the young people who were 10 to 13 years old in 1987 and recall *Harry and the Hendersons* as "their" remembered Bigfoot film have grown up to dismiss the subject. If your brain was awash in the midst of a silly film about a bearded Bigfoot that sits in your front room during those key years, a seed appears to have been planted that you should take the topic with a grain of salt.)

Which Bigfoot films will be remembered as having some im-

Author/cryptozoologist/curator/lecturer Loren Coleman and friend. (2010, photograph courtesy Loren Coleman.)

pact on future generations? Only time will tell. But will any live up to what we now call the classics?

Not everyone who sees Abominable Snowmen films or Bigfoot movies when they are at a critical age become Bigfoot or Yeti researchers, of course. Some grow up to be anthropology professors, filmmakers, firefighters, bakers, human service workers, wildlife biologists, artists, stay-at-home mothers, baseball cable production staff or cookbook authors. But most who are changed by these films talk of passion coming into their lives in a newly-realized fashion. Perhaps you are one of those folks? Explore your film memories as you read these pages.

Enjoy this quest into the deep forests and snowfields of films full of hairy hominoid beings, with Dave Coleman as your guide on a journey many of us have taken and most have emerged from changed forever for the better.

Loren Coleman, whom some call the "world's leading living cryptozoologist," is the director of the International Cryptozoology Museum in Portland, Maine. He has been involved in Abominable Snowmen/Sasquatch research, fieldwork, and media appearances since March 1960. He is the author or coauthor of 35 books, including *Tom Slick and the Search for Yeti, Bigfoot: The True Story of Apes in America,* and *The Field Guide to Bigfoot and Other Mystery Primates.*

Introduction

Some would argue that critiquing the genre I choose to call "Ciné du Sasquatch" is not only a dubious idea but a waste of a proposed genre classification (as well as paper and binding glue), a white whale of a cinematic obsession which has lead the author astray and whose proposed genre, even if granted to exist, has made no impact whatsoever on film history. Such post-publication analysis is thankfully beyond any need of defense by the author. Luckily, I need only content myself with the humbler rewards of completion and addition. "Completion" because any in-depth viewing of Ciné du Sasquatch requires a nearly masochistic taste for bad cinema (though there are *bona fide* classics and many entertaining television shows featuring Bigfoot that transcend the genre's "rank" reputation). "Addition" because whether or not any film genre has ever "changed the face of film-making" (an unreliable hypothesis at best) is irrelevant as cause to undertake (or not) a critical survey of an oft-neglected cinema, a unique filmic grouping sharing subject matter, thematic resonances, and cultural touchstones.

This book is not intended to enter the ongoing debates over whether or not Bigfoot is real or imaginary. Such real-life inquiries and conversations are the realm of cryptozoologists, zoologists, and passionate laymen, as well as debunkers, skeptics, and equally vociferous laymen on the opposite side of the arguments. Rather, this reference guide is mainly focused on the fictional treatment of Bigfoot, Sasquatch, and Yeti in film and television appearances. For those interested primarily in documentaries that treat the subject matter without artistic embellishment or poetic license, please understand that an honest appraisal of both fictional and non-fictional entries was beyond the scope and intent of this book. For the sake of accuracy, I have tried to include the documentaries for future researchers as well as lovers of Ciné du Sasquatch. However, these entries are limited to a Sergeant Joe Friday "Just the facts, ma'am" approach, whereas the fictional films and television shows receive the most attention and analysis. Also, not all fictional films receive the same in-depth analysis, as the author has chosen to focus on the entries he selfishly decided deserve the most scrutiny (not that shorter-written entries are any less worthy of their own limelight; rather, that the writer herein simply has biases and prejudices just like the reader).

Still, in terms of clear-cut distinction between all forms of Ciné du Sasquatch, it is akin to the images of the creature itself—the lines blur in and out of focus in a heady mixture of documentary, pseudo-documentary, and mockumentary states of being. In such cases where a documentary is concerned, notation is given whenever possible whether or not staged recreations of encounters or depictions of Bigfoot are of such an order as to warrant attention. Again, however, such designations (much like the author's critiques of fictional films) are as much a matter of subjective interpretation and style as objective criteria. The primary focus remains on dramatic narratives and not documentaries.

Some will also wonder: Why the interchangeable use of Bigfoot, Sasquatch, and Yeti as terms? It is true there is a profound disparity between many real-life Bigfoot and Abominable Snowmen sightings. Bigfoot (or "Sasquatch," from the Native American name) is typically described (though not always) as having dark fur and a huge stature, and preferring deep forest habitation; whereas an Abominable Snowman (or "Yeti," which is derived from the Sherpa tribal name) is typically (though, again, not always) described as having white fur and a more human-like stature (though not always), and residing in the Himalayan Mountains. In actual cryptozoological reports, however, a Sasquatch can be smaller than humans or towering over ten feet in height; it can have lightly-colored fur or dark; and it may even be reported as residing in a marshy swamp as much as behind the cloak of a dense growth of Redwood trees. Equally, a Yeti may be reported as having darker fur and exceed height expectations; and as residing in countries other than Tibet. If one then adds the eyewitness reports made by thousands worldwide per annum of various localized variations (three toes versus five, etc.) and colorful regional colloquialisms (such as "The Fouke Monster" in Arkansas or "Skunk Ape" in Florida), the list of possible names for our cryptid hominid grows to monstrous proportions.

For the sake of clarification and contrast, as far as this book is concerned, the fictional world of Ciné du Sasquatch only rarely portrays a bipedal cryptid that is *not* named Bigfoot, Sasquatch, or Yeti. These three names embody the cinematic whole for the genre's titular creatures. Even when one accounts for translations of foreign films and regional filmic productions in the United States, the holy trinity of Bigfoot, Sasquatch, and Yeti are as apt to be used as any local derivation. Why this is so is mere speculation, but may be due to commercial interests on the part of the producers: these three terms are the most widely-known worldwide, whereas local variants, such as "Yowie" (from an

Australian Aboriginal name) or "Grassman" (an Ohio-named Bigfoot), tend to produce a look of confusion on the face of the average viewer outside the respective region. As film distribution is an international concern, one then suspects the use of Bigfoot, Sasquatch, and Yeti is more or less designed to capitalize upon the global awareness of the phenomena rather than show any planned favoritism or preferential treatment.

On a less planetary-wide level, my own earliest passion for Bigfoot, Sasquatch, and Yeti cinema began with Charles B. Pierce's legendary *The Legend of Boggy Creek* (1972), billed as the "true story" (how I always liked that oxymoron in films as a child, as it promised non-stop embellishments and anything *but* documentary realism) of the so-called Fouke Monster of Pierce's rural Arkansas hometown. Besides scaring the hell out of myself and a hundred-plus other screaming kids (and more than a few accompanying adults), *The Legend of Boggy Creek* transcended the fourth wall and disabled my subconscious defense mechanisms. This was because the authentic locales Pierce featured

The haunting, silhouetted graphic from *The Legend of Boggy Creek* (1972) would become a visual landmark in the genre. The monster's facial features are barely visible in this key art from the original release.

throughout his bayou epic didn't vary significantly from the rural, piney woods area where I grew up. Fed on the mostly Los Angeles–lensed diet of Hollywood locations via television and movies up to that point, it was rare indeed that a movie "felt" as if it had been made in one's own backyard as a Southerner, let alone one featuring a cast of bucktoothed characters who spoke with accents and mannerisms as real-life as your uncle or elderly neighbor Miss Lucinda.

It was as if Pierce had "pierced" the veil and diabolically destroyed the quaint sense of isolated safety of small-town, rural America that still pervaded the country's psyche. In an era before Amber Alert child abductions and heartland serial killers were profiled daily on television, the impact of *The Legend of Boggy Creek* is perhaps difficult to understand for those who did not experience the era of its release. The suspect G-rating was a powerful lure, at once promising the safety of a typical Disney outing and yet (perhaps dishonestly) delivering the more mature, scary, monster-stalking thrills of a cryptid variation of *Deliverance*. An entire generation was baptized in the waters of *Boggy Creek*, and into the religion of the Ciné du Sasquatch that year, by "Brother Charles" Pierce, and thereafter maintained the fervor of said holy spirit, if only deeply within each privately crypto-gnostic soul.

A dual inferno raged during my formative adolescent years that only fueled my growing cryptid obsession. The national media had discovered (yet again!) the power of Bigfoot sightings and UFO encounters to generate profits. While both had been print, tabloid, and television fodder for decades, the Me Too decade brought them back with a national furor not witnessed since the 1950s (when, perhaps not coincidentally, the political fabrications being spun in Congress were met with increasingly sensationalized stories about "foo fighters" and Abominable Snowmen from equally "ordinary, God-fearing" citizens). Whereas xenophobia seemed to be the spark for such Fortean claims in the 1950s, the 1970s distrust of government produced a state of national paranoia. Following Nixon's Watergate fiasco and subsequent departure from office with his indelible peace wave on the steps of the Marine One helicopter, stunned Americans were left to ponder: If even the President of the United States were "a crook," despite his protests to the contrary, then who *could* be trusted? Xenophobic fear of the Outsider had further metastasized into outright paranoia of the Insider, your fellow citizen, as well. In such a climate, conspiratorial tales of marauding space aliens in cahoots with one's own government, and mauling forest monsters ignored by local law enforcement officials, seemed as right at home as bad disco music and skin-tight spandex pants.

The singular event that drove the 1970s hype in regards to UFOs was the so-called "Pascagoula Abduction" of two Mississippians, Calvin Parker and Charles Hickson, who claimed to have been floated aboard a flying saucer while fishing on a pier of the Pascagoula River on October 11, 1973. Their incredible story included silvery, robotic aliens who scanned them with an eye-like orb before releasing them from their hovering craft. Not since Orson Welles' infamous radio broadcast of *The War of the Worlds* in 1938, had the country been so mesmerized by the seeming imminent "threat" of an alien invasion. The national media descended upon the small coastal town with an intensity not seen since the devastation wrought years earlier by Hurricane Camille, which was highly unusual for a state otherwise largely ignored since the Civil Rights era of protests and desegregation.

For me, it was a one-two punch to my pre-teen psyche. First, Charles Pierce's Fouke Monster had rendered me incapable of sleeping anywhere near an open window for fear of being bodily snatched away; second, even fishing was now an improbable but horrific potential catalyst to an abduction scenario! If I needed any further convincing that neither woods nor wetlands were safe from lurking horrors, the fact I had lived as a toddler in the port of Pascagoula resolved any doubts: There was no place one could escape one's destiny if the slowly spinning Wheel of Fortuna capriciously landed upon "Bigfoot" or "Alien" as your intended *fait accompli*. You were a "goner" (as my friends and I commiserated about our childhood fears on the playground) should *that* black day occur, which it readily might at any given anxiety-fueled moment. And who knows? In a worst-case scenario, Bigfoot might even turn out to be an alien abductor!

Adding to our supreme belief that we would hardly survive the coming months of outdoor recreation widely (and only) available — for our small hamlet offered no malls, no playgrounds, no video arcades, no multiplex cinemas, etc. — was the local legend told by a schoolmate. It seems his older brother had not only encountered a shaggy, 7-foot hominid while hunting deer that very same year, but had been so shocked and horrified that he had dropped his prized shotgun, vowing never to set foot near the creek where said sighting occurred. The fact the older sibling had won the shotgun in a rodeo the previous year only lent credibility to the tale: What self-respecting cowboy would be so afraid of *anything* in the forest that he would sacrifice his name-engraved Remington rather than own up to his innate fear? We were convinced: Bigfoot was *real*, and so was our mortal peril. The choice was as startling as it was ominously depressing: Stay indoors and survive the boredom, or risk bodily-dismemberment via an enraged hominid by venturing outdoors even for a nanosecond. I reconciled myself to a lonely strategy of living out a bunker mentality upstairs in my pre-teen bedroom, stocked with magazines and books devoted to the phenomenon of Bigfoot, Sasquatch, and Yeti in reality and media. My measures were drastic, but then I figured to at least live to see the summer of 1974 with my concocted strategy. And lo and behold, though I experienced many sleepless nights, I survived.

My love of Ciné du Sasquatch took a pronounced break when I enrolled in the film program at the University of Southern California. Prior to my collegiate exposure to such internationally-renowned filmmakers as Kurosawa, Fellini, and Bunuel, my personal idea of a foreign film growing up as a child was *Godzilla vs. the Smog Monster* or the latest Bruce Lee import. Not surprisingly, I found a pronounced bias against such "exploitation fare" among the university faculty, many of whom had written and directed enduring classics of the American cinema in the decades prior to my enrollment. They rightfully (from their viewpoint) considered such "grade Z" moviemaking

Sasquatch's rising popularity in the 1970s was quickly exploited by Milton Bradley for their *Big Foot: The Giant Snow Monster* game. The family-friendly image of a benign Bigfoot was introduced.

as the equivalent of a street urchin comparing himself to Little Lord Fauntleroy. How *dare* any serious film student consider such "cinema trash" as worthy of intellectual critique, when one had the works of Hitchcock, Hawks, Kubrick, and other famous directors to study?

This disregard for "low art" over established landmarks of cinema was, in part, generational. Many of us post–Boomers had grown up consumers of not just the legitimate films of popular entertainment, such as *Jaws* or *Star Wars*, but a more subversive "junk culture" diet consisting of endless TV reruns of *Green Acres*, *Gilligan's Island*, and Saturday morning psychedelic-drenched fare by the Brothers Krofft; the prevailing influence of later era drive-in filmmaking by the Roger Corman factory that gave rise to women in prisons and rock & roll high schools; lurid underground "comix" swiped from older siblings featuring the works of R. Crumb and the like; and, of course, the still popular *Famous Monsters of Filmland* and newcomer *Starlog*. I remember well how difficult it was to convince our reluctant Western Genre instructor to even include Leone's landmark *The Good, the Bad, and the Ugly* in the viewing curriculum; he finally relented to generational pressure and allowed the film to be viewed in the class, but only for extra credit, via a heavily-spliced, 16mm non-scope print, and only on a Saturday morning (when most film students were just turning in rather than rising to face a new day).

Of course, many Spaghetti Westerns are now considered classic "revisionist" films within the Western genre, while many of the so-called classics I was required to view by film teachers are so obscure as to be forgotten. This is not to say the now less-regarded films or their craftsmanship have lost luster, but that popular and critical tastes are always a matter of perspective and perception. Perspective changes with the passing of the guard; perception alters as new viewers rethink old, formerly dismissed cinematic efforts. The latter often seems to focus less on popular appeal during the critiqued film's era and more upon how it prevails throughout the elapsed time in terms of its own unique outlook regarding its era of production. Dismissed "trash" such as *Plan 9 from Outer Space* become immortalized and even lead to Academy Award nominations in biographical movies chronicling their production in such films as *Ed Wood*; "great" films such as *How the West Was Won* and *Duel in the Sun* fade into historic footnote and are only occasionally mentioned alongside such replacement entries as *A Fistful of Dollars* or *The Wild Bunch*.

So it went with my love affair of bipedal cryptid cinema. And then the old flame was re-ignited, so to speak, by a sudden, unexpected encounter with a shambling Sasquatch at the movies.

For many years after graduation, as I sought employment within the dream factory of Hollywood, the idea of consciously reviving my interest in Ciné du Sasquatch was a remote fancy at best. Simply put, no Hollywood producer believed folklore tales about hairy swamp creatures were worthy of "A" level budgets. But then the out-of-the-blue box office phenomenon entitled *Harry and the Hendersons* exploded upon the commercial film world and radically reawakened my abandoned filmic flame. It was not so much the movie itself (I was too old for maximum effect of the intended younger audience) as the stunning realization that ensued: I was not alone in my appreciation of Ciné du Sasquatch. For the first time since the unexpected success of *The Legend of Boggy Creek* (a touchstone of my love for the genre, having seen it at the impressionable age of nine) over a decade earlier, Bigfoot was once again box office gold. And that meant tens of thousands of other fans for my favorite, hairy hominid were equally "out there" in the darkened cinema aisles, eagerly awaiting the next Skunk Ape epic as much as I.

Encouraged, I self-published a small, Xerox-produced fanzine

The cover art for *Argosy's Monsters* magazine from the 1970s luridly illustrates the cultural impact Sasquatch had during the decade.

The fateful issue of *Remote Jockey Digest* (1994) that started it all, with the cover story featuring "Bigfoot Cinema" as its focus.

devoted to obscure cinema and television genres called *Remote Jockey Digest*. Somewhat modeled on *Castle of Frankenstein*, *Video Watchdog*, *Psychotronic*, *Shock Cinema*, and other monster movie magazines I enjoyed, an early issue featured "Bigfoot in Cinema," complete with lobby cards, posters, and frame enlargements. As far as I know, it was one of the first-ever published in regards to recapitulating all known appearances of my favorite shaggy beast in movies and TV. Given that my modest publishing effort was only 16 pages long, the article was far from conclusive. But I received quite a lot of favorable fan mail about it, all of which made me feel much better about the growing need I had to conclusively (if not compulsively) exhaust all possibilities re: Ciné du Sasquatch entries into one reference guide. Perhaps, I reasoned, a one-off fanzine dedicated to the concept would suffice. The idea of a book never occurred to me, however; and as my fanzine efforts gave way to professional screenwriting assignments, I yet again lost sight of my ambitions to catalog the cryptid hominid cinema in its entirety.

Years later, a visiting friend and writer noticed my plethora of Bigfoot movies on VHS and DVD-R and innocently asked, "Why haven't *you* written a book about these films? You seem a natural for it." I stared at him blankly, wondering if he was attempting to bait me into another riposte (for we often enjoyed such intellectual torments in regards to one another's more esoteric tastes in "outsider" cinema), or if he was serious in his suggestion. He was serious. I realized he had a point. No one ever *had* taken the Ciné du Sasquatch genre seriously enough to offer a critique of its mysteriously enduring and widespread appeal. Despite box office triumphs, dozens of films and TV shows per decade about the subject, and enormous fan interest, the beast was considered too *déclassé* to warrant classification. I became determined to document the genre and challenge this prevailing attitude.

As a result, you hold in your hands the first-ever reference guide dedicated to a largely unbeknownst "secret cinema" genre. One held in private reserve by bad movie lovers, Generation X film school casualties, and true Bigfoot believers worldwide. It's an alive, vibrant, and absurdly irrational genre, yet one at least worthy of devout consideration, however skeptically many film lovers may greet the prospect. Why? Unlike the accounts of cryptids, which may or may not be true, fictional narratives and documentaries about such creatures exist in relative (and astonishing) abundance. Devotees of Ciné du Sasquatch know, too, the hidden appeal of the genre: It crosses lines across a diverse group of fans of all ages and races, bridging economic, cultural, and even religious norms, and all for the love of a man in the proverbial monkey suit.

I have many talented and dedicated individuals to thank for helping me with this book, and you will find them listed in the Acknowledgments. But to the numerous Ciné du Sasquatch faithful who have endured years of lambast by cynical film critics and genuine looks of sympathy from family and friends whenever you bespoke an admiration for the genre, and for those folks who kept the faith despite the ridicule in numerous fanzines and on internet websites, this book is dedicated to you. You have sacrificed much and hopefully will feel justified by this reference guide, at least in some small measure.

And who knows? Maybe one day in some future filmic studies classroom a reluctant professor will allow the inclusion of a serious study of Ciné du Sasquatch in and of itself, much the same way in which we petitioned and were allowed to include *The Good, the Bad, and the Ugly* in our Western genre class. But whatever the future outcome, I hope you enjoy reading and rereading this guide as much as I have treasured conceiving, researching, and writing it.

PART I
Ciné du Sasquatch as a Genre Convention

It's not often one uncovers a genre that is as distinct, misunderstood, and/or neglected as Ciné du Sasquatch.* Forgotten, shunned, mocked, and relegated to outsider status by even many who love the horror *oeuvre* from which it springs, Ciné du Sasquatch has nonetheless eked out a continued existence as filmic spectacle, and even a quiet if recently growing rebirth in terms of quantity and quality. In doing so, it has bequeathed a minor but substantial new genre to the field of horror cinema. Whereas a Bigfoot film or TV show was once a rarity, it is now so ubiquitous in feature films, TV shows, commercials, and fan-created YouTube parody short videos that the cryptid has arguably transcended its obscure status of folkloric beast and become an international superstar every bit the equal of Spiderman, Superman, or the like. Given Sasquatch is a public domain "every monster" and not a copyrighted figure, this commercial status is all the more remarkable, as no one corporation or individual owns the likeness.

The very notion of Bigfoot, Sasquatch, and Yeti cryptids cinematically running amok draws so heavily from previous film cycles and popular concepts of their respectively-produced eras that it is tempting to dismiss classifying Ciné du Sasquatch altogether. In this case, Bigfoot, Sasquatch, and Yeti remain lumped as they have throughout horror film history under the generic Monster Cinema category, allowing for no distinctive Ciné du Sasquatch genre traits. However, as this guide hopefully illustrates, such notions are the equivalent of disregarding the film noir genre in favor of delineating those movies as simply Suspense films and nothing more. They are tantamount to distilling all Western Cinema genre entries into a simple Action Cinema categorization, disregarding the film's distinctive, unique, and shared characteristics.

Besides, upon careful consideration, what film genre *is* free of all influence from preceding movies, books, newspapers, or political trends? Indeed, while movies dutifully free of cultural resonance are released weekly at the local multiplex, such lifeless products are invariably the ones history discards in favor of films that more accurately capture a unique place in time, regardless of popular reception (or lack thereof) during its debut era.

All truly enduring genres have various cohesive factors that make them unique and distinctive from one another. For example, the initial film noir cycle from the post–World War II era to the mid–1950s was heavily influenced by both the post-war pessimism of returning soldiers and the social realism films from the earlier Warner Brothers efforts in the 1930s, such as *Angels with Dirty Faces*. Equally influential on the genre's formation were the neo-realist films being made in Italy shortly after World War II (or, indeed, even as it was waning), such as *Rome, Open City*, which favored shooting on location over studio sets. This heavy use of location photography was not as much aesthetic choice, however, as practical reality for any filmmaker in the 1940s post–Mussolini period. Most of the country's studios had been destroyed during the war years, and there was little money for rebuilding them. Hence, realism as an artistic style was as much dictated by circumstances as by any creative necessity.

As a genre, then, film noir combines the qualities of both America's post-war malaise and foreign filmmakers' techniques (which often emphasized a more raw and energetic feel than the classically set-bound fare of the typical studio offering) with emerging production methodologies (low-light lenses and faster film stocks). As a result, film noir came to be characterized by such visual metaphors (and eventual clichés) as shadows from the blinds hitting the detective's walls at just the right angle, the dark alley that is actually pretty well-lit upon closer examination, etc. None of these were as easily possible in the decade preceding film noir. For example, in previous decades, shadows were lit into non-existence by the use of older, slower film stock, which demanded more lighting to compensate for their lack of exposure sensitivity.

With their generally gloomy psychological tone, distraught if not desperate protagonists, cinematography schemes involving an emphasis on shadows and a de-emphasis on glamour lighting, and lurid plots mirroring the "get it done by the seat of our pants" soldier mentality that ironically helped win the war itself, film noir as a genre was as gritty as their down-to-earth filmmakers. They sustain the weight of their own classification as film noir because they are characteristically and thematically united as a whole.

---

*Ciné du Sasquatch is a genre of filmmaking concerning unknown hominids. The term, of my invention, owes its origins to both an homage to the heavy French Canadian influence on the actual North American Sasquatch mythos and a tongue-in-cheek nod to the film noir genre.

In the turbulent 1960s, French New Wave critics such as Truffaut and Godard championed these cynical Hollywood films in particular, popularizing the genre under its soon-to-be enduring moniker of film noir ("black film"). Suddenly, otherwise seemingly unaffiliated B-movie crime efforts became distinctively similar in theme and tone after a judicious use of select grouping. The hallmark mood and techniques that haunt the noir themes of alienation, pessimism, and unmitigated fatality emerge intact from each work in the genre as if by magic. They were similar when grouped, in essence, because it was as if they were produced under the same aesthetic guidelines (factoring in minor and often oddly-irrelevant deviations and distinctions).

The oddity, of course, is that no overall guiding hand existed during the classic film noir production period of a dozen or so years. Does *zeitgeist* alone account for the synchronicity between otherwise unrelated films made by various studios, directors, writers, and actors over a sustained period of over a decade? If not, then *why* the similarities between literally hundreds of otherwise unrelated movies? Even the filmmakers, when interviewed, often admit to having no intent to adhere to any known dramatic dictates or prevailing lighting schemata when they were producing these works. They were mostly made under demanding schedules and with limited budgets wherein such intellectual conceits and pretensions would have been an unimaginable luxury. But then, even *if* all of film noir is but an intellectual conceit, it is all the more mysterious that the imaginary genre classification not only helps distinguish an entire set of otherwise almost "forgotten" movies but cohesively illuminates them at the same time.

Ciné du Sasquatch as a genre may never reach the vaunted heights of a now more critically accepted genre such as film noir (or, for that matter, any of the other genres in the fields of cinema research and culture which enjoy popular followings, such as vampires, demons, ghosts, werewolves, mummies, and the other filmic monstrosities). Many will consider any "man in a monkey suit" movie still *just* a "man in a monkey suit" movie. No matter the otherwise intriguing justifications for looking more deeply beneath the surfaces of the often hackneyed genre efforts themselves, such skeptics reason. As a distinct genre within horror movies, however, Ciné du Sasquatch has a lot to offer those viewers with a bit more expansive philosophy and less critical prejudice, much like the film noir genre grouping revealed unexpected, sub-textually connective themes when it was first introduced to fresh, appreciative eyes.

The cultural glimpses into rural Americana from all eras since the genre's birth alone make Ciné du Sasquatch films invaluable in terms of filmed cultural content. They offer unfettered, authentic cinematic access into impoverished backwoods and rural Americana small towns typically stereotyped by Hollywood à la *The Dukes of Hazzard* or *Lil' Abner*, but rarely realistically portrayed. Many Bigfoot films were and continue to be shot on location for authenticity purposes, if not cost savings. This gives these movies an invaluable "time capsule" snapshot of then-current trends, thinking, and culture outside the monolithic Hollywood cinema mainstream. Unable to afford the same costly studio sets or adjacent Hollywood locales, many Ciné du Sasquatch entries feature regional actors, rugged location photography, and glimpses into rarely documented folklore, customs, and local "personalities" otherwise unseen.

Digging beneath the all-too-often facile surfaces of many films in this genre, one discovers that Bigfoot as a metaphorical screen incarnation is a highly plastic, culturally adaptable litmus test reflective of its respective eras of production. The ever-changing screen incarnation of Sasquatch reveals a divergent spectrum of concurrent, more subversive or hidden attitudes towards a variety of such issues as animal rights, entrenched sexism, and environmental conservation. The enduring cinema icon is a snarling beast in one era and a benign friend to lost children in the swamps in another, who then effortlessly transforms back into rampaging beast in the next cinematic odyssey.

It's rare to see a monster mythos so flexible and apparently without rules, unlike many of the classic horror genres, such as Vampire Cinema or Werewolf Cinema, with their constraining reliance on stakes, silver bullets, crucifixes, and the like. But a closer examination of the Bigfoot genre reveals the prototypical entry (of which a majority of Ciné du Sasquatch films meet with usually overwhelmingly affirmative inclusion) inevitably consists of a carefully constructed, rarely deviating collection of underlying patterns, thematic motifs, and plot structures which place it within its own special category in horror film history.

As we shall discover, Ciné du Sasquatch has its own set of constraining rules. They're more deeply buried within the subtexts of a typical Bigfoot film than in, for example, a vampire or werewolf movie, wherein such rules are brought to the forefront of the narrative: a vampire must sleep on a bed of earth from his native country; a werewolf must avoid silver; and so on. Ciné du Sasquatch's self-defining limitations are much less rigid and apparent, but no less constraining as a genre than any other.

The Earliest Cinematic Appearances of Cryptid Hominids

It terms of cinema history, Ciné du Sasquatch is almost as old as narrative film itself. When it was released by pioneer special effects filmmaker George Méliès in 1912, *The Conquest of the Pole* was intended to rival his own earlier success with the first-ever SF blockbuster *A Trip to the Moon*, very loosely based on the work of Jules Verne. Though it wouldn't equal the earlier movie's success at the box office, the father of fantasy cinema had with *The Conquest of the Pole* unwittingly created the archetypal narrative blueprint for almost all subsequent Ciné du Sasquatch films. That is, humans invade the creature's domain, provoke or harm the creature, and fight their way back to so-called civilization, defeated as a species and realizing that Bigfoot is at least equal, if not ultimately superior to, intrusive mankind.

This thematic core of all Ciné du Sasquatch entries to follow is clearly set forth in *The Conquest of the Pole* from the outset, even as the title card appears. Note that human explorers must *conquer* rather than *explore* the terrain. This mentality clearly extends to the Yeti's portrayal as a man-eating monster in its first screen depiction. All snarling lips, drooling fangs, rolling eyes, and wildly-flying hair, it's a formidable first impression made by the gigantic snow monster.

But even by portraying the novel Yeti as beastly and non-human, there is a horrific recognition of distant kinship with the cinematic cryptid. This is one of the underlying reasons Ciné du Sasquatch is a different species from its later informative influences, such as the Killer Gorilla genre, which will be discussed in detail later. The empathetic level is high, in part because this depicted creature feels much more human and much less apelike. However nightmarishly, the monster is depicted as defending its own turf. The poor Yeti in *The Conquest of the Pole* is as much victim of its own harsh environment as are the intruding humans. It seeks to survive in reclusive isolation at the top of the world until humans arrive seeking the "conquest" of its domain. And after all, even an Abominable Snowman is still mostly a man, if by no other claim than namesake alone.

Ciné du Sasquatch founder George Méliès and design blueprints for his genre-pioneering, giant-sized animatronic Yeti monster (1912).

Herein Méliès' film has established another of the major themes that are recurrent throughout Ciné du Sasquatch: the human aspects of the portrayed cryptid give way to its baser beastly instincts because of the intrusion or provocations of the humans, underscoring the inherent loneliness contained in the concept of a shy being as intelligent as mankind but spending all waking hours actively avoiding detection. In thematic distillation, whenever mankind ventures into the cinematic worlds of wilderness redwoods, the boggy bayous, or mountaintop peaks in search of Sasquatch, Bigfoot, or Yeti, we as humans enter these sacred spaces as unwelcome visitors. The Bigfoot, however, represents the apex (no pun intended) of its own respective domain. Always it remains the alpha male of the forest, swamp, or mountain realms; in contrast, we are, as an inferior humanoid species, helpless before it until we finally learn our humiliating lesson and flee its space. Those who try to alter this basic tenet in most Ciné du Sasquatch efforts will surely and invariably pay the ultimate price.

Indeed, *The Conquest of the Pole* remains, as a title, an ironic joke at the explorers' expense, in that it's a frozen hell on Earth they find themselves stranded within. This is the new world which they've conquered. It consists of frozen fields of barren icescapes extending as far as the eye can see to a bleak horizon of jagged, inhospitable mountain peaks.

As if the cosmic laugh at their misery weren't enough, they also encounter the ravenous, giant Yeti. With its bushy eyebrows tinged with frost and maniacal eyes, the Abominable Snowman depicted is truly fearsome. But, as mentioned, the humanity of the cryptid shines through, and we as the audience become enchanted with how life-like this monstrosity behaves. Despite, or because of, its bold charm, the Yeti is the most human *being* alive onscreen during its brief cinematic birth (an impression furthered by contrasting the garish, overly-stiff *Homo sapiens* ham actors). It may be a man-eater, but from the first, Yeti is also a scene-stealer. This holds true today for modern viewers, who marvel at the monster's creation and movement ("That's amazing for its time!"), as much as it did for the 1912 audiences who were genuinely stunned by Méliès' onscreen technical wizardry.

Méliès was not indifferent to this intended consequence necessary to achieve such suspension of disbelief in his viewing public. It was as carefully prepared as any of his stage illusions performed prior to his second career as filmmaker. "It is the trick," Méliès wrote in a 1907 article about his pioneering efforts in moviemaking of the fantastic variety, "used in the most intelligent manner, that allows the supernatural, the imaginary, even the impossible to be rendered visually and produces truly artistic tableaux that provide a veritable pleasure for those who understand that all branches of art contribute to their realization."

The nascent plot from this silent movie remains the single most often used scenario in all Sasquatch genre movies. Allowing for modifications for updating and setting, almost all Bigfoot movies follow this singular "human vs. beast" narrative, which is quite interesting. While, of course, "man vs. nature" is the oldest of mythologies and clearly accounts for the partial expectation of this universal motif throughout the genre, one would be remiss not to speculate about the possible influence of underlying Jungian-styled subconscious archetypes dating back to our very origin as a species at work here. The beast as "shadow self" (as Jung called it) represents our own darker human psyches in a collective subconscious sense, which is why it frightens us when we're confronted by it in the externalized form of the "masked" monster — this dark being is our *own* worst demonic self, physically rendered incarnate and externalized into the creature, no longer merely a ravenous cryptid as the mask it wears at first suggests. Beneath the mask, in short, we see our own primitive beings in projected form.

Following this line of thought, it's then easy to see why these depicted screen hominids threaten us so: They're us, only magnified and made fantastically "more so" — literally to gargantuan proportions — neither a sub-species nor missing link in our evolutionary chain, but *co*-species to the shared title of earthly ruler. We know they are more like us upon first sight than any other animal with which we share the planet. We equally know that since they are so much like us, they are as capable of acts of unrestrained violence and monstrous destruction; only, unlike humans, they appear unhindered by any moral conscience or concern about how they will appear to the neighbors next door. As such, they evoke a figure from our collective selves and from a shared subconscious past, but unrestrained by any of the pleasantries and decorum that inhibit modern man in his rule-bound, polite society. These hominids represent and embody our past collective horror and repressed guilt over such primitive stages of social development as tribal cannibalism, human sacrifice, and other long-since buried taboos which have been repressed by the active mind but are still always lurking just below the calm waters of reason.

Méliès' visualization of the

Yeti snow giant from *The Conquest of the Pole* lends some credit to this thesis. Méliès morphs the first-ever cinematic cryptid into a kind of perverse variation of a drooling Saturn as painted by Goya, very much intent on devouring his puny human "children" alive. At black heart, this fear is also deeply buried within the genre: the fear of being eaten alive. A more primal myth would be difficult to isolate, and the Ciné du Sasquatch films which deal with an attacking beast intent on dining on humans may actually represent deeper, equally-repressed fears being collectively dredged forth from our shared, primordial past. It is an intriguing hypothesis, albeit speculative. Still, these primary images and motifs lay solidly embedded within *The Conquest of the Pole* — isolation via environment, survival vs. serving as food for the beast, and the awesome, near human-like nature of the creature — to the point they resurface again and again throughout the genre with little or no advancement or derivation, as we shall see.

Literary Influences on the Bigfoot Film Genre

Less argumentative are the obvious influences of two literary sources. The first is Edgar Allan Poe's classic work of detective

Unlike the Tarzan mythos, in Bigfoot movies, Sasquatch is lord of the jungle/wilderness domain, not mankind. Staged publicity still from *Tarzan and His Mate* (1932).

fiction "The Murders in the Rue Morgue," which was first published in 1841. The use by Poe of a frightening simian to commit unsolvable murders helped establish the notion of the sinister Killer Gorilla archetype firmly within the public's imagination.

While the notion that such a narrative twist as "the killer was an orangutan" was truly shocking may seem quaint today, it is well to recall that the first-ever mountain gorilla wasn't discovered until 1902 by German explorer Captain Robert von Beringe. This was after centuries of dismissal by many scientists and the press of reports of the mountain gorilla as being so much folklore from the superstitious natives. The newfound image of an animal so humanoid in so many traits doubtless excited the turn-of-the-century mind and appealed to a latent romantic sensibility strongly present in an era obsessed with spectral photography, psychic phenomena, and mysticism in general.

Indeed, it may very well have been the popular longing for the mythic mountain gorilla's existence triumphing over scientific skepticism that is precisely why the discovery of said gorilla is so relative to Ciné du Sasquatch. As an unproven hominid, Bigfoot labors under the same dismissal as did the mountain gorilla *before* its discovery. This is not proof that Bigfoot is real nor an attempt to persuade the reader as such. Rather, it helps explain the enduring popularity of the subject itself in the face of scientific prejudices against its very existence. It hints why Ciné du Sasquatch persists as an enduringly popular outsider cinema despite being dismissed because of the genre's inherently rural settings, impoverished residents, and subject matter itself. The mysterious, irrational impulse to believe over skeptical objections may be rationalized as leaving open the possibility of encountering such a legendary figure in one's own rural backyard (or while camping, if one is a habitual city dweller). Else, there is the depleted feeling that currently hovers over much of nature's remote areas, wherein global climate change renders once-majestic terrors of land and sea, such as polar bears and great white sharks, endangered species, and the pervasive sense that mankind has destroyed what was formerly sacrosanct and unconquerable. When all other riddles have been solved, in essence, the oldest, unsolvable ones remain embedded in the popular imagination all the more firmly.

Whatever one's belief in their real-world counterparts, Bigfoot, Yeti, and Sasquatch are as everlasting as the movies themselves, in part because cinematic audiences like underdogs. They psychologically tend to identify with any character who struggles to survive and improve his or her situation, provided it is not at the direct, illustrated expense of other onscreen characters, and especially when the underdog is battling against enormous psychological or physical odds. Hitchcock made great use of this phenomenon in many of his films, but perhaps none more so than *Psycho*. First the viewer empathizes with a woman having an adulterous affair who steals a large sum of money from her employer, and then with the shy, pathetic motel clerk who covers up his supposed mother's dark deeds after she commits each new grisly murder. As Hitchcock demonstrates so ably in *Psycho*, this intense audience need to identify will therefore momentarily transcend the moral failings of the onscreen characters; even damaged beings who would otherwise be too repulsive for

Tarzan (Johnny Weissmuller) from *Tarzan the Ape Man* (1932). The title wording alone reveals the influence the Lord of the Jungle mythos had on Ciné du Sasquatch.

most viewers — such as a serial killing, necrophilia-inclined, schizophrenic Norman Bates — are empathetic to them.

The other, more modern literary influence on Ciné du Sasquatch comes from Edgar Rice Burrough's Tarzan, first published in *All-Story Magazine* in 1912. As if he were opening up some 20th century Pandora's Box, Burrough's literate jungle man — a proper English lord who reclaims his rightful place within the aristocratic class after a youth spent among the apes — struck a nerve with the American public. Whether it was the sheer novelty (if not racist tint) of a storyline which proposes none other than a white man as lord of the Dark Continent, or simply a well-told adventure saga with enough fancy to send readers' pulses racing worldwide, since its earliest publication Tarzan remains an archetypal embodiment of the All-American heroic success story (despite the noble trappings and English background). It is, in essence, a Horatio Alger myth as if told by Kipling rather than Burroughs: A strong individual battles powerful antagonists who wish to crush him in not one but two very different worlds. Despite the odds against his very survival as a child and beyond into manhood, Tarzan succeeds because most underestimate him because of his primitive history. As a man, he is underestimated by his own kind. As an ape, he is underestimated by his own kind. It's quite a potent myth; and it's little wonder it endures so well in movies and TV shows, despite often mediocre rendering of its underlying themes.

It's worth noting, however, that most cinematic adaptations ignore or severely downplay the English nobility coursing through Tarzan's veins. Instead, they concentrate on the virility and dominance of the primal man, portraying Tarzan as Darwin's evolutionary missing link rather than the future Lord Greystoke. From a financial point of view, this filmic truncation of Tarzan into lord of the jungle and not lord of two worlds makes sense. It forces the movies to concentrate on the dynamic jungle thrills as opposed to less commercial parlor room theatrics, and — perhaps more realistically — cuts the budget in half by not having to realize both civilized and jungle worlds onscreen.

The influence of the Tarzan films, as much as the literary source, on Ciné du Sasquatch is marked but, somewhat paradoxically, also parallel to it. For in a Fortean quirk of fate, both *Tarzan, Lord of the Apes* and *The Conquest of the Pole* were unleashed on the unsuspecting American public's psyche in the year 1912. So it is arguable that it was the confluence of both events rather than each by itself that helped enshrine the early filmgoers' and readers' interest in simian species both mythic and only recently proven to them as actually existing. *Just think*, the sensationalized audiences may have mused, if the mountain gorilla was only discovered ten years earlier in 1902, what else would be found lurking in the remotest regions of the world as science and geographical exploration progressed?

What Ciné du Sasquatch owes to the Tarzan films more than anything else is actually the subversion of the Tarzan mythos itself. Whereas Tarzan is shown as the triumphant alpha male of the jungle and can best any beast therein from his origin forward, Bigfoot from first screen introduction onward is presented as the alpha predator (when necessary) of the woods, swamps, and mountaintops, and can best any beast or human therein. Tarzan, the lord and protectorate of the jungle, has been altered into Bigfoot as nature's *de facto* wilderness defender.

It's as if the transformation from Tarzan films to Bigfoot movies was intent on showing the dethronement of man as master of his environment, even the untamed ones; the Ciné du Sasquatch genre substitutes Bigfoot, Yeti, and Sasquatch for the human Tarzan role and implies we humans have done damage enough already. Like the tense relationships between Native Americans and European settlers in a John Ford western, Bigfoot and humans typically do not peacefully co-exist within any given screen space very often or very long. Whenever we uncaring, ignorant settlers (as we as humans are invariably portrayed in this genre) invade the sacred lands of Sasquatch in Ciné du Sasquatch, sacrificial blood — our own — is soon to be shed.

Killer Gorilla vs. Savage Sasquatch

An oddly relevant genre more widely known than Ciné du Sasquatch is the Killer Gorilla formula, whose prime era was from the early 1930s into the early 1950s. This Man vs. Beast genre echoes one of the main influences of Ciné du Sasquatch itself, making the two almost the same in terms of shared literary ancestry. That link is Poe's aforementioned "The Murders in the Rue Morgue," which initially planted the Killer Gorilla icon into the public's consciousness.

Still, Killer Gorilla and Ciné du Sasquatch are not to be confused as one in the same or intermingled, as each remains distinctively different within their genre limitations. Killer Gorilla movies feature known primates such as gorillas, chimpanzees, and the like, whereas Bigfoot movies posit a creature that is somewhere between human and any known gorilla species. This difference is crucial and explains how the two "species" of genres

Dr. James Brewster (Bela Lugosi) falls prey to his own scientific experimentation upon his simian subject (Emil Van Horn) while Billie Mason (Louise Currie) looks on in *The Ape Man* (1943).

diverged from the same, shared cinematic evolutionary path and became two unique film forms.

Alas for the genre in question, no matter how many gimmicks producers dreamed up for this veritable cinema staple — including such novel twists as featuring an albino as opposed to black-colored ape (*The White Gorilla* and *White Pongo*, both in 1945), shooting in the early 3-D process (*Gorilla at Large* in 1954), chemically-inducing gigantism (*Konga* in 1961), etc. — Killer Gorilla films rarely toyed with the idea of the simian in question as anything other than being a known species, however different in size, temperament, or genetic lineage.

Ciné du Sasquatch would later borrow some of the traditional trappings of some Killer Gorilla movies in terms of imagery. One potent example: the ubiquitous, terrified heroine clutched in the monster's arms. Another similarity is the typical use of anatomically-incorrect simian costumes in both genres. Ciné du Sasquatch usually features a gorilla costume that's modified

Simian actor Charles Gemora kept the Killer Gorilla genre profitable. Here he and his costume are featured on the poster art for *The Monster and the Girl* (1941), even though he's not listed in the film's credits.

to look slightly different, whereas Killer Gorilla movies take great liberty with known gorilla anatomy and limb lengths to portray the species as dramatic needs or budgets dictated. Both strain credulity, in essence, to heighten audience expectations and conform to preexisting cinematic simian imagery. But other than common ancestry and some similarities in such imagery and production techniques, the two genres really are far apart in terms of narratives and thematic concerns. And while there is some crossover from time to time between the two that effectively blurs the line, the differences remain stark.

Summing up that difference, it's as if when comparing the two cinematic simians, real and imagined, both cannot appear in the same film together. They seem to be operating under a mutual self-exclusion rule, not unlike filmic matter and anti-matter. When Bigfoot appears in a film, gorillas never appear as well. If a killer gorilla exists in a film, Bigfoot never appears alongside or in the background. It's as if there's an unspoken *quid pro quo* of mutual exclusivity between the two genres.

It's perhaps obvious why the universe of each genre restricts the possible existence of the other. One (Ciné du Sasquatch) deals with a cryptid (or unproven) creature, whereas the other (Killer Gorilla) focuses on a real (or often, with great exaggeration, a supposedly real) creature. As a result, filmmakers typically feel the need to place the unknown cryptid in the real world to convince skeptical viewers "hey, this thing *could* be out there." Conversely, they tend to place killer gorilla stories into slightly more fantastic settings and locales, trying to visually heighten the overly-familiar screen image of a gorilla-suited actor, however well-designed is said costume.

Ciné du Sasquatch emerges from the proverbial shadows of the Killer Gorilla genre in transforming the known ape into unknown cryptid. While the two are almost identical in terms of the way in which both are typically portrayed by gorilla-costumed actors, they share little beyond this singularly acute visual similarity.

King Kong's Enormous Footprint

Perhaps the most influential movie that helped shaped the ultimate creation of Ciné du Sasquatch is the work of Hollywood producing team Merian C. Cooper and Ernest B. Schoedsack. They specialized in exotic "you are there" documentary films shot in remote locations and were media sensationalists patterning themselves as the P.T. Barnum equivalents of jungle film exploitation. In the Roarin' Twenties they were just releasing their first filmed efforts. With such titles as *Chang* (1927), *Grass* (1925), and *Rango* (1931), their films from this era are the modern equivalent of reality TV (the ultimate oxymoron) programming. The producers were trying to jolt jaded viewers hardened by their economic woes and transport their mesmerized spectators into a cinematic jungle heaven and hell beyond their Depression-dulled imaginations. Exotic, never-before-seen rain forest locales and subjects, such as wandering nomadic tribes in Iran, whetted a curious public's insatiable appetite for more jungle documentary epics.

When the appeal of documentary jungle thrills began to wane,

Jungian simian symbolism: Dr. Brewster (Bela Lugosi) beats the bars of his caged, repressed Shadow Self externalized in the form of the captive gorilla (Emil Van Horn), in the Killer Gorilla film *The Ape Man* (1943).

Fay Wray helps *King Kong* writer Edgar Wallace measure the big footprints left behind by the Eighth Wonder of the World (1933).

the producers switched to making fictionalized sound films. The element of sound added creative possibilities for making more effective shock movies, as producers could control the universal experience of the film's sound and picture synchronization for the first time in history on any reliable mass scale. The young producers were intrigued and exploited sound well, filling their soundtracks with exotic bird cries, animal growls, and gunfire.

Cooper, Schoedsack, and a young producer named David O. Selznick (later to revolutionize the industry with epics such as *Gone with the Wind*) milked the formula effectively in *The Most Dangerous Game* (1932). With its spooky, isolated, jungle island setting, Fay Wray and Robert Armstrong in leading roles, and many of the same technical artists who would later work on *King Kong*, *The Most Dangerous Game* is a prescient version of the ensuing *Kong* picture itself. More germane to Ciné du Sasquatch, *The Most Dangerous Game* also eerily preechoes the Bigfoot film genre that eventually emerged decades later. The distillation of this narrative formula as haiku essence: A group of individuals find themselves cut off in the wilderness and have to fight a stalking antagonist to survive. In essence, *King Kong* was *The Most Dangerous Game* but with a cryptid monster instead of the sadistic hunter Count Zaroff, the deranged human killer.

As good as the creepy thrills of *The Most Dangerous Game* were, as evidenced by its critical and box-office reception, the producers sensed there was more to the concept if they could only add a refreshing marketing angle to a similarly-veined, subsequent effort. The magic ingredient was eventually discovered and brought forth: a giant ape falling for the girl. It was the classic tale of *Beauty and the Beast*, as referenced in *King Kong* itself with its concluding line: "T'was beauty killed the beast." With the genius of early stop-motion pioneer Willis O'Brien, animator and effects creator of *The Lost World* (1925), commissioned to bring the Kong puppets to life frame-by-frame, *King Kong* went on to become one of the most influential motion pictures ever made.

Less noticeable (and understandably so) than the worldwide commercial riches and critical praise *King Kong* has received over the seven decades since its release into the public consciousness is its impact upon the Ciné du Sasquatch genre. With its "intruders in nature versus an indigenous hominid" storyline, *King Kong* took the faint echoes of *The Conquest of the Pole* and positively rang the cathedral bells with them.

For almost all that would follow in Ciné du Sasquatch, the key elements set forth by *The Conquest of the Pole* are transplanted largely intact from a freezing to a jungle hell, but with the underlying "man vs. cryptid" myth maintained, only flipped in terms of its designed emotional manipulation. *The Conquest of the Pole* attempts to terrify with the unknown; *King Kong* attempts to gain empathy for a dethroned, heartbroken, cryptid king. Both strategies worked well for their respective eras. Thus, from the beginning of Ciné du Sasquatch, the genre has allowed a huge amount of elasticity in terms of how the creatures are cinematically incarnated — each gigantic in proportion to us humans, but, equally and importantly, as different as night from day as portrayed in these two films.

Of course, the brilliant idea to add a romance was what made *King Kong*, well, *King Kong* and therefore ironically *not* a good example of Ciné du Sasquatch, per se. But because the "footprint" was so large, *King Kong* made an indelible imprint on basic genre structures and iconographic imagery. In truth, *King Kong* created such a large wake for all movies that many once-dormant genres, such as the Killer Gorilla, were temporarily and sometimes enduringly revived. But unlike *Beauty and the Beast* and its influence on *King Kong*, the love story between cryptid and human would not transfer into the Bigfoot genre with as much obvious thematic resonance. In most Ciné du Sasquatch films, love rarely enters into the storylines unless it is between human protagonists; and if the taboo of bestiality is dared to be broken in a Bigfoot film, the concentration is less on a doomed romance between species than simply the doom of the perceived human love object in the hands of the cryptid itself. So to this extent, the romantic undertones of *Beauty and the Beast*— both as legend and cinema — has proven to be almost non-existent as an influence on Bigfoot films as a genre.

In fact, and sadly to their detriment, too many of the subsequent offerings in the Bigfoot cannon only weakly exploit the

Fay Wray reacts to off-screen menace in this staged publicity photograph for *King Kong* (1933). The latent sexual hysteria at implied or explicit bestiality later prevalent in Ciné du Sasquatch originated herein.

Poster art for the theatrical release of *The Most Dangerous Game* (1932).

tragic but humanizing connection that distinguishes *King Kong*, with its *Beauty and the Beast* sub-plot. The basic narrative arc of "man into wilderness, man versus big ape, man escapes back to civilization" is maintained in the Bigfoot genre as a whole, but, post–*Kong*, the romantic angle in most efforts is simply beyond the typically limited budgets (with some notable exceptions) and available talents. If such subject matter is contained in a Yeti film, it is most often an inherent cross-breeding sub-plot involving male cryptids and female humans, as in *Man Beast*, the John Carradine version of *Bigfoot*, *Night of the Demon*, and others in the genre. Some even go so far in the more sordid Ciné du Sasquatch films as to not merely hint at bestiality but graphically demonstrate it, as in *Beauties and the Beast*, *Search for the Beast*, and *Yeti: A Love Story* (2006).

But to say these efforts are mirroring the basically less risqué romance of ape and woman in *King Kong* is to do a real disservice to the Eighth Wonder of the World. In short, most (though not all) Ciné du Sasquatch films seek to portray the women as victims, not love objects, of the cryptid, often with brutal results.

Mythic Resonances in Ciné du Sasquatch

This is not to impugn the very genre under discussion. In fact, given that a majority of these movies were independently made, on pressure-cooker shooting schedules at often challenging locations with low or no budgets, it may speak more loudly about the enduring power of actual Bigfoot believers' unusually high tolerance for bad filmmaking in general, at least in terms of most movies in the genre. After all, fans of Ciné du Sasquatch were willing to endure decades between good entries during its infancy. And even to this date, mediocre examples top the truly entertaining ones in the genre by a wider margin than ever before (though there are some truly interesting ones being released today, as well). It is also worth noting that today's output of Bigfoot film releases outnumbers their earlier kin in volume and regularity of titles, which also accounts for the feeling an avid viewer encounters that many are recycled without variation.

It is not just that the sheer number of films and television shows has lessened the uniqueness of the genre in and of itself. Rather, it's the fact that Bigfoot has super-saturated the collective popular consciousness and therefore transcended beyond folklore into a bona fide cultural megastar status. A new season of films or TV without an appearance of a fictional Yeti, Bigfoot, or Sasquatch somewhere in the entertainment mix seems unthinkable today. As the shelves at any DVD store reveal, more and more titles continue to be released into the Ciné du Sasquatch genre in an attempt to capitalize upon the giant's ever-increasing popularity. Not since Godzilla has such an iconographic monster become ubiquitous in all forms of entertainment across the international media spectrum.

As a collective archetype, Bigfoot offers an endless reservoir of mythic resonances: passivity versus violence; self-protection versus unprovoked attack; and survival versus extinction. Similar themes and subject matter harken back to the first recorded stories of mankind. These are the basic storylines of our species. Tales that, as Joseph Campbell, expert on world mythologies, pointed out so often in his works (such as *Hero of 1,000 Faces*), universally appeared across all cultures throughout all recorded time.

This forces the critical viewer to question the deeper resonances of the genre; what is it about this particular subject matter that endures while so many others fall to the wayside? If approached from an anthropological stance, and with the necessary indulgence of granting that most, if not all, Ciné du Sasquatch filmmakers probably rarely, if ever, conceived of their efforts as anything more than routine shock-fests, one begins to see a window into the why of the genre's enduring popularity. In so many ways, the creature is the perfect embodiment of the big bad wolf of the classic "Little Red Riding Hood" or "The Three Little Pigs" folk tales. The cryptid is most often portrayed, not unlike the wolf, as a cunning, intelligent foe. Unlike the less-human and outright simian gorillas of an average Tarzan jungle film, Sasquatch and the bad wolf use their shared knowledge of the forest to lay in wait and devise traps to use against their human adversaries.

The similarities don't end there, either. The wolf is "bad" in part because it is a lone creature, which is diametrically opposed to the known reality of the species, which live and hunt in a pack. Left unquestioned but implied is the obvious: Why is this wolf solo? Similarly, why is Bigfoot most often cinematically rendered as being a loner? Again, the implied answer is: The inherent threat of the nemesis is increased by its stand-alone nature. After all, a being which chooses to go it alone must be all the more dangerous in comparison to a majority seeking the opposite advantage of strength in numbers.

Indeed, there is an underlying, almost palpable *Last of the Mohicans* feel to many of the Bigfoot efforts. They seem to pick up on the cryptid's lonely plight and, more often than not, as in *King Kong* and later examples such as *Creature from the Black Lagoon*, show the almost human side of the monster in question. As Marilyn Monroe remarks in *The Seven Year Itch*, one feels sorry for the Creature, who, like Kong, dies for love's sake. After all, one can further conclude, what rational human being hasn't acted like an irrational animal every now and again when falling in and out of love?

It is true that some Ciné du Sasquatch films portray their creatures as tribal entities, but these are exceptions rather than the rule. Importantly and somewhat ironically as well, most entries pit a lone Bigfoot against a tribe of humans. Another key contradiction lies therein: The humans are so loosely-affiliated and argumentatively individualistic they typically prove to be their own worst enemies. By bickering over what course of action to take in the face of a singularly savage monster, such as an enraged Bigfoot, the human clan is presented as collectively ineffectual. The underlying message is not buried beneath any hidden sheets of ice — the human attempts at tribal organization are so pathetically self-immolating that efforts by them to remain united are more lethal to the *Homo sapiens*' chances of survival than potential death from the creature. Extrapolating even further, a bleaker picture is formed. To wit, humankind is self-destructively doomed because of its very nature; we value individual identity over unity as a species, even when it doesn't provide either stability or sustainability. This is as true in the Eastern/Yeti form as the Western/Bigfoot incarnation, transcending all cultural barriers, as the cryptid itself does as universal archetype.

It's not exactly an inspirational, uplifting theme, granted, but nevertheless omnipresent throughout the genre. In an era of global climate change wherein human and animal species alike are seemingly at times threatened beyond any shared future coexistence, one would be hard pressed to cite a more topically-relevant subtext in any other filmmaking genre. Just another possible reason why Ciné du Sasquatch films seem ever on the increase in output while other genres in the horror film field have come and gone in enduring meaningfulness to collective audiences — they express a worldwide if subconscious dread and fear of nature's harsh, retributive judgment (as Sasquatch is usually a figure of apocalyptic revenge in its dealings with the environment-destroying humans it encounters). Like a volcano, hurricane, earthquake, or flood, the beast is but a two-legged incarnation of the natural life forces exacting planetary revenge against the so-called human masters of the world.

Of Cold Wars and Cryptids: The 1950s

Because Ciné du Sasquatch took decades to crystallize into a formal genre, many producers and directors during the 1940s never fully followed in the obvious footsteps of *King Kong* and *Son of Kong*, the intangible earlier films such as *The Conquest of the Pole*, or the Killer Gorilla genre which it so closely resembles. Rather than becoming trendsetters and introducing the American Abominable Snowman legends such as Bigfoot (printed newspaper accounts of which existed for almost a century by this point) to the American cinemagoer during the 1940s, they followed the usual retread mentality of most Hollywood studios and simply remade the same films with the same themes. As a result, *Mighty Joe Young* and *Rue Morgue*–styled gorillas demonstrating uncanny intelligence were the dominant horror film figures relating to known simians of all sizes, while the formulaic Tarzan, Bomba, and Jungle Jim adventure films filled out the production slate with more savage-styled gorillas.

In regards to the 1940s' lack of contributory films to the advancement of the nascent Ciné du Sasquatch genre, it is possible to speculate that audiences were in no mood for such horror fare given the actual horrors of World War Two engulfing the globe. However, as Universal's steady output of Gothic monster fare, such as *The Wolfman*, *House of Frankenstein*, and the like, suggest the opposite; the reality was that the dream factory had anything but an aversion to filling theaters with diversionary screams of terror. Indeed, the decade saw the rise and subsequent fall of a myriad of monster-friendly movies, not only from Universal and other major studios, but from the smaller B-moviemakers such as PRC and Monogram. Bela Lugosi, John Carradine, George Zucco, Boris Karloff, and Lon Chaney, Jr., became marquee fixtures portraying a plethora of mad scientists,

the walking dead, zombie creators, and even venerable killer gorilla enablers in both big and small studio output. When the war ended, Val Lewton and his corps of talented craftsmen, such as Jacques Tourneur and Robert Wise, followed up on the horror film's popularity and gave birth to more restrained, thoughtful terrors such as *Curse of the Cat People* and *The Seventh Victim*. And, of course, the aforementioned *Mighty Joe Young* was a major commercial success during the 1940s, albeit not Kong-sized in direct comparison.

And yet, despite the public's seemingly insatiable appetite for monster movies of all thematic ranges, not a single entry was made in the 1940s that truly can be called a Ciné du Sasquatch film. Nor were there produced any Killer Gorilla films aping *King Kong*'s success that had any impact of the Bigfoot genre. This dry decade became one of the longest stretches in celluloid history wherein the giant hominid did not make a major screen

Gorilla Woman (1935) actually had a more risqué poster that featured topless native women for more liberal markets. "Giant Monsters Enthroned as Love Gods! Startling in its Weird Action!" screams the ad copy.

appearance or see a film made that at least influenced the genre. Instead, mad scientist cinema stereotypes concentrated on serums that would change a man into a gorilla and other such variants. It was as if Yeti had vanished from the filmic lexicon altogether, and *The Conquest of the Pole* had never been made nor exhibited to enthralled audiences. Such was the power of *King Kong* and its legacy that it virtually swept away any other conception of a large, unknown bipedal "monster ape man" from the movies for nearly two decades. Instead, fantastic-sized gorillas and other gargantuan primates ruled.

All this would change in the 1950s, however, with the exploits of Sir Edmund Hillary and the "conquest" of Mount Everest in the Himalayas (which, ironically, harkens back to the earlier *The Conquest of the Pole* and its creation of the Sasquatch genre itself). For not only did the British explorer ignite the public's appetite for literally high adventure in scaling the peaks of one of the world's tallest mountains, he also brought back tantalizing tales of the local Bigfoot beastie known as Yeti, the proverbial Abominable Snowman. Due to the popularity of *National Geographic*'s coverage of the expeditions and the subsequent migration of lurid Yeti stories into radio, early television, and tabloid newsstand magazines concerning the albino monster supposedly inhabiting the snowy ridges, the ferocious Yeti was soon an internationally-known cryptid, arguably the most famous to date. The photographs accompanying the scientific reports showing strange footprints and conical-shaped scalps supposedly belonging to dead Yetis were a sensation few alert producers in Hollywood could have possibly failed to recognize as box-office gold for those willing to cinematically pan for it.

Yeti fever swept the scientific community, giving rise to what would become the first true generation of cryptozoologists. These early pioneers in the field quickly purchased a seemingly inexhaustible supply of Yeti artifacts from Sherpa villagers. Some of the sellers were apparently as canny at chicanery as they were as trail guides. It was a time when calmer heads should have perhaps prevailed; after all, given that even the locals claimed the Abominable Snowmen were scarce, one would naturally question how such a limitless supply of scalps, bones, and claws would be so readily available for commercial exploit. But with the hysteria caused by worldwide interest in the "newly-discovered" Yeti, few and far between were the scientists unwilling to buy first and examine evidence later. Should the Yeti species become legitimately recognized, they not only stood to benefit as the discoverers, but financially as well in possessing all rights to the evidence. The latter aspect, though not a motive of the many honest researchers, was an example of the Carl Denham Syndrome in real-life action for the few who did seek to exploit the newly-created marketplace for Yeti hysteria.

The Yeti artifacts, such as the scalps, turned out to be clever fakes made for quick profits, fabricated from Yak hair and animal skulls. Likewise, most of the rest of the Yeti evidence (with the exception of the photographed footprints, which endure as records of some*thing*— or someone — having produced them) melted like snowflakes under the heat of closer scientific scrutiny. By the end of the 1950s the Abominable Snowman's waning cultural impact transformed the Yeti into an increasingly obscure footnote in a decade that had been overrun and perhaps overtaxed by such zeitgeist-draining phenomena as flying saucers and the constant threat of nuclear annihilation. The remote nature of the Yeti, confined as it was to the Himalayas in far away Tibet, may have also contributed to its soon-lagging popularity in the public's mind; after all, UFOs and atomic bombs were a threat no matter where one built one's fall-out shelter, figuratively and literally speaking. As if further proof were needed of the Snowman's lagging credibility, no less than Bugs Bunny was reducing the cryptid to laughing stock in a 1961 Warner Brothers cartoon called "The Abominable Snow Rabbit," which saw the Yeti portrayed as a gigantic simpleton molded after the lumbering but loveable Lenny from *Of Mice and Men*. Though entertainingly animated by a master of the medium, Chuck Jones, the underlying message was clear — the Abominable Snowman was no longer to be taken seriously as a cinematic threat, but played for guffaws at its own expense.

But prior to this decline the Yeti was the subject of a series of fictional suspense and horror pictures that in no uncertain terms advanced Ciné du Sasquatch during one of its most fecund periods. Indeed, it is appropriate to consider the 1950s as the Golden Era of the genre for this very reason. Among these formative pictures were Lee Wilder's *The Snow Creature* (directed by Billy Wilder's brother W. Lee Wilder, no less), Jerry Warren's *Man Beast*, and Toho Studios' retitled *Half Human* (aka *Jû jin yuki otoko*). *Snow Creature* was a headline-grabbing rip-off intended by director Wilder to cash in on the current Abominable Snowman craze. Given that it was the first of the Golden Era of Ciné du Sasquatch movies released, one is perplexed by how little impact it made. Much of this is obviously due, however, to the poverty-row budget of *Snow Creature*, which features a police dragnet searching for a murderous hominid on the loose,

This supposed Yeti skull/scalp has been proven to be a fake, but many still falsely claim it is legitimate (date unknown).

with only a handful of cops ever shown for the entire city of Los Angeles. Indeed, both *Snow Creature* and *Man Beast* were quick-buck affairs. *Man Beast* filmmaker Jerry Warren bragged in interviews of sneaking onto an adjacent set created by another, unconnected production in the studio in which he directed *Man Beast* because it held a mountain monastery set which he couldn't otherwise have afforded. So he covertly shot fast scenes with his bewildered cast at night while the other producers (who only shot during the day) remained oblivious as to how their supposedly vacant sets were being utilized! Neither *Snow Creature* nor *Man Beast* made much of an impact, either commercially or on the Bigfoot film genre, save for their historical status as leaders of the pack.

Half Human was another matter. Intelligently-made by Toho Studios and featuring a well-designed suit by Godzilla special effects guru Eiji Tsuburaya, it, alas, also suffered from a fast-buck mentality by importer DCA Pictures, its American release company. Rather than keep the carefully, suspense-building tone Honda so cleverly rendered, and either dub or subtitle the dialogue to preserve quality, the tiny releasing entity instead opted to hire John Carradine as an American expert who tells the story in flashback. The DCA producers filmed Carradine in a tiny, two-room office set, using his soothing voice to explain the story in lengthy voiceovers and adding expository scenes that were spliced into the Toho footage. The effect was to nearly ruin the movie despite its clearly superior artistic origins. Nevertheless, it survived the butchery with at least enough of its horrors intact to cause a stir among the faithful who saw it, whether theatrically (where it was double-billed on the lower half of the marquee with *Monster from Green Hell*) or soon thereafter in syndicated TV. *Half Human* is a superior motion picture that deserved better than its initial American fate. Alas, because of sensitive portrayals of indigenous people throughout the feature, Toho Studios has enacted a virtual ban on the film ever being seen in public again. Much like how Disney's *Song of the South* is currently not in release in America because the parent company fears ruining its non-racist image, Toho sadly still pretends *Half Human* is merely a footnote in their catalog rather than a vital motion picture, flaws and all. This robs the film of its rightful due in cinema history, not to mention denying it a more objective assessment for its many contributions to the formation of the Ciné du Sasquatch genre.

In terms of lasting impact and overall international commercial success, none of these aforementioned efforts would achieve the enduring legacy of Hammer Studios' memorable and often chilling *The Abominable Snowman* (1957). Oddly, *The Abominable Snowman* first began as a live BBC television broadcast entitled *The Creature* (1955), only later to be translated to the silver screen. Thus it enjoys a rare double crown status in the Ciné du Sasquatch genre of having appeared in both televised and theatrical formats. Key to the success in both fields is the taut writing of the teleplay and screenplay by legendary British author Nigel Kneale. Kneale was an amazingly productive and intelligent talent, writing for over half a century for film, television, radio, and even published fiction. He is best known for his creation of the Professor Quatermass character, a scientific

variation on Sherlock Holmes, and the cult films featuring the brainy doctor known as the Quatermass series, such as *Five Million Years to Earth* (aka *Quatermass and the Pit*). These films focused on Gothic horror and science fiction elements in a blended vein not dissimilar to the American writer of the Cthulhu mythos, H. P. Lovecraft, but with emphasis placed more on the scientific rather than mystical viewpoint. An uneasy tension typically exists in these efforts in which cold, rational scientists attempt to logically explain various supernatural phenomena they encounter, only to realize that there is a definitive (albeit illogical) coexistence between the two that can never be resolved.

The sensational ratings produced by *The Creature* all but guaranteed a theatrical remake, and Hammer was quick to jump aboard. Both versions feature an English anthropologist teaming with Americans to search for the elusive Yeti in the Himalayas. Both versions were also fortunate enough to feature Peter Cushing in the beginning stage of his long, varied career portraying a variety of men of science roles (most famously Dr. Frankenstein). But whereas the live version on the BBC (unfortunately, no known kinescopes survive by which to analyze it) was designed to play within the non-budget and confining technicalities of the television medium in its infancy, the theatrical version was fully expanded with a modest but well-spent budget and convincing, haunting, and evocatively eerie sets of the Himalayan mountaintops. Combined with director Val Guest's serious tone in dealing with the subject matter (Guest had earlier directed Kneale's *The Quatermass Xperiment*) and the terrific cinematography by genre expert Arthur Grant (who also lensed superior efforts such as *The Devil Rides Out* and *Plague of the Zombies*), *The Abominable Snowman* set a high altitude standard for all subsequent Yeti films to follow, one which has only rarely been topped in the ensuing decades for both entertainment and thoughtful handling of the subject matter.

In telling its sinister, suspenseful tale of marauding humans intruding into the highest, hidden vestiges of the dying Yetis, *The Abominable Snowman* echoes the *Last of the Mohicans* theme (as previously noted) that is common throughout the genre. The difference herein is that *The Abominable Snowman* was one of the first to introduce the concept and bring it to the forefront, thus making it seminal to subsequent Ciné du Sasquatch entries. It also (like *Man Beast* and *Half Human* shortly before it) emphasized the standard plot that would become ubiquitous in the genre: the aforementioned human conquerors who invade the Yeti's mountaintop retreat only to be forced to withdraw when the Abominable Snowmen use violence against mankind.

In fact, examining both *The Conquest of the Pole* and *The Abominable Snowman* as contrasting book-ends at this point in Ciné du Sasquatch's film history reveals just how little had changed in almost half a century since the formula was introduced — at least on their respectively icy surfaces. In both films, cocksure humans arrive to best the beast in the confines of its own heretofore unexplored lair. In both, the beast gets the better of them. But this facile comparison, of course, misses all of the subtle changes Kneale masterfully brought to his well-honed screenplay.

For example, the very beginning of *The Abominable Snowman*

sets in motion the real conflict underlying all that follows, as well as acting as painlessly-crafted exposition to set the tale in motion. The Buddhist Sherpa monk who serenely warns the assembled group of prototypically self-centered Westerners about to embark on their trek to the snowy peaks not to do so, intoning in plain language (plain, that is, to anyone who is not self-absorbed and spiritually dead to the core) that one's own Shadow is as much (if not more so) a threat in hazarding such explorations as any exterior monsters. Herein Kneale makes explicit what the genre has always asserted throughout its filmic incarnations — it is the Jungian inner monster, the so-called Shadow Self. The Shadow, according to Jung, represents all that

DEMON - PROWLER OF MOUNTAIN SHADOWS.
DREADED MAN - BEAST OF TIBET ...
THE TERROR OF ALL THAT IS HUMAN!!

The Abominable Snowman of the Himalayas

WE DARE YOU TO SEE IT ALONE!
Each chilling moment a shock-test for your scare - endurance!!

A REGALSCOPE PICTURE

STARRING
FORREST TUCKER · PETER CUSHING
PRODUCED BY   DIRECTED BY   SCREENPLAY BY   BASED ON THE PLAY   Released by
AUBREY BARING · VAL GUEST · NIGEL KNEALE ·   "THE CREATURE"   20th CENTURY - FOX
                                              by NIGEL KNEALE

57 - 537

The Jungian concept of a projected Shadow Self is literally illustrated in this lurid half-sheet poster for *The Abominable Snowman* (1957).

is unknown to the conscious mind but secretly desired by the unconscious mind. Because each person is blind to his own Shadow, Jung's theory concludes, the subconscious mind freely projects the repressed, unrecognized imagery onto other living beings, like a long shadow falling upon all who come near each living person. The externalized Bigfoot represents little more than each person's projected, primordial natures prior to civilizing influence. In essence, Sasquatch is a dark mirror before which each human being might be brought face-to-snarling-face with his or her own self in a ferocious animal form. Whereupon the startled civilized human being, having recognized the darker impulses of his own masked depravities, hurriedly retreats back to the safety of civilization itself (the latter of which is a collective form of denial wherein we all mutually if silent agree to ignore all lurking evidence of our own worst impulses). This shell-shocked human being is left with the undeniable, lingering perception that it is his own world of teeming cities, and unending and often unenforceable social contracts (and therefore cruel contradictions), that is the more dangerous and less moral world in which to inhabit. The sub-human status of the wild monster is revealed in no uncertain terms to be that of a higher spiritual being, however much it survives by brute force and unfettered laws of the jungle, woods, or mountaintops. The survivor —*if* one remains — is left to ponder the paradox of his own advanced state as a human in contrast to the elevated status of the beast he once pitted. In so doing, self-pity replaces the former attitude of superiority, and the human realizes not only that in nature one finds a self-justified balance of survival needs versus actions taken, but that man as a coexisting species has much to learn before proclaiming himself the master of the world.

This is perfectly illustrated by the Westerners who reject the wise monk's advice as so much religious hokum. They talk secretly out of range of the Sherpas with a mixture of detached sense of elevated self-worth and deluded self-aggrandizement, little realizing it is the Sherpas who are the Westerners' superiors in every sense of the word save technologically, at least in this unforgiving climate. Here, it is the Sherpas who have mastered difficult terrain, low-oxygen endurance, and the spiritual fortitude to deal with the extremes of nature. Indeed, even the botanist portrayed so effectively by Peter Cushing allows himself to be persuaded of the superiority of his own intellectual abilities, to the extent that he, too, rejects maintaining a scientifically-mandated open mind to at least consider the monk's sincere warning. Kneale's appropriate use of the Eastern Sherpas (and therefore philosophy) conflicting with the Western Individualists (and their shared sense of unspoken Manifest Destiny over all before them who cannot oppose them with better technology) provides a brilliant, underlying tension that runs throughout the picture. It establishes the genre's main thematic obsession from here forward: No matter the carnage a Yeti may inflict in retaliation, there exists at least a modicum of Rousseau's Noble Savage present in the depictions of cryptids in Ciné du Sasquatch, just as there exists a pervading sense that mankind never understands (and continuously underestimates) that Mother Nature herself is a form of technology. Humans dominate their world (or so they like to imagine) through the use of guns and other weaponry; nature avenges with organic phenomena such as blizzards and biological entities like Sasquatch. Formerly confident mankind crumbles in the face of powers far greater than his puny technological crutches. In so doing, he is reduced to a stage of primitive existence yet again in the face of a cryptid being already at peace with its place in the natural order of the planet. Never is the lesson learned, however, until it is too late for either party to avoid conflict and all-too-often mutual self-destruction in the process.

Whatever reservations one may harbor towards this genre (understandably so, given the lack of critical reception most entries have engendered), *The Abominable Snowman* is an example of a well-rendered tale escaping any genre limitations imposed upon it. It entertains as a drama, and holds viewer interest as both a thought-provoking and scary adventure tale. From the crisp direction, taut script, and fine cast, to the unexpectedly touching special make-up effects by Phil Leakey, *The Abominable Snowman* is a genuinely effective shocker in the best Val Lewton manner. Shadows count for more terror-inducing impact than close-ups of any rubbery-faced masks. A single claw glimpsed as it slips under a tent at night implies far more off-screen horror than any suited actor, however well-crafted, could achieve, especially given the film's modest budget and era of production.

One of the Yeti's more mystical qualities has always been that it supposedly eludes detection by startled witnesses' cameras and therefore remains a mental construct necessary for each viewer to create in his or her own imagination when viewing a Ciné du Sasquatch effort (until, and if, the filmmakers reveal their visualization of the hominid, that is). This vacuum of existing pre-imagery can be both a blessing and a curse in any film involving fantasy, science fiction, or horror, perhaps never more so than in an age when computer-generated imagery limits no cryptid depiction save an animation team's skills and imagination. And yet, the constant cinematic dilemma remains. How much does one show of any imaginary or unknown creature, and how often before audience credulity renders the visualization itself problematic? There is no magic formula for this delicate balancing act; it is left to the skilled director's alchemical abilities to transform the less-than-desirable "need to show the monster" limitation into cinematic gold by *not* doing so unless and until absolutely necessary ... whatever the term "necessary" means in such admittedly vague criterion.

As previously mentioned, *Half Human*, *The Snow Creature*, and *Man Beast* all contributed, to greater and lesser extent, to many of the tenets of the genre; but none managed to do so with the same aesthetic completeness of form or box office returns as *The Abominable Snowman*. Hammer's film forever put Yeti on the cinematic map and therefore into the pantheon of great cinema monsters, mainly because it refused to consign itself to exploitation filmmaking and instead aimed for the pin-

This lobby card from *The Abominable Snowman* (1957) depicts the dismissive attitude Dr. John Rollason (Peter Cushing) exhibits towards the Lhama (Arnold Marle), far left. Rollason will come to learn the error of his ways.

nacled peaks of larger, crossover audience success, which it achieved to everlasting impact.

Alas, the bloom was about as long-lasting as the wolf's bane flowering season in the Himalayas — short but spectacular while it lasted. By the early 1960s, the nascent, Yeti-lead rebirth of Ciné du Sasquatch was effectively dead. The era's producers must have reasoned that, minus the audience's curiosity at a new phenomenon, there was no commercial advantage in making pictures about cryptids. Little could they foresee (or probably care, for that matter) that these series of rapidly-shot, one-off films they had all so eagerly created to fill empty theater seats and drive-in parking lots would sustain themselves beyond this first great brush with widespread audience appeal to become an entire genre unto themselves. And, in doing so, become a part of film's unique ability to record dramatically-rendered folklore for all time to follow.

It was as if the cameras had magically filmed the Himalayan culture's mythic folklore, which formerly had only been accounted for in either spoken or written legend. This transformation into popular cinema, however, made such cultural touchstones universally accessible to all; the limitations of the spoken word were transcended by the barrier-smashing power of cinema, as a picture knows no boundaries. An oral and written regional history had become, for better or worse, a cinematic one and therefore a worldwide, transcendental one as well.

Peace and Revolution: The Cryptid 1960s

Though there were a few Yeti cameos throughout the early half of the 1960s, the national zeitgeist seemed to have turned away from exotic beasts in foreign lands and inwards toward domestic issues and social unease at home. A good example is George Pal's entertaining *The 7 Faces of Dr. Lao* (1964), in which an Abominable Snowman makes an extended cameo as one of the traveling circus' odd attractions. Even by this point the Yeti is played mostly for laughs, even if its creepy appearance offers the startled town's occupants a truer reflection of their own hideous, masked inner hate than they would like to admit. But it's worth noting that even though the treatment of the shy cryptid in *The 7 Faces of Dr. Lao* is largely comical, it nonetheless maintains the themes present throughout the genre. To wit: the creature is without real malice towards humans, but humans look down upon the beast, unable to see that it is really just a mask worn by a doppelganger of themselves. As they jeer and gawk, they never see the mirror the creature represents as their worst impulses to oppress everything they feel is beneath themselves. A more crystallized illustration of this underlying tenet so ably distilled would be difficult to find at this point in the genre.

But with the assassination of John F. Kennedy, ensuing civil rights struggles, and a world focus on a space race to the Moon, film producers turned for the most part from the former cinema icon and instead concentrated on social dramas, space flight showstoppers, and alien beings — a natural progression given these flickering images more appropriately reflected the national imagination and nightmares. As if buried in an avalanche of indifference, the Abominable Snowman largely vanished from the silver screen for years during the first three-quarters of the 1960s.

And then Roger Patterson arrived on the scene.

Patterson was an amiable if egocentric Northern Californian rodeo cowboy with a passion for Bigfoot that bordered on a clinical diagnosis worthy of Obsessive/Compulsive Disorder. Devoting nearly all his adult life to finding and photographing Bigfoot, Patterson singlehandedly changed Ciné du Sasquatch forever with his now infamous 16mm, hand-held footage of a supposed female Sasquatch. Glaring as it stridently walks away, the depicted Bigfoot is a barrel-chested, breast-augmented visual shocker. It is at once obviously humanoid, and yet, somehow, uncannily not. Is it the unlikely gait; the penetrating eyes Bigfoot drills into the viewer, bulging in apparent warning; the casual way it looks over its shoulder, as if bemused by being photographed? Not unlike a modern movie clip of the Mona Lisa smile, the film begs all of these questions and many more, and yet answers none.

How a perpetually broke, rodeo-circuit cowboy could achieve such astonishing filmic results as an amateur cinematographer has become the stuff of modern folklore, every bit as revered by Ciné du Sasquatch viewers as the depicted creature itself. The debates swirled then and now, fueling an initial media sensation that has never truly diminished. Was it real or a hoax? Soon the buzz cut across the divided culture lines of Americans everywhere until few who owned a television set in the era hadn't seen it at least once, if not multiple times. The legit press and tabloid attention was even more staggering in its bombastic coverage. It was during this critical period that trend-spotting producers realized the dormant genre of Ciné du Sasquatch was ready for an exploitation rebirth.

The enticements to such producers from a financial risk perspective alone probably appeared irresistible. Given their incredible economic restraints as independent creators outside the well-financed Hollywood mainstream (which, conversely, made them dependent upon releasing what the major studios would not touch to fill the product gap), any subject matter that was pre-established and currently being hyped was always sought after in order to ride the wave of free publicity and help insure their fast-buck mentality would generate profits. The more a story was prone to appear in headlines, the more exploitable the films would be (akin to today's endless cable movies based on "real-life stories" fictionalizing actual, well-publicized cases of domestic abuse, spousal homicide, etc.). Whereas large-scale newspapers and television stations were constrained by their respective shareholders and the Federal Communications Commission decency restrictions, men's tabloid adventure magazines featuring a lurid mixture of fact and fiction, as well as drive-in movie theaters eager to offer an alternative to safer studio fare, were free and eager to exploit the ongoing Bigfoot craze in any creative way they imagined, as long as it made money for all concerned.

Whether or not the Patterson-Gimlin film (co-named after Bob Gimlin, Patterson's companion on the fateful day) is legitimate or not is beyond this volume's range and intent. From a purely cinematic perspective, however, the footage warrants inclusion for its cultural impact on the Ciné du Sasquatch genre. No matter one's opinion about its authenticity or lack thereof, Patterson as a *filmmaker* achieves a considerable feat: He filmicly captures his subject as the single most believable incarnation of a Bigfoot in screen history.

Consider the paradox: On the one hand the footage is real, and Patterson alone, against all odds, has filmed a Sasquatch when all others have failed, just as he bragged to friends he would do. On the other hand, the footage is fake, and an inexperienced filmmaker has crafted such a believable rendering of Sasquatch that it generates unfounded rumors for years that only a top-notch Hollywood special effects artist of the era (such as John Chambers, famous for his breakthrough *Planet of the Apes* make-up) could have possibly fashioned such a convincing suit worn by Patterson's depicted hominid (a charge that Chambers strenuously denied to his dying day). And Patterson films the shaggy forest demon in broad daylight and in long takes without cutaways, neither of which favors fakery.

It is very easy to overlook the significance of his genre-altering contribution, particularly in the age of computer-generated imagery and because of the "Is it real?" debate which forever engulfs the footage. But set aside prejudices in either camp and what is left is a 53-second cinema verite masterpiece. The Patterson-Gimlin footage forever raised the bar for subsequent depictions of Bigfoot, even in clearly fictionalized Ciné du Sasquatch entries. Simply stated, the film's unique ability to stun most viewers into believing that what they were witnessing was horrific and *possibly* an authentic cryptid specimen had never been previously achieved by any Ciné du Sasquatch filmmaker. Gone were the days when a cheesy-looking gorilla costume would suffice for any future cryptid films, as audiences were thereafter conditioned to accept the Patterson footage as *the* reference point for any visualization of said species, mythic or real. Producers slow to realize this, and mistakenly believing their audiences would accept such compromises as shoddy suits, were met with unfortunate howls of laughter as soon as their chintzy, seam-showing Sasquatch ambled across the movie screens post–Patterson. Not that the sleazier producers wouldn't try to pass off their low-rent sideshow simian costumes for lack of said insight or indifferent disdain for their audiences (indeed, many such low-rent productions continue to do so to this very day), but their contempt was thereafter self-revealing and doomed their efforts to true fans of the genre as fodder for mockery.

Whether what Patterson filmed that fateful day of October 20, 1967, was merely a chance moment of captured synchronicity between man and cryptid, or a carefully-staged, one-minute choreography of Bigfoot ballet, the authenticity arguments rage on, even as Patterson's short survives to enthrall each new generation of rapt viewers. In this regard, it is a kind of cryptozoological version of the Zapruder film, endlessly studied by avid skeptics and believers alike for tell-tale clues hidden in 952 frames of 16mm Kodachrome motion picture film stock. The key point, however, is not whether Patterson staged the event or not, as we, in all probability, will never know (despite many convincing arguments, investigations, and frame-by-frame studies made of it). In so many ways the inquiry is akin to a religious or philosophical debate — as sure to enrage the believers on either end of the spectrum as it is to divide the opinions of interested listeners.

What is indisputable is that Patterson's movie took the Ciné du Sasquatch genre from a land far away and placed it in the familiar settings of rural Americana. No longer was the beast to be found only in Nepal, and only by a select few hardy enough to venture to the literal ceiling tops of the world. Now, with luck and persistence, the North American version of the Abominable Snowman was as close as one's local forest preserve. In changing the face, color, and locale, Patterson established Bigfoot as an All-American legend every bit as tall as Paul Bunyan, whether or not the tales of his encounter where just that — tall tales.

Ciné du Sasquatch would never be the same.

Indeed, the effects on the genre quickly migrated into viewers' homes via television programming. Three examples, besides the endless reality speculation TV format segments in which the Patterson footage was shown while real-life witnesses to Bigfoot were interviewed, were the science fiction fan favorites *Dr. Who*, *Star Trek*, and *Lost in Space*.

Dr. Who is the unparalleled British equivalent of America's own Superman character in terms of popularity, and almost as long-lived. The fictionalized exploits of the time-traveling Time Lord have spanned the gamut of English media, from live radio dramas, early live television, feature films, comic books, spin-off novels, and even a recent remake television series. Though his list of enemies is long — including the dreaded robotic Daleks as perhaps the most infamous — it was the introduction of the Abominable Snowman one evening on September 30, 1967, in a serialized format known as "The Web of Fear" that makes *Dr.*

Who's inclusion in this reference noteworthy. The limited nature of the show's special effects budget make the rotund, semi-comical appearance of the Yetis questionable by today's standards; but what the series lacked in money, it typically strove to overcome with intriguing plots and unexpected narrative twists. "The Web of Fear" was no exception, and besides being a continuation of the groundbreaking use of a Yeti already accomplished by the British in the earlier *The Creature*, this particularly well-developed serial actually preceded the American idea of having Bigfoot turn out to be a robotic creature in the 1970s hit television program *The Six Million Dollar Man* by almost a decade. Dr. Who and his associates discover that the Yetis are actually cybernetic organisms being controlled by a vast, formless evil known only as the Great Intelligence. The Yetis were so popular with the show's loyal fans that they returned in future episodes of the series.

As for the American counterpart *Star Trek*, space cryptids made memorable appearances in two well-liked episodes during the series' initial run — "The Galileo Seven" and "A Private Little War." Indeed, in both "The Galileo Seven" (1967) and "A Private Little War" (1968) episodes a "Star-squatch" was prominently featured. One show even aired prior to Patterson's footage being recorded. "A Private Little War" features the Yeti-like Mugato, a variation on the Abominable Snowman, with white fur and simian-like appearance, but with some key additions to make it less obvious, such as a horn, spinal fins, and a long, reptilian tail.

Likewise, the campy *Lost in Space* features so many variations on hairy space hominids that it becomes nearly impossible to sort them all, at least in terms of any significant impact on the Bigfoot genre. Just a few of the shows featuring hairy galactic cryptids were "One of Our Dogs Is Missing" (1965), "The Space Croppers" (1966), and "The Keepers" (1966), though there were many others. This plethora of space ape appearances can be largely attributed to series producer Irwin Allen, who was notoriously reluctant to spend money on the show. As a result, the special effects technicians were often called upon to recycle existing creature costumes, making only slight modifications. Because Allen drew heavily from a work pool of talented young make-up effects artists employed by Hollywood special costume effects legend John Chambers, and because Chambers, in fact, constructed the initial cryptid suit upon which the endless variations were made by his protégés, it is difficult to attribute the precise origin of the show's many hominid creatures with clarity. Suffice it to say, the Emmy and Academy Award–winning Chambers was a major contributor in shaping the cinematic and televised look of cryptids throughout the 1960s and beyond.

This may account for why so many in the skeptic's corner of the debate re: Patterson's film believed John Chambers was a key player, despite his denials; as special effects contributor for the original *Star Trek* series, Chambers had actually designed very convincing cryptid suits prior to Patterson's astonishing footage ever coming to light. Given Chambers' proclivity for simian make-ups demonstrated herein, as well as in the *Planet of the Apes* series of films, this theory is not without supporters. Key among these believers was director John Landis (*Animal*

House, *The Blues Brothers*), who stated in interviews that the elderly make-up artist admitted his assistance to Patterson in crafting the Bluff Creek cryptid costume. Others in the Hollywood film community perhaps even more qualified to comment who've at various times stated their belief the Patterson footage features a costumed actor include such special effects gurus as John Vulich (*Babylon 5*), Tom Burman (*Close Encounters of the Third Kind*), Rick Baker (*Gorillas in the Mist*), and Dave Kindlon (*That Darn Cat* remake). But again, this ultimately leads one into the circular debate re: the Patterson-Gimlin film itself, and therefore loses its relevance to the genre beyond an admittedly intriguing sideshow footnote.

Less argumentative in terms of John Chambers' influence on Ciné du Sasquatch is his make-up for the aforementioned *Planet of the Apes*, *Beneath the Planet of the Apes*, and the three other sequels that followed (not to mention a short-lived television show in the 1970s). Chambers not only crafted incredibly realistic-looking simian cryptids (for despite their antecedents in biological history, the title players in *Planet of the Apes* are actually future links as opposed to missing links, and therefore an unknown, if fictitious, crypto-species), he also invented the use of foam rubber facial appliances as opposed to wax and

The stark realism John Chambers achieved with his groundbreaking make-up effects for the *Planet of the Apes* films would forever alter the possibilities of visualizing cinematic hominids (1968).

plastic prosthetics. These allowed the actors, such as Roddy McDowell and Kim Novak, to more flexibly perform without discomfort and helped prevent the adhesive-backed appliances from peeling off the actors' faces as rapidly as preceding make-up technologies. This special effects advancement provided future Ciné du Sasquatch filmmakers with yet another impressive tool with which to create more convincing looking creatures, particularly in any close-ups involving a Bigfoot. This influence continues to this very day, as even CGI-produced, digital cryptids almost invariably co-feature a latex-faced creature for close-ups and location photography.

The entire cycle of *Planet of the Apes* movies had an indirect though tangible impact on Ciné du Sasquatch as well. In essence, not unlike the Tarzan mythos in earlier times, combined with the cinematic influence of *King Kong*, the large-scale attention garnered by the Patterson film in combination with the enormous commercial success of *Planet of the Apes* made the Ciné du Sasquatch genre ripe for its greatest exploitation ever. For it didn't take producers and directors long to realize that if the intelligent cryptids of a future Earth, such as the ones featured in *Planet of the Apes*, were dominating the box office by decade's end, then why wouldn't a present-day cryptid species attract audiences as well? After all, Patterson's 16mm film apparently cost little-to-nothing to produce and was reaping serious money as a self-touring documentary peddled by Patterson's father-in-law throughout the Pacific Northwest to rented movie theaters, auditoriums, and even the occasional church — wherever the astute profiteer could find an affordable locale and set up his portable projector. Padded out to 50 minutes with additional interview footage from a BBC documentary and retitled *Bigfoot: America's Abominable Snowman*, the self-produced effort was screened to often overflowing crowds, with Patterson (alas in failing health but still game) speaking afterward to appreciative fans. If a rodeo cowboy could do it, and 20th Century-Fox film studios could do it, then surely there was room in-between the extremes for smartly-budgeted fare in the same vein?

And thus the stage (or, more accurately, silver screen) was set for the most lucrative, and therefore decisive, decade of Ciné du Sasquatch to date: the 1970s.

Disco Bigfoot: The 1970s

As the early 1970s explosion of grindhouse and drive-in fodder continued to take advantage of the relaxation of ratings restrictions in terms of sexual and violent content that the studios would rarely touch for fear of government or religious backlash, it was merely a matter of time before independent producers began peddling new Bigfoot films. Ciné du Sasquatch as a genre offered several especially alluring prospective hooks for canny filmmakers over the previous Yeti cycle of the 1950s. It was a home-grown product of American folklore, originating in the very rural regions where not only the sightings and legends originated, but where low-budget filmic adaptations could play to local rural audiences. While Hollywood studio executives scratched their heads in bewilderment and wondered how such low-budget, non-star schlock could rake in millions, regional filmmakers followed in Patterson's canny footsteps and launched Sasquatch movies of their own, often tinged with a local variant to help their movies stand out in the crowded exploitation marketplace.

The earliest attempt of the decade however, was the rank epitome of how *not* to go about the process. *Bigfoot* (1970) made all the classic mistakes the earlier Abominable Snowman films that had not learned the lessons of *Half Human* and *The Abominable Snowman* had taught: Without a script, decent production values, and — most importantly — an intelligent approach to the subject matter, Ciné du Sasquatch is an unforgiving genre indeed. Replete with unconvincing ape-like costumes, horrendous non-direction, and a ridiculous plot, *Bigfoot* squandered every chance for generating suspense for the sake of bad cornpone humor and leftover hippie protest anger at the Man. The endless shots of a purported biker gang in the film's advertising turned out to be a rather tepid assembly of bored teens dressed in flower power garb riding dirt bikes and motor scooters. It was hardly the Hell's Angels versus a Kong-sized Bigfoot scenario promised to gullible audiences. The producers even went so far as to state, "Not Since *King Kong*!" on the shoddy if amusing poster in an attempt to (falsely) align themselves with the progenitor of so much of what would become Ciné du Sasquatch. And by having a scantily-clad blonde woman captured by the tallest Bigfoot early in the movie for purposes of reproduction, the implied bestiality of *King Kong* has progressively become explicit, reflecting the slackening moral restraints of the liberated 1970s-era films.

In startling contrast to the epic failure of *Bigfoot*, which featured an all-star cast of has-beens and celebrity offspring (the latter of whose names presumably helped market the film), was Charles Pierce's *The Legend of Boggy Creek* (1972), which followed less than two years later. Pierce had spent a few years working in the exploitation ranks of the Corman factory in the late 1960s in California (often as a production designer) when he hit upon the concept of taking a local legend from his rural Arkansas hometown of Fouke and transforming it into a low-budget feature that he could then self-release to drive-ins and rural theaters.

Pierce's insight was not merely in terms of what audiences craved regarding the next evolution of Ciné du Sasquatch, but, more importantly, how to cinematically stage such a vision without compromising as badly as had *Bigfoot*. Rather than spending what little money he had on has-been actors, he committed to using free local talent. Given how little film production work had been done in Arkansas at that point from which he could draw on experienced actors, it was a bold if not outright risky strategy. As a result, Pierce decided to abandon a traditional narrative structure in which a fictionalized story is performed by highly-skilled professionals and instead concentrate his energies on crafting a pseudo-documentary tone in which the Fouke locals basically portrayed themselves in staged recreations of their supposed encounters with the beast. And rather than build an unconvincing ape suit upon which to focus (and no doubt prompt audience laughter), he devised a series of carefully-staged shocks and suspense sequences in which the creature is never fully seen with any clarity. This presence hovering just out of frame became a Charles Pierce stylistic trademark in later, more polished efforts, such as *The Town That Dreaded Sundown* and *The Evictors*. In this regard, it was as if Pierce had taken the lesson offered by *The Abominable Snowman* (that less shown is more) and transferred it to the bayou swamps — to great success.

In today's super-saturation of so-called reality TV, the impact of what Pierce did is easy to miss. Like the best of postmodern-tinged, deliberately self-reflexive films, *The Legend of Boggy Creek* calls attention to itself from the opening sequence. Pierce plays himself, standing in the ruins of his modest childhood home, and reflects on his earliest memory of the howls of the creature as he would cut across the swampy fields, hurrying to get home before sunset. Before the viewer realizes it, Pierce has segued into a flashback of himself as that very boy, racing headlong towards the safety of his home, only to become entangled in a barbed wire fence even as the so-called Fouke Monster screams from the darkening woods. Next, Pierce pulls the viewer back to the present, and, in a good-natured, deliberately deceptive manner, presents the little town in the kind of harmless light one might find in a civic council–funded travelogue promoting the city: a place where folks raise their kids, work hard, and worry about little if anything ... *until the sun goes down*, the narrator darkly intones. It is this very complex manner in which Pierce blends such cinematic techniques and forms as cinema verite, pseudo-documentary and dramatic narrative that makes *The Legend of Boggy Creek* such a milestone in the genre's development. It broke the existing genre rules and then put them back together in such a manner that made the *oeuvre* raw and urgent. By abandoning the artifice of Hollywood filmmaking norms that even the best of earlier Ciné du Sasquatch entries had mastered, and instead focusing on crafting a dense, multi-layered "you are there" tone, Pierce wisely utilized his best skills to create a largely effective bayou boogeyman shocker.

The terrible masks from *Bigfoot* (1970) relegate the effort to camp status the moment they first appear early on in the film.

Charles Pierce was as much a by-product of his era as any filmmaker, and the direct influences of the 1960s counterculture aesthetics on *Boggy Creek* are profound. For example, the do-it-yourself attitude of John Cassevettes' body of independent work is reflected in the manner in which Pierce approached the filmmaking — directing, writing, acting, and even shooting the movie himself. Likewise, the hand-held feeling of intimacy created by such French New Wave films as *Breathless* and *The 400 Blows* is incorporated to lend authenticity to the potentially unbelievable nature of the subject matter. And the commercial success of such regionally-lensed films as *Easy Rider* and *Billy Jack* showed that audiences were hungry for movies that took place outside the boundaries of the Hollywood/Los Angeles paradigm and locales. Too, the use of location-friendly equipment and faster film stock (requiring less lighting even in remote locations), which had given freedom to independent filmmakers on the West and East Coasts, likely influenced Pierce's impromptu decision to go it alone and create his early and only genuine masterpiece (though many appreciate his psycho killer movie *The Town That Dreaded Sundown*, a probable influence, along with *Black Christmas*, on John Carpenter's *Halloween*).

If, as a rule of thumb, Hollywood studios simply make retreads of the latest box office smashes produced by their rivals, then it may be similarly stated that exploitation filmmakers endlessly remake whatever their independent colleagues find works as a temporary formula for success. So when Pierce's amiable effort went on to gross tens of millions of dollars without any studio distribution mechanism behind the effort (and in an era when many big-budgeted and heavily-advertised Hollywood films didn't gross nearly as much), envious exploitation producers suddenly smelled big profits in making Bigfoot motion pictures. As it was evident Charles Pierce had not invested in professional actors, studio sets, or expensive special effects, these same producers likely reasoned the same recipe would work for their own knock-off versions set in similar locales but with marginally different cryptozoological hominids.

Consequently, as soon as Pierce's grosses were published in the various Hollywood trade papers (such as *Variety* and *The Hollywood Reporter*), the predictable onslaught of backwoods imitators followed "suit." Just a few of the feature films *The Legend of Boggy Creek* inspired include: Ivan Marx's *The Legend of Bigfoot* (1976); *Creature from Black Lake* (1976); *Sasquatch, The Legend of Bigfoot* (1977); *Revenge of Bigfoot* (1979); and *The Capture of Bigfoot* (1979); not to mention two sequels to the *Boggy Creek* franchise itself — *Return to Boggy Creek* (1977) and *The Barbaric Beast of Boggy Creek* (1985). No longer finding it necessary to even purchase stock footage of snowy Himalayan mountains in order to create a Yeti picture, and instead liberated to shoot (like the Patterson-Gimlin film) their Bigfoot epics in inexpensive, right-to-work (i.e. non-union) states and without royalties to be paid to owners of any copyrighted monster (as Bigfoot is a public domain character of folklore and therefore impossible to trademark as an icon), the bonanza of Ciné du Sasquatch entries that filled cheap production slates throughout the 1970s is no mystery. It would have been more puzzling, in retrospect, had there not been so many dashing into theaters,

given the lucrative returns these minor-budgeted films were generating.

In terms of television, the 1970s were no less influential for Sasquatch offerings. In the modern era of on-demand entertainment, YouTube, and digital video recorders, however, it is hard to recall that there was once a time when if one missed the original airing of a televised show, one had essentially missed the best chance of ever seeing said content. Of course, networks and local stations did run repeats of popular programs, but in a pre-videocassette recorder age, the average viewer had only a hit-and-miss ability to see desired content with any assurance. This must be factored into the assessment of why the 1970s were instrumental in the genre's development. Instead of on-demand, there was a pent-up demand, so to speak. Fans of certain actors or subject matter followed each piece of fan gossip in tabloids and magazines, hoping to glean information now readily (perhaps *too* readily) available on-line. Hence the intense devotion that emerged among Sasquatch aficionados during the 1970s, when the explosion of content generated enormous anticipation for each new televised offering for fear it would never be seen again if missed the first time around.

A perfect example, and one integral to the television contribution to Ciné du Sasquatch, was the syndicated hit *In Search Of*, starring Leonard Nimoy. Building on his already well-known and admired portrayal of Mr. Spock from *Star Trek*, Nimoy hosted and narrated each weekly episode, which focused on a different Fortean-styled topic. With his uncannily dead-pan delivery and the show's hallmark penchant for asking luridly unanswerable, conditionally-based questions over scientifically skeptical ones — "*Could* these hairy, bipedal creatures still be abducting human children to this very day...?" — *In Search Of* was a forerunner of today's abundance of Discovery Channel pseudo-documentaries which frequently (though not always) favor belief over skepticism.

Not only did *In Search Of* play well to markets nationwide, it offered a dynamic, well-scored montage title sequence which was very characteristic of its production era: moving blocks of colors; Saul Bass–like font design; sliding transitions; et al. More critically, the memorable opening narration ("Join us now as we go ... in search of...") played atop a few seconds of Patterson's footage, in addition to the usual plethora of fuzzy UFO pictures, ghostly spectral images, and Loch Ness Monster photographs. For the first time, Bigfoot enthusiasts could see the infamous 16mm Patterson-Gimlin footage weekly (and even more frequently, depending upon their local station's programming, as episodes were often run back-to-back). Prior to this halcyon moment, one had to have caught the Bluff Creek Bigfoot on a random television special or newscast about the creature. Because of the systematic repeat use of the Patterson Bigfoot imagery, the footage took on a life of its own and became a defining depiction of the world's most famous cryptid.

Again, it is easy to forget (with today's instant access abilities re: media), but this nascent ability to see the footage with dependable regularity once a week — albeit in a highly-truncated clip of the Patterson creature glancing back over its shoulder at the viewer — was significant in terms of the genre. It provided even the most economically-challenged armchair cryptid cinema fan with the first-ever chance to study the footage with successive viewings (even if spaced apart in time, often by a week or more). And with its wild, synthesized soundtrack playing over the barrage of images of various unexplained phenomena, *In Search Of* catered to and gratefully supplied a whole range of enthusiasts with the first show of its kind dedicated exclusively to their interests (with topics clearly off the grid in terms of normal mainstream fare).

The next significant leap in Bigfoot television appearances was literally bionic in measure — both in ratings by the viewing public and cryptid interior design. The two-part showdown between *The Six Million Dollar Man* (the space shuttle astronaut "barely left alive" until rebuilt by NASA engineers with bionic parts) and Bigfoot (played by 6-foot, 11-inch pro wrestler Andre the Giant wearing white, glowing contact lens) aired in a February 1976 episode entitled "The Secret of Bigfoot." To say it was a major success would be akin to stating Andre the Giant was tall. What Charles Pierce's *The Legend of Boggy Creek* had done for films of the genre, *The Six Million Dollar Man* did for televised Sasquatch. To wit, it launched a mini-franchise within the series, with Bigfoot returning not only to this show, but to its spin-off hit *The Bionic Woman* as well. Additionally, there was a merchandising bonanza featuring action figures and comic book appearances. Indeed, so popular are the memories of those who grew up watching this phenomenal, if not seminal, television event that the Bionic Bigfoot action figure in mint condition in the original box routinely sells for over $100 on eBay, and often for much higher.

Sasquatch's implied strength had never been in much doubt prior to these historic shows being aired, but *The Six Million Dollar Man*'s super-powered cryptid was positively Herculean in its abilities. Not only could Bionic Bigfoot leap tall cabins with a single bound, it also could toss huge boulders and logs without breaking stride. And in an echo of the earlier Abominable Snowmen who turned out to be androids in the 1960s episodes of *Dr. Who*, Bionic Bigfoot was revealed to be a beast built by aliens intent on destroying the Earth with artificially-induced earthquakes. The highlights of "The Secret of Bigfoot" (said secret being its alien bionic origins) were the fight scenes themselves, creatively staged in slow-motion and with the ever-present sound effect that signified the cybernetic strength of each combatant (often used in parodies now to denote unexpected powers in protagonists because of its ubiquitous cultural impact). Bigfoot, bionic or otherwise, had become a household name and every bit a Warhol-styled superstar.

The results were not confined only to prime time and syndication, either. Television masters Sid and Marty Krofft (producers of such popular Saturday morning series as *H.R. Puf n' Stuf* and *Lidsville*) recognized a good thing when they saw it. If *The Six Million Dollar Man* could earn big ratings and generate lucrative merchandising royalties by featuring a leisure-suited Lee Majors fighting a bionic Bigfoot (shot in inexpensive Griffith Park locales), why not a Saturday morning knock-off featuring an orphaned boy teaming up with their own version of a Bigfoot (also shot in the same inexpensive Griffith Park locales)?

Thus *Bigfoot and Wildboy* (1977) sprung into the tyke television lexicon when the prodigious Kroffts premiered it one fateful weekend morning as part of their 90-minute series *The Krofft Supershow*. "Sprung" is an appropriate word choice, as the Krofft's super-powered Sasquatch made the Bionic Man's Bigfoot abilities pale in comparison. As Wildboy watched in wonder, Bigfoot would hurl himself airborne without effort, often traversing an acre or more with a single bound. No earthly explanation was ever given for this spectacular talent. All Bigfoot needed was a cape, and part-time membership in any superhero league would have been assured.

Though the so-called crime-fighting angle was played for maximum effect in *Bigfoot and Wildboy*, deeper beneath its cliché-riddled stories were buried two remarkable anticipations in regards to Ciné du Sasquatch and Television. First, *Bigfoot and Wildboy* made explicit the underlying archetype of the Tarzan mythos so prevalent throughout the genre's history. Instead of Africa and an English infant being the only survivor of a plane crash that took the lives of his parents (as in *Tarzan*), *Bigfoot and Wildboy* had an American infant being the only survivor of a plane crash that took the lives of his parents in Northern California's redwoods. Secondly, the series reinforced the notion of Bigfoot as a symbolic, kid-friendly protector of the pristine wilderness, a noble character trait which a decade later would surface even more prominently in *Harry and the Hendersons*.

Though *Bigfoot and Wildboy* was critically lambasted, as were most of the Krofft's offerings in their debut era, the young audiences who watched them were not swayed by reviews but by the shows themselves. And while *Bigfoot and Wildboy* wasn't the ratings hit that other shows by the Krofft Brothers became (such as *H. R. Puf'n'Stuf* and *Land of the Lost*), it nonetheless lay the groundwork for the radicalized, non-threatening, family-styled version of the cinema cryptid that would commercially cleave the Ciné du Sasquatch genre in neat halves in the decades that followed.

As the 1970s closed, there was little doubt that Sasquatch was a "cash crop," at least in terms of expenditure-to-profit ratios. Hence the 1970s' huge influence on Ciné du Sasquatch, in which Bigfoot replaced the Yeti as the cinematic cryptid of choice for low-budget feature film and ratings-savvy television producers. From this point forward in the genre, the Abominable Snowman would forever play "second banana" to the more famous Bigfoot, both in terms of sheer output of films and shows, and monies made exploiting the genre.

Hibernation Until the VCR Thaw: The 1980s

As entertaining and diverse as many of the 1970s-era Ciné du Sasquatch films and television episodes were, they followed the same temporary destiny as their earlier Yeti screen cousins: virtual extinction by the close of the 1970s. While a cinematic rebirth happened, it wouldn't actually occur until the advent of widespread home video use in the early 1980s, at which point the floodgates were opened for the genre's re-emergence, owing to the large number of titles suddenly dumped onto the nascent "anything goes" frontier mentality of the emerging home video rental market.

Though dedicated film collectors had been willing to pay thousands of dollars for early home video recording machines, plus as much as $100 each for the first wave of VHS and Betamax titles, it was not until the adult video market established a lower per-videocassette player rate (via sheer consumer volume of sales) that virtually every household in America could afford at least a basic VCR. Video stores came into existence overnight, and soon every city and small town across the country had at least one local purveyor of videos for rent. The novel concept of renting a formerly ephemeral experience — a motion picture once confined only to the theater or small television screen — and forever being able to repeatedly view it revolutionized movie distribution, both for better and worse.

The studios of the era made a critical early miscalculation. Rather than help decide who would define the emerging market with product fulfillment, they held back their vast libraries of films, fearing profit losses via piracy. The vacuum thus created by the major studios allowed the independent filmmakers to re-release their backlog of often dated films (many re-titled to seem like new product, with new cover art to entice unwary viewers). It also created a huge window for upstart or independent video production, in that the prohibitive costs of theatrical distribution fell by the wayside for producers efficient enough to produce exploitable titles that went directly to the home video market. This allowed the filmmakers to forgo the costs of shooting, processing, and post-producing the expensive 35mm film stocks associated with a majority of theatrical releases. As a result, 16mm, broadcast videotape, and even Super 8mm were viewed as professionally acceptable production formats if the intent was to bypass the theaters and release the film exclusively on home video. This was largely a reflection of the videocassette format itself, which, while technically a breakthrough in its time, offered very little visual information per horizontal line compared to more robust, modern replacements (such as a Blu-Ray DVD as seen on a High Definition monitor).

Equally if not more important to these early home video–driven releases' ability to be produced cheaply was their lack of any MPAA ratings requirements. As video stores in the 1980s stocked both rated and unrated fare, much of the allure of what the uncensored videos offered was a Grand Guignol sensibility. Sex and violence were preferred by hungry video rental audiences because the exploitation titles offered precisely what the increasingly conservative Hollywood product refused to provide — an alternative. The theatrical business in the 1980s had grown increasingly conservative due to both a political reaction to the emergence of the Reagan Revolution and the multiplex mentality of not booking any "objectionable content" (in order to avoid worry about backlash from conservative groups). As long as the movies the studios released didn't offend the masses, so the reasoning apparently went, the small-time video rental stores could remain unregulated as to what subject matter they offered consumers to watch in the privacy of their own homes.

This Puritanical undercurrent that ran throughout the 1980s opened the window even wider for shock filmmakers willing to douse their casts in red-dyed Karo syrup and/or convince their female cast members to hurriedly disrobe at the first sound of danger in a dark forest. Few indeed were the direct-to-video releases of this time period that didn't feature at least some gore and softcore skin exposure as a guarantee of being released to the growing market; many were the older, less graphic movies that were re-edited with newly-shot footage of nudity and mutilation added to their running lengths so that the box art could feature said content. While few would argue that many of these efforts were little more than a race to the bottom in terms of quality viewing experience, at least some of the efforts seemed self-consciously aware of their crudity (a good example was the output of tiny Troma Studios, creators of the infamous *The Toxic Avenger* series) and therefore appealed to viewers for their sheer camp sensibility, if (often) nothing else. There was a slightly risqué feeling to the entire affair in the halcyon days of home video in the 1980s, as the rules of the game were being established in an unprecedented business model, both in terms of supply and demand. As long as units were sold to the video stores, and said units were in turn rented by the end consumer, there were no clear boundaries between what was "acceptable" and what was in "poor taste" — to the evident satisfaction of both producers willing to forgo modesty and viewers willing to take chances with even the most egregious of exploitable titles and subject matters.

Into this void where the Motion Picture Association of America held no sway (as the market was never formally regulated — and still isn't, beyond whatever the stores themselves are willing to impose upon their selections) crept many a Bigfoot and Yeti film, both old and new. Existing fans of Ciné du Sasquatch were delighted to find many of the classics and not-so-classics they'd enjoyed previously in theaters and drive-ins available for rental or ownership via videocassette. And a whole new generation of fans was exposed for the first time to a range of Ciné du Sasquatch entries, acquiring a taste for the often salacious offerings that would sow seeds later reaped in the DVD decades to follow. Unhinged and unrated, some of these films were so over-the-top in their graphic depictions of violence and cryptid bloodletting they created a new hybrid: the so-called Savage Sasquatch sub-genre, in which Bigfoot becomes a murderous monster beyond any redemption in the audience's eyes (unless they're relatives of the Marquis de Sade).

Perhaps no release during this time better illustrates the best and worst qualities of this newfound barbarity than one prototypical effort, the independently-lensed *Night of the Demon* (1980) — not to be confused with the excellent *Night of the Demon* (1957) directed by Jacques Tourneur, nor the *Night of the Demons* (1988) directed by Kevin Tenney. Made on a tiny budget by director James C. Wasson and filmed in Michigan's woodlands, the nominal plot concerns one Professor Nugent (an obvious reference to Detroit hometown favorite rocker legend Ted Nugent) who embarks upon a deep-woods exploration in search of Bigfoot, accompanied by the usual bevy of college student research assistants.

As they plunge into the dark terrain, the good professor delights in recounting various tales locals have reported in regards to the cryptid in question. None of the stories end without at least one human, if not all involved, meeting gruesomely violent death. Each flashback-rendered mini-story is told with increasing ferocity. Among those killed: two girl scouts who are dispatched via spear and mutilation; an unfortunate lumberjack dispatched with his own ax, limb-by-limb; a camper caught in his sleeping bag who is slung from tree trunk to tree trunk by the enraged beast and slowly beaten to a bloody pulp; and — in the most infamous sequence that lead to the film being banned in the U.K.— a motorcyclist who stops to relieve himself along a highway only to have Bigfoot rip off his genitals!

Though such moments are undoubtedly why *Night of the Demon* received the dreaded "Video Nasty" designation under Prime Minister Thatcher's repressive government (which literally forbade renting or selling select horror film titles — mostly imported American and Italian gore and horror films — and not only threatened but actually jailed several video store owners who refused to go along with the ban), it is worth noting that the filmmaker so overplays such moments that they border on camp. There is no doubt they are offensive by any normal stretch of mainstream filmmaking; but likewise, the Grand Guignol nature of blood-for-blood's-sake overkill mentality is no less blackly comical, provided the viewer is willing to allow for the *Sweeney Todd* sensibility running throughout the production. Whatever one's personal take or taste, the idea of someone imprisoned for viewing or renting it is, in a supposedly free republic, truly more deplorable than any fictionalized screen violence.

If the violence preceding the conclusion of *Night of the Demon* was deemed prurient by the British censorship board, one can only imagine the reaction they had upon viewing the film's non-stop, blood-spattered finale, which echoes *The Wild Bunch*, *Straw Dogs*, *Taxi Driver*, and *Rolling Thunder* for sheer excessiveness. It is staged as a crimson-soaked variation on the classic siege film, but condensed into one mesmerizing, prolonged kinetic ballet of death. To say it is memorable or objectionable depends entirely upon one's point of view, which is why the film outrages as many Ciné du Sasquatch devotees as it does satisfy others. For those who view the creature as a pacifist, a misunderstood missing link only concerned with its own meager survival, the portrayal is sorely lacking, to say the very least. For those who view the creature as a potentially savage monster, the portrayal captures more than any other in the genre's history the brute force such a powerful cryptid would be capable of inflicting on any puny humans if and when it cared to be so violently transgressive (and without the over-the-shoulder presence of Hollywood's self-censoring ratings patrol to hold back on the onscreen mayhem in graphic detail).

The finale begins with the surviving handful of students and professor stranded at a remote cabin à la *The Evil Dead* and trying to keep the attacking Sasquatch on the other side of their rapidly disappearing cabin door. Normally, a central if non-verbalized rule of horror films of this type is that sheer numbers equal, if not safety, then assurance of survival. Until and if a victim splits from the group, in essence, and walks away alone in the darkness, he or she will be spared a gruesome death scene.

Night of the Demon shatters this convention with devastating impact. The enraged cryptid blasts through the cabin doorway and begins picking off the survivors one-by-one in slow motion (reminiscent of *The Six Million Dollar Man* as if it had been directed by Sam Peckinpah). The other students and professor desperately try to help whomever among them is next in line to be attacked; but like an unrelenting grizzly bear, the cryptid's overpowering rage renders any action they take hopelessly ineffective and contributory to each would-be rescuer's own resultant death. As if the sheer brutality of watching so many main characters die so horrifically in a matter of minutes weren't enough, the director also shoots the entire scene in a small, confining space of a single room. Each bloody death lingers, slowed to a virtual standstill, a disturbing preview of the next butchered victim to come, until only the Professor is left alive — his face having been pressed into a hot stove until it looks like a grilled cheese sandwich — to relate the incredible carnage to disbelieving authorities at the hospital in which he awakens.

But unlike Peckinpah, who used rapid intercutting later popularized by MTV's rock videos, director Wasson holds on medium tight shots without much cutting away. As a result, *Night of the Demon* more closely resembles the ending of the Japanese samurai classic *Sword of Doom*, in which the unconquerable lone wolf warrior takes down an entire cadre of swordsmen inside an equally claustrophobic setting of tiny, bamboo-walled rooms. While many reviewers have rightfully ridiculed *Night of the Demon* for its amateurish acting, bad dialogue, and even shoddy production values (though this reviewer disagrees on the latter critique, given the film's low budget), it retains a sizable following among fans of luridly effective shockers and followers of Ciné du Sasquatch (at least those not minding a blood feast version of their favorite hominid) for the sheer carnage and unexpectedly nightmarish qualities it indisputably if queasily induces in first-time, as well as repeat, viewers.

But if *Night of the Demon* wears the perfect mask of personified evil for the menacing man-killer of the 1980s Ciné du Sasquatch, then surely the trendsetting *Harry and the Hendersons* (1987) is its lighthearted antithesis. A joyous, comical, family-friendly flip side to all that is dark and gruesome in *Night of the Demon*, *Harry and the Hendersons* achieved worldwide success in no small part due to the Spielberg name on the poster (though Spielberg was only an executive producer, as the film was actually directed by William Dear) and its sentimental, pro-environment stance (novel for its era, however timely now). With the Midas touch of the Spielberg name, *Harry and the Hendersons* proved Bigfoot was no longer simply a known commodity but, more importantly, a cinematically legit subject for even the top players in the industry to exploit. Yeti's B-movie-only days were history; Hollywood had finally rolled out the red carpet for America's folkloric forest denizen.

In recasting Sasquatch as a benign, essentially harmless (unless threatened) friendly giant, Spielberg and company craftily removed everything about the mythos and prior screen roles that was dark or overtly scary, and reshaped their hominid as an essentially overgrown house pet in need of adoption. While this theme had been tentatively explored before in *Return to Boggy Creek* and was therefore not entirely novel, *Harry and the Hendersons* removed any doubt as to the creature's benign motivation in regards to humans, whereas *Return to Boggy Creek* played up the Fouke Monster's more ambivalent nature until Nature herself (in the form of a hurricane) forced it to take a stand and rescue the stranded child protagonists.

Furthermore, Harry (as he's nicknamed by the Hendersons for obvious reasons) is a peaceful vegan who reacts with evident disgust to the surrounding suburbanites he encounters upon escaping from the Henderson home. Harry watches aghast as the neighbors thoughtlessly consume dead animals, oblivious to the horrid nature of their act from his point of view. He's equally repulsed by the humans' treatment of dogs, which are kept in cages or leashed into tiny back yards as virtual prisoners. The final straw for Harry comes when he witnesses the lifeless, mounted heads of his forest friends lining the household walls of the hunter-friendly community. For Harry, the human "civilization" is a hellish concrete jungle full of treachery, death and

The top-heavy, bulky nature of the Sasquatch costume is evident in this publicity still of Harry (Kevin Peter Hall) for *Harry and the Hendersons* (1987).

deceit; whereas the Redwoods Harry calls home seem comparatively sane and orderly (provided no vacationing humans slam their cars into him). There he coexists with nature in harmony. It is only man who brings disharmony and death when man intrudes into Harry's domain, and not vice versa. Harry is a true innocent. Only after dealing with humans willing to sacrifice their own well-being to assist him — in contrast to humans desiring to hunt him for sadistic pleasure — does Harry become aware of the dual, complicated nature of mankind which is so different from his own, simpler existence.

The commercial genius of Spielberg's touch is self-evident: Sasquatch has been expertly updated from a scary killing machine into a kindly, cryptid-styled revisualization of *Leave It to Beaver*, the Boomer-beloved 1950s sitcom, with Harry substituting for the Beaver as a middle class, suburban nuclear family member who encounters an endless set of predictable mishaps and lessons painfully learned. This clever adaptation worked so well, in fact, that *Harry and the Hendersons* actually became a successful family sitcom after the box office returns of the feature film were finally counted. This is perhaps a rare case of the prodigy reverting to its previous form through sheer success of imitation, as the series tapped into the *Leave It to Beaver* formula even more overtly than the theatrical version.

The *Harry and the Hendersons* movie also took the already typical theme we have seen throughout the Ciné du Sasquatch genre — that man is the true monster when he encounters the cryptid in the cryptid's domain — and complicated it one step further by portraying Bigfoot as neither mindless nor intellectually cunning (as characterized in so many previous incarnations), but as an idiot savant-squatch. That is, while Harry is never less than remedial intellectually, neither is he a mental giant (especially in comparison to his size!). Much of the film's comedy arises from the contrast between Harry's misunderstanding of what he witnesses in suburbia and the sheer banality of said environment that so many Americans take for granted. Though at times this reduces Harry to a buffoon, the overall effect is to make him childlike and gullible, not idiotic and haphazard. This thematic novelty, while echoing the central tenet of Ciné du Sasquatch in regards to the cryptid's inherent innocence, went one step further in the genre by humanizing its hominid more so than any previous entry in the genre since the moving ending of the 1950s era *The Abominable Snowman*. Rick Baker's amazing facial expressions for Harry, which he and his team rendered in the latex Harry mask via off-screen cable controls (winning him a deserved Academy Award for special makeup effects), brought a level of empathy to the titular star of Ciné du Sasquatch heretofore never achieved. And given the stereotypical nature of many of the human actors' roles as written in the *Harry and the Hendersons* screenplay, it is not a stretch to say that Harry's performance was by far the most multi-dimensional in the film apart from John Lithgow's turn as the head of the Henderson household. The impact upon an entire new generation of young viewers was as profound as Charles Pierce's *The Legend of Boggy Creek* had been nearly two decades earlier.

As this Benign Bigfoot/Savage Sasquatch duality progressed (as it would henceforward) in the genre, it was clear the major by-product of the 1980s was two-fold. One, the era popularized the iconographic cryptid into the fully-fledged media star it remains to this day. Two, Ciné du Sasquatch was now divided into two competing visions of the same namesake creature. One camp favored a sunny, PG-rated version; the other desired bloodthirsty, R-rated thrills. Naturally, die-hard devotees of the genre watched all efforts, from serious to serio-comical. But for general cinema viewers (and, to a lesser extent, television, though cable fare often depicted the aggressive Sasquatch in its showings of the violent Bigfoot films), two distinct depictions were now afoot, so to speak. One favored the more traditional rural values wherein Sasquatch was to be feared as a creature of nature, as embodied by *Night of the Demon*. The other favored a more progressive viewpoint familiar to metropolitan lifestyles wherein Bigfoot was simply a misunderstood bipedal simian to be respected (if from a safe distance), as embodied by *Harry and the Hendersons*.

This is not to say such artificial designations were consciously decided upon by either filmmakers or the viewing public. Rather, as the 1980s gave way to the increasingly politically polarizing 1990s in America, the filmic treatment of Bigfoot began to take on some of the cultural zeitgeist of the surrounding landscape. Whether by osmosis or chance, Ciné du Sasquatch was undergoing the same upheavals and thus reflecting the society in which the movies about the cryptid were produced. As a genre, therefore, it was alive and vital.

Postmodern Bigfoot: Ciné du Sasquatch from the 1990s Through the 2000s

As the two divergent strains in Ciné du Sasquatch cleaved the genre neatly in halves, the initial preference in terms of sheer audience numbers seemed to favor the Spielberg family-style approach over the more traditional monster run amok formula as embodied in *The Legend of Boggy Creek*. This was perhaps less a popularity contest decided by producers and more an astute business realization: It didn't take much monetary difference to make a family-friendly knock-off of *Harry and the Hendersons* over a bayou beastie version, given the rural settings and same basic production methodology. Since both styles were cost-effective to produce, why not capitalize upon Spielberg's success and release carbon copies of kiddy cryptic fare?

Therefore the 1990s saw a rush to emulate *Harry and the Hendersons*' box office grosses, resulting in such entries as *Bigfoot: The Unforgettable Encounter* (1994), *Little Bigfoot 1* (1997), and *Little Bigfoot 2: The Journey Home* (1997), all "aping" the basic formula. These lower-budgeted family films stayed firmly within the mythic paradigm of the genre: man's inhumanity made manifest when he ventures into the shadowy woods Bigfoot calls home. Most featured a kid who, through accident or kismet, became stranded in the woods and had to rely upon Sasquatch (or its offspring) to rescue them and lead them to safety. So whereas the earlier prototype plot for adult versions of the genre typically involved hunters, campers, and others unlucky enough to encounter an angry, territorial hominid, the family film variation typically utilized Bigfoot in a revised manner akin to

Toho's *Godzilla* series. That is, whereas Godzilla was first seen to be a world destroyer in most of the early releases, the city-smashing, mutant dinosaur hybrid was transformed in most of the later entries into a kid-friendly, Earth-defending, pro-human curiosity who raged against invading aliens and warded off other, malicious giant monsters.

Despite the seemingly radical departure in terms of style and tone, both family and fright versions of Ciné du Sasquatch remain heavily intertwined, close siblings with a shared genetic structure. More unites than divides them, as they each primarily focus on hominids in isolated settings and share an underlying, generalized characterization of Bigfoot. To wit, Sasquatch is a pro-environment, anti-human (or, at the very least, wary) recluse, highly intelligent but guided as much by its animal instincts as any consciousness. In many ways it is the embodiment of our own lost branch of humanity (or is it that we're the lost branch of Yeti-kind?). Tonally, the variation between Benign Bigfoot and Savage Sasquatch films are day and night, often literally so. But though the execution and mood varies, it remains remarkable how the cryptid itself remains constant in either vision. It may or may not befriend humanity, but whether it chooses to be accomplice or foe, the Sasquatch itself retains its aforementioned essential defining characteristics: solitary or within small tribal associations; defensively territorial; and largely impervious to and unconcerned with human beings as a species (until forced to be so). Only the humans it encounters seem to obviate between a classic fight or flight response, revealing the misapprehension our species has in regards to the idea of sharing the planet with other sentient simians.

Given that much speculation has arisen in scientific circles about why the Neanderthals went so recently extinct (less than 30,000 years ago by most estimates, which is a fortnight in terms of biological history on our planet), and how some theories favor genocide via interaction with the larger populations of *Homo sapiens* they probably encountered, does this suggest there exists in mankind an inherent fear of the Other? That, if given the choice between peaceful coexistence with another intelligent tribe of neo-humans or slaughtering them, do we as a species possess a latent inability to elect the former option? While beyond the scope of this book, it is an intriguing question. Many fictitious realizations of cryptids in movies and television answer said question in the affirmative. According to these thematic resonances of Ciné du Sasquatch, then, *Homo sapiens* simply cannot conceive of sharing the planet with *any* species, let alone simian-based ones, who threaten our domination as masters of the planet. One of the constant myths one finds in the genre is this ultimate motif: That which we cannot tame we must destroy. If so, are we trying to eradicate the intelligent Other, or simply externalizing the dark Other within ourselves and annihilating it in the form of a shadowy substitute?

As for the dichotomy between the two styles of Ciné du Sasquatch, the delicate balance of friendly versus savage slowly began to tip back into the fearful cryptid camp as the century came to a close. Whether it was the overuse of the G-rated incarnation and/or audiences hungering to see scarier versions of their favorite hominid, the *Harry and the Hendersons* portrayal waned as the major influence, replaced by more films in which viewers were subjected to an ever-increasing level of bloodshed and carnage. Perhaps this was a deeper reflection of the culture itself, driven as it was by coarsening standards of rap-fueled, gun-prevalent darker visions. After all, if the returning GIs of World War II could have their angst and turmoil mirrored in the emergence of the film noir genre, then surely Ciné du Sasquatch filmmakers could add their grip to the cliché-bound hold of the seemingly endless postmodern era?

But tempting as such analysis is — in that it explains the sudden return of the more sinister Sasquatch movies (if not how badly conceived and executed so many in the 2000s were as a viewing experience) — the more likely speculation is that most Yeti film producers were betting on the bottom line: An absence of scary Bigfoot movies meant a niche market to exploit and fill with products aimed at a sure-fire audience. In short, a plethora of family Bigfoot movies for rent at the local video store meant there was, conversely, a need for Savage Sasquatch entries.

The independent Ciné du Sasquatch filmmakers quickly adapted to the newly-emerging distribution models in the beginning of the 21st century, such as DVD, downloadable Internet files, and direct-to-consumer eBay sales. All of these formats offered a substantial aggregate niche market for low-budget productions. More often than not, these semi-professional efforts portray their hominids in a horror film mode. The reason is again mostly economic. While the studios ventured into the family versions of cryptid cinema, they were less willing to release darker versions of the creature. Thus a window was yet again left open for cunning exploitation film producers to mine the monies Hollywood simply ignored.

Heavily influenced by such earlier genre milestones as *The Legend of Boggy Creek* and *Night of the Demon*, these latest examples of Ciné du Sasquatch often visualize Yeti as borderline if not outright supernatural in strength and abilities. Equally, the beast is easily provoked by the merest of intrusions into its private domain. If earlier Sasquatch films hinted at or portrayed a cryptid reluctantly defending itself only when the extreme need arose, these newest offerings abandoned any such pretensions. In place of a Bigfoot that is motivated by territoriality or self-defense for survival, the Postmodern Sasquatch has no moral or spiritual hesitation whatsoever in dismembering humans alive without the slightest provocation or pretense of dramatic justification. We have entered the stage of the cinematic homicidal maniac in this later decadent strain of the genre in which Sasquatch has degenerated to the equivalent of Freddy Krueger or Jason Vorhees in a furry suit. That is, the creature is little more than a psychopathically-driven demon intent on racking up a body count and little else. It is a sad decline, to be sure, but one that is doubtless more a reflection of the tiresome grip of Postmodernism itself (in which characters exist as self-aware stereotypes and therefore engender little if any true audience empathy). The future promises better treatment, if the genre's constant rebirth is any indication. Let us hope for better times, rather than burying the genre simply because some versions of Ciné du Sasquatch currently offer little more than recycled gore quotas and cardboard characterizations. And, after all, it is not a genre that has typically depended upon the greatest of thespian abilities to craft entertaining visions as an *oeuvre*.

Mention herein should be made of another Spielberg classic besides *Harry and the Hendersons* that still casts a long shadow over all suspense and horror films involving the Man versus Beast theme: *Jaws* (1975). The initial success of *Jaws* resulted in a crimson-colored tidal wave of monsters from the deep — copycats devouring any humans foolish enough to venture into any ocean, lake, or shallow pond. While the prevailing mood of unrelenting terror and reduction of the Great White shark into a mindless eating machine in Spielberg's movie was effective beyond doubt, lesser filmmakers, alas, saw it as an opportunity to use cinematic short hand and simply expect the viewers to bring the *Jaws* experience into their substandard knock-offs in lieu of crafting their own novel variations. Two notable exceptions are William Girdler's *Grizzly* (1976) (which at least manages to rise above the pack with some well-shot suspense sequences) and John Frankenheimer's under-appreciated, Bigfoot-tinged, environmental horror film *Prophecy* (1979) (which basically recast its cryptid creature as a mutated bear but otherwise played the stock Ciné du Sasquatch themes and terror situations).

Again, if such assessments regarding the malaise confronting Ciné du Sasquatch appear bleak to the reader, one can easily find solace in the exceptions to the routine drudgery most films in the genre exhibit in the 2000s. For example, several examples show glimmers of light in the darkness of Postmodernism which currently cloaks the cinema's output in general, if not specifically in cryptid filmmaking. Among the noteworthy efforts are *Abominable* (2006), *The Long Way Home: A Bigfoot Story* (2007) and *Paper Dolls* (2007), all three of which demonstrate how serious directors can reshape the moribund nature pervading too many Yeti efforts. As an exemplary lot, they couldn't be more different in terms of scale, intention and filmic vision, which is why all three are worthy of critique. The trio of movies each entertains the Ciné du Sasquatch filmgoer by following in the "footprints" of the earlier successes in the genre in at least some small measure, and yet each refuses to fall victim to Xerox-styled retreads of former hits from previous decades. Too often filmmakers in the last ten years have chosen to stay firmly within the classical mold of the genre's restraints without simultaneously advancing it by giving something original back, both to the viewer and future creators of said films. This creates the pervasive feeling about too many recent Bigfoot films being at once tired *and* lacking in any innovative qualities to distinguish themselves.

As mentioned, however, some filmmakers who've approached the genre have seen fit to use the possibilities afforded by the new medium of the digital revolution and subsequent commercial freedom to endlessly meld and redefine the genre's limitations. Working on home computers and shooting in high definition video, these newest generations of Ciné du Sasquatch makers avoid the costs associated with previous Bigfoot films and focus on taking liberties with some of the commercial expectations their predecessors faced. Consequently, they may be able to finally fulfill at least some of the promise of Postmodernism as a worthwhile aesthetic beyond the conventional self-referential film citations and outright lifts that have constituted the art movement to date, at least in cinematic terms. Being self-aware *does* offer an astute director a potentially valuable, rewarding approach to the material at hand, but only if the awareness is not limited to how many quotes and situations from previous films and television shows the filmmaker can cleverly seed throughout the movie in question. Provided the creative vision is a working alchemy of new ideas mixed with classical techniques, the boundary formerly imposed on Ciné du Sasquatch as a genre begins to loosen, allowing the basic mold of *The Conquest of the Pole* from almost 100 years previous finally to be reinvented without restraint. Provided filmmakers know the genre in question in order to work both inside its parameters and concurrently outside its critically gutter-level non-appreciation by many ignorant of the *oeuvre*, the ties of limitation that once bound the genre director finally offer dramatic liberation, but only if the vision is bold enough. And only if the filmmaker is willing to take chances with both form *and* content.

Meanwhile, on the television side of the genre, a healthy rebirth of documentary series and specials produced by the Discovery Channel, the History Channel, Travel Channel, Arts & Entertainment, and so on has resulted in a virtual rebirth of Sasquatch on the smaller screen. Utilizing the increasing amounts of data compiled by serious, real-life and often Internet-based cryptozoological research teams, such series as *MonsterQuest* have made Bigfoot an ongoing subject of speculation and investigation. More pertinent to this guide, fictitious television programs, such as the critically well-received *Northern Exposure* (which featured a mysterious Sasquatch-like — though mostly human — character known only as Adam, a likely reference to the cryptid being an archaic First Man in Paleolithic terms, who was well-played by Adam Arkin as a reclusive master chef, no less!) and the Joe Dante–produced *Eerie, Indiana* (which often had a cameo Bigfoot stealing food scraps from residents' trash bins), continued the evolution of Bigfoot as something other than an animalistic aberration and instead as an instantly recognizable American icon (even when culturally disguised as the Adam character from *Northern Exposure*).

Another notable Bigfoot appearance in television programs during this era came on the web series turned television series *Sanctuary* (whose premise had a secretly-protected group of Abnormals — creatures such as werewolves and other mutants — hidden away in the titular zone, and included a lead character known as Bigfoot or "the Big Guy," who acted as a Lurch-type butler à la *The Addams Family*). Unique about *Sanctuary* in the genre was the fact Bigfoot was not just a one-off character in appearance but a series regular. And unlike *Northern Exposure*, which suggests a Bigfoot lineage but doesn't fully explain Arkin's Adam character as such, this Bigfoot was given a background and character conflict, and made a vital part of the show's success.

While brief in duration per segment, the Jack's Beef Link

Sasquatch goes ape in the wildly successful Jack Link's Beef Jerky commercial series *Messin' with Sasquatch* (2009).

series of commercials, in which human antagonists taunt a hapless Sasquatch with bites of beef jerky or pull pranks on the naïve creature only to feel its wrath in a series of comedic come-uppances, demonstrates a potent realization by the advertising world that not only is Bigfoot a well-known character but much-beloved. The series of commercials — aptly named "Messin' with Sasquatch" — portray Sasquatch as a kindly figure who (in keeping with the oldest of Ciné du Sasquatch genre thematic motifs) is quite at peace until humans invade its domicile and create havoc at its expense. The commercials also contain a more subtle context that is fascinating: Sasquatch is passé in terms of scare factor, and is continuously treated not with amazement by the various humans it encounters, but as just another wild animal. This acceptance places the cryptid into actual non-cryptid status! The humans react not with fear or even awe upon their encounter with the hairy giant — it's too well-accepted as being real by them for such emotions — but as if they've stumbled upon just another wildlife specimen they can prank for cheap laughs. That's quite an evolution (some might suggest *de*-evolution) from the earliest days of the genre wherein the egg-headed scientist-type characters had to explain to the audience what the cryptid was and how it could possibly exist. In the "Messin' with Sasquatch" ads, Bigfoot is as *de rigueur* as a bear and afforded as much respect as Rodney Dangerfield.

The Cultural Floodgates Open: 2010 and Beyond

At the time of publication, Ciné du Sasquatch shows no signs of becoming placed on any endangered species list. Quite the opposite, as high profile directors such as Sam Raimi and top box office names such as Jack Black continue to announce new feature films centered on cryptids, while large scale, multi-million dollar epics such as *The Mummy 3: The Tomb of the Dragon Emperor* already stock the local mega-chain DVD rental outlets. Downloadable and streaming video from major providers like Netflix and Amazon (not to mention the file-sharing networks which allow users to exchange video and audio files free of charge) have made many of the films and television episodes reviewed in this guide available, albeit after some diligent research and old-fashioned but always necessary good luck.

Even more exciting frontiers in Ciné du Sasquatch doubtless lie ahead. As technology in the moving image arts changes and adapts to the latest innovations (such as the immersive fields of IMAX, 3-D, and beyond into...?), it is always only a matter of time before the next cryptid tale is wrought, large or small, in films or on television, or, indeed, whatever storytelling form comes next. Like the folklore, footprints, and claimed encounters of Bigfoot, Sasquatch and Yeti themselves — which have been with mankind since the village shaman told of its existence in the woods and jungles just beyond a crackling fire — Ciné du Sasquatch will readily adapt itself, as it has done for close to a century and counting. Wherever human beings gather to hear and see any ageless tales told — cinema, television, and beyond — they will transmit the narratives and myths that are universal to our species. And one set of those timeless tales will always be cryptid-based. No matter the medium, the story will remain the same.

PART II
Bigfoot, Sasquatch, and Yeti
Films and Television Programs

Abominable (2006)

Starring Matt McCoy, Jeffrey Combs, Lance Henriksen, Haley Joel, Paul Gleason, Dee Wallace, Christien Tinsley, Ashley Hartman, Karin Anna Cheung, Natalie Compagno, Jim Giggans, Rex Linn, Phil Morris, Tiffany Shepis, Chad Smith, Paul Spadone and Michael Deak. Produced by Donna Cockrell, Theresa Eastman and Paul Spadone. Written by Ryan Schifrin and James Morrison. Directed by Ryan Schifrin. USA. Color. Stereo. 94 Minutes.

Overview: After surviving a mountain climbing accident which took the life of his wife, Preston Rogers is left a grieving, wheelchair-bound man. Undergoing intensive occupational therapy, Rogers is convinced by his medical team to return to the scene of the accident and seek emotional closure. Accompanied by his male nurse, Rogers returns to his remote mountain cabin near where his wife died for the first time since the tragedy.

Everywhere Rogers looks he finds nothing but artifacts and reminders of his formerly happy life. In order to distract himself, he begins voyeuristically surveying a cabin not far from his own, which several vacationing college sorority types have rented for a holiday. Hardened city dwellers, the females openly react with disgust to Rogers' spying on them, figuring he's just a lecherous old man attempting to get his jollies.

Despite himself, Rogers is unable to quit living vicariously through the lovely young women's seeming carefree attitudes, which is precisely what he's lost in his life's unfortunate turn of events. But while watching one young lady making a cell phone call in the darkness of the driveway outside her shared cabin, Rogers witnesses something he cannot logically explain: the woman is seemingly abducted by something shadowy and monstrous. Upon further investigation, Rogers sees Sasquatch and realizes the cryptid is alive and dangerous.

Meanwhile, a trio of hunters camp in the nearby woods. While skeptical of the frequent reports of a locally-dubbed Flatwoods Monster, they've nevertheless come armed with high-powered shotguns just in case. When Ziegler Dane, the alpha male of the group, discovers the remains of the young college woman Rogers saw abducted stuffed into the creature's isolated cave, he rushes back to his comrades to report his findings. Alas, Sasquatch attacks and decimates all three hunters before they can even make a stand against it.

Back at the cabin, Rogers attempts to convince both the local police and his male nurse of what he has seen, but no one will believe him. Realizing he is vulnerable while his nurse is in town getting supplies, Rogers survival-proofs his cabin. His efforts are hampered by his inability to navigate the tiny cabin, which was not designed for anyone in a wheelchair.

Soon, Bigfoot returns and targets the surviving women in the nearby cabin, who are isolated by inclement weather and downed phone lines. The male nurse returns and believes Rogers has become

Poster art for the original release of *Abominable.*

mentally unstable with his babbling about Bigfoot. In order to calm him, the nurse injects Rogers surreptitiously, which causes Rogers to lose consciousness. Meanwhile, the unlucky nurse comes face-to-face with the ravenous Sasquatch, whereupon it eats him alive.

After a couple of the women in the adjacent cabin are dispatched by the bloodthirsty Bigfoot, a recovered Rogers risks his own life to rescue the lone college student survivor. The two make a stand together in Rogers' cabin against the rampaging monster, but although deterred momentarily, it becomes clear the hominid will not be thwarted until both humans are dead. Rogers finally has an email he's sent to the local Sheriff's office taken seriously, but while they wait for the police to respond, Bigfoot attacks the cabin, tearing it asunder. The two remaining humans flee in a car, but Sasquatch holds the vehicle aloft by the rear bumper. Eventually the local police arrive, and an ambulance soon carries Roger and his newfound female friend to safety. However, as soon as they're alone, the isolated handful of police officers are horrified to see scores of red, glowing eyes in the woods surrounding them — the tribe of Sasquatch monsters are set for a final attack.

* * * * *

Like a deep breath of mountain air, *Abominable* dissipates the stalest of Ciné du Sasquatch clichés with a combination of fresh energy and novel narrative structure. By crafting a deft blending of a conventional siege film and Hitchcock's beloved *Rear Window*, the filmmakers largely avoid the pitfalls that so numerously dot the scattered Sasquatch genre landscape. By using a similar plot approach to Hitchcock's masterpiece, director Ryan Schifrin enables the audience to participate on two levels at once: the first is the tense, suspenseful tale itself, which is new enough not to be a carbon copy of *Rear Window*; the second (and more esoteric) comes by counting the nods to the Jimmy Stewart–starrer (in which Stewart plays a photographer with an unhealthy streak of voyeurism spying on his adjoining apartment building's neighbors). To its credit, *Abominable* works equally well on both levels.

Structurally, *Abominable* also draws upon classic siege films ranging from Howard Hawks' *The Thing* to George Romero's *Night of the Living Dead*. This is admittedly an ideal set-up for a modestly-budgeted film, as it centralizes the location to one major set and (when properly utilized) creates an atmosphere of impending doom through claustrophobia and a sense that no escape is possible, save for death. Again, by welding these two plot elements together, the writers and director have fashioned a taut yet flexible storyline that allows for plenty of incidental action and set pieces while still providing time for characterization and back story.

Such Postmodern concoctions are not as easy to execute as they are to envision. One recalls the perhaps apocryphal story in which Brian DePalma, after having directed a thinly-veiled remake of *Vertigo* called *Obsession*, asked Hitch's frequent composer Bernard Herrmann to watch the rough cut and score DePalma's film too. Supposedly Herrmann leapt up after the screening, pointed a finger at the director, and screamed, "You are *not* Hitchcock!" (before, it should be noted, agreeing to score *Obsession* anyway). However true or false the anecdote, it does encapsulate the frequent criticism of Postmodernism in and of itself as an independent art form. To wit: How much can such a work stand alone versus only work for a viewer who can supply the necessary references while watching to make the experience anything less than a confusing confection of borrowed ingredients? And if being able to participate in any meaningful manner requires previous knowledge of the referenced works, then to what extent is the Postmodern film in question an independent work of art or merely a thinly-disguised extension of another filmmaker's vision? Though these are neither infrequent nor unjust criticisms of many Postmodern movies, *Abominable* largely avoids these traps by

simply concentrating on making the best of its allusions without ever becoming enslaved by them. So while, yes, there are plenty of Hitchcock allusions planted throughout, *Abominable* thankfully never degenerates into a fan boy exercise of self-parody or pastiche.

The use of long takes to create suspense is notable, as many Ciné du Sasquatch entries rely on fast cuts to obscure cryptid costume deficiencies and therefore help maintain suspension of disbelief. Instead, *Abominable* favors lingering takes with off-screen space threatening to intrude into the frame at any moment. This heightens the edginess of the shot, much like *Jaws* did with its similar technique, in which the shark lunges into frame after the filmmakers have lulled the audience with a continuous, uneventful take. By constantly framing characters standing near windows and doorways, Schifrin places the viewer on the peripheral edge of his seat. It's a creative strategy: It holds the impressive monster suit until the conclusion for maximum impact and makes the preceding moments full of audience jumps (often set off by the well-timed mix of audio cues which sonically enhance the onscreen action). While the filmmakers didn't exactly invent the cinematic wheel here, one can still admire how they so effortlessly grease the axle and make it spin to such suspenseful effect without too many creaks or groans.

The professional cast of recognizable genre actors help tremendously, particularly Jeffrey Combs' portrayal of the bizarre local kook (Combs is best-known to cult movie fans from his turn in *The Re-Animator*), as well as perennial Ciné du Sasquatch performer Lance Henriksen as Dane. Henriksen's laconic delivery and cynical attitude adds some necessary black humor to the film, especially when his character discovers the cryptid's cave. As he eyes the gaping wound in the female victim's side and squeamishly listens to her raspy, dying cries for assistance, Henriksen merely shakes his head, never budging from his spot, and mutters, "God, that's *gross*." The utter lack of empathy would seem callous if not for the completely selfish manner in which the actor delivers the line — despite the lack of heroics, the honest viewer can envision any number of real-life acquaintances less inclined to altruistic behavior behaving precisely this way. This off-kilter quality insures *Abominable* never takes itself too seriously — a recurrent weakness in many of its cinematic brethren — and allows for a release from the tension, which only increases later by way of more unexpected shocks.

The creature design is excellent, ferociously believable as it is bulky. Not only does it have the impressive girth and monstrous eyes, but it sports a pair of wide-stretching jaws that unhinge and drop open so that the cryptid may crunch on a victim's skull! While other Bigfoot films have shown predation upon human victims, seldom have they depicted a shark-like ability to literally engulf an entire head and swallow it whole. While some will debate whether this shock moment is the film's highlight or lowlight, it is definitely a moment of Grand Guignol which produces shivers and revulsion in equal measure for most viewers. There is, however, one unexplained anomaly in regards to the costume: the film's title itself. While *Abominable* suggests the creature will sport white fur and be of Himalayan descent, the actual hominid in the film has brown fur and inhabits the Redwood environment most clearly associated with Bigfoot.

The cinematography by the late Neal Fredericks (*The Blair Witch Project*, *Laughing Dead*) is technically far above the average Ciné du Sasquatch effort and wisely only portrays the Sasquatch in night-for-night photography. Along with judicious rim lighting that makes the cryptid's fur stand out in relief against a dark background, Fredericks, along with Schifrin, creates an eerie silhouette effect in which the beast is not fully seen until the final reel. This makes the film scarier in that it invites the viewer's imagination to run wild in regards to the hominid's true visage; likewise, it doesn't disappoint because the realization is so horrific.

Again, *Abominable* does not break any new cinematic ground, but it does compile an impressively entertaining list of tried-and-true filmic techniques into a thoroughly watchable whole. Future filmmakers who wish to delve into the genre of Bigfoot movies would do well to study how adroitly *Abominable* packs its running time with characterization, conflict, and enjoyable narrative twists. As it amply demonstrates, there is still much room left in Ciné du Sasquatch to explore if the creators are willing to address the genre's limitations in order to overcome or incorporate them, rather than simply ignoring and succumbing to them.

The Abominable Snow Rabbit (1961)

Featuring the voice of Mel Blanc. Starring Bugs Bunny and the Abominable Snowman. Produced by David H. DePatie. Written by Ted Pierce. Directed by Maurice Noble and Chuck Jones. USA. Color. Mono. 6 Minutes.

Overview: Bugs Bunny and Daffy Duck take the proverbial "wrong turn at Albuquerque" and wind up in the Himalayas. The Abominable Snowman takes a liking to Daffy Duck, believing Daffy to be a cuddly rabbit. Naming him George, the Abominable Snowman decides to keep Daffy as his newfound pet rabbit until Daffy convinces the Yeti that Bugs Bunny is a real rabbit and therefore more suitable for the Abominable Snowman.

The Abominable Snowman abducts Bugs Bunny and promises to "hold him, and squeeze him and cuddle him" until Bugs tricks the slow-witted Yeti into going after Daffy again for his keepsake pet. A variety of back and forth turning of the tables occurs in which each friend betrays the other to the confused Yeti. Finally, Bugs flees to Palm Springs, but the Yeti follows. Upon arrival in Palm Springs to witness Bug's misery, Daffy is yet again taken by the Snowman as his pet. Luckily for Daffy, the Yeti melts into a puddle of water, ending their problem.

* * * * *

This beloved Chuck Jones (with co-director Maurice Noble) Warner Brothers cartoon introduced the goofy, slow-natured Abominable Snow-Man (*sic*), who was prone to mistaking any animal it encountered as being a rabbit eager to become a pet. With a drippy voice and languid speech pattern clearly patterned on Lon Chaney, Jr.'s portrayal of Lennie in *Of Mice and Men* (hence the Yeti's penchant for naming its newfound pets "George" when it captures them), the Yeti remains one of the most popular bit players in the Bugs and Daffy universe (though the Abominable Snowman didn't reappear until *Spaced Out Bugs*; the popularity was maintained simply through the endless repetition of this short which frequently ran in television syndication). Credit consummate voice actor Mel Blanc with the loveable nature of the Yeti's vocal patterns; it adds a lot of dimension to the towering snow giant.

Per the norm for this period, Jones' style is at his creative "peak" level. The lushly drawn but still Modernist backgrounds; the finely-attuned line styles in which each character's outer lines are darker shades of their inner colors (atypical in an era when most animated characters were simply black outlines with color swatches filled in); and the visually bizarre and inventive sight gags all work in synchronization to marvelous and entertaining effect. The touch of surrealism which also pervades most of Chuck Jones' finest works is also present throughout. The sight, for example, of the Abominable Snowman diving into one of Bugs Bunny's infamously long burrow trails and following after the rabbit underground is hysterical, as is the sudden, literal melting away of the Snowman by the short's end, leaving but a puddle of water where the cryptid once sat in a deck chair fanning itself in the broiling Palm Springs sun. This may be the first time a Yeti was ever suggested to be a literal ice monster, and probably the last!

From the vibrant colors which saturate the frame to the combative antics of Daffy and Bugs, and the extra bonus of an easily-confused but well-meaning Abominable (which Bugs insists on calling the "Abomina-Bubble"), *The Abominable Snow Rabbit* is easily deserving of its accolades as being placed in the rarefied ranks of best-ever cryptid cartoons. A classic.

The Abominable Snowman (1957)

AKA: *The Abominable Snowman of the Himalayas*. Starring Forrest Tucker, Peter Cushing, Maureen Connell, Richard Wattis, Robert Brown, Arnold Marlé and Michael Brill. Produced by Aubrey Baring, Michael Carreras and Anthony Nelson-Keys. Written by Nigel Kneale. Directed by Val Guest. UK. Black & White. Mono. 91 Minutes.

Overview: A well-meaning but misguidedly naive British scientist, John Rollason, and a hard-headed American sensationalist, Tom Friend, are among a group of explorers intent on rescuing stranded colleagues trapped in the peaks of the Himalayan Mountains. Despite dire warnings not to venture after their missing comrades by their friendly Sherpa host and the other monks who shelter Rollason and company in their Tibetan monastery, the rescuers precede into the treacherous, icy passageways.

After finding footprints and hearing eerie cries, it becomes apparent to both Rollason and Friend that the legendary Abominable Snowmen the monks worship are anything but mythic. Meanwhile, the originally stranded climbers return to the monastery and are shocked to learn the rescue party is now trapped themselves by a raging blizzard. Back on the mountaintop, Rollason and Friend's party are terrorized by the Yetis, creatures whose enormous footprints suggest they're true giants. When it later becomes apparent to Rollason that the reckless Friend only wants to bring back a Yeti, dead or alive, Rollason stages a bitter attempt to convince the profiteering American adventurer that the latter's quest is both folly and conceit: folly because the creatures are superior in intelligence; conceit because after Friend and his men slaughter one of the Yetis, the surviving creatures make it readily clear to the humans that their party will never escape the Snowmen's mountain hideaway alive to reveal their existence.

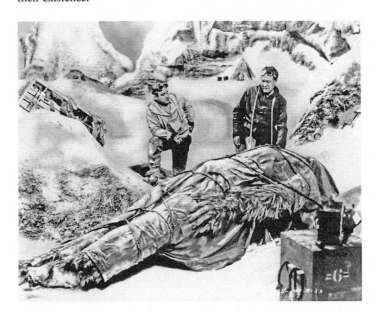

The gigantism of the Yeti is maintained but scaled down from Kong-size in Hammer's influential *The Abominable Snowman* (1957).

But Friend only ridicules Rollason, sacrificing crew member after crew member in an ill-advised attempt to bring the dead Yeti back to civilization. Friend even goes so far as to allow his best friend to serve as live bait in a cave to lure a Yeti into a trap, which only results in the man's death. Now mortally at odds with Friend, Rollason beseeches the crazed hunter to give up in order to survive their ordeal. But unwilling to forgo his insane goal, Friend pays the ultimate price. In an unexpected act of generosity, the creatures spare Rollason's life. Rollason is later rescued and returned to the monastery, the sole survivor of his ill-fated expedition. After a meeting with the knowing monk who warned against their trek, Rollason vows to keep the secret of the Snowmen to himself, worried about the creatures' fate should the outside world ever learn of their fragile existence.

* * * * *

In the annals of Ciné du Sasquatch, *The Abominable Snowman* towers like the film's namesake creatures above all others that would follow. This is because despite its brazen capitalizing upon the era's fashionable fascination with "all things Yeti" in print and book, the movie offered a stellar and still unmatched combination in cryptid cinema: an intelligent script; a believable, professional cast; taut, suspenseful direction (by Val Guest); and magnificently evocative widescreen cinematography (by Arthur Grant). A final touch that defines *The Abominable Snowman* as one of the great Yeti movies of all time is the wise decision to keep the Yetis off-screen for much of the film's running time. Whereas today's CGI-laden movies eagerly exploit the cinematic ability to display said creatures in photo-realistic detail, *The Abominable Snowman* eschews such suspense-destroying tactics in favor of creating a claustrophobic, viewer-imagined cryptid rarely glimpsed until the movie's final, unforgettable moments. Even then, Guest smartly chooses to go for an unexpected degree of pathos over mere shock of revelation.

Indeed, the uncanny feeling the image of the Yetis produces in the viewer when finally glimpsed isn't so much horror as genuine empathy. With their sad, wizened features and frightened, childlike eyes, these Snowmen seem at once all too human and yet superior to our own species in every respect — physically, psychologically, and spiritually. In no uncertain terms, the film's creators turn the tables by film's end, crafting a scenario wherein the human characters scale the heights to find an unknown monster, only to ironically discover the true beast lies lurking deep within themselves instead. The Yetis, in comparison, are revealed as Buddha-like in their simple desire to peacefully coexist with all living creatures... until directly threatened and left with no choice other than to defend themselves or perish.

Not unlike *King Kong*, the real "monster" of the plot is the Carl Denham archetype portrayed by Forrest Tucker, who is a maniacally-driven, status-seeking tabloid headline hunter of the first order. In essence, Tucker portrays and represents the Ugly American at his swaggering, arrogant worst. A self-styled John Wayne adventurer with no conscience whatsoever, Tom Friend cares little for life unless it offers him immediate satisfaction, instant fame, and endless fortune, no matter the cost. As his macho swagger and insanely selfish tactics reveal throughout *The Abominable Snowman*, Friend is amoral when it comes to allowing — even encouraging — others to pay the price with their lives for his own egotistical greed and narcissism. He uses others like pawns in a chess match, a true sociopath who is unable to feel pity or remorse for those he routinely betrays, even as they die as a direct consequence of his actions. His obsession is not unlike Ahab's to capture the great white whale in *Moby Dick*; Friend wants the great white cryptid no matter how it dooms all around him (even if he hasn't lost a leg to motivate his rage).

In contrast, Cushing plays the mild-mannered but perceptive scientist John Rollason, who slowly but surely comes to the realization that Friend is a madman on a misanthropic mission. At first enamored

(albeit unwittingly) of Friend's charismatic facade as rugged individualist and bravado-inspiring "man of action," Rollason finally sees through the boastfulness all too readily and, in doing so, is forced to reconcile his newfound insight into Friend's darker nature with his own insecurity-driven character flaws. Wanting initially to become famous, as Friend promises, as the discoverer of the world's greatest cryptozoological find of all time, Rollason willingly turns a blind eye until it is almost too late. Only when Friend finally callously tricks his own best friend and allows the man to literally die from fright by leaving him alone with a gun loaded with blanks (unbeknownst to the victim) does Cushing awaken to where the truest evil lies: not within the pacifist Snowmen but the invading humans themselves. Thematically it harkens back to the same dire warning of another classic in the science fiction genre, *The Day the Earth Stood Still*, which equally demonstrates the dangers of mankind remaining oblivious to our innate ability to sleepwalk through larger responsibilities. It may seem heavy-handed, but to its great credit, *The Abominable Snowman* never preaches but merely dramatically enacts this logic, which, of course, gives it all the more power to move an audience.

Nigel Kneale's well-observed script was based on an equally well-rendered BBC live television production, *The Creature* (1955). Not unlike the later Professor Quatermass series of movies, *The Abominable Snowman* first thrilled spellbound UK TV viewers before Hammer and American co-production company 20th Century–Fox cinematically recreated it. The story's modest albeit effective narrative conflicts transferred well from the small to larger screen. Kneale and Guest intelligently kept the focus of the filmic adaptation not on the special effects the larger budget allowed, but on creating a chilling atmosphere and foreboding sense of dread.

The spooky, desolate, craggy-ridged sets and fog-shrouded widescreen photography lend the film a much admired sense of authenticity and tension far beyond its modest budget. While realism is never overwhelmingly convincing, the creepy horror *The Abominable Snowman* takes on as the explorers meet their ends is genuinely effective. Key moments of terror are underscored visually with unexpected shocks. One great example: A crew member experiencing mountain sickness from the altitude (or so the explorers initially rationalize before they learn better) awakens at night in his tent, alone, only to see a gigantic Yeti hand casually slip inside. The clawed hand gently if curiously picks through the weaponry Friend and party have brought along. The guns look like small, ineffective toys in contrast to the off-screen Yeti's huge, grasping fingers. And while the special effects employed in the scene are only modestly effective, the psychological shock to the viewer upon seeing this moment through the hysterical man's viewpoint cannot be over-praised. In short, it packs a wallop, one of the many such effectively horrific, lasting moments.

The final make-up creation by famed Hammer specialist Philip Leakey is a masterpiece of the genre. The artful manner in which Leakey's design and Grant's shadowy lighting combine to reveal the soulful depths of the misunderstood Yeti tribe would not be equaled until Rick Baker won an Academy Award decades later for instilling similar magic into his Sasquatch creation in *Harry & the Hendersons*. Attempting to describe its emotional impact is akin to verbalizing what makes Goya's *Saturn Devouring His Children* horrifically mesmerizing — that is, the most adept turn of phrase can only hope to barely approach it, let alone capture it. As the creatures appear out of the darkness and hover over a terrified but awestruck Rollason, the viewer is wordlessly forced to rethink his or her own preceding bias against the unseen Yetis as surely as Rollason himself. This is great cinema, regardless of genre affiliation — a careful, well-designed approach that allows the picture to tell the story and which therefore elevates *The Abominable Snowman* to the true peak of its respective *oeuvre*.

Though Forrest Tucker's performance is a bit monotonous in its unmotivated audacity, Cushing's sensitive, articulate counter-balancing act as the Intelligent Everyman caught up in moral uncertainties beyond his control or imagination redeems any lack of depth on Tucker's behalf. Structurally speaking, Cushing is actually the protagonist who undergoes a profound psychological change in the best Joseph Campbell *Hero of a Thousand Faces* sense, whereas Tucker subtly acts as the film's immoral antagonist, hell-bent, with Satanic glee, on overriding Cushing's better-natured angel by using charm, threats, lies and finally outright murder when all else fails. To this extent, the Snowmen are more like a classic Greek chorus, echoing the intercine human warfare between the two leads as much as embodying the roles of "monsters" themselves. This is cleverly underscored throughout the script by the dedicated Sherpa monk who psychically sees from the movie's opening scenes the true intents and hidden natures of the supposedly "superior" Western outsiders, all of whom treat the monks and locals as ignorant savages at best. By film's end, it is clearly revealed that the monk is in telepathic communication with the Yetis as well, and has warned them of the danger soon to arrive.

Rollason can only marvel at how he has not only been out-played mentally and physically by the ordeal, but spiritually enlightened by the very culture he had earlier dismissed. He discovers a form of self-redemption as a result. He loses the ability to claim a scientific find, but he has regained his soul in the process. All in all, it is an apt exchange given his initial Faustian bargain with Friend's Machiavellian opportunist.

The Abominable Snowman (1996)

Starring Keith Barber, Byron Clark, Edward Dloughy, Joe Hanna, William Houck, Teresa Jones, Steve Stewart and the Great Antonio. Produced by Michael J. White. Written by Edward Boitano and Michael J. White. Directed by Michael J. White. USA. Color. Stereo. 90 Minutes.

Overview: A group of ordinary citizens who become stranded in remote, snow-covered mountains find themselves at the mercy of both a ravenous Yeti and a Captain Ahab–like madman obsessed with killing the cryptid at all costs—including his human companions' lives. Despite the clearly paranoid nature of their survivalist-trained leader, the group have no choice (or so they feel) but to follow his keener instincts or perish in the process, lacking the personal muster themselves to challenge the survivalist's alpha male mentality. But as they learn the survivalist will stop at nothing to accomplish his task, even using them as bait to lure the Abominable Snowman, a horrible realization sets in: They must either stand apart and make their own way, or allow the crazed survivalist to use them for his own ends.

* * * * *

Although made on a very low budget, *The Abominable Snowman* is an interesting Ciné du Sasquatch film because it is clear the filmmaker was interested in the underlying mechanics of the genre, despite his budgetary limitations. While the plot is par for the course, it does feature an interesting twist on the *Moby Dick* theme which is so prevalent in the *oeuvre*—that of presenting an obsessed human who will stop at nothing to capture or kill a cryptid.

Of course, one of the seminal influences on the Bigfoot film genre is *King Kong*. It can be argued that King Kong is ultimately more a hominid than giant ape of typical cinema presumption, in that there is no known species of mountain gorilla that remotely resembles the morphology and size of the Eighth Wonder of the World. Too, gorillas only rarely walk on their hind legs, whereas Kong only rarely resorts to using his forearms for short bursts of locomotion or balance. There is also the lurking hint of bestiality in the classic, although more romantically-inclined souls may wish to credit the fairy tale "Beauty and the Beast" as a more innocent influence of sub-textual interspecies sexuality (though it's worth noting, as this guide does, the sheer number of Sasquatch films that explicitly suggest or even depict a bipedal hominid having intercourse with human females).

But the Carl Denham character in *King Kong* is perhaps one of the most potent influences the 1933 box office hit had on Ciné du Sasquatch, at least in terms of human roles. As mentioned in the previous entry for Hammer's 1957 version (also called *The Abominable Snowman*), the archetype is a direct descendent of Captain Ahab, though for different reasons: Instead of revenge or a sense of domination over nature, Denham is interested chiefly in profligate profits. While he feels some empathy for Kong—especially after his short-sighted greed has caused the so-called beast's demise—Denham basically is driven by an innate robber baron mentality to always be the king of his own domain, as surely as Kong is king of his own world physically.

Here is where the 1996 version of *The Abominable Snowman* echoes the archetype of both Denham and the Tom Friend character portrayed by Forrest Tucker in the earlier Hammer Studios version of *The Abominable Snowman* (1957)—the newer character is a survivalist by nature and instinct, and when challenged with either fleeing in fear of the Abominable Snowman or destroying it to test his own sense of superiority, the survivalist elects to sacrifice the well-being of the others in his party in order to achieve "total victory" over his self-defined nemesis, the Yeti. In essence, he looks down upon his human companions as unworthy of redemption in comparison to the grotesque if invigorating challenge of bringing down a wild cryptid, the latter of which he respects as a force of nature every bit equal to his own sense of self-entitlement.

By no means an overlooked classic, *The Abominable Snowman* nevertheless provides some fine scares and suspense as the humans dependent upon the survivalist slowly begin to realize the nature of their predicament. On the one hand, they are stranded in the snowy mountains and unable to leave without the survivalist's skills. On the other, there is no doubt the hunter will utilize them as bait to attract the beast because it serves his ultimate goal. Sadly, despite the acknowledgment of the director of the prevailing motifs so common throughout Ciné du Sasquatch and his adroit handling of them in a B-movie setting, the film is difficult to see and has not been released onto DVD as of this publication.

The Abominable Snowman (2008) (TV)

AKA: *Snezhnyy chelovek*; *Снежный человек*. Starring Viktoriya Isakova, Aleksey Makarov, Sergei Astakhov, Natalya Shvets, Aleksandr Robak, Galina Shevyakova, Valdis Pelsh, Vadim Andreyev and Alena Kuznetsova. Produced by Sergey Danielyan, Ruben Dishdishyan, Dmitri Dobouzhinsky, Yuriy Moroz and Aram Movsesyan. Directed by Konstantin Charmadov. Russia. Color. Stereo. 100 Minutes.

Overview: This feature-length romantic comedy is about a Russian cryptozoologist and three other people whose lives become entangled while stranded in a mountain cabin during a search for the Yeti. Originally shot for Russian television and released in some Eastern European countries on DVD, it remains unreleased in the United States as of this publication date.

Adventure ("Search for the Yeti") (1987) (TV) (Doc)

Starring Chris Bonington. Series Produced by WGBH Public Television. Produced by Nelsa Gidney and David Fanning. Directed by Lawrence Blair. USA. Color. Mono. 60 Minutes.

Overview: This hour-long documentary funded by critically-acclaimed, Boston-based public television station WGBH focuses on the history of the Yeti from a scientific point of view. It features a cameo by noted Himalayan mountaineer Chris Bonington, who explains how the valleys in the northeastern sections of Mount Everest are incredibly isolated, heavily forested and could definitely supply enough food and shelter to allow the Abominable Snowman to exist. Also detailed are the tantalizing encounters between various Sherpa and Tibetan locals, as well as the evidence — photographic and physical — recovered by Western Himalayan explorers such as Sir Edmund Hillary and others.

The Adventures of Sam & Max: Freelance Police ("Little Bigfoot") (1998) (TV)

Featuring the voices of Harvey Atkin, Robert Tinkler, Tracey Moore and Patrick McKenna. Produced by J.D. Smith. Written by Steve Purcell. Directed by Steve Whitehouse. USA/Canada. Color. Stereo. 10 Minutes.

Overview: Sam and Max are freelance police who roam the world (and even the Moon in one episode) at the behest of their mysterious employer the Commissioner, whom they've never met in person. Handling a variety of paranormally-tinged cases, Sam (a 6-foot canine in the classic Sam Spade detective mold and attire) and Max (a 3-foot-tall "rabbity thing," as described by the series' producers) ceaselessly solve situations others would fail to even comprehend, partially owing to their own unique form of bonded insanity.

When they're visiting a roadside museum of backwoods Americana featuring the usual plethora of concrete dinosaurs and tourist trappings, Sam and Max spot a bus boy who is clearly a small Sasquatch cleaning up after guests in the dining room. Sam realizes the Bald Man who owns the dive must be exploiting Little Bigfoot and tells Max they must return the captive cryptid to its own hominid homelands.

Max isn't too keen on the idea. After all, what do Sam and he know about Bigfoot as a species? But bowing to Sam's pressure (if not outright abduction of the silent Sasquatch tyke), the crime-fighting duo speed away with Little Bigfoot strapped into a child-restraining seat in their stretch police car. The outraged Bald Man screams for them to stop, but they won't listen, hell-bent on accomplishing their goal of liberating Little Bigfoot.

Along the way, the mute Little Bigfoot seems completely indifferent to Sam and Max, as well as to their mission of mercy. When Max attempts to communicate with Little Bigfoot by dressing in tree bark as a Sasquatch, the child cryptid drives away in their squad car, using wooden blocks attached to its big feet to reach the pedals. Sam and Max trundle through the redwoods and eventually wind up in a mountain resort village staging an annual Sasquatch festival for diehard believers. During a film festival in which the best footage of the year is screened, Sam and Max see Sam as Sasquatch blurrily projected from Sam's earlier imitation of a bipedal hominid. But the winning entry entered by a group of backwoods types shows a brief glimpse of a Sasquatch cook-out in progress, complete with hamburger grill and a Bigfoot cook sporting a chef's hat.

Sam figures that by following the winning rednecks, he can solve the mystery as to where the Sasquatch beings can be found. He, Max and Little Bigfoot set off in pursuit. However, the pick-up driving hicks don't take to Sam and Max chasing them, and throw logs at the freelance police. After a tense chase, Sam and Max catch up to the truck and force the pick-up's drivers off the road with a "ratlin'" machine gun (a Gatling gun that fires rats). Sam pulls off the head redneck's rubbery mask, revealing them to be actual Sasquatch creatures merely posing as humans to win the annual film contest.

The police arrive with the Bald Man from the curio shop. He accuses Sam and Max of child abduction. When Sam protests that Little Bigfoot clearly belongs to the Bigfoot clan, the Bald Man introduces his wife, a cryptid female with a penchant for pink house dresses. Explaining that Little Bigfoot is literally their cross-bred son, the nuclear family is reunited. Sam and Max attend a suburban-styled barbeque party staged by the Sasquatch community, pleased the case is solved but worried that they must now devour the grub the creatures are grilling—literally, as they are offered a plate of wiggling grubs.

* * * * *

The Adventures of Sam and Max: Freelance Police is a rare case of a series of comic books and videogames being successfully translated into a television show that is arguably superior to the characters' original mediums. While both the comic book and the LucasArts adventure videogame are highly entertaining, the maniacally-paced television episodes are so densely-wrought with one-liners and evolving plot contrivances that it takes the viewer's keenest attention to keep up with them. All of which may explain why such a challenging but rewarding show never lasted beyond a single season on Fox, lacking the cruder language and situations more familiar to viewers of *Family Guy* and, to a lesser extent, *The Simpsons*.

In "Little Bigfoot" the crime fighters are placed in an atypical situation of having to act on their own recognizance rather than rely on the never-seen Commissioner to justify their irrational acts of unintentional sabotage and disorderly conduct in their pursuit of justice. The outcome, naturally, is predictably the same—total chaos. The plucky Sam, who sees himself as a cartoon version of Sam Spade but comes across more akin to Maxwell Smart, and "hyperkinetic rabbity thing" Max, who looks like a demented escapee from a crudely-rendered anime show, are a successful recombinant version of Laurel and Hardy, Mutt and Jeff, and a long line of comedic oddballs who are inexplicably teamed together (inexplicable, that is, save for maximum laughter generated in the viewing audiences).

"Little Bigfoot" was the next-to-last episode in the all too brief series. It provides equal doses of humor in both outrageous and satirical modes. The outrageousness comes from the incredible amount of zany dialogue this supposed children's show sports, causing it to resemble a Marx Brothers movie for the non-stop double entendres. The satire skewers everything from the American obsession with turning all folklore into a capitalistic enterprise (such as the roadside museum clearly ripping off *Jurassic Park*, with terrible concrete dinosaurs hastily placed outside to make whining kids force road-weary parents to stop and spend money) to cryptozoologists who occasionally take themselves too seriously in what should be, after all, a subject matter open to debate and not laced with theological dogmatism (realized to devastatingly funny effective by the Sasquatch convention Sam and Max stumble upon, which is strictly for believers only).

The Little Bigfoot character is a real charmer. With huge black orbs and pinpoint white pupils, Little Bigfoot comes across as perhaps the most huggable cryptid in Ciné du Sasquatch history. It's not just sentimental in appeal, however; the character seems dazed and confused in the world it inhabits, being neither a pure *Homo sapiens* nor 100 percent genetic crypto-specimen. Given the fast pace of the episode and the limited amount of screen time the creators can dedicate to Little Bigfoot, "Little Bigfoot" is a remarkably good example of what Bigfoot cinema as a genre can render when properly produced. It not only entertains, but manages several plot twists that are for the most part unexpected, as well as skewering the societal obsessions that accompany the real-life interest in its subject matter (the tourist trap museums and their carny-esque sideshow mentality, as well as the humorless self-righteousness of some believers who exhibit a near theological belief in All Things Cryptid). As if that were not enough to accomplish in ten minutes, "Little Bigfoot" even echoes the crossbreeding theme so common in the Ciné du Sasquatch genre with its clever dénouement. While live action Bigfoot movies tend to portray this interbreeding of the species subtext to horrific effect, "Little Bigfoot" goes for the more gentle but equally thought-provoking reversal of showing just how genetically similar such a species as Sasquatch might be if proven one day to exist.

All in all, "Little Bigfoot" is a total delight for all fans of the genre willing to withstand a small bit of self-referential laughs at their own modest expense. After all, it's not as if Sam and Max are above ridicule, either. Indeed, what is perhaps most unexpectedly delightful about *The Adventures of Sam and Max: Freelance Police* (and "Little Bigfoot" is no exception) is that it skewers both subject matter and the viewer alike in equally gentle doses. If you enjoy your laughs animated and frenetic, "Little Bigfoot" is recommended.

The Adventures of Sass Parilla, the Singing Gorilla (2005) (Cameo)

Starring Sass Parilla, Lambert, Alex Rambaud, Nik Morgan, Toniet Gallego, Andre Bonnet, Calu, Shane Morton, Blake Myers and Monty Trammell. Produced, Written and Directed by Chuck Porterfield. USA. Color. Stereo. 65 Minutes.

Overview: A singing blue gorilla named Sass Parilla fights all manner of evils, including such diabolical foes as the manifestly maniacal Black Widow. In Chapter Two ("Are We There Yeti?") of the four-part opus, Sass, his genius friend Dr. Newtonious, and Gary, the helpful everyman with a heart of gold, embark on a journey to Nepal to free Dr. Newtonious' fellow female scientist Jade Yau, who has sent her friend an emergency distress message. To speed their journey, they enlist the help of Heindrich the mute Eskimo to navigate the frozen Himalayan Mountains.

Alas for Sass, Black Widow and his evil henchman Conrad are behind the kidnapping of Jade Yau. Their diabolical intent: entrap the beloved blue gorilla and then use Black Widow's own new weapon to summon the monstrous Yeti to destroy the simian singer. The battle between the Good and the Bad is set, with an Ugly showdown looming. Can Sass Parilla save the day?

* * * * *

This series of charming short films was shot in Atlanta, Georgia, one summer and edited into a feature-length movie. Each roughly 10- to 15-minute segment features the same set of characters—Dr. Newtonious, Gary and, of course, Sass Parilla, the Singing Gorilla. Crudely made but with filmic skill, *The Adventures of Sass Parilla, the Singing Gorilla* is an entertaining mishmash of old Japanese children's action series such as *Space Giants*, *Ultraman*, and *Spectreman*, rock 'n' roll musicals, Mexican *lucha libre* films, and old Republic serials from the 1940s (like *Commando Cody* and *Captain Marvel*). With its subversively campy retro-cardboard set designs featuring obvious miniatures and flagrantly flimsy walls, *The Adventures of Sass Parilla, the Singing Gorilla* also reminds one of both *Pee Wee's Playhouse* and the live action footage found in the early Patchy the Pirate skits within *SpongeBob SquarePants*.

Admittedly adolescent in approach but unapologetically so, the film is (as a first-time viewing experience, at any rate) an acquired taste, as Sass Parilla's roughly torn-open mouth and visible human hands in the otherwise effective blue ape suit self-consciously calls attention to the movie's threadbare budget. Likewise, the hammy, over-the-top performances will strike many as amateurish and thus turn away potential viewers who insist such insipidness come in smaller doses than a feature length film. Ironically, however, those who appreciate the artistic amalgamation which the creators have lovingly stitched together will find favor with the short running

lengths of each of the four segments, as they more faithfully capture the slim storylines and blistering pace of their referenced inspirations, which were always short on plot and long on action.

Sass Parilla is something of a local legend in Atlanta, Georgia, performing at various musical venues (but *never* for hire as a singer of telegrams, his website amusingly and emphatically insists!) and nightclubs in the area. The film builds on the schtick brilliantly, setting Sass as frequent visitor to Dr. Newtonious' laboratory wherein various misadventures naturally (or supernaturally) arise. Sass' epic battle with the Yeti is imaginatively executed on an ice cave set that, while obviously fake, is nevertheless artistically rendered. The creators used their Atlanta-based warehouse location to good effect, building cheesy sets that really capture the low-budget nature of such 1970s shows as *The Ghost Busters* and related set-bound kiddy fare. The accompanying music (which is as intentionally campy as the rest of the production) also adds a level of laughter to the proceedings. Last but certainly not least, there's also Sass Parilla's own tuneful songs, which are heavy-handedly inserted into each segment (thus making them all the more amusing).

For those who don't mind watching self-parody that works for instead of making fun of the viewer (a frequent mishap of this genre, alas), *The Adventures of Sass Parilla, the Singing Gorilla* is a Ciné du Sasquatch short form delight.

The Adventures of Tintin ("Tintin in Tibet") (1991) (TV)

Featuring the voices of Thierry Wermuth, Christian Pellissier, Henri Labussière, Yves Barsacq, Jean-Pierre Moulin, Colin O'Meara and Susan Roman. Produced by Pierre Bertrand-Jaume, Philippe Gildas, Philippe Grimond, Simon Hart, Michael Hirsh, Stephen Hodgins, Patrick Loubert, Robert Réa and Clive A. Smith. Written by Amélie Aubert and Bruce Robb. Based Upon "Tintin au Tibet" by Hergé. Directed by Stéphane Bernasconi. France and Canada. Color. Stereo. 30 Minutes.

Overview: Intrepid young reporter Tintin, while vacationing in the Swiss Alps, is intrigued by reports of a plane crash in Tibet. That night he has a vivid nightmare in which his friend Chang Chong-Chen appears, crying out for help. When Tintin awakes, he is startled to discover the plane that has gone missing contained none other than Chang himself.

Convinced he has received a psychic distress call from his friend, Tintin convinces his skeptical travel companion Captain Haddock to accompany him to Tibet to investigate Chang's fate. Alas, when they find the downed aircraft's wreckage, their Sherpa guide Tharkey tells them that all hope is lost, pointing at the sinister Yeti tracks surrounding the crash. When Tharkey refuses to go further for fear of angering the Abominable Snowman, Tintin and Haddock continue alone, ignoring the Sherpa's dire warnings.

After a series of near-death experiences climbing the treacherous mountains, and with Tharkey finally rejoining their trek, the trio find themselves nearly frozen to death when their tent is destroyed by a windstorm. They arrive at a Buddhist monastery called Khor-Biyong and are befriended by a telepathic monk named Blessed Lightning. With the aid of Blessed Lightning's abilities, Tintin is informed that Chang Chong-Chen is being held captive in an ice cave by the Yeti. The other monks admonish Tintin and his companions to quit their mission after hearing of Blessed Lightning's vision, but Tintin refuses.

At the cave's entrance, Tintin waits until the Yeti leaves and then hurries inside, where he finds Chang cold and shivering. Before they can escape, the Yeti returns and growls at Tintin, alarmed. Tintin flashes a camera bulb at the cryptid and uses the Yeti's blindness to escape, with Chang in tow. The Abominable Snowman stumbles after them, but they escape back to the Buddhist monastery. There, Chang informs them all that the Yeti is actually a kind-hearted human and not an animal. Further, Chang states that he would have perished had not the Snowman rescued him from the crash and fed him. As Tintin, Haddock and Chang return to Western civilization, the broken-hearted Yeti watches from high atop the mountain as his only friend disappears from sight.

* * * * *

The delightful, enduringly popular *The Adventures of Tintin* series of graphic novels were created by Belgian artist Georges Rémi, using the pseudonym Hergé. Universal in their appeal since their first publication in 1929 in serialized comic strip format, the delicately-drawn characters were world travelers inserted into informative, well-researched storylines that often were so accurate they acted as educational introductions to many of their youthful readers to the cultures and geographical features of their various plots' locales.

Tintin in Tibet was no exception to the high standards set forth by its creator. Hergé captured the details of life in Tibet so well that the book was awarded the Dalai Lama's Truth of Light Award. This was the first time the award was ever given to a fictional work by the Tibetan government, with the 2006 cultural committee citing the book's influential effect on the Western world by portraying the customs and heritage of the indigenous people in such a favorable, positive light. Hergé claimed that this adventure began much like Tintin's in the story itself, with a dream in which the artist was lost in a world of whiteness.

Although there had been an earlier television adaptation and feature films, it was this French/Canadian co-production that first captured the magic of Hergé's unique style of artwork. Entitled *Ligne claire*, or "clean line" technique, the art emphasized a distinctive balance of line delineation in which all elements of the drawing were in harmony, rather than certain elements being emphasized via thickness and detail, as is common in most graphic novel artwork even to this day. Color was an equally important element that contributed to the popularity of Hergé's style, which was perfectly suited for early printing presses (where *The Adventures of Tintin* first made its appearance). Nelvana Studios in Canada worked closely with Hergé's estate, literally scanning some of the images from the graphic novels to use in the show, and almost invariably following the originals as storyboards for the animation, which was completed in the traditional painstaking traditional method rather than with the use of CGI.

This is a particularly moody entry in the series, as it features a worried Tintin, lots of near death experiences, and even the poignant ending in which the Yeti is revealed to be the loneliest of God's creatures, having lost his only friend (the adopted Chang) to Tintin's "rescue." While it is true that Chang Chong-Chen is barely alive when Tintin eventually reaches him in the Abominable Snowman's cave, there is more than a bit of irony in the fact that the Buddhist monks shower Tintin for his heroic efforts even as Chang bemoans the misperception that it was anyone other than the Yeti who truly gave him a second chance at life. Where others refer to the cryptid as the Abominable Snowman, Chang refuses to do so, telling Tintin that his furry friend is not an abomination but a misunderstood relative of all mankind.

Whether or not Hergé was influenced by the Hammer Films production of *The Abominable Snowman* (1957) is anyone's guess. That said, the story Hergé crafted with *Tintin in Tibet*, written three years after *The Abominable Snowman* film, shares a number of similarities with Hammer's entry. First there is the Tibetan monk who has a psychic connection with the Yeti high in the Himalayas. The manner in which the Westerners, such as Tintin and Captain Haddock, embody the usual skeptical attitude towards the Abominable Snowman echoes

that of scientist Peter Cushing in the Hammer film. Even the reversal at the end of the story in each production is uncannily similar: The Yeti is revealed not to be an aggressive monster seeking destruction but a lonely pacifist denizen merely seeking to co-exist with humanity. Had not *The Abominable Snowman* been such a box office hit in Hergé's home country of Belgium, it would be less remarkable, though the similarities are more than likely due to the limitations of the adventure story format itself than any deliberate intent by the illustrator.

Less speculative as influence upon other creative types is the mark *The Adventures of Tintin* left on Steven Spielberg, whose own production of *Harry and the Hendersons* owes more than a passing nod to the Hergé graphic novels. The adventure quest mode of most of the *Raiders of the Lost Ark* feature-length serials can be seen as influenced by the Tintin books as well, with their focus on world culture and globetrotting hero. As if in nod to the master, Spielberg has announced he is planning on directing a 3D motion-capture CGI version of *The Adventures of Tintin*, in conjunction with Peter Jackson's WETA special effects studios, for release in 2011.

All in all, *Tintin in Tibet* is a terrific adaptation of a well-realized graphic novel. Fans of Ciné du Sasquatch will definitely want to seek it out as required viewing.

Ajouba Kudat Kaa (1991)

AKA: *The Magnificent Guardian*. Starring Shagufta Ali, Hemant Birje, Manjeet Kullar, Deepak Parashar and Sonam. Directed by Shyam Ramsay and Tulsi Ramsay. India. Color. Stereo. 130 Minutes.

Overview: When a little Girl is kidnapped by a gang of thugs, her Father and Uncle must deliver a ransom in cash or face her certain death. But while the gang awaits the pay-off, the Girl manages to break free of confinement and race into the snowy wilds of the Himalayas, where her kidnappers are holed up inside a cabin.

Chased by the kidnappers, she flees into a cave, which turns out to be the home of a Yeti. The beast snarls at the men and advances on them until the frightened crooks flee for their lives, abandoning the Girl to her fate. She passes out in fright and is scooped up by the Abominable Snowman, who takes her deep into his tunnel-bound lair.

The kidnappers' Head Honcho decides to lie to the Father and tell the worried Father his daughter is still within their care, but that the Father must deliver the ransom even sooner. They set a trap and await the Father. But unbeknownst to the Father, the Uncle has followed and intervenes. Using his kung fu prowess, the Uncle helps the Father defeat the gang, forcing them to scurry like squirrels.

Meanwhile, Yeti proves to be anything but a monster to the frightened little Girl. He gently places a boulder in front of his cave entrance to shield her from the bitterly cold winds and feeds her to help maintain her strength. Back at their cabin, the kidnappers meet with a Crime Boss who views the slides they took of the Abominable Snowman. Convinced the cryptid is worth millions if secured by his henchmen, the Crime Boss orders the kidnappers to capture the beast alive and get rid of the Girl, who is the only living witness to their botched attempt to extort money from the Father.

The Father and Uncle visit a tavern of local Tibetans and secure assistance in locating the Yeti's lair. A confrontation is set in motion between the rescuing Father and Uncle, the vengeful kidnappers (lead by their Head Honcho), who are intent on redeeming themselves in their Crime Boss' eyes, and the protective Yeti, who refuses to give up the little Girl to anyone but her proper caretakers.

* * * * *

If you've never seen a Bollywood film, you've truly missed something unique in world cinema. One of the largest cinema-attending countries in the world (far exceeding America and other countries in this regard, as well as in sheer output — a staggering 900 films per annum for India, compared to the paltry 200 to 300 made by American studios and independents alike!), the sub-continent's cinematic formula is almost the same across every genre. That is, whether the film is a romance, an action film, or even a horror movie, a few musical numbers are sure to pop up. It is as if each Bollywood film is a blend of *all* possible genres, no matter the overall designation in terms of audience appeal; in this way, the producers have crafted an *uber*-genre that insures each and every film will literally have "something for everyone," rather than adhering to the rigid aesthetic distinctions so common in American films. And so a horror film like *Ajouba Kudat Kaa* will not only feature traditional elements such as monsters and violence, but moments from a children's movie, an action adventure film, and — almost inevitably — a musical number or two straight out of *Singing in the Rain* (seasoned, of course, with local flavors and spices).

Ajouba Kudat Kaa is a production of the prolific Ramsay Brothers, who cornered the Indian horror and fantasy film market for over a decade of solid output. A majority of their movies were thinly-veiled redos of American box office spectaculars, such as *The Exorcist* and *The Omen*. The source inspiration for *Ajouba Kudat Kaa* is clearly *Harry and the Hendersons*, but the resemblance is nominal; apart from the insipid melodrama of the kidnapped child being taken care of by the Yeti (a reversal of the Spielberg film), the movies could not be more different. Like all Indian films, *Ajouba Kudat Kaa* is as much an action-filled, fists-a-flying extravaganza as it is a Ciné du Sasquatch entry. For example, the film opens (after the customary slaughter of several explorers who unwittingly stumble upon the Abominable Snowman's cave and meet their deaths) with the Uncle character fighting a street duel with a thug, while the Father character takes the betting proceeds (à la *Hard Times* with Charles Bronson). After victory, the scene swiftly switches to a romance scene between the parents, and just as quickly to a children's party sequence which plays straight out of a Disney movie. Yet another dramatic turn ensues when a creepily-masked bandit appears without warning among the happy partygoers and kidnaps the Girl!

These transitions are as sudden as they read; the Indian style of filmmaking favors a surrealist (some might say choppy) editing style that constantly jumps ahead of the spectator rather than dogmatically following linear logic. While this is a valid criticism, it also helps keep the typical Hindi film's bloated running time (three hours is not unusual!) from collapsing into sheer tedium. *Ajouba Kudat Kaa* is no exception, favoring alternating moments of pandemonium, horror, humor, and musical interludes, with a dose of sentimentalism tossed in to create a completely madcap movie.

Yeti is actually (as far as Hindi films go, anyway) very well crafted. While never more than convincing as a man in a Sasquatch suit, it at least rises above the man-in-a-gorilla-suit level. Several close-ups feature what appear to be a canine's jaws and teeth being pushed through the rubber mask of the Yeti's open jaws; the effect resembles the wolf emerging from the girl's face in Neil Jordan's *The Company of Wolves*, and John Landis' *An American Werewolf in London*, albeit on a much cruder scale. Whether the filmmaker is attempting to demonstrate that the Yeti has non-human abilities, or simply scare his audience, is about as clearly delineated as the special effect itself, alas.

A final note of weirdness is the musical score. Films of this era often featured American and other countries' film scores lifted cue by cue and simply dropped into the soundtrack of their respective Hindi counterparts. Even more strangely, the scores were "borrowed" not only for Indian remakes of the foreign originals, but for any and all Hindi films! So during the running time of *Ajouba Kudat Kaa*, one is startled to hear strains from Ennio Morricone's music from *A*

Fistful of Dollars, as well as *The Good, the Bad and the Ugly*! Snippets from other scores too numerous to list are equally and suddenly dropped into the film with unexpected and jarring impact. The sound mix is akin to a needle being dropped on an old vinyl album rather than smoothly-faded transitions mixed in a professional audio lab. Where one cue ends in mid-note, another will pop up to fill its void. To say the overall effect for Western audiences is abrupt is an understatement equal to saying *Ajouba Kudat Kaa* is an atypical example of Ciné du Sasquatch. It's that and so much more. Like the dialogue itself, in which Hindi speakers will suddenly utter unexplained English phrases (one that particularly stands out occurs when the little Girl compares her Uncle the street fighter to "He-Man and the Masters of the Universe" in perfect English), this is one Yeti film unlike any other most viewers have ever seen.

The Al Hodgson Interview (2010) (Doc)

Featuring Al Hodgson. Conducted by Steven Streufert. USA. Color. Stereo. 137 Minutes.

Overview: Elderly Bigfoot expert Al Hodgson is interviewed by the owner of Bigfoot Books (a clearance center for all things published in regards to Sasquatch) in his Willow Creek, California, home. Hodgson made the fateful telephone call to Roger Patterson that resulted in Patterson and Bob Gimlim mounting their joint expedition in 1967 to the Bluff Creek area, where their famous 16mm footage was shot. A key archivist of early Bluff Creek Bigfoot plaster casts since the 1950s, and curator of the Willow Creek-China Flat Museum, Hodgson is rightfully considered a premiere contributor to the field of cryptozoology for his ongoing preservation of major evidence and memorabilia for over sixty years.

The genial octogenarian converses freely about a wide range of topics Ciné du Sasquatch documentary lovers will find intriguing. Topics discussed include the obscure Blue Creek Mountain film footage shot by Rene Dahinden in 1967, which preceded the Patterson-Gimlin film and was spliced together with the Patterson-Gimlin footage at one point; various famous and not-so-famous Bigfoot hunters he's known; the infamous claim that a family of Bigfoot creatures were slaughtered and buried to hide the secret in 1967; John Green's return to the Bluff Creek area several months after Patterson's footage was taken, where he filmed the precise locales and had assistant Jim McClarin walk the same path as the hominid seen in Patterson-Gimlin footage; and much, much more.

For those seeking historical information and verification of facts otherwise unavailable in even the best researched books on the subject, *The Al Hodgson Interview* is as invaluable as the actual Patterson-Gimlin footage itself. The complete videotaped interview can be downloaded from Bigfoot's Book Blog at *http://bigfootbooksblog. blogspot.com/2010/02/interview-with-al-hodgson-bigfoot-elder.html*.

Almost Live! (1996) (TV) (Cameo)

Starring Tracey Conway, Pat Cashman, Nancy Guppy, Steve Wilson, Bill Stainton and Bob Nelson. Produced by KING-TV. Written by Kim Evey and Barbara Klansnic. USA. Color. Stereo. 30 Minutes.

Overview: A Seattle, Washington, comedy revue show that ran from 1984 to 1999 on local television station KING-TV and featured various skits and commercial parodies, *Almost Live!* preceded NBC's *Saturday Night Live* for many years, and was later broadcast after *SNL* in the years following its cancellation. Among the many popular segments was "Bill Nye the Science Guy," which was later spun-off into a PBS series bearing the same name; and some segments were re-used later on Fox TV's short-lived comedy show *Haywire*.

One of the most enduring of the sketches was an *SNL*-styled "Weekend Update" parody of the local Seattle news called "The Late Report," which focused on everything from politics and the economy to the grunge music scene and even Bigfoot in one segment. Bigfoot, played by Pat Cashman in a ridiculous suit, responds to a report that he is being hunted by a Washington State University egghead who believes only a dead Bigfoot body will convince skeptics. Outraged at the doctor's insensitivity, Bigfoot takes him to task, pointing out that he's got a tough life as it is, what with his bad smell, constant lampooning by shows just like this one, and quacks like the Washington State teacher advocating violence against him. After comparing himself with a freshman at the same university who's had a few too many beers at a frat party, Bigfoot implores the viewers to refrain from plugging him if they should happen to encounter the friendly if misunderstood hominid while hiking or camping.

Because of the enduring popularity of both the show and Sasquatch sightings in the Washington state region, both the series and the cryptid segment are well-remembered by fans of *Almost Live!* The series was briefly syndicated in the earliest years of Comedy Central's cable debut, with most of the regional material cut from the show to make it more appealing to a national audience.

Alpine Affairs (1995)

Starring Baily, Robin Lee and Olivia. Produced, Written and Directed by Gail Force. USA. Color. Stereo. 72 Minutes.

Overview: When a ski park ranger is informed a hairy snow monster is abducting women skiers, he enlists the help of his two shapeliest assistants to track down the beast. Needing additional help, with his two sex bunnies out of the office stalking Sasquatch, the ranger is delighted when a comely young lady shows up and offers to do whatever it takes to become a park ranger herself. He quickly takes her up on her offer — and takes her sexually.

Meanwhile, the mystery deepens as the snow monster continues its assault on more females, dragging them away, never to be seen again. Two male Australian witnesses to the latest Yeti attack meet up with the two female park rangerettes, and many sexual peccadilloes ensue. Eventually satiated, one of the Australian men tracks the Abominable Snowman to a remote shack. Therein he discovers the beast has tied one of the missing women to a chair and held her captive. The Australian man frees her, and they make love. Alas, the ranger returns, with the two park rangerettes in tow. He locks them all in his remote cabin basement and tells them he has been pretending to be the Yeti. When they ask why the elaborate ruse, the ranger explains the land beneath the ski resort once belonged to his ancestors, and that there is still gold in the valley, which he intends to take, rightfully or wrongfully, as his revenge for his kinfolks being robbed of their land rights by the swindlers who built the lodge.

After tricking the ranger into a *ménage a trios*, the rangerettes overpower the sex-crazed ranger and the case is closed.

* * * * *

Alpine Affairs is a tawdry set of love connections indeed. Complete with hissing audio track, non-existent lighting, beyond-amateurish dialogue that steps into sub–Ed Woodian territory, the most unconvincing Yeti costume in recent Ciné du Sasquatch history, and a monotonously predictable barrage of non-stop pornographic sex scenes, *Alpine Affairs* makes the viewer dizzy not from stimulation, but from lack of oxygen from the heights of ineptitude on display.

Of course, where adult videos made for the cost of blank VHS stock are concerned, it is useless to complain about the comparative lack of production values. The typical male purchaser of such lurid fare cares very little about the filler in-between the hardcore sex (of which there is plenty throughout *Alpine Affairs*), and — as the Internet age of porn has proven beyond any reasonable doubt — the less time "wasted" on acting, plot, and characterization, the better ("better" being a qualified word choice in this regard). To put it bluntly, *Alpine Affairs* makes *Deep Throat* seem like it was directed by Alfred Hitchcock in comparison.

The nominal use of Sasquatch to act as a decoy to draw suspicion away from the park ranger, who is plotting to secretly mine the ski lodge for gold, is straight out of *Scooby Doo*. All that is missing is a panty-clad Velma explaining how the lawman performed his trickery to make this a complete "homage" (or, if you prefer, rip-off). That, *and* the well-endowed ranger saying as he's lead away in handcuffs, "And I'd have gotten away with it, too, if it hadn't been for you meddling, lust-filled kids!"

The cheesy snow monster suit is hilariously bad. First, the albino ape mask is five shades lighter than the dirty white ape suit, which creates the illusion that the Yeti has been wearing a ski mask or some other "sun block" device. Likewise, the ludicrous costume is played strictly for laughs, complete with a long, dangling tail! While the "director" may have entertained notions that the length of the sorry appendage cinematically signified some hidden phallic sub-text, this surely fell by the wayside when the drugs utilized during production wore off. The sight of the slackened tail swinging literally half-assed after each turn of the Snowman is, in a word, abominable.

All of the above aside, at least *Alpine Affairs* caters to its craven crowd with a sense of showmanship, however badly achieved. Compared to the tedium of pseudo-porn efforts such as *Search for the Beast*, *Alpine Affairs* makes no pretentions to being other than what it is: unadulterated hardcore. As sleazy as this renders all that is on display — and nothing is left to the viewer's imagination (save the longing for the chroma-keyed end credits) — it at least gives it one redeeming feature the aforementioned "legitimate" Sasquatch movie lacks: marginal entertainment value. Better to have tried at porn and succeeded, in other words, than failed with a reprehensible effort that renders cryptid cinema nothing more than a perverted carnival sideshow, as does *Search for the Beast*.

Altered States (1980) (Cameo)

Starring William Hurt, Blair Brown, Bob Balaban, Charles Haid and Miguel Godreau. Produced by Daniel Melnick, Stuart Baird and Howard Gottfried. Written by Paddy Chayefsky. Directed by Ken Russell. USA. Color. Stereo. 102 Minutes.

Overview: Dr. Eddie Jessup is obsessed with the possibility of uncovering ancient human pre-history via the exploration of encoded memories within the human DNA structures themselves. To facilitate his research, Jessup utilizes a sensory deprivation tank and experiments with hallucinogenic drugs to stimulate his regressive recall abilities. Against all expectations, Jessup's bouts with altered states of consciousness bring results: He begins to catch brief if elusive glimpses into the distant past of mankind's origins.

Despite the warnings of his wife Emily and colleagues Arthur and Mason, who see Jessup's self-destructive side emerging as a result of his odyssey, Jessup only accelerates his prolonged trips into the primordial past of humanity via confinement in the tank. Eventually he emerges from the tank one night having literally and physically regressed into a diminutive hominid that proceeds to terrorize two campus guards. Jessup as prehistoric Hyde roams the dark city streets until he reverts back to his normal self the next morning. Jessup continues with his now pathological experiment, despite abandonment by his wife and friends, until he nearly dematerializes into a blob of microcellular stew. At the last moment he is rescued by his wife, who acts as a kind of matter to his anti-matter and saves his life.

*****

Altered States is by no means a full-fledged entry in Ciné du Sasquatch. Rather, in a film full of brilliant sequences and thought-provoking concepts so atypical in the cinematic SF genre, *Altered States* presents a prolonged sequence that is thematically resonate within the Bigfoot genre if detached from the otherwise more hallucinogenic proceedings involving sensory deprivation tanks, self-degenerative molecular disintegration, and the like. This is the so-called "Primal Man" sequence, and it works by itself as well as it does plopped into the middle of *Altered State*'s narrative in terms of illustrating Sasquatch cinematic concerns (not to mention also providing some viscerally scary moments in an otherwise cerebral thriller).

The sequence takes place one night wherein two luckless campus security guards are startled to encounter noises outside the basement where Jessup conducts his secretive sensory deprivation tank studies. A small ape-like man who is clearly somewhat human and equally somewhat simian bursts free from the lab. To the guards' horror, the Primal Man is anything but happy with suddenly finding itself transported into the current century, and goes "ape" in a savage display of ferocity that leaves the guards shaken to their cores. The Primal Man flees into the night as they watch, helpless. Later, Jessup will revert to his human self and realize, as he examines himself covered in the blood of slaughtered zoo animals, that his is not just radical research, but physically dangerous to himself and others.

The Primal Man realization is very much a cryptid by any other name, even if many would consider him a "caveman" by more common nomenclature. But this is akin to calling all cinematic cavemen Neanderthals, when in fact many examples of other cave-dwelling hominids were known to exist throughout history, some more humanlike and others more simian-related. Not quite matching any known fossil or human ancestor, the Primal Man instead represents the "fork in the road" where we, as *Homo sapiens*, clearly diverged from our simian cousins to become (over a long evolutionary path of adaptation and genetic advancement) the modern humans we are today.

Herein the Primal Man echoes the themes so prevalent throughout Ciné du Sasquatch — to wit, Primal Man is not merely an earlier version of man, but something so closely related in terms of genetics and anthropology that we see similarities with ourselves in him, and yet — to our horror — an equal recognition of the differences. The Primal Man is, in other words, a shadowy version of us, our cinematic realization of the Other. He is bipedal and human-like in structure, but at the same time organized along an entirely different set of cultural and physical modes of existence. This is vividly illustrated by the fact the Primal Man is not a defensive, tree-dwelling coward who hopes to escape the menace of predatory life (as we might expect from a "monkey man"), but a full-on, aggressive, attack-minded creature who embodies the idea that the best defense is a good offense.

The guards see this first-hand when the Primal Man emerges from the tank not with the idea of making peace with his surroundings but conquering them. For the Primal Man does not wish to rationalize external reality as much as he does control it with sudden, savage fury. In this regard, he is more like an animal than a human being, who typically attempts first to gain an understanding of his environment (at least, that is, before destroying it if he cannot then control or conquer it). The distinctions make sense: The Primal Man has evidently achieved domination over his world of constant threat by utilizing a type of psychic furor modern human beings spend an entire lifetime attempting to suppress. Forget any hopes of a negotiated settlement, the Primal Man seems to be telling the viewer; prepare for survival of the fittest (fittest being the most able to inflict bodily damage in the shortest amount of time).

In all of the above qualities, the Primal Man is truly a cinematic half-brother to most filmic hominids. Like other cryptids in Ciné du Sasquatch, the Primal Man does not wish to engage in conflict unless territorial boundaries are unobserved by intrusive human beings. Like other cinema simian cryptids, the Primal Man will respond with ruthless aggression should any *Homo sapiens* be foolish enough to cross the imaginary yet mentally-established boundary lines. Neither the Primal Man nor Bigfoot seek to mix peacefully at the market fair; both wish to avoid any association with human beings altogether and will react violently if this innate wish is not respected. This need seems to be genetically encoded into their very weave of life, and transgressions in Ciné du Sasquatch of this clear understanding (at least, that is, clear to the hominids) always brings about death and destruction of the natural order as a direct consequence.

One might successfully argue that Dr. Jessup more closely resembles Dr. Jekyll turned into Mr. Hyde than any cryptid hominid in *Altered States*. But this misses the larger point Chayefsky, both in his novel and brilliant screenplay adaptation, as well as director Russell, echoed throughout the film — that such Victorian era moral distinctions between good versus evil simply fade into nothingness when confronted with the fog of primordial existence. The Primal Man is not interested in releasing his inner beast on the one extreme any more than he is in having a cigar, a brandy and a good philosophical discussion in front of a roaring hearth on the other; the Primal Man exists to exist, *a priori* and only, and renders all obstacles in his way to doing so obsolete or subservient to this overriding need. This is truly an "altered state" of consciousness mankind has emerged from, the creators are telling us. It is not some peaceful, innocuous hominid with good intent for all living things around him, but a resourceful, cunning killer with no restraint. It's little wonder, then, that the results of modern civilization seem so Draconian and unapologetically cruel; after all, the real question isn't whether or not the Primal Man has truly progressed, but whether or not modern mankind has. Too, the Primal Man is not shown to possess a lack of technological understanding — it can craftily open a door and adapt implements for use as a weapon — but a lack of simple self-enlightenment that always destroying before one understands may not be the wisest course of action, however much it helps (or has helped) Darwinian evolution of its species to this point.

The altered state, in essence, is going from a subconscious state into conscious realization of one's own placement along the developmental continuum. Without it, the film suggests, we are all just the Primal Man waiting to regress at a moment's notice. Which is precisely the "mask" worn by the typical hominid in Ciné du Sasquatch that the viewer encounters — Sasquatch as the Shadow Self, the Animus, the Other, all externalized masks for our darker natures wherein the rules of society (or, at least, our human society) have vanished and been replaced by a primordial force of pure, unadulterated fear and desire. Such impulses always conflict with the "better angels of our nature," but therefore represent our self-stymied longing for the simplicity of taking what we want when we desire it without the subsequent judgment or responsibility for our actions. Here one has come face-to-face with the embodiment of not just the Primal Man, but the Cinematic Sasquatch as well. We have met the hominid, and, in disguise, it is us.

American Dragon Jake Long ("Hairy Christmas") (2007) (TV)

Featuring the voices of Dante Basco, Amy Bruckner, Keone Young, John DiMaggio, Kali Troy, Charlie Finn, Mae Whitman and Jeff Bennett. Produced by Eddie Guzelian, Matthew Negrete, Jeff Goode, Larry Johnson and Christian Roman. Written by Chris Parrish. Directed by Steve Loter. USA. Color. Stereo. 30 Minutes.

Overview: Teenager Jake Long is a secret "Dragon"—a normal person with the ability to transform into a mythical protectorate of humanity since time immemorial—due to his lineage on his Chinese mother's side. Because he lives in New York with his family, he is the American Dragon. Along with his teen pals Spud and Trixie, he fights a variety of evils that spring up in the Big Apple, always keeping his identity as the American Dragon from his unknowing parents and kid sister.

When a giant pine is airlifted by woodcutters to New York's Rockefeller Center to be installed as the annual Christmas tree, it inadvertently transports a baby Bigfoot in its top. The outraged Sasquatch clan follows on foot, determined to wreak havoc in the big city when they find the guilty party who have stolen their offspring. Meanwhile, in New York City the baby Sasquatch escapes from the tree, causing quite a stir and winding up videotaped in the process. Professor Rotwood (a self-professed "mythobiologist") sees the cryptid and realizes his long-desired goal to study a Bigfoot specimen is at last within his grasp. He sets out with his equipment and bait to capture the infant hominid before anyone can beat him to it.

Word gets to Jake from his grandfather that the Sasquatch tribe is nearing the city and will destroy it as they seek out their missing infant. Jake and his two pals set out to prevent the coming chaos, but soon face not only Professor Rotwood, but a pair of Huntsboys, teen hirelings of the infamous Huntsman, who is always attempting to intervene with Jake's heroics and foil the outcome (to his own nefarious advantage). After Jake transforms into the American Dragon and almost secures the baby Bigfoot, the Huntsman maneuvers his stealth helicopter into position and snags the cryptid with a grappling hook and net. Worse for the city, the Sasquatch clan have arrived. They smash cars and destroy all in their path as they draw closer to their abducted kin.

Spud helps by clogging the intake of the Huntsman's helicopter with a fruitcake his grandmother has sent him for the holidays, which causes the Huntsman's chopper to explode. Jake catches the falling baby Bigfoot and returns it to the growling Bigfoot group, who threaten to smash him for his interference until the infant shows affection to Jake and his friends. The tribe accepts that Jake has acted nobly and leaves the city without further rancor.

* * * * *

The use of an infant Bigfoot is an ingrained staple of Ciné du Sasquatch—from *Little Bigfoot* to *The Adventures of Sam and Max: Freelance Police* and beyond, the Bigfoot genre is filled with such imagery. It is not that surprising, given that some real-life Sasquatch reports have witnesses describing seeing such families of cryptids acting together in tribal settings. So in this regard, this episode of *American Dragon Jake Long*, called "Hairy Christmas," is par for the course in terms of concept. It does, to its credit, feature a few novel visualizations of life among the hominid clan not typically seen in the genre.

One of the unexpected qualities shown is the Sasquatch clan's ability to dematerialize (or, as Professor Rotwood calls it, "invisibly cloak themselves") when threatened. This is depicted by having the Bigfoot creatures shimmer and turn translucent, becoming almost but not quite invisible. Without expository commentary, this goes a long ways towards suggesting to audiences why such a crypto-species could remain undiscovered for so many centuries by scientists and non-believers. Because the ability is visually shown and not discussed by the characters, it works quite well. Despite this ability to shapeshift and dematerialize being mentioned in some of the more Fortean Sasquatch sightings and Native American folklore, it is rarely invoked in the films and television shows themselves. This probably is because the creators want to portray the threat of a Bigfoot as physical, not amorphous or paranormal. It's not that a "ghost-squatch" couldn't be scary in and of itself if properly portrayed; rather, it perhaps stretches the already necessary suspension of disbelief beyond the breaking point to for many audiences have both a Sasquatch and such supernatural powers shown onscreen at the same time.

Another original concept is the Bigfoot tribe using trees for their homes. While this is not unique by itself, it is atypical in the genre. On those occasional instances when such tree use is shown in Ciné du Sasquatch, Bigfoot is mostly shown attacking from above and off-screen, grabbing an unsuspecting human below and yanking them upwards. Herein, however, we see the actual living conditions by which such a semi-simian species might actually utilize the dense woods they are typically reported to dwell within to their advantage, nesting in them almost like giant birds of prey. Again, many species of simians are known to live in the trees and rarely venture to the ground to protect themselves from predators, but having such a large quasi-primate doing so is not the usual genre visualization. Rather, a cave or related shelters are suggested as the creatures' domain for obvious protective reasons. The idea of such large hominids "hiding in plain sight" hundreds of feet above the forest floor again works to explain how Sasquatch might survive without detection in the modern world.

For all the imaginative touches, *American Dragon Jake Long* basically portrays the Sasquatch elders as a group of albino gorillas in the *King Kong* mold (albeit with the power to turn themselves semi-invisible). They are even shown to ultimately wreck some valuable New York City commercial real estate, even if they never climb any high rise towers. This homage to the Eighth Wonder of the World is difficult to ignore, especially given the baby Sasquatch has white fur just like Kong's own lineage in *Son of Kong*. In fact, the entire tribe of Sasquatch creatures have white fur, which makes the show's calling them (without variation) either Bigfoot or Sasquatch strangely amusing, as no one ever suggests the terms Yeti or Abominable Snowmen. Whether this is an unwitting desire to simply keep the cultural affinity entirely North American or a deliberate slight against the Tibetan legend is, naturally, merely speculation. Still, one is left wondering why, since the Asian background of Jake Long himself is so carefully stressed throughout the series, the producers wouldn't want to include the more obvious relevance to such a geographical link as the Sherpas, the Himalayan Mountains, etc.

Less speculative and more outright entertaining is the deft pun of having Professor Rotwood call himself a "mythobiologist" rather than cryptozoologist. While there is no reason to not simply have the Doctor label himself the latter, the former adds a bit of wacky charm to the show and is a first in the genre—even the name of the field of research in regards to the study of such unproven animals has been parodied herein! Most cryptozoologists have endured more than their fair share of ridicule at the very nature of their endeavor; perhaps it is only fitting then to allow them some much-deserved breathing room and invent a counter-science so as not to confuse younger viewers.

While it never breaks much new ground in terms of its television handling of the Ciné du Sasquatch genre, *American Dragon Jake Long* does offer plenty most children and early teens will find engaging. It is fast-paced, well-animated and features a believable set of likeable, modern characters who always learn a lesson by show's end and painlessly impart said message (painless, that is, to all but the most cynical viewers). "Hairy Christmas" embodies the show as a representative episode quite well, and, if not completely original, works as mild entertainment.

Among Us (2004)

Starring Bob Dennis, Hunter Mackenzie Austin, Jon McBride and John Polonia. Produced by Jon McBride, John Polonia and Mark Polonia.

Written by John Oak Dalton. Directed by Jon McBride, John Polonia and Mark Polonia. USA. Color. Stereo. 85 Minutes.

Overview: Billy D'Amato, director of numerous obscure direct-to-video, camcorder-shot cheapies (many in the Ciné du Sasquatch genre), has a real-life encounter with a cryptid after years of cynical denial of Sasquatch's existence. Realizing he has done an injustice to his subject matter, as well as to the friends he ruthlessly exploited and rarely paid to assist on his movies, D'Amato sets out on a personal odyssey to redeem himself and Bigfoot as a legitimate species.

The filmmaker approaches those he's wronged in the past, asking them to help him one last time in the pursuit of making a truly defining Sasquatch documentary. D'Amato's goal is nothing less than proving Bigfoot's existence with indisputable video evidence. But given his prior mockery of the genre and his callous alienation of his ex-girlfriend, his long-time camera operator, and his resident cryptozoology expert, D'Amato quickly learns there are greater challenges than proving Bigfoot is real — namely, engendering trust among humans who've been previously betrayed.

* * * * *

Though it suffers from a severely limited budget, amateur performances, technical deficiencies in audio and video, and the usual gorilla suit stand-in for Bigfoot, *Among Us* is not without occasional merit for ardent viewers. Although its critical reputation among aficionados of Ciné du Sasquatch hovers near the bottom of the genre, low-brow, ironic laughs are to be found for anyone not adverse to crass humor.

That's not to say the drawbacks don't outweigh the slim plusses — that is not even a fair contest, so large is the discrepancy — but at least *Among Us* has the knowing grace that it is a bad film at its core and mercifully lets the audience in on the joke with a leering wink. Though a small favor, it is more than far too many Ciné du Sasquatch entries are willing to concede, suffering as they do from an earnest and deadly seriousness which leaves the viewer to wonder about these later filmmakers' motives, mental stability, or, in more than a few cases, both.

The fictitious D'Amato is a reference to prolific Italian cult director Joe D'Amato, and, like his namesake, this filmmaker takes whatever producers offer as long as a paycheck is attached to the project. A two-bit, self-taught hustler of dubious talent and absentee ethics, Billy D'Amato has, to his infamy, amassed a number of credits involving Sasquatch, such as *Gladiator Bigfoot* (Ridley Scott's *Gladiator* but with a Bigfoot and no budget), as well as a series of gay porn videos with a log cabin setting.

Alas, the self-deluding director has fooled no one but himself, as both critics and friends alike consider his meager skills sub-par. Given the forty-plus features to his credit and their astounding lack of entertainment value, the scene in which D'Amato's ex-girlfriend Jennifer confronts him about his unending cinematic failures is poignant if not bitterly funny. She asks him if, when he saw *Close Encounters of the Third Kind* and *Star Wars* as a child, D'Amato was aware such comparative greatness would be forever beyond his own abilities. Here *Among Us* achieves a

momentary pathos; the realization is painfully apparent in D'Amato's expression that, indeed, no such truth ever entered his mind, however permanently she has now implanted it.

In many ways D'Amato is akin to a modern-day Ed Wood, Jr.— if Wood had been given a camcorder instead of a 35mm motion picture camera. With raw stock no longer a cost prohibition (as it was for Wood's equally lurid efforts), D'Amato indulges himself in his favorite fetish subject matters, much like his predecessor. Only instead of worshipping Angora sweaters as did Wood, D'Amato's obsession is a Bigfoot costume, grafted onto his every effort despite his best intentions otherwise. This unhealthy cryptid mania is actually quite true-to-life, in that many Ciné du Sasquatch fans find themselves equally unable to remain objective about the genre or its inspirational hominid namesake, and thus rings very real in an otherwise farce-driven effort.

The other characters (or, to be more precise, caricatures) are underdeveloped in terms of believability and back story. The cryptozoologist Wayne Beaubier (portrayed by co-director Jon McBride), for example, is a thinly-veiled Jerry Lewis type circa *The Absent-Minded Professor*, complete with bowl haircut, thick glasses and geeky mannerisms. Self-absorbed with his quest and a complete believer unwilling to objectively consider any evidence to the contrary, the crypto scientist believes that, despite the ludicrous manner in which D'Amato has rendered Bigfoot to date in his tawdry videos, the specimen has been done more good than harm; after all, he rationalizes to the camera, haven't viewers at least learned *some* information (however ill-informed) about Sasquatch by watching D'Amato's bad Bigfoot films?

Beaubier offers corroborating evidence of his thesis by demonstrating the correct manner in which to cast plaster when one finds a Sasquatch footprint. In lingering close-up, the so-called expert first sprinkles dry plaster into the imprint and then adds water atop the powder. Anyone who has ever mixed plaster of Paris or related alginates will quickly understand the fallacy of this approach; simply, the casting material must first be mixed together and *then* poured

Key artwork from the DVD release of *Among Us*.

into the print in order to maintain consistency. Though an admittedly small detail, it's indicative of the film itself: a crazy concoction that never blends together into a believable whole, though it admittedly delivers low-key laughs to those who appreciate the inherent absurdities present in much of Ciné du Sasquatch.

Among Us opens with a man dashing into an eerily vacant rest area on a remote highway. No sooner has he started his business than Sasquatch sneaks inside via an open window. The hapless human stares in disbelief (as will most viewers) as the killer cryptid murders him with deliberate overkill; a literal level of toilet humor is herein established from the beginning that *Among Us* rarely "floats" above and all-too often "sinks" beneath. And while Ciné du Sasquatch fans will occasionally appreciate the parody nature of the "film within a film" recreations of D'Amato's hilariously inept earlier features, the lambasted fictional films are not much worse than *Among Us* itself. For most, the required obsessive necessity to watch the entire movie will outweigh the marginal laughs.

Credit must be given, however, for the sheer durability of the filmmakers. Along with Jon McBride, the real auteurs (in the best Ed Woodian sensibility) behind *Among Us* are the twin brothers Mark and John Polonia. Having started making video features in their teens in their childhood state of Pennsylvania, they self-produced, directed, acted in and distributed over 20 horror features in their native homeland until John's untimely death at the age of 38 of a heart aneurysm in 2008. A sampling of the titles they put out: *Splatter Beach*; *Peter Rottentail*; *Gorilla Warfare: Battle of the Apes*; *Holla If I Kill You*; and *Hellgate: The House That Screamed*. Surely the fictitious filmmaker Billy D'Amato is a composite of their own life-long experiences as widely-panned, no-budget directors of schlock themselves. In this sense, they capture the poignant, real horrors of a life lead in quiet desperation, anonymously grinding out feature after feature and yet remaining in remarkable obscurity even to this day.

Ancient Mysteries (1996) ("Bigfoot" and "Abominable Snowman") (TV) (Doc)

AKA: *Ancient Mysteries: New Investigations of the Unsolved*. Featuring Leonard Nimoy, Peter Byrne, Jimmy Jackson, Byron Nelson, Jr., Roderick Sprague, Ed Edmo, Mary Schlick, Theodore Roosevelt (archival footage), Grover Krantz, Allen Mootnick, John Crane, Daryl Owen, Scott Herriott, Al Hodgson, Debra Jones and Craig Carpenter. Produced by Larayne Decoeur, Dale Dreher, Craig D. Forrest and Lars Ullberg. Written by Lionel Friedberg. Directed by Steven Talley. USA. Color. Stereo. 60 Minutes.

Overview: Leonard Nimoy returns in the 1990s in a virtual remake of the 1970s series *In Search Of* that immortalized the phrase "Could it be..?" which was a rhetorical device used by the *In Search Of* writers to basically ask questions whose answers were, more often than not, answerable by the response, "Probably not, but it sure *sounds* convincing when you ask it *that* way, Leonard." So similar was the Arts & Entertainment Television Network's series it even had Nimoy begin each show by saying, "Before we unlock the future, we must find the keys to the past. I'm Leonard Nimoy. Join me and open the door to ancient mysteries, beginning now..." (Compare this to the opening of the *In Search Of* series from 1976: "Lost civilizations, extraterrestrials, myths and monsters, missing persons, magic and witchcraft, unexplained phenomena. *In Search Of* cameras are traveling the world, seeking out these great mysteries.")

The popular "Bigfoot" episode of *Ancient Mysteries* is remarkable for the sheer amount of cryptozoologists it contains who are and were once preeminent in the field: Peter Byrne, director of the seminal Bigfoot Research Project; Grover Krantz, anthropologist and early

cryptid advocate; Scott Herriott, Bigfoot documentarian and eyewitness to his own encounters; Al Hodgson, Bigfoot researcher and curator of the Willow Creek-China Flat Museum; and many others. Even Teddy Roosevelt appears courtesy of stock footage, as his journal entry from his book *The Wilderness Hunter* relates the story of Canadian fur trappers who met a Savage Sasquatch — one to a fatal end. As a final plus, the Patterson-Gimlin footage shot in 1967 at Bluff Creek, California, is also included.

Ancient Mysteries also produced an episode called "The Abominable Snowman," featuring cryptozoologist/consultant Loren Coleman, as well as various segments exploring the history and culture surrounding the Tibetan cryptid (such as the Tom Slick 1959 and Sir Edmund Hillary 1960 expeditions into the Himalayan Mountains in quest of the Yeti). Also highlighted was the infamous "Snow Walker" footage, which at the time of production was newly-revealed as genuine but later proven to be a hoax.

The History Channel purchased the A&E Network and retitled this particular episode "In Search of History: In Search of the Abominable Snowman." The Leonard Nimoy narration was removed, as were various titles identifying the show as part of the A&E series *Ancient Mysteries*, and several factoids regarding the Abominable Snowman were added as wraparounds. Otherwise identical, this was released on home video and shown on the History Channel (aka History).

Angela Anaconda ("Camp Anaconda") (Cameo) (TV) (1999)

Starring the voices of Sue Rose, Richard Binsley and Kevin Duhaney. Created by Joanna Ferrone and Sue Rose. Canada. Color. Stereo. 30 Minutes.

Overview: The delightfully low-tech cut-out style of animation frequently used by Terry Gilliam in his Monty Python short films is employed throughout the iconoclastic *Angela Anaconda*. In an episode called "Camp Anaconda," Angela goes on her usual manic-paced recapitulation of what happened once when she and her friends decided to make her own home a "virtual camping site" after an unwanted excursion at a nearby woodsy camp, complete with local legend Bigfoot skulking around the young campers' cabins (or at least their imaginations). It's a brief cameo, but it captures the nearly hysterical intensity with which younger Sasquatch believers can conjure up the notorious wood demon and place it within a few licking flames of their campfire.

Animal X (1997) (TV) (Doc)

Hosted by Bill Kerr. Featuring Richard Greenwell, Darwin Greenwell, Jeffrey Meldrum, Mark Slack, Professor Valentin Sapunov, Senator Bill O'Chee, the Australian Hominid Research Group, the International Society of Cryptozoology, Craig Woolheater and Texas Bigfoot. Produced by Storyteller Media and the Discovery Channel. Australia/USA. Color. Video. Stereo. 30 Minutes.

Overview: This Australian-produced cryptozoology-themed series ran for three seasons and featured a plethora of well-shot, well-researched segments, usually 8 to 9 minutes in length, focusing on such cryptid phenomena as Bigfoot in Texas, Yowie in Australia, the Jersey Devil, Chupacabras, Goatman, and other animal-related unknown species. The segments were then edited into 30-minute programs consisting of three segments each.

Traveling the world to document the latest findings, *Animal X* (and its direct-to-DVD off-shoot *Animal X: Natural Mystery Unit*) is of particular interest to Ciné du Sasquatch aficionados for segments from the first season ("Episode 5: Bigfoot," "Episode 11: Yeti," and "Episode 12: Yowie"), the second season ("Episode 1: Bigfoot," "Episode 4: Skookum Expedition," "Episode 5: Global Bigfoot," "Episode 6: Skunk Ape," and "Episode 9: Yowie"), and the third season ("Episode 4: Texas Bigfoot").

The series was so popular that the Discovery Channel co-financed the second and third seasons, including a special Skookum episode in conjunction with the Bigfoot Field Research Organization. The show remains a popular favorite for many in the cryptozoology community.

Answers About Creation (1998) (Doc)

Featuring Dr. Kent Hovind. Produced by the Apologetics Group. Written and Directed by Kent Hovind. USA. Color. Video. 120 Minutes.

Overview: This is an in-depth examination of the Creation mythos, featuring Dr. Kent Hovind, in which various Biblical accounts of the world's beginning are contrasted with Evolutionary Theory. Dr. Hovind, an ardent believer in Creationism and Intelligent Design, delves into such topics as whether or not God created birds on the third or sixth day of Creation, as well as the Biblical rationale and proper spiritual placement of cryptids such as Bigfoot in the hierarchy of God's plan for mankind's salvation.

Suffice it to say, *Answers About Creation* is definitely unique in the canon of Ciné du Sasquatch, although it can at least be ironically noted that many indigenous tribes have equally imbued Bigfoot with religious significance in their respective traditions (for example, as being the Spirit of the Forest — albeit definitely *not* as a Christian deity).

Ape Canyon (2002)

Starring Gabrielle Bell, Ryan Burns, Miranda Eckert, Jon Fisher, Trevor Guthrie, Melissa Hannum, Chris Henry, Zack Levine, Clover Lutter, Anna McGriff, Doug Mitchell, Jon Olsen and Tory St. Peters. Produced by Trevor Guthrie and Doug Mitchell. Written by Frannie Flounder, Trevor Guthrie and Jon Olsen. Directed by Jon Olsen. USA. Color. Stereo. 84 Minutes.

Overview: Fancying himself the greatest stud in the Pacific Northwest, Sasquatch sexually molests every female tree hugger, camper, and nature photographer he encounters. After assaulting each victim, the horny hominid disappears into the protective cover of the woods, afraid of any long-term commitment. Apparently, every female *Homo sapiens* who has sex with such a tall, dark lover can never find satisfaction again with a mere human male.

Alas for Sasquatch, his latest victim — a restless Hooters waitress named Darcy — has fallen in love with the carousing cryptid, to the chagrin of her shotgun-toting, redneck husband Bill. Determined to reclaim his female at any cost, Bill sets out to find Sasquatch before his pining wife Darcy (who has taken to writing odes of passion to her hominid lover in her poetry journal and calling into the wilderness for Sasquatch to return to her) can re-connect with her hairy lover. Loaded for Bigfoot, Bill is prepared to blast the beast into smithereens in order to break its Svengali-like spell on Darcy... even if it means having to turn off the couple's trailer park TV set and leave their well-worn sofa to do so. But is it already too late for the wayward husband, or can he best his crypto-simian rival before Darcy begs the creature to take her as its beastly bride?

* * * * *

Like some of the earlier bestiality films in Ciné du Sasquatch, such as *The Geek* and *The Beauties and the Beast*, *Ape Canyon* seeks to expose the oft-implied "hidden" meanings lying just beneath the surface of such efforts and effectively turn them upside-down, bringing their torrid "cryptid on woman" themes to the forefront. Unlike these previously mentioned softcore pornography films, however, *Ape Canyon* is intended to play like a low-budget early John Waters film — that is, guaranteed to offend both the Religious Right *and* the Politically Correct in equally strident measures, satirizing as it does such taboo subject matter as rape, class distinctions, interspecies sex, and political divides. For some, the idea of any movie of any genre using such topics for crass entertainment value is vile and beyond the pale. Such viewers will definitely want to skip *Ape Canyon*.

For those willing to forgo any sense of moral decency and instead wallow in amoral decadence, *Ape Canyon* is a hit-or-miss "affair" that affords as many laughs as it does groans. Doubtlessly the excruciatingly low budget made the production nearly impossible to complete in any professional manner, which both detracts from the film's watchability and, ironically, imbues it with a certain passionate sense of skewering the typical studio fare afraid of offending one special interest group or another. If the idea of a female tree hugger (for but one example) being sexually molested by a horny hominid seems at least potentially comical, then *Ape Canyon* is probably worth your while for low-brow chuckles.

The bad gorilla suit is clearly designed to induce disbelief in everything that follows its initial appearance, and, indeed, in this capacity it serves *Ape Canyon* well. Unlike so many bad filmmakers dabbling in the Bigfoot film genre, at least the director demonstrates he is aware of how awful his Sasquatch's superstar appears. Many are the low-budget Ciné du Sasquatch efforts which try to pretend (to their detriment) that their equally poor gorilla costumes can be "disguised" from alert (or, rather, awake) viewers. The lust-crazed Bigfoot's obsession with masturbating while looking at glossy weekly news magazines featuring celebrities like Britney Spears perhaps offers some self-referential commentary to the audience of college-aged males most likely to enjoy *Ape Canyon*, but it's doubtful such an alcohol-fueled crowd would ever bother to analyze the film beyond its plethora of scatological one-shots.

If nothing else, director Olsen is a total showman in the old school mold. Like with many of the pioneering Sasquatch films, such as *The Legend of Boggy Creek* and *Sasquatch, The Legend of Bigfoot*, the filmmaker and his girlfriend took to the road with a digital projector and rented any theater or venue in America that was willing to book his effort. Though they only netted 15 show dates across the United States, their efforts paid off in at least one respect. Graphic artist Gabrielle Bell (who plays a nature photographer in the film) adapted the story of their stay in New York City promoting *Ape Canyon* into a comic strip called "Cecil and Jordan in New York," which was in turn made into a short segment of the theatrical film *Tôkyô!* In a roundabout way, therefore, *Ape Canyon* received a much wider distribution (albeit in fictionalized format) than its actual, original incarnation. Not bad for a low-budget, independently made feature, all in all.

Arthur C. Clarke's Mysterious World ("The Missing Ape") (1980) (TV) (Doc)

Featuring Arthur C. Clarke. Produced by John Fairley, John Fanshawe and Simon Welfare. Directed by Charles Flynn, Peter Jones and Michael Weigall. UK. Color. Stereo. 30 Minutes.

Overview: Science fiction writer and noted futurist Arthur C. Clarke held a lifelong fascination with Fortean phenomena such as crystal skulls, UFOs and, of course, cryptids. While his involvement in this 13-part series was limited to introducing and concluding each show, as well as offering a few wry but skeptical observations per topic, it nevertheless gives the proceedings an air of legitimacy otherwise lacking in many of the genre's documentaries.

Of particular relevance to this guide is the episode "The Missing Ape," dedicated to an overview of Sasquatch and Yeti. Clarke at one point concludes that if he were a betting man and forced to wager on the existence of these hominids based on the scientific evidence to date, he would place a small amount on Bigfoot, a small amount on Yeti, and keep the majority for himself. While much of the information is dated, it remains a concise if brief overview of unexplained and paranormal subjects.

Astroboy ("The Abominable Snowman") (1963) (TV)

Featuring the voices of Billie Lou Watt, Ray Owens, Gilbert Mack, Peter Fernandez, Shimizu Mari, Kachita Hisashi, Mizugaki Yoko, Muto Reiko, Yoshikawa Kazuko, Komiyama Kiyoshi, Yajima Kazuaki, Wada Fumio, Yokomori Hisashi, Sakamoto Shinpei, Kanemoto Shingo and Chiba Koichi. Produced by Hidehiko Takei, Satoshi Yamamoto and Fred Ladd. Written by Osamu Tezuka, Fred Ladd, Peter Fernandez, Ray Owens and Billie Lou Watt. Directed by Noboru Ishiguro. Japan/USA. Black & White. Mono. 30 Minutes.

Overview: Dr. Packadermus Elefun, head of the Ministry of Science, is the world's foremost expert on robotics. His crowning achievement is his robot super hero Astroboy, a flying robot child with miraculous powers of self-defense. Together they form a virtual father and son duo dedicated to solving the world's problems and defending it from tyranny and injustice.

When Dr. Elefun tests a new robotic explorer tank in the Himalayan Mountains, the experiment is interrupted by a ferocious, two-storey-tall Abominable Snowman. The Yeti destroys the robot tank and kidnaps Dr. Elefun. Astroboy receives a distress signal from the doctor's camping partners and responds, seeking his creator.

Eventually, Astroboy locates Dr. Elefun, who is being held captive by one Sam Caesar, a self-styled Roman ruler and master robot maker himself. Caesar stumbled upon an ancient, forgotten Roman city resembling Pompeii in the Himalayan Mountains and decided to inhabit the ruins himself. Designing a robot army to defend his city, Caesar has also constructed a giant robot Yeti to discourage any who would foolishly attempt to trespass into his private empire.

Astroboy is able to overcome the robotic Yeti by stripping the monster of its hide and revealing its robotic interior, but Caesar's hold on Dr. Elefun is insidious: Caesar has invited the renowned scientist to stay on in the ancient city and catalog the architecture to his heart's content. Elefun doesn't want to forgo the archeological chance of a lifetime by returning with Astroboy, but when the paranoid Caesar accuses Elefun of being a traitor to Rome, the sentence is death. Elefun is tossed into the gladiatorial arena and forced to defend himself against a fire-breathing, saber-toothed cat. Astroboy intervenes and rescues Elefun, who escapes with only a diary filled with his scientific observations from his ordeal.

Stranded in the mountains, his robotic powers depleted, and with the doctor freezing to death, Astroboy convinces Elefun he must ignite the diary in order to signal overhead search planes. Elefun reluctantly agrees. The smoke alerts a rescue plane, and the two are saved.

* * * * *

Astroboy is one of the most influential Japanese pop culture icons in manga, anime, television, and moviemaking history. The original manga comics were popular in both Japan and the United States, and the groundbreaking black and white anime series was the first in Japanese television history to be exported to foreign countries such as the United States and Europe. Given the juvenile storylines and non-stop action, it is little wonder the *Astroboy* series created anime fever in an entire first-wave generation of avid followers who gobbled up each new episode. With a unique, cartoonish style mixed with heavy doses of science fiction elements, the series was a perfect zeitgeist distillation of the technological wonders of a decade enthralled by the space race to the Moon, scientific marvels such as computers, and a still optimistic tone about the positive values of machinery.

"The Abominable Snowman" is a telling example of the original *Astroboy* series' penchant for banality and simultaneous charm. The banal quality comes from the limited animation technique (which is an acquired tastes among those who didn't grow up with it), and the charm from the wholesome naiveté Astroboy exhibits no matter how grim the situation. In many ways a robotic version of the classic Pinocchio fable minus the penchant for lying, Astroboy is any parent's ideal embodiment of the perfect child, never cynical and always wide-eyed about the wonders of life and learning. The fact that Astroboy yearns to be accepted by Dr. Elefun as a "real son" (read: actual human boy) underscores this thematic tone.

It is interesting that when Astroboy first encounters the Yeti he immediately deduces the cryptid is a fellow robot (a genuine case of it taking one to know one, it seems). This is a very novel concept for the era — that the hominid in question is actually a robotic being — and marks one of its earliest introductions in Ciné du Sasquatch. Later television series such as *Dr. Who* and *The Six Million Dollar Man* would echo this concept, but here, in 1963, one finds this novel variation on the typical formula (typically it is either a real Yeti or merely a person in a suit) to be a clever twist. While it seems quaintly obvious today, the young viewers of the era must have found the revelation surprising; one wonders, in fact, if it had any influence on the concept being introduced in subsequent Bigfoot films and television shows by impressionable watchers who later recycled the concept in their own scripts.

The bulk of the show does not actually concentrate on the Yeti, per se, but the ridiculous character of Sam Caesar, the self-styled autocratic rule of the lost Roman city he has discovered hidden in the Himalayan Mountains. While the portrayal and idea are absurd, it is noteworthy how the producers go out of their way to introduce actual historical relevance to the show's background re: Rome and its legacy. Using recreations of famous architecture, reliefs and statues, Dr. Elefun takes the viewer on a mini-tour of the empire's conquests and ultimate destruction. The narrated lecture is not only visual, but surprising for its accuracy and detail. While it doesn't propel the narrative forward, it does show why *Astroboy* was atypical for its era: It has a sense of its own responsibility to its tyke audience to educate along with entertain, though the accent is decidedly upon the latter.

For cryptid cinema fans, "The Abominable Snowman" is a nostalgic example of how the Yeti was treated by the popular media of the era, neither particularly illuminating nor without significance, given that it introduces what will become a thematic sub-text in subsequent Bigfoot entries — the robotic cryptid.

Attack of the Yeti Hand (2009)

Starring A.M. Sannazzaro, Jodi Bookout, Matthew Wheeler, Kira Dounias, Darin Maddox, Adam B. Smith, Aasem Shah, Juicee Couture, David Matz, Megan Rawley Hernandez, Alex Caparula and Philip Waln. Produced by Sarah M. Hines and Karyn Ben Singer. Written and Directed by Karyn Ben Singer. USA. Color. Stereo. 73 Minutes.

Overview: Journeyman delivery boy Ned Whiteman finds to his horror he has lost a package containing a mystical Yeti paw with the power to kill. Ned enlists the aid of Judy Terracotta, a professional security guard, in hopes of discovering the whereabouts of the missing Abominable Snowhand and retaining his imperiled job. Unbeknownst to Ned and Judy, the package's intended recipient, Hilary Montegnya, begins her own search for the stolen package, intent on securing its black magic powers for herself before the duo can solve the mystery for her.

* * * * *

Attack of the Yeti Hand is a no-budget comedy feature shot in Lancaster, California. Starring a local cast of unknown performers, it bypassed the traditional shortfall in many Ciné du Sasquatch productions (in which a full costume is often the weakest "link") by focusing on a clever "The Monkey's Paw" derivation. It was in postproduction at the time of this guide's publication and unavailable for critique.

Backwoods Bloodbath (2007)

AKA: *Backwoods Bloodbath: The Curse of the Black Hodag*. Starring Scott Ash, Ryan Buth, Erin Castrapel, Seth Chilsen, Tyler Constable, Jesse L. Cyr, Adam J. D'Amato, David Lephardt, Angela Lowe, Dwight McMillan, Josh Mijal, Amy Quinn, Julie Roy, Travis Ruhland, Rex Steven Sikes, Kyle Swartz, Phil Vacca and Joseph Walzer. Produced and Written by Donn Kennedy and Brandon Semling. Directed by Donn Kennedy. USA. Color. Stereo. 90 Minutes.

Overview: Several college students intent on partying in the dark woods of Black Forest are warned off by the superstitious locals, who talk of the legendary Black Hodag, a local Bigfoot variation that preys on just such ill-advised tourists. Undeterred, the cabin renters soon come to learn everything they were told about the dread Black Hodag is true, and, what's more, that the Black Hodag is now stalking them, intent on slaughtering them one-by-one before any can return to civilization and reveal its existence as definitive rather than mythic. Can the remaining students survive the assault on their cabin and the long night that awaits, courtesy of the hook-wielding Hodag?

* * * * *

Clearly an attempt to turn back the clock to the 1980s direct-to-video daze (probably the last great gasp of American independent filmmaking before Hollywood finally shut it down with the advent of tighter controls on DVD), *Backwoods Bloodbath* is a no-budget shock effort designed to appeal less to cineaste lovers and more to zombie gut-munching genre movie fans, as it aspires less to mainstream acceptance than immediate cult appeal. It's not altogether unsuccessful at the latter, containing as it does a plethora of amateur acting mixed with deliberately *bad* acting by more competent performers (though it becomes difficult to distinguish between the two), but becomes less entertaining if one watches it as anything other than a deliberately campy laugh-fest.

Strictly speaking, while the Black Hodag is a hominid monster, *Backwoods Bloodbath* does somewhat alter the concept of what constitutes Bigfoot. For example, the Hodag is shown to utilize weaponry (particularly a nasty hand scythe for slicing and dicing at close quarters), and it even appears to wear a long trench coat retrieved from the trash to disguise itself in the darkness. These adaptations make the film cosmetically novel within the genre, but otherwise the film so deliberately follows the typical rules of engagement that it actually plays as self-parody (along the lines of *The Rocky Horror Picture Show*). The students who rent the spooky cabin are warned about the lurking danger of the Black Hodag but blithely ignore the earnest advice to wantonly party and subsequently die in the process. Herein one sees the combining of the endless *Friday the 13th* movies and knock-offs (which cater to the Puritanical need for the viewing audience to see the "guilty" screen heroes "punished" for any carnal "sins" in which they indulge — or even think about indulging, in some cases) with

the classical Bigfoot narrative. The Black Hodag straddles the fence between the two genres effectively, for the most part, if one is inclined to accept such cross-genre blending in the first place. All too often, such hybrid attempts fail to satisfy the core audiences that appreciate each genre being spliced, let alone stand alone as an independent movie.

The extent to which the viewer believes *Backwoods Bloodbath* achieves its hodge podge stirring together of genre ingredients is largely dependent upon whether one is willing to give it credit for trying on a non-existent budget versus deducting points for the obvious deficits: shoddy sound, a video camera look and feel, amateurish acting, etc. It has some effective moments and is rarely objectionable; even the gore quota is not excessive (despite the misleading title), especially by 1980s (lack of) restraints and standards in such matters. Perhaps the best summation that can be said is that is comes so close to achieving the everyday, just-another-Bigfoot-movie-on-the-video-store-shelf effect its makers intended that it actually could fit in well with the 1980s genre fare without much commentary or alteration. Whether this is to one's liking or not answers the question of whether one should seek out *Backwoods Bloodbath*. In terms of the Bigfoot film, it is strictly retrograde; though where cinematic homage is involved, that is not always a bad thing.

The Backyardigans ("The Yeti" and "Fly Girl") (2004) (TV)

Featuring the voices of Jonah Bobo, Sean Curley, Reginald Davis, Jr., LaShawn Jefferies, Naelee Rae, Jordan Coleman, Gianna Bruzzese and Zach Tyler. Produced by Jennifer Hill, Jonny Belt, Patricia R. Burns, Scott Dyer, Jocelyn Hamilton, Ellen Martin, Doug Murphy and Robert Scull. Written by Janice Burgess, Anne D. Bernstein, Radha Blank and Scott Gray. Directed by Donald Kim. USA. Color. Stereo. 30 Minutes.

Overview: Five colorful preschool friends play together in their enclosed backyard neighborhood, pretending to be a variety of stock characters and situations from the various movies, books, and television shows they daily consume. In enacting each fantasy, the Backyardigans become the characters necessary to make the narrative come alive in their imaginations — the sheriff, the bag guys, the detective, etc. They sing and dance and learn valuable lessons in friendship and the importance of playing together as a team. At the end of each episode the conjured group vision dissipates, revealing their neighborhood backyards. Each character bids one another good night and returns to his or her respective home.

* * * * *

Children's television programming is admittedly an often difficult enterprise for adults to critique with any objective perspective, just as adult dramas mystify most tykes. That said, the monotonous tone of Political Correctness that pervades each and every episode of *The Backyardigans* renders it as diabolically adult-proof as *Barney the Dinosaur*, which this colorful but banal CGI-fest closely resembles in thematic resonance (or lack thereof). Some children love it; many more find it too cloying even for their sugarcoated dietary intake. Suffice it to say, *The Backyardigans* will never be confused with the halcyon days of the Brothers Krofft in terms of subversive puns and unmitigated boundary pushing.

In the second episode ever ("The Yeti"), the Abominable Snowman appears in the form of Pablo, who pretends to be a Yeti. His friends Uniqua, Tyrone and Tasha pretend to be hunters who pursue him, tracking the Yeti's "droppings" (actually Pablo's raisins, the Abominable Snowman's preferred snack, we are told, but the reference to the trail actually being Yeti scat is unavoidable for adult viewers) to the North Pole, where we learn the cryptid lives in an igloo. After various musical numbers and Pablo singing a Yeti song ("Stomp! Stomp! Stomp! I'm doing the Yeti Stomp!"), the friends all have hot chocolate and laugh about their silly adventure together.

Apart from the musical numbers themselves, which are so similar throughout the series as to have been written on a computer program that spits out each slight variation with minor alterations, the cryptozoological anomalies pile up throughout this episode. For example, while it is understandable the show's producers feel the need to push healthful snacks to the kid-based audience, the illogical nature of the Yeti's choice herein is obvious. How on Earth can a being that inhabits a frosty region of the world's climate depend on raisins/dried grapes for its dietary intake, when such fruit will not grow in cold climates? Likewise, the idea that the Yeti lives in an igloo may make perfect sense to the same creative team who feels it is no mean feat for *Homo sapiens* to have devised such adaptive technology as ice block dome construction in a harsh environment, but does this truly educate the tykes or simply create erroneous impressions that this breakthrough is so easy that (to rephrase the insurance company commercials) "even a cryptid can do it?" And this says nothing, of course, of the geographic distance between the Alaskan borders and Tibetan frontiers!

It may seem unfair comparison, but the same set-up in *Tintin in Tibet* shows how a more intelligent approach to both storyline and characterization created not only a superior entertainment, but a more educational one. Perhaps it is too much to expect such artistic achievement in today's more commercial TV programming, of course, but one wonders if the time spent on such supposedly "positive alternatives" as *The Backyardigans* doesn't come with a hidden backlash potential of dumbing down the intended tyke audience.

The Abominable Snowman made yet another (briefer) appearance in the second season ("Fly Girl"), which had Uniqua as a female aviator in the Amelia Earhart mold who flies around the globe giving singing telegrams to grumpy types in need of cheering. This time Tyrone imagines himself to be the Yeti instead of Pablo, but rather than call himself the Yeti, as did Pablo, Tyrone makes it a point to mention he's the Abominable Snowman. Uniqua makes the fearsome Abominable Snowman realize he'd be a lot less lonely (the real source of his anger) if he'd spend less time acting fearsome and more time having fun. For *The Backyardigans* completists, this show was adapted into a children's book, *Flight of the Singing Pilot*.

The Barbaric Beast of Boggy Creek, Part II (1985)

AKA: *Boggy Creek II*; *Boggy Creek II: And the Legend Continues*. Starring Charles B. Pierce, Cindy Butler, Chuck Pierce, Jimmy Clem and Serene Hedin. Written by Charles B. Pierce. Directed by Charles B. Pierce. USA. Color. Mono. 91 Minutes.

Overview: Professor Lockart, a noted zoologist from the University of Arkansas, enlists the help of several students on an expedition to search for an elusive, legendary Bigfoot known as the Fouke Monster, supposedly a denizen of the meandering waterways of Boggy Creek along the Arkansas and Texas border. The scientist is convinced he can locate the creature by utilizing high-tech equipment and mapped locales of where the beast has been sighted over the years.

As he and his college-aged crew of three—Tim, Leslie Anne and Tanya—interview various locals who've had encounters with the swamp Sasquatch, a picture of a ferocious, unpredictable monster emerges. Periodically leaving its creek side habitat and invading farms and homes in search of food, the beast's reputation as being savage beyond human ability to subdue or frighten grows. Nothing works to prevent it from reappearing—not the endless shotgun blasts

fired at it in the dead of night nor the howling dogs that it easily dispatches.

Setting up camp in the remotest area they can access despite local warnings to abandon their quest, Lockart and his team deploy a perimeter around their recreational vehicle with a pinging radar watching the surrounding woods. When the beast rears its ugly head, a tiny blip displays on their computer screen, showing them its exact location.

The Fouke Monster makes several attempts to breech their warning system, but it proves effective at alerting the humans, who ward it off before it can attack them. It is effective, that is, until the portable generator powering it runs out of gasoline. Tim goes outside to refill it, only to be assaulted by the Sasquatch. He escapes, with Lockart's help. Rattled, Leslie Anne and Tanya want to leave, but Lockart and Tim feel they're on to the greatest discovery in scientific history and demand to stay one more day.

The men leave the women behind for safety while they set out in search of the Boggy Creek legend, venturing deeper into the bayou after their subject. Spooked by a sudden downpour of rain and the monster's roars, the women decide to take the pick-up truck and drive back to civilization. Alas, their truck becomes stuck in mud, stranding them as the sun sets.

The men narrowly rescue the women before the beast's final assault. All four take shelter in a backwoods hermit's shack. The reclusive Old Man Crenshaw reveals his secret to them: He has captured a baby Bigfoot and is holding it hostage. Now realizing why the adult monster has been so vengeful, the researcher convinces the old man to release the creature's offspring. The four researchers watch tearfully as the cryptid family is reunited. They leave, determined not to reveal the secret of Boggy Creek.

* * * * *

By the time this last installment of the *Boggy Creek* franchise was released, interest had waned and home video was its only real market. In part this was because the mid–1980s theatrical market had been overtaken by the Hollywood studio system, which squeezed out most independent films, relegating such regional releases as *The Barbaric Beast of Boggy Creek, Part II* to an already crowded home video distribution channel.

In part, Pierce was a victim of his own earlier success with *The*

Doc Lockhart (Charles B. Pierce) confronts residents of Fouke, Arkansas, in his search for *The Barbaric Beast of Boggy Creek, Part II*.

Legend of Boggy Creek. It not only spawned a sequel (*Return to Boggy Creek*), with which he had no creative involvement, but a plethora of competing Bigfoot movie clones that literally "swamped" Pierce's own once-novel water cryptid formula. So by the time this entry ended the trilogy, few fans of even Ciné du Sasquatch noticed as it slipped from the sparse videocassette rental shelves it occupied into hard-to-find collector status (where it remains to this day).

Pierce abandons his earlier pseudo-documentary style completely, instead relying on traditional narrative cinema techniques, with an emphasis on story and characters. The problem with this approach, however, is revealed early on: Such emphasis requires good actors, fine dialogue, and taut dramatic construction. Sadly, *The Barbaric Beast of Boggy Creek, Part II* offers little, if any, of the aforementioned qualities and becomes rapidly "bogged" down in a mire of its own making.

The acting is uniformly weak, with the exception of Pierce, who casts himself in the lead role. His real-life son plays his male assistant in the movie and spends a majority of his screen time walking around shirtless (an odd decision, given how skinny he appears). The young ladies seem cast more for the shapely manner in which they fill out their tight cut-off jeans than any demonstrable thespian abilities; while they excel at looking comely in revealing garb, the more demanding talents, such as delivering dialogue and not appearing uncomfortably self-conscious in close-ups, are beyond them. Pierce is actually passable; he brings an earnest intensity to his role. It is never entirely successful, but at least he anchors the cast with his manic propensity to action and "cut to the chase" heroics.

Production values are good for such a low budget, owing to the fact Pierce shot his own movies and had an eye for nature photography. In all technical respects, *The Barbaric Beast of Boggy Creek, Part II* is a notch above the original film. Ironically, that does not make this the better viewing experience, as the limitations of the first entry are eclipsed by its superior sense of suspense. The acting is bad in both efforts, but the pseudo-documentary approach of the first allows for more suspension of disbelief, as Pierce wisely has the Arkansas locals playing themselves, not fictional roles requiring professional training.

Narrative impact in *Part II* is further hampered by the choice to spend most of the first half of the picture having Pierce recount old encounters with the Fouke Monster. While some of these are effective in and of themselves, they slow the story's natural progress and leave the viewer impatiently waiting for the promised set-up of man vs. beast. It is not a fatal flaw; rather, it creates a feeling one is seeing two different films edited into one.

The Skunk Ape is seen onscreen mostly in glimpses and shadowy silhouette, thereby keeping its impact largely intact. The ending (which finds the cryptozoologist releasing the baby Bigfoot to its mother) is maudlin. After building up the beast as a wild, savage monster, it feels anti-climatic to suddenly reveal the Fouke Monster to be just a hairy parent in search of a runaway child. Though meant to be novel, it plays as clichéd.

In the end, *The Barbaric Beast of Boggy Creek, Part II* is not so much badly made as it is tired in execution and bereft of originality. Even the "surprise ending" in which the Sasquatch is humane and unwilling to hurt humans who have not provoked it is contained in the soggy prequel *Return to Boggy Creek.* It is never boring as much as it is predictable, which is a disappointing bookend to the series from such a talented filmmaker as the legendary Charles B. Pierce.

Battle of the Planets ("The Alien Bigfoot") (1978) (TV)

AKA: *Kagaku Ninja Tai Gatchaman*; *G-Force.* Featuring the voices of Keye Luke, Alan Dinehart, Alan Young, Casey Kasem, Janet Waldo and Ronny Schell. American Version Produced by Alan Dinehart and Warner E. Leighton. Japanese Version Produced by Tatsunoko Productions. Created by Tatsuo Yoshida. Written by Jinzo Toriumi. Directed by Hisayuki Toriumi. Japan/USA. Color. Mono. 30 Minutes.

Overview: Five young Earthlings with superhuman ninja powers are recruited by the International Science Organization to combat Planet Spectra, an alien world with incredibly advanced technology and a ruthless desire to exploit the Earth's natural resources. Under the watchful eyes of their mentor, Chief Anderson, the "G-Force" (as they're informally known) repeatedly encounter a masked, androgynous Spectra villain named Zoltar, who is revealed midway through the series to be a shapeshifting hermaphrodite, as well as Zoltar's direct superior, the Great Spirit.

The G-Force fly around the globe aboard their high-tech jet the Phoenix, alert for any signs of Spectra's latest treachery. When they fly too close to Tibet, the Phoenix is forced to crash-land after its navigation systems are interfered with by outside forces. It is discovered that the Spectra forces have deployed an "Inter-Frequency Disruptor" and are utilizing it to keep the G-Force members from uncovering the precise whereabouts of their Himalayan secret base.

To further discourage the local Sherpas and any other humans from snooping, the alien fiends keep an Abominable Snowman under their mental control. Keyop, a G-Force member, infiltrates the secret base but is taken hostage by Zoltar. While the other G-Force team repairs the Phoenix, Keyop outwits the Spectra forces and sends an alert to his fellow G-Force fighters, who then storm the secret base and flush out Zoltar's evil crew.

* * * * *

Battle of the Planets was a popular syndicated American version of the even bigger hit known as *Kagaku Ninja Tai Gatchaman* in its native Japan. While its early 1970s anime seems positively crude by today's standards, *Battle of the Planets* enjoyed a significant fan base owing to its long run of 105 episodes (which allowed for long stretches of audience viewership without repeats) and charming use of colors, design and internal mythos. For the era, it was essentially a quasi-adult show in nature, and, in fact, much of the overt violence was removed and the series re-edited to become *Battle of the Planets.* Character names and organizations were changed from more threatening, mature-sounding monikers to simplistic, kid-friendly ones (such as Bergu Kattse to Zoltar, Sosai X to the Great Spirit, and Joe Asakura to Jason), all in an effort to make the series more palatable to American kids' parents in regards to its relentless action.

As with many other popular anime series from Japan that followed the success two decades earlier of *Astroboy*, *Battle of the Planets* also incorporated the universally-accessible cryptid Yeti in an episode. Given that the Asian culture has as many hominids (such as Yeti and the Orang Pendek) from which to draw popular recognition as the United States, it is entirely logical: The translation is without verbal need of exposition, as the Abominable Snowman is a well-known icon to all worldwide audiences.

Interestingly, the concept of an alien race controlling a cryptid for its own nefarious purposes is quite ubiquitous. Although the theory that actual UFO sightings in conjunction with Bigfoot encounters is generally greeted with skepticism in the cryptozoological community (a case, perhaps, of there simply being one too many probabilities heaped atop one another in violation of a Fortean version of Occam's Razor), this sub-theme is quite abundant in Ciné du Sasquatch. Oddly, it apparently exists in an effort to explain two anomalies with one hominid; but, as mentioned, it actually just adds to the disbelief most examples utilizing the two-for-one approach must overcome in the skeptical viewer. Other examples include *Terror in the Midnight Sun*, *Ultraman*, *Snow Devils*, *Dr. Who*, and *The Six Million Dollar Man.*

As far as lasting impressions go, *Battle of the Planet*'s use of Bigfoot is akin to the same manner in which the original anime "godfather" of them all, *Astroboy*, inserted the hominid into its respective episode. That is, the creature is utilized more as a gimmick than for any real narrative impact. And while *Astroboy*'s Sam Caesar villain character has ultimately created a robotic Abominable Snowman to defend his secret city, Spectra's use is eerily the same in that it is the typical "scare away inquisitive humans" rationale (a terrible idea, actually, given that the sightings would logically lead to scientific expeditions setting forth to investigate!). A final note: Though the American translators chose to call the cryptid Bigfoot, it is obviously a Yeti, given the stated location being the Himalayan Mountains. Presumably this was altered to make the creature more familiar; if so, it was an unnecessary change, as both are equally well-known in America.

The Beachcombers ("The Sasquatch Walks by Night") (1974) (TV)

Starring Bruno Gerussi, Robert Clothier, Pat John, Joe Austin, Jackson Davies, Rae Brown, Charlene Aleck, Marianne Jones, Cory Douglas, Frances Hyland, Tom Byrne, Robb Smythe, Sean Gorman and Dion Luther. Produced by Hugh Beard, Robert Frederick, Derek Gardner, Philip Keatley, Gordon Mark, Brian McKeown and Don S. Williams. Written by Marc and Susan Strange. Directed by Patrick Corbett. Canada. Color. Stereo. 30 Minutes.

Overview: Sasquatch is spotted by Nick and Hugh. The amazed boys seek the help of Sadie and Jesse to set a series of traps to capture Bigfoot. But when the cryptid overruns their campsite, the intrepid crew is forced to flee for their lives, trapping themselves in their own crudely-devised snares, nets, and pits.

After freeing themselves, they chase after the fleeing Bigfoot. They corner the creature at a cliffside, certain they've bagged their quarry. But to their surprise, Sasquatch dives over the cliffside. As the kids watch in amazement, the creature swims over to a boat and makes its getaway — piloting the vessel like an expert. It turns out the hoax has been perpetuated by Nick Adonidas' arch-rivals Relic and Jesse in an attempt to embarrass the Greek log salvager, while Relic has been selling worthless souvenirs to gullible tourists who've been excited by the talk of a Sasquatch in their area.

* * * * *

The Beachcombers was one of the most successful television shows in Canadian broadcast history, running for 17 years without a break and producing an astounding 387 episodes before it finally ceased production under the shortened name *Beachcombers*. The basic set-up had honest Greek immigrant Nick Adonidas earning a modest living by retrieving the logs that broke loose from logging boats (hence the series' title). Along with his extended family, Nick constantly battles poverty, hard times and the ever-present threat of his competitive rival Relic, who often resorts to questionable means to steal logs and other business opportunities from the Adonidas family.

Set in the seaside communities along the Vancouver shorelines in British Columbia, the series took advantage of its rugged exterior locales to great effect. Though set in modern times, the nearest American TV show in terms of success and family-life subject matter is *Little House of the Prairie*, with both emphasizing the values of family cohesion and gratitude for life's simple bounties.

As a typical "it was all just a man in a costume" subtype of Ciné du Sasquatch, the episode follows the usual bait-and-switch formula. First the audience is shown the cryptid through the protagonists' eyes as being an actual Sasquatch. Only later is the motivation for the feigned Bigfoot explained away as commercially oriented. In this case

the hoax is perpetrated by the family's business rivals to capitalize upon tourists too uncritical to know better and who already are predisposed to believe the local legends about a forest primate because of extensive media coverage.

There's little else remarkable about this Bigfoot entry, per se. The shots of the Sasquatch are kept brief and largely off-screen, so that the later revelation that it is a hoax is more believable. The idea that Relic is selling trinkets to visitors while helping stage the sightings themselves at the Greek family's expense is both cynically funny and a commentary upon the manner in which the two clans view the possibilities of life itself: One (the Adonidas family) sees it as an intriguing mystery of life; the other (Relic and Jesse) see the legend as nothing more than an opportunity to make a quick buck at others' expense, no matter the consequences. While neither is fully vindicated by their belief structure (the believers are made to feel foolish; the cynics made to look like fools when foiled), the episode does capture the lingering divide that exists between real-life cryptozoologists and skeptics, each camp dubious of the other's point of view in such matters.

The Beast (1975)

AKA: *La bête*; *The Beast in Heat*; *Death's Ecstasy*. Starring Sirpa Lane, Lisbeth Hummel, Elisabeth Kaza, Pierre Benedetti, Guy Tréjan, Roland Armontel, Marcel Dalio, Robert Capia, Pascale Rivault, Hassane Fall, Anna Baldaccini, Thierry Bourdon, Mathieu Rivollier, Julien Hanany, Marie Testanière, Stéphane Testanière and Jean Martinelli. Produced by Anatole Dauman. Written and Directed by Walerian Borowczyk. Poland. Color. Mono. 93 Minutes.

Overview: Lucy Broadhurst, the daughter of an American millionaire living in France, is set to be married to Mathurin de l'Esperance, the son of the Marquis dynasty, with whom she has maintained a correspondence affair that has remained physically unconsummated. Alas, the Marquis estate turns out to be nearly bankrupt, which is why the head of the Marquis clan is so overjoyed at the coming union — Miss Lucy's fortune means a possible rebirth of the decadent, collapsed familial fortunes. A true innocent abroad in the literal sense, Miss Broadhurst is accompanied by her mother Virginia to maintain the necessary proprieties and act as chaperone.

It doesn't take long for Lucy to realize her new family's history is drenched in tragedy and whispered legends of debauchery. Most startlingly, the former head of the estate is rumored to have had sexual relations with a beast who roams the forests surrounding the estate, as Lucy finds depicted in the surreal artwork that hangs on the château's walls (showing strange manbeasts having sex with women). The legends have it that this lustful hominid only appears every 200 years to prey upon maidens who desire his carnal advances. Determined to pry deeper into the stories, but cautioned by the Marquis family's natural reluctance to talk of such matters, Lucy begins to spy on various family members and read from the former Lady Marquis' personal diary.

Miss Lucy's journey into sexual awakening is filled with many unexpected revelations. The priest enjoys fondling the young children of the poor stable hand workers. Her sister-in-law routinely beds a black servant without much effort to disguise the tryst. As for herself, Lucy begins to have erotic dreams in which she herself is stalked in the primeval forests by the beast. As her dreams progress, they become more graphically potent and disturbing. She goes from unwilling rape victim in her initial encounters to willing participant in subsequent dream couplings with her phantasmagoric lover.

She awakens from the last extensive, troubled dream of coupling and rushes to her husband's room for comfort, only to find him dead. With her mother in tow, the Broadhursts flee the crumbling mansion, eager to return to the innocence of their former city existences.

* * * * *

Based on the short story "Lokis" by Prosper Merimée, *The Beast* is one of the most notorious feature films ever made in Europe. When it initially screened in London, a scandal erupted when it was revealed the film had been passed by the British censorship board for public showing. The film was shut down and prohibited from further exhibition immediately after it came to light in a subsequent investigation that a large majority of the film censorship board members had simply failed to attend the required ratings screening, while the few that did had slept through its duration! The entire UK censorship process was given a thorough vetting as a result, and for decades, until its DVD release, *The Beast* remained virtually unseen apart from rare film society screenings or in truncated editions, such as *Death's Ecstasy* (which had most of the sexual scenes cut or severely redacted).

With the passage of time and the DVD revolution, *The Beast* now has been rediscovered by many film lovers and critically re-evaluated. Many modern viewers find it as offensive as did the censors throughout Europe during its initial, abortive release. Still others appreciate its alluring eroticism and frank depictions of such taboo subject matters as bestiality and the uncompromising willingness the filmmaker demonstrates to forgo the usual sense of moral judgment that inevitably accompanies such subject matters. In terms of shocking uniqueness and the cinematic ability to render what is generally considered impossibly dark, one may compare Borowczyk to David Lynch. Borowczyk's painterly use of light and lack of narrative urgency is considered narcoleptic by some, and vociferously defended by others more tolerant of films lacking the usual American sense of pacing. Some argue that his visions are what is often called "pure cinema" in that he uses pictures over words and dialogue to convey his themes; this is the essence of the art form, as proven during the birth of filmmaking itself in the silent era. And as Stanley Kubrick once remarked, very little in actual filmmaking has changed, allowing even for the introduction of sound, color and other additions since then. Borowczyk would undoubtedly have agreed — hence his passion for exploring verboten topics which challenged, offended and upset more conservative viewers.

As an example of Ciné du Sasquatch, it is almost outside the genre save for the fact the beast is, for want of a better term, a true hominid. It is bipedal, it is clearly simian in origin, and though its features are wolfish, it still maintains the essence of what most viewers would characterize as falling within the Bigfoot film range for physical characteristics. But even if one discounts the direct inclusion, one is forced to admit its indirect lineage to the endless sub-genre examples within Ciné du Sasquatch which graphically depict sex between male cryptids and female humans.

In fact, this theme is so prevalent in Ciné du Sasquatch it is almost impossible to find at least a few, scattered examples in any decade of the genre that don't hint at (if not outright depict) this implicit, underlying sexuality between the species. From such earlier mainstream works as *Man Beast* and *Night of the Demon* to later adult films such as *The Geek, Alpine Affairs,* and *Perverted Stories,* this ever-present subtext is a staple of the genre's history. Given the underlying sexual tension in *King Kong* (best personified by the often cut sequence in which Kong slowly rips away Ann Darrow's garments and sniffs each piece with growing excitement), which was a major influence on the directions Ciné du Sasquatch took over the decades, this is hardly new or unexpected. As moral standards of acceptable screen depictions of formerly taboo sexuality inevitably give way to more explicit depictions, so these inherent themes are brought to the surface and explored (or exploited) with increasingly graphic details.

Borowczyk was a unique filmmaker in his peak years of Euro cinema output. Always controversial and willing to break down walls of "good taste" and artistic self-restraint, his previous film to *The*

Beast was the appropriately-named *Immoral Tales* (from which he actually deleted the extensive end sequence which makes up *The Beast* and later repurposed it by expanding the cut footage into a feature film). *Immoral Tales* artistically examined such cinematic subject matter rarities as lesbianism, incest and rape. Later efforts like *Emmanuelle V* and *Dr. Jekyll and His Women* showcase equally transgressive filmmaking at its uncensored height, though more puritanical viewers will likely find them without any merit whatsoever. As a former painter and animator, Borowczyk was the rare filmmaker who favored composition over kinetic motion, and lighting over narrative exposition. As such, his films are more akin to visual poetry and erotica than pornography or even softcore sex films (under which categories they have often been miscategorized). They defy verbal description and, like the work of Bunuel and Lynch, require the viewer to suspend preconceptions and simply participate without moral judgment. Suffice it to say that for many audiences this is simply not acceptable as cinema and therefore to be scorned.

There *is* much to shock the unprepared. The last 20 minutes of *The Beast* are an extended dream sequence in which Lucy fulfills her every erotic desire with her bestial lover, leaving no inhibition unexamined. As such, she indulges in masturbating the creature's massive penis, even encouraging him to ejaculate onto her in copious amounts, and participates in many other formerly-oppressed desires. Too, the film opens with a stud horse mounting a female horse in heat, with Borowczyk lingering in close-up on the stud's aroused genitalia. Some will be so put off by this example of animal husbandry that they will refuse to go further into the film's transgressive themes of sexual fantasies and repressed lusts. But as the sequence is seen through the startled eyes of the naïve Lucy Broadhurst as an indication of her dawning awareness of the physically aggressive nature of a sexual encounter — of which she knows little or nothing — it is entirely appropriate to all that follows (provided, of course, one finds such imagery in a narrative film morally acceptable).

In the arts, after all, the oppressiveness and authoritarianism of everyday reality often gives way to a dreamlike sense of liberation and escape; surely, this is one of the movies' greatest lures. The ability to dream while awake, communally and individually, and have such journeys guided to cathartic conclusions is what gives film its power. Given the enormous repression of sexuality, violence and other animalistic urges in the "civilized" human being, where even the admission of such darker sides remains taboo, films such as *The Beast* bring to graphic life the admittedly debased but no less passionately-fueled desires and lusts lurking in *Homo sapiens* as a species. We *are* the real beasts, after all, but with a fragile veneer of intelligence and moral restraint that makes us build laws and societies to supposedly keep such personal "demons" in check. Denial of this state of existence for mankind leads to the projection of those collective inner monsters outward onto external reality in the forms of world wars, genocidal mania, environmental depletion, and other human-created catastrophes.

In light of the realities of modern man, in other words, such "depraved" visions as the type Borowczyk presents in *The Beast* are actually quite tame. No real people are injured, and viewership is optional to each individual. Would that this could be said for the civilians and drafted soldiers who have died against their wills in the wars of the last hundred years, let alone throughout human history, and there would be a more believable, logical argument against the comparatively benign visions of "perverse" filmmakers like Borowczyk. *The Beast* is a must-see for mature, serious students of Bigfoot cinema who wish to examine the darker implications so readily dispersed throughout the genre and often masked by more puerile sensibilities behind the camera in lesser genre efforts that imply or depict bestiality. Repulsive, liberating, and illuminating, the film holds a steadily burning candle up to the darker recesses of the human sexual psyche, and refuses to look away from what is revealed.

Beastie Boys ("Triple Trouble") (2004) (TV)

Starring the Beastie Boys and Shaquille O'Neil. Produced by the Beastie Boys. Song Written by Michael Diamond, Bernard Edwards, Adam Horovitz, Nile Rodgers and Adam Nathaniel Yauch. Directed by Nathaniel Hornblower (aka MCA). Color. Stereo. 5 Minutes.

Overview: After a six-year absence, the Beastie Boys appear at a music awards show in Hollywood. As they exit their limo, a TV reporter asks them where they've been all these years. The rap group explains that they've been held by Sasquatch for the duration of their missing time. Furthermore, they state Bigfoot reeks and made for a lousy housekeeper.

Watching the event back home in his cave, Sasquatch becomes enraged at the Beastie Boys' bad manners. After trashing his own abode and then looking up the directions to Hollywood on the Internet, the cryptid storms out of his forest domain and heads for Southern California, intent on exacting revenge.

Meanwhile, the Beastie Boys don industrial work uniforms and perform "Triple Trouble," their latest song, for the live television crews. Sasquatch arrives halfway through their set and knocks them down. He straps the trio to a hand cart and dollies them back to his cave. When they're set free, Sasquatch forces them to relive their captivity and realize he was not such a bad host after all. He fixes them heat-and-serve frozen lasagna. He plays old Atari Pong with them on his ancient TV set. He even reads them bedtime stories while they listen, tucked into their sleeping bags.

After some reflection, they all return to suburbia, whereupon Sasquatch puts on sweat pants and challenges the Boys to a game of three-on-one basketball. The Beastie Boys give it their all, but Sasquatch is more than a match for them, stuffing shots with ease and knocking aside their tosses as if the ball was thrown in slow-motion.

* * * * *

The fact that the New York–born and based Beastie Boys reflect so positively on Bigfoot in their "Triple Trouble" video demonstrates the widespread appeal of the cryptid character. Sasquatch is not merely a rural or even suburban phenomena, but one that also appeals to the modern city dweller. By the time of this video's production, Sasquatch had largely transcended all attempts to be "ghetto-ized" as a marginal figure of folklore and become every bit the pop-sensation equivalent of the Beastie Boys themselves. As if further proof was needed, this song's popularity (while very good by way of sales) was topped by the video's bigger success on MTV and VH-1, and in repeated Internet viewings.

The casting of NBA all-star Shaquille O'Neil is particularly adroit. Not only does Shaq have the stature the role requires, but he brings some needed athleticism to the way the Beastie Boys have envisioned their cinematic cryptid as super agile, hip to the modern world and competitive in (naturally) shooting hoops. The costume is terrific and echoes the ones worn by Andre the Giant and Ted Cassidy on *The Six Million Dollar Man* series, as well as its spin-off *The Bionic Woman*. The interior visualization of Sasquatch's cave home as a comfortable, middle-class setting is both funny and touching. Like *Harry and the Hendersons*, it makes the creature seem downright human in the simplicity and homines of its needs. Equipped with microwave, oven, TV, videogames and books, this is one hominid who doesn't mind enjoying the proverbial *la dolce vita* while whiling away the hours in his cavernous abode.

The highlights are definitely the interaction between the Boys and Shaq-squatch upon their forced return to his lair. As the fatherly Bigfoot tends to their every need, it is the Beastie Boys themselves who seem, well, "beastly" for their earlier rude, insensitive remarks about their former captor. They may be held against their will, it is clear, but no one can accuse their kidnapper of lacking good table manners and being an otherwise top-notch host. Quaint as the cryptid's homey cave may be, even Martha Stewart would find it difficult to critique his gracious entertaining style.

All of this is successfully played for laughs, but it furthers the perception that Sasquatch is not only a figure of transcendental cultural popularity, but "one of us" in his physical and emotional needs. He is an "average Joe" just looking to get by in a world full of anxiety and pressures. Sasquatch experiences all the emotions the rap superstars themselves feel and more: rage, indignation, pride and even love. It's difficult to imagine a more humane vision of the beloved Bigfoot than the one herein contained, where Sasquatch is just the "Everyman" (or is that "Every*cryptid*"?) not seeking attention but merely trying his best to get along with the majority of his fellow sentient beings. It's quite the "evolution" from the typical Savage Sasquatch depiction, as entertaining as it is thought-provoking in terms of the genre.

The Beauties and the Beast (1974)

AKA: *Desperately Seeking Yeti*; *The Beast and the Vixens*. Starring Valdesta, Uschi Digard, Marius Mazmanian, Bob Makay, Patrick Scott, David Wheeler, Susan Wescott, John Shell, Carol Evins, Sandy Carey, Colleen Brennan, Tami Lynn, Beverly Wallace, Paul Kalin, Charles David, Brian Jacobs and Tracy Handfuss. Produced by Arthur A. Jacobs and Al Fields. Written by Gaynor MacLaren. Directed by Ray Nadeau. USA. Color. Mono. 66 Minutes.

Overview: Well-endowed women with a proclivity for stripping nude find themselves at the mercy of a sex-addicted Bigfoot in the mountains near Los Angeles. Meanwhile, vacationing lesbians Ann and Mary try to escape the pressures of Hollywood by taking a much-needed break and staying in a remote cabin in the very vicinity of the recent Sasquatch abductions, unaware they are in danger even as the horny cryptid peeps through their cabin window and spies on them cuddling together in bed.

A scummy-looking low-life spots Ann and Mary's arrival and makes a phone call to the mysterious, sinister Frenchie back in Hollywood, informing his boss of the cabin's current occupants. Frenchie laughs and tells his henchman to stay put; soon Frenchie will arrive to take care of business. Frenchie speculates that it might be even be fun, given that the women are all alone.

A couple pauses to make love in the great outdoors, but Bigfoot slays the man and steals away with the naked, screaming woman. The hormone-ravaged beast takes her back to his cave, where earlier we have seen him stash two other beauties unfortunate enough to come within his hairy grasp. One of the desperate women tries to make a break for it, but Bigfoot arrives and kills her for her escape attempt.

Ann and Mary meet a bunch of hippies skinny-dipping in a lake the next day and join in the nudist fun. Later that night they all retreat to a deserted cabin nearby discovered by the hippies. Stories are told about a spooky old Hermit who lives somewhere in the mountains — the hippies leave him food at night, and apparently the Hermit leaves them good-luck charms in exchange, which they sell to gullible tourists in the local village. One of the hippie chicks declares she believes that a Bigfoot monster is the actual charm-maker and food-taker, but no one believes her fantastic stories.

Frenchie arrives and, together with his criminal buddy, takes the entire group of young people hostage at gunpoint. After tying them together, Frenchie informs the bewildered youngsters that they have unknowingly stumbled across his hidden gold loot, for which he served seven years in prison and had hidden in the cabin the hippies inhabit. He shows them the charms they sell left each night by the mysterious stranger, which contain a gold piece embedded within as a design motif. The hippies, Ann and Mary beg for their lives, pleading innocence, but Frenchie is convinced that they knew about the gold and have been creating the charms — after all, they admit they sell them to tourists.

Frenchie takes Ann and leaves his compadre to watch over the remaining hostages. Frenchie's goal is to return to the cabin and recover the gold. While Frenchie is gone, his sociopathic accomplice begins to rape one of the hippie women. The group free themselves and attack, managing to kill the degenerate rapist. They head for the cabin, hoping to save Ann before Frenchie has his way with her and escapes with the gold.

At the cabin it becomes clear that the Old Hermit is actually alive and in possession of the gold. Outraged, Frenchie makes Ann take him to the Hermit's lakefront cabin, where Frenchie strikes the Hermit and demands the gold pieces. Alas for Frenchie, Bigfoot shows up at the same time. Ann gets loose during the struggle between Frenchie and Bigfoot. Enraged the outsider has assaulted the Hermit, Bigfoot crushes Frenchie and breaks every bone in his body. The hippies rescue Ann. The last time we see Bigfoot, the creature is stumbling along behind its caretaker, the Old Hermit, who leads the cryptid through the forest and to hidden safety.

* * * * *

Beneath many Ciné du Sasquatch movies there lurks the theme of bestiality, however well-hidden in most such efforts. From the innocuous version seen in the influential *King Kong* to the outright degenerative, poorly-rendered versions in such entries as *Search for the Beast*, the taboo of sex between species is a common subtext. In some examples, such as *Night of the Demon*, there is the implicit connection between such a mating having occurred that "explains" the existence of the cryptid itself. In still others, such as the John Carradine version of *Bigfoot*, sex-starved hominids embody the cliché of the caveman who abducts desirable females no matter their tribal affiliation or even barely-related genetic status.

The Beauties and the Beast is an incredibly cheesy example of the underlying thematic being "laid bare" (in every sense of the phrase!) for all Bigfoot cinema fans to examine (or not). Like the frequent examples of softcore sex throughout the film, the mechanics are on "open display" and therefore offer a perfect example of how the genre so often balances on the edge of descending into outright camp on the one hand, and creepy, more disturbing symbolic portrayals of darker male instincts (such as rape and worse) being suggested on the other.

As a Jungian version of the Animus released — the repressed, animalistic side of male sexual conquest — these examples in Ciné du Sasquatch can reliably be categorized as expressing a certain male "pent up rage" towards women, particularly well-endowed women who are not ashamed to display their figures. As outrageous as this may read, it is no less apparent and accepted in the Slasher Film genre, wherein the psychopathic serial killer "punishes" the promiscuous females who dare to engage in premarital sex and who inevitably wear revealing clothing to "taunt" the usually male murderer with their very femininity. The latent misogyny is so well known that it is frequently parodied in satires, most notably in Wes Craven's witty critique *Scream*. It is no less absent in the Bigfoot films that incorporate the concept.

The key difference — to the extent there is one between the genres' realization of this theme — is that in Ciné du Sasquatch there is the undercurrent (if not explicit notion) that Bigfoot is seeking not to murder the women, but to humiliate, degrade and occasionally impregnate them, thus carrying out a diabolical need to genetically cross the boundaries between species. Why this need exists is never addressed nor even hinted at in the narratives; one is forced to speculatively formulate the symbolic Freudian implications motivating such queasy but prevalent subtexts in the genre. To wit, the taboo lines of bestiality and forced sex are being cinematically exploited, while still allowing enough psychological "distance" for the male viewer to not feel as if he is a willing participant in or approving party of the grotesquerie itself.

In a puritanical society such as the United States, this admittedly theoretical explanation at least makes sense: It has long been a norm of American cinema that while violence is totally acceptable as a means of expressing manhood (in fact, it's often an indication of a lack of manliness if an individual is unwilling to engage in violence as a rite of passage), the sexual urge to conquer and dominate is forbidden unless courtly rituals are observed prior to the act, wherein the female "signals" her willingness. For the man who grows up emotionally stunted, however, the latter poses significant obstacles over the easier path to emotions expressed through violence. Hence, in at least some civilized males, there exists a frustration with the status

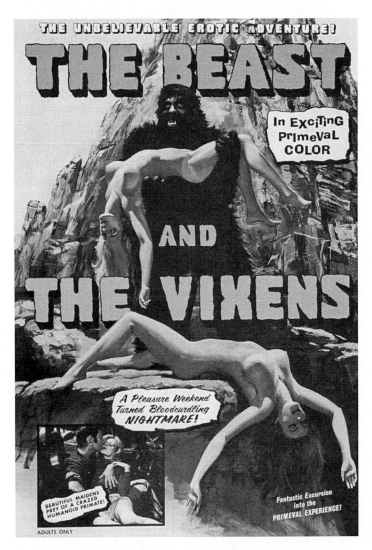

Poster art for the theatrical release of *The Beauties and the Beast* (aka *The Beast and the Vixens*).

quo which provides plenty of outlet for physical aggression, but only as long as it is directed towards same-sex members in sanctioned (that is to say socially-approved) activities such as sports and business competition. The other, more unacceptably dark sexual impulses are consequently self-repressed in men lacking the necessary communication skills; this in turn leaves a psychic and, of course, physical need unalleviated in such males. Call it the subconscious Hyde element of the unaware Jekyll viewer; these Ciné du Sasquatch bestiality films may be actively exploiting such male urges by externalizing the darker impulses and projecting them onto the "animal" figure represented by the marauding Bigfoot, who knows no sense of "decency" or boundary. Hence, the cryptid cannot be conventionally judged by civilized morality any more than the male who is living vicariously through such a depiction.

So much for the in-depth, analytical approach. The actual movie itself is nothing less than a bawdy sexual romp that's never as serious as the aforementioned didactics; moreover, it's entertaining in a campy manner. The generous amount of softcore sex seems almost quaint in an era when such imagery is prevalent on cable programming; though one cannot help but contrast how well-endowed women in 1974, with their fleshy curves and large breasts, would be considered "plus-sized" in the modern era. With Russ Meyer–style aesthetics amply on display, *The Beauties and the Beast* plays as an unintentional diatribe against the skinny screen temptress imagery of the 2000s — this is a cryptid who clearly prefers female humans with D-sized bra cups!

Technically, there is no sense the film was made as anything more than a weekend wonder, designed for a quick pay-off and nothing more. While the sex scenes are for the most part well-lit and carefully photographed (as would be expected, given the obvious Pussycat Theater–styled intended marketplace), much of the action is shot without sound and obviously post-dubbed with loose sync. The outdoor sequences of the roaming Sasquatch, oddly, are often spectacular, in that the seasonal variations in foliage against the actual mountain locales renders well on what appears to be Kodachrome film stock (which favors outdoor photography, given its slower emulsion rating).

The acting is generally dreadful, though most of the cast is required simply to appear as natural while *au naturel* rather than emote. The character of Frenchie, in contrast, is so over-the-top as to bring a genuine Snidely Whiplash flavor to the proceedings. Displaying zero vulnerability, always dominating in any scene, and a vociferous and vocal hater of all humanity he encounters, Frenchie seems to be on a personal, nihilistic quest to dismantle all spiritual qualities inherent in our species. He also hates hippies with a vengeance, which fuels his mania to destroy the innocent group of freeloaders, similar to the rednecks' violence against Captain America and Billy in the final moments of *Easy Rider* (sans the Southern accents). It is only fitting, in a perversely ironic way, that the Old Hermit — who is portrayed as representing the goodness of nature — is the unwitting cause of Frenchie's gruesome death at the hands of the enraged Sasquatch, said hominid viewing the Hermit as his caretaker and resentful of Frenchie's mistreatment of the lonely octogenarian.

The location photography of Hollywood Boulevard and Laurel Canyon in the polyester 1970s is spot-on for those who enjoy seeing the area the way it was before becoming generically "revitalized" by the corporate developments of the 1990s — there's nary a Starbucks, Planet Hollywood or the like within sight as far as the eye can see (which, given the heavy smog, isn't far). In a strange coincidence, the feeding of the creature at night by the hippies to establish a kind of truce with Bigfoot is echoed decades later in *The Wild Man of the Navidad*, which is supposed to take place decades earlier in the 1970s themselves!

While it is no lost masterpiece, *The Beauties and the Beast* never takes itself seriously enough to warrant much beyond casual derision. All but the most hardened or prudish viewers will find much to be amused by throughout its scant running time, not the least of which is Sasquatch's secret lair. The abode consists of a small crevice clearly right off a busy roadway in what looks to be a city park that is crudely covered with decrepit blankets hanging from the entrance (probably to mask the fact the actual cave is not more than a few feet deep). The cave interior — which is clearly a set, complete with cardboard walls — indicates within the opening scenes that *The Beauties and the Beast* is never going to be a masterpiece in Ciné du Sasquatch. Oddly, however, many shots of the cryptid — who is suitably bulky and more closely resembles the Patterson-Gimlin Bigfoot — are eerily effective, which may be a smart casting choice as much as anything else. Like the frolicsome nudes who cavort sans clothing throughout, the actor beneath is sufficiently well-endowed with muscular bulk to bring believability to the low-rent suit.

Behind the Cameras: The Unauthorized Story of Charlie's Angels (2004) (TV) (Cameo)

Starring Christina Chambers, Dan Castellaneta, Dan Lauria, Wallace Langham, Tricia Helfer, Lauren Stamile, Ben Browder, Chelsea Watson, Brandy Ledford, Summer Gibson-Lefaive, Bruce Altman and John DeSantis. Produced by Ted Bauman, Howard Braunstein, Matt Dorff, Michael Jaffe and Michael G. Larkin. Written by Jack Condon and David Hofstede. Directed by Francine McDougall. USA. Color. Stereo. 96 Minutes.

Overview: When Farrah Fawcett, Jaclyn Smith, and Kate Jackson are cast in *Charlie's Angels* — a new all-female private eye ABC television series produced by Aaron Spelling — they each grapple with the sudden fame and success the overnight sensation generates in their professional and personal lives. Farrah, a small-town Texas gal, struggles to stand by her man, megastar Lee Majors, even as he resents her being outside the home and refusing to have supper ready for him when he returns after a long day of shooting. Kate Jackson fights the inherent sexism of the role into which she's been cast, even as it makes her wealthy. Jaclyn Smith worries about how her friends and family will view her in a format that weekly portrays her wearing the skimpiest of outfits. Meanwhile, a Machiavellian Aaron Spelling manipulates and coerces the starlets to keep the ratings high and the money rolling in. Andre the Giant, who plays an android Sasquatch in the Lee Majors series *The Six Million Dollar Man*, is sympathetic to the feelings the women have of being cast in roles that require self-parody of one's physical attributes in an industry not known for caring how one views oneself, as long as one shows up on time for the morning's first take. With varying degrees of success, the real-life women behind *Charlie's Angels* achieve an understanding with their show — which is dubbed "Massage Parlor TV" by critics — and, to varying degrees, learn to grow beyond the series' stereotypes of themselves in their careers and personal lives.

* * * * *

As a campy, retro-stalgic trip into the 1970s, *Behind the Cameras: The Unauthorized Story of Charlie's Angels* positively revels in its own inherent cheesiness. From the choice of pop music on the soundtrack to the clothes and hot-air blown hairstyles, the telefilm refuses to ever make more than token attempts at playing its subject matter for anything more than lurid tabloid thrills. And to surprising effect at times, it achieves its limited goal in an entertaining manner.

Helping matters is the casting of the three leads, each of whom captures the physical nature of their respective Angel — the sexy, dipsy blonde one; the serious intellectual one; and the gorgeous classy one. Dan Castellaneta (best known to fans of *The Simpsons* as the voice of patriarch Homer) captures the maniacal nature of Aaron Spelling with overt glee, puffing on his pipe and manipulating the behind-the-scenes action as deftly as the filmmakers of *Behind the Camera* do their own lurid exposé. While some of the episodes are doubtlessly based on well-researched reality, the key word in this distinction is "based upon"—the show itself plays more like a Jackie Collins novel as adapted to teleplay format, complete with the melodramatic flare so often associated with Collins' works of thinly-disguised fiction.

Ciné du Sasquatch devotees will appreciate the brief cameo by actor John DeSantis as Andre the Giant (who played the android Sasquatch in the first few appearances of *The Six Million Dollar Man*). While the intent of *Behind the Camera* is to point out the ridiculous nature of much of 1970s-era television production by showing that Lee Majors could take such obviously silly material as a bionic man fighting a robot Bigfoot and still fill himself with self-importance during his 15 minutes of fame, it nevertheless will bring a probable smile to those who relish the sporadic Sasquatch episodes of the Steve Austin chronicles because it was such a touchstone to their lifelong obsession with All Things Cryptid. It's a frivolous but fun Bigfoot cameo.

The Berenstain Bears Meet Bigpaw (1980) (TV)

Featuring the voices of Ron McLarty, Pat Lysinger, Bob Kaliban, Gabriela Glatzer and Jonathan Lewis. Produced by Joseph Cates, Nancy B. Dodds, Jere Jacob and Buzz Potamkin. Written by Jan and Stan Berenstain. Directed by Mordicai Gerstein and Al Kouzel. USA. Color. Stereo. 30 Minutes.

Overview: The Berenstain Bears live in the ancestral forests of the Grizzly Bear lineage. One afternoon, Papa Bear leads Brother Bear and Sister Bear on a food-gathering mission in preparation for Thanksgiving. As the Berenstain Bears live in a valley of plenty, they have nothing to fear—nothing, that is, save the legend of Bigpaw. For an ancient Grizzly prophecy has foretold that if the bears ever forget the needy among their fellow valley inhabitants and become selfish and greedy, they will face the wrath of the vociferous Bigpaw, a Sasquatch variation that lives high atop the craggiest mountain.

Papa Bear, however, isn't much for all the hokey legends of Bigpaw. He prefers to indulge himself without limits and celebrate Thanksgiving by each course consumed rather than expressing any personal gratitude. Mama Bear, the moral center of the family, tries to counter his heartless attitude by instilling more humble values in her cubs.

That afternoon, while Papa Bear is in town, a Hedge Hog informs the populace that there's been a sighting of Bigpaw in nearby Sinister Bog. Alas for Papa Bear's nerves, that's where Brother and Sister Bear are currently harvesting wild nuts, his favorite Thanksgiving treat. Sure enough, the siblings soon encounter the 90-foot-tall hominid, who boasts (in a musical number) that he exceeds both Sasquatch and the Abominable Snowman in ferocity. Bigpaw shakes their paws and watches as Brother and Sister Bear slowly walk away, terrified but grateful Bigpaw exhibits no hostility towards them.

The grown-up bears have begun Operation Bigpaw, an attempt to marshal their forces and take on the towering avenger. Mama Bear arrives and admonishes them, singing a melody that explains that not all strangers equal danger. Realizing his wife may have a point, Papa Bear decides to visit Echoing Ledge and see for himself, accompanied by Brother and Sister Bear. Alarmed by what he's seen, Papa Bear races back down the mountain to warn his bear brethren in a call to arms. His cubs try to tell their father that Bigpaw is peaceful, but Papa Bear is so frantic he won't listen.

When Bigpaw sees the unruly mob of bears storming up the mountainside towards his cave, Bigpaw prepares a trap to defend his home. Just before he unleashes a rock tower that will crush the bear mob, however, Brother and Sister Bear try to alert Bigpaw to the mob's fury. The rocks give away and only Bigpaw has the wherewithal to save the endangered cubs from certain death. Papa Bear and the others realize that Bigpaw is their friend and thank the monstrously tall but friendly hominid for saving their cubs' lives.

Properly chastised by their adventure, the adult bears celebrate their Thanksgiving by inviting Bigpaw to be their honored guest. Papa Bear is delighted when Bigpaw gives him a treat: nuts, Papa Bear's favorite.

* * * * *

First created in the 1960s and published under the Dr. Seuss imprinter, *The Berenstain Bears* have seen numerous television adaptations, including two different series and many one-off holiday-themed specials, of which *The Berenstain Bears Meet Bigpaw* is typical. Creators Jan and Stan Berenstain have published over 300 different books relating to the grizzly family's various adventures, all roughly sketched in an ad hoc style that resembles what might be rendered by a child (by way of an adult imitating one).

Bigpaw adeptly plays upon the classic Ciné du Sasquatch concept of Bigfoot as spiritual protector of the forest. This post–*Harry and the Hendersons* role as Benign Bigfoot is so pervasive in the genre that it has become the *de facto* rendering of Sasquatch in films and on TV for children's programming. The transformation of the bipedal woods dweller from "monster" to "friendly giant" is entirely logical, of course, as it not only offers the chance to expound upon the environmental concerns so prevalent in modern kiddy entertainment but avoids scaring the tyke viewers witless with the thought of a large, hulking creature lurking in the trees.

Interestingly enough, Bigpaw considers himself superior to Sasquatch and the Abominable Snowman, going so far, in his self-centered theme song, to vocalize how "you can have them," as they're nothing compared to him! Forgetting the rarity of a talking Bigfoot in and of itself (surprisingly uncommon, given how human are many of the adaptations of the hominid)—let alone one who sings in minor key!—this is one Bigfoot who is not above having some serious but comical Ego imbalance. He stomps through the forests as the clear king of his domain, sending alligators, turtles, hedge hogs and every other animal species scurrying away in quivering fright. This, too, is a common theme of the genre, and while Bigpaw's song mocks the solemnity often associated with this distillation, he nevertheless also brings the paradigm right to the forefront. As the ancient Chinese saying intones: "The most dangerous animal in the forest is the one that remains unseen."

Habitat, too, plays a large part in the show's sense of eco-balance. For example, the mountain where Bigpaw resides is clearly a reference to the Himalayan peaks, with its nearly unreachable zenith and snowy crags; while the favorite roaming ground of Bigpaw is a swampy flatland area known as Sinister Bog, which references the bayou-type country favored by the Fouke Monster of *The Legend of Boggy Creek*. This is a highly unusual synthesis in the genre and easy to miss for all the cuteness the storyline is sugar-coated with, as nearly all examples of Ciné du Sasquatch isolate their respective hominid into either a mountainous setting (reflecting the Yeti), a redwoods forest setting (reflecting Sasquatch) or a boggy area (reflecting a Skunk Ape). It is genuinely atypical for one entry in the genre to portray the cryptid in question as both residing at the heights of the mountains *and* preferring the swamps as well. This may only be a reflection of live action films' and TV shows' budget restraints, wherein producers are forced to choose one locale or the other for cost reasons. But even within animated fare, this remains a blending of Bigfoot and Yeti backdrops that is anything but normal for the genre.

The Berenstain Bears Meet Bigpaw is no classic of Ciné du Sasquatch. Indeed, it's tough viewing for any over-the-single-digit-age viewer. But for cryptid cinema fans interested in seeing how core concepts of the genre are readily adapted into various popular culture franchises (such as the fifty-year-old Berenstain Bears behemoth), it provides plenty of insight into Bigfoot's nearly chameleon-like ability to "blend in" not only with any setting, but with any other mythos.

Best Evidence ("Bigfoot") (2007) (TV) (Doc)

Featuring John Bindernagel, Tim Martindale, Jeffrey Meldrum, David Begun, Nina Jablonski, John Turtle, Jessica Rose, James Gamble, Bronston DeLone and Dick Smith. Produced by Andre Czernohorsky, Phil Desjardins, Vanessa Dylyn, Amanda Enright, Dave Harding, Erica Lenczner, Jennifer McAuley, Erik Nelson, Richard O'Regan, Martin Pupp and Michael Sheehan. Writing by Aeyliya Husain. Directed by Mitchell Gabourie. Canada/USA. Color. Stereo. 60 Minutes.

Overview: A critical and often skeptical look at the plethora of evidence offered by some cryptozoologists and "pseudozoologists" (those who claim absolute belief in Sasquatch over any possible denial or contradiction in the evidence they present), *Best Evidence* is admittedly as much for objective viewers as for frequent viewers of Ciné du Sasquatch. As such, while often seemingly biased against any wholesale endorsement of the scrutinized claims and physical forensic items (such as hair samples and filmed footage), the show is actually more akin to a resident of Missouri, the "show me" state. That is, both arguments pro and con towards the Sasquatch as a living animal are examined in-depth, with both sides given healthy measures of serious consideration as well as critical dismissal.

Much will be made of the attempts to show the recreations of the Patterson-Gimlin film footage as being either legitimate or faked. Dr. Jeffrey Meldrum, an associate professor of anatomy and anthropology in the Idaho State University department of biological sciences, finds some compelling reasons to believe the footage could be legitimate, but comes to the conclusion after working with the Idaho State University Virtualization Laboratory on the Patterson-Gimlin film that there is at least the possibility that some of the walk could be replicated by a human being. Dick Smith, the legendary make-up effects artist who contributed to *The Exorcist* and *Altered States*, states his professional opinion that the footage portrays a costumed actor and denies the rumor that John Chambers, a fellow make-up effects technician, participated in the Roger Patterson Bigfoot suit creation (if, indeed, it is a suit). Skeptical scientists, such as Dr. John Turtle, Dr. David Begun and Dr. Nina Jablonski, conclude that most of the evidence is wishful thinking, outright hoaxes or the by-product of well-meaning but misinformed eyewitnesses.

Big and Hairy (1998)

Starring Robert Burke, Trevor Jones, Greg Thirloway, Richard Thomas, Chilton Crane, Donnelly Rhodes, Tyler Thompson, Zach Lipovsky, Zachary Martin, Stacy Grant, Colleen Fox, Gina Stockdale, Adrian Hughes, Anna McRoberts and Fred Keating. Produced by Marcy Gross, Colleen Nystedt and Ann Weston. Written by Brian Daly. Directed by Philip Spink. USA. Color. Stereo. 94 Minutes.

Overview: Picasso Dewlap is the proverbial new kid in town. Child of flower power purveyors Victor and Elizabeth Dewlap, Picasso's parents have had to move in order for Victor to forgo his career as a painter and instead work as a designer for a lawn ornament manufacturing company. Partly because of his strange name and partly because of his parent's hippie mentality, Picasso doesn't exactly blend in with the local kids, who prefer sports to artistic self-expression.

Trying to win social points for effort, Picasso joins the basketball team. However, he's anything but a natural athlete, and during an early game in the season he blows several shots that cause his school's team to lose. Victor's boss is a sports nut who can't stand to see his new employee's son as the weak link in their basketball team. His bellicose manner at the game dooms from the start Picasso's long-shot effort to win respect.

Ruminating in the forest near his home, Picasso meets Ed, a young Sasquatch. They quickly become friends, and when it is readily apparent to Picasso that Ed has a natural ability to slam dunk basketballs, Picasso comes up with the ultimate wild-card play. He convinces Ed to join their team as a player, despite Ed's initial misgivings. But when the Coach and Victor's boss see how dominant Ed is as a player, they're suddenly all for his inclusion. And as there is nothing

Cover art for the VHS release of *Big and Hairy*.

in the rule book that prohibits hominids from playing the game, no one can rightly object.

However, Ed soon misses his parents, Mom and Dad Sasquatch. As the basketball team becomes increasingly dependent upon Ed, and the junior Bigfoot longs to return to his forest home, a moral dilemma arises among the community — and, more importantly, within the Dewlap household. To wit, should Ed stay or be allowed to go free to his ancestral dwellings? And how can Picasso, who has enjoyed unexpected popularity as the "discoverer" of Ed, possibly risk his newfound fame to act on behalf of Ed to help him escape if he so chooses?

* * * * *

Some movies within Ciné du Sasquatch take a certain leap of faith in order to suspend disbelief. Examples of this type of Bigfoot film include *Sasquatch, The Legend of Big foot* and *Abominable*; one must be willing to grant the possible existence of a cryptid or the film cannot be enjoyed. And then there are the more comedic and/or family-oriented Bigfoot films that not only insist the viewer accept a cryptid as possible, but that human and hominid interaction would go so smoothly and so unnoticed as to be otherwise akin to an Olympics sporting event between nationalities in terms of cultural novelty. *Big and Hairy* is just such a long shot, and much like *Harry and the Hendersons* (which it clearly draws upon), the younger the audience, the less likely they'll have buying into the concept.

In terms of believability, *Big and Hairy* is like a last-second desperation half-court toss in a basketball game. That is, more often than not it simply collapses in on itself in terms of credulity. It's one thing to accept that Picasso, the alienated kid, and Ed, the alienated Bigfoot, form a bond; this is a likeable if far-fetched scenario but a cornerstone of every children's movie (ranging from *Flipper* to *Gentle Ben*). But even Flipper didn't play Marco Polo, after all; and neither did Gentle Ben play a mean game of darts. In essence, *Big and Hairy* asks us to believe that not only could a Sasquatch play basketball, but that it would be accepted as a legitimate player on a boy's team without much beyond a token protest.

Obviously, *Big and Hairy* is following in the "footsteps" of such animal sports films as *Air Bud*, in which a dog shows equally amazing prowess tossing hoops. There is, however, one key difference: The idea of a known animal species overcoming the barriers to besting a human, while incredulous, remain in the realm of only "nearly impossible"; whereas this film asks the audience to not only believe Sasquatch exists as a friendly species, but that they're willing to allow human interaction with their young to the extent that said youngsters are exploited for human gain in, no less, a competitively organized sport! This is, to say the least, a huge "leap" of faith and one that, sadly, *Big and Hairy* can make with only modest success and about as frequently as a referee-tossed jump ball.

Richard Thomas, most famous for his stint as John Boy on *The Waltons*, plays against his normally conservative, shy type in an atypical role as the long-haired, semi-manic artist who never shies away from expressing himself or his enthusiasm for his son's newfound social success (thanks to Ed, the slam-dunking Sasquatch). Production values are good, with crisp cinematography and decent hominid costumes (though obviously nowhere near the caliber of *Harry and the Hendersons*, given the film's modest budget in comparison). *Big and Hairy* was shot in Canada, which adds scenic beauty to the outdoors sequences, though the majority of the film takes place in the suburban locales and the school's gymnasium.

A final bit of homage has Ed watching television with Picasso and seeing Chewbacca from *Star Wars*. Ed quickly identifies with the wayward Wookie and begins imitating him, thinking Chewie is perhaps a lost cryptozoological cousin of his own kind. If there was much doubt that Chewbacca represents the most famous "space cryptid"

in Ciné du Sasquatch, this brief bit offers resounding evidence to allay it. It takes a Sasquatch, after all, to know one.

Bigfoot (1970)

AKA: *Big Foot*. Starring John Carradine, Joi Lansing, Judy Jordan, John Mitchum, James Craig, Christopher Mitchum, Joy Wilkerson, Lindsay Crosby, Ken Maynard, Doodles Weaver, Noble "Kid" Chissel and Del "Sonny" West. Produced by Anthony Cardoza and Bill Reardon. Written by Robert F. Slatzer and James Gordon White. Directed by Robert F. Slatzer. USA. Color. Mono. 84 Minutes.

Overview: Traveling salesman Jasper B. Hawks and sidekick Elmer Briggs eke out a living by peddling their wares across the rural United States, dropping in on various remote country stores to hawk their largely useless goods. But when the amiable if hefty Briggs, refreshing himself in a mountain stream, hears a Bigfoot growling and then finds giant footprints, he becomes convinced it's time to drop his partnership with his cousin Hawks. Wily Hawks smooth-talks Briggs into reconsidering, pointing out that all the tall tales about Bigfoot and such are just folklore.

Meanwhile, a gang of young toughs on motorcycles (and scooters!) tear ass through the same California foothills, getting high on more than just the altitude. When Rick and Chris, a frisky biker couple, leave the group for some one-on-one time, however, they stumble

Pressbook ad for the original release of *Bigfoot* (1970). "The Greatest Monster Movie Since *King Kong*!" falsely proclaims the misleading ad copy, illustrating the influence of the 1933 classic on the Bigfoot genre.

upon a Bigfoot burial ground and a freshly-buried creature. A savage Sasquatch attacks, beating Rick senseless and abducting the bikini-clad Chris. Regaining his senses, Rick rides his cycle down the mountain to Bennett's Country Store to seek help, only to be met with skepticism by local law enforcement officials Sheriff Cyrus and Deputy Hank when he calls them on Bennett's pay phone.

Overhearing the young man's plight, Hawks — sensing an opportunity to make millions by capturing a Bigfoot alive — offers to assist in the search and recovery of the missing girlfriend, providing needed guns, a flashlight and Hawks' own acumen as a long-time backwoods hunter. A reluctant Briggs goes along as the trio sets out into the mountain darkness in pursuit of the kidnapping monster.

They find the burial site of the Bigfoot monsters just as Rick described. Now convinced he's onto the score of a lifetime, Hawks pushes his two companions deeper into the redwoods in search of his prey. The creatures stage a surprise attack come daylight, however, and take Rick, Hawks and Briggs alive as prisoners. They're tied up, along with Chris and Joi, a female pilot who had earlier parachuted from her crashed plane, and left to fend for themselves while the Bigfoot monsters prepare them for a ritualistic slaughter. Just when all hope seems lost, the gang of biker teens and Sheriff Cyrus and Deputy Hank arrive to save the day, utilizing dynamite to seal the cave in which the Bigfoot monsters dwell and rescue the stranded humans. As they depart the mountainside, Hawks promises the naive Chris that he will make her a star by exploiting her on the talk show circuit as the woman who survived being abducted by Bigfoot.

* * * * *

Bigfoot is perhaps the most entertainingly bad Bigfoot movie of the entire "cycle" (no pun intended), though, of course, that's a "tall" order to fill. But given the strange blending of motorcycles, ridiculously bad Bigfoot costumes, has-been actors, bikini babes, and a mutant music score, the entire experience is truly a slow-paced, stupefying descent into all things torpid, but with a camp sensibility that redeems *Bigfoot* from total boredom.

The film has many distinctions, though at least half are dubious (and that's perhaps being generous). Foremost is the large amount of screen time ham-fistedly chewed, swallowed and digested by veteran character actor John Carradine. With his trademark laconic gait, wiry frame, magnetic eyes and booming bass voice, Carradine brings *Bigfoot* alive whenever he's center frame. By this point in his career Carradine was mostly relegated to cameos and one-day shooting appearances too often designed by shoddy film producers to capitalize upon his name without offering him much to do. Herein he's arguably offered his last starring role as the Mr. Haney–esque seller of claptrap who's always looking to gyp the next unwary customer.

Carradine delights in the ample screen time allotted, and while the banal script prevents any true interior characterization for him to externalize, Carradine does his best to shade his role with an unexpected sense of cynical wisdom and physical vigor. Watching the elderly actor toting his own heavy shotgun through the rugged terrain of steep canyons and dense forests, adept at not only keeping pace but leading two men less than half his age, reminds the viewer just how vital the man truly was. In a film short of believability of any kind, Carradine adds what little verisimilitude is present in *Bigfoot*, anchoring the movie not unlike Robert Shaw as Quint did for *Jaws*: at once feisty and over-the-top, yet enjoyable to watch. And at this point in the Ciné du Sasquatch genre Carradine held the distinction of being in not one but three Sasquatch movies (this, *Terror in the Midnight Sun* and the earlier *Half Human*). It's doubtful Carradine considered this equal to his work in *The Grapes of Wrath*, but it's still noteworthy at least as far as this guide is concerned.

Bigfoot is filled with second generation actor nepotism as well as old school veteran actor cameos. Robert Mitchum contributes two relatives in the roles portrayed by Chris Mitchum as Rick and John Mitchum as Elmer Briggs. Lindsay Crosby, daughter of Bing Crosby and Dixie Lee, stars as Wheels, the leader of the biker gang. Silent cowboy star Ken Maynard portrays Bennett, the dry goods store owner, and even poses in front of a poster, hanging on the wall behind him, from one of his old westerns! He appears to be drunk throughout *Bigfoot*, but perhaps it's just the altitude. *Bigfoot* offers further cameos by such vets as Doodles Weaver, who distinguished himself earlier in his career working with Spike Jones; Noble "Kid" Chissel, who had a 50-year-long Hollywood career in various bit parts; and even Joi Lansing, well-remembered for her various television roles on *The Beverly Hillbillies*, *The Bob Cummings Show* and *Klondike*.

Otherwise, *Bigfoot* is so bereft of original ideas in regards to the Bigfoot film genre that the recurrent themes so prevalent in other entries preceding it are presented in the movie as a de facto summation. For example, there is the "they must mate with human women" concept which dates all the way back to Jerry Warren's *Man Beast* Yeti opus, though *Bigfoot* puts a new patina of camp on it by having two attractive, bikini-wearing women discuss the concept. Said female victims calmly talk of their probable fate as mates for the hairy Bigfoot tribe with earnest, Ed Wood–

The disappointing suits in *Bigfoot* (1970) dated the film even in its era. After Roger Patterson's film, cinematic hominids would require better special effects to be convincing.

styled dialogue, complete with scientific lingo and mentions of the missing link theory!

Another Bigfoot genre staple — the Carl Denham/*King Kong* exploiter archetype — looms large in the greed-driven character of Jasper B. Hawks, portrayed with a fast-buck hustler mentality by Carradine. It's odd that when Carradine discovers the Bigfoot burial ground he doesn't settle for making his profit by excavating a Sasquatch corpse. One would think a dead specimen, while not the jackpot Carradine seeks by capturing a living "critter" (as he calls it), would nevertheless be of some value, especially given how much easier it would be to dig it up and avoid confronting a live monster. Of course, Carradine must have a living one (and, hey, as a secondary thought, rescue any captive human females the tribe holds), which is why his Jasper Hawks character fits so well into the Carl Denham mold. Still, the idea such a seasoned con artist would leave a silver mine behind in search of the much more difficult (if not impossible) to obtain fool's gold of a live capture seems improbable at best. The writers seem to have unwittingly stumbled onto the same reaction in crafting Carradine's response to his companions when they question how he intends to subdue a clan of the creatures with only two guns and a flashlight. "You'll see, boy," Carradine replies, "when the time is right." Remarkably, his travel mates buy into such sterling logic without further question.

A final negative is the creature costumes themselves. While one imagines the difficulty of creating a plethora of such cryptids on a low budget, the results are unbelievable and stilted. With rubber face masks of the pseudo gorilla variety and the usual sideshow furry ape suit, *Bigfoot*'s titular attractions feel ridiculously non-threatening. This problem is compounded by the producers' apparent decision to photograph much of the Bigfoot action in sunlight. While it makes for some occasionally scenic travel footage, it does no favors for the gorilla suits. It gives pause when considering the fact that the infamous Patterson/Gimlin 16mm footage achieves a far more believable impact while also shooting in broad daylight — assuming, of course, the Patterson depiction is not a real Sasquatch!

Bigfoot owes much to the preceding wave of Ciné du Sasquatch efforts such as *The Abominable Snowman* and *Half Human*, but it marks the beginning of a new era in the genre in that draws a clean dividing line between the earlier film incarnations of the "wild man" cryptid appearing mostly in snow settings as a Yeti. To wit: Following the notoriety of Patterson's California footage, the producers shift the locale to the Pacific Northwest and use the familiar Bigfoot moniker. While this is, in retrospect, perhaps the only significant impact *Bigfoot* had on the genre, it nonetheless helped set the stage for the plethora of Bigfoot-focused movies to follow in the 1970s. If for no other reason (and one would be hard pressed to come up with others), *Bigfoot* is a noteworthy Ciné du Sasquatch entry.

Bigfoot (1987) (TV)

Starring Adam Carl, Timothy Brown, Lucy Butler, Candace Cameron Bure, Jerry Chambers, Colleen Dewhurst, Gracie Harrison, Joseph Maher, Dawan Scott, James Sloyan, Bernard White and Dianne Wiest. Produced by Michael S. McLean. Written by John Groves. Directed by Danny Huston. USA. Color. Stereo. 95 Minutes.

Overview: A camping trip to the Walla Walla mountains goes awry when the children of a couple of single parents who are dating one another become lost in the woods. The kids, Kevin and Samantha, do not get along owing to their personality differences, which makes their situation all the more dire. Things turn decidedly worse, however, when the lost kids stumble across a pair of hominids who abduct them and take them to their hidden domain.

Meanwhile, a millionaire hunter named Jack Kendrix hires a local

helicopter pilot to help him find his latest prey. Kendrix's goal: capture a Bigfoot by using aerial surveillance to first spot one of the elusive cryptids and then land to hunt it on foot. His Native American pilot has doubts about the rich man's plan, believing that all the talk of his indigenous people about Bigfoot is so much nonsense. But as the wealthy man has money to burn, the guide decides to take his share and fly Kendrix wherever he wishes.

Kevin and Samantha soon learn their captors — a male and female Sasquatch — are lifelong mates grieving over the recent death of their only offspring. It becomes apparent to the children that the creatures mean them no harm. In fact, they are kind and gentle beings who feed them and make them feel as comfortable as the situation allows. Kevin and Samantha also bond, realizing they have far more in common than they previously supposed.

The worried single parents have reported their missing children to the authorities. They also enlist the help of Gladys Samco, a female anthropologist who happens to be in the mountains, in their frantic search. Initially skeptical of the mounting evidence, Samco soon realizes the hominids who've kidnapped the children are real and redoubles her efforts to help find them, as much for the missing kids' safety as the scientific value of proving Bigfoot's existence.

A race against time begins as the hunter closes in on the Sasquatch family, caring little about the well-being of the children as long as he can bag his specimen.

The benign Bigfoot motif was prominent in the Danny Huston–directed *Bigfoot* (1987), wherein hominid creatures, grief-stricken at their own offspring's death, temporarily shelter lost human children from harm.

* * * * *

It's quite a shame this effective, low-key example of Ciné du Sasquatch remains out-of-print in the legitimate home video market (though bootleg versions are available via the Internet from the earlier VHS domestic release and overseas import). Made in the same year as *Harry and the Hendersons*, it is almost the antithesis of the Spielberg production. Where *Harry and the Hendersons* is sentimental and melodramatic in equal turns, *Bigfoot* remains remarkably free of most of these obvious pitfalls. And where the Spielberg opus parodies the cryptid's possible existence for the sake of laughs as much as it entertains the notion as an actual reality, *Bigfoot* goes out of its way to modestly but effectively involve the viewer in the daily minutiae and small details that such a large species would actually face if it lived among us.

Neither movie is meant to be other than entertainment for younger audiences; and each is relatively successful in this regard. Still, despite the overwhelming popularity of *Harry and the Hendersons* and its literal genre-changing impact, *Bigfoot* is every bit as genuinely memorable. Much credit is owed to director Danny Huston, son of the legendary John Huston (who, in turn, was son of the legendary Walter Huston — talk about family dynasties!). Huston coaxes believable, naturalistic performances from his entire cast, especially the child actors and Colleen Dewhurst as the anthropologist. But with such actors as Dewhurst and Joseph Maher (as the hunter Kendrix), and even the smallest parts filled by such high-caliber actresses as Dianne Wiest, it's no wonder; the director has plenty of talent upon which to draw.

The location photography is convincing and naturalistic, which is in keeping with the film's overall tone and pacing. Again, a comparative contrast between *Bigfoot* and *Harry and the Hendersons* reveals much in terms of how two different and creative filmmakers can approach their subject matter without making the same film. *Harry and the Hendersons* sets an early tone of comic absurdity and mixes in occasional dashes of pathos to enliven the proceedings. *Bigfoot* establishes itself from the onset as a more believable drama with comic undertones. Neither approach is necessarily superior, but the result in both cases is that even within the limitations of Ciné du Sasquatch, a visionary director can render new and surprising twists from otherwise familiar genre material.

While the script does meander, it also takes pains to carefully echo and rhyme its own internal dynamics. For example, the motif of the two kids not getting along and blaming their parents (a sort of reverse of *The Parent Trap* premise, if you will) isn't terribly original. And yet screenwriter John Groves (who acquitted himself well as writer of the underappreciated children's films *The Golden Seal* and *Biggles: Adventures in Time*) deftly weaves the grieving of the Sasquatch parents into an effective moment of self-realization for the lost children, who are forced by the cryptids' suffering at the loss of their child to open their eyes to the obvious pain their own human parents must be suffering in their absence. Simple, yes, but it's layered so well that it works.

Equally worthy of praise is the way *Bigfoot* examines some of the tenets of the Sasquatch film *oeuvre* and overturns them. Case in point: The Native American 'copter pilot is not the usual mystic who believes in Bigfoot and warns the Great White Hunter of his impending doom should he fail to halt his quest. Quite the opposite, the pilot is in it for the money and uses his knowledge of the woods for selfish, capitalistic gain. This is a real rarity in the genre, wherein almost every Native appearance is accompanied by the well-meaning but trite portrayal of a magical shaman who would never betray their spiritual ancestry.

Another example is the Kendrix character, played to perfection by Joseph Maher. Many other films using the same plot device — the

wealthy hunter who wants to capture Sasquatch (such as in *Bigfoot, the Unforgettable Encounter*, to cite one of many) — overplay this stereotypical Alpha Male character to the point that he becomes Evil Incarnate. While there is much that is morally repugnant about Kendrix's vainglorious mission, Maher makes it more palatable by infusing his performance with a certain sense of restlessness. He is less a maniacal madman as a lonely human who has conquered everything that he's taken on — except, that is, himself. There is the profound sense that Kendrix wants to see Bigfoot harnessed in an unacknowledged bout of shadow-boxing with his own inner demons. It's not the sound and fury of Captain Ahab versus Moby Dick, but rather a thoughtful understatement.

The costumes for what is clearly a modest budget are, for the most part, effective. They clearly cannot compete with the technical wizardry of Rick Baker's Oscar-winning effects work on the Harry costume for *Harry and the Hendersons*. But in their own way they work just as adroitly to establish audience empathy and are charmingly likeable. It helps that they're imbued with characteristic mannerisms rather than the usual imitation of the Patterson-Gimlin "Bigfoot walk" or the lightning-fast attack of the typical Savage Sasquatch effort. The actors underplay their roles with Kabuki-styled restraint, which makes the graceful nature and non-threatening nature of the hominids visually expressed rather than simply told via exposition.

The telefilm initially aired on ABC and was sometimes shown on cable for the first few years after its initial broadcast (probably to capitalize upon the enormous success of *Harry and the Hendersons*, as well as the latter's successful run as a television series). As of this writing, however, there is no official DVD version of *Bigfoot* available in the United States or any apparent plans for such a release from the Disney Studios in the near future. That's too bad, because *Bigfoot* is a case study in how one can create a diverting family Sasquatch film without falling prey to clichéd situations and tired handling of the performers, as well as how to tell a modest but moving story quite apart from any Ciné du Sasquatch elements in and of themselves. While it unfortunately was not widely enough seen during its modest first airings to establish much in the way of genre credentials, it still entertains to this day.

Bigfoot (2006)

Starring Todd Cox, Liza Foster, Bob Gray, Bettina Steinmetz, Wes Shofner, Saverio Marinelli and Shawn Kipp. Produced by Todd Cox and Bob Gray. Written and Directed by Bob Gray. USA. Color. Stereo. 87 Minutes.

Overview: After being court-martialed for striking a superior officer and having his wife abandon him and his preteen daughter, Jack Sullivan leaves his Navy past behind and moves with his daughter back to his small-town Ohio home to start life anew. Soon he's reacquainted with his former high school drinking buddy Perkins (who is now the town's sheriff) and involved in a nascent relationship with Sandy Parker, an attractive female game warden.

Alas, all is not well in the suburbs. The locals are spooked by a series of deer mutilations which a handful of the terrified citizens attribute not to a bear (as the game warden suspects) but a legendary Bigfoot. The theory: The monster's habitat has been encroached upon by unending housing developments, thereby forcing it into a defensive posture. One embittered old man at the local watering hole is particularly vocal in his belief, pointing out that no forest predator would devour only the liver and heart of the deer remains except Sasquatch. The game warden and the sheriff remain skeptical.

Later that night, however, while escorting the drunken Perkins home, Jack sees a growling Sasquatch in his car's headlights. Now a true believer and certain of the cause of the deer mutilations, he vainly attempts to enlist the support of both Perkins and Sandy. But neither believes him: There is no such thing as Bigfoot, they say.

The next day a wildlife photographer is found dead, ripped apart, his liver and heart missing like the slaughtered deer before him. The startled Perkins suspects his ex-military friend Jack may have stumbled upon the truth, but nevertheless decides to play it safe for political reasons. He does not alert the townspeople of the danger, convinced it will end his career. With the discovery of a bear's devoured carcass, however, Sandy also begins to believe the Bigfoot scenario, despite a lack of proof.

Events spiral out of control when a young baseball player is snatched from the field during a little league game in broad daylight. An enraged local cadre of rabble rousers decides to hunt the monster themselves, heading into the woods with shotguns. They find it; or, rather, it finds them, gutting them alive, one by one, leaving their discarded bodies for Jack and Perkins to discover. They retreat, realizing the enraged beast is beyond their ability to handle.

Guilt-ridden over his abject failure to uphold his responsibilities, the sheriff drinks away his blues at the local tavern. The intoxicated Perkins stumbles outside and into the waiting grasp of the Sasquatch. It rips his beating heart out, squeezes it, and claws into the dying man's liver.

Rage overcoming Jack at the news of his closest friend's death, the ex-soldier decides to take matters into his own hands. Breaking out

This close-up of Bigfoot (Shawn Kipp) in full make-up reveals the detail that went into the creature's design. From *Bigfoot* (2006). (Photograph courtesy Troma Studios.)

his military footlocker, Jack arms himself with weaponry from head to toe and rides out on a motorcycle, intent on destroying the Bigfoot. In a showdown to the death in a rock quarry, Bigfoot is killed when it's impaled on some steel rebar, thus sparing the Ohio town further killings.

* * * * *

Bigfoot is prototypical Ciné du Sasquatch, in terms of both strengths and weaknesses. To its credit, the low-budget effort wisely invests a substantial portion of its limited funds in crafting a convincing Bigfoot costume. And while the screenplay and direction suffer from an overwhelming sense of dubious plotting and torpid pacing, *Bigfoot*'s writer, director and co-star Bob Gray (who plays the Sheriff with believability) deserves credit for a few scattered fright jumps, effectively utilizing off-screen space and sudden fits of intense violence, à la *Jaws*, to enliven the otherwise predictable proceedings.

Despite the semi-amateur nature of the production, the three leads gamely bring a serious tone to their roles that helps make them likeable if not small-town credible. They are given back-story and conflict, which is all-too-rare in most Ciné du Sasquatch entries. But the overall lack of sustained narrative tension and ham-fisted performances by the supporting players counteract all that is minimally effective about the project, leaving this *Bigfoot* with little to add to the Sasquatch *oeuvre*, apart from the novelty of its Mentor, Ohio, setting.

Logic lapses are the primary culprit; this Bigfoot is more akin to the Shape in John Carpenter's *Halloween* than an isolated forest creature only encountered in the deepest, darkest woods. It turns up with mystical frequency within busy urban settings and exhibits an ability to kill as the plot dictates, with nary an explanation as to how such a hulking brute could achieve near invisibility. Examples of these convenient plot contrivances sustained at the cost of believability include a little league baseball game (wherein Bigfoot snatches a player, unnoticed save by the protagonist) and outside the sheriff's favorite bar (wherein the sheriff stumbles into its waiting arms to be devoured).

While the film goes to great lengths to have the warden speculate that the non-stop tract home construction is the culprit in driving the cryptid's killing rage, the theory loses credibility in the face of a creature as comfortable in any downtown city setting as the forest.

Cover art for the indie DVD release of *Bigfoot* (2006). The film was subsequently re-released by Troma with new cover artwork.

This works well for comedic efforts such as *Harry and the Hendersons*; it defies credulity as portrayed in *Bigfoot*.

As mentioned, the costume itself is convincingly designed — a notable exception for most Bigfoot films produced on such constrained budgets. Director Gray wisely keeps most shots of the rampaging

Bigfoot (Shawn Kipp) is prepared for his death throes for the climax of *Bigfoot* (2006) while writer/director/star Bob Gray looks on. (Photograph courtesy Troma Studios.)

beast brief and in motion, which helps create suspense. Ultimately, however, *Bigfoot* succumbs to an inability to coherently stitch together its own myriad conflicting pieces into an effective, entertaining whole.

Bigfoot (2008)

Starring Adam Raque, Angie Everhart, Richard Tyson, Kenyon Dudley, Nicole Badaan, Andrew Chase, Brandon Gibson, Fallon Goodson and Jean Louise O'Sullivan. Produced by Osama Bastaki, Jess Mancilla and George Shamieh. Written by Sandford Schklair. Directed by Kevin S. Tenney. USA. Color. Stereo. 90 Minutes.

Overview: When a forest fire engulfs a wilderness preserve, Sasquatch is forced to flee to the suburban oasis between his world and ours. Percy Caldwell, a well-meaning but shy high school freshman, has a secret crush on Madison, the hottest girl in his class; but Percy finds Madison intimidating because of her good looks, intelligence, popularity and — most of all — unwillingness to conform to social norms. When Percy uses his off-road bicycle abilities to make fools of two local drop-out slackers named Devlin and Cletis, Madison notices his heroics and is impressed. She's not the only one — Devlin and Cletis are so taken with Percy that they give chase in their pick-up truck, intent on doing Percy bodily harm.

Percy eludes them by cutting through the rural mountainside near his home until he crashes into a ravine. When he awakens, he's stunned to find Bigfoot staring down at him. Fearing for his life, Percy runs but gets his foot stuck in a rocky outcropping. Sasquatch follows and frees him; the "monster" is really a gentle giant. Realizing Bigfoot is merely hungry, Percy feeds him and waves good-bye, heading home. Neither Brooke nor David, his parents, believe Percy's story about his encounter with a cryptid, however. Percy senses that he should leave well enough alone and quietly researches Bigfoot on the Internet.

At school the next day, Percy is stunned when cheerleader Madison stops him in the hallway. She compliments him on his gallantry and proclaims him her new boyfriend in front of her astounded social climber cheerleader friend, who says Madison can't date a "nobody" like Percy. Madison won't be told what to do and further invites Percy to see her perform with the rock band she is a part of later that night. She kisses him on the cheek and leaves Leonard, Percy's best friend, staring slack-jawed — how can this be happening? Leonard's feelings are later hurt when Percy skips their own planned band-forming practice and ducks out after school without further explanation.

Percy returns to the woods where Sasquatch is temporarily hiding. This time, Percy has brought along plenty of food for his newfound furry friend, including hot dogs with onions, which Sasquatch finds too spicey for his palette. Percy even plays guitar to soothe Bigfoot's nerves at being dislocated from his home. Their bond of friendship intensifies. On his way home, Percy runs into Devlin and Cletis, who are armed with rifles while hunting in the backwoods. Devlin moves to avenge his prior embarrassment by pummeling Percy, but Bigfoot intervenes, literally tossing the terrified redneck into the fleeing Cletis. They regain their wits and try to double back on Bigfoot and Percy to shoot the hominid, but Sasquatch tosses a log at them first, sending them sprawling on their backsides into a creek.

After a quick conference, the two brainless drop-outs concoct a plan: They will capture Bigfoot and then keep him confined on their farm in a hastily-erected cage. Once secured, they'll then auction him off to the highest bidder, thereby making a fortune. Meanwhile, Percy's budding romance with Madison continues when he invites her to his home to watch a movie with him. She selects the original version of *King Kong* for them to view.

Deciding he must introduce both Leonard and Madison to Bigfoot, Percy invites them both to accompany him the next day. Neither believes him, especially Madison, who feels Percy is playing her for a fool. Leonard goes with his best friend, humoring him.

When they arrive at Bigfoot's hiding spot, however, they find Devlin and Cletis already present, their rifles now equipped with tranquilizing darts. Percy admonishes Bigfoot to flee, but before he can, Devlin shoots him with a dart. Enraged, Bigfoot chases after the two hunters, who take refuge in their pickup. Bigfoot attacks their truck, trying to pound the roof in and grab them. Eventually the dart takes effect and Sasquatch falls asleep.

Realizing he's unintentionally been the cause of Bigfoot's capture, Percy attempts to enlist the aid of Madison, who knows where Devlin and Cletis live. She is reluctant to believe Percy, despite the digital photo he shows her on an iPhone, until Leonard steps in and convinces her it's true. When they arrive at the rednecks' remote farm and find Bigfoot caged, even Madison must admit the legendary forest creature is real. They try to pick the lock, but it takes the strength of Sasquatch to snap it off. Free once again, Bigfoot tosses Devlin and Cletis into hay bales and escapes in the bed of the farm boys' pickup truck, with Percy driving.

Alas, Cletis manages to get off a shot, which ricochets off a rock and into Sasquatch. Percy realizes he must enlist the help of his father David (who is an emergency medical technician) to save Bigfoot's life. David performs an operation and removes the bullet. Fortunately, it is only a minor wound. With Percy's urging, David and Brooke agree to return the recovering cryptid to his native habitat. They nurse Bigfoot until he is well and then load him into the family's RV. Alas, both Devlin and Cletis lay in wait down the street and covertly follow Percy, his friends, parents and Bigfoot.

When the RV takes a back highway, the rednecks make their move, attempting to run the rig off the road. Instead, Devlin and Cletis find their own vehicle upside-down and their last-ditch plan to prevent Bigfoot's homecoming thwarted. Percy shares a tearful farewell with Bigfoot, who soon joins his waiting female mate. Paw in paw, the two hominids stroll back into the deep forests as Percy watches, saddened but realizing he's done the right thing.

* * * * *

Bigfoot is the perfect book-end film to its obvious inspiration— *Harry and the Hendersons*—to see both how much and how little the Benign Bigfoot example of Ciné du Sasquatch has changed in the intervening two decades since the William Dear–directed, Spielberg-produced landmark opus (at least, that is, landmark in terms of its commercial impact upon the Bigfoot film genre). While both stories concentrate on suburban encounters with Bigfoot, *Harry and the Hendersons* moves the "boy and his dog by any other name" storyline from the deepest woods into modern suburbia; whereas *Bigfoot* neatly closes the gap, creating a reality wherein the distance between city and countryside has become so narrow as to be borderline nonexistent. Given 20 years have passed between the films, it's a telling distinction. Mankind's encroachments have become not merely a short vacation's distance away, as they were for the Hendersons, but literally intrude into the cryptid's formerly distant domain, as does the Caldwells' mountainous ranch home.

It's quite remarkable how durable the formula established by *Harry and the Hendersons* has otherwise remained. Although *Bigfoot* shifts the storyline from the point of view of the Hendersons as a family and instead focuses on the teenagers' perspective, the basic emo-

tional peaks and valleys remain the same. A classic "shaggy dog story" (or is that *Shag*-squatch story?), *Bigfoot* plays upon the conventions the viewer has come to expect in such well-worn genres as teen date movies, *Hee Haw* cornpone entries, and—yes!—Ciné du Sasquatch. To director Tenney's credit, the effortless blending of these elements into one fairly seamless whole extends from the balanced casting choices to the creature costume itself, which is literally seamless. Well-photographed and taking full advantage of its sunny screenplay, which never allows too many dark clouds to hover too long on the horizon, the entire film is fast-paced and rarely fails to make each scene count to advance the narrative.

The Bigfoot costume is remarkably similar to Harry from *Harry and the Hendersons*, so much so that one is tempted to speculate this *Bigfoot* is actually an unofficial sequel. Had Amblin (the production company behind *Harry and the Hendersons*) been smart to the potential upside, *Bigfoot* could easily have been retitled *Son of Harry* and released to the DVD market without anyone being the wiser. Although the Bigfoot herein has longer hair and is slightly smaller in stature, he bears a familiar expressive countenance to Harry, right down to the soulful eyes and ability to register shock, anger, and sadness in rapid succession. Given that the entire modest budget for *Bigfoot* was probably equivalent to what Spielberg's company spent for *one day* of principal photography, it's a testament to *Bigfoot's* production designer and related personnel that so much of what little was spent winds up on the screen.

The narrative is underdeveloped—at least from a cryptid's perspective. That is, Bigfoot remains an almost incidental element to the plot until late in the film's second half. It's not that Sasquatch isn't present throughout, as much as the romance between Percy and Madison takes center stage until the moment of the second-act crisis. This is unusual but also in keeping with the teen romance angle, which the story is heavily skewed towards in terms of dramatic development. Whereas most Bigfoot family films concentrate on making the protagonists either younger children or Splatter genre–styled *Friday the 13th* sex and dope youths, *Bigfoot* takes a much gentler ap-

Inevitably, captured cryptids wind up on display behind bars and/or shackled in chains, bringing a strong sense of moral judgment to many Ciné du Sasquatch efforts. From *Bigfoot* (2008). (Photograph courtesy Alecia Ashby.)

proach, more reminiscent of early John Hughes than Sean Cunningham. Tenney is careful to keep the focus on the younger teen cast, which makes the film very atypical in Bigfoot cinema. It's an interesting balance between the sophomoric and the sentimental, and while *Bigfoot* doesn't always maintain the groove (the Devlin and Cletis hillbilly schtick does wear a bit thin), it does a good job of establishing its tone and keeps returning to it again and again.

Like many latter-day Ciné du Sasquatch entries, *Bigfoot* comments upon the genre with knowing Postmodern prescience. For example, Madison chooses *King Kong* for when she and Percy spend their first night watching movies together on DVD. This all but acknowledges the influence the 1933 film has had on the Bigfoot genre. As if that weren't clear enough, the plot hatched by Devlin to capture and sell Bigfoot for money is the classic Carl Denham archetype so readily apparent throughout hominid cinema. It's rare, upon critical reflection, to find many examples of this genre that *don't* owe at least a modest debt to the Carl Denham Syndrome. There seems to be an unconscious motif buried in the *oeuvre* of Bigfoot movies which insists that whenever *Homo sapiens* meet a Sasquatch, grotesque exploitation is sure to follow. This externalization of the darker aspects of the human psyche when confronted by a so-called lesser, primitive being is quite damning. It's as if the genre insists that no matter how advanced we believe ourselves to be as a species, there are those among us who debase our best intentions for such ultimately banal self-delusions as ego, money, and/or hatred of the Other, which Bigfoot easily personifies. In no uncertain terms, Bigfoot thus becomes the very essence of Rousseau's ideal of the "Noble Savage" who is ignorant of the supposed superiority of technologically-dependent modern man, a true innocent but nonetheless the better angel of our own perverse natures for being so.

Those hoping to find themselves immersed in an engrossing drama that breaks new ground in Ciné du Sasquatch are probably not the ideal audience for *Bigfoot* and would therefore be advised to skip it. But for younger viewers who appreciate the youth-focus of such Disney fare as *The Wizards of Waverly Place* and the like, *Bigfoot* delivers the requisite thrills, laughs, puppy-dog crushes, and even a few lumps in the throat. With a likeable cast, professional direction, and convincing cryptid costume, *Bigfoot* demonstrates quite capably that, over two decades after *Harry and the Hendersons*, there is still plenty of mileage to be clocked by paying attention to the basics of good storytelling and technical craftsmanship.

Bigfoot: A Beast on the Run (2008) (Doc)

Featuring Tom Biscardi, Henner Farenbach, Thom Powell, Jeff Meldrum, Tom Limberg, Jason Valenti, M.K. Davis, Peggy Marx and Don Monro. Written by David Thayer and Katrin Sutter. Produced and Directed by David Thayer. USA and Switzerland. Color. Stereo. 55 Minutes.

Overview: Tom Biscardi, the self-proclaimed "millionaire" Bigfoot hunter (with 40-plus years of studying Sasquatch), is the main focus of this look at the impact of hominid sightings and investigations in the Pacific Northwest. From an amiable "Joe Average" Tom Limberg, who manages to record what he believes are the howls of a Sasquatch, to a group of non-professionals who gather in the woods on weekends to make Sasquatch "vocalizations" in hopes of luring real-life hominids, to the gatherings of various Bigfoot believers and, of course, to Biscardi's own well-funded organization, the world in a microcosm of All Things Bigfoot is documented.

* * * * *

Documentary filmmaker David Thayer scores a real bull's-eye in terms of allowing the interviewed subjects to reveal themselves in his award-winning *Bigfoot: A Beast on the Run*. In less than an hour of

Cover art for the DVD release of *Bigfoot: A Beast on the Run*.

running time it manages to keenly observe a variety of individuals involved in all forms of Bigfoot research, from merely curious individuals to full-fledged, self-inflated professionals lacking any apparent sense of humor. The former might be characterized as Thayer's own brother-in-law Tom Limberg, who has merely recorded the lonely cries of what he believes could possibly be a Bigfoot; the latter is perhaps best characterized by the self-aggrandizing Tom Biscardi, self-promoter extraordinaire and one-time friend of Ivan Marx (notorious for his fake Bigfoot photos, though Marx and his widow deny any chicanery on their part), who eerily follows in the real-life mold of Carl Denham from *King Kong* in terms of his repeated attempts to capitalize upon Sasquatch throughout his involvement with the subject.

Like the documentary works of Werner Herzog, Errol Morris, and other dryly humorous filmmakers, Thayer is not interested in grandstanding and calling attention to himself by literally becoming the focal point (as, for but one example, does Michael Moore). Rather, Thayer wisely stands back, calmly observes with his camera, and allows the subjects to state their case in their own words. This non-confrontational approach allows him to give each interviewed person just enough proverbial rope with which to hang himself or herself.

Not everyone falls prey to their own ego, however. For example, Thayer's brother-in-law (who was the unwitting genesis of the project when he recorded the howls and sent them to Thayer and others, as he simply tried to figure out what animal would make such strange vocalizations) seems an amiable, unpretentious young man merely curious to discover a possible answer to the Fortean mystery of what he has recorded. He makes a striking contrast to, for example, Tom Biscardi and his research team, who dismiss the tape's howls as those of a coyote, and Jeff Meldrum, a noted university anthropologist with a keen scientific mind, who listens to the sounds and believes they could be authentic Sasquatch howls. The wide world that separates Biscardi's flamboyant approach and Meldrum's low-key insistence on "Just the facts, ma'am" (à la Joe Friday from *Dragnet*) provides *Bigfoot: A Beast on the Run* with its inherent sense of dramatic contradiction and amiable tension.

Most Bigfoot documentaries fall into one of two opposing viewpoints: The first tends to be of the absolute conviction that Sasquatch is real and that anyone who questions the validity is off his rocker; the second is skeptical to the point that any and all claims are "debunked" (or at least ridiculed) as hallucinations, hoaxes, or a sign of mental instability. To his credit, Thayer doesn't play fully into either camp; instead, he objectively records what each person believes, which allows the viewer to come to his or her own conclusions. That said, it's inevitable that some of the subjects come across as either more or less believable, but this is largely due to their own volition and not from Thayer forcing them into taking positions they don't readily espouse.

Don Monroe, who calls himself the "Indiana Jones" of Idaho, comes across as a likeable if noncritical believer in Bigfoot. A hardened cowboy who may have spent a little too much time in the saddle and sun, Monroe presents Thayer with the opportunity to document what Monroe believes are the caves Sasquatch utilizes to migrate through the state. Leading the documentary filmmaker into one such easily accessed opening, nothing is found but signs of local teenage habitation (beer bottles, a blanket and used condoms).

Thom Powell in the Pacific Northwest has a novel strategy: rather than traipse through the woodlands, he uses his remote cabin home as a "lure" to bring Bigfoot to him. Surrounding his abode with apples and other fruit designed to be irresistible to the hairy giant's palette, and rigging cameras in the trees surrounding his homestead, Powell believes he will be the first to make verifiable contact with Sasquatch.

And Peggy Marx, widow of Ivan, is interviewed at her decrepit farmhouse, where she adamantly maintains that every last photo and film she and her husband made of Bigfoot are authentic, and that any talk to the contrary is simply wrong.

But without much doubt, it is Tom Biscardi and his Searching for Bigfoot, Inc., outfit of entrepreneurs who play out over the documentary as the most unreliable and self-invested in catching a cryptid — less for scientific gain than self-enrichment. Repeatedly throughout the doc Biscardi brags that he and his organization will capture Bigfoot "before this movie is released." Alas, Biscardi's prediction (like his two previously-exposed hoaxes) falls as flat as a Sasquatch's arches. Given this track record — both in 2005 when he promoted a pay-per-view webcam on the popular AM talk radio show *Coast-to-Coast* promising viewers the ability to see the first confirmed Sasquatch corpse (Biscardi later claimed he was "hoodwinked" by the woman who had previously revealed the details about said specimen), and later in 2008 with the infamous Georgia Bigfoot body in a refrigerator hoax (after a nationally-televised press conference, the rubber-suited costume was revealed for what it was by Matthew Whitton and Rick Dyer, the two men responsible for its creation) — Biscardi's credibility in such matters is about as rank as the supposed Georgia cryptid.

Never one to take what he perceives as personal or professional criticism without becoming litigious in response (despite being involved in two major hoaxes in less than 3 years!), Biscardi even threat-ened to sue Thayer because Biscardi believed his own words came across poorly in *Bigfoot: A Beast on the Run*. Given how Biscardi's assistants constantly brag about the machinery they employ over any sense of said equipment's legitimate value in actual field locations (as one example they hold up a fast sports car, claiming it is to be used by Biscardi to quickly lead their caravan, which includes a Hummer, to any reported forest sightings, no less!), it's little wonder Biscardi tells Thayer again and again that Biscardi's efforts to bag a 'Squatch are "money in the bank," as this seems to be his primary objective. Biscardi even goes so far as to say that his bringing in a specimen is not only "money in the bank," but something that will be bigger than King Kong and Godzilla — two fictional screen characters!

While it is never definitive, *Bigfoot: A Beast on the Run* is definitively entertaining and informative, technically well-produced and strikingly photographed. There is a montage of Bigfoot commercial enterprises seen midway through the film (which shows the endless motels, curio shops, carved statues, highway museums and roadside tourist traps in the Pacific Northwest), which is as revealing as any of the interviewed researchers in terms of the stand-alone economics of Bigfoot as profitable engine in a region starved for such enterprises. Too, by straddling the divide between believers and skeptics, Thayer enables viewers on all sides of the debate to see both the weaknesses and strengths of their respective positions. This is a unique perspective in Ciné du Sasquatch and all the more laudable for it. While some cynics and believers will be offended, it refuses to capitulate to either viewpoint. One can only hope future documentaries about Bigfoot will employ equally admirable restraint, as it makes for superior filmmaking on the documentary front.

Bigfoot: Alive and Well in 82 (1982)

Starring Ivan Marx. Written and Produced by Ivan Marx. USA. Color. Stereo.

Overview: Though *Bigfoot: Alive and Well in 82* is often listed in the Ivan Marx trilogy of self-produced Sasquatch films, no one this author interviewed or corresponded with had ever actually seen it. Apparently it was a self-released effort Marx made in an attempt to once again garner attention for his previously discredited photos and films of Bigfoot. After six years of inactivity, Marx suddenly resurfaced with this no-budget effort. It was quickly followed by the Tom Biscardi co-produced documentary *In the Shadow of Bigfoot*.

If indeed Marx's intent with *Bigfoot: Alive and Well in 82* was to alert other Bigfoot hoaxers, con artists, and profiteers about the ongoing market in cryptid moneymaking opportunities, it may have served its purpose. Biscardi signed on as enabler shortly thereafter and was the driving force behind the still available *In the Shadow of Bigfoot* (still available, that is, from Mr. Biscardi himself at his website for the princely sum of $35 per DVD-R!), the latter of which is a poorly-made recapitulation of Marx's career as an early Bigfoot hunter and his most recent "evidence" as to the hominid's indisputable existence. But given that Biscardi has thrice been the self-admitted hoaxer of Bigfoot media-hyped events, any serious devotee of Ciné du Sasquatch will probably lose little sleep from knowing *Bigfoot: Alive and Well in 82* remains in oblivion. Some things are truly best left forgotten.

Bigfoot: America's Abominable Snowman (1968) (Doc)

Featuring Roger Patterson, Bob Gimlin, Al DeAtley, Dr. Grover Krantz and Dr. Louis Leakey. Produced by Al DeAtley. Written and Directed by Roger Patterson. USA. Color. Mono. 136 Minutes.

Overview: Using the footage he shot with Bob Gimlin, Roger Patterson explains how he studied Sasquatch, plaster-casted footprints of it, and — of course — captured the most famous 16mm footage in cryptozoological history. Introduced by his brother-in-law Al DeAtley, Patterson reveals the locales and methodologies important to him as a hominid hunter.

*　*　*　*　*

Some films in the Ciné du Sasquatch genre are so rare as to be (at the time of this book's publication) non-existent. These rare movies are the Holy Grail of the genre. One film fitting this description is *The Revenge of Bigfoot*, alternately known as *Rufus J. Pickle and the Indian*, which to date has not resurfaced after its initial theatrical runs in any known format. As far as documentaries go, however, none can top *Bigfoot: America's Abominable Snowman* for complete and utter obscurity. No prints, videos, or even frame enlargements are known to exist, either legitimately or on the bootleg circuit frequented by Bigfoot film fans. It is as if the thirty-plus 16mm prints made of the film were destroyed after their one-year circuit, primarily in the Pacific Northwest region, in a self-financed tour managed by DeAtley in order to capitalize upon Patterson's growing fame and the notoriety of the Patterson-Gimlin footage.

What little is known about the film is largely due to Greg Long's controversial "exposé" *The Making of Bigfoot* (Prometheus Books, 2004), courtesy of extensive research Long conducted into the film's short life span. Basically, according to Long's sources, Patterson shopped the Patterson-Gimlin footage around Hollywood with the help of a press agent, getting some nibbles from interested studios (including a rumored near-offer from a young producer named Aaron Spelling, who would later go on to produce *The Six Million Dollar Man* and *Bionic Woman* series, which featured a Sasquatch!). Nothing panned out, however, except one offer from the BBC. In exchange for editing the footage into a professional, 52-minute television special for exclusive airing in England, the BBC would give DeAtley and Patterson the completed special for non-television showings in America. Realizing this was the best deal on the table, they took it.

After they viewed the 16mm production, DeAtley approached American National Enterprises (an independent distributor of nature wildlife documentaries out of Salt Lake City, Utah) about whether or not they would be interested in purchasing the film, adding some footage, and then releasing it using their novel "four-wall" technique (wherein the distributor rents an independent or small-chain theater owner's facility and keeps all ticket sales, rather than splitting the box office with the owner, as is customary). The elderly members of ANE didn't believe in the film and passed on the offer. Unfazed by their rejection after learning of their methodology, DeAtley paid a Seattle-based editor $3,500 to edit the film, with additional footage written and directed by Patterson to pad it out to its final running time.

Using only portable 16mm projectors, and touring throughout Washington, Oregon, and other Northwestern states, DeAtley soon realized he had a sure-fire moneymaker. To sweeten the draw in some small towns where *Bigfoot: America's Abominable Snowman* screened, DeAtley had Patterson himself show up for a question-and-answer session (whenever Patterson's failing health permitted; sadly, Patterson would die not many years later in 1972). In the lobby of each theater or rented hall where the film was shown, copies of Patterson's self-printed book about Bigfoot (which DeAtley also paid to have published) were sold to further increase profits. As the film's intake grew (actually out-grossing a live Simon and Garfunkle concert in Salt Lake City), DeAtley reinvested much of the earnings to strike additional prints so that he could more effectively blanket a region and therefore exponentially increase ticket sales.

Oddly, given the enormity of the film's success, DeAtley abandoned

the film as a self-distributor in the wake of the infamous "Minnesota Iceman" hoax, in which a supposed "real life" hominid encased in a block of ice being toured around the country was revealed to be a fake that was constructed in Hollywood. In the weeks after the news broke, interest in *Bigfoot: America's Abominable Snowman* plummeted, with DeAtley losing an estimated $100,000 before he finally pulled the plug on further screenings (although he also claimed in Long's book that he more than doubled that in profits). Perhaps it was because Patterson sold the rights to the one-minute Patterson-Gimlin footage contained within *Bigfoot: America's Abominable Snowman* (ironically, to none other than ANE, who had initially rejected the feature itself!) that the feature no longer seems to exist. Too, there was no way of DeAtley surmising in 1969 that a future in home video existed two decades down the road as motivation for him to preserve the feature-length film. Given that the Patterson-Gimlin footage wound up in courts for many years in an ongoing rights struggle in which there were many losers and few winners, DeAtley may have felt ambivalent about hiring lawyers to retain the rights to include the footage on what had been a profitable business venture in its day. He hardly needed the money, being a self-made millionaire prior to the financing of Patterson's feature film.

Whatever the rationale, it is truly sad that *Bigfoot: America's Abominable Snowman* does not exist for at least archival research purposes. Whatever its qualities as a film (or lack thereof), it is a real "missing giant" of a movie, shedding light as it doubtlessly would on a plethora of early attitudes, perspectives, and evidence regarding Patterson's veracity and motivations for his obsession with Sasquatch. Until such time as someone can produce a copy for viewing purposes, it remains a lost treasure awaiting re-discovery.

Bigfoot: Man or Beast? (1972) (Doc)

AKA: *In Search of Bigfoot*. Featuring Rene Dahinden, John Green, Grover Krantz, Sam Melville, Robert W. Morgan and J. English Smith. Produced, Written and Directed by Lawrence Crowley. USA. Color. Mono. 90 Minutes.

Overview: Renowned cryptozoologist and independent filmmaker Robert W. Morgan is the main focus of this documentary quest to unearth physical evidence and a hopeful encounter with a "Forest Giant" (Morgan's phrase for unknown hominids) in the Mount St. Helens area in Washington state. Along with his small band of hippie assistants, he travels by van into the forests of the mountainous wilderness, interviewing various locals who've seen Sasquatch.

At one point a gathering of the then-elite cryptozoologists in America meet at a park and have a spontaneous conversation about Bigfoot. In attendance are Morgan, John Green, and Rene Dahinden. As they discuss the creature's existence and need for definitive proof, a heated argument unfolds as to whether or not it is morally justifiable to shoot a Sasquatch, with the debate splintering along "yes, in order to convince a skeptical scientific community" versus "no, it would be akin to homicide, given the near *Homo sapiens* status of the being."

The Patterson-Gimlin footage is shown and critiqued, with Grover Krantz weighing in (as he almost inevitably did during this period of Ciné du Sasquatch documentaries). The ending comes when Morgan and his flower-power entourage are forced to abandon their expedition just when they believe they're on the verge of a major breakthrough after Morgan falls and breaks some ribs. Worse yet, a forest fire sweeps through Mount St. Helens and forces them to flee for their lives. Morgan breaks down crying as he informs them of his decision to cut their losses, and the posse surrounds him, offering a group hug so characteristic of the era. Vowing to return to finish the quest one day with additional funding, Morgan and crew vacate the area as the smoke billows up behind them.

Sadly, Mount St. Helens erupted the following decade, and a major portion of the scenic beauty Morgan canvassed vanished with it. In this regard, *Bigfoot: Man or Beast?* is a worthwhile watch for historical reasons alone, as Crowley makes good use of the natural splendor prior to its demise. One can only speculate, of course, as to the fate of any Sasquatch inhabitants of the area.

Robert W. Morgan would later write, direct and even act in *Bloodstalkers*, a fictional Skunk Ape movie, as well as pen *Soul Snatchers*, an autobiographical tome about his years spent documenting Bigfoot. For many years he also hosted an Internet radio program devoted to interviewing witnesses and cryptozoologists about hominids. Writer and director Lawrence Crowley re-released *Bigfoot: Man or Beast?* four years later, with 20 additional minutes tacked onto the end, as *In Search of Bigfoot* in order to capitalize upon the success of the Leonard Nimoy TV program (it has no direct connection other than utilizing the similar title). Crowley also produced *Mysteries from Beyond the Triangle*, concerning a team of psychics who explore the Bermuda Triangle in a yacht.

Bigfoot: The Making of a Documentary (2006)

Written, Produced and Directed by Chris Penney. USA. Color. Stereo. 60 Minutes.

Overview: Two female college students decide to finish their thesis by documenting the long history of sightings of a Bigfoot in the dense woodlands of Michigan. They hire a small, local videotape crew to follow them into the forests. Alas, their guide — a supposed expert who knows the terrain — turns out to be a fraud. Worse yet, the legend is anything but a myth, as the unfortunate researchers and video crew soon learn to their fatal horror. Only the raw video of their ordeal is ever recovered to last as a post-mortem testimony to their demise.

* * * * *

In filmmaking, there is the homage, the remake, and the rip-off. This is not to denigrate films falling within any of the three classifications (for example, *The Bride Wore Black* by Truffaut is an obvious Hitchcock homage; remakes are occasionally as good as their predecessors; and even rip-offs — as Hollywood endlessly demonstrates each year by cloning whatever is popular — have their place in the entertainment scheme of things). But basing a film too closely upon the original source risks losing originality to the degree that viewers simply have a difficult time suspending their disbelief (not to mention ire) that they're basically witnessing the same vision as before without enough demonstrable change. So it goes with *Bigfoot: The Making of a Documentary*, which is so heavily based upon *The Blair Witch Project* that the only novel additions are a cryptid instead of a witch and color instead of black and white.

The film utilizes the same sense of voyeuristic, if not *verboten*, thrill of seeing a snuff video which is, conversely, clearly a fictional treatment shot in a deliberately exaggerated *cinema verite* style: handheld camera work; blurry, under-lit shots; amateurish performances; and long, meandering takes to supposedly represent raw footage before it has been professionally edited. A sense of genuine terror is intended to be felt by the viewer because the usual narrative "fourth wall" techniques, such as intercutting, interpretive lighting, a certain veneer of professionalism in production values, invisible direction and competent acting, are replaced by a sense of impending peril that precludes the videographer from such niceties. Alas, when the footage is consistently lit with a flashlight (as in *Bigfoot: The Making*

of a Documentary), what is left for the viewer to experience is literally nothing more than perpetually black screen imagery with an underlying radio-styled audio play to conjure what is missing visually. While in theory this can work to good effect, *Bigfoot: The Making of a Documentary* exhausts the minor novelty of such a technique early on, leaving little for even the most ardent Ciné du Sasquatch enthusiast to find entertaining.

Again, originality is not necessarily the most important aspect in making these "You are there!" no-budget horror films, as both *The Blair Witch Project* and *Paranormal Activity* proved with literal hundred-million-dollar box office grosses. Indeed, *The Blair Witch Project* is basically an homage/rip-off of Ruggero Deodato's 1980 gruesome gore-fest *Cannibal Holocaust* (in which an anthropologist recovers the filmed footage made by an unlucky earlier expedition of explorers of cannibal-infested jungles); and *Paranormal Activity* owes much to such "reality TV" series as *Ghost Hunters* and the like, with its reliance on off-screen space, grainy home video footage and rickety haunted house sound effects. The key difference is that the makers of these successful efforts realized the severe limitations they were facing and compensated to the best of their respective abilities to generate scares and suspense despite them. *Bigfoot: The Making of a Documentary* simply ignores them and, as a result, excludes the audience's participation on any significant level because it presumes they haven't seen *The Blair Witch Project* or its sequels. This proves to be a deadly mistake, reducing the effort to little more than an exercise in fan-based recreation of its source.

Bigfoot: The Unforgettable Encounter (1994)

Starring JoJo Adams, Matt McCoy, David Rasche, Crystal Chappell, Clint Howard, Rance Howard, Alan Wilder, Neal Matarazzo, Tohoru Masamune, Darrell Mapson, Brian Avery, Derek Barton, Douglas Bennett, Zachery Ty Bryan, John Cade and Gary Maloncon. Produced by Scott McAboy and Gilbert Alexander Wadsworth III. Written and Directed by Corey Michael Eubanks. USA. Color. Stereo. 88 Minutes.

Overview: When a young boy, Ben, is lost in the wilderness during a camping trip, the local sheriff, Nick, and his posse begin a frantic search. Meanwhile, reports of a savage Sasquatch attacking a group of hunters set the local townsfolk abuzz. The talk reaches fever pitch when uber-wealthy collector of crypto evidence Chad Frederick authorizes his assistant Gary to post a million dollar reward for the first person in the tiny town who can bring in the beast. Soon the town is overrun by every redneck in a five state vicinity, each armed to the teeth for Bigfoot, dead or alive.

The lost boy accidentally steps into an ankle-bruising hunter's trap. When a bear charges the pinned youth, Bigfoot leaps to his defense. After a vicious battle, Bigfoot triumphs, although he's wounded. Sasquatch leads Ben to a nearby waterfall, where the injured Bigfoot washes his wounds and Ben cleans his own ankle gash. The stranded Ben soon realizes the monster is actually a gentle if powerful ally.

Meanwhile, Samantha, a female cryptozoologist, and her eager team of young researchers arrive from their university to hopefully intervene, realizing Bigfoot is in grave danger. She attempts to enlist Nick the sheriff in her quest, but Nick is more interested in recovering the missing boy. Frustrated, Samantha rents a helicopter and scours the forest from above, desperate to locate the cryptid before it is blown to smithereens by the money-crazed hunters who now fill the woods in search of bounty.

Ben and Bigfoot trek through the wilderness, only to find their new friendship abruptly interrupted when the well-intended crypto team spots the creature from their chopper and shoot Sasquatch with tranquilizing darts. Over the boy's protests, they airlift their specimen and lock it in a cage. The locals gather and gawk at the helpless beast. Upon seeing the boy among the faces in the crowd, Sasquatch silently begs for the lad to free him, but the boy is unable to act due to the surrounding locals.

Wracked with guilt, Ben convinces his best friend to assist him in setting Sasquatch free. They sneak past the guard in front of Bigfoot's cage and silently demonstrate how it can use its enormous strength to bend the cage's bars. Bigfoot does so, and the boys lead him into the woods, where the monster shows his gratitude before disappearing. Meanwhile, disappointed no hunter has bagged the beast, the billionaire collector arrives on the scene, determined to personally handle the search. He ups the ante to two million dollars, sending the weary gunmen back into the woods, intent on killing Sasquatch for the reward.

Now convinced the billionaire will lead to Bigfoot's demise, Nick joins forces with Samantha and Ben. The boy leads them to an area he knows to be the home grounds of Sasquatch, whereupon they tranquilize the creature for its own good, intent on relocating the slumbering giant to a protected federal sanctuary. But Frederick hires a rag-tag bunch of local mercenaries and, acting as their leader, stalks his sought-after prize, intent on killing anyone in his path, man or monster. A race against time ensues, with the wealthy hunter intent on heading off the sheriff before he can set Bigfoot free in its new habitat.

* * * * *

As far as family-friendly Bigfoot movies go, *Bigfoot: The Unforgettable Encounter* is a well-made piece of "Skookum hokum" molded within the large footprints left by Spielberg's *Harry and the Hendersons*. While it never rises above predictable children's fare, it nevertheless offers good production values for its meager budget, a likeable cast, a well-constructed Bigfoot costume and good location photography. And although both pictures are different in tone, they share an attempt to mythically blend the cryptid legend with suburban and urban environments while maintaining soft PG ratings.

In each, the creature is first seen in the wilderness, only to be later transposed into a city setting before eventual release back into his redwood forest home. Therein lie the differences: *Harry & the Hendersons* aims for outright comic effect in most sequences; *Bigfoot: The Unforgettable Encounter* favors the more traditional boy's adventure sensibility (akin to a Hardy Boys storyline). Both films also offer similarly rendered Sasquatch creatures, right down to the make-up which favors built-in expressions realized by sophisticated foam latex and control cables, so that each can emote without the mask looking rubbery. Given the budget in comparison to Spielberg's production, *Bigfoot: The Unforgettable Encounter* acquits itself reasonably well, though Rick Baker (winner of an Academy Award for his *Harry* creature design) probably didn't lose any sleep over the competition.

Bigfoot: The Unforgettable Encounter offers the underage viewer plenty of entertainment value. The action is plentiful, the cast mostly professional, and the creature effects largely successful (if a bit overused in close-up, which reveals the inherent flaws).

There are several suspenseful moments that transcend the corny narrative and offer genuinely scary thrills. The opening sequence, for example, is set outdoors during a lightning storm and is as effectively terrifying as any sequence in most Ciné du Sasquatch entries aimed at the adult market. Equally, the moment wherein the lost boy first realizes he's being stalked in the woods at night is truly eerie — the Sasquatch moves from behind a tree, silhouetted by moonlight, growling. This scene is as chilling as any found in *The Legend of Boggy Creek*.

But despite some striking location cinematography, *Bigfoot: The Unforgettable Encounter* suffers from a clichéd story and several notably weak performances, not least of which is the female cryptozoologist, whose monomaniacal intensity restricts the character's range from exasperated to *ultra*-exasperated. The ruthless billionaire role is equally overplayed by character actor David Rasche but doesn't impact the film as negatively because he is largely relegated to the final act. On the opposite end of the acting scale is Matt McCoy, in the first of three Ciné du Sasquatch credits he would add to his resume (the other two being *Little Bigfoot* and *Abominable*). Whenever McCoy is onscreen, *Bigfoot: The Unforgettable Encounter* lives up to its unforgettable moniker, and father and son Rance and Clint Howard also acquit themselves well. The film's director, Corey Michael Eubanks, is best known in the industry as a stunt man.

In terms of Ciné du Sasquatch, *Bigfoot: The Unforgettable Encounter* is really not much of an advance on the "Squatch out of the woods" twist of *Harry and the Hendersons*. In fact, the Bigfoot herein doesn't really make it to civilization or suburbia as much as it does into a small town for a night. Still, it treads in *Harry*'s large, deep "footprints," and as such provides a bridge forward for subsequent variants to come, such as *Little Bigfoot*. For family fare and cryptid cinema, the viewer could do a lot worse. It bears a notable resemblance in set-up and plot mechanics to the Walt Disney version of *Bigfoot* made in 1987, which was directed by Danny Huston, but is nowhere near as subtle or emotionally effective as that superior effort.

Bigfoot and Wildboy (1977) (TV)

Starring Ray Young, Joseph Butcher, Joel Bailey, Steve Bond, Sorrell Booke, Robin Dearden, John Milford, Deborah Ryan, Leonard Stone, Carel Struycken and Chris Knight. Produced by Donald R. Boyle, Sid Krofft, Marty Krofft and Arthur E. McLaird. Directed by Leslie H. Martinson, Donald R. Boyle, Irving J. Moore, Charles R. Rondeau and Gordon Wiles. USA. Color. Mono. 30 Minutes.

Overview: When a young boy grows up an orphan in the wilds of the California redwoods, he is adopted by a mentoring Sasquatch. Together the duo forms an inseparable team. As he grows into a young man known as Wildboy, he and Bigfoot staunchly defend their vast wilderness sanctuary against a non-stop variety of invaders, both natural and supernatural, including a vampire, aliens, a mummy and even another Bigfoot.

* * * * *

Sid and Marty Krofft were the creatively warped producers behind such subversive children's television fare as *H.R. Puf'n'Stuf*, *Lidsville*, *Sigmund & the Sea Monsters*, and *Land of the Lost*. Featuring trademark psychedelic-drenched colors and phantasmagoric set design, their output was covertly deviant in subtext. While parents saw innocent fairy tales rendered with zero budgets and off-putting banality, children raised in a post-hippie culture quickly related to the hidden messages sprinkled throughout the average Krofft Brothers series. Even the titles were a knowing wink at the viewer: *Puf'n'Stuf* ("puffing stuff") and *Lidsville* (a "lid" being a marijuana slang term in the era). A decade later *The Pee Wee Herman Show* would echo the outrageous mix of camp and adult sensibility masquerading as children's entertainment, but the Krofft Brothers invented the formula.

Early pioneers in the use of a video blue screen technology called Ultimatte (which allowed the brothers to create inexpensive special effects combining rubbery creatures with human actors shot against blue screen) the Krofft Brothers produced much of their output in a studio to avoid expensive location photography. In this regard, *Bigfoot and Wildboy* was an exception, as it was shot on film stock and lensed almost entirely in and around Griffith Park, California. It also featured a more serious tone than most of the Krofft output (with the exception of *Land of the Lost*, which employed published science fiction writers to add verisimilitude). For the Krofft Brothers to deviate from their established formula and take risks with outdoor photography and the expense of shooting on film as opposed to video indicates they sensed commercial potential in their cryptid/boy combination.

To hedge their bets, the producing team initiated the *Bigfoot and Wildboy* franchise as self-contained, 8-minute-long episodes within their showcase *The Krofft Supershow*. This 90-minute variety behemoth was chock full of live musical acts (Kaptain Kool and the Kongs initially, later replaced by the Bay City Rollers) as well as over-the-top comic book character mini-shows such as *Dr. Shrinker*, *Wonderbug*, and others. During the second season of *The Krofft Supershow*, *Bigfoot and Wildboy* debuted in a revamped *The Krofft Superhour* (so called because the network demanded 30 minutes be cut from the show's budget). Alas, the golden era of the Krofft Brothers was coming to a close, and ratings had dwindled. ABC soon canceled the variety show altogether.

To its credit, however, ABC sensed potential in the *Bigfoot and Wildboy* episodes and ordered a dozen 30-minute episodes from the brothers as a summer replacement series. Intent on pushing the boundaries of their Sasquatch and son concept, the stories grew more outlandish by the week, as a sampling of the show titles reveals: "Eye of the Mummy"; "Space Prisoner"; "The Other Bigfoot"; and "Return of the Vampire." Alas, even the legendary Krofft Brothers were unable to curtail the declining ratings, and the series was dropped. Nevertheless, a generation of tykes fell in love with the outrageous series and took some solace from the fact the titular duo was featured in a series of comic books that continued their adventures.

Most viewers recall the unique transportation methodology employed by Bigfoot. Rather than lumber along, this friendly forest dweller bounded skyward and flew through the air as if shot from a circus cannon straight into the clouds. This stock shot was endlessly repeated throughout the series, edited into each episode when convenient. Accompanied by Bigfoot's memorable yell ("Bah-Yah-*Bah!*"), the fantastic leaping ability was never explained. Rather, it seemed patterned on the success of the leaping ability suggested by the popular Bionic Bigfoot featured in *The Six Million Dollar Man*, only taken to the extreme. The difference was marginally justified in *The Six Million Dollar Man* by way of explanation that its cryptid was actually a bionic robot with enhanced powers. No such explanation was offered in *Bigfoot and Wildboy*. This cryptid's ability to leap several stories at will seemed as immensely improbable as the teaming of the pair itself. But without a doubt this remains the most agile Sasquatch in the genre's history, however dubious such a distinction.

Actor Ray Young played Bigfoot. While his most frequent credits were for such TV series as *Wonder Woman*, *Quantum Leap*, and *Bonanza*, he had smaller roles in feature films like *Blood of Dracula's Castle* and *Coffy*. Joseph Butcher's career has encompassed not only portraying Wildboy, but guest appearances on *The Waltons*, *Knot's Landing* and *55 Degrees North*, as well as the seminal exploitation film *Hollywood High*.

Bigfoot and Wildboy remains a treasured memory for the cryptid

The low budget of *Bigfoot and Wildboy* necessitated shooting on existing sets, such as this standing Western town, and in Griffith Park. Still, the extensive outdoor settings were unusual for the Kroffts.

cinema fans that grew up watching it..By extracting the Tarzan mythos (which is integral to Ciné du Sasquatch as an underlying piece of the genre's construction) and inverting it to have the "wild boy" adopted not by apes but by a cryptid, *Bigfoot and Wildboy* reveals the true elasticity of the so-called rules in this enduring *oeuvre*.

Episodes by Season

First Season: 1. "Sonic Projector"; 2. "Black Box"; 3. "Abominable Snowman"; 4. "UFO"; 5. "White Wolf"; 6. "Amazon Contest"; 7. "Secret Monolith"; 8. "The Trappers."

Second Season: 1. "The Secret Invasion"; 2. "Space Prisoner"; 3. "The Birth of a Titan"; 4. "Bigfoot vs. Wildboy"; 5. "Meteor Menace"; 6. "Earthquake"; 7. "Eye of the Mummy"; 8. "The Wild Girl"; 9. "The Other Bigfoot"; 10. "Return of the Vampire"; 11. "Outlaw Bigfoot"; 12. "Spy from the Sky."

Bigfoot at Holler Creek Canyon (2005)

AKA: *Holler Creek Canyon*. Starring Melisa Breiner-Sanders, Anna Bridgforth, Chris Darder, Danny Darder, Tom Davis, Jennifer Deceder, Nathan Faudree, Gentry Ferrell, Ron Jeremy, Johnny Ostensoe, Amy Poague, Brian Poague, John Poague, Kenny Poague, Lois Roll, Valerie Saunders, Julienne Springer, Johnny Sullivan and Tammie Taylor. Produced by Chanda Fuller, Jean Poague and John Poague. Written by Barbara Kymlicka and John Poague. Directed by John Poague. USA. Color. Stereo. 99 Minutes.

Overview: A group of college students are invited by their classmate Jill to stay at the cabin of Jill's divorced parents during spring break. Located deep in the Virginia woodlands, the cabin is outfitted with all the modern conveniences, including electricity, baths and all the comforts of home. Along the way, the students encounter a strange hermit who threatens them when they ridicule his "children" (plastic dolls hanging from trees outside his roadside camper cabin), and a surly convenience store owner named Ranger Rik. Ranger Rik warns them a rogue bear is on the loose and has killed two campers. He advises them to use extreme caution, pulling a handgun and shooting a bear poster inside his own store. Alarmed by Ranger Rik's maniacal turn, the campers leave with beer and sundries in hand.

During their stay, Matt tries to smooth things over with reluctant Jill, his ego hurt because Jill has broken up with him over her suspicions of Matt's constant infidelity. Meanwhile, Danny and Viv enjoy rough sex while Danny borrows geeky Chris' video camera to secretly record himself in bed with Viv without her knowledge. Ranger Rik spies on the couple through their open window, using his own camcorder to record their sex acts for his later pleasure. After sex, Danny tries to maneuver Viv into have a *ménage a trios* with Jill, but Viv grows angry at the suggestion. Rebuffed, Danny storms out, telling Viv he's heading for Daytona in Florida to catch the last of spring break there.

As he makes his way through the woods, Danny steps into a bear trap. Unable to free himself, he remains immobilized when Sasquatch attacks and rips him to pieces. The next day the remaining campers search everywhere for Danny but cannot locate him. They visit Ranger Rik and catch him masturbating to the video he's taken of

Pre–Production artwork for *Bigfoot at Holler Creek Canyon*.

Danny and Viv in bed the previous night. In response to their worries, Ranger Rik agrees to scour the woods and look for any trace of Danny.

Ranger Rik shoots and kills a grizzly bear while deep in the forest. The noise summons Bigfoot, who gives chase. Ranger Rik tries to hide by lying down in a shallow ditch, but Sasquatch leaps atop him. With one hairy fist Bigfoot crushes the store owner's head like an overripe tomato. Back at the cabin, Viv explains that she and Danny had a fight and that Danny has simply left for Daytona. The students relax, realizing the mystery is solved. But Chris is not so sure. He has studied video footage he's taken of Jill earlier when they first arrived and is convinced it reveals the shadowy figure of Bigfoot in the background. He tries to convince the rest of the students of his theory, but they refuse to believe him.

That night Matt makes a move on Jill, while Chris is seduced by the horny Bree, who has a crush on him despite Chris' constant rebuffs. Later, however, Matt awakes and surprises Viv outside as she smokes a cigarette. The two have been having an affair under Jill's nose the entire time. Matt insists they continue their tryst and carries her deep into the woods. She ties him up and leaves him naked after teasing him, intent on scaring him. But by the time she comes back, Matt has been slaughtered by Bigfoot, his orbs popped from their sockets and his throat slashed. Viv runs for her life but winds up falling prey to the beast when he grabs and pulls her screaming from inside the outhouse she attempts to hide within.

The next morning the surviving trio discuss where Viv and Matt could have gone. Chris and Bree confess they suspect Viv and Matt are lovers, but Jill refuses to believe it. Chris suggests they explore a cave both he and Jill used to play in as children, as that seems a logical place for Matt to have taken Viv for sex. When they arrive at the cave, they discover the possessions of their missing friends. Chris, Jill and Bree run back to the cabin. Jill packs up, insisting they must leave. Chris objects, wanting to return to the cave and get more footage. When Bree hears Chris tell Jill that he considers Bree just a one-time affair because she doesn't share his interests, Bree grabs his camera and goes back to the cave to prove her abilities to him. She is attacked by Bigfoot.

Jill insists they must go to the cave and see about Bree. Chris confesses his love for Jill, but she only considers him a friend. Disappointed, Chris nevertheless accompanies Jill. They find Bree held in a bear trap, and the rest of their friends gutted and hanging upside-down like slaughtered cattle. Bigfoot attacks before they can help the limping Bree outside. Jill drives an axe into the beast and the students make it back to the cabin.

Alas, the creature follows them. Bree is killed inside, and Chris follows soon thereafter while Jill attempts to start a four-wheeler for their escape. She drives away as Chris' arm is ripped from its socket by Bigfoot, realizing there's nothing she can do for him. She sets Bigfoot ablaze with gasoline and leaves the cryptid in flames, screaming. Jill pauses beside Holler Creek Canyon, exhausted, to gather her wits. Bigfoot, severely burned, roars as it appears before her. Jill revs the four-wheeler and takes off. The bike crashes into Bigfoot and sends the beast falling into the waters far below.

Later that night three park rangers confront Jill about the ludicrous nature of her claims that Bigfoot slaughtered her friends. They insist the killer must have been a grizzly they recently shot. Jill refuses to budge. The rangers ignore her and decide to call the incident a bear attack. Just then, Bigfoot crashes through the walls and kills them all.

* * * * *

Whether or not the viewer finds favor with *Bigfoot at Holler Creek Canyon* will largely depend upon his or her nostalgia for the Slasher genre of the 1980s. If one is too young to have seen the genre first-run, never enjoyed the gore quota, or simply disliked the genre itself, then *Bigfoot at Holler Creek Canyon* is like camping in the swamps without a can of Off!— endless misery and a longing for it to finish. Indeed, many reviews have stated as much, lambasting the film for its numerous lapses of logic, amateurish acting and lack of Bigfoot screen time in favor of focusing on the college students and their preoccupation with sex and drinking.

These are fair criticisms, and *Bigfoot at Holler Creek Canyon* certainly has its share of foibles, even for the most tolerant fan of Ciné du Sasquatch. But as a nostalgic trip down memory lane to a time when exploitation films were often encumbered by such drawbacks but still entertained, the film has some positive qualities as well. For example, there is often genuine suspense generated by the various stalk and slash sequences when the creature is on the attack. Too, there are some much-needed laughs provided by the campy cameo by Ron Jeremy as Ranger Rik (Jeremy is the porn star known for his generous "endowment to the arts"). As a nod to Jeremy's modest thespian abilities, the director allows him to stay clothed throughout the film's running length, and to his credit, Jeremy does a likeable if perennially sleazy job of playing the lecherous, gluttonous voyeur (given his X-rated career, this is admittedly not much of a stretch). Never really believable with his thick East Coast accent and over-the-top style (nor the fact that he wears Crocs rubber sandals to go hunting for Bigfoot in the woods!), Jeremy nevertheless seems to be enjoying himself and brings humor to an often too-serious effort.

Likewise, the director creates a droll, off-the-wall cameo for himself as the hermit who taunts and terrorizes the college students not far from their cabin. With his bizarre penchant for crafting dolls that he hangs from trees and calls his "children," and his shaved, penciled-in eyebrows and garish eye shade that resemble Divine's from any early John Waters film, this is one backwoods bandito that is every city dweller's worst nightmare come to life. While the character is superfluous to the overall plot, director and actor Poague does a good job of bringing his part to vivid life in an homage to *The Texas Chainsaw Massacre* redneck school of acting.

The technical level is generally good, taking advantage of the actual Virginia locales to create suspense. Much like the *Friday the 13th* series, which this closely resembles in terms of set-up and execution (so to speak), *Bigfoot in Holler Creek Canyon* creates a believable level of isolation that helps the attack sequences seem almost inevitable. Not all of the "one-by-one" killings work, but overall they provide a cumulative sense of "body count" for which the 1980s Slasher genre was known. And at least the filmmaker delivers some of that quality for those who like blood with their baths.

Where *Bigfoot in Holler Canyon* deviates from the classic formula is inverting the sex-to-violence ratio. Whereas such films as *Prom Night* and their ilk often tantalize with nudity and implied sex but linger on and exploit the violence, *Bigfoot in Holler Creek Canyon* inverts the paradigm, focusing on the sex over the violence. Though novel, this is actually detrimental to the film's overall impact; the softcore nature of the sexual encounters is never more than gratuitous in nature and works to weaken the narrative impact, slight as it is (as is usual in the Slasher genre). If the film were more sexually graphic, it would tip over into the sub-genre of Ciné du Sasquatch in which reside such efforts as *Beauties and the Beast* and *Alpine Affairs*. Too, the minimal plot focuses so heavily on the young cast, rather than on Bigfoot thrills, that the film often plays more like a drama with Bigfoot exploitation sequences suddenly inserted. And the finale unwinds in an awkward back-and-forth manner, extending the resolution with several false climaxes that do nothing for the film's overall suspense (even if the "shock ending" works quite well in a manner similar to *Friday the 13th* and the original *Carrie*).

Still, it offers its fair share of nominal scares and laughs, flaws and

all. *Bigfoot in Holler Creek Canyon* is neither the worst nor the best in a genre full of misfires. Fans expecting anything other than a mild diversion from the usual Bigfoot fare will doubtless be disappointed. Others willing to forgo any pretensions and forgive many false steps may find there is much to enjoy in *Holler Creek Canyon*.

Bigfoot FAQ (2006) (Doc)

Produced, Written and Directed by Jay Michael. USA. Color. Stereo. 45 Minutes.

Overview: Bigfoot FAQ (or "Frequently Asked Questions" from the Internet abbreviation) is designed as a primer for cryptozoological fans and Sasquatch eyewitnesses in dispelling long-standing rumors surrounding the hominid, as well as inform the casual viewer about the various theories and facts in real-world Bigfoot exploration. Among the many issues it explores are: where to see Bigfoot; how to investigate a sighting; can Bigfoot talk; is Bigfoot an alien; and is Bigfoot seen more during the day or at night? CryptoVideography, the independent company behind this production, also produced *Bigfooting in Oklahoma* and *Swamp Apes*.

Bigfoot Lives! (2007) (Doc)

Featuring Tom Biscardi, Tommy Biscardi Jr., Robert "Java Bob" Schmalzbach, Steve Kulls, Hiriam Upham, Don Monroe, Hans Mobius, Tim McMillenm, Becky Sawyer and Mike Sell. Produced by Todd Douglas Bailey, Tom Biscardi and Rob Piecuch. Written and Directed by Todd Douglas Bailey. USA. Color. Stereo. 81 Minutes.

Overview: Bigfoot hunter and self-proclaimed millionaire Tom Biscardi and his intrepid band of Team Bigfoot members visit several states across America in search of the elusive hominid. Along the way, Biscardi interviews several eyewitnesses and documents physical evidence, including a Paris, Texas, locale wherein Biscardi digs for the skeletal remains of a Bigfoot; a Minnesota visit to Don Monroe, who believes Bigfoot uses the local underground caves near his ranch to hide while migrating across the state; an Arizona interview with a hunter who claims to have shot Sasquatch but became too frightened by its wounded screams to track it further; a New York state interview with Hans Mobius, who took a photograph on his Clarence, New York, horse farm of a rampaging Bigfoot behind Mobius' John Deere "Gator" mini-truck; a re-enactment of Mike Sell's encounter with a Sasquatch at night; and an Idaho discussion about the reported "Hand of Unknown Origin" which Biscardi and his researchers believe may be from a mauled Sasquatch.

* * * * *

The name Tom Biscardi is synonymous with notoriety within the cryptozoological community. Some believe Biscardi to be an ardent and dedicated researcher who has tirelessly sought the elusive bipedal creature as his life's work. Others, however, are inclined to see the former Las Vegas promoter as a Carl Denham-esque, self-aggrandizing showman intent on capitalizing on Sasquatch at every turn. While the former must rely on Biscardi's diligence and crack (or crack*pot*, depending on one's point of view) Team Bigfoot, the skeptics have at least some evidence Biscardi has perpetrated hoaxes in the past.

The first black mark is that he was a long-time acquaintance of Ivan Marx, who is generally dismissed by most in the field as a hoax master. While Peggy Marx denies that her husband ever knowingly deceived anyone (see *Bigfoot: A Beast on the Run*), the fact that Biscardi still maintains Mr. Marx's legitimacy — even going so far as to offer Marx's infamous and debunked "cripplefoot" Sasquatch photos as proof in this very documentary — offers the first strike against Biscardi's claims of legitimacy. The second problematic Biscardi hoax is the *Coast-to-Coast* radio debacle in 2005, in which Biscardi promised all who were willing to pay over the Internet exclusive webcam access to view his unearthing of a Bigfoot body in Happy Camp, California. After collecting said revenues and then confessing he was "hoodwinked" by the woman who claimed to have knowledge of the cryptid's burial spot (one wonders how it is that Biscardi would go so far as to collect monies *before* he investigated the matter thoroughly), Biscardi eventually offered to return the money to those who paid him via his website (but only after George Noory, the radio show's host, demanded Biscardi do so or face legal reprisals).

But the final and most damaging strike against his veracity was the nationally sensationalized "Georgia Bigfoot Body in a Freezer" hoax, in which a deputy sheriff named Matt Whitton and a used car salesman named Rick Dyer claimed to have a dead Sasquatch stored in a old freezer. This scam was *the* major news story of 2008, and when word spread of Biscardi's claim to have uncovered the ultimate scientific proof of Sasquatch's existence, literally thousands of media outlets worldwide covered the event in anticipation. The well-regarded, serious-minded *Cryptomundo* website was so besieged by traffic it was effectively off-line for days on end, so great was international curiosity.

All of the preceding should warn those serious about the subject matter of hominids to be extremely cautious, if not outright dismissive, of such Biscardi-produced titles as *Bigfoot Lives!* The fact that Biscardi interviews Hans Mobius, who was revealed by a local store clerk in his hometown to having personally purchased a gorilla suit days prior to his "sighting" (Biscardi conveniently doesn't bother to mention such damning evidence) only furthers the disreputable backlash that honest cryptozoologists face in a skeptical world. Bigfoot may live, all right; but for Tom Biscardi, it appears more as an unending source of revenue than any legitimate avenue of scientific inquiry.

Bigfoot Meets the Thing (1979) (TV)

Featuring the Thing/Benjy Grimm, Kelly, Betty, Miss Twilly, Ronald Radford, Spike, Stretch, Turkey and Dr. Harkness. Produced by Hanna-Barbera Studios. Directed by Ray Patterson, George Gordon and Carl Urbano. USA. Color. Mono. 11 Minutes.

Overview: Centerville High School student Benjy Grimm is actually a teen superhero incognito. By slamming together two rings on either hand and saying, "Things, do your thing!" he transforms into the Thing, a rocky monster with super strength.

One weekend Benjy is invited along with his friends — rich kid Ronald Radford, snob Betty, and Betty's sister Kelly — to go skiing on the nearby slopes. Biker deadbeats Spike, Stretch, and Turkey warn the wholesome teens that Bigfoot will abduct them if they dare invade its mountain domain. Spooked but undeterred, Benjy and friends head for Ronald's cabin.

Spike and his grease monkey pals decide to teach Benjy and company a lesson. They buy a Bigfoot costume and prank the frightened teens by hiding outside their cabin windows and growling. Unbeknownst to Spike, Stretch and Turkey, however, a real Bigfoot sees Stretch in the Bigfoot costume and falls in love. Stretch is abducted for some Sasquatch loving until Benjy Grimm transforms into the Thing and rescues the undeserving but grateful biker gang. The Thing takes pity on Bigfoot and stuffs the phony cryptid costume with snow so that Bigfoot may keep it as if it were a legitimate mate.

* * * * *

In an age when the top grossing films of all time regularly have the Marvel Comics stamp upon them, it's difficult to recall an earlier era when Marvel suffered through the worst possible cinema and television adaptations. Before Sam Raimi resurrected *Spiderman*, and that franchise was followed by the endless other filmic incarnations (such as *The Fantastic Four*, *X-Men*, *Iron Man*, and so forth), there was nothing to which Marvel could point with any semblance of pride, save the usual Saturday morning fare such as *The Fantastic Four*, Nicholas Hammond's baggy-pants *Spiderman* television series, or Reb Brown in the low-budget feature film *Captain America*. Fans of Marvel were embarrassed by these early efforts, and Marvel itself seemed embarrassed in turn.

The Thing is typical in regard to the first wave of Marvel adaptations: faithful to the source in name only. Whereas the actual Thing character was a team player in the comic book series *The Fantastic Four*, created by accidental exposure to cosmic rays, this Hanna-Barbera production abandoned the entire back-story, changed Grimm from a tragic figure into a Shaggy-styled teen, and even made the venerable rock man's plight — never being able to predict when he would return to human form — simply a matter of connecting two rings together at his leisure in order to transform into the Thing and vice versa. Adding insult to injury, the tough, streetwise, Bronx-born Ben Grimm was transported to a nameless, bland suburban landscape and plopped into an equally cardboard Centerville High School (the "center" being in the middle of Cliché City, USA).

Using limited animation and even less-inspired writing, *The Thing* is a classic example of how Hanna-Barbera Studios had declined by this period in their otherwise vaunted history. While the studio would undergo a revitalization in the coming decade, at this point it was strictly a paint-by-numbers outfit cranking out the most insipid drivel imaginable. Gone were the halcyon days of *Scooby Doo, Where Are You?* Instead, a new generation would suffer through the likes of *The Thing* as a sad place holder until a new infusion of cash and management brought the Hanna-Barbera name back to filmic prominence.

If poor Ben Grimm suffers from this fiasco's failed attempt to "mainstream" his appeal for teens, Bigfoot fares far worse. Portrayed as a furry idiot, and reduced to lumbering around while barely able to walk and breathe simultaneously, this is one simpleton Sasquatch (even given the children's series market). And yet, as if bestowing upon him some necessary human attributes, Bigfoot can miraculously speak English, albeit with the usual Tarzan-styled pidgin abbreviations and contractions. The unexplained contradiction of having this cryptid at once too stupid to recognize a stuffed costume as a nonliving entity and still be able to speak a human language is beyond comprehension; suffice it to say that no one questions the discrepancy (probably because they're too amazed by the sudden appearance of the Thing himself, despite the fact Benjy Grimm and the Thing, à la Clark Kent and Superman, are never far from one another).

For an 11-minute cartoon, *Bigfoot Meets the Thing* is a remarkable compilation of some of the worst elements in all-too-many Ciné du Sasquatch entries. There is the typical "it was just a guy in a suit" cliché, which in this case is shown to (surprise!) disguise the revelation that there is also a real cryptid lurking nearby. Equally predictable is that Bigfoot turns out to be a "loveable goof with a heart of gold," which is, sadly, the norm for any children-aimed depiction of a hominid. The fact that this Bigfoot comes across as even more stupid than the moronic leads Benjy, Betty, Ronald, Spike, Stretch, Turkey and the rest is a formidable achievement by the show's creative team; it could not have been easy to write down to a level even lower than the precedent set by the starring simpletons.

And yet they manage to render one of the most brain-dead Bigfoot realizations in the genre's history. The fact the kids even need the Thing to intervene during the final moments to deal a blow to Bigfoot is a sadder commentary on their own lack of mental acumen. At least

Bigfoot has the common sense to appear only once during the brief-but-still-too-lengthy run of the series, which fittingly included a later show actually entitled "The Thing Goes to the Dogs." In the immortal words of Stan Lee, "Nuff Said!"

Bigfooting in Oklahoma (2007) (Doc)

Featuring Esther Schritter. Produced, Written and Directed by Jay Michael. USA. Color. Stereo. 45 Minutes.

Overview: Bigfoot researcher and Oklahoma resident Esther Schritter recounts her life-long obsession with and experiences of Sasquatch, including the first time she witnessed the elusive cryptid as a child when it peeked into her parents' kitchen window and glared at her as she sat, terrified, in her highchair. Also detailed are Schritter's later encounters with Bigfoot as she grew to maturity in the remote areas of the state, and the profound impact Charles B. Pierce's *The Legend of Boggy Creek* had upon her as a child. Many other eyewitnesses are interviewed and detail their own first-hand sightings. Also included is video footage shot by Schritter which features what she claims to be Bigfoot. *Bigfooting in Oklahoma* is from CryptoVideography, the same small company that produced *Bigfoot FAQ* and *Swamp Apes*.

Bigfoot's Reflection (2007) (Doc)

Featuring John Bindernagal, Robert Pyle, John Green, Bill Miller, John Kirk III, Tomas Steenburg, Richard Noll and Mel Skahan. Produced by Frederic Bohbot and Evan Beloff. Written by Darryll B.D. Walsh and Evan Beloff. Directed by Evan Beloff. USA. Color. Stereo. 60 Minutes.

Overview: Dedicated to covering the Sasquatch from a cryptozoological and field researcher's perspective, *Bigfoot's Reflection* concentrates on the Pacific Northwest area of the U.S. The filmmakers spend time analyzing 50 years worth of evidence, as well as journeying to remote areas of the wilderness to show how rugged the landscape often is and how it could sustain a large bipedal hominid.

Bigfootville (2002) (Doc)

Featuring Cindy Bear. Written and Directed by Bruce Burgess. UK/USA. Color. Stereo. 46 Minutes.

Overview: Tulsa, Oklahoma, television news reporter Cindy Bear accompanies British film producers as they cover 800 square miles of Oklahoma wilderness, along with several witnesses who claim to have encountered a 9-foot-tall hominid in the area. Though much of the documentary focuses on rural forest locales, many Oklahoma small towns are featured, including Sapulpa, Ada, Smithville, Broken Bow and Disney. Among those interviewed are law enforcement officials and residents who claim direct contact with the cattle-mutilating cryptid. Night vision and infra-red cameras were utilized in an attempt to record video of any sightings, but the only reported anomaly is some stones being tossed at the documentary crew by an unseen assailant (which some attribute to Sasquatch). Independently made, this documentary first aired on the Travel Channel in 2002.

The Bionic Woman (1977) ("The Return of Bigfoot Part 2") (TV)

Starring Lindsay Wagner, Richard Anderson, Martin E. Brooks, John Saxon, Stephen Young, Severn Darden, Ted Cassidy, Sandy Duncan, Stefanie Powers, Lee Majors and Charles Cyphers. Produced by Harve Bennett and Craig Schiller. Written by Kenneth Johnson. Directed by Barry Crane. USA. Color. Mono. 47 Minutes.

Overview: Jamie Summers, a tennis professional, is nearly killed after a skydiving accident. Top secret government man Oscar Goldman and genius scientist Dr. Rudy Wells rebuild her in exchange for her agreement to act as their secret spy. They implant a bionic-powered right arm, legs, and hearing aides that enable her to clearly hear minute sounds at great distances. After the surgery is completed and she is healed, Jamie discovers she can now run faster than a speeding car, jump high obstacles, physically overpower non-enhanced humans, etc.

When Steve Austin, the original Bionic Man, suffers radiation poisoning after battling an android Sasquatch of alien design, Jamie seeks out the aliens behind the robotic Bigfoot in hopes of obtaining a drug used by the aliens called Neotrax that could save Steve's ebbing life. She desperately searches throughout the Northern California woods in quest of the invaders, who are attempting to mine the Earth's volcanoes for precious if planet-destroying energy supplies they need to survive. But as she draws near, she finds the same robot Sasquatch who nearly killed Steve now preventing her from obtaining the medicine. A confrontation looms between Bionic Woman and Android Sasquatch as Jamie fights to complete her errand of mercy. And even if she defeats Sasquatch, she still must befriend the aliens who have turned renegade against their superiors in hopes of stopping the bad aliens from destroying the Earth.

* * * * *

This two-part episode of the Bionic franchise was split, with the first half airing on *The Six Million Dollar Man* show, and the conclusion airing on *The Bionic Woman*'s opening episode of the latter series' second year. Subsequently, however, the two-part episodes have been packaged together in syndicated runs of *The Six Million Dollar Man* rather than *The Bionic Woman*. This is odd, given that the second half of the two-parter has Steve Austin virtually comatose and places the emphasis on Jamie Sommers, which, of course, made a lot more sense when the first half had the Bionic Man lead-in to support it.

Besides the camp value of seeing Sandy Duncan — the perennial "nice girl next door" — playing a "nice alien next galaxy," the episode offers many memorable Ciné du Sasquatch moments, though most are unintentionally hilarious. One example: the sight of the helpless Sasquatch under John Saxon's leaden command, which consists primarily of Saxon saying repeatedly: "Attack! Sasquatch! *Attack*!" While Saxon gamely varies the vocal intonations, there really is a limit to how effectively any thespian can deliver the same line over and over before it devolves into self-parody. Speaking of which, the series' trademark overuse of having Jamie run, jump and strike blows in slow motion, accompanied by the jazzy, upbeat Muzak blaring underneath, slows the pacing considerably. While intended to show the supreme agility of a bionic person, the effect of endless shots of Jamie running through the California forests, hair bouncing like something out of a Breck shampoo ad, is simple tedium. Doubtless it was a cost-effective way to save on having to stage action, as what would normally take the Bionic Woman a few seconds to accomplish (for instance, jumping out of a hovering helicopter to land far below without injury) stretches into half a minute or longer. But *The Bionic Woman* uses this technique so frequently it becomes almost surreal. The result is often akin to a Japanese *kaiju* film, such as *War of the Gargantuas* (which, given the slight resemblance the Sasquatch costume has to the battling twin Toho titans, is not a flattering comparison). Whereas the *kaiju* ("strange beast") films work because all of the creatures are supposedly giant-sized (and therefore their motions slowed to suggest scale), herein it simply reveals much of the obvious use of stunt doubles, wire-rigged foam boulders and seam lines in the Bigfoot costume.

The dialogue in the first battle sequence between Jamie and

Sasquatch is typical of the effort's juvenile tone. She mutters to the advancing creature even as it growls with clearly malicious intent, "Oh boy, Steve said you were big, but *this* is ridiculous!" It has all the convincing reality of a looped line from a porno actress opposite John Holmes during the same era. In truth, it reminds one of the campy tone used by Lorenzo Semple Jr.'s screenplay for the *King Kong* remake starring Jessica Lange. Still, for what it's worth, the confrontation is well-staged for the small screen, and features a bevy of traded blows, hurled boulders and even Jamie retreating to a tree top while the enraged Sasquatch topples it over and brings her crashing back to Earth. It is suggested that without Sandy Duncan's kindly intervention as the good alien Gillian seconds before Sasquatch pulverizes Jamie, the Bionic Woman would be in the same expensive junk heap as her male counterpart. In this sense, given that Sasquatch bests both bionic humans in one two-part show, there can be little doubt as to who is the superior being, at least in terms of brute strength. Even an "enhanced" *Homo sapiens* is no match for an android Sasquatch!

As for how it falls into the thematic spectrum of Ciné du Sasquatch, "The Return of Bigfoot" two-parter actually uses two common motifs: one is the Savage Sasquatch, as exemplified by the destructive hominid under the evil Nedlick's control, and the other is the Benign Bigfoot, as the android cryptid is revealed to be so at the conclusion. Because Gillian, Bigfoot's creator, has sacrificed her own supply of Neotraxin to save Steve Austin's life and therefore fallen into a coma herself, Sasquatch is shown to be remorseful when released from Nedlick's dominance, thus demonstrating that beneath the savage exterior there is a sentient, caring being who only harms humans when forced to do so against its will. This dovetails nicely with the genre's two major strains of cryptid depiction—as both vicious defender of its domain against intrusions *and* kindly towards our own species. It is to the show's credit that the episode does this so adroitly in one entertaining narrative arc.

For those wishing to relive a simpler time when the mere appearance of a well-designed cryptid costume was enough to make the average Ciné du Sasquatch fan giddy with joy, "The Return of Bigfoot" is a nostalgic treat. Along with the earlier, non–Bionic Woman costarring episodes with Sasquatch in *The Six Million Dollar Man* series, these hour-long television programs were major contributors to the Bigfoot genre's growing acceptance by the viewing public. As such, they are vital examples of the popularization process of hominids in the filmic culture and—campy flaws and all—vital in the *oeuvre*'s evolution.

Birdman and the Galaxy Trio ("Monster of the Mountains") (1967) (TV)

Featuring the voices of Keith Andes, Don Messick and John Stephenson. Produced by Joseph Barbera and William Hanna. Written by Neal Barbera and Phil Hahn. Directed by Joseph Barbera and William Hanna. USA. Color. Mono. 30 Minutes.

Overview: Endowed by the Sun god Ra with extraordinary powers—including the ability to shoot pulsating solar energy beams from his fists and create temporary force fields to shelter himself and others from harm—Birdman fights for the justice-loving people of the world via his affiliation with the Inter-Nation Security organization. Along with his eagle helper Avenger and sidekick Birdboy, the trio fly around the globe to defeat a variety of supernatural and superpowered foes, such as Dr. Freezoid, X the Eliminator and Mentok the Mind Taker.

Strange sightings of a giant monster have been reported in Tibet by frightened Sherpas. Birdman and company wing their way to the Himalayan Mountains to investigate. The villagers' accounts of an attacking Abominable Snowman prove to be true, as Birdman discovers himself when the Yeti attempts to bury him, Birdboy and Avenger alive under an avalanche of snow. Escaping via the use of his solar shield, Birdman tracks the Yeti back to its cave, where he discovers the true nature of the hominid—it is a robot designed by the evil Chang, who wishes to frighten away the Sherpas in order to mine the priceless uranium buried in the mountain.

Birdman, Birdboy and Avenger make short work of both Yeti and Chang, delivering Chang to the relieved Sherpas. Birdman instructs them to prosecute Chang for his crimes using their own local form of justice, and the superhero trio leaves, flying back to the United States.

* * * * *

Few who saw the short-run series *Birdman and the Galaxy Trio* will ever forget the campy cry the titular hero yelled each time he launched himself airborne: "Birrrrrrd... MAN!" Although designed by Alex Toth (who was key to the memorable design of *Space Ghost* and *Jonny Quest*, as well as *Space Angel*), *Birdman and the Galaxy Trio* (the latter were Vapor Man, Gravity Girl and Meteor Man, who appeared in their own separate episodes of the series) lacked the edginess and "cool factor" of the more successful Hanna-Barbera collaborations. Perhaps it was the nature of Birdman's name, costume and powers; while it is tempting to say they were strictly for the birds, the reality is that most adolescents didn't equate feathered species with incredible abilities and preternatural powers (however incorrect this may be in a zoological sense). Sadly, too, no matter how sleek the eagle Avenger was, the addition of Birdboy was perceived as a weakness by many tyke viewers. And then, as mentioned, there was the anemic battle cry Birdman felt compelled to voice with embarrassing regularity, when most self-respecting superheroes would've perhaps refrained out of a sense of pride (or shame).

This evident perception even by the producers themselves was gamely overcome—or at least attempts were made to do so, with varying degrees of success—by pitting the heroes against an imaginative series of arch villains and creatures. While this was equally true for *Space Ghost*, *Birdman and the Galaxy Trio* was particularly dependent on whether or not each episode featured an interesting antagonist, lacking as it did the high-tech secret headquarters and phantom cruiser of the aforementioned show. As such, Chang and his robotic Yeti rank among their lesser foes, as Chang is portrayed as a human without any diabolical powers (save the ability to construct an Abominable android). One is left to wonder: If Chang has such incredible skill, why doesn't he simply create advanced robots for industrial applications and/or retire on the intellectual copyrights for his design work alone? Surely this would be an easier task than frightening away Sherpas, fighting super-powered adversaries and mining potentially lethal uranium? Presumably the series creators believed the youngsters watching wouldn't subject their super villains to such scrutiny, but the ploy of having yet another Yeti passed off as simply "my superior robot creation" is anti-climactic, to say the least. In an era when robotics were still a crude dream, surely a King Kong–sized android would have had some economical value (for show business if nothing else).

Birdman and the Galaxy Trio enjoyed a revival (of sorts) in the self-parodying remake known as *Harvey Birdman: Attorney at Law*. This series featured a courtroom format in which various Birdman villains were either tried or acted as judges, as well as other Hanna-Barbera characters making cameos in various legal-related troubles. In many ways the remake captured the absurdity of the original character far better, playing the concept for laughs rather than the thrills that were all too often absent in the 1967 incarnation.

Bloodstalkers (1978)

AKA: *Blood Stalkers*; *The Night Daniel Died*. Starring Ken Miller, Toni Crabtree, Jerry Albert, Celea Ann Cole, Herb Goldstein, Robert W. Morgan, John R. Meyer, David Faris Legge, Stan Webb, Lane Chiles and Joe Hilton. Written by Ben Morse. Produced and Directed by Robert W. Morgan. USA. Color. Mono. 90 Minutes.

Overview: Two couples vacation in the Florida Everglades, ignoring the warnings of a local known only as the Old Man, who tells them they're entering "bloodstalker" territory. But Daniel, the insistent leader of the vacationers, informs the Old Man the cabin they intend to stay in belonged to his father and nothing will stop them, especially some superstitious folklore about legendary monsters. Daniel's girlfriend Kim is sufficiently spooked and pleads with Daniel to abandon their plans, but Daniel holds firm. The other couple awakens in the back seat to witness the confrontation. Mike and Jeri are unnerved as well, but for different reasons. Mike feels the trip to date has been a bust, as the couples have done nothing but endlessly drive, while Jeri feels she is wasting her time in a hick paradise instead of enjoying the bright lights of the big city. Daniel shushes them all and leaves the Old Man and his cohorts — a savage bunch of rednecks by the names of Jarvis, Lester, and Pip — eating his car's tailpipe exhaust, determined more than ever to reclaim his family's property from such local idiocy.

The cabin is decrepit beyond belief. Mike, Jeri and Kim complain when Daniel informs them they must park their station wagon a hundred yards away from the cabin because the driveway has become overgrown with vines and low-hanging branches. Despite the lack of electricity, Daniel convinces the other three to set up a crude camping environment inside the flimsy, four-walled shack. Daniel and Kim decide to go skinny-dipping in a nearby waterhole as the sun sets, while Mike and Jeri retire inside the cabin to make out.

But while Daniel and Kim are enjoying the cool swim, a bloodstalker enters the water from the opposite shore and swims towards them. Kim sees the Bigfoot creature, but Daniel misses it. Soon enough, however, the howls of the Sasquatch alert them to the fact they're not alone in the woods. They race back to the cabin, interrupting Mike and Jeri, who are startled by their abrupt return. Daniel convinces a distraught Kim that they only heard a large bobcat or swamp panther, and promises to hunt it down the following morning. The couples relax, enjoying a meal and getting drunk on beer. Daniel unexpectedly gushes forth about how much he values the friendships he has with Kim, Mike and Jeri, and then stumbles to bed, embarrassed by his outburst. While Kim joins Daniel to soothe him, Mike explains to Jeri that Daniel is a Vietnam veteran and once inadvertently slaughtered a hut full of civilians during combat operations. Haunted by his mistake, Daniel has subsequently managed to reconstruct a private life only at great personal cost to himself and those with whom he comes into contact, hence his emotional instability at dinner.

A bloodstalker suddenly smashes the window, grabbing Jeri. Mike is too terrified to react and watches, frozen in place, until Daniel rescues Jeri and hacks at the bloodstalker's hairy arm with his knife. Daniel tells them that they're surrounded by the creatures, and that unless they take drastic action, they will not survive until dawn. They have only a handful of bullets in Daniel's pistol and no other weaponry save an axe. Daniel devises a plan — he will slip outside and attempt to drive the station wagon closer to the cabin. But when he does so, Daniel discovers the vehicle has been stolen.

Daniel makes a desperate decision, with the group's approval: He will attempt to reach the small town nearby and summon help, while his friends remain behind in the cabin to make a stand. Using the skills he learned as a soldier, Daniel races through the forest, ex-

hausted. Meanwhile, the bloodstalkers attack, forcing Mike, Kim and Jeri to battle for their lives. They repel the beasts until one slips in through the attic unnoticed. In the small town, Daniel finds the locals unwilling to help in any way. He believes he has found a savior when he encounters a preacher at a black church, but the preacher turns him away, shame-faced. Unable to run much farther, Daniel eventually encounters a local deputy, who takes him back to the ravaged cabin.

Inside, Daniel's worst fears are realized. All three of his friends have been horribly killed, their bodies left posed in grotesque displays. The deputy finds a number of animal skins in the cabin's attic and realizes someone has been poaching the lands, using the structure as a base of operation. The deputy is unexpectedly killed by one of the three rednecks employed by the Old Man, who turns out to be the ringleader of the poaching operation. The redneck goons are revealed to have been staging the bloodstalker attacks in a Bigfoot costume designed to frighten any locals from investigating their illegal fur trade. Filled with sudden rage and becoming a one-man slaughter machine, Daniel murders Jarvis, Pip and Lester before blowing the Old Man away with a rusty shotgun at point blank range.

While the stunned townspeople watch, Daniel staggers through their dilapidated city, his shotgun draped across his shoulders like a crucifix. Bloodied, bruised, broken but determined to leave them to rot in their own indifference and bury their own dead, Daniel moves on without pause.

* * * * *

Bloodstalkers is the sole fictional film made by Bigfoot researcher Robert W. Morgan, who appeared in many documentaries about his favorite cryptid, such as *The Mysterious Monsters*, *In Search of Bigfoot*, and *Bigfoot: Man or Beast?* Bald and bearing an intensity that reminds one of a younger Donald Pleasance, Morgan has never abandoned his lifelong interest in the subject matter, hosting webcast programs about cryptozoology, as well as making plans for a remake of *Bloodstalkers* itself. Despite its limited distribution, the film has garnered a small but devout cult following, and Morgan even has a small role as one of the killer rednecks.

As far as Ciné du Sasquatch movies go, *Bloodstalkers* resorts to the "ultimate cop out" of having the cryptids revealed to be simply humans in costumes. This is a classic revelation in the genre, of course, and can be witnessed in other entries, such as *Shriek of the Mutilated* and *The Long Way Home: A Bigfoot Story*. Such a plot twist needn't be reason for exclusion from the genre, however, as the films employing this narrative contrivance still explore the impact on human society of encountering supposed hominids, no matter if they are revealed as fake in their respective cinematic universes. It is this quality — the examination of species interacting and the sociological outcomes of those interactions — that truly renders a film either within or outside the Ciné du Sasquatch canon, as these qualities define the genre rather than whether or not the cryptid was "real" or "imaginary."

Bloodstalkers has an unusual sense of character development for such a low-budget hominid-themed film. The bloodstalker cryptids are less the central focus and more a peripheral menace that produces the characters' interactions and conflicts. While the writing is limited to two-dimensionality in terms of depth, this is still one dimension more than in many Bigfoot movies. Additionally, the acting and direction limit the earnest attempts made to strike a balance between a standard-issue monster movie and creating concern for the victims' plight. Still, using authentic locations, and depicting a rural poverty that is unquestionably harsher than most, adds a great deal of believability to the film's sense of tension. Like with *Deliverance*, the viewer feels these characters come from their setting rather than being imported for day-player rates as professional actors. This works for and against *Bloodstalkers*, but, on the whole, adds a level of verisimilitude lacking in many other cryptid films.

Borrowing a cue from *The Legend of Boggy Creek*, the director rarely shows the actual monsters with any clarity, preferring to keep them in the shadows or photographed only at night. Given that the night-for-night cinematography is actually quite good for the most part, this adds a gritty texture to the mise-en-scène that reminds one of the similarly-filmed *Creature from Black Lake*. The first fully-glimpsed appearance of a bloodstalker, set during the couple's night swim in a lake, is chillingly effective because the director keeps the creature always in silhouette, yet always advancing on the unaware swimmers (first by surveying them from above on a rocky outcropping and then later covertly wading into the murky waters and heading directly for them). Likewise, many of the siege moments inside the cabin produce the necessary jumps for which this genre is so well-known, including the ubiquitous "cryptid's arm smashes through a window" moment that has become a hallmark of Ciné du Sasquatch.

The sequence in which Daniel finds no one willing to help in the small town is reminiscent of *High Noon* or *Bad Day at Black Rock*. The bitter irony that Daniel and friends arrive to use Daniel's own land, but the community wherein his property is located turn their collective backs on him, speaks volumes about why the town has effectively died out. And while the point has already been made, the encounter with the black preacher outside the small church in which Daniel pleads for his friend's lives while the congregation inside sing hymns to God's mercy is particularly effective. Rather than play the scene with the usual verbal overkill, Morgan simply has the chorus' songs play over the dialogue, which is mixed below the audio threshold, and holds on the two men's faces — Daniel as he silently begs for help, and the preacher as he sternly but shamefacedly shakes his head no. Talk about your town without pity! Even the so-called spiritual leaders in this dead burg have abandoned all hope. This bleak outlook reminds one of the later *The Wildman of the Navidad*'s equally acerbic observation that the real monsters aren't the bloodstalkers but the human beings who refuse to help one another. It's not subtle, but it is the high point of *Bloodstalkers*, and a rare moment of profound humanity in a genre not known for displaying such humanitarian concerns.

Likewise, the ending sequence in which Daniel — a haunted Vietnam War veteran — is forced to witness his friends' twisted bodies, posed in rigor mortis, and re-experience the horrific déjà vu of his inadvertent atrocities against Vietnamese citizens during his service period is unexpectedly complex. This kind of sub-text and characterization is unusually rich for Ciné du Sasquatch, and even while the actors don't completely succeed at making it totally believable, it is to their and Morgan's credit that they were willing to stretch the boundaries of the genre anyway. It is interesting to note, however incidental, the prevalence of combat veterans in Bigfoot movies: the likeable if emotionally-damaged Pahoo in *Creature from Black Lake*; the trio of old timers in *Sasquatch Mountain* with wartime records; etc. There is an intriguing hint that such veterans realize the nature of confronting the darker sides of their own personalities and, as a result, have an emotional simpatico with the cryptids they're inevitably pitted against. For these vets, in essence, Sasquatch offers an unexpected chance at personal redemption — if only the war-weary men can recognize the possibility before they begin slaughtering yet another life form they truly don't understand.

The final shot, in which Daniel strides out of town bearing his shotgun like Christ carrying his cross, is both heavy-handed and an effective summation of this unusually sober Sasquatch movie. While it plays as maudlin in a *Billy Jack* manner, it also embodies the film's theme of societal disintegration quite well. There is no sense that the

darkly ironic alternative title for this film — *The Night Daniel Died* — is not as worthy as *Bloodstalkers*, for by the end it is clear Daniel has survived the lion's den twice, but lost all of his humanity in the process of his second go-round. In a play on words, Daniel is the only survivor, and yet he has died spiritually along with the rest of the uncaring, selfish townspeople around him. That's pretty strong stuff for a genre known more for biting its protagonists than its thematic bite. In this sense, fans of the Bigfoot genre will find much to contemplate that is unusual and provocative in *Bloodstalkers*, even if the film in its entirety is not successful. It's just different enough to warrant at least a one-time viewing experience, however flawed.

Bloody Rage of Bigfoot (2010)

Starring Andrew Baack, Louis Diaz, Steve Galayda, Ingrid Gregerson, Bob Rogers, Kathie Napholz, Michelle Ruiz, Ron Feyereisen and Mario Sanchez. Produced, Written and Directed by James Baack. USA. Color. Stereo. 3D.

Overview: Bigfoot contracts rabies from a half-dead raccoon hit by a car. As the rabies virus progresses, so does the deterioration of his mind. He wanders deep into the woods and encounters a racist militia group, and attacks them without further provocation.

At the same time, two young Goth girls from a local high school are experimenting with black magic. After they use a vicious street pimp in a human sacrifice as a burnt offering, they successfully conjure a hideous demon beyond their control. The rabid Bigfoot and the hell-spawn "Demonfoot" find one another, and a battle to the death ensues.

* * * * *

Writer, producer and director James Baack has been in production on this, the world's first 3D entry into Ciné du Sasquatch, for over two years. As the director of C-grade anti-films such as *Brandy or Freedom* and *Pus-E the Clown*, Baack's *The Bloody Rage of Bigfoot* promises to be short on logic and production values but long on campy exploitation thrills, per the abby norm for his output. Highlights (or lowlights, depending on your mood) include Sasquatch fighting Demonfoot with flares, music by Electric Gutpile, and the shoot-out between the cracker survivalists and Bigfoot, in which the cryptid deftly handles an Uzi with devastating precision, à la Tony Montana.

Boston Pizza Sasquatch Commercials (2007) (TV)

Starring John DeSantis. Produced by the DDB Canada Ad Agency. Directed by Daryl Gardiner. Canada. Color. Stereo. 30 Seconds.

Overview: Louie the Sasquatch is hired as the new spokesperson for the Boston Pizza International eatery. Alas, putting a hominid in a workplace environment can be fraught with peril, no matter how you dress him up with name tag and tie. Louie quickly takes a liking to the on-tap beer dispensers, accidentally blasting himself in the eyes with alcohol. He wipes his stinging eyes clean with the startled manager's tie, grunting in pain. Two co-workers watch from a safe distance and remark of their new 7-foot-tall mascot, "Seems like a nice guy."

This charming commercial was part of a 17-million-dollar ad campaign that appeared in print, on radio, and on TV to promote the pizza brewpub throughout Canada. 6-foot, 11-inch actor John DeSantis inhabits the well-conceived costume with graceful charm, having previously appeared as Lurch in *The New Addams Family* TV series.

Bugs Bunny's Bustin' Out All Over ("Spaced Out Bunny") (1980) (TV)

Featuring the voices of Mel Blanc and Paul Julian. Produced by Chuck Jones and Mary Roscoe. Written by Chuck Jones. Directed by Chuck Jones and Phil Monroe. USA. Color. Stereo. 6 Minutes.

Overview: Bugs Bunny stars in a triptych of shorts. In the second segment—"Spaced Out Bunny"—Bugs is abducted by Marvin the Martian when Marvin tricks Bugs into eating a drugged carrot. When Bugs awakens, he's on Marvin's home world and now the "pet" to Hugo the Abominable Snowman, who is Marvin's own pet crypto specimen.

Hugo decides in regards to Bugs that he will "hug him and squeeze him and name him George" (just like during Bugs' previous encounter with Hugo decades earlier in the Himalayan Mountains), but the Earth-based bunny has different ideas. He convinces the Abominable Snowman that what Hugo really is lacking is a toy robot—in other words, Marvin the Martian himself. Hugo agrees and takes Marvin to be his own plaything. Marvin objects, which results in a humiliating spanking from Hugo.

Bugs, wanting to return home, whispers a suggestion into Hugo's ear. Hugo agrees and dons Marvin as his new Mickey Mouse–styled wristwatch and then hurls Bugs (who's inside a flying saucer) like a Frisbee back to Earth.

* * * * *

Chuck Jones first introduced the Abominable Snowman character in the classic short "The Abominable Snow Rabbit" in 1961. Although the ending of the cryptid's first appearance had him literally melting into a puddle of water, he's inexplicably back, good as new, under the care of Marvin the Martian in "Spaced Out Bunny."

This time the Abominable Snowman has been christened Hugo, but otherwise he's the same dim-witted but sweet-natured Yeti who only wants a huggable pet for his very own to love. As in "The Abominable Snow Rabbit," Mel Blanc provides the syrupy voice that gives the towering hominid his benevolent character. Of course, said benevolence is a matter of perspective. For those such as Bugs Bunny, who happens to be at the mercy of the pet-loving Yeti, Hugo's insistence on keeping his temporary target of choice is filled with lurking dread. It's not that Hugo means badly; rather, Hugo has no sense of his own power to easily harm during his acts of "loving" and "squeezing" his object of affection.

Strangely (given it was probably the furthest thing from creator Chuck Jones' mind), "Spaced Out Bunny" seamlessly fits in with Ciné du Sasquatch themes during its brief running time. For instance, it echoes two different motifs common in the Bigfoot film genre. The first is the infrequent (but not rare either) "Space Sasquatch" visualization, as seen in such examples as *Terror in the Midnight Sun*, *Snow Devils*, and Chewbacca in the *Star Wars* films. The other is the buried but lurking fear the creature represents to humans because the Abominable Snowman is superior in strength and cunning. In other words, whereas even the most ferocious land-based predators, such as a polar bear or lion, represent animalistic danger, the hominid conveys a deeper, more primordial anxiety. It is, after all, genetically our closest living relative. Not only that, it shares with us many characteristics: It walks upright, it is basically humanoid and it survives with its intelligence rather than brute force only. This means that on the deepest level the hominid is in competition with us for supremacy of the planet. Worse yet, it has several advantages we lack, not the least of which is its preternatural ability to remain undetected.

Of course, this is all so much subtext (and hardly present save for its basic presence) in "Spaced Out Bunny," which Jones wisely keeps briskly-paced to amuse rather than lecture. Still, when all is said and done, there is a slightly sinister quality to Hugo's unstoppable (if not abominable) desire to dominate other living beings of superior intelligence and reduce them to his personal playthings. This is a kind of karmic justice being served on sentient beings such as Bugs and Marvin, who have vastly superior technology and intellectual capacity upon which to draw, but find themselves at the mercy of Hugo despite their inherent advantages. And while the classical "trickster" figure of the rabbit, which Bugs incarnates to perfection, *always* eventually outwits his opponent, it comes here not with the usual ease and lack of concern on Bugs' part (as, for example, when he's matched against Daffy or Elmer Fudd). Indeed, in both their encounters under Jones' direction, the Abominable proves to be Bugs' equal in terms of persistence and level of threat, often reducing even the normally confident Bugs to a worrisome wit's end state rarely seen in other Warner Brothers' entries. Jones wisely if subconsciously makes the most of the very isolation that accompanies any Abominable Snowman scenario—whether it's in the most remote mountaintops on Earth or the confining depths of outer space—to heighten the level of dread and unease, and produce superior animation shorts.

Building a Thrill Ride: Expedition Everest (2006) (TV) (Doc)

Featuring Adonis Stevens, Eric Ditman, Alexie Schauerte, Tom Myers and Jayson Talbert. Written by Lisa Feit. Produced and Directed by Yehuda Goldman. USA. Color. Stereo. 45 Minutes.

Disney's "Imagineers" create dread in the *Expedition Everest* thrill ride by showing just shadows of the Yeti as riders approach a final face-to-face showdown with the beast.

Overview: *Building a Thrill Ride: Expedition Everest* takes an inside look at the building of the Florida-based Walt Disney World theme park adventure ride "Expedition Everest," one of the most popular of recent creations for attendees. Disney's team of "imagineers" first take a real-world expedition of their own to the Himalayan Mountains to study the culture and obtain authentic artifacts that will be incorporated into the ride. Paintings, carved statues, blankets and many other Sherpa-made art work is acquired and shipped back to Orlando for utilization.

A fictional set-up is created for the ride that gives visitors a narrative thread upon which to hang their thrill ride experience, which is the distinction that sets Disney's parks apart from the normal rollercoaster-type affair. Supposedly, riders are informed, a group of cut-rate entrepreneurs have purchased old mining cars that tunnel through Everest with an eye towards capitalizing upon the notorious cryptid legend. Alas, the Carl Denham–esque owners have refused to hype the fact that the Yeti is real and not very happy its home has been turned into a theme park. As the mine cars race through the rickety tunnels and around blind bends, riders become increasingly aware that the Abominable Snowman is alive and plotting their demise.

Featuring behind-the-scenes footage at the processes employed by the normally secretive Disney corporation, *Building a Thrill Ride: Expedition Everest* is a rare opportunity to see the inner workings of the immense amount of planning, engineering, art design and thorough testing that goes into the brief but entertaining whirl through a state-of-the-art ride. The animatronics utilized to create the massive Yeti, which appears to grab at the passing mine cars at the ride's climax, are also well-documented and offer an instructive course in the mechanical considerations that go into the building of such a rigorous "robot" that is subjected to hundreds of repetitive motions daily.

Buzzkill ("Bigfoot, Biggerfoot") (1996) (TV)

Starring Dave Sheridan, Travis Draft, Frank Hudetz and Vince D'Orazi. Produced by Paul Cockerill, Greg Johnston and Lesley Wolff. Written by Travis Draft and Dave Sheridan. Directed by Jason Sands. USA. Color. Stereo. 30 Minutes.

Overview: Merry pranksters pull so-called "buzzkills" or rude pranks on unsuspecting victims and videotape the results without the targeted subject realizing they're on hidden camera.

* * * * *

In many ways (both for better and decidedly worse) *Buzzkill* was a forerunner of all the modern prank TV shows that would follow: *The Tom Green Show*, *Jackass* and *Punk'd*. But who would argue that Allen Funt's *Candid Camera* isn't the *real* influence on all of these so-called "reality TV" series, anyway? Minus the increasingly vulgar tone and often tasteless nature of the pranks and pranksters themselves, there's really nothing new under the "sun gun" (a type of light used to simulate the sun's rays for daytime videography) in any of these shows, even granting their often outlandish sense of entertainment value.

"Bigfoot, Biggerfoot" followed the typical *Buzzkill* format: Rather than simply expose victims to a prank, the writers actually scripted narrative twists to occur during the event's unfolding to further complicate the victims' reactions. Often this consisted of a "Shemp" or insider in on the prank who acted as if he or she were ignorant but was actually a planted participant. This allows the chosen targets less time to critically analyze and deduce they were being punked, as events unfold so quickly and (to their point of view) unexpectedly.

In this hilarious episode, groups of volunteers are escorted into the woods to examine evidence of a recent Sasquatch sighting—footprints, broken branches, etc.—little realizing they are being "stalked" by an actor in a Bigfoot costume. When the victims least expected it, the costumed cryptid would leap out of the bushes and attack the group. After the initial screams and sudden bursts of flight, one member in the group would suddenly "fight back" and begin clobbering the suited Sasquatch over the head with a fallen log or tree branch. The staged counter-attack was so vicious that the once-terrified explorers were suddenly faced with the realization, as the Sasquatch screamed in human misery, that they were "witnessing" a poor hoaxer caught in the web of his own deceit. The question they quickly faced: Do they allow the planted explorer to continue to assault the obviously fake Bigfoot or intervene to stop the violence? As the reader might expect, reactions were as varied as the motley group itself.

Ironically, MTV cancelled *Buzzkill* after concerns arose over the possibility of litigious actions on behalf of the pranked victims, owing to the show's success. This didn't keep the networks from revamping the formula later, however, in series such as the aforementioned *Punk'd* and *Jackass*, nor even a novel variation also using Bigfoot in the puppet-based crank phone call series *Crank Yankers*. It's a case, one concludes, of he who laughs loudest laughing all the way to the bank.

Captain Planet and the Planeteers (1990) (TV) (Cameo)

Featuring the voices of David Coburn, LeVar Burton, Joey Dedio, Janice Kawaye, Scott Menville, Kath Soucie, Whoopi Goldberg and Frank Welker. Produced by Thom Beers, Nick Boxer, Andy Heyward, Larry Houston, Robby London, Will Meugniot, Barbara Pyle, Cassandra Schafhausen and Lisa Salamone Smith. Written by David Ehrman, Phil Harnage and Ted Turner. Directed by Jim Duffy, Will Meugniot, Vincent Davis and Stan Phillips. USA. Color. Stereo. 30 Minutes.

Overview: When Gaia, the spiritual force of Earth, discovers that mankind and various villains are wreaking havoc on her carefully-constructed environment, which sustains all life, she retaliates by recruiting five human youngsters. Empowering each with a magical ring that imbues them with the power to fight wrongdoers, the Planeteers (as they're known) live on Hope Island with Gaia and train under the watchful eyes of Captain Planet. When an environmental catastrophe arises, Captain Planet and the Planeteers arrive on the scene to offer help and combat such evildoers as Verminous Skumm, Duke Nukem, and Looten Plunder.

* * * * *

Ted Turner, creator of CNN and TBS, placed his personal belief structure on the line when he not only financially backed *Captain Planet and the Planeteers*, but helped devise the series' mythology and characters, and even wrote some episodes! To observe that this is an anomaly among uber-capitalists of his stature is a profound understatement. And while inevitably preachy, owing to its context as a Super Green concept, the show's broader mission to help educate children about their own responsibility and power to help prevent Earth's deteriorating climate was at least commendable. While adult critics typically snickered at what they perceived as the show's patronizing tone, who is to say whether or not it actually contributed to the largely pro-green, anti-pollution trend among the latest generation of adults who may have actually watched *Captain Planet and the Planeteers* and been influenced at an impressionable age? Surely if one low-budget, non-studio feature such as *The Legend of Boggy Creek* can launch an entire generation of cryptozoological interest among its viewers, then a long-running TV show could offer the same influence.

In terms of Ciné du Sasquatch, however, *Captain Planet and the Planeteers* is but a "foot"note. In one episode the Planeteers put the Earth itself on trial at Gaia's request, hoping that if nothing else, crooked attorneys who enable environmental polluters will be taught a lesson via their own craftily-written legal loopholes. During the trial a silent but serious-faced Sasquatch is shown in the jury box, evidently displeased with the deforestation his domain has undergone at the greedy hands of developers praying for acquittal. It's a brief but damning cameo, long on implication albeit short on screen time.

The Capture of Bigfoot (1979)

Starring Stafford Morgan, Katherine Hopkins, Richard Kennedy, George "Buck" Flower, Otis Young, Wally Flaherty, Randolph Scott II, Janus Raudkivi and Randolph Rebane. Produced by Bill Rebane, M. Dan Stroick, William D. Cannon, Peter Fink and Elwyn O. Jarvis. Written by Ingrid Neumayer, Bill Rebane and John F. Goff. Directed by Bill Rebane. USA. Color. Mono. 92 Minutes.

Overview: When two locals are slaughtered in the desolate, snow-blanketed Wisconsin mountains, a man named Olsen — a small-time entrepreneur who dreams of striking it rich — believes "the Legendary Creature of Arak" (the local Indian name for Sasquatch) is the responsible culprit. Twenty-five years earlier the same "legend" had slaughtered townsfolk, only to escape capture, so Olsen is as sure of his local history as he is of Arak's gold mine status for the lucky

Poster art for the theatrical release of *The Capture of Bigfoot*.

"owner" of said creature. Sensing his fast buck chance is close at hand, he hires a covert crew of trappers to capture the beast alive so that he can exhibit it and transform his tiny ski hamlet into an internationally famous resort.

During the hunt the woodsmen wound Little Bigfoot, Arak's offspring, but fail to capture the parent creature itself. Unobserved by the men, a boy witnesses the shooting of the immature Bigfoot and rushes home to inform his adult sister Karen. She in turn enlists the help of Steve Garrett, a local game warden, with whom she is romantically involved.

Word spreads in the tiny town of Olsen's insane attempts to capture Arak and exploit the beast for profit. Cooper, the town's sheriff, warns Olsen to call it off, fearful of an even higher body count should the search continue, but the single-minded businessman will not be deterred.

An elderly drunk named Jake seeks the help of an Indian shaman, who gives Garrett an amulet that will protect the wearer from Arak's wrath. Meanwhile, Olsen ensnares Arak and holds the monster against its will in an abandoned mine shaft. Garrett intervenes, helping Arak to freedom. Olsen engages the warden in a life and death struggle, which Olsen loses, consumed by flames as the mine shaft explodes. Arak rejoins its offspring. They share a poignant moment, exchanging looks with Garrett, Karen and her little brother, before wandering back into the wilderness.

* * * * *

Bill Rebane, the Wisconsin filmmaker who brought such notorious drive-in fodder as *The Giant Spider Invasion*, *Monster a Go-Go* and *Rana: The Legend of Shadow Lake* to quasi-life, began his career as a regional booker of film rentals for the major Hollywood studios. Deciding to return to his roots in Wisconsin, he built his own mini-studio and, utilizing family and friends in his community, created a

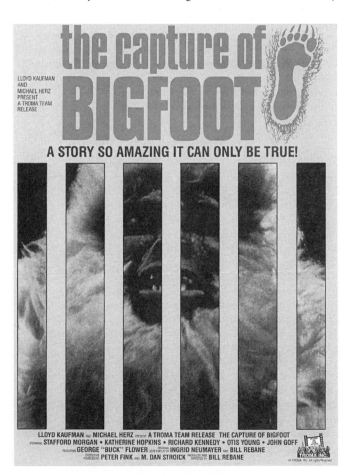

Promotional flyer for the Troma Films VHS release of *The Capture of Bigfoot*. (Courtesy Troma Studios.)

thriving if modest exploitation fiefdom of his own. Like other regional independents before and after him, such as Larry "Texas" Buchanan, Don "Baltimore" Dohler and Earl "North Carolina" Owensby, Rebane gambled that audiences would appreciate any locally-lensed entertainment as a contrast to the steady diet of films coming only from tinsel town. More often than not he was correct, as his box office receipts proved.

As long as each picture was micro-budgeted, it produced enough revenue to cover expenditure costs and finance the next film in the cycle. While never producing box-office spectaculars that earned the national film rentals achieved by Hollywood, Rebane nevertheless carved out a niche market for himself and his tiny studio that the majors, needing vastly larger grosses per picture in order to maintain their stranglehold on monopoly distribution practices, simply couldn't enter without losing money (losing money being as antithetical in studio practice as a corporate ex–CEO leaving behind a non-depleted employee pension fund). So rather than take a loss, the studios simply turned a blind eye, much as they did with Roger Corman.

As a result, Rebane and the other "states right" (or territorially-divided but not nationally-oriented) producers enjoyed considerable freedom both artistically as well as financially, having no studio-dictated censorship to answer to and being able to keep a majority of the profits for themselves. This in turn funded the local economies where such mini-studios were located, requiring as they did skilled labor, raw supplies, and related services. Throughout the 1960s and into the early 1980s this model was not atypical, however difficult to sustain. Not until the arrival of videocassettes in the 1980s did the system become untenable. As drive-in theaters closed nationwide, they left only the tiniest of windows open for Rebane and other once-thriving independent producers through which to theatrically screen their product.

The Capture of Bigfoot is not only a typical Ciné du Sasquatch effort, it is a prime example of Rebane's own output: Take a sensationalized concept that the majors wouldn't touch (a cryptid or a giant arachnid, for example) and make it as quickly and cheaply as possible into an exploitable feature film. The goal was less quality oriented than simply having a final product to screen at drive-ins, where the movie would play to a weekend crowd of necking teens before moving on to the next drive-in nearby, thus avoiding any need for critical recognition or praise. More important than any true entertainment experience, in short, was an enticing poster and preview reel that inevitably promised more than the feature delivered.

In order to create a more legitimate sense of professional production values, Rebane used the tried-and-true exploitation formula of casting former marquee names or character actors underutilized in Hollywood due to age and placing them in smaller roles, while filling out the lead parts with local talent. This allowed him to put recognizable names on the posters and in the previews without incurring the cost of paying top salaries. In *The Capture of Bigfoot*, Rebane casts veteran character actor George "Buck" Flower, a later favorite of John Carpenter in such films as *Starman*, *They Live* and *Escape from New York*, but who also had a long line of prior credits in such drive-in fare as *Ilsa, She Wolf of the SS*; *The Daring Dobermans*; and *Delinquent School Girls*.

As far as Ciné du Sasquatch goes *The Capture of Bigfoot* shares a myriad of common traits: amateur acting, bad dialogue, stilted characters, leaden pacing, unbelievable special effects and hackneyed plotting. The only redeeming quality that elevates the film is the location photography, which, to Rebane's credit, is shot entirely in snowbound cabins and forests. Not unlike *Snowbeast* (which it resembles, given the ski lodge setting mixed with an "Abominable Snowman on a rampage" plotline), *The Capture of Bigfoot* possesses an authentic sense that the setting is indeed remote and isolated.

Apart from this salient quality and the always entertaining "Buck" Flower cameo (who's woefully underutilized but screen-dominant whenever present), *The Capture of Bigfoot* is a wooden (or is that Ed Wood-ian?) exercise in tedium. The focus is sadly not on Arak, but on the ill-conceived and badly performed human characters, all of whom are closer to monotypes than stereotypes. Scant screen time is given to the titular capture or cryptid itself, and far too much is wasted delineating annoyingly "cute" bits of human interaction (such as a tiresome sheriff, played by Wally Flaherty, who literally spends his screen time imitating Humphrey Bogart and John Wayne, despite other characters telling him his impersonations are horrible).

Likewise the obsessed Olsen is a one-note Johnny from frame one, as played by Richard Kennedy, another drive-in veteran chewing scenery as if it were beef jerky. He also appeared in *Invasion of the Blood Farmers*, *French Emmanuelle*, and *Fangs*, but this is his biggest-ever role in terms of screen time, if not ham-fisted delivery. He plays his character like Ahab stalking the great white whale. The problem with this performance is that there is no motivation for Olsen's pathological need to capture Arak. Unlike Captain Ahab, who lost a leg; Captain Hook, who lost a hand; or even Captain Quint from *Jaws*, who lost hundreds of his fellow shipmen to sharks in the sinking of the U.S.S. Indianapolis; Olsen is not seeking metaphysical revenge. He mumbles at one point about a half-baked scheme to use the captured monster to put his nowhere Cedar Park hamlet on the map and transform it into the premiere ski resort of its type, but it's all so much banal conceit. Never is Olsen portrayed as anything less than hell-bent in his desires, and as a result, even one of the hunters he hires mumbles shortly before the capture of Arak that "Olsen has gone crazy." Given there's no doubt Olsen is deranged from the beginning, one is left to wonder just how observant these supposed "hardy backwoods types" truly are not to have noticed their employer's mouth-frothing mental instability much earlier, especially as he endlessly and remorselessly sends them to their grisly fates, courtesy of Arak.

"Buck" Flower fares much better. His untimely death is the most effective moment of horror in *The Capture of Bigfoot*, mainly because Flower humanizes his brief cameo and thus creates viewer empathy. Olsen runs him over and kills him on a deserted mountain roadway when he chances upon the grizzled hermit. Flower runs down the middle of the icy path until Olsen finally catches up (why not leap aside to safety?), which is uncharacteristically idiotic, given that Flower's Jake is the one character who comes across as intelligent. What little charm the movie possessed disappears with Flower's death, and the remainder skis downhill faster than any vacationer Olsen ever imagined hitting the proverbial slopes.

Two genre notes are worthy of mention in regards to *The Capture of Bigfoot*. First is the presentation of Arak. The viewer is lead to believe from both the one-sheet theatrical poster and the film's title that the cryptid will be Bigfoot. Yet the creature bears no resemblance to either the usual Bigfoot description or the dark-haired monster on the poster. Arak is shown to be white and furry, more accurately resembling a Himalayan Yeti. The Arak costume appears to be more an albino snowsuit than animal hide, which probably served at least one practical purpose — it kept the actor inside warm during night location shoots in snowy locales. The Arak mask is slightly better detailed than in many other Yeti movies, but it still more closely resembles a standard white gorilla mask than anything else.

The other noteworthy aspect is the theme song. Charles Pierce's *The Legend of Boggy Creek* and its influential use of country ballads to set the mood cannot be underestimated, as *The Capture of Bigfoot* illustrates during its opening moments. Not only did Pierce create many iconographic moments in Ciné du Sasquatch with his 1972 genre-defining effort (the rarely glimpsed creature; the rural assaults on cabin-bound inhabitants; the ubiquitous moment wherein Bigfoot smashes a grasping hand through a window), he also pioneered the use of a folksy theme song to decry man's inhumanity to nature and thus imbue his creature with a sense of pathos even before the title credits end. Like Howard Hawks' use of a theme song in his classic westerns, such as *Rio Bravo*, it is designed to at once evoke an era and locale, as well as sum up the film's themes in a lyrical haiku. Alas, the crooner who warbles Rebane's title song makes it feel like "paneful" window dressing. Not only is the song bad in a camp sense, but it begins the film with a ridiculously hokey false note from which *The Capture of Bigfoot* sadly never recovers.

Caveman (1981) (Cameo)

Starring Ringo Starr, Barbara Bach, Dennis Quaid, Shelley Long, Jack Gilford, Ed Greenberg, John Matuszak, Avery Schreiber and Richard Moll. Produced by David Foster and Lawrence Turman. Written by Rudy De Luca and Carl Gottlieb. Directed by Carl Gottlieb. USA. Color. Mono. 91 Minutes.

Overview: Atouk the caveman lusts after Lana, the beautiful mate of his tribe's brutish leader, Tonda. Tired of the needless competition, Tonda banishes Atouk into the wilds of prime dinosaur-hunting territory to fend for himself. Lar, Atouk's equally dumb friend, is also thrown out of his former tribe. Together the two attempt to forge survival skills without the help of their former cave people.

As they make their way through the dry, desolate lands, Atouk and Lar stumble into a series of misadventures, including an encounter with a long-limbed Abominable Snowman in the cryptid's cave. Each step along the way brings additional members into their outcast tribe of rejects (all of whom have been excommunicated from their former clans: a gay caveman couple; a blind caveman; a dwarf caveman and other assorted misfits. The nascent band of brothers learn to survive the harsh climate by discovering the secrets of fire, how to roast dinosaur meat and even how to defend themselves against the peabrained "terrible lizards" that formerly preyed upon them.

Dissatisfied with his banishment from his former tribe, and emboldened by his newly-acquired leadership skills, Atouk returns to his former tribe to challenge the brute strength of Tonda and hopefully win the sexy Lana for his own mate.

* * * * *

Ringo Starr is perhaps the ultimate acquired taste in comedies. As a former Beatle, his likeable if underwhelming personality was perfectly balanced against the other three Fab Four members in *A Hard Day's Night* and *Help!*, offering lightweight comic relief. But minus the serious anarchy of John Lennon and the puppy dog charm of Paul McCartney (not to mention the wizened, sleepy-eyed presence of George Harrison), Ringo's solo appearances tend to run the gamut from bad to tolerable. *Caveman* is, surprisingly, one of the highlights from his otherwise less successful if sporadic post–Beatles cinematic career, along with his fun (if Peter Sellers–shouldered) turn as Youngman Grand, Esquire, in *The Magic Christian*.

The film is a pastiche of caveman movie clichés that often feel strained even for such an obviously campy outing. The plot is a straight lift from *One Million Years B.C.* (itself a remake of the 1940 Hal Roach film *One Million B.C.*), starring Raquel Welch, with the Tumak character (played in the Welch version by John Richardson, and by Victor Mature in the 1940 version) here portrayed by Starr, renamed (barely!) Atouk. Instead of having to unite the Rock Tribe and Shell Tribe, as Tumak strives to do, Atouk must refine a group of misfit cavemen rejects into one cohesive unit for survival. And whereas the earlier films played the human vs. dinosaur battles seriously (a ridiculous concept, of course, in terms of any credible scientific evidence), *Caveman* plays them for laughs (the dinosaur mo-

ments are definitely the source of some of the belabored film's best jokes).

The sequence wherein Ringo Starr and his motley crew stumble into the ice cavern of the Abominable Snowman is a brief but memorable highlight. The strange yet comedic design by special effects artist Chris Walas (who also did *The Fly* costume for the David Cronenberg version) features a hominid with exaggeratedly long limbs, two saber-tooth tusks, and long hair (like a cryptid hippie's shag). As it stumbles along the icy floor of its cave as ineffectively as Atouk and his fleeing tribesmen, genuine moments of comedy arise. Though lasting but a few minutes of screen time, the sequence (along with some of the charming stop-motion dinosaur scenes begun by Jim Danforth before a falling out with producers lead to the animation being completed by Dave Allen and Jim Aupperle) is among the least offensive in a movie rife (or is that ripe?) with fart and poop jokes. When the Yeti is left alone and realizes its newfound playmates have deserted it, it sadly sighs and slumps its shoulders, slowly shuffling away to yet again while away the lonely hours as the perennial Other and Outsider. It's a bleakly comical moment, but one that also touches a chord of pathos that frequently arises in portrayals of cinematic hominids — the *Last of the Mohicans* syndrome incarnate.

No new ground is broken in terms of Ciné du Sasquatch in *Caveman*, but it's good for cheap laughs and amusing dinosaurs if the viewer is in a tolerant mood.

Celebrity Deathmatch ("Loch Ness Monster vs. Bigfoot") (1998) (TV)

AKA: *MTV's Celebrity Deathmatch*. Featuring the voices of Maurice Schlafer, Len Maxwell, Mills Lane, Jim Thornton, Chris Edgerly, Masasa Moyo, Steve Austin and Debbie Matenopoulos. Produced by Eric Fogel, Morghan Fortier, Tally Barr and Ed Robinson. Written by Eric Fogel, Matt Harrigan, Aubrey Ankrum, Jed Elinoff, Scott Alan Thomas, Tally Barr, Reid Harrison, Alan P. Cross, Randolph Heard, Scott Prendergast, John T. Reynolds, Scott Sonneborn and Jed Spingarn. Directed by Andrew Horne, Jack Fletcher and Dave Thomas. USA. Color. Stereo. 30 Minutes.

Overview: Various celebrities meet in a wrestling ring, whereupon they fight to the death. A set of announcers offer color commentary to television viewers while audience members cheer and boo the celebrities.

* * * * *

Before *Robot Chicken* there was *Celebrity Deathmatch*. Each episode would bring together claymated (and foam latex models designed to resemble claymation) celebrities from the worlds of movies, music, sports and TV, with occasional politicians and assorted examples of the famous and infamous. The battles were typically short-lived and brutally violent, and often resulted in the bloody deaths of not only the combatants but of audience members as well.

In "Loch Ness Monster vs. Bigfoot," the two most well-known cryptozoological specimens in the world enter the ring in what is billed as the "Largest *Clay*-Per-View" event in TV history. With Sean Connery in the audience cheering on the Scottish legend, and guest announcer "Stone Cold" Steve Austin of the World Wrestling Federation offering technical analysis for home viewers, Nessie launches into action as soon as the bell sounds. Unprepared for the Loch Ness Monster's sudden whip of its tail, Bigfoot is cleaved neatly in half. Blood splattering from both halves, the wounded Sasquatch falls to the mat and is quickly pronounced the loser. Abandoning the wrestling ring, Nessie scoops up Fran Drescher in the audience and spirits her away to make love. Later in the show he returns to assist in a battle between David Letterman and Jay Leno.

Despite the deliberately crude nature of the animation (and content as well), "Loch Ness Monster vs. Bigfoot" is a funny segment. It ironically points out how rarely any two variant forms of cryptid creatures are ever present together onscreen (leave it to MTV to break the "Fortean species" barrier!). While it's reminiscent of the type of well-executed fan-based video one might find on YouTube, only an uptight fan of Ciné du Sasquatch would fail to laugh at the unexpectedly rapid demise of their favorite hairy hominid. Given the gargantuan size advantage enjoyed by Nessie, the outcome was definitely predictable (albeit premature), even by *Celebrity Deathmatch* standards. While the violence is never much worse than *Robot Chicken* (upon which this series had an obvious influence), it's not for the very young.

Charmed ("Wendigo") (1999) (TV)

Starring Shannen Doherty, Holly Marie Combs, Alyssa Milano, Ted King, Jocelyn Seagrave, Billy Jayne, J. Karen Thomas and Christina Milian. Produced by Sheryl J. Anderson, Tony Blake, Constance M. Burge, Peter Chomsky, Paul Jackson, Brad Kern, Jonathan Levin, Betty Reardon, Les Sheldon, Aaron Spelling and E. Duke Vincent. Written by Edithe Swensen. Directed by James L. Conway. USA. Color. Stereo. 60 Minutes.

Overview: The Halliwell sisters — Prue, Piper and Phoebe — are modern-day witches, each attuned to respective supernatural abilities and dedicated to fighting evil wherever they encounter it, all the while maintaining a facade of normal, everyday citizens. But when Piper is attacked by a vicious cryptid while attempting to repair her car's flat tire one night in a city park, and saved at the last moment by Billy, a total stranger, the sisters realize their lives are about to take the usual turn into solving another paranormal case.

Billy confesses to the sisters that he had lost his fiancé to the same creature while camping in Michigan and has been tracking it across the countryside. FBI Special Agent Ashley Fallon arrives at the hospital where Piper is recovering, as does local inspector Andy Trudeau. Fallon confirms the creature has indeed been involved in a series of unsolved homicides nationally, though Trudeau remains skeptical.

After she is released and recovers at home, Piper decides to help Billy, despite warnings from Prue and Phoebe not to get involved until she's feeling better. Piper is grateful, however, to Billy for risking his life to save hers and wants to use her white magic to thwart another preventable homicide. She meets with Billy and gathers enough information to consult a book of witchcraft, which helps her identify the mysterious creature as a Wendigo. According to the lore, a Wendigo — a kind of Sasquatch with the ability to transform from human to beast for three nights in a row once each month — is the culprit. Worse, the Wendigo devours its victims' hearts by ripping them out while the victim is still alive. It also needs a rare blood type, which limits its potential human hunting pool.

Billy has a conversation with Agent Fallon wherein he tells her Piper has discovered that the guilty cryptid is a Wendigo. When Billy lights a cigarette, causing Fallon to recoil in horror, Billy — knowing a Wendigo fears flame — realizes she has been the shape-shifter all along. The Wendigo snaps his head and leaves him for dead in a parking lot, intent on next killing Piper to keep her identity a secret.

Alas for Fallon, Trudeau visits Piper first, arriving moments before her. Fallon peppers Piper with questions, trying to determine if Piper has guessed the identity of the Wendigo. But Piper has become ill with the virus of the Wendigo's bite and is unable to mentally focus. Trudeau urges her to rest. He and Fallon agree to stake out the local park, realizing that this is the third night and that the Wendigo will most likely strike where it has attempted to previously feed. Fallon brazenly discusses the possibility of having sex with Trudeau, but

Trudeau — who has previously dated Prue and is therefore preoccupied with Piper's condition — is a bit put off and refuses to take her up on her offer, citing professional obligations to their current case.

Prue and Phoebe realize Piper is now infected and will become a Wendigo herself. Worse yet, Phoebe's psychic ability shows her Agent Fallon's true identity as the murderous monster. Prue and Phoebe handcuff Piper to a pipe in the attic and race to the park to save Prue's former boyfriend, Inspector Trudeau. As soon as they're gone, however, Piper transforms into a Wendigo herself and smashes through the attic's window, fleeing into the night.

At the park, Trudeau comments on how ironic it is that he has the same rare blood type as Piper, which makes him a potential victim of the Wendigo himself. Moments later, Fallon turns into her Wendigo form and knocks Fallon unconscious, hovering over him to feed. Prue and Phoebe arrive at the park, armed with a flare gun to do battle for Trudeau's life. The Wendigo tries to attack them, but the sisters fire flares, each of which temporarily blinds the beast and forces it to retreat into the protective tree line. With only one flare left, Prue and Phoebe realize they have placed themselves in a hopeless situation.

Without warning, a second Wendigo — obviously Piper in her cryptid form — arrives. Neither Prue nor Phoebe know which Wen-

Piper Halliwell (Holly Marie Combs) is stalked by the Wendigo in this staged publicity shot for *Charmed*.

digo is Fallon. Phoebe fires the flare at Piper, believing she has fired it at Fallon. Piper uses her special witchcraft power of freezing objects to make the flare hover in place, and then she redirects it into the chest of Fallon. The Fallon Wendigo falls to the ground, writhing and screaming, before it vanishes in a puff of smoke. Piper transforms back into her human form, and Trudeau, though unconscious, is alive. The sisters later celebrate with drinks at the bar where Piper works as manager.

*****

Charmed lead a charmed life as a television series, running for 8 consecutive years (albeit with cast changes during the tenure). Another Aaron Spelling production in a long line of storied successes, *Charmed* was like a modern variation of Spelling's own *Charlie's Angels*—but with three nubile witches in place of the three nubile detectives. Using all sorts of excuses and innuendo in every episode to highlight the attractive comeliness of the three protagonists and their relaxed sexuality (in this episode, for example, Phoebe just happens to have a pair of handcuffs in her bedroom when the sisters need to restrain Piper; Prue asks why Phoebe has them, whereupon Phoebe nonchalantly shrugs and grins, embarrassed by the obvious answer). With generally lighthearted if workmanlike scripts, the show was an undeniable success, especially among young females who found the trio to be worthy role models in their relentless pursuit of using their "white wiccan" powers for good (if not equally the Halliwell sisters' striking sense of style and fashion accessories).

"Wendigo" is an above average example from the series, coming as it did in the first season when the concept was still fresh. Although riddled with plot holes and some forced exposition in regards to the Wendigo's nature (for example, it must devour victims of a certain rare blood type and only during a full moon, but *only* if killing a victim will metaphorically destroy the love bond between said victim and an associate... whew!), the show works hard to keep a fast pace and add turns to the narrative. Alas, the "whodunit" aspect is obvious from the beginning, as there are no other viable suspects in the story besides FBI Agent Fallon. From the moment she strides into her introductory shot, the arch portrayal by Jocelyn Seagrave as Fallon leaves little doubt about her true nature. The revelation that she is the Wendigo is made early on as well, which reduces suspense.

The idea of a Wendigo is interesting in terms of Ciné du Sasquatch because it is a rare incorporation of the "shape shifter" example of a cryptid. Most posit the Bigfoot in question as either natural but unknown, or supernatural but of one corporeal form. Herein the Wendigo is much more like the classic werewolf, transforming during a full moon and seeking out those it loves most to destroy first, if possible. This is very unusual in the Bigfoot genre and a positive, in that *Charmed* handles it well in terms of clarity and originality. It would have been a lot easier, after all, if Piper had simply been attacked by a Sasquatch, however unmotivated. Though convoluted at times, "Wendigo" nevertheless entertains as a familiar but well-crafted hour-long television show dealing with a homicidal hominid.

The depiction of the Wendigo is almost werewolf-ish, which is appropriate, given the basic lift of the lycanthrope legend. Less understandable is the entire "it must eat the heart of the one it loves" idea mixed with the "it must drink the blood of a certain rare blood type" concept; surely one or the other necessity was enough (with confusion being the outcome as written). It is interesting to speculate that these ideas originated with the Algonquian Natives who are recorded as the creators of the Wendigo myth; their version involves a ghastly fear of turning into a Wendigo if a person devours human flesh. Such an act of cannibalism can lead to one being possessed by the spirit of the Wendigo. The description of the Wendigo, however, is so far removed from Sasquatch as to bar inclusion as a cryptid. Among the Cree, Ojibwa, Saulteaux, Innu, Naskapi and Montagnais

tribes, the being was described as resembling an emaciated, elongated corpse with mummified flesh tautly stretched across the monster's bones. *Charmed*'s "Wendigo" follows the gaunt skin idea but otherwise plays the cryptid as distinctly Bigfoot in bodily form, with head-to-toe hair and a bulky body to match.

As an interesting bit of trivia, director James Conway had previously served as an associate producer on the Peter Graves–hosted *The Mysterious Monsters* Bigfoot documentary, which is a fondly-remembered entry in the Ciné du Sasquatch genre. He occupies a rare niche in Ciné du Sasquatch, one shared by only a handful of other filmmakers (such as Robert Morgan, with his documentaries and *Bloodstalkers*) who have made both fictional and factual movies or TV shows about cryptids.

Chill Out, Scooby Doo! (2007)

Featuring the voices of Rene Auberjonois, Jeff Bennett, Mindy Cohn, Grey DeLisle, Kim Mai Guest, James Hong, Casey Kasem, Alfred Molina, James Sie and Frank Welker. Produced by Joseph Barbera, Margaret M. Dean, Vera Morales, Sander Schwartz and Joe Sichta. Written by Thommy Hutson, Adam Scheinman, Joe Sichta and Catherine Trillo. Directed by Joe Sichta. USA. Color. Stereo. 90 Minutes.

Overview: When the Mystery, Inc., gang decides to take a little down time away from solving cases, they head for Paris. Daphne, Fred and Velma arrive earlier than Scooby Doo and Shaggy, owing to Scooby and Shaggy taking a new cut-rate airline that offers unlimited meals while in flight. Alas, the airline is but a cargo plane charade run by Alphonse LaFleur, the world's self-billed greatest hunter. LaFleur is only transporting the duo of ravenous crime stoppers to the Himalayan Mountains in order to use them as bait for the Yeti, which he intends to shoot. Before Shaggy and Scooby can escape, LaFleur throws them out of the plane inside a box. The box deploys a parachute, and LaFleur parachutes after them. During the drift down to Mount Everest, however, Scooby and Shaggy are separated from the hunter.

Meanwhile, Professor Jeffries, an American seeking the lost kingdom of Shangri-La, and Pemba, his Sherpa guide, encounter the legendary Abominable Snowman and barely escape with their lives. They soon meet up with Shaggy and Scooby inside a Buddhist monastery. There the High Lama is alarmed when he learns that Scooby Doo has accidentally uncovered the monks' deepest-held secret: a priceless gem that wards away the Abominable Snowman from harming them. Furthermore, the High Lama intones that they must be wary if they go higher into the mountains, as the Yeti will surely destroy them as guardian of the lost valley.

Shaggy and Scooby, frightened, initially wish to heed the Lama's warning. Their wits are somewhat calmed when LaFleur arrives, admits his true identity and offers them protection with his various high-tech hunting weaponry. Professor Jeffries soon convinces them that the only way Shaggy and Scooby have of possibly contacting Fred, Daphne and Velma is to scale the mountain to a weather station outpost. There the only satellite service available can be utilized to alert the worried Mystery, Inc. members as to Shaggy and Scooby's safety and whereabouts. The worried canine and hipster agree, not knowing Fred is already driving Velma and Daphne in a rented van towards Mount Everest (though they've already become lost themselves owing to a faulty map).

A snowstorm hits the mountains while Shaggy, Scooby, the Professor, LaFleur and Pemba journey to the weather station. Minga, Pemba's sister, accompanies them after Pemba has warned her not to do so owing to the dangerous cryptid. An encounter at night with the Snowman, however, splits Shaggy and Scooby from the rest of their party. They arrive alone at the weather station, only to find that the smooth-talking, music-spinning deejay who broadcasts from the isolated hut is none other than Del Chillman. Del is a renowned cryptozoologist who the Mystery, Inc., team encountered while stalking the Loch Ness Monster.

With Chillman's help, the team of motley sleuths are soon together again. But can they stop the Abominable Snowman from attacking them when they try to return to civilization? And who is behind the attempts to steal the priceless gem that protects the villagers below from the hominid?

* * * * *

Scooby Doo and pals have racked up three Ciné du Sasquatch encounters in their filmic and televised adventures. The first came in the original animated 1969 TV series *Scooby Doo, Where Are You!* in an episode called "That's Snow Ghost." The next was in the 1972 hour-and-a-half-long reincarnation of the first series called *The New Scooby Doo Movies*, in an episode called "Scooby Doo Meets Laurel & Hardy," which featured the so-called Ghost of Bigfoot. And finally there was this 2007 feature-length production, which is perhaps the most impressive of the lot (at least in terms of technical achievement, devotion to actual Yeti lore and the Abominable's screen time).

Having the gang meet up with a Yeti seems only natural (or is that *un*natural?), given the plethora of vampires, werewolves, ghosts, goblins, aliens, zombies, mummies and other monsters and/or thugs pretending to be as much in order to "get away with" their criminal activities (the latter being the classic and oft-repeated "revelation" at the conclusion of the original series, in which the bad guys were unmasked or shown to be hoaxing the scares) Scooby, Shaggy, Fred, Daphne and Velma battled over the four decades of their existence. Arguably one of the most successful franchises in Saturday morning animation history, the characters have emerged from their modest but successful initial run as cartoon spook busters into full-fledged icons in motion pictures, DVDs, toys, games and even theme park rides. In short, they are every bit the equal to their hominid counterpart, Sasquatch, in terms of cultural pop appeal and instant recognition.

Chill Out, Scooby Doo! has several advantages over the older series, not least of which is that it offers higher production values than the Hannah/Barbera shows. While the duo are acknowledged in the credits, the animation and production chores were actually handled by Warner Brothers, who own the rights to the characters. The increased monies and digital animation techniques allow for more complex shots and color shading that is superior to the limited, jerky movements seen in the original two series. This makes for a very saturated look for *Chill Out*, which helps makes the characters seem much more fully-realized and literally fleshed out. While the storyline is not the most original, it's generally pleasing to the intended audiences of young Scooby Doo lovers, as well as the more tolerant "first generation" older fans.

One nice touch is the continuity between this effort and *Scooby Doo and the Loch Ness Monster* via the Del Chillman character, who is a cryptozoologist. The recognition factor of what a cryptozoological investigator does is so well-known in the culture by this point in Ciné du Sasquatch that only the merest of cursory explanations has to be offered to unfamiliar viewers about what the field of study represents and its intended goals. This is quite a change from the days when Bigfoot movies never even utilized the word "cryptozoology" (if they referenced the token scientist's profession, they usually characterized them as being anthropologists). Del Chillman offers a fun, lighthearted way for children to immerse themselves in the mysteries of the unknown without having to rely on the Mystery, Inc., gang for exclusive exposition. Fred and Daphne seem incredulously naïve to the reality of cryptozoology, given their long history of encounters with Sasquatch and Snow Ghost; they even profess during the

Parisian scenes prior to their departure to the Himalayas to have never heard of the Abominable Snowman! Given that they encountered a Yeti in "That's Snow Ghost!" and later Bigfoot's Ghost in "Scooby Doo Meet Laurel & Hardy," one has to question just how severe are Fred and Daphne's short-term memory problems. Fred cannot even mouth the word "abominable" without error, which truly strains believability given his endless encounters with every weird creature in existence (including cryptids) prior to this adventure. Surely this is a case of the writers failing to properly research and exploit the characters' prior episodes; it would have made the premise all the more entertaining if the amateur sleuths realized this wasn't the first time they'd battled a Yeti.

It's a small drawback to what is an otherwise enjoyable cartoon outing. The voice talents of character actors par excellence Rene Auberjonois (the 1976 *King Kong* and *The Eyes of Laura Mars*); as the French hunter LaFleur, and Alfred Molina (*Spiderman 2*'s Doc Ock) add panache to what are thankless roles. But for sheer, gravel-voiced impact, none top James Hong (*Big Trouble in Little China* and the indelible Mr. Chew from *Bladerunner*) as the High Lama. Hong's instantly recognizable intonations give the animated monk leader a sense of sinister dread no amount of animation could imbue. With a career stretching back to the 1950s, and almost 350 film and TV credits to his name, he is truly the elder statesman present, even given the others on hand in *Chill Out, Scooby Doo!*— indeed, that's perhaps the highest compliment to his impressive abilities. Too, one would be remiss if the perennial value of Casey Kassem as Shaggy wasn't noted, as Kassem's scratchy vocals are the essence of the bony slacker's characteristic high-pitched delivery of such signature expressions as "Like, wow, man!" and "Zoiks!"

For those Ciné du Sasquatch fans who don't mind a lot of slapstick and puns (not to mention a snack-obsessed, pseudo-talking dog), *Chill Out, Scooby Doo!* offers a lighthearted Yeti experience that is well-animated if predictably tame. It's perfect for both the budding young crypto as well as nostalgic-minded adults.

Chilly Beach ("Not Without My Yeti") (2004) (TV)

Featuring the voices of Steve Ashton, Damon D'Oliveira, Dwayne Hill, Robert Smith, Samantha Espie and Mary Lawliss. Produced by Daniel Hawes. Written by Brian Hartigan. Directed by Edin Ibric. Canada. Color. Stereo. 30 Minutes.

Overview: Dale and Frank, two Canadian xenophobes, have spent their entire lives in Chilly Beach, a remote tourist trap town that rarely sees a tourist, let alone entices one to actually stay long enough to spend money. Chilly Beach's bad reputation for travelers may derive from its having been literally built atop an ice floe that is perpetually moving somewhere in the northernmost Canadian waters. Having lived mainly on a mass consumption of beer and endless hockey games, Dale and Frank are decidedly provincial in a manner as extreme as their environment, but are positively worldly in comparison to the rest of the eccentrics who barely populate their frozen wasteland of a small town.

When Angus, an irate Scottish-accented hunter with a dislike for all humanity, captures a Yeti, hopes are reborn in tiny Chilly Beach that their long-cherished desire to become a destination rivaling Disney World may at long last be within their frozen grasp. While the Abominable Snowman is caged for display, Angus falls victim to Celebrity Stockholm Syndrome, at first becoming a resentful prisoner to his sudden fame but then pleased that he can charge fast bucks for little more than autographing photos of his captured Yeti. Alas, all plans to exploit the creature for further material gain come to a crashing halt when the Yeti's enraged family smash the tiny village to smithereens and free their imprisoned relative, leaving the town in ruins and its seemingly existential fate as the frozen hell hole of the Earth.

* * * * *

Clearly influenced by the animated success of *South Park* and its look at the myopia that pervades its titular Colorado town, *Chilly Beach* is like a Canadian redux of its more famous Southern cousin, right down to the deliberately crude animation style, off-color humor (although nowhere near as raunchy in language or scatological references) and Swiftian satire of all things sacred to Canuck culture. As such, a lot of the jokes play too inside for many American viewers, but as the show was primarily aimed at Canadians and produced by Canadians, this seems a trivial critique at best.

Dale and Frank, the bone-headed but well-intentioned lead characters, are reminiscent of Bob and Doug McKenzie, who achieved fame via *SCTV* with their Canadian public access parody show "The Great White North" and later their own theatrical movie *Strange Brew*. Like Bob and Doug, Dale and Frank spend their wintery days obsessed with hockey stats, swilling beer and generally remaining as oblivious to any outside influences as their alcohol-addled brains can defend them against. When the occasional bear attack occurs in "downtown" Chilly Beach and some helpless local is eaten (which is a running gag akin to *South Park*'s having Kenny being killed every episode), the chuckleheaded duo summon their wits long enough to scurry to safety. As soon as the threat level decreases, they slump back into their mental hibernation.

The Yeti that Angus captures is truly massive, as drawn by the animators. Not unlike the Bumble from *Rudolph, the Red-Nosed Reindeer*, it is a towering behemoths of a hominid, not to be trifled with unless one is eager to tempt fate. Easily 15 feet in height and immense in girth, the Snowmen are depicted as having their own language (which is presented in subtitles) and are basically your run-of-the-mill small-town types. One of the female cryptids, for example, wears perpetual hair curlers like they were a cap and berates the timid males (not unlike the treatment Fred Flintstone constantly received from the domineering Wilma). The Yetis show evident disgust at having to wreak havoc in the human community to liberate their captured family member, as if it were akin to having to bail out a drunken relative from jail late one night. They scare the terrified citizens of Chilly Beach with an ease bordering on outright boredom because it is all without effort and clearly so *de rigueur* for them.

Though *Chilly Beach* is squarely aimed at Canadian viewers, fans of Ciné du Sasquatch will find some amusing moments in the treatment of the Yeti tribe, simply because of the universality of the cryptozoological community. If anything, "Not Without My Yeti" demonstrates the ubiquitous nature of the Abominable Snowman figure, which long ago transcended the Himalayan Mountains of its origin and rapidly spread across the globe — even to a tiny, self-described backwater burg like Chilly Beach.

Choose Your Own Adventure: The Abominable Snowman (2006)

Starring the voices of William H. Macy, Frankie Muniz, Felicity Huffman and Mark Hamill. Directed by Bob Doucette. USA. Color. Stereo. 85 Minutes.

Overview: Based on the popular series of "Choose Your Own Adventure" children's books, this first-ever adaptation to home video is a visually dense, technically well-produced piece of DVD interactivity. *Choose Your Own Adventure: The Abominable Snowman* introduces the younger viewer to many key cryptozoology concepts and terminologies in an easy-to-navigate, intriguing adventure story format. The plot follows the three North family children — Ben, Marco, and Crista — as they journey to Nepal in search of their missing uncle, who is voiced by co-producer William H. Macy. Naturally, all roads with clues relating to the vanished explorer eventually lead back to the Abominable Snowman, who is key to the mystery.

Like the beloved "gimmick" books upon which this movie is based, *Choose Your Own Adventure: The Abominable Snowman* is not for all tastes. That the viewer must choose at key plot points and said decision affects the story's outcome (slightly, at any rate, as all roads lead inexorably towards the same pre-determined finale) will bore some who wish merely to entertain their tykes or themselves with a passive storyline that unfolds conventionally. But those who wish to jazz up their crypto-viewing and engage younger watchers will find the well-designed interactivity a breeze to use and never intrusive beyond merely offering a way to spice up what is otherwise a conventional Sasquatch outing. The animation is very anime-influenced, with a bold separation of outlined characters from their backgrounds that is almost the visual antithesis of the influential *Adventures of Tintin* series, which featured a blended style of equal line width throughout its meticulously illustrated panels. It just displays the fluidity of Ciné du Sasquatch in that two vastly different aesthetic approaches can work equally well without denigrating the underlying tenets of the genre. With wonderful voice talents that included Mark Hamill and Felicity Huffman, *Choose Your Own Adventure: The*

Cover art for the DVD release of *Choose Your Own Adventure: The Abominable Snowman*.

Abominable Snowman is a good example of Bigfoot films transcending the formal narrative conventions via interactive choice but still maintaining the underlying themes and obsessions of Ciné du Sasquatch.

Clawed: *The Legend of Sasquatch* (2005)

AKA: *The Unknown*. Starring Dylan Purcell, Brandon Henschel, Miles O'Keeffe, Jack Conley, Chelsea Hobbs, Casey LaBow, Nathaniel Arcand, Michael Bailey Smith and Cooper Huckabee. Produced by Bill Bragg, Chuck Colclasure, Joel Eisenberg, Dick Fisher, Karl Kozak, Victor Lou and Andre Johnson. Written by Karl Kozak and Don J. Rearden. Directed by Karl Kozak. USA. Color. Stereo. DVC Pro HD. 85 Minutes.

Overview: Two high school seniors are paired together by their biology teacher. Richard is an academic nerd who is shy with the opposite sex; Jay is a failing jock who can bed any cheerleader but lacks brains enough to pass his exams. Their assignment is to finish a joint presentation in class about any locally endangered species or receive a failing mark.

Despite there being no love lost between them, the jock and the whiz kid decide to make the best of their situation and go camping. Their goal is to find evidence of a local bear that has recently been suspected of killing a hunter. Since no bears are thought to exist in the region any longer, they decide it's the perfect subject for their study.

Jay brings his female cousin Jenny along, knowing Richard has a secret crush on her. The good-looking athlete also brings along his sexy blonde girlfriend Shea. While Jay and Shea spend their time making out in their tent, Richard and Jenny awkwardly make small talk about their intended assignment — photographing the rogue bear willing to attack humans — over the groans emanating from the nearby tent.

Unfortunately, there is no killer bear at work but a savage Sasquatch. Ed, a local redneck and brother of the murdered hunter, vows vengeance, assembling a cadre of his drunken, shotgun-toting buddies and heading into the forest in search of the monster. Sheriff Kassel gets wind of their plan and confronts the redneck avenger. He warns the grieving, bitter hunter that the town does not need any further bloodshed, especially perpetrated by a trigger-happy, inebriated posse. Ed feigns compliance and then uses the cover of darkness to enter the restricted forest with his buddies, hell-bent on destroying the killer grizzly.

Pressure mounts as the tiny town's businessmen react to the negative publicity their fair city receives from the media. They demand the sheriff find the responsible animal and slaughter it before the tourist season is effectively ended by rumors of a "monster bear" preying on campers. Realizing his elected position is in jeopardy, Sheriff Kassel sends his ranger deputy, Eagleheart, into the woods to track the culprit for him. Because he is of Native American descent, Kassel figures Eagleheart has the best chance to uncover the marauder's lair. Eagleheart stumbles upon tell-tale signs that alert him to the deeper reality: Sasquatch is the real killer, not a bear. Knowing from his heritage that the beast is practically indestructible, the deputy ranger tries to warn Sheriff Kassel to keep all locals out of the woods, but Eagleheart's radio transmitter is out of range because he is so deep in the woods.

Meanwhile, the camping teens are alarmed by campfire tales Richard recounts of the area's bloody pioneer history. As white settlers moved into the woods, they massacred Native Americans and claimed their lands. In a move of spiritual retaliation, Bigfoot slaughtered the offending immigrants, ever the protector of his worshipful people. Soon the woods attained a local legend as being cursed by a monstrous forest demon willing to dismember anyone who trespassed in its domain.

Terrorized by the spooky stories of the past, the teens retire to their tents, trying to forget the chills running down their spines. But that very night a growling Bigfoot attempts to grab Shea, who narrowly escapes becoming a victim. Come morning the frightened teens decide to abandon their mission and trek out of the forest before sunset. Alas, they become lost along the way and are forced to spend another night in the woods. While setting up camp again, Richard discovers the half-buried body of a dead Sasquatch. Moments later they're attacked by a living Bigfoot and scatter into the woods in different directions.

The vengeance-seeking Ed and his party of hunters stumble across a gruesome discovery of their own: a lost member of their pack who has been half-eaten. As the long, dark night progresses, both the teens and the hunters attempt to escape the cryptid's domain, but by dawn's early light only Ed remains alive from his original party, while all four teenagers have survived. The scattered teens try to find one another in the daylight, still lost. Ed takes Jenny hostage until Eagleheart offers himself in exchange. Convinced the Native American lawman is to blame for all the deaths that have occurred, Ed makes the deal, whereupon he shoots the deputy ranger to death.

Richard grabs a fallen gun and aims it at the wild-eyed redneck. Ed taunts him, saying the geek lacks the guts to actually fire. Richard blasts Ed and rescues his newfound love. The teens are reunited and happy to have survived their ordeal. Before they can stumble back to civilization, however, they notice Sasquatch staring from the bushes, no longer savage but seemingly at peace with them. They videotape the benign creature's face before it disappears into the wilderness.

Back at home, Richard and Jay present their report to their skeptical biology teacher, who threatens to fail them. But while they're at home watching TV, the teens are shocked to see their video footage being shown. They realize the biology teacher has sold the footage to the media without their permission and only feigned disbelief in order to profit from the footage himself. Ironically, the video is deemed a fake by a noted cryptozoologist, and the biology teacher is summarily fired from his post.

* * * * *

Clawed: The Legend of Bigfoot is a tried-and-true Ciné du Sasquatch effort with the genre's usual hallmarks: a small-town setting; an overwhelmed sheriff; the disbelieving city folks; a Native American who believes Sasquatch is the culprit because of his mystical heritage; beer-guzzling hunters so witless they may as well be dead from their rednecks up (and soon become so, courtesy the cryptid); a rampaging hominid who attacks without provocation; and isolated teenagers trying to flee for their lives.

Not that *Clawed: The Legend of Bigfoot* is without mild entertainment values sprinkled throughout the clichéd trappings. Postmodern film lovers will find amusement in deconstructing the myriad of prior films referenced throughout the movie. For example, the rural town sheriff having to face off against his irate constituents in a town hall setting, all of whom demand summer business over tourist safety, is pulled straight from the shark's mouth in *Jaws*. Other films bearing an influence on *Clawed: The Legend of Bigfoot* include *Deliverance*, the Burt Reynolds 1970s-era Dixie films such as *Gator* and *White Lightning*, and the plethora of 1980s teen chillers such as *Fright Night*, wherein the horrors are mostly implied rather than viscerally rendered à la the gorier fare such as *Friday the 13th*. Indeed, and to its credit, *Clawed: The Legend of Bigfoot* eschews the usual teen body count formula and allows all four protagonists to emerge frightened by their ordeal but physically unscathed.

Compared to many killer cryptid films in the genre, such as *Night of the Demon* and *Shriek of the Mutilated*, *Clawed: The Legend of Bigfoot* seems positively tame, as the aforementioned efforts revel in their graphic, Grand Guignol–styled deaths. This is both endearing and problematic, however. It's admittedly refreshing because *Clawed* plays against expectations; conversely, the film is less successful as a horror entry in that the hominid's threat is reduced. It appears as if Sasquatch has so refined its victim selection process that one is never in danger unless one is a drunken hunter carrying firearms. On the other hand, if one is a basically decent teenager, or at least not prone to casual sex, Sasquatch is a forgiving monster (apart from perhaps a few minutes of terror inducement) and will therefore allow one to survive.

It's not that altering this formula would necessarily have made *Clawed: The Legend of Bigfoot* any less predictable, per se. But it's hard to deny that as a result of the division between morality and lack thereof being so starkly on display, the viewer is left with the obvious conclusion that anyone who is flawed will perish, while those without character problems will survive. It deflates tension because the lines between good and bad are so distinctly drawn and never waiver. Contrast this with the death of Alex Kittner (the boy who is eaten alive while riding an inflatable raft) in *Jaws*, wherein the shocking death of a true innocent shatters the audience's comfort zone and creates a resulting "no one is safe" feeling. *Clawed: The Legend of Bigfoot* teases that it may venture into equally bloody waters, but it pulls back early on and remains conventionally bound to stock situations and characters.

The film has some plusses lacking in most recent Ciné du Sasquatch entries. One is the beautiful cinematography, which captures the rural nature of the setting with total believability. Location photography such as this goes a long ways towards adding realism to the story's inherent improbability, visually suggesting how easy it would be for a large, unknown hominid to remain undiscovered in such a dense, impenetrable forest. Too, the cast is very likeable, if stereotypical, and the costume is well-made. But for other than mild scares and genre conventions illustrated, *Clawed: The Legend of Bigfoot* remains a mundane viewing experience. Non-genre fans may actually find its treatment of its cryptid more enticing than true Bigfoot film lovers in that the beast is rendered more as a generic movie monster than a specifically-delineated hominid.

Clutch Cargo (1959) ("Mr. Abominable") (TV)

Featuring the voices of Richard Cotting, Margaret Kerry and Hal Smith. Produced by Dick Brown. Written by Clark Haas. Directed by Phil Booth. USA. Color. Mono. 5 Minutes.

Overview: Clutch Cargo, dashing world adventurer and aviator, travels the globe to offer heroic help to all who need his services. Along for his journeys are his young ward Spinner and a dachshund named Paddlefoot.

En route to visiting the Himalayas, Clutch Cargo sets down his plane due to a blizzard and is greeted by a local Sherpa named Gung Ho. Gung Ho is troubled: His prized, mystical blue yak has been abducted by someone or something. Gung Ho's large assistant believes it is the work of the Yeti, but as no one alive but the assistant has ever seen the cryptid, doubt remains.

Intrigued, Clutch decides to lend his assistance to the recovery efforts for the blue yak. He, Spinner and Paddlefoot scale the mountains. To their surprise, they encounter a fur-clad man who speaks perfect English. The man, whose name is Smith, tells his sad story: He once owned a profitable factory in Ohio, but after it burned to the ground he moved to the desolate Himalayan Mountains to become a hermit.

Smith reveals he has seen the blue yak in a pen nearby. But when

Cover art for the DVD release of *Clutch Cargo*.

the Clutch Cargo team surveys the crevice wherein the yak was located, they discover it has disappeared. They report their findings to Gung Ho. Clutch decides to take to the air and survey the impenetrable valley to gain further insight. While in flight, he sees that the yak has been returned to the pen. Upon landing, the team treks to the pen, and Gung Hu is joyfully reunited with his sacred yak.

However, a fur-clad caveman who looks exactly like Smith conks Smith on the head and assumes Smith's place in the recovery party. After Clutch, Spinner and Paddlefoot discover an ice tunnel that is the obvious entry and exit route for the yak's mysterious comings and goings, the impersonating "Smith" attempts to smash them with a boulder. Paddlefoot saves the day, and the impersonator is revealed to be Gung Ho's assistant. Gung Ho thanks Clutch Cargo and company. They fly away, taking the real Smith with them, who has decided to return to civilization after his many years in exile.

* * * * *

Before *Jonny Quest* dominated Saturday morning airwaves five years later, *Clutch Cargo* was a popular syndicated children's show very much in the style of the old serials from the 1930s and 1940s. Each crudely-animated but well-drawn episode lasted 5 minutes, with five of the episodes strung together to make one longer show if the station airing the series so desired. The production was the brainchild of Clark Haas, who wrote all 52 episodes, and the handiwork of fledgling Cambria Studios, who would later bring tykes *Space Angel*, *The New 3 Stooges* and *Captain Fathom*. Haas, who was a professional jet pilot prior to his interest in animation, clearly demonstrates his love of aviation in the show by not only making Clutch an appealing, winsome alter ego but embedding many accurate technical details about aircraft in a series otherwise completely fantastic in terms of realism.

This episode is typical of the *Clutch Cargo* series as a whole, with each of the first four mini-episodes ending in a cliffhanger. Per the continuing formula, the week's fifth show summed up the prior 5-minute adventures into one neat whole, capped with a fitting climax à la an old serial. "Mr. Abominable" has a double-meaning in that the moniker refers not only to a Yeti but to the reclusive character Smith, who has abandoned his Ohio roots and retreated to a life of quiet solitude as a hermit in the vast Himalayan Mountains. Smith explains his motivation as being the loss of his factory in a tragic accident, but such an explanation raises more questions than it answers. For instance, why would an average citizen of the USA suddenly move to such a desolate locale? The chances of survival are astronomical, and yet he adapts without stated discomfort. While it's true regions of Ohio have their cold spells, the idea that Smith could easily make such a transition is surely more unbelievable than the notion of there being an actual Yeti.

Alas, "Mr. Abominable" goes one step further, suggesting that there *is* a real Abominable Snowman who "looks exactly like Smith." In a scene that defies credulity, Smith is knocked unconscious by an identical lookalike — complete with the beanie cap Smith favors wearing! The narrator tells us that no one can tell them apart, and indeed both characters are clearly the same animation cell, so that much is true. But the idea that this obvious human being could somehow be mistaken for a cryptid in any way, shape or form is ludicrous; this is clearly a man dressed in a fur hide and wearing a twirling beanie cap. Worse, the so-called Yeti is at last revealed to be none other than Gung Ho's assistant, whom we've seen in the show's beginning and who looks nothing like the later Abominable Snowman. To call such lapses "continuity errors" begs the definition of the phrase; this is outright laziness on the creators' behalf. Of course, naming a protagonist Clutch Cargo and a guest character of Asian descent Gung Ho (with no hint of sarcasm or parody) indicates the show's staff weren't particularly concerned with much beyond meeting what must have been a grueling deadline.

Haas was — to his credit — quite candid about *Clutch Cargo*'s cost-cutting mechanics. In an interview in the December 24, 1960, issue of *TV Digest*, he stated, "We are not making animated cartoons. We are photographing 'motorized movement' and — the biggest trick of all — combining it with live action. This enables us to produce film at about one-fifth what it costs Hanna and Barbera. Footage that Disney does for $250,000 we do for $18,000." The so-called motorized movement was nothing more than employing the artists to simply paint the characters against a clear overlay cell and pull the cell across a static background as if they were moving, further utilizing such foreground objects as rocks, bushes, and whatnot to obscure the fact the characters' non-moving legs could not be seen. In-camera techniques were often employed, such as filming live action elements in conjunction with the cells (i.e., studio smoke, flames, etc.).

The most notorious (and equally well-remembered) technical aspect of *Clutch Cargo* is definitely the Syncro-Vox format developed by Cambria Studios co-owner Edwin Gillette. Gillette, a former news cameraman, created a process whereby a live actor's lips were filmed and then superimposed onto a static animated character's face. This gave the illusion, for better or worse, of the characters having the ability to speak long stretches of dialogue without the costly need to animate each vowel, as Disney, Hanna-Barbera and the other traditional studios did. While the effect has garnered its share of critics, for the time it enabled a tiny studio like Cambria — which employed less than a dozen workers — to produce a half-hour of syndicated television fare every week.

As far as Ciné du Sasquatch entries go, however, "Mr. Abominable" begs the question not once, but twice — first by employing the ruse of having a human mistaken as a cryptid and explaining it as a case of mistaken identity, and second by having a character then pretend to be a Yeti on top of the earlier chicanery! To add further confusion, the resolution reveals that the Yeti does not physically resemble the human impersonator at all. As a mish-mash of Abominable Snowman themes, "Mr. Abominable" is well-titled; still, cryptid cinema fans will probably enjoy the quaint production methodology, even if it's ultimately revealed that the hominids depicted are merely human beings.

Colonel March of Scotland Yard ("The Abominable Snowman") (1956) (TV)

Starring Boris Karloff, Peter Bathurst, Ivan Craig, Alec Mango, Doris Nolan and Olaf Pooley. Produced by Hannah Weinstein. Written by John Dickson Carr and Leslie Slote. Directed by Bernard Knowles. UK. Black & White. Mono. 30 Minutes.

Overview: Colonel Perceval March, a one-eyed, eyepatch-wearing detective, heads the so-called Department of Queer Complaints, an organization funded by the British government to handle all cases deemed too outré for Scotland Yard's regular officials. A specialist in solving supposedly unsolvable crimes with a supernatural tinge, Colonel March maintains a keen air of skepticism at all times, refusing to believe in otherworldly solutions when more probable answers are to be found on Earth itself.

In his latest case, members of the Himalayan Mountaineering Club have reported being stalked by an Abominable Snowman, which they believe may be a result of their previous expeditions to the Tibetan mountains. Fearing for their lives, they call upon Colonel March to protect them from possible violence. The only evidence they have of their claims is a footprint of the cryptid found outside their club's door, which precisely matches similar casts they've found during their expeditions. Colonel March is reluctant to believe the stories; he theorizes it may be all an elaborate prank.

But when he himself receives an apparent visitation one night in his own study, and later finds the familiar Yeti footprint outside his door, March must confront the possibility that his theory of a hoax just may be incorrect. Undaunted by the "scare away" visit, March pushes further into his investigation, which makes certain members of the club suddenly very nervous.

* * * * *

John Dickson Carr, a British novelist and short story writer, specialized in locked room murder mysteries — the type of peculiarly puzzling whodunits in which the body of the victim is found in a setting which is seemingly impossible for a human to have entered to commit the homicide in question. Using Carter Dickson as his pseudonym, he created, among many characters, Colonel March, the eye-patched investigator whose keen logic and analytical mind refused to be intimidated by calls for belief in the supernatural when more readily accessible explanations for various crimes were readily available. In many aspects, March was like Sherlock Holmes, but with the same focus as Professor Quatermass of the popular BBC series — a man of science battling a world of superstition.

The Department of Queer Complaints (which reads as unintentionally comical today) was an early forerunner of similar organizations seen in such later American series as *Project Bluebook* and *The X-Files*. But a key difference between *Colonel March* and these later series is that *Colonel March of Scotland Yard*'s protagonist was a skeptic, not a believer. Even though there were often red herrings which made Colonel March waver in his stoicism, he eventually triumphed over the forces of darkness by proving they were located more correctly in the hearts of men rather than monsters.

This series was very inexpensively produced in its day, owing to the fact live television was viewed as such an ephemeral medium. Indeed, the various episodes that have survived are often so badly preserved as to be hardly watchable, save to the most avid or curious of fans. "The Abominable Snowman" is one such episode, alas, and has never been officially released in any high-quality version on DVD.

Understandably, this half-hour of mystery focuses more on the humans involved rather than any actual cryptid depiction. Given that the sets are obviously constructed from the flimsiest of materials (they literally shake when characters enter and close doors behind themselves), it is only the calm, professional presence of Boris Karloff as Colonel March that elevates the episode to even marginal interest for Ciné du Sasquatch viewers. As a kind of British version of Peter Falk's later Columbo character (but without the *déclassé* mannerisms), Karloff makes a fine, believable Colonel March, but most viewers will see through the mystery element far in advance of the production's ending. The fictitious Himalayan Mountaineering Club is obviously a reference to Sir Edmund Hillary and his expeditions to both Mount Everest and the South Pole.

The Conquest of the Pole (1912)

AKA: *À la conquête du pôle.* Starring Georges Méliès and Fernande Albany. Written by Jules Verne and Georges Méliès. Produced and Directed by Georges Méliès. France. Black & White. Silent. 12 Minutes.

Overview: A group of French scientists and explorers meet to determine the precise machinery and survival skills needed for an expedition to the frozen North Pole. After some debate, they regroup in a factory, where the necessary flight machine — a hybrid plane with a helicopter lift added — is designed and manufactured to their exact specifications. After some ballyhoo, they start their voyage. Along the way, they encounter astral bodies such as stars and comets (personified by human actors). After landing on the ice flows, they encounter the *géant des neiges* (the giant of the snows), an Abominable Snowman who smokes a pipe as large as any of the humans themselves. After the beast ravenously devours a few of the unlucky ex-

The first-ever cinematic Yeti rears its ugly head. From the film that began Ciné du Sasquatch — *The Conquest of the Pole* (1912).

plorers in its massive jaws, the group manages to escape and return to their homelands.

* * * * *

Without George Méliès' contributions to fantastic films there would not have been — or at least there would have been a delay in the creation of— movies as filmgoers know them today. In fact, over one century later it can be convincingly, if sadly, argued that very little has changed from when Méliès was at the height of his creative output as a filmmaker (wherein he concentrated more on filmic illusions than believable stories or characterizations — a common complaint about today's CGI-laden visual spectaculars).

As a former stage magician, Méliès saw the value of cinema as an extension of his skills in performing illusions — a far cry from the documentaries made by other early filmmakers (the only other form utilizing the process when Méliès began making his short narratives). His initial output was confined to creating "magic lantern"–type trick films to fill the time he needed to set up each new complicated live stage illusion. But when he noticed that audiences were as entranced by the silent films as by any of his costlier and laborious live stage acts, Méliès realized a new potential for what he'd formerly viewed as merely a distraction —films for films' sake, to be viewed as a medium in and of itself.

For over a decade he was the true master of his art form. His earliest films, such as *Le Voyage dans la lune* in 1902, were internationally renowned, mystifying audiences globally who could not understand how such filmic illusions were created. Again, the parallel between today's wowed audiences for such films as *Avatar* make such seemingly quaint reactions more understandable; one has but to imagine a time when there was no television, Internet or other visual moving image distractions that audiences could entertain themselves with to understand their amazement.

Although time and more sophisticated filmmakers introducing more complicated filmic techniques and sustained narratives (such as D.W. Griffith in America) would take their toll on Méliès and render his films a relic of the past, he nevertheless revolutionized film as an art form. And just as importantly, he created the very prototype of Ciné du Sasquatch with this silent short.

As was previously pointed out in the overview section, *The Conquest of the Pole* contains the very essence of all other Yeti films that followed in its large footprints: the invading humans who fall victim to a defensive cryptid on the hominid's home turf; the recognition that the Yeti is not so much monster as missing link in the *Homo sapiens* lineage; and even the archetype of the Savage Sasquatch, which is still the predominant incarnation of most Bigfoot films to this very day. The visual conceits that would seem to indicate this Snow Monster is perhaps less simian and more human — such as the fact it puffs a pipe!— are more in line with Méliès' stylistic preference to romanticize his imagery than any indication this is other than an early forerunner of the cinematic Yeti. Witness, for example, the famous image Méliès used in his moon voyage film — in which the Man in the Moon is portrayed quite literally as being nothing less than the very Moon itself, complete with eyes, nose and mouth. In the same film the viewer is treated to stars that have comely maidens swinging upon them in the heavens, and mermaids underwater when the astronauts return to Earth and splash into the ocean. Indeed, during a remarkably brief career as a cinemagician, Méliès exhausted an incredibly vast range of possible mythic deities, monsters, and related fantasy subjects — he clearly realized how perfect the motion picture medium was for bringing to life phantasmagorical imagery.

The Abominable Snowman depicted by Méliès was one of the most elaborate special effects ever constructed for a film up until 1924, when Fritz Lang created a dragon to fight in his epic silent version of *Die Nibelungen: Siegfried*. The skill Méliès demonstrates in

The Conquest of the Pole with his cryptid is truly awe-inspiring and genius in its originality. With its elaborate wooden structure, mobile jaws, eyebrows, and pulley mechanisms bringing it to life (operated by unseen stagehands), it is every bit the forerunner of later screen miracles such as the bust used in *King Kong* for close-ups; and the crude beginnings of animatronics (as it would later come to be called) is also on display beneath the yak-covered fur. Herein Méliès' contributions to cinematic sleight-of-hand cannot be fully grasped unless one is willing to step back and appreciate the innovations he conjured — seemingly out of thin air, like a rabbit from a top hat — that would later become standard trick effects technology for almost a century of uninterrupted usage by countless other filmmakers.

Corwin's Quest ("Realm of the Yeti") (2006) (TV) (Doc)

Featuring Russell A. Mittermeier, Joe Rohde and Jeff Corwin. Produced by Jeff Corwin. USA. Color. Stereo. 120 Minutes.

Overview: Daredevil risk-taker Jeff Corwin takes on the legendary Yeti, the Abominable Snowman, in this two-hour special. Never content to make his life any easier than possible (or risk his ratings plummeting should he do so), Corwin handles every native specimen he encounters, no matter how relatively dangerous to his continued well-being, all in a tawdry sideshow revue, thereby testing his own health insurance options as well as the viewer's nerves. Whenever the narrative stalls out, Corwin "juggles" handfuls of squirming mortality to spice up the show's sense of urgency — giant insects with quivering, poised stingers; monster snakes able to inject enough venom to kill a grown man within minutes; or, scariest of all, enraged primate species like spider monkeys, chimpanzees, and the like who have been "domesticated" and mistreated to the point of descending into a cross-species-shared Helter Skelter desire for revenge against any and all mankind.

In "Realm of the Yeti" Corwin first visits the Makalu Barun National Park in Nepal. His task: document real-life encounters between trusted eyewitnesses and the Snowman, bringing the viewer along on his mission. Unfortunately, Corwin falls victim to Newbie Cryptic Syndrome, an unfortunate malady that sees Corwin rushing off to Nepal before conducting even cursory research into cryptozoology. This causes him to derail his own investigation when he uncritically buys into the notion that the supposed Yeti scalp housed in a locked glass-paneled ceremonial box in Khumjung is legitimate evidence of the Abominable Snowman's existence. Had he fact-checked the history of the relic, which was well-known and widely debunked as a fake at any number of websites accessible at the time of this production, he could have saved himself much grief. As cryptozoologist Loren Coleman wrote on the April 16, 2006, *Cryptomundo* blog, in a piece entitled "Yeti Yes, Corwin Hardly Bearable":

> Needless to say, it has been known since first seen by Westerners in the early 1950s that this "skullcap" is a replica, a ritual object, and not something even claimed by the locals to be made from a Yeti. They told Sir John Hunt, Ralph Izzard, Tom Slick's team, and others who came to see it that it was "made in imitation of Yeti." Furthermore, most casual Yeti researchers have understood this, and since 1960, also known that the skin that was used to make the skullcap is from a four-legged Himalayan animal, called the serow (*Nemorhaedus sumatraensis*).

When options run out for capturing that magical moment Corwin sees as vitally necessary to end the debate — High Definition digital video of Sasquatch that makes the Patterson-Gimlin film of 1967 forever "quaint" by comparison — Corwin further stumbles when he chooses not to recognize the Yeti skullcap as a fraud. An example of "Spend Now, Research Later" mentality, Corwin's stumble casts a shadow over his own objectivity in this particular episode.

Not that scientists and researchers shouldn't promote their own ideas and receive worthwhile consideration from an admiring segment of the public. Philanthropy is a source of the risky venture capital required to map unexplored continents, deep sea dive into underwater mountains, and even fund Bigfoot expeditions in the real world. In fictionalized form in a prototypical Ciné du Sasquatch movie, such philanthropy turns greedy in basic conception — the archetype being Carl Denham from the original *King Kong*, who looks down upon his huddled masses of audience members and can only think about how to orchestrate his next epic capital adventure in response to all the suffering and deprivations around him (how to make a superior "product" that will con a few million Joe Suckers into parting with the cost of an admission ticket).

This potent exploiter of hominids is so fundamental to Ciné du Sasquatch that the genre could not exist without this central figure. This P.T. Barnum–ish, self-aggrandizing blowhard huckster represents the *worst* of ourselves in regards to how we treat the less-aware animal life around us; therefore, and fittingly, it takes on a nightmarish, Jungian projection the size of King Kong himself when it is Kong's domain which is invaded, Kong who is carried away in chains and stripped of the one he loves, and Kong who must ultimately sacrifice even his declining nobility in order to let folks gawk at him and feel superior. In so many ways (though he doesn't mean to be as abrasively so), Corwin remains the quintessential Carl Denham type — selectively capable of being well-meaning, but preferring to seize every opportunity in terms of business gain that will all but insure increased instability for all concerned.

"Realm of the Yeti" also includes footage of Russell A. Mittermeier, President of Conservation International, who shares his viewpoints about the *Gigantopithecus* species being perhaps the most probable Sasquatch "explanation" (even as Mittermeier distances his own professional belief in such a possibility by stating the odds are very long against this being an actually living, remnant species, as most theorize the *Gigantopithecus* died out 20,000 or more years ago), and video clips from Hammer's landmark Yeti film *The Abominable Snowman*. Overall, "Realm of the Yeti" is a missed opportunity, producing a feeling of "what might have been" upon subsequent viewings. Much of the information is neither novel nor well-presented. Enthusiasts will have a harder time letting Corwin's production off the proverbial hook than viewers who are simply seeking the latest pleasant few minutes of Ciné du Sasquatch research and theory handed to them on a pithy platter. There are many better documentaries about Yeti that contain far better information.

Courage the Cowardly Dog ("Courage Meets Bigfoot") (1999) (TV)

Featuring the voices of Marty Grabstein, Lionel G. Wilson, Simon Prebble and Billie Lou Watt. Produced by John Dilworth, Risa Neuwirth and Robert Winthrop. Written by David Steven Cohen, William Hohauser and John Dilworth. Directed by John Dilworth. USA. Color. Stereo. 10 Minutes.

Overview: Courage the Cowardly Dog lives on a remote farm with his elderly owners Eustace and Ma Bagge. One night Courage spots what he believes to be Bigfoot prowling outside, going through the couple's garbage; but as is typical for the pair, his masters cannot understand Courage's frantic warnings.

Later that evening Courage witnesses Bigfoot attempting to steal a freshly-baked pie Ma has left in the open kitchen window to cool.

Courage tries to stop the theft, but is coated in the pie when Bigfoot releases it and flees. Ma Bagge finds Courage and assumes he is the culprit.

The next night Eustace watches a local television show dedicated to strange, unexplained phenomena. The host explains there's been a Bigfoot sighting and offers the viewers a reward and lifetime membership in a local museum for anyone who captures the cryptid. Delighted to have something to alleviate his boredom, Eustace sets out in search of Bigfoot and his reward.

While he's gone, however, Bigfoot enters the farm house while Ma Bagge naps. Courage and Bigfoot have a food fight in the kitchen as Courage tries to repel the invader. When they accidentally coat each other with bananas and other tropical fruit, they wind up dancing together, à la Carmen Miranda in a South Seas musical. The song and dance number is interrupted by the return of Eustace and an angry mob of citizens carrying torches. They demand the surrender of Bigfoot.

Courage tries to tell the heartless mob that Bigfoot is a harmless being, but no one will listen. An old woman staggers forth and calls Bigfoot her son. Bigfoot clutches her forlornly — clearly, it is actually his mother. Touched by the mother and son display, the mob loses its furor. Eustace, however, refuses to give in, wanting his reward. Ma Bagge beans him with a rolling pin and demands Bigfoot be set free. When Eustace remains steadfast, the mob chases after him, enraged that he could be so cruel. Bigfoot and his mother go home, and Courage has a slice of pie with Ma Bagge on the front porch.

* * * * *

For just a ten-minute episode, "Courage Meets Bigfoot" is action-packed and — more to the point — highlights (albeit in a comical manner) many of Ciné du Sasquatch's most common themes. For example, it showcases the perception that Bigfoot is a creature to be feared, which is reversed by show's end to reveal the creature as nothing more than a scared, semi-simian being needing love and compassion just like any human. The fact it takes Courage the Cowardly Dog to recognize the human qualities in Bigfoot, while the mob of *Homo sapiens* are intent on lynching the cryptid, is ironic; apparently they're too far removed from their own species to see the similarities, especially when engaged in the thoughtless mob mentality.

The visualizations throughout "Courage Meets Bigfoot" are highly stylized but charming in their originality. Courage is a very expressive character, at once full of fear and then a few seconds later grimly determined to "do the right thing" in the face of long odds to protect his newfound friend Bigfoot. Clearly, this is no cowardly canine at all, just one all too familiar with the vagaries of human conduct in the face of the unknown. This is perfectly represented by the mob itself, which is tellingly drawn as a single entity and never as a group of individuals. The artists literally render them a faceless, formless mass of silhouetted torch carriers who stretch across the frame from one side to the other. The only salient detail visible in their otherwise black form are their angry, murderous eyes. Though made funny by the story's actions, it is a chilling depiction of yet another theme in Ciné du Sasquatch: the Us versus Them mentality that so pervades any encounter with a cryptid when *Homo sapiens* are involved.

Bigfoot is an absurd hominid with a bulky body, huge feet and hands, and legs and arms far too skinny in proportion to the rest of the design to make it much of a threat (except perhaps to itself when it gets itself into situations such as facing a human mob reacting out of fear). In the course of a few minutes, Bigfoot is shown first as a scary series of shadows, then a growling monster intent on scaring Courage into allowing it to eat his owners' foodstuffs, and then as a timid, friendly cryptid needing the nervous pooch's assistance to save its very hide. That's quite a range for any Bigfoot film, let alone a short subject. Would that many features had adopted such an unexpectedly complex visualization of Bigfoot, and the genre as a whole would be much richer and poignant.

The expressive use of sound and color make this show atypical. For those who like their animation rendered in the classical Warner Brothers or Disney mode, *Courage the Cowardly Dog* may be too artsy for their tastes. More clearly influenced by the Czech style of animation, which favors abstract design and camera angles over simple outlines and fluid motion, it is an acquired taste; but like the pies Courage devours throughout, it is well worth it and filling. It's never explained how the elderly lady who is Bigfoot's mother ever came to be such a person — Bigfoot is clearly not a human being in any way, shape or form — but then again, it's never really made logically clear how a dog can talk, walk on two legs, and dance the cha-cha, either. Like all comic satires, "Courage Meets Bigfoot" takes, well, a little *courage* in letting go and trusting in the concept's necessary suspension of disbelief. The reward for Ciné du Sasquatch viewers willing to do so is a fun, well-executed example of television Bigfoot cartooning at its best.

Crank Yankers ("Birchum Is on the Hunt") (2005) (TV) (Cameo)

Featuring the voices of Adam Carolla and Bill the Store Owner. Produced by Rob Anderson, Daniel Kellison, Jimmy Kimmel and Jonathan Kimmel. Written by Reed Agnew, Darren Belitsky, Aaron Blitzstein and Tim Burns. Directed by Bill Berner, Bobcat Goldthwait and Hugh Martin. USA. Color. Stereo. 3 Minutes.

Overview: Birchum, an embittered Vietnam veteran, is on the hunt for Bigfoot. Claiming to have seen "Ses-quatch," he calls the Little Bigfoot Shoppe and asks Bill, the store's proprietor, if Bill has ever seen Bigfoot. Bill relates how he encountered the cryptid in both Louisiana and Missouri in 1972. Birchum explains he has heard that Bill was attacked, but Bill denies it, saying he only witnessed a Bigfoot attack some hunting dogs, whose heads were ripped off.

Birchum suggests Bill accompany him on a hunting trip to "bag one of them Bigfeet," but Bill is hesitant: Is Birchum *sure* he's seen a real hominid, or could it be a human in a costume pranking him? Birchum, who explains he has killed men during his Vietnam years, irately reiterates he knows the difference between a Sasquatch and a man. Bill, sensing Birchum is perhaps mentally unstable, hesitates to commit to the hunting trip. When Birchum tells Bill the main reason Birchum needs an "extra set of eyes" is for human bait, Bill definitely loses interest. Birchum tries to sweet talk Bill by suggesting they could snuggle together in one sleeping bag and a shared tent, but Bill loses interest completely and says good-bye.

Moments later, Bigfoot — who has been sneaking around the store unobserved by the engrossed Bill — tries to buy cigarettes and condoms. Bill is willing to sell Bigfoot the condoms but cards the cryptid on the smokes, pointing to a sign that restricts cigarette sales to minors. With a heavy sigh, the underaged Bigfoot leaves, empty-handed.

* * * * *

Crank Yankers was a popular if rude prank show that ran for years on Comedy Central. The show was an off-color mixture of *Sesame Street*–styled puppets and prank phone calls, the latter of which the puppeteers recreated as if they were live (when, in fact, the calls had been made earlier and edited for maximum comic impact).

Cryptozoology fans lacking a sense of humor will find precious little to laugh about in "Birchum Is on the Hunt," but less easily offended Ciné du Sasquatch followers will probably enjoy the satirical nature of the prank call itself, as well as the comic shenanigans of the unnoticed Bigfoot wandering around in the store's background. Provided one doesn't mind a mean-spirited sense of humor, the Adam Corolla–voiced Birchum character is a cantankerous riot, and the puppetry is first-rate.

The highlights/lowlights (depending on one's point of view) include Birchum, a crotchety old man prone to racist slurs and non-politically correct verbosity, describing Bigfoot ("All's I know is it's got beady red eyes, is covered with hair, walks like an old Jew and it needs to *die!*"), and the various items Bill the shop owner has for sale in his Sasquatch-themed curio store (such as an actual "Bigfoot Dingleberry" specimen for $25.98 and a cereal called "Yeti Nuts"). A funny video on Birchum's television set shows an obvious recreation of the Patterson-Gimlin footage but done by the producers as a clear parody (at which Birchum constantly aims his gun's crosshairs for target practice as he talks). Also amusing are the various mounted trophy heads Birchum has on his wall, such as a unicorn and Cookie Monster; a blank mounting plate is also seen with Bigfoot's name on a plaque, only awaiting a head to complete the feisty hunter's collection.

There's a reason Carolla, Jimmy Kimmel, and the rest of the pranksters had to travel to Nevada to stage their original prank calls: it is the only state in America that legally allows the use of recorded conversations of this type made by only one-half of the two parties involved in the call. In short, it shielded the series from legal liability should any irate recipients of the *Crank Yankers* treatment wish to sue Comedy Central. Proof positive the lawyers representing the network were concerned about such a possibility (besides requesting they use Nevada as the recording state) comes in the form of the show's name change. Originally to be called *Prank Puppets*, the network demanded the title be altered, fearing this indicated "clear malicious intent" on the part of the creators. How anyone could believe otherwise after watching even only this segment of the outrageous series — title change or not — is as unbelievable as many of the phone calls themselves.

Creature from Black Lake (1976)

AKA: *Demon of the Lake*. Starring Jack Elam, Dub Taylor, John David Carson, Dennis Fimple, Bill Thurman, Jim McCullough Jr., Roy Tatum, Cathryn Hartt, Becky Smiser, Michelle Willingham, Evelyn Hindricks and Joy N. Houck Jr. Produced by Jim McCullough Jr., Jim McCullough Sr. and William Lewis Ryder Jr. Written by Jim McCullough Jr. Directed by Joy N. Houck Jr. USA. Eastmancolor. Mono. 95 Minutes.

Overview: Rives and Pahoo, two college buddies taking an anthropology class, decide to spend the summer break in the swamps of Louisiana searching for evidence of a legendary cryptid. Shortly after arriving in a small town with a history of creature sightings, they meet a friendly local named Orville, who instantly bonds with them, as he's the same age (albeit from a radically different culture). Orville invites them to have supper with his kinfolks, provided they do not mention the creature until Orville has got the okay to do so from his grandfather. But Pahoo does just that in a mistaken moment of mirth, upsetting Orville's grandmother. Orville's grizzled grandfather, Bridges, relates that she and the family encountered the creature one day in the bayou and have lived in fear of it ever since. Their fears are well-founded, as the young men — sleeping in the Bridges' barn later that night — hear the beast screaming in lonely frustration, scaring them all almost to death.

Realizing they're upsetting their hosts, the boys move out and onward with their investigation. They meet two local cuties named Becky and Michelle, who seem interested in participating in some mutual hanky panky, but Becky's father — Sheriff Billy Carter — is unhappy to learn two "Yankees" are trying to make time with his

daughter and her best friend. He advises them to move along and not stay in the town stirring up folks with their nosy research. The pair of explorers camp in the wilderness after lying and saying they will leave. Becky and Michelle visit them at their campsite and begin to make out with the boys, but Sheriff Carter surprises them all and arrests the boys for trespassing and failing to heed his warning to leave town.

Meanwhile, a backwoods hermit named Joe Canton is visited late one night on his bayou house boat by the creature. The shaggy-haired Sasquatch attempts to batter its way inside Canton's hovel until Canton blasts at it with his shotgun. Rattled, Canton stumbles into town the next day and blathers about the creature attacking his home. Sheriff Carter arrests the obviously drunken Canton and tosses him into the jail cell, which he shares with Rives and Pahoo. When they learn of Canton's claims, they eagerly ask him for all the information Canton can provide them. He goes one step further, inviting them to his house boat to investigate the evidence and his stories firsthand. They eagerly accept, despite Sheriff Carter warning that if he catches them again inside the county limits, things will go far worse for them.

Canton's remote home proves the ideal embarking point for Rives and Pahoo to journey deeper into the fetid waters in search of the beast. Canton advises them of a particular area in which he has frequently seen evidence of the creature, and they follow his directions, setting off alone to face down the water demon. They find a dry piece of land and set up camp, patiently waiting for any sign of the cryptid. Pahoo's nerves fray and he suggests they leave, afraid the creature will harm them both. But Rives is obsessed and refuses to go. The two researchers argue, and Pahoo announces his plans to leave the next day.

But the creature attacks them that very night, nearly killing Pahoo and forcing Rives to fight the beast one-on-one for his life. The boys survive the long night when the monster abandons its siege as the sun rises. Pahoo awakens in the local hospital to find Rives teary-eyed and apologetic. Their friendship renewed, and despite having gathered no evidence of any real value, they vow to return the following summer armed with cameras and determined to prove the cryptid is real, once and for all.

* * * * *

Creature from Black Lake is a lightweight entry in the Ciné du Sasquatch genre, but unexpectedly entertaining as a result. Whereas many entries make the mistake of taking their subject matter far too seriously — as if such grim determinism will allay any viewer's doubts about Bigfoot — here the filmmakers were clever enough to keep the cryptid convincingly savage and scary while loading the balance of the film with healthy doses of regional realism and character-driven humor. The pleasant jambalaya thus concocted is a more believable and amusing blend. Never campy per se, *Creature from Black Lake* nevertheless adds welcome dollops of broad humor to alleviate boredom, but smartly keeps such comic relief centered on the human cast and never the terrifying creature itself.

Helping matters significantly are the two grizzled character actors present, each of whom is given ample screen time to show how experienced pros can elevate such material. Dub Taylor plays a classic redneck whose son has befriended the two outsiders, and Jack Elam portrays the backwater hermit who has seen the "critter" on more than one occasion. Both actors are veterans of countless Westerns and therefore lend an earthy, saddle-worn reality to the proceedings.

Dub Taylor's perennially hoarse, belligerent presence rings especially true, particularly in his defensive nature regarding the creature. While he is more than happy to relate a flashback to the young researchers about his family's own frightening encounter with the cryptid (for a non-refundable cash fee, of course), Taylor forbids any mention of the hominid in front of his nervous wife, who has never fully recovered from the shock. Of course, it doesn't take the loud-mouthed pair of students long to blurt out a question about the creature over a home-cooked meal provided by Taylor's mate. Suffice it to say, Taylor roundly berates them before unceremoniously kicking them out of his house.

Jack Elam later takes in the cryptozoologists when he discovers the reason they're in the small Southern town. His own memories of the monster are as terrifying as Taylor's; clearly, whatever else the students have uncovered, it is clear that the creature is anything but a pacifist. With the monster willing and able to kill to aggressively defend its territory, Elam stresses to the two that it is not to be tangled with lightly. Alas, the old man's words fall on deaf ears, as the students decide to push further into uncivilized countryside in hopes of an encounter of their own. Elam's prescient warning that nothing good can come of their expedition is graphically proven during the exciting, suspenseful final reel, wherein the beast demonstrates its penchant for destruction.

Equally adroit in his role as Sheriff Billy Carter (!) is character actor Bill Thurman. Thurman made a career out of playing a kind of poor man's Ben Johnson — the kind-eyed but expressionless man's man — often in lawman and western roles. He's perfectly cast herein and handles his scenes with a believable mixture of concern for his daughter and the researchers, mixed with a stern sense that the two young men are in way over their heads in terms of what they might be facing. Thurman's innate sense of veracity was used in many features, including the opening of *Close Encounters of the Third Kind*, Larry Buchanan's classic *The Trial of Lee Harvey Oswald*, exploitation grindhouse fare such as *Hip, Hot and 21* and *Spiked Heels and Black Nylons*, and serious-minded movies like *The Last Pic-*

Rives (John David Carson) and Pahoo (Dennis Fimple) interview Orville Bridges (Jim McCullough, Jr.) and Grandpaw Bridges (Dub Taylor) about their encounters with the *Creature from Black Lake.*

ture Show and *Places in the Heart.* As far as screen time goes, Sheriff Carter in *Creature from Black Lake* is one of the largest roles he ever had throughout his varied career, and one of the reasons the film stands out.

Creature from Black Lake also benefits from authentic location photography by Dean Cundey. The now-famed cinematographer would shoot John Carpenter's *Halloween* the same year. Throughout *Creature from Black Lake* Cundey uses balanced widescreen compositions and a blue gel lighting scheme for night-lit scenes that would become an early hallmark of his style (very similar to the look he achieved in *Halloween*). His talent as director of photography gives the film a polished, higher-end look than its modest budget suggests.

As for the cryptid itself, the costume is not particularly convincing when briefly shown for the first time in the final showdown. As if to compensate, the director seems to have deliberately kept his Bigfoot mostly confined to shadowy glimpses and back-lit silhouettes. The more effective strategy employed throughout shows only a clawed hand rising from the water or an over-the-shoulder shot from the creature's point of view looking at unsuspecting humans as they pass by in a boat. This off-screen presence is remarkably similar to the manner in which the Shape from *Halloween* often intrudes into frame unexpectedly, and while this film is nowhere near as effective as that Slasher classic, this creative staging for the camera definitely adds suspense.

The creature's face is rubbery-looking, but, interestingly, the design suggests a combination of human and simian features (rather than ape-like, as in most Ciné du Sasquatch entries). Given how ineffectively the mask photographs, it was wise of the editor to relegate the close-ups to a few brief cuts.

Overall, *Creature from Black Lake* follows its clearest precedent, Charles Pierce's *The Legend of Boggy Creek*.

Rives (John David Carson) and Pahoo (Dennis Fimple) await a final confrontation with the *Creature from Black Lake.*

That said, the films are very different in execution and tone. Whereas *The Legend of Boggy Creek* uses non-professional cast members and a pseudo-documentary approach, *Creature from Black Lake* is a more traditional creature feature with fictional narrative and a largely imported Hollywood cast. As far as Bigfoot movies go, the film's major drawback — a tendency to over-reach for dramatic heights the actors and scenario never quite achieve — is ably offset by the movie's overall effectiveness, in particular the concluding sequence, which is as tense as any in the genre. Flaws and all, it remains one of the high points of Ciné du Sasquatch in terms of the Disco Era of its production, the 1970s. Though often terse and failing to offer much in the way of subplots, *Creature from Black Lake* stands out as a well-produced indie feature.

Creepshow ("The Crate") (1982)

Starring Hal Holbrook, Adrienne Barbeau, Fritz Weaver, Robert Harper, Don Keefer, Christine Forrest, Chuck Aber, Cletus Anderson, Katie Karlovitz and Darryl Ferrucci. Produced by Salah M. Hassanein, Richard P. Rubinstein and David E. Vogel. Written by Stephen King. Directed by George A. Romero. USA. Color. Stereo. 35 Minutes.

Overview: When Horlicks University janitor Mike discovers an ancient crate stenciled with the date 1834 under the stairwell in a basement hallway, he immediately calls his supervisor, Professor Dexter Stanley, to alert him to the find. Professor Stanley rushes over to see what could be inside, half-convinced it's nothing more than a crate of rotting back issues of *National Geographic* magazine. They pry open the crate, only to discover a Yeti-ish creature inside — one very hungry after its prolonged hibernation. It attacks and devours Mike, leaving a helpless Professor Stanley to watch in horror. Stanley staggers upstairs and enlists the aid of graduate student Charlie Gereson, who believes the older man is simply drunk, stoned or both. But when Charlie finds the chewed up shoe of the dead janitor near the crate, he suspects Professor Stanley may not be exaggerating. Alas for Charlie, the cryptid attacks and shreds him to pieces, just as it had killed the janitor earlier.

Meanwhile, not far away, in his on-campus home, henpecked husband Professor Henry Northrup fantasizes about killing his bitchy wife Wilma, who drunkenly insists that everyone call her Billie. Like Walter Mitty, however, Northrup cannot imagine putting his fantasy plans of doing away with the obnoxious Wilma into practice. Wilma leaves him for her regular night of bar-hopping after the usual catty insults to his manhood. Not long thereafter, Professor Stanley arrives at his friend's home in a state of panic, babbling incoherently about what has happened in the basement at the university.

After calming his colleague with a few drinks, Northrup — who believes Stanley is telling the truth — comes up with a plan. Slipping a sleeping aid into Stanley's drink, which causes him to pass out, Northrup heads to the university, leaving a note to Wilma for her to find on her return home. While he cleans up the blood and evidence in the basement, Wilma discovers the note, swallows the bait, and heads over to the university, falling into Northrup's trap.

Northrup lures Wilma into the stairwell hiding place where the creature lives inside its crate, but becomes impatient when the monster doesn't attack. Northrup bangs her head against the crate and yells loudly, hoping to enrage the Yeti. Nothing happens. Wilma laughs at him, mocking his pathetic attempt to dominate her. Suddenly, the monster springs forth and devours her alive. After it's over, Northrup locks the crate and hauls it away, dumping box and beast into a flooded quarry. But after the crate sinks to the bottom, the Yeti bursts free and swims towards the surface, very much alive and hungering for its next victim.

* * * * *

In an anthology filled with many grimly amusing and blackly horrific segments, *Creepshow* achieves a definite sense of playfully ironic fun with "The Crate" segment. Much of the credit is owed to the choice casting. Hal Holbrook plays the cuckolded husband to weary perfection, expressing far more with a hangdog look of accepting resignation at Wilma's latest insults than with any of his minimal dialogue. Equally effective is Adrienne Barbeau as Wilma (aka "Billie"), who staggers under the influence and hams up her performance as the cheap, foul-mouthed spouse. So shrill and hateful is Barbeau in the role that when Holbrook imagines killing her for the first time (by pulling a gun at a cocktail party and blowing her brains out in front of the other guests), his fantasy concludes with the shocked partygoers actually applauding his actions, and one offended male even muttering with relief, "Good shot!" Given the violence Holbrook has just exhibited, the laughter the punch line produces in most viewers indicates that a potentially tasteless gag has been well-executed (so to speak). It could have reeked of misogyny; instead, it plays as justified comeuppance, albeit stylized as a daydream to lessen the graphic gore.

Romero directs with a penchant for allowing the camerawork to remain largely unobtrusive until a transition or attack occurs, at which point he highlights the action with such self-conscious cinema techniques as comic book-panel framing, page-flipping wipes (to suggest an actual comic book's pages being turned), and intense primary colors of red and blue. Every time the cryptid attacks, normal colors suddenly transform into crimson and cyan, providing a visual shock akin to the manner in which Dario Argento stages the gruesome witch murders in *Suspiria* with equally lurid color palettes. It's great fun and captures the nature of the horror comics which the film at once parodies and pays homage to.

Makeup maestro Tom Savini (*Friday the 13th*, *Dawn of the Dead*) renders a particularly effective Yeti creation. With a mouth full of fangs, and claws as sharply pointed as daggers, this is one Abominable Snowman that truly lives up to the first half of its name. It is interesting to note that the creature is never directly called a Yeti or Snowman at any point in the segment's duration. In fact, the graduate student even mocks Professor Stanley's description of the beast as being nothing more than a Tasmanian Devil — until he encounters the hominid first-hand in his dying moments. Too, Stephen King's original short story from 1975 (also called "The Crate"), which he

The Tom Savini–crafted, Yeti-like creature from "The Crate" segment of *Creepshow* in all its fang-faced glory.

adapted into the script, describes the cryptid as being more akin to a wolverine. But given the fact the crate in which the beast has been stored is marked with "Arctic Expedition 1834," and its physical resemblance to a Yeti in most respects (including being bipedal and able to function as a hominid), it is difficult to consider the creature as being anything other than a Sasquatch. The white, shaggy fur and ape-like face are clearly a deliberate nod to it being a Yeti, not to mention the polar origin.

How such a hominid could survive for over a century being bound inside a chain-locked crate is never explained (nor even speculated upon). Professor Stanley even goes so far as to reassure the jittery janitor Mike as they open the crate for the first time that anything that might have once been inside would surely be dead after such a long time. But not only is this Abominable quite healthy, it immediately goes on an understandable feeding binge, dispatching three human beings in a matter of hours without a trace of their bodies left (save for small pieces of dropped body parts here and there). Even if the creature were capable of hibernation, the 147 years of suggested slumber seems beyond any realm of possible scientific belief; indeed, the same (non)logic prevails when the cryptid is dropped into the water by Northrup after he's used the beast to dispatch his nagging wife. It not only doesn't drown, but—belly full of three digesting *Homo sapiens*, no less!—bursts free from the crate and easily swims to freedom. This plays more for exaggerated comic effect than shock. But this is true tonally of much of the segment, wherein Barbeau tells Holbrook she's going to "wear his balls like earrings" (among other verbal pleasantries). If ever a character "had it coming," as the expression goes, surely Barbeau's Wilma is deserving of her gruesome demise. "Just tell it to call you Billie!" Northrup concludes as it finishes her off to O. Henry–esque, blackly comic effect.

Well-done and without pretentions of being anything other than what it is—a Hitchcock-styled exercise in grim horror and suspense—"The Crate" is not only a high point of *Creepshow* but also an effective half-hour of Ciné du Sasquatch, showing how a lighter tone can combine with gory shocks to make an effective Bigfoot genre short.

Creepy Canada (2002) (Multiple Episodes) (TV) (Doc)

Featuring Terry Boyle and Brian O'Dea. Produced by Brian O'Dea and Indra Seja. Written by Karen Gordon. Directed by Bill Burke, Chad Archibald, William Burke and Simon Gebski. Canada. Color. Stereo. 30 Minutes.

Overview: Originally airing on the Outdoor Life Network, *Creepy Canada* was a 40-episode series lasting several years that focused on a variety of paranormal and cryptozoological subjects, mostly relating to sightings and investigations confined to the Great White North. Host Terry Boyle (and, briefly, Brian O'Dea in the third season for some episodes) narrated the various topics with a definite bias towards sensationalizing the subjects, if not outright promotion of events as being factual. Still, comments from skeptics such as Dr. James Alcock are occasionally interspersed with the eyewitness accounts to offer plausible counter explanations, such as faulty memories and group hysteria.

The show is heavy on staged recreations, which tend to dominate the visual format at the expense of any information being offered. The Bigfoot suit used throughout the production is above average, featuring an unusually accurate large-shouldered hominid (most sightings remark on the girth of the chest, shoulders and hips) and a slightly altered gorilla mask. Most recreations show the cryptid stomping through the Canadian wilderness, hunting for game near the abundant waterways in the country, and occasionally wielding

weaponry, such as large sticks or rocks. Eyewitnesses will tell the camera what they've seen as the show's producers recreate the encounters with a variety of MTV-styled fast cuts and montage editing, overlapping the fictional recreations with the talking heads.

Each episode is comprised of multiple reports, thereby insuring a variety of topics, with never a single expanse dedicated to only one subject. This allows the editors to recycle many shots of the Bigfoot creature throughout the series and save on production costs. Episodes that will interest Ciné du Sasquatch viewers include: Episode Four, Season One ("Sasquatch"); Episode Seven, Season Three ("The UFO/Bigfoot Invasion"); and Episode Eleven, Season Three ("Bigfoot Alberta" and "The Great Dismal Swamp"). Fortean phenomenon fans will find *Creepy Canada* more rewarding due to the in-depth examinations of oft-unheralded ghost stories with a distinctly regional sensibility.

Cry Wilderness (1987)

Starring Eric Foster, Maurice Grandmaison, Casey Griffin, John Tallman, James Bryan, Faith Clift, Roger Davis, Jeff O'Haco, Lee Pavlo, Logan Richards and Marvin White. Produced by James Ernest Davis, William F. Messerli, Gene Ruggiero, Jay Schlossberg-Cohen and Philip Yordan.

ERIC FOSTER CASEY GRIFFIN JOHN TALLMAN

CRY WILDERNESS

SOMETIMES WE FIND FRIENDS IN THE MOST UNLIKELY PLACES.

DVD

The deceptively alluring poster from *Cry Wilderness* places Bigfoot in a much larger role than how it appears in the actual film.

Written by Jay Schlossberg-Cohen and Philip Yordan. Directed by Jay Schlossberg. USA. Color. Mono. 93 Minutes.

Overview: Young Los Angeles boarding school lad Paul Cooper spends a magical summer in Northern California with his estranged park ranger father Will. Paul spends a lot of time alone in the forests, enjoying the sense of isolation. Soon he meets and befriends Sasquatch, who also prefers solitude. Paul offers Bigfoot Coca Colas as a treat, which the cryptid particularly enjoys. After a tearful farewell, Paul returns to Los Angeles at the beginning of the next boarding school session.

During a heated discussion with his principal over Paul's constant telling of outrageous stories, Paul spills his tale of his secret summer Sasquatch encounter. The headmaster is so angered by Paul's continual defiance and lying that he threatens to have the boy kicked out. Later that night Paul has a phantasmagoric nightmare in which Bigfoot warns Paul that his father is in severe danger but doesn't know it yet. Awakening and feeling the dream is a portent of things to come, Paul steals away from the boarding school and hitchhikes his way back to Northern California.

When the boy arrives in Northern California, however, Paul learns that his father has brought in both a U.S. Marshal and a local Native American tracker to help uncover and destroy an elusive predator that is killing the area's protected wildlife. Paul tries to warn his father of his vision, but Will isn't in the mood. The marshal, who is also a big-time game hunter, and his in-the-know Indian guide actually suspect they're hunting Sasquatch after they overhear Paul's story. But realizing Will doesn't believe Paul, the duo concocts a story about an escaped circus tiger being the actual culprit as a convenient cover. Sasquatch's psychic dream sent to Paul turns out to be a premonition, just as Paul suspected. The three men set out to destroy the "tiger," with the marshal/hunter and his accomplice plotting to do whatever is necessary to kill the Bigfoot for profit — and, if need be, allow Will to perish in the process should he object to their goal. Realizing he has unwittingly placed his own father in mortal danger, Paul tags along to attempt to avert certain disaster; but can such a small boy outwit two seasoned experts and save his unsuspecting father's life — not to mention Bigfoot's as well — in the process?

* * * * *

After the enormous success of *Harry and the Hendersons*, it was only a matter of months before independent filmmakers rushed their own low-budget knock-offs into production. After all, and as the history of exploitation films within the Ciné du Sasquatch genre prove again and again, whenever cryptid cinema scores at the box office with an audience, rip-offs are sure to follow. Alas, some are more worthwhile than others, and, sadly, *Cry Wilderness* is an example of a lesser effort in Bigfoot films.

The problem lies within the core of the script, which is a bit surprising given the pedigree of at least one name involved: the inestimable Philip Yordan. For those unfamiliar with the legendary screenwriter's name or output, Yordan, the son of Polish immigrants, went on to write 66 Hollywood and Off-Hollywood feature films (and perhaps more, using pseudonyms). With such credits to his name as *The Big Combo*, *Johnny Guitar*, *El Cid*, *Houdini*, *Detective Story* and *55 Days at Peking*, it's no stretch to say the Academy Award–winning scriptwriter wrote for some of the biggest names in the business: Charlton Heston, Kirk Douglas, Alec Guinness, Tony Curtis and Joan Crawford, among many others. Therein, however, lies the rub: Many of these credits are actually "front" jobs for Hollywood blacklisted writers like Bernard Gordon, Ben Maddow and other pro–Communist Party members who were prevented from working in Hollywood under their own names in the destructive aftermath of the McCarthy-led HUAC (House Un-American Activities Com-

mittee) inquisition. Often, such as in the case of *Johnny Guitar*, Yordan would have little or nothing to do save lend his name to the project, as Ben Maddows actually wrote the majority of the script (with non-credited rewrites by Nicholas Ray, as well). At times, Yordan—who ran a virtual "crank 'em out" assembly line of blacklisted writers working for him — had several such talents all working on various projects at once in a single room! But always, to insure sales, the ubiquitously generic "Written by Philip Yordan" would appear on the actual title page. The oft-told tales — perhaps, as in all things Hollywood, a bit apocryphal — even became the basis in part for the well-received Martin Ritt film *The Front* in 1976, with Woody Allen acting as a Philip Yordan stand-in.

Sadly, that talent doesn't help *Cry Wilderness*, which feels as dashed out as many of the later efforts from the one-man scriptwriting factory. By this point in his career, Yordan was collaborating with this film's director on low-budget films mostly bound for home video and/or international-only distribution. Schlossberg-Cohen also worked with Yordan on the cult favorite *Night Train to Terror* and the little-seen but equally fan-appreciated *Carnival of Fools*. *Cry Wilderness* owes, at least in part, its existence to the earlier distribution of *Night Train to Terror* in that *Night Train to Terror*—which is an anthology film — was actually just three shelved feature films that Yordan, as script doctor, compacted into 20- to 30-minute segments, complete with a hastily-written wraparound. The wraparound, which featured John Phillip Law and Cameron Mitchell as God and Satan taking a train ride and discussing the three stories as proof of good or evil inherent in the human species, seemingly inspired the pair to look to pad *Cry Wilderness* with a lot of stock nature footage of wild animals. This reduced the production costs substantially. Not surprisingly, *Cry Wilderness* has begun to enjoy a limited "so bad it's good" cult reputation, though most just find it tediously predictable. Nowhere near as outré as *Night Train to Terror*, it nonetheless will entertain fans of the Ed Wood school of filmmaking who enjoy gawking at technical deficiencies, bad acting and plot holes large enough to hold a Bigfoot track. And speaking of trains: In a bizarre case of a few degrees of Hollywood separation, Philip Yordan frequently fronted for Bernard Gordon (*Johnny Guitar* and *Day of the Triffids*), who was responsible for the Bigfoot-on-a-train film *Horror Express*! It's truly a small planet in the world of Bigfoot films.

The Curse of Bigfoot (1977)

AKA: *Teenagers Battle the Thing*. Starring Bob Clymire, Jan Swihart, Bill Simonsen, Ruth Ann Mannella, Ken Kloepfer, Mary Brownless, Phil Catalli, Jackey Neyman and Augie Tribach. Written by James T. Flocker. Produced and Directed by Dave Flocker. Color/Black & White. USA. Mono. 88 Minutes.

Overview: Dr. Bill Wyman, a high school teacher, is having a difficult time keeping his students interested in his lecture on Bigfoot, despite showing them clips from a Hollywood horror film to set the tone. He invites Norman Mason, an older man clearly suffering from mental instability, to lecture to the class. The elderly man relates a tale of woe in which he took a group of student archeologists into the woods, whereupon they stumbled upon the tomb of Bigfoot. After removing the Sasquatch corpse from the cave, however, it came to life and began slaughtering them. Forced to fight for their survival, they eventually set the beast ablaze with the help of local lawman Sheriff Walt. The ordeal was so traumatic that the expedition's survivors — himself included — have been under intense psychiatric care and will need to remain so for the rest of their lives to avoid depression and suicide. Soberly reflective, Dr. Wyman's students realize Bigfoot is real.

* * * * *

Many low-budget independent films of decades past were often re-released with different titles. To fool distributors, new scenes were sometimes shot and edited into the existing features, and new title cards were added with an alternative title. But it's very rare when a film made 17 years earlier, as was the case with *The Curse of Bigfoot*, is converted into a newer one and even utilizes the same actor — in this case, Ken Kloepfer, who ages in front of the viewer's eyes without the aid of any make-up trickery.

In 1958, the filmmaking team of brothers Dave and James Flocker made *Teenagers Battle the Thing*, a black and white, nearly hour-long movie. This mini-feature concerns Kloepfer's character Norm Mason, who leads an expedition of teenage students into the woods in search of archeological artifacts. When they enter a previously undiscovered cave, they find it is a tomb for an ancient Indian mummy. Removing the corpse, they soon realize what a mistake they've made when the mummy awakens from its 1,000-year slumber and begins to kill everyone it encounters. With the help of local Sheriff Walt, they eventually trap the creature and set it ablaze, burning it to death (again).

The film was never properly released, being seen only at a few local showings by the brothers. Watching the footage, it's no mystery why: *Teenagers Battle the Thing* feels more like the student-produced film it is than any serious attempt by even a modest independent filmmaker attempting to cash in on the drive-in market of the 1950s that routinely played such fare. With static camera-on-a-locked-tripod direction, disinterested non-performers whose chief asset was an ability to avoid looking directly into the camera lens, a ridiculous excuse for a mummy costume, and no production values, the film justifiably sat unreleased and unseen for almost two decades.

Cut to the 1970s. The Sasquatch craze is in full swing. *The Legend of Boggy Creek* has made its landmark impact in Ciné du Sasquatch and on the public at large. A sequel and countless knock-offs have been released to audiences hungry for cryptid thrills. Television offers such popular series as *In Search Of*, *Bigfoot and Wildboy* and, of course, the ratings colossus pairing of Bionic Bigfoot and Cybernetic Steve Austin in *The Six Million Dollar Man*. Against such a backdrop, it's easy to grasp why the Flockers decided to dust off their older film, shoot new scenes, add some nature footage to pad the length and release the newly-crafted results as *The Curse of Bigfoot*.

Alas, from the "trick" opening, which turns out to be a monster movie being screened by the professor in an attempt to jolt his jaundiced students, to the technical limitations on display (or, rather, semi-display, as much of the film is terribly under-lit), and concluding with the flashback within a flashback narrative, *The Curse of Bigfoot* proves to be the Curse of the Viewer.

The cryptid is actually only in the film for a few minutes. The real monster of the show is the Indian mummy, which is inexplicably simply referenced as being Bigfoot. Flocker adds a boring half-reel of forestry footage to set the stage and intercuts interminable shots of the teacher and students endlessly hiking through a non-matching locale. At every point where it becomes clear the mummy is not Sasquatch, the professor narrates to explain that, yes, it *is* Bigfoot. Alas, the attempt to hypnotize the audience into denying what they're seeing fails. The papier-mâché nature of the mummy's rigid mask looks nothing like a cryptid and therefore makes no sense. Perhaps the filmmakers believed the film would be shown at drive-ins where the ambient light would help wash out such revealing details. But as the movie was quickly sold to independent TV markets, such wishful thinking melted away in the bright glare of the cathode rays.

Often considered one of the worst Bigfoot movies ever made, *The Curse of Bigfoot* really shouldn't be held up as such, because technically, it's not actually a Bigfoot movie but a *pretend* Bigfoot movie. If looked upon as a typically bad, misleadingly-titled horror film of the era(s), this viewer has seen much worse. Still, unless one is seeking a sure cure for insomnia when all medicinal prescriptions have failed, *The Curse of Bigfoot* should be avoided except by ultra-completists and those who love movies so bad they're marginally good.

The Daily Show (Multiple Appearances) (TV)

Hosted by Jon Stewart. Featuring Vance DeGeneres, Stephen Colbert, William Zapuncic, Ray Crowe, Jim Baum, Dave Shealy and Don Keating. USA. Color. Stereo. 30 Minutes.

Overview: Comedy Central's popular *The Daily Show* with Jon Stewart has featured several cryptid segments during its decade-plus run. The latest was during the August 9, 2007, show in a reoccurring segment called the Subaru Random Road Trip with a 30-second focus on roadside "shrines to towering man-beasts." The MTV-styled promotional spot shows graphics of Bigfoot against state roadmaps of Washington, California, Oregon, Florida, Arkansas and Oklahoma, along with the names of the various attractions promoting hominid photo opportunities for sightseeing tourists in their Subaru vehicles.

On March 4, 1999, in a segment called "Big Foot-Long," field reporter Vance DeGeneres visits the Poconos to interview elderly William Zapuncic, who claims to have encountered a hot dog–hungry Sasquatch back in 1962. Describing the cryptid as possessing huge eyes and a "classical Greek nose," the retiree relates how Bigfoot attempted to take three "weenies" from his backyard wiener roast ("because they smelled so good") until Zapuncic shouted out for the startled creature to stop.

A little over a month earlier, on February 17, 1999, *The Daily Show* had Stephen Colbert in a segment called "Bigfoot Fetish" on location in King County, Washington. There Colbert interviewed Jim Baum, a horse ranch owner. Baum relates how he could not develop his ranch to his liking because county officials have placed Sasquatch on the endangered species wetlands list. Over Baum's skepticism, Colbert suggests that the fact no one has ever seen a Sasquatch on Baum's property is convincing proof the species *is* endangered and needs protection. Next Colbert turns to wildlife expert Ray Crowe, who expresses doubts about the King County prohibition on wetlands development because he believes the Sasquatch species is so plentiful. Estimating that Bigfoot outnumbers the local bear population 10 to 1, Crowe maintains there is abundant proof of the American Abominable Snowman's existence, citing for one example the fact that there are numerous holes along the rural trails where he believes Bigfoot has pulled large rocks out of the ground.

The Daily Show had previously reported on the Skunk Ape in Florida as well, interviewing Dave Shealy, who, along with his brother Jack, has been studying the smelly swamp hominid all his adult life. The brothers' modest "Skunk-Ape Research Headquarters" outside of Ochopee, Florida, doubles as a tee shirt and souvenir shop, as well as a campground entrance for tourists. And not to leave Ohio out of the loop, Don Keating, cryptozoological researcher of the so-called Grassman, has also appeared on *The Daily Show* in his basement Bigfoot headquarters, explaining how the evidence of Sasquatch in his state is simply too overwhelming to ignore.

Danger Mouse ("Bigfoot Falls") (1991) (TV)

Featuring the voices of David Jason, Terry Scott, Edward Kelsey, Brian Trueman and Jimmy Hibbert. Produced by Brian Cosgrove, Mark Hall and John Hambley. Written by Keith Scoble and Jimmy Hibbert. Directed by Keith Scoble. UK. Color. Stereo. 25 Minutes.

Overview: Secret agent Danger Mouse is the world's greatest rodent detective. Along with the assistance of his incompetent but well-meaning aide Penfold, Danger Mouse takes on a variety of arch fiends, creatures intent on world destruction, and related assignments from his immediate superior Colonel K.

After a series of sightings of a scary Sasquatch in Canada, the Colonel sends Danger Mouse and Penfold north to investigate and apprehend Bigfoot if necessary. Penfold is less than thrilled, afraid the hominid won't look favorably upon their mission, but Danger Mouse is not worried, having bested aliens, demons and worse in past adventures. Alas, the overly-confident Danger Mouse doesn't realize that "Beeg-foot" (as his proper English accent renders the hominid's name) is indeed big — as in huge — towering over 40 feet tall. Their first encounter results in the creature stomping Danger Mouse into a pancake, and the second has Danger Mouse being tied into a rodent pretzel.

Hopping into their secret agent flying car, they track Bigfoot to his cave lair. Danger Mouse confronts Sasquatch, reeling off a long list of offenses for which the secret agent must arrest the puzzled hominid. Bigfoot explains that he's not really to blame, that it's the result of his pedicure problems owing to his extremely large feet. Between his fallen arches, ingrown toenails and corns, Bigfoot explains he often blacks out from the pain while walking and stomps various log cabins and the like while in a trance-like state.

Danger Mouse decides to enlist the aid of a bona fide RCMP — not a Royal Canadian Mounted Police office, but rather a licensed Royal Canadian Mounted Pedicurist. As luck would have it, a small tribe of Blackfoot natives have taken just such a pedicurist hostage. After Bigfoot frightens the whooping natives away, Danger Mouse frees the pedicurist to attend to Sasquatch's feet. As Danger Mouse and Penfold depart, several French Canadian underground gnomes (which the narrator labels "metrognomes" and then laughs at his own witticism) pop their heads out of the ground to watch the super spies fly away in their winged car.

* * * * *

Danger Mouse, from England, is similar in style and tone to the old *Bullwinkle* cartoons produced by Jay Ward in America. With very limited motion and repetitive use of the same poses for the main characters, each episode focuses on verbal hi-jinks and situational comedy over fluid animation and visual storytelling. Alas, whereas Ward's cockeyed creations had a certain zany flair for riposte humor and unexpectedly adult elements of satire, *Danger Mouse* is much more cast in the traditional kiddy mold, its tone watered down to be innocuous and tolerable to any age range — any, that is, save for those viewers over the age of 10, for whom the series will be an endurance test.

"Bigfoot Falls" is a lesser entry in the long-running show's history, and that's because it never quite manages to incorporate Bigfoot in a cohesive manner. The first half of the episode is spent with the typical exposition favored by the spy genre, with Danger Mouse and Penfold receiving their orders from Colonel K, flying in their aerocar to the exotic scene of distress, and stumbling around for awhile before actually encountering Sasquatch. The pace picks up when Danger Mouse tackles Bigfoot head-on, but the size differential between them renders moot any notion that Danger Mouse can do anything more than lecture such a gigantic foe that is so beyond his reach, literally and figuratively.

In fact, when Danger Mouse and Penfold finally do have their first conversation with Bigfoot (who speaks with a drippy Cockney accent for unexplainable reasons, given that Bigfoot is characterized as being a native Canadian) in the beast's cave home, lecture is precisely all that Danger Mouse does, citing a list of punishable offenses for which he insists the creature must surrender. Disappointingly, Bigfoot agrees

he's been bad without the slightest protest and apologizes, but blames his actions on his unendurable foot agonies, which cause him to go "ape" and level mountain tops, crush trees, etc. The ridiculous manner in which Bigfoot speaks ("It's me feet what causes it!") is only lacking the exclamatory "Gub'nor!" to complete the stereotype, and the idiotic mentality the giant maintains is only superseded by Penfold's constant moronic behavior.

On the subject of stereotypes, the portrayal of the Canadian Blackfoot tribe is beyond one-dimensional and dangerously close to racism. Complete with war paint and hands patting "Woo woo!" over their mouths, eagle feathered headbands and attire more appropriate to Navaho natives from the Southwest portions of the United States (where the climate is warm), this vision of a hostile group of "Indians" would doubtless be censored had this show been exported to America or Canada. It's akin to portraying an African in black face eating fried chicken, or a Brit going on about "tea and scones, old chap" while speaking with an upper-class snob accent, checking his pocket watch on his tweed vest, and twiddling his handlebar moustache. It's notable that for all of its mockery of Canadians, the French, the Blackfoot tribes and even cryptids, Danger Mouse and Penfold never seem to quite receive the same amount of satirical excess themselves (unless one factors in the pair's incorrigible stupidity).

Lacking much in the treatment of Bigfoot in terms of novelty, "Bigfoot Falls" is appropriately named. This episode falls flat on its mousey face owing to a lack of creativity, stilted dialogue, banal Bigfoot realization, and — worst of all — an ongoing lack of simple but necessary entertainment value. If you're a fan of *Danger Mouse*, you'll find it a treat, but for Bigfoot film fans there's nothing here you've not seen before and better rendered elsewhere.

Dark Stalkers (1995) (TV)

Featuring the voices of Kathleen Barr, Scott McNeil, Gary Chalk, Ian James Corlett, Lisa Ann Beley, Kyle Labine, Laura Harris, Saffron Henderson, Lisa Harris, Colin Murdock, Michael Donovan and Venus Terzo. Produced by Daniel S. Kletzky and Kenzo Tsujimoto. Written by Katherine Lawrence and Brooks Wachtel. USA. Color. Stereo. 30 Minutes.

Overview: Evil galactic overlord and planet collector Pyron has decided to rule the Earth. In order to achieve his dark quest, he summons Demitri, lord of the vampires, to be his assistant. A loose affiliation of bad monsters are enlisted by Demitri to help in his quest: Morrigan Aensland, an alluring but lethal succubus; Anakaris, a Pharaoh mummy with super powers; Lord Raptor, a rock n' roll zombie king; and Bishamon, a supernatural samurai. Meanwhile, a feline human warrior named Felicia assembles her own good group of counter-insurgent fighters to defend their home world: Bigfoot and his nephew Hairball; Johnathan Talbain, the ferocious fighting werewolf; Victor von Gerdenheim, a Frankenstein-like creature; and Rikou, a merman with aquatic super powers. In the neverending struggle between the forces of darkness and light that ensues, who will survive to either enslave or free the planet?

* * * * *

Capcomm first introduced the venerable *Dark Stalkers* as a videogame called *Vampire* in Japan but translated into the more marketable *Dark Stalkers* in America. Much like their successful *Street Fighter* games, *Dark Stalkers* featured up to 10 playable characters and 2 non-playable "bosses," which enabled great variety among users who were accustomed to the usual 2- or 4-player modes of other videogames. The new game quickly exceeded Capcomm's hopes and became a sensation that lead to the inevitable franchise of merchandise, spin-offs, and, of course, requisite cartoon series.

For both the videogame and the animated series, Capcomm developed an entire back story for the venerable cryptids. For example, though drawn as the white-furred creature more typical of the Yeti sightings in the Himalayan Mountains, the *Dark Stalkers'* hominid lived in the basin of the U.S. Rocky Mountains along with approximately 100 of its own rarified kind (which is odd, because there are so fewer white-haired hominids reported in North America than the Far East). Nor is Sasquatch a primitive, non-verbal being as depicted in most scenarios. In fact, they have named their village Crevasse (after the nearly-inaccessible opening that humans lack the ability to scale) and even have an international postal mail system called "Makai Postal" or Stone Postal! The Yetis can thus communicate in 4 days with anywhere on Earth by sending messages to one another. In summation, *Dark Stalkers* envisioned Sasquatch as a sophisticated, intelligent hominid species quite the equal to *Homo sapiens* in many aspects.

Despite the relatively developed mythos, *Dark Stalkers* as a cartoon series often received fan derision for its simplistic storylines and relatively crude animation. Some fault the cultural differences that haunted the U.S.-based but Japanese-funded show, specifically pointing fingers at Kenzo Tsujimoto, Capcomm's marketing director, who was responsible for the translation of the game into a sustainable narrative of ongoing adventures as a cartoon. Rather than address many understandably difficult problems between the two countries, Tsujimoto apparently resorted to simplification of the core concepts, watering down the unique flavor of the videogames and downplaying their relatively complicated mythology into a more kiddy-friendly format. As far as the Sasquatch character went, this was minor though ironic. "Sasquatch" simply became "Bigfoot" but otherwise remained the same, which is remarkable given that "Yeti" is the more fitting name for the portrayal of the snow-favoring hominid tribe.

Although the series ran only 13 episodes on the USA Network and was subsequently cancelled owing to fan indifference, *Dark Stalkers* was a perennial local TV syndication favorite because of the high recognition value of the videogame among the younger viewers, as well as its relatively benign content. The animation company who produced it, DiC Entertainment (pronounced "Deek" Entertainment), was a formerly French-based company which had moved to Burbank, California, in the early 1980s, whereupon it cranked out numerous cost-saving Saturday morning cartoon series. Among the better-known (or more notorious, depending on your opinion) were the first season of the *Care Bears* series, as well as *Inspector Gadget*, *The Real Ghostbusters*, *Rainbow Brite*, *Mary-Kate and Ashley in Action* and *Swamp Thing*. Generally known for its poor product in terms of stylistics and puerile content, the DiC adaptation of *Dark Stalkers* followed the company formula to a fault, which is why fans of the videogames objected so strenuously. In terms of the Sasquatch tribe, among the more egregious examples of the dumbing down were the manner in which they formed a circle and spewed streams of what appeared to be icy vomit skyward to form a protective dome above their heads. They also spoke like inbred hillbillies, took literal pie shots to the face, and utilized a limited locomotion that all but insured their fight scenes were kept to a minimum. This is a rare case wherein the videogame treated the Sasquatch legend far superior to the cartoon show based upon it, even down to the quality of the animation itself.

Demonwarp (1988)

Starring George Kennedy, David Michael O'Neill, Pamela Gilbert, Billy Jayne, Hank Stratton, Colleen McDermott, Michelle Bauer, Shannon Kennedy, John Durbin, Jill Marin, Joe Praml, Larry Grogan and Bruce Barlow. Produced by Richard L. Albert and Mark Amin. Written by Bruce Akiyama, Jim Bertges and John Carl Buechler. Directed by Emmett Alston. USA. Color. Stereo. 91 Minutes.

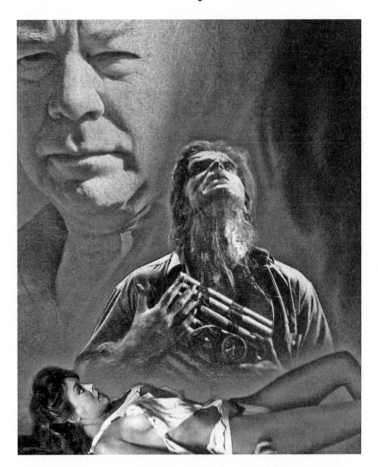

Cover art from the VHS release of *Demonwarp*.

Overview: In the desolate Old West, a wandering preacher witnesses the crash-landing of a UFO mere yards from where he stands. A century later, Bill Crafton attempts to spend some quality time with his daughter Julie in a remote cabin in an area known as Demon Woods, little realizing they are being stalked by a Savage Sasquatch hovering just outside the windows. The beast bursts inside and knocks Bill aside. It then grabs Julie, killing her in front of Bill's wide-stretched eyes before he passes out. Bigfoot drags Julie's corpse away.

Months later a group of college-aged vacationers arrive at the same cabin. One of them is Jack, whose Uncle Clem owns the rental retreat. The others — Carrie, Tom, Cindy, and Fred — joke about the rumored killings in Demon Woods to creep themselves out, but the kidding stops when they arrive at the cabin and find its door smashed off the hinges. Inside the place has been vandalized, or so Jack theorizes. A shotgun blasts from the front yard. Carrie, Tom, Cindy, and Fred rush outside the cabin to find Bill Crafton. He holds them at gunpoint and tells them the cabin is dangerous, even going so far as to explain his daughter's disappearance. He warns them about the killer Bigfoot, but before he can order them to leave the area, Jack grabs Crafton's gun. Crafton stumbles away, realizing he cannot make them believe his story nor their own impending mortality.

Later that night Jack explains the truth behind his coming to the cabin. His uncle has gone missing, and there's been no sign of him for weeks. As a result, Jack has brought guns and intends to find whatever abducted his uncle. Sufficiently spooked by the day's events, they all go to bed. While Jack and Carrie make love, Fred and Tom decide to play a prank on Cindy. Fred dons a Bigfoot costume and taps on the window outside the bathroom while Cindy showers. Tom comforts Cindy when she screams and runs into the hallway. Alas, believing Fred is still joking, they refuse to open the door and let him back inside when he claims a real Sasquatch is approaching him. Bigfoot grabs the costumed Fred and carries him away.

Jack and the rest search outside for their vanished friend, finding nothing but parts of his costume. They retreat into the cabin, but the Bigfoot attacks again. This time it knocks Jack aside and kills Tom, carrying his body away with him. By the time Jack recovers and tries to shoot at the Sasquatch, it is long gone. Realizing they cannot remain in the cabin any longer unless they wish to meet their inevitable deaths, they decide by dawn's light to set forth, heading for a nearby logging road which will carry them to a small town.

Meanwhile, Betsy and Tara search the area looking for a pot stash Betsy's brother has planted. Alas, it has been trampled flat. Shrugging it off—along with their clothes—Betsy and Tara sunbathe on the spot, unaware Bigfoot is eyeing them from behind a nearby tree. Not far away, a wildlife photographer finds the remains of Bigfoot's earlier victims, and soon after the creature itself. It chases him through the forest until finally slamming his arm into a hunter's trap and jabbing a makeshift spear into his gut, stirring his intestines as the photographer dies screaming. The sunbathing beauties fare no better. Tara's head is ripped off, her blood splattering Betsy, while Betsy runs for her life, abandoning her friend to her fate.

Jack saves Carrie and Cindy from stepping into another hunter's trap. Clearly someone has gone through the forest and set dozens of them, hoping to capture Bigfoot. A sudden movement makes Jack take aim and shoot into the woods. An irate Crafton lifts his head, joining them. He explains he's been hunting Bigfoot and even wearing a yellow hat so that the cryptid can spot him that much easier. In addition to setting the traps, he's also rigged dynamite at various points, along with tripwire, hoping to blow Bigfoot to smithereens. They all agree to band together for safety when Betsy arrives, naked save for her bikini bottom, and incoherently mumbling about Tara's fate.

Bigfoot attacks, knocking Jack unconscious. Crafton tries to take a shot but cannot, for Sasquatch holds Betsy aloft. Crafton tries to lure the Bigfoot into tripping a bundle of dynamite, but the beast outwits him. It kills Crafton and carries off Betsy, alive and screaming. By the time Jack awakens, he is alone in the forest, with no sign of Carrie or Cindy. He finds Crafton's body and follows the tracks of the departing Bigfoot after collecting the bundles of dynamite and placing them in his backpack.

Soon Jack encounters zombies walking through the forests, each of whom obliviously ignores him. He follows them into a cave, whereupon he encounters Bigfoot and shoots him to death. To Jack's horror, Bigfoot transforms into his dying Uncle Clem, who explains to his nephew with his dying breath that he had no choice, as he was being controlled. Jack wanders deeper into the cave, where he finds Fred, still alive but bound. Inside a sealed doorway leading to the interior of the crashed UFO, the preacher rips the heart out of a strapped-down Betsy and offers it to the demon alien known as Astreth, who is the mastermind behind all that has occurred.

Fred tells Jack to leave while he can, but Jack is determined to save Carrie and Cindy. Alas, Cindy is already a zombie, as is Tom. An alert is sounded, and Jack is overwhelmed by a zombie horde. Just before Carrie can be sacrificed and her heart fed to the ravenous demon alien, Jack attacks and kills the preacher. He and Fred fight off the zombies who flood the control room of the ship, but in the process Fred is injected by the alien demon with the Bigfoot-transforming serum. Carrie is freed, and Fred begs them to leave him behind, showing them his arms—already he is becoming Bigfoot. Holding the sticks of dynamite to his chest, Fred waits until Jack and Carrie are free of the cave, and howls as the explosives go off,

destroying the ship, the zombies, himself and the cave. Jack awakens in bed with Carrie, having had a nightmare about the incident. Zombies pop up from the bed and claw at him. He awakens again and finds that Carrie has turned into a zombie. He awakens a final time and stares into space, traumatized.

* * * * *

Even though it's ridiculously bad for most of its running length, *Demonwarp* has gained a minor "so bad it's good" cult following since its original home video release in the 1980s. This is largely due to the younger teen set who saw and rented it during its first VHS debut. Lacking their own equivalent of *Half Human* or *The Legend of Boggy Creek*, they were surprised to see a hominid rendered so bloodthirsty (and with a penchant for decapitating humans). Many of this generation whose only previous exposure to Sasquatch was the family-friendly *Harry and the Hendersons* write today, in various nostalgia-laced reviews, of the uneasiness *Demonwarp* created in them, even as they admit they found it cheesy and unbelievable when they first watched it.

Normally a film as violent as *Demonwarp* would have been rated R and therefore seen by few pre-teen and teenaged viewers. But as this was a direct-to-video effort and therefore bypassed MPAA ratings scrutiny, it was easily rented by underage viewers. There was and remains no actual ratings code for home video stores in the USA, and despite the largely corporate takeover of the market decades later with the introduction of DVD, even the studios realized the benefit (albeit too late to control it initially) of having an ancillary market to sell their movies after theatrical revenues had been exhausted. Besides, it was a statistical fact that the single largest source of revenues for video rental stores was adult porn, which meant a "hands-off" in terms of any enforcement of obscenity or ratings controls on the VHS market, save in isolated cases.

Vidmark (as in "video market") specialized in these kind of direct-to-video releases, and *Demonwarp* is typical of their output: a "name" actor or two to help foreign market sales (in this case, George Kennedy shortly before *The Naked Gun* and its sequels revived his moribund career), lots of softcore-styled nudity and simulated love-making, plenty of gore, modest but professionally competent production values, and a science fiction or horror concept to insure global buyer appeal. Equally important to the Vidmark formula for success was what was *not* included in their average effort: well-written screenplays, good direction, believable acting, and a well-rounded entertainment experience. Not unlike the Roger Corman/New World-styled titles upon which they were based (but meeting with much less success, both in terms of quality, subversive nature and windfall profits generated), Vidmark movies were designed to be cut into action-filled, niche-marketed trailers so that video store owners would buy them to fill shelf space. If the final product was actually watchable from opening titles to final credits, of course, so much the better, but this was rarely the case.

Part of *Demonwarp*'s problem is the script, which is awash with competing and often contradictory concepts. It first begins as a flying saucer mystery. Then it shifts a century forward and restarts as a typical Ciné du Sasquatch entry, with Bigfoot on a killing spree for no explicable reason. Later it devolves into a "shocking surprise" involving the walking dead, Bigfoot as a werewolf-ish transforming entity, aliens attempting to repair their spaceship, and human sacrifices to a demon overlord! (And the latter multiple twists all occur within the last 30 minutes of the film, no less.) To say it is one of the most unusually-plotted Bigfoot films in all the genre is a definite understatement, as even after multiple viewings it is difficult to summarize the narrative turns taken in *Demonwarp*.

According to special effects make-up artist and director John Beuchler in an email exchange with this writer, *Demonwarp* had a very troubled production history. Initially he was set to direct the film, but complications (after he'd built the Bigfoot suit and a couple of the other creatures) lead to his leaving the project, along with Jack Palance, who was initially set to play the Crafton role eventually taken by Kennedy. Emmett Alston was hired to direct after Beuchler's departure, which meant the project was a for-hire effort he evidently cared little about as director. Indeed, according to an interview with Jim Bertges (who was hired to do a two-week rewrite on Beuchler's script) on *The Unknown Movies* website, Alston (also the director of B-movie dreck *New Year's Evil* and *Nine Deaths of the Ninja*) mostly read the trade newspapers on the set while his director of photography actually set up most of the film's shots, rehearsed actors, etc. The results bear out Bertges' claims, as the acting is uniformly unconvincing and bland.

In terms of Ciné du Sasquatch and its recurring motifs, *Demonwarp* features a few novelties, not least of which is the "werefoot"—the Bigfoot who can transform from human to Bigfoot status and vice versa. The television series *Charmed* would later use the same premise (in an episode called "The Wendigo"), but as obscure as it is, *Demonwarp* preceded it. But the illogical and unexplainable contrivances throughout *Demonwarp* in terms of Bigfoot genre filmmaking offer little else to recommend. Part of the problem, of course, is the reported $225,000 total budget, of which $15,000 went to George Kennedy for 3 days of work as Crafton. Interestingly, one of Kennedy's requirements to appear in the film was that his daughter play the Tara role, even though Kennedy was reportedly upset her character's head was torn off by the Sasquatch during the shoot. Though off-screen, that incident pretty much encapsulates the strained rationale present throughout *Demonwarp*. There is no reason offered why an alien would need to employ zombies (nor by what mechanism, either) to rebuild its spaceship, nor why or how Uncle Clem is needed as a Bigfoot monster to roam the woods and kill indiscriminately.

Perhaps Beuchler's original script was referencing both Carpenter's *The Thing*, with the alien rebuilding its ship, and *The Six Million Dollar Man* having aliens employ Bigfoot to protect their mountain hideaway. If so, this was lost in the Bertges rewrite and left as plot holes that no (Big)footprint could possibly fill. The shots of the zombies using spare parts from a personal computer circa the 1980s to repair the obviously wooden walls of the spaceship set are laughable. One wonders what kind of alien (who is also described as a demon for reasons not divulged either!) is so incompetent as to need sub-human slave labor to fix a space craft clearly made out of drywall.

Finally, the Bigfoot suit is over-utilized. While it looks impressive, given that it was made for a reported $6,000 (which included two other creatures as well), the director shoots it in lingering close-ups in daylight so much and so often that it becomes ludicrous early on in the movie. One particularly bad trademark of this cryptid's screen appearance is a snarling lip on the left side of its mouth. Clearly an interior cable is being pulled to expose the fake fangs beneath, but the effects crew yank it so often it appears that this hominid suffers from Bell's Palsy. With its quivering, rubbery lip flapping in every shot, slime dripping from inside the gaping jaws, and incessant need to attack anything that moves in its vicinity, this is definitely one screen Sasquatch in desperate need of veterinary care for rabies.

While fans of cult starlet Michelle Bauer will appreciate her topless cameo, and fans of B-movies the use of the Bronson Cave location (also seen in older fare such as *Robot Monster* and countless others, as well as *Abominable*, another notable Ciné du Sasquatch entry), *Demonwarp* is too tediously nonsensical to qualify as anything more than a "minorpiece" of 1980s direct-to-video hokum.

Destination Truth (2007) (Multiple Episodes) (TV) (Doc)

AKA: *The Monster Hunter*. Featuring Josh Gates, Dr. Shrestha, Jeff Meldrum, Dr. M. J. Hajianpour, Kong Tobar, Sal Lou, Nick Ray, Rochom P'ngieng, Bechara Gholam, Evan Stone, Gabe Copeland, Mike Morrell, Rex Williams, Vanessa Joy Smith and Erin Ryder. Produced by Michael and Neil Mandt. Written by Michael and Neil Mandt, Joshua Cook and Nick Scown. Directed by Neil Mandt. USA. Color. Stereo. 45 Minutes.

Overview: Host and "extreme explorer" Josh Gates travels the world in search of popular mysteries and myths, attempting to document the latest and perhaps newest information about each topic he and his crew profile. Each trip begins with a typically disastrous attempt to simply make it to the designated locale, as Gates and crew overcome a seemingly unending set of obstacles merely to arrive intact. After finally accomplishing landfall, they begin exploring their episodic topic in earnest, if a bit exhausted by the grueling travel itself.

Many hominids have been featured. In an early episode called "Malaysia: Bigfoot," Gates journeys to Malaysia's Endau Rompin National Park in search of a Malaysian Sasquatch. He interviews a researcher who claims to have taken in-depth notes from local eyewitnesses. But as these witnesses are city dwellers, Gates feels it necessary to venture deeper into the jungles to document more recent and reliable sightings. In Endau Rompin he dubiously profiles a couple of eyewitnesses who seem unreliable at best and outright liars at worst. Undeterred, he pushes his native guides into the rain forest until they bolt in panic when he discovers hominid footprints and broken branches. Now alone with his camera crew, Gates records an audio growl of something in the woods. When word spreads about his findings, however, the Malaysian government requires Gates leave his plaster casting of the footprint with them. They do allow him to make a replica of his casting, however, which he provides, along with his audio recording, to various experts. None can identify the species who made the tracks and growls with any certainty, which Gates concludes means there may indeed be something to the Malaysian Bigfoot stories.

In the "Nepal: Yeti" episode during season two of the series, Gates and his team travel to the Himalayan Mountains to track the elusive Abominable Snowman. When they arrive in Nepal they are greeted by a Dr. Shrestha, who espouses a scientific belief that the bipedal Yeti is a nearly extinct species which has managed a modest comeback in its numbers owing to an increased awareness among locals and visitors that it is truly endangered. Encouraged by Shrestha's enthusiasm, Gates and crew head to a tiny village called Lukla, which is located a few days from the valley lying in the Himalayas where they believe they are most likely to encounter the cryptid. Alas, despite having a Sherpa guide who leads them to a monastery that reportedly has a Yeti scalp on display, the local monks threaten Gates if he attempts to utilize his cameras inside their holy place. Eventually a local woman agrees to speak on behalf of the disappointed team and manages to convince them Gates means no harm. The crypto-team videotape the scalp, which is deposited inside a locked case, but Gates' pleas to have but a solitary hair from the object for DNA analysis are rebuffed. Fortunately, the team later captures a thermal image at night of something moving, as well as casting footprints apparently made by a Yeti the next morning. Dr. Jeff Meldrum is consulted back in America. Meldrum concludes that the thermal image is useless because it is too indistinct, but that the Yeti footprint casts are significant because they are detailed and difficult to hoax.

"Cambodia: Wild Man" finds Gates and company travelling to the Far East to investigate the stories of a Wild Man living in the Cambodian jungles and, in particular, the claims made by journalist Nick Ray, who first published an account of a young girl who was held captive by the Wild Man for eighteen years. Gates eventually meets the father of the girl, whose name is Rochom P'ngieng, but the young woman is so traumatized by her ordeal she has not spoken since breaking free of the Wild Man's clutches. She does manage to show Gates some drawings she has made, which spurs the producer deeper into the jungles with his intrepid crew. They have some spooky close encounters with something, but because of the dense blackness of the wilderness they are not able to record any images of the Wild Man, despite their innate belief he was near them at times.

In "Brazil: The Mapinguary," the focus is upon a supposedly remnant species of a giant sloth, but the native depictions of the creature actually resemble a Sasquatch with claws and pointy fangs. Gates' expedition is inconclusive, and, owing to the density of the jungle, he and his crew are unable to detect any thermal images of a creature.

But in the episode entitled "The Yeren" Gates has more luck, interviewing a park ranger who has seen the Chinese version of Bigfoot, as well as tour guide Wang Dong, who, along with five tourists and a taxi driver navigating a remote mountainous road, encountered a black-furred, bipedal Yeren.

The popular series has also featured shows highlighting other cryptids, such as Yowie ("Australia: Yowie"), Orang Pendek in Sumatra ("Orang Pendek"), Skunk Ape ("Florida: Swamp Ape"), and Bhutan's Yeti ("Bhutan: Yeti"). Even more remarkably, many of its shows have featured creatures virtually unknown to most Western viewers, such as El Pombero, Nahuelito, Tokeloshe, and a host of others that — while not hominids — are equally fascinating in terms of documenting the truly stunning diversity of Fortean monsters populating the world, each with its own sworn adherents and unwavering eyewitnesses. Shot in a loose, handheld style reminiscent of both *The Blair Witch Project* and countless paranormal exploration TV shows, *Destination Truth* is an entertaining part-research, part-recreation concoction that remains wholly engrossing, even to non-believers who will revel in the sheer abundance of cryptozoological specimens they've never heard of prior to seeing this series, as well as the exotic travel footage to what are truly some of the most remote corners of the globe.

Dexter's Laboratory ("Sassy Come Home") (1997) (TV)

Featuring the voices of Jim Cummings, Christine Cavanaugh, Kath Soucie, Kat Cressida, Frank Welker and Jeff Bennett. Produced by Donna Castricone and Linda Simensky. Written by David Smith. Directed by Genndy Tartakovsky. USA. Color. Stereo. 7 Minutes.

Overview: Dexter, the boy genius, has a laboratory in which he crafts his ongoing experiments. Alas, his huge-footed sister Dee Dee is always gaining access (despite Dexter's attempts to keep her out) and ruining his latest breakthrough.

When their family goes camping, Dexter decides to use the opportunity to slip away and document the existence of Bigfoot. But Dee Dee finds Bigfoot first. Mesmerized by Dee Dee's enormous feet, the two instantly bond, much to Dexter's chagrin. Dexter takes photographs with his 35mm film camera and races back to his lab to develop them. Realizing her newfound friend Bigfoot will be forever exposed if Dexter processes the negatives, Dee Dee sets out to ruin the photographic evidence before her brother reveals the existence of the shy, hidden hominid.

* * * * *

Dexter's Laboratory was a Hanna Barbera creation that aired on Cartoon Network during the revitalization era of the venerable animation studio that also created *The Flintstones*, *Scooby Doo* and *Jonny Quest*. *Dexter's Laboratory* featured a rough-hewn style of drawing

and a sensibility seemingly equal parts child version of Jerry Lewis' *The Nutty Professor* and grotesque exaggerated cartoon style of *Ren and Stimpy*. With his average, normal, suburban American parents (though Mom tended towards obsessive-compulsive) and his cloying but crafty sister Dee Dee, Dexter was also clearly a forerunner of the later *Jimmy Neutron* series. But whereas *Jimmy Neutron* geared its humor much less towards the adults who might be watching, *Dexter's Laboratory* was genuinely aimed at young adults as well as the obvious kiddy viewers. This perhaps explains how Seth McFarlane, one of the early directors of *Dexter's Laboratory*, later went on to create the raunchier *Family Guy* series for Fox TV.

The Bigfoot depiction in "Sassy Come Home" (an obvious play on *Lassie Come Home*, with Roddy McDowall) is very human-looking, almost like a Neanderthal with slightly more hair covering his face. With his well-groomed moustache and neatly curled hair, he definitely seems more closely related to the *Homo sapiens* race than the usual hominid rendering. The preordained love match between Dee Dee, her colossal shoes, and Sassy's own huge feet is sweetly realized. In one comical montage, they slap their feet together as wild, psychedelic colors flow out around them like something out of *The Yellow Submarine*.

The classic cartoon characterization of Sasquatch being lonely is made explicit in "Sassy Come Home." When Dee Dee informs Sassy she must return to her domestic suburban homestead, Sasquatch literally bursts into frantic sobs and becomes inconsolable. This recurring motif is present in many Ciné du Sasquatch entries, perhaps owing to the original and perhaps most influential comic book Yeti appearance in *Tintin in Tibet*, which ends with the Yeti mournfully watching the departing Tintin (whose life the cryptid has earlier saved) from high atop his Himalayan crevice. It's present in a majority of cartoons featuring a hominid, including such satirical ones as *The Abominable Snow Rabbit*, which features Hugo the Yeti so in need of something living to love he's willing to forcibly enslave Bugs Bunny or Daffy Duck as his pet.

This vision of Sasquatch as the Ultimate Lonely Being is not so deeply buried beneath the child's psyche, though it may take recalling one's own childhood to fathom the ubiquitous nature of it. From a child's point of view, it is very probable the creature strikes a note of melancholy, owing to the cryptid's extreme isolation in setting and/or portrayal as inevitably alone or in small groupings edging towards extinction. Younger viewers tend to identify with the plight of any lonely character (hence the allusion to Lassie, the abandoned collie, in the title of this episode), experiencing as they do such extremes of emotional polarities by nature and the complicated rules set by adults which they must learn and master. In no uncertain terms, the isolated Bigfoot represents a perfect externalization of a child's worst fears of being abandoned or orphaned and left to defend for oneself in a cruel, uncertain world. A nearly human being like Yeti struggling to survive in the wilderness with an IQ nowhere near as masterful as a grown person's surely embodies the perfect distillation of a child's subconscious shadow-self, with all its attendant unspoken fears, unrealized tensions and nightmarish worries.

Indeed, Carl Jung would have a difficult time envisioning a more succinct symbolic representation — hence its enduring popularity and widespread utilization throughout animated and child-oriented Ciné du Sasquatch fare, even when, on the surface, played for laughs. Many a child-friendly fable contains latent images and moments of horror, after all. One has but to conjure Hansel and Gretel being eaten alive by an old woman in the woods, or Pinocchio's transformation into a braying donkey at the hands of once-kindly strangers, to immediately surmise that children are particularly aware of the lurking horrors inherent in all storytelling.

Dino Boy in the Lost Valley ("The Mighty Snow Creature") (1966) (TV)

Featuring the voices of Mike Road, John David Carson and Don Messick. Produced and Directed by William Hanna and Joseph Barbera. Written by Bill Hamilton. Created by Alex Toth. USA. Color. Mono. 6 Minutes.

Overview: Dino Boy, Ugh the Caveman, and Bronty the Brontosaurus are visiting a tribe of peaceful cave people at the foot of Snow Mountain. Suddenly, a huge Snow Creature attacks, scattering the terrified villagers. The Snow Monster abducts a brave little girl and retreats to the top of Snow Mountain with his captive.

Unfazed by the monster's size, Dino Boy, Ugh, and Bronty chase after the hominid. The Snow Creature deposits the girl in a cave and covers it with a boulder. While Ugh battles the Yeti, Dino Boy frees the girl. Bronty races up, offering Dino Boy and the girl a ride to safety down the mountainside. The Abominable Snowman gives chase.

Boulders rain down on its head, however, knocking it senseless. High above, the formerly scared villagers have now teamed up to toss boulders down onto the stunned creature. Beaten, the Snow Monster returns to its mountain retreat. The tribal people thank Dino Boy and Ugh for saving the girl and teaching them the benefit of group cohesion in defending themselves.

* * * * *

Hanna-Barbera cartoons and cameo cryptid appearances seem to be a match made in animation heaven. From the late 1960s original version of *Scooby Doo, Where Are You!* to the most modern, CGI-continued adventures such as *Chill Out, Scooby Doo!*, Bigfoot appears repeatedly in the Hanna-Barbera catalog. It's not just the venerable Scooby Doo and Shaggy that meet Yeti, either. *Birdman and the Galaxy Trio* featured a Yeti, as did the producing duo's premiere Saturday morning success, *Jonny Quest*. Later series, such as *The Berenstain Bears* and *Dexter's Laboratory*, also featured hominid cameos and guest shots. If it can be said that the Hanna-Barbera team had their fingers on the pulse of America's youthful television-watching audience with their endless parade of hit shows, then it can equally be deduced that the pair knew the value of Yeti in terms of pop culture appeal.

The towering Snow Creature of this episode is a nearly King Kong–sized cryptid with a penchant for smashing whole, uprooted trees into villagers' grass huts and a ravenous appetite for human sacrifices, particularly little children. In terms of actual reportage of some ancient lore regarding Sasquatch, this fits in with tales of women and especially children being taken by the "wild men of the woods" before anyone could react to prevent such kidnappings. So accustomed to this are the pacifist tribal cave people depicted here that they actually refuse to even give chase, telling Dino Boy and Ugh, "No one ever returns from Snow Mountain." Naturally, Dino Boy, Ugh, and Bronty refuse to allow such an intimidating history deter them, setting off immediately to rescue the missing child.

Whereas some Abominable Snowmen are presented as very human looking, with shaven faces to produce a more *Homo sapiens* kinship, this Snow Creature's visage is fully hair-covered, making it resemble a giant Muppet as much as a large simian. With its two lower-jaw fangs, gaping mouth, and popped eyes, the cryptid shown could be a Jim Henson design, albeit rendered in crude animation rather than with sophisticated animatronics. There is no attempt to humanize the hominid herein; it means to kill, maim and abduct with impunity, and never demonstrates the typical qualities of defending its turf against invading humans, a hallmark motif of the Bigfoot genre. Rather, from the very opening this Yeti storms into the peaceful humans' village, rips up trees, attempts to crush the scattering cave people, and never makes any attempts at understanding nor compassion. While many live action Savage Sasquatch feature films use this one-dimensional portrayal of an Abominable Snowman, it is rare in the cartoon versions. When presented, Yetis in animation fare tend to be either loveable, goofy, or (on those occasions when they're hostile) simply misunderstood. Not this Snow Monster. He ends the short, 6-minute cartoon the way he began it — savage and carnivorous — only taught a lesson by the now unified villagers. One gets a sense, however, that the Snow Creature will return to test the newfound alliance, having demonstrated its capacity for brutality in countless previous attacks.

While it's not much in terms of pushing the envelope of Ciné du Sasquatch, "The Mighty Snow Creature" at least lives up to its episode's name. Unlike many children's versions of the legend, this cryptid would prefer to consume any human as form emotional attachments. Such a Savage Sasquatch portrayal is again very rare in the typically G-rated cartoon versions.

The Dinosaur and the Missing Link: A Prehistoric Tragedy (1915)

AKA: *The Dinosaur and the Baboon*. Starring Wild Willie the Missing Link, Duke, Stonejaw Steve, Theophilus Ivoryhead and Miss Araminta Rockface. Produced by Thomas A. Edison and Herman Wobbler. Written and Directed by Willis H. O'Brien. USA. Black & White. Silent. 6 Minutes.

Overview: Wild Willie, a bipedal hominid, decides to go down river one fine day and capture some snakes for dinner. Mistaking a dinosaur's tail for a serpent, Willie pounds the flopping tail with a boulder. Seeing that this particular "snake" has two long necks (Willie fails to realize he's stoning a baby brontosaurus), the cryptid leaps atop the serpent's back and commences to wailing on it from its "front" side.

A comely cavewoman named Miss Araminta Rockface is frightened by the scene as she floats down the river in her boat. She screams for help, fearing the battle will harm her. Meanwhile, Willie is thrown from the bucking brontosaurus and left for dead on the ground. A timid caveman named Theophilus Ivoryhead approaches the prone Bigfoot, cautiously nudging it until he's convinced the beast has actually expired. He and two other cavemen carry the limp Sasquatch back to their camp, where Theophilus accepts Miss Rockface's passionate kisses and bravely tells her, "Yes, yes — a mere trifle! He irritated me, and I was forced to kill him!"

* * * * *

While generously renowned for his contributions to the art of motion picture special effects with his pioneering use of stop-motion in the features *The Lost World* (1925) and *King Kong* (1933), it was actually this early short film which established the career of Willis H. O'Brien. Using the earliest known example of claymation — the animation of 3-dimensional figures made of wire frames and clay bodies to provide the exterior flesh and fur — *The Dinosaur and the Missing Link: A Prehistoric Tragedy* was equally critical to the formation of Ciné du Sasquatch. In this short film (not unlike *The Conquest of the Pole*, made in France in 1912) one encounters all the familiar motifs that will later come to dominate the Bigfoot film genre for nearly a century to come.

O'Brien's short film is an impressive display for its era if for no other reason than it is entirely set-bound, employs no optical tricks (save the time-consuming process of minute movement per frame of photographed film that O'Brien was literally inventing as he made this short), and renders its punch line tale with the trademark sense of O'Brien's notable Irish humor (which was frequently on display in his later work). Indeed, so impressed was Edison that he put O'Brien under contract to make 8 more one-reelers for his Edison film company, though none had the impact of this early example of the animator's unique genius.

O'Bie (as he was affectionately known to friends) had a difficult life. Starting out as a cartoonist in San Francisco before becoming a sculptor for marble casts, he soon began to experiment with the stop-motion technique after several short, conventional, two-dimensional cartoon-styled works. To say his work was immediately impactful is an understatement, as the techniques he would create out of thin air and much diligence would revolutionize the art and industry of special effects, inspiring (and in some cases mentoring) others to follow: Ray Harryhausen, Jim Danforth, Dave Allen, and Phil Tippett to name but a few. Alas, just when it appeared O'Brien would experience the just rewards and fame from *King Kong*'s release in 1933, his divorced first wife Ruth shot their two children to death and turned the gun on herself, attempting suicide. Though she survived, she later died of cancer. Subsequently, O'Brien was forever haunted by a sense of tragedy that severely impacted his professional and personal life.

Thereafter, with the notable exception of *Mighty Joe Young* in 1949 (in which a severely alcoholic O'Brien was assisted by young protégé Ray Harryhausen, working on his first full-length feature), which won a technical Academy Award for Best Visual Effects (even though RKO insisted on receiving the credit publicly, O'Brien was also given an Oscar in private), his major contributions were behind him. Along with Harryhausen, and on his own, he struggled for years with many abortive projects: a stop-motion version of *Frankenstein*; a dinosaur epic called *Creation*; Viking warriors riding prehistoric eagles in *War Eagles*; and a cowboys versus dinosaurs epic titled *The Valley of Gwangi* (which was later produced and animated by Harryhausen after O'Brien's death). O'Brien even conceived an early Yeti film project which he labeled *Baboon* as the working title, but which was about the Abominable Snowman and set in the Himalayan Mountains.

In terms of Ciné du Sasquatch, *The Dinosaur and the Missing Link: A Prehistoric Tragedy* is a forerunner in many details. First, while the cryptid was called a baboon for the film's subsequent re-releases, this was likely as much to avoid the controversy surrounding Darwin's Theory of Evolution as to clarify what precisely the Missing Link itself was in terms of zoology. There is no way the depicted hominid can be anything but a cryptozoological specimen, no matter the change of title: It walks upright; it is roughly the size of a man but slightly larger; it is clearly unafraid of snakes (avoidance of which is a hallmark of most simian species); and it seeks to hunt and then slaughter an animal to devour. No baboon species has been documented as engaging in any such behaviors; but even if they had, the clear conception O'Brien renders is that this is a half-man, half-simian crypto species. In short, it is the first American Bigfoot ever rendered in a motion picture, complete with having the so-called grand-sized feet.

The Dinosaur and the Missing Link: A Prehistoric Tragedy embodies another crucial aspect of core thematic concerns to the Ciné du Sasquatch *oeuvre*. That is, when *Homo sapiens* meet a hominid — dead or alive — they will exploit it for selfish gain. In this humorous film, said exploitation is presented as the butt of a comical joke, with Theophilus(!) the caveman using its corpse to lie to his potential mate Miss Rockface and increase his desirability. But almost 20 years later, Carl Denham would do the exact same thing, albeit less to be seen as an alpha male with increased sexual prowess as much for power, fame, and money (which, of course, imbue the male owner with even *more* alpha male dominancy than merely relying on genetic predisposition). In other words, in both *The Conquest of the Pole* and *The Dinosaur and the Missing Link: A Prehistoric Tragedy*, two basic tenets of the genre are inherent in the first examples ever: Man must conquer all that is like him (especially all that is *too* much like him), and man must exploit said conquest for personal or tribal gain. The reverberations for the next century of Bigfoot-related films cannot be underestimated, for they are central to all that follows in Ciné du Sasquatch. Indeed, one will be hard-pressed to find many examples of the genre that do not touch upon these basic motifs.

Dr. Pepper Commercials ("We Exist") (Cameo) (TV) (2010)

Produced by Deutsch LA. Directed by Ken Lidster. USA. Color. Stereo. 30 Seconds.

Overview: The Dr. Pepper soda empire hired the influential Deutsch LA ad agency to produce a series of "We Exist" commercials featuring mythical creatures who attend an ongoing support meeting designed to bolster their collectively low self-esteem. It seems that the Easter Bunny, the Tooth Fairy, Santa, and even Bigfoot are taking an ego-bruising beating because everyone believes they are fantasy characters and not real flesh and blood creatures, as they know themselves and one another to be. The commercials employ a deliberately low-tech, Rankin Bass–influenced "look" of stop-motion puppet animation designed to invoke *Rudolph the Red-Nosed Reindeer*. In "Unbelievable," the Dr. Pepper Delivery Man holds a contest at the local support group meeting as the creatures try to decide who is the most unbelievable of them all, with Bigfoot chosen as the judge to pick the most unbelievable. When the confused cryptid selects the Dr. Pepper Delivery Man as the most unbelievable of those present and holds him aloft for the others to view, the human soda delivery man wryly smiles — point well-taken.

While the humorous tone guarantees that none will be offended, some Sasquatch purists will likely experience some mild chagrin that Bigfoot is lumped together with what are clearly nonexistent myths of obvious human origin, such as the Tooth Fairy. What is missing from such a viewpoint, of course, is that Bigfoot is in group therapy precisely because the commercial posits a world where the cryptid *is* real, and the outside world only believes Bigfoot is mythic. Therein lies the knowing craftiness of the "We Exist" spots — they can at once poke gentle fun at what are clearly popular folk tales, and at the same time suggest the beloved myths underlying the jests are actually real. The successful ad campaign continues to this book's publication date, often appearing in the drink aisles of your local supermarket as cutout standees and the like.

Dr. Who ("The Abominable Snowmen" and "The Web of Fear") (1967) (TV)

Starring Patrick Troughton, Frazer Hines, Deborah Watling, Jack Watling, Wolfe Morris, Charles Morgan, Norman Jones, David Grey, David Spenser, Raymond Llewellyn, David Baron, Reg Whitehead, Tony Harwood, Richard Kerley, John Hogan, Nicholas Courtney, Tina Packer, Jon Rollason, Ralph Watson, Jack Woolgar, Richardson Morgan and Roger Jacombs. Produced by Innes Lloyd and Peter Bryant. Written by Mervyn Haisman and Henry Lincoln. Directed by Gerald Blake and Douglas Camfield. UK. Black & White. Mono. 180 Minutes.

Overview: The Doctor is a time traveler who uses his TARDIS (Time and Relative Dimension in Space) transporter, disguised as an English-style police booth, to journey through time and space, helping to avert disasters and right wrongs. A member of the Time Lords, an extraterrestrial race who invented the TARDIS technology, the Doctor frequently visits Earth on various missions.

In "The Abominable Snowmen," a routine trip to the Himalayan Mountains allows the Doctor to reveal to his travelling companions,

Jamie McCrimmon and Victoria Waterfield, that he had visited this area before over 300 years ago. He instructs them to seek a "Holy Ghanta" and cryptically informs them he hid the holy relic on his last voyage for reasons that will soon become apparent. Meanwhile, Professor Travers, who is exploring the mountains with a cohort, is terrorized by an Abominable Snowman, who has apparently also killed his friend.

The Doctor visits the Detsen Monastery while Jamie and Victoria recover the Ghanta and an ancient sword. The Doctor stumbles across Professor Travers' dead friend. Meanwhile, tired of waiting in the TARDIS for the doctor's return, Victoria and Jamie venture outside to explore the snowy mountains, whereupon they find Yeti tracks. At the monastery, Travers recognizes the backpack the Doctor carries as belonging to his dead companion. Even though the monks who've taken in Travers have informed him the Yeti is responsible for the killing, Travers blames the Doctor in a fit of hysteria. The armed monks take the Doctor hostage, forcing him to face justice. The chief of the warrior monks, Khrisong, explains that some of their own have been slaughtered as well. The protesting Time Lord is tossed into a cell.

Victoria and Jamie discover the Yeti's cave and explore it. The Abominable Snowman rolls a boulder in front of the entrance, sealing them inside. Khrisong demands a trial to prove the Doctor's guilt, but the reigning peaceful monks object. In the cave, Victoria and Jaime discover a pile of strange, silvery orbs and steal one, fleeing after a fight with the Yeti. They meet Thonmi, a peaceful monk, and give him both the Ghanti and the silver sphere. Thonmi tells the ancient guru ruler of the monastery named Padmasambhava about the Doctor. The guru recognizes the Time Lord from his previous visit, but does not want the Doctor to interfere with something called the Great Plan. Nevertheless, Padmasambhava tells Thonmi to release the Doctor.

The Yetis attack the monastery. The beasts are finally repelled, but a slain hominid is revealed by the Doctor to be a robot, with the silver sphere Jamie and Victoria recovered being its source of power. Padmasambhava, meanwhile, orders all monks to leave Detsen because the Great Intelligence is almost ready to materialize and wants no humans present that could harm it. A vastly superior mind presence from another dimension, the Great Intelligence has been working for centuries to manifest itself physically on Earth to rule the planet. Realizing what he now faces, the Doctor enlists the aid of Khrisong to protect the monastery from being overrun by Yetis.

Abbot Songsten, who is the Great Intelligence's choice for human embodiment of its astral spirit, betrays the other monks and allows the Yetis into the sacred grounds. The Doctor uses Thonmi, Victoria and Jamie to distract the Great Intelligence while he smashes the equipment the force from beyond is using to control the attacking Yeti robots. While most of the Abominable Snowmen are thwarted, some still run errant on their own. Eventually the Doctor triumphs and saves the monastery, banishing the Great Intelligence (at least for a while). The centuries old guru Padmasambhava dies in the Doctor's arms but thanks him for his heroic stand. The trio departs in the Tardis, saddened but grateful they've at least thwarted the Great Intelligence in this round.

A few episodes later, in "The Web of Fear," Professor Travers is revealed to have survived his ordeal in Tibet and returned to London, where he has donated a supposedly lifeless corpse of a Yeti to a museum. Travers accidentally discovers how to control the Yetis with the silver sphere and warns Silverstein, the museum's curator, to dismantle the Snowman exhibit when the sphere goes missing. Silverstein won't hear of it. Shortly after the distressed Travers leaves, however, the sphere smashes into the Yeti and reanimates it, whereupon it attacks and kills Silverstein.

The Doctor, Victoria, and Jamie land in an underground railway station in the Tardis, only to find the station abandoned and covered with creepy webs. It is clear the Underground hasn't been used in some time, which makes no sense to the Doctor, as it should be working perfectly. They hide in a recessed area while soldiers march inside the tunnel, unwinding cable. The Doctor follows but instructs Victoria and Jamie to remain behind. When Victoria becomes trapped in a giant web, the soldiers return and capture her and Jamie. Meanwhile, at the Charring Cross station, the Doctor observes a Yeti wielding a strange gun of some kind. Soon another Yeti appears, also toting a gun. They both spray several shipping boxes with the weird webs while the hidden Doctor observes their actions.

Victoria and Jamie are taken to Staff Sgt. Arnold, who questions them as to why they were present in the tunnels. Anne Travers, Professor Travers' daughter, is also present. The Yetis set off an explosion which causes the webs they've spun to grow into a super mass of fungus. Soon the entire underground tunnel system is nearly encased in the sticky strands. Anne alerts Professor Travers, who is reunited with Victoria and Jamie. Travers marvels at their lack of aging since the

Cover art featuring an Abominable Snowman from a novelization of the Yeti narratives that appeared on *Dr. Who.*

Tibet expedition so many years previously, not realizing that the Doctor has the ability to travel through time via the TARDIS.

Eventually the Doctor and the rest of his team, plus Travers, meet and agree the Yetis must be under the control of the Great Intelligence again. The Doctor attempts to get to the surface to grab some parts to make a device that will interfere with the Yetis' control mechanisms, but he barely survives an Abominable attack in the process. He retreats below ground, telling all concerned that the Yetis are too powerful on the surface now. Yetis burst into the room in which they're holed up with Professor Travers, the latter of whom is now under the control of the Great Intelligence. The sinister dimensional being uses the possessed Travers' body to issue an ultimatum: Either the Doctor submits to having his brain drained, or the Great Intelligence will do so to Victoria and Jamie. The doctor is given a short amount of time to decide, as the Yetis leave. The Doctor decides to make a last-ditch attempt to repair a broken sphere that controls the Yetis and use the robot creatures against the Great Intelligence itself.

Piccadilly Circus underground station is the HQ for the Yetis and the Great Intelligence. There the hominids have constructed a glass pyramid to house their control spheres, and from which they plan to launch a massive army of Yetis to overrun London. Realizing he cannot beat the mental overlord's time limit, the Doctor surrenders to the Great Intelligence to have his mind washed. Jamie prevails however, using a damaged Yeti and ordering it to smash the glass pyramid. This causes a chain reaction which destroys the Yeti army. The Great Intelligence is beaten again, but the Doctor is disappointed the evil mind has not be totally destroyed, merely driven away to plot another day. He, Victoria, and Jamie vanish in the TARDIS.

* * * * *

According to the *Guinness Book of World Records*, *Dr. Who* is the longest-running science fiction TV show in history, and — in terms of production costs vs. lucrative returns — one of the most successful as well. Beginning in 1963, and characterized by its imaginative use of more traditional science fiction plots (as opposed to American TV programs, which tend to rely more on science fantasy, emphasizing the action over the technological possibilities) and creative special effects on the lowest of budgets, *Dr. Who* has conquered not only the fictional realms of space and time, but the entire international TV market, spawning endless comic books, fan magazines, novelizations, merchandising, and movies. As a testament to its enduring appeal, the character of the Doctor has been portrayed by 11 different actors during its 4-decades-plus existence, including Tom Baker, who is the most familiar Doctor to American audiences (owing to a brief U.S. syndication on PBS during the post–*Star Wars* craze).

It is as noteworthy that most American viewers lack knowledge of the *Dr. Who* series, which is so well-known in England and throughout much of the world. Part of the problem may have been that unlike most one-hour science fiction TV shows in America (*Lost in Space* or *Star Trek*, for example), *Dr. Who* was a serialized show running 25 minutes per day, 5 days a week, with a week's worth of such episodes constituting the storyline in total (although, it should be noted, only one week's worth of original content was produced per month). For example, "The Abominable Snowmen" afforded viewers the fun of tuning in each day to see the story progress until the culmination each Friday when the plot climaxed. This is antithetical to United States programming methodology, which has traditionally favored one hour or less per week, with self-contained stories that establish a conflict and neatly resolve it by closing credits. Even in the rare two-part episodes on American TV, there was never anything quite akin to the *Dr. Who* style of elongated format. While the show could meander as a result, and often felt padded by American "keep it fast and keep it simple" standards, it had the positive effect of allowing

viewers to luxuriate in each new story in much the same way that traditional soap operas do in the States. Perhaps only Dan Curtis' *Dark Shadows* series ever came close to the same technique on American TV; but despite that show's popularity, it's safe to say that it lacked the long-term impact that *Dr. Who* has enjoyed.

If *The Six Million Dollar Man* and *Bionic Woman* shows in the States established Sasquatch as a household name beyond any pop culture doubt, the same (if not more) can be said of *Dr. Who* and the popularization of the Yeti in the rest of the English-speaking TV world. So well-liked were the Yetis in their initial appearance in "The Abominable Snowmen" that they reappeared less than three months later in "The Web of Fear," as well as being revived for use in the unofficial "interim" *Dr. Who*–related one-off *Downtime* (which didn't feature the Doctor but had all the other major characters, settings, etc.). The Abominable Snowmen remain, along with the alien robot Daleks, among the show's favorite villains, inspiring some fans to go so far as to make their own versions of the so-called "missing episodes" of the series featuring the Yeti. The existence of the missing episodes is a result of the fact that the BBC broadcast the show live, with filmed content, in the earliest days (of which this was the fifth season) to reduce costs, and that kinescopes (16mm filmed transfers of the original live video broadcasts) have been lost (somewhat ironically, given the show's premise) in time.

Along with the earlier TV success of *The Creature* on the BBC in 1955 (which was made into an even more successful feature film by Hammer Studios as *The Abominable Snowman of the Himalayas* in 1957), "The Abominable Snowmen" and "The Web of Fear" rank among the most influential in British history in terms of Ciné du Sasquatch. These shows gave a tangible if fantastic realization of the otherwise distant expeditions being undertaken by such noted English explorers as Sir Edmund Hillary in the faraway mountains of Tibet. They also bear an enormous influence on their American cryptid counterparts, since before Sasquatch overtook the top slot for United States–set Bigfoot genre films, American movies focused on the Yeti rather than its North American relative. Not until Roger Patterson's historic 16mm "Patterson-Gimlin" film would the focus shift from Tibet to the Pacific Northwest of America (and into the rest of the states). Tellingly, even then Roger Patterson often hedged his bets by first introducing his accounts with the term "North America's Abominable Snowman" to capitalize and build upon preexisting recognition among the public.

The fact *Dr. Who* revealed its Yetis to be robots controlled by an otherworldly intelligence was also history-making. While this has come to be an accepted, almost clichéd idea in many Ciné du Sasquatch entries, it was novel in the era. In fact, many would argue that *The Six Million Dollar Man* basically copied this concept by having aliens use a robotic Sasquatch in the 1970s. Whether or not the influence is direct, the Bionic Man and Woman certainly followed in the large "footprints" left by the Yetis from *Dr. Who* (though, historically speaking, it was the Japanese anime series *Astroboy* in 1963 that first utilized the concept of a robotic Yeti; *Dr. Who* remains the first live-action incarnation of the idea, however, and had greater impact in England and most of the English-speaking world).

The depiction of the Yetis (while beloved by *Dr. Who* fans) is somewhat comical to most new viewers of the older episodes. This aligns with a frequent (largely American) criticism of the BBC series, which is that *Dr. Who*'s special effects often lacked the panache of their Yank counterparts. While undoubtedly true as a generalized statement, if one considers the scant budget the BBC spent on the show during the earliest runs, the criticism can be somewhat tempered. Sterling pound note for note, *Dr. Who* demonstrates an imaginative albeit distinctly British sensibility in terms of visual effects and their realization. Not unlike *Alice in Wonderland* mixed with *Monty Python*, there is an absurdist sense of comical interplay between viewer and effects that requires a bigger leap of faith than most American shows of the respective era. The TARDIS, for example, is a simple police booth on the outside, but once the characters step inside, it becomes a much larger room. While this is obviously achieved by simply cutting from the exterior booth to an interior set, it works on the level of playfulness many more reality-oriented, hardware-driven American SF efforts fail to attain.

Likewise, the rotund, slow-moving Yetis may appear off-putting to American viewers upon first glimpse. It's as if the *Dr. Who* creature costume designers took the "Snowman" aspect very literally, as the Yetis resemble nothing so much as fur-covered snowmen with dark, furry faces. Yet despite their deliberative movements, the cryptids are anything but friendly — under the direction of the Great Intelligence, they mercilessly slaughter humans on a scale heretofore unprecedented in Ciné du Sasquatch. While the show's budgetary constraints prevented the visualization of such mass destruction, "The Web of Fear" goes so far as to suggest a veritable Yeti army is in the process of being created to overrun and enslave Londoners. This level of aggression is so rare to the genre it wasn't until *The Mummy 3: Tomb of the Dragon Emperor* that it truly was visualized onscreen — and even then in more modest ambition in terms of sheer numbers of hominids and overall scope.

Dr. Who remains a popular franchise to this day, with a new series still in syndication in worldwide markets (albeit produced on a much higher level and with more state-of-the-art special effects). Still, for those interested in the field of Bigfoot cinema, these two keys episodes from 1967 and 1968 remain indispensably critical in understanding just how the Sasquatch mythos transcended all filmic and television barriers, and, in so doing, became a cultural mainstay.

The Don McCune Library ("Sasquatch") (1977) (Doc)

AKA: *Sasquatch Syndrome*. Featuring Don McCune, John Green, Mark Pittinger and Rod Puller. Produced, Written and Directed by Don McCune. USA. Color. Mono. 80 Minutes.

Overview: Seattle, Washington's KOMO-TV on-air personality Don McCune was a multi-talented writer, producer, host, director and even actor (as star of KOMO-TV's *The Captain Puget Show*). As part of a series he made entitled *Exploration Northwest*, McCune would explore subject matter of particular local interest and document the various personalities involved in their respective regional activities.

In 1977 and then in 2003, McCune produced and hosted two different Sasquatch docs. First was "Sasquatch Syndrome" in the 1970s, and then later a continuation and updating of that 30-minute effort's main focus, the appropriately-named "John Green" episode in the 2000s. "Sasquatch Syndrome" featured an analysis of the Patterson-Gimlin footage, a visit to the Mount Baker region where a hunter named Rod Puller displays Bigfoot tracks he found after hearing the cryptid cry out, and an interview with John Green about his life's work studying the elusive forest hominid. In 2003, John Green attended the International Bigfoot Symposium at Willow Creek, California, and McCune's camera was there to capture the buzz as Green highlighted his 44-year career as a cryptozoologist. Green showed the 1977 "Sasquatch Syndrome" to his eager audience before giving a multimedia presentation.

A few years after his death, McCune's widow had both "Sasquatch Syndrome" and "John Green" edited into one 80-minute DVD under the more generic title *The Don McCune Library: Sasquatch*.

Downtime (1995) (TV)

Starring Nicholas Courtney, Elisabeth Sladen, Deborah Watling, Jack Watling, Beverley Cressman, Mark Trotman, Geoffrey Beevers, Peter Silverleaf, John Leeson, Miles Richardson, James Bree, Kathy Coulter, Jonathan Clarkson, Miles Cherry, Alexander Landen, Richard Landen, David J. Howe, Tony Clark and Conrad Turner. Produced by Keith Barnfather, Andrew Beech, Paul Cuthbert-Brown and Ian Levine. Written by Marc Platt. Directed by Keith Barnfather and Christopher Barry. UK. Color/Black & White. Stereo. 65 Minutes.

Overview: Detsen Monastery in Tibet is the home of not only the mysterious Great Intelligence (an alien presence from another dimension) but robotic Yetis. The otherworldly Abominables serve the Great Intelligence by keeping away curiosity seekers and stopping any who would try to interfere with the Great Intelligence's goal to take control of the Earth. Though successfully bested by Dr. Who in the past, the scheming, mental power-being has never abandoned its desire to break fully into the human dimension.

Victoria Waterfield once helped Dr. Who banish the Great Intelligence but is now undergoing a mental crisis, tormented by visions of her deceased father, Professor Travers. She journeys to Detsen after a dream in which she sees her late father beckoning to her with a promise of reunification. Alas, it turns out Travers is possessed by the Great Intelligence, which is merely using his visage to manipulate Victoria into helping spread its malignant influence over the world in its latest attempt at global domination. Some 15 years later, Victoria has spent her considerable family fortune to open the New World University in London, a radical spiritual campus supposedly dedicated to the enlightenment of troubled youth. In actuality, it is a front cult for the Great Intelligence, which has transformed the students into brainless automatons. Called "Chillys" by outsiders because of their computer-like manner, they nevertheless cling to the belief they are on the verge of a return by "Chancellor" Travers, which will signal the beginning of a new dawn in human evolution. Victoria herself is equally under the Intelligence's spell, having been promised spiritual enlightenment in exchange for her services to the ethereal mastermind.

The Great Intelligence desires to consolidate its power by taking possession of Brigadier Lethbridge-Stewart, a retired military genius and former head of U.N.I.T. (UNified Intelligence Taskforce). U.N.I.T.'s primary mission is to combat all paranormal and alien hostilities as a covert wing of the United Nations. The Intelligence takes possession of Lethbridge-Stewart's daughter Kate and her son, little realizing it has merely taken Lethbridge-Stewart's grandson instead of the older man himself.

Meanwhile, Sarah Jane Smith, an investigative reporter friendly to U.N.I.T. and a long-time secret accomplice to Dr. Who, becomes aware of the New World University's sinister mission when she is contacted by them and asked for information about Lethbridge-Stewart. She advises U.N.I.T., which prompts the secret organization to launch its own counter-espionage attempt to gain critical data, lead by Sarah Jane and Lethbridge-Stewart himself. Eventually Lethbridge-Stewart orders U.N.I.T. soldiers into the hallways of New World when he discovers the "Chillys" have all been rendered immobile in strands of web courtesy of the Great Intelligence. The besieged uber-mind launches a counter-attack of Yetis, who rush to fight the human troopers head-on. An all-out battle for control of the city erupts, until Victoria turns on her former mentor and helps destroy the university's mainframe. The Great Intelligence is crippled and defeated in the ensuing explosions, sparing London from further danger.

* * * * *

The popular *Dr. Who* franchise has enjoyed an enduring history at the BBC. Fans adore the series, which is why every time the long-running show has been cancelled, it inevitably is revived at some later point. While *Downtime* is not an official *Dr. Who* entry per se (lacking as it does the venerable good Doctor himself), it nevertheless cleverly incorporates some of the titular series' mainstay protagonists and villains in one action-packed storyline. Chief among those popular antagonists include the disembodied Great Intelligence (a loose adaptation of the Cthulu Elder Gods mythos by H.P. Lovecraft into more concrete science-fiction terms) and the robotic Yetis (android cryptids being a sub-genre of Ciné du Sasquatch in and of itself, along with the "it turns out it's all just a man in a gorilla suit" sub-genre of Bigfoot films). While the synthetic Snowmen are bound to the Great Intelligence as mechanical henchmen, they nonetheless embody the threat of the nebulous, unseen force of the Great Intelligence. Lacking a physical incarnation, the Great Intelligence would play as nothing more than a voiceover menace which occasionally takes possession of human beings to control its destiny in the physical world. But with the addition of the Yetis, the dimensional demon is both an abstract and specifically incarnate horror that cannot be avoided on any plane of existence.

The Yetis in *Downtime* are transformational. That is, they can change from human to Yeti and back again. But unlike some films and TV shows in Ciné du Sasquatch, this is not because of a curse or genetic condition, but because the Great Intelligence wields so much power in the physical world that it can utilize technology in ways humans cannot yet imagine. This is a very novel variant in Bigfoot films, but it is not without at least some influence from the Killer Gorilla genre. That is, often a mad doctor in the latter genre will experiment upon a man and deliberately or inadvertently revert him backwards in evolution into a simian, or the process will be played forward in time by starting with a simian and bringing it forward to *Homo sapiens* status. Some examples of the first type (human-to-ape) include *The Ape Man* and *Altered States*. Examples of the latter (ape-to-human) include *The Island of Lost Souls* and *Captive Wild Woman*. And as previously mentioned, android hominids are seen in such Ciné du Sasquatch efforts as *The Six Million Dollar Man*, *Robot Monster*, and the original *Astro Boy* cartoons.

Drawing Flies (1996)

Starring Jason Lee, Renée Humphrey, Jason Mewes, Carmen Llywelyn, Martin Brooks, Gloria Ingram, Kristin Mosier, Sheryl Brooks, Joey Lauren Adams, Kevin Smith, Chris Pastras, Brian Pearson, Ethan Suplee, Lisa Zimmerman, Paul Zimmerman, Scott Mosier and David Keeps. Produced by Lisa N. Cohen, Mark Cohen, Matthew Gissing, Malcolm Ingram, Jonah Loeb, Marie Loeb, Scott Mosier and Kevin Smith. Written and Directed by Malcolm Ingram and Matthew Gissing. Canada. Black & White. Stereo. 76 Minutes.

Overview: Five slackers in Canada live month-to-month on welfare relief, never actively seeking any form of work or meaning in their pointless existences. But when all save one fails to qualify for their checks, doom is at hand. The landlord will soon evict them, and they have no place to call home, collectively sharing a dive apartment and unable to scrape together enough money to put a deposit on another pad.

Donner is the de facto semi-charismatic leader of the tiny group. Stoned and feeling the blues on the night before their eviction, he has a vision of Sasquatch. Convinced the creature is beckoning him to follow, Donner lies to his four friends and convinces them that the best solution to their troubles is to get out of Vancouver and backpack to a cabin his uncle owns in the wilderness. After much bitching, they load up their van and undertake the journey.

Tensions mount as Donner explains the cabin is further than he remembered. The troop are forced to abandon their van and trek on foot for days on end. Every day Donner disappears for stretches of

time and then returns to the bewildered group, unwilling to account for his mysterious absences. Eventually the dope-smoking, booze-swilling group begin questioning Donner's leadership.

After an encounter with a group of strange men who wear diapers as a form of primal therapy, the group loyalty disintegrates rapidly. One is injured when he falls from a tree. Donner admits his strange disappearances are because he has been searching not for the cabin but evidence of Sasquatch. Two members depart; two others remain for the time being with Donner (out of fear for his sanity).

Donner finally explains to the remaining friends he is on a vision quest. He believes he has been psychically summoned by the Bigfoot tribe to become one of them. Further, Donner is certain that if he will but undergo the trial of initiation and not give up, he will be inducted as a full-fledged member of their community. Realizing Donner is hopelessly crazy, his remaining two friends leave him alone in the woods, covering himself with what he claims is Sasquatch dung and awaiting induction.

Back in Vancouver the four friends meet up at a party. All have since found steady if low-paying gigs. No one has seen Donner, however. In the remote wilderness, we see Donner has indeed been befriended by a Sasquatch tribe. He bemoans the loss humanity has undergone by becoming civilized and offers laments for his fallen friends, telling his new cryptid family how sorry he feels for them that they're missing paradise on Earth with him.

Cover art for the DVD release of *Drawing Flies*.

* * * * *

Drawing Flies is a controversial film in the Kevin Smith *oeuvre*. While it is true Smith only executive produced the film, he does appear as his *Clerks* and *Mallrats* character Silent Bob in a brief cameo in *Drawing Flies*. Many of the cast members are holdovers from *Mallrats* as well. Long unseen due to almost no distribution, save rare film festival screenings, *Drawing Flies* was finally released on DVD after many years to mixed reviews from fans of View Askew (Smith's production company). Many appreciated its quirky, meandering storyline; others found it pointlessly tedious.

As Ciné du Sasquatch entries go, *Drawing Flies* falls into the parody category, alongside such other comedic Bigfoot movies as *Harry and the Hendersons*, *The Sasquatch Gang* and *Tenacious D & the Pick of Destiny*. Though it has its share of serious undertones, *Drawing Flies* largely goes for the laughs, some of which are obvious and some of which are well-observed character bits. Though unevenly paced, it has many plusses for patient Sasquatch film fans willing to view it through a cracked genre prism. Chief among these are an early comic performance by Jason Lee (who has since gone on to bigger roles in *My Name Is Earl* and *Alvin and the Chipmunks*), some occasionally nice black and white cinematography, and a twist on one of Ciné du Sasquatch's most cherished themes.

Much of the first act takes place in Vancouver, setting up how clueless the five leads are in terms of their pointless lives. They attend rave-style parties, sell dope for food money, and rely on cheating the welfare system in order to pay their rent and utilities. Living in a collective, grimy apartment and seemingly challengingly one another to continue failing in their lives as a means of prolonging their miserable inability to mature beyond youth itself, there is a lot of realism within the sometimes strained facetiousness. These characters often pretend to be desperate as a means of alleviating their shared boredom, but in reality they truly *are* desperate in a spiritual sense. Like many of their generation, the expectations of life (careers, marriage or related adult life arcs) seem a distant impossibility and are undesirable as a result. Lacking any form of leadership or self-motivation, they have basically drifted into a situation wherein Donner (Jason Lee) is their quasi-hero and director, though his role is unspoken and therefore ripe with interpersonal conflicts and unexpressed jealousies.

Some of this aimless youth formula works very well, à la *Clerks* and *Slackers*. Other parts play as pretentious self-indulgence by a group of otherwise well-off white kids who seem unappreciative of how easy their lives are laid out for them compared to many who struggle to achieve what they take for granted. Life is a matter of perspective, of course, but the group's complete lack of inclusion of a world larger than their own grimy flat is particularly annoying at times. Thankfully, the first-act turning point shatters this when the soulful Donner has a vision in which he hears the proverbial "Call of the Wild" and responds to the spiritual awakening laid before him by a hallucinogenically-summoned Bigfoot.

Donner's goal is never fully explained, unfortunately, which — while it provides some needed narrative tension — places the viewer in the dark as to his true motivations in misleading his flat mates. One wonders: Is he going homicidally psychotic, or merely indulging himself at their expense? This lack of concern for their welfare, and his own unchallenged ability to lead the group, is as bewildering as it is emotionally frustrating, and may be why many fans of View Askew's Kevin Smith–directed films are less than satisfied with *Drawing Flies*. It is true that the second act loses much of its nascent momentum because the filmmakers have either deliberately lead the viewer astray and/or failed to deliver the necessary exposition to build audience interest in the trek. Whatever their motivation, the viewer is left to passively watch the inevitable break-up of the group as they degenerate into predictable intercine disagreements.

The conclusion is as unsettling as it is surprising. While the outcome is never fully without the ability to be anticipated one way or another (because the filmmakers have posited the ending as an either/or possibility: Is Donner's vision real or imaginary?), it still has an emotional poignancy. As Donner sits around the campfire with his newfound Sasquatch family, one is left to ponder deeper questions: Are we to believe Donner is merely clinging to his refusal to accept maturity and substituting a hermit-ish retreat from reality and civilization like some kind of cryptozoological version of Ted Kaczynski? Or is Donner essentially correct when he bemoans the loss by *Homo sapiens* that refuse to live beneath the stars as he and his cryptid tribe do, allowing nature to take care of their survival without conflict and worry?

It is an unsettling question, both philosophically and in terms of the characters we have seen in the previous 70-odd minutes. The four "civilized" characters retreat just as much as Donner does in the end — only back into their own unsettled realities instead of the wilderness. And while they acquiesce to the lure of day jobs and economic pressures, there is little sense that they have achieved any-

The insert accompanying the DVD release of *Drawing Flies* adroitly features a mock *Weekly World News*–styled promo card.

thing more than bland conformity with their decision to abandon Donner's challenge to them to remain in the wilderness with him. They gain little from their capitulations, in short, other than semi-relief from the pressures of unending boredom. Donner, however, seems truly content to live the primitive but spiritually-fulfilling existence of being a primal throwback with his Bigfoot brothers and sisters. The film calls into question whether one is better off taking the path of one's own unique destiny, no matter how bizarre the outcome, or following the path of least resistance, as have so many others before the individual pondering such a dilemma. Because it doesn't answer the question per se, *Drawing Flies* is an open-ended experience, forcing the viewer to answer the moral quandary for him or herself.

The theme that humanity is corrupted and fallen from grace, whereas Bigfoot is purer and without Original Sin, is very much within the Ciné du Sasquatch range of thematic motifs so often illustrated in the genre. Interestingly, *Drawing Flies* reverses the usual condemnation of *Homo sapiens*, which is typically shown by having them slaughtering Sasquatch, by painting humans as spiritual zombies, alive but not awake to their own emotional emptiness. The Bigfoot beings are presented as a peace-loving tribal clan that refuse to engage in violence and seeks only to be left out of mankind's plans for planetary supremacy — hence their initial reluctance to accept Donner into their family until he proves himself worthy of their unquestioning allegiance post-induction. This is very much akin to the *Little Big Man* and *Lawrence of Arabia* story archetypes, wherein a rootless Western man is reborn within a less technologically-obsessed culture whose naturalistic existences are ironically threatened by the newcomer's own Western society.

This is novel territory for Ciné du Sasquatch and the most fascinating aspect of *Drawing Flies*, even though the filmmakers (to their credit) do not philosophically pander to make the point. Rather, they simply present the scene and end the movie with it. Again, whereas much of the low-budget, independently-made film misses more than it hits, the originality of the ending renders the film as thoughtful viewing for serious fans of cryptid cinema. It demonstrates that there is still power in the basic tenets of the genre's construction, provided the filmmakers are aware of them enough to flip them on their head and therefore make them refreshingly relevant again.

Duck Dodgers ("The Six Wazillion Dollar Duck" and "Bonafide Hero") (2005) (TV)

Featuring the voices of Joe Alaskey, Bob Bergen, Amy Brassette, Chris Edgerly, Michael Patrick McGill and Henry Winkler. Produced by Spike Brandt, Tony Cervone, Paul Dini, Tom Minton, Bobbie Page and Linda Steiner. Written by Mark Banker. Directed by Spike Brandt and Tony Cervone. USA. Color. Stereo. 30 Minutes.

Overview: Daffy Duck plays Duck Edgar Dumas Aloysius Dodgers — aka *Duck Dodgers in the 24½ Century* — in a parody of the classic *Buck Rogers* space opera. When he is unfrozen after a deep cryogenic sleep lasting three centuries, Duck Dodgers is recruited by the Galactic Protectorate to defend Earth against all interstellar foes. Along with his faithful sidekick, known only as the Eager Young Space Cadet, who is played by Porky Pig, Dodgers does whatever is requested of him, albeit reluctantly and often after great avoidance, by Dr. Ignatius Q. "I.Q." Hi, the Protectorate's chief brainiac.

In "The Six Wazillion Dollar Duck," an accident occurs while Duck Dodgers is testing the latest experimental rocketship — Dodgers nearly electrocutes himself to death by simply touching the faulty exterior entry button. Left with only pieces of his former fowl self,

Dr. I.Q. Hi restores Dodgers using cyborganics — the melding of cybernetics with avian flesh. Restored to a super version of himself, Dodgers is thrilled. He can now leap, lift, and hurl heavy objects, and all in slow motion, no less.

In order to speed his recovery, Dodgers is teamed with Steve Boston, a six wazillion dollar human cyborganic experiment who is currently retired from active duty. Boston helps Dodgers understand and utilize his newfound powers by winning an Indianapolis speed car race (the two enhanced beings simply outrun the super-charged vehicles to win the race), tossing a football stadium back and forth between them as easily as a pigskin ball itself, and resting on the beach to soak up some rays. Alas, their vacation is short-lived when Marvin the Martian launches an invasion fleet to steal both Boston and Dodgers in an ill-advised attempt to bypass having to do the actual cybernetics research himself.

In an act of derring-do, Duck Dodgers and Steve Boston dismantle the Martian robots. Dr. I.Q. Hi relates to them a tale of a former experimental cyborganic being called Bigfoot who was earlier kidnapped by the Martians, as well as Jamie Winters, the six wazillion dollar woman (and Boston's wife). Dodgers, Boston and the Space Cadet blast off for Mars, intent on rescuing Jamie and Bigfoot. Meanwhile, Marvin convinces Queen Tyr'ahnee ("tyranny") to enlist the services of Dr. Maniac, despite the mad scientist's reputation for being mentally unstable. Dr. Maniac outlines a bold plan: allow Boston and Dodgers to enter Marvin's hidden fortress and then entrap them, thus making Mar's menagerie of Earth's cyborganic beings complete.

The trio of Dodgers, Boston, and Space Cadet easily gain entrance via a cave marked "Ordinary Cave Entrance" and bypass a cadre of Martian robots, who gracefully allow them to pass, fearing further damage. Inside Marvin's lair, Dr. Maniac forces Bigfoot and Jamie to wear funny animal balloons on their heads. Marvin admits Dr. Maniac is a cousin of his fallen on hard times to an angry Queen Tyr'ahnee, but it's too late — Dodgers and Boston start a battle royale. Using a mind-control device, Marvin forces Bigfoot and Jamie to fight Dodgers, Boston, and the Eager Young Space Cadet. The Earthlings triumph and return to their home planet. When Dr. I.Q. Hi inquires as to why Bigfoot, however, is not with them, they explain Dr. Maniac has convinced the none-too-bright hominid to work with him in a Pancake Warehouse chain serving up short sides of breakfast to hungry space travelers.

In the episode "Bonafide Heroes" — a take-off on a reality TV show that focuses on a different crime-fighting superhero each week, à la *This Is Your Life* — Dodgers is profiled by host and movie star Kirk Manlord, who is also hyping his latest feature opus, *ManBeast RageWar IV*. Various interviews are conducted with Dodger's associates, including Dr. Maniac and Bigfoot, both of whom are shown incarcerated in the Galactic Protectorate Penitentiary in orange jumpsuits. Both are short-changed, and poor Bigfoot isn't even allowed to growl so much as a monosyllable before the prison guards haul them away.

* * * * *

Chuck Jones was no stranger to Ciné du Sasquatch devotees, having created the popular *The Abominable Snow Rabbit*, featuring Hugo the talking Yeti, in the 1960s. After several short sequels, Warner Brothers finally set the wacky quacker Daffy Duck to play the titular *Duck Dodgers in the 24½ Century* in a series of his own. Imaginative, well-executed, and blending the best of conventional cel animation with computer enhancements, *Duck Dodgers* proved to be an acclaimed cartoon series for the venerable Looney Tunes franchise.

It also was the second time Daffy Duck encountered a cryptid. The previously mentioned *The Abominable Snow Rabbit* co-starred

Daffy and an Abominable. In *Duck Dodgers* the hominid is Bigfoot. And not just your typical forest dwelling hominid, but a cybernetically-enhanced (Dr. I.Q. Hi calls his version "cyberorganics" in a sly reference to recent health food trends) Sasquatch, no less. In a parody of *The Six Million Dollar Man*, said Sasquatch in "The Six Wazillion Dollar Duck" is eventually used by aliens (rather than created by them) for their own nefarious purposes. The aliens in *Duck Dodger's* case use cherry pie to lure Bigfoot to their side. When Dr. I. Q. High mentions that Bigfoot couldn't resist pie, Dodgers knowingly intones, "Who could?"

The entire episode is a funny homage to the beloved 1970s series, as it includes not only the Steve Austin character (herein known as Steve Boston) and Jamie Summers (aka Jamie Winters), but even the trademark slow motion cybernetic/cyberorganic movements. In fact, at one point in their mission Porky Pig, as the Eager Young Space Cadet, timidly asks Steve Boston why each time he uses his powers they're always reduced to slow motion. When Boston admits he doesn't know, Dodgers chimes in, "Because it looks so cool!" This funny bit of postmodern humor is telling of the serio-campy nature of fans' nostalgia for *The Six Million Dollar Man* as a series, in that it reveals how lame much of the so-called action scenes were, even during their era of broadcast.

Bigfoot, it is revealed, was the first of the cyberorganic experiments conducted by Dr. I. Q. Hi. A former janitor at Galactic Protectorate headquarters, Bigfoot seemed a likely choice given his close genetic proximity to human beings. This is an oblique reference to the recurrent motif in Ciné du Sasquatch (as well as cryptozoology itself) that supports the concept that Bigfoot is most likely a separate but close genetic bipedal relative from our own branch of evolution. As for depiction, while embellished with the typical cartoon exaggeration, Bigfoot is shown to be a classic cryptid hominid, complete with hairy face, half-man and half-ape physiognomy, and possessing a near-human level of intelligence (or, in regards to some Looney Tunes characters, a higher-than-average level of intelligence, as most of the players are less than brilliant).

The cryptid's appearance in "Bonafide Heroes" is so brief it's only worth mentioning as cameo status. Still aligned with the deranged Dr. Maniac, it's pretty clear from the expression of contempt on Bigfoot's face, however, that, should the beast see freedom, it plans on terminating its association with all mad doctors, at least in the foreseeable future.

Eddie Murphy Delirious (Bigfoot skit) (1983) (TV)

Starring Eddie Murphy, James Argiro, Gus Loundermon, Brian O'Neal, Kevin O'Neal and Clint Smith. Produced by Daniel A. Bohr, Eddie Murphy, Richard Tienken and Robert D. Wachs. Written by Eddie Murphy. Directed by Bruce Gowers. USA. Color. Stereo. 69 Minutes.

Overview: During his raunchy stand-up performance in Climax, Michigan, cameras rolled as then up-and-coming young talent Eddie Murphy used this HBO-produced comedy special to take full advantage of the cable network's uncensored status. With excessive use of expletives that would put Tony "Scarface" Montana at a loss for four-letter words, Murphy truly went over the proverbial top and a few miles higher, including during one skit about his brother's wife.

According to Murphy, his sister-in-law is so large she breaks the steps leading up to Murphy's home every time she comes over to visit. He laments that she's so ugly and hairy-faced that she scares the hell out of his kids, who have nightmares in which Aunt Michelle is coming to get them. After thinking it over, Eddie declares he's figured it out. Michelle is not Puerto Rican, as his brother has main-

tained. Nor is the phrase "Goonie goo goo" that she keeps repeating Spanish, as Murphy was lead to believe.

In fact, Murphy declares, his brother has married a Bigfoot. *That's* why she has a moustache down to her chest. That's why their kids have 17-inch Afros when they're only youngsters — because they're half–Bigfoot. So in the spirit of his own brother having lied to him about "meeting his wife on a camping trip" (which may, ironically, turn out to have been the partial truth of the matter), Murphy decides to tell him to take his Bigfoot-speaking wife, climb in their "Goonie goo goo" Bigfoot van with the kids, and get the hell off his property, never to come back.

Dressed in skin-tight, Day-Glow orange leather, like some neon version of Elvis (it was the 1980s, after all), Eddie Murphy's manic delivery and profanity-laced diatribe about the horrors of having a Sasquatch-in-law is hilarious. Influenced by equal parts Richard Pryor and Rudy Ray Moore in terms of outlandish comic genius, *Eddie Murphy Delirious* is both a great time capsule view of the Reagan era and a font of water cooler–readymade funny quotes. As schtick goes, it's hard to beat for sheer performance or punch lines in one tightly-packed skit.

Oddly, Murphy's routine also touches upon on the basic motifs of Ciné du Sasquatch, hence its inclusion in this reference guide for more than novelty value alone. By castigating his brother for marrying a Bigfoot and trying to pass her as human, he takes the classic theme of interspecies sex between *Homo sapiens* and hominid so prevalent in so many serious, fictional Bigfoot films to the next ludicrous but logical degree: Not only is his brother ashamed and lying about his preference for bestiality, but he's hiding the nature of his half-bred children as well. Given how the supposed "shock value" of this concept is employed in movies such as *Night of the Demon*, *Man Beast*, and others in the genre, it's actually refreshing to hear Murphy's outrageous take on what is clearly an absurd premise. In his own bizarrely amusing way, the stand-up comic takes the *a priori* extreme of the inbreeding motif and "deliriously" twists it in upon itself.

The Edge of Reality ("The Quarry") (2003)

Starring Dan Bailey, Bill Chaput, Bruce G. Hallenbeck, Mary Kay Hilko, Jeff Kirkendall, Leo Nicotera, Ron Rausch and Gary Secor. Produced by Joe Bagnardi & Jeff Kirkendall. Written by Joe Bagnardi and Bruce G. Hallenbeck. Directed by Joe Bagnardi. USA. Color. Stereo. 78 Minutes.

Overview: An anthology horror film told in three tales, *The Edge of Reality*'s concluding segment is called "The Quarry" and focuses on a Savage Sasquatch. It is loosely based upon the supposedly true-life campfire story Teddy Roosevelt used to tell about two Canadian fur trappers, one of whom had his neck snapped and throat eaten by Bigfoot.

Jack Greene and Scott Donahue are two desk jockey businessmen who are so bored in their big city jobs they're willing to do anything for a change of pace. When Jack becomes obsessed with tales of a cryptid who roams the forests near their urban landscape, the two men visit an old codger who talks their ears blue with tales of the hominid's encounters with local residents. Deciding this is just the ticket to end their doldrums, the two men set out to camp in Bigfoot's literal stomping grounds in hopes of catching a glimpse of it.

Alas, their plan backfires when the two men feel they're being watched by something unseen, scaring them both witless. While one wants to remain for a longer time, the other is impatient to leave. The next morning they pull up stakes and head back towards civilization, but when they temporarily split up — one to relieve himself and the other to scout their location on a nearby hilltop — Bigfoot attacks, killing one man and leaving the other to wander about amidst his companion's strewn belongings, pistol readied, and praying he will not be the next to die.

* * * * *

For a no-budget movie, *The Edge of Reality* is not without entertainment value. While it has the typical home video look and feel of a glorified camcorder feature, at least it can be said the filmmakers were seriously attempting to craft suspense and tell stories for their viewers, which is definitely in the plus column in terms of many competing entries in no-budget Ciné du Sasquatch films (such as *Search for the Beast*). To their credit, portions of the *Twilight Zone*-ish anthology work quite well, complete with "The Quarry" writer Bruce G. Hallenbeck acting as a cemetery-wandering host, à la Rod Serling.

Alas, "The Quarry" is perhaps the weakest of the three segments, lacking much in the way of narrative structure for anyone who's ever seen more than a handful of Bigfoot fright films. While the choice of locale is convincingly remote and woodsy, and the music often tense and well-composed, the segment relies too much on the banter between the two city dwellers turned amateur cryptozoologists to be effective as a horror movie. It reminds of the joking camaraderie utilized to great effect in both *An American Werewolf in London* and *Return of the Living Dead*. Alas, lacking the same quality of performers and — most crucially — unexpected shocks to counter the humor, "The Quarry" falls flat in contrasting the two tones.

The Bigfoot costume is the typical gorilla suit but with one interesting variation. Instead of the usual ape mask, the special effects artist has cleverly used a black ski mask hood with tufts of hair added to the cheeks and forehead of the cryptid actor to blend into a seamless whole. Along with bloodshot eyes and werewolf fangs, it gives Bigfoot a much more sinister appearance than is normal in such semi-pro efforts. The red contact lenses in close-up, along with the actor's expressively spooky stares, actually lifts these brief moments into a scare territory the rest of the film just can't inhabit. As soon as the director shows the wide shots of the creature, however, the lumbering, slow-moving gait of the stiff-limbed Sasquatch reduces this powerful ocular effect to near zero in terms of suspense. Never as bad as some no-budget efforts, and yet lacking any real novelty (apart from the creature's face), "The Quarry" is a slightly below-average short that hints the filmmakers could've done much more with more time, a bigger budget and professional actors.

Eerie, Indiana (1991) (TV) (Cameo)

Starring Omri Katz, Justin Shenkarow, Mary-Margaret Humes, Francis Guinan, Julie Condra, John Astin, Belinda Balaski, Harry Goaz, Archie Hahn, Gregory Itzin, Doug Llewelyn, Steven Peri, Dan Stanton and Don Stanton. Produced by Jose Rivera, Gary Markowitz, Walter Barnett and Michael Cassutt. Written by Jose Rivera, Karl Schaefer, Matt Dearborn, Vance DeGeneres, Julia Poll, Michael R. Perry and Michael Cassutt. Directed by Joe Dante, Bob Balaban, Bryan Spicer, Tim Hunter, Sam Pillsbury and Ken Kwapis. USA. Color. Stereo. 30 Minutes.

Overview: When Marshall Teller's family uproots from a noisy New Jersey urban city and relocates to the small town of Eerie, Indiana, the teen immediately notices how strange the locals are in many regards. For example, Elvis lives in a nondescript tract home on Marshall's newspaper delivery route. Bigfoot visits and digs through his family's trash can for food when no one is looking (save Marshall). In short, despite its attempts to pass itself off as Everywhere, America, his new town is, in actuality, the center of the weird universe. It's up to Marshall to explore and record the odd environment and make sense of it all, if that's even possible.

* * * * *

With a youthful spirit, creative advisor (and sometimes director) Joe Dante and a host of talented directors, such as actor/director Bob Balaban, Bryan Spicer, and Ken Kwapis, *Eerie, Indiana* was a critical success that never quite achieved the necessary ratings to go beyond its 19-episode run. Though it had a hardcore fan following who loyally lobbied the network for its continuance, the series existed in an uncomfortable niche somewhere between the outright comedy of the TV version of *Harry and the Hendersons* and a teen-friendly version of *Twin Peaks*. Always sweet-natured and never too frightening, *Eerie, Indiana* instead concentrated on character development and a *Twilight Zone*-like sense of fantasy over scares.

The opening narration centered on Marshall's dislocation blues at having been uprooted from New Jersey and plopped into the middle of All-American nowhere. As he tours his new neighborhood on his bicycle, the viewer is treated to such sights as an overweight, disheveled Elvis staggering down his concrete walkway to fetch the morning paper in his ratty bathrobe, and an orange-furred Bigfoot rummaging through the Teller's street-side trash cans, annoyed whenever it doesn't find a tasty treat. Though offering only a single shot from a low angle, the cut of Sasquatch grimacing in hungry disappointment always generated a laugh during the opening intro, and may have been an influence on the later Jack Link's *Messin' with Sasquatch* commercials, which had a similar tongue-in-cheek approach to Bigfoot.

The Empire Strikes Back (1980) (Cameo)

Starring Mark Hamill, Harrison Ford, Carrie Fisher, Billy Dee Williams, Anthony Daniels, David Prowse, Peter Mayhew, Kenny Baker, Frank Oz, Alec Guinness, Des Webb, Jeremy Bulloch and James Earl Jones. Produced by George Lucas, Gary Kurtz, Rick McCallum, Jim Bloom and Robert Watts. Written by Leigh Brackett, Lawrence Kasdan and George Lucas. Directed by Irvin Kershner. USA. Color. Stereo. Panavision Anamorphic. 127 Minutes.

Overview: The rebel alliance representing the failed Republic is in full retreat as the dark forces of the Empire attack without mercy, seeking to crush the remaining hold-outs. Luke Skywalker survives an encounter with a cryptid known as a Wampa on the ice planet of Hoth, and then seeks spiritual training from Yoda on the jungle world of Dagobah. Realizing his friends Han Solo and Princess Leia are in peril, Luke abandons his training before he is finished and seeks to free his comrades from captivity in the cloud city of Bespa. There he discovers Darth Vader has set a trap, and that the evil Sith lord is actually his biological father.

* * * * *

Luke Skywalker finds himself suspended upside-down, feet frozen in ice, and prepped for slaughter in the suspenseful opening of *The Empire Strikes Back*. The creature, known as a Wampa, who has imprisoned Luke in its ice cavern is, for all practical purposes, portrayed as an Abominable Snowman, right down to the characteristic snow-colored fur; shaggy, yak-like head hair; and remote, mountain-dwelling cavern in a blizzard-bound climate. The only noticeable variation on the Yeti of legend are a set of tusk-like horns that protrude from each side of its head where the ears are located and extend forward towards its jaggedly-fanged mouth.

Utilizing the Force, Luke summons the strength to grab his light saber and slices his way to freedom. Seconds thereafter, he similarly slices off the Wampa's arm, thus sparing himself certain doom. So while it is true the Yeti that Luke destroys is from a galaxy "far, far away," no Ciné du Sasquatch fan could fail to appreciate that this bipedal beast is the Abominable Snowman's distant relative. The visualization is so briefly rendered onscreen (literally a matter of seconds in total), it is difficult to clearly argue one way or the other; but the intent to draw upon the Yeti of myth and sightings in *The Empire Strikes Back*'s tense opening is demonstrable enough to warrant inclusion in this guide as a definitive cryptid cameo.

For "factual" reference, the Star Wars mythologies place the Wampa as existing only on the icy sixth planet of the Hoth system. The production history of the creature is interesting in that it presents a case study of how difficult even specialists like George Lucas' empire of talent from his ILM (Industrial Light & Magic) workshop have had bringing a satisfactory vision of a Yeti-like creature to cinematic life. In the original 1980 release of *The Empire Strikes Back*, the suit is barely glimpsed, reduced to mere seconds of screen time owing to technical difficulties with the design. The Wampa is only shown in one full-frontal shot as it strikes at the camera from Luke's point of view, claws slashing and mouth growling (and this was a puppet designed to overcome the problems with the suit). The other brief edits show the creature in quick, shadowy cutaways, including a particularly unconvincing side shot of the Wampa "walking" past the camera that appears more like the creature is rolling on skates, due to the stiff, unmoving motion of its musculature (probably a piece of footage salvaged from the unsuccessful Wampa creature realization itself spliced in to make at least some usage of it).

Known for his sense of perfectionism and detail, Lucas must have been bothered by the artistic compromises, for in the 1997 digital edition of *The Empire Strikes Back*, the Wampa is shown again in newly-created shots in a well-lit version of its ice cavern home. The Wampa went on to achieve the ultimate prestige award within the Lucasfilm hierarchy of creatures when it was released in many forms as collectible merchandise, including a highly-detailed action figure that came in a box set with the Hoth-gear-clad Luke Skywalker. It has also made brief cameos within the vast array of Lucas video games, and even in the animated television series *Star Wars: Clone Wars*, wherein Count Dooku employs a Wampa (among several other aliens) to test the powers of his female apprentice Asajj Ventress.

The bipedal Wampa from *The Empire Strikes Back* hails from the ice planet Hoth, but its Yeti-like source origins are strictly Earthbound.

Encounters: The Hidden Truth (1994) (TV) (Doc)

Hosted by John Marshall. Produced by Kathryn Kaycoff, John McLaughlin, Andy Schatzberg and Gary Tellalian. Directed by John Jopson. USA. Color. Stereo. 60 Minutes.

Overview: As a lead-in series for Fox's much more successful *The X-Files*, which followed *Encounters: The Hidden Truth*, this series was a low-budget way for the network to capitalize upon eager viewers too anxious to wait a full hour until the intrepid secret government agency's duo went about their fictional exploits. Shot in the news magazine format popularized by *60 Minutes* (but in a more tawdry style, befitting the network which aired *Alien Autopsy* as a sincere exposé), each episode featured a few segments devoted to UFOs, Men in Black, ghosts, and, of course, Bigfoot (which received multiple segments owing to the hominid's popularity).

Encounters with the Unexplained (2000) (TV) (Doc)

Hosted by Jerry Orbach. Produced by David W. Balsiger, Jerry K. Rose, Charles E. Sellier Jr., Evelyn R. Manangan and Gail Fallen. Written by Joseph Meier, Sharon Dymmel, Susan Horwitz and Gary Raad. Directed by David Priest. USA. Color. Stereo. 60 Minutes.

Overview: Hosted by *Law & Order* regular Jerry Orbach, *Encounters with the Unexplained* was an *In Search Of*–styled documentary series focusing on Fortean phenomena such as UFOs, cryptids, mysteries of the Holy Bible, and related topics. With 53 episodes produced for syndication, and running for 3 years, it was a successful if familiar excursion into the unknown frontiers of human and paranormal activity.

The only episode of interest to Ciné du Sasquatch viewers is "Bigfoot Sightings: Real Monster or Urban Legend?" Oddly, one would have to question if Bigfoot could technically be classified as an urban legend per se, given that it has existed for centuries prior to the establishment of any civilization that could be classified as urban.

The Fairly Odd Parents (2003) ("Snowbound") ("Mile in My Shoes") (TV)

Featuring the voices of Mary Kay Bergman, Tara Strong, Daran Norris, Susanne Blakeslee, Carlos Alazraqui, Grey DeLisle, Frankie Muniz, Ibrahim Haneef Muhammad, Gary LeRoi Gray, Jim Ward, Faith Abrahams and Tom Kenny. Produced by Butch Hartman, Fred Seibert, Scott Fellows and George A. Goodchild. Written by Scott Fellows. Directed by Sarah Frost. USA. Color. Stereo. 30 Minutes.

Overview: Timmy Turner is an average 10-year-old kid who is suddenly granted the ultimate wish-fulfillment fantasy — the guardianship of two fairy godparents, Cosmo and Wanda. Imbued with the powers to grant Timmy his every wish (subject to the rules of Fairy World and the stringent codes of conduct therein), Cosmo and Wanda ceaselessly spend their careers as Timmy's spiritual guardians, first transforming his heart's desires into reality and subsequently attempting to undo the damage Timmy's ill-conceived wishes create. Though he never heeds nor learns, Wanda constantly warns Timmy to carefully consider his wishes.

In the episode called "Snowbound," Timmy's father is worried when he believes his wife is visiting the Sky Lodge ski resort to console her ailing aunt and won't return his constant phone calls to check on her safety. In reality, Timmy's mother has conspired with several other moms on the block to get away from their husbands and children in order to relax and unwind. When Mr. Turner sees on TV that the Abominable Snowman is on the loose in the Sky Lodge area, he panics, fearing for his wife's safety. He picks up Timmy's teenaged babysitter Vicki on the way out of town to watch over Timmy as he drives the three of them to Sky Lodge.

Vicki enjoys some snowboarding action (Timmy is her makeshift snowboard) on the top of the snowy peaks until an avalanche occurs when she yells at Timmy for being nice to her. The resulting tumult sends them plummeting into an icy cavern, where they are trapped without hope of escaping. Timmy thinks to wish himself free with his Fairy Odd Parents but finds them frozen into God-sicles due to the extreme temperatures. Realizing he must rise to the occasion on his own, Timmy consoles Vicki. Touched by his unexpected kindness and fearful her life will soon be over, Vicki confesses she doesn't mean to be so horrible to him all the time but has major issues from her childhood that make her behave badly towards everyone in her life.

Meanwhile, at the Sky Lodge Mr. Turner has barely noticed that Timmy and Vicki are missing, being so obsessed with tracking down the elusive Yeti. When he discovers a trail of ice cubes on the lodge floor that he mistakes for Abominable Snowman scat, Mr. Turner follows until he skids on them and falls down some stairs. Back in the cave, the Abominable Snowman arrives, livid that its home has been invaded by Timmy and Vicki. Timmy manages to escape the lair through an air hole in the ceiling, but Vicki is left to her fate. Thawing his Fairly Odd–sicles in the sunshine, Timmy begs them to grant him a wish to save Vicki's life. Neither Cosmo nor Wanda can believe it — they know Timmy despises Vicki and wonder what has changed.

Vicki is cornered in the rear of the cave near a pile of pizza boxes as the Abominable Snowman advances on her. A drill machine wished into reality and driven by Timmy bores through a cave wall. Timmy rescues Vicki in the nick of time from the Yeti, and they sled down the slopes, only to be followed by the Abominable Snowman atop a pizza carton. Timmy and Vicki race into the Sky Lodge and slam the door shut behind them. Reunited with his mother, Timmy is happy again. A knock on the door reveals the Yeti, holding pizzas. Timmy reacts with horror, but the Snowman removes his mask. It turns out he is the "Abdominal" Snowman — a hunky, well-built bodybuilder whose entire schtick to increase his pizza delivery business is to play up the Yeti angle. The Nordic stud explains that he was trying to tell Vicki and Timmy of this when they were in his cave pizza shop, but he couldn't get his ultra-tight mask off in time, hence the growled mumbling.

Everything seems resolved until Vicki slams a pizza box on Timmy's head, angry at him as usual. She screams at him for not introducing her to the Abdominal hunk, who she thinks is cute. Vicki's screams trigger another avalanche, this one covering only her. When Mr. Turner awakens from his fall and sees Vicki covered head-to-toe in snow, he believes she is the real Yeti and grabs a snow shovel. As Vicki races for her life, Mr. Turner gives chase, determined to bag the elusive hominid.

Bigfoot made an ultra-brief cameo in "Mile in My Shoes," in which Timmy is forced to see what it's like to be a Fairy Odd Parent in order to learn a lesson in comeuppance, having taken Cosmo and Wanda for granted once too often. While he's sliding down the steep learning curve in terms of inter-dimensional transport, he accidentally poofs into a strange netherworld. There he faces Bigfoot, who looks perturbed at Timmy's sudden intrusion. "Fairy world?" asks a bewildered Timmy, confused by the cryptid. "Hairy world!" growls Sasquatch. Timmy quickly vanishes, heading into another fantasy world — to Bigfoot's relief.

* * * * *

The Fairly Odd Parents was a success from the moment it debuted as a short segment within the *Oh, Yeah! Cartoons* show on Nickelodeon. Created by Butch Harman, *The Fairly Odd Parents* remains one of the most popular and longest running shows on Nickelodeon's lucrative schedule, trailing only *SpongeBob SquarePants* and *Rugrats* in longevity. Featuring a zany pace and absurdist sense of humor, as well as a veritable smorgasbord of off-the-wall celebrity cameos (such as Adam West, Norm Macdonald, Alec Baldwin, Brendan Fraser and Gene Simmons), *The Fairly Odd Parents* is a shining example of a show that can appeal both to kids and young adults alike, with many in-jokes and double entendres clearly aimed at more mature viewers to balance the childlike sense of fantasy.

While the Bigfoot appearance in "Mile in My Shoes" is but a glorified cameo, "Snowbound" offers Ciné du Sasquatch watchers many memorable moments. The hysteria with which Mr. Turner reacts when he inadvertently mistakes the pizza delivery commercial for an actual news report on Yeti sightings near the ski lodge is a self-referential nod to many of the tenets of the genre. Not only does the ski lodge setting reference two well-known entries in the *oeuvre* (*Snowbeast* and *The Capture of Bigfoot*), but "Snowbound" contains the less-than-unexpected ending in which the Abominable reveals itself to be a man in a suit. In this case, the comic novelty is not the usual twist (as depicted in *Shriek of the Mutilated*) but a clever parody of the growing commercialization of Yetis in the media. Realizing he needs a competitive edge to distinguish his pizza delivery business, the delivery dude of "Snowbound" decides that capitalizing upon the Abominable Snowman (aka Abdominal Snowman, as he dubs himself) is a surefire way to get tourists to choose his small company over larger national chains.

This is not only a pretty viable commercial strategy (as witnessed by the real-world ad campaigns for Boston Pizza featuring Sasquatch, Pizza Hut's literally-named Bigfoot Pizza, and Jack Link's *Messin' with Sasquatch* series), but it plays upon the Carl Denham Syndrome originated with *King Kong*, albeit indirectly and subversively. While the scheming entrepreneur doesn't intend to capture a Sasquatch to exploit, he nonetheless is more than eager to use the pop icon status of the hominid to create customer awareness of and desire for his product. Substitute a ticket sale to see the creature (à la Denham) for the pizza delivered by a faux Bigfoot and one is left with the same impulse to exhibit and commercialize the cryptid for self-gain. This is such a long-running theme in the Ciné du Sasquatch genre that it's nearly impossible to find an entry in which this archetype is not present to at least some degree. Even when this mythic character is portrayed for laughs, as in *Harry and the Hendersons*, there is nevertheless a sinister undertone present. How could there not be, after all, when it so clearly embodies the darker side of the human psyche? Here we are encountering not the unknown in the dark woods and unexplored mountaintops, but the well-hidden but known darkness in the deepest recesses of our own internal midnight forests and the shadowy canyons of our shared human psyches.

On a lighter note, "Snowbound" portrays its Yeti as a lean, angular creature with the characteristic red, glowing eyes so prevalent in many reported real-world encounters. With its crimson orbs being the only visible feature in its blank black countenance, this is one Abominable Snowman that truly conjures, in a comic manner, a more horrific visualization of Sasquatch. Contrast this with the image of Hugo from *The Abominable Snow Rabbit* and countless other children's cartoons, and it's readily apparent that most depictions of the Yeti tend to favor a less scary visualization in favor of the goofy, loveable version. It is to *The Fairly Odd Parents'* credit that it manages to both craft a sinister Snow Monster and then parody the expected clichéd ending (whereupon the cryptid is revealed to be a man in a suit) with entertaining aplomb. While not believable in the slightest, "Snowbound" perfectly captures many basic motifs in the genre.

Family Guy ("I Never Met a Dead Man") (1999) (TV) (Cameo)

Featuring the voices of Seth MacFarlane, Alex Borstein, Seth Green, Mila Kunis, Mike Henry, Lori Alan, Erik Estrada, Butch Hartman, Aaron Lustig, Joey Slotnick and Frank Welker. Produced by Lolee Aries, David A. Goodman, Seth MacFarlane, Daniel Palladino, David Zuckerman and Kara Vallow. Written by Chris Sheridan. Directed by Michael Dante DiMartino. USA. Color. Stereo. 30 Minutes.

Overview: Peter Griffin and his family — Lois, his wife; Chris, his teenage son; Meg, his preteen daughter; Stewie, his infant son; and Brian, their pet dog — live an average American, middle-class lifestyle in Quahog, Rhode Island. Average, that is, if your dog talks, drinks martinis, and dates a blonde human girlfriend while driving a Prius. Among the many anomalies in their dysfunctional domicile, the Griffins try to express love and remain tightly-knit, despite the pressures of modern culture, underlying tensions, and strange neighbors who systematically undermine any chance of family cohesion.

In "I Never Met a Dead Man," Peter gives a driving lesson to his daughter Meg, during which she inadvertently knocks out the local Quahog television transmitter. As a result, an angry mob of citizens suddenly surround the pair, irate that their sets have gone dark. Peter refuses to accept any responsibility, instead blaming a nearby Bigfoot, who is minding his own business in the adjacent park's forest. Bigfoot quickly denies any part in the accident, stumbling on his words as he proclaims his innocence, clearly afraid of a lynch mob mentality on the part of the humans.

* * * * *

For all of its controversies and cancellations, *Family Guy* remains a remarkably accurate parody of all that is dysfunctionally American in culture and politics. Little wonder, then, that this, only the second episode in the series, featured a brief cameo of Sasquatch. After all, the series' creators grew up in the halcyon post–*Legend of Boggy Creek* and *The Six Million Dollar Man* days in which Bigfoot was already an American pop icon. Ironically as well, there is no doubt, nor surprise, expressed by either Peter Griffin when he attempts to blame Bigfoot nor the crowd, which doesn't buy the blame game. They willingly accept that Bigfoot is real — a part of their community — *and* his perfectly-spoken explanation that Griffin is lying. Compare this to most Bigfoot cameos in which the creature engenders either fright, flight or both. By now in the evolution of Ciné du Sasquatch, one may depict a cryptid as commonly as the old *Daniel Boone* series did a bear or mountain lion. To wit, Bigfoot has become an animal species to be respected, and one expected to be seen at any given time.

It's also worthwhile to note how easily Peter Griffin presumes to frame the Sasquatch, as the Other, for the accident. There is a clear racist subtext herein by which Peter believes he can automatically assign blame to those in his community who are perceived as "lesser beings" by the citizenry. The hapless Bigfoot stammers in abject fear as the focus turns upon him, as if he's had long, painful experience

with such mob mentality and its ugly outcomes in terms of his personal well-being. It's hard not to view this as a satirical nod to the Rodney King–styled moments in American history wherein equality and racism have not culturally aligned. To both Quahog's credit and Peter's shame, however, the angry mob doesn't accept Griffin's pathetic attempt to shift the focus and basically ignores the cryptid altogether. While it bodes well for Sasquatch (in that he's at least come to the point of being accepted as an integral member of the Rhode Island commonwealth in which he resides), one does wonder: What if the creature *had* been somehow accidentally involved, such as darting in front of Meg Griffin while she was driving? *Family Guy* is adroit at implying both this darker possibility and producing laughs all at the same time. Like an animated, postmodern version of *All in the Family* (which it oddly resembles at times — minus the talking dog), the show has drawn a true bead on its target subjects.

Fear Runs Silent (1999)

Starring Stacy Keach, Billy Dee Williams, Suzanne Davis, Dan Lauria, James O'Shea, Riley Bourdeaux, Robert Jayne, Ethan Erickson, Jim Great Elk Waters, Stephen R. Hudis, Victor W. Amato, Daniel L. Brison, Travis De Renzo, Raymond W. Hampton, Dublin James and Craig Irwin. Produced by Serge Rodnunsky, Jim Rodnunsky, David Forrest, Pierre Lorillard, Scott Putman, Beau Rogers and Gerald I. Wolff. Written and Directed by Serge Rodnunsky. USA. Color. Stereo. 90 Minutes.

Cover art for the DVD release of *Fear Runs Silent*.

Overview: High school student Kerry is suffering from recurring nightmares and the resultant clinical depression. Unable to shake the intense feeling her dreams are actually psychic flashes of horrors to come, she enlists the help of a local hypnotherapist in hopes of uncovering the root source of her emotional disturbance.

During her hypnotic regression, events become a jumbled, indecipherable blur. Past, present and future — all somehow tangentially if mysteriously connected to visions of a savage Sasquatch — unfold in a dreamlike state of confusion, leaving Kerry to wonder if she is losing her mind.

In her nightmare/reality, Kerry and her high school biology class are viciously attacked by a Bigfoot tribe moments after arriving at a remote mountaintop cabin on a field trip. She is abducted, along with her best friend Jennie, by a Bigfoot, and both women are deposited in its lair alongside their half-devoured biology teacher, Mr. Hill.

Meanwhile, the rest of the surviving students barricade themselves inside the cabin, only to discover the beast has broken into the basement. They manage to keep the monster at bay, but only after the creature impales another student with a long spear.

Kerry and her shaken friend escape the Sasquatch's cave and rejoin their fellow students in the cabin. Sheriff Hammond arrives with his deputy in tow, believing the students have broken into the cabin illegally. But when his deputy is speared to death, the sheriff realizes the truth. He rushes to his squad car to retrieve a shotgun, only to be stabbed in the head by a spear.

Seizing their only chance, the students race to Hammond's car, hoping to drive to safety. An entire tribe of the monsters emerges from the surrounding woods, swarming the car and dragging several students to their deaths. The survivors make their getaway, only to plunge into an unseen river.

Kerry staggers out of the ordeal, battered and bloodied, despite having watched her best friend slide over a raging waterfall to her demise. Kerry finds her brother still alive, but her boyfriend has now become a Bigfoot himself. She pulls him over the waterfall with her, killing them both in an act of self-sacrifice.

Kerry awakens from her hypnotherapy session and realizes her creepy therapist has been attempting to plant false memories in her mind, spinning a scenario in which her stepfather has sexually abused her since she was a child. Disgusted, she leaves, embittered by the experience, and vows to face her inner turmoil on her own, without professional help.

But as she boards the van for her biology class field trip the next morning, just as she has in her lethal visions, she wonders if she is experiencing simple déjà vu or a premonition of bloodshed and death.

* * * * *

Fear Runs Silent has generally received harsh treatment at the hands of those few Ciné du Sasquatch viewers who've been able to actually see it — an accomplishment in and of itself given its lone direct-to-video release by a small independent DVD distributor. These fans (primarily via Internet reviews) often express negative reactions to the film's endless "dream within a dream within a dream" structure, as well as the suggestion the Bigfoot monsters may or may not be a figment of the heroine's imagination.

Other critical lambasting understandably focuses on the wasted talents of the headline actors: Stacy Keach and Billy Dee Williams. Given their respective stature in movies and television, it is admittedly disappointing they are relegated to the briefest of cameos. This is most likely due to the film's budget, which probably allowed for only a few days' rates for such expensive actors, while the bulk of the film relies on the cast of unknown, less-expensive players. Given the youthful actors largely acquit themselves well (especially the leads), this is the least of problems affecting *Fear Runs Silent*.

Admittedly, these are fair reactions from a purist Bigfoot fan's point of view, but they discount the often tense, maddening sense of chaotic dream logic that pervades the film. Not unlike *A Nightmare on Elm Street*, *Fear Runs Silent* uses extensive, prolonged nightmare imagery to create a surreal sense of terror. Even when the acting, story and believability evaporate, the kinetic power of the editing (similar in impact to the dense, fragmentary style of Donald Cammel's *White of the Eye*, Nicolas Roeg's *Don't Look Now* and Dennis Hopper's *Easy Rider*) goes a long ways towards keeping viewer interest. Serge Rodnunsky, who also directed and wrote, edits the entire film with a manic intensity that shreds most individual shots into less than a second in length. This is virtually unprecedented in Ciné du Sasquatch, which favors linear narrative and coherency over endless flashbacks and surrealism, and goes a long way towards making *Fear Runs Silent* an atypical, sporadically-entertaining effort.

The production values are high for such a relatively unknown movie. Convincingly shot on the snowy plateaus of the Big Bear, California, region, *Fear Runs Silent* benefits from a sense of verisimilitude most of its counterparts lack. Especially realistic is the opening sequence wherein a young couple is attacked during a driving snowstorm while attempting to navigate an isolated roadway. So effective is the cinematography and staging, it feels as if the film crew actually braved the highly-unpredictable elements in crafting this first harrowing Sasquatch scene. As the howling winds reduce visibility to near zero, little viewer imagination is required to suspend disbelief; the cloak of snow, the craggy canyons, and the towering trees renders the possibility of such a cryptid far more believable.

Viewers seeking catharsis via a traditional storyline and characters, however, are in for a tedious, exasperating experience. But given the plethora of otherwise straightforward Ciné du Sasquatch entries, this is precisely what empowers *Fear Runs Silent* with what little novelty it possesses. It is fair to label this film the most heavily edited entry in the entire genre. Indeed, cuts generally come every second, and this frenetic style is maintained and even accelerated during attack sequences. Perhaps in a post–MTV editing landscape this is not so remarkable, but consider: The film's structure continuously time-shifts as well as introduces fantasy imagery not literally supported by the narrative itself. This confusing, dense approach to filmmaking is visually tiring but equally involving, in that one is never quite sure what it supposedly real and what is not in the unending kaleidoscope.

Like Oliver Stone's excessive *Natural Born Killers*, the technique is, flaws and all, intermittently effective as cinema. This is because of cinema's unique ability to break all rules of conventional dramaturgy (such as narrative linearity and three-act structure) and, with a simple series of alternating edits, create its own poetic sense of reality. Herein *Fear Runs Silent* is an editor's show reel, albeit at the expense of characterization and any deeper meaning achieved by its flashy technique. Still, the audacious strategy makes an otherwise clichéd story and characters palatable. Director, writer, and editor Rodnunsky — who started out as a choreographer and dancer for the American Ballet Company, and worked with Mikail Baryshnikov, Agnes De Mille, and George Balanchine — is a formidable low-budget talent, having completed over 17 features since his move behind the camera.

The creature make-up is mostly effective though overly utilized in too many extreme close-ups of its yellow eyes and drooling mouth. The depicted cryptid is also one of the most agile in all of Ciné du Sasquatch, running the gauntlet of steep, snowy crevices at inhuman speeds and launching itself horizontally airborne as it attacks, thereby rendering any possible defense all-but-impossible due to its sheer speed. This may reflect the director's previous career as a choreographer.

The final assault, in which the faceless, silhouetted creatures attack the cabin and squad car, is reminiscent of the manner in which John Carpenter portrayed the gang members in *Assault on Precinct 13* and the subterranean dwellers of *Escape from New York*: Minus any defining characteristics, they take on the universally shared horror of a faceless mob preying upon lone individuals. In particular, the finale, with the monsters swarming over the car even as the survivors attempt to flee, seems patterned on the taut ending of Leon Klimovsky's underrated *The Vampires' Night Orgy*.

Alas, the filmmakers' best creative intentions never fully overcome the weaknesses of story and characterization. The dialogue is often annoyingly banal, even if given leeway for the teenage idiom. Further straining credibility are such obvious touches as naming the high school Sasquatch High and having screaming cheerleaders chant "Go Sasquatch, Go!" Combined with the director's apparent predilection for photographing the lead actress in her underwear for a majority of the film's length, *Fear Runs Silent* is toppled by its own hubris. It is too disjointed to work as narrative, and too predictable to work as art-house cinema either.

A final interesting if minor note about this Bigfoot's approach to killing: Unlike most films in the genre which portrays Sasquatch as a bare hands predator prone to ripping apart its victims, *Fear Runs Silent* portrays its creatures as true weapon builders, at least as far as the lethally effective gigantic spears they toss. Apart from such unusual depictions of the hominids in the "Galileo Seven" episode of *Star Trek*, this is atypical. It posits Bigfoot as being more akin to a Neanderthal man than a mindless, non-human monster. One only wishes, in retrospect, that the filmmaker had been able to adroitly exploit the other creative elements as effectively as this innovation. As it is, *Fear Runs Silent* actually runs shallow as an occasionally visually exciting failure.

Felix the Cat ("Abominable Snowman") (1958) (TV)

Featuring the voices of Jack Mercer, Pierre Guillermo and Mae Questel. Produced by Joe Oriolo and Pat Sullivan, Jr. Written by Joe Oriolo, Joseph Sabo and Joe Stultz. Directed by Joseph Oriolo. USA. Color. Mono. 8 Minutes.

Overview: Crafty, cunning Felix the Cat is no feline's fool. When his arch rival the Professor attempts to steal Felix's magic bag while Felix is visiting Alaska, the nefarious supermind plants Yeti tracks in the snow. Felix plays along, pretending he's hot on the cold trail of the Abominable Snowman, realizing all along the Professor is behind it.

The Professor dons a makeshift outfit of ice and snow and pretends to be the snow monster long enough to distract Felix and snatch the charismatic cat's secretive sack. But when the Professor runs away to enjoy his newfound treasure, he encounters the real Abominable Snowman, a towering, ill-tempered hominid who doesn't take kindly to strangers. The fearful Professor screams for Felix to help. Felix dons icicles as skis and slides down the slopes until he rescues the old man from the Yeti. The two intruders race to safety, with the Professor burrowing under the ice all the way home while Felix transforms his magic bag into a submarine. Felix navigates under the North Pole in his magic submarine, garnering attention worldwide, while the jealous Professor looks on at home and then pounds his head against the wall in anger.

* * * * *

Felix the Cat was a popular silent film star created by Pat Sullivan Sr. and Otto Messmer. While proper credit has always been in dispute between the two — with Sullivan arguing he created Felix, and Messmer the same while in the employ of Sullivan — one historical fact remains unchallenged: Prior to the rise of Mickey Mouse, Bugs Bunny, Donald Duck, Porky Pig and a host of other cartoon superstars that prospered in the decades that followed, Felix the Cat was the first cartoon character to have truly recognizable commercial appeal. Beginning in 1919, with distribution by Paramount Studios, *Felix the Cat* was a hit with audiences worldwide and a surefire laugh-getter for audiences of all ages. So popular was the cat star, in fact, that Paramount released a daily comic strip to capitalize on the film's recognition (and not the other way around).

While Felix's filmic fortunes declined with the release of sound, circa *The Jazz Singer* in 1927 (it seems the public was somewhat taken aback when their lovable cat hero spoke for the first time), the character's merchandising never truly faded. By the 1950s, Sullivan's son and Joe Oriolo (the long-time assistant to Sullivan Sr., as well as creator of *Casper the Friendly Ghost*) decided to produce a series of cartoons in color for television, which was a bit daring for its era given a majority of viewers were still tuning in via black-and-white sets. Each half-hour "chapter" consisted of three 8-minute segments, each segment featuring a different mini-plot and theme. "Abominable Snowman" was the third segment in the first-ever 30-minute episode, which indicates the notoriety of the Snowman in terms of popular culture.

Given the time frame of the late 1950s, when *Felix the Cat* was produced for TV, it's little wonder that a Yeti was featured so prominently. Ripped straight from the headlines of the world press, and various feature films (such as *Half Human, Man Beast,* and *The Abominable Snowman*), the icy cryptid was a renowned phenomena. Having said as much, it's interesting how many liberties "Abominable Snowman" takes with what was generally assumed to be common knowledge about the hominid at that point in time. For example, the show takes place in Alaska rather than the Himalayas, but makes no accounting for the difference, as if they have the same cultural and folkloric history of Yeti sightings. Given that "Abominable Snowman" features clichéd, non-stop imagery of Inuit tribesmen building igloos, ice fishing, and the like, but doesn't bother to correctly place the Abominable Snowman as a reference to the Tibetans who most famously popularized it, it's culturally telling of the general ignorance of Alaska's native tribal people by those residing in the lower 48 states.

This in and of itself wouldn't be so surprising save for the way the animators also render the state of Alaska during the short's final moments. When the Professor is shown speeding under the ice fields (much in the same manner Bugs Bunny would later utilize in "The Abominable Snow Rabbit"), the state of Alaska is drawn on a map as hovering above Canada, with the United States drawn below Canada! Even given that Alaska didn't attain statehood until 1959, this seems ridiculously ill-informed by way of general geography, especially for a show aimed largely at children. While few will deny entertainment owes nothing to education and vice versa, the distortion is so complete as to be utterly preposterous. Then again, given the depiction of the Yeti as a 40-foot-tall man literally made of ice, holding out expectations of anything beyond child-friendly laughs for this episode of *Felix the Cat* is as improbable as the drawn map of Alaska. There's a reason, after all, that Felix's TV adventures are largely dismissed by knowledgeable fans of the silent film incarnation as being inferior. It's not only the limited animation and simplistic storylines (which fare poorly compared to the Sullivan-Messmer collaborations made decades earlier), but the sloppy attention to details and believability. Even for a cat who talks, there are lines that must not be crossed if the audience, children or not, are to be expected to suspend disbelief.

Foot: Phantom of the Forest (2008)

Animated by Vance Reeser. Written and Directed by Kirk Demarais and Mike Becker. USA. Color. Stereo. 17 Minutes.

Overview: Mike, a 10-year-old boy, grows up fatherless in rural Washington state during the 1970s. When he learns his deceased father was stalking the "phantom of the forest"—Bigfoot itself—Mike decides to dig deeply into his mysterious dad's background in order to determine for himself whether or not the mythical monster is real.

* * * * *

This old-fashioned, emotionally sweet short film was made as a labor of love by several professional talents in order to showcase their abilities. With lush animation more traditional to cell animation (though rendered with CGI), and a storyline more akin to *E.T.* or a good *Hardy Boys* mystery than cynical postmodern efforts, *Foot: Phantom of the Forest* focuses on the 10-year-old protagonist's point of view of the intriguing world of Sasquatch and the mysteries lying ahead in his life as he matures from child to young adult. The setting of the 1970s as backdrop helps propel the sense of narrative urgency, as so much is happening in the media around the lad to reflect his local fascination: endless Bigfoot movies, TV specials and series about Sasquatch, and magazines (such as *Argosy*) hyping the latest Yeti expeditions and updates.

The film played at the 2008 San Diego Comic Con International Independent Film Festival and was simultaneously released on DVD by FunKo, packaged with a unique collectible Bigfoot Wacky Wobbler toy tie-in resembling the cryptid featured in the film, in a limited edition of less than 500 copies.

The Force Beyond (1978) (Doc)

Hosted by Donn Davison. Featuring Orson Welles, Captain Gerald Noven, Dr. Don Elkins, Michael C. Heleus, Ed Herlihy, Dr. George Wald, Peter Byrne, Rene Dahinden, Count Peter Turrolla, Peter Tompkins, Jack Horkheimer, Grace Robertson, Joe King, Gregory Abbott, Dr. Paul Mahler, Jim Lorenson, Coral Lorenson, Ashley Montagu, Bernard O'Connor, Colman Von Koviczky, Charles Hickson, Dr. Leo Sprinkle, Frederick Tourin, John T. Fahey, Elwood Fox, Arthur Denny and John Fox. Produced by Donn Davison and Edward L. Montoro. Written by Barbara Morris Davison, Donn Davison and William Sachs. Directed by William Sachs. USA. Color. Mono. 85 Minutes.

Overview: A veritable overview of over-the-top Fortean phenomena, this documentary look at Bigfoot, the Devil's Triangle, psychic surgery, UFOs, and more is a treasure chest full of leading experts in their respective fields of controversial research. For Ciné du Sasquatch fans, the highlights include cryptozoologists Peter Byrne, who has spent over four decades in the field searching for Sasquatch, and the equally well-known and well-respected Rene Dahinden. Byrne began his post–RAF career hunting big game cats and the like in India before migrating to crypto-hunter status in 1960 when he was underwritten by a wealthy Texas oil man to bag a Bigfoot in the Northern California mountains. Dahinden, who died in 2001, spent even more time researching hominids, beginning in 1956 when he met the prominent Bigfooter John Green. Having just migrated from Switzerland a few years earlier, Green seemed to spark an infectious life-long obsession in the Swiss emigrant. Dahinden would go on to document many first-hand encounters with Sasquatch throughout the Pacific Northwest, as well as become a major believer in and eventual rights owner of the Patterson-Gimlin film footage of 1967. Both men are given ample screen time in *The Force Beyond* to make their case in regards to their beliefs Bigfoot is an actual creature, which makes this documentary compelling for real-life enthusiasts, however sensationalized and patronizing its overall tone.

Some other notable footage is embedded in what is admittedly a luridly-conceived effort. Rare footage of Charles Hickson, one of the two fishermen who claimed to have been abducted by aliens in a flying saucer off the shores of Pascagoula, Mississippi, in the early 1970s (which launched the entire decade's subsequent UFO mania), is included; in it he talks about his successful polygraph test and the experience itself. Newsreel clips of Orson Welles sheepishly apologizing to the nation for his 1930s *The War of the Worlds* radio broadcast hysteria is priceless and hard to find. Likewise, interviews with such figures as Walt Andres, then-director of MUFON, and Bernard O'Connor, editor of *UFO Magazine*, are of interest to aficionados. Jack Horkheimer, the director of the Space Transit Planetarium in Miami, also speaks about his belief that aliens exist throughout the cosmos. A year later he would host the popular PBS syndicated TV show *Jack Horkheimer: Star Hustler*, in which he advised viewers of upcoming eclipses, star sightings, and related astrological phenomena to witness for themselves.

The name of *The Force Beyond* co-producer/writer Donn Davison is familiar to lovers of bad Ciné du Sasquatch from his earlier opus *The Legend of McCullough's Mountain* (for which he purchased an older, non–Bigfoot film and inserted new stock shots of a cryptid to

A short film by Mike Becker & Kirk Demarais

FOOT

PHANTOM
of the FOREST

OFFICIAL SELECTION
SAN DIEGO COMIC CON
2008 INTERNATIONAL
FILM FESTIVAL

Poster art for the animated short video "Foot: Phantom of the Forest."

capitalize upon the Bigfoot craze of the 1970s), wherein Davison performed P.T. Barnum–like hosting duties as a self-billed "World Traveler, Lecturer and Psychic Investigator." (He left off his resume the fact he was a notorious exploitation film huckster and owner of the legendary Dragon Art Theater in California, which was an early pioneer cinema dedicated to X-rated fare.) In *The Force Beyond* he promises in the film's opening scenes to reveal incontrovertible, "never-before-seen film footage" (always a dubious claim, in that surely the photographers, labs, and presumably even producer, such as Davison himself, would have viewed the footage in question at least once each) of UFOs taken by Russian jet pilots and smuggled out "from behind the Iron Curtain!" Eighty minutes later and just before the end credits, he unspools the 16mm footage and tells the projectionist to let it roll. It turns out to be several blurry lights moving against a pitch-black background — hardly discernable at all, let alone incontrovertible proof.

Edward L. Montoro, *The Force Beyond*'s co-producer, is equally infamous in cult film circles. As head of Film Ventures International, the former Georgia-based commercial airline pilot barely survived a 1968 plane crash and decided a career change was in order. Montoro cranked out outlandish drive-in hits such as *Grizzly*, *Hometown USA*, *The Dark*, *Beyond the Door II*, and *The Incubus*. Lawsuits seemed to

Be prepared for a new force to invade your life...and your mind!

Who really determines the fate of mankind?

THE FORCE BEYOND

Enters a dimension never experienced by man.

Edward L. Montoro presents THE FORCE BEYOND Featuring Don Elkins, Peter Byrne, Renee Dahinden and Frances Farrelly. Written by Donn Davison and William Sachs. Produced by Donn Davison. Directed by William Sachs. Color by Movielab. A Film Ventures International Release.

Poster art for the theatrical release of *The Force Beyond*.

follow wherever he went, with director William Girdler (*Grizzly*, *The Day of the Animals*) one among many suing him for shares of profits, as well as major studios suing him for infringement of their copyrights owing to similarities. When his wife eventually divorced him for half his estate in California, and he'd racked up enormous medical bills after a lengthy illness, Montoro drained his bank accounts — and those of his investors — disappearing à la D.B. Cooper, never to be seen nor heard from again. In an ironic sense, Montoro would've been a perfect subject for one of his own bizarre films, given his nine-lives talent to constantly reinvent himself with "a force beyond" most average persons' abilities.

Forest Story (1977)

Produced, Written, Animated and Directed by John Dods. USA. Color. Stereo. 10 Minutes.

Overview: In an ancient forest there lives a terrible Monster, so fearsome that all the other forest animals tremble whenever it roars. From its bone-littered cave, the Monster sometimes wanders the primeval woods in search of prey upon which to feed.

Meanwhile, elsewhere in the magical forest, Big Grog and Little Grog — father and son apple eaters who refuse to harm other animal life — are gathering a basket of apples. Big Grog shows Little Grog how to correctly stack the fruit in the basket and leaves his offspring to gather apples deeper in the forest. As soon as he is alone, Little Grog playfully kicks the basket and sends it soaring far away.

Alas, the Monster finds the basket and sniffs it. Detecting the delectable aroma of Little Grog on the basket, the Monster's eyes narrow and his fangs flash as it mentally pictures a pile of after-dinner Little Grog bones.

Little Grog knocks a difficult-to-reach apple from a high tree top. The apple rolls and bounces, leading the little creature deeper into the darker regions of the forest without him realizing it. To Little Grog's surprise, he sees a row of apples, neatly aligned, all leading up to a cave's mouth and disappearing inside it. Little Grog happily eats his way towards oblivion, never realizing the Monster awaits him inside the cave's shadows.

Just when it appears Little Grog will become the Monster's dinner, the frightened young Grog leaps to safety, avoiding the Monster's grasp. As the Monster gives chase, it hurls boulders at Little Grog and breathes fire at its fleeing prey. The beast follows Little Grog all the way back to the Grogs' cave. Only by springing a makeshift catapult made from a tree does Big Grog save the day, hurling the Monster skyward. The Monster flies all the way back at its own cave, landing with a mighty thump. Throughout the forest, every ripe apple falls at once to the ground. Big Grog and Little Grog happily gorge themselves, delighted by the turn of events.

* * * * *

Stop-motion animator John Dods began his journey towards professional stage, film, and TV makeup effects master the way many youngsters did — by making his own home movies. While these Super 8mm and 16mm efforts typically emulated the works of Ray Harryhausen and other animators of renown during that era, Dods' superior efforts were a stand-out from the start. Whereas many would-be animators settled for jerky movement, clay models, and poor storylines, Dods quickly established himself as a demanding perfectionist from the beginning, concentrating on smooth animation, foam latex puppets with ball-and-socket armatures every bit as professional as those built by working animators twice his age, and well-developed plots with likeable characters.

Forest Story is perhaps his ultimate stop-motion effort to date, taking the animator over four years to complete. A delightfully magical bit of moviemaking, it features meticulously crafted sets, terrific lighting, and imaginative models made with an eerie sense of fantasy mixed with a touch of cartoonish reality that feels CGI in effect decades before such technology would become the norm. Like the best stop-motion films, *Forest Story* transports the viewer into a completely artificial world that can only exist in cinema (and as the purest examples of cinema itself), demonstrating Dods' remarkable control over the medium in every aspect possible.

The lineage of depicted creatures is amusingly contrasted, especially between the pacifist apple eaters and the carnivorous cryptid. In terms of Ciné du Sasquatch, the "Grogs," as Dods calls his rotund hominids, could best be thought of as embodying the very essence of the Benign Bigfoot archetypes. They are shy, retiring vegans who studiously avoid contact with other species and maintain a strict code of "live and let live" as their inherent philosophy. The Monster, in comparison, is the perfect distillation of the Savage Sasquatch mythos, a hellbent hominid who stops at nothing to devour any denizen of the forest it inhabits. Indeed, when we first see the Monster it snatches one of three terrified birds to eat, leaving only a plume of cascading feathers in its wake.

Even the typical reported encounters with Sasquatch in the real world follow suit in *Forest Story*, with the Monster tossing boulders after Little Grog as the small cryptid runs for its life. And while few,

The dreaded Bad Bigfoot forest monster from John Dods' delightful *Forest Story* short film.

if any, reports feature Sasquatch spouting flames or sporting horns atop its saggital crest (as does the Monster), the Monster nevertheless encapsulates the entire history of Ciné du Sasquatch's typical depictions of a Savage Sasquatch in terms of its cinematic abode: a cave deep in the forest with tons of bones littering the area. So while neither the Grogs nor the Monster is ever referred to by name as a species, their visualizations leave little doubt as to their mythic origins.

Forest Story is a truly magical example of Ciné du Sasquatch and an ideal illustration of how universal the genre is in terms of its ability to be cinematically realized in almost any form, be it horrific, dramatic, as documentary, or even animated via stop-motion. It unfolds like the best of children's fairy tales, with its built-in morality and lesson-learned scenario, but at the same time acts as a perfect Bigfoot movie for adults who desire a nostalgic trip backwards in time when a delightful patch of playful sunlight in the woods could just as quickly become a terrifying blight of darkness and shadow when overhead clouds suddenly obscure the sun.

In a fitting bit of irony and well-deserved reward for his years spent toiling on this labor of love, Dods would go on to become the award-winning make-up effects artist who nightly transformed the Beast in Disney's long-running Broadway smash *Beauty and the Beast*, the stage adaptation of its hit animated feature film. Mr. Dods toured the world with the internationally-travelled production, applying the satisfying Beast illusion literally thousands of times over the years. And yet as wonderful as that experience was, the fact he has announced on his website that he intends to eventually produce and animate another Grog short film speaks volumes about his enduring love of Ciné du Sasquatch.

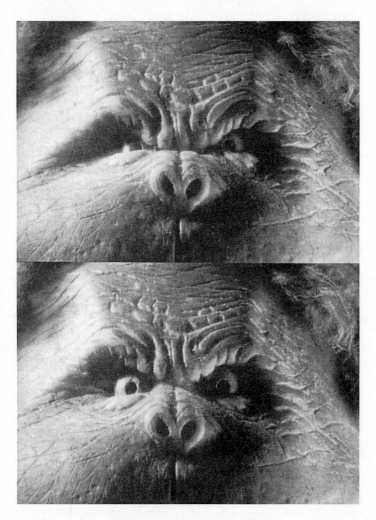

Two extreme close-ups from *Forest Story* show the enormous attention to detail animator John Dods lavished on his starring stop-motion Bigfoot creatures.

Friends ("The One with the Yeti") (1998) (TV) (Cameo)

Starring Jennifer Aniston, Courteney Cox, Lisa Kudrow, Matt LeBlanc, Matthew Perry, David Schwimmer, Helen Baxendale, James Michael Tyler and George Newbern. Produced by Shana Goldberg-Meehan. Written by Alexa Junge. Directed by Gary Halvorson. USA. Color. Stereo. 22 Minutes.

Overview: While Rachel and Monica are searching in the basement of their apartment for a waffle iron, they encounter a hairy man in the dark. Believing him to be a Yeti, they activate a bug bomb and toss it at Bigfoot, racing away under cover of the spraying fog. Later they discover, to their horror, that the supposed Sasquatch was actually Danny, a new neighbor, who has just moved into their building after a four-month-long trek through the Andes, hence his hairy countenance. When Danny knocks on their door to apologize for scaring them earlier in the basement, he is clean shaven and handsome. Rachel realizes her mistake, instantly attracted to the man who she earlier doused with a bug bomb.

* * * * *

When no less than *Friends*, one of the most successful TV shows in the history of the medium, uses a title such as "The One with the Yeti" without the need to explain it to the viewing audience, one can rest assured that Ciné du Sasquatch has not only come of age, but has gone positively mainstream.

Furthering this impression is the dialogue, such as Rachel's terrified replay of her encounter to Joey: "It was like this crazy-eyed, hairy beast man! He was like a, like a Bigfoot or a Yeti or something!" To this Rachel adds a moment later, after Monica explains their use of the bug bomb, "I-I-I just pulled the tab and I just fogged his Yeti ass!" Never does anyone have to justify either woman's description; in fact, Rachel is able to build upon it to the extent she can even recount her self-defense by way of her assault on the hominid's *derrière*.

It's all for laughs and immediately revealed to be perhaps the ultimate case of mistaken identity, but it again demonstrates how far Sasquatch has come in terms of cultural fame — from trite explanations of speculative hominid existence circa the early 1970s TV shows to the mass knowledge and prevalent belief in the possibility only two decades later on *Friends*. The brief moments in the basement in which Rachel and Monica encounter their supposed cryptid are shot to reinforce this perception in the viewer's mind, with shadowy lighting, the fog of the bug bomb, and the general sense of menace that Bigfoot could be hiding in such an urban space. It's a generational flashback to the terrors induced by such fare as *The Legend of Boggy Creek* and *The Mysterious Monsters* — twenty years after the fact being regurgitated as comic relief.

Frostbiter: Wrath of the Wendigo (1996)

Starring Ron Asheton, Lori Baker, Patrick Butler, Devlin Burton, Tom Franks, Alan Madlane, John Bussard, David Wogh, John Mietelka, Bill Siemers, Matt Hale, Mike Missler, Vicki Howard, Bret Julyk, Irina Dvorin and Joel Hale. Produced by Tom Chaney, Rick Cioffi, Steve Quick and David Thiry. Written by Tom Chaney, Rick Cioffi and Steve Quick. Directed by Tom Chaney. USA. Color. Stereo. 106 Minutes.

Overview: Hunters encounter an old man called the Guardian who has spent 100 years preventing a murderous Wendigo from breaking a circle of skulls and being set loose upon the remote Michigan woods wherein the Guardian resides. Dave, one of the hunters, destroys one of the skulls, and soon enough the beast is wreaking havoc, along with a cadre of demons and chili monsters assisting it.

* * * * *

Some films and TV shows, such as *Charmed*, depict the Wendigo as a Bigfoot creature, while others stay true to the Native American legends which more often than not cast the being as a wind demon who can assume skeletal human form in order to commit cannibalism. *Frostbiter: Curse of the Wendigo* is closer to the latter than the former, which is why it's technically outside the Ciné du Sasquatch genre — but included here so as to distinguish it from the plethora of Sasquatch-related Wendigo visualizations.

The Wendigo creature by Dave Hettmer and Richard Jacobsonis is a stop-motion creation that is quite good for the film's reported overall budget of $25,000. Featuring a skeletal equine body but with a white, hominid upper body and head with antlers, it conjures images of the centaur brought to life by Ray Harryhausen for the finale of *The Golden Voyage of Sinbad*. But despite the trappings and title, *Frostbiter: Curse of the Wendigo* remains a non–Bigfoot film, especially in terms of Yeti genre conventions, and is included strictly for clarification.

Futurama ("Spanish Fry") (1999) (Cameo) (TV)

Featuring the voices of Billy West, Katey Sagal, John DiMaggio, Lauren Tom, Phil LaMarr and Maurice LaMarche. Produced by David X. Cohen, Brian J. Cowan, David A. Goodman, Matt Groening, Alex Johns, Eric Kaplan, Claudia Katz, Ken Keeler, Bill Odenkirk, Michael Rowe, Dan Vebber, Patric M. Verrone, Ron Weiner and Mili Smythe. Written by Ron Weiner. Directed by Peter Avanzino. USA. Color. Stereo. 30 Minutes.

Overview: Series regular Fry goes camping, only to have his nose removed by aliens who consider human noses a delicacy. His friends Bender and Leela attempt to help Fry get his errant nose back before it is consumed. They manage to recover Fry's nose, but as a direct result his penis next lies in jeopardy of removal. Bigfoot intervenes to save the day (and Fry's anatomical correctness), but a park ranger, who is keen on seeing a specimen of Sasquatch brought to scientific light, attempts to amputate one of Bigfoot's feet as just such evidence. The aliens halt this attempt, delivering a stern speech about the need to respect all of God's creations throughout the galaxy as they are, without alteration, even if it means forsaking all future eating of human's anatomical extremities. Bigfoot is eventually released back into the wilds, and Fry is saved from jeopardy. The park ranger makes off with a secret snippet of the hominid's hair he's taken, determined to see the world recognize the creature as real, once and for all.

* * * * *

Often a loose strand of speculative sighting dates joined together, there nonetheless exists a minor group of Bigfoot-UFO eyewitness sightings which overlap with some degree of peculiarity in rare instances (in others they seem merely exaggerated or speculative, at best). Though details vary greatly, as in all such hominid and flying saucer reports (owing to witness particulars and the veracity of their allegations), the generally consistent fact present in so many of these reports suggests Bigfoot and UFO sightings being made in the vicinity together at the same time are substantial evidence of a joint Fortean event. In some cases the connection is obvious, as when witnesses report seeing both cryptid and UFO evidence at the same time. But more generally, it is a post-event analysis made by someone studying the reports in triangulation that uncovers possible connections between the UFO sightings and Bigfoot encounters.

Not surprisingly, therefore, this trend has been picked up and used in Ciné du Sasquatch movies and TV shows. For example, *The Six Million Dollar Man* episodes featuring a Bionic Bigfoot also had a subplot which designated ruthless aliens as the actual puppet masters behind the Sasquatch's every move. *Terror in the Midnight Sun* filled an entire feature film with a similar treatment, though the Yeti in question was shown to be 100 percent giant hominid rather than robotic. And then there's the influence of *2001*, which in its "The Dawn of Man" sequence featured a trembling tribe of hominids encountering alien greatness so vast it literally changes the destiny of the early humanoids' history as a species. These are all very potent cultural embodiments of the concept of an alien-hominid connection, dispersed in merely these three cited examples across two different mediums, various genres, and even international arenas of production.

The belief that primitive humans (and therefore, possibly, earlier hominid species) were visited by space aliens is a deeply held one, and, much like the Bigfoot icon itself, may be found in as many different cultural representations as there are cultures.

None of this would appear to matter much save for the fact this episode of *Futurama* so adroitly weaves these existing strands of strangeness together into one funny, Bigfoot-relevant episode. While Bigfoot doesn't really appear until the waning moments, the lead-up is entertaining and worth the wait, particularly for series regulars who will appreciate this particularly raunchy episode of the often adult-themed show. The park ranger's deranged need to get proof of Bigfoot (even if it means maiming the poor creature) is emblematic of the progression in Ciné du Sasquatch for those who would be witnesses to "the cause" of Bigfoot — they want proof, hard proof, and nothing *but* the proof. This myopic mission is mostly a clever retelling of the ever-present Carl Denham archetype so inherent in the genre. In most versions this character exploits a hominid for fame and fortune. In this funny inversion, it is a park ranger — a figure who may otherwise have previously been sympathetic to Bigfoot's precarious position in the delicate balance of nature, but who now has become so blinded with proving Bigfoot real that he's become a poor man's substitute for Carl Denham. In both scenarios it is worth noting that Bigfoot is the intended recipient of the short end of the stick — caged, exhibited, and even amputated in this episode of *Futurama*. It's all for laughs and plays mainly as such, but "Spanish Fry" also knows the rules of Ciné du Sasquatch and abides by them with model narrative efficiency.

The Geek (1971)

Starring Mycle Brandy, Queen Amora and Lynn Holmes. USA. Color. Mono. 50 Minutes.

Overview: Three young couples go in search of Bigfoot in the remote wilderness. After trekking to a secluded spot where they suspect they might find Sasquatch, they pitch camp. A married couple wanders away and makes love outdoors. After they're done, they head back to camp. All of the hikers retire for the evening. Another couple makes love in their tent.

The next day they all head deeper into the woods to find Bigfoot. Soon they find tracks. They film the evidence with a 16mm camera. Suddenly, Sasquatch appears, grunting and groaning. The amateur cryptozoologists decide to offer one of the young ladies as bait. Bigfoot takes a liking to her and forcibly rapes her. Eventually the onlookers rescue her, but while they're not looking, Bigfoot abducts another female and rapes her as well.

The men take the creature on in a fight. Bigfoot easily knocks them off and shambles away. One of the men is helped to his feet and solemnly mutters, "One day, I'm going to get that bastard!" They all head back to civilization.

* * * * *

The Geek is a true anomaly in Ciné du Sasquatch, as rarely seen as it is discussed, even among Bigfoot film completists. Clearly shot on a nothing budget in a matter of days and lacking even the most rudimentary filmmaking abilities, it is little wonder the crew behind its making chose to forgo recognition. To this day, in fact, the director, writer and producer remain incognito, which is probably for the best, given the backlash they'd face if friends, family and coworkers ever learned they were behind the production of this film.

The opening title shot encapsulates everything that is trying about the film. Consisting of a sheet of rolled plastic held in front of the camera lens with the titles hand-painted on them, the credits are literally partially off-screen as the director has someone lift them so that they appear to crudely scroll upwards. While the plastic sheet wobbles in and out of focus and slips sideways to render much of the writing incomprehensible, terrible stock music blares in low-fidelity monaural, clearly mixed with the single speaker system of most adult movie theaters of its era in mind.

The narrator tells us that the story we're about to witness is entirely true, and that it is based on scientific research! Given that the camera person cannot achieve consistent focus nor correct lighting exposure, this claim seems extravagantly indulgent. There is nothing remotely scientific involved in the entire enterprise of *The Geek*, unless one counts the curiously correct pronunciation by the narrator of the word "Neanderthal" (as in, *Nee-And-Der-Tall*, which is the correct Germanic style), which for 1971 was definitely ahead of its time (the word is still mispronounced by most Americans to this day). Ironically, the narrator concludes that the Neanderthal was not the missing link suggested by Darwin, but that Bigfoot was said species. So far, so good (in terms of theoretical science, at least), but then he concludes by saying: "Known as Bigfoot to many, and of course, to countless others as the Geek!" Given that a "geek" is historically based upon the notorious carnival act in which a man bit the head off a live chicken and has subsequently devolved in modern nomenclature to indicate a nerdy intellectual type, this makes absolutely no sense whatsoever. Nor is there any history of the use of the word "geek" for hominids in any cryptid literature, film, or reporting. In short, *The Geek* has just committed its first of many cinematic perversities.

The film was clearly shot mostly silent and post-dubbed, not that there's more than a handful of dialogue sequences over its nearly hour-length running time. Most of the first half-hour is spent showing endless shots of the couples hiking into what the narrator claims is the wilderness of Oregon (though it more obviously resembles someone's cleared ranch lands). The sparse landscape is almost entirely devoid of trees, which one would think was a major disadvantage for a creature that towers over humans in height and therefore has no place to hide from detection while in the open. Likewise, the pasture seems without tall grass or weeds, though from the hippie-like appearance of the six human protagonists, it may well have been they smoked it all during production.

After an unendurable series of tedious takes, the couples finally begin their sexual escapades, which is, of course, the true commercial reason for the film's existence. Here *The Geek* again fails to arouse viewer interest, either figuratively or literally. Part of this is attributable to the unflattering long takes the director chooses to employ while his actors are having sex. The only cuts occur when the hardcore footage has been snipped out (most likely by the projectionists of the time who were notorious for doing so before returning the film to the distributors), which causes a bizarrely unsettling jump cut effect/flash forward in the sexual activity. The other reason the sex scenes play as ineffectually as they do is that they're shot in broad daylight and with unenthusiastic performers. Given that "stars" Mycle Brandy, Queen Amora, and Lynn Holmes all were professional porno players in their day, it's surprising how lame they are in terms of their screen presence. This may be due as much to a lack of directorial vision and proper staging as the performers' faults. At any rate, the whole enterprise feels so sleazy in terms of its voyeuristic "let's hurry up and get this shot before the local cops bust us" mentality that only the most inveterate of pornography lovers would find it appealing.

When all else fails, of course, one can always bring on the horny cryptid, which is what the creators of *The Geek* do at the 35-minute mark. This astonishing turn of events and sudden, manic pace is as unbelievable as the sex-crazed Bigfoot costume itself. Within moments of arriving on the scene, the Sasquatch takes the offered bait — one of the female campers — and proceeds to rape her while the others look on without reaction. One of the men even films the incident and boasts afterwards when queried by another, "Yeah, I got it all on film!" In the interim, the Bigfoot has forced the woman to the ground and sodomized her for an excruciating amount of screen time. While clearly designed for the porno crowd to "synchronize their watches," in terms of appeal there's simply nothing pleasant about a grunting, groaning, badly-suited Sasquatch committing bestiality on the poor victim, who seems so ashamed by this sequence she keeps her face (understandably) turned away from the camera. The callous nature with which the men react (including her boyfriend), who wait until after the encounter to do anything, veers beyond absurd into outright misogyny. The boyfriend consoles her as he helps her back to the group with such sensitive remarks as, "Shhh, it's okay. You'll be all right," never once defending his lack of action to save her from the assault!

When Bigfoot repeats the same stunt with the second victim, however, *The Geek* goes from stupefying to sickening, even in terms of camp. For this second go-round, the woman is clearly shown enjoying the rape, putting up no resistance and offering expressions of pleasure. It's difficult to imagine in today's post-feminist climate such a scene not being condemned and prone to outright censorship, but as in all such sexist imagery, the era and intended market for the film should be kept in mind. One does have to wonder, however, at the mental well-being of the audience who found this material erotic; but, of course, as the Internet's widespread revelation of every known sexual deviancy has demonstrated, there's nothing too bizarre to garner at least some marginally prurient interest.

The film concludes with the men inexplicably deciding it's time to take action and fight the beast, *mano a hominido*. They encircle Bigfoot and run at him, one at a time, as he knocks them aside in some of the worst-staged stunts in cinematic history. After pounding them into submission (one could speculate on deeper psycho-sexual meanings hidden within this sequence, but, thankfully, that's beyond the need of this critique), Bigfoot lumbers away as lethargically as he first shambled into the film. The concluding line, as the beaten male glares at the departing cryptid and utters, "One day I'm going to get that bastard!" is a genuine laugh-inducer. The film abruptly cuts to a title card with "The End" handwritten on it, and, mercifully, *The Geek* is completed.

There's no denying the potential cult qualities inherent within *The Geek*. Not only does it feature Mycle Brandy, who would later appear in the cult favorite *Flesh Gordon*, but it hovers on a technical level far below even the worst Ed Wood production. Too, the grotesque nature of the final minutes, wherein Bigfoot runs amok, is both shockingly campy and unexpectedly ludicrous. But getting to (and through) these moments is an endurance test that few, if any (even ardent fans of Bigfoot cinema or adult films), will find rewarding. It's a curiosity piece, no more (and often much less); and as such, it may be regarded as a relic perhaps unworthy of more than a passing nod.

The Ghost Busters (1975) ("The Abominable Snowman") (TV)

AKA: *The Original Ghostbusters*. Starring Forrest Tucker, Larry Storch, Bob Burns, Ronny Graham, Richard Balin and Lou Scheimer. Produced by Norm Prescott, Marc Richards, Richard M. Rosenbloom and Lou Scheimer. Written by Marc Richards. Directed by Norman Abbott. USA. Color. Mono. 30 Minutes.

Overview: Dr. Centigrade, a diabolical mad scientist, wishes to end the continual frosty emanations of his nefarious cryptid companion the Abominable Snowman. So he devises a plan to transplant a live human heart into his Yeti sidekick, figuring this will transform the beast into a warmer, finer-furred friend. Dr. Centigrade sets his sights on his arch rivals the Ghost Busters, a trio of spirit-capturing specialists consisting of Kong (a crotchety older gent) the zoot suit-wearing Spenser and Tracy (a beanie-wearing gorilla).

* * * * *

This delightfully cheesy Saturday morning live action sitcom was the epitome of the type of television programming aimed at children in the 1970s. Courtesy of Filmation Associates (the prolific company which also produced *Isis, Shazam, Jason of Star Command, Ark II* and the animated version of *Star Trek*, among many others), *The Ghost Busters* consisted of a reunion of two of the stars from the primetime sitcom *F-Troop*, Forrest Tucker and Larry Storch, here accompanied by mute gorilla companion Tracy, who was played by simian suit expert Bob Burns. Every week the trio of sleuths received an assignment from a mysterious Zero after visiting a convenience store, at which their newest tape-recorded orders were hidden in various common household products. After listening to each new challenge (invariably involving zombies, vampires and the like), the product would then explode in the face of the hapless Spenser (Larry Storch), nearly ruining his trademark zoot suit.

Inevitably, the villainous monsters and supernatural beings they faced were housed in an abandoned castle on the "outskirts of town" (which probably made many young viewers wonder what American burg it was that had such a structure so close to the city limits; the town is never specified). The Ghost Busters would arrive, bumble through various entrapments, free one another at the last possible moment, and then—using Kong's (Forest Tucker) specially-made, ghost-destroying, dematerializing gun belt—trap the evil presence. The formula varied very little in the 16-episode run of the series, as much of it was shot back-to-back in order to economize production costs.

The set-up of "Abominable Snowman" is really quite ridiculous, even by the relaxed story standards of *The Ghost Busters*. Dr. Centigrade's goal to transplant a human heart into the Yeti in order to make the Yeti emit less coldness is both preposterous and contradictory. Surely if a cryptid such as the Yeti existed in the snowy tops of the Himalayas, the last biological development it would need or evolve would be the ability to make itself colder instead of warmer! With that in mind, however, there is some comic irony in the fact that the selected transplant donor (though he is not aware he will be donating his heart) should be Forrest Tucker's character named Jake Kong. Why not Tracy the gorilla instead? After all, Tracy's supposed genetic similarity to the Yeti would make him a more appropriate fit, as the two seem more closely aligned.

But this fits in with the series' set-up, in which things are always screwed up, starting with the characters' names themselves. For example, why is the gorilla named Tracy and the human leader of the trio named Kong? And the irony of having Forrest Tucker as the intended organ donor is funny to those steeped in the history of Ciné du Sasquatch—Tucker was the antagonist intent on bagging a Yeti in the hallmark 1957 film *The Abominable Snowman*, so it's only fitting he should now find himself hunted by a Yeti. It's doubtful that anyone but those on-set and the actor himself appreciated this subtle inside reference, as the intended audience would have been unlikely to have seen Tucker in the earlier Hammer movie. But it does make for an interesting Ciné du Sasquatch "foot"-note.

Bob Burns is worthy of a mention in terms of Ciné du Sasquatch as well. He continued the tradition set forth by simian costume expert Charles Gemora (who virtually created the "gorilla man" as an archetype seen in countless Hollywood movies featuring stars like Abbott & Costello, the Marx Brothers, Hope & Crosby, the Little Rascals, and others). Burns never received the acting opportunities Gemora pioneered for himself, but was nonetheless the major go-to "gorilla man" for many low-budget TV and film producers throughout his long career. Burns appeared as his own creation Kogar the Ape in *Rat Pfink a Boo Boo* and *Lemon Grove Kids Meet the Monsters*, as well as on *The Lucy Show* with Lucille Ball. As an avid collector of movie memorabilia, with an emphasis on fantasy, horror, and science fiction films, his personal collection remains one of the most unique and valuable in the world. He has authored a pictorial coffee table book showcasing his immense collection called *It Came from Bob's Basement: Exploring the Science Fiction and Monster Movie Archive of Bob Burns* (Chronicle Books, 2001), which is recommended to fans of cryptid cinema if for no other reason than the many simian costumes and props he owns (including one of the original ball and socket armatures used by Willis O'Brien in the original *King Kong*). Equally important, Burns nurtured a lot of talent who went on to make major contributions to the fantasy, horror and SF film genres, such as Oscar-winning special effects artists Dennis Muren, the Skotak Brothers and Rick Baker (who won his first Academy Award for his *Harry and the Hendersons* Sasquatch suit). In no small part, Burns carried forward the Killer Gorilla genre with his many appearances, though he typically portrayed his Kogar the Ape as a more gentle incarnation (which in and of itself was a precursor to the Benign Bigfoot that would later become so prevalent in Sasquatch films).

In a bizarre bit of history, the Ivan Reitman film *Ghostbusters* clearly (or perhaps unintentionally) borrowed not only the name and basic set-up of *The Ghost Busters*, but even the dematerializing belt device (it is slightly modified for the Reitman film to have nozzles, backpacks, etc.). Columbia Pictures eventually settled out of court with Filmation rather than risk the further embarrassment a trial would bring, and both sides then fought a war of attrition in which Columbia began calling their franchise *The Real Ghostbusters* in a Saturday morning cartoon series designed to capitalize upon the successful Bill Murray film; while Filmation put out its own cartoon series called *The Original Ghostbusters* — designed to capitalize upon the Murray film as well. All rancor aside, it is worth noting that neither party acknowledged the earlier film *Spook Busters*, which was made in 1946 and starred the Bowery Boys as a group of young men who start their own extermination business and battle a mad scientist intent on switching Sach's brain with a gorilla in a haunted house. The only connection to Ciné du Sasquatch lacking in the latter film is Charles Gemora as the "gorilla man" actor!

Ghosts: True Hauntings in Montana (2003) (Doc)

Produced, Written and Directed by David F. Curran. USA. Color. Stereo. 36 Minutes.

Overview: This regionally-produced independent documentary features recreations of two local ghost legends collected by the filmmaker. The first is "The Mailbox" and the second is "Kelly Saloon." Also included are supposedly real photos of Montana's own Bigfoot, hence the interest to Ciné du Sasquatch fans. Rounding out the disc in the Director's Special Edition are additional local ghost legends accompanied by slideshow photos.

Giganto: The Real King Kong (2005) (TV) (Doc)

Narrated by Edward Herrmann and Stan Bernard. Starring Joseph Frascella, Steve Stark and John Keppler. Produced by Doug Hajicek, Carl H. Lindahl, Dan Nyberg, Michael Stiller and Jeffrey C. Weber. Written by Dale Bosch and Doug Hajicek. Directed by Doug Hajicek. USA. Color. Stereo. 60 Minutes.

Overview: This interesting, well-researched documentary focuses on the actual species known as *Gigantopithecus blacki* or "Giant Ape." While the *King Kong* title tie-in is a bit spurious, the theory held by some cryptozoological researchers that this extinct Asian primate may have lingered on in small numbers and thus explain many Bigfoot sightings is, however far-fetched, at least scientifically plausible. Given *Gigantopithecus* were nearly ten feet in height when standing fully erect, 1,000 pounds in weight, and covered in black hair/fur, any modern human being encountering such a relic hominid would doubtless describe said cryptid as Sasquatch-like (for want of a better adjective). Though the species is believed to have become extinct approximately 500,000 years ago, *Giganto: The Real King Kong* reviews the possibilities of its continued existence with in-depth DNA testing, 3D model CGI recreations, and other scientific processes needed to establish objective data and findings.

The first version of *Giganto: The Real King Kong* appeared on the Arts & Entertainment Network in 2005, hosted by Edward Herrmann. Three years later it was included in the popular History Channel series *MonsterQuest*, with additional footage and new narration by Stan Bernard (though Herrmann's original narration was retained), as the opening episode of that series' second season.

Godzilla and the Super 90 ("The Sub-Zero Terror") (1978) (TV)

AKA: *The Godzilla Power Hour*; *The Godzilla Show*; *The Godzilla/Globetrotters Adventure Hour*; *The Godzilla/Dynomutt Hour*; *The Godzilla/Hong Kong Phooey Hour*. Featuring the voices of Ted Cassidy, Jeff David, Al Eisenman, Hilly Hicks, Brenda Thompson and Don Messick. Produced by William Hanna, Joseph Barbera and Doug Wildey. Directed by Ray Patterson and Carl Urbano. USA. Color. Mono. 90 Minutes.

Overview: Dr. Quinn Darian heads an investigative oceanic task force aboard her high-tech vessel the Calico under the guidance of Captain Carl Majors. Along for the adventures are Dr. Darian's nephew Pete, the ship's first mate Brock, and Godzooky, the bumbling young cousin of Godzilla. Godzilla is never far away, either, typically intervening whenever the crew of the Calico find themselves in mortal danger.

Dr. Rourke, a former colleague of Dr. Darian's, joins the ship in search of a reputed geothermal power supply located in the Himalayan Mountains. The Calico anchors near a dormant volcano, which instruments reveal is the source of the suspected energy fluctuations. A skyscraper-sized Yeti starts an avalanche, intent on burying the crew members. Godzilla rises from the depths and saves them in the nick of time.

Refusing to be intimidated, Dr. Darian and friends guide their boat inside the volcano via a hidden cove and discover an interior land populated by a race of people called the Watchuka, human-sized hominids who are clearly the basis of the Abominable Snowmen legends. Suspicions are aroused in Dr. Darian when she discovers a monstrous steam engine, which she realizes is the means by which the hidden race have built their secretive civilization. Worse still, when the Calico team members stumble upon the Watchuka's true motivations — they intend to release an army of snowmen held in suspended animation to conquer the outside world — they are taken hostage, one by one, until all hope seems lost.

Gadzooky helps Pete and Brock liberate Dr. Darian and Dr. Rourke, forcing the outraged Watchuka to summon the assistance of the Great Watchuka, the earlier-seen gigantic Yeti. The Great Watchuka attempts to crush the fleeing Calico team, but Godzilla intervenes again, providing the humans precious time to board their ship. Godzilla and the Great Watchuka battle for dominance, triggering the volcano. Godzilla bests the giant Abominable Snowman and uses a huge boulder to seal the volcano's opening. With the Watchuka now unable to carry out their plan and the Calico crew safe from danger, Godzilla sinks beneath the waves.

* * * * *

The Hanna-Barbera animation titans set the record in terms of sheer number of hominid portrayals throughout their vast *oeuvre* of kiddy-oriented fare. Yetis appear in a virtual litany of the producers' most popular (as well as less popular) series: *Johnny Quest*; *Scooby Doo, Where Are You?* and its various spin-offs and sequels; *Birdman and the Galaxy Trio*; *Space Ghost and Dino Boy*; *Dexter's Laboratory*; *The Grim Adventures of Billy and Mandy*; and more. Never let it be said that Hanna-Barbera didn't realize a good antagonist when they saw it, as their constant recycling of Bigfoot demonstrates. Too, the constant Bigfoot barrage, courtesy of their cartoons' use of said cryptid, had a huge impact on tyke viewers during the halcyon 1970s when Bigfoot was popularized in mass culture. This would be the same generation enthralled by *The Legend of Boggy Creek* at their local matinee, Sasquatch on television with *The Six Million Dollar Man*, and in popular magazines such as *Argosy*, which featured the latest hominid headlines. The non-stop blitz across all media formats in no uncertain terms stimulated an entire generation of real-life cryptozoologists, as well as hardcore lovers of Ciné du Sasquatch.

Godzilla was another beloved icon, even if by the 1970s the Toho Studios had relegated their iconic star to self-parodying knock-offs such as *Godzilla on Monster Island* and *Godzilla vs. Megalon* (which portrayed Godzilla as little more than a friendly helper to little kids worldwide). While the Godzilla films of the 1950s and 1960s could still be called juvenile, they at least had a seriousness that was painfully absent in later entries. So it was with great hope (and subsequent disappointment) that the esteemed Hanna-Barbera duo tackled an American animation adaptation of the beloved beast in 1978 with *The Godzilla Power Hour* on NBC. With limited animation, generally poor plots, and the particularly offensive introduction of Godzooky, the annoying flying cousin of Godzilla (who many still consider the worst character in Hanna-Barbera's library, rivaled only by the equally annoying, pint-sized Scrappy Doo), many child-aged fans of the *kaiju* films ultimately refused to watch the American cartoon incarnation.

Matters weren't helped by NBC's constant reshuffling of the series' numerous titles, broadcast time slots, and formats. *Godzilla* the animated series was presented in a variety-style format with wraparound segments featuring a diverse range of characters, such as Jana of the Jungle, Jonny Quest, the Super Globetrotters, Dynomutt, and even Hong Kong Phooey! Little wonder with such a mélange of ill-fitting and confusing cohorts that Hanna-Barbera's *Godzilla* was a slow-motion flop, even though some fans who grew up watching it now consider it a guilty pleasure. To its credit, the show did survive several seasons, which, given the sub-par treatment by the network, was a testament to the character's enduring appeal; it was a true case of even bad Godzilla being better than no Godzilla.

"The Sub-Zero Terror" episode appeared under the *Godzilla and the Super 90* title (the "90" being a reference to the running time in minutes, as reruns of *Johnny Quest* were included to pad the show's length) after NBC decided to revamp the original version of *The Godzilla Power Hour*. In terms of how it plays into and with the motifs of Ciné du Sasquatch, this episode is both typical of how the Yeti is often portrayed in animated fare, as well as how Hanna-Barbera itself often utilized hominids. To wit, they almost invariably favored a gigantic rendition of the Abominable Snowman versus a scaled-to-human version (unless the Yeti would later be revealed to be a human

wearing a disguise, as was the case in the *Scooby Doo* franchise). While this makes some narrative sense for the *Godzilla* series (as it gives Godzilla a foe of equally huge proportions), it often seemed more for sheer exaggeration in other Hanna-Barbera series (such as *Space Ghost and Dino Boy*). It seemed to be less a case of basing the cryptid on actual reports as much as on the original *King Kong* movie, right down to the character's scale.

This episode actually manages to have its frost-covered cake and eat it, too. Both human-sized *and* towering Snowmen are depicted. The Watchuka are seen as both a threat to Dr. Darian (and the Calico crew) and to Godzilla (when the King of the Monsters must engage with the so-called Great Watchuka, which is the skyscraper-sized version of the hominid). It's a strange, unexplained phenomena that the Watchuka come in such a range of adaptable heights, but then again, in a series wherein Godzooky is not much larger than humans and Godzilla is 400 feet tall, it is perhaps begging the point to apply any critical rationale regarding size.

Still, it is never even suggested why such a severely depopulated species as the Watchuka would want to attempt to conquer the entire planet when they are entirely self-sufficient and non-threatened in their hidden lair. Given they are few in numbers — despite their building of an army of Snowmen with which to engage the human civilization outside their relatively small domain — and even with the Great Watchuka at their beck and call, it is ridiculous to think they could mount much of an effort against a modern military force of even the most basic nation-state, let alone the combined global might of said nations. Indeed, the Watchuka are no match for the handful of *Homo sapiens* they encounter on their own home turf, and are easily defeated by none other than the goofy Godzooky himself! Given their lack of true muscle, they perhaps owe more of a debt of gratitude to Godzilla for sealing them inside their volcano hideaway than they seem willing to acknowledge, as Godzilla's action spares them further humiliation at the hands of the world's military superpowers. In more succinct, brutal terms, the Watchuka wouldn't have provided even a minute's worth of CNN coverage time if they'd faced American-styled "Shock and Awe" bombardment circa the start of the Iraqi War.

A Goofy Movie (1995) (Cameo)

Featuring the voices of Bill Farmer, Jason Marsden, Jim Cummings, Kellie Martin, Rob Paulsen, Wallace Shawn, Jenna von Oÿ, Frank Welker, Kevin Lima, Florence Stanley, Jo Anne Worley, Brittany Alyse Smith, Robyn Richards, Julie Brown, Klee Bragger, Joseph Lawrence, Pat Buttram, Wayne Allwine, Herschel Sparber, Dante Basco, Sheryl Bernstein, Corey Burton, Pat Carroll, Elizabeth Daily and Carole Holliday. Produced by Gaëtan Brizzi, Paul Brizzi, Leslie Hough, Patrick Reagan, Dan Rounds, Michael Serrian and Will Waggoner. Written by Jymn Magon, Chris Matheson and Brian Pimental. Directed by Kevin Lima. USA. Color. Stereo. 78 Minutes.

Overview: Goofy, a hardworking dad, believes he's losing touch with his teen son Max. Max is intent on impressing a cute cohort named Roxanne who he's had a crush on since grade school, leading him to impersonate a famous music star named Powerline one day at school. Roxanne is swayed by Max's talent and accepts his invitation to the school dance. But Max's principal is convinced Max's breaking of school decorum will lead the errant youngster straight into a life of crime and eventually the electric chair. Convinced by the principal's overly-hysterical phone call, Goofy decides to take time away from his job as a child photographer and spend some quality one-on-one time with Max while they drive across country on vacation.

During an extended camping trip sequence, Goofy and Max are

fishing when Goofy's sirloin steak bait hooks none other than Bigfoot. Goofy reels him in, believing the catch to be a three-pounder, at the least. Sasquatch leaps from the water mere feet from a terrified Max and Goofy, roaring in indignation. The pair run for their lives, with Goofy videotaping the incident the entire way. Alas, Goofy accidentally drops the camera, and he and Max are forced to hide in their car while Bigfoot ransacks their camping gear, seeking food.

Night falls, but Bigfoot remains nearby, toying with headphones while he dances to the Bee Gee's "Stayin' Alive" hit song. Goofy and Max, stuck in their car because Bigfoot has thrown away the keys, are forced to spend a tense night together. Each realizes they've been hard on one another, refusing to truly listen and openly communicate. As soon as they bond, however, Bigfoot noisily climbs atop their vehicle and falls asleep. Goofy bids his son a goodnight and soon falls into deep slumber as well. Max listens to Goofy and Bigfoot trying to out-snore one another with eyes wide open, unable to sleep for their combined noise.

* * * * *

Goofy has long been one of the favorite Disney characters, and *A Goofy Movie* immediately establishes why the appeal has lasted for seventy-odd years. Whereas Donald Duck can seem abrasive and Mickey Mouse downright patronizing, Goofy's self-deprecating charms always seem to engender a sense of endearment in most viewers, young or old. Perhaps it's the syrupy, self-conscious voice Goofy employs. Or maybe the beguiling likeability comes from his wide blinking eyes, which alternately seem on the cusp of an enlightenment that never arrives and a confusion that never abates. Or maybe it's just his sincere, self-effacing manner, which suggests self-esteem issues in personal worthiness that transcend the 2-D nature of his rendering. Whatever the reasons, Goofy is loveably laughable, a true clown with a heart of gold.

The combination of sentiment and laughter can easily transform into maudlin entertainment, but for most of its brief 78-minute running time, *A Goofy Movie* manages to have the best of both at heart and onscreen. The sequence involving Bigfoot's cameo, which lasts over 5 minutes, is the film's highlight, featuring a slobbering, simple-minded hominid who makes Goofy look like Albert Einstein in comparison. But while the Sasquatch is portrayed as a comical figure, he still retains a distinctively fun sense of individuality, which elevates the cryptid from mere fool archetype into a gregarious character full of a need for instant gratification and respect (as being dominant in his own domain). When Goofy or Max inadvertently interfere with either need, Bigfoot goes comically haywire, intent on destroying anything and anyone in his path.

In some clever ways the creators have basically made Bigfoot an overgrown infant by reducing his desires to a child's penchant for wanting what it wants and wanting it *now*. This impertinence mixed with impatience plays particularly well for comedy when placed within the body of a giant hominid, as the threat level of said "baby," should he become angry, is all the more damaging. Like the old joke asks: "Where does an 800-pound gorilla sit? Anywhere it wants!" Such is Sasquatch in *A Goofy Movie*.

Disney's best animated films always achieved a kind of hyper-surrealism in terms of fluidity of motion, rarely matched by competitors until the arrival of CGI. *A Goofy Movie*, while no *Beauty and the Beast* or *The Lion King*, is nevertheless genuinely top-notch in terms of technical animation achievement. It's very likely this is the finest rendering of Bigfoot to date in any strictly animated medium, as the Disney studio employed literally hundreds of artists and animators to bring the visual kinetics to life. Just watching the few seconds of Bigfoot shooting up from under the water, Goofy's fishing bait clenched in the cryptid's teeth, while the water runs down the hominid's fur in rivulets in a convincing, realistic manner, illustrates

the level of artistry and professionalism on display throughout this short feature film.

Voiced with a hilarious sense of self-delight by actor Fred Welker (who also did the feline star of the *Garfield the Cat* TV series) in a series of indecipherable but self-explanatory grunts and groans, Bigfoot's cameo in *A Goofy Movie* ranks highly in the Ciné du Sasquatch genre not only because it so impressively renders the creature, but equally illustrates two major tenets present throughout the genre. One, it demonstrates the underlying motif that when *Homo sapiens* (or in this case, personified *Homo sapiens*!) meet a hominid in the hominid's setting, the humans usually come out on the losing end of the match. Two, while Bigfoot may vigorously defend said territory, it typically does so only to the extent that the invasive humans admit defeat and allow the beast to reign supreme in its domain.

By capitulating and locking themselves in their car for the night, and thereby allowing Bigfoot to tease them for his own amusement (at one point Bigfoot places Goofy's socks on his hands and renders a puppet show outside their car's window to mock their fear), they are demonstrating submission to their own Animus and darker, more primitive side of their psyches, as embodied externally by the cryptid literally outside their exterior, protective shell (the car). The fact that said showing of humility directly leads to both Goofy and Max having a long-needed communication breakthrough moments later is no accident. Because each has to forgo his Ego and Super Ego, both are able to finally allow their deeper subconscious instincts to relay their actual, heartfelt love for one another as father and son. It all plays as coy comic relief, when in fact, and true to Ciné du Sasquatch's genre rules, the scene perfectly reveals the mechanics of the genre itself.

While some criticized *A Goofy Movie* as a lesser Disney effort upon its initial release, it has gone on to enjoy quite a following among both children and adults. The universality of its themes — coming of age, father and son relationships, and family vacations — are well-captured for such a seemingly facile cartoon. Goofy's self-recriminations and haunting sense of doubt at having failed his son's emotional development are both unexpectedly complex and completely believable, thus giving the film a darker, more somber undercurrent than the otherwise glib proceedings would suggest are present. Resultantly, and not too surprisingly, the Bigfoot cameo is often cited by many fans of *A Goofy Movie* as the highlight of the entire effort.

The Grim Adventures of Billy & Mandy ("Here Thar Be Dwarves" and "Be A-Fred, Be Very A-Fred") (2004) (TV) (Cameo)

AKA: Grim & Evil; Evil Con Carne. Featuring the voices of Richard Steven Horvitz, Grey DeLisle, Greg Eagles, Vanessa Marshall, Jane Carr, Rachael MacFarlane, Jennifer Hale, Dee Bradley Baker, Phil LaMarr, Martin Jarvis, Debi Derryberry, Diedrich Bader and Maxwell Atoms. Produced by Maxwell Atoms, Louis J. Cuck, Brian A. Miller, Jennifer Pelphrey and Shaun Cashman. Directed by Robert Alvarez, Maxwell Atoms, David Brain, Julie Hashiguchi, Brian Hogan and John McIntyre. Maxwell Atoms, David Brain, Julie Hashiguchi, Brian Hogan, John McIntyre; USA. Color. Stereo. 22 Minutes.

Overview: Billy and Mandy are two ordinary American 10 year olds living in Anywhere, USA. When Billy's pet hamster is dying, the Grim Reaper appears to take the pet's soul. To the Reaper's surprise, Billy and Mandy are completely blasé and show no fear. When they ask the Reaper to spare the hamster's life, the Reaper responds with a challenge: If they can beat him at his favorite game in the otherworld of Limbo, he will do as they ask — and the Reaper will stay with them "forever and ever" as their household best friend.

In the mists of Limbo the Reaper reveals his challenge — none other than a low-straddling game of Limbo itself, set to Caribbean music, in which he is an undisputed master. But a quick-thinking Mandy tricks Grim by releasing their hamster on the soul collector, causing him to fail. Despite himself, the Grim Reaper relocates to Billy and Mandy's home and subjects himself to a quieter life of domestic servitude. But the Grim Reaper's fantastical background never completely leaves him, and he is often called upon to perform various supernatural tasks.

In "Here Thar Be Dwarves" viewers are shown why Billy is afraid of going on a picnic in the woods owing to an earlier childhood trauma. In a repeatedly shown flashback, we see Harold, Billy's father, donning a Bigfoot costume and kidnapping Billy while the family was on a camping trip. While his father eventually revealed the prank to his frightened son, Billy has been suffering post-traumatic stress symptoms as a result. Thus, when Grim, Billy, and Mandy encounter magical elves and dwarves while on a picnic deep in the woods, Billy's sense of past terror is triggered again and again, leading him to freeze with fear.

In "Be A-Fred, Be Very A-Fred" an annoying green monster who resembles a child-aged elephant with tiny tusks is the winner of a corporate contest and therefore gets to spend a day with the Grim Reaper. The monomaniacal Fred Fredburger, as he calls himself, can hardly utter anything save "Yes!" to any question, repeatedly announce and then spell his name with some difficult remembering the letter "g" when he does so ("My name is Fred Fredburger. I can spell my name real good. F-R-E-D F-R-E-D-B-U-R- ... er... G-E-R. Fred Fredburger! Yes!"), and demand endless amounts of frozen yogurt and nachos, the only two foods he will eat.

The miserable Grim Reaper tries everything in his power to thwart Fred Fredburger's visit and send the tiresome tyke home early, but Fred misses every slight and insult, oblivious to the tactics. When Grim finally caves in and takes Billy, Mandy, Fred, and himself to an amusement park to cap the day, however, Fred Fredburger is thrown from the rollercoaster while it's at its highest peak and goes sailing into the horizon, to Grim's exclamation of "Holy Moley!"

Moments later, in a remote mountaintop cave somewhere in the Himalayas, Fred finally lands. To his surprise, a group of Yetis bearing an uncanny resemblance to Fred greet him in English and ask their new arrival if he likes frozen yogurt and nachos. Delighted, Fred wanders back into their cave with them, explaining how much he enjoys their offered treats.

*   *   *   *   *

Though Bigfoot appears in glorified cameos at best, *The Grim Adventures of Billy and Mandy*'s use of hominids is nevertheless a perfectly valid illustration of how Ciné du Sasquatch has become accepted by the viewing public, especially among children. Whereas earlier cartoon adventures like *Jonny Quest* and the like had to have at least one or two lines of exposition in regards to a cryptid's appearance, by the time of this series, such characters were so stock as to need no explanation at all. They are not only immediately known to the protagonists involved, but induce both a sense of fear, as with Billy, and friendliness, as with Fred Fredburger when he meets the Abominable Snowmen and instantly bonds with them over his favorite food groups.

Both visualizations show the bipolar disparity between the classic Savage Sasquatch and Benign Bigfoot realizations typical to the genre. In "Here Thar Be Dwarves" the flashback in which Billy's father deliberately dons a Sasquatch costume to scare the hell out of his son perfectly encapsulates the around-the-campfire nature of many classic horror tales. Likewise, when Fred Fredburger meets the kindly Yeti

clan, their non-threatening, mutually-beneficial encounter posits the friendly hominid myth so prevalent in films like *Harry and the Hendersons* and *Return to Boggy Creek*, as well as TV shows like *Tintin in Tibet*.

Besides this, both segments' cryptid cameos provide genuine laughs not at the expense of Ciné du Sasquatch, but in general recognition of how prevalent the Yeti has become in the public's consciousness. This is a credit to the show's creators, and not unexpectedly so, given the entertaining nature of *The Grim Adventures of Billy and Mandy*, which many adults will sheepishly admit they enjoyed just as much as the intended younger demographic audience.

Hair of the Sasquatch (2008)

Starring Jan Bos, Rodger Cove, Alex Dafoe, Jeremy Dangerfield, Lindsay Maxwell, Howard Siegel, Dale Wolfe and Dylan Wolfe. Produced by Rodger Cove and Dale Wolfe. Written by Rodger Cove. Directed by Dale Wolfe. Canada. Color. Stereo. 79 Minutes.

Overview: Two documentary filmmakers embark on a Canadian odyssey to investigate the history of Sasquatch sightings in the Great White North. What they initially find shocks them: While there are a plethora of stories, the commercial aspects of the legendary cryptid far outnumber (literally and figuratively, in terms of dollars grossed) the reported sightings. An entire tourist industry has evolved that peddles Sasquatch Burgers, Sasquatch Inns, Sasquatch merchandise, professional sports tie-ins, beer commercials, and beyond. Dismayed but determined to document the reality versus what they hoped to find, the filmmakers interview the various hucksters and profiteers who feed off Bigfoot without a thought as to how they're damaging and damning the real possibility the creature may actually exist and become just another extinct species even as the hucksters race to make a buck off a dying breed.

Eventually, however, the Bigfootsploitation community inadvertently tips off the documentarians about a certain local man named Steve Hastings, which seems to offer a much more tantalizing take on their subject matter. Hastings, it has been rumored, once disappeared for four days while on a hunting trip, only to reemerge entirely unscathed and claiming he'd encountered Sasquatch. Intrigued, the filmmakers agree to Hastings' terms for cash in exchange for an exclusive interview on videotape regarding his closely-held meeting with the beast.

Hastings' initial reluctance gives way to intimate details of his days in the company of what turns out to have been a female Sasquatch. Hastings returns with the camera crew to the cave where the female hominid kept him "hostage" and alive, struggling emotionally with some dark secret as he hesitantly reveals only partial details about the ordeal. Eventually the filmmakers — surmising the obvious implication — use a ruse to trick one of Hastings' friends who knows the real story into spilling the details. In turns out Hastings had willing sex with Sasquatch!

The filmmakers can't believe their good fortune: They have stumbled upon the most sensational Bigfoot report since the infamous Patterson-Gimlin film of 1967. They ignore the moral questions of prodding Hastings towards further revelations about his experience, preferring instead to turn a blind eye and allow his relationships with friends, family, and his wife to fall apart even as he delves deeper and spews forth more lurid details. As the world of carefully constructed lies about his missing time crumbles around him, Hastings realizes his mistake, but what can he do? He's told it all and to a video documentary duo, no less. Stuck between a cave and a hard place, Hastings must take desperate actions before the entire world knows his story.

* * * * *

There's a nearly forgotten story that once haunted the back issues of *Argosy* magazine and the likes about a logger in the Pacific Northwest who claimed he was abducted by a female Sasquatch and forced to sexually pleasure her for days and nights before he managed to escape his enforced slavery. The man stumbled into a sheriff's office to report the incident, afraid he would be fired for missing time from his job. Covered in what he claimed were hickeys given to him by the cooing cryptid, the man further revealed to the startled lawmen that the reason she had been attracted to him had been her sighting of his enormous penis. As the doubtlessly bemused police officers took notes, the logger maintained that he had gone skinny-dipping to cool off in a backwoods creek when the female Sasquatch sighted him and his well-endowed member. Taken by force to a cave of such cryptozoological beings, the female Sasquatch forced him to perform while the male Bigfoot monsters jealously eyed his comparatively larger anatomical specimen.

Of course it's none too surprising the man's story fell apart when an investigation revealed that he'd actually been holed up in a local motel on a drinking bender and merely needed a cover story to keep employment (a losing bid, alas, as he was terminated, for obvious reasons, shortly thereafter). But while this particular claim was proven false, many are the reports of abduction by Bigfoot with the intent of cross-species sex at the core of the affidavits. Perhaps the most famous is that of Albert Ostman from 1924, in which the camper claimed he was slung over a Sasquatch's shoulder while in the remote wilderness of British Columbia and carried back to a tribe of the creatures. While he was held there for seven days on end, Mr. Ostman concluded the intent of his abduction was to mate with the young female of the bunch, who was as reticent about romance as she was flat-chested. Only by tricking the cryptids into eating his chewing tobacco and making them sick did Ostman gain enough time to outrun his captives and race to safety. It may very well be this story that the logger later based his own fabrication upon, as it was widely reported in the press and various other news outlets — and included Ostman's claim that the alpha male cryptid's penis was only two inches in length.

Both stories were probable inspirations for R. Crumb and his infamous "Whiteman Meets Bigfoot" comic strip, which first appeared in *Home Grown Funnies* in 1971. The underground cartoonist's Whiteman character was a classic WASP businessman too uptight for his own good who is abducted by a large-chested, free-loving female Bigfoot while Whiteman is camping. After several rounds of lovemaking with the voracious Lady Squatch, Whiteman taps into his "inner light" and realizes the error of his ways in being such a prejudicial jerk prior to his liberating bout of backwoods bestiality. Deciding he's through with civilization and its repressive ways, Whiteman takes up with his hominid gal for good in a kind of Hippie retelling of Henry David Thoreau's Walden Pond–era rejection of all things material. The resonance of this comic tale has been so widespread that not only was it produced in the 1980s as a one-act play at Humboldt State University, it was almost produced as a Hollywood adaptation, to be directed by Terry Zwigoff, the close friend of the artist who directed the well-received *R. Crumb* biographical documentary. Alas for followers of Ciné du Sasquatch, the project was abandoned as being too risqué for mainstream audiences.

What this has to do with *Hair of the Sasquatch* is tangential, to be sure, but not so the bestial subtext present in many Ciné du Sasquatch efforts: *Man Beast*; *Night of the Demon*; *The Beast*; *Yeti: A Love Story*; *The Geek*; *Alpine Affairs*; etc. In essence, almost since the genre's birth the sordid but ever-present sexual deviancy sub-current of "man on ape" sex (as Senator Rick Santorum might have dubbed it) has persisted. As previously referenced in this guide, the precedents for this lie in the underlying influences of the genre itself: the implied sexuality of the classic fairy tale *Beauty and the Beast*; the large imprinter of *King Kong* and its depictions of Kong's obsessive lust for Ann Darrow; and so forth. So it's only fitting that by the time *Hair of the Sasquatch* arrived within the genre's postmodern period, such underlying motifs were brought to the very forefront and given a critically-needed examination.

The context in which the viewer watches *Hair of the Sasquatch* unfold is itself a familiar postmodern device. Rather than tell a purely fictional account, the filmmakers begin their pseudo-documentary tale as an earnest attempt to sketch the characters of the tourist trap valley in which Sasquatch has been converted by money-minded locals into a virtual cash crop. This section is adroitly accurate in detailing the avaricious nature of mankind when it confronts a phenomena such as cryptids or UFOs. Rather than conduct themselves seriously, the film suggests, *Homo sapiens* instead tend to look for and exploit the least common denominator: cash on the barrel. Interviewing a plethora of motel owners, burger joint workers, and even so-called Bigfoot experts, the documentarians uncover, to their dismay, an unending stream of self-styled hucksters and snake oil salesmen out to make a buck at Bigfoot's expense.

Whereas many lesser effort might have settled for parody and created the characters we encounter out of whole cloth, *Hair of the Sasquatch* cleverly utilizes actual persons and situations in these opening scenes to give the film a true verite feel. They visit the set of a Kokanee beer commercial shoot in progress, which has for years marketed their product by using Sasquatch as an official pitch hominid. They feature the owners of such enterprises as the Bigfoot Inn, Bigfoot Burgers, and the like, revealing a sordid underside to the cryptomania which has overtaken any sense of respect for the true wonder of the possibility of Sasquatch and replaced it with a driving need to make more money off the next van of gullible tourists than the con artist next door.

Only later, when the filmmakers stumble upon the rumored stories of Steve Hastings and his long-whispered encounter with a Bigfoot, do they see any daylight in terms of their documentary gaining anything more than an unpleasant revelation of capitalism triumphant. At this point *Hair of the Sasquatch* takes a surprising turn into an odyssey of personal confession that viewers of reality TV fare will quickly recognize. Ironically, as Hastings' dark secret of bestial sex with a female Sasquatch is revealed to them, the filmmakers fall prey to the very sense of exploitation they were disgusted by in the film's opening moments. Realizing they've stumbled upon a great new "angle" with which to exploit the Bigfoot genre, they dig deeper, even going so far as to use trickery to force the reluctant Hastings family and friends into spilling sordid details. We have documented the enemy, one might paraphrase in regards to the documentarians' actions, and they are us.

This clever turn of events leads to predictable if dramatic confrontations and decisions involving moral choices among the onscreen players, but it's the gradual succumbing to the very cash-obsessed mentality they once despised that makes the viewer contemplate the Ciné du Sasquatch genre as a whole. How often have fans of this oft-ridiculed body of work felt sheepish in defense of their hominid choice of cinema for this very reason? For every serious documentary and well-constructed dramatic rendition of Bigfoot filmmaking, there exists an abundance of cheaply-made, fast-buck mentality efforts to which non-believers can point and ridicule. For every *The Legend of Boggy Creek* there is Ivan Marx's scandalous *The Legend of Bigfoot*. For every serious scientist or cryptozoologist using scientific methodology featured in a documentary, there is the lurking visage of a grinning Tom Biscardi, thrice-debunked hoaxster, in his own self-produced efforts promising to deliver a Bigfoot specimen only to be proven a peddler of a gorilla costume in a Georgia freezer.

Hair of the Sasquatch is well aware of these contradictions in Ciné du Sasquatch. It even plays upon them, having the real-life interviewees who've unwittingly steered the fictional documentarians to the fictional Steve Hastings re-appear in the film later to react to the staged events with complete believability (or, it must be said, with as much believability as they're capable of rendering as non-professional performers). In doing so they reveal just how easily their adopted beliefs as to the creature's existence (or not) can be altered as long as they're receiving free promotion via the filmmakers interviewing them yet again. Not unlike a vacuum cleaner sucking up its own hose and disappearing into itself, the film becomes self-cannibalizing, blurring fiction and fact repeatedly until the line is no longer clear — nor even relevant to what the filmmakers are clearly indicating is the "lie-within-a-lie" theme of the overall viewing experience.

The film is not without its drawbacks. The acting in the Hastings family scenes at times stretches credibility. The filmmakers tend to make the common mistake many "mockumentaries" do by lingering on long stretches of handheld, shaky-cam footage in order to convince viewers of the reality of what they're watching. The best documentaries tend to be incredibly if invisibly well-edited. In fact, documentaries, even more than narrative features, rely on astute choices and pacing, as they have so little to fall back upon, lacking professional actors, rehearsed dialogue, forced situations, manipulated conflict, etc. This tends to reveal the amateur nature of the performers in such overly-naive efforts, and *Hair of the Sasquatch* is no exception in this regard.

Still, the film's short running length and witty perception render it a worthwhile effort in a genre not exactly known for acute self-analysis. By using the bestial subtext present in its own narrative device, *Hair of the Sasquatch* cleverly revels in the deeper questions lurking within genre as a whole — to wit: Where does one draw the line between being an observer, a voyeur, and even an enabler of the various exploitation elements rampant within Ciné du Sasquatch? And does such an uncritical lack of perspective harm ourselves as an unintended result? Not bad for a small-budget, no-frills documentary.

The Hairy Horror (2009)

Produced, Written and Directed by George Kuchar. USA. Color. Stereo. 10 Minutes.

Overview: George Kuchar provides the following programming notes to accompany any showing of his recent work, describing *The Hairy Horror* as being about "a chance encounter with a sober student [which] reveals the mystery of a woodland wonder that has left a mark on his youthful psyche just as it leaves huge footprints on the forest floor. A short meditation on a tall terror in the trees that shade shadowy giants from the glare of sanity."

The essence of "The Hairy Horror" is not Bigfoot, per se, but, as in Kuchar's previous short film which fell within the Ciné du Sasquatch genre — "Yolanda" (about a woman slowly losing her sanity as she dwells on the possibility of graphic sex with Sasquatch), a look at the meditations that go on in the human psyche when exposed to the very concept of bipedal hominids unknown to us, and how our rational mind struggles to comprehend this as even a remote possibility while our subconscious screams with hominid joy at the chance to project onto the potent Sasquatch mythos.

Shot in fluid, long takes that slowly dissolve into one another, and set to ominous strains of Bernard Hermann's best Hitchcock suspense scores, "The Hairy Horror" is not Bigfoot in terms of titular significance but the *Homo sapiens* who mull over the hidden hominid's possible existence as a means of escaping from day-to-day pressures and

realities. Those who don't like non-mainstream entertainment will soon grow bored with it, even if its brief ten-minute running time certainly passes entrancingly enough. This short film is a hypnotically-shot, postmodern study of human emotions set to discordant music and featuring as its nominal subject matter an archetypal hominid — one that ranks as a true Jungian superstar and reigning psychological example of how our own human shadow-selves are externalized into beastly forms in order for us to wrestle with our own darker instincts.

Half Human (1958)

AKA: *Jujin Yuki Otoko* (1955); *Half Human: The Story of the Abominable Snowman*. Starring Momoko Kochi, Akira Takarada, Akemi Negishi, Sachio Sakai, Nobuo Nakamura, John Carradine, Russell Thorson, Robert Karnes and Morris Ankrum. Produced by Tomoyuki Tanaka and Robert B. Homel. Written by Takeo Murata. Directed by Ishiro Honda and Kenneth G. Crane. Japan/USA. Black & White. Mono. 63 Minutes (U.S. Version) and 94 Minutes (Japanese Version).

Overview: Three skiers in the remote mountains of Japan are trapped inside a cabin by a raging blizzard. While trying to phone for help, one of the trapped skiers sees the Abominable Snowman outside the frost-covered window. Meanwhile, at a nearby resort lodge down the mountain, the skiers' friends welcome Chika, a local mountain girl, inside to warm up from the storm. The phone rings and the lodge skiers answer, hearing the trapped skiers in the cabin up the mountainside screaming in terror as they're attacked by the Yeti.

Their friends rush to the assaulted cabin only to find it torn asunder. Two skiers are dead, but one is missing. As soon as the snowstorm abates, the remaining skiers mount an expedition to search for their missing friend. Unbeknownst to them, however, some ruthless profiteers, lead by a man named Oba, overhear the skiers' plans and covertly follow the party, intent on exploiting any chance to capture or kill an actual hominid for money. After several nights of setting camp as they scale the mountain, the search party is visited one evening by the creature, which frightens Machiko when it peers inside her tent. Takeshi, one of the male search party members, chases after the Yeti but loses its path. He winds up inadvertently stumbling into

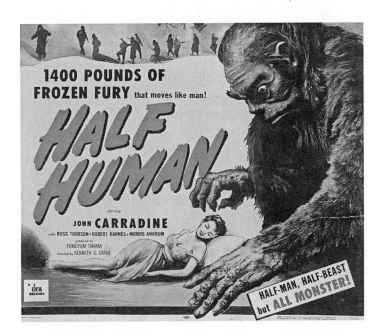

Theatrical lobby card for the original release of *Half Human*.

Oba's camp and is thrown over the side of a cliff by Oba in order to keep Oba's shadowy stalking of the search party a secret.

Chika, the mountain girl we have seen at the beginning, returns to her village of Ainu people high in the cliffs, where she finds her fellow dwellers have discovered Takeshi and left him tied to a cliffside to be devoured by buzzards. Horrified by the treatment of the foreigners, Chika appeals to her elderly Grandfather, but he savagely strikes her and reminds her of her place within the tribal structure: to do as told, not question his authority. Dispirited by her cruel treatment and the primitive nature of her people towards outsiders, Chika wanders away into the wilderness, bereft of hope. She encounters Oba and his henchman there. Realizing she actively feeds the Abominable Snowman as part of a ritualistic appeasement of the worshipped cryptid by the Ainu tribesmen, Oba convinces Chika to trade information as to the creature's hiding place for a ring he wears. Not really wanting to help them but afraid of defying their clear intent to gain the information she holds one way or the other, Chika accepts Oba's offer and tosses a rock in the direction of the beast's hidden cave. Oba penetrates the lair and captures the Snowman's offspring, a smaller version of the cryptid, dragging it away in chains.

When Chika returns to her village, the Grandfather discovers the ring and quickly deduces she has traded it for the Snowman's whereabouts. He beats her yet again and forms an impromptu posse of Ainu villagers, ordering them to seek out Oba before he can disturb or harm the giant hominid. Alas, when the gun-wielding Oba shoots the Grandfather, nearly killing him, the effort is effectively halted. Enraged by the invasion of its territory and abduction of its young, the adult Yeti attacks the Ainu village. It topples over the Grandfather's hut, killing him in the process, while the rest of the villagers scatter in terror.

Oba tries to flee in a truck that carries the younger Yeti caged in the flatbed, but the roaring Snowman pursues. It stops the truck and topples it over, smashing the cage and setting its offspring free. Oba

attempts to shoot the parental cryptid, but his errant bullet instead kills the child cryptid. The grieving, blood-simple Snowman attacks Oba, lifting him high and then tossing him, screaming, over a precipice. Taking the lifeless body of its child, the defeated Abominable leaves the scene, heading back to its lair.

Takeshi secures the assistance of Chika to lead the remaining ski party to the Yeti's cave so that they may hopefully find the missing skier. Along the narrow pathways, however, they are blocked by a landslide, clearly created by the creature to slow their progress. By the time they find the lair and enter it, there is no sign of the Abominable Snowman. They do find the missing skier's body, however, along with a note explaining with his dying words of the wrong that has been done to the cryptid and how badly he feels about his involvement, however tangential and unintended. Realizing the creature may one day return to its cavernous home, the search party decides to keep the precise location secret even as they report their findings to the proper authorities back in Tokyo.

* * * * *

The history and significance of *Half Human* in the development and maturation of Ciné du Sasquatch should not be underestimated. While the bastardized American version released by tiny DCA in the United States is bereft of the film's finest qualities, even the theatrical release company who brought Americans the outrageous *Plan Nine from Outer Space* and *Monster from Green Hell* (which *Half Human* was often double-billed with upon its initial U.S. release) couldn't completely ruin the raw, cinematic spookiness of Ishiro Honda's 1955 masterpiece. Too, at least some credit (however much Toho fans are reluctant to give it) is due DCA, despite the harm they did to *Jujin Yuki Otoko* with their crude editing of the film's most basic narrative sequences and the additional, completely unnecessary American-photographed exposition of John Carradine and Morris Ankrum. For had DCA not taken the gamble on releasing the early Japanese *kaiju* monster films of Toho, it is very likely Godzilla and all their other famous rubber-suited ilk would have never become so well-known and beloved. This is because DCA also released their own version of the equally-butchered original *Gojira* film. Similarly padded with new scenes (this time featuring a then fresh-faced Raymond Burr), DCA's release of the film, retitled as *Godzilla, King of the Monsters*, truly started the whole phenomena stateside. So while no one who has ever seen the original versions of either of Honda's atmospheric, brooding Monster Noir thrillers could rightfully claim the DCA variants are superior, at least DCA had the market sense to realize they would play to American audiences when the major American studios rejected them without a second thought. Only after DCA's success did Warner Brothers, and eventually other major studios, consider releasing Toho products in America, and even then they basically followed the DCA formula by either inserting additional American actors or, later in the co-production phases, simply casting American actors, such as Russ Tamblyn (*War of the Gargantuas*) and Nick Adams (*Frankenstein Conquers the World* and *Monster Zero*), in the films as inte-

The lonely air of majesty that special effects designer Eiji Tsuburaya brings to the Yeti creation of *Half Human* has rarely been surpassed in terms of sheer screen pathos.

gral players so that they appealed to domestic and international markets.

This is not to excuse the excesses of DCA as much as to indicate the probable rationale behind much of the decision-making as being partly institutionalized (and therefore unrecognized) racism. It had only been a little over a decade since America had been the first and only country in world history to drop an atomic bomb on civilians (at the close of the Second World War), and anti–Japanese sentiments lingered deeply over Pearl Harbor, even though the Americans had triumphed in the conflict. The racist portrayals of Japanese citizens as buck-toothed, glasses-wearing "Yellow Peril" that had permeated the American cinema, newsreel and later TV culture in the World War II propaganda years and subsequent Cold War era had not been erased, if even dealt with, as a national issue of conscience. The labor camps to which Japanese citizens were forced to relocate was still a shameful secret most Americans refused to accept as a darker side of the U.S. war against fascism; and rare indeed were the films imported from Japan in the 1950s that were not ghetto-ized to small showings on the East and West Coast (much the same way the works of early African American filmmakers, such as pioneer Oscar Micheaux, were shown to segregated black-only audiences in small venues in the South and industrialized North in the 1930s). In fact, there is speculation that *Jujin Yuki Otoko* (a rough translation would be "Monster Snowman") probably played at such venues in Los Angeles and San Francisco, and other metropolitan "specialty cinemas" in the U.S. before DCA acquired it, redubbed it, and altered it into *Half Human* nearly three years later (though these showings would have strictly been aimed at Japanese audiences and without English subtitles — definitive records are lacking, as such screenings rarely used printed advertising materials, and instead relied on exterior marquee exposure, to save costs).

The original film *Jujin Yuki Otoko* was not without its own controversies in its homeland. Because of the racist manner in which the Ainu people are presented in the film (as barbaric simpletons — in a manner similar to the way Native Americans and African Americans were portrayed in early Hollywood films), Toho has all but disowned the picture in subsequent years. Even to this day there has sadly been no official release of *Jujin Yuki Otoko*. Instead, there exists in the gray markets of collector-exchanged DVDs a very crude transfer (perhaps made illegally in Japan in either a print lab or at a television station) of the film, minus subtitles and only in the original Japanese language. While this makes it difficult to understand portions of the story, Honda's cinematic techniques are so visual as to effectively convey the basic story even to non–Japanese-speaking viewers. While it has the slower pace most Japanese film watchers will recognize as characteristic of the era, *Jujin Yuki Otoko* remains infinitely better than *Half Human* as the most fully realized version of the tale, even with the lack of translation and generally poor image quality of the only known bootleg outside of Toho's control.

The film's fate to date is not unlike the manner in which Walt Disney's *Song of the South* remains officially unavailable in the U.S. due to its racist content, but is licensed to distributors in Japan, where it remains hugely popular. But one is forced to wonder: How much longer will corporate decision-makers hold onto such cultural artifacts rather than release them, flaws and all, so that audiences can learn from the past rather than be sheltered from it? Had not DCA taken the gamble with *Half Human*, this film would not exist to American audiences, which would have been a tragic blow to the entire field of cryptozoology (and at least one prominent researcher — see Loren Coleman's introduction to this guide for the complete details), as well as the entire genre of Ciné du Sasquatch.

In order to understand the film's legacy, one must remember that the Boomer generation in America had been inundated with news stories and TV reports of the Abominable Snowman as related by various English and American expeditions into the Himalayan Mountains during the 1950s. But despite the photographic evidence of footprints, recovered scalps purported to be Yeti crests, and even eyewitness sketches of the hominid, few films or television shows had actually utilized the creature in a fictional film format. As a result, the pent-up demand was enormous for an entire generation of post–World War II viewers who'd been weaned on the news accounts but had no moving depictions of the fabled beast. Along with *The Abominable Snowman* from Hammer and a handful of other low-budget American independent films, such as Jerry Warren's *Man Beast*, DCA's minor hit firmly established the Bigfoot genre as a viable variation in cinema.

While it's true Ciné du Sasquatch was overshadowed by the giant mutation films such as *Them!* and its countless clones, as well as the flood of alien invaders after the smash success of *The Thing from Another World*, the nascent Bigfoot genre nevertheless gained a fertile foothold with the successive releases of these 1950s Abominable Snowman films. Many were the childhood viewers who became enthusiasts of both the cryptid field and genre cinema as a result of this early exposure, even if their hunger was to remain largely unfulfilled by way of subsequent films until later. Because many of these 1950s-produced Sasquatch movies would eventually wind up in television syndication, where they were often shown repeatedly year after year, they not only developed cult followings but introduced the Bigfoot genre to an ever-increasingly wide berth of nascent but avid followers.

Along with the Peter Cushing version of *The Abominable Snowman*, *Half Human* is often considered the premiere Yeti film of its time, and rightfully so, especially when one views it in its original Japanese form. But the differences between the two films are as stark as their cultural origins, and therefore each reflects two very different approaches to their hominid subjects and the genre as a whole. Though both films portray the Yetis as creatures best left alone by *Homo sapiens* because of their innate strength and superior cunning, *The Abominable Snowman* all but visualizes its hominids as true pacifists who gamely attempt to avoid harming humans until their own survival is at stake. *Half Human*, however, makes it clear from the opening scenes that its Snowman is an animal which, though intelligent and human-like, will attack without provocation — as it does when it kills the skiers. In so many ways, the Benign Bigfoot versus Savage Sasquatch divide which will later become starkly apparent in Ciné du Sasquatch was firmly established by these two seminal films.

Another key distinction between the two films is the manner in which they treat the visualization of the creatures themselves. In *The Abominable Snowman* the viewer is left in the literal dark, forced to mentally conjure a complete picture of the Yetis until shown a shocking medium shot of their faces at the picture's conclusion. While glimpses of their clawed hands and the like are briefly shown throughout, director Val Guest relies on mood and the nearly surreal Himalayan landscapes of light and shadow to play upon the viewer's mind in lieu of a full-on approach. Honda, however, chooses to reveal his Yeti much earlier in *Half Human* and rely upon the impact of its scary design and super-sized appearance to evoke dread and horror. Though he's careful to use night photography for most of the scenes involving the Yeti, Honda nevertheless is not shy about lingering on the suit's dramatic appearance to create a mood of fear, as this is one Abominable that lives up to its moniker. In terms of both ferocious ability and horrific visage, the costume (which was created by Toho's genius of special effects, Eiji Tsuburaya, who also did a majority of the other *kaiju* films, such as *Godzilla*, *Rodan*, and *The Mysterians*) is a nightmarish concoction of brutal ape strength and bug-eyed Neanderthal-like brows, along with devilishly pointed ears and a mouthful of fangs. Though today's effects may render it quaint, it must have been quite a shock for younger audiences in its heyday, resulting in many sleepless nights as they turned its fiendish image over and over in their minds. Even today it has a sinister impact that is not easily defined, lingering as one of the great examples of scary Sasquatch costumes in the genre's long history.

Much has been made of the watered-down version DCA released, as critiqued in the preceding sections. But even with the additions of John Carradine on a cramped office set to narrate and guide the American viewer through the adventure in flashback, and the unnecessary padding of Morris Ankrum performing an autopsy on the Yeti's offspring in an adjacent room, the basic storyline remains intact. The key differences are that the Kenneth Crane–directed version truncates the Japanese version's events, often reducing the original's effect to a second-rate redux. Equally bothersome is the lack of the Japanese music score, which has been replaced with typical stock music of the 1950s SF variety, and the typically rubbery-lipped dialogue replacement, which, while definitely necessary in the era for theatrical showings, is pretty dismal as far as dubbing goes by today's standards. Still, the mood and cinematography go a long ways towards making both versions effective in their own right, a tribute to Honda's ability to create a vision strong enough to survive the Americanization process.

In either version, there are lingering images which haunt the viewer long after the house lights go up. For example, the lair in which the Yeti resides is a vast, labyrinthine connection of tunnels, holes, and steaming vapor pools that almost rivals the original *King Kong* for sheer visual beauty. The shots of the creature in this environment are as powerful and majestic as any ever created in the Bigfoot genre, and elevate the film with a transcendent sense of visual poetry, externalizing the lonely plight of the Snowman. One can actually believe this creature exists when placed in such a setting, as it seems so appropriate for such a hulking hominid, in much the same way Moby Dick seems so at home in the ocean's darkest depths. There is a Dantelike sense that one is seeing Lucifer in the deepest ring of Hell in these moments, with the creature striding through its domain with an almost vindictive sense of joy at ruling in Hades rather than serving in the human society of Heaven as some sideshow freak. It's little wonder *Half Human* made such a lasting impact on its largely childfilled audience members — it captures pathos and horror with equally adroit ease.

This heavily-retouched promotional still from *Half Human* renders the creature almost unrecognizable from its actual cinematic counterpart.

So profound was *Half Human*'s legacy that it would not be until 1967 and the one-minute Patterson-Gimlin film that anything would quite rival it. Thereafter, only *The Legend of Boggy Creek* and then *Harry and the Hendersons* mounted a serious challenge to the impact of *Half Human*. Even to this day it is rare to see a more thoroughly well-crafted and believable rendering of the major themes of Ciné du Sasquatch than in this Toho effort. While countless bad Bigfoot films, and many entertaining ones, have been made in its wake, it stands alongside the aforementioned landmark films as one of the touchstones of the genre's history; as such, it should be considered required viewing by all enthusiasts. It is true one longs for a restoration of the original *Jujin Yuki Otoko* with proper translation and a much-deserved digital transfer; but until such time, *Half Human* is a good glimpse of a finer effort buried beneath the inferior Americanization.

Hanabari (1952)

Starring Dhiraj Bhattacharya, Bipin Mukherjee, Pranoti Ghosh and Gautam Mukherjee. Produced, Written and Directed by Premendra Mitra. India. Black & White. Mono. 75 Minutes.

Overview: An old dark house, long abandoned, is visited one stormy night by a stranded young visitor seeking shelter from the monsoon raging outside. To his horror he sees an apparition of what appears to be a cryptid monster, slightly gorilla-like but more resembling a dark-furred Yeti. Undeterred, an uncle and his nieces move into the mansion. Soon a series of unexpectedly dire occurrences begin, such as whispered stories about the former owner who used to don a gorilla monster suit to frighten any who would come near the house, an unsolved murder, and even a secret tunnel beneath the mansion.

A detective is soon on the case, convinced the supernatural encounters can be rationally explained. He uncovers clues that the former owner, who was a painter by trade, may have had more motivation to scare potential house guests than anyone formerly suspected.

* * * * *

As *Hanabari* is ultimately not a true Yeti film, it is only included here for its brief, early scare scenes in which the appearance of a cryptid is implied. As the detective quickly uncovers the clues in what is a classic Old Dark House mystery, and the viewer learns the mansion's owner was utilizing a gorilla skin to frighten tourists and visitors, the suggested Abominable Snowman connection evaporates. At this point in the plot *Hanabari* becomes more properly classified as a Killer Gorilla effort with supernatural overtones, which was a familiar subset within American movies in the 1930s and 1940s.

The ultimate shared influence between *Hanabari* and Ciné du Sasquatch is actually literary, not filmic: Edgar Allan Poe's *Murders in the Rue Morgue*. Not only is Poe's tale considered to be the first modern detective story, but also the progenitor of the supposedly "unsolvable" locked room murder mystery (in which the victim is found killed inside his or her own abode with all methods of escape potentially used by the murderer secured and locked). The solution — that a trained orangutan was the true culprit — was a shocking revelation in its day and helped establish the format that would later become even more popularized by such followers as Arthur Conan Doyle with Sherlock Holmes and the like.

Hanabari is notable for its influence on Bengali film production, as it was a huge hit in its country and therefore paved the way for future Indian Yeti efforts such as *Ajouba Kudat Kaa*. Complete with musical numbers and well-photographed Universal-styled horror sets circa the 1940s, and equal parts comic slapstick and light horror, it can best be considered a better version of its Killer Gorilla counterpart *Bela Lugosi Meets a Brooklyn Gorilla*, but with a tad more hominid tossed in to divert the audience.

Harry and the Hendersons (1987)

AKA: *Bigfoot and the Hendersons.* Starring John Lithgow, Melinda Dillon, Margaret Langrick, Joshua Rudoy, Kevin Peter Hall, Lainie Kazan, Don Ameche, M. Emmet Walsh and David Suchet. Produced by William Dear, Richard Vane and Steven Spielberg. Written by William Dear, Bill Martin and Ezra D. Rappaport. Directed by William Dear. USA. Color. Stereo. 110 Minutes.

Overview: While vacationing in the Washington state mountains, the Henderson family accidentally runs over Bigfoot in the family sedan. Uncertain how to treat the humongous hominid, they strap it to the top of their car and return home to the Seattle suburbs with it, believing they've at first killed the towering man-beast. The Bigfoot soon revives, however, and lays waste to their living room and kitchen. Realizing he's actually a gentle giant and bewildered by his new domestic quarters, the Hendersons nickname him "Harry" and welcome him into their home.

Alas, a French Canadian hunter by the name of Jacques LaFleur

Kevin Peter Hall as Harry from *Harry and the Hendersons* (1987) plays Bigfoot as an errant idiot savant, a true pacifist unless threatened by humans.

has figured out what has happened when he finds a license plate belonging to the Hendersons and some furry evidence embedded therein. He begins tracking down the Hendersons, believing they know more than they are letting on with their blanket denials when he shows up unexpectedly on their doorstep and nosily inquires about their recent vacation.

Meanwhile, Harry escapes confinement and goes on a controlled rampage throughout the Seattle suburbs the Hendersons call home. Realizing that LaFleur will track Harry down and kill him unless they intervene, the Hendersons mount a frantic and ultimately successful search to locate the errant Sasquatch and return him to his forest abode. As Harry waves good-bye and the family sadly reacts, they are heartened to see other cryptids welcoming back their missing loved one. The bittersweet reunion makes the Hendersons realize that they've done the right thing in returning the hominid home.

* * * * *

So ubiquitous has been the influence of *Harry and the Hendersons* on Ciné du Sasquatch that it is difficult to imagine a time when the Benign Bigfoot icon, as embodied and trail-blazed by Harry, wasn't omni-present in the Bigfoot genre. But prior to this Spielberg-produced effort, most films were as likely to portray a Savage Sasquatch or, at the least, a highly ambivalent hominid. While cartoon versions such as *The Abominable Snow Rabbit* (which portrayed its Snowman as a loveable if unwittingly dangerous simpleton) and live-action cameos in such films as *The 7 Faces of Dr. Lao* (which showed its hominid as shy and retiring unless provoked to self-defense) existed prior to *Harry and the Hendersons*, it took this William Dear–directed film to forever alter the perception (or at least the family-friendly one) of Bigfoot in popular culture. After the smash box office success of *Harry and the Hendersons*, as well as its 3-year TV series follow-up, the depiction of Bigfoot as a threatening menace best left to its own kind and not to be interfered with would be a stereotype of the past. While it's true a similar motif is expounded in Dear's film — that ultimately Harry belongs in the wild and not as a domesticated family pet (as John Lithgow verbalizes towards the movie's conclusion) — *Harry and the Hendersons* declares its message with such a sentimental streak that it's impossible not to view the effort as *E.T.* with a Sasquatch substituted for the stranded alien. Indeed, the predicaments, conflict, and plot progressions are nearly identical in both films, with an unearthly or at least unknown species infiltrating and mucking up an otherwise dysfunctional if well-meaning lot of lost American suburbanites, all of whom learn a much-needed lesson via sacrificial love in order to reestablish their nuclear family bond. It's akin to the credo stating that "if you love someone, set them free; if they love you, they will return." While the return half of the saying is left off-screen in both movies, the first half is tacked into not just the subtext but the actual message of each respective effort.

Again, this "Bigfoot as loveable, huggable pet" theme is not entirely new to the genre. *Return to Boggy Creek*, for example, featured a menacing swamp hominid which rescued hurricane-stranded children deep in the storm-ravaged bayou towards that film's end. The difference, however, is that the Fouke Monster is presented as a true Savage Sasquatch prior to this sudden conversion to childhood savior. In other words, the film has it both ways rather than relying solely on the concept that Bigfoot is not much more than a highly intelligent bear locked in a pseudo-human's body. *Harry and the Hendersons*, by contrast, never treats its Sasquatch as anything more than a well-meaning pacifist, and one manageable by human intervention even when aroused to anger (at least by the humble Hendersons). This is a novel variation on the genre's key tenet — that Sasquatch is a dangerous being, even if it may occasionally be seen as helping or at least not actively conspiring to harm *Homo sapiens*.

Not everyone believes this landmark turn of events in the Ciné du

Sasquatch *oeuvre* is a positive. Loren Coleman, contributing editor of the influential *Cryptomundo* website, as well as noted cryptozoologist, accomplished author, and writer of this guide's introduction, believes the simplification of the world's favorite hominid into little more than a glorified teddy bear has had a negative impact on the genre. In a posting entitled "How Kids' Films Destroyed Sasquatch Research" on *Cryptomundo*, dated March 3, 2010, Coleman states:

> It is a finding of sociological/media research that the impact of images and films during the critical ages of 10 to 13 will influence mature individuals' world views. Therefore, if you figure that 10–13 year olds during the 1987–1997 period are now 23 to 36 years old, no wonder there is a growing wave of silly skepticism regarding the study of Sasquatch. Bigfoot was portrayed during that era with less than serious intent. Intriguingly, most people that grew up with the Patterson-Gimlin footage (1967) as their prime imagery cornerstone are now 43–56 years old. For those that wish to debate my theory, as supported with the above example [*Little Bigfoot*], I give you as Exhibit #1, the film *Harry and the Hendersons* (1987).

Coleman's point is well-taken. In this author's research, and in interviews with several directors of Bigfoot films, the anecdotal evidence bore out this hypothesis. Those who were mostly influenced by either *The Abominable Snowman* with Peter Cushing or *Half Human*, or by the secondary surge of fictional films featuring Bigfoot (such as *The Legend of Boggy Creek* or *Sasquatch, The Legend of Bigfoot*) almost two decades later, tended to characterize their obsession with a sense of foreboding one might associate with, say, the hunt for the elusive giant squid or related phenomena. Those who came of age during the post–*Harry and the Hendersons* phase, however, tended towards a much more playful, urban legend–type belief in hominids as fantasy over fact. Of course, this is far from a scientific conclusion and merely based on a handful of random samplings; still, the theory deserves further scrutiny as the true-life field of cryptozoology matures.

For better or worse for the future of cryptozoology, *Harry and the Hendersons* was a turning point in Ciné du Sasquatch, if for no other reason than it marked the beginning of Hollywood's realization that Bigfoot was big box office. When mega-moneymakers like Steven Spielberg capitalize on a subject matter, the rest of Tinseltown quickly follows. While Bigfoot has always been an option for independent film producers, who took advantage of the dearth of mainstream studio films about Sasquatch, after *Harry and the Hendersons* the major studios were no longer afraid of finally and financially exploiting the beast's inherent commercial appeal.

This widespread acceptance would have the effect of lifting the formerly sub-par status of the Bigfoot film (with mainstream media thinking that Bigfoot only appealed to the rural audiences) to new-found heights never dreamed of before by aficionados of Sasquatch movies. From the endless commercials, merchandising, and ubiquitous appearances across TV, films, and beyond, Bigfoot cinema had arrived. Perhaps only Elvis' post-mortem rivaled Sasquatch in the popular imagination; but unlike Presley, Sasquatch at least held out the possibility of a real-life sighting (some would argue, of course, as much for Elvis, but that's another story). This sensibility — that Bigfoot might actually be *real* and therefore worthy of the cultural zeitgeist's fascination — has never wavered since. In fact, as the increasing movie and TV appearances prove, Ciné du Sasquatch has only increased in terms of sheer output and instant recognition factor.

Hollywood execs talk of a certain celebrity's "Q score" (aka Quotient score) among the public in terms of instant recognition. Bigfoot's Q would certainly rank among the elite of pop icons, such as Spiderman, Superman, and the like. Rarely has a figure in popular public

mythology achieved such bona fide superstar status — not even Paul Bunyon, Pecos Bill, and Brer Rabbit, all three of whom would leave most folks scratching their heads beyond sheer name recognition if asked to further detail each of these once-popular folkloric figures. *Harry and the Hendersons*, along with its successful TV spin-off, is one of the main reasons why Sasquatch made this transcendent leap in the public's mind.

However one may feel about said popularization, it was perhaps inevitable given the building phenomena of a non-stop combination of real-world sightings and larger-budgeted film and TV appearances. And credit should be given where it is honestly due: *Harry and the Hendersons* remains one of the most impressive technical achievements in terms of cinematic realization of a hominid. Oscar-winning make-up effects guru Rick Baker designed the impressive creature costume, which featured a novel use of air bladders and facial pulley wires to create Harry's wide range of expression. Because the costume's mask allowed Harry actor Kevin Peter Hall to use his eyes for emotive purposes, in conjunction with dozens of effects technicians just off-screen augmenting them with the carefully choreographed foam latex wire-pulling, the entirety of Harry's persona came to life in a manner unmatched, before or since, in the genre's history. For his impressive work on *Harry and the Hendersons*, Rick Baker won the Academy Award that year, marking only the second time in the history of Ciné du Sasquatch that an Oscar had been bestowed upon a film in the genre (the other being for *The 7 Faces of Dr. Lao*). Sasquatch movie-making had truly come of age.

Harry and the Hendersons (1991) (TV)

Starring Bruce Davison, Molly Cheek, Carol-Ann Plante, Zachary Bostrom, Kevin Peter Hall, Dawan Scott and Brian Steele. Produced by Sheree Guitar, Jill Lopez Danton and Lin Oliver. Written by Sheree Guitar, Marc Sheffler, Sam Denoff, Bob Fraser, Harriet B. Helberg, Sandy Helberg, Alan Moskowitz, Daryl G. Nickens, Lin Oliver and Mike Scott. Directed by Nick Havinga, Don Amendolia, Scott Baio, Bruce Davison, Tony Dow, Dwayne Hickman, Richard Kline, Lee Lochhead, Howard Murray, Donna Pescow, Jeffrey Wheat and James Widdoes. USA. Color. Stereo. 30 Minutes.

Overview: In a continuation of the feature film, the Hendersons yet again house the beloved Harry, gamely attempting to keep his identity secret lest he become exploited by both the scientific and media communities. At first their job is made even more difficult by snooty next-door neighbors and the usual antics of Harry trapped in a suburban domicile.

In an unexpected turn of events, Harry is exposed to the public at large, and the Hendersons must adjust to the fact that their "family pet" is now world famous. With the constant television crews, paparazzi stalkers, and scientific inquiries, Harry's life becomes a living hell of non-stop media requests and zoological studies. Eventually the Hendersons learn to cope with their hairy hominid being a celebrity and even adjust to it, relieved that at least they no longer need keep his identity a secret nor worry he will be harmed or abducted, as his fame guarantees a certain level of protection.

* * * * *

While critics were forgiving of much of the sentimentalism that marred the theatrical version of *Harry and the Hendersons*, no such luck attended the first season of the sitcom adaptation. For the most part mercilessly savaged, *Harry and the Hendersons* nevertheless managed to keep its audience share and limp back into a second season, albeit with some changes in cast and crew. Most significantly, and sadly, actor Kevin Peter Hall contracted AIDS from a tainted blood transfusion and passed away after only four episodes in the first season of production. He was 35 years of age, and while few would have recognized him outside his expressive costume and make-up, there is no denying Hall brought what little charisma the hominid possessed to the TV series, which lacked the freshness of concept and was plagued by the weaker sitcom screenplays of its limited format. Hall was an all-star monster actor of the first order, having brought to life such memorable creatures as the mutant bear in *Prophecy* for John Frankenheimer, the alien hunter for John Tiernan in *Predator*, and even the gray alien in the campy *Without Warning*. He likewise played Big John in *Big Top Pee-wee* and had a host of other monster-type roles. The Harry suit was taken over by Dawan Scott initially, and then later by Brian Steele, who went on to become something of a monster actor himself in such films as *The Relic*, *Hellboy*, *Terminator Salvation* and *Predators*.

But the biggest problem with the series was not the lack of a steady performer in the role of Harry, nor of the largely seasoned and professional cast members (such as Bruce Davison), but the ridiculous and unsustainable construction of the series itself. Unlike the theatrical incarnation, in which the suspension of disbelief could be maintained for the better part of an hour, *Harry and the Hendersons* was destined to run for 72 episodes! The sheer amount of manipulation and plot contrivances necessary to keep Harry from becoming a known quantity to the Hendersons' neighbors, local police, and government officials was so convoluted as to defy credibility in even the most generous of viewers.

Another problem facing the cast, crew, and writers was the lack of character development in Harry himself. While he could be charming, confused, annoying, or even just plain stupid, the lack of progress reduced the hominid to little more than an oversized jester forced to comically react to the unfolding situations going on around him. While understandable, given how constrictive the concept was, this made *Harry and the Hendersons* a farce on the order of something more befitting Saturday morning status than prime-time, where a broader range of viewers expected more in the way of adult accessibility beyond mere strained shenanigans. Sadly, even the children were probably let down by Harry's stale predicaments, in that most were set-bound affairs that relied on dialogue rather than action.

Given that Harry was effectively mute, this meant his character was forever a second "banana," no matter what the situation!

The creators seemed to realize their dramatic predicament and altered the format so that Harry was discovered by the world at large (or at least Seattle), but this created its own set of problems. While the Hendersons are shown having to adjust to their newfound status as housekeepers of the only known cryptid in "captivity" (or at least residence), the strain of believability was yet again tested. Even the most ardent fan was forced to question the logic and desirability of such a narrative twist. After all, if the premise of the show was to showcase the comic downsides of harboring a Sasquatch in a typical suburban family home, how on Earth could said family ever remain anonymously average if they're renowned as "those folks who have the Bigfoot in their living room" week after week? Perhaps with more time the show's writers and producers could have milked this Sasquatch scenario for more humor, but with the show constantly under the pressure to be "fixed" (and facing production changes, such as recasting and format changes), *Harry and the Hendersons* proved to be a limited success that duly (and finally dully) ran its course.

It's somewhat ironic that actor Tony Dow, best remembered as older brother Wally from the iconic *Leave It to Beaver* sitcom, directed some episodes of *Harry and the Hendersons*, as did teen idol Scott Baio from *Happy Days* and *Joanie Loves Chachi* fame. Doubtless the warm, lessons-learned formula of such sitcom hits was what the Amblin-backed series desired to recreate. But the key to those series was expert writing and a sense of progression within the main characters' storylines that *Harry and the Hendersons* sadly never was able to manifest. While it remained a marginal fan favorite for those who enjoyed its sense of absurdity, à la *Bewitched* with a Bigfoot, the series faded quietly away after its third season, having served its purpose and at once outlived its time slot.

In terms of Ciné du Sasquatch, the truly remarkable retrospective accomplishment of *Harry and the Hendersons* is how little it contributed to the genre's advancement. While the feature film altered the genre for both good and ill, the television series was a practical non-starter in terms of its perception and impact. Surely it introduced the hominid themes to a range of youngsters who'd enjoyed the theatrical feature or were new to the concept, but the lack of cultural culmination rendered it the equivalent of a cryptid eunuch. It was like a shadowy version of the feature movie but without the testosterone to distinguish itself as a stand-alone entity.

Episodes by Season

First Season: 1. "The Arrival"; 2. "The Day After"; 3. "Cool"; 4. "Harry Goes Home"; 5. "Whose Forest Is It Anyway?"; 6. "The Father-Son Game"; 7. "Bagging the Big One"; 8. "Harry the Hero"; 9. "Roots: The Herb"; 10. "The Mentor"; 11. "The Bodyguard"; 12. "Harry & the Homeless Man"; 13. "Harry Goes Ape"; 14. "Pet Psychic"; 15. "The Bigfoot Who Ate Seattle"; 16. "Harry, the Masked Wrestler"; 17. "When Harry Met Sammy"; 18. "Harry and the Cheerleaders."

The *Leave It to Beaver*-esque quality of the *Harry and the Hendersons* theatrical concept made it well "suited" for quick adaptation into a TV sitcom.

Second Season: 1. "The Ransom of Bigfoot"; 2. "Retrospective"; 3. "The Terror of the Trees"; 4. "Sara Sings the Blues"; 5. "Mom"; 6. "Halloween"; 7. "Brett Hits Home"; 8. "George's White Light"; 9. "Working Stiffs"; 10. "Love Mask"; 11. "The Blue Parrot"; 12. "Winning"; 13. "'Til Theft Do Us Part"; 14. "The Genius"; 15. "Wild Things"; 16. "Fatherhood"; 17. "Sara Spills the Bigfoot Beans"; 18. "Moonlighting"; 19. "The Green-Eyed Bigfoot"; 20. "The Ichthyologist"; 21. "Selling Out"; 22. "The Girl Who Cried Bigfoot"; 23. "The Busybody"; 24. "I Got Your Birthday Right Here."

Third Season: 1. "Yo Richie!"; 2. "The Candidate"; 3. "The Bride and the Gloom"; 4. "Born Again"; 5. "The Old Bigfoot"; 6. "The Outing"; 7. "Harry Henderson National Park"; 8. "Breaking Up Is Hard to Do"; 9. "Blood Is Thicker Than Karma"; 10. "Pitch, Pitch, Pitch"; 11. "Harry, the Mascot"; 12. "The Big Kiss Off"; 13. "The Frenchman"; 14. "Laid Up"; 15. "Harrywood Babylon"; 16. "Witness"; 17. "Harry the Hostage"; 18. "The Ex-Terminator"; 19. "Beauty and the Beast"; 20. "Big Feet, Small Minds"; 21. "Surf's Down"; 22. "Follow Your Art"; 23. "Them Bones"; 24. "The Three Faces of Brett"; 25. "Ernie Confidential"; 26. "Uncle Mack Comes Back"; 27. "Skin Deep"; 28. "The Write Stuff"; 29. "The Long Goodbyes Part 1"; 30. "The Long Goodbyes Part 2."

Harry Knuckles and the Pearl Necklace (2004)

Starring Phil Caracas, Nancy Riehle, Emma Maloney, Jeff Moffet, Josh Grace, Ian Driscoll, Patricia Bellemore, Nancy Bouzi and Shana Sosin. Produced by Odessa Filmworks. Written by Ian Driscoll. Directed by Lee Gordon Demarbre. Canada. Color. Stereo. 116 Minutes.

Overview: When a Bionic Bigfoot steals a valuable pearl necklace from the Canadian Museum of Nature, super agent Harry Knuckles (aka Special Agent Spanish Fly) is called upon by his government to recover the goods. Befriended by his paunchy pal El Santos (a lucha libre star in his own mind), Harry embarks on a complicated quest to root out the true culprits responsible for the crime. He quickly deduces the sweet-natured Sasquatch needs the radioactive pearl necklace to power itself and is therefore only tangentially to blame. In their misadventures, the leisure suit–clad Knuckles and Santos battle Virtual Girl in a swimming pool, Attack Nuns in panties and bras, and Lesbian Flesh Eaters; have a drinking contest with Troma Films' head honcho Lloyd Kaufman; and even beat Harry's own formerly unknown twin brother. Throughout it all, and aided and abetted by such supporting players as Cassie Nova, the Unknown Gas Station Attendant, and his own fistful of hairy mitts, Knuckles and Santos triumph at every turn (or, at least, manage to stay alive until their next action-packed duel with death).

* * * * *

Canadian filmmaker Lee Demarbre revels in the kind of 42nd Street cinema cheesiness Quentin Tarantino would doubtless produce if restricted to making such efforts as *Grindhouse* and *Kill Bill* on the budgets his own larger-budgeted movies' caterer spent for an average crew breakfast. Demarbre's earlier cult mini-epics — *Harry Knuckles and the Treasure of the Aztec Mummy* and *Jesus Christ, Vampire Hunter* — were prequels to this Harry Knuckles "franchise" follow-up (suffice it to say that no Happy Meals were part of the marketing blitz), which finds the sweat pants and hair band–wearing Harry facing off against a bionic Bigfoot in what is perhaps the ultimate homage to *The Six Million Dollar Man* meets *Bruce Lee Fights Back from the Grave*.

Relentlessly and unapologetically cheesy, *Harry Knuckles and the Pearl Necklace* is a bittersweet kung fu slap to the viewer's face, at once designed to parody the excesses of the average chop-socky Hong Kong kung fu export circa 1974 and equally as guilty as the skewered

sources in its occasional bouts of tedium, plot contrivances, and sheer buffoonery. But with its deliberately bad dubbing, over-the-top use of zoom shots, and comically-staged fight sequences, it still entertains, especially for fans of early Jackie Chan and Bruce Li (not Lee) efforts. If the lucrative *Austin Powers* trilogy had been focused on the endless zero-budget rip-offs of *Enter the Dragon* instead of poor man James Bond clones, *Harry Knuckles and the Pearl Necklace* might have been the end result: a delight for those in the know about such genres, and a probable strike-out for any whose taste and knowledge fails to encompass grindhouse cinema.

There's really not much relevant about the Bigfoot's extended cameo in terms of shedding light on Ciné du Sasquatch, save for its very inclusion. By tossing in Sasquatch and the bionic reference, *Harry Knuckles and the Pearl Necklace* acknowledges and draws upon a shared cinematic and televised shorthand that all Gen X viewers will instantly identify. If camp is the art of utilizing kitsch while simultaneously parodying the effort — surely a postmodern art form if ever there was one — then *Harry Knuckles and the Pearl Necklace* is a retro act of vindication for endless hours (mis)spent by an entire generation at the movies and glued in front of their cathode-ray small screens. By referencing Sasquatch as an icon of the 1970s, the filmmaker is tacitly admitting the almost passé nature of cryptid cinema as part of the era's zeitgeist.

What would a good exploitation film be, he seems to be asking, *without* a Bigfoot in at least a few scenes? His point is well taken, as the Sasquatch scenes are some of the funniest in the film. Other sequences minus the cryptid sometimes veer from self-parody into self-immolation, especially when the film ventures into original characters beyond the scope of the Me Decade. Then again, and perhaps to their unwitting credit, this was precisely the resulting conclusion of many of the kung fu and exploitation films of the 1970s (or at least the more self-aware of the lot).

Heart of Dorkness: Behind the Scenes of "My Name Is Bruce" (2009) (Cameo) (Doc)

Starring Aaron Allen, William Boggs, Bruce Campbell, Mike Campbell, Tracy L. Connors, Mark T. Elliott, Mike Estes, Dan Hicks, Michael Kallio, Rachel Lipsey, Ben L. McCain, Dawnn Pavlonnis, Timothy Patrick Quill, Ted Raimi, Kurt Rauf, Mike Richardson, Jackson Rowe, Craig Sanborn, Sasquatch, Brent Streeper, Grace Thorsen, Mark Verheiden, Erin Walters and James Wilder Hancock. Produced by Mark T. Elliott and Michael Kallio. Written and Directed by Michael Kallio. USA. Color. Stereo. 60 Minutes.

Overview: This hour-long documentary that accompanies the DVD release of *My Name Is Bruce* is a short feature about the movie in which Bruce Campbell plays himself being mistaken for Ash from the *Evil Dead* trilogy and forced to battle Guan Di, an ancient Chinese evil unleashed by idiotic teenagers. Like the feature film itself (which Campbell also directed), *Heart of Dorkness* features a brief cameo by Sasquatch (though Bigfoot's appearance is longer in this making-of film than in the movie it profiles). *Heart of Dorkness* interviews long-time friends, family, and colleagues of the well-regarded actor, profiling his long-standing Michigan roots, his genial nature, and his willingness to help out indie filmmakers throughout his career. Both *My Name Is Bruce* and *Heart of Dorkness* are filled with insider jokes aimed at Ultimate Bruce Campbell fan boys, so it's almost pointless to recommend them to those who are unfamiliar with his nearly 30-year-long career in a variety of B movies, TV series, and cameos in bigger-budgeted films (like his auteur friend Sam Raimi's *Spider Man*). But for those who've seen a majority of his work and are impressed, *Heart of Dorkness* is a must see that fortunately is included on the feature's home video release.

Honey, I Shrunk the Kids: The TV Show ("Honey, He's Not Abominable ... He's Just Misunderstood") (1998) (TV)

Starring Peter Scolari, Barbara Alyn Woods, Hillary Tuck, Thomas Dekker, A.J. Bond, Don Enright, Bruce Hunter, Andy Maton, Clint Morris, Jacalyn O'Shaughnessy, Rick Overton and Tom Shorthouse. Produced by Leslie Belzberg, Ed Ferrara and Dan Studney. Written by Ed Ferrara and Jim Lincoln. Directed by Chad Gottlieb. Canada. Color. Stereo. 60 Minutes.

Overview: Amy goes for an off-road mountain bike ride but has an accident. She is rescued from her lonely predicament by Bigfoot, who follows her home when she is well enough to leave his cave. Alas, Bigfoot's walkabout has alerted the media, who are looking everywhere for the cryptid to exploit the hominid for ratings.

The Szalinski family realizes they must return the favor Bigfoot has shown Amy and therefore decide to hide the errant Sasquatch until they can help him return home. Alas, just when Wayne Szalinski, the inventive head of the household, believes he's taken matters into hand and solved the problem, a Yeti shows up as well. Bigfoot and the Abominable Snowman don't get along, which only makes the situation worse for the inventor of the infamous shrinking ray.

* * * * *

The phenomenal success of the original *Honey, I Shrunk the Kids* lead to theatrical sequels and this Canadian-produced TV series. While none of the original cast members from the features reprised their roles, *Honey, I Shrunk the Kids: The TV Show* (surely one of the worst titles in television history for sheer clumsiness) managed to capitalize upon the franchise for 66 one-hour syndicated episodes, which is impressive given how limiting the concept would seem at first glance.

This episode reminds one of the *Harry and the Hendersons* TV series for obvious reasons: Both are sitcoms, both feature a suburban family attempting to hide a Bigfoot from the media until they can return it to its native habitat, and both rely on the same schtick familiar to viewers of such seminal examples of the form as *Leave It to Beaver.*

Where "Honey, He's Not Abominable ... He's Just Misunderstood" achieves some degree of novelty in the Ciné du Sasquatch *oeuvre,* however, is in having Bigfoot meet the Abominable Snowman. This is a rare occurrence in the genre, despite its seeming obviousness in retrospect. Most efforts in the hominid cannon feature one or the other — or, as a variation, a group of like-species tribal Sasquatch creatures or Abominable Snowmen.

But unique indeed is the idea that the two are distinctively different to the extent that they are not blended into the same cryptid by most producers. With rare exceptions, the titles "Bigfoot" and "Yeti" are almost interchangeable in most Ciné du Sasquatch films. Another common motif in the genre is having the poster show one type of cryptid but the film depicting another (e.g., *The Capture of Bigfoot,* which shows a brown-furred Bigfoot on the poster but whose actual screen hominid is clearly a white-furred Yeti).

This anomaly aside, however, "Honey, He's Not

Abominable ... He's Just Misunderstood" could almost be a two-part episode of the Amblin-produced *Harry and the Hendersons* TV series, as if Harry suddenly met his Tibetan cousin. It's amusing as a concept, but at one hour it runs its novel concept into the snow-covered ground far earlier than the end credits. Too, it offers nothing unique to the Bigfoot film or TV cannon apart from this one clever deviation, and thus adds little to the genre as a whole.

Horror Express (1972)

AKA: *Panic in the Trans-Siberian Train.* Starring Christopher Lee, Peter Cushing, Telly Savalas, Alberto de Mendoza, Silvia Tortosa, Julio Peña, Ángel del Pozo, Helga Liné, Alice Reinheart, George Rigaud, Hiroshi Kitatawa and Juan Olaguivel. Produced by Bernard Gordon and Gregorio Sacristán. Written by Arnaud d'Usseau and Julian Zimet. Directed by Eugenio Martín. Spain. Color. Mono. 90 Minutes.

Overview: An erudite anthropologist named Sir Alexander Saxton uncovers the remains of a frozen cryptid in the remote mountains of Manchuria in 1906. Realizing the priceless discovery may be impounded by the local authorities should he declare his find, Saxton decides to board the Trans-Siberian Express in China with the creature hidden in a large crate and smuggle it back to his native England for further study. At the ticket station he has a chance encounter with Dr. Wells, an eminent scientist in his own right and colleague of Sir Saxton. Though they travel together as old friends, Saxton is initially reluctant to entrust Wells with the secret safely stored in the train's cargo bay.

During the long cross-continental railway trip, the Yeti awakens and escapes from confinement. Soon it is killing passengers and psychically projecting its essence from one human to the next, using each to hide from the growing awareness by the train's survivors that they are in horrific danger. Wells deduces the creature is an ancient alien life form after examining drops of its eye tissue under a microscope, and that is has furthermore been frozen in the unknown hominid life form for over two million years, simply waiting to thaw and attack the first species it can inhabit.

Poster art for the Spanish theatrical release of *Horror Express.*

Before the remaining passengers can formulate a survival strategy, Captain Kazan, a Cossack officer, boards the train with his soldiers in tow, seizing control. Disbelieving the creature story until it is too late, the cynical Kazan and his cadre are slowly taken over by the creature's psychic essence, which transforms them all into a horde of white-eyed zombies intent on killing Saxton, Wells and the handful of survivors. A last-minute decoupling of the train from the zombie soldiers sends the living dead over a cliff and spares the human passengers, leaving them to ponder the horrific nature of what they've endured.

* * * * *

Not a Yeti film in the traditional sense, *Horror Express* nevertheless briefly features one of the scarier realizations of a savage Sasquatch in the genre. This is achieved by keeping the cryptid off-screen for most shots and relying for impact not on a costume (which is still quite frightening whenever briefly glimpsed) but on a haunting musical theme which accompanies it. Italian filmmaker Martino does use sudden shock cuts of the beast to create jumps, but they're infrequent and all the more powerfully effective for it. A hairy, grasping claw here and the monster's baleful red eyes there result in creating more suspense than had Martino taken the more obvious approach of repeatedly showing the Yeti.

The fine casting of Christopher Lee in the Sir Hillary–esque role as the stiff upper-lipped anthropologist Sir Saxton, and Peter Cushing as traveling gentleman scientist Dr. Wells, works to great effect. It also makes one wish other producers had more often contrived to put the two exceptional talents together onscreen more often as cohorts rather than as arch rivals, as was the norm during their careers. They play off one another with amusingly wry energy, a clear nod to their real-life mutual affection. Telly Savalas also makes an appearance as the scene-chewing Captain Kazan halfway through the film and offers grim comic relief with his campy performance.

The real draw of *Horror Express* (at least in the first half) is not the cast, however, but the Abominable Snowman–like hominid. Though its fur is brown, making more akin to Bigfoot than Yeti, this large, aggressive cryptid is definitely of the take-no-prisoners mentality. It also acts with clear intelligence, deftly picking a lock in one scene with deliberative skill and stunning its first victims by laying clever

traps. Only later does the viewer learn the beast is only a shell of its former Yeti being when Dr. Wells deduces the animating force is not the hominid itself but an alien life form which inhabits it (making *Horror Express* the first and only Ciné du Sasquatch film to suggest a zombie cryptid). Cushing's theory that the alien inhabited the then-living Yeti in order to survive after crash-landing its flying saucer in the frozen Siberian wastelands turns out to be accurate. But by this point in the narrative the creature has long since abandoned its hominid form and moved on to hiding in the unsuspecting human passengers.

At this juncture in the movie, *Horror Express* abandons its relationship to Ciné du Sasquatch and settles into a more traditional, if occasionally effective, version of *The Thing* (either version) set on a train. It is still entertaining, but the original Ciné du Sasquatch premise of the film, focusing on the Yeti, falls away, leaving only the more traditional zombie horror movie in its wake.

While its action-packed scenario remains centered on the Abominable Snowman, however, *Horror Express* attains a kind of Gothic-influenced, near-operatic intensity. The Gothic flavor comes from the Victorian-styled settings of the train's interior; the operatic excess arises because, not unlike *The Phantom of the Opera* itself, the creature is only glimpsed by way of a hairy claw or shadowy shape. The shrill, high-pitched whistling theme accompanying its appearances is also very much in the Italian opera mode — almost like a musical aria written for the creature. The train's lush sets were craftily re-utilized by the film's producer from his previous collaboration with director Martino and Telly Savalas called *Pancho Villa*, which had filmed in Spain two years earlier.

Producer Bernard Gordon was one of the original blacklisted Hollywood screenplay writers from the 1950s Communist witch hunts lead by Senator Joe McCarthy. He was forced to write under a pseudonym (as Raymond T. Marcus) afterwards for such genre films as *Earth vs. the Flying Saucers*, *The Day of the Triffids* (for which writer Philip Yordan acted as front man) and *Zombies of Mora Tau*, which makes *Horror Express* a kind of wonderful amalgamation of Gordon's best science fiction and horror themes (although the actual script for *Horror Express* was written by his frequent collaborators Arnaud d'Usseau and Julian Zimet, who also crafted the cult favorite *Psychomania*).

Because it was shot with many Italian crew members (though filming was done in Spain), one is tempted to think of *Horror Express* as the world's first Spaghetti Yeti film (a nod to the so-called Spaghetti Westerns so lovingly popularized by Sergio Leone). While *Horror Express* was actually not the first Italian cryptid film (*Snow Devils* holds that distinction — perhaps the film's only redeeming feature), it remains the best (as *Yeti: Giant of the 20th Century*, made years later, proved beyond all doubt) and is a genuinely scary film experience, strange plot twists and campy performances included.

Hunt for Bigfoot (1995) (Doc) (TV)

Hosted by Clu Gulager. USA. Color. Stereo. 60 Minutes.

Overview: Long-time character actor and occasional independent filmmaker Clu Gulager hosts a syndicated TV show examining the usual suspects. As Gulager narrates, several recreations are staged in which Bigfoot attacks or bothers woodsy locals, including a teenage couple parked in a lover's lane. A psychic is called upon to ascertain the whereabouts of Bigfoot, and skeletal

The red-eyed, mummy-faced monster from *Horror Express* takes its latest victim in a moody, well-produced example of a Spaghetti Yeti.

remains of a supposed cryptid are shown, with the documentarians proclaiming their authenticity (given such remains would have been worth more for the DNA rights than 100 such syndicated hours of television, this is a dubious claim at best).

Generally considered by serious cryptozoologists and Ciné du Sasquatch fans as one of the worst-produced television "exposés" on Bigfoot, *Hunt for Bigfoot* seems more motivated to track down syndicated TV revenues than produce any meaningful evidence, theory, or analysis of the subject matter at hand. The production values are very low, the videography less than stellar, the Sasquatch suit threadbare, and the effort by the talented Gulager to avoid looking embarrassed understandable. *Hunt for Bigfoot* remains a rare title that is generally unavailable outside of collectors' sources on the Internet.

Hunt the Dogman (2006) (Doc)

Featuring Bart Nunnelly, Linda Godfrey, Rose Jenkins and Jan Thompson. Produced, Written and Directed by John L. Johnsen. USA. Color. Stereo. 60 Minutes.

Overview: Wildlife videographer turned cryptid documentarian John Johnsen uses a straight-forward approach to shed non-fiction light upon several regional Fortean phenomena: the Dogman of Kentucky, the Beast of the Land Between the Lakes, and the Spottsville Monster. While sightings of the Dogman tend to describe the creature as a bi-pedal, half-man/half-dog hominid, there is enough counter

Cover art for the DVD release of *Hunt the Dogman*.

evidence to suggest it may be a variant of Bigfoot, given its erect walking posture. The Beast of the Land Between the Lakes and the Spottsville Monster fall into the more traditional Sasquatch genre, hence this documentary's inclusion.

Johnsen focuses on eyewitnesses who recall their ordeals with the cryptids, including interviews with Bart Nunnelly, who wrote the Fortean-themed book *Weird Kentucky*. Nunnelly's mother is also interviewed, wherein she recounts seeing the Dogman once outside her modest childhood home. An older gentleman who prefers to be known only as "Roy" describes his own encounters with the hominid, including seeing a portal during a near-death experience through which the hairy creatures were coming and going as he lay dying. Linda Godfrey, a researcher who has spent much of her time documenting the Dogman sightings, presents her evidence of Dogman sightings from Wisconsin, Texas, Alabama, and beyond. The "Gable Film" (which supposedly shows a Dogman attacking the camera operator) is shown and critiqued. Kentucky resident Jan Thompson details her encounter with the Beast of the Land Between the Lakes and its possible link to the unsolved murders of a family of four campers in the area during the 1980s.

Because of his extensive background as a professional wildlife photographer, Johnsen's documentary captures his Kentucky bluegrass state with a sense of both delicate beauty and harrowing foreboding. He has also produced and directed the Bigfoot documentaries *Keeping the Watch* and *Spotlight On: The Patterson-Gimlin Film*, with researcher M.K. Davis.

Hunters of Unknown Animals (Doc) (TV)

Featuring Bill Dranginis, John Kirk, Michael Archer and Professor Tran Hong Viet. Produced by Mona Lisa Film. France. Color. Stereo. 60 Minutes.

Overview: This pilot episode focuses on cryptid hunters around the world who are in search of evidence for their respective obsessions. Profiles include John Kirk's quest to find the elusive Canadian version of the Loch Ness Monster known as Ogopogo; Australian scientist Michael Archer's attempt to restore the vanished Tasmanian tiger from an embryo; and Professor Tran Hong Viet's successful proving of the existence of a saola, a species of mountain antelope thought extinct. Of interest to Ciné du Sasquatch fans is the inclusion of interviews and footage of William Dranginis, the Virginia man who has devoted his life's energies to documenting more conclusive proof of Bigfoot after his own close encounter with one.

Dranginis claims that while hunting for Confederate artifacts in the rural Virginia woods with friends—one of whom served three tours in Vietnam and was a special agent at the time for the Federal government—they witnessed a large hominid sprint out ahead of them on a remote trail, leaping upward, and pivoting off a pine tree before disappearing into the thickets. Dranginis and his fellow startled companions were able to find footprints and other physical evidence the next day to back their claim, but nothing conclusive.

Convinced that what he saw was authentic, Dranginis eventually converted an RV into a Bigfoot research van, complete with high tech night surveillance equipment and video cameras. He documented many locals who'd also seen the creature but were previously too afraid of being ridiculed to come forward with their eyewitness accounts. Some were seasoned hunters who swore never to set foot in the woods again after what they saw, terrified of a second encounter with a less-peaceful denouement. Because of his law enforcement background and low-key nature, Dranginis comes off as a credible convert.

Dranginis has since been featured in several other Bigfoot documentaries, and maintains the Virginia Bigfoot Research website, which contains reports of local sightings, photographs, and other evidence he has amassed since beginning his quest.

Hyde & Sneak (1962) (Cameo)

Featuring the voices of Grace Stafford and Dal McKennon. Produced by Walter Lanzt. Written by Bill Danch. Directed by Paul J. Smith. USA. Color. Mono. 5 Minutes.

Overview: Chief Inspector Seward Willoughby (aka Secret Agent 6⅞) is small in height but large in detective prowess. Often sent to overcome the worst bad guys on the planet, the irreducible Willoughby was often beaten in the "short" run but never bested by credits' end. With his trademark laconic style, droopy handlebar mustache, and lidded eyes, Willoughby is a globetrotting spy every bit the equal of James Bond, even at half the stature.

In *Hyde & Sneak* the Chief Inspector is in London, hot (or is that cold?) on the trail of Vampira Hyde, a renowned burglar of precious jewels. But Vampira is as clever as Willoughby is tenacious. When Willoughby tracks her to a tea shop and believes he has her cornered, she slyly takes a pill which transforms her into a Kindly Old Lady. Aghast at his mistake, Willoughby releases her, only to see her reappear later when the potion wears off. Realizing he's being played for a sucker, Willoughby baits Vampira by hiding inside a giant false diamond and springing upon her when she tries to steal it. As she's lead away, Willoughby's curiosity gets the better of him. He swallows the remaining pills, determined to see if they're really as effective as Vampira maintains. To his horror, he rapidly cycles between several instant transformations, including a snorting gorilla, a bizarre alien from outer space, an Abominable Snowman, and even Woody Woodpecker before the short ends.

* * * * *

Sounding like the cartoon character Droopy (and even resembling the syrupy-voiced canine in diminutive form), Inspector Willoughby was a short-lived theatrical series of cartoons produced by the Walter Lantz Studios for Universal, who distributed them. The character never fully caught on, but was clearly designed to capitalize upon the 007 craze sweeping cinemas around the world.

The Abominable Snowman's cameo is but a brief couple of seconds in length, and, as such, is included here merely for historical purposes. But given the brief appearance, it does indicate the growing recognition of the cryptid in and of itself, as the visualization needs no verbal or expository cues in order to clue in the audience. Given this was in the era when Bugs Bunny and Daffy Duck met *The Abominable Snow Rabbit*, and Felix the Cat had a run-in with the *Abominable Snowman* in his own short film, it also indicates the growing popularity of Yeti among animators across the Hollywood cartoon spectrum, who realized a good thing when they saw it in the public zeitgeist. The Abominable proved an irresistible icon even at this early stage of hominid cinema's metastasizing cultural influence.

In Search Of (1976) (Multiple Episodes) (TV) (Doc)

Featuring Leonard Nimoy. Produced by Jon D. Ackelson, Annette M. Bettin, Seth Hill, William Kirnick, Jeffrey Pill, Alex Pomansanof and Barbara Wegher. Written by Jon D. Ackelson, Annette M. Bettin, Deborah Blum and Leonard Nimoy. Directed by Nicholas Webster. USA. Color. Mono. 30 Minutes.

Overview: Leonard Nimoy is the host of an investigative series of half-hours examining such Fortean topics as UFOs, cryptids, psychic phenomena, and related experiences in the unknown. Using inter-

views, recreations, and actual photographs and filmed footage when available, *In Search Of* focuses on a different topic each week to study in-depth.

* * * * *

Spurred on by the Neilson ratings success of *In Search of Ancient Astronauts* in 1973 and *In Search of Ancient Mysteries* two years later, TV producer Alan Landsburg decided to launch a weekly series based on their popularity with viewers. Rod Serling was invited by Landsburg to host the continuing franchise, as he'd done in the previous specials, but his death forced the producer to instead go with Leonard Nimoy, the cult favorite from *Star Trek*. While *Star Trek* has since scaled the heights of spin-offs, remakes, series, and sequels beyond anyone's imagination, in the mid–1970s Nimoy's career was — like his former Enterprise crew mates — decidedly Earthbound. In no small manner, *In Search Of* helped Nimoy reestablish and reconnect with his already devoted fan base, as well as introducing him to a new generation of viewers who'd been too young to fully follow his earlier 1960s work in *Star Trek*.

In Search Of was also a landmark in its serious consideration of paranormal and cryptozoological phenomena via an ongoing, weekly format. While earlier TV news shows had featured Bigfoot stories and Yeti sightings, none had devoted itself to such regular exposure of Fortean subject matter exclusively. Had not the series — which focused on such a wide-ranging catalogue of topics as Amelia Earhart, ESP, Incan treasures, flying saucers, firewalkers, ghosts, and on and on — been as popular as it was from its debut, there arguably would have never been such later, better-produced efforts as *MonsterQuest*, *Animal X*, and the rest, all of which owe an enormous debt of gratitude to *In Search Of* in terms of investigative formatting and atypical, non-sensationalized tone.

Each week also had another huge influence on viewers: For many, it was their first repeated exposure to the infamous Patterson-Gimlin footage, which appeared briefly in the series' opening credits montage. While only a brief glimpse was shown, it nonetheless firmly established what a "real Sasquatch" would look and walk like for an impressionable young audience. Combined with the earlier shock inundation of *The Legend of Boggy Creek* and the concurrent rage of Bionic Bigfoot in *The Six Million Dollar Man* prime-time series (as well as the *Bigfoot and Wildboy* Saturday morning alternative), one can easily understand why so many later Ciné du Sasquatch fans cite this as the Golden Age of the genre.

There are four particular episodes from the original run of the series that Bigfoot fans will appreciate. "In Search of Bigfoot" (aka "Bigfoot") was the usual overview of the subject matter, featuring eyewitness accounts, scientists pro and con, plaster casts, and filmed evidence. "The Swamp Monster" was a look at the Fouke Monster featured in *The Legend of Boggy Creek*, concentrating on the local eyewitnesses who've claimed contact with the hominid. "Monster Hunters" examined crypto hunters, such as Peter Byrne, who were combing through the vast Pacific Northwest forests to uncover Sasquatch. And "The Abominable Snowman" was a concise presentation of the history of Yeti sightings in Tibet, along with interviews with and stock footage of some of the explorers who mounted expeditions to Mount Everest, which triggered much of the early speculation.

The original series was syndicated instead of broadcast on network television. This meant it was hit-or-miss for many viewers, as time slots for such materials tended to be very flexible for station managers (which was their appeal, as they were not beholden to network affiliation and guaranteed schedule placement for national or regional advertisers). Alas, in an era prior to videocassette recorders becoming inexpensive and widely available, this also meant faithful fans had to go in search of *In Search Of* themselves. But owing to the fondness with which many recalled it, it was put back into production (with slightly better production values) in 2002 on the Sci Fi Channel (since retitled Syfy). This short-lived revival lacked the magic (and Nimoy) but did feature one episode entitled "Catacombs/Bigfoot/Rennes," which devoted time to a recap of the Bigfoot phenomena. The original series was also repeated on the A&E Network in the 1990s.

In Search of Yeti (2009)

AKA: *YetiKo KhojiMa*. Starring Laxman Basnet, Dibyaswar Gautam, Pamela Alisa, Sunita Gandharba, Swami Krishna, Pema Sherpa, Rajan Khatri, L.B. Thapa, Uttam Newa, Lal K. Shrestha, Akur Khadka, Hari Acharya, Samriti Thapa and Samresh Thapa. Produced by the Visual Production Center. Directed by Santosh Dhakal. Nepal. Color. Stereo. 110 Minutes.

Overview: Yet to be released in the United States, *In Search of Yeti* is the first-ever Nepali-produced take on the Yeti legend, making it quite unique in the history of Ciné du Sasquatch. Given the nearly endless number of Western versions of the Himalayan hominid, it may seem somewhat surprising it took this long for such a production to be mounted. This is due less to cultural reverence for the iconic Abominable Snowman as it is to the fledgling film industry in Nepal itself.

In Search of Yeti is not a docudrama or a historically self-validating, cultural by-product, but an entertainment for a mass audience. As such, it is described by its producers as being first and foremost an action film dealing with the discovery of and then struggle with the Yeti by a group of profiteers intent on destroying the pristine Himalayan wilderness. Impoverished but attempting to emerge into the modern age, the Sherpas and other indigenous tribes are besieged by natural disasters, which tempts them to forsake their cultural ties in exchange for easy money.

The creators hired stunt director Roshan Shrestha to train many locals to act as stunt people in the making of the film, creating a small industry in and of itself. Intent on featuring the natural splendor of

Behind-the-scenes snapshot taken by the cast and crew of *In Search of Yeti*, the first-ever Abominable Snowman movie filmed entirely in Nepal.

the Nepali region, the producers shot most of the film on location. Among the locations — many seen for the first time in a modern cinema undertaking — that *In Search of Yeti* utilizes is the rural area of Langtang, where, local legends insist, the Yeti originated and still exists. Other scenic locations included Lete, Ghasa, and Tukuche in Mustang; Tiplyang in Myagdi; Siddha Cave in Bandipur Tanahu; Dhampus, Sikles, the Annapurna Range, and Pokhara; and Kathmandu and Dhulikhel in Kavre.

To increase the likelihood of successful international distribution, the producers staged all of the action and fight sequences at altitudes of over 4,300 meters in order to give them a natural sense of grandeur akin to a James Bond film. While this placed considerable strain on the stunt performers due to the naturally thin air available, the producers felt it was necessary in order to heighten the story's realism. To date, it is also the first time anyone in cinema history has ever attempted such an ambitious fictional narrative in the mountainous locales. Designed in part to highlight the developing tourist industry in Nepal, as well as cement the cultural affinity the region has for the Yeti, the movie (with its Westernized style) was intended to help Nepali-produced films break out of their regional-only status and secure more worldwide audiences. By all accounts it is one of the most ambitious productions ever undertaken by the nascent film industry in Nepal, which speaks volumes about the awareness of the Abominable Snowman globally, as well as the perceived commerciality of Ciné du Sasquatch.

In the Shadow of Bigfoot (1983) (Doc)

Featuring Tom Biscardi, Ivan Marx and Dr. Warren Cook. Produced and Directed by Tom Biscardi and Ivan Marx. USA. Color. Stereo. 85 Minutes.

Overview: Wherever the name Ivan Marx appears in Ciné du Sasquatch, his infamous hoaxed crock-umentary *The Legend of Bigfoot* immediately springs to mind. A self-made monument to the proposition that all lovers of Bigfoot and Bigfoot fictional films are morons, Marx was a semi-professional nature photographer and full-time con man whose poorly-staged Bigfoot photos and filmic efforts cast disrepute upon an already often ridiculed subject matter.

Combining the co-producing and co-directing names of Tom Biscardi *with* Ivan Marx is a surefire recipe for Barnum and Bailey–level veracity. Tom Biscardi is perhaps most notorious for his involvement as promoter of the Georgia Bigfoot hoax of 2009 (in which a Sasquatch suit was placed into a non-functioning freezer — à la a modern restaging of the famous Minnesota Iceman prank — until all involved, including Biscardi, were forced to admit the fabrication) and his pro–Bigfoot documentary *Bigfoot Lives!* Biscardi actually sought out Ivan Marx *after* Marx was forced to go on the run by Bigfoot hunter Peter Byrne, who had funded Marx to shoot film of the elusive beast, only to have Marx deliver obviously staged footage. Rather than refund the monies owed and admit deceit, Marx and his wife instead abandoned their rural trailer home and split the area, never to be seen nor heard from by Byrne again. The fact Biscardi sought out and found Marx after Marx had lost all credibility in the cryptozoological community (save for Marx's own profit-making ventures) speaks volumes about Biscardi's probable motivation.

Whatever Biscardi's rationale, the results, as demonstrated within *In the Shadow of Bigfoot*, cast a long shadow of doubt over Ivan Marx's ability to offer any new evidence to redeem his discredited reputation. Instead, *In the Shadow of Bigfoot* seems designed to rebuke the majority of scientists, cryptozoologists, film critics, and general skeptics who had earlier and rightfully passed judgment on Marx as a hoaxster (and a poor one, at that). Likewise, it equally appears positioned as an attempt to reboot the Ivan Marx franchise of exploiting Bigfoot for profit and enshrining Marx as a pivotal figure in American Yeti research of the 1950s on the West Coast. This last is actually true: Marx was an early believer in Bigfoot sightings, along with John Green, Rene Dahinden, and other key figures in the field. However, it's equally true that Marx was the first to attempt to cash in on the others' serious commitment to document rather than exploit their research subject. Somehow, when all others failed, Marx was consistently able to capture photographs of Bigfoot as easily as most wildlife photographers snap pictures of hawks or deer.

Shot on videotape, amateurishly produced, and marketed directly to home video, *In the Shadow of Bigfoot* is an aptly-titled enterprise, as viewers are left entirely in the dark to speculate on both men's firmly-stated and endlessly repeated belief that Bigfoot *is* real — without any evidence to back such a claim. Given the lack of proof to justify their nearly religious fanaticism, one can truly say, "The ladies doth protest too much," even if they be gentlemen capitalists. Biscardi's motives are perhaps best illustrated by his website, which now offers the DVD-R version in a white paper sleeve for $34.95 (including free shipping, no less!), and states: "This particular film has been selling on eBay, in its original VHS form with original packaging, for as high as $250. Now you can have a much clearer digitally remastered copy of this video, without waiting weeks for one of the rare offers for the old VHS version on eBay." But, as the "digitally remastered" version of *In the Shadow of Bigfoot* all too clearly reveals, some documentaries are best left in their original format. After all, this entry into Ciné du Sasquatch is analogous to an 8-track cassette in terms of being archaic and deservedly forgotten. No amount of enhancement can alter the basic lack of content.

The Incredible Hulk ("The Antowuk Horror") (1978) (TV)

Starring Bill Bixby, Jack Colvin, Lou Ferrigno, William Lucking, Debbie Lytton, Lance LeGault, Dennis Patrick, Myron Healey, Bill Deiz and Gwen Van Dam. Produced by Chuck Bowman, Nicholas Corea and Kenneth Johnson. Written by Nicholas Corea. Directed by Sigmund Neufeld Jr. USA. Color. Stereo. 48 Minutes.

Overview: The small town of Antowuk, Utah, is dying from lack of tourism to support its empty ski lodge, its lake fishing, and camping grounds. Dr. David Banner, who transforms into the Hulk when angered, is working for Harlen Bates, a small-time hunting supply retailer, in order to hide out from the law and Jack McGee, a reporter determined to expose Banner's dark secret. Bates, a widower, and his daughter Samantha are considering closing up and moving out. One day a drunken Bates taunts Banner. The rage builds in Banner and he transforms into the Hulk, almost destroying Bates' shop. Bates and his friend Brad, owner of the ski lodge, try to resist but are tossed aside like rag dolls by the Hulk, who escapes the town.

Banner returns when he has regained his human form only to find Bates has stirred up the town with the idea that they should publicize their Hulk encounter in order to draw in tourists. To further their goal, Bates and Brad head into the woods to try and capture the Hulk. Hours later, Brad staggers into town and claims Harlen Bates was abducted by the Hulk. He leads the Sheriff and other town officials to the scene of their confrontation, indicating the large foot-

prints and other physical evidence to corroborate his story. Banner, who knows better because he *is* the Hulk, confronts Brad when the two are alone, accusing him of hoaxing the story to bring in the media. Brad denies it, suspicious: Just how is Banner so certain unless he has inside information about the Hulk? Realizing he cannot blow his cover, Banner backs down.

In order to further the coverage, Bates dresses up as a Bigfoot-type hominid and smashes through a traveling carnival, creating mayhem. He overturns the Sheriff's truck and races away, gloating in hiding with Brad as he boasts how this will put Antowuk on the map for sure. Meanwhile, Banner is forced to tell Samantha that her father is obviously the hoaxer, and when he presents her with evidence, she reluctantly comes to the same conclusion. Banner asks her to lead him to her father so that he can coerce Bates into forgoing the stunt before a professional hunter who has arrived in town shoots Bates while he's posing as the Antowuk Horror.

When Banner confronts Bates in his latest act of monster hoaxing, however, Bates is in no mood to consider backing down. He throws Banner aside and callously continues with his effort. Enraged by the pain, Banner transforms again into the Hulk. The Hulk and the Antowuk Horror fight, but the Hulk easily overpowers his human foe. Alas, Samantha falls over the edge of a cliff and hangs on for her life while they struggle. They hear her cries for help and respond. The Hulk lowers Bates by his ankles until Bates can retrieve his daughter. The game hunter takes a shot and grazes the Hulk's shoulder. With Samantha now safe, the Hulk leaps down the mountain and is preparing to smash the hunter when the police arrive. Fleeing into the woods, the Hulk vanishes, leaving the witnesses stunned: While Bates is clearly a hoaxster, there *was* a real monster — the Hulk — after all. Having saved the town, Bates realizes he must learn to live without

Bruce Banner (Bill Bixby) and his alter ego Hulk (Lou Ferrigno) meet a Hoax-squatch in the 1970s TV series *The Incredible Hulk*.

the anger he's felt since his wife's death and build upon the newfound opportunity the press has afforded Antowuk. David Banner bids farewell to Samantha and heads out on his existential quest to find solace, alone yet again.

* * * * *

Though it was but a moderate ratings hit during its initial run, *The Incredible Hulk* enjoyed an intensely loyal following among its dedicated viewers. Partly this was due to the casting of Bill Bixby, who brought a likeable charm to his forever wandering character of Dr. David Banner, and the mute but physical presence of the green-colored Lou Ferrigno, who remains a well-respected bodybuilder to the stars (he helped Michael Jackson get in shape for his return in 2009). Between the warmth of Bixby's tragic hero and the convincing rage of Ferrigno's bulky Hulk, the low-budget effort proved to be far superior to the other Marvel Comics TV adaptations of the era, such as *The Amazing Spiderman* and *Captain Marvel*. While it took great liberties with the original origin story, at least *The Incredible Hulk* maintained the basic flavor of the Jekyll and Hyde dynamic of the comic book series, whereas the latter two adaptations never seemed able to please either fans, viewers, or critics.

"The Antowuk Horror," alas, is definitely far from the best of the series, which occasionally rose to the heights of good melodrama. The biggest drawbacks are the lack of suspense regarding Bigfoot (the plot "twist" that it's a hoax is revealed moments after its first sighting in the script) and the lack of any meaningful involvement of the David Banner character. The latter was a frequent problem in the less successful episodes of *The Incredible Hulk*, especially when writers forgot to solve the inherent problem of the passivity of Banner, a plot device needed to prevent him from transforming into the monstrous side of his personality. This could be a good dramatic device, but it creates an imbalance: How does one incorporate the more interesting dynamic of the Hulk himself? The comic books often achieved this by simply substituting action and a greater focus on the Hulk portion; whereas, due to its limited budget, the TV series was forced to devote more time to Banner in human form. Given the episodic nature — in which Banner had to literally move from town to town every show — this meant setting up new characters each week and stalling the inevitable Hulk transformation as long as possible. It was no easy task.

Still, more successful series such as *Kung Fu* and *The Fugitive* utilized this very formula to great success on many occasions, so it was not impossible. Given the rather limited effects technology available in the 1970s, especially for a TV production such as this, one can argue that *The Incredible Hulk* did as good a job as could be expected. Certainly there are moments of genuine pathos, perhaps none so memorable as the weekly ending, in which a forlorn Bill Bixby would leave his latest acquaintances and set out again on a his lonely trek. The plaintive, melancholy piano accompaniment by composer Joseph Harnell was very memorable and added to the closing moments each week.

The Bigfoot creature (aka the "Antowuk Horror") is the clichéd version so frequently seen in Ciné du Sasquatch: the man in a costume, typically held as a "surprise" until the movie or TV show's ending, when it is revealed to the astonishment of all. Though predictable, "The Antowuk Horror" would have been stronger had the writers decided to go with this plot structure, as there is no sense of drama in waiting for the Hulk to confront a mere mortal merely *dressed* as a monster. The epic battle is anything but, with the Hulk easily quashing the puny Bates. When Bates' daughter is in peril and the Hulk turns good guy, another predictable plot point is dutifully carried out, again without much emotional impact. The hunter actually squeezes off one shot and wounds the Hulk, causing him to bleed. This is quite contrary, of course, to the comic book legend

and recent filmic features wherein the Hulk is practically impervious to bullets, missiles, and even tank fire. The illogical nature of the Hulk's shoulder gash is even contradicted by the dialogue of the amazed townsfolk when one utters, staring at the fleeing Hulk, "Man, it would take a cannon to take *that* thing down!" moments after the hunter wounds the angry green giant with a glancing shot!

The make-up for the monster is also disappointing. Basically, the actor wears a fright wig, black greasepaint under his eyes, and a furry chest piece, along with arm extensions that give his elbow-to-fingertips a simian-styled elongation. The numerous close-ups, despite being briefly edited, do little to hide the deficiencies of the make-up both as a weak design concept and its subsequent poor realization in application. Definitely not a highlight of Ciné du Sasquatch, Bigfoot's pseudo-appearance in *The Incredible Hulk* nevertheless points out the continuing popularity of Sasquatch during what was the genre's Golden Age of exposure (some might even argue *over*-exposure) in television and filmic mediums, when the shaggy hominid was plugged into any situation that would withstand a cryptid cameo, for better or worse.

The Incredible Hulk ("Man to Man, Beast to Beast") (1996) (TV)

Featuring the voices of Neal McDonough, Lou Ferrigno, Genie Francis, Philece Sampler, Luke Perry, John Vernon, Clancy Brown, Peter Strauss, Kevin Schon, Matt Frewer, Mark Hamill, Richard Moll, Thom Barry, Shadoe Stevens and Lisa Zane. Produced by Saban Entertainment and Stan Lee. Written by Len Wein. Directed by Tom Tataranowicz. USA. Color. Stereo. 30 Minutes.

Overview: Dr. Bruce Banner, aka the Hulk (when enraged), stumbles through the Canadian wilderness, nearly frozen to death, in an attempt to escape the perils of civilization. His quest is to find his old colleague and sympathetic friend Dr. Walter Langkowski. Dr. Langkowski, Banner knows, has also been experimenting with gamma radiation treatments in a remote section of the Great White North. Befriended by a local boy and lead to his old colleague, Banner seeks Langkowski's help in ridding him of his Hulk alter ego. But during the process, Banner learns Langkowski made a tragic error earlier and has been hiding the secret. By using himself as his own guinea pig, with an experimental serum Langkowski has created a genetic instability wherein he randomly transforms into the legendary Sasquatch. After a battle between the Hulk and Sasquatch, Langkowski reverts to human form and realizes he is a menace to civilization after having nearly killed Banner's young benefactor. Vowing to remain in the remote woods until he can solve his dilemma, Langkowski exiles himself, leaving Banner to face yet another dead end in his efforts to solve his own shape-shifting dilemma as the Hulk.

* * * * *

While it took three tries to finally produce a successful Hulk animated TV series (earlier attempts being made in the 1960s and 1980s to less than stellar fan reactions), this 1990s UPN-aired incarnation generally met with substantial favor among fans of the original Stan Lee comic books. Partly this was because Stan Lee oversaw the production and had a hand in the storyline's creations (some of which were unofficial adaptations of earlier published comic books — this episode, for example, was based upon *The Incredible Hulk* Vol. 2, Annual No. 8).

Sasquatch is portrayed as the equivalent of a were-hominid, which is not without precedent in the Bigfoot films and TV shows. Still, it's far rarer than simply depicting the Abominable Snowman as a completely distinct hominid species in and of itself. One can view "Man to Man, Beast to Beast" as a kind of doppelganger episode in which both Banner and Langkowski, decent men of honorable character, are forced to do battle with their respective shadow selves, externalized into monsters (à la Dr. Morbius in *Forbidden Planet*). As humans, both men are friends and morally good; as beasts, both are enemies who succumb to rage and primitive instincts over rational thought and concepts of ethics. So despite the mirror image theme and were-hominid uniqueness, "Man to Man, Beast to Beast" fits quite adroitly into Ciné du Sasquatch's prevailing motif of the Yeti as the embodiment of *Homo sapiens* minus the restraint of civilization, as well as the subsequent hypocrisy of said society. For better and often for worse, Sasquatch as symbol represents the unfettered state of man's being, freed from any religious or philosophical constrictions. This is aptly illustrated by Langkowski's realization when he reverts back to his human form that he is unfit to live among mankind, as he cannot be trusted (nor trust himself) to obey the rules of civilization while in his more regressive state as Sasquatch.

Into the Unknown (1997) (TV) (Doc)

Hosted by Jonathan Pryce. Canada. Color. Stereo. 30 Minutes.

Overview: Actor Jonathan Price hosted this syndicated TV series that focused on a variety of Fortean phenomena, with a particular interest in UFOs, but occasionally delving into the cryptozoological arena with shows on the Loch Ness Monster, giant sea serpents, thunderbirds and, of course, hominids. Generally, each of the 55 episodes produced focused on one topic, though occasionally they were segmented and joined together to form a complete episode.

Of particular interest to Ciné du Sasquatch documentary viewers are the three shows profiling Bigfoot, Yeti, and related bipedal cryptids. "Chinese Wildman" is an overview of the mystery of the continual sightings of the Orang Pendek, or "short person," which reportedly inhabits the remote jungles of Sumatra and Southeast Asia. Included are eyewitness interviews and evidence of fossil remains. "Unknown Creatures" focuses on both Bigfoot in North America and the Yeti in Tibet, as well as a segment on reported sightings of gigantic snakes in the Amazon jungles. Finally, "Strange Beasts" features a segment dedicated to the *Gigantopithecus* and claims that it still exists in remote areas of China, along with a shorter piece about giant cats.

Is It Real? (2005) (Multiple Episodes) (TV) (Doc)

AKA: *National Geographic's Is It Real?* Featuring Will Lyman, Ian Gregory, Dr. Jeff Meldrum, Bob Heironimus, Dr. David Daegling, Dr. Peter Tse, Shara Bailey, Todd Disotel, Igor Burtsev, Wallace Swett, Adam Davies and Andrew Ferguson. Produced by Michael Cascio, Martha Conboy, Noel Dockstader, Eleanor Grant, French Horwitz, Michael Rosenfeld and Chris Sondreal. Written by Cara Biega, Noel Dockstader and Eleanor Grant. Directed by Cara Biega and Noel Dockstader. USA. Color. Stereo. 60 Minutes.

Overview: For much of the modern era of hominid sightings, there has been the National Geographic Society looming somewhere in the background, reporting the evidence and eyewitness accounts. From the earliest published reports of the Abominable Snowman (accompanied by photos of supposed Yeti footprints from Mount Everest expeditions) to present-day documentary productions, *National Geographic* has truly been one of the veritable cornerstones of accurate, unbiased explanations and presentations of existing evidence in regards to Bigfoot-reality-vs.-hoax.

The *Is It Real?* series is a critical examination of the most up-to-date information, photos, castings, and filmic "proof" of various reported but unproven phenomena, using expert analysis, new digital technologies to reexamine old evidence, and staged, scientifically-monitored recreations to put existing accounts under a new light. While the results are not always flattering to many Sasquatch aficionados (as many cherished theories and evidence have been dismissed during the course of the series in regards to hominids), at least it can be said *Is It Real?* examines its subject matters from a position of objectivity rather than outright skepticism or passionately-held belief. As fans of documentary entries in Ciné du Sasquatch know all too well, such unbiased attempts to prove or disprove Bigfoot sightings are rarer than the actual species itself. The show often manages to offend both extremes in the Great Divide of belief versus dismissal: Many in the skeptical community find *Is It Real?* too lenient on the cryptozoological community, while many in the latter group find the show far too critical. Given the criticism, it's easy to see why balanced, reflective examinations such as this series are not more common, which is, sadly, a loss for all involved (as no one who believes wishes to be deceived by proven hoaxes and false evidence; likewise, disbelievers would welcome any scientific proof to justify the search for Sasquatch).

There are three episodes in the two-year run of *Is It Real?* that apply to Ciné du Sasquatch. The first is "Bigfoot," which examines the North American cryptid via a primary focus on the Patterson-Gimlin film—which *Is It Real?* suggests is the most likely piece of evidence ever presented of the possible existence of Sasquatch. The show is not without a dry sense of humor in its approach. For example, narrator Will Lyman opens the episode over a montage of Bigfoot creatures with the following introduction: "He's tall, he's dark, and he's having a bad hair day from hell." While serious cryptozoologists may find the remark indicative of a bias against the veracity of claimed Sasquatch sightings, it actually sets the stage rather adroitly for the coming hour, as it neatly demonstrates the divide that exists between those who have claimed an encounter with Bigfoot and the often skeptical sense of humor that accompanies such reports by non-believers or Yeti Agnostics.

Dr. Jeff Meldrum, something of a documentary mainstay in the genre, reports that he believes the evidence is overwhelming as to the high probability Bigfoot is real, while Dr. David Daegling argues just the contrary—that evidence can be faked and scientists fooled by it, despite their best efforts. The show begins in Six Rivers National Forest in Northern California with scenic cinematography that is not difficult to capture given the impressive vistas and remote locale. The tiny town of Willow Creek, California, is shown on the morning of its annual Bigfoot Parade, a largely tourist-driven attraction designed to capitalize on the fact that this area of California has had more physical evidence and eyewitness accounts reported than anywhere else on Earth. Park ranger John McDonald argues that if we're searching for life on other planets without any evidence to date, why *not* Bigfoot and other cryptozoological creatures? Rebecca Cape, a fire watch volunteer with 20 years of experience, believes there is plenty of coverage available to sustain a cryptid population, whereas Benjamin Radford, an editor for *Skeptical Inquirer*, cautions that the reports should be taken with a grain of salt, as they nearly always lack corroborating evidence.

Next comes the real focus of the documentary: the Roger Patterson footage. The narrator says, "Eyewitness accounts are one thing. Eyewitnesses who conveniently, perhaps *too* conveniently, have a film camera with them is another." Staged shots of Roger Patterson and Bob Gimlin (portrayed by lookalikes) are shown riding their horses in a recreation leading up to the famous Bluff Creek encounter in 1967. Here is where many believers fault the episode for its characterization of Patterson as a broken, destitute man, dying of cancer, who is frustrated that Hollywood won't bite on his idea of making a

Bigfoot feature film. Describing Patterson in such admittedly unflattering terms does go a long way towards positioning the viewer to disbelieve anything that follows. The problem is, what follows is so damaging to the veracity of the Patterson-Gimlin film itself that even the most ardent supporters of the footage surely must give pause if they're objective in any sense of the word.

Bob Heironimus, a long-time friend of Patterson's, speaks openly about the fact he was hired by the dying cowboy to wear a suit and fake the footage. Were the claims merely of the "he said, he said" variety, they would not be very conclusive. But some truly shocking footage follows, as Heironimus demonstrates his decidedly distinctive walking gait. From a distance and in silhouette against the setting sun, it is almost as if one is seeing the Patterson-Gimlin film minus the depicted creature's familiar furry outline. Sitting with his buddy in a local cafe, Heironimus laughs that his unique gait is so unusual that many who knew him back in 1967 came up to him after seeing the footage, clearly realizing who was inside the costume. Further suspicion is cast upon the Patterson-Gimlin film when *Is It Real?* shows a split-screen between the Patterson Sasquatch on one side and Heironimus today on the other, matched in motion as they walk in the same direction. It is eerily like looking at a mirror image when one accounts for the difference in the suit's bulk and, of course, the decades following that have taken their toll on Heironimus' aged body. While there is little doubt at least some mimics could learn to fake the gait of the most famous filmed Bigfoot in Ciné du Sasquatch history, one is left with some unsettling questions. To wit: Why would Heironimus bother, given he was a friend of Patterson's until Patterson died? Heironimus claims no financial gain from his admission, and even his harshest critics, as the show points out, have not accused him of cashing in on his claim to be the suit's wearer. And what are the odds that a friend of Patterson's, who is slightly hunched in his natural gait, would learn to copy the shown Sasquatch if not for material gain? Heironimus seems anything but agile, especially in his elderly years. The coincidences pile up, which begs the question of the Patterson-Gimlin film's authenticity in light of Heironimus' confession. Again, one is forced to reexamine the footage anew, which, in a bizarre way of course, only makes it more relevant to those who believe *and* those who dismiss.

Less contentious in the series were the other two hominid episodes, called "Ape-man" and "Russian Bigfoot," which deal with the Orang Pendek and Baltic Bigfoot, respectively. "Ape-man" was photographed in the jungles and remote villages of Sumatra and focused on the frequently reported sightings of the "short person" by farmers and residents. Described as being barely over two feet in height, the bipedal hominid has been reported for over a century by both natives and Dutch explorers alike. Dr. Peter Tse sets motion detection cameras and interviews eyewitnesses in hopes of shedding light on the cryptid. Attention is also focused on the so-called "Humanzee"— an incredibly intelligent chimpanzee known as Oliver. Oliver's caretaker, Wallace Swett of Primarily Primates in San Antonio, Texas, is profiled, wherein he reveals he had Oliver's DNA tested, with results proving conclusively that he is 100 percent chimp in origin.

"Russian Bigfoot" explores the world of the Almas, the most common moniker for Sasquatch in the Baltic states. Russian Bigfoot researcher Igor Burtsev proposes the theory that many of the sightings of Almas could be of Neanderthals that never went extinct but somehow survived in small numbers in the vast wilderness areas of the former Soviet Republic. New York University anthropology professors Shara Bailey and Todd Disotel examine human and Neanderthal skulls to elucidate the comparative differences and similarities between the two species, which are generally considered having co-existed until approximately 30,000 years ago (a very short time indeed by evolutionary standards). A British cryptozoologist by the name of Adam Davies is profiled in his search of the Mongolian no man's lands for the Almas, joined by his colleague Andrew Sanderson. Showing the wry, dry humor characteristic of all three hominology episodes, the narrator echoes the opening of the first "Bigfoot" show in "Russian Bigfoot" with the mantra "He's hairy and scary." It's not just a facetious phrase, as both "Bigfoot" and "Russian Bigfoot" feature their share of spooky recreations of various cryptid encounters.

Isis ("Bigfoot") (1975) (TV)

AKA: *The Secrets of Isis*. Starring JoAnna Cameron, Brian Cutler, Joanna Pang, Scott Colomby, Neil J. Schwartz, Albert Reed and William Engesser. Produced by Arthur H. Nadel, Norm Prescott, Richard M. Rosenbloom and Lou Scheimer. Written by Michael Reaves and Marc Richards. Directed by Arthur H. Nadel. USA. Color. Mono. 30 Minutes.

Overview: When high school teacher Andrea Thomas takes her class on a picnic in the mountains, two of her students — Cindy Lee and Lee Webster — claim to have seen a large, hairy monster on the prowl. While her male teacher counterpart escorts the students to safety, Thomas stays behind to investigate the sighting. She secretly transforms into the mighty Isis, a super-powered goddess, and flies high above the treetops.

Isis discovers huge footprints but no other evidence of Bigfoot. Meanwhile, tired of being ridiculed for his claim, Lee Webster returns to the woods with a camera, intent on getting a photograph.

The supposed creature turns out to be a lonely hermit of enormous stature who's frightening in appearance owing to his size and wild hair. When the photography student Webster accidentally tumbles over the edge of a cliff and is rescued by the quick actions of the hermit, the boy realizes his savior is merely a misunderstood outcast. The recluse tells Webster he's retreated from society after years of enduring cruelty and harassment, favoring solitude over ridicule.

Webster accidentally drops his camera down a ravine, and the hermit attempts to retrieve it for him. During the descent, the giant stumbles and hangs on for his life. Isis appears in the air above and rescues the thankful hermit. Safely back on solid ground, Isis invites the shy mountain man to visit with his fellow humans for companionship, reminding him that not all humans are insensitive and prejudiced. He agrees to consider it.

* * * * *

The ghetto of children's TV programming that dominated early Saturday morning in the 1970s was populated by crudely-rendered skip-frame animation, low-budget live action comic book adventures, and just enough interstitial educational segments (such as the acclaimed *School House Rock*) between shows to avoid further scrutiny from the Federal Communications Committee (earlier FCC hearings resulted in toy and cereal advertisers being subjected to newer, stricter rules in order to establish a more equitable balance of entertainment and education).

As a result of the FCC's mandates, network executives were forced to seek out the safest content possible, carefully reviewing the scripts submitted by producers so their respective networks weren't cited for violations. Enter prolific Filmation Studios, a large-scale provider of quality children's fare in both animated and live action formats. In almost diametrical opposition to the more subversive, surreal productions of their chief rival the Brothers Krofft (such as *H.R. Puf'n'Stuf* and *Lidsville*), Filmation concentrated on more innocuous productions, such as *Valley of the Dinosaurs*, *Tarzan*, and even a cerebral if disappointing animated version of the *Star Trek* series.

The Filmation formula is perfectly distilled in *Isis*, for better and worse. A basic knock-off of *Wonder Woman* with Linda Carter (minus the budget), *Isis* is a lighthearted attempt to emulate the success of

Filmation's earlier hit featuring male comic book superhero Captain Marvel—*Shazam!* By running both series back-to-back, Filmation dominated the hour in which the two shows aired. But in comparison to Captain Marvel, Isis never quite took off (despite her ability to fly). This may be in part because Captain Marvel had decades' worth of printed comic book adventures from which to draw, both for stories and fans, whereas Isis was an original creation.

But as this episode of *Isis* clearly reveals, another key reason the immortal female heroine never matched her male counterpart were deficiencies in writing and production values. While neither series appeared to be expensively produced, *Isis* was as revealingly bare as star JoAnna Cameron's comely outfit, despite the actress' game attempt to bring a warm sense of likeability to her under-written role.

This episode—deceptively but deliberately called "Bigfoot"—is emblematic of the show's shortcomings. The bait-and-switch approach chosen by the producers (first suggesting there is an actual cryptid, only to reveal the suspected hominid is really a reclusive mountain man with a long beard and large feet) is disingenuous and defies credulity. It is never explained how the teenagers who clearly witness the supposed Bigfoot in the opening moments (an event that conveniently happens off-screen) fail to recognize the "beast" as human. Given the hermit wears a plaid shirt, overalls and large timber boots, it begs the question as to how they could even imagine such a person was a Sasquatch.

It is interesting to note, however, the great lengths the episode

goes to educate young viewers about the various theories and beliefs re: Sasquatch. An open door is left swinging widely for the possibility of an actual Bigfoot existing (or not), as no one (save the class clown, who predictably learns a lesson in humility by the end credits) dismisses the creature outright. Presumably this was crafted by writer Michael Reeves to lessen the disappointment of the suggested Sasquatch being revealed as a human being. Given the media frenzy surrounding Bigfoot during this time period, it's no wonder Reeves was disappointed when he pitched the original concept to the producers as a tale about the mysterious cryptid known as the Wendigo (a legendary Native American forest demon that was a distant relative of Sasquatch with a taste for human flesh) but was shot down. Arthur Nadel, the series' executive producer, wouldn't allow any additional fantasy elements to be introduced into the franchise, feeling that one fantastic element—Isis herself—was enough for the tyke audience to buy into. Reeves had been forewarned that this rule might sink his story pitch by his scriptwriting mentor Russell Bates (also a writer on the show), and so Reeves had the Bigfoot turn out to be a hermit. Nadel purchased the story on the spot once the creature turned out to be human in origin.

Alas, this minor effort to at least address the creature's relationship to the field of cryptozoology (which occurs in a lab scene between Isis in her human guise of biology teacher and the principal of her school, who lectures her about keeping an open mind to the reality Bigfoot) does little to alleviate this episode's inherent lethargy of pacing and lack of suspense. Production values are sub-par even by *Isis*' modest standards, and depictions of Isis' flying effect (a stock shot used in every episode, with little or no variation) consists of little more than an obviously off-screen fan blowing her hair to suggest flight. The visible, shaking matte lines framing Isis against a static sky are as unconvincing as the plot itself. As it exists, *Isis* initially capitalizes on its titular King Cryptid but completely capitulates midway through by revealing Bigfoot to be a human hermit, shrugging off the mantle of genuine Ciné du Sasquatch.

Jack Link's Beef Jerky *Messin' with Sasquatch* Commercials (2006) (TV)

Starring Sasquatch. Produced by the Carmichael Lynch Agency. USA. Color. Stereo. 30 Seconds.

Overview: Sasquatch just wants to be left alone, but no matter how hard the cryptid tries, pesky humans always stumble into his domain. Typically they do so while he's sleeping and pull cruel pranks on him. Other times the human interlopers bait him with Jack Link's Beef Jerky or other food and beverages. Always there is a pay-off involved, with Sasquatch the butt of the joke—that is, until Sasquatch has his revenge on the puny humans, using his enormous strength to wreak havoc and earn the last laugh.

* * * * *

One of the most successful ad campaigns in the last few years on television, apart from Geico's long-running Caveman ads, has been the Jack Link's Beef Jerky *Messin' with Sasquatch* series. By establishing a formula and mini-narrative from the very first 30-second spot (humans meet Bigfoot; humans prank Bigfoot; Bigfoot gets revenge), the makers of what are called "snack meats" in the industry have scored mightily. With annual sales totaling over $2 billion, Jack Link's ranks alongside Slim Jim as one of the most successful distributors of beef jerky products in a global market. It's a remarkable success story considering the company's creator, Jack Link, began the business selling out of the back of his pick-up truck in 1985!

The company was already a star on the rise prior to the *Messin' with Sasquatch* ad series; in fact, meat snack competitors often re-

JoAnna Cameron made a believable, winsome lead as the heroine *Isis*.

marked on the inexplicable success of the company, given that Jack Link's spent so little on product advertising. After the series, however, an entire mini-industry grew up around their forever-punked Sasquatch, including tee-shirts, a website that allows visitors to create their own Sasquatch videos, collectible merchandise, and so forth. Given that Sasquatch is a public domain character (meaning no one company can claim any exclusive right to use the character in a capitalistic venture, and can only copyright *their* distinct version of it), such success demonstrates the high public awareness Bigfoot enjoys among the general population. By carefully building upon that superstar status, the Jack Link's commercials cunningly exploit the built-in audience favorability ratings for Sasquatch and seamlessly associate their product with those sentiments.

Key to the success of the formula is establishing empathy for the picked-upon primate within the first 10 seconds of each commercial spot. By demonstrating the Benign Bigfoot aspect of Sasquatch's nature — i.e., the creature only wants to be left alone — and having intrusive humans take advantage of the cryptid to embarrass and humiliate him, the ad-makers cleverly manipulate the viewer's sense of fair play. The next 10 seconds of each spot furthers this sense of injustice by showing the callous humans laughing at their own deceitful natures, upping the desire in the viewer to see justice done. As a result, the final 10 seconds, in which Sasquatch exacts his revenge, not only works as comedy relief, but completes a deceptively sophisticated narrative that has been compacted into a half-minute's running length. As Stanley Kubrick once remarked about filmmaking, one can learn a lot about how to tell a story in 30 seconds from watching well-made commercials — a story is set up, characters are introduced, and a conflict is resolved. There are many Ciné du Sasquatch features in this guide that fail on all three counts; whereas each *Messin' with Sasquatch* ad captures these narrative basics (though to various degrees of success).

The suit design is crucial, as well. Although it owes a large debt to Rick Baker's Academy Award–winning design for *Harry and the Hendersons*, this Sasquatch has its own distinctive features. Chief among these are some rather sinister-looking beady eyes and canine-type fangs. While these work to comic effect when the beast is being taunted, they also add a moderate scare factor when Sasquatch goes on the rampage to right the wrongs perpetrated against him. The solid corporeal performance by the actor wearing the costume also makes this Sasquatch seem a dangerous cryptid, as one immediately gets the impression of enormous strength that is being self-restrained — until the hominid is bothered by some pesky human, at which point all bets are off. In this regard, Sasquatch is not unlike the Hulk character and his refrain "you won't like me when I'm angry."

The series began in 2006 with "Shaving Cream," wherein three male friends hiking through the forest discover a snoozing Sasquatch. After a brief exchange of amazed looks, the trio pull a prank on their new discovery: They squirt shaving cream into his open hand and then tickle his nose with a long strand of grass. Sasquatch swats at his nose, which splatters the shaving cream all over his face. The young men dash out of the forest onto a logging road, laughing at their cleverness. One stops to gather his breath, however, and before he can react, Sasquatch is upon him. Swinging his gigantic arm, Sasquatch sends the hiker flying across the road like a sack of feathers. The comical effect — enhanced by computer graphics to make the hiker soar like Superman after he's hit — cannot be rendered in words, but is truly hysterical. Comeuppance is served with a wicked right-handed swing, and a commercial star is born!

A web-only commercial was also placed on the Jack Link's website during this time — "Salt Shaker," in which two hikers see Sasquatch cooking wild game over a fire. One of them sneaks up on the unsus-pecting Sasquatch and unscrews Bigfoot's salt shaker without being noticed, which then predictably spills all over the roasting meat. Sasquatch pummels the hiker while his friend mouths "Asshole!" to the video camera he is holding to record the prank.

"Water Bowl" was another web-only spot, with a trio of hikers discovering Sasquatch asleep. They heat a pan of water and then stick the sleeping cryptid's fingers in the warm liquid. After a few moments, Bigfoot awakens to the sound of his own urine streaming all over his lower, off-screen legs. The hikers stumble away, laughing, one of them mumbling, "Where'd he go?" Before they can react, Sasquatch emerges from behind them, growling, and attacks. While it lacks the visual pay-off of the first effort, it nevertheless establishes the commercial series' theme of pranks and redemption.

In 2007 the company released "Pickup," which is in many ways the definitive summation of the series in terms of comedic impact and production values. Two friends are driving on a remote mountain road when they see Sasquatch. The solitary cryptid is strolling along, minding his own business, apparently lost in deep thought. One of the friends — a particularly smirking type — leans out the window and offers Sasquatch a friendly ride in their car, using a patronizing tone more fitting for a child than an 8-foot-tall Bigfoot. Sasquatch accepts the offer and moves to open the back door when the driver pulls away, leaving the enraged hominid to roar as he chokes on the car's dust. The friends laugh, and then the car once again slows. "Sorry, buddy ... hey, we're sorry," claims the smirker, again waiting for Sasquatch to join them as a hitcher. Again they pull away, laughing and sputtering, "Sorry, buddy!" as if it is the height of all witticisms. Suddenly a hairy arm thrusts through the front windshield. The relentless bully is savagely pulled through the window, hoisted high in the air, and then tossed into the forest by Sasquatch. An extended 45-second cut of this popular ad was also shown in which Sasquatch sits in the front seat after tossing the bully and bangs on the dashboard, demanding the driver continue with the journey. Once again the split-second timing and editing make the final pay-off hilariously funny.

Also in 2007 was the introduction of a web-only commercial called "Watch Face." This time, two friends encounter Sasquatch fishing with his hands like a bear in a wilderness stream. One of the two pranks Sasquatch by aiming his watch into the sun and bouncing the rays into the beast's eyes, blinding him. As they laugh, however, Sasquatch aims a caught fish and hurls it. It lands with a solid thud right in the watch-flasher's groin, and he doubles over in pain.

Yet another commercial entry was "Joy Buzzer," which featured a young couple (the first time a female is seen in the popular series) who stumble upon Sasquatch per the typical set-up. The boyfriend winds up a joy buzzer and offers a handshake to Sasquatch. Thankful for the kindly gesture, the cryptid screams in pain as the guy laughs, looking back over his shoulder at his amused girlfriend. The enraged Bigfoot grabs tighter and hurls the helpless hiker head-over-heels into the brush. His terrified girlfriend beats a hasty retreat, abandoning him.

In 2008, Jack Link's added to the canon with "Cold One," in which two golfing buddies witness a tired and hungry Sasquatch chasing a rabbit onto the golf course they're playing upon, only to give up when he loses the bounding hare. With a sly grin, one of the golfers offers Sasquatch a cold beer — but only after secretly shaking it. The beer shoots foam all over the enraged cryptid, and the two buddies drive away in their speeding golf cart, doubled over with laughter. Little do they anticipate the ferocity, however, with which an angry Bigfoot can react, which he demonstrates by slamming into their golf cart and sending them tumbling to the ground. An extended cut of this commercial features additional shots of the men taunting Sasquatch — who is unable to figure out how to open the can — and telling him, "C'mon, you can do it." Bonus footage from this ad also appeared on the website showing Sasquatch playing with a golf club and bouncing a ball up and down on it until he grows bored, as well as Sasquatch leaning against a tree and cuddling the rabbit he was earlier chasing, all the while parodying the gentle giant nature of the mentally-challenged Lenny character from *Of Mice and Men* (also parodied in the Bugs Bunny short "The Abominable Snow Rabbit").

Also on tap in 2008 was "Flaming Bag"— another internet-only ad in which three buddies discover Sasquatch's cave. They set alight a paper bag containing their own crap, drop it in front of the cave, and, as they scramble away, yell, "Ding dong!" Sasquatch emerges, surprised to find the fiery sack, and stomps it out, coating his infamous giant foot with feces. The human trio hop into their boat on a nearby lake to make their getaway, unaware Sasquatch is watching them from above on a cliffside. With a roar, Sasquatch throws a handful of his own scat at them, which splatters the chest of the main prankster.

Yet another commercial spot was "R.C." The title refers to radio control, as in the radio-controlled flyer a father and son are shown operating in the wilderness. When they spot Sasquatch, they dive bomb him in a funny homage to *King Kong*. Peeved by their insolence, Sasquatch makes a Tarzan-like call to a nearby hawk, which swoops down after the fleeing family. The father stops long enough to regret his decision when the hawk expels a torrent of fecal matter onto his shirt front. While still humorous, it is fair to say the campaign had reached its peak at this point, mainly due to the fact the formula and subsequent pay-offs are so predictable. It's a case of being so successful at realizing the pastiche that it no longer works, save as self-parody. As if realizing this, the company posted bonus footage from "R.C." on their popular website — MessinwithSasquatch.com — that showed Sasquatch swatting at the buzzing plane, à la *King Kong*, the video going to black & white, with vertical streaks running through it as if it were old film stock. Again the pay-off is less inventive, however amusing the production techniques.

"Towel Slap" was a web-only variation in which two couples are swimming in a lake when they observe Sasquatch crouching down, unaware of their presence, as the thirsty cryptid slurps water. One of the young men laughs and grabs a wet towel, sneaking up behind the bent-over beast. With a vicious snap, the man cracks Sasquatch across his derrière, inflicting a painful sting. While the man laughs it up, Sasquatch turns, grabs him by his swimming trunks, hurls him through the air and holds onto the trunks, thus sending the bare-assed bad boy naked through the air in front of his stunned friends.

Finally (as of this writing, at least), "Mud" features three off-road bike riders who encounter Sasquatch as he struggles to light a fire. They maliciously wait until he finally has his modest campfire going, and then one of the bikers deliberately skids into a pile of mud beside it. The mud splatters the fire, extinguishing it. The bikers ride away, laughing, but Sasquatch uproots a tree and tosses it at the culprit. The biker is thrown head-first over his handlebars and slams into a tree.

The series and website show no sign of losing their appeal, even if the formula has become tiresomely predictable. As if to keep the gold-mine open and thriving, the ad company behind the commercials has placed digital avatars of Sasquatch and assorted human pranksters online at their site and encourages visitors to download them and make their own *Messin' with Sasquatch* variations. After they're done, they can upload them to YouTube and other video-sharing websites — which, of course, is akin to free advertising for Jack Link's.

All in all, the *Messin' with Sasquatch* commercials have proven not only an exceptional success for Jack Link's, but an iconographic entry into the American lexicon itself. Although Sasquatch remains a sep-

arate, distinct cryptid on its own account, the phrase "Messin' with Sasquatch" is now ubiquitous in pop culture and has transcended its television set origins as surely as Bigfoot has gone beyond common folklore into a full-fledged media star.

Journey to the Center of the Earth (1993) (TV) (Cameo)

Starring David Dundara, Anthony LaStrella, Farrah Forke, Kim Miyori, John Nevillem Jeffrey Nordling, Tim Russ, Carel Struycken, Fabiana Udenio, Justina Vail, F. Murray Abraham and Francis Guinan. Produced by John Ashley, William Dear, Dale De La Torre, David M. Evans, Robert Gunter and Marvin Miller. Written by David M. Evans and Robert Gunter. Directed by William Dear. USA. Color. Stereo. 90 Minutes.

Overview: Professor Harlech believes he can uncover preexisting tunnels that lead to the center of the Earth if he can but build a machine that will dig deeply enough to connect with the natural subterranean infrastructure. Alas, during the maiden voyage of his nuclear-powered drill machine, the engine melts down and the launch ends in death and disaster. Years later the professor's nephew is undaunted, sure he can correct his uncle's minor mistakes and build a successful drill colossus. He does just that with the help of investors and drills down into the Earth's core. Along the way he meets a variety of folks who wish to join him aboard his exploratory drill tank, including a Yeti who is taught the human language after wearing an electronic thinking cap devised by the humans as a means of communicating with the mute Abominable Snowman. Yeti joins the crew as the drill machine sinks further and further beneath the Earth's crust in search of adventures unknown.

* * * * *

NBC initially flirted with making this 1993 adaptation of the Jules Verne classic an ongoing series. In fact, the two initial episodes were later edited together to form this solitary release when NBC quietly broadcast the two-hour television movie and just as quietly shelved it without further ado. Despite the misleading cameo by F. Murray Abraham as the progenitor of the entire adventure, most of the movie is a routine, dreary retread of overly-familiar clichés (as this Victorian-era SF genre has been overly-mined for decades to, with very few exceptions, equally dreary effect). With anachronistic dialogue and a ridiculous sense of science (which, problems aside, Verne at least attempted to address in his work with imaginings that were scientifically feasible for the times), *Journey to the Center of the Earth* was doomed to sink into a cinematic legacy littered with the bones of noble failures as well as crass exploitations, hovering dangerously close to the muddy bottom waters of the latter categorization.

The biggest problem is that the script is never very interesting. Hence, a lot of screen time goes by without much in the way of viewer excitement before the Yeti appears. The Yeti upstages all and helps erase a lot of the previous banality; but despite the charm of the costume and performer inside, there is simply not enough juice in the teleplay to rescue the already sunken premise. Still, the "Flowers for Algernon"–type instant-transfer ability to converse with human beings via the thought cap the Yeti dons (while completely unbelievable, as is all that has transpired to that moment in the movie) is at least fun, in that serious roles featuring a fluently speaking hominid are rare. Because the creators clearly intended this to be an ongoing series (this two-hour compilation even ends on an open note with the stalwart crew sinking deeper into the Earth's crust as the credits roll), it is equally clear they were intending to make the Yeti a major supporting player — hence the speech ability being so carefully set up in these opening episodes.

Talking hominids do pop up on occasion, especially in children's programming. But these are not very common, either, with a majority of films and TV shows portraying Bigfoot as a non-speaking, guttural-growling man beast. A hominid being able to communicate via speech is an always-controversial assertion, even when made by a qualified anthropologist; this is because it is rare to find a hominid skeleton so intact as to have the neck pieces present, let alone any vocal chords (as the fleshy organic matter decays too quickly for fossilization, unlike the slower decomposition of bone). It is a best-guess scenario until such time as an intact frozen hominid is found which can be dissected to better understand whether or not prehistoric men shared with modern humans the ability to speak, sing, and tell stories. There are some tantalizing clues about some of these mysteries, as with the cave paintings made by Cro-Magnons who clearly were utilizing their painted tableaux to convey their equivalent of the latest Hollywood widescreen epic; the paintings may have been designed in relief, in fact, so that a shaman could flicker the torches used to light the ceiling to create undulation in the image — not unlike a modern 3D movie effect.

Other than this Dr. Doolittle realization of a hominid, however, there is not very much original about *Journey to the Center of the Earth*, especially in terms of the Bigfoot film genre, nor is the execution so imaginative as to rise above the mediocrity of the storyline. It did mark director William Dear's second cinematic encounter with a hominid — the first being, of course, his mega-successful *Harry and the Hendersons* for Spielberg. Despite the warmth Dear brings to the Yeti character in this effort, it is a far cry from the budget and quality of even *Harry and the Hendersons*. Otherwise, alas, *Journey to the Center of the Earth* sinks beneath the crust and slowly descends to the bottom in every sense of the word.

Julius and Friends ("Yeti, Set, Go!") (TV) (2002)

Featuring the voices of Mikey Kelley, Christina Pickles and Jason Schwartzman. Produced by Tim Rummel. Written and Directed by Obie Scott Wade. USA. Color. Stereo. 4 Minutes.

Overview: Julius (Jason Schwartzman) the Sock Monkey and his kooky pals vacation on the ice powder to get in some much-deserved snowboarding. Alas, Julius winds up snowballing down the slopes in a near-avalanche with his bewildered friends following head-over-heels. Soon they're face to face with the legendary Abominable Snowman, who "seizes unwary snowboarders and grinds their bones in his teeth." The blue-horned, goateed Yeti, however, turns out to be a cream puff, all howl and no bite. Soon he's pals with his newfound friends, Julius and company. Hip to the fact they won't blow his cool, the Yeti offers them a ride on his back, and, as they hold tightly, the hominid slides down the slopes belly first, offering Julius and friends the best downhill run of their lives.

The *Julius and Friends* franchise is a gentle comedy of manners aimed at a young skill-set. But with Jason Schwartzman's warmly hesitant voice talent shining through in the title role, the series nevertheless wins over all but the most cynical of adult or child viewers. It's a rare, well-paced show, free of any obvious morals or badly-written lectures. Instead, a form of non-violent character conflict emerges as each character interacts with one another as friends in each new challenging environment they find themselves inhabiting from show to show. "Yeti, Set, Go!" is fairly typical of the Benign Bigfoot model — as befitting a children's series — codified to make Sasquatch a non-threatening entity who spiritually embodies a "watcher over the woods" folkloric role. Still, the artists apparently had fun with their version of a Yeti, which is much more akin to a

postmodern riff on Sendak's *Where the Wild Things Are*, with its striped shirt, devilish horns, and goatee on its pointy chin, than any usual white gorilla depiction. This hipster Yeti is decidedly *not* your Grandpa's Abominable, which again illustrates the transcendently fluid nature of the underlying Bigfoot archetype embedded within Ciné du Sasquatch.

KaBlam! (1996) (TV)

Featuring the voices of Julia McIlvaine, Noah Segan, Mischa Barton, Mo Willems and Danielle Judovits. Produced by Kevin Kay, Will McRobb, Robert Mittenthal, Chris Viscardi, Richard Winkler and Mo Willems. Written by Will McRobb, Robert Mittenthal, Chris Viscardi, Matt Harrigan, Mo Willems, Robert McNally-Scull, Michael Pearlstein and Krystine Kryttre. Directed by Mo Willems, Jesse Gordon and Mike DeSeve. USA. Color. Stereo. 30 Minutes.

Overview: When Nickelodeon television decided to introduce an entirely new line of animation series to its network in 1996, none was as beloved as *KaBlam!* Conceived as an anthology format in order to feature a variety of short segments, the show debuted in an era when the only true hit the network had under its belt was the mega-popular but controversial *The Ren & Stimpy Show*. While Comedy Central had *South Park*, MTV had *Beavis & Butthead* and Fox had *The Simpsons*, Nickelodeon was languishing behind these networks due to a kids-only perception among the critical teen male audience. Matters were not helped by the tonal changes that were mandated by executives on *The Ren & Stimpy Show*, which so infuriated creator John Kricfalusi he left the show in a well-publicized and acrimonious split.

Nickelodeon sensed the time was right to regain the foothold they had established but lost in the tussle with Kricfalusi. *KaBlam!* was the result. Hosted by two buddies named Henry and June, each episode featured the two crudely animated characters flipping through a comic book, appropriately named *KaBlam!* As they arrived at each new segment, a new mini-series would begin. Some segments were longer, such as the popular "Action League Now!" which was a forerunner of today's successful *Robot Chicken*, utilizing action figures as the protagonists. Others, such as the hilarious "Prometheus and Bob" segments — in which an alien named Prometheus lands in Earth's prehistoric past and tries to teach a caveman named Bob various methods of advancing the human species, to repeated catastrophic failure — were often less than a minute in length.

As the show's hosts, Henry and June have a small supporting cast of characters that would interact with them. Chief among these was a Mr. B. Foot. Mr. Foot is an easily provoked Sasquatch prone to losing his temper (but only at June and never at Henry). Though gruff and prone to violence, Mr. Foot is actually shown to be a cryptid with a heart of gold, as well as a great drummer when given the chance. He only spoke in one episode ("A Little Dab'll Do Ya"), choosing to otherwise express himself physically. Mr. Foot even helped his pals Henry and June work off some of the buddies' couch potato fat with the assistance of diet guru Richard Simmons in "Sasquatch-ercise."

Other character segments that appeared within *KaBlam!* included "Angela Anaconda," "Life with Loopy," "Sniz and Fondue," "The Off-Beats," "Randall Flan's Incredible Big Top," "The Brothers Tiki," "The Girl with Her Head Coming Off," "The Adventures of Patchhead," "Jetcat," "Race Rabbit," "Fuzzball," "Garbage Boy," "Emmett Freedy," "Stewy the Dogboy," "The Little Freaks" and "Dr. Worm." As the titles suggest, Nickelodeon was open to experimenting with an amazing amalgamation of animation styles, tones and viewer interests. Alas, not long after the series began (at least as far as *KaBlam!* was concerned), *SpongeBob SquarePants* debuted and became the sensation that Nickelodeon had always hoped to achieve with

KaBlam! but never had. The show limped along in the ratings but was soon cancelled.

Keeping the Watch (2006) (Doc)

Featuring Dan Jackson, M.K. Davis, Chanda, Carol Solomon, David Shealy and Lloyd Pye. Produced, Written and Directed by John L. Johnsen. Color. Stereo. 60 Minutes.

Overview: Former wildlife photographer John L. Johnsen turned videographer of cryptid phenomena wore all the production hats while making this non-skeptical look at the Bigfoot field of research — writing, producing, shooting, directing, editing, and even self-distributing. Designed for true believers only, *Keeping the Watch* is less about producing scientific evidence to convince cynics than simply allowing those who have had extensive experience in the field to present their own pro–Sasquatch viewpoints.

Highlights of *Keeping the Watch* include: Mississippi-based researcher M.K. Davis, best known for his extensive analysis of the Patterson-Gimlin footage, using digital enhancement techniques; Carol Solomon, a Florida resident who details the dead livestock she has found on her cattle property, along with Sasquatch footprints; contrasting views of the Skunk Ape by two different Floridians in the form of Dan Jackson, who claims to have abandoned his own field work after a horrific encounter with the swamp ape, and David Shealey, who leaves the impression of having perhaps hoaxed his information; Lloyd Pye, who gives insight into various world hominid sightings, such as the Alma and Orang Pendek; and Chanda, a young woman based in Illinois who wishes to remain surname-anonymous but believes her studies of Bigfoot's migratory propensity will change the world.

The filmmaker has also produced two other previous Bigfoot documentaries: *Hunt the Dogman*, an examination of cryptids in Kentucky; and *Spotlight On: The Patterson-Gimlin Film*, with the aforementioned M.K. Davis.

The Kids in the Hall (1989) (TV) (Cameo)

Starring Dave Foley, Bruce McCulloch, Kevin McDonald, Mark McKinney and Scott Thompson. Produced by Donna Aprile, Jeffrey Berman, Joe Bodolai, Joe Forristal, Lorne Michaels, Cindy Park and Pam Thomas. Written by Dave Foley, Bruce McCulloch, Kevin McDonald, Mark McKinney, Scott Thompson, Paul Bellini, Brian Hartt and Norm Hiscock. Directed by John Blanchard and John Paizs. Canada. Color. Stereo. 30 Minutes.

Overview: The popular Canadian series *The Kids in the Hall* was a Monty Python–esque comedy sketch show that was shown in America by both HBO and then CBS in a late-night run. In the second season, show number thirteen, a news parody segment called "Fact! Bigfoot" featured a female reporter who breathlessly leaned into the camera to scream, "It's a fact! Bigfoot has a wonderful singing voice!" Bigfoot is then shown singing an intense aria from an emotionally-charged opera. Afterwards, the reporter wipes her tear-stained eyes and shakes her head with awe. "Wasn't that beautiful?" Though ultra-brief as a cameo, the segment nevertheless produced laughs, as was par for the course for the often hysterical comedy troupe. Despite their series' cancellation, the group still performs live on stage and does occasional TV specials.

King Kong (1933) (Influence)

Starring Fay Wray, Robert Armstrong, Bruce Cabot, Frank Reicher, Sam Hardy, Noble Johnson, Steve Clemente and James Flavin. Produced by Merian C. Cooper, Ernest B. Schoedsack and David O. Selznick. Written by James Ashmore Creelman, Ruth Rose, Merian C. Cooper, Edgar Wallace and Leon Gordon. Directed by Merian C. Cooper and Ernest B. Schoedsack. USA. Black & White. Mono. 104 Minutes.

Overview: When film producer Carl Denham realizes he needs new thrills in order to distract the weary audiences of the Great Depression who consume movies as the ultimate form of cheap escapism, he decides to take a chance on a mythic creature as subject matter for his next adventure picture. Recruiting a starving young actress named Ann Darrow from the streets of New York to star, Denham charters a ship and heads for the foreboding, little-visited Skull Island, where the so-called Kong resides.

By reputation, Kong is a monstrous cryptid worshipped by the isolated human tribe who populate the island. Upon arrival, Denham, Darrow, and John Driscoll, one of the crewmen on the ship, lead a small reconnaissance team deep into the terrain of Skull Island, where they encounter the natives. Denham and company are transfixed by the towering wall the inhabitants have erected around their village, which cuts them off from Kong. The natives are transfixed by Ann Darrow, whose Caucasian features and blonde hair seem exotic to them. The Chief of the tribe attempts to barter for Ann, but Denham won't have it. They return to their ship and plot their next move. Alas, Ann is kidnapped by the islanders that night and offered in sacrifice to Kong.

Kong takes the screaming Ann Darrow and instantly falls in love with her. A gigantic hominid closely resembling a monstrous-sized gorilla, Kong is the ultimate alpha creature of the island, which is populated by dinosaurs and other prehistoric organisms which went extinct elsewhere in the world tens of millions of years ago. Denham and Driscoll return to the island, armed, to recover Ann, heading into the dangerous jungle in search of her and her captor. Along the way they battle various creatures, not least of which is Kong himself, who dispatches many of Denham's men when Kong catches them as they cross a treacherous ravine over a fallen log. Shaking the men off the log to fall screaming to their deaths below, Kong leaves the lone survivors — Denham on one side of the gulf and Driscoll on the other — to their fate. Denham, cut off from Kong and Driscoll, heads back to bring more men. Driscoll pursues Kong to his mountaintop cave.

While Kong is distracted after saving Ann from a pterodactyl, Driscoll rescues her. They dive into a river below and escape. Kong, enraged, follows. The humans scurry through the jungle, with Kong in pursuit. Just as the huge hominid makes his way into the village and destroys it in his frantic search for Ann, Denham and his crew lure Kong to the shores of Skull Island and bomb him with sleeping gas. Kong awakens in New York City, where Denham exhibits him like a circus specimen to a well-hyped Manhattan audience who've paid top dollar to witness the unveiling of "the Eighth Wonder of the World," as Denham has dubbed his prize.

Alas, the reporters ignore Kong's growls when the beast presumes their snapping of flash bulbs for photographs of Ann is a threat to his beloved. Believing her in danger, Kong breaks free of his restraints and goes on a rampage, destroying any and all who happen to cross his path. He derails a commuter train and tosses a woman he finds sleeping in her apartment, whom he mistakes for Ann, to her death when he realizes his mistake. Bi-planes are sent to strafe Kong, who has since found Ann and taken her to the top of the Empire State Building. Snarling in defiance, Kong snags a couple of planes and hurtles them into the building. Eventually, however, the pilots riddle his body with bullets. Swooning in his death throes, King Kong takes a final, longing look at Ann and topples over the edge, falling to his doom.

As the crowds mass around the bleeding hulk of Kong, someone remarks that it was the planes that got him. "Oh no," intones Denham knowingly, "'twas Beauty killed the Beast."

* * * * *

It's difficult to posit a cinematic icon more enduringly popular and universally beloved than the towering cryptid in *King Kong*. Worldrenowned, the subject of its own sequel, two major Hollywood remakes, and countless derivative cinematic knock-offs, *King Kong* is arguably one of the most famous motion pictures ever made in the history of the medium. From its classic but fairy-tale simplistic storyline, to its exquisite production design and groundbreaking special effects, the film is the epitome of transcendent narrative filmmaking at the height of its Hollywood powers. It was a record smasher at the box office in its era, and remains one of the most popular of the classic films ever released, still able to garner audiences whenever it is shown at revival screenings or on cable TV.

Likewise, it is impossible to imagine Ciné du Sasquatch without the impact of *King Kong*. While arguably outside the Bigfoot genre in technical terms, *King Kong* nevertheless is the single most seminal influence on hominid cinema, a strangely prototypical imagining of many of the staples that would later spin off and become Ciné du Sasquatch at its core.

In *King Kong*, the viewer is confronted with perhaps the ultimate mythological underpinning of all that would later be echoed in Bigfoot filmmaking: the unknown giant ape-like creature which is a fantastic blending of *Gigantopithecus* and *Homo sapiens*; the Carl Denham archetype of the Western "Great White Hunter" as exploiter of said hominid for material gain, regardless of the moral consequences and cost to human life; the beguiling human female which the hominid cannot ignore, even at risk of its own existence; the dominance of the creature in its own world until it encounters modern man as intruder, destroyer, and bringer of death; and the abject horror at confronting the Other and realizing in the end that it was but a nobler externalization of all that is within us that is dark, unexamined, and unrecognized. There would be variations and additions to all of these motifs in the Ciné du Sasquatch genre for sure, but none would ever mark it as deeply and as sustainably as *King Kong*.

Kokanee Beer Commercials (1992) (TV)

Commercials Produced and Directed by the Beakbane Marketing Agency. Color. Stereo. 30 Seconds.

Overview: Kokanee Beer is a product of the Columbia Brewery located in British Columbia, Canada. In 1992 the company hired Beakbane Marketing from Toronto to help broaden the beer's regional appeal into the Pacific Northwest of America, as well as nationally throughout Canada.

At first, a new label featuring the Kokanee Glacier was created by nature photographer Alec Pytlowany. Within each label a small representation of Sasquatch was hidden as a ploy to market an ad campaign similar to the popular *Where's Waldo?* children's books, with the concept asking, "Can *you* locate Sasquatch?" Concurrently, a series of television commercials featuring Sasquatch were produced and aired throughout the intended marketing areas. The campaign was humorous and enormously popular from the beginning, and the company even began to call their cryptid by the name Mel the Sasquatch.

Featuring a different slant with each new commercial, the Kokanee Beer spots soon became every bit the forerunner of today's Jack Link's Beef Jerky commercials, only produced on a more economical budget. Numerous spots were made and continue to be produced even to this day. René Dahinden, one of the foremost Bigfoot researchers in modern cryptozoology times, signed on for a year to be official spokesman for the brand. His best-remembered spot showed the tiny, plaid-shirted Dahinden sitting in a chair outside of his scenic Canadian wilderness home (which was a modest trailer permanently parked near a lake). As Dahinden is queried by the off-screen announcer as to what beer Sasquatch prefers, the oblivious Dahinden fails to notice his trailer is being ransacked by the hominid, who steals away with Dahinden's supply of Kokanee Beer.

Other spots had Sasquatch relaxing at home in his spacious cave and kicking back with a tasty Kokanee Beer, extolling the virtues of the brew. Yet another showed Sasquatch not only crashing a wedding party, but abducting both the bride and the ample stash of Kokanee Beer being served to the guests. More recent efforts parody Dahinden in a playful manner with a fictional Kokanee ranger portrayed by John Novak. The ranger is obsessed with discovering the whereabouts

King Kong as powerful archetype of hominid sacrifice. Note the cross motif recurrent throughout this shot: Kong's pose; the inverted crosses in the support tresses; etc. It became a familiar Bigfoot motif, as well.

The superior production values Kokanee Beer brought to the small screen is apparent in this publicity shot from one of their long-running Bigfoot TV commercials.

of Sasquatch, who he is certain is stealing the precious supply of Kokanee products. Of course, the thirsty hominid always thwarts the persistent Novak's efforts to stop him. After this series of spots ran its course, the company sponsored a "Should the ranger live or die?" website campaign which allowed Kokanee drinkers to decide the ranger's fate. Alas for the doomed crypto-hunter, he was voted "off the island" and met his match in a parody of the last episode of *The Sopranos*.

Sasquatch continues to appear on the bottles and cans of Kokanee Beer. The filmmakers of the pseudo-documentary *Hair of the Sasquatch* interviewed the cast and crew of a Kokanee Beer commercial while the Kokanee team was on location in Canada. The footage was included in *Hair of the Sasquatch* as part of the documentary portions of the otherwise fictional feature to demonstrate just how commercial Sasquatch has become in terms of exploitation, along with the various local variations on Sasquatch Inn, Sasquatch Burgers, and related tourist traps.

While the Kokanee Beer spots have never achieved the American notoriety and fame of the aforementioned Jack Link's Beefy Jerky equivalents, it's hard to imagine that they weren't a direct influence on the latter efforts, even if neither Kokanee nor Jack Link's were the first (or last) commercials to capitalize on Sasquatch.

As part of a long-running Bigfoot tie-in, Kokanee Beer labels sometimes featured hidden hominids. If you look closely at the mountain art, you may see a Yeti's face in the rugged snowscape.

Kolchak: The Night Stalker ("The Spanish Moss Murders") (1974) (TV)

AKA: *The Night Stalker*. Starring Darren McGavin, Simon Oakland, Keenan Wynn, Severn Darden, Randy Boone, Johnny Silver, Jack Grinnage, Brian Avery, Don Mantooth, Ruth McDevitt, Ned Glass, Virginia Gregg and Richard Kiel. Produced by Cy Chermak. Written by Alvin R. Friedman, David Chase and Jeffrey Grant Rice. Directed by Gordon Hessler. USA. Color. Mono. 60 Minutes.

Overview: Intrepid newspaper reporter Carl Kolchak investigates a series of homicides in which the victims are found with their chests crushed and Spanish moss strewn around their broken corpses. Suspicious that Chicago Police Captain Joe "Mad Dog" Siska is withholding information from his reading public, Kolchak digs deeper into the case, eventually uncovering a connection between the moss murders, a bayou monster, and a comatose patient.

The troubled patient has been undergoing a series of R.E.M. tests at a sleep research institute to better understand his mysterious condition. During the extensive periods in which he is unconscious at the center, he has been dreaming to life the so-called "Peremalfait," a Cajun swamp monster which enacts his vengeful fantasies for him against anyone who ever wronged him while he was awake.

Kolchak soon finds himself the target of the creature when it realizes the reporter has discovered its vulnerable human alter ego. Realizing no one will believe his fantastic story, and that he must now defend his own life without assistance, Kolchak invades the sewers beneath the city the monster calls home. Armed with a wooden spear carved from wood native to the monster's Louisiana origins, Kolchak destroys the beast, saving himself and sparing the metropolis from further slaughter.

* * * * *

While not a typical Ciné du Sasquatch entry, "The Spanish Moss Murders" nevertheless warrants inclusion in the genre because of the origin of the featured cryptid. Known by the Cajun immigrants who are the unwitting bringers of the beast to Chicago as the dreaded Peremalfait (as they call it in Louisiana), the swamp monster remains, despite the science trappings (the sleep research center and R.E.M. machines), a glorified Bigfoot.

There are some minor physical variations — it's covered by Spanish moss to better camouflage its movements in the bayous — but otherwise, as described by the Cajuns to Kolchak ("a wild man who predated our ancestors before they first settled the swamps" that "reeks of rotten flesh"), this is the same cryptid known in Florida as the Skunk Ape: an enormous, bipedal, hairy "wild man" who uses the swamps for transit. Even the use of Spanish moss is not unknown to the genre — *Return to Boggy Creek* later visualized its Fouke monster draped in the web-like substance.

The premise offered the producers of the popular if short-lived TV series a clever way to incorporate Sasquatch without having to remove Kolchak from the inner city setting which was as much a character as the hero himself. Using the sewers also reduced the implausibility of a rampaging monster failing to draw attention to its murder spree while surrounded by a teeming mass of humans. In this sense, "The Spanish Moss Murders" pre-dated many of the later Sasquatch-in-Suburbia movies, from the comical (*Harry and the Hendersons*) to the literal (*Suburban Sasquatch*). And though it is generally forgotten today, *The Snow Creature* from 1954 featured its Yeti escaping confinement in the foothills surrounding Los Angeles, becoming one of the earliest examples of this formulaic twist on Bigfoot in the Big City.

The TV episodes back story of a displaced Cajun community in Chicago — all members of which know of the Peremalfait (Creole for "Cajun Bad Man") — provides a believable context within which the patient can bring the monster to life through his dreams. In simplest terms, the creature represents the ultimate boogie monster of the man's heritage of oft-repeated folklore. It's therefore natural he would envision the beast while undergoing a nightmare, as it is authentic to his cultural roots.

The added twist (that the dreaming man is subconsciously projecting his darker side by externalizing the bayou monster) is reminiscent of the Dr. Morbius character in *Forbidden Planet*, who likewise brings to physical life the depths of his own repressed Id in an attempt to destroy those he believes threaten his daughter with her sexual awakening.

This Gothic play on the so-called "plastic visualizer," as used by Dr. Morbius, however, is never fully explained in "The Spanish Moss Murders." Kolchack theorizes that the sleeping suspect is the source of the Peremalfait, but in structural terms the theory is what Hitchcock called a MacGuffin — a deliberate misleading of the viewer with a red herring that goes nowhere but distracts from plot holes that would otherwise stand out. In this episode of *Kolchak: The Night Stalker* the MacGuffin directs attention away from the obvious questions (for example, why is a Cajun swamp cryptid in Chicago?) and towards the mystery of how merely dreaming of the beast brings it to life. It is a nifty parlor trick that doesn't obscure the show's basic conflict — Kolchak versus Sasquatch (by any other name).

Though frequently plagued by anemic teleplays and less-than-stellar support from the ABC network that produced it during its brief run, *Kolchak: The Night Stalker* had a loyal fan base and enjoys a substantial cult following to this day. Fortunately, "The Spanish Moss Murders" was definitely above average as far as entries went, and is fondly remembered by Kolchak enthusiasts. Partly this is due to the sudden, vicious attacks committed by the creature, which are unexpected in their urban locales. Equally powerful for visual horror is the sewer hideaway used by the Peremalfait; the black waters and scurrying rats create a claustrophobic sense of confinement akin to sequences in *Aliens*. In fact, the shot of the monster slowly rising from the fetid sludge is eerily like the alien beast that makes a similar entrance behind the little girl Newt in the Cameron film.

The bayou cryptid is portrayed very effectively by character actor Richard Kiel, the gentleman giant perhaps best renowned for his role as the steel-fanged Jaws in *The Spy Who Loved Me* and *Moonraker*, but who was equally a stand-out (literally) in minor roles on TV, such as *Star Trek*, and in films, such as *Butch Cassidy and the Sundance Kid*. Kiel also starred in another *Night Stalker* episode, as El Diablero in "Bad Medicine," and he posed for John Chambers for his infamous "Burbank Bigfoot" suit in the 1960s. Though his face is obscured beneath moss in "The Spanish Moss Murders," Kiel brings an imposing sense of physicality and cunning to the role that a lesser actor would have missed. This could not have been easy, given the confining nature of the costume and the water-filled tunnel setting of the tense confrontation finale. One can only imagine the dank costume's aroma after hours of shooting in waterlogged conditions on a claustrophobic set under hot studio lights. In terms of Ciné du Sasquatch, Kiel's cryptid is as well-acted as any in the genre's history.

Also making an extended cameo is character actor Keenan Wynn as the hardened police captain "Mad Dog" Siska, who's attempting to exorcise his explosive temper via courses in anger management. Of course, the badgering Kolchak (played to iconic perfection by Darren McGavin, replete with seersucker suit and porkpie hat) elevates Wynn's blood pressure whenever the two share a scene, as Kolchak gamely attempts to wheedle whatever information he can out of the apoplectic lawman.

"The Spanish Moss Murders" also echoes, with subtle understatement, the Native American belief sometimes associated with reported sightings of Sasquatch that the beast has a psychic ability to manifest

Kolchak (Darren McGavin) meets El Diablero (Richard Kiel) in TV's *Kolchak: The Night Stalker*. Kiel would also appear as a Skunk Ape in the following week's show "The Spanish Moss Murders."

itself and dematerialize at will, leaving no trace (save, in this case, a handful of moss). Though "The Spanish Moss Murders" couches this cryptid's ability to do so within the framework of a human's dreamlike phantasms, it nevertheless illustrates this seldom-spotlighted disappearing ability. It's easy to understand why most filmmakers avoid portraying the prescribed power — it makes the unexplained but natural hominid mystically paranormal, thus requiring the viewer to buy into the concept twice.

It's to *Kolchak: The Night Stalker*'s credit that it not only stretches Sasquatch boundaries in the aforementioned manner, but does so without destroying crucial suspension of disbelief. Credit goes to the cast, teleplay writers Alvin Friedman and David Chase (for their lean writing), and director Gordon Hessler, who directed many television movies, such as the notoriously campy *KISS Meets the Phantom of the Park*, and the cult features *Scream and Scream Again* and *The Oblong Box*. All in all, "The Spanish Moss Murders" ranks as one of the series' highlights for most fans, and that's not bad for a 50-minute piece of weekly hokum that often — but not in this particular episode — sank under its own illogical excesses.

Land of the Lost ("Ancient Guardian" and "Abominable Snowman") (1974) (TV)

Starring Spencer Milligan, Wesley Eure, Kathy Coleman, Philip Paley and Ron Harper. Produced by Sid and Marty Krofft. Written by Sam

Roeca and Peter Germano. Directed by Joe Scanlan. USA. Color. Stereo. 30 Minutes.

Overview: Rick Marshall and his two children, teenager Will and pre-teen Holly, are on a routine expedition mapping geological phenomena for Rick's scientific research when the greatest earthquake ever known opens a rift in the river they're navigating and plunges them 1,000 feet below into an alternative dimension known only as the Land of the Lost. In this non-linear time zone construct, ancient, modern, and futuristic elements are thrown together in a hodge podge of anachronistic disorder. The Marshall family encounter a strange mélange of otherworldly beings while they attempt to escape the confines of their metaphysical domain, including Pakunis (a small-statured hominid species), Sleestaks (a once intelligent race of half-human, half-reptilian beings reduced through savagery to an aggressive sub-species of their former selves), and a variety of dinosaurs who thrive in the jungle plateau setting.

* * * * *

The imaginative uber-realization of Sid and Marty Krofft's ultimate Saturday morning program, *Land of the Lost* lasted but three seasons but forever changed the genre of kid-level programming. Whereas their previous efforts, such as *H.R. Puf'n'Stuf* and *Lidsville*, had subverted the formal expectations of most romper room set creations with their bizarre acid-drenched sets and stoned characters, even the Krofft Brothers had played it safe within the expected boundaries of soft fantasy, inane plots, cheesy musical numbers, and outlandishly over-the-top acting styles. But with the dawn of *Land of the Lost*, the Kroffts dared do what no children's series had previously attempted (and few have followed): make an at once entertaining but serious-toned science fiction Saturday morning TV show.

While the results were often less than spectacular owing to the extremely modest budgets (which were pushed to the edge of the creative envelope by the show's imaginative scenario and reliance on special effects heretofore beyond the scope of such a tyke-oriented show), *Land of the Lost* nevertheless was a milestone for the era. Begrudging adult critics often admitted, in otherwise patronizing reviews, that the series deserved credit for its ambition alone, and

the intended viewer demographic appreciated the show's complex mythology, surrealistic storylines, and attempt to treat them as intelligent rather than moppets to be bombarded with endless sugary cereal commercials (not that such advertisements didn't surround the show during commercial breaks, of course). It would have a profound impact on many Generation X fans of the series, leading them into a lifelong interest in such Fortean phenomena as UFOs, parallel dimensions, unexplainable mysteries, and hominology — all owing to the inclusive nature of the show's approach to such subject matter.

While only two episodes explicitly dealt with Yeti — "Abominable Snowman" and "Ancient Guardian" — the regular appearances by the mythic Pakuni tribe (consisting of Cha-Ka, Ta, and Sa) firmly established the idea of bipedal hominids from the show's first episode. Remarkably, the Pakuni were portrayed as diminutive pre-humans with a simple but fluid language, the ability to make tools, and the general tendency to act like humans circa tens of thousands of years prior to our ascent. Unlike most such cryptids, the Pakuni were not simply uttering stage gibberish, à la the typical *Tarzan* treatment of non-whites, but speaking a language created for the original series by Victoria Fromkin, a linguist who based her Pakuni lingo on the Kwa language of the West African tribesmen. In fact, "Pakuni" means "people" in the Kwa lexicon. Fromkin eventually established over 200 hybrid words of part–Kwa/part-invention for the Pakunis to speak, which gave their dialogue an added charm. Many were the children watchers of *Land of the Lost* who later imitated the lingo owing to its real-life emphasis on consistent word choice, strangely nasal intonation, and ante-penultimate stressing of certain vowels. In short, it was a language that became recognizable to frequent viewers as being as such, with the Pakuni never violating the rules of their own verbalizations. This is quite a feat for a children's series of any era, let alone as early as 1974, when the show debuted on NBC.

Much of the credit for the show's earliest success lies with science fiction writer David Gerrold. In a 2005 interview conducted by writer Valerie Kuklinski for the *Daily News* of Los Angeles, Gerrold claims he basically created the entire concept based on a series of science fiction images from various paperback and comic book covers cut and pasted onto a large presentation board by Sid and Marty Krofft, each image containing key artwork as to how they wanted the series envisioned. An entertaining and expansive world of fantasy, science fiction, and even mild horror was thus brought to life with an internal consistency and logic that feels much the same as similar mythic worlds created by Frank Herbert, J.R.R. Tolkien, Edgar Rice Burroughs, and other renowned fantasy writers. Whereas most shows, even in the adult realm of science fiction and fantasy, of the era played fast and loose with the rules of reality (as well as their own internal consistency), *Land of the Lost* promoted the idea that each week's newest show would follow and build upon the complicated mythos of the previous week. In this manner, each new episode offered novelty via a new plot or characters, while building upon its larger story are on a far grander scale. This had never before been attempted by a kid-oriented television show (and, as previously mentioned, very few adult ones either).

To foster this vision, Gerrold brought aboard many fellow science fiction writers to bolster the series' credentials as an alternative

The cheesy video matte lines visibly present were part of the inherent charm of Sid and Marty Krofft's outrageous *Land of the Lost*.

to the usual ghetto of children's fare. Among them were truly accomplished and well-respected authors, such as D.C. Fontana, Larry Niven, Norman Spinrod, Theodore Sturgeon, and Ben Bova, some of whom were working in the field of teleplay writing for the first time in their careers. While Gerrold would ultimately depart, owing to the usual "creative differences" with the Kroffts (doubtless arising from the complexity of storylines he insisted on utilizing, not to mention atypical demands for quality writers), during *Land of the Lost*'s first season, the concept was self-sustaining and proved durable even with the subsequent and inevitable watering down of his brilliantly flexible scenario in subsequent seasons.

Besides the Pakuni, another bipedal crypto species was introduced in the third season of *Land of the Lost*. These were basically Abominable Snowmen that were shown to be the protectors of the Altrusians, the former Sleestak ancestors who were intelligent, could talk, and were basically similar to the human species — but in bipedal lizard form. The Yeti beings were called Tapa and Kona, and were left by the Altrusians high in the mountains where the Altrusians kept their vast reservoir of accumulated knowledge in the Library of Skulls. Because the Altrusians believed their knowledge was dangerous to most who would possess it, they deliberately kept Tapa and Kona in the mountain fortress as guardians to insure no one lacking the intellectual ability to outwit them would ever possess the sacred Library's secrets.

The Yeti guardians — who served a similar purpose and were probably based upon the Yetis in the *Dr. Who* series, save for being flesh and blood rather than cybernetic — were first encountered by Holly in "Abominable Snowman," in which her magical unicorn vanishes and she enlists Cha-Ka's help to find it. Cha-Ka and Holly follow the trail until it vanishes in the frozen wastelands of the mountaintops near the Library of Skulls, which Holly knows to be forbidden to her and the Marshall family because of Enik's, the talking Altrusian Sleestak, warning. But determined to find her unicorn, she ventures into the icy caverns, only to come face-to-face with a guardian Yeti named Tapa, who traps them, per its instructions. It falls upon Rick and Will Marshall to rescue Holly from the Abominable Snowman's grasp.

In "Ancient Guardian," the Marshall family takes a Sleestak totem from the icy caverns where the Abominable dwell, little realizing it is the magical item that prevents the Yetis from descending from their caves and roaming the valleys. When Rick Marshall figures out that Kona, another Abominable guardian of the Library of Skulls, doesn't want his family as hostages except to restore order, he insures the stolen totem is restored to the Library of Skulls, thus also insuring the protective Yetis do not escape ever again.

The realization by Holly that the Snowmen are not aggressive by nature, but only because they are charged with an important task by their taskmasters the Altrusians, changes her and her family's perception of the hominids entirely. No longer afraid of the cryptids, but realizing they serve a vital role in the overall balance necessary to maintain their habitat, the Marshalls learn that even frightening elements of the Land of the Lost must be seen in their overall context in order to gain any understanding as to their rightful existence. Though heavy-handed, it's a motif recurrent in Ciné du Sasquatch and points to the show's prefiguring of both *Return to Boggy Creek* and *Harry and the Hendersons* in terms of the increasing cinematic and television acceptance of a Benign Bigfoot in temperament (versus a Savage Sasquatch by mere default existence).

The actual creature costumes are about par for the Krofft course. The hominid's arctic white fur suit is fairly convincing, but the manner in which the full-head mask covers the actor and droops down with a clearly visible separation between the head and shoulders renders the illusion transparent. The mask resembles a ski mask with open eyes and nose, with facial makeup that is unconvincing. Still, as low-budget Abominable Snowman realizations go, the genre has seen much worse.

The Kroffts were doubtless impressed with the favorable reaction toward *Land of the Lost* in terms of cryptid usage, and it was instrumental in their decision to launch *Bigfoot and Wildboy*, yet another successful human and hominid pairing by the Kroffts. So culturally impactful was *Land of the Lost* that it was remade in the 1990s, and later as a theatrical movie in 2009, although neither the TV remake nor the movie captured the serious undertone and imaginative likeability of the original. Given how much was stacked against *Land of the Lost* in 1974 when it was launched in terms of diminished expectations, it is a testament to Gerrold, the Kroffts, and the entire production team behind the series that it succeeded as well as it did, forever altering the landscape of children's programming.

LandSAR Commercial (2009) (TV)

Produced by Phil Liefting and Film Construction, Inc. Directed by Nic Finlayson. New Zealand. Color. Stereo. 30 Seconds.

Overview: Dave is backpacking in the New Zealand mountains when he slips and falls. Disoriented, he hangs upside down, his hands bloodied. A huge Yeti arrives, gently scooping him up and carrying him to safety. The Abominable Snowman builds the injured hiker a roaring campfire that night to protect the human from the elements and drapes him in a wool hide to keep him warm. Leaning over, the Yeti says, "Dave, there's no such thing as a Yeti." Dave awakens, still in his injured position from his fall, and realizes he needs to call LandSAR (Land Sea and Rescue) by tapping 911 on his cell phone, which is within easy reach.

* * * * *

This clever, extremely well-produced commercial spot is at once moving and comical in the best tradition of successful public service announcements. The expressive, massively bulky Abominable Snowman suit is one of the best ever designed, and the director takes great pains to keep its visibility brief to sustain believability. The soaring music that accompanies the panoramic helicopter-filmed shots of the Yeti carrying the injured hiker while the two crest the snow-covered mountaintops is truly great, as is the sudden payoff punch line when the Yeti leans into a spooky, fire-lit close-up and announces to the startled man he's merely dreamed everything. While cryptid fans may be a bit miffed by the implied message, the execution is so wonderfully imaginative that it is clear the producers have a soft spot for their hominid star, whether they "want to believe" or not. Look for this highlight in the long history of Ciné du Sasquatch commercials on the Internet.

Legend Hunters ("Bigfoot") (2007) (TV) (Doc)

Featuring Jim Lansdale, Ken Gerhard, Chester Moore, Derek "Bamm Bamm" Snell, Lynn Johnson and Lee Hales. Produced by the Travel Channel. USA. Color. Stereo. 60 Minutes.

Overview: On the border of West Central Louisiana exists a 400-plus acre reserve known as Monster Central. So-named because of the numerous sightings of Bigfoot within the rural acreage, the area is favored by Southern cryptozoologists because of its easy access and private ownership by one Jim Lansdale, who is also a participant in the GCBRO (Gulf Coast Bigfoot Research Organization).

The Travel Channel's resident monster experts (aka the Legend Hunters) travel to Monster Central to investigate for themselves. Ken Gerhard and Derek "Bamm Bamm" Snell, monster hunters, embark from Houston, Texas, and travel deep into the Louisiana thicket in search of "Wooly Boogers" (a local Bigfoot moniker). There they interview Lynn Johnson, who claims to have seen a Wooly Booger in the Monster Central area in the 1990s. Also interviewed is Shawn Gregory, who relates how he's seen two different hominids over the years in the region, as well as Jim Lansdale, who relates how he and his son had their own encounter with Sasquatch on a rural road that runs through the mossy woods.

Along with Jim Hales, the team sets out to install motion-detection cameras in the trees in hopes of snapping digital images of a Bigfoot. A rifle-armed Chester Moore declares he will not settle for merely snapping pictures of a smiling Sasquatch, but will bag Bigfoot with a bullet in order to convince skeptics. He then vanishes into Monster Central in search of his prey.

Alas, nothing comes from the adventure save some scintillating details about former encounters and sightings. Lansdale shows a couple of typically indecipherable photos, taken earlier, that show a blurry figure which may or may not be Bigfoot. Audio recordings of what several research members believe are "Bigfoot vocalizations" are made; but lacking any proof as to the origins of the cries, their sounds remain inconclusive. Also shown are crude teepee structures which some believe are made by the Wooly Booger as a form of temporary shelter, though no DNA or hair samples are found or collected. Additionally, several witnesses claim to have found "tree sculptures" (limbs bent in weird positions at heights difficult for a human to reach) that indicate Bigfoot's presence (at least to believers). Lastly, unidentified scat is found in a large pile, though, again, no genetic testing is presented afterwards to indicate whether or not it is from a known species or something more mysterious.

While technically okay, *Legend Hunters* suffers from a case of the "overly familiars," in that it offers very little one hasn't encountered in numerous TV shows dedicated to such phenomena. The less-than-serious tone doesn't add veracity either, at times making the amateur monster sleuths appear decidedly self-deluding. While this is all probably encouraged and staged by the filmmakers to enliven footage of grown men wandering through the woods without much conflict, it detracts from the only real novelty at hand: the fact that Monster Central remains so relatively unknown in the Ciné du Sasquatch genre, in either documentary or dramatic form. Given the enormity of the area, the number of documented sightings, and the ease of access, one would hope and believe the definitive Monster Central doc is yet to be created. The potential far outweighs the results to date.

The Legend of Bigfoot (1976) (Doc)

Starring Ivan Marx and Peggy Marx. Produced by Ivan Marx, Don Reese and Stephen Houston Smith. Written by Paula Labrot and Harry Winer. Directed by Harry Winer. USA. Color. Mono. 92 Minutes.

Overview: Ivan Marx, a pro tracker of wild game turned quasi-professional wildlife cinematographer, uncovers mounting evidence that Bigfoot is real. Despite taking 16mm footage of Sasquatch he considers beyond critique, scientists and skeptics alike dismiss his movie as a poorly-staged hoax.

Enraged but undaunted, Marx sets out to prove his personal theory that Bigfoot is a migratory animal. By roaming the Pacific Northwest and filming as many locations as he can where Sasquatch has been reported as active, Marx pieces together the puzzle of how and why the hominid makes the annual trek from the Northern California redwoods to the Alaskan wilds.

Determined to document his findings with filmic evidence, Marx and his wife Peggy drive to Alaska. They set up camp and await their proof. Sure enough, a family of Bigfoot creatures soon appears and allows Marx to freely film them. Convinced he has now proven his theory, the cameraman returns to the lower states to exhibit his evidence to skeptics. But will they believe?

* * * * *

Ivan Marx was once considered a legitimate Sasquatch hunter going back to the 1950s before defrauding several serious cryptozoologists with his now discredited "Cripplefoot" hoax film in the early 1970s. But by the time Marx self-produced *The Legend of Bigfoot*, he was clearly bitter about the entire experience. This is borne out by the strident tone he maintains throughout this amateurish production, if not the cynical nature of the film's bogus "Bigfootage" as well. By insisting any skeptics are simply fools and all believers are saints, Marx is his own worst enemy in winning converts to his cause. Passionate viewpoints are one thing, blind dogma presented as sacrosanct fact quite another.

The more radically Marx insists there is no conceivable way his theories re: Bigfoot could possibly be wrong, the less the objective viewer is inclined to exhibit anything but justifiable skepticism. After all, science is distinguished from dogmatic faith by a central tenet. To wit: A scientific theory can be, and often is, proven wrong (to the embarrassment of the theoretician); whereas faith need never fear such revelation, as it is based upon unassailable *a priori* belief. While it is true many scientists hold onto cherished theories well beyond popular acceptance, Marx's hatred of anyone with learned credentials undermines his overwrought argument. So much for the merits of maintaining an open mind, Marx seemingly implies.

Nothing of what is blandly presented in *The Legend of Bigfoot* would be as risible as it ultimately plays had not Marx so flagrantly exploited his legitimate background and friends, shamelessly capitalizing upon their sincere research (often at great cost to themselves out of pocket). One such serious cryptozoologist was none other than Peter Byrne, who has spent decades studying the phenomena at great personal cost. According to Byrne, Marx was a salaried employee for only three months at Byrne's influential California Bigfoot Project when Marx suddenly, miraculously photographed *and* filmed a Bigfoot. Skeptical but hopeful, Byrne agreed to a deal wherein he would advance $25,000 to Marx for exclusive rights to the 16mm film and photographs if Byrne was able to authenticate the footage and photos. The original, sealed can of 16mm film was delivered unopened (by legal agreement) to Byrne's lawyer until the authentication process could be completed. When Byrne and his fellow associates quickly determined the footage was faked, they paid a visit to Marx's rented tar paper shack home to question him about the matter, only to find that Marx and wife Peggy had hastily departed ahead of them. When Byrne's lawyer opened the sealed can of original film he possessed, it turned out to be spliced footage from old Disney cartoons! Undeterred, Marx would surface again five years later with *The Legend of Bigfoot* to further capitalize upon the cryptid, only this time as a self-identified expert.

That Marx purports to have been a skeptic, if not outright disbeliever, early in *The Legend of Bigfoot* (factually incorrect, given his extensive prior background research and his earlier involvement in scamming Byrne), only to undergo a sudden, miraculous conversion a few scenes later, strains the almost nonexistent credulity. It has all the hallmarks of a planted "sinner" who spontaneously admits the error of his ways at a religious tent revival, even as the collection plates are hurriedly passed among astonished attendees.

This "bait and switch" approach is ludicrously delivered by Ivan Marx in the opening minutes of *The Legend of Bigfoot*. After being told by cattle farmers that ongoing mutilations of their herd is the result of Sasquatch, and having earlier been told of the creature by Native Americans claiming its existence, Marx derisively retorts:

"Bigfoot? I'd had about a belly full of *Bigfoot*!" Marx has his own encounter with the creature shortly thereafter, which he recreates cinematically with an extended run through the woods from his own point of view, heavily shaking the camera, with nary a cryptid in sight. Now convinced (and convinced the viewer is, too), Marx sets up his Bolex camera and soon records a limping Bigfoot, which Marx attributes to the beast having polio.

The footage is truly mind-boggling in that Marx could've conned anyone, especially himself, into ever believing his so-called "Cripplefoot" film would survive even the most casual of scrutiny by any objective viewer. He sorely laments: "And the so-called 'experts' tried to dismiss my film as a hoax. What did these so-called 'experts' really know?" Perhaps not much, but at least enough to disregard the phony evidence Marx insists is incontrovertible.

Working himself into a frothing tirade, Marx blasts these skeptics: "I'd show *them*!" He calls them on the carpet, explaining what hypocrites they were for denouncing his footage and then profiting on it by showing it on their lecture circuits. This may be the most ingratiating commentary he offers — that his faked footage would be used as a visual aid for anything other than a skeptics' convention for cheap laughs is difficult to imagine. One wonders how these lecturers obtained copies of Marx's film if they did not pay him for 16mm prints in an era before inexpensive video duplication. A more likely scenario for Marx's evident disenfranchisement is that he missed the gravy train, à la Roger Patterson, who actually did make money on the lecture circuit for a while showing his more credible film. Marx includes his widely discredited footage without explanation as to why the viewer should go against the condemning tide (perhaps with profit as the motive, as it serves as cheap padding to stretch *The Legend of Bigfoot*'s running time).

This theme of money resurfaces constantly throughout the production. While in Northern California, Marx and his wife Peggy film themselves strolling across the magnificent driftwood beaches. In contrast to the imagery, a wretched Marx intones with angst that "money was running out, and *fast*!" How, he wonders aloud, will he ever get the Sasquatch footage the world has been awaiting if said economic hardship continues?

Marx never posits the plight of the creature nor the possibility he may buy additional film stock at some future date. One would hope a true believer such as Marx claims to be would not frame the admittedly difficult task he's set for himself in financial terms only, however dire his money troubles. And yet as Marx shows himself driving through the western U.S. in his sputtering VW Bug in supposed search of the elusive hominid, the underlying seediness of his low-rent venture is as apparent as his threadbare Bigfoot costume. Combined with his incessant whining about a lack of production funds, it brings the probable underlying motif for *The Legend of Bigfoot* to the forefront: a desperate attempt by Marx to cash in on Sasquatch one last time. Alas, even though this effort is self-revealing in this aspect, Marx would twice more dip into the well he already self-poisoned with two additionally suspect documentaries.

The ridiculous nature of *The Legend of Bigfoot* never abates. As soon as the couple arrive in Alaska and set up their modest tent, they naturally feel they're being observed by some unseen entity. Marx grabs his camera and films two glowing orbs in the distance, which he immediately attributes to Bigfoot. More astute viewers will likely conclude they are large photoflood lights, as they hover unevenly and vary in distance and height from one another. Unless the cryptid in question had severe ocular strain, the more likely scenario is that Marx or his wife was holding aloft photofloods, as this is much closer to what is portrayed in the footage — despite Marx's narrated protests to the contrary.

Marx does great disservice to any credibility he hoped to establish

with *The Legend of Bigfoot* by endlessly repeating shots wherein he has clearly set his camera on a tripod and walked slowly away from it, often vanishing into a wooded area. While this occasionally provides some scenic relief from the tedium, it also clearly shows a very pronounced limp in the filmmaker's gait. By showing himself over and over (surely becoming the most filmed backside in all of Ciné du Sasquatch), he emulates the bad magician who repeats his trick until all present have figured out the secret.

In terms of sheer economy, this "set up and shoot" approach works well, in that Marx can literally self-produce most of the film's scenes without additional help (as he appears to have done in most scenes, apart from his wife's occasional acknowledged assistance). The problem, of course, is that after seeing Marx's trademark gait (akin to a poor man's John Wayne), it doesn't take analysis of the Zapruder film level to notice that Marx's footage of Bigfoot employs the same stiff-legged stride as the filmmaker himself. So while some have maintained that his wife Peggy wore the gorilla suit while Marx filmed the efforts, the cinematic evidence seems more likely to convict Marx himself as the cryptid performer.

His associates were correct to be wary. The real legend behind *The Legend of Bigfoot* is that Marx "borrowed" heavily from them, provided less than stellar footage, and then vanished shortly thereafter without bothering to repay his "loans" to anyone. Worse yet, having such a once-prominent cryptozoologist reduce himself to the level of parody set back all serious researchers in the field, as Marx's shenanigans cast a long shadow over everyone he left holding the empty bag. The fact Marx later became a mentor to infamous Bigfoot "researcher" (read: profiteer and known hoaxster) Tom Biscardi doesn't add to Marx's legacy either. Undeterred by ridicule from his former associates, Marx went on to co-produce two more equally ludicrous Bigfoot exploitation features: *In the Shadow of Bigfoot* and *Bigfoot: Alive and Well in '82*.

There is occasionally scenic footage worthy of watching in *The Legend of Bigfoot*, and Don Peake's eerie, plaintive score elevates what is otherwise beyond redemption. Peake also later scored Wes Craven's *The Hills Have Eyes* and *The People Under the Stairs*. Likewise, first-time director Harry Winer (which at first seems like a good pseudonym for the perpetually bitching Ivan Marx in his pathetic Bigfoot costume — a truly "hairy whiner") went on to forge a respectable career directing sitcoms on television. But on balance, and even including the talent behind the camera (Marx excluded), only a rube would fall for Marx's carny-esque schtick, which in terms of veracity and placement within Ciné du Sasquatch is a bona fide sucker's bet. Campy laughs aside — and there are plenty for the less critical viewer — *The Legend of Bigfoot* is truly a heaping helping of steaming Sasquatch scat.

The Legend of Boggy Creek (1972)

Starring Vern Stierman, Chuck Pierce Jr., William Stumpp, Willie E. Smith, Lloyd Bowen, B.R. Barrington, J.E. "Smokey" Crabtree, Travis Crabtree, John P. Hixon, John W. Oates, Judy Baltom, Mary B. Johnson, Phillip Bradley, Dennis Lamb, Loraine Lamb, Glenn Carruth and Bunny Dees. Produced by L.W. Ledwell, Charles B. Pierce and Earl E. Smith. Written by Earl E. Smith. Directed by Charles B. Pierce. USA. Color. Mono. 90 Minutes.

Overview: A grown man reflects on his childhood spent in the small Southern town of Fouke (pronounced "Fowk"), Arkansas, and the supposed monster that haunts the region. He remembers how, as a youngster cutting through the deserted fields at sunset, endangered he felt whenever he heard the lonely wail of the creature in the distance.

The residents of Fouke, many playing themselves, recreate for the camera their personal encounters with the so-called Fouke Monster. According to local folklore, the Fouke Monster travels by way of the meandering Boggy Creek, which surrounds the tiny town and offers the creature easy access to the nearby human population. Almost like the creek itself, there is a natural ebb and flow to the sightings, which are as mysterious and unexplainable as the creature — some years pass without any encounters, while others are filled with unnerving contact between men and beast. Unfortunately for the citizens of Fouke, the ferocity of attacks seems to increase every time the Fouke Monster returns from its long absences.

After many suspenseful recreations of Fouke townspeople witnessing the frightening cryptid, the film concludes with a particularly grueling night siege in a small trailer home. Several young married women spend time together in the home, where one is nursing her newborn child, while their husbands are away at work on the night shift. First there is a harrowing moment wherein the young ladies attempt to load an empty shotgun as the Fouke Monster stumbles along the outside of their house trailer, searching for a way inside. As the gun shells fall to the floor amidst the chaos, the women work themselves into a screaming panic. The husbands return to find their wives shaken, and are understandably upset. Seeking revenge, the men lay down a barrage of "suppressing fire" around the cabin's perimeter, shooting at anything that moves. Finally, the Fouke Monster makes a surprisingly resilient last-stand lunge, grabbing one of the men and forcing him to smash through the cabin's front door in order to escape the vice-like grip of the creature. In shock, the families carry the man to the local emergency room, and all vow never again to set foot anywhere near Boggy Creek.

* * * * *

No amount of criticism leveled against Charles Pierce's filmic output — and the sheer number of less than favorable reviews could fill volumes — have kept his one bona fide "monster"-piece from achieving box office gold and revered status among Ciné du Sasquatch fans. *The Legend of Boggy Creek* made over $20 million during its original release (when major Hollywood fare often didn't gross as much), created a mini-series of sequels, and was a progenitor of much of the cryptid cinema that followed in its soggy footsteps. Without its financial windfall, there very likely would not have been follow-up films like *Sasquatch, The Legend of Bigfoot; Creature from Black*

Lake; The Revenge of Bigfoot; Screams of a Winter Night and *Shriek of the Mutilated*. All owe a huge debt to Pierce's seminal trailblazer — if not for subject matter then certainly for establishing independently-shot, non-actor docudramas made in regional locales as being able to make money rivaling any other genre in the 1970s, including biker films, kung fu epics, and the usual plethora of vampire and werewolf flicks.

In no uncertain terms, *The Legend of Boggy Creek* also redefined Ciné du Sasquatch, transforming the genre's geographical association from primarily one of a Yeti/Himalayan context to a more familiar Bigfoot/North American vantage point. This was particularly potent and new to the Bigfoot genre — instead of a distant location and foreign culture, filmmakers were suddenly free to exploit inexpensive American locales and public domain folklore. As a result, the commercial potential of the average Ciné du Sasquatch feature became much more expansive and economical to produce, and much more likely to find a target audience who had heard about legendary hominids in their own areas of the country and were eager to see them visualized in motion picture format, most for the first time ever.

It is not that other films (such as *Bigfoot*, starring John Carradine) hadn't tried this approach prior to *The Legend of Boggy Creek*. But these efforts typically made the mistake of keeping their approach distinctly Hollywood in tone and execution: cheap sets, obvious

Charles Pierce (center, back to camera) directs the final cabin siege on location in rural Fouke, Arkansas, in this rare behind-the-scenes still from *The Legend of Boggy Creek.*

A young hunter encounters *The Legend of Boggy Creek.* Pierce was a master of using off-screen space and depth of field, as this promotional still enlarged from an actual film frame vividly demonstrates.

Griffith Park locations, B-movie casts, etc. The genius Pierce demonstrated with his bayou epic was to shoot in his home state of Arkansas and take advantage of the scenery (most of it rarely, if ever, featured in Hollywood filmmaking, thus imbuing the production with an exotic flair). Another prescient stroke was having the actual witnesses to the Fouke Monster recreate their own personas instead of hiring actors to do so, which gives the accents and weathered faces a sense of verisimilitude so often lacking in the West Coast dream factory's efforts in this genre. In an era where "reality television" is pervasive, it is perhaps difficult to remember there was once a time when such techniques as handheld cameras, non-professional "actors" and existing locations were considered a radical departure from the usual studio approach of anchored cameras, professional actors, and meticulously-lit sets. So radical was it, in fact, that this methodology was called *cinema verite* and considered nearly *avant garde* if utilized in any production save one originating in France and directed by Godard or Truffaut. In a strange way, then, it was Pierce's blending of these then–New Wave techniques with the classical docudrama format that provided *The Legend of Boggy Creek*'s impact for 1972 viewers.

Arguably only *The Abominable Snowman* and *Harry and the Hendersons* have had such an effect on Ciné du Sasquatch. The earlier Yeti film did so by creating the most believable and atmospheric entry up to that time; the latter Bigfoot film revitalized the genre by sweeping aside the Savage Sasquatch figurehead and making the Benign Bigfoot a viable commercial concept. What *The Legend of Boggy Creek* did — besides scaring the hell out of an entire generation of 1970s cryptid cinema kids — was to bestow a kind of Mark Twain "tall tale" quality on the genre. Pierce updated Twain's Huck Finn into Travis Crabtree, the boy who can hunt and fish without adult supervision in the resplendent Arkansas bayou even though he's barely of age. Like Huck, Travis is the embodiment of the all–American nature boy, as unshakable in his sense of pioneer integrity as the Fouke Monster is of being the alpha male in its own dark domain. They are like cinematic doppelgangers of one another: Travis Crabtree represents all that is pure and innocent about the snaking Fouke River; the Fouke Monster all that is ominous and threatening. This offers a way into the material that few other cryptid filmmakers ever perceived prior to *The Legend of Boggy Creek*— as a kind of American folklore rendered incarnate — though it would quickly be absorbed and rendered into a filmic cliché by so many subsequent Bigfoot films (including *Return to Boggy Creek* itself) that it would lose its impact.

Though lovingly photographed by Pierce utilizing a Techniscope widescreen format (which enabled filmmakers to shoot two frames for every one on the original negative and thus economically double their footage during the processing phase), *The Legend of Boggy Creek* does have many technical deficiencies. Some scenes are woefully underlit, particularly in the night-for-night encounters. The choice Pierce makes to keep the creature at the periphery of the frame (via telephoto lenses) is deft however, because it allows him to shift focus rapidly from one visual plane to another, often to devastating effect when he suddenly reveals the Fouke Monster lurking unnoticed in the murky foreground or background space. Audiences of the era were constantly put on the edge of their seats with these kinds of shock "rack focus" cuts, which Pierce would make a hallmark of his style in later works such *The Town That Dreaded Sundown* and *The Evictors*.

Pierce also intelligently keeps the creature costume mostly out of view, which, given that in its brief screen appearances it appears to be the usual gorilla suit, adds suspense that earlier films in the genre, such as *Bigfoot* (1970), lacked. With the hominid always photographed in soft focus tantalizingly out of the range of crystal sharp vision, the viewer is left to conjure mental images of what the beast truly looks like, which heightens involvement. It's safe to say that Pierce got his money's worth from the unique poster design, in that the audience brings the terrifying image of the Fouke Monster slithering out of the river, silhouetted against a rising full moon, into the theater with them. While no such scene appears in the actual film, Pierce's clever marketing and use of this salient image to brand *The Legend of Boggy Creek* made it as ubiquitous in the cinemagoers' minds as the image of the huge shark on the poster for *Jaws* (which is so out of proportion to the young lady it is about to devour that it would be, as depicted, a 100 feet or more in length!). It's a pretty good sleight-of-hand trick, given that both films rarely show their antagonist with much clarity. Herein the audience is almost subconsciously implanted with an image of horror and then mercilessly forced to visualize it over and over again (lacking any onscreen variant); the effect is like a version of filmic post-traumatic stress disorder, in which a painted image supplants the projected one and forces the watcher to undergo a continuous frightening re-experiencing of the initial shock. Low-budget filmmakers should take note, even if most directors rarely have the kind of creative influence over the poster's design as did Pierce and Spielberg.

All of this may strike the first-time or non-critical viewer of *The Legend of Boggy Creek* as so much "heady film talk," especially for what is generally perceived to be a simple, technically-primitive exploitation film. But all of this and more is there for anyone willing to critically examine Pierce's groundbreaking film and admire what lurks below its murky surface, so to speak. In no uncertain terms, *The Legend of Boggy Creek* is the ultimate example of a "shaggy bog" story triumphing over limited means and oft-dismissed subject matter. In recent Bigfoot genre films, such as *The Long Way Home: A Bigfoot Story* and *The Wildman of the Navidad*, the influence of Pierce's enduring work is lovingly reflected in homage; but its more subtle, long-lasting impact can be seen in virtually any post–*The Legend of Boggy Creek* film made that features a Savage Sasquatch motif.

The Legend of Desert Bigfoot (2005) (TV)

AKA: *The Last Chance Detectives: The Legend of Desert Bigfoot*. Starring Ryan Calhoun, Crystle Lightning, Davin Jacob Carey, David Netter, James T. Callahan, Brian Frejo, Raymond Guth, Sherry Hursey, Don Jeffcoat, Alan Johnson, Steve Kanaly, Kevin Kraft, Peg Stewart and Jody St. Michael. Produced by Stephen Stiles. Written by Robert Vernon and Douglas Lloyd McIntosh. Directed by Robert Vernon. USA. Color. Stereo. 53 Minutes.

Overview: Four youngsters in Ambrosia, Arizona, pattern themselves after the Hardy Boys and Nancy Drew (or perhaps a devout version of Scooby Doo and company), using passages from the Holy Bible to spiritually guide themselves as they set about trying to solve local mysteries. In "The Legend of Desert Bigfoot," an old-timer in their community named Eli Patterson claims to have been attacked by Bigfoot on his desert property. Other campers in the popular recreational area claim to have been frightened by the same hominid around their campfire, while still another trailer home resident has circumstantial proof that his double-wide was attacked by the creature while he was inside, praying to God to spare his life.

Intrigued, the four junior detectives set out to prove or disprove the sightings. At first no one takes them seriously, but their sincere Christian tenacity wins their cause over to others in their small community who are impressed by their spirit of adventure. After interviewing the various people who have seen the creature, Jake — the lead detective — is convinced the only way the group will ever encounter the cryptid is to lay in wait for it along a suspected pathway it utilizes for travel. Meanwhile, Jake rescues a dog that is near dehydration from the mean-spirited Eli Patterson. Patterson has left the poor canine near death and muzzled outside his trailer home. Convinced he's doing the right thing to save the dog's life, Jake takes the dog to the vet without Patterson's knowledge. Indeed, the vet confirms the worst: Had Jake not done as he has, the animal would have soon died. The vet agrees to nurture the dog back to health, whereupon Jake will return the dog to Patterson.

Back on the trail, the four kids share with one another a Christian perspective on the trials and tribulations they've endured on their latest adventure. Jake feels he may have sinned by rescuing the animal and asks his mother her perspective. Indeed, she confirms, Jake has disobeyed God's commandment that "Thou shall not steal." Far better, she tells her distressed son, that he should have never stolen Mr. Patterson's dog and instead left its fate up to God, who is in charge of all. Jake does precisely this, and then returns to the group as they finally have their unexpectedly poignant encounter with Bigfoot.

* * * * *

The Last Chance Detectives series of books are Bible-based children's mysteries published by Tyndale House Publishers, who specialize in Christian-themed tomes. This filmic adaptation was produced by Focus on the Family, whose website states as their mission: "To co-operate with the Holy Spirit in sharing the Gospel of Jesus Christ with as many people as possible by nurturing and defending the God-ordained institution of the family and promoting biblical truths worldwide." As one might expect, the messages of each story tend to be forefront and not disguised in any subtext, as is best exemplified by the subplot in *The Legend of Desert Bigfoot* when Jake rescues a dog from an abusive owner but is later informed by his mother he has done a sinful thing because — no matter the justification — he has gone against the expressed will of God by breaking one of the Ten Commandments.

Herein lies a problem with the production that many will find difficult to morally justify and others downright repulsive: Even though Mike has been told by the vet that the stolen dog would have died without immediate help (the cruel owner, Mr. Patterson — note the surname — has deliberately muzzled the dog and refused to offer the pet water in the desert heat), his mother's admonishment is taken to heart by the boy and validated by the filmmakers. This is not just objectionable as a lesson, but seems contrary to what many Christian followers would say is lawful, given that such mistreatment of animals by their owners is illegal in most states in America. Arguably, of course, Mike should have only called the local animal enforcement authorities to report Mr. Patterson's actions and hoped for the best outcome. But because the vet to whom he takes the animal confirms Mike's worst fears — that the dog would've died in a matter of hours had Mike not acted as he did — all but the most ardent supporters of so-called "tough love" philosophies will question why Mike is condemned as the sinner when Mr. Patterson is without a doubt an animal torturer. Thus the viewer is left to ponder which is worse — to steal an animal which is being slowly tortured to death by its owner, or allow such a heinous act of cruelty to occur in order to keep faith with God's ordained commandments?

Of course, this moral dilemma is supposed to be the heart of the story in and of itself: that no matter how we might view the actions of others, God's plan for us all prevents any of us from taking His laws into our own hands for any reason, even the salvation of a mistreated pet. But contradictorily, *The Legend of Desert Bigfoot* attempts to have it both ways, for had not Mike rescued the dog, there would be no dog over which a moral dilemma could be argued. In essence, Jake would have died, and the subplot — which is really the film's main plot minus the Bigfoot cover story — would have been for naught. By arguing, as Mike's mother does, that Mike committed a worse "crime" by stealing than the old man did by torturing his dog

to near-death (she insists Mike should have simply trusted God to handle the matter for all concerned), *The Legend of Bigfoot* firmly places itself in a camp most secular viewers will find as morally objectionable as more conservative Christians find it justifiable.

While it would be easier to dismiss this kind of harsh religious perspective if the overall production were not so anchored in Biblical maxims, as it is, *The Legend of Desert Bigfoot* is awash in such perspectives. Again, for some this will make the production all the more delightful, offering as it does a morally correct, Judaic perspective on lessons learned, while others will find it heavy-footed, so to speak, and insufferably immoral. Indeed, despite Focus on the Family's stated goal to "model for our children how to humbly follow the teachings and spirit of Jesus at home and in the community," *The Legend of Desert Bigfoot* feels much more at home wandering Moses' parched deserts of uncompromising moral absolutism in search of the promised land, or Abraham's requirement by Yaweh to unquestionably sacrifice his son Isaac, than it does with the more forgiving aspects of stewardship stated by Jesus in the New Testament, who admonishes against cruelties to animals in the gospels of Luke and Matthew, and warns about the vanity of animal sacrifices.

The Legend of Desert Bigfoot is well-produced on a modest budget and acquits itself well in terms of the cable airings on Christian networks by delivering the requisite content of faith-based teachings. However, the fact that the Southern Poverty Law Center cites the producing organization, Focus on the Family, as a known hate group might give pause to most Ciné du Sasquatch fans who do not share the film production company's strongly held anti-gay bigotry. Among other gay-bashing activities (according to the SPLC website), Focus on the Family has proposed that gay people are "diseased perverts" with a stated program to molest children and demolish America; they have distributed pamphlets falsely alleging that gay people were much more likely than others to be serial murderers, child molesters, and intentional disease-spreaders; and the organization spends an average of $130 million *per year* at their 47-acre campus in Colorado to combat both women's rights issues and the "homosexual agenda" they claim is rotting America's spiritual core.

Given such a pedigree, one wonders if all but the most ardent Christian extremists would want to consider *The Legend of Desert Bigfoot* as anything more than dogmatic propaganda. It offers zero insight into the themes, motifs, and central tenets of the genre of Bigfoot films, supplanting them instead with a discriminatory religious zeal for True Believers who seem bent on enforcing a doctrine of self-stated "dominion" (i.e. the non-separation of church and state in America, where only white males rule). Of course, it's little wonder the film never seriously considers cryptozoological phenomena; it which would be contrary to many of their followers' convictions, as they're equally at war with Darwinian Evolution. Given Focus on the Family's radical political agenda, one suspects (with at least some supporting evidence in the production of *The Legend of Desert Bigfoot*) that the use of Bigfoot was merely a convenient hook for a more classic Jack Chick–styled, bait-and-switch tactic to enrapture followers and hopefully gain converts. While it is not the first example of an entry in Ciné du Sasquatch exploiting the hominology phenomena for self-evident financial gain, it is certainly one of the more noxious, and the only known example of a fictional Bigfoot film to offer religious salvation in exchange for human and humane intolerance.

The Legend of Grassman (2010)

Starring Max Meyer, Matt Funke, Jeidy Melendez, Stephan Meyer, Jory Moore, Rich Shevchik and Dennis Meyer. Produced by Dennis Meyer and Tyler Meyer. Written by Dennis Meyer. Directed by Tyler Meyer. USA. Color. Stereo.

Overview: After a mysterious attack on a home in rural Ohio, a group of hunters and cryptozoologists head deep into the woods, hoping to find proof of what they believe is responsible — the legendary Grassman, Ohio's elusive Bigfoot. When they encounter the cryptid, they must fight their way out, one-by-one, as the creature kills them to keep its existence secret.

* * * * *

In post-production as of this book's publication, *The Legend of Grassman* is an action-adventure–styled horror effort shot on location in Ohio. Independently lensed on a low budget, it concentrates on the classical "enter the woods and get out alive" scenario so frequently seen in Ciné du Sasquatch. Based solely upon the previews posted on the filmmakers' blog, *The Legend of Grassman* looks to be a fairly moody telling of the Buckeye Bigfoot tales, complete with a convincingly bulky and sinister-looking cryptid costume apparently modeled upon the classic creature seen in the Patterson-Gimlin film.

The Grassman is relatively obscure in terms of Bigfoot cinema, with most movies focusing on Sasquatch in the Pacific Northwest, the bayou Bigfoot of Louisiana, and the Skunk Ape of Florida. The only other fictional feature using the Grassman exclusively was the 2006 version of *Bigfoot* directed by Bob Gray.

The Legend of McCullough's Mountain (1976)

AKA: Blood Beast of Monster Mountain; McCullough's Mountain; The Legend of Blood Mountain; Demon Hunter. Starring George Ellis, Erin Fleming, Edward Yastin, Ernest D'Aversa, Glenda Brunson, Cheryl Goldberg, Wanda Lee Hunt, Linda Faye, Mary Nell Santacroce, Zenas Sears, Peggy Dorris, Virgil Hopkins, Donn Davison, Florence Doolin and Sarah Pablecheque. Produced by Don Hadley and Frank Winecoff. Written by Bob Corley and Donn Davison. Directed by Massey Cramer and Donn Davison. USA. Color. Mono. 76 Minutes.

Overview: There is a legend about a certain mountain in Georgia inhabited by a killer Bigfoot. According to over a century of local oral history, 100 people have ventured to the top of Blood Mountain (aka McCullough's Mountain) and never been seen again. Only traces of blood splattered across the lonely crags are ever found; no bodies have ever been recovered.

After a series of local sightings of the Mountain Monster, an intrepid newspaper copy "boy" (actually well into his middle-aged years) named Destoink Dooley convinces his editor to allow Destoink to cover his first-ever assignment — an exposé of the legendary creature. The editor scoffs at Destoink's preposterous belief in said cryptid, but allows him to report on the subject — provided Destoink does it on his own time and without pay. Destoink thanks the editor by accidentally knocking over the editor's treasured box of Cuban cigars and stepping all over them as he tries to retrieve the expensive smokes. Later that night Destoink dreams of his worldwide fame at having broken the story and his editor's newfound appreciation and gratitude, as well as becoming a lady's man as a handy by-product.

The next morning Destoink hops in his 1930s convertible automobile and races to McCullough's Mountain to interview locals who have seen the monster. But he finds few willing to go on record about the Blood Beast for fear of being ridiculed by outsiders and dismissed as cranks. Finally, with the help of a friendly merchant, Destoink makes contact with the Doctor, an "outlander" (as the cloistered locals refer to any not born in the area) who has spent the last few years studying the mountain's peculiar geological features. Although the Doctor scoffs at the idea of a living simian of unknown origin, he does relate several tales of the creature's supposed reign of terror to Destoink over dinner, even as the learned man of science dismisses

them all as so much local superstition. The Doctor's servant insists the stories are true; he only laughs at her.

But when his own comely research assistant is abducted by the monster from Destoink's convertible after they narrowly avoid hitting it, even the Doctor finds himself wondering if he's been too rash in his skeptical dismissals. Before the local law enforcement can render aid, Destoink and his old friend — now a game warden — are reunited in a feverish hunt for the Bigfoot. The warden shoots the Sasquatch, causing it to drop the abducted research assistant and run for its life. The woman's bloodied body is recovered, and the grieving Doctor realizes that with key eyewitnesses — Destoink and the game warden — as well as the body before him, he can no longer deny the existence of the Blood Beast.

A search party is hastily organized. Because Destoink carries no firearm, he is left behind in a flimsy cabin with the Doctor's daughter to guard her safety. While Destoink searches the game warden's vehicle for a weapon, however, Bigfoot attacks, forcing Destoink to take action (despite his own cowardly nature). Using a portable flamethrower he finds in the game warden's trunk, he douses the roaring monster in flames. The fiery hominid staggers over the edge of the mountain and plunges to its death. The survivors gather and watch the burning body with relief and a sense of dread ... are there more of the creatures in the mountains, or has Destoink killed the only one?

* * * * *

The Legend of McCullough's Mountain is a truly amazing entry in the annals of Ciné du Sasquatch. In the 1976 release edition (reviewed here), it is an amalgamation of Bigfoot terror movie, regional yokel comedy, and pseudo-documentary of the *In Search Of* variety, with a self-billed "world traveler, lecturer, and psychic investigator" host, Donn Davison, who interviews alleged witnesses of the McCullough's Mountain Bigfoot first-hand. The resulting mish-mash of old footage mixed with talking head–styled reportage by Davison is awful — and yet intermittently entertaining in a grade–Z manner for patient viewers of camp.

The history of the movie alone is as mind-boggling as reports of any Sasquatch. The film was originally produced as *The Legend of Blood Mountain* in 1965. In its initial incarnation, it was a very typical regional film created to be shown in the Southern movie theaters of America. Producers of such regional fare (others include Bill Rebane in Wisconsin, Earl Owensby in North Carolina, and Larry Buchanan in Texas, to name but a few) would maintain strict budgets, with an eye towards rapidly recouping their films' costs on fast turnarounds via theatrical releases, most often in only a few hundred theaters. By cycling the same handful of 35mm prints from one theater circuit to the next until all potential display venues were exhausted, such novelty films attracted enthusiastic local audiences. These efforts remain largely and sadly unknown to many film fans, even those with tastes in the esoteric and B-movie category, because many were not distributed beyond their initial limited theatrical release dates and never saw subsequent light on VHS or DVD. Never acquired by Hollywood studios for distribution and rarely released abroad, many remain invisible even to this date, save for Internet websites and magazines such as *Psychotronic* or *Shock Cinema*, which are devoted to such obscure schlock filmmaking.

As *The Legend of Blood Mountain*, the film is actually not a Bigfoot movie per se, but simply a classic monster movie of the generic variety. The creature was originally depicted as more of a phantom bogey creature along the lines of the Mothman, featuring insect-like double tails on either side of its man-like form, a strange cornucopia resembling a giant beehive atop its head, protruding, wild eyes, and a dark stretch-leotard body suit. Referred to as the Blood Beast and Mountain Demon throughout in the 1965 version, these references were later altered in the 1976 incarnation to capitalize upon the Bigfoot craze. In the 1976 version, Donn Davison filmed himself interviewing various witnesses to the creature who claimed they saw Bigfoot. All shots featuring the former Blood Beast from the 1965 version were crudely edited out and replaced with several stock shots Davidson hastily (though rather eerily) filmed of a Sasquatch silhouetted against a perpetual bank of fog. These shots endlessly repeat throughout *The Legend of McCullough's Mountain* (retitled as such to play upon Charles B. Pierce's successful *The Legend of Boggy Creek* franchise) whenever the original, shoddier Blood Beast appeared, resulting in a schizophrenic feel to the film. Weirdly, the newly-photographed scenes are often technically better than the original footage, which results in the occasionally effective new Sasquatch inserts adding impact to an otherwise tedious viewing experience. Whether or not the improved technical quality is the result of the remade version utilizing an inferior print of the original 1965 film rather than the 1965 version's negative is, however, impossible to gauge. Suffice it to say that neither version—1965 nor 1976—is technically proficient beyond a merely acceptable level.

As a narrative in and of itself, *The Legend of McCullough's Mountain* is a cliché all Ciné du Sasquatch fans will recognize from its stock ingredients: the reluctant townfolk wary of city slickers who might ridicule their stories of the creature; the skeptical scientist who insists the tales are but local superstition; the intrepid reporter determined to get to the bottom of the story; the pretty women who offer little reason to be there save to become the inevitable victim when they go sunbathing or swimming; and the monster which attacks with no discernible motive save sheer viciousness. Still, the outlandish, near *Hee Haw* guffaws rendered by George Ellis alone in the lead role as the overweight buffoon Destoink Dooley elevate the dismal amateur level of acting to low-brow vaudeville, reminiscent of Lou Costello on a non-budget. Wearing spats, a purple blazer, and a porkpie hat (as well as driving a vintage 1930s convertible automobile), Destoink is like a stylish character straight out of *Lil' Abner*, at once a dandy *and* a nincompoop. Saying he's the stand-out amidst the cast of self-conscious "amateur night in Dixie" thespians surrounding him is indeed faint praise, but at least whenever Destoink is onscreen the film has a schlocky, likeable tone. One is thankful he is able to offer a variety of facial expressions and voice inflections; the rest of the cast are as monotonous in their mask-like visages as they are monotone in their dialogue delivery.

There is a reason George Ellis as Destoink acquits himself well. By no means a stranger to show business on the regional level, Ellis hosted a Saturday morning children's television show in the Atlanta area wherein he portrayed none other than ... Destoink Dooley! So in many ways, the original version was created rather craftily to capitalize upon the show's success and name recognition, not to mention the opportunity to advertise on the series itself ("See Destoink in his new feature motion picture, kids!"). Reportedly produced for $750,000 (a not inconsiderable sum for the era for a regional picture), *The Legend of Blood Mountain* had an initial run of approximately 450 Southern theaters on Saturday matinees and grossed $1.5 million before it was retired from distribution. For its time, this was a considerable success, and even with costs deducted, the filmmakers must have felt they'd hit a small jackpot.

Lacking additional outlets in an era before videocassettes and whatnot, Ellis and his partners left well enough alone, save for occasional rentals of the film to television (where its G-rated nature and lurid title doubtless made for easy programming). Ellis and his brother retired from production and turned to running an art house movie theater in Atlanta, which introduced many patrons to films they would have otherwise never seen in a time when cable and DVDs were still a generation away. Then, in the 1970s, Donn Davison and

his California partners purchased the rights from Ellis' company with the intent to remove all references to a blood monster and replace them with Bigfoot. To help pad the running length of the newly-rechristened film—*The Legend of McCullough's Mountain*—Davison acted as an "on the scene" reporter and had himself filmed interviewing various locals as they described their encounters with Sasquatch. These so-called "real life" witnesses seem dubious at best and obvious local amateurs at their worst. Most offer about as much authenticity as an Ed Wood playbill.

Additionally, Davison hosted an introductory sequence wherein he explains that Bigfoot sightings are both a historical fact and worldwide phenomena, citing examples of the Russian Alma, the Himalayan Yeti, and the Canadian Sasquatch, among others. Lurid paintings of red-eyed Bigfoot cryptids are intercut with Davison's spiel, until he finally explains that the film to follow is fictitious but factually-based (a ludicrous assertion, given the outlandish, cornpone nature of the Destoink Dooley sequences that follow).

Davison was no stranger to exploitation filmmaking. A former national Yo Yo champion and professional stage magician, he was adept at pulling off no-budget miracles in the indie film arena. Perhaps best known for his Fortean pseudo-documentary *The Force Beyond* (which "examined" such phenomena as psychics, UFOs, Bigfoot and the Devil's Triangle), he also produced, directed and/or starred in such drive-in fare as *Secrets of the Gods*, *Honey Britches*, *Moonshiner's Woman* and *She Freak*. He also ran the XXX-rated Dragon Art Theater in California and was a producer for Edward Montoro's notorious Film Ventures, Inc. Davison was never short of work, acting as voiceover talent for low-budget exploitation film previews, radio spots and even filmed promotional shorts hawking "How To" sex manuals which were sold to gullible audience members in the lobby after watching "actual birth footage" movies (luridly bad films that inserted clinical birth scenes in order to skirt legal objections to on-screen nudity). It is safe to say that when Mr. Davison billed himself as a "world traveler" he was at least half right—surely few filmmakers ever traveled in as many shady worlds of business and hucksterism as he did throughout his amazing, patched-together career!

Davison's portrayal as himself in the movie is never less than jaw-dropping; he asserts, for example, that there can be little doubt of Sasquatch's existence and infers the more likely explanation for the lack of scientific evidence is that scientists are engaging in a hush-hush conspiracy to keep the public from a state of shock should they discover the Truth. As if to prove his point, he tells the story from Teddy Roosevelt's hunting memoirs in which two fur trappers encounter Sasquatch, leaving one of the men dead. Davison's telling is deadpan until he grows excited recounting how the hunters "smelled the *smell* of a rotten *smell*." Still, at least it can be said Davison admits his epic is merely a recreation; which is more than can be said for Ivan Marx's *The Legend of Bigfoot* released the same year, in which the cynical Marx expects the audience to believe his badly-stitched ape costume is actually a real-world cryptid specimen.

As previously mentioned, the movie's Sasquatch suit is for the most part well-filmed. Davison wisely chose to keep the fog machine pumping and the back-lighting dramatic, which silhouettes the creature and highlights its furry outline. One problem with the reshoot approach, however, soon becomes apparent: There are never any master shots of the main characters interacting with the Bigfoot. Rather, Destoink reacts to something off-screen, and then the editor cuts to the newly-photographed shot of Sasquatch, and then the film cuts back to more reaction shots of Destoink. While the technique becomes obvious after a time, it should be fairly noted that Davison's sleight-of-hand as a magician must have been a plus in assisting the film's editor in pulling off an entire feature in this manner.

The melodramatic musical score is a stock library selection that reminds one of endless 1950s creature features that sported the same cues. The newly created 1976 version features an opening theme song sung by Tim York with an obvious tip of the hat to Pierce's *The Legend of Boggy Creek.* At one point the curious lyrics state: "Some say he breathed fire like a dragon/Some say he's a giant ape with a human soul." One is struck by the anomaly of comparing Bigfoot to a fire-breathing dragon—an image definitely not present in the film!

In whatever version the Ciné du Sasquatch lover sees *The Legend of McCullough's Mountain*—whether as the original *The Legend of Blood Mountain* or the later Davison redux incarnation *McCullough's Mountain* (shortened for promotional reasons)—be forewarned: The film is as difficult to track down as any legendary Bigfoot. And though it is no lost masterpiece, it quaintly captures the 1970s Sasquatch frenzy as a nostalgic time capsule.

The Legend of Sasquatch (2006)

Featuring the voices of William Hurt, John Rhys-Davies, Jewel Restaneo, Blaire Restaneo, Joe Alaskey, Brian Cummings, June Foray, Lance LeGault and Frank Welker. Produced by Bill J. Gottlieb and William Hurt. Written and Directed by Thomas Callicoat. USA. Color. Stereo. 74 Minutes.

Overview: When John, Kristy, and Maggie Davis move as a family into a cabin in the mountains near Seattle, Washington, young Maggie soon discovers a cave that is home to a family of Bigfoot creatures. At first scared of the cryptids, owing to their horrifying reputation, Maggie soon learns they are gentle, loving bipedal hominids who merely want to exist and persist—just like her own family. Never harming any humans, and good stewards of their environment, they become worthwhile companions and play friends for Maggie, especially Baby Sasquatch, with whom she forms a deep bond.

Alas, a new dam being built in the area threatens the Bigfoot clan's cave, promising to sink it underwater. Having lived in the caverns all their lives, the creatures are understandably concerned that their entire way of living is threatened. The hominids turn to Maggie and her human family for assistance in protecting their habitat, but can the Davis family stand in the way of larger corporate interests and maintain the status quo of the secret Bigfoot tribe's way of life? Or will the successful construction of the dam doom the creatures to exposure and exploitation by humans as sideshow media freaks?

* * * * *

One can feel especially uncharitable when reviewing such a well-intentioned effort as *The Legend of Sasquatch* and concentrate on its flaws rather than its merits. On balance, its appeal is very limited to the youngest of audiences and their patient parents. There are a variety of reasons this is so, but the main one is that it's simply noneventful for the most part, despite the high caliber of talent involved. In a word, it's surprisingly dull.

The main drawback for all but the first-grade set is the limited computer animation. Given that William Hurt and John Rhys-Davies were involved (with Hurt even a co-producer), one would have hoped the animation company would have perhaps set the bar a bit higher than what amounts to some very average technique. Largely stiff and devoid of movement, most of the characters are posed in shots rather than moving within them, which creates a stilted effect. Another problem is that the design favors a pseudo–*South Park* look. The figures are generated as if to appear "cut out" of paper and animated in a two-dimensional style. This is *not* how they were animated, as the entire process is clearly CGI. But the flattened, quasi-2D perspective only makes the lack of motion by the characters all the more tedious. Whether this anemic animation style is a result of

Cover art for the DVD release of *The Legend of Sasquatch.*

a lack of budget, art direction, or both is impossible to say, but it makes *The Legend of Sasquatch* slow going from a viewer's perspective.

The animation might seem more acceptable had the storyline been a bit less mundane. But the plot is so reminiscent of a plethora of Benign Bigfoot children's films and TV shows that *The Legend of Sasquatch* remains is predictable from start to finish. Even with the likeable, genuinely warm voice talents of Hurt and Rhys-Davies, the film feels stifled in key areas: animation quality, narrative arc, and emotional dramatics. Tyke audiences are less likely to notice or care, however, provided they've not been exposed to earlier versions of this plot by viewing *Harry and the Hendersons, Little Bigfoot,* and the like. But as these types of family-friendly Ciné du Sasquatch entertainments are plentiful and run constantly on cable TV, as well as being readily available on DVD, even some of the youngest viewers will no doubt be familiar with this archetype and story approach. This is truly a lost opportunity because with Hurt's and Rhys-Davies' names, *The Legend of Sasquatch* has the rare distinction in the Bigfoot genre of having Oscar-winning talent in the thespian column (while Rick Baker won the Oscar for *Harry and the Hendersons* for make-up, it's far rarer to have Academy Award winners such as Hurt—who won for *The Kiss of the Spider Woman*—on the acting side of the margin).

In the plus column, the scenic background imagery and musical score are moodily evocative. Too, the gentle approach to the Bigfoot clan as kindly, huggable, overgrown Teddy Bears will appeal to parents who tire of the endless spectacle of explosions and super hero movies all too common in much of what passes as children's programming today. However, this very same Gentle Giant rendition of Sasquatch is also potentially problematic, in that it somewhat reduces the mystery of the creature to just another plush toy ready for the marketing department to take over. While the creatures depicted are undeniably cute, there is something to be said for at least a modicum of campfire creepiness, even if only from a mythological standpoint. It lends an air of cautious majesty to the darker, less-explored areas of the unknown forest regions, and therefore represents our own sense of wonder at the deeper mysteries of human existence.

There was a reason that native shaman performers often wore frightening masks to represent the eternal beings of the spirit world — not because the beings were evil, per se, but because the reaction evoked a sense of profound horror and commiserate reverence in the tribal followers. Without this spark, one wonders if children will lose the thrill of participation in something grander and more complicated than their own zone of comfort? After all, many are the children who were scared by an effectively told ghost story at a friend's sleepover who went on to become paranormal investigators and writers of horror fiction. Likewise, many prominent filmmakers and artists cite the profound sense of dread early encounters with raging cinematic monsters produced within them as children at the local matinee, which lead to their own lifelong fascination with monsters, real, imaginary, and in-between. Fear and fascination, in other words, are often bound together as polar opposite of the psychological experience, particularly in the subconscious mind, which refuses to analyze and instead relies upon impression to formulate its imagery.

Perhaps this is all too much to ask from a "simple" children's effort like *The Legend of Sasquatch*. It doubtlessly served at least to fulfill the expectations of some of the viewership, as the film won "Best Feature Film Animation" at the International Family Film Festival, as well as being only one of a handful of Official Selections at the Kids First! Film Festival. It may be only a case of expectations, after all, as to whether or not one finds it successful on its own modest terms. Provided one is willing to forgo any lasting impression and view it as a harmless bit of entertainment, *The Legend of Sasquatch* delivers a mildly diverting hour and 14 minutes. Those wishing for a bit more bite in their Bigfoot, however, are advised to seek mythological impact elsewhere.

Legend of the Honey Island Swamp Monster (2008) (Doc)

Featuring Dana Holyfield, Evan, Lloyd Pye, Billy Mills and Yvonne Ford. Produced, Written and Directed by Dana Holyfield. USA. Color. Stereo. 66 Minutes.

Overview: In 1974, Harland E. Ford, a former FAA flight official, made the startling claim that he had seen a 7-foot-tall creature in the bayou of Honey Island Swamp, Louisiana, where he lived. While Ford's claim garnered much media attention in the 1970s, including an appearance with Leonard Nimoy on *In Search Of*, Ford passed away before offering anything more than tantalizing plaster footprints he made of the hominid ... or so it was believed until the making of this independent documentary.

Decades later, Ford's granddaughter, Dana Holyfield, returned to her Louisiana roots after a stint in Hollywood as an actress and producer of independent films to follow up on the many witnesses who also claimed to have seen the creature. Motivated in part by the exposé conducted by crypto enthusiasts M. K. Davis and Jay Michael (who

claimed probable hoaxing on the part of Ford after they recovered a shoe with a resin cast molded to the bottom which they believed belonged to Ford and was used to create the tracks), Holyfield wanted to set the record straight, feeling that the hoax theory was simply inaccurate. Because her grandfather had passed away, Holyfield interviews his best friend and co-witness to the Honey Island Swamp Monster — one Billy Mills.

Mills relates how he and Ford were searching for an abandoned hunting camp in the 70,000-acre thickets of the Honey Island Swamp back in 1963, which Ford had earlier spotted from the air during a routine surveillance in his airplane. To the men's surprise, they rounded a corner and found themselves face to face with a cryptid on all fours. When they shouted their surprise, the Skunk Ape reared on two legs and ran from them in bipedal fashion. Though they pursued the bayou Bigfoot with guns readied, it eluded them. Then in 1974, while duck hunting in an area near their first encounter, the two men spotted tracks the beast had just left, along with the freshly-slaughtered remains of a wild boar. After returning the next day to make a plaster cast of the tracks, Ford contacted the Louisiana Wildlife Commission to make his startling report: Honey Island Swamp was home to a genuine Swamp Sasquatch.

Holyfield also conducts interviews with a Cajun gentleman (who wishes to be known only as "Evan") who relates his experience with the creature while rowing a canoe back into the most remote areas

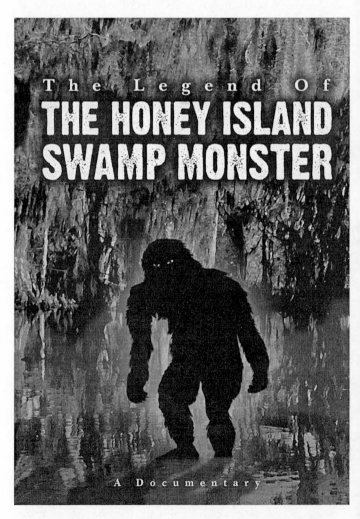

Cover art for the DVD release of *The Honey Island Swamp Monster.*

of the swamp, which proves an effectively believable setting for a cryptid encounter given its difficult, isolated geography. Cryptozoologist Lloyd Pye cameos to analyze and break down his belief in the authenticity of the three-toed plaster casts, which some have remarked somewhat resemble tracks made by an alligator (of which, naturally, the Louisiana swamps have many).

Perhaps the most intriguing aspect of the documentary is the interview with Ford's surviving widow, Yvonne Ford. Quite elderly and frail, she impresses as quite authentic in her retelling of her husband's exploits, at one point producing an old Super 8mm 50-foot reel of film she says she found while rummaging through his possessions in preparation for Ms. Holyfield's documentary. Mrs. Ford claims it is footage her deceased husband made of the Honey Island Swamp Monster but never released to the public. Holyfield believes she may have the "smoking gun" of proof in her possession and has the footage transferred to digital video. In a frame-by-frame analysis, the footage shows what appears to be a large, indistinct creature darting between the trees. While far from conclusive, it provides *The Legend of the Honey Island Swamp Monster* an eerie conclusion, leaving it up to the Ciné du Sasquatch viewer to decide (as per the norm for the genre) if it is real or fabricated.

Holyfield is an entrepreneur in the mold of Charles Pierce, which is evident from the manner in which she titles the production and independently markets it. She was interviewed for Fox News and had clips from the show featured on Sean Hannity's program, among other promotions, proving it was not just her grandfather who had the knack for drawing national attention to regional news stories. In addition to being a filmmaker, she is also the author of a book upon which the documentary was based (*Encounters with the Honey Island Swamp Monster*), as well as several popular Cajun-inspired cookbooks, including *Cajun Sexy Cookin'* ("Hotter Than Cayenne!" touts the cover's subtitle), which features a plethora of scantily-clad Cajun gals cooking lean, healthy Cajun recipes (the latter of which may seem like an impossibility unless one takes into account the amply-endowed but tonally-shaped women on display, pouting in provocative positions as they yank outboard boat engine chords and the like). Whatever one's feeling about the visual conceit and said juxtaposition between the food and the women, there's little doubt the selected models each do justice to the "honey" moniker in the Honey Island Swamp name. And though *The Legend of the Honey Island Swamp Monster* has technical deficiencies owing to its do-it-yourself low budget, it nevertheless provides an authentic glimpse into an often-neglected culture that seemingly breeds tales of boggy beasts as frequently as it does bevies of beauties.

Legend of the Sandsquatch (2006)

Starring Trent Haaga, Hilary Schwartz, Josh Cornell, Ward Roberts, David Reynolds, Danny Saxton, Aubrey Jensen, Brendan Early, Mike Korich, Noah Naylor, Amanda Ward, Katie Rhine, Travis Betz and Michael Powers. Produced and Written by Tom Devlin and Lola Wallace. Directed by Lola Wallace. USA. Color. Stereo. 90 Minutes.

Overview: When elderly Frank goes missing from his desert shack of a home, his granddaughter Sue decides to investigate. A punk rock emo girl at black heart, Sue is depressed (per normal) by her latest relationship gone sour and glad to have the distraction of her missing Grandpa Frank upon which to focus her energies and lift her spirits. She runs into Garrett, an old school friend who has always had a secret crush on her, and, lacking anything better to do owing to his own slacker lifestyle, he eagerly accompanies her on a road trip into the desert to search for her missing grandfather.

Flashbacks reveal that Grandpa Frank first encountered the Sand-

squatch while he was a young man on a desert foray with a group of his friends. The entire cadre were attacked and horribly killed by the 10-foot-tall Sandsquatch, with only Grandpa left as a survivor of the massacre. Since that fateful day, Frank has dedicated his life to repeatedly returning to the same desert spot where his buddies were murdered. He keeps a journal of any and all sightings and clues he finds, hoping they will add up to solving the mystery of the cryptid's existence.

Sue and Garrett don't find any sign of Frank but do locate the journal. After spending time reading it, they decide to return to the desert with their own small party of hominid hunters, armed with an arsenal of weaponry, and destroy the Sandsquatch. Meantime, Sue's on-again, off-again boyfriend, the lead singer in a punk band, decides to play a prank upon her and dress in a gorilla suit. Not surprisingly, he pays the ultimate price when the real creature rips his head off.

Possessing the abilities to move at superhuman speed and hypnotize its victims, the Sandsquatch proves to be a formidable foe. One by one the twenty-something hunters are dispatched in a series of gruesome decapitations, violent limb removals, and other gory deaths. Will anyone survive their horrific ordeal?

* * * * *

Though it touches upon many tenets of Ciné du Sasquatch, including, of course, the play on words in the title ("Sandsquatch" for Sasquatch), *The Legend of Sandsquatch* is actually a pseudo–Squatch movie. Towering 10 feet tall but razor thin, like an emaciated zombie, the Sandsquatch's hairless body more resembles an alien monster from the old Baltimore-lensed Don Dohler B-movie *The Alien Factor* than an actual cryptozoological specimen. With flaring legs that look like a scorpion's from the knees down, and leathery human visage, this cinematic cryptid resembles Bigfoot with a serious case of the mange *and* starved nearly to death.

As it does, however, attempt to render itself as a novel variant on the Bigfoot film, *Legend of the Sandsquatch* merits inclusion in this guide. And it does mimic many of Ciné du Sasquatch's main tropes: the wayward group of youthful types who are dispatched one-by-one after they invade the hominid's domain; the back story wherein a lone witness has earlier encountered the monster and lived to tell about it — to the complete disbelief of others; the cave dwelling where pieces of various victims are found in skeletal and flesh-rotted remains; and even the splatter film motif so common in most Savage Sasquatch movies post–*Night of the Demon*, which, while far from the first Bigfoot movie to portray the hominid as bloodthirsty (there's also *Shriek of the Mutilated* to consider), was definitely the progenitor of the fertile combination of the "gut bucket meets Bigfoot" formula that is still a potent sub-genre in Ciné du Sasquatch today. A final nod to the genre comes in the creature's ability to hypnotize its victims, which — while never as effectively realized — is an homage to *The Abominable Snowman*, with Peter Cushing, and the later *Horror Express*, also with Cushing.

Because of the well-endowed young starlet and manic camera energies, *Legend of the Sandsquatch* often feels like it was helmed by the offspring of Russ Meyer directing an early Sam Raimi screenplay. With its butch emo girl bouncing through the desert armed to the hilt in her leather boots, tight tank top, and cut-off pants, and endless scenes of various expendable victims having their guts ripped out or heads torn off while still alive, a better moniker for this film would have been *Faster, Sandsquatch ... Kill, Kill!*

Alas, despite the obvious references, *Legend of the Sandsquatch* never matches the ferocity of its intent with actual execution of cinematic energy, and often limps along through dull stretches of exposition until the requisite final-act bloodbath. Clearly a low-budget labor of love, it is sadly stillborn in terms of novelty or genre appeal;

and as it technically falls narrowly outside Ciné du Sasquatch in strictest terms, it's recommended only for self-admitted gore hounds and those interested in the unusual fact it was directed by a female filmmaker who's made a series of equally lurid horror films.

Lissi and the Wild Emperor (2007)

AKA: *Lissi und der wilde Kaiser*. Featuring the voices of Michael Herbig, Christian Tramitz, Rick Kavanian, Lotte Ledl, Gerd Knebel, Monika John, Waldemar Kobus and Henni Nachtsheim. Produced by Michael Herbig and Michael Waldleitner. Written by Alfons Biedermann and Michael Herbig. Directed by Michael Herbig. Germany. Color. Stereo. 85 Minutes.

Overview: Yeti nearly falls to his death one day in the Himalayan Mountains. Hanging by a sliver of ice over a lethal crevice, Yeti is relieved when the Devil appears and offers the dangling hominid a second chance at life. The Abominable Snowman agrees before even considering further, terrified by his mortal predicament. Only later does the intimidated Yeti learn the deal comes with one condition: that Yeti must kidnap the most beautiful woman in the world for Satan's own pleasure, bringing her down to the fieriest depths of Hell.

Meanwhile, Prince Franz returns to his parents' castle kingdom to show off his newly-wed bride Lissi. Alas, between Franz' emotionally frigid, dominatrix-obsessed mother, the Empress Dowager; the depressive Emperor with his constant headaches; and the other dysfunctional members of his royal family, Lissi soon learns her new home will be chock full of interpersonal drama. But all plans are put on hold when the Satan-empowered Yeti kidnaps Lissi one dark night and spirits her away, setting off pandemonium in the once docile kingdom. It falls upon Prince Franz to muster the courage of his stated convictions and rise to the occasion in rescuing her. But how can even a stalwart stud like Franz hope to overcome both Sasquatch *and* the very Devil himself in order to liberate Lady Lissi?

* * * * *

While generally unknown in the United States, German comedian and parody filmmaker Michael Herbig is a homegrown hero, having long since established a beach head in Hun viewing homes with his popular if scathingly satirical comedy show *Bullyparade*. The long-running success of *Bullyparade* and the notoriety it provided enabled Herbig to branch out into larger-funded theatrical movies. In two previous features he skewered over-produced, empty-headed Hollywood action films as well as the clichéd nature of epic superhero movies, which currently dominate the summer months of cinema-going seemingly without abatement.

Lissi and the Wild Emperor is his most ambitious effort to date, featuring *Shrek*-influenced CGI animation and storyline to produce an episodic parody of what may best be described as the epitome of a Dreamworks, Disney, or Pixar Studios animation effort mixed with healthy doses of largely local humor for the Vaterland. This may well be the reason it has yet to be imported to the United States, as translating and dubbing some of the regional humor is a tricky proposition; still, one wishes it had been, if only to show that world animation in the digital age is universally well-produced. Indeed, if one reckons the overall quality, this may be the Silver Age of the art form (which, in the previous forms of magic lantern shows and zoetropes that often consisted of drawn silhouettes rather than photographs, is literally older than the motion picture format itself).

The Yeti is played with a growling voice and angry demeanor, especially when the poor creature finds himself suddenly beholden to none other than the Prince of Darkness. The animation style is far different from Pixar's *Monsters, Inc.* and their depicted Abominable Snowman. Whereas that being was almost soft and cuddly, this Yeti is slim by comparison, but still quite clumsy physically (given the propensity to show animated Yetis as butterfingers, it must be a genetic shortcoming). It's all strictly for laughs, playing openly upon the classic *Beauty and the Beast* paradigm, which has always been an iconic if indirect influence on the Bigfoot film genre.

Basically an innocent caught in a bad exchange, Yeti in *Lissi and the Wild Emperor* is your Everyman hominid charged with a thankless task sure to raise the ire of the humans even more than usual (borrowing the Ogre vs. human theme from the *Shrek* films)—kidnapping royalty, no less. The poor cryptid sap knows what awaits him in terms of scorn, retribution, and *Homo sapiens* cries for Abominable blood, but what choice does the creature have, bound as it is to none other than Satan himself?

Lissi and the Wild Emperor was not as big a hit as Herbig's previous two box office smashes, but it still performed well in Germany and other European countries. It shows that while Germanic entries in Ciné du Sasquatch are rare, the universality of the character is such that the hominid may be utilized not merely for the shock value of its own appearance or notoriety, but as "just another character" in the narrative. In a postmodern sensibility, this is the ultimate proof that the character has infiltrated the public consciousness, for it demonstrates the creators feel it safe to experiment with the Yeti's very inner essence, pitting his hominid soul against the Father of All Lies. This is a radical notion in one key respect for the Bigfoot film genre: It posits that hominids are so much like us that they have eternal damnation or salvation to fear or look forward to upon the expiration of their current biological forms. This is a first for Ciné du Sasquatch, as never before has a Yeti been forced to choose between Hell and Heaven quite so literally or in such a starkly existential manner. For all that it matters, the filmmakers seem to suggest the poor Yeti is being given a chance to avenge itself upon the human race for all the evils that *Homo sapiens* have heaped upon its own cryptid species. But, endearingly, the Yeti is not as "hell bent" upon performing such a task as a human charged with the same divinely-backed power play might have been. For the Yeti, simply having to interact and deal with humans is stressful enough, without having to figure in how to avenge his own species on top of it all, however justified such a lofty notion may sound. This is a good illustration of how the beast in the Yeti is unable to rise to the occasion as rapidly or deadly as a human, and, equally, how the human side of the Yeti, which values peace and harmony, makes the beast slow to use violence to settle conflicts, which humans are frequently all-too-ready to embrace for a "justifiable war" and the like.

Little Bigfoot (1997)

Starring Ross Malinger, P.J. Soles, Kenneth Tigar, Kelly Packard, Don Stroud, Chris Finch, Matt McCoy, Caitlin Barrett, Francis Fallon, Steve O'Connor, Gregg Brazzel, Timothy D. Baker, Gerald Okamura, Randall Shiro Ideishi, Jefferson Wagner, Dean Raphael Ferrandini, Kurt Bryant, Kristine Bergman, Aimee Gideon, Johann Benét, Joseph S. Griffo, Kelly Hirano and Erika Page. Produced by Scott McAboy, Joseph Merhi, Richard Pepin and Amy Sydorick. Written by Scott McAboy and Richard Preston Jr. Directed by Art Camacho. USA. Color. Stereo. 92 Minutes.

Overview: While on vacation, a single mom raising a family of three unruly teen and pre-teen kids stumbles across a Baby Bigfoot in some heavily-deforested Oregon woods. Because the creature is threatened by the evil logging company who will stop at nothing to see the hominid dead (said company owners realizing the forests will be designated a protected habitat should Little Bigfoot live to be listed as an endangered species), the children take Little Bigfoot into their summer cabin home with them to offer shelter.

Realizing the kids have intervened but unsure of their identity, the logging company ups the reward to $50,000 for any hunter who can bring in Little Bigfoot, dead or alive. It's up to the three children to create a diversion and somehow reunite Little Bigfoot with his mother Sasquatch before the hunters can kill it. Using their bikes, and even commandeering a pickup truck, the kids continually outwit the fumbling pursuers until a final showdown that threatens the lives of both the children and the creatures.

* * * * *

If insipid has another name, then it must be *Little Bigfoot*. While some will find the screwball shenanigans harmless enough to be utilized by unimaginative babysitters bored of showing their wards the latest Disney offering, most viewers will be challenged to stay awake for the duration of the running time without frequent adrenaline-boosting shots of strong Turkish coffee. Never less than semi-competent, and yet never rising above it either, *Little Bigfoot* is the equivalent of *Harry and the Hendersons* without the latter's sense of pacing, comic twists, involving art direction, and groundbreaking animatronic costumes. In summation, the film comes up as short as its leaden namesake.

Little Bigfoot was produced by the infamous PM Entertainment Group, whose combined output singlehandedly achieved the dubious distinction of never releasing a truly breakout film of any reputable quality in their entire history of almost 100 releases. Among the more notoriously inept titles PM Entertainment released were *Cellblock Sisters: Banished Behind Bars*; *Alien Intruder*, with Maxwell Caulfield; *Undercover Angel*, with Yasmine Bleeth; and *Skyscraper*, with Anna Nicole Smith (as both star and co-producer). Given that the PM Entertainment producers often had name actors and even occasional name directors working on their projects (including Academy Award–winning filmmaker John G. Alvidsen — winner in 1976 for best director for *Rocky*— who changed his credit on the PM Entertainment release *Inferno* to "Danny Mulroon" after viewing the first cut), it's quite amazing their product wasn't better. Even so, many of their films sold quite well internationally, and a handful even became perennials on American cable stations such as HBO and Showtime. Indeed, before their collapse in 2002, the company had even constructed a multi-million-dollar production facility (which may have actually contributed to their collapse), with plans to increase their already profligate output. While theirs was a meteoric rise to a short-lived history (lasting a little over a decade), PM Entertainment averaged nearly 10 feature-length films per year, which is a remarkable record for such a small company.

As for *Little Bigfoot*, perhaps the best thing that can be said for it is that it lead to only one sequel, the inevitable *Little Bigfoot 2: The Journey Home*. Remarkably, the sequel was shot and released the same year as the first film, which gives one an idea of the churn factor present in the average PM Entertainment effort (and the lackluster quality therein). P.J. Soles, sadly, stars as the mother; but the clichéd nature of the script can only remind one of her wasted talent after earlier charming cameos in such cult classics as *Rock n' Roll High School*, John Carpenter's *Halloween*, and Brian DePalma's *Carrie*. Likewise, lead child actor Ross Malinger, who starred in *Sleepless in Seattle* and *Kindergarten Cop*, is unable to generate any interest, save for the most indiscriminate moppet crowd, with his cloying performance as the Boy Who Would Rescue Little Bigfoot. Matt McCoy — a Ciné du Sasquatch regular, with lead parts in *Abominable* and *Bigfoot: The Unforgettable Encounter* — plays a smaller role with at least a modicum of endearing humor as the small-town sheriff, a reprise of his befuddled lawman character from *Bigfoot: The Unforgettable Encounter*.

Worst of all, however, is the reprehensible Little Bigfoot itself. While it's no fault of the actor who portrays the cryptid (little person character actor Joseph Griffo, who has appeared in *Fear and Loathing in Las Vegas* and *Epic Movie*), the suit is a hairy Oompa Loompa wannabe costume with a terrible animatronic oversized head set atop it. The bug eyes, which seem designed to evoke E.T.'s equally large orbs, are as lifeless as a pair of painted softballs — and just as convincing. While one empathizes with the special effects team's doubtless lack of budget, the results are so laughably inept that clips of *Little Bigfoot*'s baby hominid appear with frequency on such derisive websites as YouTube and the bad film shrine known as EverythingIsTerrible.com.

For genre motifs, *Little Bigfoot* keys into so many of the same elements as *Harry and the Hendersons* that it is virtually identical. For example, the bad guys (including one who wears a pirate eye patch!) are all stereotypical goons straight out of bad biker movie, while the pro-green, suburban family are so sweet-natured as to be faultless. This is the epitome of bad screenwriting, in that it allows for no internal character conflict for either the protagonists or antagonists. As a result, *Little Bigfoot* plods along between predictable action stunts and the usual vehicle chases until it putters to its thankful but hackneyed conclusion.

Little Bigfoot 2: The Voyage Home (1997)

Starring Stephen Furst, Taran Noah Smith, Michael Fishman, Chuck Borden, Tom Bosley, Melody Clarke, Steve Eastin, Nick Finch, Joseph S. Griffo, Kelly Hirano, Kevin LaRosa, Steve Nave, Erika Page and Dani Shear. Produced by Art Camacho and Raymon Khoury. Written by Art Camacho and Richard Preston Jr. Directed by Art Camacho. USA. Color. Stereo. 93 Minutes.

Overview: A single dad who sells insurance for a living decides to stage the ultimate family getaway and takes his two kids and their best friend along for a wilderness vacation. But their trip to Oregon is anything but peaceful when Little Bigfoot rears its mug while the family is camping. It turns out the baby Sasquatch was separated from its parents by hunters, which inspires the kids to keep Little Bigfoot as their pet, even when Dad moves them all into a motel after the scary encounter. The kids refuse to reveal their secret Sasquatch and plot how to best return the errant hominid to its frantic parents.

Meanwhile, a land owner named Cavendish is intent on wiping out any and all traces of any Sasquatch creatures so that he can legally possess huge tracts of acreage belonging to a group of beleaguered Native Americans. To this end, he's hired an Indian game tracker who can follow Bigfoot with uncanny ability owing to his tribal knowledge of the cryptid's means of survival. The Native tracker and several rednecks with rifles are given explicit orders: find Little Bigfoot and terminate him with extreme prejudice.

As the net slowly closes in around them, the kids realize they must enlist the help of their father if they wish to prevent Little Bigfoot from becoming a Cavendish throw rug. Dad is obviously surprised, but when he sees that it's a life or death decision on behalf of the tiny hominid, he springs into action. He and the family spirit Little Bigfoot back to the woods in hopes of finding its parents, but not before a hunter shoots the baby Bigfoot. Before it can die, however, the Native Tracker has a change of heart and uses a spiritual chant to restore the dying Sasquatch. During the resulting chase through the woods by Cavendish and his men, a cave with Chinook paintings on the inside is discovered, which invalidates Cavendish's plan to buy the land. Little Bigfoot is reunited with his grateful parents.

* * * * *

Just when you thought it was safe to go back to the forest, *Little Bigfoot 2: The Journey Home* arrives to convince you that an extended holiday in the most crack-addicted slums of any major American metropolis beats even the tiniest chance of experiencing yet another sighting of Ciné du Sasquatch's most annoying hominid. A virtual remake of *Little Bigfoot*, *Little Bigfoot 2: The Journey Home* is a sentimental tyke tear fest which makes one long for the Shakespearean complexities of *Harry and the Hendersons*.

Stephen Furst substitutes for P.J. Soles as the single parent who decides to bond with his family by whisking his city-slicker brood away from videogames and shopping malls. Best remembered for his work as Flounder in *Animal House*, Furst gives an honorable performance in what is a terribly underwritten role, riddled with the clichés one has come to expect from the Benign Bigfoot formula (as exemplified by *Little Bigfoot* itself). Likewise, the young cast — all seasoned professionals, given their ages, with *Home Improvement*'s Taran Noah Smith, *Roseanne*'s Michael Fishman, and *Unhappily Ever After*'s Melody Clarke — dutifully deliver their campy dialogue to the best of their abilities. Also on hand are *Happy Days*' Tom Bosley in the thankless small-town sheriff role played by Tim McCoy in the original, and Steve Eastin from *The Hidden* and *The Hidden 2* as uber-bad Cavendish. The problem here is not the cast, but the dreadfully lackluster screenplay's juvenile wordplay, co-written by triple threat writer, producer, and director Art Camacho, which forces them all to sound like one-dimensional monotypes, whatever personal energy they bring to their roles.

Little Bigfoot and *Little Bigfoot 2: The Journey Home* were probably shot back-to-back, as they were released in rapid succession. This is apparent in the location photography, which features the same Southern California wilderness scenery and small town setting. While it does give each film at least a modicum of production values (because they appear to be largely photographed on location rather than in the confines of a studio), this is akin to saying the icing is sweet on an otherwise tasteless cake. Half-baked but overcooked, just like its predecessor, *Little Bigfoot 2: The Journey Home*'s only journey was a deservedly swift ride to home video land. Given its puerile storyline and tepid execution, this was probably the film's only hope for finding an audience anyway. As of this writing, it was widely available, paired with *Little Bigfoot*, in a low-cost double feature set of hominid hilarity at many discount outlets, though one shudders to imagine viewing them back-to-back unless one's children suffer from frequent bouts of insomnia — in which case a few minutes of watching either should work magic to put them under.

The Little Documentary That Couldn't (2007) (Cameo)

Starring Michael Alexander, Carol Ashley, David Boller, Andy Brendle, MarLee Candell, Axelle Cummings, Brian DeCato, Gabriel Diani, Denver Dillon, Brett Galde, Mara Grimes, Jake Hanover and Catherine Kamei. Produced by Sean P. Keenan and Ken Saba. Written by Shawn Brazeau, Matt Lambro and Ken Saba. Directed by Richard Hartman and Matt Lambro. USA. Color. Stereo. 80 Minutes.

Overview: Michael Chordus, a struggling actor in Los Angeles, believes that by shedding light on the constant battles thespians face in tinsel town he can empower those who suffer in his situation. Alas, the more he tries to show the nobility of enduring for one's art and craft, the less he believes in his own documentary efforts. The results are predictable and reveal the high level of narcissism and self-denial inherent in most of his circle of friends/actors — all of whom are working day jobs in order secure small gigs as stand-ins and extras to bolster their non-existent credits on their skimpy resumes. Michael quickly surmises that even his documentary film is a failure in the making.

Determined to salvage the time, money, and energy he's wasted in shooting the first two-thirds of his unfinished personal epic, Chordas hits upon the idea of deviating from his original storyline of "a day in the life of an actor" and instead focusing on one of the female

protagonist's ex-boyfriend, invading their personal space at every turn. At one point we see a glimpse of the kind of dreck many of these talented but desperate actors are forced to work on when Chordus' camera visits the set of a no-budget Bigfoot video effort. The rented gorilla suit and bad direction the nascent exploitation filmmaker gives to the hapless actor playing Bigfoot (including having Bigfoot bang himself in his own hairy gonads to enliven the staged shots) send the already dismal production straight into Ed D. Wood Jr. territory, minus the production values Wood typically achieved with no budget.

* * * * *

While the cameo status of Bigfoot in *The Little Documentary That Couldn't* is basically a one-off sequence, it's still quite funny and fits in well with the film-within-a-film structure of the mockumentary. Basically a low-key, self-deprecating look at the trials and tribulations of breaking into the acting world in self-absorbed La La Land, *The Little Documentary That Couldn't* takes an overly familiar premise and does a good job of adding some refreshing, Woody Allen–styled characters who form a loose-knit circle of dysfunctional friends, all of whom are doomed to never receive anything remotely resembling their proverbial big break.

The Bigfoot sequence is a hilariously cheesy example of the stresses of low-budget filmmaking in the guise of a behind-the-scenes look at what it means to be a method actor stuck in the lower rungs of Hollywood hell. Forced by the psychotic director to smack himself in his own testicles, the Bigfoot actor — his all-too-human neckline clearly visible beneath the rubbery gorilla mask — dutifully pounds himself into painful numbness in a perfect externalization of the emasculation experienced by every actor who ever started at the bottom of the celluloid heap with hopes of one day seeing their name in lights. It's also brutally funny.

The Little Documentary That Couldn't won several independent film festival awards for its charming, unpretentious nature. But it's the knowing examination of Ciné du Sasquatch and its less noble exploitation genre efforts (such as *Search for the Beast*) that rely upon sex and Sasquatch in equally tawdry measure that rings particularly true. While this film is wise enough to parody how bad many of these no-budget, video-shot features are in terms of passing off a gorilla suit as a hominid, one wishes that the directors of the "serious" titles *The Little Documentary That Couldn't* mines for guffaws had bothered to realize just how ridiculous it is to expect modern viewers to accept such vaudeville "monkeyshines" in terms of incompetent cryptid costume construction *before* they'd made their own contributions (or lack thereof) to the Bigfoot film *oeuvre*.

Little Nicky (2000) (Cameo)

Starring Adam Sandler, Patricia Arquette, Harvey Keitel, Rhys Ifans, Tommy "Tiny" Lister, Rodney Dangerfield, Robert Smigel, Reese Witherspoon, Dana Carvey, Jon Lovitz, Kevin Nealon, Michael McKean, Quentin Tarantino, Carl Weathers, Blake Clark, Rob Schneider, Clint Howard, Lewis Arquette, George Wallace, Henry Winkler, Ozzy Osbourne, Regis Philbin, Sylvia Lopez, Sid Ganis, Todd Holland, David Sardi and Joseph S. Griffo. Produced by Allen Covert, Michael De Luca, Robert Engelman, Jack Giarraputo, Michelle Holdsworth, Adam Sandler, Robert Simonds, Rita Smith and Brian Witten. Written by Tim Herlihy, Adam Sandler and Steven Brill. Directed by Steven Brill. USA. Color. Stereo. 90 Minutes.

Overview: One of Satan's sons, named Little Nicky, is half-angel, half-devil and therefore the odd demon out in Hell, where his two brothers, Adrian and Cassius, resent his half-breed and often sweet nature. When Adrian and Cassius escape to the Earth's surface to wreak havoc on the eve of Daddy Satan's retirement as lord of the underworld, it falls to Little Nicky to right all wrongs before hell literally breaks loose and one of his errant siblings inherits the crown as ruler of Hades.

* * * * *

Basically a one-scene wonder, Bigfoot appears in *Little Nicky* as a horned horror with cloven feet but otherwise unmistakable hominid attributes. Confusingly called Gary the Monster in the film itself, but referred to as Bigfoot in the shooting script, *Little Nicky*'s cryptid monster was produced by McFarlane Toys as an articulated figure for collectors, in collaboration with the film's many producers.

Oddly, *Little Nicky* has several tangential connections to Ciné du Sasquatch, despite the flop nature of the film itself, which was nominated for — and won — the infamous Razzie Award in the year of its release in numerous categories, including Worst Actor of the Decade (Rob Schneider), Worst Actor (Adam Sandler), Worst Director (Steven Brill), Worst Screenplay, Worst Supporting Actress (Patricia Arquette), and Worst Picture. Not only does it feature an appearance by little person character actor Joseph Griffo (who played the diminutive Little Bigfoot in *Little Bigfoot* and *Little Bigfoot 2: The Journey Home*), but also the presence of Carl Weathers (who later played a cryptozoologist in the hilarious *The Sasquatch Gang*) and Clint Howard (from *Bigfoot: The Unforgettable Encounter*). Equally strange, it was Quentin Tarantino's borrowing of the *Little Nicky* Bigfoot costume one Halloween as a gag while on a talk show that inspired *Abominable* director Ryan Schifrin to hire the same special effects costume designer to create his cinematic cryptid! Not bad for a film that basically has very little Ciné du Sasquatch screen time for its hominid and was generally panned upon release as one of the worst films of the year.

The Long Way Home: A Bigfoot Story (2007)

Starring James Cromer, James "Bubba" Cromer, J. Lewis Cromer, Helen Marini and Pat Patterson. Produced by James Cromer and James "Bubba" Cromer. Written and Directed by James "Bubba" Cromer. USA. Color. Stereo. 72 Minutes.

Overview: D.J. Galloway, a Miami reporter on the rise, has a nervous breakdown and loses his job shortly after covering Elian Gonzalez's Cuban extradition, owing to his bipolar disorder. Unable to secure employment as a writer, Galloway self-medicates with booze, stuck in a clinical depression. Hanging out in beach bars, he happens to catch a news broadcast about a series of Bigfoot sightings in his tiny North Carolina home town of Indian Camp Mountain. Lacking ambition or a job, but desiring a second chance, Galloway heads home, hoping to cover the story and regain his reputation as a first-rate journalist.

Among those he interviews upon his return to the mountainous rural burg is his father, Big Jake Galloway, who happens to be the sheriff. Big Jake is not only an avowed believer in Sasquatch, but has previously spent time hunting another cryptid, known as the Lizard Man, in nearby South Carolina. Mindful of his son's career setback, the father encourages Galloway in the younger man's quest.

Other residents the reporter interviews include a reclusive, snake-handling fundamentalist who claims to have been visited by the hungry Bigfoot at night, as well as a host of other Appalachian backwoods types, all of whom espouse their own egocentric but heartfelt theories about the hominid and why it has suddenly appeared. Even as he completes his initial investigation, more sightings occur. Galloway is thrilled, believing his long-awaited comeback is just around the publishing corner.

Alas, a visit to a drag queen friend at a local nightclub alerts Galloway to the truth behind the sightings: a few buddies of the reporter, having heard of his Miami troubles, have staged the Bigfoot sightings in an old gorilla costume. Their intentions are sincere if misguided, hoping Galloway will use the renewing energies of his hometown to regain his footing (so to speak). But the writer is devastated, realizing his newly-restarted career has been built on a house of marked cards.

Equally difficult for Galloway is informing Big Jake that the sightings are fake after the two have recently begun to repair their formerly estranged relationship. His father is a true believer, having sighted the creature himself, and is convinced beyond doubt that what he witnessed was not a man in a monkey suit. Adding to the mystery is the strange fact that the sightings of Bigfoot have continued, even after his friend's wife burned the ape costume.

Galloway, unable to reconcile the discrepancies, builds a campfire in the woods and tries to contemplate his conundrum. Before he can arrive at an answer, however, he is attacked and killed by Bigfoot.

* * * * *

The Long Way Home: A Bigfoot Story is one of the more unique, heartfelt entries in recent Ciné du Sasquatch. At once a semi-convincing, no-budget effort that takes advantage of its local cast of

This window display for a North Carolina showing of *The Long Way Home: A Bigfoot Story* features the Bigfoot costume used by the filmmaker. (Photograph courtesy James "Bubba" Cromer.)

eccentrics in a manner similar to early John Waters films (such as *Pink Flamingos* and *Female Trouble*), it equally pays tribute to Charles Pierce's *The Legend of Boggy Creek*. By combining these influences but adding a deeply personal perspective clearly based on the filmmaker's own struggles, *The Long Way Home: A Bigfoot Story* often transcends its technical limitations and regional trappings to become a surprisingly effective independent film of its own accord, provided the viewer is willing to accept the camcorder-styled production values.

Despite the largely non-professional cast, the often haphazard, thrown-together feel of the videography, and occasionally weak moments, the movie works more often than not in the best tradition of such locally-produced regional fare as *Gal Young'Un*, *Killer of Sheep*, and *Chan Is Missing*. Like these efforts, *The Long Way Home: A Bigfoot Story* favors naturalism and authenticity of setting to attain a sense of believability most Hollywood efforts rarely achieve. For no amount of voice coaching could ever come close to capturing the gritty, hard-lived accents the residents shown in *The Long Way Home: A Bigfoot Story* display time and time again.

That's not to say that the film doesn't have drawbacks, as it clearly does. The amateur cast, the low-budget gorilla suit and the shot-on-video look all give it a crude feel at times. But the talent behind the project shines through in a manner that can only be captured by off–Hollywood projects like this. More often than not, the entertainment value outweighs the technical drawbacks. More jaundiced viewers might dismiss the non-professional cast as audience members straight off the set of a Jerry Springer taping, or criticize the accents as being thick enough to warrant subtitles. But those willing to suspend judgment for the film's short duration are likely to be pleasantly surprised, for as a simple slice of true Americana, *The Long Way Home: A Bigfoot Story* is surprisingly entertaining. So many films with hundred-million-dollar budgets lack even this modest quality, let alone a sense of humanity beneath the relentless effects and non-stop explosions (of which this film thankfully has none). For all its shortcomings, *The Long Way Home: A Bigfoot Story* sounds as real to the ear as it looks to the eye.

This is partly due to James "Bubba" Cromer and his knack for finding larger-than-life characters who, if nothing else, know how to portray themselves. Cromer tends to hold on his performers for long takes, which helps reveal their personalities far more effectively than quick, mocking cuts played for *Hee Haw* laughs would have. In exposing the very limitations of one's "constant persona"— the social mask all humans wear to conceal the often awkward inner core of conflicting emotions and doubts—the director enters the same aesthetic territory explored by Andy Warhol, Rainer Werner Fassbinder and Werner Herzog. The harder Cromer's so-called stereotypes try to maintain the façade of their own down-home personalities while struggling to remember dialogue, the more their human frailties are exposed for the camera (and viewer). The effect is akin to watching an amateur juggler wearing only a modest fig leaf that keeps slipping while he's performing; the more the humiliated acrobat desperately attempts to redirect attention back to the juggling, the more he inadvertently "exposes" himself. With its cast of hammy performers chewing up the scenery as if at the local talent show, *The Long Way Home: A Bigfoot Story* is awash in these kinds of over-the-top acting styles until the whole film spills its deeper contents (a juxtaposition of raw emotions, wounded psyches and real-life pathos) smack into the startled viewer's lap.

Like Paul Morrissey's similarly crude, Warhol-financed efforts such as *Flesh* and *Trash*, Cromer mines these personalities to such ridiculous effect that the line between self-parody and parody blurs. Too often this tricky balancing act implodes and produces bad camp; here it reproduces the shocked horror lurking just beneath the façade of every human being. This forces the viewer to confront the voyeuristic quality of cinema itself, as one continues viewing, despite the excesses of personality, because it's simply too difficult to turn away.

It's no secret to commercial filmmakers that most cinemagoers prefer to hide behind the invisible fourth wall between actors and viewers and watch from a vaunted position within the self-protective, audience-superior position. This enables the viewer to absorb emotions normally too disturbing otherwise, in that viewers may realize that much of what they find repulsive they hide as well. *The Long Way Home: A Bigfoot Story* constantly breaks down this metaphoric wall with its chaotic mix of clashing personalities, reminding the viewer that the harder one stares into the film itself, the deeper it stares back.

The movie is an uneasy pastiche of Ciné du Sasquatch and personal filmmaking that blends cultural clichés and novel approach to defy expectations, despite its severely restrained budget. And in art, as in life, the whole is usually more revealing than any one individual piece. *The Long Way Home: A Bigfoot Story* will not be to the taste of many fans of cryptid films who prefer more traditional narrative-styled approaches. But it demonstrates an uneasy if strangely fitting wedding of something old and something new, thus injecting new life into the Bigfoot genre on its own modest terms. In this regard, one can only hope future directors and writers will study it before they set out to make their own Ciné du Sasquatch entry and avoid the common pitfalls of many of the more recent Bigfoot genre efforts.

Lost in Space (Multiple Episodes) (1965) (TV) (Influence)

Starring June Lockhart, Mark Goddard, Marta Kristen, Bill Mumy, Angela Cartwright, Guy Williams, Jonathan Harris, Bob May and Dick Tufeld. Produced by Irwin Allen. USA. Color/Black & White. Mono. 60 Minutes.

Overview: Irwin Allen's crowning achievement, however cockeyed he may have worn it, was the beloved *Lost in Space*, the weekly television series that detailed the exploits of a star-lost family and their robot attempting to survive and find their way back in time and space to their own dimension of origin. The inherent *Leave It to Beaver* quality of having a young boy grow up facing challenges the universe itself hurls at him and his unprotected family, and with only his mother's sage advice and his robot's stern warning cry ("Danger! *Danger*, Will Robinson!") to protect him, was irresistible when combined with the alien-monster-of-the-week formula the show frequently indulged in as part of its long-running history. And several of these space cryptids were noteworthy in terms of their influence on Ciné du Sasquatch, even if the actual depicted hominids are not Sasquatch per se.

Part of the reason *Lost in Space* maintains a tangential but often-remarked-upon link to Ciné du Sasquatch is that published rumors over the years have speculated that *Lost in Space* special effects contributor John Chambers, who designed most of the simian monster suits seen on the show, also created a Bigfoot suit as a hoax for an unnamed private client at his Burbank, California, studio in the 1960s. Whatever Chambers' intent (if anything other than professional) for the so-called Burbank Bigfoot suit he built, legend has it that he was making this costume for none other than Roger Patterson (for Patterson's own infamous mini-opus). This has been vehemently denied by almost everyone who would go on record over the years, including Chambers himself, who maintained until his dying breath that he did *not* create a Bigfoot suit for Patterson. Given how little money Patterson had throughout his life to finance his peculiar obsession with Sasquatch, it is doubtful he could have afforded the services of a top-notch talent like John Chambers anyway, who already had more work than he could handle with such series as *Mission: Impossible*.

The other reason *Lost in Space* ranks as an influence on Ciné du Sasquatch is that through sheer repetition of hominid space monsters on offer, the series began to establish how normal the idea of Bigfoot was, even if moved into the depths of outer space. What was important in the transportation of Sasquatch from Earthly backwoods hominid into star-dwelling cryptid was that it subtly demonstrated the mythic value of Bigfoot. Space cryptids such as these would hereafter become a norm rather than an exception, cumulating in the climax of this concept with the success of 20th Century–Fox's *Planet of the Apes*, which took it to its logical conclusion by situating humans as the inferior species in terms of the social hierarchies arranged by talking apes for ape society's benefit. While technically only an influence as well, *Planet of the Apes* made the idea of bipedal simians as humanity's equal a mainstay theme of its own five-picture series (not to mention TV show and remake).

Several noteworthy episodes of *Lost in Space* feature space cryptids. Among these are: "Fugitives in Space," which features a simian-faced hominid named Creech; "One of Our Dogs Is Missing," in which Judy Robinson is menaced by a hairy bipedal cryptid resembling Sasquatch while the family is stranded on a desolate planet; "The Keeper," which guest-starred venerable SF icon Michael Rennie as a guardian of intergalactic species best kept on the leash, including one that is suspiciously like Bigfoot; and "All That Glitters," another typical episode in which a menagerie of alien monstrosities are paraded around, with one of them being a hominid stand-in. Others that feature a slightly different looking space cryptid include "The Space Croppers" (which has a werewolf's head but whose body design and fur construction heavily resembles that of the Patterson-Gimlin creature), "The Oasis" and "The Magic Mirror," although these offer very brief cameos.

As *Lost in Space* sped through its budget and time constraints in an insatiable need for new monsters each week, the costumes were often recycled. So it is very possible many of the space cryptid appearances are basically the same costume, only modified for whatever requirements the new shooting schedule required (and to avoid recognition from a previous episode).

Lost Tapes ("Bigfoot," "Swamp Sasquatch" and "Southern Sasquatch") (2009) (TV)

Starring Meredith Louise Thomas, Bill Oberst Jr., David Sawyer, Gerald Brodin, Jason Ellefson, Loren Coleman, Dallas Tanner, Joe Nickell, Jessica Lynch Alfaro, Craig Stanford, Jayson Matthews and Charlie Newton. Produced by Gary Auerbach, Amy Cron, Tina Gazzerro, Patrick Keegan, Douglas Segal, Fred Villari, Chris Chaffin, Kevin Tao Mohs, Sarah Barresi, Todd Darling, Margaret Goodman, Amy Brown, Kelly Le Castre, Bo Palinic and Brian Snedeker. Directed by Doug Segal. USA. Color. Stereo. 30 Minutes.

Overview: Purporting to be a series of found videotapes which are presented in edited format, *Lost Tapes* is a fictionalized cryptid encounter show in which various Fortean-type monsters are shown having typically fatal meetings with humans in remote settings. Since most of the videotapes are recovered post-homicide, the viewer is forced to piece together the mystery of the incidents based mostly on the camcorder footage mixed with alternating clips of various cryptozoological experts commenting upon the profiled hominid.

* * * * *

Imagine *The Blair Witch Project* mixed with *In Search Of* and, viola, *Lost Tapes* is readily grasped both in format and tone. Combining the now hackneyed handheld approach of the former theatrical sensation with the latter TV series' utilization of expert commentary from cryptid witnesses, dedicated hominid hunters, and serious scientists, *Lost Tapes* tries to capitalize upon spooky sensationalism over factual presentation by blending the line between real, pseudo-real, and outright fabrication. The editorial strategy is simple: By interspersing the bogus enacted "found" footage with existing interviews of eyewitnesses and experts, the staged segments are supposed to gain credibility by way of the documentary footage.

This is, of course, an old TV and filmmaking concept — that of the so-called dramatic reenactment used by crime shows and the like to enable direct viewer participation. Even such classic Ciné du Sasquatch TV series as *In Search Of*, and films like *The Legend of Boggy Creek*, utilized this technique; so in and of itself, it's not very controversial. Where *Lost Tapes* crosses the boundary for some is in its relentlessly hyped status as being comprised of true stories. Some in the Bigfoot film and TV camp feel the show does damage to the serious crypto research by never clearly delineating fact from fantasy, while others just enjoy the creepy sense of verisimilitude *Lost Tapes* imparts.

For most viewers tuning in to the series for the first time, it is difficult to believe that any objective watcher would have a problem distinguishing what are clearly semi-professional performers seemingly improvising their videotaped confessions from the grainy, heavily-processed stock footage of various cryptozoologists (such as Dr. Grover Krantz, for but one example) intercut throughout each episode. It may be simply a matter of formal degree: rather than clearly draw a

June Lockhart is menaced by one of the many space hominids that frequented the popular *Lost in Space* TV series.

line between the fiction and documentary shots, *Lost Tapes* employs a constantly-shifting viewpoint in which a few documentary interviews are shown before dissolving into the fictional characters and then back to real-life talking heads, ad nauseum. Whereas *In Search Of* labeled such recreations with the stock "Dramatic Reenactment" disclaimer, *Lost Tapes* actively deconstructs any semblance of difference in order to heighten viewer suspense. While a novel effect, it quickly grows tiresome (and self-defeating) in that it begs the question: If cryptid encounters are so easily staged for a fictional series, are the documentary segments just as easily hoaxed? It's this uneasy alliance between truth and fiction that many find confusing if not outright bogus. But despite such trepidations, the series has proven popular on the cable channel Animal Planet, with two seasons already having aired and a third in the works as this guide goes to press.

"Bigfoot" aired during the first season. Rachel Glen, a fictional park ranger, discovers that poachers are setting wire snares to trap black bears, several of which she has found dead when her videotaped journal of her activities begins the show. Along the way, however, her suspicions grow as to the true nature of the strange noises she's heard. They do not resemble, she tells the camera, any known animal species she has ever encountered in the woods. Her surveillance cameras are tampered with, as well. She discovers a lair she initially believes to be a black bear cave — until she finds strangely human-looking hair samples, which she sends to a colleague for DNA analysis.

Surprisingly, the samples are from a primate of unknown origin. She continues her vigil, hoping to find who or what is causing the decline in the bear population, particularly when she discovers a poacher's hidden camera in the woods and sees that the poacher has been stalking her with the device. After several nearly-lethal encounters with the poacher, who is intent on seeing Rachel fail in her mission, Rachel is forced to make a stand in her cabin against the poacher when he attacks. Fortunately for the ranger, Bigfoot attacks the poacher and saves her life, even as the cryptid savagely ends the hunter's own existence. Convinced to leave well enough alone, and grateful to her unseen savior, Rachel abandons any further search.

Also shown in the first season was "Swamp Sasquatch," about the fabled Honey Island Swamp Monster supposedly inhabiting the Louisiana bayous. In this episode, Dr. Chapman, a naturalist, is commissioned to study the alligator population post–Katrina. Accompanied by her nephew Ethan, they are soon lost in the swamps when an alligator destroys their GPS equipment. Fortunately, they run across Bud, a local swamp rat, who has set up camp and invites them to share his modest tent. He warns them that it is not safe to be in the bayous after dark, owing to the legendary Honey Island Swamp Monster, which will attack humans without provocation. Dr. Chapman is naturally skeptical, but is a bit taken aback when Ethan accidentally crushes a few extremely large eggs they discover nearby, as she cannot readily identify the species that laid them.

That night the creature reaches into Bud's tent, grabbing at the frightened fisherman. Dr. Chapman, Ethan, and Bud flee before the Swamp Sasquatch can destroy their camp. Stumbling through the darkness, they fire shots wildly behind them in hopes of discouraging the beast from further pursuit. Their strategy apparently works, as they all survive and are eventually rescued. Properly chastised, and realizing there is more to the stories than mere folklore, Dr. Chapman resolves to continue her studies in pursuit of documenting the existence of the Honey Island Swamp Monster so that the scientific community will no longer scoff at the possibility of unknown hominids dwelling on the planet.

Not to be confused with the first season's similarly-titled episode, the second year saw the airing of "Southern Sasquatch," about the Fouke Monster (known most famously from Charles Pierce's land-

mark *The Legend of Boggy Creek* and its lesser sequels). "Southern Sasquatch" follows the grim expedition of Matthew Barton and his soon-to-be brothers-in-law, Corbin and Levi Knox, on a routine hunting trip into the remote Boggy Creek region in hopes of bagging deer. After Levi takes a shot at a mysterious but unidentified shape, the two brothers decide to play a trick on Matthew and fool him into leaving their deer stand, sending him on an errant quest into the woods on a snipe hunt. The creature attacks, however, and then disappears after Levi and Corbin shoot at it. They search for Matthew but find no sign of him anywhere.

Realizing they've stumbled into the legendary Fouke Monster, they attempt to find Matthew and flee, but the creature assaults Levi before they make any progress. Corbin panics and runs away, leaving Levi to his grisly fate. In an unexpected twist, Matthew is found by the fleeing Corbin. Drawing strength as a pair, they venture forth together to double back and rescue Levi, but to no avail: They find Levi's lifeless body hanging suspended from a tree limb. The creature springs forth, having used Levi's corpse as bait, and savagely mauls the horrified Corbin. Unable to prevent Corbin's grisly fate, Matthew retreats to the deer stand, hoping to climb to safety. Instead, he finds that the rope ladder has been ripped apart. The boggy beast nears, growling. Later, when the three men's mutilated remains are discovered, authorities conclude they were attacked and mauled by a bear.

All three episodes are remarkably similar in dream-like tone and formatting, with the narrative flow hazily mixing into the documentary footage of scientists and the like commenting upon the respective creature's reported area of habitation and physical characteristics. While they each work as effective mood pieces, each has flaws in terms of plot holes. For example, the DNA evidence of the hair samples is never followed up in "Bigfoot" (one would think such valuable evidence would be preserved and documented for the scientific community); while the strange egg shells, implied to be the Honey Island Swamp Monster's own spawn, receive no further genetic analysis by Dr. Chapman in the "Swamp Sasquatch" episode. But for forgiving fans of Ciné du Sasquatch who are in the mood for easy thrills versus intellectual challenges, *Lost Tapes* is a painless if gimmicky half-hour's worth of entertainment. It never advances the Bigfoot genre per se, (relying instead upon said recreations to basically remake earlier bigger-budgeted films), but at least it imparts a sense of the awe, mystery, and underlying horror often attendant with the study of cryptozoology, which doubtless makes the subject matter so widely popular.

The Lost World (1925) (Cameo)

Starring Bessie Love, Lewis Stone, Wallace Beery, Lloyd Hughes, Alma Bennett and Bull Montana. Produced by Jamie White and Earl Hudson. Written by Sir Arthur Conan Doyle and Marion Fairfax. Directed by Harry Hoyt. USA. Black & White. Silent. 106 Minutes.

Overview: Eccentric world explorer Professor Challenger finds a diary from a survivor of a visit to a forgotten South American plateau filled with sketches of living dinosaurs. Determined to prove that dinosaurs still exist, he embarks on a treacherous journey to explore the hidden land, accompanied by a reporter, a hunter, the daughter of the original journal keeper, and a handful of servants.

Once they penetrate the so-called lost world, they discover the journal was truthful, encountering living thunder lizards at every turn. Among the monster-sized reptiles are an Allosaurus, a Pteranodon, and a Brontosaurus. Making matters worse, a bipedal hominid known only as the Ape Man attempts to crush them with boulders, and attacks them whenever it feels they are vulnerable to its surprise ambushes. They eventually kill the creature by shooting it.

Challenger insists on bringing back the Brontosaurus to convince skeptical Londoners of his incredible find, whereupon the beast breaks free and causes havoc. When the Brontosaurus attempts to cross London Bridge, its massive weight causes the structure to collapse, dropping the dinosaur into the River Thames. The prehistoric specimen vanishes beneath the river's waters as Challenger mourns the scientific loss, oblivious to the harm his actions have caused the English metropolis.

* * * * *

Without Arthur Conan Doyle's *The Lost World*, many of the critical motifs so central to Ciné du Sasquatch may never have crystallized as concretely as they did after its release, both as novel in 1912 and subsequent silent movie in 1925. Chief among these is the concept of a cryptid existing near mankind-dominated geographical locales but tantalizingly hidden from view. Another is that the hominid is the alpha being of its own world until unsettled by the intrusion of modern *Homo sapiens* and bested. Yet another is the exploitation aspect in which a Caucasian figure (herein portrayed as an explorer accompanied by an Anglo hunter) wants to take a specimen of the newly-discovered life form back to civilization, only to meet with disastrous consequences when said goal is accomplished.

Of course, most of these tenets appear in *King Kong*, as well as the Bigfoot genre. But given *King Kong*'s enormous impact on Ciné du Sasquatch, denying credit to *The Lost World* would be an oversight akin to ignoring the influence of the Tarzan mythos, or the later Patterson-Gimlin 16mm footage, on the cinematic hominid *oeuvre*. Simply stated, without the enormous success of *The Lost World*, there would never have been a *King Kong*, which in turn would have severely delayed the introduction of many key creative concepts that would become indispensable to the standard Sasquatch movie.

For but one example, it was Doyle's showing of O'Brien's stop-motion dinosaurs prior to *The Lost World*'s filmic incarnation that sparked initial interest in the later cinema incarnation. This fateful screening occurred in 1922 at the Society of American Magicians, where O'Brien's test reels of battling dinosaurs were unveiled to stunned professional illusionists, including Harry Houdini, who could not figure out the methodology by which Willis O'Brien had brought such figures to seeming "life" on the silver screen. Even such respected newspapers as the *New York Times* ran stories the day after the screening proclaiming "if fakes, they were masterpieces."

The Lost World also featured a very recognizable iconic figure central to Ciné du Sasquatch: the hominid that attacks humans invading its territory. The so-called Ape Man of *The Lost World* is a definite Bigfoot being by any other name, albeit much more human looking than many of its later cinematic cousins. With its muscular hominid body but clearly simian facial structure, the Ape Man is a ferocious, intelligent species, fully the match for any human being it encounters in cunning and physical prowess. Lacking the prototypical gorilla suit bulk and ape mask so characteristic of the Killer Gorilla films that would follow in the wake of *King Kong*, the Ape Man is much more like a human-looking simian in his upright stance, bipedal gait, and shortened forearms. In many aspects, the Ape Man is *the* prototypical screen visualization of many Ciné du Sasquatch cryptids to follow, albeit lacking the height later attributed to many real-life Bigfoot sightings.

In terms of Bigfoot cinema, it's worthwhile to note the influence of often forgotten animator Willis O'Brien in terms of the key stages of the genre's development. Though perhaps unwittingly on his part, O'Brien was significant in three vital Ciné du Sasquatch aspects: first with his early cryptid introduction in *The Dinosaur and the Missing Link: A Prehistoric Tragedy* in 1915; then in 1925 with the Ape Man in *The Lost World*; and lastly, of course, in 1933 with *King Kong*. By experimenting with techniques of hominid visualization and size,

O'Brien was a true pioneer not only with stop-motion effects technology, but in helping to define how Hollywood would forever portray hominids. His Missing Link character was a smaller-than-human bipedal being, whereas the Ape Man was normal *Homo sapiens*–sized and King Kong monster-sized. In an era where such visualizations are borderline cliché, it is well to remember that a lone filmmaker such as O'Brien was able to so readily cement the epitome of a cinema cryptid with just three early efforts. His legacy lives on in the next Bigfoot movie the reader will view.

The Lumberjack of All Trades (2006)

AKA: *The Lumberjack of All Trades: Bigfoot Massacre*. Starring Ken Johnson, T. Chris Bosies, Sammy Barnes, Warren Bloodsworth Jr., Bob Connelly, Don Atkinson, Matt Ripa, John Taylor, Josh Taylor, Graham Caldwell, Kurt Ludwick, Jim King, Richard Bird, Paul Klaverweiden and Jordan Nichols. Produced by Deborah J. Dawson and Dave Schwarten. Written by Matthew LaCurts and Eric Walter. Directed by Eric Walter. USA. Color. Stereo. 71 Minutes.

Overview: A grizzled old gold miner known only as the Prospector by the local redneck citizens of tiny Townville, Maryland, awakens the wrath of a Savage Sasquatch while camping in the creature's domain. The cryptid attacks the townsfolk and mercilessly slaughters them in an act of retribution for its sacred grounds being despoiled by the Prospector. Sheriff Hanson and Deputy Allen are hopelessly out of their depth in handling the disturbance, so it falls upon Mark the Lumberjack and his white trash brigade of Bigfoot bounty killers — manly man Brick McPhearson, mechanic Greasy Joe, and Winston the old war vet — to save the day. But can an axe-wielding, beer-guzzling maniac lumberjack and his killbilly brigade thwart a Scary Skookum hell-bent on eating the flesh of every human it dismembers alive?

* * * * *

A true no-budget cult oddity, *The Lumberjack of All Trades* is the kind of B-movie parody that separates the highbrows from the lowbrows in terms of tolerating over-the-top campiness, prolific and ridiculous gore, and postmodern schtick. For those who find anything less than well-staged, believably acted, and cleverly written comedies beneath their standards, *The Lumberjack of All Trades* will be an endurance test nothing short of the Ludivico Treatment undergone by Alex the Droog in *A Clockwork Orange*. Those who enjoy the most ridiculous of camp, however, as typified by the earliest and crudest films of Russ Meyers, John Waters, and 99 percent of Troma Films overall output, will definitely find much to like and laugh about (and at) in the breezily-paced film.

A good analogy to the formal construction of *The Lumberjack of All Trades* is the old *SCTV* Canadian comedy series that starred Joe Flaherty, John Candy, Eugene Levy, Andrea Martin, Martin Short, and many others. Like *SCTV*, the entirety of *The Lumberjack of All Trades* supposedly takes place as a late night horror film playing within the framework of a local TV station, complete with fake station ID tags, local commercials, etc. Not unlike parody films such as *The Groove Tube*, *Kentucky Fried Movie*, and *Amazon Women on the Moon* (but with a constant cast of characters instead of the aforementioned films' skit approach), *The Lumberjack of All Trades* hits and misses its intended comedic marks; but more often than not, it offers some genuinely funny Bigfoot guffaws.

The non-stop gore is so overwrought, for example, that all but the most ultra-sensitive viewers will quickly realize it is all for the Grand Guignol effect. For example, when Bigfoot is mauling one helpless motorist the monster has just dragged out of his car, the Lumberjack and pals bear down on the hominid in their 18-wheeler, intent on mowing it over. But the snarling Sasquatch quickly plucks some handy viscera from his thrashing victim's chest cavity and hurls it onto the big rig's windshield, thus bloodily reducing the driver's visibility and slowing the assault. In yet another scene, the Lumberjack axes a surprised character to death in front of a group of local men, women, and children, repeatedly hacking the body to smithereens as the stunned crowd looks on, aghast. The director clearly relishes the buckets of fake blood with which he coats each and every bystander in a montage of rapid cuts — the little old lady, the grizzled war vet, and even a couple of suburban moms with children — all of whom wind up doused like stand-ins for Sissy Spacek at the climax of *Carrie*. Like the obvious cherry-flavored Kool-Aid they're splattered with, such humor is clearly an acquired "taste" and will doubtless turn off some squeamish Ciné du Sasquatch viewers who prefer a more reverential tone in their Bigfoot outings.

That said, this author found the "running of the bulls" parody sequence à la Pamplona, Spain, a true visual highlight. In this genuinely funny scene, the Townsville residents are surprised by a sudden Sasquatch attack in broad daylight. As the terrified citizens flee en masse (a dozen or so, due to budgetary constraints), the Bigfoot follows fast on their heels, swatting them aside one by one. Some crash into mailboxes, others are mercilessly trampled in the street. Men, women, children ... none are spared from the hominid's avenging wrath. And the lumbering, shoulder-padded gorilla-style Bigfoot actually works for its pathetic cheesiness, as the filmmakers wisely don't pretend it's anything but a dime store concoction designed to garner cheap laughs. To their credit, they also suitably endow their cryptid with a massive chest, impressive height, and expressive rubber mask, which is more than some low-budget, serious-minded Ciné du Sasquatch movies accomplish on their limited budgets. At times the effect is subtly horrific, in that it is just as easy to imagine some demented redneck dressing up as Bigfoot, à la Leatherface, and committing these homicides in a booze-induced psychotic rampage as it is a Savage Sasquatch. Thankfully, most of the comedy is so exaggerated — in a *Benny Hill Show* manner — that it's clearly not the intent of the director to do more than emulate H. G. Lewis circa *2,000 Maniacs* or *Blood Feast*.

As a knowing wink at the lesser efforts of Bigfoot movies and drive-in exploitation fare of the 1960s and 1970s, *The Lumberjack of All Trades* proves an amiable if low-key diversion. Fans of either type will find a knowing nudge of nostalgia embedded within the otherwise tawdry proceedings that redeems it for all but the most critical of viewers. Faults and all, at least it can be said of the effort that it deliberately rather than unintentionally parodies itself, which is the cornerstone of producing an effective homespun comedy for practically no money.

MacGyver ("Ghost Ship") (1987) (TV)

Starring Richard Dean Anderson, Dana Elcar, Katey Wright, Michele Goodger, Nicholas Rice, Byron Chief-Moon, Len George, Chief Khotlacha, Ken Kirzinger, Blaine Lamoureux, Lon Katzman and Bill Stewart. Produced by Calvin Clements Jr., Stephen Downing, Michael Greenburg, Hudson Hickman, Stephen Kandel, John Rich, John Whelpley and Henry Winkler. Written by Stephen Kandel. Directed by Michael Vejar. USA. Color. Stereo. 60 Minutes.

Overview: MacGyver, a resourceful government agent with the ability to craft ingenious solutions to sudden life-threatening problems using only the barest of tools and his wits, is hired, along with a team of fellow "spotters," to help place geographic satellite downlinks across the dense Canadian wilderness. The task is difficult because there are no roads and no shelter, and requires each team member to act independently, using their survival skills, in order to rig each GPS system in a coordinated and extremely limited time frame.

But the mission is crucial because it will enable all future travelers to be rescued should they become lost.

All begins well until MacGyver is diverted from his mission when he stumbles upon a lost young woman who is unable to speak. Unsure if she is mute or simply in shock, MacGyver convinces her, with kindness, food, and hand gestures, to lead him back to where she first became lost in the wilderness. To his surprise, MacGyver finds himself staring at an abandoned freight ship in a nearby uninhabited harbor. The young woman becomes frightened, but, determined to investigate further, MacGyver builds a makeshift raft and kayaks over to the ship, which is anchored in deep water. He boards the rusting hulk and quickly ascertains it is of Russian origin. Before he can uncover more clues as to what went wrong, he is attacked without warning by a Savage Sasquatch.

The monster chases MacGyver throughout the dilapidated interior of the ship's cargo section, nearly killing him at several turns. MacGyver finally outwits the beast and paddles his boat back to shore. The young woman has vanished, so MacGyver chases after her, fearing for her safety. Meanwhile, the Sasquatch slips into the water and heads after them. In the woods, MacGyver catches up with the young woman and convinces her that they stand a better chance of

MacGyver (Richard Dean Anderson) against a *Close Encounters*–styled backdrop in this publicity still from the TV series *MacGyver*.

surviving if they stick together. After a makeshift meal, the young woman reveals she can speak English and her name is Joanna. She tells MacGyver she was a stowaway on the vessel, and didn't speak because she feared he was associated with the crew of the Russian ship. MacGyver is amazed not only that she can talk, but that Joanna suggests the crew of the ship is alive and well. If so, where are they now?

It turns out the Russian ship is a tanker with a converted hold filled with empty barrels, and that the crew are planning on tapping into the nearby Alaskan pipeline, filling their jerry-rigged barrels aboard their ship, and then selling the black market crude to the highest bidder. MacGyver soon realizes the Sasquatch is actually just one of the Russian pirate crew members dressing up in order to frighten away any unwelcome visitors (such as himself) while the rest of the ship's crew are busy tapping into the oil pipeline. Alas, he and Joanna stumble into the crew while trying to escape.

The crew tries to kill MacGyver and take Joanna hostage. Using a rigged trap, MacGyver is able to take down the Sasquatch crew member and rescue Joanna. He wires up the GPS unit he has deployed to send a distress signal. This alerts the officials who have been worried about his disappearance and failure to report in on his mission's progress. They deploy an emergency rescue helicopter to the GPS MacGyver has activated. MacGyver and Joanna make their way to the landing chopper and narrowly escape. The Russians are arrested, and MacGyver is once again the hero of the day.

* * * * *

MacGyver was a surprisingly successful action/mystery series which ran for 140 one-hour episodes during its seven seasons on TV and garnered a worldwide fan base. Much of the credit is due to the likeable, low-key nature of star Richard Dean Anderson, who was the antithesis of the swaggering, suave Bond-styled super agent; rather, he was a naturalist New Ager who valued intelligence over brawn, and cleverly improvised tricks and traps to free himself from the weekly trials and tribulations. Where most TV detectives and agents used a gun and their fists, MacGyver trended towards thoughtful analysis and patient clue gathering, becoming a kind of pro-green Sherlock Holmes. Though not above using physical force when necessary to protect himself or defend his cohorts, MacGyver was more akin to the David Carradine character in *Kung Fu*, only utilizing such crude methods when all other, more reasonable efforts had been previously exhausted. This unique, charming undercurrent, combined with above-average writing and direction, were the key ingredients to the series' long-term success.

"Ghost Ship" is fairly typical of both the show's strengths and weaknesses. The weaker elements come from the usual overly-familiar nature of the series, which has become nearly self-parodying in today's culture, owing in no small part to *Saturday Night Live*'s mercilessly accurate take-off on the plaid shirted, mullet-wearing detective's ability to save the day in the nick of time (or rather not at all in the *SNL* sketch's twist ending in which MacGyver is always a second too late, thus resulting in an enormous fireball finale in which all involved perish). But for its first few years of airing, *MacGyver*'s formula was indeed refreshing.

The more successful aspects of "Ghost Ship" are the hominid treatment in the first half-hour of the episode. Up until the point MacGyver determines the cryptid is just a man in a costume with the clichéd Ciné du Sasquatch motivation of scaring away innocents from uncovering the criminals' activities, "Ghost Ship" is effectively moody, suspenseful, and believable. As was always the case with *MacGyver*, location shooting (in this case, remote wilderness areas) adds a spooky level of authenticity to the proceedings, which culminate in the truly nail-biting stalking sequence aboard the eerily abandoned freighter. Here, as Sasquatch ducks and darts in and out of the rusting overhead

tangle of pipes, and between endless rotting wooden crates, "Ghost Ship" achieves a rare note of genuine horror few Bigfoot TV efforts of the era ever attained. While the suspense lessens once the creature is revealed to be a costumed human, until that mid-point revelation, "Ghost Ship" is on par with the excellent "The Spanish Moss Murders" from *Kolchak: The Night Stalker* for sheer intensity and scariness. Partly this is because the direction is efficient and taut, allowing the viewer to experience the encounter with Bigfoot through MacGyver's eyes. As he boards the ship for the first time and the visual evidence mounts as to the cryptid's unseen presence, the pay-off is a real jump-out-of-your-seat moment, wherein the creature smashes its hairy arm through the captain's port hole and grabs at the genuinely terrified MacGyver. During the following moments, "Ghost Ship" is as exciting as any televised Ciné du Sasquatch entry in the genre's long history.

The ending attempts to have it both ways: MacGyver is told that the eerie Bigfoot cries he heard previously in the forest were simply tape recordings utilized by the pirates, who broadcast them through a bullhorn to make them loud enough to echo throughout the dense woodland. To prove her point, his supervisor plays the recordings, which relieves MacGyver, as this was the one piece of the puzzle he could not fathom previously. However, just as he and his female superior share a laugh, a lonely, distant cry sounds forth from the woods on the horizon. MacGyver and his cohort share a stunned look — is this a real hominid responding, or...? It's not totally unexpected, of course, but nevertheless makes a nice coda to what is a generally well-realized episode of the series. As far as Ciné du Sasquatch is concerned, *MacGyver*'s "Ghost Ship" is a notable exception to the general exploitation pattern of far too many TV shows utilizing a cryptid cameo, as it features a well-photographed sense of menace, a believable Sasquatch costume, and even moments of unqualified terror. It's therefore as good a slice of Bigfoot TV as it is a popular show on its own, acquitting itself well on both counts.

Making Wolvy (1996) (Doc)

Featuring Louis Kiss, Jody Mullenax, Todd Tucker and Brian Steele. Produced, Written and Directed by Scott Essman. USA. Color. Stereo. 24 Minutes.

Overview: A behind-the-scenes documentary about the unreleased short fictional film *Wolvy*, this insightful "making of" video chronicles the ambitious special effects filmmaker Todd Tucker utilized for his still-unreleased movie. *Wolvy* was an attempt by Tucker to produce the beginnings of what he hoped would be a director's reel and lead to employment in the special effects business (as well as feature-film financing for his concept). Even though *Wolvy* itself sadly never saw the light of day on its own, much of it is included in this well-executed effort.

The titular character, Wolvy, is a bipedal werewolf who is into wrestling with a passion not seen since Blue Demon or El Santo donned tights and masks. Among the other fantasy characters featured (all created by Tucker in his spare time and involving an amazingly complicated level of prosthetic latex makeup effects and animatronics) is Gus, a four-armed, childlike Abominable Snowman who enters the ring to demonstrate his superior moves against the cocksure Wolvy, the latter of whom believes he's the Jerry Lawler of cryptid body-slammers. An obvious over-the-top (as in the ring's ropes!) comedy, *Making Wolvy* is a must-see for fans of both special effects creation on a low budget and Ciné du Sasquatch fans who want to see the only quad-armed hominid in the genre's history (as dubious a distinction as that may be). Included are comments by Academy Award–winning makeup artist Greg Cannom, as well as step-by-step demonstrations of how Tucker and his crew brought the creatures to life.

Man Beast (1956)

Starring Rock Madison, Asa Maynor, George Skaff, Tom Maruzzi, Lloyd Nelson, George Wells Lewis, Jack Haffner, Wong Sing and Brianne Murphy. Written by B. Arthur Cassidy. Produced and Directed by Jerry Warren. USA. Black & White. Mono. 67 Minutes.

Overview: When Connie Hayward's brother goes missing in the Himalayas, she enlists the help of her friend Trevor Hudson to mount a search party. Luckily, a scientist by the name of Dr. Ericson has just departed for the mountains himself on an unrelated trip. Realizing Ericson may hold the key to helping her in her quest, Connie employs local mountain-climbing expert Steve Cameron to lead her and Trevor to the base camp of Dr. Ericson. Ericson agrees to include the search party. Proving of particular value to Ericson's expedition is Varga, a Sherpa guide who is an expert in the various trails and pitfalls of the dangerous mountain.

Along the way, tensions boil over as the group uncover evidence

Poster art for the theatrical release of *Man Beast*.

that Connie's brother was not merely exploring the terrain, but intent on uncovering the whereabouts of the fabled Yeti said to inhabit the area. The party is attacked by the club-wielding creatures while sheltering in a dark cave, which only proves to the human explorers their mission has value beyond uncovering the mysterious disappearance of Connie's brother. Eventually they are made to realize that Varga has been tricking them all along; posing as an ignorant native, he is actually a highly intelligent college-educated man. Beyond that, to the surviving party members' horror, they learn that Varga is also a half-human, half-hominid being, birthed of a *Homo sapiens* and Abominable Snowman coupling. The terrified Connie is informed that such interbreeding has been going on in an attempt by the Yetis to infiltrate any expeditions trying to uncover their secret hiding place in the Himalayan mountains, and that her fate will be to give birth to such half-breeds. Varga falls to his death after a struggle, while Connie and Trevor escape with their lives, shattered by what they've uncovered but realizing no one will ever believe them.

* * * * *

Jerry Warren is often "credited" with being one of the worst filmmakers in Hollywood (or, rather, off–Hollywood) history. Even the much-lambasted Ed D. Wood Jr. had an all-star biopic made of his life, after all; but there are no reported plans as of this writing to produce such a testament to the career prowess of Warren. Many of his later films (such as *Frankenstein Island*, *The Wild World of Batwoman*, *Attack of the Mayan Mummy*, and *Face of the Screaming Werewolf*) were pastiche editing jobs in which Warren purchased one or two low-budget Mexican horror films, shot a few new scenes with fading American genre actors (such as Lon Chaney Jr. or John Carradine), and unleashed the newly-assembled mongrel upon a disbelieving matinee and drive-in public. To describe most of these later efforts as "bad" is a failure to grasp the essential definition of the term, as a relatively mild term such as "bad" posits a positive opposite, such as "good," in contrast. In the Jerry Warren world, however, the opposite of "bad" would be "worse."

How then to account for the relative entertainment value of *Man Beast*? Many critics have credited the brief running time, which, at barely over an hour (with credits), surely is a major plus. Others have cited the relatively suspenseful screenplay by B. Arthur Cassidy, which is also worthy of mention, especially given that he never wrote another produced television or film screenplay. Still others remark upon the stock footage, which adds an air of production gloss to what is a nonexistent budget. All of these are astute as far as it goes, but one additional note should be added to the brew: Warren was probably inspired at the time he produced and directed *Man Beast*. Being his first film, he had yet to develop the cynical veneer that would coat his later films. Whereas W. Lee Wilder couldn't muster enough self-belief to make *The Snow Creature* watchable throughout, the cash-strapped Warren triumphed, making his film an enjoyable if threadbare hour-plus of hominid hokum for non-critical viewers. If Orson Welles achieved his greatest cinematic triumph with *Citizen Kane* as his first film, then it's fair (though admittedly contentious) to say Jerry Warren equally "peaked" atop the Himalayas (which were actually stock footage of said mountains mixed with Warren-filmed sequences of his cast in the hills of Bishop, California) with *Man Beast*.

The film posits a major thematic motif in terms of Ciné du Sasquatch, as well. That is, Varga admits his he is a half-human, half-hominid byproduct, and that human women are captured for interbreeding purposes. Owing to the creepy cinematography and hamfisted but suitably eerie performance by actor George Skaff (whose intermittent on-again, off-again career would see him working with Hitchcock on *Topaz* and subsequent appearances on TV fare such as *The Rockford Files*, *Wonder Woman*, *Delvecchio*, and *Columbo*). While this subtext has always been implicitly present in the Killer

Gorilla genre, and in such Bigfoot influences as *King Kong*, it was *Man Beast* that took it to its logical conclusion and brought the bestiality to the forefront of the narrative (at least, that is, at the film's conclusion). It must have provided quite a shock for conservative 1950s audiences unconditioned to such overt sexuality in their fantasy films to see and hear a character talking of this as if it was the most normal activity imaginable. While it is true that aliens taking Earth women for mating was a staple of the science fiction films by this point, the one-less-removed level of such pseudo "race mixtures" probably hit more than a few nerves in the pre–Civil Rights era. Given that the 1950s were marked by a puritanical emphasis on segregation of race, politics, and the like, *Man Beast* is positively transgressive. This act of subversion is made all the more unusual in that the audience is shown the results first-hand when Varga reveals he's been masking his "otherness" all along; in effect, he has "passed as white" the entire length of the film, bringing into question the validity of the inherent racism of the day if none of the humans could tell the difference before his revelation. What good, Varga's masquerade poses, has been the human (and, specifically, the Western WASP human) air of superiority if it only enabled Varga to turn the tables on them all the more readily?

Indeed, throughout *Man Beast* the humans come across as insufferably arrogant and self-dividing. They constantly quarrel and display non-stop condescension towards Varga and his "simple people" until he reveals to them he has been college-educated at their own universities. While this initial confession sets the white intruders on their collective heads at first, they soon regain their superior airs because he remains, after all, their hired servant, no matter how "uppity" his manner or education. In other words, as long as Varga "remains in his place" as a lower class worker, no harm is done in his having educated himself in their "superior" ways and customs. While it can be argued this reading derives from the amateurish performance of the actors in *Man Beast*, who refuse to play their characters as anything more than stereotypical, the looks of horror on their faces when they realize how deftly Varga has used their colonialist attitudes against them is hard to dismiss.

This theme matches the other tenet present in *Man Beast* that is a hallmark of Ciné du Sasquatch: humans looking to invade the ho-

minid's territory always assume a superior position as a collective species to the "primitive animal" whose domain they self-righteously infiltrate. Only after encountering the cryptid on its own turf do the *Homo sapiens* come to realize they're at best equal and in many cases inferior to their bipedal rivals, at least as long as they remain on the Yeti's turf. This sudden reduction in status as the dominant species on the planet always comes as a profound and unsettling shock to the humans involved; they struggle with their self-absorbed identity as God's chosen species after their encounter with a Sasquatch. Cinematic hominids seem to represent the footnote to God's original blessing. They are the reminder that while *Homo sapiens* may be dominant, they are not without rivalry to the title of Masters of the World, even if in most cases humans eventually triumph over hominids.

Man Beast features a less-than-convincing Yeti suit, especially the dome-shaped heads. But their bulky form is menacing in and of itself, and Warren keeps them mostly in the dark, which helps hide the deficiencies. Unlike most cinematic hominids, the creatures wield clubs with aplomb. This is rare in Ciné du Sasquatch, which typically depicts the Abominable Snowman as a non-technological being. Apart from the occasional hurled stone, most screen Yetis simply use their teeth and claws to destroy their prey. Why this should be so is a matter of speculation the movies themselves don't dwell upon, but given that most *Homo sapiens* ancestors developed at least minimal tool-making skills, it is worth pondering. Even chimpanzees are known to use sticks to forage for insects to eat. Surely a bipedal hominid species would have at least advanced to the stage of spears and the like?

Despite the fact Warren would quickly fade into obscurity as a filmmaker, he can be acknowledged (at least in the Bigfoot film canon) as having created a genuinely entertaining and modestly successful Yeti film. Given the dismal creative failure of *The Snow Creature* prior to *Man Beast*, and that Hammer's *The Abominable Snowman* was still a year away, *Man Beast* surprisingly marks the best American effort of the 1950s dealing with a cinematic Yeti. While this is faint praise, given the lack of competition, it is still impressive in context, as Warren was walking a low-budget tightrope upon which many would have been unable to balance. The fact *Man Beast* is even watchable, let alone moderately suspenseful, is to his credit.

The Man from U.N.C.L.E. ("The Abominable Snowman Affair") (Cameo) (TV) (1966)

Starring Robert Vaughn, David McCallum, Anne Jeffreys and Leo G. Carroll. Executive Produced by Sam Rolfe. Written by Kirshna Shah. Directed by Otto Lang. USA. Color. Stereo. 60 Minutes.

Overview: To be a superspy in the 1960s was to be the male epitome of cool: One had unlimited power to kill without worry, travel globally without personal costs or care, a bevy of model-beautiful women waiting in every exotic destiny, unlimited gadgetry, and really groovy threads. The popular NBC series *The Man from U.N.C.L.E.* maintained just the right balance between outright camp and suspense in the classic Hitchcock mold (this is very much a spy recasting of Hitch's *North by Northwest*, with the fictitious George Kaplan spy character made real via the suave duo of Robert Vaughn and David McCallum as government agents — even Leo G. Carroll is on hand to reprise his head agent role from Hitchcock's comic-suspense masterpiece). As a result, it ran for many seasons, as well as spawning theatrical releases, comic book tie-ins, and the inevitable spin-offs, sequels, and remakes.

"The Abominable Snowman Affair" is less tawdry than its title

The intrepid explorers from *Man Beast* brave the Himalayas, actually mostly stock footage intercut with second unit Southern California mountain shots assembled by director/editor Jerry Warren.

might imply. Indeed, the word "Affair" was added to every *The Man from U.N.C.L.E.* episode title in order to capture that "shag-a-delic" feel more recently attributable to Austin Powers than Napoleon Solo. The Bigfoot cameo is brief but self-referentially poignant, and occurs when Agent Illya Kuryakin (David McCallum) must enter the politically restricted land of Chupat in the Himalayas in order to make contact with a clandestine agent therein. Ironically, in order to avoid drawing attention to himself among the Sherpas who frequent the trails, Illya dons a Yeti costume! Thus passing as just another Abominable Snowman sighting to any locals he might chance upon, the U.N.C.L.E. agent easily crosses from neutral into enemy territory without drawing a second glance. While preposterous, the idea is so comically beguiling it works to produce a knowing laugh.

Ciné du Sasquatch fans will get a kick of recognition out of the suit McCallum uses in the brief cameo. It is the same costume designed by Academy Award–winning special effects artist William Tuttle that was previously seen in the MGM film *The 7 Faces of Dr. Lao.* While it doesn't look any better for the wear and tear, the costume is as immediately familiar as a Robby the Robot cameo from the same era. Though the rest of the episode pays mere lip service to the Yeti, this episode is worthwhile for die-hards who wish to see Tuttle's wonderful Yeti suit receive tribute via the judicious budgetary recycling that once marked successful TV productions.

Manbeast! Myth or Monster (1978) (Doc)

Featuring Peter C. Byrne and Ted Williams. Produced by Alan Landsburg and Nicholas Webster. Written by Nicholas Webster, Diana Webster and Anthony Potter. Directed by Nicholas Webster. USA. Color. Mono. 90 Minutes.

Overview: Alan Landsburg made a fortune out of popularizing Fortean phenomena in the 1970s with such landmark TV series as *In Search Of*, with Leonard Nimoy, and documentary specials such as *The Outer Space Connection*. A Korean War vet turned filmmaker, he revolutionized the television documentary format with his helming of the Mike Wallace–hosted series *Biography*, which practically created the news journal format that would become *60 Minutes*.

This obscure, hard-to-find documentary has yet to be released on DVD. It is well-remembered, however, because of the effective direction by Nicholas Webster involving the Bigfoot sequences and the convincing make-up effects by a young Rob Bottin, who would later devise the spectacular effects that made John Carpenter's *The Thing* so repulsively effective. Bottin later created the memorable hominid for *Tanya's Island*, another well-regarded (but fictional) Ciné du Sasquatch entry. Bottin's contributions greatly elevate *Manbeast! Myth or Monster*, allowing the director to linger on the creatures while at the same time deliberately obscuring them in shadows to maintain their eerie effectiveness. And unlike many documentary films, *Manbeast! Myth or Monster* actually shows a family of Bigfoot creatures — from the opening frames, no less. As they stride across the darkened foreboding landscape during a primordial dawn sequence straight out of *2001*, we see a large male, a curvaceous female (with the tiniest hourglass waistline in Bigfoot genre history), and even several younglings. Given how this image immediately creates empathy for the cryptids, it's surprising how few other documentaries in the *oeuvre* have copied it.

Of course, that may be a reflection of the low budget so many Bigfoot documentaries face, thus forcing the filmmakers to concentrate their limited resources on a single costume. The production budget for *Manbeast! Myth or Monster* was relatively high for the era — at one million dollars — and the increased spending allowed producer Alan Landsburg to fly his crew around the globe to such authentic locales

as Nepal, the Pacific Northwest, and Louisiana to thoroughly cover his subject matter. At one point his beleaguered film crew was actually stuck high in the Himalayan Mountains for over a week during a blizzard.

Despite its lurid title, *Manbeast! Myth or Monster* is actually quite objective for an early documentary in the field, refusing to outright endorse any belief system as much as document the eyewitness stories. To this end, Landsburg and his team of creative writers sifted through over 130 different recorded encounters with bipedal cryptids and settled on a dozen to recreate cinematically. Some, such as the Honey Island Swamp Monster, are familiar to Bigfoot devotees, but others are fresh to Ciné du Sasquatch. Among the highlights are the reenactment of two Nepal hunters trapped inside an Abominable Snowman's cave; the mysterious case of a Washington snow skier who vanished without explanation, his ski trails suddenly interrupted by large footprints; and a recreation of an Alma (a Russian derivative of Bigfoot) encounter inside a snowbound cabin at night.

The latter is best-remembered by younger viewers of *Manbeast! Myth or Monster* because of the scary intensity of the sequence. It chronicles the report by a Russian researcher who was alone in her two-story, snowbound cabin one night. Awakening from a deep sleep, she claimed she sat upright in her bed and turned to see the Alma rocking in a chair across the room, growling at her with ferocious intent. Her screams sent it fleeing down the steps, never to be seen again. The tale has the eerie feel of a ghost story, in part because of the bizarre imagery of a Bigfoot rocking in a chair! The director shoots the scene for maximum impact, keeping the creature in the far corner of the room opposite the researcher and lighting Bottin's scary makeup so that only the most basic features are revealed. This pattern is maintained throughout the film, to the creatures' advantage: In daytime scenes they're always photographed in silhouette against the sun; in night sequences the lighting is indistinct so that features are difficult to ascertain. It adds a level of drama otherwise lacking in the stories alone.

It is truly sad that *Manbeast! Myth or Monster* is so hard to see today. It not only works as a successful though often scientifically inaccurate account of hominids circa the 1970s, but equally as a docudrama, given the myriad recreated encounters. Along with *The Mysterious Monsters*, this remains one of the better efforts of the era.

Meet the Vancouver 2010 Mascot Commercial (2010)

Produced by the Vancouver Organizing Committee for the 2010 Olympic and Paralympic Winter Games. Canada. Color. Stereo. 4 Minutes.

Overview: In order to help promote the 2010 Vancouver Winter Olympics and the Paralympic Winter Games, the Canadian government produced a series of "child-friendly" mascots — Miga, Quatchi, and Sumi. Quatchi (short for Sasquatch) was a benign Bigfoot character who promoted the idea of winter sports, particularly ice hockey. Quatchi was rendered in an anime style similar to the Powerpuff Girls, and was supposedly obsessed with becoming a top-notch goalie in his chosen competition. Alas, because of his girth, Quatchi was often inept at blocking speeding pucks and consequently imparted the lesson to kids (or so organizers claimed) that practice makes perfect.

Quatchi was heavily commercialized leading up to and during the Olympic Winter Games of 2010, especially throughout Canada. The stuffed mascot collectible doll of Quatchi was a big Canuck seller, as were tee-shirts and related Quatchi-themed merchandise. The official Vancouver Winter Games website highlighted Quatchi, making the cryptid their de facto branded identity. Quatchi's enduring charm may lead to further adventures down the ice field, given how enormously successful the ad campaign was for the producers.

The Mighty Boosh (2005) ("Call of the Yeti") (TV)

Starring Julian Barratt, Noel Fielding, Michael Fielding, Dave Brown, Rich Fulcher and Barunka O'Shaughnessy. Produced by Spencer Millman and Alison MacPhail. Written by Julian Barratt and Noel Fielding. Directed by Paul King. UK. Color. Stereo. 30 Minutes.

Overview: Howard Moon and Vince Noir form a comedy pair of nitwits eking out a lurid living in a tiny Dalston, England, flat. While daydreaming of scoring big with their horrendous musical two-man band, they work their dreary day jobs as employees at the horrible tourist trap enterprise known as the Zoo-niverse. Bollo the gorilla and shaman Naboo the Enigma join them as flat mates after they quit the exploitative Zoo-niverse. Together, the four oddballs have an amazing series of adventures, usually in far-flung, exotic locales that would, in reality, be beyond their meager means of achieving.

In the "Call of the Yeti" episode, Howard invites Vince, Bollo, and Naboo to a remote cabin for some downtime in the wilds. However, Vince is mistaken for a female by Kodiak Jack, the cabin's owner, and spends his time thwarting Kodiak Jack's amorous advances. Wanting to be alone with Vince, Jack tells Howard of the supposed Yeti inhabiting the nearby woods. Seeking to fulfill his "inner wildlife photographer" ambition, Howard takes off alone to capture images of the Abominable Snowman, only to be captured by the Yeti and put under its hypnotic spell. Meantime, while shopping for supplies, Naboo learns that the annual Yeti breeding night is nigh, which results in the local villagers staying indoors for fear of being abducted. Fearing for Howard when he doesn't return, Vince, Naboo, and Bollo set out to find their missing flat mate. Alas, the trio is also placed in a somnambulistic trance by the Yeti. All four captives are strapped down in order to be sexually sacrificed to the Yeti population, but Kodiak Jack arrives in the nick of time to thwart the pagan hominid ritual. Unfortunately, Kodiak Jack falls prey to Yeti rape while his freed comrades escape.

The Queen of the Yetis gives chase, determined to have Howard at any cost. The four friends barricade themselves in their cabin, but the Queen forces her way inside. She steps upon Vince's overstuffed suitcase, however, and shoots through the cabin's roof from the resulting explosion of force. Spared but determined never to mess with a Yeti again, the chastised but cryptically-chaste flat mates return to their English apartment, grateful for the modern horrors of civilization in comparison to the sinister mating calls of the wild.

* * * * *

A popular mainstay of recent British television, *The Mighty Boosh* is a surreal sketch comedy show that plays like Monty Python's *And Now for Something Completely Different*, albeit with a continuing set of characters rather than an episodic series of interconnected segments. Each show features a different and ridiculously improbable locale for the two dimwitted flat mates Howard and Vince to circumnavigate and typically extract themselves from in the face of mortal peril. Mixing a perverse set of *This Is Spinal Tap* moments, wherein the viewer is left aghast at the maniacally untalented musician's attempts to make a success of their monotonous band, with a variety of fantastic creatures and settings, *The Mighty Boosh* works largely as an absurdist,

Promotional artwork for *The Mighty Boosh*.

postmodern variation on the overly-familiar sitcom. Refusing to take itself too seriously (or the trite sitcom formulas so well known to any viewer over the age of five), the series manages to be both charming and chuckle-inducing despite (or because of) the over-the-top nature of the characters and their inept lack of self-perception.

"Call of the Yeti" is typical of the series, which has the characters embarking on an excursion to anywhere but their dreary English flat in search of relief from the crushing boredom of their going-nowhere lives. And, of course, where Howard and Vince are involved, any such transition will inevitably involve them in events and situations beyond either their control or comprehension. Howard, ever the more practical and seemingly intelligent of the pair (but who is actually just more self-deluding in a "normal" everyman manner), fancies he'll use his buddy's cabin to launch his long-repressed career as a wildlife photographer. Vince, the rock and roll long-hair and less intellectually-inclined partner (but who is, conversely, more apt to imagine an outlandish way to help the duo escape their prescribed fates when in peril), simply looks forward to a commune with nature. Both are quickly foiled in their respective plans; Howard is hypnotized by the Himalayan hominid he seeks to photograph in a bid to spectacularly launch his newfound passion, and Vince is mistaken by Kodiak Jack, the cabin's owner, as a desirable woman.

In many ways this particular episode resembles the classic 1980s comedy *Withnail & I*, particularly the long middle section of that film in which Withnail and Marwood escape their English flat and crash in a cabin owned by Uncle Monty, Withnail's family relation. Similarly in *Withnail & I*, Uncle Monty takes an immediate liking to the handsome Marwood, little caring that Withnail's partner is clearly not homosexual nor interested in experimenting with Uncle Monty. But given the influential cult nature of *Withnail & I*, there's every reason to believe "Call of the Yeti" is a tongue-in-cheek homage rather than unintentional rip-off. And, of course, *Withnail & I*, for all its absurdities, didn't dwell on any cinematic cryptids, upon where this episode of *The Mighty Boosh* concentrates the largest part of its plot.

The mythology in "Call of the Yeti" also plays into the crossbreeding bestiality motif so frequently apparent in Ciné du Sasquatch. In this show, the Yetis actually do their mating with humans every five years, thereby reducing their chance of being discovered by the human populace and held accountable for their actions. The human villagers, nervous on the eve of the mating night but unwilling to risk bodily dismemberment to prevent it (or worse fates — as sexual slaves to an Abominable Snowman!), always look the other way and simply allow a few campers or visitors to be sacrificed in their place, spreading the word among themselves to keep well clear of Piney Ridge (where the Yetis dwell). Though played for humorous effect in "Call of the Yeti," it follows Bigfoot film genre conventions, echoing the *Man Beast* and *Night of the Demon* examples of implied interbreeding between *Homo sapiens* and hominids. The sexual attraction Kodiak Jack has for the unwilling Vince is a well-executed narrative rhyming of the Yeti's sexual desire for Howard, thus neatly dovetailing both plots.

The visualization of the Yetis is quite unique in the genre. Instead of the rubbery gorilla masks so common in most low-budget TV series featuring an Abominable Snowman, the creatures wear skull masks over their countenances. So in an ironic twist, the totems the natives carve depicting Yeti faces actually display the disguising masks. The lesser tribal Yetis wear white skull faces while the Queen Yeti has the visage of a Chinese demon, complete with red face, wild popping eyes, and snarling fangs. It's a funny gag, mainly because *The Mighty Boosh* is such a modestly-produced series that it would have otherwise been unable to depict the cryptids in any convincing manner. So the stone-faced realizations represent a comic concession to this constraint and make a positive out of it, displaying the show's continuous creativity.

No real explanation is ever given as to why Yetis would be in the English countryside instead of Nepal, but then again, no rationale is ever offered for why Howard and Vince have a flat mate who is a gorilla *and* speaks perfect English. It's a case of suspension of disbelief being critical to appreciate the humor of *The Mighty Boosh*, without which there would be no humor at all (or series, for that matter). For those who enjoy the kind of absurdities so prevalent in English "telly" comedies, however, *The Mighty Boosh* is a genuinely funny half-hour of Ciné du Sasquatch.

Mighty Mightor (1967) ("The Snow Trapper" and "Attack of the Ice Creatures") (TV)

AKA: *Moby Dick and Mighty Mightor*. Featuring the voices of Barry Balkin, Bobby Resnick, Don Messick, Norma McMillan, John Stephenson, Paul Stewart, Bob Diamond and Patsy Garrett. Created by Alex Toth. Written by Eddie Brandt and David Scott. Produced and Directed by Joseph Barbera and William Hanna. USA. Color. Mono. 30 Minutes.

Overview: Mighty Mightor is the flying, super-powered caveman defender of his tribe of cave people. His alter ego is a young man named Tor, who has been given a magical club by a grateful hermit which transforms the lad into Mightor whenever trouble arises. Along with the help of Tog (his faithful pet dinosaur), Sheera (his girlfriend, who suspects but does not know Tor is also Mighty Mightor), Lil Rock (his kid sidekick), and Ort (his friendly flying dragon), Tor and Mightor fight a never-ending battle for truth, justice, and the prehistoric way.

* * * * *

Those master purveyors of kiddy cryptid cartoons, the Hanna-Barbera production studio, featured a vast array of hominids within their long line of Saturday morning success stories. From *Jonny Quest* to *Scooby Doo*, and *Birdman* and beyond, their impressive output would almost invariably feature the appearance of at least one Sasquatch or Yeti by any other name. Whether this was because of the popularity of the Abominable Snowman in popular news accounts of the day, or simply because large, furry, white hominids were rela-

tively easy to draw for time-pressed animators (one gets the feeling both probabilities were incentives), the dynamic duo of cel animation for TV simply couldn't resist cryptid inclusions in their *oeuvre*.

Mighty Mightor (talk about alliterative names!) was created by stalwart graphic illustrator, comic book artist, and animation designer Alex Toth, whose other creations include the aforementioned *Jonny Quest*, as well as *Space Ghost* and the earlier *Space Angel* series for tiny Cambria Studios. As far as Mightor is concerned as a character, he is basically identical to the old *Shazam* comic book series featuring Billy Batson, who transforms into Captain Marvel when danger calls. The only difference (besides *Mighty Mightor* being set in the prehistoric past) is that instead of an old cave hermit giving young Batson a magical ring that transforms him into the good Captain, Tor is given a club by an old cave hermit which shape shifts him into muscular Mightor.

Not to wear a good thing out, Hanna-Barbera actually topped themselves with this iconic effort, featuring not one but two different Yeti variants in the first season alone. In "The Snow Trapper" episode, legends abound within the caveman community about a tribe of fearsome monsters known only as the Snow Trappers. Lil Rock encounters the Abominable Snowmen and discovers they're anything but folklore, which sets in motion Mightor having to intervene on Lil Rock's behalf to free him from captivity. And in the "Attack of the Ice Creatures" episode, a bizarre, talking hominid known as Gorr leads his band of what are basically Yetis on a relocation expedition into the valley where Tor and his people reside. Gorr displaces a giant iceberg into the valley with the intent of inhabiting the iceberg's peaks and crevices while enjoying the more favorable source of easy prey in the animal-populated lowlands. Mightor intervenes, of course, setting off a volcano in order to redirect its spewing lava into the iceberg and melt its base. Realizing their frozen domain is doomed, Gorr uses his mystical powers to cause the iceberg to reverse its course. He and his tribe of hominids retreat atop it, leaving the lowlands safe again for Tor's clan.

The depictions of both the Ice Creatures and the Snow Trappers are almost identical to each other: large, menacing, Abominable Snowman–styled monsters. Gorr and his followers have one salient feature that distinguishes them from the Trappers (besides the ability to speak): Gorr's hominid variants have a raccoon-like mask of dark fur around their eyes that droops down either side of their faces like a handlebar mustache. In contrast, the Snow Trappers have much larger eyes, fanged mouths, and long, claw-like fingers. Otherwise, it's as if the animators took the Trappers and stenciled black eye masks onto them to create the Ice Creatures. There is never any doubt as to each species being Yetis because of their icy domains and large feet, even if the series goes to great lengths to give each of the cryptid tribes different names and customs.

The Mighty Peking Man (1977)

AKA: *Goliathon*; *Colossus of Congo*; *Hsing Hsing Wang*. Starring Li Hsiu-hsien, Evelyn Kraft, Hsiao Yao, Ku Feng and Lin Wei-tu. Produced by Chua Lam and the Shaw Brothers. Written by Kuang Ni. Directed by Ho Meng-hua. Hong Kong. Color. Stereo. 90 Minutes.

Overview: Danny is dismayed when his girlfriend cheats on him, so he flees to the slopes of the Himalayas as a hired big game hunter to seek solace in the wilds. Lost in the jungle, he encounters Utam, a gigantic Yeti that towers over the tall tree tops. Spared certain death at the hands of the Mighty Peking Man by the timely intervention of Samantha — a beautiful blonde woman who grew up alone in the jungle after her parents' plane crashed with her on board — Danny is grateful but mystified by what he's encountered.

When a poisonous snake bites Samantha on the thigh, Danny saves her life by sucking the venom out of her wound. This endears him to both Samantha, who finds herself falling in love with him, and Utam, who is obsessed with the blonde jungle goddess. Samantha is dubious when Danny insists on leading her back to civilization, but coaxes Utam to follow the human duo out of the jungles and back to Danny's hunting party. The Mighty Peking Man is captured and chained aboard a ship while Samantha watches in dismay, horrified by Danny's acquiescence to a sleazy promoter intent on exploiting Utam back in Hong Kong.

During their voyage, a storm rises and Utam is released from his chains long enough to prevent the ship from smashing against a dangerous outcropping of rocks. The group arrive, with great fanfare, in Hong Kong, whereupon Danny's brother, a TV producer, interviews them, thereby insuring enormous interest in Utam. Danny reconciles with his old girlfriend, much to Samantha's chagrin. She runs away from Danny, eventually finding herself nearly raped by the slimy promoter inside a hotel room while the enraged Utam watches from just outside the window, where he is chained. Utam breaks free, scoops up Samantha, and chases after the hysterical promoter, eventually crushing the man to death.

With Samantha in his grasp, Utam climbs atop the Jardine House, the highest structure he can find in Hong Kong, seeking solace and safety. Alas, helicopters are dispatched to rid the city of the menace of the Mighty Peking Man. Utam is strafed to death with bullets. He sets Samantha down and dies, but she is also killed in an explosion. Danny sadly watches, realizing he's had a hand in both their deaths.

* * * * *

After the international success of *Infra-Man*, Golden Harvest movie mogul Runme Shaw, one-half of the prolific Shaw Brothers, decided a *King Kong* knock-off was in order. Combining a female Tarzan with the venerable Kong plot, the Brothers Shaw unleashed *The Mighty Peking Man* on the world. Sadly, it was not the box-office spectacular of *Infra-Man* in terms of garnering widespread audience interest, but given its similarity to Dino De Laurentiis' recent *King Kong* remake (which had spawned a slew of knock-offs to the point the market was overly-saturated for giant hominid films, particularly given that most were inanely produced for a fast buck), this was not surprising. The lack of name cast members in the United States didn't help matters, nor did its release by tiny World Northal in North America (a specialist in Asian action and martial arts movies), who retitled the film *Goliathon* (for reasons known only to the studio, but perhaps to avoid litigation at the hands of De Laurentiis). Equally mysterious but probably for similar reasons, the film's giant cryptid was shown on the poster as a white-haired Yeti rather than the King Kong lookalike that actually starred in *The Mighty Peking Man*.

The thematic resemblance to *King Kong* is so complete that the deviations from the formula are more remarkable than any parallels. Chiefly, the jungle woman element is borrowed from another Bigfoot film genre influence, Edgar Rice Burrough's *Tarzan*; and with the change of sex of the Lord of the Apes, as well as the regional differences owing to the production locales, *The Mighty Peking Man* is a mighty close offspring indeed. The romance between Danny and Samantha is straight out of any of the *King Kong* films, as is the Carl Denham figure (although in *The Mighty Peking Man* he has gone one step beyond the normal exploiter of a giant cryptid to become an outright sociopath, as illustrated by his attempted rape of Samantha). Another swipe from *Kong* has the giant creature seeking higher ground from which to defend itself, only to tragically fall to its death. One minor, albeit tragic, difference is that Samantha is also sacrificed, giving a twist to the old adage which ended King Kong: "'Twas civilization that killed beauty *and* the beast."

As a filmic experience, it's easy to view *The Mighty Peking Man* as camp from today's perspective. It has many of the cult hallmarks requisite to such lionization: the ludicrous nature of the "homage" (which is really a Xerox of the *King Kong* source material); the bad dubbing and technical limitations (though many of the special effects are often quite innovative, given the low-budget nature of the production); the scantily-clad and stunningly attractive Russian-born Evelyne Kraft (who sadly died of a heart attack in 2009), whose character insists on wearing the same fur bikini whether in the Nepal jungles or in the concrete jungles of downtown Hong Kong; and the generally bad but intentional humor which runs throughout. Still, as Quentin Tarantino's theatrical re-release of the film in 1999 under his Rolling Thunder banner shows, *The Mighty Peking Man* is not without its fans. No less than Roger Ebert (who was also a big fan of the earlier Shaw Brothers' *Infra-Man*) gave the film a three-out-of-four-stars rating, citing its "certain level of insane genius" in his review of the movie.

In regards to Ciné du Sasquatch, *The Mighty Peking Man* plays out remarkably similar to *Yeti: Giant of the 20th Century*, which also posits a monstrously large Abominable Snowman as its civilization-

Poster art for the theatrical release of *Goliathon*. The Yeti is portrayed with white fur but was dark-colored in the film. This (and vice versa) is an inexplicable but frequent Ciné du Sasquatch occurrence.

bound cryptid. Both clearly demonstrate the genre's central tenets of having a hominid as master of its lost world who is captured and returned to man's world to meet its doom. Of the two films, *The Mighty Peking Man* is much better produced than *Yeti: Giant of the 20th Century*; but given the fact they were made literally worlds apart (the former in Hong Kong and the latter in Italy and Canada) and at roughly the same time, it's remarkable how each identifies and decides to explicitly exploit the Ciné du Sasquatch connection rather than merely portray their titular monsters as giant gorillas. This shows a canny knack that Bigfoot filmmakers have demonstrated throughout the genre's history in terms of wedding existing Sasquatch mythology to currently popular film cycles (in this case, the wave of *King Kong* clones flooding the world cinema markets). Equally it shows that the relative size of the Abominable Snowman in movies is completely flexible, unlike reported sightings in reality. Whether it's a tiny *Little Bigfoot* or towering *Mighty Peking Man*, cinematic cryptids have great leeway in terms of height, but are restrained by the same common qualities in terms of genre limitations.

Missing Link (1988)

Starring Peter Elliott, Michael Gambon, Brian Abrahams, Clive Ashley, Fred T. Baker, Adrian Brett, David Daley, Jim Dvorak, Dave Holland, Gary Kettel, Mike Kidson, Will Menter, Chris Redsell, Colin Thompson, Andy Warrington, David Damaseb, Johannes Bees and Aloysius Nariep. Produced by Peter Guber, Dennis B. Kane and Jon Peters. Written and Directed by Carol Hughes and David Hughes. USA. Color. Stereo. 91 Minutes.

Overview: The last of a dying species of hominids journeys across the African continent after Stone Age humans slaughter his tribe at a watering hole. The lonely ape-man encounters all sorts of life — lions, turtles, zebras, elephants, and other exotic animals — but never hears an answering cry to his wail of distress. He eventually makes it to the ocean, and the narrator informs us that he will face certain extinction, lacking any hope for a mate, and that mankind has only succeeded in destroying what may have been the better genetic strain of itself, given how cruel *Homo sapiens* are towards any other hominids.

* * * * *

While it's technically not within the Ciné du Sasquatch genre, owing to the fact the ape-man star of *Missing Link* is identified as being an example of the *Australopithecine* species, the film is worthy of notation as a pseudo-example of Bigfoot filmmaking in that it so clearly crystallizes the major themes of the genre in a way that is at once sobering and forthright. Because the film is rendered without dialogue and is presented as a pseudo-documentary, *Missing Link* often feels more like an episode on the Discovery Channel than a feature-length film.

Despite the designation of the ape-man as a known species of hominid, *Missing Link* presents the same dynamics of the typical Bigfoot movie — but in reverse. Rather than having the human beings invade the dominant cryptid's territory, the depicted ape-man is the weaker of the two species from the initial encounter forward. Rather than witnessing the *Homo sapiens* retreat in horror as they realize they've come across a lost species every bit their equal in terms of cunning and strength, *Missing Link* shows the diminutive ape-man barely escaping with his life after watching the rest of his small tribe being slaughtered by the proto-humans. It's never even a battle, as the humans are weapon-bearing, organized for ambush, and ruthlessly predatory. In a strange way, *Missing Link* has the Ciné du Sasquatch roles adroitly reversed, with the passive hominid in retreat for its life and the domineering humans attempting to kill it at every turn.

This is similar to what some paleontologists believe may have hap-

pened when, for example, Neanderthals met Cro-Magnons, as portrayed in Jean M. Auel's best-selling novel *The Clan of the Cave Bear*. That is, the more human Cro-Magnons killed off the less savage Neanderthals, who may have actually been more intelligent (though brain capacity in and of itself is no predictor of intelligence per se, it's worth noting that Neanderthals had a larger brain than modern *Homo sapiens*). Certainly Neanderthals were nothing like their typical Hollywood counterpart, as most scientists now agree they were advanced enough to bury their dead in ceremonial shrines, use tools, and even possibly possess language skills. Of course, there is no proof that Cro-Magnons or any other species of pre-human beings systematically or unintentionally (via competition for limited resources, for example, or through disease) killed off Neanderthals, despite the fact Neanderthals are generally believed to have become extinct about 30,000 years ago (a very recent date in geological terms).

Ciné du Sasquatch frequently implies, if not explicitly states, a similar explanation both of how a hominid species such as Bigfoot may have become nearly extinct (they were forced to retreat into isolated regions in order to survive contact with mankind) and why they are naturally aggressive towards *Homo sapiens* when humans enter their sanctified domains. Not that Sasquatch needs much in the way

Missing Link is a rare example of a diminutive hominid film. The creature is realistically presented, à la those in *2001: A Space Odyssey*. The genre's recurrent image of a silhouetted cryptid is predominant in this theatrical release poster.

of justification for savagely defending its territory, given that most cinematic transgressors of the *Homo sapiens* variety come armed with weaponry and fully intent on murdering any hominid who crosses their path, often for economic reasons (a desire to exploit the species or its dead body as a freak show exhibit).

Seeing the flipside of the equation that *Missing Link* portrays makes astute Bigfoot film lovers immediately aware of the reverse parallels — the little ape-man in *Missing Link* is the antithesis of a similar creature depicted as Primal Man in *Altered States*. Whereas Primal Man as a pre-human is nothing but aggressive and willing to attack species twice its size with murderous intent, the *Missing Link* ape-man is only interested in exploring its environment in a gentle, prodding manner that is both sweet-natured and pre-scientific. As the narrator suggests, the loss of its genetic contribution to our own "superior" *Homo sapiens* DNA pool may be to our detriment, as we seem helpless as a species to prevent self-annihilation owing to our inherently violent nature. This, too, is a neat echoing of the Ciné du Sasquatch motif of mankind being the ultimate exploiter of its fellow animal species, even those (such as chimpanzees or bipedal hominids) who are so closely related to us as to be "missing links" in our own heritage.

Missing Link's technical qualities are excellent, including the cinematography and ape-man make-up by Rick Baker, who won an Academy Award for designing Harry of *Harry and the Hendersons*. No stranger to hominid cinema, Baker also did effects for *Schlock!* the remake of *Mighty Joe Young*, Tim Burton's *Planet of the Apes*, Dino De Laurentiis' *King Kong*, and many others featuring gorillas and simian hybrids. The long stretches of inaction and lack of narrative focus may bore some less patient viewers, but those seeking excellence over excitement will find it a satisfying experience that warrants multiple viewings.

The Monster and the Stripper (1968)

AKA: *The Exotic Ones*. Starring William Austin, Sleepy LaBeef, Ron Ormond, Tim Ormond, June Ormond, Kathy Clifton, Georgette Dante, Peggy Ann Price, Ronald Drake, Lynn Fontane, Marilyn Gallo, Jack Horton, Chuck Howard, Lee Hysinger, Diane Jordan, Curtis Keen, Patty Kelly, Red Lane, Pauletta Leeman, Ed Livingston, Diane Marshall, Harris Martin, Sonja Massey and Gene McFall. Produced by Ron and June Ormond. Written and Directed by Ron Ormond. USA. Color. Mono. 91 Minutes.

Overview: Nemo, a sleazy, Roy Orbison–lookalike nightclub owner along New Orleans' infamous Bourbon Street, is in trouble. His stripper acts aren't bringing in the tourists and locals the way they used to, and Nemo owes money to the local mob. When word comes that a local legend called Swamp Thing has resurfaced, Nemo knows what must be done: trap the creature and exhibit it in his nightclub to bring back the crowds.

Realizing that backwoods bayou expeditions are a bit out of his range, Nemo hires four local experts to do his dirty work for him. After two of the hunters are savagely slaughtered — one by having his arm ripped from its socket, whereupon the enraged swamp cryptid uses it for a club to beat him to death — Swamp Thing is taken prisoner. He is soon filling Nemo's nightclub with startled customers, who down their Hurricane drinks while ogling various strippers who perform and arouse the caged Swamp Thing sharing the stage with them.

Forced to perform a variation on the old carnival sideshow attraction known as the Geek by the exploitative Nemo, Swamp Thing rips the heads off chickens and devours them whole in front of gagging audiences in addition to his more benign duty as mere stage presence. Alas, a rivalry between the jealous strippers who vie for

Nemo's attention results in a melee in which Swamp Thing breaks free of his cage and rips the breast off one particularly well-endowed stage dancer. Nemo takes Mary Jane — a fresh young stripper to whom the monster has grown attached because she's kind to him — hostage in an attempt to stop Swamp Thing's rampage. Alas for the club owner, Swamp Thing crushes Nemo's head to a bloody pulp and escapes, thus ending its own sordid exploitation at the hands of mankind.

* * * * *

Ron Ormond was a exploitationer-turned-Christian filmmaker whose career spanned decades, first as a Hollywood B-movie director of westerns for the likes of Lash LaRue, then as the helmer of 1950s drive-in quickies such as *Mesa of Lost Women* (and this burlesque-inspired Southern swampfoot classic), and — after narrowly surviving a plane crash that almost killed him and his producing partner/wife June — finally as a maker of regionally-distributed Christian "scare films" in which tent revival attendees were shown the pitfalls of their errant ways, usually with horrific footage of the literal hell that awaits them upon expiration (*Burning Hell*, in fact, is perhaps their best example of this underappreciated genre, with its lurid, Fellini-esque

Theatrical poster for *The Monster and the Stripper* (aka *The Exotic Ones*). Ad copy: "SEE the MONSTER Beat a Man to Death with His Own Arm!"

low-budget depictions of the agonies and torments of a Baptist-envisioned Hades, narrated by the Mississippi-based Reverend Estus Pirkle).

Monster and the Stripper is a bizarre attempt by the Ormond family (Ron, June, and their son Tim, who all contributed to and starred in this effort) to capitalize upon the outrageous sex films of Russ Meyers, mixed with the blood-and-guts violence of H. G. Lewis' output. For a film that features non-stop stripper acts, it's curiously remarkable that no actual nudity is shown, only scantily-clad dancers performing and backstage shenanigans in dressing rooms. The gore, however, is never less than abundant, including the hilariously inept but well-photographed sequence in which the hunters first attempt to capture Swamp Thing. In this amazing series of shots, Swamp Thing emerges as one of the most savage hominids in Ciné du Sasquatch history up to that point in the genre's history, depicted as an arm-ripping monster that uses one poor hunter's own bloody limb to beat the screaming redneck to death. This kind of over-the-top, in-your-face violence plays as Grand Guignol to most viewers, but still manages to shock with its outlandish sense of literal overkill.

The creature is actually closer to man than monster, looking like a huge inbred backwoods hillbilly with a wild hairdo, drooling fangs, and hairy chest. Swamp Thing is also modest, as screen cryptids go, wearing a strategically-placed loincloth at all times. With Swamp Thing portrayed by country music and rockabilly legend Sleepy LaBeef (who has, in his 60-year long career, shared the stage with the likes of Elvis, Roy Orbison, Carl Perkins, George Jones, and Kenny Rogers, and was an admitted inspiration for such later artists as the Beatles and Bruce Springsteen), *Monster and the Stripper* may be the only entry in Ciné du Sasquatch's long history to have cast a genuine musical star as its lead hominid. At six feet, seven inches in height, LaBeef is certainly right up there in terms of requisite screen stature for playing Bigfoot. While his performance is wooden, his towering presence — particularly when contrasted against the generally smaller-statured female dancers — effectively imbues his Swamp Thing character with the same kind of eerie, outsized menace Richard Kiel would later bring to his cryptid roles, such as in the well-done "The Spanish Moss Murders" episode of the original *Night Stalker* TV series.

The unusual, studio-bound production of *Monster and the Stripper* actually works to its advantage, giving the film a lurid, Hammer-styled mood. The bayou sets are obviously just that, but the saturated lighting scheme, which features a vivid pseudo–Technicolor feel that George Romero would later capture in his *Creepshow* feature, creates a surreal feeling that is not easy to dismiss. Since most of the film is shot entirely in a small studio, this claustrophobic quality is maintained throughout; but rather than the Ed Wood effect so common with such productions, *Monster and the Stripper* uses its confines to produce a sense of dreamlike logic. It's as if Ormond is portraying a fairy tale for wicked adults and therefore lighting the film with the kind of overly-bright colors one associates with low-rent honky tonks and garish whorehouses. Red is the prominent color throughout, from the crimson drapes adorning Nemo's tastelessly-furnished nightclub dive to the frequent blood spurting from various body sockets. Not until Kubrick's *The Shining* had such a careful study in red been so cinematically rendered, and it works remarkably well given the film's lack of budget.

Thematically, *Monster and the Stripper* hits on all the classic motifs of Ciné du Sasquatch, with a clear nod to *King Kong*. The Carl Denham character is embodied in this incarnation by Nemo the nightclub owner, but Nemo's motivations are the same as Denham's: capture a cryptid and display it for money. If anything, Nemo remains a

slightly less pretentious (at least morally speaking) version of Denham, as Nemo never kids himself about bringing new thrills to his audience by way of self-deluding justification (as does Denham in the original *King Kong*). Rather, Nemo is a sleaze purveyor without any pretense of being otherwise, and knows that a swamp monster means boffo box office, period. To this end, Nemo is a purer version of Denham, comfortable with leaving the poor Swamp Thing caged for the duration of its life as long as the hominid brings in the yokels to buy his overpriced drinks. Indeed, Nemo goes one degrading step further by forcing the ravenous, deliberately-starved Swamp Thing to devour his live chicken meal in front of horrified but entranced crowds who cannot take their eyes off the bloody sight. Whether intentional or not, Ormond has distilled the thematic obsession of Ciné du Sasquatch, demonstrating that when it comes to cruelty, *Homo sapiens* will stop at nothing for mere entertainment, while the captive cryptids maintain a Noble Savage nature (in that they have not chosen to profit from the misery of humans but only killed in self-defense).

Monster and the Stripper was almost a lost film in Ciné du Sasquatch history. After its production, the Ormonds were forced to abandon the film to the laboratory that developed it because of a lack of completion funds. Only after it was released on VHS in a limited edition in the 1980s was it given the proper if modest attention it deserves. It is highly unusual, quite unlike anything else in the entire Bigfoot canon; and while never truly original nor successful on anything other than a camp level, it nevertheless is a genuine oddity worth watching, especially by Ciné du Sasquatch viewers.

Monster Auditions (2009) ("Roz") (TV)

Featuring the voice of Ona Nurkkala. Produced by Donna Andrews and Stu Connolly. Written by Doug MacLeod and Stu Connolly. Directed by Suren Perera. Australia. Color. Stereo. 1 Minute.

Overview: This series of short one-minute cartoons features candid, one-on-one interviews with various monsters in which they reveal their deepest, most intimate fears, secrets, and aspirations. Included in the ten-part series were spots dedicated to Bigfoot, a vampire, a gill man creature, a zombie, the blob, a human fly, and more.

The "Roz" episode shows a female Sasquatch (or Yowie in Down Under lingo) sitting on her sofa, wearing a pearl necklace and lipstick, addressing the complete lack of privacy she experiences owing to the

Roz the Celebrity Yowie from the Australian animated series *Monster Auditions*.

constant paparazzi exposure in the media. Roz delves into the pressures of the celebrity lifestyle, which few outside the hominid community ever understand. For example, she comments upon the ceaseless criticism of her dietary habits, which she reminds astute viewers have not changed over the eons for her species. Roz also expresses lingering resentment about the size of her feet, which are completely normal for any Sasquatch, male or female.

Monster Auditions were shown in Australia on the Oz equivalent of PBS. Rendered in a quirky blending of traditional animation, Flash, and photographic backgrounds, they each have a different perspective on contemporary Australian society, utilizing the monsters as a comedic conceit in order to more fully satirize whatever dysfunctional behavior they're parodying. "Roz" is a pointed look at the "horrors" of celebrity culture, with Roz portrayed quite wittily as the typical pop diva who laments being in the public spotlight even as she narcissistically denies how much she lives *for* it. The series has been renewed for additional episodes in the coming year. Hopefully they'll be exported, but for now, interested Ciné du Sasquatch fans can find them as streaming videos on the Internet.

Monster Beach Party (2009)

AKA: *Stomp! Shout! Scream!* Starring Claire Bronson, Cynthia Evans, Jonathan Michael Green, Edward Hastings, Christopher Hines, Mary Kraft, Alex Orr, Adrian Roberts, Bill Szymanski and Travis Young. Produced by Arma Benoit and Evan Lieberman. Written and Directed by Jay Edwards. USA. Color. Stereo. 79 Minutes.

Overview: Merriville Island, slightly north of Florida along the Eastern seaboard, receives a surprise visitor — a stowaway Skunk Ape who has hitched a ride atop its own thatched hut. Far from home and dumped on the tiny island surrounded by seawater, the Bigfoot creature ponders its next move as a freshwater hominid. Meanwhile, the hurricane that has uprooted the Bigfoot and sent it through turbulent waters to tiny Merriville Island now races further into the Floridian East Coast seaboard, guaranteeing foul weather on the sparsely-populated island.

The traveling all-girl group the Violas experience motor trouble on their way to Florida to play a bar gig. They receive assistance first from a visiting egghead scientist, John Patterson, and then from a friendly grease monkey, Hector, who owns his own repair shop. While potential favors are discussed in return for free car repairs — such as the Violas playing a free set at Hector's party that evening (the *only* kind of *quid pro quo* discussed by the class act known as the Violas, if you *please*) — a series of murderous mutilations occur throughout the tiny town, all at the hands of the Savage Sasquatch. John Patterson reveals he's been stalking this particular hominid species (dubbed Skunk Apes for obvious reasons after one whiff of its natural essence) since he was a child and lost his parents to them while the family was exploring the Florida Everglades National Park on vacation. Clearly obsessed with the Southern Swamp–squatch beyond any level that is psychologically healthy, Patterson nevertheless seeks dramatic closure in the classic melodramatic manner. By using emotional transubstantiation, if you will, he attempts to assuage the grief he suppresses over his parents' death at the hands of these foul Skunk Apes and his own self-disgust (a classic case of "survivor's guilt" raging throughout his damaged soul — why was *I* spared when my parents were taken by those creatures?).

Matters come to a head when Hector insists on having his Beach Blanket Blow-Out Party despite the local authorities pleading with him to postpone until after the slaughtering Sasquatch is dispatched. As the Violas take to the stage and blast out lyrics dedicated to youthful indiscretions, it is little wonder the titular Monster goes "ape"

and grabs charismatic lead singer Theodora, grooving off into the beach's wilderness with his screaming female captive slung over his furry shoulder. An epic showdown between elected town officials, a visiting cryptozoologist, a girl-group rock band, a local mechanic with a heart of gold, and a monster hell-bent on destroying all kids trying to enjoy the summer fun ensues. And given the loony-bin assortment of rednecks, roustabouts, and religious types present under even the best of "normal" circumstances, can eccentric Merriville Island keep its shaky collective head above the troubled waters rising high? Or will the formerly sleepy town implode under the strain of a homicidal hominid?

* * * * *

A quaint, quasi-campfest softball entry into Ciné du Sasquatch, *Monster Beach Party* has an eerie, born-of-a-love-of-the-genre ability to mimic a bygone era of more innocent exploitation filmmaking — a time in which all that was needed for a certain production start date was a few bikini-clad babes, some beach locations, and a guy in a gorilla costume. *Monster Beach Party* nostalgically recalls a "more innocent era" in which it seemed reasonable that a girl rock group called the Violas could drive from New York City down to Florida in the middle of an oncoming hurricane and *not* expect to meet with assorted terrors on the road. And in a time when Torture Porn has left its grisly mark upon horror films, *Monster Beach Party* seems like a tale of terror made and distributed by Ward Cleaver's local Lions' Club Charity Feature Filmmaking Grant. It is a deliberate attempt to eschew much of the brutal ugliness that followed the Kennedy Assassination and Vietnam escalation both abroad and at home. Instead, as the filmmakers of *Monster Beach Party* might say, imagine a time warp wherein you somehow missed this particular mid–1960s artifact over all the years of cult movie film searches and are now in for an entertaining drive-in picture rediscovery (of course, it is actually a more recent feature film simply assuming the kitschy style of an AIP surf blanket bonanza, complete with a Skunk Ape Sasquatch). It does beg the question: How is it American Independent Pictures actually *missed* stirring together such a slew of elements in the era of *Dr. Goldfoot and the Bikini Machine*, when anything could and did go? It seems a golden opportunity missed, one that the creators of *Monster Beach Party* wanted to rectify. And so the conceit is carried forward from frame one to the closing shot with a kind of mesmerizing monomania. Indeed, it actually feels in sections as if *Monster Beach Party* were an old 35mm grindhouse feature that had been dug up, intact, from beneath an old movie theater. *Monster Beach Party* goes for a kind of self-imposed rigidity and deliberate mockery of limitations of production means to produce laughs. It always looks professional (to its credit, given the strains on the film's modest budget) and well-shot, which elevates *Monster Beach Party* to a higher status than many Ciné du Sasquatch films made for dozens of times its cost. Those who like a tad more acerbic wit mixed with their camp fare are apt to be disappointed, at least over the long haul. Rather than incorporate the wilder, freestyle methods of Richard Lester circa *A Hard Day's Night* or the deliberately over-the-top outrage of John Waters, *Monster Beach Party* feels as if one has literally stumbled upon a local legend — some "lost" 1960s drive-in feature that neither transcended nor succumbed to its time period and region of production.

The gorilla/hominid suit is substandard, as per the norm (and as intended). After all, everything in *Monster Beach Party* is supposed to make the viewer feel as if he or she had stumbled upon a rare showing on late-night cable. This imaginative approach often works to give the slim production a much more expansive look, as the deliberate cheesiness is well-maintained across a broad spectrum of locales and sets, making it feel like a legitimate period piece as well as Ciné du Sasquatch musical. The film's original release title (*Stomp! Shout! Scream!*) was changed to *Monster Beach Party* presumably for commercial reasons. However, the first moniker is more true to the campy tone of the film. The opening song performed by the three-piece Violas is "Stomp! Shout! Scream!" and is illustrated with comic book–styled panels and chintzy lettering, all appropriate for the look and era the filmmakers so successfully invoke. While the rest of the film never equals the powerful opening title sequence, it nonetheless makes a game attempt at staying focused on its basic premise: that you're back at the drive-in, or seeing it for the first time one astonishment-filled night on some obscure satellite channel. So while it can be faulted for being too earnest — at the expense of betraying its camp origins, *Monster Beach Party* never flip flops completely either. There's much to enjoy in this proverbial cool ocean breeze tale of a Skunk Ape trapped on a vacation island in the summer heat. Add the light-headed, "groovy" Motown soundtrack, and one can easily understand why *Monster Beach Party* draws fans into its widening cult circle.

Sasquatch movie fans won't be quite as smitten, however. It does faithfully recreate the sense of outrageous fortune at having been ripped off by the latest Bigfoot exploitation filmmaker (when it can feel like one is seeing the same bargain-basement gorilla suit passed down from one generation of bad Bigfoot-filmmakers to the next). But there is no expectation, given the tone of *Monster Beach Party*, that the creature will be anything *but* a badly-detailed gorilla suit from the film's onset; and wisely, the creators of *Monster Beach Party* refuse any shoddy attempts to "disguise" or hide the monster suit's obvious primate costume origins. Doing so would have failed and betrayed the mimicked era's 1960s film aesthetic (as said drive-in monster fare often brazenly revealed their monster suit's shortcomings in the blazing heat of an overhead sun).

The icing on this cryptid cake is the likeable regional cast. They all bring a lot of quality community theater feeling to their work, which means the viewer is being treated to far, far superior performances than in the more common scenario of a cast composed of the filmmakers' friends, investors, and relatives. It is funny how often low-budget films overlook such valuable resources as seasoned, local theater actors when they're so widely available; perhaps it is a case of the filmmakers not being able to house and feed actors, which could be problematic with a seasoned cast of talents as opposed to "employing your friends" on weekend shoots.

With its freewheeling, anything goes point-of-view, *Monster Beach Party* shows a lot of attention to detail and production design far better than many in the Ciné du Sasquatch genre. Admittedly, the movie is very uneven in mixing its drama and comedy, alternately stopping and starting, building some momentum and then losing some, etc. But one should remember that *Monster Beach Party* is a successful "Mod Era" oceanside rock musical (with or without its Skunk Ape plot). Since the film is working as a crossover, much can and *should* be overlooked in terms of storyline and character performances. If nothing else, it highlights the enduring plasticity of the Bigfoot film genre, showing yet again how the central motifs of Ciné du Sasquatch can be engineered by skilled screenwriters and filmmakers into wilder, more-unexpected re-imaginings. This is a positive sign that Ciné du Sasquatch lovers will be happy to note: The genre which is most flexible to reinvention is most likely to be among the best-preserved for future generations.

Monster Hunters: Ordinary People on an Extraordinary Mission (2002) (TV) (Doc)

Produced by Sheera von Puttkamer. Written and Directed by Peter von Puttkamer. Canada. Color. Stereo. 100 Minutes.

Overview: Canadian filmmakers Sheera and Peter von Puttkamer focus on six different "monster hunters," all from ordinary walks of life but who spend their free time in the wilds looking for traces of elusive cryptozoological specimens. The focus is on the mundane daily aspects of their search rather than sensationalized recreations of past reports and flashy graphics. By keeping the documentary at a realistic level, the filmmakers allow the viewer to see into the often grueling nature of what it means to be an armchair crypto-hunter. Among the obvious difficulties are finding sympathetic friends and family members; financially justifying the expenditures on limited incomes; and the outright hostility and rejection any findings are met with by so-called "legitimate" scientists.

Among the crypto species profiled are the Yowie of Australia, the Jersey Devil, the Cadborosaurus (a Nessie-type creature), the Chupacabra, and others. Some of the researchers reveal a serious, poignant side by offering up sketches, eyewitness accounts, and the scant but compelling evidence they've managed to collect over the years of their personal odysseys. Some come across as either self-indulgent or outright delusional, including the Yowie hunters who seem more eager to play Indiana Jones with their latest tech gear and survival equipment than amass crucial clues, or the Chupacabra hunters who admit that they rely exclusively on psychic visions of where they may find such a beast rather than topographical maps or even the latest sightings. But for the most part, the amateurs seem as whole-heartedly dedicated to their respective hunt as any mainstream scientists who are passionate about their own, more socially-acceptable areas of study.

The show was broken into two segments and aired on the Discovery Channel before the filmmakers edited it into this 100-minute distillation. As a feature-length documentary, it was screened to good reviews at the New York International Film Festival and won two Platinum Awards at the 2002 Worldfest in Houston, Texas. Though the film is less sensationalized than most efforts in the cryptozoological doc field, hardcore Sasquatch believers and Ciné du Sasquatch fans will enjoy the non-condescending approach, in which von Puttkamer allows them to speak for themselves rather than offer onscreen judgments on their respective sanities. The widescreen cinematography is often breathtaking, featuring wilderness vistas not typically seen in the usual low-budget Bigfoot doc. The same director also made the well-regarded *Sasquatch Odyssey: The Hunt for Bigfoot* in 1999, featuring Rene Dahinden, John Green, Dr. Grover Krantz, and other luminaries in the Bigfoot crypto field.

Monster in the Woods (2008)

Starring Jana Regan, Seth Holbrook, Dennis Doiron, Paul Drinan, Carolyn Higgins, Peter Paton, David Wallace, Cheryl Mercer-McCullough, Laura Graham, Peter N. Dudar, Tony Ezzilio, Nanette Henning, Snooj Dowdy and Loren Coleman. Produced by John Lane and Olin Smith. Written by Al Lamanda. Directed by Andy Davis. USA. Color. Stereo. 85 Minutes.

Overview: When a series of reports on a Maine Sasquatch are splashed across a television show called *The Paranormal Files*, a pair of university-funded cryptozoologists named Anna and Kline arrive to investigate. The local citizens of the small Maine town don't take lightly to the barrage of reporters in search of an easy headline and, mistaking Anna and Kline for more big city types out to ridicule them, treat them with hostility.

The cryptozoologists interview a local chicken farmer. While searching his land, Anna is nearly run over by a Bigfoot as it darts straight at her and then steps over her. She uses her camera to take a last-minute picture of the cryptid, which they send to their mentor back at the university. Pleased but pressed for funds, their mentor urges them to gather physical evidence to go along with the photograph, hoping this will keep his department financially stable.

Meanwhile, a 7-year-old local girl named Maura Lapanne confesses to Sheriff Paterson that she has been having strange dreams in which the female Sasquatch has been in psychic communication with Maura. Ever since Maura correctly predicted the manner of her own father's death, the citizens have regarded her spooky powers with considerable awe. When a happenstance meeting between Anna, Kline, Maura and Maura's mother occurs in the town diner, the cryptozoologists realize they have stumbled upon their best lead.

The problem is that they're not alone in their quest. Multimillionaire Jack Killington has decided to stalk the elusive Bigfoot, having also heard the reports on *The Paranormal Files*. Anna is incensed; she explains to Kline that Killington is only interested in self-promotion and exploiting Sasquatch for his own egotistical needs. When it is inadvertently revealed that Killington and Anna once had an affair, Anna's anger becomes transparent to Kline, who has begun to develop a romantic interest in her himself. But Killington says that they have no choice but to work *with* him when he informs Anna and Kline he has funded the university with a generous grant in exchange for their supervisor promising that the duo will assist the playboy hunter.

Killington offers a million-dollar reward to any local who brings in the hominid dead or alive, therefore filling the Maine woods with every redneck capable of toting a gun (and some who are too drunk but venture forth anyway). The cryptozoologists realize they must act fast if they're to save the endangered species from becoming a mere sideshow attraction in Killington's carnival of conquests.

* * * * *

Monster in the Woods opens with a title credit song that is both hilarious and reminiscent of such Ciné du Sasquatch classics as *The Legend of Boggy Creek*. Sung in an off-kilter hillbilly manner, equal parts fiddles and fun, the theme song definitely gives the opening moments a needed lift, preparing the viewer for the serio-comic approach to follow. Sadly, the rest of *Monster in the Woods* wavers between strained comedy and earnest seriousness, a none-too-successful approach to the genre in general, and herein specifically.

The largest problem is the cast. While amateur casts in Bigfoot films are a common lot (see the aforementioned *The Legend of Boggy Creek* for one good example of how such locals can be integrated into the film successfully), *Monster in the Woods* makes the mistake of integrating regional thespians with local "talent" that never quite gels together in terms of the range of acting styles on display. For example, the two young leads, Jana Regan and Seth Holbrook, both do a decent job of helming a majority of the film's scenes, even if there is some occasionally clunky dialogue they're required to deliver with straight faces. That's no deal breaker in terms of success overall, of course; many are the Bigfoot films that have less talented personnel in front of the camera. But by combining their already polished theater backgrounds with an ad hoc, unsteady mixture of amateurs who are gamely trying their best (and mostly hamming it up in the process), *Monster in the Woods* loses its balance early on and much of its hard-fought verisimilitude along with it.

Part of the problem in the film's lack of cohesion is due to the script. While there are many moments that work, too many false scenes and on-the-nose type moments abound. The local humor of the Maine setting is both played up and overplayed, depending on the moment. There is nothing bad about incorporating regionalism in Ciné du Sasquatch efforts, as by and large, there have been many examples in the genre that have done so quite enticingly. When executed with a tight rein by the filmmakers, it can even add a sense of

believability that the best special effects cannot do alone. There is a feeling in which the setting becomes authentic, in essence. Alas, *Monster in the Woods* plays at once as a parody of thick Maine accents circa a vintage "Pepperidge Farm Remembers" television commercial and equally attempts to portray the locals as being simply decent but mentally dense. In this regards, it plays like Maine's most famous horror author's adapted cinematic works, Stephen King: there is the good (*The Shining*) and the not-as-good (*Maximum Overdrive*). It is a difficult and delicate proportion to achieve and maintain, so fault not the filmmakers for at least attempting the nearly impossible when well-funded masters such as King himself cannot always succeed at it. While recent Bigfoot films such as *The Long Way Home: A Bigfoot Story* and *The Wild Man of the Navidad* have shown how backwoods regionalism can be utilized to charmingly add character—and characters—to a low-budget film, *Monster in the Woods* is unable to keep the integration from harming its own sense of dramatic purpose.

The creepy girl with the psychic connection to the Bigfoot is perhaps the most original element in the movie, and resembles Mr. King's fictional Maine stories in the best "senses" of the word. Though the role is a tough one, young actress Carolyn Higgins is suitably spooky and stone-faced, as any child would rightfully be in such a predicament. Other elements fare less well, especially the monomaniacal Jack Killington, who is as clichéd as his name (he suffers from the Carl Denham Syndrome and reminds one of the equally hell-bent characters filling the same role in *The Capture of Bigfoot* and *Bigfoot: The Unforgettable Encounter*, to cite but two obvious examples). Speaking of names, the inclusion of a Sheriff "Paterson" (pronounced as "Patterson" in the film, despite the credit's alternative spelling) is surely no coincidence, as demonstrated by the raised eyebrows this moniker elicits from several cast members. These kinds of postmodern attempts at humor can work if they're subtle, but when played for obvious laughs, they tend to fail and remove the viewer from the experience.

The Bigfoot costume is regrettably of a rather standard gorilla type, but the filmmakers are intelligent enough to keep the close-ups to a minimum and not linger on the deficiencies. Some shots, such as the opening where the creature is standing in a high window and peering down at the screaming little girl, are quite effective; others, as when the Bigfoot steps over our heroine cryptozoologist, are less so. As a team, the two leads play their roles to hit-or-miss success in the well-worn pattern of *The X-Files*, but at least one cryptozoologist comes across as authentic and believable: real-life crypto expert Loren Coleman. Coleman is featured in the film's opening moments within a fictitious *The Paranormal Files* television show that is the reality TV equivalent of *MonsterQuest*. He convincingly recounts the rare but documented cases of actual Savage Sasquatch attacks that have occurred throughout history, setting the tone for the "nature of the beast."

If only *Monster in the Woods* had maintained this level of professional acumen, the overall film would have been a much better example of Ciné du Sasquatch. Still, it at least has the distinction of being the only Maine Bigfoot film in the genre's history, and regional viewers of cryptid cinema will definitely enjoy it for that reason alone, if no other.

The Monster of the Volcano (1962)

AKA: *El monstruo de los volcanes.* Starring Ana Bertha Lepe, Joaquín Cordero, Andrés Soler, Jorge Russek, Salvador Lozano, José Dupeyrón, Carlos Suárez, Antonio Raxel and Victor Alcocer. Produced by Adolfo Grovas, Jesús Grovas and Rafael Pérez Grovas. Written by Federico Curiel and Alfredo Ruanova. Directed by Jaime Salvador. Mexico. Black & White. Mono. 76 Minutes.

Overview: In the remote Mexican mining village of Popocatépetl, legends persist of a buried treasure once belonging to Moctezuma that lies somewhere inside the hidden tunnels of a nearby dormant volcano, protected by an Abominable Snowman with hypnotic powers. A well-educated engineer from a well-to-do family insists it is all just so much peasant superstition until a series of unsolved murders occur among the menial laborers who are conducting excavation work inside the abandoned tunnels for an upcoming mining project. Faced with a work shortage owing to the locals being unwilling to risk their lives at the hands of what they believe to be a Yeti, the engineer realizes he must take some action to solve the homicides. Before he can act decisively, however, his fiancée is kidnapped by the creature and taken back to its volcanic lair. Mounting a rescue, the engineer and several brave hunters confront the beast on its own turf. The beast is bested and falls over the edge of the volcano's mountainous peaks.

* * * * *

With over 100 feature-film credits to his credit, stretching back into the 1930s, venerable Mexican auteur Jaime Salvador still impresses with not one but two Ciné du Sasquatch entries (this and its sequel, *The Terrible Giant of the Snow*). While they were probably shot back-to-back (given they were released in 1963 within months of one another), it's a rare feat indeed that *The Monster of the Volcano* and *The Terrible Giant of the Snow* each met with success at the box office in Mexico, leaving one to ponder why the beast didn't surface yet again in more sequels (*Blue Santo vs. the Snow Giant* anyone?). Both films also enjoyed later success in endless repeats on Mexican television stations, where they still appear today in late-night slots.

The two films are often mistaken for one another, and with good reason. The sequel uses a lot of the same cast, the same director, the same producers, the same technical crew, and even recycles much of the footage of the village, the mountains, and even the hacienda that is the main setting for much of the dialogue-driven scenes. Both feature the scientist who believes in the creature and the stalwart hero who denies its existence, and both feature the same Yeti suit. Oddly, it resembles the *Dr. Who* depictions of Yetis more than the usual albino gorilla suit utilized in most low-budget cryptid films featuring an Abominable Snowman. The Yeti herein is rotund, with more girth than height, and clearly an actor wearing what appears to be a Chuck E. Cheese–type costume, complete with visible sleeve attachments where the arms meet the body and detachable head mask. While surely passable for the era, it seems woefully unconvincing to modern audiences, who will be equally unimpressed with the beast's lumbering gait (which appears to be the result of the actor's inability to see out of the mask, as he carefully taps his foot in front of him each step he takes on the rocky terrain).

To its credit, much of the night photography is very stylish, in an old Universal Studios manner, complete with dark pools of shadows and rich contrasts of light. Alas, most of the Yeti scenes are photographed on location and in the daylight, which puts an unfortunate glare on the costume's literally unseemly shortcomings. The idea that the Yeti has hypnotic powers is interesting, but seems appropriated from Hammer's *The Abominable Snowman* more than any original invention on the part of the writers, as *The Monster of the Volcano* doesn't really utilize the concept for any narrative impact, as did the Peter Cushing film. *The Monster of the Volcano* also illustrates the universal nature of Ciné du Sasquatch in that all the motifs are maintained, despite the Mexican setting and folklore: The beast falls for a beautiful human female; the creature is dominant in its volcanic territory until it interacts with mankind, at which point its days (and nights) are numbered; and the hominid is all but *Homo sapiens*' equal in intelligence and cunning.

MonsterQuest (2007) (Multiple Episodes) (TV) (Doc)

Narrated by Stan Benard. Featuring Todd Disotell, Jeffrey Meldrum and Loren Coleman. Produced by Doug Hajicek, Will Yates, David Bell, Dale Bosch, Dan Nyberg, Michael Stiller and Jeffrey C. Weber. Written by Doug Hajicek and Dale Bosch. Directed by Doug Hajicek. USA. Color. Stereo. 45 Minutes.

Overview: One of the most popular cryptozoological series in recent TV history, History Channel's *MonsterQuest* was unfortunately cancelled midway through season four by the network. Given the enormous fan base and serious if entertaining nature of the show, one wonders if the cable network may have erred in their judgment, as the list of crypto specimens to be explored was far from complete. Whatever the network's decision factors, the existing series (which is also available on a collected DVD set) remains a high water mark in terms of overall execution, credibility, and production value for hominid exploration on a TV series. While molded somewhat on the *In Search Of* format (as are most such series), *MonsterQuest* was one of a handful of latter-day remakes which actually improved upon the venerable Leonard Nimoy classic and pushed the creative envelope in terms of how cryptozoology is treated in television production. With complicated field research, a sizeable budget, and CGI recreations of the various cryptids featured, *MonsterQuest* proved a ratings bonanza for the History Channel, often running in consecutive blocks of hour-long programming for marathons with staggering regularity. Despite the wide availability of home recording devices, such as digital video recorders and the like, *MonsterQuest* seemed to inspire a dedicated loyalty among hardcore cryptid fans that resulted in each scheduled marathon block or new episode debut receiving immediate and enormous buzz on various Internet sites. In short, it was as much a means of social gathering (albeit virtual) for many dedicated viewers as it was a source of entertaining information.

Among the many Bigfoot creature episodes produced, the tone was set early on with the second episode ever, which was called "Sasquatch Attack." Set in a remote Canadian cabin — the site of eyewitness accounts of prior Bigfoot visitations — the episodes spooky tone and use of high-tech computer graphics to depict the hominid created both a sense of verisimilitude and Fortean intrigue. The careful scripting by the series' producers, in which evidence is treated as neither conclusive nor fabricated, also helped, as it gave both believers and skeptics a way "in" to the series without feeling neglected. Jeffrey Meldrum, who has appeared on many such TV series, analyzed the evidence collected by the *MonsterQuest* team and concluded much of it pointed towards authentication of an unknown hominid existing in the region.

The first season also saw the use of an all-female exploration team in search of Bigfoot in Washington state, with the idea that the scent of a woman, so to speak, could be an attraction to male Sasquatch creatures. Despite the somewhat spurious nature of the premise, much evidence is presented to support the hypothesis, as well as in-depth analysis of the Patterson-Gimlin film from 1967 via digital microscope. And while it was not strictly Bigfoot-related, the episode called "Russia's Killer Apemen" featured noted cryptozoologist Loren Coleman speaking about the notorious Joseph Stalin–approved "army of apes" research in which Stalin envisioned a half-man, half-ape army of super-strength simian soldiers defending the Russian homeland. Despite the ludicrous nature of the subject matter, the show reveals actual documentary evidence that it was no mere myth, but an actual scientifically-based attempt to crossbreed humans and simians. Coleman also addressed the Honey Island Swamp Monster of Louisiana and similar so-called Skunk Apes in an episode entitled "Swamp Beast," which featured an attempt to track a Skunk Ape in the boggy bayous with bloodhounds scent-attuned to sexually-charged pheromones from actual ape species.

Not to let a good thing lay unexamined, *MonsterQuest* launched season two with "Sasquatch Attack II," a follow-up to the previous year's showcase about a Canadian cryptid known for its visitations to a particular remote cabin. This time around, the crew arrives with night vision cameras and other equipment to better track their intended subject, while DNA analysis is performed on hair samples collected from a wooden porch plank. In "Wild Man," the series sent a team to explore the possibility of a reddish-orange haired bipedal hominid in remote Hubai, China. The government officials claim to have collected a plethora of actual hairs from the creature, which adds veracity to the numerous eyewitness accounts. The intriguingly named "Bigfoot in New York" show featured an in-depth accounting of the Monster of Whitehall, an upstate Sasquatch sighting reported by police officers in 1976 that has never been fully or officially explained. Over 30 years after their initial report, the officers involved agree to a polygraph test to determine whether or not they fabricated the incident, while noted zoologists attempt to piece together the continuing sightings of the Whitehall Monster.

Season two also saw the introduction of the "Legend of the Hairy Beast," which focused on the ubiquitous and enduring folklore among many Native Americans in regards to Bigfoot, predating any exposure to Western civilization. Interviewing actual tribal leaders in the Klamath River region of Oregon reveals the depth of their belief in Sasquatch, including ancient cave artwork, oral histories, and a continuing series of eyewitness accounts. Closer to the American heartland, "Grassman" featured a look at the Ohio version of Bigfoot with the colorful name of Grassman, which, as Loren Coleman explains, is but a regional nickname for the famous hominid. Known to create forts out of grass and to have a nasty disposition when it comes to interacting with humans, the Grassman evidence is reviewed and explored, including an attempt to stalk the creature at night with aerial surveillance via infrared cameras.

Season three saw another hominid lead-off with "Abominable Snowman." The show featured an in-depth review of the historical evidence and sightings of the Yeti, as well as a dangerous mission to scale the heights of the Himalayan Mountains where much of the earliest Abominable Snowman encounters and artifacts were originally collected. "Critical Evidence" was a hard-edged look at the latest Sasquatch evidence gathered from around the United States in hopes of distilling the most reliable data about the well-documented hominid. As an overview of previous sightings and evidence, as well as an up-to-date recap of accounts and videos made after the famous Patterson-Gimlin film, "Critical Evidence" put much of the recent evidence to scientifically-based analysis, attempting to separate the hoaxes from the hominids.

"Mysterious Ape Island" concentrated its Sasquatch focus on a piece of land in the Pacific Ocean 70 miles off the coast of Seattle, Washington. Known as Vancouver Island, the densely-forested land mass has a long history of Bigfoot sightings, including Native Americans who warned their children of its ferocious nature, as well as eyewitnesses who claim to have seen it devouring fish along the coastlines and attacking sleeping campers at night. The *MonsterQuest* team investigates and comes to the startling conclusion that Bigfoot may be an aquatic species that can swim just as well as it can travel the dense woods on legs. "Monster Close Encounters" profiled the increase in Savage Sasquatch encounters, in which eyewitnesses report Bigfoot as anything but benign, whether their head-to-head meeting involved simply seeing the hominid while driving a remote roadway or being chased by it while on foot in the forests. Polygraphs are given to some, while bite force tests are run to see how much power the reported Sasquatch creatures would need to cause some of the

reported damage they've inflicted. And the third season concluded with the venerable Fouke Monster in a show called "Swamp Stalker." Kayaks and canoes are used to penetrate the dense, hard-to-access backwaters of the meandering Fouke River and ascertain if the historical reports of an aggressive hominid in the tiny Arkansas town are fact or fantasy.

The final year of *MonsterQuest* saw the airing of "Sierra Sasquatch" and the intriguing new evidence from California eyewitnesses that not only is the Bigfoot creature stepping up its aggressive nature, but travelling in packs to enforce its territorial domain. And while "Hillbilly Beast" wasn't technically a Sasquatch episode, the closely-aligned nature of the Kentucky bluegrass cryptid with Bigfoot accounts makes it intriguing viewing for cryptozoology fans.

While admittedly produced as much for entertainment as any hard scientific value, *MonsterQuest* nevertheless achieved a rare balance between outright fantasy and serious science. Never residing wholly in either camp, *MonsterQuest* instead attempted to remain as objective as possible in its handling of hominids, while favoring the possibility over improbability that giant hominids really do roam our unexplored wilderness areas. It is missed by fans and Ciné du Sasquatch devotees alike.

Monsters! Mysteries or Myths? (1975) (TV) (Doc)

Narrated by Rod Serling. Featuring Robert Morgan, Dr. Grover Krantz, Sir Edmund Hillary, Lord John Hunt, Peter Byrne, S. Dillon Ripley, Dr. T. Dale Stewart, Jim Craig, Colleen McKay, Louis Allway, Dan Maloughney, Oliver Potter, Richard Rainer, David James and Richard Kiel. Produced, Written and Directed by Robert Guenette. USA. Color. Mono. 46 Minutes.

Overview: Rod Serling hosts an in-depth look at Bigfoot, Yeti, and the Loch Ness Monster, using archival footage, photographs, expert testimony, and eyewitness recreations. Co-sponsored and partially shot at the Smithsonian National Museum of Natural History in Washington, D.C., *Monsters! Mysteries or Myths?* remains skeptical but informative as to the possibilities, with many interviewed scientists expressing outright disbelief, while others caution their fellow researchers to keep open if critical minds.

When this CBS prime-time special first aired in October of 1975, it was an instant media sensation. The Neilson viewership ratings remained unmatched for decades, with literally tens of millions of Americans having watched this one-hour examination of the cryptozoological phenomena (the first real introduction to this burgeoning field for many). The narration by Rod Serling, much beloved from his earlier *The Twilight Zone* and *Night Gallery* stints, lent the production an instant air of spookiness and credulity, setting the proper mood of balanced fact and speculation.

One of the highlights of *Monsters! Myth or Mysteries?* was the sequence in which a camping trip by several boy scouts is interrupted by a meandering Sasquatch that invades their tented area late one night. Portrayed by actor Richard Kiel (who was fresh — or at least freshly-scrubbed — from playing the bayou-lurking hominid in the "Spanish Moss Murders" episode of the *Kolchack: The Night Stalker* TV series the year before) makes a convincing cryptid in this brief but memorable scene, rummaging through the boys' backpacks and supplies, clearly in search of something to eat. The screaming boys startle the Sasquatch and send it running, but not before several of the young men get convincing looks at the creature. While the sequence may seem tame in today's saturated market of gore and violence, it was a real groundbreaker in its era. Coming as it did during the height of the UFO craze and post–Watergate weariness, *Monsters!*

Myths or Mysteries? was a major contributor to the explosive sudden fascination with All Things Cryptid throughout the country.

The show was later padded with additional scenes and re-edited to feature length for a theatrical tour in North American cinemas as *The Mysterious Monsters*. Because Rod Serling had died in 1975, Peter Graves was hired to replace his narration for the theatrical version, which mainly expanded the original one-hour TV documentary with additional Fortean mysteries, such as psychic phenomena and the Bermuda Triangle, rather than use more cryptid sequences. The film was a moderate success, and was quickly cycled back to television, where it also did well despite being largely the same production as *Monsters! Myths or Mysteries?* The film's producers also published a paperback book bearing the movie version's film poster on the cover, which was sold in lobbies for additional profits (a not uncommon technique in the era of four-walling motion pictures).

But despite the similarities, there is something more satisfying in the simple purity of *Monsters! Myths or Mysteries?* which lingers in the mind's eye, than the more sensationalized approach of *The Mysterious Monsters*. The leaner narrative of the former, the sublime narration by Serling, and the zeitgeist of a stunned nation all witnessing the same hour's worth of programming in one night made it the generational equivalent of Orson Welles' *War of the Worlds* radio broadcast (which, perhaps not coincidentally, was also broadcast on CBS and also during the Halloween season). And while it did not result in panic-stricken masses fleeing to the hills for safety, it did lead to an immediate increase in reported Sasquatch sightings and even a Bigfoot abduction claim by a woman shopper in the Pacific Northwest. More importantly, Bigfoot was suddenly a big American media topic of conversation, from the living rooms of viewers watching this documentary to the producers in Hollywood who saw the astounding ratings bonanza a public domain "mythic monster" could generate on a low budget. The influence was contagious, resulting in a flurry of copycat productions, both independent of the Hollywood studios and within them, and on TV as well as in movie theaters.

Monsters Inc. (2001) (Cameo)

Featuring the voices of John Goodman, Billy Crystal, Mary Gibbs, Steve Buscemi, James Coburn, Jennifer Tilly, Bob Peterson, Frank Oz and John Ratzenberger. Produced by Darla K. Anderson, John Lasseter, Kori Rae and Andrew Stanton. Written by Andrew Stanton, Daniel Gerson, Robert L. Baird, Rhett Reese and Jonathan Roberts. Directed by Pete Docter, David Silverman and Lee Unkrich. USA. Color. Stereo. 92 Minutes.

Overview: In a parallel world to our own, children's imaginary monsters are actually real. So real, in fact, that the monsters' world is literally powered by the screams of the terrified human kids whenever their various nightmare fears come through their closet doors. When two lovable but goofy scare-team monsters unwittingly uncover a nefarious plot being conducted by upper management in the nightmare factory, they are banished to the Himalayan Mountains, whereupon they are temporarily befriended by a kindly Yeti.

* * * * *

Though the Abominable Snowman in *Monsters, Inc.* makes little more than a glorified cameo appearance, the Yeti nevertheless makes a charming impression. His loveable role further blurs the storyline's already complicated set-up of "when worlds collide." Given the wavering line between the fantasy world of the scare monsters and the human world in which the creatures invade, the Abominable Snowman has one "big foot" in each plane; it is a monster to real-world humans, and just another humanoid beast to the scare monsters in their world.

The Yeti comes across as a kind of Joseph Campbell–type figure, embodying the coming transfiguration of the artificial divide between the monster vs. human universes and its collapse, or at least blending into a cooperative, unified whole. Misunderstood and an outsider in the human world, and non-existent in the monster's fantasy world, the Yeti acts as an unwitting cultural ambassador or hidden helper to the two stranded monster characters, offering them assistance along their heroes' journey. In doing so, the Yeti redeems the concept of "monster as perennial outsider," which the two protagonists feel as stranded beings in the human universe until their successful return to their own world of monsters.

Mainly, however, the Yeti functions as a comic foil to offer some much-needed levity during the final act of *Monster, Inc.*'s otherwise darker finale. In doing so, this delightful Abominable Snowman remains one of the genre's most amusing and noble incarnations, one guaranteed to delight viewers of all ages.

The Mothman's Photographer (2006) (Doc)

Featuring John Keel, Marcella Bennett, Faye DeWitt LaPorte, Tom Ury, John Frick, Harriet Plumbrook, Robert Godbey, Gary Chester, Ed Oundee, Ken Alton, Mercedes Yaeger, Jerry Deloney, Scott Ward, Neal Mindrum and DJ Novocaine. Produced and Directed by Andy Colvin. USA. Color. Stereo. 30 Hours.

Overview: Frequent contributor/guest on the conspiracy-based radio talk show *Beyond the Grassy Knoll*, amateur researcher/Mothman expert Andy Colvin self-produced this amazing 30-hour DVD and CD (a 5-disc set) for those interested in Fortean phenomena, ranging from the Mothman prophecies, Bigfoot, UFOs, 9-11 visions, Men in Black, alien abductions, ESP, World Bankers, Frightwig Man, psychic events, plasma-energy beings, the Philadelphia Experiment, quantum anomalies, thunderbird sightings, and beyond. In no uncertain terms, it is the most comprehensive amalgamation of video and audio recordings of such materials ever created, and would work well as a college-level study guide due to its in-depth nature and variety of interviewees.

Of particular interest to Ciné du Sasquatch fans will be his interviews with Neal Mindrum, a Cincinnati graphic artist who claims to have encountered an "invisible" Bigfoot in 1982 in New York's Bear Mountain State Park, as well as the long discussions with John Keel, a renowned if controversial Fortean investigator with a belief in UFOs and bipedal cryptids. Considered something of an underground classic by those interested in such "beyond the realm" topics, *The Mothman's Photographer* was also self-published as a book by Colvin as *The Mothman's Photographer: The Work of an Artist Touched by the Prophecies of the Infamous Mothman*.

MSNBC's Countdown with Keith Olbermann ("Seeing, but Believing?") (2007) (TV) (Doc)

Hosted by Keith Olbermann. Featuring Bob Kiviat. Produced by MSNBC. USA. Color. Stereo. 5 Minutes.

Overview: Keith Olbermann's mostly political program, *Countdown* occasionally featured cultural spotlight segments and a focus on sports. One such segment in 2007 was called "Seeing, but Believing?" and featured TV producer Bob Kiviat, who created the Fox Channel debunking show *The World's Greatest Hoaxes: Secrets Finally Revealed*. Kiviat's hoax program focused on the allegations that Bob Heironimus wore a Sasquatch costume in the famous Patterson-Gimlin film from 1967. In this interview, both Olbermann and Kiviat discuss the supposed baby Bigfoot captured in the so-called "Jacob's Creature" photograph.

Kiviat, who not only produced the ratings hit *Alien Autopsy* for Fox (which supposedly showed an Area 51 alien being dissected by government scientists), as well as its subsequent revelation as a hoax for his own *Greatest Hoaxes* series, would seem to be an ideal candidate for understanding how to go about duping an often-gullible American public (or at least those who would admit to watching Fox as a reliable source of information). Olbermann agrees with Kiviat that Heironimus was the party who wore the suit, and goes on to express skepticism that the depicted Jacob's Creature isn't a Photoshop wonder. Cryptozoologists Loren Coleman and Jeff Meldrum have expressed their belief the photo shows a mangy bear, and many Internet websites devoted to Bigfoot have shown side-by-side comparisons between a yearling bear cub and the supposed Jacob's hominid that seem to lay the matter to rest for all but the most fervent believers (of which Olbermann, who can barely suppress a smirk throughout, is clearly not).

The Mummy 3: Tomb of the Dragon Emperor (2008)

Starring Brendan Fraser, Jet Li, Maria Bello, Michelle Yeoh, John Hannah, Luke Ford and Anthony Wong Chau-Sang. Produced by Sean Daniels, Jim Jacks, Bob Ducsay, Stephen Sommers and Chris Brigham. Written by Alfred Gough and Miles Millar. Directed by Rob Cohen. USA. Color. Stereo. 112 Minutes.

Overview: Rick O'Connell and his bored millionaire wife Evelyn are thrilled when offered a chance to deliver a precious gemstone on behalf of the British government, post–World War II. Their adventure leads them to China and eventually Nepal, where they encounter their missing son Alex. Alex has become embroiled in an ancient mystery involving a so-called Dragon Emperor and an army of the dead the Emperor can summon if in possession of a sacred stone — the very gemstone his parents are carrying, naturally. Soon they find themselves face to face with not only the revitalized Dragon Emperor (who can shapeshift into a multi-headed dragon) but his army of 10,000 dead soldiers. Fortunately they are able to rely upon the help of a band of Yetis who are willing to fight on the side of O'Connell and

company if it means destroying the dreaded rule of the Dragon Emperor. In the climactic showdown atop the Himalayan Mountains, the Abominable Snowmen prove a decisive advantage for the British adventurers.

The Mummy 3: Tomb of the Dragon Emperor is a technical tour de force that, alas, suffers from the typical hallmarks of such beyond-bloated summer spectacles — bad storytelling and overly-produced special effects. So while the aesthetic panache the CGI artists bring to the movie's surface is alluring, the content is so lacking as to make one feel as if one has inadvertently stepped inside a Universal Studios tour attraction for *The Mummy* franchise. Again, whether one finds the spectacle visually exciting enough to compensate for the woefully underdeveloped storyline will determine the quality of any viewing experience; little else can be critically said (perhaps so much the better).

Whatever one's preference, *The Mummy 3: Tomb of the Dragon Emperor* does offer a genre-breaking use of an entire army of Yeti warriors during the film's climax. To see the horde of Abominable Snowmen, so lifelike and photorealistic, is the culmination of every Bigfoot and Yeti film preceding this effort. And while it is equally true the narrative and emotional impact achieved is very little in comparison to the impressive Yeti visualizations, the filmmakers deserve recognition for having finally achieved the digital equivalent of the impressive work done by Rick Baker in the latex field with *Tanya's Island* and *Harry and the Hendersons*. Through countless shadowy glimpses of onscreen Yeti to full-on white gorilla suits of the worst sideshow quality, Ciné du Sasquatch has finally reached a point in its history where depicting the creature is no longer the biggest challenge. Instead, the relative ease with which any image may now be cinematically evoked highlights the deeper underlying necessities of the form: The story, characters, and conflicts themselves must be just as astonishing, or all is for naught. There is enough entertainment value present in *The Mummy 3: Tomb of the Dragon Emperor* to keep it from being totally unwatchable, and yet one finds more wonder and genre-bending efforts made for micro-budgets (such as *The Wild Man of the Navidad* and *The Long Way Home: A Bigfoot Story*) far more compelling because they manage to tell more effective stories, despite having anemic production values in comparison to studio-produced fare.

At the end of *The Mummy 3: Tomb of the Dragon Emperor*, an entire army of CGI-rendered Yetis joins forces with outside humans to defeat a common enemy.

My Friend the Yeti (2001) (TV)

AKA: *Ein Yeti zum Verlieben*. Starring Oliver Stokowski, Ines Nieri, Sophie von Kessel, Peter Rühring, Wilfried Hochholdinger and Kristina Van Eyck. Produced by Carolin Haasis and Doris Zander. Written by Martin Rauhaus. Directed by Thorsten Schmidt. Germany. Color. Stereo. 98 Minutes.

Overview: German zoologist-turned-cryptozoologist Tim Bergmann is experiencing a career funk — he has begun to believe in the Yeti, but no one in the scientific community will take his obsession seriously. Then comes his big break — footprints uncovered in the Himalayas that lead Bergmann to convince a skeptical female reporter named Christine Wendler and his new boss at the zoo to fund an expedition to uncover the truth. Needing valuable publicity before an IPO with which he hopes to finance the dilapidated zoo, Bergmann's boss agrees to underwrite the trip. Accompanying Bergmann and Wendler is Charlie, Bergmann's 12-year-old daughter, who still mourns her mother's passing years earlier, as does her lonely father.

The Yeti is indeed captured, but it turns out to be a younger cryptid instead of a full-grown adult. The plight of the homesick hominid touches Charlie, who identifies with its sense of profound alienation at being kept behind bars in a cage while Bergmann and Wendler plot how best to extract the creature from Nepal without the government authorities intervening. Adding to the conflict is Bergmann's boss, who turns out to be a morally dubious capitalist intent on crafting the zoo facility into a Disney-styled Yeti theme park, with the captive Snowman as the centerpiece attraction. Realizing he has inadvertently placed the beast's best interests in the hands of a greedy developer who will never allow the Yeti to live with any sense of dignity, Bergmann (with Charlie's influence) has a change of heart and wonders if he should help return the hominid to its wildlife sanctuary. But will the driven Weldler be able to put her Yuppie ambitions for fame and fortune aside to assist them, or will she sell out her own soul in order to deliver the young Yeti to the corporate magnate for a shot at her own show?

* * * * *

While comparisons to *Harry and the Hendersons*, as well as the *Little Bigfoot*, are inevitable, *My Friend the Yeti* is actually a well-crafted family film that delivers laughs and lumps in the throat, at least for the younger viewing set for which it was intended. And while it is highly predictable, scriptwriter Martin Rauhaus at least develops his stock characters with a certain amount of flair, imbuing them with believable human conflicts and emotions. For example, rather than play the cryptozoological character as the absent-minded professor type, Bergmann is actually well-rounded, having both a serious side in terms of his daughter's well-being (he realizes he has been neglectful since his wife's passing and feels guilty about not spending more time with Charlie) and an unshakeable need to prove the existence of the Yeti beyond any reasonable doubt (which causes him great embarrassment and a sense of low self-esteem). Likewise, his daughter Charlie is not merely a moppet who is only swayed by cheap sentimentality, but a girl who's been hardened somewhat by the life lessons she's been dealt, which has made her wiser than her years but still emotionally fragile because she's been unable to accept her own mother's death. Thus when she meets the captured Yeti, her back story is neatly mirrored in the Abominable's own sense of being on display without a way of escaping its fate. By helping to free the Yeti, Charlie is undertaking the painful but necessary steps to resolve her own troubled sense of deeply-held pain.

Still, *My Friend the Yeti* doesn't wholly avoid the many pitfalls typical of the Benign Bigfoot sub-genre. For but one example, the greedy zoo owner is the epitome of the Carl Denham Syndrome so firmly established in the original *King Kong*. He's taken to the same extremes as most arch-villains in kiddy Bigfoot movies, presumably to offer an easy target for scorn. One wonders, however, that had the creators crafted this stereotypical antagonist as well-meaning and intent on saving the zoo, would the dramatic construction have been superior for most viewers? In other words, had the same level of depth been offered to the greedy capitalist by showing that he's well-intended but simply misguided in his approach, would *My Friend the Yeti* have been any less potent emotionally? It may seem a minor point, but one hopes for better in a narrative with this overly-familiar set-up than playing to the obvious expectations; indeed, such is the difference between a retread and a re-imagining of a tale perhaps told once too often. Likewise, the reporter who falls for the cryptozoologist, despite her instincts to the contrary, is a cliché of convenience; but rather than dwell on establishing this as realistic, the filmmakers intelligently decide to simply play it for laughs.

The cryptid costume is stylistically reminiscent of some of the furry creatures in *The Neverending Story* and its sequels. It's both enchanting and fantastic beyond realism, which is not a problem given the story's treatment of the subject matter. While this definitely places *My Friend the Yeti* in the comic camp in terms of approach, it equally manages to be touchingly expressive, owing a lot to its large, soulful eyes and sad countenance. Given how badly *Little Bigfoot*'s title cryptid looked on film, at least it can be noted that *My Friend the Yeti*'s technical effects wizards achieved a level of empathetic identification with their hominid creation.

There's nothing new under the Himalayan sun herein, but neither is the material allowed to sit in the rays so long as to become overheated. It's well-directed and fast-paced, making the lapses in logic and characterization less noticeable as the storyline rapidly moves on to the next set piece. All in all, it's a superior example of the often badly-constructed kid-friendly cryptid cinema variant, and deserves recognition for taking a trite tale and making it highly watchable.

My Pet Monster ("Little Bigfoot") (1987) (TV)

Starring Sunny Besen Thrasher, Stuart Stone, Jeff McGibbon, Alyson Court and Dan Hennessey. Produced by Michael Hirsh, Peter Hudecki, Patrick Loubert and Clive A. Smith. Written by Alan Swayze. Directed by Laura Shepherd. Canada. Color. Stereo. 30 Minutes.

Overview: Max, his sister Jill, his best friend Chucky, and his secret pet Monster plan a camping trip. But when the only available adult who can lead them into the forest is Mr. Hinkle, their grumpy scout leader, their enthusiasm fades. Thankfully, Mr. Hinkle announces that he's intent on shooting Bigfoot (with a camera, he adds) and having the photograph published in *Scout Monthly* magazine, thus making him famous. With hopes of encountering Sasquatch, the kids and Mr. Hinkle set forth into the wilderness. The only problem is, Monster is forbidden by Max to come because Max is afraid that Mr. Hinkle will snap a picture of the loveable creature and reveal his existence to the world.

As soon as the kids and Hinkle leave, however, Monster hops on a bike and follows. He is pursued by the fearsome Beastur, another monster from their shared dimension of Monster Land, who wants to bring the errant Monster back home. Monster escapes his adversary Beastur and lands atop Mr. Hinkle's van. The kids are delighted but warn Monster to keep out of sight of Mr. Hinkle. After setting up camp, Mr. Hinkle and Princess, his poodle, stalk Bigfoot in the nearby woods. But Mr. Hinkle only manages to photograph himself

Charlie Bergmann (Ines Nieri) holds the paw of *My Friend the Yeti*.

as an angry bear mauls him, and then a two-fisted romeo who Mr. Hinkle startles behind a bush while the man and his girlfriend are making out.

Later that night the kids tell themselves scary stories until everyone retires to their tents, frightened now by the darkness engulfing them. When Bigfoot screams, the kids shake and shiver, wishing they'd remained home. A long night of fright slowly passes. At dawn there is no sign of Bigfoot, but neither is there any sign of Monster. Realizing he has slipped away in the dark, the kids resolve to find Monster before Mr. Hinkle sees him, and set out in search of their blue-furred friend. Meanwhile, Monster quite literally bumps into Little Bigfoot. The young cryptid is distraught, however, because he's become lost in the woods and can't find his way home to his tribe. Max, Jill, Monster, and Chucky agree to help Little Bigfoot.

Before they can, Beastur appears out of a black vortex from Monster Land and attacks, attempting to drag Monster back to their home world. Little Bigfoot kicks Beastur with his massive feet and sends Beastur flying back into the vortex, whereupon the door closes, thus saving Monster's life on Earth. They regroup and plan to search for Little Bigfoot's parents, but Mr. Hinkle shows up. Max and the rest prank Mr. Hinkle by shaking various trees and bushes until they lead him astray, whereupon they renew their search for the hominid's home.

Alas, a surprise return by Beastur puts an end to their rescue operation. Beastur pursues the kids and Monster to a dead end. Using quick wits and overt politeness, Monster tricks Beastur into stepping through the Monster Land vortex door first, thus sealing Beastur's fate (temporarily) while Monster flees. Mr. Hinkle spots Monster and believes him to be Bigfoot. The scout leader chases Monster but falls into a river that leads to a waterfall. The kids and Monster form a human/monster chain and dangle from a tree branch to rescue Mr. Hinkle and Princess before they tumble over the watery abyss. But they lack enough height to reach Mr. Hinkle until Little Bigfoot adds himself to the equation. The day saved, Monster leads Little Bigfoot back to his mother. Max, Jill, Chucky, and Monster look on with tear-filled eyes as the two hominids are reunited.

* * * * *

After the success of a furry blue stuffed toy named My Pet Monster in the 1980s, the toy's makers, American Greetings (primarily known for their greeting card sales), decided to create a one-off video special. Due to the success of that effort, a limited-run animation series was commissioned, with the creative chores handled by the Saturday morning giant Nelvana of Canada. Nelvana almost didn't survive long enough as a company to do *My Pet Monster* after passing on doing the animation for *Heavy Metal* in favor of *Rock and Rule*, the latter of which bombed at the box office while the former was a modest hit worldwide. However, with the success of a *Strawberry Shortcake* children's morning series based on Mattel's line of girls' dolls, and then the runaway worldwide hit *The Care Bears* franchise, Nelvana became one of the most successful animation studios in North America.

My Pet Monster was never more than a footnote in the famous company's history, but owing to the popularity of the actual Monster toys, it remains a nostalgic favorite as a TV show to those who grew up owning the creaky-voiced collectible. As for Ciné du Sasquatch relevance, the episode "Little Bigfoot" actually prefigures the *Little Bigfoot* movies made years later in plot and tone so much one wonders why Nelvana didn't sue the production company of said feature films. Not only is the concept identical, but the plot is the same, right down to having city kids on a camping expedition stumbling across a lost Sasquatch youngster and helping it find its way home to Mama Bigfoot. For whatever reasons, *My Pet Monster*'s rendition of "Little Bigfoot" has one advantage the live-action movies lack: It's mercifully only 30 minutes in length! Would that both *Little Bigfoot* and *Little*

Bigfoot 2: The Journey Home had employed such brevity, they might have fared well in direct comparison to the Nelvana effort.

It's true there's nothing new under the sun, especially where Benign Bigfoot shows in the kiddy TV realm are concerned. In this regard, "Little Bigfoot" is as clichéd and predictable as one would expect, right down to the sentimental execution and crudely limited animation. Only the least discriminating of tyke audiences will find "Little Bigfoot" anything more than a thankless time-waster between other, more engaging Saturday morning fare. The element of having a baby hominid is so thoroughly pushed into the background of this episode, in fact, it may as well have been eliminated. Most of the show is taken up with Mr. Hinkle's insipid camping lessons and the constant struggle by Beastur, the bad monster, to lure Monster back through a black vortex which will return the pair to Monster Land, their native habitat. In some perhaps unintended ways, this actually anticipates *Monsters, Inc.*, right down to having the lead creature be a blue-furred monster who bonds with kids on the Earthly side of the equation. Still, the similarities are superficial, and one cannot help but note that such doorway devices separating two worlds in children's fantasy novels, short stories, TV shows and movies are quite common, going back to Alice and her adventures through the looking glass.

There's not much "there" there in "Little Bigfoot," and that's the problem as well as the innocuous charm of it. For most viewers it's a completely dispensable entry in the canon of Ciné du Sasquatch, neither contributory nor completely inept. But for those who merely desire some inane escapism and pretty, pastel-colored backgrounds, there's nothing contained within its scant running time that will cause much consternation. Like much Bigfoot evidence itself, it's all in the eye of the beholder.

Mysterious Encounters (2003) (Multiple Episodes) (TV) (Doc)

Featuring Autumn Williams. Produced by the Outdoor Life Network. USA. Color. Stereo. 30 Minutes.

Overview: Autumn Williams is a long-term Sasquatch researcher and personal witness to multiple Bigfoot sightings. The founder of the popular Oregon Bigfoot website and blog, Ms. Williams has appeared at many national conferences and symposiums related to cryptozoology and the hunt for hominids. One of only a handful of dedicated female cryptozoologists who've achieved true renown, she has recently taken a sabbatical from active Sasquatch research (though she plans to remain an active contributor to her website), in part because she is concentrating on writing a book about her past work and in part because she believes the field has become too overrun with disingenuous types who are more interested in making money than any true investigation of the subject matter.

Ms. Williams and her team of assistants covered a variety of cryptids rarely featured when this series first aired. Using high-tech gear now common in such shows as *MonsterQuest* and the like, Ms. Williams and her team would arrive at a particular location, conduct eyewitness interviews, deploy a variety of testing apparatus, and then conclude each show with an analysis of the collected data. Among the gear utilized to search for Bigfoot and its related cryptid cousins were cameras that were motion-activated, thermal imaging and/or infrared in spectrum. More traditional methods included hunting dogs, scent traps, low-altitude balloons, and blasting simian howls via loudspeakers in suspected hominid areas to hopefully attract responses. Occasional reenactments were staged in order to gather evidence and provide a sense of the horrific nature of encountering a cryptid in a lonely setting, such as a remote roadway or deep in the wilderness at night.

A variety of regional bipedal cryptids were given the weekly spotlight. During its year-long run, *Mysterious Encounters* featured half-hour episodes with the following titles: "Texas Thicket Monster" (aka the Caddo Monster); "Redwood Forest Giant"; "Oklahoma Wildman"; "Bigfoot of Bluff Creek"; "California Creek Devil"; "Tsiako Beast"; "Mountain Devil"; "Mount St. Helens"; "Creature of Cumberland"; "The Creature of Whitehall"; "Louisiana Swamp Creature"; "Alabama Booger Monster"; and "Florida Skunk Ape." After the series was cancelled, Ms. Williams also produced a documentary called *Oregon Bigfoot: Search for a Living Legend.*

The Mysterious Monsters (1976) (Doc)

Featuring Peter Graves, Peter Hurkos, William Stenberg, Dr. Sidney Walter, Jerilou Whelchel, Dr. Geoffrey Bourne, Dr. Lawrence Bradley, the Rev. Father Brusey, Peter Byrne, John Cobb, Tim Dinsdale, John Green, Grover Krantz, Ed McLarney, Robert W. Morgan, Roger Patterson, Robert Rines, Adrian Shine and Eric Shipton. Produced by James L. Conway, Frances Guenette, Robert Guenette, Raylan D. Jensen and Charles E. Sellier Jr. Written and Directed by Robert Guenette. USA. Color. Mono. 86 Minutes.

Poster art for the theatrical release of *The Mysterious Monsters.*

Overview: Host/narrator Peter Graves explores the Fortean worlds of cryptids, UFOs, psychic phenomena and beyond. Prominent Bigfoot researchers, such as Peter Byrne, John Green, Robert Morgan, and Grover Krantz, share and critique various field evidence, including photographs, plaster footprint casts, and the controversial Patterson-Gimlin footage. The Abominable Snowman is also given in-depth examination, including an interview with a Sherpa girl who claims she was attacked by a Yeti, as well as film and photographs of supposed Yeti scalps and a mummified claw. Other strange phenomena examined include the Loch Ness Monster, Peter Hurkos describing how psychic detectives ply their trade, speculation about visitation from ancient alien civilizations, and the power of hypnotism. Many of the hominid sequences include recreations utilizing fairly convincing cryptid costumes.

* * * * *

For a complete overview of *The Mysterious Monsters*, the reader is advised to review the entry for *Monsters! Myths or Mysteries?* In essence, this feature-length documentary is a re-editing of that monumentally successful CBS-broadcast Bigfoot television special which achieved the highest ratings ever in American TV history in its era, a record which remained untoppled for decades. Filmmaker Robert Guenette took the basic format, most of the footage from *Monsters! Myths or Mysteries?*, and padded it with additional scenes newly shot, most of which concerned not Bigfoot or cryptids but paranormal subjects such as psychic research and UFOs. This enabled the venerable exploitation masters at Sunn Classic Pictures based in Salt Lake City, Utah, to four-wall the resultantly retitled *The Mysterious Monsters* throughout America during the summer of 1976, thus capitalizing on the vast numbers of kiddy matinee crowds owing to the summer vacation from school. While this seems an obvious gambit in hindsight, it is well to remember that until the smash success of *Jaws* just a year previously, summer was considered one of the worst times for Hollywood studios to release movies because it was generally assumed children would rather be outside playing rather than indoors watching movies, and adults too busy on vacation to venture into theaters for entertainment.

Peter Graves was hired to replace Rod Serling as host and narrator. Serling had voiced the popular *Monsters! Myths or Mysteries?* but sadly died shortly after it aired. Realizing it would be tawdry to use a sound-alike, all of Serling's narration was removed and Graves dubbed it anew, along with the original material created especially for *The Mysterious Monsters*. The result is largely seamless, and while Serling's stentorian vocals are missed, at least Graves acquits himself with an adroit seriousness. Ciné du Sasquatch fans will find most of the non–Bigfoot material less involving, but the hominid sequences are quite informative, well-researched, and non-sensationalistic, particularly given the filmmakers clearly are in the camp of the believers rather than the skeptics. Throughout the documentary, for example, Graves continuously announces that the overwhelming evidence re: Bigfoot is so conclusive that there can no longer be any scientific doubt as to its existence — a contentious and wishful boast at best, even more than three decades after its theatrical release.

The technical qualities are quite good for such a low-budget effort, particularly the Tom Burman–created hominid costumes. Burman is the special effects makeup artist who worked with legendary Hollywood effects master John Chambers, and, as Chamber's helper, created the original *Planet of the Apes* make-ups, as well as several of the space cryptids seen in such key Ciné du Sasquatch TV series as *Star Trek* and *Lost in Space*. One particularly well-remembered scene by young viewers of the film takes place in a young wife's remote home late one night. Engrossed in watching a TV program, the woman fails to notice a shadow which falls behind her on the curtained window only a few feet away. Moments later a hairy arm smashes through the glass and grabs at her, attempting to pull her outside. She flees, screaming for her startled husband, who yanks open his front door only to find the beast towering in front of him, a horrific expression on its face as it stares down at the terrified man.

Theaters showing *The Mysterious Monsters* were often accompanied by Sunn Classic Picture sales agents who hawked the paperback version of the movie, also written by Guenette and bearing both the film's title and iconic poster image on its cover. Guenette would go on to become a prolific producer and director of behind-the-scenes documentary specials about successful motion pictures, such as *SPFX: The Empire Strikes Back*, *The Making of Star Wars*, and *Great Movie Stunts: Raiders of the Lost Ark*, before his passing in 2003. He was a co-founder of the International Documentary Association, won two prime-time Emmy Awards, was nominated for two daytime Emmy Awards, and was cited by the International Documentary Association as a Pioneer Award Recipient in 2001.

"MONSTRUOS
MISTERIOSOS"
("The Mysterious Monster")
Producida por:
CHARLES E. SELLIER Jr.
Dirigida por:
ROBERT GUENETTE
Color / MDF

Sasquatch remains aloof in the foothills in this staged publicity still from the Mexican theatrical release of *Mysterious Monsters*.

Often considered one of the best Bigfoot documentaries of the 1970s, owing to its inclusion of many respected researchers, suspenseful recreations of hominid encounters, and accurate distillation of the Sasquatch sightings and gathered facts for its time period, *The Mysterious Monsters* is required viewing for all serious Ciné du Sasquatch viewers who favor sampling documentaries as well as fictional incarnations of Bigfoot.

The Mystery of the Sasquatch Triangle (2007) (Doc)

Featuring Linda Wygle, Chuck Storrie, Terry and Treba Jahn, Rod Zorger and Richard Mye. Produced and Directed by Don Keating. USA. Color. Stereo. 92 Minutes.

Overview: This Ohio Bigfoot researcher Don Keating production is dedicated to a white-furred hominid sighted in the so-called "Sasquatch Triangle," composed of Coshocton, Guernsey, and Tuscarawas Counties in Eastern Ohio. This area is known for its frequency of Bigfoot encounters, particularly a rogue albino cryptid locals dub the Ohio Abominable Snowman for obvious reasons.

Included in the documentary are eyewitness accounts of the bipedal creature from Ohio residents, such as Terry and Treba Jahn, and Chuck Storrie. Also featured is an audio recording of a purported Ohio Yeti vocalizing in the night, as well as a home video of what is supposedly a white hominid in the forest (though the imagery is quite blurry — through no fault of the filmmaker, who includes it for analysis only). The DVD version of *The Mystery of the Sasquatch Triangle* also includes Keating's previous shorter non-fiction film *Ohio's Abominable Snowman?* dedicated to similar sightings.

The New 3 Stooges (1965) ("Abominable Snowman") (TV)

AKA: *The Three Stooges — Cartoon Classics*. Starring Moe Howard, Larry Fine and Curly Joe DeRita. Produced by Dick Brown. Written by Cecil Beard, Edward Bernds, Homer Brightman, Barbara Chain, Sam Cornell, David Detiege, Art Diamond, Nick George, Pat Kearin, Jack Kinney, Jack Miller, Lee Orgel and Warren Tufts. Animation by Chick Otterstrom, Kay Wright and Bob Maxfield. Directed by Edward Bernds, Sam Cornell, David Detiege and Edwin Rehberg. USA. Color. Mono. 4 Minutes.

Overview: Larry, Moe and Curly Joe embark on a photographic expedition to the Arctic to capitalize upon the wonders of nature. Along the way they encounter the legendary Abominable Snowman, who turns out to be a lonely, English-speaking Yeti who only wants to entertain the Stooges if they will befriend him.

The Stooges, however, are more excited about the possibility of taking its picture than forming any emotional bonds. Alas, the Yeti is a shape-shifter par excellence, and transforms into various human impersonations, such as a cowboy and sideshow huckster, in order to impress them. Securing a shot of the Yeti as a Yeti proves to be an impossible task for the Stooges, despite their best efforts. Before they can accomplish their mission, the Yeti is signed by a Hollywood talent scout, and the Stooges are left behind and stranded in the Arctic, missing their literal and figurative boat.

* * * * *

By 1965 the Stooges franchise was in serious decline. While Moe Howard was able to successfully keep the act afloat with various lower-budgeted endeavors, such as the feature film *Snow White and the Three Stooges* and combination live-action skit/cartoon segments such as *The New 3 Stooges* television show (from which this is episode 112 in the series), the trio of physical comedians were all in bad health and advanced age.

To its credit, *The New 3 Stooges* was pretty much the same old Stooges as always, albeit toned down in terms of physical humiliation endured by each Stooge owing to the intended juvenile audience. Each cartoon was introduced by a short (typically one-minute-long) live action sequence in which the Stooges performed a skit that was relevant to the subsequent cartoon. So in "Abominable Snowman," for example, we find the Three Stooges in a nature setting attempting to take a picture of a rare bird in order to make some much-needed cash. This thematically sets up the animation to follow, wherein the Stooges are distressed to learn the Abominable Snowman has the ability to basically do vaudeville schtick and shapeshift into various human personages at will. What they desire is the beast in the raw; what they get is Shecky Green in a Yeti suit!

The animation is technically very crude, owing mostly to the production company behind it. Cambria Studios was a tiny West Hollywood outfit that also produced such low-budget fare as *Space Angel* and *Clutch Cargo*, the latter series featuring the infamous Synchro-Vox format. Syncro-Vox was a cost-saving technique in which human actors' lips were photographed speaking dialogue and then superimposed atop the animation. This saved the animation team from having to redraw each vowel or syllable of spoken text, thus saving time and money. While never technically believable, it did render a surreal effect which is often parodied today via video matte technology, wherein a celebrity's head shot has another performer's lips green-screened over the actor's facial image. For its time, it was a novel variant and allowed enough financial return for Cambria to produce *The New 3 Stooges* among their later fare (though the Stooges show used conventional animation and not the Syncro-Vox format).

The Three Stooges were no strangers to simian cameos in their short two-reelers prior to their Ciné du Sasquatch entry.

As far as cryptid cinema goes, "Abominable Snowman" is basically a copy of the more successfully rendered Bugs Bunny encounter with a Yeti in "The Abominable Snow Rabbit," complete with English-speaking hominid of clearly limited intellectual capacities. Like in the earlier Bugs Bunny short, this Yeti is playful and basically harmless in nature, desiring human contact more than avoiding it. The one novel variation — and what a variant it is! — is that in the Stooges' version the Snowman can *literally* transform himself into various human disguises. Though probably a coincidence, this parallels the old Native American legends of Sasquatch having an ability to shapeshift into different animals. Nevertheless, it places the episode into the pattern of Ciné du Sasquatch themes, as this ability is sporadically encountered in other television and feature film productions. The ruthless Westerner embodied by the Hollywood mogul (who wishes to sign the Yeti to a talent contract and whisk the creature back to civilization to exploit it for gain) equally fits the paradigm so frequently encountered in Bigfoot filmmaking, as illustrated by such previous cinematic incarnations as *The Abominable Snowman* and *Yeti: Giant of the 20th Century.*

Only hardcore Three Stooges and Ciné du Sasquatch fans will find much to enjoy in this brief short, but these audiences should find little to dislike about the effort: It's briskly-paced and at least renders the cryptid as likeable rather than in rampage mode.

NewsRadio ("Apartment") (1999) (TV) (Cameo)

Starring Dave Foley, Phil Hartman, Stephen Root, Andy Dick, Joe Rogan, Maura Tierney, Vicki Lewis, Khandi Alexander and Jon Lovitz. Produced by Julie Bean, Bernie Brillstein, Kell Cahoon, Brad Grey, Alan J. Higgins, Sam Johnson, Josh Lieb, Chris Marcil, Drake Sather, Tom Saunders, Paul Simms and Kent Zbornak. Written by Tom Saunders, Kell Cahoon, Sam Johnson and Chris Marcil. Directed by Skip Collector. USA. Color. Stereo. 23 Minutes.

Overview: Lisa Miller and Dave Nelson, employees of TV news station WNYX, both find an apartment for lease independent of one another and decide to fight over who can rent it. Meanwhile, Joe's boss Jimmy decides Joe must update the WNYX website with something more interesting than a posted picture Joe has put up of a pregnant Bigfoot. Max Lewis, a co-worker, passes by the computer and happens to notice the picture of the pregnant cryptid. Alarmed, Max asks if it is not actually a photo of himself, shirtless, while sunbathing in the park. Joe denies the charge and Max leaves, uncertain, whereupon Joe thanks Beth, who's standing nearby, who supplied him with the photo of Max. "Keep the photos coming," he intones.

This amusing play on Jon Lovitz's inability to distinguish himself while topless from a pregnant hominid is a funny reference to the infamous breasts apparent in the Patterson-Gimlin film footage, wherein the pendular boobs of the beast are frequently cited as proof of the cryptid's sexuality. Lovitz cups his "man boobs" at one point and utters, "This wouldn't be the first time I've been exploited this way," as a further coda to the punch line. It's played merely for chuckles but aptly demonstrates how deeply saturated the Patterson-Gimlin footage has become in the national psyche (a comedian can riff upon the reference without the need to explain it). Indeed, the actual photograph posted on the website is never seen by the viewer, only reacted to and referenced by the horrified cast members.

Night of the Demon (1980)

Starring Joy Allen, Bob Collins, Barrett Cooper, Michael Cutt, Shane Dixon, Lynn Eastman-Rossi, Rick Fields, Melanie Graham, Paul Kelleher, Jody Lazarus and Jennifer West. Produced by Jim L. Ball. Written by Mike Williams. Directed by Paul C. Wasson. USA. Color. Stereo. 97 Minutes.

Overview: Professor Nugent has survived a horrendous encounter with Sasquatch and lived to tell the local sheriff about it while recovering in a Michigan hospital. "Those horror stories that you've heard from the forest," Nugent begins, referring to the various newspaper accounts of a Savage Sasquatch wreaking havoc in the area, "they're all true."

We then witness a reenactment of one such moment of terror. A fisherman has his arm ripped from his body during broad daylight for the audacity of utilizing Bigfoot's favorite fishing hole in the middle of the woods. Carla, the fisherman's daughter, appears in Nugent's anthropology class later to relate the tale of her father's unfortunate encounter with Bigfoot. Nugent convinces some of his students to go along with him on an expedition deep into the wilderness area where the stories are coming from in hopes of finding leads as to the creature's whereabouts. Carla is glad for the expert help of Nugent, but warns the students of another recent encounter which resulted in the deaths of two locals.

Flashing back to said incident, we witness a young couple making love in the back of a van which is parked in a remote lover's lane. The van's doors are ripped open without warning and the man is dragged to his death by a howling-mad Sasquatch. The dying, bloody romeo attempts to crawl across the front windshield, upside-down, and escape with his life, but the creature pulls him back atop the van's roof and finishes him off. The screaming woman dies of a massive stroke, unable to deal with what she has seen and what awaits her as the next intended victim. Properly sobered, Nugent's students realize their undertaking is not without risk, but are so inspired by the professor's overriding passion for his task they refuse to be deterred.

Following various leads, Nugent and company make their way up a winding river and park their boats, trekking the rest of the way into the wilderness on foot. That night, after setting up camp, Nugent relates another tale of misfortune in which a sleeping camper was assaulted by the hominid, which we witness in flashback. After grabbing the helpless man inside his sleeping bag, Bigfoot swings the pinned camper around and around, eventually releasing him. The centrifugal force slams the screaming camper into a tree branch, impaling him upside-down and left barely alive to face a painful, lingering death. Also detailed are the deaths of two young girl scouts who are lost in the woods and meet their grisly deaths as well.

Professor Nugent and his crew of college kids visit the only town in the area and interview locals who are willing to talk about Bigfoot. Most offer various and often contradictory tales of the creature's existence, but the name "Crazy Wanda," who is characterized by the citizens as a backwoods loner, appears throughout the various accounts as a common thread. Realizing they may have stumbled upon their first real clue, Nugent leads his crew up the mountainside in search of the female hermit. Wanda proves to be a veritable gold mine of information, but how much of her ramblings can be believed? For example, she claims to have birthed a deformed child that her father tossed into the woods owing to its mongoloid nature many years prior, but Wanda's glassy-eyed stare and babbling nature make Nugent suspicious of her sincerity. Besides, what possible connection could such a feral child have to Bigfoot if Wanda is a human, anyway?

The group ventures deeper into the wilderness. Nugent tells the exhausted group another tale of a Sasquatch encounter gone awry as they sit around a blazing campfire. We witness Nugent's retelling in flashback as a motorcyclist stops to relieve himself as he smokes a joint. To the biker's horror, Bigfoot reaches out and grabs the biker's penis, ripping it off! The biker dies in agony as his crotch spurts streams of blood. Shivering with fear, the students bed down for the night, wondering if they've perhaps gotten in over their heads, despite their good intentions to help Nugent solve the series of homicides.

That night they're awakened by a ritual going on in the nearby forest. Nugent and one of his students investigate, and they see a young woman apparently about to be raped by one of the black-clad men who encircle her. Nugent sets fire to the woods and diverts the participants, who flee with the girl. In the morning Nugent is angered to learn that the expedition's boat has been cut loose from its mooring, thus effectively stranding his expedition in the woods. Two of the students decide to move away from the others and fool around, but during their love play, Bigfoot claws the male's exposed back, thus sending the lovers racing back to their group. Realizing they must somehow find help, the terrified Nugent and company decide to seek out Wanda's cabin.

They find it, but, to their horror, the creature is just behind them. They implore Wanda to offer some assistance, but she merely sits and rocks in her chair, oblivious and evidently at peace with whatever happens. Nugent leads the students in a heroic last stand, barricading the tiny wooden home. But Bigfoot will not be deterred. The monster smashes through the flimsy door. One-by-one the students are disemboweled, impaled, crushed and slaughtered by the enraged Sasquatch. Nugent is grabbed by the towering fiend and has his face pressed down onto a hot stove. In the emergency room where Nugent concludes his tale of misery, he rips off his bandages to reveal his melted half-face, imploring the sheriff to do something before more innocents are killed by the cryptid creature. Nugent passes out, and the sheriff and doctors theorize Nugent was actually responsible for the murders and is simply a schizophrenic in denial of what he has done.

* * * * *

It's difficult, even with the above overview, to capture the incredible sense of jaw-dropping gore and subsequent shock *Night of the Demon* produces in even the most jaded viewer of Slasher films. With a sense of sleazy voyeurism unmatched by the majority of hardcore porn efforts, the filmmakers linger on every violent death with a kind of unblinking sense of fatalism that defies easy description. Death alone is never an easy thing, most horror films posit as a given; but for the creators of *Night of the Demon*, death itself is the *easy* way out. It's the squirming, madness-inducing finality leading up to said relief from the world's miseries that one must really fear and (at least in this cinematic Grand Guignol) endure before the promise of release via expiration.

Again, none of this is without precedent in the horror films made before or since *Night of the Demon*. And nothing is as violently gory within *Night of the Demon* that would rival H. G. Lewis' *Blood Feast* or *Two Thousand Maniacs*, for example. But within the relatively gore-free genre of Ciné du Sasquatch, *Night of the Demon* was and remains either a milestone or a low-point, depending upon one's stomach for such onscreen mayhem. Bodily dismemberment, castration, rape, impalement, child homicides ... it's as if the Marquis de Sade and Pier Paolo Pasolini had combined forces to write and direct the ultimate sadistic Bigfoot movie!

While the movie sank into virtual oblivion upon its modest videocassette release in America, it caused quite a stir in Great Britain. Banned as a so-called "Video Nasty" by the Thatcher regime, along with 71 other specifically-named horror films, all copies of *Night of the Demon* were yanked from rental or sale to the public, with actual imprisonment possible for any videocassette purveyors caught by the British government's undercover police disseminating said specified "profane" movies! It's difficult to imagine such a reaction, save for in the most conservative of localities in America — indifference being the more likely outcome, if not picketing and boycotting of said store owner until the title was removed — but under the provisions of the Video Recordings Act 1984, enforced removal and jail time were the actual outcomes in regards to the banned titles. Along with *Night of the Demon*, a small sampling of other notorious Video Nasties prohibited from viewing by UK citizens included: *Blood Rites*; *The Boogeyman*; *Cannibal Apocalypse*; *Dead & Buried*; *Don't Look in the Basement*; *The Evil Dead*; *Andy Warhol's Frankenstein* (aka *Flesh for Frankenstein*); *Last House on the Left*; *Love Camp 7*; *Tenebrae*; and *The Werewolf and the Yeti* (which, given this last-cited title, meant the Brits had effectively made history not only for state-sponsored censorship of movies, but for banning two separate Ciné du Sasquatch entries). Eventually many of the titles were edited for gore content and resubmitted for approval for distribution, but it's equally true that several of these titles remain technically illegal to view to this day. Even some screenshots captured on home computers of scenes from these banned movies have been deemed illegal and thus criminal to possess as of this writing. *The Werewolf and the Yeti* has technically never been re-released, thus making it (at least in Britain) the one Ciné du Sasquatch movie which could land viewers in the stony lonesome for having it in their Bigfoot collection.

Issues of redaction and freedom aside, there will be a supposed number of viewers of *Night of the Demon* who will thoroughly understand, if not tacitly support, the Margaret Thatcher government's position. This is understandable if one is not either a Splatter film fan or a follower of Bigfoot movies, as the violence will be considered in poor taste and extreme to those used to tamer Hollywood fare. However, issues such as these aside, *Night of the Demon* is key in Ciné du Sasquatch's history as a genre, for it marks both the turning away from its most recent commercial precedent — the Benign Bigfoot of *Harry and the Hendersons* — and a shift back towards the threat implied by Charles Pierce's *The Legend of Boggy Creek* (only taken to the nihilistic extreme). Whereas Harry was a befuddled hominid merely in need of a return to nature to reestablish his innate goodness, the Demon of *Night of the Demon* is a corrupt, loathsome hominid willing and preferring to demolish all human lives at the first moment of contact — sadistically so and without need of provocation. Sleeping, fishing, having sex, becoming lost, or simply stopping to relieve oneself on a beautiful roadside — all are tantamount to an instant death sentence to this cinematic cryptid, who brooks no intrusion without rendering immediate, morbid punishment. To say that Wasson as director has inverted the Benign Bigfoot paradigm into its opposite Savage Sasquatch mode is an understatement; he literally reinvigorates the genre's darker impulses in a single, extremely influential motion picture.

Dismissed outright when it first appeared on the home video scene, *Night of the Demon* has since become a cult film of growing significance. The makers of *The Blair Witch Project* cite it, along with Pierce's *The Legend of Boggy Creek*, as a major influence (indeed, the sequence wherein Professor Nugent and his team investigate and interview townsfolk in *Night of the Demon* about their local killer Sasquatch bears a remarkable resemblance to the opening scenes of *The Blair Witch Project* in tone and execution). The film was to revitalize the sinister nature of Sasquatch as a murderous monster, in contrast to the friendly, happy-go-lucky Bigfoot of the Spielberg factory's making. This schizophrenic divide exists in an uneasy dichotomy to this day, with the two camps seemingly growing only further apart in the bipolarity of their hominid depictions.

Critics rightly cite the poor performances and tepid pacing in some sequences to deride *Night of the Demon*. These arguments are not without merit. But just as the same arguments did not stop *The Legend of Boggy Creek* from becoming a milestone in this genre, neither did they impede *Night of the Demon*. In fact, the notoriety of the movie has only grown yearly, especially as Ciné du Sasquatch viewers come to see its major inspiration on the Savage Sasquatch milieu. It still retains its power to brutalize and shock the viewer, which may be dismissed by upper-crust critics as vulgar and common, but nevertheless insures the film an equally vociferous crowd of B-movie defenders who "get" the deliberately transgressive nature of Wasson's intent. If there is any doubt of the latter, one only need to examine the slaughter of not one but *two* girl scouts in *Night of the Demon* as proof positive (or is that negative?) the director wanted audiences thoroughly scandalized by the violation of the cinematic staple that children will rarely be subjected to overt graphic violence, even in horror movies. *Night of the Demon* yanks any preconditions away in this regard, mercilessly showing first the stalking and then savage murdering of the girls in unsparing detail. By the time the film's slow-motion, Sam Peckinpah–influenced duel to the death between hominid and *Homo sapiens* erupts in a truly deplorable but

mesmerizingly violent coda, it becomes obvious to repeat viewers of the film that no other ending could possibly have worked. Like *Taxi Driver*, *Straw Dogs*, and *Rolling Thunder*, everything in the picture has built to this last non-stop slaughter in terms of catharsis. What is so unexpected is that it works as well as it does, uncomfortably reminding the viewing audience that despite our often-stated staunch opposition to real-world violence, we are, as audiences, clinically unable to avoid the thrill of bloody denouements when properly manipulated by the filmmakers. Like Pavlov's dogs, we salivate despite ourselves, only for showers of crimson rather than biscuits.

Never for the easily offended or faint-hearted, *Night of the Demon* is a juggernaut that goes for the viewer's jugular without warning or moral excuse-making. With its wraparound sequence in which the protagonist is in a hospital and blamed by the doctors for the atrocities that occurred, it reminds one of *Attack of the Mushroom People*. And like in that Honda-directed classic, the folks who encounter the horrors of isolation in the wilds are as much victims of unknown "demons" as they are their own hubristic natures. They don't fall prey to Bigfoot; they actively if subconsciously conspire *with* the monster to meet their grisly fates. In this manner, *Night of the Demon* perfectly distills both the bestiality aspects of the crossbreeding motif so prevalent in the genre and graphically illustrates the visceral "Bigfoot as superior" theme in one blood-soaked swoop. The externalization of Sasquatch as man's darker, unexamined Animus lurks just below the surface throughout *Night of the Demon*, just as it did in Toho's *Attack of the Mushroom People*. To paraphrase the old Walt Kelly *Pogo* mantra, "We have met the savage Sasquatch, and he is us."

Night of the Sassy (2005)

Starring Brian Bertsch, Greg Carlson, Brady Daley, Robin Garland, Adam Hagen, Sally Jacobson and Shannon Jacobson. Produced by Greg Carlson, Matt Dreiling and Mike Scholtz. Written and Directed by Greg Carlson. USA. Color. Stereo. 15 Minutes.

Overview: Sally is a vivacious young woman who has a sexually-tinged obsession with all things Sasquatch. Her slacker boyfriend is as indifferent to her interests in the cryptid as he is to her experiencing a satisfying orgasm when they make love. But after a tender encounter with a gentle, foreplay-believing Bigfoot while on a camping trip, Sally realizes her future lies not with her boyfriend but with her hominid lover. She abandons her former life and heads for Alaska, in search of Sasquatch for scientific and erotic reasons.

* * * * *

This amusing, off-beat short film — while strictly for adults — encapsulates many of the motifs of Ciné du Sasquatch without missing a comic beat. While played for garrulous laughs, *Night of the Sassy* offers the typical bestiality theme in reverse, with the human female falling for the hominid rather than vice versa. While there has been an element of this in some Bigfoot films (most notably *The Beast*), the long shadow of *King Kong* still looms over most efforts, keeping the human female's interest platonic (although again, some exceptions, such as *Tanya's Island* and even a gay twist in *Yeti: A Love Story*, occasionally occur, wherein the border is pushed into outright mutual sexual attraction). Still, it's rare to find a Sasquatch movie that begins with the woman character already in lust with the creature. It's a head-over-heels redo of *Beauty and the Beast*, for certain, with Bigfoot as the shy, awkward Belle and Sally as a feminine form of the Beast, aggressive and eager for a tryst to fulfill her forbidden passions.

Shot in 16mm in Fargo, North Dakota, and Morehead, Minnesota, *Night of the Sassy* is a clever, engaging short film that played in a couple of festivals but is sadly unavailable in any legitimate DVD release or included in any compilation of short films as of this publication date, although limited edition silkscreen prints of its colorful poster are available from the graphic artist who created it via his website at Punch Gut Studio.

Nightbeasts (2009)

Starring Zach Galligan, Apesanahkwat, Audra Wise, Robert Miano, Sonny Skyhawk, Billy Daydoge, Donn Angelos, Holly Wilson, Patty Toy, Chad Trager, Kevin Glashan and Lloyd Kaufman. Produced, Written and Directed by Wes Sullivan. USA. Color. Stereo. 80 Minutes.

Overview: A divorced, middle-aged Charles Thomas takes his estranged boy Tim on a father/son camping trip, concerned the boy's mother Patricia is slowly poisoning Tim's feelings with her constant bad-mouthing of Charles. But the father-and-son weekend outing turns outlandish when they stumble into the rare but periodic return of a hidden Bigfoot tribe living in the woodlands where Charles owns a cabin. It turns out the local Native Americans maintain an uneasy alliance with the frightful creatures by staying well within the confines of their narrow tribal land whenever the hominids venture forth, and maintaining a non-interference policy when any rampaging Sasquatch monsters devour any white people who just *happen* to be outside the Indians' Protected Magic Circle.

Charles and Tim realize their only hope is to make it to Charles' cabin, where there is a phone line which will enable him to call outside authorities for help. Louis Freebird, an elderly Indian rainmaker, accompanies the two outsiders, realizing his mystical knowledge of Sasquatch may save the father and son from their own ignorance of the menace they're about to face. Meanwhile, Sheriff Horace Jimmerson and his dim-witted deputy assistant Clarence survive a Bigfoot ambush on their patrol vehicle while responding to the numerous reports of Sasquatch sightings. Forced to flee, Sheriff Jimmerson and Deputy Clarence retreat to Charles' cabin as well. There the assembled humans endure a terrifying siege as the Sasquatch monsters lay waste to the two-story structure, intent on killing all the embattled humans inside.

Eventually Patricia decides, because she's not heard from her son or Charles, that she will drive up to the cabin to check on Tim's condition. Her car's headlights reveal to the cabin survivors that bright lights harm the Bigfoot creatures' ultra-sensitive, bat-like eyes. And despite the fact Patricia drives a convertible, there is still a chance they can all escape in the car. After blasting a myriad of the monsters with their shotguns, the men folk and Patricia pile into her car. Even as they speed away, the creatures race after the departing vehicle, clawing at the terrified passengers and driver. They arrive safely at a lakeside rescue center and are welcomed by a boat captain who ferries them back to civilization.

* * * * *

Nightbeasts is an often suspenseful and mostly entertaining shocker directed in a decidedly old-school style (and all the better for it). While it's not without its limitations and moments that stretch beyond even the necessary upfront "givens" of the genre (acceptance of the hominid premise and a B-movie sensibility that throws most rules out the shattered windows), *Nightbeasts* largely avoids the pitfalls inherent in many Ciné du Sasquatch efforts. With a healthy sense of mordant humor, fast-moving set pieces, and some genuinely creepy moments, it follows in the footsteps of Joe Dante's *The Howling*, as *Nightbeasts* transforms, like a wolf hidden in a sheep's hoodie, from a self-aware quirky variant on a submerged horror western into its own mythic, even elegiac treatment on the postmodern state of the Bigfoot film genre. Whereas *The Howling* uses the idea that a self-help therapy group has overtaken a large patch of Northern California

old growth forest area to use as their secretive werewolf colony (which, in turn, is really masquerading as the ultimate nature-based "primal scream" psychiatric treatment to lure in new members), *Nightbeasts* has a secret order to the unfolding nature of things that is revealed as tribal construct.

Like many postmodern cryptid creature flicks, *Nightbeasts* not only assumes but is predicated upon the fact that audiences will bring a full-range of clichéd cultural expectations to the viewing experience. Indeed, it trades upon these expectations like a Bigfoot version of Wes Craven's *Scream* (though, admittedly, it is not as on-the-nose with its genre-tweaking dialogue). From the knowing casting of Zach Galligan (whose brightest prior cinematic moments are staged within siege-styled night battles against foraging *Gremlins*), to the frequently wry humor, and even lovingly including such ubiquitous horror film staples as fog-shrouded forests and a cat that jumps suddenly into frame for cheap shock value, *Nightbeasts* is thoroughly postmodern. It even offers a cameo appearance by perpetual big-city Lothario and Troma Studios CEO Lloyd Kaufmann, who forgoes his renowned sartorial acumen for this role as a helplessly self-deluded Park Ranger who dies screaming while wearing khaki shorts, pith helmet, and regulation tee shirt, no less.

Nightbeasts also takes time to examine, nullify, and even enshrine new viewpoints in the Ciné du Sasquatch *oeuvre*, though like with

THEY COME OUT AT NIGHT

NIGHTBEASTS

TREEHOUSE PICTURES PRESENTS "NIGHTBEASTS" ZACH GALLIGAN AUDRA WISE APESANAHQUAT SONNY SKYHAWK ROBERT MIANO BILLY DAYDODGE HOLLY WILSON CHAD TRAGER DONN ANGELOS MUSIC BY JASON SOLOWSKY PRODUCED, WRITTEN AND DIRECTED BY WES SULLIVAN

Promotional poster artwork for *Nightbeasts*.

all stylistically-driven cinematic fare, this is all buried in the sub-text and only occasionally comes to the forefront. Like the classic Western movie, it deals with interracial tensions in regards to assimilation and the dominance of a class of people; it examines the impact culture often unwittingly plays on the political decisions, character conflicts, and related dramatics upon which depend the narrative itself; and it forces both "sides" of the cultural divide to peer with less-biased eyes at their own sobering reflections in the proverbial cracked mirror. Like how such moralistic folklore is brought Biblically forward in many of the Western genre's finest examples as a dramatic excuse to invoke God-licensed fury against the Other (typically, the Other is presented as the Native American), *Nightbeasts* drags ethnically-dependent cultural taboos into the campfire light, using the opportunity to catalogue a myriad of issues on either side of the culturally-driven fault lines between present-day Native and Anglo societies. All parties will be given the rude raspberry as comeuppance by film's end. As in *The Searchers*, there exists a line beyond which no one can judge, save to offer that, indeed, some souls are lost on *both* sides of the artificial divides that emerge between human societies.

In *Nightbeasts* modern tensions are everywhere: the failure of the American Dream; the disappointments of a dissolving marriage and child estrangement; race wars forever simmering just beneath a fractured crust of barely-suppressed rage; an alienation from the mainstream culture and its endless "Buy Me!" by-products; and even the souring of Native Americans themselves, some of whom have maintained a balance between tribal spiritual values and the more unforgiving world of "White Men," but some of whom have given in to their experience-based cynicism and begun to sell themselves and their fellow tribesmen short during hard times. The latter theme of tribal values betrayed is an interesting acknowledgement that no matter how perfect one's political stances, there still remain those who would seek only to profit from said values like so much parasitic dead weight, never putting the group's larger concerns at the forefront.

Everywhere in *Nightbeasts* there exists a foggy malaise of indifference and cynicism that prevents even a son and a father from connecting, let alone the rest of the world so bleakly sketched. It's a hard luck story from every character's point of view, which again makes it emotionally reflective of many Western films. It shares a similar viewpoint with countless cinematic and TV entries wherein a band of White Men suddenly find themselves under threat of extermination, drop their culturally-driven and political differences to work together, and make a stand for survival against overwhelming odds (two of many examples are Howard Hawks' *El Dorado* and John Wayne's version of *The Alamo*). Rarely, if ever, is the Other presented as anything else but deserving of retribution, and is often shown as having perpetrated an act of taboo-shattering violence (and therefore worthy of the wrath of the vengeance-seeking European settlers). In this sense, *Conquest of the Pole* and *Nightbeasts* share a theme that stretches from the very beginning of Ciné du Sasquatch in 1912 and continues almost a century later. This shared bond is the depiction of the story from the *Homo sapiens'* viewpoint, which forces the cryptid in *Conquest of the Pole* and the cryptids in *Nightbeasts* to don the fearful mask of a demonic, sub-human version of killer hominids. Said inhuman beasts can only *justly* be dealt a mortal blow by mankind *if* mankind is sufficiently awake enough to even guide the "implementation" process (perhaps best iconographically visualized by *King Kong*'s climactic machine-gun death of Kong at the wings of whirling warplanes high atop the Empire State Building). *Nightbeasts* goes one further by having one of the experienced Indian characters explain that the lively Sasquatch tribe are individually "dumb as a sack of nails" and only ever achieve success when they work under the silent command of an alpha hominid of their own kind who issues the group's orders. At such a time, however, they are formidable. This is

a reversal of the typical Ciné du Sasquatch portrayal in which the cryptid is beyond human imagination in terms of physical bulk and abilities. In *Nightbeasts*, the faceless, anonymous Sasquatch tribe members are like the endless parade of super-tall Martians who ran up and down the neon-green tunnels of the original *Invaders from Mars*—convincing because no individual is ever distinctive from the overall clan of Sasquatch creatures themselves. They have a pack mentality, and *Nightbeasts* sufficiently captures their appropriately lumbering gait and unimaginative methods of attack, which inevitably involve them sacrificing themselves as much as "taking down" any humans present. There is a sense from the Native American elder that he feels much empathy for Sasquatch not as the Spirit Being of the Forest but as a kind of self-defeating species doomed to slowly wind its way to extinction, sooner if not later. These are clearly ominous omens of possible societal hardships for the Indian man to be justifiably concerned with, based on his historical experience.

Contrary to such sensibility, however, is the film's willingness (even eagerness) to gently mock everyone who makes a claim of moral superiority by way of affiliation to one human tribe and its spiritual values over another. The Indian tribe depicted are largely destitute and seem as uncertain about their future as the rest of the onscreen *Homo sapiens*. This is where *Nightbeasts* excels as a traditional narrative in the B-movie vein. It offers stereotypes, as is inherent in the B-movie horror tradition, but comments upon them in a wry manner at the same time. The Indian Folk Dancer mocks the handful of Caucasians who've paid to be in attendance by telling them to remember Indians are still considered more hip than a white dude because Indians are seen as cool, reflective, and possessing a pragmatic desire to co-exist, facing as they did annihilation in an earlier failure to secure a lasting peace. The implicit criticism, mixed with a biting sense of personal failure in the sad faces of the fallen Natives as they've watched themselves slowly whittled away from once heroic custodians of North America to little more than parking lot sideshow relics in only a few destructive generations, is the real "monster" in *Nightbeasts* that drives so much of each character's respective Id: a sense that each persona represents the failed compromises of life when the future seems just more of the same and the past no longer worthy of self-examination for fear of where that would lead. The proverbial "lone cowboy," played by Galligan, is a cinematic lost cousin to Joe Buck from *Midnight Cowboy*. No doubt Galligan's modern-day cowboy is a better educated, street-smart version of the naïve Joe Buck, but the archetypal protagonist remains intact. Here is Joe Buck if he'd returned to small-town America, gone through an economic downtown that wrecked his entire sense of well-being (and ability to support his family), and eventually divorced his less-than-friendly wife. Galligan crafts his sad-faced persona like a Gary Cooper imitation mixed with a layering of Kurt Russell's deadpan cynicism circa *Escape from New York* to create a finely-etched portrait of the everyman buckling under endless "double dip" recessions and the American Dream gone awry.

The creature visualizations are numerous and well-done in *Nightbeasts*. Rather than rely on lingering close-ups, the director wisely shoots his cryptids as shadowy glimpses of beings constantly in motion, darting in and out of the frame unexpectedly. The manner in which these mini-shock moments unfold is through a series of rapid vignettes. Each moment typically presents its informative and dramatic content from a few well-chosen angles and quickly shutters to black. This compression of time under the force of a lurking calamity, building towards an explosion, draws a parallel between *Nightbeasts* and Kubrick's *The Shining*. This eerie sense of a disaster looming helps both films build an inevitable sense of proper Gothic dread. Indeed, in *Nightbeasts* there is a noticeable lack of true surprise in the lead characters' encounters with Sasquatch. Not that the filmmakers stage it in this manner; rather, the characters accept the reality of Bigfoot with the blasé attitude of having won a $5 lottery ticket and being offered $4 cash for it if they'll but sell it now. "It just *figures*" is the general reaction in so many words and actions when the truth of Sasquatch's existence is made known to a new generation of Native American caretakers. "It just *figures*" is the overall reaction by the Indian community when they learn their tribal chief cut a less-than-honorable deal with the Nightbeasts themselves to avoid harm for his people (but at the direct expense of others). "It just *figures*" is Zach Galligan's tired cowboy's tepid response to the utter destruction of his plans to reunite with his son, leaving them both in mortal peril in the process.

Zach Galligan as the quasi-depressive father Charles Thomas has been shaken to the core by all that has suddenly ended for him — marriage, family, and any long-term, secure working scenario — and left adrift in a self-deprecating fog of personal miasma. The "rise to the challenge of survival" tone of *Nightbeasts* actually works to awaken Thomas' repressed, animalistic side, which had been slumbering until the sudden cryptid rampage. Charles Thomas' crushed Super Ego and humbler Ego have been all but eliminated by events just prior to the movie's beginning; he has been among the walking wounded in hellish times, and that is never an easy personal depth from which to recover sans major scarring. Thomas has plenty of those scars. Basically borderline when *Nightbeasts* starts, Thomas' own need to reassert "control" over his surroundings in defiance of the Bigfoot tribe's taking it for their own sacred roaming grounds is actually a positive, Howard Hawks–styled male apotheosis rebirth from the smoldering ashes of prior failure. This is, of course, the symbol of the Phoenix, the majestic bird arisen from the ashes of former ruination and now redeemed in the new glory of living reincarnation. In so many ways, the siege is the "Great Awakening Call" to Thomas, and even as the Postmodern Cowboy he cannot fail to rise to the occasion as his prototypical predecessors might have stoically done: group loyalty at the moment of crisis, standing side-by-side, à la John Wayne and Robert Mitchum in *El Dorado*. At one point in *Nightbeasts* the men folk and Thomas' son all arm themselves with shotguns and go on a Bigfoot kill spree in order to clear a potential pathway for their escape. As they march silently beside one another, shotguns blazing, the Sasquatch monsters falling as victims of a sudden gun massacre, the less-jaded viewers are lead to recall the "Cowboys vs. Indians" mythos of an earlier era sadly marked by violent race relations. Here the Indians have long since abandoned any true sense of moral superiority over "The White Man" or any other such formerly necessary political baggage, à la Chief in *One Flew Over the Cuckoo's Nest*. Not that these Natives are cynical and refusing to carry their load out of sheer laziness, an earlier stereotype hopefully recognized as now thankfully bygone. Indeed, what is refreshing about *Nightbeasts* is how such tenuous differences between us as self-proclaimed Americans vanish when suddenly confronted with the threat of an entirely new species who is possibly as smart as we are, if not smarter, because we are always the last to discover it and not vice versa.

For the most part well-shot and spookily-staged to draw out suspense, *Nightbeasts* is as scattershot as a well-aimed round of buckshot — dead on when it strikes the center of the target (such as the cryptids being described as "dumb as a sack of nails" by the cocky humans even as the creatures are successfully breeching the humans' cabin with each new wave of attacks) and a bit more defuse when smattering around the edges of the broader targets (such as the over-the-top *Forrest Gump*–styled Deputy Sheriff character who makes *Hee Haw* seem like Tennessee Williams in comparison). But any free-spirited, albeit homage-oriented, show like *Nightbeasts* will never be to all filmgoers' tastes. Indeed, this is why, like so many entries in Ciné du Sasquatch, *Nightbeasts* is definitely going to appeal to the

Savage Sasquatch film fans more than to the Benign Bigfoot lovers, the latter of whom often prefer to see the hairy hominid as an externalization of Mother Nature's more beatific protective powers — as spirit protector rather than carnivorous predator of human flesh. It is truly the vegan vs. carnivore viewpoint in terms of cultural preference that is at play herein, however self-knowingly.

But if you *do* enjoy scary Sasquatch movies more than kids hugging the Big Guy at the end of the film and shedding tears because "My Summer with Sasquatch" is coming to a late August ending, then *Nightbeasts* should definitely be on any diehard's to-see list. It's never definitive, but then again, it never fumbles entirely either. It is well-paced, well-structured, and clearly driven by its narrative, however modestly envisioned, to the point that it could have actually withstood an expanded running time had the filmmakers wished or been able to shoot additional sequences, expand existing scenes, etc. Most Bigfoot films and TV shows could use a healthy editing session, so in this case *Nightbeasts* is an at-home crowd pleaser for genre-loving audiences looking for an "escapist Sasquatch" B-rental title. Consider the ending scene wherein the handful of survivors must flee (in a convertible, no less) a snarling pack of snapping Sasquatch creatures who chase after them at high speed — a scene which could have played as camp but instead has a lingering, haunting quality of suburban horror as the ferocious creatures drool and snarl, fully intent on shredding the last ounce of *Homo sapiens* they can get their claws on. It's a great last image. For those eager to see Ciné du Sasquatch stretched atop a new, astonishingly pliable narrative canvas, *Nightbeasts* offers a good postmodern example: a lot of jump scares mixed with the usual B-movie hokum in equally entertaining doses.

No Burgers for Bigfoot (2008)

Starring Jonathan Grant, Brittany Joyner, Lucas Ross, Keenan Garrett, Twyla Gonzales, C. Douglas Grant, Nancy Heinbach, Monica L. Jones, Donald J. Krejsek, Ty McCarthy, Aubree Mckamie, Tom Monnot, Aubrie Ross, Jamie Ross, Abby Schmidt, Delores Wheeler and Raychel Winstead. Produced by Jonathan Grant. Written by Jonathan Grant, Brittany Joyner, Drew Overholt, Lucas Ross and Ryan Staples Scott. Directed by Jonathan Grant and Josh McKamie. USA. Color. Stereo. 94 Minutes.

Overview: Independent filmmaker Michael Justice is gut-sick from the injustice that his career and Bigfoot have suffered. A wounded soul, he determines to make his new Bigfoot epic, "The Return of Bigfoot," the greatest Ciné du Sasquatch *short* film ever made. Putting together financing isn't easy these days, so Justice has to compromise with product placement, which he finds in the form of Bovagina, a stud bull enhancer pill produced by a local company. Alas, slipping a bovine sexual performance drug into the story without drawing attention to itself proves a difficult challenge for the indie filmmaker during the writing phase. After much deliberation, Justice settles upon using a pump-action water gun to visually remind the audience of the product's intended use.

The surly, cynical crew is obliviously indifferent to the low-rent nature of "The Return of Bigfoot" (the short-film-within-a-feature-film being directed by Justice). To prove he's not biased, Justice hires a production assistant who is a black female. Justice and the rest of the all-white crew proceed to walk on pins and needles whenever the young lady approaches, revealing their true colors.

The actual production phase is a series of catastrophes. The director complains about a mourner at a cemetery, outraged that someone would ruin a shot for his godsend of a short film simply to bemoan the passing of some deceased loved one. A female lead's Russian-tinged accent becomes Russian-tinged Russian the longer the production grinds on, making sound continuity for her scenes a nightmare and her dialogue incomprehensible even to the bewildered crew. Eventually the nightmare of making the short film concludes, but then there is still the premiere at the local film festival to face for the ego-driven filmmaker, which offers its own share of challenges to overcome.

* * * * *

No Burgers for Bigfoot is like *This Is Spinal Tap* but with a skewering of independent filmmakers instead of heavy metal rockers. By filtering the entire movie through the uber-ridiculous personality of the self-inflated Michael Justice (played by the multi-talented writer, director and producer of *No Burgers for Bigfoot* himself!), the tone is set early on for continual comic derangement. Justice stands before the cameras in his suburban backyard, plaid shirt unbuttoned to reveal his hairless chest, and cockily tells the world how he's got a special message of world-saving importance to relate with his new Bigfoot opus. In launching the film-within-a-film in this manner, *No Burgers for Bigfoot* succinctly summarizes the doomed nature of the short film, which even suffers in the title department (as the confused crew continually ask, "But why 'The Return of Bigfoot' if there wasn't a first movie?"— a question for which Justice has no answer).

As the filmmakers state, it's not a movie about Bigfoot, but about the pretentiousness that inhabits so many who enter the arts (in this case it's independent filmmaking), who have clearer ideas of self-aggrandizement than they do creative, artistic visions. In fact, the creators of *No Burgers for Bigfoot* comically illustrate the pitfalls of having unfettered ambition but no talent. Michael Justice is all bravado and little brains, despite his pretense of being an intellectual. He never questions his own fallible premise for his short film: He is making a pro-green movie wherein he contradictorily portrays Bigfoot, a beloved icon of environmentalists and the very New Age audience he hopes to reach, as a rampant killer hominid spewing blood and guts everywhere. The bone-weary crew never voice much in the way of critique of this obvious problem which negates "The Return of Bigfoot" as a workable premise; instead, they blindly, dully work to bring the premise to cinematic reality. In this manner, they are the ultimate unquestioning foot soldiers which Hollywood power agent and studio head Michael Ovitz once famously quipped will kill on demand as long as the orders come from on high.

Even if it really lacks a central focus on Bigfoot as a hominid character, *No Burgers for Bigfoot* still shows how uniquely personal and flexible the Ciné du Sasquatch genre can be in the hands of talented, risk-taking filmmakers who are not shy about addressing the inherent awfulness of too many Bigfoot films and TV shows. It takes real moxie to work in a genre that for most of its history hasn't even been credited as a legitimate branch of cinema. The comic laughs that are mined from *No Burgers for Bigfoot* therefore feel based in real world experiences on low budget films. More universally, it captures the horror of being cornered at a cocktail party and subjected to an onslaught of some self-professed expert's perfect opinions, which he passes as fact beyond question, and the subsequent sense of wanting to commit hara-kiri rather than face another agonizing moment listening to such a blowhard pontificate further. That's not an easy feeling to translate into any medium, and the fact that Jonathan Grant et al. does it so well speaks volumes about the nature of their talent. The film also rather accurately parodies those in any field of endeavor who would dare to don the official mantle of expert, especially when it has been laid upon the recipient's shoulders by the recipient himself. In a media age wherein everyone can be a CNN iReporter and the like, turning themselves into instant video viral celebrities, and one in which talking heads with impressive credentials and broadcast-friendly facades dominate the media landscape, this type of narcissistic expert character becomes an ubiquitous presence. This is all the more reason such buffoonery is a worthy target of satire, and largely why *No Burgers for Bigfoot* generates worthwhile laughs at the expense of cretinous dilettantes everywhere.

Northern Exposure (1990) ("Aurora Borealis: A Fairy Tale for Big People") (TV)

Starring Rob Morrow, Barry Corbin, Janine Turner, John Cullum, Darren E. Burrows, John Corbett, Cynthia Geary, Elaine Miles and Adam Arkin. Series Created by Joshua Brand and John Falsey. Written by Kevin Murphy. Directed by Fred Gerber. USA. Color. Stereo. 60 Minutes.

Overview: Recent New York City university graduate Dr. Joel Fleischman owes the state of Alaska four years of his services in exchange for the scholarship the state (which he's never even visited) provided to help him complete his medical training. Hating the remote small town of Celily, Alaska, where he must practice, Fleischman at first avoids becoming friendly with any of the strange assortment of locals he's forced to treat, hoping that they'll so dislike him the state will either cancel his contract or assign him to a larger city, like Anchorage. Alas, the prior lack of quality medical care all but insures Fleischman will be stuck in the frozen hinterlands no matter how craftily he attempts to alienate himself from his patients.

* * * * *

The mysterious "monster" character named Adam is kept off-screen for much of the early part of *Northern Exposure*'s first season episode called "Aurora Borealis: A Fairy Tale for Big People." Viewers only learn of the unknown character via the eccentric locals of Cecily, Alaska, as they relate stories of Adam to Dr. Fleischman to explain mysterious footprints, missing items, etc., all of which they attribute to their local Bigfoot variation, who they claim has been committing such acts of vandalism for over 15 years. One night Dr. Fleischman finds himself stranded on a dark, windswept road when his vehicle breaks down. He's taken hostage by a lonely, doe-eyed hermit who lives in the woods.

It turns out the hermit is a former Vietnam war veteran who has retreated to Alaska after the conflict because he despises mankind for what he witnessed and was forced to do during his tour of duty. Because of his extremely large feet and hairy body, and his huge snow-shoes and furry parkas, he is often mistaken for a Sasquatch in the driving snowstorms so common to the area (and which he often uses to his advantage as a natural cover to forage for necessary supplies). Realizing Adam has taken him in not to harm him but to save him from freezing to death in his car, Dr. Fleischman warms to the gentle giant and vice versa.

Adam is actually not a true cryptid, but the manner in which *Northern Exposure* misleads, and even leaves unsettled several of its clues about Adam's true nature and origin, is not only typical of the quirky nature of the series, but equally tantalizing for the implicit possibilities. Does Adam have something to do with the majority of the hominid sightings, or is it merely a coincidence? And what about those unusually large feet? Are they a sign he may possess a latent genetic strain that links him to some unknown bipedal ancestors of humankind?

Adam would go on to make several cameo and guest appearances throughout the later four seasons of *Northern Exposure*, adding to the show's already character-rich milieu. As with this first-ever appearance, there is always a mysterious element associated with his character that never quite resolves itself. This deliberately vague sense of specificity in regards to Adam made his character somewhat magical, not unlike the mythic monster folks believe him to be related to. A well-written and well-produced series, *Northern Exposure* garnered major fan and critical attention before a premature retirement after its fifth season.

Not Your Typical Bigfoot Movie (2008) (Doc)

Featuring Dallas Gilbert, Wayne Burton and Tom Biscardi. Produced by Jay Delaney and Jeff Montavon. Directed by Jay Delaney. USA. Color. Stereo. 63 Minutes.

Overview: Dallas Gilbert and Wayne Burton, two middle-aged men in Portsmouth, Ohio, dedicate themselves to researching and filming Bigfoot whenever personal finances, broken-down vehicles, and physical and mental health allow. Calling themselves "Bigfoot partners" in research, the duo form an inseparable bond based on documenting the greatest cryptid mystery left for mankind. With a website, local newspaper attention, and even out-of-state crypto conference appearances to their credit, Dallas and Wayne seem to be making unexpected headway against the enormous odds they face daily — such as Wayne avoiding having his home foreclosed upon by the bank and Dallas battling the emphysema which plagues him.

Hope for a break-out of their regional cryptozoological obscurity looms when Tom Biscardi, infamous promoter of the Georgia-Bigfoot-in-a-Freezer hoax, arrives on the scene to supposedly help Wayne garner attention for Wayne's "Black Bigfoot" 35mm photograph by having Wayne appear on an Internet radio talk show dedicated to Fortean phenomena. Alas, Wayne follows Biscardi's instructions to sensationalize the facts surrounding the hominid photo during the interview. The on-air host busts Wayne for his dishonesty, thus causing a prolonged rift between Wayne and Dallas, as Dallas' credibility in the Bigfoot community becomes suspect as a result of the bad publicity.

The two men seem destined to end their relationship until Biscardi makes good on his promise to show in Ohio and research their findings with Wayne and Dallas. Their hopes renewed, the two locals roll out the red carpet for Biscardi. Alas, their savior turns out to be less than they had hoped for in terms of his desire to work with the two Ohio natives, leaving them out of the research loop. Depressed but determined not to let Biscardi's dismissal thwart them, the two friends dedicate themselves yet again to pursuing their passion, whether or not they ever receive any attention for their efforts.

* * * * *

It's very satisfying to see Ciné du Sasquatch mature as a genre and begin to realize both the pitfalls and possibilities of its postmodern era. *Not Your Typical Bigfoot Movie* references both qualities — the bad and the good — beginning with its very title. The bad is, not unexpectedly, that disreputable persons and lingering negative assessments prevail in and about Bigfoot researchers; the good is that within these self-sustaining communities, which are grassroots-driven and maintained, there is an open door policy where all who are without scorn are welcome to participate and add their own energies to bolster the awareness about cryptozoology. Much as amateur astronomers contribute a vast wealth of information every year about the solar system without much recognition from the professionally-funded scientific universities, so do unpaid crypto hunters help sustain the search and appreciation for unknown species of all kinds, not merely hominids.

The filmmakers are wise to avoid lecturing the audience about such distinctions by non-critically focusing on two humble, working class protagonists: real-life Bigfoot hunters Dallas and Wayne. Dallas has spent the better part of a decade and a half taking videos (which he lovingly calls "films" throughout the documentary) of bipedal creatures. Alas, a majority of the Bigfoot images are indistinguishable from shadows in the forest, begging the question: Does Dallas see something the viewer simply cannot, as several of his friends suggest, or is he merely off his rocker? There is plenty of evidence to support

either conclusion. For example, Dallas (who is slowly dying of emphysema) claims spiritual powers of healing by laying hands on his friends, but relies on conventional medical technology to slow the progress of his own disease. Likewise, he comes across as sincere and likeable in countless scenes, only to be followed by smaller bits in which he claims four different doctors have told him that he has "sheep DNA in my brain." But because the documentarians are not interested in passing simple judgment on either Dallas or Wayne, offering them instead "as is" (complex, contradictory personalities in motion, as are we all who call ourselves human), feelings of audience superiority are short-lived.

As for Wayne, he is presented against the kind of working class background so typical of Ohio and Michigan post-automobile industry heights and steady, unionized employment. Indeed, Portsmouth's fading welcome sign reads: "Portsmouth — All America City" for those few passersby who may have strayed off the interstate and wonder why they're surrounded by abandoned factories, weed-choked lawns, decrepit homes, and unending economic blight as far as the eye can see. Wayne himself disparages his lifelong hometown,

Poster art for the theatrical release of *Not Your Typical Bigfoot Movie.*

pointing out that no jobs exist in the heartland burg any longer. Like in a Michael Moore documentary gone to Sasquatch, the audience is firmly grounded in the doldrums and disappointments of the two men by presenting them within the context of their depressed (and depressing) environment. Lacking jobs, trapped in a dying American dream, and struggling with constant poverty, Dallas and Wayne have abandoned all hope in reality and given themselves over to the only lifeline that seems at all hopeful, however long the odds: hitting the jackpot financially and redeeming their mutual low self-esteem by proving Bigfoot is real. "Just think," says Wayne about his van (which lacks heating in the brutal Ohio winter) as he attempts to lift his own sagging spirits, "my van might one day wind up in a Bigfoot museum or something like that."

Again, it is easy to initially dismiss and mock Dallas and Wayne. After all, Dallas can be seen at the doc's beginning as a toothless old New Age Bigfoot guru and Wayne his self-delineating "loser" buddy who has failed to force his way into Sasquatchology. Numerous times throughout *Not Your Typical Bigfoot Movie*, Wayne derides himself as a complete and utter wash-out in life. "If there's any message I'd want anyone to get from my life, it's don't end up like me. Don't do what Wayne Burton done and wind up a loser," he intones, shortly after revealing how he attempted suicide many years earlier by slashing his arm, showing the massive scar tissue to the camera. And Dallas, who refuses to accept any criticism of his passions as anything more than ignorance on the behalf of others, has to endure his otherwise loving wife telling the camera, as the two sit on their sofa, that Dallas' eldest son considers Dallas a nut. Dallas half-heartedly argues, but the tears welling in his eyes as he realizes he can no longer deny even his own family members' belief that he has lost touch with reality — even though they love him without question — pushes him into a reluctant silence of painful inarticulateness. But whereas such moments might seem to make the chronicled duo nothing more than pathetic "losers," as Wayne harshly (and incorrectly) labels himself, the exact opposite effect is created in all but the most cynical viewer. One begins to see the underlying desperation as nothing more than learned frailty from a lifetime of having lived through seeing every once-cherished dream slowly wither on the vine into the bitter remains of personal despair. The lyrics from Bruce Springsteen's

Dallas Burton and Wayne Gilbert, best friends and Ohio-based Bigfoot researchers, are the focus of *Not Your Typical Bigfoot Movie*. The title itself references the clichéd nature of many Bigfoot efforts.

"Born in the U.S.A." come to mind: "You end up like a dog that's been beat too much/Till you spend half your life just covering up."

The arrival of Tom Biscardi injects a natural antagonist into the movie, in contrast to the pure, sweet-natured motives of Dallas and Wayne. Dallas, who has convinced himself beyond doubt that Biscardi is the answer to the pair's hopes of fame and fortune, bombards Biscardi's well-funded Bigfoot research organization with endless photos via email until Biscardi's attention is captured by one in particular: the 35mm snap Wayne made of the Black Bigfoot. This is somewhat ironic in that it was this first-ever photo Wayne took which lead him to initially seek out Dallas (a known local cryptozoology devotee) for counsel as to what Wayne had photographed. Dallas smothers his resentment that the one photo that interests Biscardi is his friend Wayne's, in hopes of making up for the fact Dallas had earlier attended a Tennessee Bigfoot conference without his resentful junior partner in tow. Biscardi arranges for Wayne to appear on an Internet radio talk show in which Wayne will extol the history of his Sasquatch photo. But, as Wayne later relates with tears in his eyes, Biscardi convinces the media-shy Wayne to alter some key facts about the photograph's taking. For example, when Wayne favors being honest and mentioning the fact he took the photo years ago, Biscardi insists he make it sound jazzier by claiming it was "in the last few months." Likewise, Biscardi tells Wayne the precise distance Wayne was from the cryptid — 300 feet — so that the encounter will be less likely to be perceived as questionable. The naïve Wayne awkwardly does as he is told, only to become trapped in his own lies by the radio show's host, who bluntly goes to a commercial break after effectively calling Wayne a liar, thus ending the interview.

This is a key moment to understanding the movie's impact, in that it creates an understandable rift between Wayne, who regrets his well-intended but foolish mistake, and Dallas, who has to live with the predictable consequences of having his own photographs of Bigfoot tarred with the same dubious brush as Wayne's Black Bigfoot image. It also offers further proof — as if any were needed, based on his past media hoaxes in regards to Bigfoot — that Biscardi is prone to play fast and loose with the facts, at least if Wayne's version of events is to be believed. Given the simple nature of Wayne's earnest personality versus the portrayal of Biscardi as an egomaniac (Biscardi even threatens to sue Wayne in front of a stunned Dallas "no matter how little he's got" — a favorite technique of Biscardi to silence critics), one is left with little doubt as to the accurate version of events, as least as far *Not Your Typical Bigfoot Movie* renders the facts.

Oddly, Biscardi unwittingly acts as the perfect dramatic lynchpin for Dallas and Wayne to realize that their bond of friendship and mutual respect is far more important to them than any recognition or monetary gain the professionally-funded Biscardi might provide. After Biscardi pays Dallas a visit to spend several days "Bigfooting" in the Ohio woods, tensions mount the very first night out when Dallas insists on chanting an "authentic" Native American Bigfoot call to attract the beast. Biscardi hisses "Shut up!" to the startled Dallas and bitterly complains that the two amateurs are mucking up his pro team's investigation. "This is what we do for a *living!*" he growls, clearly upset. It's a telling line, and reveals much about the approach Biscardi envisions for his pursuit of Sasquatch. The next day, as the camera records their obvious disappointment and heartbreak, Dallas is unable to reach Biscardi via telephone, only to discover Biscardi and his team have gone to the locations Dallas and Wayne showed them without the Ohio researchers in tow. Embittered, Dallas and Wayne put a brave face on their sense of betrayal, realizing that they've been played as fools by Biscardi without so much as a phone call to explain his abrupt termination of their participation. It is difficult to watch this section without feeling an enormous sense of empathy for Dallas and Wayne, which is as much a credit to their own unpretentious natures winning over the viewer's heart as to the filmmakers, who carefully set the stage for this inevitable exploitation with sublime foresight as to the probable outcome of encountering Biscardi.

Had *Not Your Typical Bigfoot Movie* ended on such a sad note, it would be *The Last Picture Show* of Bigfoot movies. That would not be bad, of course, and indeed there is a Sam the Lion (Ben Johnson) and Sonny Crawford (Timothy Bottoms) quality to the relationship between the older mentor Dallas and the younger, depressive Wayne; neither man seems complete without the other to lean upon in a landscape otherwise bereft of love and hope. But wisely, the filmmakers linger after Biscardi's departure and allow the viewer to see the healing that has occurred between the two after their grueling visitation by the California team. Having had their friendship tested by turmoil and conflict, Dallas and Wayne have become closer than ever before, like all great human relationships that endure the daily tragedies and storms of life.

In this regard, *Not Your Typical Bigfoot Movie* transcends the genre and becomes a moving testament to the most basic but necessary of human needs: to have one's soul known and loved by another human being, whatever one's inherent flaws and failures. It's hard to imagine a more touching coda to the genre to date, and indeed this sense of loyalty over belief has become something of a new wrinkle in the genre's development. Other examples that recognize this sense of mutual dependency as the underlying gravitas between participants in a quest for a cryptid include *The Long Way Home: A Bigfoot Story*, *The Sasquatch Gang*, *The Wildman of the Navidad*, and *Drawing Flies*. These filmmakers have recognized that the earlier paradigms of Ciné du Sasquatch — believer vs. skeptic, scientist vs. hunter, monster vs. man, etc.— must be examined anew if the genre is to remain alive and emotionally involve the viewer. In doing so, they are all but commenting upon the Bigfoot genre itself, gently indicating how clichéd mundane distinctions have become and attempting to reinvigorate the genre by introducing a new character-based orientation to the proceedings. While each succeeds and fails on its own individualistic terms, it is nevertheless a profoundly welcome exploration of and expansion on the themes and archetypes of Ciné du Sasquatch. In short, they indicate a healthy future for an undying genre of popular filmmaking.

On Bigfoot's Mountain (2007) (Doc)

Featuring Stan Johnson. Produced by Dick Criswell. Directed by Joan and Dick Criswell. USA. Color. Stereo. 120 Minutes.

Overview: Paranormal investigator and personality Dick Criswell interviews Oregon native Stan Johnson against a chroma-key background of an alien landscape. Johnson talks at length about his encounter with a Sasquatch in Oakland, Oregon. Eventually the two men leave the studio and slowly trek to the top of the mountain where Johnson claims to have stumbled upon Bigfoot. After talking about the incident further and offering no corroborative or physical evidence, the documentary mercifully ends.

While Criswell is a known commodity on the old *Coast-to-Coast* radio show with Art Bell, this amateurish production leaves much to be desired, such as editing, a tripod, qualitative information, discernable audio, and a running time of less than 15 minutes (as anything beyond that is superfluous, given the lack of content). In all, it doesn't help matters that one is left with the lingering suspicion the producer spent less producing the master than he does on mailing each DVD to those who spend the $14.95 plus shipping to order it on-line. Unimaginative, to say the very least.

On the Fringe ("Fouke Monster" and "In Search of Bigfoot") (2009) (Doc)

Produced, Written and Directed by Justin Minor. USA. Color. Stereo. 25 Minutes.

Overview: One of the fortunate aspects of home video technology is that formerly bypassed filmmakers can inexpensively access desktop editing to produce professional-quality results. One of the *un*fortunate aspects of the same set-up is that anyone else can do the same, talented or not. Herein witness *On the Fringe*, an aptly-titled amateur "TV series" that is really just a compilation of overly-long YouTube videos strung together to warrant (as in the filmmaker should have been arrested) two self-distributed DVD releases, each running 25 minutes in length.

Episode One ("The Fouke Monster") has the director, Justin Minor, and his buddies packing up their vehicle and driving to Fouke, Arkansas, hometown of the legendary *Boggy Creek* cryptid. As they drive on what feels like an endless road trip, they relate stories about seeing Pierce's film and growing up devoted believers in the Fouke Monster. After finally arriving in the small town, they are basically shunned by everyone they randomly approach in the streets. Not surprisingly, the Fouke residents have long since tired of being treated as idiots by total strangers bearing video cameras that ride into town and expect them to talk on cue about a creature that many have no clue even exists. Miffed, but reading the rejection as actually wary yokels who are "in the know" but don't want to divulge their secrets for fear of being ridiculed, the filmmakers call it an outing.

Episode Two ("In Search of Bigfoot") sees the company once again hitting the road, leaving behind Fouke not dispirited but hopeful their next rendezvous in Southeastern Oklahoma will yield more positive results. They discuss their ambitions, recorded sightings, and fascination with the subject inside their vehicle for the majority of the video's length, before finally arriving in Oklahoma in time to grab some shots of the lonely wilderness area. After parking on the road side, they trek into the forest and set up camp, hoping to videotape Bigfoot. Alas, their efforts are in vain, though they do claim to feel as if they were much closer this time around than on their previous Fouke excursion. Both of director Justin Minor's "documentaries" are definitely in a minor key, though at least the DVD cases have appropriately spooky box art.

One Step Beyond ("Night of the Kill") (1959) (TV)

Starring John Newland, Fred Bell, Dennis Holmes, John Marley and Ann McCrea. Produced by Collier Young and Merwin Gerard. Written by Merwin Gerard. Directed by John Newland. USA. Black & White. Mono. 30 Minutes.

Overview: Davey Morris disappears from his rural ranch home for three days in the remote mountainous wilderness. His frantic parents search with the help of many local residents until all are exhausted from the effort, but still no one finds any sign of their missing son. Distraught, all but a handful of the most dedicated neighbors and Dr. Frazier, a local country doctor, resign themselves to young Davey's probable fate and abandon the search. But when all seems lost, Davey is found sitting high atop a cliffside in perfect health — not hungry, nor thirsty, nor harmed.

Questioned about his disappearance, Davey tells his incredulous parents that he was not missing but merely playing with his friend. Davey goes on to tell them his newfound pal is a 16-foot-tall creature that his folks quickly surmise is Bigfoot. They refuse to believe him, but there are lingering doubts despite their rationalizing it as all so much fantasy on the boy's part: How did Davey manage to get so high on the cliffside? And who fed and protected him in a rocky forest area full of predators?

Deciding to leave well enough alone and be thankful for their blessings, Davey's parents take him home and try to put the incident behind them. But the very next morning they discover Davey missing yet again, his second-story bedroom window open and a foul, lingering odor present. They frantically search the farm until they locate Davey just outside the barn. He explains to them his friend visited early in the morning and lifted him outside his window to play, whereupon Davey showed the visitor the meat-curing shed to help feed his guest. At first the parents scold Davey for his persistent lie, but when they enter the shed they see huge slabs of beef with massive bites taken out of their sides. They also find monstrous-sized footprints in the mud, verifying Davey's story.

Realizing there may be something to the boy's encounters, Davey's father organizes a small posse of local men with guns to protect his family should Bigfoot return that night. Sure enough, the giant towers over the trees, looking down at the men until blasted at by the terrified locals. Howling in pain, the creature retreats and the men give chase, determined to destroy it. Davey tries to prevent them from killing his innocent friend, but the men won't hear of it, fearing for their own families. Unable to kill the cryptid with their guns, they set fire to the dense underbrush near the night visitor's cave entrance, intent on burning it from its cover. But by dawn's light, they find no trace of it: no bones, no hide, nothing. It is as if the hominid has vanished with the smoke.

* * * * *

ABC and corporate sponsor Alcoa produced *One Step Beyond* as an answer to the enormous popularity of Rod Serling's *The Twilight Zone* on CBS. Though never the ratings bonanza of Serling's series, *One Step Beyond* nevertheless enjoyed a popular following in its day and even several "steps beyond," owing mostly to the fact that many episodes were not copyrighted properly and fell into public domain, thus making them widely shown in syndicated television format. And while Serling took home the Emmys for his creation, *One Step Beyond* enjoyed a surprisingly enduring critical reputation every bit the equal to *The Twilight Zone*, with some fans still preferring the ABC series, citing the better quality writing and overall scare factor. Whatever one's preference, it is indisputable that both were quality anthology format programs that employed a plethora of deserving talent behind and in front of the cameras.

If there was a chief difference, it was that *The Twilight Zone* favored outright fantasy and science fiction stories (many tinged with latent horror elements), whereas *One Step Beyond* featured storylines supposedly based upon reported incidents that were dramatically recreated. Otherwise, the similarities were startling, including having a genial host who introduced each story and concluded each episode with a moralizing epilogue. John Newland, *One Step Beyond*'s version of Rod Serling, was every bit Serling's equal in terms of presence and loquaciousness. And if Serling was the living ad spot for the cigarettes he chain-smoked while on-camera, Newland was his equal as a non-smoker in at least one truly startling episode about magic mushrooms, when — as the cameras rolled — he ingested actual mushrooms used by shamanic Indians in Mexico (which were the focus of the episode) and reported firsthand on the psychedelic "trip" that followed! Bearing in mind this was in 1961, prior to the hippie movement, it is not surprising that this particular show was not only controversial, but, according to Newland, the most popular ever aired in the entire *One Step Beyond* series. A final caveat by way of comparison with Rod Serling was that while Serling wrote many of *The Twilight Zone* shows, Newland single-handedly directed all 80 episodes of *One Step Beyond*'s entire three-year run from 1959 to 1961!

"Night of the Kill" is an interesting, well-written episode focusing on Bigfoot, though the cryptid is never referred to as such directly, but rather through the host's inference that the episode concerns the legendary creature roaming the "Oregon forests" of the United States. This is interesting, in that Sasquatch never physically appears onscreen throughout the show's length. It is only described as being as tall as a two-story home and the height of a poplar tree. The characteristic huge footprints are found and cast in plaster, and the parents smell the tell-tale odor so often reported, but otherwise the viewer only ever hears Davey's recapitulation of what his "friend" looks like and the reactions of the horrified posse members, who are so shocked they cannot at first believe what they've witnessed.

Russy Metty, the renowned cinematographer who worked with such filmmaking legends as Orson Welles, John Huston and Stanley Kubrick, shot the episode in understated black and white. The episode features many depth-laden compositions that were a signature of his earlier work with Welles, and while Newland obviously was equally involved in staging the actors, the manner in which the cast constantly move from the background to the foreground, into an extreme close-up and then away again in long, fluid takes is very typical of Metty's earlier collaborations with Welles in such films as *The Stranger* and *Touch of Evil*. The style is most effective in "Night of the Kill" because it creates an eerie sense of off-screen space; it is as if the hominid could be just out of frame, lurking and preparing to strike. Given that neither hide nor hair of the Bigfoot is ever shown — not even a shadowy glimpse — this is a remarkable achievement. The viewer is left to conjure the cryptid in his or her own imagination.

In terms of Ciné du Sasquatch, "Night of the Kill" echoes the genre's core observation that man is far more dangerous to any rare species than said species is to man. Only Davey realizes this and tries to warn the blood-simple adults that Sasquatch means them no harm; indeed, the boy knows he would not have survived his ordeal in the forest had not Bigfoot taken him in and literally saved his life. Davey rightfully finds it morally repugnant that the men find it necessary to destroy the harmless hominid when it has never harmed any of them; but, of course, fearing what the "dangerous animal" (as Davey's mom describes it) *might* do rather than what it has done, all of the humans, save Davey, favor killing it as soon as possible. This is very much akin to the theme of *Harry and the Hendersons*, made almost three decades later, albeit with the sub-text trumpeted much more loudly in the later 1980s effort. Newland and company make the point, nonetheless, that the only thing that dies the night in question is Davey's innocence and trust in his fellow man; how else to rationalize to himself as a young boy their cruel need to destroy what they don't (or won't) take the time to understand?

For an entry in the cannon that doesn't even depict Bigfoot, "Night of the Kill" is one of the better examples of Ciné du Sasquatch from its era. Indeed, it's no exaggeration to say that its mature handling of the subject matter and refusal to play the tenets of the genre as frivolous or for camp value makes it one of the finest in television history in regards to an intelligent approach to the subject matter.

Oregon Bigfoot: Search for a Living Legend (2005) (Doc)

Featuring Autumn Williams, Kelly Berdahl, Jeff Johnston, Mike Nave and Jack Peters. Produced, Written and Directed by Autumn Williams. USA. Color. Stereo. 113 Minutes.

Overview: Autumn Williams, founder of OregonBigfoot.com as well as star of the Outdoor Life Network hominid series *Mysterious Encounters*, treks into the Oregon forests in search of proof of one of the most-sighted cryptids in North American history. Along with her research assistants Kelly Berdahl and Jeff Johnston, she sets up camp and awaits a possible encounter with Bigfoot. Alas, she only experiences some strange rapping on sheet metal one night, but feels she may be getting closer.

Mike Nave and Jack Peters join the group shortly thereafter and help the team deploy equipment, such as infrared cameras, in hopes of aiding in her quest. Although no footage is captured, they do record more audio of the strange sounds. A reenactment of the famous Teddy Roosevelt "Bauman Incident," which told of a Sasquatch encountering two fur trappers, is staged. Included on the DVD are portions of Ms. Williams' presentation "Women in Sasquatch Research" to the 2005 Bellingham Sasquatch Conference, out-takes, and a field guide to the high-tech equipment used during their trip.

Ostroznie, Yeti! (1961)

Starring Jarema Stepowski, Stefan Bartik, Ludwik Benoit, Bogusz Bilewski, Anna Czapnikówna, Mieczyslaw Czechowicz, Wieslaw Golas, Józef Nowak, Roman Polanski, Czeslaw Roszkowski, Zygmunt Zintel, Michal Zolnierkiewicz and Saturnin Zórawski. Written by Andrzej Brzozowski and Ornette Coleman. Directed by Ornette Coleman, Andrej Brzozowksi and Richard Pluciński. Poland. Black & White. Mono. 66 Minutes.

Overview: When zoologist Professor Karol, an eccentric but passionate believer in the Yeti, receives word an actual Abominable Snowman has been captured, crated, and transported back to Poland, he immediately dashes to the airport, intent on taking the cryptid specimen before the news media and gangster/profiteers can put the poor creature on display. Alas, because he bypasses customs and refuses to go by the book, the Polish airport police promptly arrest the Professor and jail him for breaking the law.

Worse still for the Professor is that the crate supposedly bearing the hominid is empty. The gangsters believe the learned scholar has stolen the creature and is hiding it. They send word to make the Professor talk at all costs, wanting to use the Yeti for their own nefarious purposes. The Professor, who is chained to a lowly thief while held in prison, picks his handcuff and is able to sneak out while the distracted guards fail to notice. Meanwhile, a series of unsolved crimes in and around the vicinity of the Snowman's escape are blamed on the still-unseen hominid as public hysteria grows — when and where will the monster strike next?

In the end the situation is cleared up when it is revealed the crate was labeled incorrectly when it left India. In fact, it was supposed to contain another kind of animal, not a Yeti. Realizing they cannot arrest a man for stealing an empty container, the police (as well as the disappointed gangsters) drop their pursuit of the Professor.

* * * * *

A fast-paced farce in the British Ealing Studios tradition, *Ostroznie, Yeti!* (literally: *Caution, Yeti!*) is a well-acted comedy which often feels like a Monty Python movie with its broad, surreal tone. The film is full of narrative twists, sudden reversals, and an unrelentingly critical eye towards the absurdity of the Polish system and its Communist-era obsession with red tape and rule-following at all costs. It often feels quite subversive for 1961, as if the creators realized that by utilizing a fantastic premise such as a Yeti they would be freer to satirize the Soviet system with far more impunity.

While an actual Abominable Snowman never appears (it's all merely a clerical error on the original shipping manifest, you see), there is a cameo by none other than Roman Polanski in a very small part as a taxi cab driver. Billed in the credits as "Raymond" Polanski (probably a simple mistake, given he was an unknown bit player at the time), it makes for an amusing crypto-appearance in its own right of a true cinematic genius who would later craft such superior

Hitchcock-influenced thrillers as *Knife in the Water*, *Repulsion*, *Rosemary's Baby*, and *Chinatown*. The cinematography and sets are first-rate for such a low-budget production, and the cast is filled with first-rate character actors. For those who enjoy a touch of zaniness with their Ciné du Sasquatch outings, *Ostroznie, Yeti!* offers inoffensive entertainment (though it is difficult to see in the United States, never having enjoyed an official release Stateside).

The Other Side (1994) (TV) (Doc)

Featuring Will Miller and Dana Fleming. Produced by Ron Ziskin, Shukri Ghalayini, Sandy Frank and Leslye A. Gustat. Written by Ron Ziskin and Mack Anderson. Directed by Rob Fiedler. USA. Color. Stereo. 30 Minutes.

Overview: Although the stage-bound *The Other Side* was taped in front of a live studio audience each week, various topics were occasionally given the filmed reenactment treatment to help boost the show's low-budget production values. Such was the case when the short-lived series focused on Bigfoot. Most of the series, however, was dedicated not to cryptid sightings but paranormal, Forteanstyled phenomena such as ghosts, possession, alternative medicines, psychic powers, and related non-cryptozoological events.

Pampalini Łowca Zwierząt (1977) (TV)

AKA: *Pampalini I Yeti*. Produced by Barbara Malik. Written by Lezsek Mech and Bronistaw Zeman. Directed by Jan Hoder. Polish. Color. Mono. 10 Minutes.

Overview: A popular children's animated series in Poland, *Pampalini Łowca Zwierząt* (translation: *Pampalini the Animal Hunter*) chronicles the adventures of Pampalini, a crusty adventurer who is decidedly old-school in his animal capturing methodology. Preferring to go it alone and stake out his game with only his survivor's wits and minimal gear, each show finds Pampalini managing to bungle capturing whatever exotic specimen he may be hunting.

In "Pampalini I Yeti" he drags his ski sled up the slopes of the Himalayan Mountains in search of the elusive Yeti. After he sets up his tent, it doesn't take long for the Yeti to find Pampalini rather than the other way around. The Abominable Snowman zippers the helpless old man inside his tent and promptly makes off with Pampalini's entire supply of canned goods. Pampalini gets out and spies the beast retreating to its cave through his binoculars. While the creature is outside, Pampalini sets up a portable TV he just happens to have with him. As soon as the Yeti returns, the grizzled hunter activates his remote control, displaying a looped image of himself being chased by a lion during a previous expedition.

The Abominable Snowman is bemused to the point of distraction, laughing at the silly human's antics. Pampalini douses his handkerchief with ether and holds it in front of the Yeti's nostrils, making the hairy giant pass out. The hunter secures the sleeping cryptid to his sled but accidentally sets the sled into motion. Pampalini chases after it until the sled slams into a snow bank, which awakens the Yeti. Pampalini trips on his own feet and snowballs down into the waiting Abominable's grasp. Plopping the confused human on his sled, the Yeti kicks it down the mountainside, sending Pampalini sledding home with a bittersweet sense of failure.

* * * * *

While certainly not a highlight in Ciné du Sasquatch animation, "Pampalini I Yeti" (translation: "Pampalini and Yeti") is far from the worst. In terms of television animation, the quality is equivalent to the Jay Ward *Rocky and Bullwinkle* series made in the U.S. a decade earlier: limited in motion but playfully sketched and colorfully rendered. Like all such shows, most of the action occurs off-screen in between the sound effects which illustrate the non-visualized event, an effort to economize such low-budget productions' strained finances.

While Pampalini is the classical bumbling oaf, the Yeti is actually quite atypical in terms of realization. For starters, this beast wears clothes! With a sleeveless vest and what appear to be blue jeans covering its legs, the Yeti seems drawn to resemble a classic hippie from the preceding decade as much as a cryptid. The creature also has brown/black fur and what is apparently a thickly-drawn beard (it's difficult to tell precisely because of the minimalistic design of the characters), which puts it at odds with most Yetis, who are depicted as white in color to more easily blend in with their snowbound setting.

A minor entry in Ciné du Sasquatch, it nonetheless indicates the widespread cultural appeal of the Sasquatch character as well as the common worldwide belief many share that the creature is real, not mythic. As witness, consider this fact: Of the remaining 12 episodes of *Pampalini Łowca Zwierząt*, none of the other animals featured were cryptozoological in terms of catalogued species — an elephant; a lion; a hippo; an anteater; a crocodile; etc. Yeti is slipped into the line-up without explanation that it is crypto in origin, which again implies the acceptance by many of its actual status as real, albeit as of yet(i) unproven.

Paper Dolls (2007)

Starring Rob Benitz, David Blair, Andra Carlson, Fox Clark, Lynn-Wood Fields, Gill Gayle, Gatlin Hardy, Kent Harper, Sarina Hart, Tony Hernandez, Dan Hickey, Mike Houser, Rian Jairell, Jasmine John, Angela Millhone, Josh Mintz, Life Noell, Jaime Perkins, Nathaniel Peterson, Adam Pitman, Dane Sjoden and Adam Stilwell. Produced by Adam Stilwell, Kent Harper, David Blair and Adam Pitman. Written by David Blair, Adam Pitman and Adam Stilwell. Directed by David Blair and Adam Pitman. USA. Color. Stereo. 98 Minutes.

Overview: Nate and Travis are two typical American teens who decide a sudden road trip to Canada through their pristine home state of Montana will do them good. Alas, while making their way through the lonely roads cutting through the remote forests, they take a supposed shortcut that leads to a sudden dead-end — in front of their car's headlights stand a line of cryptid hominids blocking their path. Each beast is locked arm in arm like a series of horrific paper dolls. The boys try to retreat, but the creatures attack. Nate is dragged screaming from the vehicle while Travis recovers just enough to flee in the besieged car.

Travis calls upon Chris, Nate's older brother, and begs him to bring firepower. Chris responds, arriving with enough guns to fight a small army. They track down the monsters but are forced to make a survival stand inside a flimsy shack. Laying down protective gunfire, Chris buys Travis enough time to once again escape with his life. Alas, Chris is not so lucky and finds himself following and falling into his dead brother's footsteps.

Travis is disturbed beyond immediate psychiatric recovery by his ordeal. But his ordeal is only just beginning, as a local sheriff doesn't believe a word of the troubled young man's story. In fact, the lawman believes Travis has murdered the victims and concocted a fantastic story to literally "cover his tracks" and blame Bigfoot for the crimes. Recreating Travis' every move, the suspicious sheriff finds loopholes that indicate to him that Travis is actually a murderer with motive to have killed and enough imagination to create a clever alibi in blaming an unseen hominid. In a tense stand-off between the two, Travis defends his story even as the sheriff shreds it, bit by bit, until even Travis is left wondering if he's experiencing a psychotic breakdown and actually killed his own friends.

* * * * *

Paper Dolls is an unusually well-structured example of Ciné du Sasquatch. It's that rare Bigfoot movie that truly crosses over from enthusiasts-only viewer potential into broader horror and psychological thriller appeal. It's one of a handful of Bigfoot films that takes on the general feeling among many skeptics and non-believers that anyone claiming to see a Sasquatch is suffering from a mental disorder and turns the premise upside-down to entertaining and suspenseful effect.

The film actually begins quite slowly, apparently another "teens slaughtered by Bigfoot" movie in the endless *The Blair Witch Project* mold. It opens with an extended camcorder viewpoint in which a randy young man hides a videotape camera in order to privately record his having sex with a high school beauty. Inside a tiny cabin the two make love while a party dies out all around them, having been staged at an abandoned summer campsite filled with such shelters. Without warning, Sasquatch breaks down the door and kills the girl with a sudden fury of blood and howling. By the time the boy can react, his girlfriend is dead, mutilated beyond recognition.

After this opening sequence, *Paper Dolls* settles down into a more traditional narrative. Travis and Nate become the central focus, and just as well: The film's opening, while crucial to the story's later rev-

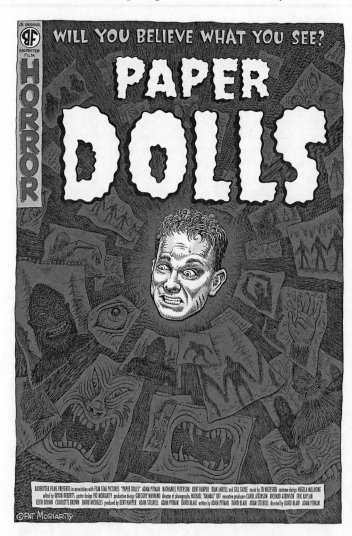

Poster art for a special screening of *Paper Dolls*. The image was created by graphic illustrator Pat Moriarity to echo the old E.C. Comics' covers. (Graphic courtesy Pat Moriarity.)

elations, unfortunately conditions expectations in perhaps too many viewers that may explain why the film is so little-seen, despite its superior nature. One has the feeling the overly-long opening may have mistakenly convinced some less objective distributors that the film would remain on the "grainy cam" production level, which it decidedly does not. Shot in high definition video in the Glacier National Park in Montana, *Paper Dolls* actually has a hauntingly beautiful look, using the deep shadows and thick forests for maximum impact. One wonders if minus this footage, or with it severely truncated, *Paper Dolls* might be available as of this printing from Netflix or your local DVD retailer, a fate more deserving of its qualitative difference over many of the Ciné du Sasquatch entries which *have* gained distribution both before and after *Paper Dolls'* production.

Not unlike the equally fine *The Sasquatch Gang*, *Paper Dolls* employs a *Rashomon* structure to complicate its narrative and forever cast doubt in the viewer's own mind as to what has been witnessed. But whereas *The Sasquatch Gang* uses the Kurosawa framing device for broad, comic effect, *Paper Dolls* repurposes the multiple viewpoints in a more traditional, dramatic attempt to literally alter the viewers' perceptions of the overall possibility that Bigfoot could exist, or even did exist in the earlier sequences of the film itself. One is left constantly having to reflect on the earlier encounters through the "but is it all in Travis' cracked mind?" perception.

During the tense encounters between the Sheriff and Travis, Roeg's *Bad Timing: A Sensual Obsession* frequently comes to mind in terms of probable influences. With the country lawman substituting for Harvey Keitel's metropolitan police detective, and Travis the troubled teen for Art Garfunkle's disturbed psychiatrist, these unexpectedly tense and effective moments lift *Paper Dolls* into a level of filmmaking that is truly novel in the genre. While touches of this can be found in *Fear Runs Silent* as well, therein it is haphazardly presented in MTV-styled flash cuts that render the effect almost negligible. *Paper Dolls* actually slows its exciting pace down during this one-on-one confrontation between the two combatants in order to take the film in a whole new direction. This is always a risky strategy because it can wreck a movie's momentum if not done with sensitivity. But *Paper Dolls* uses it to great psychological effect, making the film suddenly double-back onto itself in an ingenious manner, revealing just how carefully-crafted the preceding narrative has been laid down for maximum shock value.

It reminds one of the granddaddy of all such literary efforts, *Crime and Punishment*; and while clearly not the intellectual rival of Dostoevsky or his masterpiece (nor intended to be so), it is to the credit to both *Paper Dolls* and its creators that so much layering and complexity is accomplished so adroitly with clearly limited means. This is particularly true with the presentation of the Sasquatch monsters themselves, who are as eerily photographed during their initial attack upon Travis and Nate in their stranded vehicle as any such creatures in Ciné du Sasquatch history. The weird imagery of the cryptids all joined together like a literal barrel of monkeys, standing perfectly motionless across a dark country road in order to block traffic, is as creepy as the best scares contained in *The Legend of Boggy Creek* or *Night of the Demon*. Shot in silhouette so that each cryptid is but a large, shaggy outline, this sequence is nightmarish in intensity and achieves a terrifying feel that nothing that follows can ever quite top. In that sense it's a bit like Janet Leigh's murder in *Psycho*—potentially anti-climactic for the rest of the film. Nonetheless, like Hitchcock's film, *Paper Dolls* is still armed with its share of surprises to follow to warrant astute viewing until the end credits.

The acting is uniformly good, though some of the minor characters show their inexperience a bit more than the leads. Still, many are the professionally-budgeted Sasquatch movies made in the last few years that would have a hard time matching the intensity and believability

of *Paper Dolls* in terms of its acting talent on display. But it's the overall vision of *Paper Dolls* as a complicated jigsaw puzzle that makes it so unique in the canon of Bigfoot films — and all the more puzzling that it has received such scant recognition and/or distribution. It deserves both in wide measure, and hopefully in time some smart distributor will come to realize the oversight and make a financial windfall rectifying it. *Paper Dolls* is deserving of the praise by the few who have seen it and reviewed it favorably, and will be appreciated by all Ciné du Sasquatch enthusiasts for its mature, rational handling of the subject matter.

Penn & Teller: Bullshit! (2006) ("Cryptozoology") (TV) (Doc)

Featuring Penn Jillette, Teller, Scott Norman, Sierra Fisk, Gene Hatcher, Christian Levatino and Jerome Vital. Produced by Jon Hotchkiss, Penn Jillette, Joshua E. Kessler, Star Price, Teller and Aaron Yampolski. Written and Directed by Star Price. USA. Color. Stereo. 60 Minutes.

Overview: Las Vegas stage magicians Penn & Teller offer their jaundiced, admittedly biased point-of-view on a variety of topics. Past subjects have included the Holy Bible, the I.R.S., the War on Porn, P.E.T.A., and many others, both commonplace and controversial. "Cryptozoology" offers a cynical, mean-spirited critique of the entire field of researchers of Bigfoot, the Loch Ness Monster, and the like. Penn slashes and burns every possibility that any sighting of any cryptid was ever real and disparages every single cryptozoologist as a person who has "too much time on his hands," while his mute partner Teller nods a lot like an accompanying mime to compliment his excitable partner. Several cryptozoologists are interviewed and then ridiculed as imbeciles and self-deceiving fools. Along the way, Penn & Teller stage various comical scenes of Bigfoot with a rented Sasquatch costume from a professional North Hollywood special effects house. Their conclusion: It's all a big fake.

* * * * *

While admittedly funny at times in a caustic, cynical way, *Penn & Teller: Bullshit* is definitely not for those seeking an objective viewpoint on any of the subject matter covered. As professed Libertarian political believers and members of the influential Libertarian think tank (i.e. policy propagandists) the Cato Institute in Washington, D.C., the duo is not without an agenda to promote, as they freely admit in interviews (when pressed on the matter). Believers in nongovernment intrusion or regulation of drugs, guns, prostitution, and nuclear energy, one can quickly see why they're favorites in Las Vegas, Nevada.

With this in mind, one can approach their episode dedicated to "Cryptozoology" with a keener sense of understanding of their stacked critique. It is never so much as skeptical (a position which at least allows the possibility of the subject matter under discussion to actually exist) as it is an attempt to actively debunk any and all claims of cryptozoological specimens as utter bullshit, to use the series' own frequent proclamation. Therein lies the outrageous shock value humor (akin to a Mutt n' Jeff version of Howard Stern) as well as the problematic position the two hosts take.

For example, the show actually opens with Penn admitting in voice-over that past specimens of unlikely, formerly cryptid species have been uncovered by zoologists. Throughout the show he mentions that it is estimated by reliable scientists (of which, of course, he would not include any cryptozoologist) that there are over 10,000 undiscovered species of ants worldwide, and that we as humans know virtually nothing of the marine species living below 1,000 feet of ocean water. But without missing a beat he specifies that any claims about any other species, such as Sasquatch, the Loch Ness Monster, supposedly extinct animals, etc., are absurd beyond consideration. This is contradictory, as *any* of the 10,000 species of ants he proclaims may be found at any moment are, by definition, crypto by default *until* they're found and catalogued. For the rotund host, the difference is that, as he explains it, finding a new ant species is hard work, whereas the search for a hominid is, by implication, child's play.

Nothing could be further from the truth, of course. One only has to look to any of the many expeditions documented in a handful of the non-fiction movies and TV specials reviewed in this guide to understand how penetrating the deepest of redwood forests for weeks on end or scaling the heights of the Himalayan Mountains is far from an easy undertaking. Indeed, one of the cryptozoologists Penn most heavily scoffs at is Scott Norman, who devoted the majority of his life to exploring some of the most remote countries in the world in search of a possible living aquatic dinosaur species. Penn's basis for satire seems based less on any evidence or theories Norman offers as much as on the fact Norman wore a hat, lived modestly in an apartment, and "had lots of time on his hands." Alas, only a few years after this embarrassing show attempted to discredit him, Scott Norman was dead at the age of 43 from a probable blood clot, thus refuting Penn's assertion that the humiliated cryptozoologist possessed much valuable time to waste.

Given equally harsh treatment are Richard Freeman and Jonathan Downes, who run the Center for Fortean Zoology in England. The duo — who have a penchant for dressing in black leather and assorted Gothic regalia — are hired by Penn and Teller to investigate Loch Ness for the famous monster which many believe inhabit its murky

Penn Jillette and Teller, hosts of Showtime's scathing exposé-styled show *Penn & Teller: Bullshit!*

depths. It's ironic that Penn and Teller lament how overly-commercial cryptozoology is as a whole, all the while literally financing two researchers that they lambast as incompetents. Why not hire more reputable zoologists instead of cryptozoologists if one's goal is anything more than lambasting whoever is hired? Why not, for that matter, hire less comically absurd cryptozoologists? Not that Freeman and Downes are deliberately attempting to sabotage their task, but it's clear that they're playing along with the basic comic conceit, realizing that Penn and Teller are far from serious in their quest. This is the disingenuous nature of the show that makes it an easy target for critics who decry the series' title in regards to the manipulated content each show employs. Were Penn and Teller willing to hire serious experts and contest their findings, they would find themselves having to offer serious rebuttals; instead, they find the most bumbling of targets and/or portray their interviewed subjects in the least favorable light possible.

Penn and Teller: Bullshit! is as subtle as its title, and likewise about as in-depth in regards to its treatment of subjects and subject matter. If adolescent mockery is what one seeks, à la the ugliest of schoolyard humor, then this Showtime-sponsored series offers non-stop entertainment. For those who have even a modest belief in Sasquatch as something other than a source of ridicule, however, it is generally quite insensitive and as adamantly one-sided as the subject matter it attempts to debunk. Merely proclaiming loudly that "it's all bullshit" and offering nothing in the way of counterproofs or arguments (other than smug superiority) does produce its share of bitter laughs, no doubt. But then again, so does tripping a blind man at the bus stop for those who find the darkest impulses of human nature side-splittingly hilarious. In this regard, one is left to wonder by show's end: Is one better off with the so-called fools who believe in Bigfoot as a possibility, or with the court jesters who believe they know more than everyone else simply because they can and do mock them? Neither is a pleasant choice, but then again, pleasant is not the word to describe *Penn and Teller: Bullshit!* when the best word is already in the title itself.

Perverted Stories #35 ("Bigfoot") (2002)

Starring Alaura Eden, Melanie Jagger, Taylor Lynn, Sage, Brian Surewood, Rick Masters, Jay Ashley, Johnny Thrust, Mr. Pete and Pylan Blake. Produced by Jeff Steward. Directed by Jim Powers. USA. Color. Stereo. 104 Minutes.

Overview: In 1974, female cryptozoologist Joanne Green ventures alone into the woods to search for Bigfoot. While she is setting up camp, the horny hominid attacks, molesting her and forcing her into a sexual encounter which she ultimately enjoys, despite her initial reluctance.

* * * * *

A fifteen-minute segment of a four-part porno compilation, *Perverted Stories #35*'s "Bigfoot" has all the subtle qualities one would expect from a production starring such obvious *non de plumes* as Johnny Thrust, Brian Surewood, and Mr. Pete. Shot on what appears to be camcorder-quality home video, the production values are non-existent. During the sex scene, the roar of nearby traffic can be heard in the background (that is, when the ridiculous Bigfoot actor isn't grunting and groaning so loud he is over-modulating the camcorder's built-in microphone). Likewise, the crude slit that has been made in the front of the costume to accommodate the hominid's sexual organ is as laughable as the segment itself is offensive. Whether or not the heroine's moniker, Joanne Green, is a play on cryptozoologist John Green's own name thankfully remains a mystery, but the coincidental aspect would seem unlikely. After all, no names are generally given in the typical porn outing save descriptive — Blonde, Pizza Delivery Man, etc.— and it's hard to credit the producers with anything beyond the mundane.

Without giving it any due credit (as it is overdrawn in that department from the moment Sasquatch appears, fondling himself, as he lusts after the woman cryptozoologist), "Bigfoot" does fit within the often sleazy sub-cult of cryptid sex films that persists throughout Ciné du Sasquatch. Some of these efforts are serious looks at the underlying sexual tension implicit in the genre itself (and seen outside the genre in the influential *King Kong* via Kong's obsession with Ann Darrow). Some genre examples include *The Beast, Man Beast*, and even *Night of the Demon*. Many, however, are more in line with *Beauties and the Beast, The Geek*, and *Alpine Affairs*— tawdry adult efforts designed to exploit the subject matter in the most pornographic manner possible for their respective eras of production.

With its underlying theme of "rape is actually good for the woman"— in the form of bestiality, no less —*Perverted Stories #35* lives up to only half of its titular moniker. While it is truly perverted (the box art labels its hominid protagonist as "Snatchsquatch"), there is hardly any narrative present to qualify as a story — unless one includes the literal progression of changing sexual positions as a three-act structure (though there is most definitely a climax to the rising action, at least in visual terms).

Given the other 15-minute tales include such titles as "Momma's Boy," "Coma," and "It Happened in the Desert," one must admit that at least "Bigfoot" has an almost novel variation on the tried-and-true tryst formula, though it's hardly a redeeming feature. This is a truly awful and sordid example of Bigfoot being as exploited as the unfortunate young starlet onscreen.

Petrified Beast of the Frozen Zone (1990)

Starring Chuck Gerchow, Bruce Gilbert, Fred Hopkins, Ray Houser, Vanessa Love, Pouneh Partowkia, Victoria Princeton and Ken Smith. Produced by Fred Hopkins. Written by Fred Hopkins and Bruno Moultrock. Directed by Fred Hopkins. USA. Color/Black & White. Stereo.

Overview: Indie videomaker Fred Hopkins took *Man Beast* and other "found footage" from various Yeti movies, re-edited them, and added additional, newly-shot footage to create this reconstituted Sasquatch adventure.

Basically a glorified home movie, it nevertheless made the rounds during the pre–Internet days as a VHS fan-circulated underground video. The additional scenes were shot with an amateur cast in and around Seattle, Washington. Though the title is well-known to many ardent Ciné du Sasquatch fans, very few have ever seen it. It appears to be not only out of print but harder to find than Bigfoot itself.

Picket Fences ("Abominable Snowman") (1994) (TV)

Starring Tom Skerritt, Holly Marie Combs, Costas Mandylor, Lauren Holly, Kathy Baker, Justin Shenkarow, Adam Wylie, Fyvush Finkel, Ray Walston, Kelly Connell and Don Cheadle. Produced by Jonathan Pontell, Alice West, Robert Breech, Michael Pressman, Steve Robin, David E. Kelley, Jack Philbrick, Ann Donahue, Geoffrey Neigher and Mark B. Perry. Written by David E. Kelley. Directed by Bill D'Elia. USA. Color. Stereo. 42 Minutes.

Overview: Rome, Wisconsin, is a small town peopled with eccentric characters. The folks of Rome try to maintain an open mind (and heart) towards their fellow residents, but sometimes the conflicts spill over into the lap of Sheriff Jimmy Brock. When Howard, a senior citizen suffering from Alzheimer's, sees a vagrant known only as the Potato Man leaving his supply shed one night, Howard imagines he's seen a Yeti because of a recent TV special about the hominid. Sheriff Brock arrives at Howard's house just in time to find the old man aiming a working cannon at the shed and declaring he's about to blast the Abominable Snowman to smithereens. Howard's son tries to calm his father, but the cannon goes off. The shed is destroyed, and the ensuing ruckus causes Howard's son to have a massive heart attack.

* * * * *

Though titled "Abominable Snowman" (perhaps for ratings purposes), this episode of the critically-lauded *Picket Fences* doesn't actually feature any onscreen cryptid. Howard, the old man suffering from a mental disorder, believes a homeless man he's seen exiting Howard's shed is actually a Yeti not because the homeless man resembles the creature, but because Howard has recently seen a documentary on television which has confused his sense of reality.

While it plays for laughs, it doesn't do much to keep those real-world Bigfoot eyewitnesses who don't have Alzheimer's or related mental impairments from perhaps feeling as if they're being unfairly critiqued and/or lumped in with those who do. Given that the fictional town of Rome, Wisconsin, is already populated with a citizenry clearly exhibiting every known clinical mental condition known to mankind, however, one wonders if one more claiming to have only seen a Yeti wouldn't be the least of Sheriff Brock's worries, if not an outright relief.

Pizza Hut Bigfoot Commercial (1993) (TV)

Starring Hayley Joel Osment. USA. Color. Stereo. 30 Seconds.

Overview: Although it never technically shows a hominid, Pizza Hut capitalized upon the namesake of Bigfoot itself with the introduction of their Bigfoot Pizza in 1993. The ad opens with a roaming shot of a woodsy, suburban community, clearly intended to be Sasquatch's point-of-view. The narrator breathlessly intones that "recently an object has been sighted" as the commercial then cuts to a series of eyewitnesses who describe the object in various hyperbolic terms. Eventually the object in question is delivered to a waiting family's door — it's not Sasquatch, but the Bigfoot Pizza in a box. After showing a logo for Pizza Hut and the product, an animated Bigfoot's hairy leg and foot stomp the pizza into a pulp.

While only a variation on the Bigfoot name, this ad was very popular in its year of release, even being shown during the coveted Super Bowl commercial slots, which are the most expensive and typically highest-viewed ads per year on broadcast TV. Young actor Haley Joel Osment (who has but a brief cameo) was discovered at a shopping mall audition and granted this, his first role. He would later receive an Academy Award nomination for his memorable turn as the child who "sees dead people" in *The Sixth Sense*. Although a successful commercial, the actual Bigfoot Pizza product didn't last very long and was soon retired.

Planet Cook (2004) (TV)

Starring Kevin Woodford and Luke Bromley. Produced by Nigel Stone, Mellie Buse, Roy Milani and Kevin Woodford. Written by Tommy Donbavand, Simon Grover and Nigel Stone. Directed by Iain McLean. UK. Color. Stereo. 22 Minutes.

Overview: Captain Cook, a quick-preparation chef extraordinaire, and his sidekick Boumer, a colorful Yeti, prepare recipes that child and pre-teen viewers can emulate themselves with the help of their parents. Kevin Woodford, a renowned chef in England, is the host and plays Cook, who—despite the similarity in names—is not a direct reference to the world explorer Captain Cook of historical record. The Yeti is played strictly for laughs, sporting as it does bright orange fur, a light green skin, and pants as it bumbles along, mostly staying out of the way until it gets so bored it gets itself into some merrymaking troubles from which Cook must extract it. Though it features some CGI-rendered characters and a touch of the fantastic, *Captain Cook* is basically a studio-bound children's TV show with a "how-to" slant. While it may help British tykes to better understand the basic food groups, as well as how to fix bangers 'n' mash for themselves, its use of Boumer as a Yeti figure is almost random in terms of impact; the character could easily be any other species, with no discernible dramatic or comic difference.

Pop-Tarts Yeti Commercials (2004) (TV)

Produced by the Leo Burnett Ad Agency. USA. Color. Stereo. 30 Seconds.

Overview: A rather rotund Yeti is seen hawking the new Pop-Tarts frozen variety, which the hominid suggests can be stored in a freezer until ready to eat on hot summer days. In each instance the children who are listening to the guttural growling of the Abominable Snowman watch stone-faced until he finishes his product pitch, at which point they run screaming in abject terror. Cued by their panic, the Yeti screams as well and races for shelter.

When the Battle Creek, Michigan–based Kellogg's Pop-Tarts company decided to convince consumers that their product is more than a breakfast-only foodstuff, they hired the Leo Burnett Ad Agency to deconstruct the pastry's image. Using a comical but slightly horrific Yeti, the ad makers came up with the concept of the beast showing up in a variety of domestic settings, calmly pitching the benefits of eating Pop-Tarts any time of the day, and then causing a mass exodus after the initial shock of the hominid's sudden appearance wears off on the stunned humans present. The formula worked well, but whether or not the success was due to the ads or simply the suggestion that kids eat more Pop-Tarts is, of course, open to debate.

Less unmistakable is the creepy nature of the cryptid. While some will see a harmless hairball, others will notice the dark, menacing circles under the Yeti's eyes, its rather demonic-sounding garbled language, and the overall sense of menace present throughout the series. The creature's unearthly lingo is subtitled so that one can read the pitched message, but there is a disturbing quality to the actual hominid mutterings than will leave at least some kids slightly spooked. Of course, this is all resolved by the Yeti becoming as terrified of his human audience as they are of him when they react by screaming, suggesting that even a towering Abominable Snowman can become scared. Still, in terms of underlying threat, this is one Yeti few Pop-Tart eaters would welcome in their kitchen, morning, noon, or especially at night. Kellogg's spent over $25 million on the series, which ran on radio, TV, and in print media.

Power Rangers: Operation Overdrive (Multiple Episodes) (2007)

Starring James Maclurcan, Caitlin Murphy, Samuell Benta, Rhoda Montemayor, Gareth Yuen, Dwayne Cameron, Rod Lousich, David Weatherley, Kelson Henderson, Gerald Urquhart and Ria Vandervis. Produced by Bruce Kalish, Koichi Sakamoto and Janine Dickins. Written by John Tellegen, Jackie Marchand and David Garber. Directed by Jonathan Brough, Britta Johnstone, Vanessa Alexander, Mike Smith and Charlie Haskell. USA/New Zealand/Japan. Color. Stereo. 22 Minutes.

Overview: Based on the Japanese super sentai series *Gôgô sentai Bôkenger*, *Power Rangers: Operation Overdrive* follows five young people who are given super powers in order to discover the whereabouts of several vanished magic crystals and prevent them from one day falling into the wrong hands. From their base camp in San Angeles, they travel around the world fighting villains and pursuing neverending adventures looking for the missing jewels, which will give their possessor untold abilities to destroy the planet. Their DNA having been modified by their financial backer, Andrew Hartford, the newly-created heroes are given code names—Red Ranger, Blue Ranger, Black Ranger, Yellow Ranger, and Pink Ranger. Soon they are joined by Mercury Ranger, an extraterrestrial with the power to morph his physical form into mercury and back again.

The Power Rangers' main nemesis is called Flurious. Relegated to a mountainous abode and forever cursed to inhabit a body made of ice, Flurious is attended by hideous helpers he calls Chillers in his mission to gain possession of the magic jewels so that he might transform himself back into human form. Flurious is also served by his chief aid, Norg, who is the last Yeti left alive on Earth. Although Norg attempts to gain Flurious' tacit if not outright approval, it is never forthcoming, leaving Norg to dwell on his constant sense of futility and low self-esteem. Norg repeatedly bungles Flurious' plans, despite his best efforts—in effect, acting as an unwitting accomplice to the Power Rangers.

* * * * *

The amazing success of the *Power Rangers* series internationally is truly staggering. In this incarnation, as *Power Rangers: Operation Overdrive*, the franchise marked 15 years in continuous production. Given the simplicity of the storylines, the cardboard characterizations, and the ridiculous nature of the non-stop action, one would be hard-pressed to imagine a less-probable success story, though it must be admitted that both the Disney and Toei studios get much of their limited budget onscreen. If nothing else, *Power Rangers: Operation Overdrive* has an impressive array of mostly CGI-styled effects combined with a visceral pace that rivals anything ever shown in the genre for sheer carnage and MTV-blister cuts of subliminal intensity. The series also makes good use of its three-country shooting locales, featuring a wide variety of scenery photographed in California, New Zealand, and Japan.

The Norg character is portrayed by actor Kelson Henderson very much in the *Harry and the Hendersons* gentle giant mode. With his conical forehead rivaling that of Beldar's from *The Coneheads*, a perpetually goofy expression of pained confusion, and a pair of oversized overalls covering his massive gut, Norg is far from representing the best of his species (even if he's the last known Abominable Snowman in existence). If Norg's innate lack of intelligence is any indication, one senses very quickly why his kind have vanished from the chain of living animals. A bigger mystery is why an obviously super-intelligent being like Flurious would bother with the hopelessly incompetent Norg. It seems to be the unwritten rule of super-villainy that superior types rely on inferior minions to muck up their best-laid plans. In this regard, Norg plays the comical buffoon quite nicely, if predictably, in each and every episode in which he appears.

As an adjunct and sidekick, Norg fulfills the lesser role required of his character but reduces the proud, fierce independence of most screen and TV hominids to the level of court jester, minus the fool's hat (though his ridiculous overalls stand in quite well in terms of self-mockery). This is a sad but inevitable outcome of the over-abundance of Yetis appearing in TV series and movies. Eventually the mythic power of the creature loses its inherent ability to threaten or even offer a sense of mystery, at such point the stereotype degenerates into a Brer Bear kind of archetype. While this is commonplace in the many Yeti commercials which play to the lowest common denominator in order to sell products, it's unfortunate to see Ciné du Sasquatch so thoroughly debased in terms of cultural imagery. Still, in the age of postmodernism, in which it is presumed the audience knows every possible variation pertaining to each mythical character, any other outcome would be preposterously unlikely. Nothing is sacred in postmodern entertainment, and therefore all archetypes must be overturned to become amusing fodder for an aesthetic that refuses to take anything (most assuredly its own indulgent narcissism) with any seriousness or self-insight.

Primal (2007)

Starring Sean Brennan, Andrea Brokaw, Tommy Clark, Bethany Davis, Popeye Fontaine, Michelle Franklin, Brian Girard, Jack Griguoli, Jermaine V. Hatley, Paul Hovermale, Ana Kelly, Josh Levy, Dawn McElhare, Mike Mcgrath, James Piper, Marcy Secora, Biz Urban and Eric Weller. Produced by Chad Brokaw, Greg Hoyt and Patrick McManus. Written and Directed by Steffen Schlachtenhaufen. USA. Color. Stereo. 81 Minutes.

Overview: An estranged brother and sister are reunited when she travels to his remote wilderness park ranger station to visit him, with her fiancé in tow. The ranger is a hermit by choice, never having fit in with society, and therefore enjoys the solitude of his work. He has also been secretly photographing Sasquatch, showing his imagery to his impressed sister. Meanwhile, a group of college students who've been hired by a oil and gas company to survey the private lands adjacent to the national park where the ranger is stationed set off to explore the deep woods. Alas, they soon learn that their maps have been covertly altered by the oil execs who wish to conduct an illegal catalog of the resource-rich wilderness sanctuary in hopes of paying off politicians later to gain drilling rights to the protected lands. The leader of the exploration team balks at first, but when the chief executive applies pressure, the reluctant young man agrees to keep his group in the dark and hike into the prohibited area.

They are not alone. Sasquatch stalks the group and patiently waits for them to split up to perform their tasks. As soon as they do, the savage Sasquatch begins systematically slaughtering them one by one. Eventually the diminishing group realizes they're being targeted not by a rogue grizzly but by Bigfoot. They attempt to flee the forest, but the ferocious hominid stays hot on their trail, killing more of the team members. Back at the ranger's station the brother is alarmed when his sister and future brother-in-law disappear into the deep woods on a hiking trip and fail to return on time. He sets out in search of them and helps them avoid certain death by blasting the Bigfoot with his guns.

Calling in an air rescue helicopter, the ranger, his sister and her fiancé make their way to the rescue destination point, along with the remaining handful of surveyors sent by the oil corporation. The park ranger dies saving his sister in an act of self-sacrifice that also destroys the cryptid, thus guaranteeing his sister and her soon-to-be fiancé will escape with their lives.

* * * * *

Many reviews of *Primal* have listed it as the worst Ciné du Sasquatch entry ever made. This is far from accurate. In fact, compared to such truly amateurish efforts as *Search for the Beast* or *Suburban Sasquatch*, *Primal* is positively professional in scope and ambition. What it lacks is originality and a better budget. Had the filmmaker had either or both, *Primal* would have definitely risen much further in the canon of Savage Sasquatch films.

The script is anemic to a fault, but at least it makes a modest attempt at crafting a back story for the brother and sister protagonists. It's true this conflict is largely too muted and slow to be effective, but at least it demonstrates the writer had knowledge of the need for

Cover art for the DVD release of *Primal*.

such narrative tension, even if he failed to capture it. The plot, however, is *Primal*'s primary failing. The straight-shot approach in which a group of humans venture into the wilderness only to be picked off as they reverse course to flee for their lives back to civilization has never been more flagrantly distilled into a "fight and flight" formula. Apart from the minor sub-plot in which the sister attempts to beguile the brother into attending her wedding back in the big city, there is not much to forestall the utterly predictable outcome of the film's story. In essence, the humans run, Bigfoot picks them off, and they run some more. While some rare examples of adventure cinema have achieved notable success with a variant on this structure (such as Cornel Wilde's *The Naked Prey*), most are doomed to meet the same fate as *Primal* and sputter to the inevitable foregone conclusion.

The cryptid is a long-haired version of Sasquatch with super-long arms equipped with claws. While clearly stiff appendages being held by the cryptid actor, à la a pirate hook in a low-budget sails-and-swords action film, they still provide modest shock value when first glimpsed. They are razor-sharp and truly spindly, much like the vampire's dagger-like digits in the original *Nosferatu*. But the overuse of these unmoving claws eventually reduces the horror to cliché. They soon come to resemble digging implements used by a suburban gardener more than the talons of a terrifying beast. This is also true of the footage of the Sasquatch itself. Initially startling, it soon becomes irritating because the filmmaker holds on it too long, without much sense that familiarity truly breeds contempt (at least as far as horror film icons are concerned). An attempt to render this less problematic is made by applying stutter frame effects to the footage, as if it were from an old movie, complete with jittery frames going awry. Alas, the effect is more akin to a cinematically-induced seizure in which the viewer is made to undergo a sensory shakedown.

Primal's prime problem lies in its construction more than its execution. With a better storyline that offered more twists and characterization complexities, this might have been a far more interesting effort. As it is, it still has some modest entertainment value. To its credit, it is shot on location, features some moody and appropriately eerie landscape cinematography, and offers the occasional fun scare (courtesy of the cryptid). But for fans of Ciné du Sasquatch accustomed to the mechanics of the genre, there's not much *Primal* urgency to see it as anything other than derivative.

Prophecy (1979) (Influence)

AKA: *Prophecy: The Monster Movie.* Starring Talia Shire, Robert Foxworth, Armand Assante, Richard Dysart, Victoria Racimo, George Clutesi, Burke Byrnes, Tom McFadden, Everett Creach, Charles H. Gray, Lyvingston Holmes and Graham Jarvis. Produced by Robert L. Rosen. Written by David Selzter. Directed by John Frankenheimer. Color. USA. Stereo. 102 Minutes.

Overview: Dr. Robert Verne and his pregnant wife visit a Maine paper mill that is potentially polluting the pristine waters nearby. While they conduct their investigation for the Environmental Protection Agency, however, a series of unexpectedly brutal murders occur in and around the plant. At first a rogue grizzly bear is suspected. But in time it becomes apparent that something far more

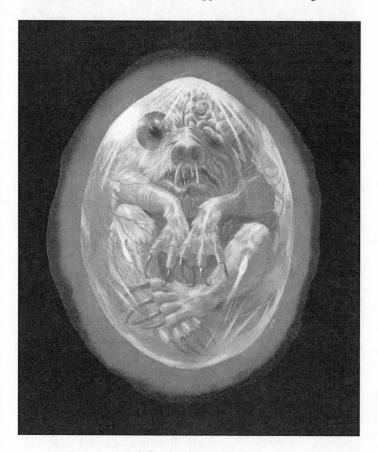

Poster artwork for the theatrical release of *Prophecy*.

monstrous and unpredictable is responsible for the mounting homicides.

* * * * *

Technically speaking, *Prophecy* is not an example of Ciné du Sasquatch. However, up until mid-way through its second act it is virtually indistinguishable from a Bigfoot movie; in fact, the film exploits all the mechanics of the Bigfoot film genre. It features a band of humans who travel deep into the woods only to encounter a monstrous, bipedal cryptid who quickly slaughters them as they try to flee back to society. It espouses an environmental message in which mankind is clearly denigrated as an unworthy steward of the wilderness, therefore earning the wrath of the avenging creature. It features Native Americans who warn that the beast is a part of their mystical heritage and therefore an unstoppable force of Mother Nature. And it even offers the standard scenes of unsuspecting campers being killed without warning by an unseen menace. In fact, up until the mutant bear is revealed as the actual monstrosity half-way through its running time, *Prophecy* could just as well be one of the biggest-budgeted Sasquatch movies ever produced.

All the hallmarks are present in these early scenes. The opening, which is quite tense and scarily effective, shows several hunters racing through the forest with their baying hounds as they corner ... *something* in a nearby quarry. When their dogs are suddenly silenced, the men lower themselves into the pit only to meet their own grisly demise. Later, in a scene that is both horrific and marginally campy, a family sleeping under the stars is awakened to the same beast, who is in no mood for trespassers. The youngest member of the family, zipped into his sleeping bag, attempts to hop away before meeting his doom, only to be flung head-over-heels by the monster as it slashes its claws into his side. This moment is so eerily like so many in the Ciné du Sasquatch canon that it's worth noting that the influential *Night of the Demon*, made a year later, featured almost precisely the same sequence with a sleeping camper who is hurled around and over the Sasquatch's head until he is released, screaming as he flies into a tree branch and becomes impaled, slowly dying. It would be hard to believe the filmmakers hadn't seen and been influenced by *Prophecy*, as its first 45 minutes are so well-executed that *Prophecy* ranks among the best of the 1970s "nature runs amok" movies that were once so common.

Frankenheimer is often criticized for the deficiencies of *Prophecy*, and they *are* present. But for over half its running time and even beyond, there are scares and jumps with such regularity that its indirect influence upon the Bigfoot genre as a prototype of how to craft an effective "monster in the woods" movie is undeniable. Had the budget been bigger and Tom Burman's often sub-par monster suit effects been better designed, *Prophecy*'s impact on Ciné du Sasquatch would've been even greater.

PSI Factor: Chronicles of the Paranormal ("Forbidden North") (1997) (TV)

Starring Paul Miller, Nancy Anne Sakovich, Barclay Hope, Colin Fox, Maurice Dean Wint, Matt Frewer, Nigel Bennett, Peter MacNeill, Joanne Vannicola and Soo Garay. Produced by James Nadler, Seaton McLean, Peter Aykroyd and Christopher Chacon. Written by Damian Kindler and Peter Aykroyd. Directed by Ken Girotti. Canada. Color. Stereo. 30 Minutes.

Overview: A Canadian version of *The X-Files*, *PSI Factor: Chronicles of the Paranormal* featured a group of experts from the Office of Scientific Investigation and Research (O.S.I.R.) who investigated sightings of and encounters with a variety of Fortean-styled phenomena. In "Forbidden North" the team interviews a logger who claims to have been attacked by Sasquatch. At first the O.S.I.R. researchers believe a resistance organization called Planet Alert may have staged the attack with a Bigfoot suit. However, after reviewing the evidence — including a recent attack on one of the female members of Planet Alert and the destruction of their facilities — the investigators begin to wonder if perhaps the loggers truly *are* the guilty culprits. After all, what better way to discredit the Planet Alert force than to blame them for violence by staging an attack on one of their own lumberjacks? Soon, however, it becomes apparent that there are at least two of the hominids at work when one costumed Planet Alert radical dressed as Bigfoot is found dead from what all evidence indicates was a real Savage Sasquatch mauling.

The O.S.I.R. team is left with lingering doubts from their limited first-hand evidence, which consists mainly of the "not quite definitive" gray zone that drives all concerned to share expressions of consternation. The show concludes in a stalemate between the two political sides — the roadway being cleared through the pristine wilderness loses funding during the legal entanglements, while the Planet Alerters have to live up to the fact that even though they internally rejected the errant "camouflaged, costumed cryptid" approach espoused by the same two radical members they then later denounced, the group of well-meaning protestors also *did* allow a cover from which the Bigfoot hoaxers could infiltrate the surroundings, map the lay of the land, and then act with an agenda which includes violence. The Planet Alert leadership correctly shuns the two "at any and all costs" cultural jihadists in favor of peaceful protest. But the group doesn't bother to report the renegade duo as armed and dangerous, which jeopardizes Planet Alert's mission and needlessly risks their own members in attendance, each of whom could be innocent passersby to sudden stray gunfire, mob violence, etc. These are not your typical "Bleeding Heart Elves" but more akin to "Rugby Lovin' Trolls" who are more than willing to abandon their morals just as fast as the logging company does their own when push comes to shove. It's a sobering, more *Twilight Zone*–ish assessment of the stewardship of the planet's resources, in which no one — not the "tree huggers" who love Bigfoot enough to die impersonating one, nor the "got mouths to feed" macho men who depend on the non-stop harvest of old growth forests for a living — can really rationalize their internal strife over this basic "Respect Animal Rights" (or not) viewpoint. It cleaves and divides as neatly as a Psycho-Squatch on steroids, reducing each side to bellowing human bullhorns who endlessly attempt to "convince" the Other of the error of their ways (at 90 decibels and climbing per outburst!). Eventually the project is called off, and the surrounding intelligence-gathering ops staged by O.S.I.R. are designated by command to remain active in status but top secret (non-existent) in nature.

* * * * *

This likeable, dry-witted, Fortean-styled government explorers series featuring tales of covert cryptid investigations (and beyond) was a modest yet mostly successful attempt to create a Canadian-friendly version of *The X-Files* (which would have been difficult under any circumstances, given that a majority of the Fox Network series was lensed in Vancouver, Canada). With multi-talented producer, writer, and actor Dan Aykroyd working with his brother Peter, *PSI Factor: Chronicles of the Paranormal* begins with a plus in the production column simply because the resulting series makes it self-evident the two siblings are thoroughly enjoying themselves — working together on a tongue-in-cheek but still seriously wide-eyed examination of the modern versions of Jersey Devils, Nessies, and MoMos running loose across North America. And with Dan Aykroyd transforming his gentile imitation of Rod Serling from the old skit days during *Saturday Night Live* into a suave, dapper International Man-in-Black-about-town based on his own comic persona, the co-

writer of *Ghostbusters* demonstrates his sincere interest in paranormal phenomena and cryptozoological research (as does his involvement in this series by basically co-producing it from the ground floor up). To his credit, Peter Aykroyd takes a blackly humorous approach to soft pedal the subject matter, as it could otherwise quickly degenerate into something far, far less interesting, with its "Us vs. Them!" internal strife, feuds, etc. That *PSI Factor: Chronicles of the Paranormal* showcases the no-frills approach taken by government-employed scientists who only want to do their jobs well (not becoming heroes in the process) and keep the standards of their chosen professions as high as possible is remarkable. It's rather like a youthful version of *House* in this regard; the clinical nature of the expository dialogue is livened by the deep sense of dedication and passion held by the cool but never detached investigators, each a specialist in his or her own field of endeavor. As befitting Aykroyd's personal belief in Fortean phenomena, *PSI Factor: Chronicles of the Paranormal* posits Sasquatch as a likely species during its final voiceover, just one whose existence is yet to be proven to the satisfaction of O.S.I.R. team standards. But as if to underline with a visual *wink, wink, nudge, nudge*, the director shows several objective angles throughout the show that are hidden from the fictional protagonists but witnessed by the viewer, thus cinematically portraying the hominids as reality-based.

Even the Sasquatch creatures are dramatically split in this somber tale of civilization and its lack thereof once humanity is artificially thrust back into the great wilderness. For example, the O.S.I.R.'s early investigation indicates there is probably both a Mama and Baby Sasquatch. Later, however, with the discovery of the corpse of the fallen human posing as cryptid, the only other logical suspect remaining for the killing becomes the actual Sasquatch, as supported by eyewitness accounts and physical evidence. In an ironic twist, the O.S.I.R. team is stymied before coming to a conclusion due to the unexpected bankruptcy of the road-making company. This is odd, however, because although it ends the tension due to the current political state of affairs, there has been, after all, at least *one* human murdered by a Bigfoot — and team O.S.I.R. have watched the horrifying videotape that virtually proves it, shot by the dying imposter's own whirring camera. And yet when the conflict is ended because the legal complications shut down the road construction (which has a lethal effect on lost kick-backs, promised dates of completion, and other work-related matters), the thoughtful but exhausted members of O.S.I.R. basically shrug off the revelation via a voiceover that states the case was dropped soon after the construction company went under. Likewise, the case is erroneously attributed to a "probable fatal mauling by bear" in the team's files, though they know that the Bigfoot creature has all but been proven to exist. They seem to conclude: Why bother making for more paperwork (even if it is generated in bytes rather than paper reams) when you know it won't make a difference to your own government one way or the other?

This weary, by-the-book attitude is where *PSI Factor: Chronicles of the Paranormal* resembles an earlier series about government lifers forced into "harm's way" with their weekly encounters with civilians, one that featured Jack Webb, another huge Aykroyd influence. The show was *Project Bluebook*, based upon the actual declassified portions of the infamous "Project Bluebook" investigation report eventually released by Congressional order. Project Bluebook was the Air Force's years-long study of reported flying saucer phenomena from 1952 to 1969. Echoed by *PSI Factor: Chronicles of the Paranormal's* portrayal of how the special agents tend to feel artificially dehumanized whenever they're forced to interact with a politically polarized public (because they must, as members of O.S.I.R., maintain a fragile, internally-shared sense of objectivity), *Project Bluebook*, under Webb's creative control, was another in a series of semi-*Dragnet* redos, only with uptight government Air Force agents cataloguing the vast wasteland of North American contactees and abductees rather than uptight city detectives bringing in the latest small-time hoodlum. Most of these "marginal civilian riff-raff types" (as Webb might have labeled them after a few stiff rounds) come across as lost, if not stillborn, souls, rarely meeting up with the personal sense of superiority earned by Webb's ever-present contemptible look of "I've already seen it all, mister — *twice*!" In fact, the cold, psychologically psychotic manner in which Jack Webb brazenly glares back at the intimidated civilians he must routinely "interact with" (as if they're aliens of some kind in and of themselves) makes one wonder if Webb's character even cares about some extraterrestrial invaders anymore, or if he ever did. Clinically detached from humanity at large, Webb becomes the perfect scapegoat for the gods' own amusement when he's forced to constantly intersect with alien-witnessing individuals, one after the other, and basically decide whether the witnesses are pathological liars, criminals with nefarious intent, all of the above, or legitimate contactees.

This "just the facts, ma'am" mentality plays out to *PSI Factor: Chronicles of the Paranormal*'s favor. The intellectuals who value their own expertise and share good feelings about being a valuable asset in a serious team effort seem psychologically more Earthbound than the higher-flying hi-jinks of some restless government "X" agents on other popular shows of this ilk who risk their careers at the drop of a restricted cold case file. The team members of O.S.I.R. are, first and foremost, dedicated Company Men. Their task is not to question authority; their mission is to investigate and come to conclusions, some of which may or may not see public light for decades to come, depending on how their employers — the government itself— wishes to handle sensitive elements buried within each file. This "respect the knowledge, not the conjecture" attitude levels the playing field between often-divided Ciné du Sasquatch viewers — those who prefer Benign Bigfoot vs. Savage Sasquatch — and helps make "Forbidden North" a less predictable episode. It even explores legitimate scientific scenarios and theories by which an unknown hominid of Bigfoot's reported size could sustain itself on indigenous plants and animals (for such a large, free-roaming creature would need a lot of energy to exist, would keep active as a warm-blooded mammal, etc.). The latter, which is bandied about during one of the O.S.I.R. team meetings, strikes a realistic chord about the veracity of research, and puts aside the perception that interweaving actual science with hoarier entertainment fictions means Professor-Ed-the-Talking-Head time. Instead, when properly handled, this kind of fascinating detail makes the entire premise of unknown cryptids much more tantalizing and probable than the stereotypical outright dismissals of any scientific proof, etc. The O.S.I.R. team believe one should *not* explore the known perceptions of the scientific inquiry at hand; they see it as imperative they not fall prey to the inevitable human contagion factor present whenever they arrive on location to investigate a Fortean phenomena and remain open-minded to any and all possibilities, however far-fetched or mundane. Makers of future TV series and movies about cryptozoologists and scientists who conduct field research would be wise to watch as many episodes of *PSI Factor: Chronicles of the Paranormal* as they could before actually beginning the writing of said series or motion picture. There is much to be gained from the Canadian-lensed locales and realism of the muddy, perpetually difficult terrain the loggers and road crew are attempting to penetrate. At times one can clearly see the cast members struggling to stay afoot in ankle-deep mud turned to goo in the deep forest settings, winds splattering rain onto already soaked-through costumes as the storm rages on. It makes the monster sequences seem more threatening, as there is a palpable sense that this is truly no man's territory — a place where nearly-vanished hominids could make a stand against extinction.

The "actual" Bigfoot (as opposed to the hoaxed one) is depicted as curiously similar to the cave man archetype. It was most recently used, for example, in *Sasquatch* (aka *The Untold*), complete with a bald, domed head, human-looking eyes, and distinctive bipedal locomotion. These depictions of Sasquatch typically present the hominid as much more closely aligned to *Homo sapiens* than the usual Bigfoot monster, which is more simian in comparison. Though the creature creators for "Forbidden North" probably had no conscious intent, they actually generated an unwitting recreation of the very first Ciné du Sasquatch moment in history — *The Conquest of the Pole* in 1912, which could have just as easily been subtitled "Forbidden North" for all the differences between the Yeti movies. This is the primordial hallowed grounds of the Bigfoot film genre's birth. With each subsequent rebirth in an ever-expanding market explosion of All Things Hominid, the rules are being rewritten with new, ever-changing complexity.

Quantum Leap ("The Beast Within — November 6, 1972") (1992) (TV)

Starring Scott Bakula, Dean Stockwell, Pat Skipper, Eileen Seeley, Sean Sullivan, David Tom, Mike Jolly, David Denney and John Hillard. Produced by Donald P. Bellisario. Written by John D'Aquino. Directed by Gus Trikonis. USA. Color. Stereo. 60 Minutes.

Overview: Dr. Sam Beckett becomes lost in time when an experiment he conducts goes awry. Unable to solidify in the space/time continuum with any prolonged stability, he leaps from one quantum event to the next, each time hoping to find a way back into his own time frame. In each new time paradox, Beckett finds himself landing "inside" a host human being, whom he must quickly identify and then help through his or her own personal crisis in order to survive long enough to escape into the next quantum leap himself. With only the help of Al, a fellow scientist who projects himself via hologram into Beckett's current quantum reality and advises him of each new incident's probability of success or failure, Beckett attempts to correct whatever moral conflicts he faces on behalf of each person he inhabits.

"The Beast Within — November 6, 1972" sees Beckett leaping into the human known as Henry Adams. A former Vietnam veteran now living as a recluse in the woods of Washington with his shell-shocked buddy Roy, Henry assists Roy, who was a "tunnel rat" in the war and suffers from Post-Traumatic Stress Disorder. In particular, Roy needs medications that keep him from having mental seizures owing to his shattered psychology (and having barely survived a Viet Cong bullet to his head). Alas, while raiding a young boy's bedroom one night for money for medications, the boy — named Daniel — mistakes the fur coat–wearing Beckett for a Bigfoot. The alarmed boy screams, alerting his mother Karen and stepfather Luke.

Luke, it turns out, is the small town's sheriff. He investigates and realizes it is Henry Adams and not Bigfoot who has broken into Daniel's room. But Daniel won't hear of it, recalling a time when his father John and he saw a Sasquatch while on a camping trip when Daniel was younger. Luke, who served in Vietnam with Henry, Roy, and Daniel's father John, suffers survivor guilt over having witnessed John's death and subsequently returning Stateside to marry Daniel's grieving mother. As a result, Luke denies the boy's claims of Bigfoot and insists as sheriff that it is his mission to arrest both Henry and Roy for breaking the law. But during a flashback to Vietnam, we see that Luke himself lead indirectly to John's death by refusing to follow an order given to him by John as his commanding officer.

With Al's help, Beckett learns that Roy will die unless he receives medication soon. But Al also informs Beckett that historical records indicate Beckett as Henry Adams will be arrested if he attempts to secure said meds while in town. Meanwhile, Daniel runs away from home with a camera, intent on capturing an image of Sasquatch and proving he and his deceased father were not liars when they claimed to have seen the forest giant. After a long night in the forest alone, Daniel stumbles into Beckett's and Roy's camp. Beckett as Henry implores Daniel to stay put while Beckett steals into town for Roy's necessary pills. But once there, Beckett is arrested and jailed by Luke the sheriff, who does not care to be reminded of the guilt he carries over John's death. Karen eventually strikes a bargain with Beckett to let him out of the unattended jail in exchange for leading her to Henry's campsite and her son.

Almost at the site, however, Karen accidentally skids her van in a ditch to avoid hitting a deer. Beckett as Henry leads her to Roy and the boy. Alas, Daniel has fallen into some rocks deep inside a crevice while attempting to take Roy's picture. Roy is finally coaxed by Beckett into squeezing into the crevice and rescuing Daniel, despite Roy's long-held phobia about ever entering anything that remotely reminds him of his tunnel rat missions in Vietnam. Daniel is taken to a nearby hospital, bruised but okay, while Luke admits his culpability in John's death to Karen. Karen forgives him. To their surprise, Karen's van has somehow moved from the ditch where it was lodged back onto the road. Beckett and Al watch as Daniel, Karen, Luke and the rest vanish, taking the boy to recovery.

Beckett wonders how the van was moved. Just then, an astounded Al points into the woods. There they both see a white, furry Sasquatch leaving the scene, having just lifted the van and set it onto the road.

* * * * *

Like many TV shows featuring Bigfoot, *Quantum Leap* exploits the lure of a cryptid tale well-told rather than actually featuring a true hominid as its focus. This is understandable given the difficulties of budget and tight shooting schedules hour-long television shows (particularly of this era) faced in terms of completing one episode after another with little time, money, and ability to build a convincing Bigfoot costume. "The Beast Within" sees Beckett mistaken for Bigfoot by a myopic lad who isn't wearing his glasses when he makes his sighting of the creature. Combined with the youth's earlier encounter with a Bigfoot, it makes sense that the lad would be predisposed to jump to such a conclusion, even if Beckett doesn't particularly look like anything other than a human wearing a ratty bearskin parka.

Most of the show is about the Vietnam veterans and their inability to resolve survivor guilt and resume normal lives after their tours of duty. Only in the show's literal final minute does Bigfoot rear its furry head. Having tied up the loose ends of the story's plot, Dr. Beckett wonders aloud how Karen's van was righted from its precarious position in a roadside ditch and conveniently placed back onto the remote logging road. When Al gasps and points to the nearby Sasquatch making its way back into the forest, the answer is provided. Up to this point, however, the viewer has been more or less conditioned to believe that Daniel has fantasized his sighting of Bigfoot as a means of keeping alive his memory of his deceased dad, with whom he had his hominid encounter many years earlier.

The cryptid depiction is unusual in one degree: It is very top-heavy and barrel-chested beyond the normal Ciné du Sasquatch costume. The suit emphasizes the massive girth of the pectoral muscles to the point Bigfoot seems akin to a power-lifter at a local gym, complete with muscular shoulders. Like so many movies and TV shows, "The Beast Within" applies the Bigfoot name to what is more traditionally known as a Yeti (i.e., having white fur rather than a brown, black, or dark reddish hue). This is a common occurrence in the genre, which also sees its share of black-furred Bigfoot labeled as Abominable Snowmen. It's as if producers wish to hedge their bets and evoke both hominids. Of course, the reality is that such confusion may just be a matter of blind luck. If, after all, one can hire an effects artist who has a preexisting suit of one color rather than another, why *not* simply let it slide? Cryptozoological accuracy is far from paramount in most fictional shows about hominids — that much is certain.

While it's not a bad episode of *Quantum Leap* by any means, "The Beast Within" is not particularly outstanding as a Ciné du Sasquatch entry owing to the fact it is basically a drama with a cryptid on the fringe of the plot to give it exploitation appeal. As mentioned, this is a very common strategy; and as far as "pseudo-squatch" efforts go, this is as good as any like it. The story is entertaining and features a nice twist ending. Still, only fans of *Quantum Leap* will be particularly engrossed, owing to the otherwise predictable nature of the narrative in terms of Bigfoot television entries.

Quest for the Yeti (2004)

Starring Malcolm Freeman, Amy Earhart, Dick Edwards, Andrew Lynch, Roberto Lemmo and Steve Monroe. Produced, Written and Directed by Victoria Arch. USA. Black & White. Stereo. 42 Minutes.

Overview: This short comic film parodies the quest by several Himalayan mountain explorers to find the elusive Yeti while Sir Edmund Hillary simultaneously, yet unbeknownst to them, attempts to scale the heights of Mt. Everest. Little is known beyond the film's production (at an estimated cost of $13,000) and subsequent disappearance after initial screenings; but with character names such as "Harry Bottoms" and "Daisy van Plank," it's a good bet the effort was a stretch, especially at nearly three-quarters of an hour's running time.

The Red Files ("Bigfoot Attacks!") (TV) (2004)

Created by Ron Bonk. Directed by Tim Ritter. Color. USA. 4 Minutes.

Overview: A middle-aged rural couple take a long detour along a remote country road, bickering as they drive. The truck predictably breaks down, forcing Hal, the husband, to check the engine while his nagging wife complains about the odor of a skunk ... or...? Next they glimpse something in the nearby trees. Eyes? Fangs? Hal feigns bravery, but his quaking hands tell all as the bobbing flashlight illuminates the scary monster that is now stalking them. "How did it move so *fast*?" are his last words as the beast rips him to pieces in front of his horrified spouse. She gathers her wits long enough to realize she must now make a survival stand on her own against the Savage Sasquatch somewhere in the darkness around her.

Nothing much more than a mood piece, "Bigfoot Attacks!" is nevertheless a perfect distillation of every Savage Saquatch entry in the genre, boiled own to 4 overheated minutes of sheer panic and scares. It lacks the finesse of a larger-budgeted affair, but for sheer recapitulation of the underlying folklore quality so inherent in the genre itself, "Bigfoot Attacks!" concisely sums up the relative strengths and weaknesses of Ciné du Sasquatch in the current era. Strong on suspense and technique but bereft of anything more than stereotypes and stock situations, "Bigfoot Attacks!" is as emblematic as its title. "Bigfoot Attacks!" can be found as a short bonus film on the DVD called *Strawberry Estates*.

The Red Green Show ("Bigfoot Defense") (2000) (TV)

Starring Peter Keleghan, Steve Smith, Patrick McKenna, Rick Green, Jeff Lumby, Wayne Robson and Bob Bainborough. Produced by Steve and Morag Smith. Directed by William G. Elliott. Canada. Color. Stereo. 4 Minutes.

Overview: A parody, à la *SCTV*, *The Red Green Show* is a combination fishing, hunting, and home improvement show that featured an ensemble of character actors playing various outdoors and "manly men" stereotypes, such as Red Green and Ranger Gord. The latter hosted a segment within the overall show itself which portrayed the lonely ranger as a virtual hermit ensconced within his fire watch tower in the remote Canadian wilderness. Always eager to greet viewers and temporarily allay his solitude, Ranger Gord dispensed survival and camping tips for those wanting to make the manly best of their outdoor adventures.

Ranger Gord also showed cartoons that were instructional in nature. Gord claimed to have written, produced, directed, voiced and animated them himself (he had a lot of spare time on his hands, after all). One of these was called "Bigfoot Defense" and featured a first-hand account of how Real Men deal with any attacking Sasquatch they're likely to encounter at any given moment while in the wilds. Red and Harold Green join Ranger Gord to demonstrate as Gord explains the correct fighting techniques to repel Sasquatch, which basically include using surprise drop-kicks before the hominid expects it. Alas, Bigfoot gets the better of the poor schmucks and repeatedly uses his monstrous-sized feet to demolish Red and Harold.

Though the hominid appears only in a brief cameo, "Bigfoot Defense" is a humorous satire of the educational films students once endured in stuffy science classrooms, right down to the deliberately stiff animation. In all, over 23 total cartoons were made for the Ranger Gord portion of *The Red Green Show*, which ran from 1999 to 2006 on both the CBC in Canada and various PBS stations in America.

Reflections of Evil (2002) (Cameo)

Starring Damon Packard, Nicole Vanderhoff, Beverly Miller, Dean Spunt, Chad Nelson, Lana Turner, Tony Curtis, Joey Heatherton, George Hamilton, Josue Clement, Tim Colceri, Elliott Joseph Brakeman and Greg Bajakian. Produced, Written and Directed by Damon Packard. USA. Color. Stereo. 180 Minutes.

Overview: Bob, a disgruntled, impoverished, obese young man reduced to living with his Grandmother and selling cheap watches to passersby in downtown Los Angeles, witnesses a series of apocalyptic horrors in his daily rounds as seller of time pieces: corpses left in the streets; raving homeless men wielding machetes; police brutality; chemical trails covertly sprayed into the skies by his own government; etc. Dispirited, alienated, and lonely, Bob struggles to make sense of any of it, only to find himself more confused than before his failed efforts at comprehension. Everywhere he turns, rage and destruction are the order of the day — the only order at all in an increasingly lawless society. As the mentally deficient and swelling ranks of impoverished humanity spill over and drown the landscape, Los Angeles becomes a vision of Hell on Earth, complete with ghoul-faced zombies, mass casualties in all forms of public transportation, and an overall sense of impending doom as citizens lose the last semblance of control over their fragile, communal reality.

During one particularly surreal evening, Bob hallucinates a visitation by the ghostly spirit of his dead sister, who accidentally overdosed on drugs many years prior, when Bob was a young boy. She seems to be reaching out to him, as if in silent warning, but Bob cannot make heads nor tails of her phantasm's appearance. Outside his home, however, a storm rages and the wind blows, creating a scary light show in the house's windows. The apparent visage of Sasquatch is clearly visible in silhouette outside the glass plates during particularly violent flashes of lightning, growling in fury before quickly vanishing.

Eventually Bob is joined by his sister while he aimlessly wanders like a ghost through the Universal Studios Tour, fondly remembering his more innocent childhood as he's confronted by the modern horrors of relentless corporatism, numberless consumer zombies, and a poisoned planet slowly dying before its killers' collective eyes.

* * * * *

Though the Sasquatch cameo in *Reflections of Evil* is brief, it is also quite effective. Like much else of this independent feature film's notorious love affair with All Things 1970s (such as its sampling of old "Movie of the Week" promotional trailers and Polyester Decade pop music), Bigfoot is included for its cultural shock value, forcing the audience into recalling the horrific impact the legendary hominid once had in the so-called Me Decade in films and on TV. In so many ways the utilization herein is almost entirely postmodern, included more to instantly reference a bygone era than to present any viewpoint of its own or update the genre itself.

It's a minor appearance, but the haunting visual intensity of the creature's brief flashes of snarling anger impress via clever staging and spooky back-lighting. The long, shaggy fur of Sasquatch is never seen save in silhouette, and full-facial glimpses of the beast are rendered indecipherable owing to the fast cutting on display. But if anything, such techniques only more fondly recall the intended 1970s approach to depicting Sasquatch, including *Kolchak: the Night Stalker*'s "The Spanish Moss Murders" episode in which Richard Kiel portrayed a skunk ape.

A genuine cult oddity for any number of positive reasons (not the least of which is its clear affection for Ciné du Sasquatch, further amplified by the director's appearance in the short film "Yeti Vengeance" as a sex-obsessed camera operator), *Reflections of Evil* perfectly recreates the feeling one had living in the 1970s and experiencing a wonderful Last Gasp of creative greatness slowly, hideously giving way to the more sinister, defeated reality of the 1980s and beyond.

Return of the Forest Monster (2003)

Starring Chris Crowson, Raighne Davidson, Vance Kotrla, Mike Newhouse and Jeff Smith. Produced by Travis Gordon. Written and Directed by Vance Kotrla. USA. Color. Stereo. 75 Minutes.

Overview: Jeff, Roy, Morgan, Dave and Kid Gorgeous go camping outside of Austin, Texas. They are attacked by the Forest Monster that dwells outside their cabin. Dave is killed. The rest escape back to Austin. They spend a restless week mostly contemplating how weird it was that their friend was killed by a Forest Monster.

Eventually, Kid Gorgeous and Roy get bored and propose going back to the scene of slaughter to kill the Monster in revenge. They survive a kidnapping attempt by two angry frat brothers and convince Morgan and Jeff to return with them to the cabin. There they face the Lugo, the Forest Monster, in a battle of *mano a monstro* wherein only the strongest will live.

* * * * *

Return of the Forest Monster isn't really a Bigfoot film, but, oddly, neither it is *not* a Bigfoot film. The technical mumbo jumbo unearthed by the idiot students attribute the beast in question (aka the Lugo) as having been created centuries earlier by a battle between warring wizards. But given the depiction and the fact that many Ciné du Sasquatch films also posit that Bigfoot is a mystical spirit of the woods as well as a physical being, this does not disqualify the film from maintaining all the aspects inherent in the genre as a whole. Chief among these are the kids venturing into the forest who encounter a bipedal cryptid, the hominid slaughtering them, and their fight and flight for survival.

The film is not low-budget but rather no-budget. This is evident across the board, from the camcorder-style videography (calling it cinematography would be an injustice to all directors of photography who've ever bothered to light a shot or mount a camera on a tripod), amateurish acting, non-scripted dialogue, and leaden pacing. The Lugo is bottom of the barrel in terms of Bigfoot movie appearances. It is literally a young man wearing a gorilla face mask and fuzzy black sweater, along with long shorts and sneakers. No attempt is made by the filmmakers to ever disguise the ridiculous nature of their cryptid, which is perhaps *Return of the Forest Monster*'s only redeeming feature. It can be truthfully said that the cast and crew did not take any of the proceedings seriously, and, consequently, neither should any viewer.

Return of the Forest Monster does have a quirky charm often apparent in regional undertakings such as this effort, which was shot in Austin, Texas, and takes advantage of the many scenic possibilities offered by the area. However, the lack of lighting in the night scenes is a real drawback in terms of visual clarity. The audio was recorded directly on the camcorder's microphone, which makes for intermittently bad production sound. Provided one is willing to overlook and/or endure such technical deficiencies, *Return of the Forest Monster* does have some amusing moments and occasionally effective misdirection. There is a low-key nature to the proceedings reminiscent of Richard Linklater's *Slacker* (a clear influence) but without that film's complex sense of possibilities and its ebb-and-flow narrative construction. It feels largely improvised on the spot, and, as such, meanders more than it makes its points. It's not the worst Ciné du Sasquatch movie, but it should be viewed with a huge sense of college humor and perhaps the accompanying chemical enhancements.

Cover art for the DVD release of *The Return of the Forest Monster*.

Return to Boggy Creek (1977)

AKA: *The Legend of Boggy Creek 2*. Starring Dawn Wells, Dana Plato, David Sobiesk, Marcus Claudel, John Hofeus, Jim Wilson, Richard Cusimano, John Fiero, Vic Vead, Ray Gaspard, Laura Wilson and Louis Belaire. Produced by Bob Gates, Robert Buford, Jamie Coulter, Robert A. Geist, Joe Hathoot, Clyde H. Jones, L.W. Ledwell Jr., Stephen H. Ledwell and Ken Wagnon. Written by John David Woody. Directed by Tom Moore. USA. Color. Mono. 85 Minutes.

Overview: Jolene, a widower, and her three children — Evie Jo, John Paul and T-Fish — live on the edge of the infamous Boggy Creek in Fouke, Arkansas, constantly struggling to make ends meet in an impoverished if culturally rich Cajun fishing village. When a visiting Little Rock wildlife photographer believes he's seen the legendary Fouke Monster, he enlists the help of local tour guide Bruno to trek into the bayou's backwaters to help him photograph the elusive beast.

Meanwhile, Jolene's children follow the photographer and Bruno in their own boat, hoping to catch a glimpse of the creature themselves. A hurricane strikes before the men or children can return to safety, stranding them in the swamps. In a desperate bid for survival, the children take refuge from the battering storm in an abandoned, decrepit boathouse. Soon they discover they have inadvertently invaded the Fouke Monster's domicile, complete with skeletal remains and other stolen items.

The children attempt to flee, despite the raging winds, in a skiff, but before they can escape, the beast returns, roaring in apparent outrage. To their shock, the Bigfoot grabs hold of the tiny boat's tow line and pulls them and the stranded men to safety. Realizing the creature is actually benign, the rescued humans decide to keep the Fouke Monster's existence a secret rather than risk it being hunted to extinction by outsiders.

* * * * *

Throughout the decades since its poorly-distributed initial release, *Return to Boggy Creek* has been generally dismissed by Ciné du Sasquatch enthusiasts as a vastly inferior sequel to its superstar predecessor, *The Legend of Boggy Creek*. Little seen and only briefly available on home video during its limited VHS release, *Return to Boggy*

The legendary Fouke Monster nears its derelict-houseboat-turned-beastly-lair at the conclusion of *Return to Boggy Creek*. Note the arm extensions designed to make the creature more simian.

Creek is even dismissed by Fouke Monster progenitor Charles Pierce himself. Director, writer and star of the first and third *Boggy Creek* films, Pierce claimed no authorship or ownership of the second installment, owing to a falling out with *Return to Boggy Creek*'s producers, to whom he initially licensed rights to the sequel. Given the sheer number of producers credited to the second film and Pierce's notoriously independent penchant for wearing all the creative hats himself, it is easily understandable why the series' progenitor would wish to step away from such a mixed jambalaya of competing visions — nine separate producers are listed for *Return to Boggy Creek*!

Nevertheless, *Return to Boggy Creek* is far from the unmitigated disaster of genre reputation. In fact, it is technically well-photographed and far superior in many aspects to the rougher, *vérité* Pierce-photographed *The Legend of Boggy Creek*. Likewise, the cast is largely professional, deftly combining national and regional actors with the typical smattering of grizzled locals to add authenticity and save money. The latter is a hallmark of the success of the first *Boggy Creek* film, and the formula was continued into the trilogy's conclusion.

When *Return to Boggy Creek* was produced, Dawn Wells was the marquee name among the modest cast members. Forever known as Mary Ann, the sweet-natured castaway on *Gilligan's Island*, Wells (as Jolene) brings a much-needed level of professional believability to the film's otherwise emotionally-vacant center. Portraying the widowed mother of three children, and fearing her missing husband was killed by the monster five years earlier, Wells is well-cast and earthy in a difficult role that too often sabotages logic and leaves her scrambling to paper over gaping plot holes. Her skillful range allows her to do just that, and holds viewer interest despite the tedium of the plot.

A case in point is the back-story itself. While everyone in the tiny fishing community believes the missing husband met his demise at the claws of the Fouke Monster, Wells' doting mother figure inexplicably allows her children to blithely play in the backwaters of the bayou with nary an expressed concern. Wells smartly glosses over such frequent lapses of credulity by centering her performance on Jolene's sense of overwhelming exhaustion as mother, cook, breadwinner, house cleaner, and even caretaker of her semi-invalid father. This helps distract from the story's contradictions and gives the film its singular strength: a protagonist around whom the viewer may anchor at least a modicum of emotional investment.

In the years since its production, however, it is Dana Plato (in her first-ever starring role) as Evie Jo, the eldest of Wells' onscreen children, who has gained the most notoriety from appearing in *Return to Boggy Creek*. Her debut role casts her as a boggy version of Scout from *To Kill a Mockingbird*, a young girl growing into womanhood, with the trappings of a tomboy, in a rural setting and with a deceased parent (in this case reversed, so that the father figure is missing instead of the mother). Like Scout, Evie Jo must act as both sibling and part-time parental enforcer to her younger brothers, and also like Scout, she must face up to the local "boogeyman" (not in the form of Boo Radley, but the Fouke Monster itself). While the comparison weakens when considering the execution, it is nonetheless present just beneath the surface and echoed throughout the film's duration; the Fouke Monster even rescues the kids from certain doom at the film's finale, echoing Radley's sudden heroism in *To Kill a Mockingbird*.

Plato is a classic example of a child movie actress seemingly unable to cope with the nearly-impossible transition to adult-aged performer. Forever typecast (not unlike Dawn Wells herself, but at a much younger age) by the success of her role of Kimberly Drummond on the television sitcom *Diff'rent Strokes*, young Plato was never able to transition beyond her initial young stardom into becoming a mature actress. Part of her career woes were simply bad luck: She au-

Jolene (Dawn Wells), a lonely widow, searches for her missing children who have disappeared into the swamps in *Return to Boggy Creek*.

ditioned for the Princess Leia role in *Star Wars* but was turned down; she was selected by director Louis Malle to star in *Pretty Baby* but turned it down herself, fearing typecasting (the film launched Brooke Shields' career); and she was let go from *Diff'rent Strokes* as a regular when she became pregnant because producers didn't want her character's wholesome image "ruined" by the reality of her condition. She eventually fell into a personal spiral of drug abuse, nude *Playboy* pictorials, and even armed robbery of a convenience store in later years

Evie Jo (Dana Plato) stares at the off-screen Fouke Monster with a mixture of fear and reverence in *Return to Boggy Creek*.

before her death by overdose. In an era of celebrity worship fueled by the likes of the Internet and *TMZ*, her career seems as untimely as it was prescient to all that would follow. One is left to speculate if she was not an eerie precursor to today's salacious starlets and their daily barrage of licentious behaviors for the photo hounds and a sad, voracious appetite by the reading public — even if, of course, this uneasy exploitation has been a part of show business since its inception.

Whatever her legacy, Dana Plato carries herself with confidence as Evie Jo, especially considering her novice status and the script's clichéd dialogue. Her raw talent shines through and makes tolerable the film's lengthy running time devoted to her. It is easy to surmise why Hollywood agents casting for talented tykes quickly signed her shortly after *Return to Boggy Creek*'s release. Though not widely seen, the film must have proven to be a young actor's dream demo reel. There is hardly a scene in the movie that doesn't have Plato in it. This gives *Return to Boggy Creek* a (tragedy-tinged) cult following today, as it features not one but three genuine cult favorites for fans to relish: Dana Plato, Dawn Wells, and, of course, the Fouke Monster.

In terms of Ciné du Sasquatch, *Return to Boggy Creek* is a noteworthy failure. While most Bigfoot movies (including the original *The Legend of Boggy Creek*) portray the monster as hell-bent upon destruction without rationale, *Return to Boggy Creek* introduces the more pacifistic characterization of the cryptid as sentient and, more importantly, an instinctual protector of children in peril within its domain. Never as overly sentimental as *Harry and the Hendersons* and all the related Benign Bigfoot movies that followed the Spielberg film's success, this Boggy Creek denizen is nevertheless a redeemer of its own native folklore rather than simply a scary incarnation of its own lurid past. While presented as a man-stalker in the opening scenes, by the film's conclusion, the creature is rescuing the children from a hurricane. By risking its own life in doing so, the Fouke Monster transforms from horror icon into the more family-friendly Sasquatch depicted in so many movies to follow.

This "large step" forward is unevenly handled in *Return to Boggy Creek*. In part, this is because the creature itself is so marginally developed as a character. It is difficult to sustain much empathy when the reversal at the climax is so sudden and unmotivated. In the rough, however, the film introduces what would become a major new wrinkle in the Ciné du Sasquatch formula. Because it is one of the first to present this new genre twist, *Return to Boggy Creek* warrants respect for its early recognition of the inevitable trend to humanize the creature and offer it sympathy as well as condemnation, catering to a family-friendly audience in the process.

While it is never successful as an effectively chilling Ciné du Sasquatch entry per se, patient children will find at least some entertainment value in *Return to Boggy Creek*. In tone and setting it very much attempts to be progressive within the severe limitations of its own genre confines. As such, it offers mild thrills and a Nancy Drew sense of mystery younger audiences not entirely jaded by today's CGI-laden fare may find absorbing, especially the way in which the film's viewpoint is confined largely to the younger protagonists and their perspectives on events.

A final concept briefly introduced in *Return to Boggy Creek* worthy of mentioning is the visual realization of the monster's hidden lair. In a majority of Ciné du Sasquatch films, the cryptid is depicted as living in the dense woods free of the necessity of shelter (*The Legend of Boggy Creek* is a prototypical example). And even in the rare films Bigfoot is shown to have a home, it is typically a cave setting (*Half Human* and *The Abominable Snowman*, for example). *Return to Boggy Creek* posits the novel concept of having the cryptid inhabiting an abandoned house boat and collecting human artifacts as "decorations" and curiosity pieces. This odd perspective on Sasquatch is so rare as to be almost nonexistent in the genre otherwise; it imbues the creature with a sense of longing and loneliness only hinted at in the first *Boggy Creek* entry. It is but one more reason *Return to Boggy Creek* warrants viewing. It may be a failure as a general release, but it contains many nascent themes the genre itself would later incorporate and explore more successfully.

The Revenge of Bigfoot (1979)

AKA: *Rufus J. Pickle and the Indian*. Starring Rory Calhoun, Mike Hackworth, T. Dan Hopkins, Patrica Kane, Jeffrey L. Cox, Mike Downs, Sara Hughes and David Bohn. Produced by Joe Glass and Harry Thomason. Directed by Harry Thomason. USA. Color. Mono. 85 Minutes.

Overview: Bob Spence is a tolerant good ol' boy living in Texarkana, Arkansas, trying to earn a modest living as a rancher. He takes in a Native American from the area to provide shelter to the man as well as secure his services as a desperately-needed ranch hand. Alas, a local bigot, Rufus J. Pickle, won't hear of it and sets his black heart on driving the Indian helper out of town. Enter a local Bigfoot who is anything but intolerant. The hominid decides Rufus J. Pickle must suffer the same torments of the damned as he is inflicting on Spence's guest. In the resulting chaos, the town is turned upside-down and the citizens terrified witless as a battle between Bigfoot and Pickle erupts into full-scale tit-for-tat.

* * * * *

There are several Ciné du Sasquatch movies that are practically, if not definitely, lost to all modern viewers. This would not be unexpected for some of the earliest films in the genre, such as *Conquest of the Pole* or Thomas Edison's *The Dinosaur and the Missing Link*. Oddly, however, both of these silent efforts are well-preserved and can easily be viewed online with the click of a mouse button. Alas, the later-era efforts tend to become the most difficult to locate, owing to their pre-videocassette production, particularly when they're regional efforts such as *The Revenge of Bigfoot*. For what scant information about this Arkansas-shot independent feature film is known, the vast majority is culled not from primary modern viewings but second-hand from those who saw its brief theatrical run as *Rufus J. Pickle and the Indian*, or its even more marginal re-release as *The Revenge of Bigfoot*.

Lensed in Texarkana, Arkansas, in the summer of 1978 by Harry Thomason, who also directed *The Day It Came to Earth* and later produced Emmy Award–winning sitcoms for network television (like *Designing Women* and *Hearts Afire*), *The Revenge of Bigfoot* starred Rory Calhoun, a veteran character actor of numerous TV shows and movies. Calhoun got his break portraying Bill Longley in the long-running 1950s western *The Texan*. He later starred as Darios in Sergio Leone's directorial debut *The Colossus of Rhodes* and in a diverse range of prime time one-off roles in such shows such as *Bonanza, Gunsmoke, I Spy, Gilligan's Island, Police Woman* and *Hawaii Five-O*.

Otherwise, little else is known about *The Revenge of Bigfoot* save sporadic accounts posted online by locals who participated in its production. According to these sources, the filmmakers utilized locals for extras, including for a sequence in which a honky tonk is filled with celebrating drinkers. As they leap from their seats with startled horror, Bigfoot smashes through the bar's main window, causing havoc as the terrified extras scream and flee for the exits. Another sequence involved a posse of armed hunters heading into the woods to shoot Sasquatch, bearing the usual assortment of flashlights, hound dogs, and double-barreled shotguns.

Thomason evidently never desired to see his effort preserved in any known video, DVD, or cable screening format, as there is no record of it ever having survived its initial severely-restricted theatrical showings in the Deep South and a handful of Midwestern drive-ins. Oddly, given his seeming reluctance to acknowledge the film (requests by the author to his production office in Hollywood were ignored), the director did make a joint appearance with fellow Arkansan filmmaker Charles B. Pierce at a retrospective showing of *The Legend of Boggy Creek* in 2008 at the Little Rock Film Festival to discuss both his and Pierce's cinematic opuses as they related to Ciné du Sasquatch. Alas, despite being well-attended, no transcripts nor audio or video recordings were made of the historic appearance, and *The Revenge of Bigfoot* was not screened, as Thomason merely acted as the host for the event.

Rocky Mountain Bigfoot (2004) (Doc)

Featuring Steve Boettcher, Michael Shermer and Jeff Meldrum. Produced and Directed by Mike Trinklein. USA. Color. Stereo. 60 Minutes.

Overview: One part documentary and one part travelogue, *Rocky Mountain Bigfoot* begins as an overview of the subject itself. Mike Trinklein, an Emmy Award–winning director, interviews Michael Shermer, noted founder of the Skeptics Society and writer for *Science* and *Skeptic* magazines (the latter of which he also serves as editor-in-chief). Surprisingly, Shermer doesn't fully discount at least the possibility that Sasquatch exists and may one day be found. However, his remarks are couched in his stated belief that most reports are outright hoaxes and mistaken sightings of known species. Still, the fact Shermer allows even the remote possibility is worthy of note, especially given how critical the Skeptics Society has been of cryptozoology to date.

Next up is Professor Jeff Meldrum, a familiar face and heir apparent to Dr. Grover Krantz as the "face of pro–Sasquatchology" in a plethora of Bigfoot documentaries such as this one. Always likeable and articulate, Meldrum is unknowingly given a fake Bigfoot footprint casting by the *Rocky Mountain Bigfoot* crew, complete with hoaxed dermal ridges. Alas, to the pranksters' dismay (but to his credit), Meldrum quickly deduces he's been had and announces that the casting is not legitimate. The Idaho State University professor also reviews the vast catalog of existing Bigfoot evidence in the form of sightings, hair samples, castings, and the like.

The latter half of *Rocky Mountain Bigfoot* delves into the expedition mounted by some college-aged students to document the eyewitness accounts of Bigfoot encounters in Utah and Idaho. This section is far less involving, as it spends too much of its running time showing the nascent cryptozoologists setting up camp, fumbling with their gear, and reacting with certain dread when a flock of geese sound off, convinced they're under attack by a Savage Sasquatch.

Because the video production level is so weak at times, it is difficult to recommend *Rocky Mountain Bigfoot* as an exemplary model of the Ciné du Sasquatch documentary. Especially in the latter half, far too much of the talking head syndrome is in effect, with the filmmakers missing a golden opportunity to capture the grandeur of their scenic surroundings. *Rocky Mountain Bigfoot* is for die-hards only.

Roswell Conspiracies: Aliens, Myths & Legends (1999) (TV)

Starring Scott McNeil, Peter Kelamis, Janyse Jaud, Dale Wilson, Lee Tockar, Eli Gabay, L. Harvey Gold, Saffron Henderson, Alec Willows, Alex Zahara and Richard Newman. Produced by Kaaren Lee Brown, Stephanie Graziano and Joe Pearson. Written by Marcy Brown, Dennis Haley and James W. Bates. Directed by Dan Fawcett, Joe Pearson, Brad Rader and Tom Tataranowicz. USA. Color. Stereo. 30 Minutes.

Overview: Centuries ago the Earth was invaded by various hostile life forms. Over the decades that have passed since, superstitious folklore has labeled these alien entities as supernatural but Earth-based phenomena: ghosts, vampires, werewolves, and the like. In the modern era, humans in various allied intelligence agencies uncover the nefarious invasion and realize that aliens intent on world domination still walk among us. The shocked spies form the Global Alliance, a multi-national, top-secret task force whose mission it is to uncover the invaders and defeat them at every turn.

As the Global Alliance mission matures, the agency recruits one Agent Ti-Yet (an anagram of "Yeti"), an untrustworthy but necessary member of the alien Abominable Snowman astral creatures. Because both Sasquatch and Yeti species are alien creatures fighting the Alliance, neither is ever fully trusted the human organization. However, because Agent Ti-Yet has knowledge of a weapon that can defeat the lycanthropic race of werewolves, the Snowman-turned-confidante is tolerated, albeit begrudgingly.

* * * * *

Much like its clear influences, the theatrical *Men in Black* motion pictures and the TV series *The X-Files*, *Roswell Conspiracies: Aliens, Myths & Legends* is a contemporary version of the old *U.F.O.* television series produced by Gerry Anderson in which an elite, secretive human spy agency tracks and combats hostile aliens intent on taking over the world. While most of these aforementioned shows attempt to have the agents surprised each week by what they encounter and uncover, *Roswell Conspiracies* builds its gallery of nefarious extraterrestrials much more like *Men in Black*, in which the aliens are well-known to a select few (hence the Roswell reference).

Unlike *Men in Black*, however, in which a majority of the aliens are well-adjusted and not intent on harming Earthlings, *Roswell Conspiracies* posits that a majority of its invaders are bent on planetary takeover. In this regard, the Global Alliance is more akin to Her Majesty's Secret Service (of Bond franchise fame), with the aliens being the equivalent of S.P.E.C.T.R.E. (SPecial Executive for Counterintelligence, Terrorism, Revenge and Extortion). Operating out of a hidden headquarters on the outskirts of Roswell, New Mexico, the Alliance tracks the various extraterrestrials in an attempt to thwart their plans before they can bring them to fruition.

The series incorporates many common mythologies from around the world, including banshees, Viking deities, cyclopses, and both Sasquatch and Yeti, which are explained as being both alien and divergent, with the Bigfoot variants unable to withstand the cold extremes the Abominable aliens prefer. All are revealed to be unearthly in origin. This is a clever way of re-utilizing what are overly-familiar monsters and myths, filtering them instead through a high-tech espionage formula. While not entirely successful, credit should be given to *Roswell Conspiracies* on several fronts, not the least of which is its involved sense of self-referential world-building. Not unlike a complicated game designed for role-playing by gamers, the series created a full-fledged sense of back-story and interaction between the various life forms that was entertainingly complex. There is always intrigue afoot (so to speak) between the Bigfoot and Yeti camps, for example, and few of the aliens are reduced to one-dimensional stereotypes so common to this type of animated series.

Another plus is the high-quality animation and stylistic design. Clearly patterned on the film noir style embodied by the original Max Fleischer–animated *Superman* cartoon series from the 1940s, *Roswell Conspiracies* concentrates on layouts that evoke mood and sustain suspense, heightening the lighting effects and casting the characters into shadow-swallowed landscapes and settings. The fluidity of the animation is not complete, but it is far superior to the jerkiness one associates with most Saturday morning fare. Again, composition and judicious prefiguring of angles via storyboarding gives the show a sense of production value superior to most independently-produced, syndicated animation series. In particular, the bipedal hominids are well-rendered, with the Yetis appropriately threatening and massive in bulk. They are truly a menace to the puny-sized humans, towering over the frightened agents who are quick to use force when encountering them.

All-in-all, one would be hard pressed to find much fault in this seldom-seen, barely-remembered series. While the storylines are never more than superficial, at least *Roswell Conspiracies* has in-depth characters from which to draw, and well-drawn characters at that. This places *Roswell Conspiracies* a full hominid head above most animated cryptid characters in Ciné du Sasquatch, and makes it worthwhile to those who seek an alternative albeit admittedly fantasy scenario in which Sasquatch, Bigfoot, and humanity could all possibly coexist. Action-filled and exciting, it's like an old-time serial in pacing and style.

Route 30 ("What I B'Lieve") (2008)

Starring Curtis Armstrong, Nathalie Boltt, David Cowgill, Dana Delany, David DeLuise, Christine Elise, Alicia Fusting, Ed Gotwalt, Wil Love, Dan Poole, Kevin Rahm, Robert Romanus, Carl Schurr, Darrell Vaught and Lee Wilkof. Produced by John Putch, Michael D. Sellers, Jonathan Taylor and Jamie R. Thompson. Written and Directed by John Putch. USA. Color. Stereo. 88 Minutes.

Overview: *Route 30* tells three stories that all occur along Lincoln Highway in southern Pennsylvania. In one of the three tales (entitled "What I B'Lieve"), Bigfoot chases a local young man who tries to flee their unexpected encounter on his motorbike, with disastrous results. He crashes and then tumbles down a mountainside to narrowly escape without severe injury. He's left with lingering back pain, however, and eventually seeks out a Christian Scientist to both cure him of his unending agony and rationalize his earlier encounter with the cryptid. The elderly Church of Science believer suggests all pain is imaginary, a diseased byproduct of an unhealthy mind, and that if one would put such negative thoughts away and believe in God's plan for salvation, all aches (and disappointments) would vanish. When the young man finds himself flopping on the floor in pain, even after giving the new philosophy his "best foot forward" effort, the Bigfoot-encountering biker is left to wrestle with deeper, darker demons: he feels like God is punishing him, and his numerous life's failures now feel more like judgment rather than a rite of passage to something better. With so much baggage, it's no wonder the poor man feels a permanent pain in his lower vertebrae; whether it is physical or spiritual, both body and mind are equally stressed in the ultimate theater of the viewer's mind's eye.

Eventually realizing there hasn't been a really great new Bigfoot film since the Patterson-Gimlin footage of 1967, the three buddies of "What I B'Lieve" become inspired enough to mount an off-road expedition into the state park where the creature was earlier sighted, in high hopes they'll be able to document the hominid in action (only this time with crystal clear results). Alas, their initial panic causes them to drop the camera when they actually do encounter the cryptid, and all three flee in holy terror, screaming. Only later will the trio discover that it was all actually a classic variation on a typical episode of *Where Are You, Scooby Doo?*—a goofball mutual friend has been donning the scare suit in an attempt to keep folks away from the several hemp plants he's been raising on state park grounds. The most enterprising of the buddies sees potential in the solution of the mystery, however: Why not market the expectations over the results, anyway? In short, sell the *In Search Of* sizzle.

Soon their homegrown Bigfoot DVD spectacular ("Bigfoot Is Back, *Boy!*") becomes a regional sales phenomena owing to Internet

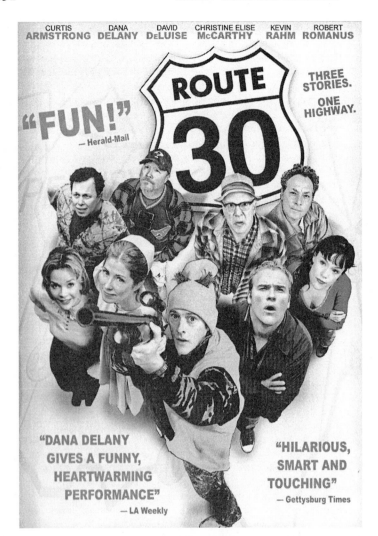

Cover art for the DVD release of *Route 30*.

interest and several news appearances by the self-styled cryptozoologists on local TV, whose stations are always eager to promote any human interest stories that are not the usual tried-and-true formula (and videotaping Sasquatch is definitely outside the norm). Though fame is fleeting, and money is not their only motivation, the three friends find that they have a new creative outlet that promises to bring them even more outrageous adventures in the years to come.

* * * * *

Route 30 is a likeable, low-key independent feature made up of three storylines. Each mini-film is tied together by its Route 30–based locale, a colorful stretch of highway running through Pennsylvania and beyond into the Western U.S. "What I B'Lieve" is the only Ciné du Sasquatch entry of the three tales told, but all three stories have that gentle, Robert Altman–esque quality of intimate observation that unites them, à la *Short Cuts*, into a larger whole that examines the overall experience. Well-cast, well-written, and well-directed, *Route 30* is a genuinely entertaining example of low-budget, character-based filmmaking the likes of which is sadly missing from today's overly-commercial marketplace. It harkens back to early John Sayles films, when good writing, fine acting, and a sense of authentic locale were more important than a derivative concept or excessive gunplay.

"What I B'Lieve" (the contraction is a play on the regional Pennsylvania dialect of the depicted characters, akin to saying "bleeve" as if phonetically spoken) captures a very modern sense of the all-surrounding, impermanent-feeling suburban culture, which, as seen through most characters who inhabit *Route 30*'s various locations, means bleak job prospects, tough times with too much time left on idle hands, and anxiety about the rapidly-fading memory of achieving any form of personal happiness, fueled by the increasingly long wait in line at the always open local quickie mart to cash one's long-overdue government "relief" check. It strays across that "lives of quiet desperation" line as it temporarily halts here and there to delineate a few of the lost souls we meet along the highway, and that's what gives "What I B'Lieve" it's strength: it feels sincere and anything but a brutal satire of Ciné du Sasquatch. Rather, it's an off-key but oddly funny character study set among a small circle of friends, like a Bigfoot variation of *Return of the Secaucus 7* by John Sayles. Folks who once took a lot of things for granted in their early 20s now look back in their 40s in mild shock, stunned by the sheer amount of their own personal debris trailing behind them. Bigfoot offers just another excuse to nostalgically perpetuate these protagonists' own childhood obsessions with crypto hominids. And these Cryptozoological Kings are just as eager to sincerely explore the mystery as they are willing to cash in on it with their *Bigfoot Is Back, Boy! The DVD*. They are a band of brothers, all right, these Bigfoot bounty hunters and motel-preferring outdoorsmen, and the fun of having an excuse to hang out together and earn themselves a little weed money in the process doesn't dampen the enthusiasm for the shared social proceedings, not even the least bit.

It's hard to explain the appeal of "What I B'Lieve" in regard to Ciné du Sasquatch at this point in the genre's history. In one sense it's clearly elegiac, filled with a sense of characters wistfully experiencing some weekend "kicks-peditions"—spur-of-the-moment fun plans about as well-advised as the less than mentally stellar friend risking *his* life to grow hemp in a state park (he uses a costume "diversion" as Sasquatch, which might have more probably drawn an expert bead through a high-powered scope in deer hunting country). Still, the off-kilter tone promises that even in the remote "jungle outposts" of suburbias nationwide, there are many stories never told that deserve their moment of fame. It also helps when independent filmmakers (such as the ones behind *Route 30*) infuse their production with such refreshing novelty and candor, especially in the acting department, where *Route 30* excels in quality.

"What I B'Lieve" also rewrites the genre in minor but noticeable ways, showing the vitality of Ciné du Sasquatch and that the genre is still alive and well—provided a filmmaker is willing to address the inherent limitations. Addressing these clichéd genre concepts and altering them, even as some basic tenets of the genre may well be incorporated and maintained here and there—these are the processes that lead to the endless variations that insures creativity within the Bigfoot film (and well beyond into all medias of popular culture). "What I B'Lieve" has a postmodern sense of self-irony about the whole Bigfoot sub-plot; but then again, what is fun and unexpected is that these actors and actresses bring it to life—skillful professionals making it is "look easy" under a very well-coordinated director who lets it unfold without stepping all over it.

"What I B'Lieve" is a distinctive, well-executed example of how Ciné du Sasquatch is really a genre still in the prime of its popular culture life. A few years or more might pass, and the bipedal hominid will suddenly reemerge from the deeper, undisturbed waters of our collective unconsciousness, thus reigniting the Ciné du Sasquatch cycle yet again, as it has self-regenerated for almost a century of motion picture history.

At this point in the Ciné du Sasquatch genre and with its nearly 100-year anniversary date approaching in 2012, one can readily see how amazingly flexible the Bigfoot genre is in form. It can be con-

structed as a classic adventure story, like Hammer Studio's *The Abominable Snowman*; as playful melodrama in *The Seven Faces of Dr. Lao* and its loving Himalayan exile; or even take the more tongue-in-cheek, low-key comedic approach of *Route 30*. All variations have their weaknesses, of course, but, more notably, each has its unexpected strengths. They all tell simple morality tales, but in complex adult societies where the rules blur with astonishing regularity. These grey areas invite the ultimate grey antagonist into the three films—the figure of Sasquatch as the Protective Guardian of the Woods. In this incarnation, Bigfoot tends to retain a distinctive Eastern philosophical tinge when presented in its more traditional Yeti backgrounds. The Buddhist monks and Sherpa guides who orchestrate the commercial flow of goods and humans along the treacherous, unmapped ice passages of the Himalayan Mountains render the Yeti archetype as very much an epic distillation of the harsh realities of life at the top of the world. The Abominable Snowman is a very unforgiving primal force in an often brutal, rigidly-caste system of human and natural order. As a mountain god (in so many words), Yeti has no concern nor desire to either meddle in human affairs or be troubled by them when they go awry. And, in closing reference to *Route 30*'s sweetly-rendered "What I B'Lieve," the same Bigfoot terror when first encountered can later morph into deeper, more interesting spirit quests in search of understanding: "Why *me*, of all people?" and "What do I do *now* that I know, but everyone else would think me a liar?"

These subtle strains of dawning awareness and sense of old habits falling by the wayside (in part to make room for the new ones soon to fill the void) is part of the reason "What I B'Lieve" works as a good "flip-side" to both *The Long Way Home: A Bigfoot Story* and *The Sasquatch Gang*. All three of these Bigfoot films attempt to postmodernize the tenets of Ciné du Sasquatch. *The Long Way Home: A Bigfoot Story* takes the immediacy of the videocam personal journal format and uses the device to largely effective results; it's documentary realism in tone only—in reality, it's *fictitious* docu-realism. *The Sasquatch Gang* covers some of the same territory (right down to the convenience of finding Sasquatch at your local state park) but for more laughs, dialing its humor up to nearly over-the-top levels (right down to its original release name, *The Sasquatch Dumpling Gang*, wherein said "dumpling" refers to a supposedly real Bigfoot scat sampling recovered by the loopy protagonists, which they use as a master mold to make limited edition plaster castings of the 'Squatch dumpling to sell on eBay—with some success). In "What I B'Lieve," the balance is down the middle. The tone is much more mature, but given that the cast members are largely two to three times older than the youthful leads in *The Sasquatch Gang*, this is only appropriately. And only appropriately up to a certain point, because these are still Bigfoot movies, albeit better than average examples. This means there will be a certain tongue-in-cheek snarkiness on the part of the doubters, cynics, and skeptics represented by their respective archetypes as pre-built within the drama itself. These characters are sure to be the first to laugh off any possibility of Bigfoot as actual, and the last to accept the overwhelming evidence that Sasquatch is alive, well, and more than likely challenging their right to survival. The sheer number of the genre's current outpouring is staggering too. Even in the exploitation heyday of drive-ins, low-budget producers never created such a plethora of product from which an independent outdoor exhibitor could choose as the average DVD store and Netflix videostream on-demand outlets offer today.

For better or worse, "What I B'Lieve" is more than likely the first in a style of new wave renderings of intimate Sasquatch tales (wherein obvious commercial conflicts are replaced with more self-conscious examinations of Bigfoot and its cultural influence). This is a hopeful sign the Ciné du Sasquatch genre has not stalled but is undergoing its usual metamorphosis, with such "butterfly heavy" comedies as

Route 30 a perfect "road marker" to indicate how far the genre has evolved and mutated. The Bigfoot film genre is both subsumed within "What I B'Lieve" and nearly consumed *by* it, too, as the clichéd set-ups and flashbacks told by other hominid witnesses (in this case a cloven-hoofed wood demon that stalks the unfortunate owners of stalled cars along remote stretches of Route 30) harken back to the classic films of the genre from which some of its neo-realistic tone is lifted (*The Legend of Boggy Creek*; *Sasquatch, the Legend of Bigfoot*; *The Mysterious Monsters*). It's "all good" in today's parlance, though; only a vital genre can be so effortlessly explored by a variety of filmmakers with hugely divergent agendas and means. The fact that "What I B'Lieve" is diametrically the opposite of, for example, *The Long Way Home: A Bigfoot Story* in terms of style and approach is the best proof of Ciné du Sasquatch's endurance rather than demise. For as is made abundantly clear by its sheer volume alone, Ciné du Sasquatch retains and often transcends many divergent cultural threads and its own genre motifs, and yet allows for much flexibility in almost all other aspects of production. Talented filmmakers see the opening and wisely go through it; the Muses may not inspire indefinitely, after all, and, as potently demonstrated, the genre endures.

Rudolph, the Red-Nosed Reindeer (1964) (TV)

Starring the voices of Burl Ives, Billie Mae Richards, Paul Soles, Larry D. Mann, Stan Francis, Paul Kligman, Janet Orenstein, Alfie Scopp, Carl Banas, Corinne Conley and Peg Dixon. Produced by Jules Bass and Arthur Rankin, Jr. Written by Robert May and Romeo Muller. Directed by Kizo Nagashima and Larry Roemer. USA/Japan. Color. Mono. 60 Minutes.

Overview: Rudolph is born into a family of flying reindeer who power Santa's annual pilgrimage to bring toys to children on Christmas Eve. Alas, Rudolph's nose glows bright red (for unexplained reasons), leading to Rudolph's alienation from his fellow "normal" flying reindeer friends.

Deciding he'll never be accepted at the North Pole, Rudolph sets out as a youngster to explore and find his place in the world. Along the way he is befriended by Hermes, an elf from Santa's workshop who wants to be a dentist instead of a toymaker (and thus is not welcome any more than Rudolph and his shiny nose), as well as Yukon Cornelius, a hearty fortune seeker who is well-equipped to deal with the difficulties of life in the frozen north.

Chief among those difficulties is the ferocious Abominable Snow Monster, a towering Yeti who feeds upon reindeer in its cavernous lair. After a series of unrelated adventures, Rudolph is eventually captured by the Bumble (as Yukon dubs the beast) and set to be devoured, along with Rudolph's family and childhood sweetheart, Clarice. Only the timely intercession of Hermes and Yukon spares Rudolph and family their lives. By the tale's end, Yukon has humbled the Bumble and introduces the newly-circumspect cryptid to Santa's workshop, whereupon the Bumble places the star atop Santa's huge Christmas tree.

* * * * *

In many odd ways, *Rudolph, the Red-Nosed Reindeer* is as important to 1960s Ciné du Sasquatch as any other entry except Patterson's footage of his Bluff Creek Bigfoot. This is because *Rudolph, the Red-Nosed Reindeer* was an immediate hit when first shown to American audiences and became a perennial yuletide television tradition along the lines of Frank Capra's *It's a Wonderful Life*. Because a substantial sub-plot of the fabled reindeer's quest involved confrontation with a Yeti — albeit a towering one far taller than typically depicted in either films or television — an entire generation of youngsters grew up with

a very seminal image of an Abominable Snowman (or Snow Monster, as *Rudolph, the Red-Nosed Reindeer* calls it) that was at once terrifying for small children but ultimately comforting (since by show's end the Bumble had been "humbled" and was for all practical purposes an overgrown teddy bear seeking human affection and social acceptance).

Over the decades of the ebbing and flowing of Political Correctness in American history, *Rudolph, the Red-Nosed Reindeer* has frequently been a target of irate groups who feel it is derogatory towards those with handicaps or ethnicities. Indeed, with its harsh outlook on life (in which even Santa treats Rudolph with condemnation for an accident of birth), the criticism is not without merit. After all, not only Santa, but Rudolph's father Donner refuses to accept Rudolph's genetic proboscis and attempts to cover it with mud to avoid embarrassment; in Donner's eyes his son is, in so many words, a misfit. So strong was this theme and resultant negative parental reaction that General Electric, the sponsors of the show, insisted on replacing a popular, if sad, song called "We're a Couple of Misfits" with a more innocuous tune from 1965 until 1998, when the original song was finally returned to its rightful place in the production, where it remains in most versions to this day.

What many may have been missing, however, is that there is no one in the storyline who is not a misfit in the strictest sense of the word's meaning. To wit: Santa Claus is a neurotic toymaker who frets day and night over making his production schedule at the expense of his own health and well-being; his wife frets over Santa's weight and emotional stability to the point of becoming co-dependent on his status; Donner and his wife are little more than latch-key parents who insist on conformity always, even while they completely avoid any medical attention being paid to Rudolph despite his obvious cosmetic birth defect; Hermes is an unhappy Everyman Elf caught in a job he hates but who dreams of bigger things; Yukon Cornelius is an outsider with an obsession to find gold or silver at any cost to his personal safety; and, of course, there's the island of

The Bumble from ***Rudolph, the Red-Nosed Reindeer***. A smaller-scaled Rudolph puppet is grasped by the hungry Abominable Snow Monster to emphasize their size difference. (Photograph courtesy Rick Goldschmidt.)

misfit toys itself, upon which Rudolph and friends find themselves (and, vis-à-vis, self-acceptance) shortly before the story's dénouement.

Though the sub-text is deeply buried in the snow drifts, the Abominable Snow Monster is equally alienated from his environment and therefore a misfit too. The Bumble rages and roars to provoke terror, but it turns out to be so much bark and bluff intended to partially fill the aching loneliness it feels at being the last of its kind (as no other Bumbles are ever shown or suggested to exist). In essence, the Bumble is a shy cryptid who only wants shelter from the cold and some much-needed companionship. It is not until Hermes removes its teeth while it is knocked unconscious that the Bumble realizes his sad situation — without his ferocious fangs, the Bumble is nothing but the largest misfit of them all. Without its reputation, in other words, the Bumble is the ultimate outsider — loathed but not feared; and merely ignored, not respected.

This admittedly saccharine theme is nonetheless entirely in keeping with Ciné du Sasquatch, wherein a major tenet frequently invoked by films and television shows within the genre centers on the potent sense of isolation the Yeti experiences as a species on the verge of extinction. In a majority of films, the Abominable Snowman is seen as a nearly human creature that longs for social contact and, lacking it, often turns predatory against invading *Homo sapiens* who treat it like an animal to be shunned or destroyed. Rarely given a chance to demonstrate its ability to peacefully coexist, the Yeti is forced into an often reluctant struggle for survival. It's true this theme is comically rendered in *Rudolph, the Red-Nosed Reindeer*, as indeed it is in most children's versions to soften the pathos. Yet, equally, the motif is ever-present throughout Ciné du Sasquatch when the hominid is not reduced to a savage monster lacking compassion.

The Bumble inspired a legion of worldwide fans, which is only fitting, given that *Rudolph, the Red-Nosed Reindeer* was actually stop-motion photographed in Japan, not the United States, as has often been believed by fans of the Rankin/Bass company. This is not to belittle the tiny American studio's penchant for crafting the storylines, storyboarding the shots or recording the voice tracks of such celebrity actors as Burl Ives and Fred Astaire, which was all done in North America; rather, it indicates their level of expertise in the matter of international co-production was so astute that few fans of *Rudolph, the Red-Nosed Reindeer* realize to this day just how global in scope the original production was as undertaken by Rankin/Bass.

So popular was *Rudolph, the Red-Nosed Reindeer* that it launched a two-decades-long output from Rankin/Bass which saw such equally-mesmerizing (though never besting) entries as *Santa Claus Is Comin' to Town*, *Here Comes Peter Cottontail*, and *The Year Without a Santa Claus*. More germane to this guide, the Rudolph character was visited again in two Rankin/Bass productions (minus the Bumble, alas), as well as the non–Rankin/Bass feature-length movie featuring the style of the earlier stop-motion characters (including the Bumble) — *Rudolph the Red-Nosed Reindeer and the Island of Misfit Toys*. The Bumble was also seen as a mute player in a 30-second Aflac Insurance commercial in 2009; it was done in the stop-motion style and featured Rudolph, Santa, Yukon, Herme, and other characters. In 2010 the popular late-night parody series *Robot Chicken* also included a series of Bumble cameos.

Rugrats ("The Legend of Satchmo") (1993) (TV)

Featuring the voices of E.G. Daily, Christine Cavanaugh, Nancy Cartwright, Kath Soucie, Cheryl Chase, Tara Strong, Cree Summer, Dionne Quan, Melanie Chartoff, Jack Riley, Michael Bell, Tress MacNeille,

David Doyle, Philip Proctor, Joe Alaskey and Julia Kato. Produced by Arlene Klasky and Gabor Csupo. Written by Matt Vitz. Directed by Jim Duffy. USA. Color. Stereo. 15 Minutes.

Overview: Grandpa takes the kids on their first camping trip without Stu, their father. To play it safe, however, Stu only allows his aging father to set up camp in the backyard. Determined to replicate the experience he remembers from when he was a kid, Grandpa tells the terrified kids the legend of Sasquatch. Later that night the kids decide to search for "Satchmo," only to mistake their father Stu for the beast when Stu ventures forth to check on his kids, worried because of his own camping trip the previous year in the real outdoors.

* * * * *

This episode of *Rugrats* is actually more of a knowing nod to the legends surrounding Bigfoot as frequently told by and to youngsters around a raging campfire rather than a full-on episode of Ciné du Sasquatch, as the cryptid doesn't actually make a physical appearance. Rather, Stu, the concerned father, is mistaken for "Satchmo" (as the kids call Sasquatch, unwittingly mispronouncing the name after Grandpa says of the hominid, "Some people call him Bigfoot ... some call him Sasquatch ... the rest just call him Sir!") when he ventures into the camping area to reassure himself his children are enjoying their first-ever camping experience without the near-trauma he himself experienced while on his first venture roughing it, which was only a year prior, as it turns out.

Though the laughs are gentle and the scares benign, "The Legend of Satchmo" does lovingly capture the magical viewpoint wherein such hand-me-down legends as Bigfoot come alive in the minds of children, who lack the skepticism of their older kinfolk in such matters. For the kids involved, the mere telling of the tale brings Satchmo to life as vividly as any movie or actual sighting. This fantasy time within a younger child's life is too often ignored as a part of the underpinning of early obsession by many fans of Ciné du Sasquatch who were "indoctrinated" at a precocious age by hearing of a local legend regarding a bipedal cryptid. This is why this particular *Rugrats* episode is so accurate as well as entertaining. Even one's own backyard becomes a possible monster sighting zone when one is still young enough to see every shadow transformed into a lurking hominid, and each scrape of one's tent becomes the tell-tale claws of a sinister Sasquatch preparing to strike without mercy. Thus "The Legend of Satchmo" is a perfect early introduction for kids who show an interest in cryptozoology, as well as a nostalgic trip backwards for adults not too hardened to remember when camping out was a life-or-death struggle of epic magnitude that was not to be undertaken lightly.

Ryūsei no Rokkuman Toraibu (2007) (TV)

AKA: *Shooting Star Rockman*; *Mega Man Star Force*. Directed by Yūko Sera, Kencho Ishikawa, Masayuki Nomoto, Akira Takahashi, Shingo Adachi and Shintetsu Takiyama. Produced by TV Tokyo. Japan. Color. Stereo. 15 Minutes.

Overview: In the year 220X, Geo Stelar, an Earth-born super hero, and Omega-Xis, his otherworldly partner from FX Planet, fight invading aliens to protect Geo Stelar's home planet. By literally combining into one being (via a process known as "electromagnetic wave change"), the recombinant Mega Man (their shared identity) has increased powers to defeat the marauding extraterrestrials who are bent on destroying the invisible EM Wave World that exists in mankind's future. Said EM World is a futuristic version of the Internet but advanced to the point where humanity is as interconnected to it for survival as they are dependent upon oxygen to breathe.

The lost continent of Mu vanished long ago in Earth's history, but several rogue species from it still exist on the planet, scattered in hiding and patiently awaiting their opportunity to regain control of the human species. These Unidentified Mystery Animals (aka "UMAs") can morph into shared existences with willing *Homo sapiens* and wreak havoc. Mega Man, with the help of Doctor Vega, learns the UMAs are secretly working on opening a fissure into the Mu world and allowing the conduit to become the central vanguard of their new plot to conquer the Earth. An all-out battle between the mysterious lost creatures and Mega Man ensues, with the winner determining the fate of the world.

* * * * *

Ryūsei no Rokkuman Toraibu was launched by the influential Japanese videogame company Capcom for the Nintendo DS platform as *Mega Man Star Force*. Basically designed as a form of advertising for the videogames, *Ryūsei no Rokkuman Toraibu* was shown as a series of continuing 15-minute short form anime segments that appeared on Tokyo TV to introduce the characters, concepts, and narrative arcs of the videogame's milieu and popularize them among the handheld player's user base. The stealth marketing was successful, launching not only the game series but two years' worth of anime series as well as a line of manga. The second season of the franchise was called "Tribe" (aka "Toraibu") to distinguish it as a separate take on the first year's *Mega Man Star Force* episodes, with the focus shifted from outer space invaders to more earthly enemies. These residents of the lost continent of Mu were similar to the Cthulu Mythos of so-called "Elder Gods" created by H. P. Lovecraft, consisting of a mythic cadre of vanquished supernatural monsters intent on a return which will supplant the now-dominant human species.

The series posited that one of the remnant Mu denizens was the Abominable Snowman. Their evil leader, Yeti Blizzard, was a constant source of trouble as it battled Mega Man to obtain an artifact known as the Sword of Berserker, which bestowed upon its possessor enormous power. During the epic battle between good and evil, Mega Man and his allies eventually trace Yeti Blizzard to the Himalayas. There they uncover the lost civilization of Mu and battle Yeti Blizzard until the cryptid is defeated and dies, thus preventing it from securing the sword.

The interesting use of both Ciné du Sasquatch motifs and videogame-styled anime is like a cultural blending of *The X-Files, Astro Boy, The Matrix*, and the earlier animated series *Roswell Conspiracies: Aliens, Myths & Legends*. In fact, both *Astro Boy*'s encounter with an Abominable Snowman in its original anime run and *Roswell Conspiracies*' use of a clandestine Yeti tribe working against humankind feel like possible influences upon *Ryūsei no Rokkuman Toraibu*. The *Astro Boy* episode even has a lost city located inside the Himalayan Mountains, as does the Capcom-produced *Tribe* show; while the *Roswell Conspiracies* narrative makes a similar use of portraying the Yetis as a superior race of beings who are actually outer space aliens. While both concepts — hidden cities inside the Himalayans and outer space aliens using Earthly hominids for nefarious gain — are not novel to either *Astro Boy* or *Roswell Conspiracies*, the specificity of their depiction in *Ryūsei no Rokkuman Toraibu* seems calculated.

Regardless of influence, the result is largely successful, owing to the interesting mix of multi-cultural folklore and hard science fiction. The Yeti Blizzard character is drawn with a serious intent instead of for comic effect, which bestows upon it the level of threat necessary to make it a dramatically satisfying villain (at least, that is, as far as anime goes) — which was not for the earlier *Astro Boy* episode in which the robot tyke encountered a comical Abominable Snowman. The episodes that are key to Ciné du Sasquatch and best capture the spirit of the enterprise as a whole because they feature the Yeti storyline most prominently include the opening episode, "The Inheritance of Mu," followed by show number 5 ("The Yeti of the Himalayas") and

episode 6 ("The Mu Ruins of the Himalayas"), in which Mega Man confronts Yeti Blizzard and destroys the winter beast.

Sabrina, the Teenage Witch ("Witch Way Out") (2002) (TV) (Cameo)

AKA: *Sabrina*. Starring Melissa Joan Hart, Nick Bakay, Nate Richert, Caroline Rhea, Beth Broderick, Michelle Beaudoin, Paul Feig, Jenna Leigh Green, Lindsay Sloane, Alimi Ballard, Martin Mull, Jon Huertas, China Jesusita Shavers, Soleil Moon Frye, Elisa Donovan and Trevor Lissauer. Produced by Paula Hart, David Babcock, Tod Himmel, Kenneth Koch, Melissa Joan Hart, Torian Hughes, Trish Baker, Suzanne Gangursky and Bill Rosenthal. Written by Adam and David Hamburger. Directed by Brian K. Roberts. USA. Color. Stereo. 30 Minutes.

Overview: Sabrina Spellman, a normal teenager, discovers on her 16th birthday that she is anything but average. She is, in fact, a teenage witch, and is entrusted to her aunts Hilda and Zelda Spellman to learn the ways of witchery without inflicting too much damage on her surroundings or herself. Aided by Salem, her talking black cat, Sabrina ages into a young adult and masters her powers, entrusting only a few mortals with the secret of her abilities along the way.

In "Witch Way Out" Sabrina meets a charming, handsome art gallery dealer named Victor, who she instantly likes. Deciding she's mature now and beyond needing her magic powers, Sabrina stores them in a Tupperware container so she can attend a gallery opening to which Victor has invited her. Alas, her friends Morgan and Roxie refuse to let her go alone, acting on the buddy system. When Victor invites Sabrina to an after hours party at his home, however, Sabrina confronts her cohorts and alienates them by insisting she's now a grown-up who doesn't need chaperones. Offended, they leave her as she wishes.

At his mansion Victor is so well-connected he has the Goo Goo Dolls playing his private party. Impressed, Sabrina overhears Victor talking to a wealthy collector who states that Victor's private basement collection is the finest he has ever seen. While Victor is preoccupied, Sabrina slips into the basement to see for herself. To her shock, Victor is a collector of rare paranormal beings, including a mermaid, a leprechaun, a roaring Sasquatch, and an empty cage with a sign marked "witch" on it. Realizing she is the literal object of his interest, Sabrina tries to cast magic to solve her problem, but remembers she's left her magic mojo at home. She frantically calls Morgan and Roxie on her cell, but neither take her seriously, still angry at her rejection of their company.

Victor surprises Sabrina and drags her down into his basement zoo, explaining he's been searching the world over for a genuine witch — including Wichita, Kansas — with no luck until he stumbled across Sabrina. She is jailed, and all looks hopeless. Meanwhile, her friends figure out her predicament and rush to help her. Sabrina's powers are restored, and she transports Victor into the cell with Sasquatch, whereupon Bigfoot beats the wealthy monster collector without mercy. After allowing the cryptid to thrash Victor for a while to teach him a lesson, Sabrina sends all of the magical creatures back to their respective homes, thus ending Victor's evil scheme.

* * * * *

Sabrina, the Teenage Witch was a very loose adaptation of the Archie Comics character, given a much more familiar sitcom setting and tone. In essence, it played very much like a younger-set version of *Bewitched*, the classic Elizabeth Montgomery comedy TV series from the 1960s. While *Sabrina* lacked *Bewitched*'s better quality writing, direction, and (not least importantly) Montgomery's comely vision of a witch in suburbia, it nonetheless managed to enjoy a successful run of seven years — truly a lucky number for *Sabrina*'s many fans, who watched lead actress Melissa Joan Hart grow from spunky teenager to mature adult during the show's span.

This episode's appearance by Sasquatch was brief indeed, but memorable. The costume is suitably impressive for a low-budget sitcom, with the creature towering over the tiny Hart in a most convincing manner. Too, when the caged leprechaun tells the bewildered Sabrina that Victor, the evil collector, keeps the hominid well-fed on a diet of campers, the writers demonstrate they're well aware of just how preposterous is the conceit of this episode — if not the entire series — and how to deftly craft camp comedy from the material. It's also quite satisfying to see the roaring Sasquatch savagely beat the playboy Victor and throw him around inside the relatively small cage. Unlike most such scenes, the violence is played strictly for laughs and therefore allows for an unrestricted sense of overkill by the actor portraying Bigfoot as he exaggerates his pounding of the staggering Victor.

By this point in *Sabrina, the Teenage Witch* the title was as misplaced as Hart's older persona itself. With Hart now clearly an adult in her mid-twenties, the series attempted to play upon the obviousness of Hart's maturity and more robust figure by having her move out on her own, become a young professional, and seriously date men in hopes of finding true love. While the attempt was noble, the comedy is resultantly strained and the series' modest charms threadbare by this, the show's final, season. Wisely, the producers (including Hart, who produced some of the episodes as well) seemed to realize the material had long since played out and mercifully retired the concept. As for Ciné du Sasquatch, *Sabrina, the Teenage Witch*'s use of Bigfoot is strictly by the book, even if said book is the *Necronomicon*. It's good for a few laughs but little else.

Sasquatch (2002)

AKA: *The Untold*. Starring Lance Henriksen, Andrea Roth, Russell Ferrier, Philip Granger, Jeremy Radick, Mary Mancini, Taras Kostyuk, Erica Durance, Rob Clark and Scantone Jones. Produced by Rob Clark, Mike Curb, Craig Denton, Bergman Lustig, Carole Curb Nemoy and Glen Reynolds. Written by Jonas Quastel and Chris Lanning. Directed by Jonas Quastel. Canada. Color. Stereo. 92 Minutes.

Overview: When wealthy industrialist Harland Knowles' private jet crashes in the remote Canadian wilderness with his only daughter is onboard, the millionaire hurriedly assembles an expert team to accompany him into the forests in search of his missing offspring. Lacking definitive proof of her demise, Knowles hangs onto the slim hope she somehow survived, along with the rest of her flight companions. A self-made man, Knowles puts his rescue group members on edge with his perfectionist insistence on running the emergency operation his way no matter how unorthodox or demanding his methods.

Critical time passes without initial success; it's as if the jet has vanished from the face of the Earth, as it is nowhere near where its coordinates suggest it should have crashed. Unbeknownst to Knowles and his team, Sasquatch has observed their arrival and begun to stalk them as they move deeper into its territory.

Inevitable tensions arise among the group of would-be rescuers. Knowles in particular fuels their suspicions, as they come to believe his secretive manner suggests he has ulterior motives beyond finding his daughter. Adding to their woes is the forced admission by their hunting guide that he's been a virtual shut-in for months in his New York City penthouse, too alcoholic to function because he's developed agoraphobia — a definite handicap for a renowned hunter who makes his living fearlessly confronting the unknown at the behest of his wealthy clientele.

Soon one of the group's female scientists is attacked at night by Bigfoot and dragged screaming from her tent. She escapes, super-

ficially wounded and convinced, despite what the others believe, that they are not being stalked by a bear but by Sasquatch. Next, the jet wreckage is discovered, but far from where it should have been found. Inside, Knowles' daughter has left behind a camcorder which reveals the fate of all aboard the craft who survived — they were besieged by a Sasquatch tribe and forced to make a losing stand against the roaring cryptids. After dragging the wreckage away to confuse any humans who may arrive to help, the creatures dragged the humans out, one by one, until even Knowles' daughter met the same fate as all the rest — devoured alive by the angry monsters.

Knowles is devastated but refuses to turn back, despite confirmation of the tragic demise of his daughter and the other members of the doomed flight. Questioned by the rescue team, he admits the other motive he's kept from them for his desperate search: the only working prototype of a new Knowles Industry invention — a DNA analyzer called the "Huxley" — was also lost in the crashed flight. He must return with the Huxley in order to keep his financial empire intact. Without disclosing it to the rest of the team, however, Knowles has actually found the Huxley and hidden it away in his own gear. Knowles' intent slowly dawns on the rest as they make their way deeper into the woods — he seeks revenge against the creatures, not the Huxley.

But the Sasquatch that is tracking their every move will not allow them to escape nor track it any more deeply into its domain. It begins to kill off the team members as they attempt to outmaneuver it, and they fall prey to the monster's superior instinct for survival. The remaining team members realize that Knowles has the Huxley and that the reason the Sasquatch will not allow the industrialist to leave with it is because Knowles' daughter has placed a hair sample into the Huxley. Since such DNA proof would reveal the existence of the hominids, the creature must prevent the knowledge from reaching the outside world in an attempt to preserve its merely mythic status. The team argues with Knowles that they must leave the Huxley behind and allow the species to survive without detection — it is the only way the creature will allow them to escape. Knowles refuses, arming himself with his rifle and bidding them farewell. They leave and make a dash for freedom.

Knowles finally comes face to face with his pursuer. Before he shoots it, Knowles and the creature share a knowing moment between themselves. Each seems to recognize what the other has lost in the tragic encounter — Knowles a daughter, and, as it turns out, the Sasquatch its own mate when the jet crashed into the woods and inadvertently killed it. With a stalemate now in effect, Knowles abandons the Huxley and leaves the forest, realizing he must keep the story to himself in order to rectify the damage he has already done to all involved.

* * * * *

Sasquatch has some noteworthy values many recent genre entries lack. It was shot on location in authentically rugged locations, which gives it a feeling of plausibility that many of the lower cost Ciné du Sasquatch efforts lack. It also offers some blackly humorous twists, such as a hunter who is agoraphobic and terrified of the wilderness (but who doesn't reveal this fact until his dependent team members are well into the worst of their desperate circumstances, thus lengthening their already long shot for survival). Alas, this also works against *Sasquatch* at times, as the comedic level rubs against the serious tone the film is also attempting to maintain. Even Hitchcock, a master of such tricky suspense and comedy balancing acts, occasionally failed when he went over-the-top in such efforts as *The Trouble with Harry*. And for all its good intents, of course, *Sasquatch* is far from *North by Northwest* in this regard.

Sasquatch has the value of a seasoned cast, though the script's severe limitations force the viewer to keep this in an overall trade-off perspective — as professional as many of the actors are, they cannot overcome the weakness of the roles written for them. Veteran character actor Lance Henriksen enjoys a rare lead role which he clearly relishes, and fans of his steely-eyed personage will not be disappointed by the immense amount of screen time given him. His intense scowl and weathered features seem made for a Sergio Leone western (he'd make an excellent Lee Van Cleef replacement in any remake of *The Good, the Bad, and the Ugly*). Too, knowing his character is suffering from the loss of a loved one, à la *The Searchers*, is a good if too-familiar plot device which adds some much-needed sympathy for Knowles as a protagonist. Henriksen brings the lingering pain and sadness to credible life throughout *Sasquatch*, and as a result, this is the rare Ciné du Sasquatch entry that features a likeable, well-motivated lead character instead of a mere cipher.

Andrea Roth is equally good in the film, playing the ultimate power-grabbing bitch, a role she seems to relish. A career TV actress with credits ranging from *Robocop*, *Forever Knight*, *Rescue Me*, and *CSI: Miami*, Roth plays a conniving hustler and blackmailer who will stop at nothing to force Knowles into sharing his new Huxley DNA analyzer's profits with her. A one-woman forest femme fatale, she delights in her arch villainess portrayal, eyes bright and shining, lips fully poised, even as she chews Knowles' own black heart out. Though the character is two-dimensional at best, Roth's unadulterated, sneering nastiness in the face of securing an economic fortune with a fast kill has the kind of conniving brutality not often seen outside of film noir.

Alas, *Sasquatch* was a very rushed production, as the disappointed director reveals on the DVD's commentary track. He also laments that he was only made aware that the title of the film had been changed from *The Untold* (the production's shooting title) to *Sasquatch* a few minutes before the studio session in which he records the director's commentary — definitely poor timing on the producers' part. Nor is he pleased with the additional editing he observes for the first time as he watches the film. One has to wonder if the producers had any common sense or great concern about the final film if they failed to even let their director know about any of them until he is recording the DVD commentary!

For all its good intentions, *Sasquatch* mostly stumbles over its own limitations. Too often the expository and largely unbelievable nature of the dialogue works against the story's best interests, with characters frequently speaking about plot contrivances instead of establishing character conflicts. And apart from Henriksen and Roth, the rest of the roles are clichéd in terms of the genre, typically underwritten and overly familiar in nature. There is the Expert, the Nerd, the Dumb Blonde, etc., with little given in the way of character development or insight. Nor is the plot novel (even if it's true to the formula of the genre, with the characters first having to battle their way into a harsh environment before battling their way back out to survive the pursuing Savage Sasquatch). To its credit, there are some minor plot twists that are unexpected, particularly the DNA analyzer having decoded the Sasquatch hair sample and thus providing irrefutable proof of the creatures' existence. Alas, these scattered attempts to deviate the overall narrative away from what is a predictable outcome fail on the whole as *Sasquatch* limps to its conclusion.

The actual cryptid suit is unique in that it doesn't resemble the usual gorilla mask and suit of most low-budget efforts. Rather, the effects team has created a "wild man of the woods" variant which emphasizes not only the empathetic nature of the creature but also suggests its closely-shared genetic history with *Homo sapiens*. It has an unusually rounded, bald skull (most Bigfoot masks and make-up designers tend to emphasize the sagittal crest associated with primates, a characteristic often noted in Sasquatch sightings), thus implying a

The empathetic Sasquatch (Taras Kostyuk) from *Sasquatch* is more human-like than most Ciné du Sasquatch depictions.

connection between itself and mankind. The director cleverly withholds the close-ups of the creature until the final moments of the film, and shoots the majority of its appearances à la *The Legend of Boggy Creek* — with telephoto lenses and quick glimpses of the cryptid as it darts in and out of cover, thus obscuring any lingering looks at it.

Some reviewers have suggested the creature's "heat vision" ability to see at night is a lift from *Predator*, but this is an effect that predates both features (one example is Michael Wadleigh's underrated *Wolfen*, which utilizes a similar infrared technique when the viewer is shown the wolves' points of view). And indeed, this technique has become so over-utilized in the Bigfoot film genre as to have become a visual cliché. Still, it at least suggests how it is possible that such a large-scale monster as Sasquatch could retain the element of surprise while stalking humans at night in a densely overgrown forest — the cryptid could move quietly until it was upon its unwitting prey.

Mildly disappointing — but understandably so, given its 12-day shooting schedule (in a forest locale no less) — *Sasquatch* comes and goes without making much of a lasting impression, at least in terms of Ciné du Sasquatch itself. As entertainment, however, it's competent but rarely more. Given the talent involved, however, one wishes a better script and a longer shooting schedule had been available, as this might have given the film a shot at rising above the ranks of merely average.

Sasquatch: Legend Meets Science (2003) (TV) (Doc)

Featuring Dr. Daris Swindler, Dr. Esteban Sarmiento, Professor Jeff Meldrum, Dr. Robert Benson, Officer Jimmy Chilcutt, Dr. Craig Newton, Dr. Russel Ciochon and Dr. John Bindernagel. Produced and Directed by Doug Haijcek. USA. Color. Stereo. 60 Minutes.

Overview: Originally broadcast by the Discovery Channel, *Sasquatch: Legend Meets Science* was later re-edited by producer and director Doug Haijcek to include additional materials. In essence, it is an attempt to examine the best available evidence at the time of its production by various experts in their respective fields and render scientific observations based on their in-depth appraisal.

Among the many featured scientists are: primate specialist Dr. Daris Swindler of Washington State University and Dr. Esteban Sarmiento of the American Museum of Natural History in New York City, who examine the infamous Skookum Cast collected by the

Bigfoot Field Research Organization and render their opinions; anthropologist and renowned Bigfoot expert Jeff Meldrum from Idaho State University, who also critiques the Skookum footprint; Dr. Robert Benson, an acoustical expert from Texas A & M, who analyzes supposed Sasquatch vocalizations recorded during Bigfoot expeditions in the wilds; Officer Jimmy Chilcutt, a fingerprinting expert, who explains about the dermal ridges that he believes authenticate the footprints he's cast at several Bigfoot sighting areas; Dr. Craig Newton, a scientist who specializes in DNA sampling from BC Research in Canada, who discusses the inherent problems and advantages of one day providing proof using genetic testing of hair samples and related genetic markings from a Sasquatch; and Dr. Russel Ciochon, who covers the presumed extinct *Gigantopithecus* species as a possible Bigfoot explanation.

Of particular interest to Bigfoot aficionados will be the digitally-enhanced analysis of the famous Patterson-Gimlin film from 1967, as well as frame-by-frame clarification of the 1994 Paul Freeman and 1996 Memorial Day video footage, both of which purport to show Bigfoot. Jeff Meldrum also published a non-fiction book called *Sasquatch: Legend Meets Science* as a companion tome to the DVD.

Sasquatch Assault (2009)

AKA: *Assault of the Sasquatch*. Featuring Kevin Shea, Greg Nutcher, Sarah J. Ahearn, Cristina Santiago, Andrea Sáenz, Alex Exum, Hank Torrance, Jason Criscoulo, Cuyle Carvin, Shawn C. Phillips, M. Kelley,

Poster art for the marketing of *Assault of the Sasquatch* (aka *Sasquatch Assault*).

Michael Wrann, Sari Gagnon, Paul Melluzzo, J. Matthew Root and Kerry McGann. Produced by Andrew Gernhard, M. Sridharan and Kevin Shea. Written by John Doolan. Directed by Andrew Gernhard. USA. Color. Stereo. 90 Minutes.

Overview: Grizzled poacher Terry Drake accidentally snares a live Bigfoot. He tranquilizes the beast, but only after it attacks and kills Drake's two young hired helpers. Game warden Ryan Walker, a former big city cop who now works the relative safety of the wilds, arrives with his partner and arrests the gray-haired poacher. Walker drives the truck into the outskirts of the nearby big city and to a jailhouse he knows can book and process Drake. It is the same jail facility where he used to be employed.

Drake is placed in solitary confinement, which is easier to accomplish than even Walker had hoped because the other cells are all empty. It turns out this is the last night of operation for the soon-to-be-closed facility, hence its nearly abandoned status. Meanwhile, Sasquatch bursts free from Drake's truck, where the creature has been slumbering. Disoriented, it hides in the urban jail's downtrodden alleyways. It is spotted by two amateur cryptozoologists, a Laurel and Hardy duo named Don and Murph, who videotape the cryptid with their camera. Determined they are on the trail of the greatest mystery ever to be resolved, the hysterical Don and laconic Murph set out to track down the beast and gather even more definitive proof of Bigfoot's existence.

A murderous psychopath named Colletti is arrested and brought into the nearly-closed jail. He is revealed to be the same man who murdered Walker's wife back when Walker was a big city cop, though Colletti only served 8 years in prison because he tricked the prosecutors into believing he was only an accomplice to the act. Walker is naturally furious to see the man who killed his mate free again, but relieved that at least Colletti has been arrested, which should put him back behind bars for probation violation if no other reason. Jessica, Walker's daughter who was traumatized as a young girl when she witnessed her mother being killed by Colletti, spits on him behind bars and vows revenge for the pain he has caused her through the years. He laughs in her face and curses her.

Jameson, a rookie cop with a crush on Jessica, waits until she is gone and then warns Colletti to never again insult the love of his life. Colletti takes advantage of the rookie's mistake and pins him against the cell bars, killing him in cold blood. Setting himself free of the cell, Colletti escapes into the bowels of the closed station, but not before shutting off all electricity to the comatose facility. The survivors regroup after realizing they're now all alone without the ability to communicate. Worse, Drake's confiscated trailer containing the Sasquatch is now empty; the monster is on the prowl. Meanwhile, teen cryptozoologists Don and Murph run into Sasquatch — quite literally when the hyperactive Don plows into the upright hominid while failing to watch where he's headed. Sasquatch takes his revenge by ripping off Don's face and then impaling the fleeing Murph with a dislodged traffic sign pole. The horrified survivors stranded in the station watch as Murph slowly dies, unable to help him.

Eventually, Sasquatch begins preying on the station occupants, picking them off one by one. However, Colletti proves to be an equally cunning nemesis, interfering in events in such a way that many innocents fall victim to death by Bigfoot. After much death and destruction, Colletti pays the ultimate price for his murderous arrogance at the claws of the creature, as does Drake. With Drake's death settled and the monster's score evened, Sasquatch lumbers off into the dark alleyways of the big city, having made the adjustment to its new environment. The grateful few station survivors who make it to dawn and a new chance at life marvel at the events they've endured, staring at the empty space where moments previously the world's most famous cryptid once stood.

* * * * *

John Carpenter's classic exploitation film *Assault on Precinct 13* (itself a police station updating of the stand-out Western siege film *Rio Bravo* by Howard Hawks) is given a Bigfoot makeover in this fun, lightweight, but still quite entertaining example of postmodern Ciné du Sasquatch filmmaking. Both Hawks' and Carpenter's films feature a shared conceit of having law enforcement officials having to barricade themselves in their own facilities in order to withstand a siege from external forces. But whereas these films use precise, ever-tightening series of bravado set pieces to sustain their laconic narratives, *Sasquatch Assault* is a rambling, more episodic affair. It prefers, and quickly establishes, the

Sasquatch (Jason Criscoulo) roams the shadowy alleyways of a decaying urban police station in *Sasquatch Assault*. (Photograph courtesy Andrew Gernhard.)

more classical exploitation film's sense of striving for shock over suspense, and laughs over any leaden seriousness.

In many ways, *Sasquatch Assault* plays like a knowing throwback to Lloyd Kaufman's Troma Studios. There is a deliberate tongue-in-cheek quality to the proceedings that, while never completely venturing into camp, gives the overall production a remarkably funny veneer. This is atypical in far too many Bigfoot films, much to their detriment. A sense of humor when dealing with the fantastic and monstrous in cinema goes a long way towards establishing a rapport with viewing audiences. Yes, a leap of faith is required, but rewards are forthcoming as a result of its granting. Though violent and occasionally violence-filled, *Sasquatch Assault* is more energetically likeable than terrifyingly scary, which is again why its humor works so effectively, as the tonal balance is maintained in favor of laughs over gore throughout most of its running time. It will appeal to the cult fans who appreciate such outings as Stuart Gordon's *The Re-Animator* and *The Human Centipede*— horror films laced with a mordant sense of black humor and featuring occasionally shocking violence to keep the viewer off-balance.

It never rewrites Ciné du Sasquatch as a genre, but *Sasquatch Assault* does show a sensibility that suggests its makers are well aware of the *oeuvre*'s pitfalls. Much of this delightfully askew sensibility is achieved by the comic mania of Shawn C. Phillips, who plays his ADD-riddled crypto-hound with all the earnestness one might expect from cub reporter Jimmy Olsen if he had imbibed a few espressos too many on the way to work one morning. While onscreen, Phillips rips into his material with an unrestrained sense of sheer hysteria reminiscent of Jack Nicholson's early screen role in Roger Corman's *Little Shop of Horrors*. Given how many of the other performers are scenery chewers, it's no small feat for Phillips to turn his sweating, overweight wreck of a human being into such a likeable slob. Other fun, over-the-top performances include Kevin Shea as Drake, who is all rotten teeth and seedy pirate (a kind of Snake Plissken 20 years past his prime), and Andrea Sáenz as Amy Steel, an ex-stripper with a lethal penchant for self-defense. The rest of the cast are equally professional and acquit themselves well, which gives the overall film a competency often lacking in low-budget Ciné du Sasquatch movies.

The creature visualization is quintessential in terms of later-era Bigfoot incarnations. With long, shaggy fur and a snarling, ape-like face, this is one nasty-looking hominid. The touch of having Sasquatch wear a crude necklace of past hunting souvenirs, such as victims' bones and whatnot, is both ghoulishly effective and unusual in the genre. It creates a sense that the hominid is more human in nature than animal, in that it shares the *Homo sapiens* habits of

Amy Steel (Andrea Saenz) prepares to fight to the death when she is forced to withstand a frenzied *Sasquatch Assault*. (Photograph courtesy Andrew Gernhard.)

collecting totem fetishes (which, ironically, both soldiers and serial killers often do as well) and exacting vengeance against a deserving set of enemies. Alas, in this instance the enemies are any and all human beings the creature comes into contact with, as it has the predilection for reacting with lethal force more often than not. In fact, every human involved, save Drake, seems to have no idea how dangerous and savage a Sasquatch can become if provoked or captured. Drake alone has respect for what he has brought into conflict with the modern world, slightly echoing the Carl Denham character's sense of appreciation for the tragedy of King Kong's demise while denying all personal responsibility. Drake is much like this, only gruffer and foul-mouthed, and his self-interest and callous reaction to the deaths he has indirectly caused (just like Carl Denham) is only matched by his greed, his only motivating factor in life. When Sasquatch finally dispatches Drake, there is a palpable sense that some sense of moral order, however perverse and tenuous, has been restored to this fictitious cinematic world. In a bizarre way, it is as if *King Kong* has been reversed, with Denham paying for his arrogance with his life and Kong left alive to explore the city at will, having already adapted to the new environment.

The Sasquatch Gang (2006)

Starring Justin Long, Jeremy Sumpter, Addie Land, Joey Kern, Rob Pinkston, Michael Mitchell, Hubbel Palmer, Jon Gries, Ray Santiago, Jeff D'Agostino, Carl Weathers, Stephen Tobolowsky, Veanne Cox, Jon Heder, Rebecca Lowe, Katie O'Grady, Don Adler, Val Landrum, Todd Skousen, Hayley Skousen and Scott Coopwood. Produced by Craig Anderson, Dana Brunette, Jeremy Coon, Randy Holleschau, Adam Kassen, Mark Kassen and Kevin Spacey. Written and Directed by Tim Skousen. USA. Color. Stereo. 86 Minutes.

Overview: Told in a series of interwoven and often intricately interlaced flashbacks, like a cinematic reincarnation of *Rashomon* meets graphic novel, *The Sasquatch Gang* details the story of a handful of small-town locals who discover what they believe to be a "dumpling" left by a squatting Sasquatch. After recovering the scat sample, an innocent, fantasy game role-playing nerd named Gavin and his like-minded fantasy-obsessed friends decide to alert the media and see if there really is a Bigfoot living in their nearby state park. Meanwhile, we also meet Zerk Wilder, an all–American unabashed Tea Party–styled super patriot and heavy metal rocker dude who is in debt to his creditors. So far has Zerk fallen behind on his payments that his beloved Pontiac Firebird has been added to the repossession team's hit list, meaning Zerk's wheels could be taken at any moment. Along with his shirtless buddy Shirts Jokum, a corn-dog eating simpleton, Zerk decides to cash in on the Sasquatch hokum that is brewing in the community and circumvent the nerd trio of Gavin and his circle of geek buddies. His plan: raise the fast cash necessary to pay off his Firebird debt by selling plaster cast replicas of the Sasquatch dumpling itself on eBay.

The expected media circus arrives and increases until a self-promoting cryptozoological "expert" named Dr. Artimus Snodgrass shows up to verify the evidence by examining the dumpling itself. While the live TV cameras roll, Snodgrass sniffs the dumpling and then proclaims it authentic hominid scat, to the town's shouts of happiness. A quick glimpse of the actual Sasquatch by the still-innocent Gavin and his friends puts the proverbial icing on the cake as the summation of what has been the best bonding experience of their shared friendships.

* * * * *

It seems sometimes as if *The Sasquatch Gang* cannot be mentioned without the obligatory link to *Napolean Dynamite*, which much of the key talent behind *The Sasquatch Gang* previously worked upon.

While there is a similar sense of nostalgia for a teenage time when everything still seemed possible, *The Sasquatch Gang* is much less deadpan and much more narratively dense. There is a lot of plotting going on in the film that is invisible until cleverly riffed on later in the story. This kind of layering of repeating motifs and visual gags is what gives *The Sasquatch Gang* its very refreshing sense of playfulness. For once it doesn't feel as if the talent behind the lens is an adult trying to calculate how to play down to his teen audience, but rather how best to capture the awkwardness and alienation without giving in to despair and lessening the comic lightheartedness. That's a tough balance to establish and maintain, and to the filmmakers' credit, they do a wonderful job of keeping the story moving along with absurd leaps and bounds whenever the film threatens to become predictable.

The cast is terrific. As Zerk Wilder, Justin Long captures the youthful restlessness and seething boredom as the rebel without a cause (and soon to be without his Firebird if he doesn't come up with the cash) with a comic intensity as sincere as his mullet hairdo. Long is no stranger to the genre, having also had a turn as one of the gang of Sasquatch nature photographers in *Strange Wilderness*. But here he's given a full range of scenes to show how much better he can flesh out a characterization. Likewise for his absent-minded but well-meaning buddy Shirts Jokum, played to perfection by Joey Kern. Not since Sean Penn brought to life the authentic memories of his childhood surfer friends as Spicoli for *Fast Times at Ridgemont High* has an actor inhabited a teen dolt so convincingly. Carl Weathers is clearly enjoying his cameo at Dr. Snodgrass, the Carl Denham archetype that's here used only for laughs. Snodgrass is like the actor's own Apollo Creed character from the *Rocky* films: a self-loving, hustling media whore always sniffing for the next crypto chance to get on camera. The satirical nature is obvious and never mean-spirited which is laudable, as there exists a faction within the Bigfoot believers' community who fit the Dr. Artimus Snodgrass bill a little too closely for comfort. Still, it's a case where a few bad apples should not reflect on the rest of those honest and sincere believers just because they share a common faith.

The execution in terms of comic timing and deft characterization is beyond what might be expected from a second-time feature filmmaker. The direction and pacing are very self-assured and without visual excess, concentrating on the characters and telling the story in simple, believably comical turns. The Sasquatch suit was a loaner from one of the crew members who is a fan of the cryptid and therefore had his own costume to lend to the production for its fleeting cameo. Given its private (versus professional) nature of creation, it outshines many bigger-budgeted films whose hominid costumes were no more realistic for the difference in monies spent. *The Sasquatch Gang* features a color-saturated framing device that literally makes the picture play like a comic graphic novel. This device also allows the filmmakers to move without chronological restriction in the narrative, as the focus veers from one set of characters to another, as if one were flipping pages in a graphic novel. In lesser hands it would play as little more than so much cinematic window dressing; instead, the director uses it to compress time, examine differing narrative points of view, and help maintain the clarity of the story's overall arc. For once, the framing device helps, not harms, the overall film.

Those who object to a Ciné du Sasquatch effort in which the hominid doesn't even appear (save for a brief cameo) may feel slighted, as if the film is playing upon their expectations and not delivering the cryptid goods. For viewers who only seek a Savage Sasquatch and the commiserate flow of blood that it brings, there will be little to hold their interest in *The Sasquatch Gang*. Its gentle but prodding sense of character humor will probably not satisfy, nor even be apparent to, this segment of the viewing audience. For most viewers, however, a pleasant, lighthearted comedy of manners and mannerisms await in a goofy but enticing satire. Technically well-crafted at every level, *The Sasquatch Gang* (formerly called *The Sasquatch Dumpling Gang* before distributors became nervous about the possible Disney wrath re: that studio's own *The Apple Dumpling Gang*) is a rarity: a Bigfoot movie that is also a real crowd-pleaser.

The Sasquatch Hunters (1997)

Starring Courtney Hall, John A. McDermott, Paul Reasbeck, Melinda Kaye Messenger, David Richmond, Ron Thronson, Vince Parenti, Jeff Ferreri and Lia Johnson. Produced by Brian Fujii and Marc Messenger. Written by William Mertz and Marc Messenger. Directed by Marc Messenger. USA. Color. Stereo. 73 Minutes.

Overview: Three competing groups are profiled, all with direct ties to Bigfoot research. The Bigfoot Society is an amateur group of hardcore converts; the American Hominid Association is a government-funded watchdog agency; and the renegade band known as the Michigan Cryptozoological Institute is funded by a wealthy eccentric who is dedicated to making social in-roads for Bigfoot and fellow hominid species as they take their debut turn in society's spotlight. Each of the three groups is wackier than a cult of suicide bombers. The filmmakers are not singling out Bigfoot believers per se, as much as they are using Bigfoot believers as a way to explore the comic obsessions of Americans from all walks of life who are caught up in any unusual hobby, fascination, or trade.

For example, the small-time group known as the Bigfoot Society has a hard time just keeping its members from brawling when they get together. To say there is some personality conflict is an understatement. Whenever anyone attempts to resolve the unstated conflict, however, the other society members react dysfunctionally, either ignoring the problem or enabling it. Soon one tearful researcher implores his fellow researcher to go 'squatching with him at the friend's trailer home front door, and then savagely turns on his friend when he won't come outside, railing against his friend's shortcomings, loudly and vocally, in front of the other stunned members. As the obstacles to proving the reality of the elusive hominid mount, so do the pressures on the competing strains of Bigfoot field researchers, causing laughter and nervous tension at the same time. Which group, if any, will triumph and produce the critical breakthrough physical evidence before they all file for bankruptcy?

* * * * *

Very loosely structured like a series of videotaped improvisational comedy scenes, *The Sasquatch Hunters* is a semi-professional but seriously funny look at the comedic dysfunctionality of a range of humans failing at the very obsessions with fame and glory that define them as American searchers — from amateurs who undertake an activity out of love, to highly paid professionals who hold in contempt any who are not of their income rank and privilege status, and to nutty fringe cult members who believe Bigfoot must be welcomed into American society with full dignity and respect. How each little tribe of *Homo sapiens* navigate the treacherous traps set for them by their own members out of petty jealousy or spite is the source of most of the loose, freewheeling comic fun that enlivens *The Sasquatch Hunters* and makes it memorable for such a modest-budgeted picture. Though relentlessly shot in a verite camera manner that can be tiring, *The Sasquatch Hunters* also manages to use it for devastating comic effect, using the swooping camera to close in on an actor's face and reveal subtle thoughts of betrayal and impatience, all of which go towards elevating the comic stakes and dramatic payoff.

The film is well aware of the Ciné du Sasquatch genre's stereotypes and thrives in presenting its own variations. They include a stern adventurer type, like a 1970s Robert Morgan updated for the picture's modern setting; a Grover Krantz clone who defends the Patterson-

Gimlin footage and most footprint casts as legitimate evidence; and, of course, the sincere True Believers themselves, who mean no harm and only wish to contribute to the betterment of mankind's understanding with their voluntary efforts. The latter, of course, provides for a wellspring of unintentional humor at the expense of the Bigfoot Believers as they encounter and overcome the skepticism of their fellow society members. And it's not just the hominid believers, either, who are harassed, for the government agents soon feel the heat themselves when the public begins making small protests against the wasting of taxpayer dollars on such nonsense as hominid patrols. It is not unlike watching a spiritualist believer struggle with his faith as he wanders among the lost souls of a major metropolis, as each set of Bigfoot camps deals with their respective setbacks in their chosen field of shared endeavor. The feeling is palpable that by far the hardest part of researching Sasquatch is having to come into contact with ourselves first, as we're the largest obstacle in our own way to any investigation. Indeed, when Sasquatch finally rears his hirsute head in the finale and boards a nearby UFO for galaxies unknown (having had enough of humans relentlessly stalking him for profit), it feels exactly right — like the coda that followed every Elvis Presley concert that the legendary man of the moment has indeed left the building, ladies and gentlemen.

With its long, hand-held takes and measured laughs in small doses, *The Sasquatch Hunters* is a quirky gem of fun, rough around the production edges but with lots of glimmering little carats beneath the flaws. It has never been officially released, but is worth the search to Ciné du Sasquatch fans who will appreciate its quirky, offbeat examination of their own society's foibles and flaws, as well as strengths and acts of redemption. It is fun and lighthearted, but with unexpected poignancy now and again to give it a bit of gravitas.

Sasquatch Hunters (2005)

Starring Matt Lattimore, Amy Shelton-White, Kevin O'Connor, Gary Sturm, David Zelina, Juliana Dever, Stacey Branscombe, Rick Holland, Samuel Mongiello, Thomas Webb, Paul Wensley and Matthew Tait. Produced by Jenny Hinkey, Alain Matz, Martha Post, Erwin Tepper, Fred Tepper, Silvia Tepper and Tom Zimmerman. Written by Alain Matz, Fred Tepper and Tom Zimmerman. Directed by Fred Tepper. USA. Color. Stereo. 88 Minutes.

Overview: Dr. Helen Gilber, a young woman cryptozoologist, and Dr. Ethan Edwards, a middle-aged male paleontologist, seek clues to the possible existence of a North American ape after a colleague shows them a bone fragment belonging to an unknown primate species found in the United States. After pinpointing the location where the bones were found, the duo venture into the remote woods in search of additional evidence.

In order to insure their safety in the wilderness, they request the assistance of a cadre of park rangers, who range from experienced to novice in their professional status. Soon after embarking, the group discovers a slaughtered bear, left uneaten and hanging from a high tree's limbs. No known predator attacks and leaves its prey untouched in this manner save for deranged humans, surmise the park rangers, which triggers worry among the team: Is a madman loose in the forest? Equally unsettling is the complete lack of animal wildlife in the area; it's as if they've been scared away.

Eventually the expedition uncovers a primitive burial ground. They dig through the unmarked graves, uncovering massive skeletal remains of the sought-after primate species. The remains are obviously not ancient, suggesting there may still be living specimens. The paleontologist believes the bones resemble those of the monstrous *Gigantopithecus*, an extinct primate species unearthed in China.

Unfortunately for the team members, the Sasquatch tribe retrieves and re-buries the bones during the night, none-too-pleased with the humans and their violation of the sacred burial site. They attack the expedition in a merciless series of assaults in an attempt to reclaim their invaded territory. One by one the humans are slaughtered as they make their way back to civilization, until only a few are left as survivors.

*****

By now, even the most casual reader will have likely noticed the singular pattern which prevails in the plot descriptions of the average Savage Sasquatch entry. With only modest variation on the formula, the scenario typically plays out with a team of humans invading the domain of Sasquatch, only to be picked off one after another as they flee to safety. Indeed, this very formula (with only minor variation in the run-for-one's-life ending) is found in the first ever cryptid movie from almost a century earlier — Méliès' seminal *The Conquest of the Pole*.

While the above distillation may seem reductionist to the point of absurdity in describing so many Ciné du Sasquatch films, the fact remains that this is the general plot of nearly every Bigfoot film of the Savage Sasquatch type. While individual entries often change minor details (varying locations, different character stereotypes and diverse depictions of Bigfoot), the banal reality is that most alterations to the formula are less directed towards plot and more towards the needless variants of well-established "slaughter mechanics" from such film series as *Friday the 13th*, *Saw*, and their endless carbon copies. If the viewer seeks an accurate body count, in other words, then detailing the typical Savage Sasquatch movie as such makes sense.

One can equally fault (for but one example) Agatha Christie's works (such as *Ten Little Indians* or *And Then There Were None*) using the same criteria: They, too, invariably entail a group of isolated individuals who are systematically murdered one by one until an expedient solution is devised by a sleuth in the proverbial nick of time. Fair enough, but the key difference lies in execution and novelty. The usual murder mystery follows a generalized formula, but the particulars and characters tend to vary greatly, thus giving the reader or viewer a basis from which to solve the puzzle presented. The average entry in the Savage Sasquatch movie, in contrast, steadfastly refuses to deviate from the tried-and-true clichéd approach, rarely, if ever, offering originality or surprise. It is as if the filmmakers have never before seen a previous Ciné du Sasquatch offering, and so walk in the same footsteps as all preceding entries. Imagine if film noir directors and writers centered almost every film they made on a protagonist who has been unknowingly poisoned and only has a handful of days left alive to find out who and why he is a dead man walking (as in *D.O.A.*, the seminal noir directed by cinematographer Rudolph Maté). This is the problematic stance filmmakers who make any cryptid cinema foray face unless they are well-versed in the genre's precedents.

Naturally, many horror films use stock situations and characters in order to invoke audience terror, and so faulting Savage Sasquatch filmmakers for incorporating these crossover elements is indeed setting a high standard to overcome. But how many films in this field can be made before some talented filmmaker realizes that only the most nascent film viewer has not seen a scantily-clad woman walking through the darkest woods with only a flashlight at her bare side, nor viewed countless clones of the same cat-and-mouse stalking sequences in which the human victim is finally ripped limb-from-limb by the monster Bigfoot? No amount of clever compositions or even a well-designed Sasquatch suit can offer much in the way of entertainment value unless, and if, the writers are willing to change the narrative paradigm of the genre.

It is easy to see the pitfalls of the genre when reviewed in succession, as this guide so frequently makes clear; it is much more difficult for screenwriters to devise novel approaches when dealing with "fight or flight for your life" variations. But without a doubt, this lack of narrative originality is why so many entries in the Savage Sasquatch mode fail before the writers even type "Fade In" on page one of their scripts. Without an original concept or novel twist on the formula, there is at least a modicum of truth in the observation that if you have seen one film of this variety, you have seen them all. All, that is, save the fortunate few (such as *Paper Dolls* or *The Legend of Boggy Creek*, for but two examples of successful variations) that conceptually approach their telling and execution with careful forethought and recognition of the genre's severe limitations.

With the preceding in context, *Sasquatch Hunters* is so prototypical of the weaknesses of the Savage Sasquatch sub-type that it is, for all practical purposes, archetypal. There is the stock cast of characters: the cryptozoologist; the park rangers; the bimbo; the skeptic; and, last but not least, the relentlessly murdering Bigfoot which is never given any justification nor rationale for attacking any and all humans from frame one. In essence, should any Ciné du Sasquatch enthusiast wish to cull forth a quintessentially bland "Bigfoot Attacks" movie, then *Sasquatch Hunters* is a perfect example in vision and execution. The only noticeable distinction it has is the computer-generated cryptids themselves, which resemble video game simians by way of *Gorillas in the Mist*. While this high-tech manner of portraying Bigfoot is initially visually intriguing, the repetitive use of the same few angles employed again and again reduces the novelty by film's end. It's as if the filmmakers could only afford three or four shots of the cryptids and simply edited them into the film whenever necessary.

The acting is another proverbial bag of bones, as skeletally threadbare as the remains uncovered in the Bigfoot burial grounds. The haphazard manner in which the team just happens to unwittingly camp beside the graves at night (only to awaken to find them the next morning) is perhaps every real-life cryptozoologist's fantasy, but it makes for poor believability in terms of the actors' ability to deny their own disbelief. The core dramatics in *Sasquatch Hunters* are so underdeveloped the viewer may find him or herself longing for the subtle nuances of an average entry in the Jason Vorhees or Michael Myers series. Forget stereotypes; *Sasquatch Hunters* only manages *mono*types for its characterizations. To paraphrase the venerable Popeye, each character in *Sasquatch Hunters* may truthfully say, "I yam what I yam"— and, sadly, often even less.

It is unfair to fault only the actors, though they're certainly responsible for their fair share of the film's overall tedium. The writing and direction are consistently tepid and set the tone from the outset. Too often the actors stand in a circle, endlessly spouting bad dialogue of the "Let's get the hell out of here!" and "Quiet! Did you hear that?" variety, and rarely react to onscreen events with any dramatic tension.

Technically, *Sasquatch Hunters* is moderately successful. At times, however, the outdoor cinematography, though well-done, has the "shot in a state park" look of sparse vegetation, well-marked trails and visitor parking lots conveniently located just off-screen, none of which is helped by the noon-time lighting schemes. Likewise, the night-for-night scenes are occasionally so poorly lit that it is difficult to distinguish enough information within the frame to delineate actors from the inky pools of the background. While this conceivably could have been suspenseful if properly photographed, *Sasquatch Hunters* evidently lacked the necessary lighting equipment, experienced crew and/or robust budget to accomplish any effective mise-en-scène during its undoubtedly rushed production.

Sasquatch Hunters is not the soggiest bottom in the Ciné du Sasquatch swamps by any stretch of the imagination, but neither is it near the top. Rather, and uncomfortably so, it is stuck in the proverbial middle grounds of mediocrity, where good intentions all too readily turn bad, and insufficiencies of budget and originality result in scant entertainment value and predictable outcomes.

Regarding the latter, *Sasquatch Hunters* is a virtual compendium of everything cliché in the genre as a whole. From the white trash hunters who are slaughtered while intoxicated in the picture's opening sequence, to the requisite, empty-headed, blonde babe who quickly strips to shower under a waterfall while under the lustful gaze of the randy park ranger; and from the kindly but ineffective crypto-researchers, to the rampaging creatures who kill, kill, *kill* without provocation, *Sasquatch Hunters* places itself in its own cross-hairs of ineptitude as often as any of the hunters do the depicted Bigfoot monsters. And all too often it manages to commit cinematic suicide in the process, sabotaging its own meager suspense with implausibility and the monotony of the plot. As a blueprint for how not to make a movie in this genre, *Sasquatch Hunters* is like a tract home: virtually indistinguishable from its countless brethren; lacking in anything save cookie cutter execution; and as predictable on the inside as its outside. For even hardcore Ciné du Sasquatch viewers the fatigue it creates will generate a restless itch to grab the remote and utilize the fast forward button.

Sasquatch Lake ... The White Bigfoot Video (2000) (Doc)

Featuring Don Keating, Daniel Perez, Peggy Tillman and Veronica Burchette. Produced and Directed by Don Keating. USA. Color. Stereo.

Overview: Eastern Ohio Bigfoot Investigation Center founder Don Keating is joined by Center for Bigfoot Studies chairman Daniel Perez as they return to Sasquatch Lake, Ohio, an area in which Keating unwittingly filmed a supposed white Bigfoot on August 2, 1992. Keating claims a creature ranging from 9 to 10 feet in height walked down a gravel road less than 100 yards away from him as he recorded the event on his home camcorder. Keating and Perez visit the scene of the incident and measure several different areas in which the cryptid was videotaped, attempting to gain scientific insight into its stride length, weight, height, etc. Also featured are Fortean researchers Peggy Tillman and her sister Veronica Burchette.

Sasquatch Mountain (2006)

AKA: *Devil on the Mountain*. Starring Lance Henriksen, Cerina Vincent, Michael Worth, Rance Howard, Craig Wasson, Tim Thomerson, Raffaello Degruttola, Karen Kim, Frank Rivera, Chris Engen, Melanie Monroe, Kate Connor, Alex Ballar, Candace Raquel, Bob Harter, David Keller and Tiny Ron. Produced by Mike Curb, Carole Curb Nemoy, Dustin Rikert and Michael Worth. Written by Michael Worth. Directed by Steven R. Monroe. USA. Color. Stereo. 90 Minutes.

Overview: A motley gang of small-time robbers knock off a rural Arizona bank, killing a lawman in the process. Wearing gorilla masks to disguise themselves during the town's annual Sasquatch Festival and blend in with the other mask-wearing participants, they make their way with the loot in a getaway van. But on a remote highway they collide with a woman driver who is also just passing through the tiny city. Cornered by the local Sheriff and his two-man crew, and without means of escape due to their crashed vehicle, the bandits shoot their way out of the situation, fleeing into the nearby woods.

Unfortunately for the criminals, the mountainous Arizona terrain is home to a savage Sasquatch. Alerted by the gunfire, the monster attacks, killing one of the wounded thieves who has been left by his gang. Meanwhile, the Sheriff organizes a posse to track the bank robbers after they take the woman driver hostage to insure their safe get-

away. The posse consists of several ex–Vietnam vets who once served together "in country" during the war but have drifted apart since their return Stateside.

The gang discovers the dreaded cryptid at the same time as the trackers when Sasquatch goes on a rampage, killing with indiscriminate zeal. The survivors of the beast's homicidal rage find an abandoned cabin and make a last stand against Bigfoot. They are soon joined by the remaining trackers, who make a temporary pact with the criminals to band together in order to defeat the Sasquatch. They wait out the long night together, huddled in fear; but when Sasquatch attacks, they are forced to flee through the woods in hopes of reaching safety.

But with the stolen money and the need for justice driving a wedge between them, the band of fleeing humans find themselves unable to keep their pact during the long, dangerous trek back to civilization with the killing cryptid on their heels. They splinter before they reach the highway, which allows Sasquatch to more easily dispatch them. A final stand-off with the survivors results in the creature being allowed to go free, as they realize it is far more human (including

Eli Van Cleef (Tim Thomerson) is the Vietnam vet with a chip on his shoulder and a Sasquatch *over* his shoulder in this publicity still for *Sasquatch Mountain*. (Photograph courtesy Michael Worth.)

having paid a huge price in the loss of its own kind) as than previously surmised.

* * * * *

It is amazing how many of the same motifs replicate themselves throughout Ciné du Sasquatch. Though there are serious entries, silly entries, parody send-ups, and low-budget knock-offs, they invariably follow in the deeply-cast footsteps of the genre's narrow constrictions.

Chief among these self-defining genre elements are the down-home Sheriff and his bewildered, understaffed crew; a Sasquatch that attacks with nearly supernatural ease and efficiency; a group of terrified humans (usually though not always young) having to first navigate their way into the difficult terrain of the Bigfoot in question, only to have to then flee for their lives as the cryptid kills them off one by one; a skeptical character who is sure Bigfoot is just a tall tale, and who is usually the first to be dispatched; an expert who knows all about cryptozoology, either through years of tireless study and/or a personal encounter with Sasquatch; a Native American character or descendant who has special knowledge of Bigfoot as a spiritual demon of the forest due to his ethnicity; stock shots of a soaring eagle or hawk; spooky, hand-held shots from Bigfoot's point of view as it stalks its human victims; scenes of entrapment in a remote cabin, tent or similarly crude shelter; a past history in the locale involving sightings and/or deaths attributable to Sasquatch; and night-for-night assault sequences to hide any cryptid costume deficiencies.

This is not to say, however, that every Ciné du Sasquatch film has all of these elements; clearly, some do not, or perhaps they feature novel variants on the formula which makes them unique in the genre (and often memorable as a result). But like holidays and found money, these atypical exceptions are few and far between.

Sasquatch Mountain is a strange hybrid of most of these elements, occasionally rendered effectively and others times routine. It is at once typically all things Ciné du Sasquatch and a blending of action sequences straight out of a hard-boiled John Woo gangster film mixed with a Hallmark Channel sentimentality. Or, more accurately, it's a rare, mostly entertaining escapee from the SyFy (aka Sci-Fi) Channel, the same network who picked up this film when it was called *Devil on the Mountain* and gave it the more "high concept" (read: Tivo-

friendly) title of *Sasquatch Mountain*. As SyFy Channel efforts go, *Sasquatch Mountain* is actually far above their average. Of course, anyone who has sat through the usual bland SyFy Channel offerings consisting of giant snakes, man-eating sharks, marauding octopi, rock creatures, and Men in Black clones, that's the epitome of a qualified statement. Still, as a well-cast, fast-paced variation on Ciné du Sasquatch, *Sasquatch Mountain* offers much that is positive.

The effective opening sequence features Lance Henriksen (the triple threat star of *Sasquatch*, *Sasquatch Mountain* and *Abominable*) and his onscreen wife stranded by a remote roadside, waiting for emergency assistance. While joking around and videotaping their comical (to them) predicament, she shoots a blurry image of Bigfoot in the woods nearby. Moments later she is tragically killed when a car smashes into her as Henriksen helplessly watches. Much like the opening of *The Changeling*, starring George C. Scott, this evokes both horror and instant empathy on behalf of the grizzled character actor, and the director wisely holds on Henriksen's inscrutable, hangdog face to drive the emotional impact home.

While this opening scene is eerily tragic, the rest of the first act quickly shifts into a more familiar heist film, losing tension as the narrative moves to the small Arizona town which is celebrating its annual Sasquatch Festival to lure in passing tourists. The appearance of the "Bigfoot Gang" as they exit their Route 66 motel hell alters the film's tone from suspenseful horror to black comedy. The characters are such perfect amalgamations of action film stereotypes — hunky charmer, Eurotrash depressive, yuppie investor, Asian dominatrix, white trash slacker — that the viewer is likely to feel he or she has inadvertently sat atop his remote and switched to the Tarantino Channel.

Though it's amusingly clever when the gang dons their gorilla disguises to go incognito during the town's vaunted cryptid fest and carry out their bank heist plan (how to tell them apart from all the other ape mask-wearing tourists?), *Sasquatch Mountain* can't easily escape the hackneyed quality of its forcibly-banded-together antagonists. No believable explanation of how such a perfectly diverse assemblage of the modern equivalent of the anti–Mod Squad came together is ever offered. Indeed, it's as if when they emerge from their motel rooms they're emerging fully unformed and unconcerned about their seeming lack of stability as a group. No doubt this can be

effective when carefully handled, à la *The Wild Bunch* or *The Magnificent Seven*, with layered, nuanced character conflicts and back story. But here this decidedly motley crew feels like they're straight out of cliché casting central. As *Sasquatch Mountain* wears on, this inherent problem of such a politically correct gang of hoods becomes magnified — to the movie's detriment.

Again, though uneven and not without its faults, *Sasquatch Mountain* has much that is praiseworthy. Kudos go to both the creature costume designer Karen Rau and actor "Tiny" Ron, who portrays Sasquatch. The creature is believably portrayed as towering in height and menacing in bulk. Much of the credit goes to director Steven R. Monroe, who convincingly stages the human/Sasquatch encounters so that the gargantuan size of the cryptid is emphasized via low angles; dark, shadowy glimpses in the trees; and cramped doorways, à la the original *The Thing*, which force the creature to squeeze its massive girth through them in order to attack the cabin-bound victims. Not since *The Abominable Snowman* has a cryptid monster seemed such a menace in physical size alone. Given the relatively low budget and short 18-day shooting schedule, this is remarkable, and demonstrates that a lot of forethought and astute planning went into the film's pre-production phase.

The impressive size difference between Bigfoot and the punier humans gives *Sasquatch Mountain*'s hominid portrayal a scarier edge than most. (Photograph courtesy Michael Worth.)

Sasquatch Mountain is also well-cast. Besides Henriksen, there's veteran character actor Rance Howard on hand as the grizzled but kindly sheriff in one of his largest screen roles in years. Another well-known cult film favorite is Tim Thomerson (the *Trancers* series), who plays one of the cryptid trackers — named Eli Van Cleef. Too, there is a *Lonesome Dove* quality to the banter and bickering between the cadre of former soldiers now reunited for one last mission. Though it never gels beyond dramatic conceit, it nevertheless gives Howard, Thomerson and Henriksen a shared back story to play upon as actors. Though faint praise, perhaps, it's high praise indeed when considering the usual paltry back stories of most characters in a Ciné du Sasquatch film, where the color of a protagonist's hair or shirt substitutes for any meaningful characterization.

Craig Wasson also stands out as the bank-robbing yuppie more comically concerned with his stock investments than any killer Bigfoot threatening him and his gang — at least until his ammo begins to run out. He also has a military background (making Sasquatch the only major character which hasn't been in the army), thereby explaining his expert shooting abilities that otherwise seem absurdly unrealistic. It is not an easy role, and he acquits himself well. It's satisfying to see this under-utilized actor receiving some well-deserved screen time. He plays his befuddled, angst-ridden character herein almost as adroitly as he did Jake, the panty-sniffing voyeur in Brian DePalma's memorable *Body Double*. And writer/co-producer/star Michael Worth does a very credible job with his role as bad guy turned lesson learned Vin Stewart, which must have been quite difficult given the multiple hats he was forced to wear under the pressures of low-budget shooting.

Sasquatch Mountain is well-shot, though the MTV-styled compression editing and fast-forward speed effects are over-utilized. The high desert mountain forests offer an atypical, shadowy landscape wherein such a darkly-rendered creature could conceivably coexist with the occasional human intruder. Helping the illusion is the filmmakers' choice to craft the creature with black fur and limit most of its appearances to brief silhouettes; in most shots the viewer glimpses only a massive bulk in motion, its hair a glowing outline rimmed by sunlight. Combined with "Tiny" Ron's physically expressive attempt to emulate and build upon the lumbering gate of Roger Patterson's infamous Bigfoot, *Sasquatch Mountain* deserves accolades for at least rendering its creature as scarily effective.

If only the cohesive narrative elements had been as effectively captured, *Sasquatch Mountain* would have become a rare Ciné du Sasquatch unqualified success. As is, however, it's a mildly diverting example of Bigfoot filmmaking with one too many diverse ingredients tossed into the pot to make it more than interesting viewing.

Sasquatch Odyssey: The Hunt for Bigfoot (1999) (TV) (Doc)

Featuring Dr. Grover Krantz, Betty Unger, Jack Lapseritis, Robert M. Pyle, Jim Hastings, James Stewart, Gloria Stewart, Henry Franzoni, Rob Butler, Ray Crowe, Toby Lindala, Janos Prohaska, Gordon Strasenburgh, Harry Schumacher, the Rev. C. Edward Linville, Lilian Perry, Matt Dunlap, Baron Alexander Leopold von Kleist, Florent Barille, Wayne Alfred, Peter Byrne, Rene Dahinden and John Green. Produced and Written by Julie Lee and Sheera Von Puttkamer. Directed by Sheera Von Puttkamer. Canada. Color. Stereo. 70 Minutes.

Overview: A documentary look back by award-winning Canadian filmmaker Sheera Von Puttkamer, *Sasquatch Odyssey: The Hunt for Bigfoot* is a self-revealing tale of the decades of strain, fractions, and — just as remarkably — harmony, peace, and friendliness endured by the so-called Four Crypto Horsemen: Grover Krantz, Peter Byrne,

Rene Dahinden and John Green. These four gentlemen were each members of the Tom Slick–financed expedition known as the Pacific Northwest Bigfoot Expedition of 1960 to 1962. Rather than cause confrontations, à la reality TV, Von Puttkamer applies patience and understanding, which yields unexpected results once a bond is created between filmmaker and the subject being interviewed. One gains a sense of the immense impact — positive and negative — each man has felt while following their passions to the literal ends of the Earth.

The film is not without intentional humor, nor does it avoid entertainment. The inclusion of actor James Stewart and his wife Gloria as "Purveyors of the Yeti Finger" — a specimen Stewart claimed was a legit acquisition from the Nepal region — adds a welcome touch of off-the-wall, jaw-dropping quirkiness, as does the addition of some priceless Bigfoot "time capsule" film clips, such as the interview with retired State Trooper Jim Hastings discussing his Bigfoot sighting, and author Jack "Kewaunee" Lapseritis who is on hand in part to promote sales of his latest book, *The Psychic Sasquatch*. But when the Ciné du Sasquatch chips are down, it is the Four Cryptos who hold court and make *Sasquatch Odyssey: The Hunt for Bigfoot* a unique look at the painful, humiliating, and often illuminating quest each man loved enough to endure the others' eccentricities. *Sasquatch Odyssey: The Hunt for Bigfoot* won Best Foreign Documentary Feature at the 1999 New York International Independent Film and Video Festival.

Sasquatch Science: Searching for Bigfoot (2006) (Doc)

Featuring Dr. Jeffrey Meldrum, John A. Bindernagel, Gordon Strasenburgh and John Green. USA. Color. Stereo. 150 Minutes.

Overview: This two-disc DVD is basically a compilation of various distinguished Bigfoot experts speaking at a cryptozoological conference. Omni-present Dr. Jeff Meldrum (surely one of the most interviewed Bigfoot experts in the history of Sasquatch documentaries) gives a slide show presentation detailing how he goes about distinguishing legitimate from fake Bigfoot castings by using the so-called "Midtarsal break" as a litmus test. John A. Bindernagel criticizes field guides to zoological species for not including at least the possibility of bipedal hominids, along with relevant data and photos. Gordon Strasenburgh concentrates his presentation on the cultural universality of Bigfoot across time and locales, suggesting this alone is proof worthy of serious consideration of Bigfoot's existence. John Green, a renowned and early cryptozoologist who dedicated his career to researching Sasquatch, discusses his lifelong study of the cryptid and his criticism of the mainstream media for their usual pandering towards him and the subject matter.

Short on production values (as it is basically a video recording of the conference and produced on a shoestring budget), *Sasquatch Science: Searching for Bigfoot* nonetheless will prove interesting to dedicated enthusiasts of cryptozoological documentaries that are long on information and in-depth speaker exposure.

Sasquatch ... The Evidence Mounts (1998) (Doc)

Featuring Richard J. LaMonica, Richard Myers and Marc DeWerth. Produced and Directed by John Horrigan and Don Keating. USA. Color. Stereo. 40 Minutes.

Overview: This is an independent documentary produced by Don Keating concentrating on sightings of Bigfoot in the Ohio area. Keating is the publisher of the now defunct *The Monthly Bigfoot Report*

Newsletter, founder of the Eastern Ohio Bigfoot Investigation Center, and self-funded videomaker of several other Buckeye State–centered Sasquatch documentaries, including *Sasquatch Lake ... The White Bigfoot Video*. Keating has frequently appeared at national Bigfoot conferences and on such programs as *MonsterQuest* discussing Grassman (the Ohio moniker for Bigfoot).

Sasquatch, the Legend of Bigfoot (1977)

AKA: *Sasquatch*. Starring George Lauris, Steve Boergadine, Jim Bradford, Ken Kenzle, William Emmons, Joe Morello, Lou Salerni and Gustave Johnson. Produced by John Fabian and Ronald D. Olson. Written by Ed Hawkins and Ronald D. Olson. Directed by Ed Ragozzino. USA. Color. Mono. 102 Minutes.

Overview: A small band of seven researchers set out to canvas the majestic Peckatoe River in the notorious Valley of the Bigfoot in the British Columbia wilderness in search of Sasquatch. Among the team members are Chuck Evans, leader of the expedition; Barney Snipe, the comic relief cook; Josh Bigsby, the grizzled field hand who has spent a lifetime tracking the dense redwood forests; Dr. Paul Markham, a respected anthropologist with a passion for cryptozoology; Techka Blackhawk, a Native American guide who offers valuable knowledge of what signs to look for in seeking Bigfoot; and Bob Ver-

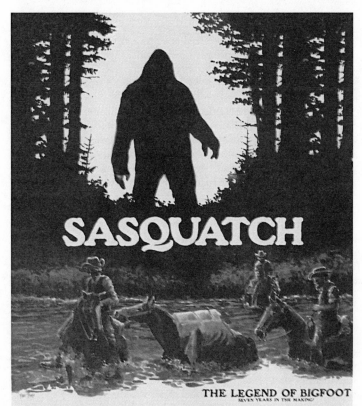

Poster art for the theatrical release of *Sasquatch, the Legend of Bigfoot*.

non, a cynical New York City crime scene photographer who is only along for the ride because he is being paid to take photographs by the newspaper subsidizing the expedition. Dr. Markham takes an immediate dislike to Vernon's skeptical attitude, concerned the disbeliever will jeopardize the mission with his negativity.

The deeper the team traverses into the wilds, the harsher their environment becomes. To relieve the boredom and fatigue of their difficulties, crotchety Josh Bigsby tells various stories of previously documented encounters with Sasquatch in the area. Despite Vernon's guffaws, Bigsby is a firm believer that Sasquatch is real and inhabits the very woods they're invading.

Over the course of their months-long journey, Bigsby recounts several notorious stories casting the roaring hominid in a decidedly savage light, which are recreated by actors in period costume. One recreation is the infamous Ape Canyon siege published in newspaper accounts in the 1920s in which miner Fred Beck and several friends survived a night of terror when a tribe of Sasquatch creatures bombarded their remote cabin with boulders. Also shown is the true-life journal entry made by none other than Teddy Roosevelt in which the President recounts a tale he's heard about two Canadian fur trappers who encountered an especially brutal Bigfoot. The end of the trapper's terrifying nightly visitations by the stalking Sasquatch resulted in the daytime murder of one of the trackers, his neck grotesquely broken, while his partner was temporarily away from base camp gathering their traps so that they could flee the mountainside.

Sufficiently spooked by the folklore (or is it?), the hardy group finally reach their destination and erect a base camp. To monitor the dark woods surrounding the clearing the crew set a perimeter of tripwires around their tents. In the event any Sasquatch attempts to invade their space, a monitor will flash, alerting the team that not only is a cryptid approaching, but from what direction. The system works better than any of the team members could have envisioned when several scary attempts are made by more than one Sasquatch racing through camp. The skeptical photographer is roughly handled when he attempts to relieve himself in the bushes and encounters a waiting Sasquatch. By dawn's early light the creatures have ceased their attack, leaving the bewildered survivors to ponder what they have endured. Alas, no photographic evidence has been collected, even if footprints have been cast to help prove their version of events. Frightened but encouraged, they all vow to return to renew their quest at a later date.

* * * * *

Sasquatch, the Legend of Bigfoot is notable in the genre for the strange yet fascinating tonal blend it achieves. At once a classic family-friendly nature film *and* a pseudo-documentary of the Schick Sunn Classics International type so prevalent in the era (such as *In Search of Noah's Ark* and *The Lincoln Conspiracy*), *Sasquatch, the Legend of Bigfoot* is also at times a rather intense horror film. While it bears superficial resemblance to Pierce's seminal *The Legend of Boggy Creek* in this respect, it varies significantly in its outdoor adventure tale format, which is more akin to the "man versus nature" first-hand tales *Argosy* magazine routinely published which initially helped popularize Bigfoot with the American reading public.

Remarkably, and against all odds (especially given the film's modest budget), *Sasquatch, the Legend of Bigfoot* skillfully balances the multiple genre formats with assured directorial ease. Though it's never entirely seamless, director Ed Ragozzino does a professional job of stitching the various documentary recreations, fictional narrative, and nature film elements together to create an entertaining whole. The result is often very suspenseful, especially given the film's G-rated nature. It's a shame Ragozzino never dabbled in feature film directing after this effort, as his talent is on display throughout what had to be a difficult location shoot in the remote Three Sisters mountain wilderness of Oregon. The filmmakers had to mule-pack all their equipment in and out of the dangerous canyon passages themselves and without mechanical support. A popular voiceover talent for commercials, and a Northwest regional theater director until his passing in 2010, Ragozzino definitely renders a sense of true isolation and eerie loneliness throughout *Sasquatch, the Legend of Bigfoot*. Given that the entire film was shot in an environment where it seems plausible a hominid could actually remain undetected by humanity, it was a wise choice on his part to use the setting to create believability when the storytelling and acting occasionally fail to achieve the same sense of authenticity.

The film's highlights are the recreated encounters with Sasquatch from historical records. These sequences are told in flashback by the old codger character Josh Bigsby, reminiscent of the character portrayed by Walter Huston in *Treasure of the Sierra Madre*. Bigsby's grizzled, uncouth bluntness makes him the true "wise old man" of the story's structure and gives the film an additional sense of verisimilitude. Though the film often goes overboard in having character actor Jim Bradford play his sidekick chef character Barney Snipe too broadly via his cantankerous outbursts and ineptitude, the cast generally does well for what are clearly non-professionals for the most part.

Still, the recreations achieve a nightmarish intensity at times that frightened an entire generation of filmgoers in the 1970s. Credit goes not only to the director for keeping the cryptids mostly off-screen to heighten suspense, but composer Al Capps, whose spooky, *Jaws*-influenced bass score really elevates the film's driving sense of terror. Capps is an unheralded musician and producer, having worked in near obscurity on generally forgotten independent films such as *Buffalo Rider*, and on better known Hollywood features like *Sharky's Machine*, *The Cannonball Run* and *Stroker Ace*. He also co-wrote the enduring song "Half Breed" (along with Mary Dean) for Cher, as well as produced her *Half-Breed* album, which sold over 500,000 copies during its release in North America. The venerable tune has been sung on such television shows as *The Sonny & Cher Comedy Hour*, and utilized in movies as diverse as *Lords of Dogtown*, *Flawless* and *Dance Me Outside*. For lucky attendees smart enough to purchase it, the producers of *Sasquatch, the Legend of Bigfoot* sold a promotional 45 rpm-sized (but actually a 33 rpm recording) soundtrack in theater lobbies. This rare collectible features the music cues on the A-side and weird Sasquatch howls on the B-side. It is a perennially sought after item on eBay and other collector websites, which is a testament to how dramatically it impacted the youngsters who vividly recall to this day how many sleepless nights they endured because of the score's menacing sense of impending doom. In a genre such as Ciné du Sasquatch, where musical scores are often indistinguishable from one another (or simply library music cues), *Sasquatch, the Legend of Bigfoot* enjoys a distinctive position as having one of the most effective soundtracks ever created for a cryptid film. Even the ending theme song, "High in the Mountains" (which, despite its 1970s time frame, is *not* a marijuana reference), has a catchy pop sensibility that captures the *Last of the Mohicans* feeling so prevalent in the best entries of Ciné du Sasquatch.

The film is also notable for the inclusion of the Roger Patterson footage taken at Bluff Creek. Utilized very early in the movie to set the tone for all that follows, the glimpse of the hairy Bigfoot as it languidly but purposefully strides from the camera creates the visual impression of the cryptid's size and girth. The director is careful to keep most views of Sasquatch in subsequent shots to brief glimpses of an arm here or legs there. Particularly effective are the tracking shots through dense forest vegetation in which the camera concentrates only on the thick, muscular legs of the hominid as it easily pushes through vines and over fallen trees. By building upon the impact of the earlier Patterson footage and forcing the viewer to participate in imagining what is kept off-screen, Ragozzino effectively captures the reality of how such a large hominid could pose a mortal threat to the relatively befuddled and undersized humans who struggle to move through the same geography. Accompanied by Capps' menacing music, these shots elevate the film above simple exploitation into true terror territory.

Sasquatch, the Legend of Bigfoot was "four-walled" across the country by the film's producers. This process involved the film being booked heavily within one area, with inexpensive television and radio ads hyping the movie's limited window of availability ("Now showing for two days *only!*"), before the small number of theatrical prints were cycled into the next region. Also part of the four-wall process was the film venues being rented by the producers themselves rather than the producers merely renting a print to the owner, as was customary. This allowed the producers to maximize their profits, while theater owners were happy to have a guaranteed fee and keep concession stand sales from packed audiences. As previously detailed, the producers were often on hand in the lobby to sell additional merchandise (such as the film's soundtrack), often with a promotional display that enticed reluctant patrons to spend with the promise that proceeds would go towards financing further expeditions in search of Sasquatch. This was clearly a ruse designed to play upon Sasquatch believers' faith and vindicate their armchair cryptozoologist status. This author purchased a copy of the soundtrack from just such a lobby representative and fondly recalls the genuine enthusiasm which he exhibited towards not only the young buyer but subject matter as well.

Despite stretches of travelogue tedium, *Sasquatch, the Legend of Bigfoot* remains one of the most beloved Bigfoot efforts of the 1970s. No doubt part of the film's popularity is owed to its hard-to-see status, as the movie was only ever available in extremely limited numbers during its one-time videocassette release and has only recently been released onto DVD (though it's merely a VHS transfer and not the true widescreen version of the film). As a result, many fans of Ciné du Sasquatch remember their original experience with the motion picture as youngsters — without the jaundiced, more critical eye of adulthood. This is often reflected in various reviews in which those who never saw *Sasquatch, the Legend of Bigfoot* theatrically in widescreen (where the pristine cinematography and booming soundtrack added immeasurably to the filmgoing impact) often espouse a less flattering assessment of the film (understandably so, given that they're viewing a poor quality videocassette transfer). But for aficionados who appreciate the serious treatment afforded to the subject matter and can recall how terrifying the film was in its day, *Sasquatch, the Legend of Bigfoot* remains an all-time "must see" in the genre.

Savage (2009)

Starring Tony Becker, Lisa Wilcox, Martin Kove, Shane Callahan, Anna Enger, Robert Pralgo, Kim Wall, Ron Prather and Rico Ball. Produced by Bo Buckley, Christopher Cook, D.J. Perry and Justin Soponis. Written by Jordan Blum, Lynn Drzick, Nancy Gideon and D.J. Perry. Directed by Jordan Blum. USA. Color. Stereo. 95 Minutes.

Overview: When a fire sweeps through the Bear Mountain National Park in North Carolina, park ranger Owen Fremont is forced to deal with a myriad of conflicting problems: a shortage of manpower; campers wanting refunds; incoming firefighters; leaving his pregnant wife Ellen alone in their remote cabin; and, worst of all, a series of unsolved missing persons cases, some involving the firefighters themselves.

The fires haven't prevented others coming to the area, however.

Among the newest arrivals are Gabrielle and Mitchell Hanley, two fugitives on the run from a convenience store hold-up gone awry in Florida, and cryptozoologist Dale Davis, who has alienated friends and family and spent himself into bankruptcy with his obsession of proving Bigfoot to be a real species. To this end, Davis has hired self-professed "monster hunter" Jack Lund, a Bear Mountain backwoods local and cynical profiteer. Unbeknownst to Davis, Lund mostly stages evidence, such as fur samples and footprints, to capitalize upon the gullible.

When Ranger Fremont finds the bodies of several mangled firefighters, he realizes he is dealing with something beyond his experience. While some believe it is the work of the legendary monster in the woods, Fremont resists such nonsense, preferring to believe either a human or bear is the culprit. But as the evidence mounts and bodies pile up, it becomes harder for Fremont to deny the existence of Bigfoot as the killer.

Mitchell is attacked and slashed to death by the cryptid. Gabrielle flees and is rescued at the last possible moment by Davis and Lund. She is hysterical and unable to travel, so the two men set up camp for the night. The next morning Ranger Fremont arrives to arrest Gabrielle, having uncovered her criminal warrants after checking up on her and her husband. She leads the skeptical lawman to the body of Mitchell, which finally removes all doubt from Fremont's mind as to the actual identity of the killer.

Alas, as Fremont escorts the handcuffed Gabrielle to headquarters for processing and to radio for back-up, Bigfoot smashes into Fremont's truck, overturning it. The creature attempts to maul them through the window but is unable to reach them because of the severe angle of the ditch-bound vehicle. Meanwhile, Lund and Davis encounter the cryptid, with devastating results — both are attacked by Bigfoot and slowly die even as it drools over them. Gabrielle and Ranger Fremont arrive by foot at Fremont's cabin; they gather his wife and prepare to make a run for town. But the hominid attacks first, cornering them in the attic. In an act of self-sacrifice, Gabrielle allows the couple to flee outside before igniting a ruptured gas line. The cabin roof explodes, killing her and the cryptid.

As they huddle in the ruined remains of their dream home, Fremont realizes a greedy developer has started the forest fire in an effort to buy up land at wholesale prices. The ranger decks the developer and quits his job, vowing he and his expectant wife will begin life anew somewhere else.

This behind-the-scenes photograph taken pre-wire removal reveals how the filmmakers of *Savage* enabled their tree-leaping Bigfoot (Jack Harrison) to effortlessly travel the woods. (Photograph courtesy Jordan Blum.)

* * * * *

For a low-budget movie, *Savage* makes the absolute most of its location photography, professional cast and inventive Bigfoot creature. While it follows familiar Ciné du Sasquatch pathways, it still manages to entertain and sustain viewer interest, owing largely to the multi-layered screenplay. That is not to say the script is overly complex; indeed, as such thoughtful earlier films as *The Abominable Snowman* demonstrate, a simple, well-developed linear narrative is more than sufficient for a movie of this nature. What is required has less to do with novelty and more to do with such staple but necessary audience-involving qualities as character, conflict and unexpected twists. *Savage* manages all of this without obvious labor and is often quite successful at doing it seamlessly. At times, however, the film strains viewer belief — but never to the breaking point like so many films in the Bigfoot *oeuvre* have done in the past.

Savage is helped quite a bit by the strength of the lead performances. While it is true one is dealing with stereotypical characters for the genre — the skeptical lawman; the nerdy scientist; the greedy developer; the hot babe in distress — at least they are well-acted. This helps the audience roll with the lesser elements (certain plot contrivances and a few minor structural deficiencies) and stay emotionally

The self-referential title of *Savage* indicates it lies firmly within the Savage Sasquatch mode of hominid portrayal. (Photograph courtesy Jordan Blum.)

attached to the characters, which goes a long way towards making any Bigfoot movie a success. Given that the genre often suffers from a lack of empathetic characters, this quality alone makes *Savage* exceptional among Ciné du Sasquatch entries.

Veteran character actor Tony Becker brings a likeable if low-key charm to his role as Ranger Fremont. With such TV credits as *The Texas Wheelers*, *The Waltons* and *Little House on the Prairie* as a child actor, and later adult roles in *Tour of Duty* and *For Love and Honor*, Becker has a distinctively believable outdoors quality. Rugged but emotionally vulnerable, he seems like he has just ridden off the set of a western movie into this role. Equally effective in her down home style is Lisa Wilcox, who plays Fremont's wife. Horror fans will perhaps best remember her from both *A Nightmare on Elm Street 4: The Dream Master* and the reprisal of her role as Alice in its sequel *A Nightmare on Elm Street 5: The Dream Child*. Her prolific credits include guest roles on *Star Trek: The New Generation*, *Knots Landing* and *Bill & Ted's Excellent Adventures*, as well as *General Hospital*.

Martin Kove chews up the scenery in a role reminiscent of Eli Wallach's from *The Good, the Bad and the Ugly*, right down to the obsession with smoking stubby cigars. Wearing a perma-stain set of false teeth, a three-day growth of beard and wild, tangled hair, Kove is a dry-land version of Captain Quint from *Jaws*. As a ruthless profi-

teer conducting phony Bigfoot expeditions, with which he lures "suckers" into paying his bills by planting false evidence for his customers to find, Kove's character is a direct descendent of Carl Denham from *King Kong*. But rather than grand ambitions like Denham's plan to make a fortune, Kove's Jack Lund character is strictly interested in turning a fast buck at every opportunity, no matter how small the situation or dollar sign. This exploitation angle is very common throughout Ciné du Sasquatch and seems to embody the darker side of humanity's need to not just kill what it does not understand, but also cage it and place it on display. It is not without some irony that, for an "advanced" species, we are the only beings on Earth that justifies entrapping other forms of life and exhibiting them for amusement.

Shane Callahan's portrayal of the cryptozoologist is typically nerdish, but at least he is sketched in as having paid the price for his intense beliefs. Too often in the genre, crypto researchers are portrayed as being either inevitably correct (they just *know* they're right *a priori* and all around them are eventually proven wrong in their skepticism) or insufferably scientific to the point of becoming a parody of the Professor from *Gilligan's Island* (they are blissfully unaware they are dealing with a dangerous animal species because of their cold, analytical detachment). Callahan manages to find a fum-

Actress Anna Enger plays Gabrielle Hanley in *Savage*. Here she kids for a behind-the-scenes photograph with the creature costume's glove. (Photograph courtesy Jordan Blum.)

The lean hominid of *Savage* is a nimble, intelligent predator, highly capable and frequently homicidal. (Photograph courtesy Jordan Blum.)

bling halfway point between the two that is both human and fragile. Whether he's pleading with the monster hunter Lund to treat him as an equal rather than as a greenhorn city boy, or explaining how he's lost everything to his belief—family, friends and fortune—this is one crypto researcher who does not appear completely insensitive to the harsh reality he faces (both in discovering an actual cryptid species or getting a reluctant humanity to accept his findings). This is much more accurate than most realizations of cryptozoologists in films.

The most unique aspect of *Savage* is the way the filmmakers visualize the creature itself. Particularly impressive are the bounding leaps and jumps it makes. Unlike the bionic approach in *The Six Million Dollar Man* and its cumbersome, slow-motion movements, the *Savage* creators stress Bigfoot's agility in the forest. Whether it is leaping from tree limb to tree limb like a primate, or dropping momentarily onto all fours to increase its speed and stability, the creature costume is not only well-designed but convincingly filmed. Several shots feature the screaming Sasquatch racing along like a charging mountain gorilla, hands temporarily acting as feet in front of it (though it remains bipedal for the majority of the film). This must have been an extremely difficult shot to accomplish in the dense woods and without making the forearm extensions look ridiculous. The special effects artists do a good job combining a few rare, understated green screen compositing shots with the on-set, wire gimbal suspension of the cryptid actor. It's an amazingly kinetic and athletic performance, and it gives *Savage* some really dynamic chase scenes unique to the genre.

Thematically, *Savage* fits the mold well. The cryptid, while brutal and not to be trifled with, is typically adverse to human contact. Only when the massive forest fire drives it (and all other wildlife) from its native habitat does it become offensive rather than defensive in posture. With the revelation that the greedy developer actually started the fire in order to "smoke out" existing land owners and force them to sell to him on the cheap (a goal which he accomplishes, despite the hero punching him for his arrogance in the movie's concluding moments), the motifs of Ciné du Sasquatch wherein the beast is truly as much victim as aggressor is confirmed. Were it not for the human real estate mogul, none of the deaths—human or wildlife—would have occurred. By setting the forest ablaze (which leads to Bigfoot having to flee for its life amidst the devastation, and seek new prey for food), it is once again mankind (or, at least, one evil member) who invokes the wrath of Sasquatch.

This is not coincidental to the film, but carefully layered and structured throughout, right to the bitterly ironic ending. For the developer has envisioned the once primeval forest lands as prime tourist grounds. His commercial scheme—conversion of the woods into a hillbilly hunting paradise that is one-part Branson, Missouri, and two-parts "shoot 'em if they move!"—is rightfully christened Hunter's Heaven, complete with a half-dozen corporate logos beneath the imitation wood welcome sign. In the final seconds of *Savage*, we see a line of cars, exhaust spewing and horns honking, as they await entrance into the "renovated" tourist trap. Guns are visible in every window's rear-mounted rack; impatient hunters guzzle beers in anticipation of the coming slaughter. It begs the question (and provides the chilling answer as well) as to who is the true *Savage*, even as we hear the lonely wail of a Bigfoot over the fade out to this sad visual coda.

Sawtooth (2009)

Starring West Ramsey, Kody Roza, Maggy Roza, Caleb Salmon and Dariusz Slowik. Produced by Justin Buettner and Keenan Johnston. Written and Directed by Justin Buettner. USA. Color. Stereo. 86 Minutes.

Overview: Three teenagers set out to investigate the infamous Sawtooth Ridge mountains after they're unfairly disciplined for a schoolyard bullying incident and suspended for a week. Carlos and Jamie are childhood friends wrestling with young adulthood who share a passion for Bigfoot. Lynn, a gutsy young woman who dreams of being the U.S. Navy's first female S.E.A.L. member, is a newer addition to the small circle of friends. While Lynn remains skeptical of Sasquatch's existence, she enjoys camping and eagerly accompanies the two males on their impromptu expedition.

Alas, their journey proves less than successful. Along the rugged trail they come face to face with not only the unpleasant realities of being so desperately alone in the middle of deep, virtually uninhabited woodlands at night, but of more sinister forces at play in the forest around them. Two pot farmers, for example, become trigger-happy when the trio of Bigfooters stumbles into their secret weed garden. A fast-thinking Lynn saves the day, proving to be every bit the S.E.A.L. she imagines she will one day become. She rescues Jamie and Carlos, and the bewildered buddies race back to their campsite, worried the pot growers have followed them. Ominously, however, one of the growers whispers to his accomplice, "Sawtooth Ridge will take care of them."

Lynn is missing one morning when Carlos and Jamie check her tent. Blood covers all of her scattered personal items, but there is no sign of her. The two young men follow a gruesome trail of blood through the dense undergrowth until it suddenly ends without warning. Exhausted by their ordeal, Carlos and Jamie return to their camp, only to find that Bigfoot has completely destroyed it in their absence. They take turns staying standing guard until the dawn finally arrives. Realizing they must take action or die of dehydration, the two set out to return to their vehicle. But the long trek is interrupted when they encounter Sasquatch. They run for their lives, but Jamie falls and severely breaks his leg. Carlos tries to help his lame friend hobble back to civilization, but the rugged terrain is unforgiving of their desperate plight.

The Sasquatch creatures prove to be formidable, dogged enemies. They relentlessly pursue both young men through the woods, refusing to allow them sleep or nourishment. Whenever Jamie and Carlos attempt to slow down, the hominids bombard them with rocks and sudden attacks from out of the blue. Eventually depleted physically and mentally, the two friends are reduced to blindly running through the forests as best they can as the conniving cryptids close in around them, prepared to finally kill them after a long, cruel game of cat and mouse.

* * * * *

Sawtooth is a well-observed low-budget take on many of the Bigfoot genre's most classical themes, but filtered through the lens of a "this camcorder footage from their trip was all that was ever found of the missing party" narrative set-up. As a device, this is overly-familiar by now, but the episodic nature of *Sawtooth* nonetheless offers some entertaining and occasionally absorbing human drama as the luckless expedition members come to realize they will probably never see their loved ones again. A little of this goes a long way, and to its credit, *Sawtooth* manages to maintain the balance between outright melodrama and suspense pretty well for a first-time directorial effort.

To his credit, writer-producer-director Justin Buettner dispenses with the intrusive nature of supposedly "found video footage" by having his onscreen characters quickly tire of the novelty of an omnipresent videocamera. Soon they simply place it in front of themselves and forget about it, going about their normal routines. This adds a refreshing bit of distance to the usual handheld, jerky shots so common to this approach but which *Sawtooth* largely avoids. This is achieved by having the film unfold in a series of long takes that are well-paced and well-staged, adding visual density and interest to what are usually "what you see is what you get" cinema compositions when video verite is the desired stylistic look. *Sawtooth* uses off-screen space, sound effects, and sudden intrusions of the creature into the frame in much the same manner as the recent box office success *Paranormal Activity* did, using the limitation of visual information and the manipulation of sound to the filmmakers' advantage. In an era of over-produced fantasy film epics lasting three hours or more, it is easy to appreciate the raw naturalism of a small, personally-realized film such as *Sawtooth*. It is true that a zero-budget effort like *Sawtooth* cannot possibly hope to compete on a fair playing field with any Hollywood-produced movie in terms of production values or pretty faces hired, but the crew and cast of this home-grown effort manage quite well without all the hoopla. The deficiencies are never so heavy as to outweigh the overall watchability of *Sawtooth*, and given the genre's over-abundance of indie-made camcorder DVD efforts, that's not a small accomplishment.

As in *The Long Way Home: A Bigfoot Story* and *Not Your Typical Bigfoot Movie*, the filmmakers have crucially addressed the many drawbacks of working in Ciné du Sasquatch, not least of which is the sheer plethora of examples of previous cinematic failures which litter the genre. By cannily examining these negatives for flipside positives, these three efforts demonstrate the untapped potential still waiting in the genre's unexamined corners. For despite its technical drawbacks and lack of huge budget, *Sawtooth* is that rarity of independent filmmaking—a Bigfoot movie with some heart that is not without merit as a shocker. The ending sequence, for example, is a tour de force of long takes in which the protagonists are wordlessly reduced to human prey, reminiscent of Cornel Wilde's *The Naked Prey* in terms of the sheer sense of kinetic desperation it invokes in the viewer. The glamour is stripped from it, and what is left is a brutal examination in a few fleeting moments of the stalk and slaughter method a canny group of hominids might actually utilize if they were working in silent concerto. As the two Bigfooters learn to their final horror, the stories about Sawtooth Ridge are actually based on a literally monstrous reality.

Scare Tactics ("Bigfoot Attacks") (2003) (TV)

Featuring Sarah Colonna, Sven Holmberg, Nicole Gordillo and Tracy Morgan. Produced by Christine Blake, Oscar H. Beltran, Becky Jacobus and Leif Sandaas. Written by Doug Perkins, Russell Arch, Scott Hallock and Kevin Healey. Directed by Mike Harney. USA. Color. Stereo. 30 Minutes.

Overview: In a state park in Overton, Nevada, a group of friends in a rented RV stay in a primitive camp spot far removed from other campers. While hidden cameras roll, some of the group decide to play a prank and suggest a late night thrill ride along the desolate country roads. They seek to film the reaction of their unsuspecting pals at the sudden sight of a bloody, mutilated tent and scattered camping supplies. The group stops to investigate, the unaware victims convinced they have stumbled into a bad horror movie come to life.

And as in a bad horror film, Travis suddenly decides to go outside and look for some missing friends who cannot be accounted for in the darkness surrounding the lonely RV. He spots a huge hominid and turns off his flashlight to spare himself from attack. Racing into the RV, Travis mutters in terror about what he's just witnessed, but his duped friends—who've seen it all unfold through the window of the RV itself—need no further convincing. Panic sets in as the frightened city dwellers attempt to secure the RV's many open windows, unlocked doors, and other vulnerable entry points. Travis realizes he

has lost his keys while eluding Bigfoot in the darkness outside. He grabs a shotgun and races outside, determined not to be held hostage by a hominid. Alas, the beast overpowers him and shoves him into the RV's main picture window, causing the frightened victims to scream in horror as they watch their friend's body slam against the exterior glass. Travis manages to get inside, nearly in shock. He claims he's bleeding. Suddenly, Sasquatch attacks, slamming its massive bulk against the RV. The enraged monster flings itself into the RV's window, howling. Finally, the prank is revealed to the relieved but outraged friends. The actor playing Sasquatch enters the van and greets the laughing participants.

* * * * *

There's an element of sadistic voyeurism in all prank and hidden camera television productions. At some level, some poor human or group of humans is made to suffer for the spectator's grim amusement. This knowing level of audience complicity is akin to Grand Guignol in Parisian theater productions, in that the audience must admit the ridiculous nature of the graphically-staged deaths in order to become unsettled by their own collective ghoulish morbidity.

So it goes with *Scare Tactics*, an often funny if formulaic hidden camera show with better than average production values for its ilk. The set-ups are often compelling, and the reactions are usually genuine. In this particular episode the inside prankster gang assembled just the right balance of young talent who are photogenic and gullible. The terror tactics of many classic Ciné du Sasquatch movies are reenacted throughout the secretly-scripted event, including having a person wander outside with a shotgun to face off with a hominid (*The Legend of Boggy Creek*), showing a missing person slam into a van's window and being pinned in place by brute force (*Night of the Demon*), and even the beast itself finally assailing the structural integrity of the vehicle's windows in a last-ditch effort to assault the humans inside (almost any Bigfoot movie in the genre featuring a siege inside a cabin/cave/etc., such as *The Legend of Boggy Creek*, *Night of the Demon*, and many more).

The cryptid costume is slightly above average, which helps. The glimpses of the creature are photographed in such a way to make it easy to see why the RV victims being pranked thought they were witnessing a bear attack until Travis, the assaulted hero, claws his way back inside the safety of the camper van and swears it was Bigfoot. Decorum evaporates at this point as the pranked victims degenerate into screaming hysteria. What is remarkable is how much this reality bit resembles the same fictional sequence in *The Legend of Boggy Creek*, wherein the young women inside a remote cabin have to fight off an attacking Fouke Monster. It's to Pierce's credit he elicited such realistic performances of terror from his amateur cast members; after all, as *Scare Tactics* proves, it takes much skillful imagination on the director's part to manipulate folks into actually being horrified where Bigfoot is concerned; but as the segment also vividly shows, the results are mesmerizing when staged to perfection, as was this bit of punk hominid humor.

Schlock! (1973)

AKA: *The Banana Monster*. Starring John Landis, Saul Kahan, Joseph Piantadosi, Eliza Roberts, Tom Alvich, Walter Levine, Harriet Medin, Eric Allison, Charles Villiers, Ralph Baker, John Chambers, Gene Fox, Richard Gillis, Forrest J. Ackerman and Susan Weiser. Produced by George Folsey Jr., Jack H. Harris and James C. O'Rourke. Written and Directed by John Landis. USA. Color. Mono. 80 Minutes.

Overview: Schlockthropus, the last living specimen of its kind, emerges from his cave home in the suburban hills of sunny Augora, California, very much alive. Schlock (as the hominid is dubbed for convenience—and as a knowing nod to *Trog*, which is *Schlock!*'s main target for parody) explores the modern world with earnest curiosity. But his innocence turns tragic as his encounters with startled home owners leaves the human participants dead. Soon victims' bodies are popping up all over the once safe Canyon Valley area, usually found with empty banana peels lying nearby. Eventually, law enforcement officials spread the word that the residents of Canyon Valley have a prowling night murderer in their midst, unaware the true killer is a homicidal hominid.

Schlock soon falls in love with a blind woman named Mindy who erroneously believes Schlock is a kindly guide dog and therefore treats him with affection rather than scorn and hatred, as do all other humans he encounters in his travails. He is mesmerized by Mindy's innocence, even if she annoys him with her constant tossing of a stick and expectation that he fetch and return the branch to her as she enthusiastically utters, "Good dog!" Eventually, Schlock realizes that, with the human authorities closing in on him, he cannot remain in Mindy's vicinity, and so he kidnaps her, unable to live without her and face his abject loneliness any longer. However, before Schlock can retreat into his cave with Mindy and enjoy domestic bliss, the National Guard troops arrive. In an ending reminiscent of *King Kong*, Schlock is riddled with bullets until his species is no more.

* * * * *

Schlock! is an amazing debut feature film, especially when one considers the enormous amount of work John Landis heaped on his shoulders as the film's writer, producer, director, star and holder of other primary production jobs. Made for $60,000 of his own saved monies, and helped to completion with funding by independent film producer Jack Harris, *Schlock!* is often overshadowed by John Carpenter's *Dark Star* as one of the era's cult film legends — the rare case of a semi-professional effort being released for a limited theatrical

run to compete with larger-budgeted studio fare. While this still occasionally (if rarely) happens today, it is more likely that a studio will acquire the film and then release it themselves rather than an independent distributor like Harris booking a film into independent theater chains himself. The comparison between *Dark Star* and *Schlock!* is not without merit, in that both were made for $60,000 (at least in their initial 16mm formats), both were labors of love, and both required monies from Jack Harris to extend their respective lengths into a releasable feature rather than an extended short, which is what they were when Harris became involved. Though *Dark Star* is the more visually arresting, with its amazing special effects and directorial integrity, *Schlock!* was just as much a harbinger of the talent to come from its 21-year-old director in terms of comedic timing and skillful use of set pieces for maximum laughs.

Schlock!'s much-lauded opening satirizes the man-apes of Kubrick's *2001: A Space Odyssey*. The quality of Baker's work on the Schlock suit is very good, given Baker's paltry $500 budgetary allotment. While nowhere near as animated and expressive as his later work in *Harry and the Hendersons* (whose costume construction costs alone were easily ten times the entire production cost of *Schlock!*), the lean hominid suit still allows actor John Landis to display a remarkable range of physical comedy skills. Much of how effective *Schlock!* is or isn't moment to moment largely depends upon Landis' languid realization of the unhurried Schlockthropus as he wanders about the Southern California Valley locales, stumbling from one misadventure into the next. The docile, seemingly self-unaware Schlock tries to navigate his landscape with respect for others, but is constantly belittled, assaulted, and forced to defend his own personal hominid space by the non-stop parade of annoying humans in his path. No scene better captures this than when Schlock is crossing a busy street

after waiting his turn at the traffic light. An obnoxious motorist pulls up to Schlock, almost running him over, and berates the beast to watch where's he's going in the future. The way in which Landis has Schlock slowly burn and seethe with resentment beneath the rubbery mask is reminiscent of Ernie Kovac's genius use of monkey masks on his old live TV programs. As the helpless driver watches, Schlock sets the human aside on the pavement, rips apart the man's car piece-by-piece, and leaves the demolished vehicle with a triumphant look of "take that!" directed squarely at the depressed man. The timing is straight out of Laurel and Hardy, the dismantling like something Jonathan Winters did in *It's a Mad, Mad, Mad, Mad World*, and the result is cinematic hilarity. There's a silent film aspect to much of *Schlock!* reminiscent of the early comedy one-reelers put out by Hal Roach, as well as a Three Stooges sense of physical violence being played for laughs.

Schlock! does suffer from the

Writer/director/producer John Landis even starred as the hominid *Schlock*, who preys upon unsuspecting LA Valley residents. Landis paid Rick Baker $500 to design and construct the Bigfoot costume.

padding needed to extend it to theatrical length. Some sequences are left to run longer than Landis probably intended, and would have probably been trimmed had he not been required to let them play long to meet Harris' distribution needs. Often these comic set pieces are good in and of themselves, but simply feel like they go on too long. One example is the funny but overlong first encounter between Schlock and the blind woman he falls in love with. The scene plays as an echo of two scenes from the Boris Karloff version of *Frankenstein*—the little village girl who meets the Frankenstein monster by the lakeside and who is accidentally drowned after a game of playing flower toss; and the blind hermit who offers the bewildered monster temporary shelter from the pursuing humans. Schlock is stunned the beautiful blind woman will allow him to get so close to her—until he realizes she's without sight. And in comedic turn, she believes Schlock is a gentle companion dog who she can trust with her safety. The fetch game they play in this scene is terrifically acted by Landis inside the latex and fur suit. At first, Schlock tenderly retrieves the stick, happy to receive the fawning attention; soon, however, Schlock grows tired of the idiotic repetition of the game and openly glares at the unseeing woman, as if contemplating her mental capacity rather than her blindness as being a serious drawback to further communication between them. Schlock dutifully gets the stick even after this realization, however, bound as he is by a sense of kindness and love towards the helpless woman and desiring her return affection. But as his anger grows, Schlock makes threatening gestures, such as a back slap from his hairy hand, as she launches the stick for the Nth time and enthusiastically claps for him to "Fetch, boy, fetch!" The hominid quivers between wild desire for possessing the woman and the straight-jacketed feelings of being in a steady relationship in a brilliant pantomimed routine of love and hate. The only problem is, the sequence goes on far past its comic potential, and the viewer is left to wait until the next episode in the narrative. But because the film is so amiable and charming, it manages to get through the duller stretches.

Cult film fans will appreciate the many insider cameos. Forry Ackerman makes a cameo in a movie theater showing a triple bill of Jack Harris' own earlier releases—*Daughter of Horror*, *The Blob*, and *Dinosaurus*. Poor Schlock, who is easily frightened, finds the act of watching a horror film shattering to his already shaky nerves, an unexpectedly sweet reaction given all the bloodshed he himself has caused.

Schlock! is very much an episodic narrative of its time, reflected in moments wherein an old lady tells Schlock to cut his hair and get a job. Landis earned part of the budget by working on *Kelly's Heroes* while it filmed in Yugoslavia, which is where he may have developed a taste for massively-staged scenes of comedic overkill. Some might consider it outside Ciné du Sasquatch because Schlock is so clearly not Bigfoot (as described in some eyewitness accounts). Then again, Schlock *is* a bipedal hominid by any other name, including, of course, the hilarious "Schlockthropus" moniker coined by Landis for the film's star. In many ways, because of the dexterity of Landis' performance as Schlock, this is one of the best-acted Sasquatch monsters in cinema history. Whereas most actors seem to struggle beneath their padding and latex masks, Landis practically wears the costume as a second skin, utilizing body language ranging from slouching and slinking to crouching, crawling, monkey-walking, and so forth. It's an astonishingly complex performance, and one easy to take for granted until one considers Landis is directing his first theatrical feature on a ultra–low budget while wearing a hairy cryptid costume in the blazing heat of the Southern California summer sun. *Schlock!* is a comic commentary on Ciné du Sasquatch on its fringe edges all right, but still a must-see for Bigfoot film fans.

Scooby Doo Meets Laurel and Hardy (1972) (TV)

AKA: *The Ghost of Bigfoot*. Featuring the voices of Don Messick, Casey Kasem, Frank Welker, Nicole Jaffe, Heather North, Larry Harmon and Jim MacGeorge. Produced and Directed by William Hanna and Joseph Barbera. Written by Larz Bourne, Heywood Kling and Sidney Morse. USA. Color. Mono. 60 Minutes.

Overview: When Scooby Doo and the gang decide to head to Vermont for a ski vacation, they encounter a stranded Stan Laurel and Oliver Hardy on the icy roadside. According to the unemployed Laurel and Hardy, their jalopy was nearly struck by a large, icy boulder. Fred offers them a ride to the ski mansion, which seems eerily abandoned. Inside, Mr. Burgess, the owner, informs them that because of the threat posed from Bigfoot, no one save his long-term tenant Mr. Crabtree, an old man in a wheelchair, will stay in the lodge.

Determined not to be intimidated, the mystery-solving teens book two rooms, one for the men and one for the women. Meanwhile, Laurel and Hardy hire on as bellboys in exchange for room and board. Stan sees Bigfoot in the pair's bathroom medicine cabinet, but when Ollie looks, there's nothing there. Shaggy and Scooby Doo make sandwiches in the dining room to calm their nerves after all the Sasquatch talk, only to see the beast howling at the window before they can ingest their food.

When Thelma and Daphne also see Bigfoot howling outside *their* window later that night, the gang, plus Laurel and Hardy, resolve to solve the mystery. But not before Fred, Daphne, and Velma insist on spending the next sunny morning skiing to take advantage of the fact they have the entire hillside to themselves. At the mountain's top they meet a mysterious Hans, the ski instructor, who wears extremely large boots. Laurel and Hardy ride a toboggan down the treacherous slopes while Scooby and Shaggy ride a single pair of skis. Later that night, however, when Laurel and Hardy attempt to serve Mr. Crabtree his dinner in his room, they discover the reclusive octogenarian missing, apparently the victim of Bigfoot.

Fred and the rest insist on exploring the mansion without Mr. Burgess knowing it. Scooby, Shaggy, and Stan are reluctant, while the rest are eager to solve the puzzle. With Ollie assisting, Fred, Daphne, and Velma uncover a secret passageway, along with a series of dusty footprints. Scooby and his team eventually enter another secret passage and suddenly coming face-to-fur with Bigfoot when the creature stomps into a hidden storage room. The rest of the gang hear the ruckus and rush to Scooby's and Shaggy's aid, only to discover the cryptid has vanished. But when Stanley plays the nearby piano, Bigfoot pops out, having hidden inside it. The monster rushes away, disappearing into a false wall.

Fred finds a list of license plate numbers left behind by the hominid and figures out the clue when he confers with Mr. Burgess. It turns out that many of the guests' cars have been stolen over the years. All of the license plate numbers on the list match the stolen vehicles. Realizing Bigfoot is somehow involved, they set out in their van to see if they can find further clues. As they drive the back roads, Bigfoot passes them, driving a flatbed semi filled with stolen cars. The gang gives chase, but Bigfoot drives faster, eluding them. Eventually they come to an abandoned car lot which is filled with rusty wrecks.

Ollie sees activity in the second-story window. They prop a ladder against the wall and Stan climbs to peer inside. Bigfoot scares him, disappearing over the hill via a back exit. The mystery-solving gang follow until they're lead to an old sawmill. Inside there are dozens of stolen cars; clearly this is a chop shop. Bigfoot attempts to flee, but Scooby's fast actions thwart the cryptid, causing him to stumble and fall. Scooby rips off his feet and Fred takes off the monster's mask, revealing Mr. Crabtree as the guilty party. Fred states that Crabtree was only pretending to be handicapped and has been using the Bigfoot costume to scare away authorities from investigating the car theft ring he runs. Hans, the ski instructor who seemed the most likely suspect, arrives and reveals he's actually an undercover cop who has been trying to solve the crimes himself. With another case closed, the gang spends the week skiing for free, courtesy of a relieved Mr. Burgess, whose business is once again booming.

* * * * *

The Hanna-Barbera production team was always big on Bigfoot in their nearly unmatched output of Saturday morning children's fare. Scooby Doo and company alone has thrice visited the fertile grounds of Ciné du Sasquatch—first in the original hit series *Scooby Doo, Where Are You?* with "That's Snow Ghost," then with this entry a few years later, and finally in the television feature *Chill Out, Scooby Doo!* In every case, the hominid depicted—whether referred to as Bigfoot or Yeti—is the classic white-furred Abominable Snowman most historically associated with the Tibetan cryptid. While this makes sense because *Chill Out, Scooby Doo!* is actually set in the Himalayan Mountains, and (to a lesser extent) in "That's Snow Ghost" because its Sasquatch is supernatural (with ability to fly through the air), it is a bit of a stretch in *Scooby Doo Meets Laurel and Hardy* to call the beast Bigfoot, as the hominid is clearly more akin to a Yeti.

Scooby Doo Meets Laurel and Hardy bears more than a passing resemblance, in fact, to its predecessor, "That's Snow Ghost," right down to the manner in which both cryptids are revealed to be humans in costumes using the fear Sasquatch strikes in the hearts of locals to mask their criminal activities. This is, of course, a recurrent plot contrivance of almost every episode in the first two series featuring Scooby Doo and Shaggy, so much so that the later live action theatrical films parodied it mercilessly. And with good reason, for no modern adaptation would be complete without the villain, at long last unmasked by Fred or Velma, uttering the immortal phrase: "And I would've gotten away with it, too, if it hadn't been for you meddling kids!" It is the equivalent of "He's *dead*, Jim!" for *Star Trek* fans.

Scooby Doo, Where Are You? ("That's Snow Ghost") (1970) (TV)

Featuring the voices of Don Messick, Casey Kasem, Frank Welker, Stefanianna Christopherson and Nicole Jaffe. Produced by Joseph Barbera, William Hanna and Lewis Marshall. Written by Ken Spears, Joe Ruby and Bill Lutz. Directed by Joseph Barbera and William Hanna. Color. Mono. 30 Minutes.

Overview: When the Mystery, Inc., crime solvers go on a much-needed vacation to a remote ski lodge, the lodge turns out to be the literal "stomping" grounds for a Yeti known locally as "Snow Ghost." The frightened locals explain that the Snow Ghost moniker is derived from the cryptid's preferred method of locomotion—it seemingly glides through the air at will over great stretches of frozen landscape—and hence their belief the creature may be paranormal in origin.

At first, Shaggy and Scooby Doo are predictably leery of remaining to "enjoy our ski vacation" as the others seem so intent upon accomplishing (for Shaggy and Scooby, even the slightest hint of monsters or the like always triggers an immediate fear-based response to do whatever will directly impugn the teen team's ability to solve the latest in a long series of crimes masked by monsters, aliens, zombies, etc.). And sure enough, as the team of mystery-busting comrades soon unearth, there appears to be a motive *and* a masquerade going on behind this latest attempt to fool the law. To wit, Snow Ghost is revealed by reel's end as being just another costumed villain intent

on scaring away meddlesome intruders like Mystery, Inc., and who masqueraded as the local folkloric beastie in order to protect his own criminal secret hidden deep within a nearby abandoned mine—one involving a fortune in precious bullion the bad guy wants to greedily keep for himself.

* * * * *

Scooby Doo, Shaggy, Fred, Daphne, and Velma were fated to encounter a variation on Bigfoot, Sasquatch, and Yeti on three separate occasions during their original and revival Saturday morning animation incarnations. "That's Snow Ghost" is by far the most prototypical of the hominid hat trick, retaining as it does the still novel freshness of the whole *Scooby Doo* concept (a sort of Maynard G. Krebs meets The Old Dark House combination), complete with talking canine tossed in just in case there was any doubt as to the show's intent from frame one: broad entertainment. This formula still retains a modicum of believability in this episode as a result of its early production within the now endless Scooby Doo shows and films, provided one gives wide latitude to the numerous plot holes, some of which are far wider than the jagged crevices gaping between ice sheets.

Part of the charm of the series, of course, was how it appealed to the young viewers who might have otherwise been frightened from watching if the monsters had proven to be real. By each episode's resolution, however, even the less-attentive viewing tykes could discern that the guy in the reptile monster costume at the end being carried away by a sheriff (when the villain *wasn't* the sheriff!) was the same guy that had innocently warned Shaggy in the opening scenes not to stay at the haunted hotel one second more than was absolutely necessary ... *not on your life!* In essence, it provided a safety switch that was built into each *Scooby Doo, Where Are You?* episode and insured that even if the comical shenanigans proved too intense for a more sheltered generation, there would always be Velma or occasionally Fred to explain the solved mystery to the bedazzled locals—"How *do* those little whipper-snappers *do* it, anyway?"—while the slowly stewing villain awaited his moment to utter a variant on the line, "Yeah, and I'd have gotten away with it, too, *if* it hadn't been for you meddling kids!"

Much that was "novel" in *Scooby Doo, Where Are You?* was actually just classic genre reworking of the aforementioned Old Dark House mysteries and the like, which had all been staples of low-cost filmmaking (given that they could be produced on studio sets, with built-in lights and the ability to record then-cumbersome live sound without exterior noise). As a result of their familiarity, even by early 1970s standards, many of these hoary devices were given the "Scooby Doo Treatment" and made much less stodgy—kind of like a *Dr. Horror's Friday Night Live Spook Show!*, the type of which was once staged live at drive-ins or B-movie hardtop theaters in small towns and growing suburbias. The costumed host Dr. Horror (or an equivalent) would introduce a couple of tired B-movies, all the while promising a finale no one would ever forget—the live invasion of *this very movie theater* by actual monsters! And unlike today's oft-flat 3D films at $20 per ticket, these cunning producers knew how to deliver their advertised thrills. At the arranged signal, the "monsters" (actually locals and/or scrubs hired to rush the crowd while wearing the appropriate latex monster mask and outfit) emerged from behind the screen curtains and rampaged up and down the aisles. They acted as if they were causing great harm, but, of course, no one was ever even touched, let alone injured. These sideshow-type affairs lasted into the late 1970s because they produced reactions in their audiences. The hysteria of a formerly collected young audience who is suddenly certain they all now face mortal peril because of "monsters loose in the aisles!" was a sight to behold. This level of showmanship would be considered so much vulgar pastiche today, and yet it is with this very dismissal that one would overlook *Scooby Doo, Where Are You?*

and therefore miss its minor but significant contribution to Ciné du Sasquatch. Given how popular "That's Snow Ghost" was as one of the original *Scooby Doo* episodes, which has been seen now almost non-stop in TV syndication for decades (not to mention on VHS and now DVD), it would be impossible to gauge the accurate impact this *one* show alone has had on fans of Bigfoot movies and TV series since its 40-plus-years-ago premiere, save to surmise that even at its most modest it probably acted as a great stimulant towards keeping interest high in fictitious Bigfoot portrayals in the media. After all, reruns of "That's Snow Ghost" were far more numerous than infrequently shown Yeti features or one-time cryptid cameos in other TV series, owing to the popularity of the *Scooby Doo* franchise and the shorter, 30-minute-per-episode running time.

The levitating Yeti effect as used by the creators behind "That's Snow Ghost" results in truly one of the weakest scientific explanations given by Velma in all of the many episodes of *Scooby Doo, Where Are You?* Staggered viewers are told by the sleuths that Snow Ghost's actor used nearly invisible skis to accomplish his hovering act, but this goes against not only common sense, but everything that has been seen in the episode. Whenever Snow Ghost "flies" towards someone (such as Shaggy), the hovering hominid is shown to truly possess the secret of levitation. So when the explanation is offered, it's a case where the logic is more tortured than the fantasy mechanism itself, as audience members are told to be believe that a man wearing a bulky creature costume and mask, with small slits for eye-holes, would have the wherewithal to always position himself so that he would precisely "float" in front of curious passersby. Too, it totally ignores the forward motion a skier characteristically makes while soaring downhill. These telltale stabilizations and body adjustments to accommodate the forces of gravity would give away the con job instantly, which is why the explanation is so ridiculous, even by *Scooby Doo* standards. One must bear in mind, however, that the protagonist of the series is, after all, an English-speaking canine mutt with an IQ equal to at least one of the human crew's (that would be Shaggy, though Fred can come across as quite dense, too, partly because of his jock-gone-to-pot persona).

While Hanna-Barbera Productions would often feature cryptids in their numerous shows, "That's Snow Ghost" is a superior incorporation, rivaled only by the more adventure-themed *Jonny Quest* episode set in a Tibetan monastery haunted by Yetis. While the actual content depicted in "That's Snow Ghost" does little to advance any of the major themes of Ciné du Sasquatch, the popularity gained by the Bigfoot genre via constant repeats of this memorable episode shouldn't be underestimated. These kinds of "normal appearances" alongside the Old World folklore forces of darkness, such as the vampire, werewolf, or zombie, are actually quite healthful for Ciné du Sasquatch overall, as they point towards a day when the Bigfoot film will be accepted on its own, with the legitimate trappings and proven advantages inherent in such a genre realization tempting savvy producers, directors, and writers to delve into the *oeuvre* with critical insight. Every time the line-up of "monsters" included not only a mummy, alien, or ghost, but Bigfoot as a worthy member of that elite roster of Ultimate Monsters, Sasquatch as a "common folkloric belief" was given more legitimacy by default.

Serious cryptozoologists may well see this as a step backwards rather than forward. Many would consider grouping Bigfoot with zombies or banshees a step down into the realms of Elvis sightings and Bat Boy photos. Fortunately, *Scooby Doo, Where Are You?* seemed to arrive on the late 1960s scene as if had always known its audience and vice versa, which meant a lot of jargon was on display mixed with some "fresh blood" in the monster gallery to liven up proceedings beyond the usual Gothic ailments. Ciné du Sasquatch was constantly encroaching upon the mainstream from its perennial edge of

regionalism; Hanna-Barbera Productions, with their unusually high dose of Yetis in their output, were a major reason this was so, as their sporadic but consistent usage of Bigfoot definitely helped raise an entire generation's awareness of the ground-swelling hominid phenomena.

Scream of the Sasquatch (2006)

Starring Andrew Schaffer, John Varesi, James Varesio, Greg Walker, Rudy DelRosario, Brian Muir, Myer Avedovech, Regina Varesio, Steve Michaels, John Guy, Maria Varesio, Crow Taylor, Jeff Jacob, Eric Roley and Beverly Gilray. Written by Guy Gilray, Andrew Schaffer and John Varesio. Produced and Directed by Guy Gilray. USA. Color. Stereo. 90 Minutes.

Overview: Young, proud, and dirt poor after his years as a Bigfoot hunter, skinny Frank VanderSchmidt is the rare breed of would-be cryptid slayer who likes to go it alone with only his wits and a high-powered rifle. His personal quest: shoot and kill a Sasquatch. As Frank concludes while being interviewed on camera, no one will believe anything less than a smoking 'Squatch corpse, and so that's what Frank is intending to bag. His steely persistence, mixed with his complete inability to register that he may be wasting valuable years of his young life basically acting like a hermit, makes for a compelling, always believable character. Frank is not much interested, however, in

Cover art for the DVD release of *Scream of the Sasquatch*.

anything beyond restocking his tent with survival supplies, cash handouts if one is interested in helping his Bigfoot research, and making sure he's on the prowl for any hominid afoot.

Meanwhile, middle-aged married man Ron Warren is also a Bigfoot researcher, but much more a weekend warrior type compared to Frank's near-survivalist methodology. Ron is a hardcore believer based on the fact he's had not one but two life-changing glimpses of Sasquatch in the wild. In terms of his approach to researching Bigfoot, he conveniently believes in the "hold your ground" strategy, which means Ron basically pulls up his camper to the same outdoor spot for years on end. Ron's strategy: sit patiently, grill steaks, drink brews, and wait for the beast to come to him. Ron's family tries to stick with him, particularly his teen son Mike, but his wife is beginning to think it may be a good time for a trial separation.

Slowly, both hunters' strategies are shown to contain flaws. Frank begins to wonder if it's all worth the high personal cost, wavering at times as he ekes out a living as the world's least successful hunter (having not killed his prey even after years of effort) and endures the harsh outdoor elements in his battered tent. Meanwhile, Ron grows estranged from son Mike when Mike uncomfortably admits on camera during an interview that he doesn't believe in Bigfoot, even though he believes his father saw something. Eventually driven to personal desperation with the break-up of his marriage and his own son's growing doubts as to his sanity, Ron vanishes one weekend in the woods, leaving his family wondering what has happened. Ron reappears after a week, claiming he was helped by a Bigfoot.

Sensing his rival is gaining on his only potential shot at fame (that is, shooting a Sasquatch), Frank decides to step up his game and go deeper into the wilderness than he normally might, concerned as he is that Ron will soon have Sasquatch in his camera sights and steal Frank's thunder. To his stunned amazement, Frank almost immediately sees Bigfoot on the horizon. Taking careful aim, he blasts the hominid in the chest. The creature staggers, screaming, until it is revealed to be none other than Ron in a Bigfoot costume. Ron's screaming son Mike drops his camera with which he's been taking hoax pictures to sell and races to his dying father's side. Later it is revealed that Ron acted out of desperation, hoping that his wife would rejoin the family if he could prove his ruinous obsession was real after all. He dies a hero to his family but leaves a sad pall over the community with his needless death.

* * * * *

If so many of the Bigfoot reports are ultimately resolved as being humans in costumes, then why have no credible reports emerged of a man dressed as Bigfoot being shot by hunters and landowners? The probability that someone donning a costume and running along a ridge line in the woods during deer season *not* being targeted by at least one zealot with a loaded rifle seems staggeringly remote indeed. So even if it makes for an abruptly comical shock ending, the violence that brings closure to *Scream of the Sasquatch* seems real-world appropriate in these gun-happy times, and does beg the question: If so many of these reported sightings are hoaxes perpetrated by a man in a monkey suit, why hasn't any accidental death gone along with it? Every year hunters die in accidents far more unlikely, from being struck by errant bullets to dropping or mishandling loaded weapons which discharge, and even to human error, such as Dick Cheney's when he blasted his friend's face while hunting on a private reserve. If a vice president can fall victim to accidental gun injury statistics, what are the odds at least one hoaxster would not have been shot from afar by now? It does make one ponder, both about the likelihood of Bigfoot's existence and the lack of intelligence of any prankster who would don a costume within a few hundred yards' range of gunfire just to earn a cheap, anonymous laugh.

Scream of the Sasquatch will not be to every Ciné du Sasquatch

fan's liking, as it stares without blinking at the two disparate Bigfoot believers and sees a plethora of character flaws in both. Frank is resilient to the point of self-sacrifice, and Ron sacrifices his family's well-being in order to maintain his own deluded fantasies of relevance via his "work" on Bigfoot. Neither paints a particularly healthy portrait of hominid research. Of course, Ciné du Sasquatch fans and cryptozoologists alike *are* accustomed to the ridicule that comes with the territory, having each developed tough hides to withstand the judgments of others. Seeing two more archetypes presented at their comic expense is not exactly an insult to the genre or true believers, especially when one grows to feel a bit attached to the lonely Frank (whose sense of competition is his only undoing and leads to tragic consequences) and at least empathy for the father-and-son Bigfoot weekenders. A moody comedy mixed with deadpan angst, *Scream of the Sasquatch* remains a gentle laughfest many genre fans will appreciate if constant laughs are not a prerequisite.

Screams of a Winter's Night (1979)

AKA: *Howlings of a Winter's Night*. Starring Matt Borel, Gil Glasgow, Patrick Byers, Mary Agen Cox, Robin Bradley, Ray Gaspard, Beverly Allen, Brandy Barrett, Charles Rucker, Jan Norton, Malcolm Edmonds, Nicole Salley, William Goodman and Jean Sweeney. Produced by S. Mark Lovell, Richard H. Wadsack and James L. Wilson. Written by Richard H. Wadsack. Directed by James L. Wilson. USA. Color. Mono. 91 Minutes.

Overview: A group of college students decide to take a winter break from school and stay in a cabin in the woods with a notorious reputation. Many years earlier, the original cabin's occupants were killed one winter's eve by a local Native American wind demon which supposedly inhabits the ancient woodlands. Most of the students are skeptical, but one among them, John, is obsessed with the cabin's murderous history. He fuels the anxiety of all present by citing endless facts about grisly homicides and serial killings that have happened in such remote settings in the past, setting everyone's nerves on edge.

Deciding to make the best of their first night together, they tell one another the scariest urban legends they each know, hoping the ghost stories will break the tension and put their fears into perspective. One of the tales told concerns a small cryptid creature known as the Moss Point Man, a four-foot-tall Bigfoot. It stalks the lonely bayou backroads in search of prey, which it finds when a young couple goes parking in its territory one dark night. The man realizes he has stupidly allowed the car to literally run out of gas instead of using that as his make-out line. He sets out on foot with gas can in hand for the nearest farmhouse, instructing his terrified girlfriend to keep the doors locked and wait for him. She protests, but he leaves her yelling at his back as he disappears into the gloom.

As soon as he is alone on the wood-lined road, however, he realizes he is being stalked by the Moss Point Man. He races as fast as he can back towards the car, but the creature gains on him, running parallel to him through the dense woodlands. The man dives into the roadside bushes, hoping to avoid the monster. Back at the car, the woman hears growling noises. She is frightened when the Moss Point Man leaps at the windows, attempting to pull her from the vehicle. Eventually the hominid ceases its attack, but the woman hears sounds from atop the car's roof which sound as if the creature may be clawing its way inside. She slowly sticks her head out of the window, only to see her dead date swinging from a mossy vine, blood dripping from his wounds onto the car's rooftop. She screams and the Moss Point Man rushes her. When she is found the next day, the terrified woman is tied to a tree trunk, alive but shocked beyond words. She has been secured by a mossy vine. When she recovers and tells her story, no one will believe her.

*****

Shot independently in Louisiana, *Screams of a Winter's Night* was a modest regional moneymaker in its state of origin. The twenty-something college students who produced it self-distributed their film by creating four 35mm prints and driving them from one theater to the next. Attracted by the notices indicating that a self-made movie turned a profit, Dimension Pictures picked it up for peanuts and released it throughout the country, particularly in the Northern and Eastern sections of the United States. As a result, the film made a healthy profit, though the indie filmmakers themselves saw none of the monies, as distribution deals notoriously deduct endless and largely bogus net costs from monies earned. Said costs never or rarely abate until and *if* the distributor decides to have mercy on the creators for personal, moral or ethical reasons (while this has undoubtedly happened on some rare occasions, existing documentation is hard to come by; the majority of the evidence indicates that distributors rarely if ever share the windfall with the filmmakers outside of a scheduled court room appearance).

Nevertheless, as a result of the successful exploitation campaign, *Screams of a Winter's Night* had a very small but dedicated impact on a generation of Ciné du Sasquatch viewers who were attracted by the film's PG rating. The equally limited but well-rented videocassette release later in the 1980s by the small outfit VCI out of Oklahoma further established this now well-regarded film's reputation. It is no classic by ordinary Hollywood production standards, but it has many positive qualities to its credit and has become something of a minor cult item in the intervening decades since it first scared audiences.

The wraparound and set up itself make *Screams of a Winter's Night* one of the first of the so-called urban legend movies. Today, with endless specials on television and websites (like the well-documented Snopes.com) dedicated to both debunking and legitimizing such popular folklore — usually told verbally prior to the rise of the Internet, where now it is sent from one recipient to the next via email — it is hard to remember that this very persistent form of viral communication once lacked a sociologist's fancy designation or available resources to check fact against fiction. As a result, the tales told in *Screams of a Winter's Night* have a peculiarly familiar feeling owing to their established status as preexisting tales told around the campfire. Oddly, however, rather than making the stories clichéd in tone, this familiarity adds a built-in sense of dread to the telling of each legend. As one of the first motion pictures to tell the stories in filmic form (and thus make them visual rather than aural in nature), the film's lack of polish and professional acting actually helps, supplying a necessary dose of suspension of disbelief.

This dovetails perfectly with much of Ciné du Sasquatch of the era, and why the genre has remained remarkably virile even when each new year sees dozens of new cryptid films and television shows flood the market. Simply stated, audiences love hearing tales they know and love seeing them visualized in screen imagery, whether real or folklore (the verdict is out as of this writing regarding Sasquatch; take your pick — it alters the actual impact on audiences very little either way, provided the film adaptation is generally faithful to the shared mythic concepts and well told as a filmed entertainment).

With this in mind, it's only fitting that *Screams of a Winter's Night* opens with a "Small-squatch" story that combines both Bigfoot and the old horror story told about the date who winds up dead in a treetop directly above the car. While countless variations of this story exist (the author heard it as a frightened child with the variant being a babysitter who tells the children in the stranded car to remain inside no matter what happens), the ending is always the same. There is a scratching or bumping sound on the rooftop, an ignored warning by the missing person not to look outside, and the final shock — the missing friend/babysitter/date is a murder victim, typically hanging by the neck or even by the ankles, his or her feet or knuckles rhythmically sliding back and forth against the car's roof as the wind slowly causes the body to twist and turn. There really is no way of knowing how ancient this story is if one accounts for technological changes; indeed, it is possible it goes back to the days (or nights!) of the horse and buggy (or even beyond).

The story is probably designed to scare young lovers away from the comfortable confines of the back seat. As such, it works remarkably well, positing the lurking horror of teenage pregnancy in the form of all the emotional underpinnings such a real-world experience might entail. To wit, the abandonment by the male figure who leaves the woman behind in the car (symbolic, if one takes it to the next level, of being stranded alone with her unborn child without the male's support); the dripping blood on the rooftop (representing either the loss of virginity or birth process itself); and even the male found hanging by his neck or upside-down, tied with a single vine or rope to a tree limb (obviously, this is an image of a child at birth, complete with umbilical cord). While it is easy to dismiss such analysis as so much pop psychology, the skeptic risks having no alternate explanation as to why certain situations and myths endure when others fail to be carried forth from one generation to the next. Sheer happenstance and a love of a good horror story are doubtlessly also contributing factors, but in an age where movies, horror books and the Internet make such gothic stories overly abundant, the encoded subtext of such myths nevertheless transcends the format of telling. In so many words, the story cuts through the media saturation because it subconsciously addresses the deeper, more primal fears all humans in the fragile dating years are prone to experience, and provides a collective catharsis for such ever-present anxieties.

If *Screams of a Winter's Night* were not so self-consciously about the art of storytelling itself and more the usual gorefest one often encounters in Bigfoot cinema, it would be useless to suggest that these deeper meanings lurk within the subtext of what is otherwise a conventional horror film. Nor is it fair to label this particular treatment of Bigfoot as anything more than average, as is the film itself. Rather, it is the peculiar quality the film imparts to the viewer that makes it worthwhile — it is restrained and Gothic rather than overblown and visceral. At least, that is, until the incredibly visceral ending sequence, in which the helpless college students are literally blown away. In this memorable scene, the entire cabin is attacked by an unseen howling wind demon. Amidst the roars and chaos that ensues, in which the cabin itself finally explodes as if caught in the vortex of a tornado from Hell itself, *Screams of a Winter's Night* earns it namesake. As the cast die one by one in a matter of horrific moments under crumbling beams and an exploding fireplace, the film suddenly achieves an unexpectedly surreal sense of terror that is nearly operatic in intensity. The long, sustained aria leading up to this crescendo pays off in viewer impact and is why the movie is well-regarded by such filmmakers as Quentin Tarantino, who introduced his rare 35mm print at the Grindhouse Film Festival in Los Angeles a few years ago.

Along with the suspenseful opening, in which a radio-styled play comprised entirely of audio is enacted against a black screen and white-lettered titles to introduce the back-story of the haunted cabin, *Screams of a Winter's Night* exceeds any expectations all but the harshest critics of such indie-made fare are likely to have. Though rare and hard to see as a result, it rewards patient and less-critical viewers with a sense of foreboding and dread.

Search for the Beast (1997)

Starring Rick Montana, Steven Steele, Holli Day, Kimberly L. Cole, David F. Friedman, Annalise Pierce, Trixie, Stupid D. Klowne and Jeffrey

Pierce. Directed by R. G. Arledge. USA. Color. Stereo. Videotape. 82 Minutes.

Overview: After a series of brutal murders deep in the Okaloosa wilderness of Alabama, Dr. David Stone, anthropologist, becomes convinced Sasquatch is behind the madness. Milton St. John, a wealthy supporter of Stone's university, offers Stone $100,000 if Stone will help track down the cryptid, which the local newspaper suggests has been responsible for up to 47 deaths. Eager to be of assistance (and be paid, at that), Stone agrees, though he's not too keen about the one condition St. John makes: Stone must allow St. John to send along an accompanying force of hired muscle to protect Dr. Stone, just in case the going gets dangerous. Setting aside his reservations, Dr. Stone realizes he'll never get a better chance to search for the beast and plays along.

As soon as Dr. Stone is out of earshot, St. John calls his hired goons and tells them to destroy the beast and kill Dr. Stone and his lovely college-aged assistant Wendy Williams. After hanging up, St. John studies a framed photo on his desk, openly weeping. The picture is of his deceased son, who Milton St. John believes was slaughtered by the Sasquatch, hence the older man's motivation to enact his revenge.

The rowdy group of irregulars St. John has hired are straight from the back page ads of a *Soldier of Fortune* magazine. Gun-toting men and women of dubious character with thick, Southern accents, they all tote high-powered weapons and eagerly snicker among themselves, realizing Stone's days are secretly as numbered as are the beast's itself. While camping and exchanging stories about the horrors of Bigfoot, Wendy and Dr. Stone share a tent. She admits she's always been attracted to her professor and acts on her emotions, making love with him.

The gun goons become separated from Dr. Stone and Wendy after they have an extended shoot-out with the snarling cryptid, which they manage to miss despite a barrage of bullets. Dr. Stone and his assistant set off deeper into the wilderness to find the lost survivalists. When it becomes apparent to the redneck gunners that they're the intended victims of Sasquatch and not vice versa, they take matters into their own hands, kidnapping Wendy and leaving Dr. Stone as bait for the beast to allow them time to escape. But Stone frees himself and gives chase. Before the ordeal is over, only Dr. Stone and Wendy survive, while the rest perish at the behest of the beast or Stone himself, who shotguns one of them to death in an act of vengeance. The pair escapes the forest and hail a passing truck. Meanwhile, a couple of young lovers are attacked by the beast, and the monster mounts the unsuspecting young woman.

* * * * *

Despite much competition for the title, *Search for the Beast* is probably the worst Bigfoot movie ever made. Given the sheer number of "Bad-squatch" films in the lower rungs of cryptid cinema viewing hell, that's quite an achievement. Against all odds, however, *Search for the Beast* manages to run its course with nary an original nor well-executed moment of even marginal entertainment. Whether it's the atrocious porn-styled acting, the neo–Godardian (not!) jump cuts, the rinky dink Bigfoot costume (tantamount to a gorilla suit found at a 99 Cents store the week *after* Halloween markdowns), the cheesy home video look, the amateur night in Dixie non-direction, the offensive sex scenes or the torpid pacing, *Search for the Beast* staggers the viewer with one jaw-dropping moment after another of bad film-making technique.

Even the most ardent fan of Ciné du Sasquatch will find it difficult to sit through *Search for the Beast* to formulate any honest appraisal. Put another way, if you watch this "effort" (as in Herculean) and don't worry about the mental health of all involved in its making (let alone your own state of mind afterwards), you are far more unkind than any harsh words this critique could catalog against the creators themselves; all should seek immediate, unqualified help from the nearest available psychiatrist. There is a dangerous, mordant quality that perversely pervades the picture that isn't just squirm-inducing but outright displays latent sociopathology on the part of its so-called director, one R.G. Arledge. This film feels as if a camcorder were placed in the hands of a serial killer recently escaped from a maximum security prison and whose low-grade charisma subsequently charmed enough gutter-level "actors" picked up hitchhiking along the way to participate in his misogynistic vision, so atrocious are the results. Mindless and mindlessly so, *Search for the Beast* induces a schizoid stupor from the opening moments and never relents.

What passes for a plot is quintessential for the genre and includes all the relevant clichéd characters: the believer scientist; the ruthless businessman; the sleazy bimbo; the paramilitary rednecks; and, of course, a cryptid that kills without rational explanation (save perhaps that the actor inside the stifling-looking excuse for a costume was probably close to having a psychotic breakdown given this was obviously shot in the heat and humidity of a grueling summer season, as witnessed by the sweat-stained cut-offs and ragged tee-shirts the cast wear throughout). The storyline vanishes approximately halfway through, at which point *Search for the Beast* lapses from comatose exposition into narrative incomprehensibility. Long, long stretches are spent at this point showing the cast wandering through the forest and gawking at various poorly-lit, handheld shots of such "exotic" wild-life specimens as a frog and a deer. After an endless amount of such padding, the film finally winds to a merciful though repulsive finale.

What can be said about the cast save that most had the common sense to use such clever thespian pseudonyms as Holli Day or Stupid D. Klowne rather than their actual names (where was this modicum of reservation and critical thinking skills when they first agreed to appear in *Search for the Beast*, one is left to ponder)? As Dr. David Stone (appropriately named, given his performance), Rick Montana is several notches below Swedish wrestler-turned-actor Tor Johnson in believability. This is not surprising, given that Montana's previous credits include acting and directing in his own no-budget *Redneck Revenge* as well as small roles in *Invisible Mom 2* and *Bikini Hoe-Down*. Less excusable is exploitation filmmaking king David F. Friedman's cameo as one Milton St. John, though, to his credit, he turns in what becomes the only passable performance. He actually seems to be enjoying himself, but this may be as much from the relief of semi-retirement — or that it clearly only took an hour or less to shoot his scene. If the latter, he had the peace of mind in knowing that his return to retirement lay just around the corner. No such luck, alas, for the *Search for the Beast* viewer, as Friedman's scene occurs early in the film, leaving well over an hour to endure.

The remainder of the amateurish, understudy-quality cast are virtually indistinguishable from one another; all wear the same vapid expression of a deer caught looking far too long into the headlights and rendered brain dead from the experience. At least one can state such metaphorically illuminated deer are at least visible; the same cannot be said for the human actors, as they are so badly lit that most times they are simply silhouetted faces against a perennially green background of foliage.

The Bigfoot costume is like something out of a bad junior high school comedy revue. The two "actors" who take turns portraying the creature both have skinny legs and arms, but their bellies are enormous in comparison. Either they were consuming mass quantities of beer prior to the shoot in a low-budget variation of Robert DeNiro preparing to play Jack LaMotta in *Raging Bull*, or — the more obvious probability, given the lumpy shape — a pillow has been hastily stuffed into the costume's cavernous gut to pad it out. Making matters far, far worse is the lame photography of the costume, consisting of long takes and close-ups in broad daylight. With its comical expression, goofy ping pong eyeballs, and rubbery countenance, the face mask appears to be of the common store-bought variety, though one suspects (hopes?) the filmmakers shoplifted the item rather than squander its one dollar retail price. This may read as harsh criticism, but like everything else in *Search for the Beast*, the mask is criminal in intent.

The editors seem to have acknowledged just how pathetic the footage of the stiff-legged Sasquatch appeared. They consistently apply a video filter designed to make the footage strobe as if intermittently freezing. Rather than creating a mood of unrelenting terror as intended, however, the opposite effect is achieved. Instead of seeing less of the mask, the viewer is "treated" to what amounts to a series of frozen close-up tableaux of the dime store monster in a strobic, seizure-inducing display of limited animation that rivals the worst Saturday morning cartoon efforts for sheer jerkiness.

But nothing is so degraded — and degrading — in *Search for the Beast* as the manner in which the filmmakers treat the female characters. It is nothing short of cinematic sadism. From the opening in which the slutty camper eagerly exposes her ample breasts, dimly lit by a flashlight, inside a tent while her male companion remains clothed, to the lingering sequence in which a diminutive woman hiker undresses and showers in a waterfall for endless minutes to no narrative advancement whatsoever while the beast heavily pants on the soundtrack, and especially to the final sequence in which a female hiker is dressed like a school girl in red-striped stockings, pigtails and short mini-skirt (while camping!), *Search for the Beast* induces a sleazy feeling of voyeurism that's truly indefensible. The shots of the candy-striped stocking girl having doggy-styled sex with her boyfriend — already grotesquely uncomfortable given the crude manner in which it is shot, revealing the actress' clear display of displeasure throughout — turns nightmarishly nauseous as the boyfriend is killed by Bigfoot, whereupon the cryptid takes the boyfriend's place without the woman even noticing the difference! It takes a real sociopath to imagine such a scene as anything other than deplorable; it takes a psychopath in the director's chair to actually shoot this as the final image of his film. To his credit, it does capture the utter contempt on display for the viewing audience by the creator. But it also leaves a feeling of degradation in any non-incarcerated watcher.

While it harkens to the Bigfoot sex films preceding it, such as *Ape Canyon, Beauties and the Beast* and others, the lack of talent, imagination and skill on display throughout renders this debacle unwatchable by even the most ardent fans of anything but hardcore pornography minus that genre's erotic content. All things considered, the filmmakers need look no further than their own cracked mirrors to find the sex-obsessed, titular monster staring back at themselves; their *Search for the Beast* begins and ends with their own deplorable inspirations to memorialize this work of sado-masochism as their legacy. And while such vitriolic hyperbole often induces some fans of Grade-Z cinema to seek out the referenced titles, this one should truly be avoided at all possible costs. This entry in the genre is unwatchably bad and offers nothing in return save remorseful self-degradation. The only true search will be for the DVD player's "eject" button.

The Secret Saturdays (Multiple Episodes) (2008) (TV)

Featuring the voices of Phil Morris, Nicole Sullivan, Sam Lerner, Diedrich Bader, Fred Tatasciore, Will Friedle and Corey Burton. Produced by Fred Schaefer and Scott Jeralds. Created by Jay Stephens. Directed by Scott Jeralds. Canada. Color. Stereo. 30 Minutes.

Overview: There exists a hidden branch of the study of science known only to a handful of initiates. It belongs to those who are members of the Secret Scientists, a cult of scientists who live in a hidden base designed as the last great hope of mankind should the planet face sudden extinction or invasion. Zac Saturday and his fellow Saturday family members willfully investigate any anomalies that suddenly arise in regards to cryptids across the globe. As the family Saturday travels the globe at the behest of the Secret Scientists, they encounter a variety of so-called "folklore" myths that turn out to be snarling, dangerous "specimens" when they confront said beasts in a life-or-death struggle. Making matters worse for the Saturdays, an evil man named V.V. Argost, host of a Fortean-themed TV show called *Weird World*, competes with a masked mastermind of cryptid abduction named Van Rook, among other foes, to make the Saturday family's latest attempts to gain knowledge and thwart destruction all the more difficult.

* * * * *

Very much a postmodern tribute to Hanna-Barbera's influential Alex Toth–designed series *The Herculoids* and *Jonny Quest*, *The Secret Saturdays* brings to the forefront cryptozoology like never before, in that the entire Saturday family is into the subject. This is a novel introduction to Ciné du Sasquatch, as slyly as it may have entered. Much like *Jonny Quest* and his familial entourage never had to worry about the cost of all the cool gadgets they inevitably wrecked by each show's end, *The Secret Saturdays* is set in a wonderland wherein costs and liability issues remain blissfully off-screen. To protect and serve, while someone else (conveniently never shown) foots the bill, is the order of the day.

The style is Anime all the way, but there is enough Westernization in the static nature of the shots to insure it stays focused on the narrative. The tone is very *Scooby Doo, Where Are You?* mixed with *The Groovy Ghoulies*. The technical quality is excellent (making good use of modern, cost-cutting technologies available on the digital production and post-production front) and video-recorded with a demonstrable desire on the part of the creators to give back much of the sense of dumbfounded "Cool!" they uttered when watching 1970s Hanna-Barbera output as tykes themselves. With the strangely muted, almost pastel color scheme, as well as the stark imagery itself, drawn with an admiring sense of genuine, loving cinematic memories, *The Secret Saturdays* is a welcome addition to Ciné du Sasquatch. While the series never enjoyed the huge success of other cable staples such as *SpongeBob SquarePants* or *Jimmy Neutron, Boy Genius*, it was well-reviewed and well-received among its small but loyal audience until it was finally cancelled by the network without much explanation.

Writing quality tends to be variable during the early production phases of any new TV series, as it takes the various creative teams time to synchronize, nurture, and narratively guide the series' dramatic possibilities. As such, *The Secret Saturdays* is above average, always trying to at least offer an imaginative new way to portray some of the classic Ciné du Sasquatch scenarios via clever dialogue, cinematic composition, effective editing, etc. If nothing else, the color range used throughout *The Secret Saturdays* and its stylistic influences (a cross between Alex Toth and modern Manga) gives it the ultimate cult film appeal: It rewards repeated viewings; has a genuinely well-realized directorial vision; and was simply "too much to get" for some audiences of its day.

The Yeti is drawn like a white-furred variant on Igoo the Rock Ape from the campy favorite *The Herculoids*. At once super cool-looking and very Anime-tinged, *The Secret Saturdays*' Abominable Snowman is nonetheless also quite mysterious, a parallel being with one foot on either side of two different co-existent realities. This mystical, ethereal approach gives the Yeti a quality that is very much in line with the "Spirit Man of the Woods" tag given to Sasquatch by many indigenous people — at once majestic yet equally sinister. Whatever one's taste in such animated hominid undertakings, *The Secret Saturdays* can only be faulted by those who allow for nothing less than full-motion, hand-drawn cel animation for each and *every* undertaking—a decidedly unrealistic and self-defeating rule of aesthetic limitation if ever there was one. While it remained safely ensconced within the Men in Black, post–*X-Files* world (albeit with super-powers), *The Secret Saturdays* is nevertheless a refreshing pseudo–Anime series that still maintains high interest for fans of both documentary and fictional Ciné du Sasquatch, as it includes the best of both worlds. The actual protagonists are professional cryptozoologists by trade. The Secret Scientists who employ them value their expertise and therefore hire the Saturdays because of their vast storehouse of personal and professional experience within the field. Rarely have cryptozoologists been portrayed as working within a field deemed so worthwhile *and* not been seen as holding the stereotypical "outside the mainstream" viewpoint. Here they are the heroes, front and center, and with superhero powers to boot! It *is* the ultimate progression in terms of Sasquatch portrayal, in that nearly a century into the genre itself, shows such as *The Secret Saturdays* have flipped the genre's precepts on their heads. By the time of *The Secret Saturdays'* production, postmodernism has made it easy to envision the superheroes as basically good if anonymous neighbors living next door rather than eccentric, multi-millionaire, self-torturing souls hanging out in their own impenetrable private subterranean bat cave. These protagonists are not merely cryptozoologists, they're a true "family," with all the inherent psychological advantages and drawbacks. Again, in a genre where characters are often not even given internal conflict with which to work, this is a minor but noteworthy achievement. Likewise, the Yeti has evolved from background predator to vital element of the Saturday family's success, which—though not as unprecedented as the cryptozoologists becoming bona fide heroes—still shows that the Ciné du Sasquatch genre can be inverted, stretched, and re-formed in innumerable patterns.

Secrets and Mysteries ("Sasquatch") (1988) (TV) (Doc)

Featuring Donald Cyr, John Andreson, Robert E. Stone, David Goudsward, Ed Krupp and Edward Mulhare. Produced by Glenn Kirschbaum and Craig Haffner. Written by Erik Nelson. Directed by Joe Dea and Graeme Whifler. USA. Color. Stereo. 30 Minutes.

Overview: Velvety-smooth host Edward Mulhare takes the viewer on an in-depth tour of each week's new subject matter. In "Sasquatch" the filmmakers feature serious and respectful interviews with field experts and researchers. Mulhare worked forever in the shadow of Rex Harrison after replacing him on the Broadway run of *My Fair Lady* but was his own accomplished actor, as was proven by Mulhare on the original *Battlestar Galactica*, by playing Captain Daniel Gregg for 50 episodes of *The Ghost and Mrs. Muir*, and appearances on other great one-hour format TV classics such as *The F.B.I.*, *Cannon*, *The Outer Limits*, *Knight Rider*, and *The Girl from U.N.C.L.E.*, as well as quality features like *Von Ryan's Express* and *Our Man Flint*. That's a lot of experience and charisma honed to perfection, and Mulhare makes an admirable if more "stiff upper-lipped" variant on Rod Serling as the loquacious host, especially with a subject worthy of his keenly sly delivery, which enables Mulhare to keep those on both sides of the argument entertained.

Secrets of the Unknown ("Big Foot") (1998) (TV) (Doc)

Featuring Edward Mulhare. Produced by Warren Carr, Michael Grais and Mark Victor. Written by Michael Grais and Mark Victor. Directed by Gilbert Shilton. USA. Color. Stereo. 22 Minutes.

Overview: Silken-voiced character actor Edward Mulhare, star of TV's *Knight Rider* and *The Ghost and Mrs. Muir*, plays a more genial version of Leonard Nimoy as host of another in a long series of *In Search Of* redos. While technically well-photographed, *Secrets of the Unknown*—and in particular "Big Foot"—suffers from a lack of novelty and the usual, unconvincing cryptid recreations via gorilla suit. Little in the way of new information or insight is offered on the subject matter, rendering most of "Big Foot" of interest to none but novice viewers. Several eyewitnesses are interviewed, but nothing in the way of definitive evidence is catalogued. The *Secrets of the Unknown* series originally aired on ABC before being released on home video. Other episodes cover the usual Fortean array of topics, such as UFOs, Nostradamus, pyramid power, lake monsters, psychic energy and the like. There were 26 of these half-hour shows produced.

Sesquac: The Story of Sasquatch (2007)

Starring Bryan Davis, Brandon Zelensky, Ryne Yarger, Kristi Gormont, Dave Gormont, Curt Henry, Courtney Hughes, Katy Dorsey and Hannah Thompson. Produced by Bryan Davis and Brandon Zelensky. Written by Bryan Davis, Curt Henry, Ryne Yarger and Brandon Zelensky. Directed by Bryan Davis. USA. Color. Stereo. 43 Minutes.

Overview: Sasquatch and his suburban neo-punk buddies hang out in a low-down, *Mean Streets* style while ripping off some chill moves on their boards in mid-air, doing a full-length Olympic pool for a few work-out laps, and seeking to let it all hang out in trendy nightclubs 'til dawn. Unfortunately, Sesquac is a numero uno target for the Paparazzi, who are constantly in the hirsute hominid's face, snapping digital pictures and grinding out digital video. They're not at Sasquatch's throat merely to get tabloid pictures or cell phone video uploads for outfits like TMZ.com; rather, some work for a new reality TV series which aims to expose Sesquac's heretofore private life with the ladies. As if *this* wasn't stressful enough, Sasquatch is also in the middle of a suspected love triangle involving a jealous husband and his actress wife, the latter of whom Sesquac happens to know from work. Ironically, Sesquac is innocent of any fooling around, but his past is rapidly catching up with him and threatening the worst possible reprisal—becoming yesterday's Tweet topic of thumb-versation: stale news.

* * * * *

Basically a short series of videos edited together into a nearly feature length odyssey, *Sesquac: The Story of Sasquatch* is an amateurish attempt to find some beer-guzzling, bong-igniting, profanity-laden humor in Sasquatch by presenting the cryptid as "just one of the gang"—and the one who just happens to have camera crews and paparazzi constantly interrupting the hominid's planned "normal" life.

It's like a Bigfoot version of *Buckaroo Banzai Across the Eighth Dimension*. Just as Buckaroo could be a multiverse of character possibilities—rock guitar god, brilliant scientist, etc.—so Sesquac is attempting to be the Renaissance Hominid by pounding his skateboard against various institutional guardians, keepin' it real with his home boys, clubbing, swimming, etc. The difference, of course, is that *Buckaroo Banzai* had a brilliant cast of eccentric character actors and a legitimate production budget, whereas *Sesquac: The Story of Sasquatch* lacks an experienced cast, crew, and financial resources. As a result, all but the most forgiving Ciné du Sasquatch aficionados will find *Sesquac: The Story of Sasquatch* to be little more than a glorified short film that's much too long (at 45 minutes) to make an impact. There are some laughs, but nothing much beyond them.

7 Faces of Dr. Lao (1964) (Cameo)

AKA: *Seven Faces of Dr. Lao*; *The Secret World of Dr. Lao*. Starring Tony Randall, Barbara Eden, Arthur O'Connell, John Ericson, Noah Beery Jr., Lee Patrick, Chubby Johnson and Péter Pál. Produced by George Pal. Written by Charles Beaumont and Ben Hecht. Based on the novel *The Circus of Dr. Lao* by Charles G. Finney. Directed by George Pal. USA. Metrocolor. Mono. 100 Minutes.

Overview: In the American Old West, a traveling carnival arrives in a small town to help relieve the boredom of local residents. The mysterious owner and solo operator of the carnival is known as Dr. Lao, an elderly albeit spry Asian gentleman. His fantastical sideshow of attractions holds up a dark mirror to the various townspeople who venture into the circus; all are shown distorted versions of themselves in an apparent warning of their various failings and vanities. Among the menagerie of monsters is an Abominable Snowman, as elusive as it is shy.

During the circus' stay in town, Dr. Lao befriends a fatherless young boy and, through patient counseling and displays of kindness, helps the child come to understand that where there is love in life, magic is always sure to follow. As he departs, Dr. Lao leaves the boy — and indeed the entire citizenry — better off than when he arrived, having taught all who would open their hearts and minds to an undeniably better moral code of existence that stresses balance, fairness, and concern for your fellow living beings (be they human, hominid, or animal).

* * * * *

George Pal's delightful visualization of the Yeti in *7 Faces of Dr. Lao* is admittedly brief in screen time but long in impact. And none can say the famed director and/or producer of such beloved fantasy fare as *The Time Machine* and *The War of the Worlds* didn't literally and figuratively have his very essence invested in the Abominable Snowman he cameos — the part is portrayed by his son Péter Pál! As a mute, voyeuristic Yeti, the cryptid depicted is more human-like than many other Ciné du Sasquatch figures, a curious cross between the classic image of the reclusive Himalayan Snowman and the more fearsome aspects of Pal's earlier Morlocks in his own screen adaptation of Wells' *The Time Machine*.

While Tony Randall steals the overall show with his Peter Sellers–like ability to flawlessly portray multiple roles, the Yeti is an adroit scene stealer in its two highlighted scenes as well. Much credit is due to make-up effects artist William Tuttle, who won a well-deserved Academy Award for his efforts, which was given to the long-time MGM in-house artist a full 17 years before the Oscar was annually awarded for Best Makeup. Tuttle was no stranger to fantasy cinema and television, having worked on *The Twilight Zone*, *Forbidden Planet* and Pal's *The Time Machine*, as well as non-fantasy efforts such as Hitchcock's *North by Northwest* and musicals such as *Seven Brides for Seven Brothers* and *An American in Paris*. With such credentials, it is no small exaggeration to suggest that, along with Rick Baker's later contribution to the Ciné du Sasquatch genre with *Harry and the Hendersons*, William Tuttle was one of the most renowned make-up artists ever to create a filmic cryptid.

The character of the Yeti is also compelling: Rather than the usual monster-out-to-devour portrayal, this likeable (though fearsome-looking) Abominable Snowman is quite the opposite. It hides from human contact as much as possible, a benign helper rather than a center stage attraction of the circus. This is much more in line with the real-life descriptions of the Yeti (as being passive unless threatened) than so many earlier genre incarnations, such as in *Man Beast*, *The Snow Creature*, and *The Monster of the Volcano*. Indeed, *7 Faces of Dr. Lao* stands alongside *The Abominable Snowman* in terms of empathetic cryptid depiction.

The shy Abominable Snowman (Péter Pál) from *The 7 Faces of Dr. Lao*. William Tuttle's imaginative make-up designs won him an Oscar.

As the film makes abundantly clear, the real villains of *7 Faces of Dr. Lao* are never the sideshow oddities but the sleepwalking townspeople themselves. The humans all succumb to various foibles — greed, intolerance, desire, and violence — when faced with their Jungian Animus selves in the shadowy forms Dr. Lao portrays so well. Much like Gene Wilder as the titular hero in *Willy Wonka & the Chocolate Factory*, the good doctor forces the reluctant residents to realize that the real "freaks" are themselves, because they alone possess the power, and therefore responsibility, to affect social change and render justice. This is clearly within the thematic core of earlier Ciné du Sasquatch entries, wherein humans are nearly always presented as intruders into the world of the Yeti, and who little realize they bring with them all too often the worst — not the best — of human nature. Only after they face the purer savagery of the Abominable Snowman and its instinctive fight for survival against the invaders and their superior technologies (along with the humans' inevitable need to exploit either the cryptid's resources or its very existence in and of itself) do any human survivors reach an understanding: The Abominable is located more deeply within their own souls than within any external projection they render upon the cryptid they face down.

It is a sobering conclusion, one perhaps unexpectedly rendered all the more poignant because it is so gently but convincingly illustrated in a so-called kiddy movie such as *7 Faces of Dr. Lao*. But as classic fairy tales and seemingly simple myths reveal upon closer introspection, the deeper truths are often encoded within sugar-coated lumps of candy where human truths are concerned. As such, Pal's film represents a continuation of the themes ever-present in Ciné du Sasquatch to this very date, which is all the more remarkable given that the Yeti has only two fleeting scenes in the entire film.

Shaawanoki (1990) (Doc)

AKA: *Shaawanoki: The Skunk Ape—Florida's Bigfoot*. Featuring Peter Byrne. Produced by Peter Byrne, Ronnie Roseman and Andreas Wallach. USA. Color. Stereo. 60 Minutes.

Overview: The Seminole Indians of Florida had a word for the mysterious, man-like monster that would appear at night and steal the human fishermen's strung-up catch of the day—"Shaawanoki" or "Man of the Swamps." Legendary crypto-hunter and Bigfoot researcher Peter Byrne helms one last steady effort as the Main Headline Attraction, which, given his amazing career, was well-deserved. If anyone could lay claim to a crypto–Cousteau title as adventurer and explorer in terms of hominology, Peter Byrne definitely had a serious stake in the outcome, a stake he'd professionally earned with thousands of hours of skeptical scientific analysis, eyewitness interviewing, and making available said relevant data to various conferences, websites, scientific and Fortean journals, and media outlets with a regularity that at the least indicated the Man in Charge was no slacker nor shyster.

Peter Byrne actually records some elders of one Seminole tribe disputing the idea that Shaawanoki was a bipedal hominid; if anything, the Seminoles adamantly defend the term as referring not to a swamp Bigfoot, but to either a giant snapping turtle or an alligator species large enough to cause human fatalities. Byrne also treks into the treacherous, largely unexplored terrain of Florida that many Americans have no idea even exists, and makes a very convincing case as to how a hominid species of the Skunk Ape's size could at least find all the food and shelter it would need to exist without detection.

Byrne and his team also don Yeti costumes in order to dramatically stage several historical Skunk Ape/human encounter moments. These recreated incidents are based upon research by none other than Byrne himself, who was known for his serious documentation of subjective witness veracity, investigated facts, verified dates and places, corroborating physical evidence (if any), etc. It must have been quite gratifying for a man who spent much of his adult life in search of one hominid after another to have the pleasure of selecting which Skunk Ape stories were so noteworthy as to be incidents forever memorialized in a documentary video, when the vast majority of reports are simply never known to the general public. This is not the most exciting Ciné du Sasquatch documentary by far, but Byrne's likeable low-budget passion for his subject matter outweighs the lack of production value on the whole.

The Shabbos Bigfoot (2006)

Starring Heidi Schooler, Patrick Coleman Duncan, Andrew Goldenberg, Darren Joel, Susan Grace, Leo Weltman, Rebecca Metz, Kerry Ham-

mond and Armand Tripp Jahangiri. Produced by Arnie Benn and Patrick Coleman Duncan. Written and Directed by Patrick Coleman Duncan. USA. Color. Stereo. 22 Minutes.

Overview: A cryptozoologist is invited to a Seder by his girlfriend. Alas, her Jewish family is less than impressed when they learn of her paramour's profession. He defends cryptozoology with a passion, tolerating their ridicule until the Seder starts. But as the religious ceremony proceeds, the cryptozoologist laments the superstitious nature of such fairy tale beliefs as God, lacking any concrete evidence of His existence. An ironic, funny conversation ensues.

This short film plays upon the hilarity of those who see their own faith-based beliefs as sacrosanct while laughing openly at others whose religious tenets they find unacceptable. While the cryptozoologist is never portrayed as an outright religious believer per se, his undying devotion to Bigfoot (or, as he corrects one of the Jewish family members, "We in the business prefer to use the Native American name—Sasquatch")—lacking any definitive evidence to offer as conclusive proof of the cryptid's existence—transforms science into religion. The Jewish family, in contrast, cannot understand how a grown man can believe in such "nonsense" as a hairy hominid roaming modern-day forests and mountaintops. Likewise, the cryptozoologist is skeptical of an unseen God who manipulates the fate of mankind just because an ancient religious tradition says it is true.

Had the filmmaker played the Jewish family as orthodox to a fault, *The Shabbos Bigfoot* would not have been as satirically biting. But because the family is clearly very modern and observes the holiday more out of cultural respect than any deeply-held religious belief, it further begs the ironic question of the comedic short: Who is to say what pairs of animals Yaweh did or didn't include on Noah's Ark, after all? Likewise, the egg-headed cryptozoologist is so full of his own beliefs that he cannot see the fallacy of his own position as having violated one of the fundamental basics of his own "religious faith" in the scientific method—he puts a priori belief ahead of objective evidence.

Shot on a very low budget, *The Shabbos Bigfoot* is still a worthwhile short film for those Ciné du Sasquatch fans who appreciate the real-world complexity of stating a belief in a cryptid species and the ensuing reactions that often accompany said statements. The cast, in particular, are especially well-selected for their roles and bring an immediate sense of professionalism to what is a modest but entertaining effort.

Short Man of the Forest (2007) (Doc)

AKA: *Search for the Orang Pendek*. Featuring Murray Collins, Debbie Martyr and Jeremy Holden. UK. Color. Stereo. 88 Minutes.

Overview: Primatologist Murray Collins travels to the jungles of Sumatra to investigate the sightings of the Orang Pendek ("short man of the forest"), whose reported encounters have been going on for centuries in the remote wilderness there. Among those Collins interviews are Debbie Martyr, who has spent over 15 years in Sumatra and is now head of the Tiger Protection and Conservation Unit there; as well as Jeremy Holden, her former partner in the project who is a professional photographer. Both Martyr and Holden claim to have seen the elusive Orang Pendek on several different occasions, though Holden was never able to photograph it. They do collect some physical evidence, however, including castings of footprints left by the hominid. Though often described as very short in stature, the Orang Pendek walks mostly in an upright bipedal fashion, according to witnesses, which all but eliminates the probability it is an Orangutan being mistaken for a cryptid hominid by untrained observers (as Orangutans are unable to sustain such locomotion save in very short bursts).

Shriek of the Mutilated (1974)

AKA: *Mutilated*; *Scream of the Snowbeast*. Starring Alan Brock, Jennifer Stock, Tawm Ellis, Michael Harris, Darcy Brown, Jack Neubeck, Tom Grail, Luci Brandt, Ivan Agar, Marina Stefan, Harriet McFaul, Jimmy Silva and Ed Adlum. Produced by Ed Adlum. Written by Ed Adlum and Ed Kelleher. Directed by Mike Findlay. USA. Color. Mono. 86 Minutes.

Overview: Dr. Ernst Prell, a college professor, has an obsession with Yeti, which he is certain exists in the upstate New York wilderness area. In the past he has lead various expeditions into the forests there, only to see them slaughtered by the creature while he remained the only survivor. Because no one believes him, Dr. Prell is determined beyond reason to capture or at least prove the Yeti is real. To this end, Prell stages trips every seven years with any foolhardy students in his class who are willing to risk life and limb for fame and glory (not to mention a guaranteed A in his course).

At a party held by a group of the volunteer students the night prior to departure, however, a drunken guest named Spencer St. Claire and his depressed wife April attend (despite the fact St. Claire is much older than the gathered group). He warns them that he is a survivor of Dr. Prell's earlier expedition, which ended in tragedy, and that the students are in mortal danger should they take the trip. He bellows that the Yeti is all-too-real and all-too-savage, and that they have no hope against it. Embarrassed and humiliated by her bellicose husband, April St. Claire drags him home to their dingy apartment, whereupon she berates him for being an abject failure who cannot get his life together. His anger fueled by booze, St. Claire cuts his wife's throat and plops into a warm bath, still wearing his blood-stained clothes. As he drinks straight from a bottle, April revives herself just long enough to crawl into the bathroom with a toaster, plug it in, and toss it into the tub with her dying breath. Her husband dies screaming, electrocuted.

Meanwhile, the students leave early the next morning with Dr. Prell, unaware of the tragic deaths of the St. Claires. After a drive into the wilderness area of Boot Island, New York, they arrive at a gated mansion owned by wealthy, eccentric Dr. Karl Werner, who shares Dr. Prell's fascination with tracking down the elusive, murderous Abominable Snowman. Their first night in the mansion, Dr. Werner entertains them with tales of the Yeti's past transgressions and his belief the beast actually inhabits the vast acres surrounding his aristocratic island stronghold. The students are unsettled not only by the stories, but also by the hulking, mute manservant Laughing Crow, whom Dr. Werner explains is a Native American descendent.

The students attempt to maintain their composure, but one-by-one they fall prey to the lurking Yeti in a series of grisly attacks. Dr. Prell finally convinces the survivors that they must use the corpse of one of the murdered female students as bait for the ravenous cryptid and then kill it when the Yeti is feasting. But this morbid strategy backfires, and soon the ultimate horror is revealed: The Yeti is but a suited fiction carried out alternately by Dr. Prell and Dr. Werner as a pretext to lure students to the mansion for a once-every-seven-years ritual cannibal cult sacrifice, at which an international gathering of elite power types feast upon the student corpses and thereby leave no trace of them for discovery.

* * * * *

Shriek of the Mutilated has been largely dismissed by many fans of Ciné du Sasquatch as not being a legitimate Yeti film because of the "surprise" revelation at the final reel. But in and of itself, the genre is not free from the hoary "it was actually just a man in a suit" trick ending, as several other Bigfoot movies have revealed. And besides, *Shriek of the Mutilated* has all the other defining characteristics of the genre as a whole: bad acting, atrocious dialogue, an unconvincing

The patchwork Yeti costume reveals its threadbare origins during the final assault sequence of *Shriek of the Mutilated*.

Yeti costume, unbelievably inept attack sequences, and a low-budget love of lurid violence for violence's sake.

Not that the film lacks redeeming features. For example, if the viewer is lucky enough to locate one of the rare VHS editions via the Internet, s/he will be treated to the inanely catchy pop Muzak tune "Popcorn," the epitome of 1970s stock music cues. This over-used ditty quickly became a staple of every local television talk show and newscast in the country during the Polyester decade, offering as it did a perfect distillation of gleeful, upbeat tempo mixed with complete non-offensiveness — not unlike its namesake product. Director Mike Findlay features it in *Shriek of the Mutilated*'s opening reel during an extended (read: padded for running time) party sequence. While a popcorn machine spews fluffy kernels to the "Popcorn" theme (wink, wink, nudge, nudge — *get it?*), college kids drink and dance to a swirl of psychedelic colors that feel more appropriate to the 1960s than the film's production era. This actually offers hungry viewers a chance to pop some corn of their own and not miss anything as far as the film itself is concerned. Alas, the DVD edition of the film overdubs the "Popcorn" theme with tedium-inducing stock music, which ruins the effect Findlay was obviously seeking. So while often retaining the violence, which was cut from the television syndication version, avoid the DVD version if you can locate the videocassette, if for no other reason than to make the party sequence bearable as a viewing experience.

But do make it back in time for the sequence that follows, in which a drunken Spencer St. Claire and wife April have it out in their roach-infested apartment after Spencer makes an ass of himself at the party by warning the students that the Yeti is real and will kill them all. Four sheets to the wind and tired of his wife's complaints that he will never overcome his tragic past (he was nearly slaughtered by the beast), Spencer does what any domestic violence-prone mate would do and slits April's throat with a gratuitous excess of pleasure. The next cut (pun intended) is perhaps unintentionally hilarious — Spencer now sits in the bathtub, chugging alcohol, uselessly scrubbing his bloodstained shirt with a sponge! Meanwhile, the dying April crawls into the kitchen (this despite her throat having been cut!), retrieves a toaster, slithers into the bathroom, plugs the toaster in, and tosses it into the tub, frying Spencer to a well-done crisp.

What this morbid yet darkly humorous sequence has to do with the Yeti — or anything that follows in *Shriek of the Mutilated*— is never even remotely delineated. Still, in terms of its unmitigated gall, it's the highlight of the movie and genuinely unexpected (in a Coen Brothers circa *Blood Simple* manner). The scene feels lifted out of an early John Waters shock comedy, such as *Hag in a Black Leather Jacket* or *Multiple Maniacs*, so audaciously out-of-context is its tone and absurd in its realization in comparison to the rest of the film.

Sadly, the remainder of *Shriek of the Mutilated* is a predictable riff on the Agatha Christie "old dark house" formula, which is as ineffectively disguised as the obviousness of the Yeti suit. The students are, for all practical purposes, unrelentingly stupid and exhibit little in the way of charm, likeability or character motivation. For example, when warned by Dr. Werner of the Yeti's horrific need for human flesh, the stud of the four-student assembly takes guitar in hand and sings a ditty with a lyrical refrain that goes: "He'll turn your threesome into a twosome." If that by chance reads as amusing, rest assured the ham-fisted delivery by the crooner, his awful guitar plucking and creaky vocal styling — not to mention the other students marveling at the singer's immense witticism — render the effect wince-inducing. One shares Dr. Werner's disdainful looks, if not because of the students' rude contempt for his hospitality being so egregiously rebuffed, then for their appreciation of such untalented songwriting and baleful performance ability. Actor Tawm Ellis plays Dr. Werner not unlike David Lochary did Raymond Marble in *Pink Flamingos*— as an insufferable but somehow dapper snob; Ellis even bears an eerie resemblance to the silver-haired cult favorite Lochary, who sadly died of a drug overdose too early in his cult film career. Along with Ivan Agar, who portrays the mute Laughing Crow with a terrific sense of physicality, Ellis is definitely the film's thespian highlight.

The Sasquatch costume is particularly inept, resembling a furry jumpsuit with a white fright wig and plastic fangs. Producer Ed Adlum had the thankless task of bringing the bulky, padded-looking

The flesh-eating Yeti (Ivan Agar) crashes through a window in *Shriek of the Mutilated*. The visual motif of hominids bursting into homes through windows and doors repeats throughout Ciné du Sasquatch.

costume to life. He gives it the old college try (appropriate to the main characters' educational status), but the lack of any muscle definition beneath the floppy white fur renders his task hopeless. The creators seemed to have realized the lack of credibility in this regards during post-production, as the opening attack sequence is printed in negative; everything white is turned to black and vice versa. The effect does mask the lack of believability; alas, it does so at the expense of comprehensibility, as the resulting footage is so dark that it's nearly impossible to decipher what is happening onscreen.

As bad Ciné du Sasquatch movies go, *Shriek of the Mutilated* does have a few worthwhile suspense moments: the aforementioned St. Claire double homicide sequence, for example, as well as the final Yeti attack sequence itself, which is handled with eerie aplomb. Findlay stages it with a female student peering out the window and watching as — on the horizon line in the distance — the Yeti races towards her, leaping over fallen logs and bounding through the snow drifts with determined agility. The manner in which Findlay intercuts the languid, deep focus shot of the Sasquatch and the woman's passive, frozen terror creates a sense of nightmarish unreality akin to something in a David Lynch movie. While anyone else in her position would flee, the woman simply stares with growing dread until the beast is upon her window, whereupon it smashes through in an attempt to gain entry to her as she presses against the back wall, too stunned to react and run. As she succumbs to the shock and slowly dies of a heart attack, *Shriek of the Mutilated* reaches a surreal moment of genuine horror resembling a similar moment of cardiac arrest in Clouzot's *Les Diaboliques* (which it was perhaps referencing). Unfortunately, it is brief in endurance and not the film's climax.

A final, sadder note was Findlay's tragic fate shortly after directing the film. Having invented a 3-D camera utilizing a new technical process, Findlay was on his way to meet with some foreign investors who were willing to back his device and bring it to fruition. Alas, the helicopter he charted that departed the Pam Am building (perhaps most famously seen in *Coogan's Bluff* in the opening and closing New York City shots) to fly to meet with the financial backers malfunctioned, killing all aboard in the ensuing crash. It was a strangely unsettling ending for the filmmaker whose final film featured such unrelentingly ghastly murders as seen in *Shriek of the Mutilated*.

The Shrieking (2008)

AKA: *Something in the Woods*. Starring Anna Bridgforth, Nathan Faudree, Jordan Finn, Logan Hunter, Justin Johnson, Christopher Kahler, Kaitlyn Kennedy and Dana Leuth. Produced by David Passine, Tony Urban, Karen Hunt and Emily Fenneuff. Written and Directed by Shawn Hunt. USA. Color. Stereo. 85 Minutes.

Overview: Four young friends take a camping trip to get the city out of their blood for a few relaxing days. Along the way they encounter evidence of a three-toed Bigfoot lurking in the remote woods where they pitch their tent. Soon they're under siege by a ravenous Bigfoot, which begins killing them one by one, as the survivors blindly flee the dark woods and hope for salvation either at the hands of rescuers or by eluding the pursuing homicidal hominid.

* * * * *

Though still in post-production and awaiting a DVD release at the time of this writing, *The Shriek-*

ing is a classic example of Ciné du Sasquatch if for no other reason than the plot is *the* quintessential Bigfoot movie approach — humans arrive as dominant in the cryptid's domain, but are soon fleeing for their lives, having turned submissive to the alpha hominid on its own turf. This basic tenet of Ciné du Sasquatch is so firmly entrenched within the narrative construction of *The Shrieking* that it would not exist as a movie without it. Indeed, as have many recent Postmodern Bigfoot movies dealing with teens and a Savage Sasquatch, the formula is almost identical to the *Friday the 13th* films — only with Bigfoot substituting for Jason. This seems to be a nascent indication of how much power *Night of the Demon* has lent the Grand Guignol–drenched Bigfoot film genre in terms of the marauding monster versus woodland pacifist image; it certainly seems as if the recent spate of Attack-squatch movies are motivated by at least a knowing wink in the direction of the Savage Sasquatch variant, of which *Night of the Demon* is really the first powerful prototype.

Another Bigfoot synchronicity occurs in the casting of actress Anna Bridgforth, whose low-key charm was the definite highlight of the earlier *Bigfoot at Holler Creek Canyon*. Bridgforth plays basically the same role here — the smarter, more instinctually aware female lead who senses the dangers before they become idiotically manifest (as some of her less brainy cohorts apparently still can't accept the concept that *they* are what's for dinner). Bridgforth possesses a likeable, congenial personality that filters through her muted delivery and neo-punk attitude, and imbues her performance with just enough longing to make the Emo Girls in attendance giddy with recognition, too. Hopefully one day soon *The Shrieking* will be released and Ms. Bridgforth will be offered another role in a yet-to-be-announced Bigfoot thriller.

Sightings (1992) (Multiple Episodes) (TV) (Doc)

Featuring Tim White, Christopher Chacon, James A. Swan and Geoff Callan. Produced by Steve Kroopnick, Linda Moulton, Joe Dea and Henry Winkler. Directed by Christopher Carson, Paul Nichols, Essy Niknejad, R.P. Sekon, Steve Feld and John Jopson. USA. Color. Stereo. 22 Minutes.

Overview: This early Fox hit show featured a news anchor format and a look at Fortean phenomena. It began as a one-hour special for the network called *The UFO Report: Sightings* that was so popular the executives at Rupert Murdoch's fledgling media empire were quick to convert it into a half-hour series of equally lurid looks at such topics as cryptozoology, UFOs, angels, near death experiences, ghosts, and the like. Slickly-produced and popular, it featured a slam-bang, MTV-styled editing style that kept it lively, if at times mindlessly so.

The episodes and segments relevant to this guide are: "Legendary Monsters," which focused on Bigfoot and the Loch Ness Monster; "Iceman Update," a segment about the Minnesota Iceman hoax which many believed was an actual hominid frozen in ice for years; "Bigfoot," an entire episode dedicated to Sasquatch; "Sasquatch," a short segment about the Pacific Northwest sightings of the hominid; "Bigfoot Update," a basic rehash of the earlier segment with a few new shots; "Update — Bigfoot in Ohio," about the Grassman; "One Missing Link," a segment about possible evolutionary hominids that genetically splintered off from *Homo sapiens*; "The Call Of Sasquatch," a segment about the vocal recordings that have been made of screaming Sasquatch monsters; and various non-catalogued updates and news tidbits in their "News Update" segments.

While the short 22-minute running time, repetitive use of graphics to pad the length, talking heads at the anchor desk reading copy, and

multiple segments per episode allowed for very little in the way of in-depth information (rather like the network equivalent of "official" news coverage), at least it can be said *Sightings* popularized Bigfoot and related subject matter at a time in the early 1990s that saw a sudden increase in viewership of such topics. The show was eventually sold into syndication and increased to an hour-long format before finally ceasing production in 1997.

The Simpsons ("The Call of the Simpsons") (1990) (TV)

Featuring the voices of Dan Castellaneta, Julie Kavner, Nancy Cartwright, Yeardley Smith, Harry Shearer, Hank Azaria, Albert Brooks and Maggie Roswell. Produced by Richard Sakai, Matt Groening, James L. Brooks and Al Jean. Written by John Swartzwelder. Directed by Wesley Archer. USA. Color. Stereo. 30 Minutes.

Overview: When Homer Simpson buys a used motor home for his family, little does he realize he is about to set in motion a series of events that will lead his small town into a series of hysterical Bigfoot sightings. While on their initial outing in the RV, Homer pilots it over a cliff, forcing everyone in his family to leap out in the nick of time. Homer and Bart become separated from the rest and are forced to struggle to survive in the wilds. At one point both take a mud bath and are subsequently mistaken for Bigfoot by a hiking couple. The terrified hikers take a snapshot of Homer and send it to the Springfield TV station, whereupon Sasquatch mania strikes. The woods are flooded with reporters and hunters hoping to be the first to "kill or capture" a cryptid. Homer is eventually mistaken yet again as a hominid by some hunters and shot with a dart, which causes him to pass out. When he awakens in a cage, he learns that he's been subjected to a series of genetic and anatomical tests by scientists. A German zoologist offers his opinion to the gathered TV crew that the creature (Homer) they've captured is sub-par in terms of human intelligence, but that he's yet to conclude whether or not the specimen is a missing link or, indeed, Bigfoot.

* * * * *

Perhaps even more remarkable than the history-making, two-decades-long run of *The Simpsons* is the startling fact that it only once featured an episode concerning Bigfoot. Given how much Sasquatch is a part of popular American culture, it seems incredulous that only in the first season did the creators see fit to star a hominid Homer in their series. Be that as it may, "The Call of the Simpsons" definitely acquits itself well as a fine example of Ciné du Sasquatch, even if the depicted cryptid is actually just Homer covered in mud and sporting a mouthful of bees that prevents him from speaking with any clarity (some might argue, of course, that the nominal head of the Simpson household rarely, if ever, speaks with any true clarity on any given occasion — a decidedly difficult proposition to argue against).

The satire underlying all episodes of *The Simpsons* is present throughout "The Call of the Simpsons," from Homer's jealous obsession with keeping up with his neighbors (it is Ned Flanders' purchase of a motor home that drives Homer Simpson to buy an even larger RV) to the typical way in which Americans use the Great Outdoors as nothing more than an excuse to blindly consume without thought. The further targeting of the media's relentless attempts to sensationalize even the most incredulous of scanty information — in this case represented by the picture of Homer, covered in mud, being misrepresented as Bigfoot — is spot on as well. It is a common motif in Ciné du Sasquatch that if and when the media is presented, they are a mindless, frothing, videocamera-toting paparazzi posse. In a symbolic manner, the portrayal of the electronic news outlets as willing to exploit any hominid without critical thought or concern is a reformation of the Carl Denham Syndrome, but personified as a group rather than a lone individual. It is worthwhile to keep in mind that though Carl Denham is the Great White Hunter archetype that insists on bringing King Kong back to New York City, it is the mob mentality of the gathered press, with their flashing camera bulbs, that actually triggers Kong's murderous rampage throughout Manhattan. This mythic overtone is often presented in more modern incarnations as television reporters who mob any captive cryptid and/or seek to exploit the creature for ratings, without regard to its well-being.

The Six Million Dollar Man (Multiple Episodes) (1976) (TV)

Starring Lee Majors, Richard Anderson, Stefanie Powers, Severn Darden, Hank Brandt, Penelope Windust, Donn Whyte, André the Giant, Charles Cyphers, Ford Lile, Chuck Bowman, Martin E. Brooks, John Saxon, Stephen Young, Sandy Duncan, Geoffrey Lewis, Tony Young, Ted Cassidy, Katherine De Hetre and Regis Cordic. Produced by Harve Bennett, Kenneth Johnson, Lionel E. Siegel and Richard Landau. Written by Kenneth Johnson and Gregory S. Dinallo. Directed by Alan Crosland, Barry Crane and Rod Holcomb. USA. Color. Mono. 60 Minutes.

Overview: Colonel Steve Austin is a test pilot for a shuttle aircraft that goes awry. Barely alive, he is surgically saved by a range of nuclear-powered bionic implants, all of which give him increased powers beyond the normal human range. In order to return the $6 million the U.S. government has spent on his recovery, Austin becomes a key member of the Office of Scientific Investigation as an undercover agent, using his newfound abilities to help save the Earth from aliens, espionage, saboteurs, and — in "The Secret of Bigfoot," "The Return of Bigfoot," and "Bigfoot V" — a robotic Sasquatch.

"The Secret of Bigfoot," a two-part episode, begins with two of Steve Austin's longtime friends disappearing while placing seismic detectors in the Northern California wilderness. Recently, it seems, a puzzling series of earthquakes have shaken the California coast line. Austin goes in search of his missing comrades, only to find a set of giant footprints. After meeting a Native American who tells him of the legend of the wild man of the forest, Austin suspects the culprit behind the kidnappings may be Bigfoot. He follows the tracks, which leads to a face-to-face encounter with Sasquatch. The two battle for supremacy until Bigfoot, surprised by Austin's superhuman strength, flees.

Eventually Austin traces the fleeing hominid back to its lair, which turns out to be the secretive headquarters of a group of hostile aliens intent on destroying the Earth. Their methodology is to trigger long-dormant fault lines beneath the surface and thus indiscriminately kill millions of unsuspecting humans. Austin battles Bigfoot until it is revealed the creature is actually a robotic monstrosity designed by the aliens to act as protector and decoy. A final slugfest occurs, with Austin barely triumphing and escaping with the former captives after thwarting the aliens' plans.

The aliens return, however, in "The Return of Bigfoot," also a two-part episode. At first Austin is the only logical suspect in a series of high-profile robberies in which the criminal utilizes bionic power to commit the thefts. Soon, however, Austin begins to wonder if Bionic Bigfoot could somehow be the culprit, even though he vanquished the robotic hominid in his earlier encounter with it. Gillian, a female alien traveler, approaches Austin and informs him that Nedlick, also an alien being of her own kind, has formed a rebellion of like-minded invaders who are intent on conquering the Earth yet again. As Austin suspected, Nedlick is utilizing Sasquatch to finance the purchase of vast amounts of technology in order for Nedlick and his cadre of evil aliens to detonate a slumbering volcano beneath the West Coast and thus wreak havoc.

At the end of this two-part episode, Austin's bionic mechanics are in danger of melting down, thus rendering him incapable of stopping Nedlick and his renegades from accomplishing their nefarious plot. Only a substance used to power the Bionic Bigfoot can save Steve Austin, but can Jaime Sommers, the Bionic Woman, take over where Austin left off, infiltrate the aliens' hidden lair, and recover enough of the substance in time to save the Six Million Dollar Man's life?

In the final appearance by Sasquatch in the series,

Col. Steve Austin (Lee Majors), aka *The Six Million Dollar Man*, faces an adversary worthy of his bionic powers in the tree-hugging Sasquatch (Andre the Giant).

"Bigfoot V," Steve Austin is stunned when anthropologist Hope Langston photographs Sasquatch roaming the Northern California forests yet again, despite the fact he believed the cryptid had returned with the space aliens upon their departure. Austin visits Langston's campsite in hopes of investigating her sighting and gaining information from her about its whereabouts, but she's suspicious of his motivations, as against her wishes, two former associates of hers have decided to track and capture Sasquatch. Their plan — hold the creature in a cage and exhibit him à la *King Kong* for maximum profit, no matter what the danger to themselves or the paying public.

Eventually Austin finds Bigfoot, but his old friend turns on him and attacks. A battle ensues, with Sasquatch temporarily victorious. The hominid flees, heading directly into a trap set by the two hunters. Austin must intervene in order to save Bigfoot and keep the alien technology from falling into the wrong hands.

* * * * *

Without doubt, Ciné du Sasquatch's major contributing force of popularization during the 1970s were these series of episodes of *The Six Million Dollar Man*. While it is truly a worthwhile debate as to whether Sasquatch helped the Bionic Man or vice versa, the unequivocal fact is that together the two proved to be a dynamic duo, at least as far as TV ratings are concerned. So popular was the initial two-part episode "The Secret of Bigfoot" during the third season that another two-parter was ordered and produced by the network to follow up at the beginning of the fourth season. The second half of "The Return of Bigfoot" actually split apart the saga into the first episode of the spin-off series *The Bionic Woman* (though when shown in syndication "The Return of Bigfoot" is included as a two-part episode of *The Six Million Dollar Man*). The strategy worked, helping launch *The Bionic Woman* to stellar debut ratings (no doubt at least partially attributable to the presence of Bigfoot).

The initial appearance of Sasquatch sparked such a furor, in fact, that Mattel introduced a Bionic Bigfoot action toy not long thereafter. This highly sought after collectible remains a valuable eBay item to this day, often fetching in excess of one hundred dollars if in mint condition and in the original packaging. Also helping popularize the craze for Bionic Bigfoot were the numerous print appearances aimed at the pre-teen target audience. A full-page color comic book advertisement done in the familiar graphic panel format presented the adventures of Colonel Steve Austin, including his encounter with Bigfoot, and appeared in many Marvel and DC publications of the 1970s. Likewise, *Dynamite*, a now-defunct but once popular full-color magazine distributed to a captive audience of school children via Scholastic Press (who sold only to educational institutions, thereby guaranteeing exposure to the key demographics in any children's market) hyped the Bionic Man character. These and other fan-oriented publications insured that the popularity of Bigfoot via *The Six Million Dollar Man* spread well beyond the initial cathode appearances and into the mainstream pop culture. Many were the 1970s-era playgrounds full of kids imitating the epic Austin vs. Bigfoot battle royale after the two-parter's ratings-smashing premiere (evidence that any sociologist who still doubted the direct influence of TV programming on child behavior would have shamefully had to ignore despite its overwhelming obviousness).

Much of the reason for *The Six Million Dollar Man*'s success was casting. Both Lee Majors and Lindsay Wagner brought likeable, low-key charm to their roles that kept their respective series from teetering over the edge into either outright camp or melodrama. Never dependent upon acting per se for its impact, *The Six Million Dollar Man* nevertheless had a fine supporting cast of players, all seasoned pros who knew how to play their stereotypical characters well within the realms of believability. Likewise, Andre the Giant (well-named for his 6-foot, 11-inch height) made a suitable Goliath to Majors'

David in "The Secret of Bigfoot," with Andre's pro wrestler's agility an added plus. In a demanding role that required girth, height, and a certain amount of athletic ability, Andre established the physicality of the bipedal bionic with lasting effect. Indeed, though veteran character actor Ted Cassidy would reprise the role in subsequent appearances on the show ("The Return of Bigfoot" and "Bigfoot V") and acquit himself well, it was Andre the Giant who most memorably introduced the character to the American viewing public. Cassidy, best remembered as the towering Lurch from *The Addams Family* TV series, was also a renowned voice actor in the TV industry and provided his own growling for his Bigfoot character. Given that the series was most often shot on location in sunny Southern California, it must have been an uncomfortable role for both actors. Indeed, behind-the-scenes photos reveal how Cassidy would remove the gloves and feet from the costume in order to help cool his body during breaks in the production.

The now clichéd use of slow motion for the generally excellent stunt work throughout the show was also novel for the time. While slow motion was used in other series during action scenes (for example, the David Carradine–starring *Kung Fu*), none came close to *The Six Million Dollar Man* for total amount of running time per episode using the over-cranked process. Taken with the accompanying sound effect of Austin's bionic mechanisms whirring loudly (with their familiar stuttering echo of "dee-dee-dee-dee-duge") whenever he leapt over a tall obstacle or delivered a punishing bionic blow to a foe, the series was widely parodied for its constant use of these two effects, eliciting knowing laughter throughout the 1970s. But this was merely a testimony to the series' amazing success, for few, if any,

Sasquatch (Andre the Giant) in a staged photo from *The Six Million Dollar Man*. His performance was far more physically threatening than Ted Cassidy's later portrayals as the Bionic Bigfoot.

who watched TV in the era didn't immediately recognize the one-two combination of slow-mo and sound effect.

The Bigfoot appearances in *The Six Million Dollar Man* echoed two prior Ciné du Sasquatch themes. Space hominids had previously appeared in the genre on TV's *Lost in Space* and *Star Trek*, and in silver screen fare such as *Terror in the Midnight Sun* and *Snow Devils*, any one (or more) of which may have influenced the creative team behind "The Secret of Bigfoot" to make Sasquatch the aliens' intergalactic guardian, a role the man beast played in the aforementioned efforts. Likewise, a Yeti who turns out to be a robotic construction has been seen earlier in the Bigfoot TV genre, dating all the way back to the original *Astro Boy* anime series in 1963. Indeed, in terms of sheer mechanical construction, the very first Yeti to ever appear in Ciné du Sasquatch history — the snarling, pulley-operated contraption of Méliès' two-story high Abominable Snowman in *Conquest of the Pole* in 1912 — was literally a semi-robotic creation in and of itself.

The novelty factor which was so key to the success of "The Secret of Bigfoot" quickly dissipated with the beast's subsequent cameos, mainly because the stories merely repeated the basic gimmick and didn't elaborate upon or advance it to any significant degree. Nevertheless, their cumulative effect was without parallel in Ciné du Sasquatch during this era. While hundreds of thousands had witnessed the cinematic impact of the wildly successful *The Legend of Boggy Creek*, and millions more during the record-shattering ratings phenomena of the Rod Serling–narrated *Monsters! Mysteries or Myths?* these were one-offs in nature and not subject to the same cultural zeitgeist as *The Six Million Dollar Man*, which was an established success already at the peak of its popularity when "The Secret of Bigfoot" enthralled the viewing public. With successive repeats and additional cameos by the Bionic Bigfoot, over a hundred million viewers worldwide would eventually experience their first introduction to a fictional narrative in which Bigfoot was such a key ingredient. As a result, *The Six Million Dollar Man* launched Sasquatch from its modest folkloric standing into the realms of cultural superstardom. Never again would Sasquatch need an explanation when appearing on big or small screen; from this point forward, Bigfoot was a cinematic and television "given" in terms of cultural recognition.

In a turn of a well-known historical phrase, it was "the 'Squatch that launched a thousand imitators" as well. To this day the reverberations still echo, however faintly, like a distant pulsar emitting continuous radiation. In particular, the visualization of Bigfoot as having long, shaggy, brownish fur and a bushy, neo-dreadlock hairstyle atop a rounded head — instead of the more common dark, short fur and bony head crest resembling that of a silverback mountain gorilla (as famously shown in the Patterson-Gimlin film) — set the pattern for most subsequent incarnations. Even the Academy Award–winning make-up effects of Rick Baker for the seminal *Harry and the Hendersons* would "ape" the look of "The Secret of Bigfoot" and its depiction of Sasquatch, at least in terms of body style and fur length. It was as if Andre the Giant/Ted Cassidy costume had become the de facto standard Sasquatch in Hollywood thereafter. And as Hollywood goes, so goes the rest of the world in terms of media imitation. In no uncertain terms, the airing of these five episodes over a few years altered Ciné du Sasquatch forever, thus making them milestones of the genre.

Skullduggery (1970)

Starring Burt Reynolds, Susan Clark, Roger C. Carmel, Paul Hubschmid, Chips Rafferty, Alexander Knox, Pat Suzuki, Edward Fox, Wilfrid Hyde-White, William Marshall, Rhys Williams, Mort Marshall and Michael St. Clair. Produced by Saul David. Written by Nelson Gidding. Directed by Gordon Douglas. USA. Color. Mono. 105 Minutes.

Overview: During an exploratory expedition to the jungles of New Guinea, adventurer-for-hire Douglas Temple and female archeologist Dr. Sybil Greame discover an unknown species of hominids, quickly dubbed "the Tropi" by Greame. The outside world is initially enthralled by word of such a discovery but interest quickly fades. The Tropi are tribal, small in stature, and seemingly a missing link between *Homo sapiens* and an earlier species of primates.

Alas, Vancruysen — the wealthy financier who has backed the initial expedition for Greame — quickly turns the race of eager-to-learn Tropi into little more than slaves for his profitable mining business when a major store of phosphor is also uncovered during the expedition. Vancruysen loves the fact that he can eliminate the costs and controversy of employing human labor and instead exploit the all-too-willing Tropi as "less than human" workers (and therefore not technically slaves). After several Tropi fall victim to Vancruysen and his henchmen, however, Greame threatens his burgeoning empire by blowing the whistle on his mistreatment of the newfound species. Vancruysen takes the legal position that the Tropi are nothing more than animals and therefore cannot be given human rights nor protection against his efforts, even up to and including their deaths during the mining process. A long, drawn-out courtroom battle ensues, with the fate of the Tropi hanging in the balance.

* * * * *

Based on the French novel *Les Animaux Denatures* (aka *Ye Shall Know Them*) by Vercors, *Skullduggery* is an oft-overlooked film in Ciné du Sasquatch, partly because it is a more serious-themed entry than the usual horror-toned effort, and more critically because the depicted hominids are not the classic towering "monsters" of a majority of entries in the genre. Nevertheless, in any appreciable terms, it is in some ways one of the most remarkable Ciné du Sasquatch visualizations of its era, and warrants contemplation for the many themes upon which it touches that are inherent in the genre's very definition.

Key to *Skullduggery*'s obscurity is the fact that it is at best an unevenly written and directed film. During its initial release, much was made of the miscasting of Burt Reynolds as well. In retrospect it is clear why the producer took the chance of casting the then relatively untested Reynolds in such a serious leading role — the rogue adventurer character must have seemed the one sure-fire commercially desirable "in" as a way to market the hodgepodge melodrama masquerading as action film (which it is not, despite being marketed as such in 1970). Reynolds would go on to acquit himself much better in John Boorman's *Deliverance* not many years hereafter in largely the same "manly man's" role, but the very qualities he captures in that more well-received (and deservedly so) screen role are equally present in *Skullduggery*— a biting sense of sarcasm, a brute physicality, and an explosively violent temper. In *Skullduggery*, however, Reynolds plays it over-the-top, whereas in *Deliverance* he subdues these qualities and his level of intensity in order to better serve the material.

Nothing Reynolds can be faulted for, however, would have made much difference, as *Skullduggery*'s largest problems lay in its unbalanced narrative construction. The film opens as a standard Tarzan-styled adventure tale, transforms into a philosophical thriller full of interesting contrasts between so-called "civilized humanity" and "primitive humanity" (or quasi-humanity, as even the film itself reserves judgment as to the Tropi's standing in terms of being technically classified as proto-humans or merely gifted primates until well into the second act), and finally ends as a protracted courtroom melodrama that seems more appropriate as a mediocre TV episode of *Perry Mason* than a fitting conclusion to such an intriguing premise. This is doubtless because the screenwriter attempted to stay true to the novel; however, there are times when screenplay adaptations require more than a literal recreation in filmic terms; *Skullduggery* is a classic case where it would have been much more dramatically effective had the various factions been forced to resolve their conflicts not by being removed to a stuffy magistrate's office, but by actions in the very jungle setting which begs the question the trial sequences grapple with in less interesting terms: If we are the invaders exposing the Tropi's heretofore hidden existence, and seek only to crassly exploit them as slave labor, who is the real threat?

This and other questions are brought to the painful forefront by the legal machinery in the courtroom scenes, which actually reduces their emotional impact. By relegating the emotional struggle between acceptance of a new quasi-human species (and therefore, it is implied, ourselves as less than God's gift to world supremacy) and condemning them to bestial slavery and commercial exploitation (not unlike we have done with the decimation of the gorilla and other primate populations worldwide for their furs and "bush meat") to a legal debate, *Skullduggery* robs the viewer of the catharsis it has so erratically but sometimes effectively built up to that point in the storyline.

Every concept that is crucial to Ciné du Sasquatch is embedded within *Skullduggery*. Indeed, because it so willingly extrapolates on these concepts and dissects them in the finale, as barristers argue about them, *Skullduggery* is a kind of Bigfoot version of *Inherit the Wind* (which dealt with the infamous "Scopes Monkey Trial") — a moral look at the pitfalls of believing in the dominance of our species over all other living beings, whether vastly or nearly imperceptibly different from us as *Homo sapiens*. As in *Inherit the Wind*, religious beliefs regarding mankind's innate, deserved supremacy over all other life forms is brought into philosophical examination by others in our species who question if such an attitude is nothing less than genetic chauvinism at its worst. It is difficult to imagine a more timely debate in an era that sadly still obsesses over such non-issues as "Evolution vs. Creationism" (as if both are mutually incompatible, and therefore one must triumph over a reasoned, balanced approach to either) to the point of altering science textbooks into religious tracts. It equally impossible to separate this basic tension from all that underlies Bigfoot films and TV shows as a genre.

Herein many Ciné du Sasquatch viewers will face their own intrinsic positions in terms of the implications of the genre. Some will claim that such notions are not contained in the genre because such thinking smacks of "liberal humanism" and the like; others will defend these concepts as the core of what makes Ciné du Sasquatch so interesting and relevant in the face of today's often anemic entertainments (which too often eschew controversy for commercial blandness) — the manner in which, for example, *Skullduggery* examines its own biting sense of race relations implicit in the material; our stewardship of the environment; and our long, brutish history of enslaving ourselves and other species for material profit. Whatever one's point of view, there is plenty in *Skullduggery* to chew upon. It is an interesting, intelligent failure, and a blistering if dramatically compromised indictment. These themes are self-evident in many Bigfoot films, of course, but rarely do the filmmakers offer more than an almost cynical, calculated lip service to the philosophical nature of such concepts. Too often in Ciné du Sasquatch the tree-hugging side is as stereotypically presented as

the bloodthirsty hunter side. In *Skullduggery*, both sides are given equal opportunity to present their case, and both come up far short of any easy assessment, pro or con. In actual fact, *Skullduggery* concludes with the rather depressing realization that both sides are simply conceited and unable to compromise in order to achieve any kind of societal balance.

This is probably why *Skullduggery* bombed at the box office when it first appeared and remains an ignored but worthwhile entry in Ciné du Sasquatch: In essence, it takes no easy path towards resolving either the pro-peaceful or pro-dominant arguments that characterize human society. *Skullduggery* uneasily suggests we are the bigger problem as a species than any relic society of pseudo-humans could ever present to us; that we are the cause of global deterioration and extinction of an ever-increasing number of life forms, which will ultimately lead to the demise of our own. It's a far cry from the rosy optimism of *Harry and the Hendersons* or even the Noble Savage iconography inherent in *The Leggy of Boggy Creek*. The skulls, the title implies, which will be dug up by some future species will be our

The diminutive hominids from *Skullduggery* are known as the Tropi tribe, but are actually small-statured cousins to Sasquatch.

own. As far as nihilism goes in Ciné du Sasquatch, *Skullduggery* is perhaps the ultimate statement to date on the ridiculousness of believing that humanity has *any* solution whatsoever to offer any life form on the planet—except, perhaps, an insane version of Hitler's Final Solution for us all. Little wonder most would rather leave its unsettling proposition unexamined. *Skullduggery* stands as the genre's bleakest yet most mature work, however uneven its execution and unsatisfying its outcome.

Skunkape (2009)

Starring Sam Abbott, Herb Britt, Molly Malone and Kurt Nolen. Produced, Written and Directed by Kurt Nolen and Chao Vang. USA. Color. Stereo. 16 Minutes.

Overview: A hunter attempts to track an elusive Sasquatch that he blames for the death of his loved ones, but he soon finds himself the hunted. This short film was co-directed, co-written, and co-produced by professional Steadicam operator Kurt Nolen, who works extensively in the North Carolina film production community. Though never released commercially, it has screened at various film and video festivals, including the 2010 Carolina Film and Video Festival.

The Snow Creature (1954)

Starring Paul Langton, Leslie Denison, Teru Shimada, Rollin Moriyama, Robert Kino, Robert Hinton, Darlene Fields, George Douglas, Robert Bice, Rudolph Anders, William Phipps and Jack Daly. Written by Myles Wilder. Produced and Directed by W. Lee Wilder. USA. Black & White. Mono. 71 Minutes.

Overview: An American botanist and his companions are forced to deviate from their planned plant-gathering expedition when their head Sherpa claims his wife was abducted by a Yeti. Despite the Americans' protests, the Sherpa guide insists he must rescue his wife

before the Abominable Snowman devours her. Against their will, the reluctant Yanks accompany the Sherpa tribesmen. They eventually find the Yeti's lair, hidden within a crevice in the Himalayan mountaintops. The missing Sherpa wife is rescued, but the humans' intrusion so enrages the savage Yeti that the hominid accidentally brings down the entire ice cavern on itself, its female mate and lone offspring. The male Yeti survives, but his family perishes.

The botanist scientist realizes this priceless scientific discovery must be given to a proper, first-rate zoology institute in order to best accelerate mankind's knowledge of the heretofore unknown species. An American hunter in his initial Himalayan exploratory party hears the Man of Science's noble ambitions and snickers, attempting to convince the botanist to make some fast bucks off the hominid by touring it around. But the incorruptible Noble Scientist again refuses to prostitute his services when he's clearly serving the larger needs of his own species' knowledge. Vindicated by his unwavering faith in the Goodness of Rational Mankind (it was 1954, after all, and such concepts were still very much cut and dried affairs, despite the post–film noir cynicism which permeated much of the era's melodramatic and fantastic film genres), the botanist builds a huge, self-powered cooling container large enough to house the cryptid and transport it back to the United States, alive and well.

The botanist's plan seems to be working perfectly until the plane touches down in Los Angeles. There the local Customs and Immigrations officials are perplexed as to how to accurately describe the contents of the self-cooling cage—is this an animal, like an ape, or a primitive version of a man? If they admit the creature as a man, then he is suddenly a non-affiliated alien at the height of the Cold War, in which not being able to prove political and national lineage was often a capital offense. And yet if they admit Yeti as an animal, have they deprived the creature of its rights as a human being? This conundrum is basically used to justify moving the creature's crate into a temporary holding facility until the immigration clerks can determine the beast's status. There it tips over its confining crate, smashes free, and assaults a terrified guard who is oddly not the least prepared to deal with the menace under his charge. The ragdoll guard is tossed aside but survives; a lady who just happens to be standing in the proverbial wrong spot is not so lucky and is killed by the monster moments later.

The frantic botanist agrees to partner up with an up-and-coming Los Angeles beat detective who has been assigned to the missing Yeti case. They form a two-man task force charged with protecting the beast man if possible, but using lethal force if necessary to preserve human life. Examining all reports of the at-large cryptid via radio triangulation, the two men soon deduce the creature's strategy—it is using the sewers beneath the city to travel undisturbed. The botanist and detective head into the sewers in hopes of capturing the Abominable. They witness the cornered creature put up a fierce struggle against a snare net until it actually seems to gain the upper hand against a small squadron of L.A. police officers. But when it threatens to kill again, the creature is mercilessly shot to death, blasted repeatedly at point blank range until it succumbs in agony, screaming.

It is nearly dawn. It's been a long day's night chasing and putting down the Yeti. The radio in the squad car crackles one more time. The detective's wife has just given birth. The jubilant detective offers the botanist a drive home, as it's on the way

Poster art for the release of *Snow Creature*. Ad copy: "Millions gasped when they read about it in *Life*, *Time* and *Argosy* Magazines!"

to the hospital maternity ward. Accepting, the botanist and detective kid about whether or not the detective should name his newly-born son after the botanist or not.

* * * * *

Many viewers have incorrectly designated *The Snow Creature* as the first-ever Ciné du Sasquatch or Yeti film. Some have further erred in stating *The Snow Creature* was the first fictional motion picture to star a Yeti. There are several precedents to all aspects of Bigfoot, Sasquatch, and Yeti that predate *The Snow Creature* by many, many decades, including *Conquest of the Pole* (1912), *The Strange Case of Captain Ramper* (1927), and even prototypical influences such as *King Kong* (1933).

But uber-distinctions aside, it *is* the first Modern Era Yeti movie; and as such, it is the prototype. But how such a mundane B-programmer can encapsulate all the tenets of Ciné du Sasquatch and yet do so without making any of the elements entertaining is a curious dichotomy. One sees the influence of *King Kong* still reverberating the later film's "invasion" of the Himalayan Mountains (instead of Skull Island), the abduction of an unwilling human woman by the aggressive male Sasquatch, and the eventual liberation of the captive human woman from the reclusive mountain cavern home of the cryptid.

Still, the mighty *King Kong*'s looming appearance aside, *The Snow Creature* did introduce some novelties to the genre. It was the first fictional narrative to correctly depict the utilization by Western outsiders of local Sherpa guides to explore the nearly impenetrable Himalayas, where even the most experienced climbers and explorers have met with disaster and disappointment upon its fabled, majestic peaks. It should be noted that director Lee Wilder chose to use Japanese actors as the Sherpas, complete with Japanese names and language. Given how little most Americans knew about Sherpas in that era, this racial bait-and-switch is not so much driven by racism as it is by economics. After all, drive-in theaters were the obvious targets for such a low-budget oddity. There is little reason then, from a strictly commercial point of view, why such complexities as the "correct Sherpa dialect" should register as a priority when production funds were severely restricted.

Another Ciné du Sasquatch contribution *The Snow Creature* makes is in scaling down its hominid to a more realistic large human size rather than Kong-sized monster of epic proportions. While the creature costume is less-than-convincing, Lock Martin, who plays the towering, mute Snow Creature itself, at least has the height to make the creature seem *almost* dangerous. Though his face is never seen in Martin's most-lauded film from the 1950s — *The Day The Earth Stood Still* — it would be difficult to imagine the movie having even remotely the same in impact without the neo-zombie locomotion Martin brought to the passive-until-provoked Gort, especially considered he was covered head-to-toe in a sweltering rubber suit under hot studio lights! He makes a few deft maneuvers in his less imaginative Snow Creature costume, but as most of the shots are endlessly repeated throughout the running time, their effect wears thin as the editor dutifully slots in yet another of the same shot of the creature emerging from the same generic black background. Most times, Martin seems to be trying to hide his face in the shadows, as if making it difficult for the camera to capture his identity (no matter what assurances the producers made that no one would recognize him). Given the result, it's no small wonder Lock Martin (who also played one of the disturbing green goliath tunnel aliens in the original *Invaders from Mars*) listed *The Snow Creature* at the bottom of his monster-suit resume.

Yet another genre vet making his paycheck appearance here is character actor Paul Langton, who also appeared in 1950s B-movie hokum like *Invisible Invaders* (often credited as inspiration for the quasi-remake *Night of the Living Dead* by George Romero), *It: The Terror from Beyond Space* (often credited as inspiration for the quasi-redo *Alien* by Ridley Scott), and, giving his finest onscreen moments as actor, *The Incredible Shrinking Man*.

And let's not forget the father/son team of W. Lee Wilder and Myles Wilder, both so impressed by their kin Billy Wilder's epic success with such studio fare as *The Lost Weekend* and *Double Indemnity* that the elder brother W. Lee liquidated his business as a handbag manufacturer and used the proceeds to relocate his family to Hollywood to become a triple threat "writer, producer, and director" of his own B-movie empire. One can only speculate how embarrassed Billy Wilder was to have such a significantly less-talented brother (at least at making films; no records exist to attest to the quality of W. Lee's handbags) attempting to capitalize upon the younger man's famous name. Given W. Lee only produced a trio of these kind of films before retiring from the business, it is easy to imagine that W. Lee's grandiose plan backfired; it is very doubtful that Billy Wilder was instrumental in helping his older brother in terms of introductions, business partners, or even personal loans. Meanwhile, Myles Wilder went on to enjoy a successful if modest career writing children's animation fare such as *Hong Kong Phooey* and many others.

While *The Snow Creature* was *not* the first Yeti movie, it was uncannily accurate at capturing all the worst in Abominable Snowman movies that would follow in its wake. Incredibly, *The Snow Creature* not only catalogs these inane quirks of the worst of Ciné du Sasquatch (endless use of stock footage in mountain scenes; badly-executed cryptid costume; turgid characterizations; lethargy in pacing and direction), it distills them into a potent example of how *not* to make a Yeti movie. While it is rare for such a failure not to doom the genre over which it presides as an early contributor, *The Snow Creature* made such a negligent impact that it can be said to have made *no* impact other than the fact of its existence. This may have been a big blessing to Ciné du Sasquatch in a time when producers had to rely on listings in such trade magazines as *Daily Variety* and *The Hollywood Reporter* to verify movies that had been released in years prior that had similar themes and titles, box office results, etc. Nowadays this kind of info is easily obtainable via the Internet, but in a time before such technology, when being the first means opening the door for others that will surely follow, *The Snow Creature* at least had this much positive influence on the genre it helped establish — it showed other producers that someone else had bet upon the Big Hairy Fellow as profitable. That meant they could follow someone else's blazed trail rather than spend precious dollars to craft their own market, which in the save-a-buck mentality of the 1950s exploitation filmmaking ("every producer for himself") ethos meant producing and releasing B-pictures similar to those that audiences had shown a liking for in terms of content and execution. Consequently, *The Snow Creature* definitely made it easier for U.S. companies to release films such as *The Abominable Snowman of the Himalayas*, *Man Beast*, and *Half Human* in the years that followed the 1954 release of *The Snow Creature*. While this may be *The Snow Creature*'s sole positive legacy, given that the film *did* cast the first set of modern-era Ciné du Sasquatch tracks, it deserves its spotlight.

Snow Devils (1967)

AKA: *Gamma I Quadrilogy Vol. 4*; *La morte viene dal pianeta Aytin*. Starring Giacomo Rossi-Stuart, Ombretta Colli, Renato Baldini, Enzo Fiermonte, Halina Zalewska, Furio Meniconi and Goffredo Unger. Produced by Joseph Fryd, Antonio Margheriti, Walter Manley and Ivan Reiner. Written by Bill Finger, Antonio Margheriti, Renato Moretti, Ivan Reiner, Charles Sinclair and Aubrey Wisberg. Directed by Antonio Margheriti. Italy. Color. Mono. 90 Minutes.

Overview: Gamma I is the premiere space protection league in the galaxy, defending Earth astronauts and government personnel wherever in space they may fall into harm's way. The Earth has undergone enormous climatic change, leading the Gamma I scientists to an unthinkable conclusion: The Earth will soon be flooded by the melting glaciers. Enormous energy beams originating from the Himalayas in Tibet, as well as the sudden destruction of a scientific outpost there by some unknown bipedal creature, lead the scientists to further deduce there may be a connection between the recent events. A team is dispatched to the frozen mountaintops to investigate and determine if there is any reality in the reports of a Yeti.

The team's leader is Commander Rod Jackson, who is rudely called off a much-needed break on Earth while vacationing in a tropical paradise and sent to the frigid mountain range overnight. He is accompanied by Captain Frank Pulasky, his second-in-command and best friend. Tagging along, despite their objections, is Lisa Neilson, whose fiancé was murdered in the assault on the outpost which left all scientists stationed there dead. While waiting for Sharu, their Sherpa guide, to make arrangements to create a diversionary cover for the Gamma team, the space patrol's helicopter is sabotaged beyond repair. Forced to scale the mountain on foot, the Gamma I members ascend the legendary mountain range in search of the Yeti and the pulsating power source.

Soon they are captured by blue-furred hominids who take them to their inner sanctum hideaway inside the mountains. There the startled Gamma team is told by the green-faced Agron, the leader of the cryptids, that they are actually from the planet Attina and have been stranded on Earth for centuries. Finding the world's current climate too warm for their liking, the immigrant Attinans have decided to melt the polar caps, flood the planet's surfaces, and then reverse the cycle, bringing on a new ice age which will cover the entire planet in ice — hence the pulsating energy blasts coming from the aliens' enormous power generator. When the world is once again in the grip of another ice age, the furry hominids plan on repopulating the planet with their kind and reducing humankind to minority status.

At first, escape seems impossible, given the physical dominance of the oversized alien hominids. But when a chance meteor storm bombards the Earth, Commander Jackson sees his opening and takes it, staging a break-out. He and his stalwart companions are able to bury the errant aliens beneath an avalanche of boulders and end their plans for world domination.

* * * * *

In the early 1960s, when the Age of Space actively gripped the world's collective imagination, several Italian film producers decided to capitalize on the fever with a series of four intergalactic adventures featuring the heroic exploits of Gamma I, an elite organization comprised of the world's best minds and risk takers, and charged with defending the Earth's interplanetary space routes. While the quartet of pictures was released in the United States every one or two years until the supply was exhausted, they were never marketed, nor shot, as sequels. Rather, they took place in a near future when Gamma I would be a logical version of a police patrol with a more militaristic edge; and they shared characters, narrative set-ups, and locations. And more importantly from an economical point of view, the four films shared many of the same sets, props, and costumes, as well as creative cast and crew behind the scenes, including the director himself.

In actuality, all four films were shot back to back, and then held back by the producers so as not to flood the international film market. While this is not uncommon with Hollywood epics today owing to the exorbitant costs of assembling acting talent for extended durations of production time, it was quite novel in the 1960s for a science fiction

series of movies. More typical of the era (and now) was the initial successful release of a film determining whether or not a sequel would be produced, let alone two additional entries after that. This demonstrated that the producers were very astute in betting that the commercial reality of the Space Race would sustain throughout the 1960s, thereby creating an inexhaustible hunger among worldwide audiences to see movies about fictionalized space heroes and their exploits. Quality issues of the films aside, it took commercial far-sightedness on the producers' part to follow such a risky strategy.

Key to the success of the series was hiring Italian genre specialist director "Anthony M. Dawson" (as he often Anglicized his name for commercial reasons), aka Antonio Margheriti. Margheriti was a competent if unimaginative professional, rather akin to prolific American filmmaker William "One Shot" Beaudine, who shifted very easily from one genre to the next without making much impact either coming or going. Still, one needn't be Orson Welles to have a career in the film industry; and indeed, as demonstrated by Welles' own inability to obtain consistent financing for his efforts, in many ways one is better off in terms of career longevity by taking the Margheriti path of least resistance. And just because he was workmanlike in his direction and pacing doesn't mean Margheriti lacked the ability to add a level of perverse charm to the otherwise juvenile proceedings. The frequent use of scantily-clad space babes in all four pictures (which became increasingly 1960s Mod as the four films were produced and the latest fashions influenced the costuming) gives them a certain campy flavor reminiscent of Pussy Galore and her flying squadron of jumpsuit-clad beauties in *Goldfinger*. Not that the films were completely sexist — just mostly (though women were often shown to be in commanding roles over subservient men in the Gamma I hierarchy, which was quite novel for the time).

The Snow Devils (or Blue Devils as they're called, owing to the distinctive blue fur of their hides) are actually alien beings, but because Yeti mythology doesn't preclude space cryptids as a possible explanation for their existence (however far-fetched), this doesn't disqualify the film as a bona fide entry in the Ciné du Sasquatch canon. In fact, SF trappings aside, *Snow Devils* is basically a classic Abominable Snowman movie with the added burden of having to offer an unbelievable explanation for the Yeti as alien visitor. Narratively, the film falls into the classic Ciné du Sasquatch pattern: First the humans trek into the Yeti's territorial grounds; next they're harassed or taken captive; and finally the survivors fight their way to freedom, with the hominids intent on destroying them as the humans retreat in terror. Even though *Snow Devils* is set in a futuristic time, its mechanics remain very much 20th century in terms of hominid outlook and genre construction.

The alien Yeti are an unusual depiction, and though this film is obscure, it may have been echoed by the 1980s comedy *Earth Girls Are Easy*, in which the blue-furred Jeff Goldblum alien wears a similar outfit and head gear as the *Snow Devils* visitors. The Snow Devil faces are actually painted in green rather than blue (perhaps to suggest an otherworldly nature), and, unlike in most Bigfoot films, they are able to speak with human beings. Apart from those instances in which human beings turn out to be wearing a cryptid costume, speech is a genuinely scarce quality possessed by other cinematic hominids. Even when presented as more human than Bigfoot-like, most screen hominids tend to have a rudimentary vocabulary of grunting and monosyllables at best. Likewise, most Sasquatch beings are visualized by filmmakers as having no ability to converse with humans beyond shrieks and growls.

While *Snow Devils* was moderately successful and helped "launch" the other three pictures into equally respectable box office profits, it had remarkably little impact on the Bigfoot film genre itself. Perhaps this has to do with the movie's relative obscurity; indeed, it made the rounds quietly on a drive-in double-bill and seems to have otherwise sat on the shelf. While shown occasionally on cable channels such as Turner Classic Movies on cult film nights, it remains difficult to see, lacking any official release on DVD to date. As demonstrated by the influence of *The Legend of Boggy Creek* in the years after *Snow Devils'* release, and *The Abominable Snowman of the Himalayas* a decade earlier, sustained availability of the picture in question is necessary in order for audiences to be influenced in the first place. As *Snow Devils* lasted about as long as a late Spring snowfall during its brief run, it made zero impact on the genre, despite being one of the earliest color Yeti films made. The brief cameo made by the Abominable Snowman in *The 7 Faces of Dr. Lao* technically precedes *Snow Devils* in terms of release dates, but the Gamma I series began filming two *years* before George Pal's fantasy picture was released to theaters in America. It is therefore possible Margheriti's blue hominids were being photographed before Pal even began pre-production on his epic.

In turns tedious and marginally interesting, *Snow Devils* is a rarity that exists in the genre without much fanfare or influence. For die-hard completists of Ciné du Sasquatch and fans of Italian space opera films, *Snow Devils* offers compelling reasons to watch. But for those outside these narrowly-defined sub-groups, most will find it simply too boring by today's fast-paced standards to endure, and the Yetis too non-threatening to be taken seriously, despite their suggested technological prowess.

Snowbeast (1977)

Starring Bo Svenson, Yvette Mimieux, Robert Logan, Clint Walker, Sylvia Sidney, Thomas Babson, Jackquie Botts, Kathy Christopher, Jamie Jamison, Richard Jamison, Liz Jury, Richard Jury, Rob McClung, Annie McEnroe, Victor Raider-Wexler, Prentiss Rowe and Michael J. London. Produced by Wilfred Lloyd Baumes and Douglas S. Cramer. Written by Joseph Stefano. Directed by Herb Wallerstein. USA. Color. Mono. 86 Minutes.

Overview: Rill Lodge, a rugged Rocky Mountain ski resort, is celebrating its 50th anniversary of being open to the public. Owner Carrie Rill, a former beauty queen, and her grandson Tony are faced with their worst nightmare, however, when word spreads that a Yeti monster is stalking the woods, eager for any chance to slaughter vacationing humans.

Amidst the simmering chaos, as Rill attempts to keep the media from exaggerating the story and ruining the entire ski season, Gar Seberg, a former Gold Medalist in skiing, and his TV reporter wife Ellen arrive at Rill Lodge. It turns out Gar has hit some rough times and wants to convince his old pal Tony to hire the former Olympian as a ski instructor. Tony agrees to hire Gar — not to teach skiing but to help Tony track the creature and end its reign of terror before it ends the ski lodge.

Eventually the Snowman is trapped in a remote cabin for a life-or-death stand-off with the human hunters. Gar and Tony triumph, saving the lodge, though its reputation will forever have a dark stain surrounding the bloody events that unfolded during the half-century celebration of the lodge's founding.

* * * * *

For cultural impact, timing is everything, and *Snowbeast* was a big winner in this regard. Not only was the potent 1970s wave of national obsession re: All Things Bigfoot at an all-time high when *Snowbeast* first aired on prime time as a movie of the week, but *Snowbeast* was perfectly pitched to the largely adolescent demographic that was most apt to be enraptured by such a hominid storyline. The tension is well-sustained throughout, and the teleplay by renowned *Psycho* screenplay writer Joe Stefano reasonably maintains a sense of veracity by isolating the horror events in a remote setting (just as *The Shining* would years later), therefore making it more believable that authorities would be slower in responding to mortal threats. The casting is varied for a low-budget TV movie, with the lovely Yvette Miemeux donning a shapely ski suit early on to reveal that she has maintained her attractive figure almost twenty years after *The Time Machine* (which also featured her battling ravenous hominids with white fur and a bipedal posture — the dreaded Morlocks — only these are merely *Homo sapiens* who have mutated due to radiation exposure).

Again, luck plays a good part in any undertaking, and in this sense Stefano's choice of using a ski lodge setting and its surroundings proved adroit. While such a "Yeti meets the visitors of a ski lodge" plot had already featured in the "That's Snow Ghost!" episode of *Scooby Doo, Where Are You?* this was the first feature-length movie to wed ski bums with a bipedal cryptid run amok. It is a possibility rife with inherent campiness, and therein *Snowbeast* can at least take a bow for avoiding some of the more painful pitfalls so frequent to Ciné du Sasquatch, not least of which is a risible costume on the order of a Dollar Store mark-down item. The suit used in *Snowbeast* is definitely well made for the 1970s M.O.W. variety and remains off-screen for most of the film's running time; only rarely is the monster shown in its full head-to-Big-toe glory.

For most other shots, the director uses a variety of classic cinematic tricks: a familiar, post–*Halloween* stalk-and-slash creature p.o.v. as it darts behind fallen logs and gnarled tree trunks to spy on its next human victim; onscreen space that reveals no hint of the creature which is suddenly intruded upon by one significant portion of the hominid (clawed hand; snarling, fanged mouth, etc.); and a few repeated shots of the monster outside the ski lodge's snow-frosted windows, howling as it spots all the tasty humans inside, even as the humans begin to scream when they realize *they* are now the other white meat. One of the best scares, in fact, occurs when a skier grabs onto some bushes at the last second to keep himself from soaring over a precipice to his doom. The young man gasps, believing he has survived certain death; then a shadow falls across his face. As he looks up into the sun, a giant paw full of bony fingers covers his wide-stretched mouth and eyes, ripping into his features as the monster roars in delight. As the blood trickles onto the snow, the scene fades to black (and a commercial break).

Others would quickly follow, riffing on the ski lodge aspect, including *The Capture of Bigfoot* by Wisconsin's own indie filmmaking magnate, Bill Rebane. But whereas in this and other Yeti films the ski lodge seems almost an afterthought, included as so much décor, it is central to the success of *Snowbeast* in that it grounds the sense of dread in the likeable small community of civic-minded citizens who are one payday away from hard times. The once-vaunted ski lodge is celebrating its 50-year anniversary, with attendance dwindling because the owners cannot afford to keep up the monthly costs *and* make the necessary but financially ruinous upgrades needed to attract new and wealthy clients. Such a real-world dilemma means lots of dramatic conflict. The lack of such crucial grounding often mars otherwise entertaining Ciné du Sasquatch efforts, and *Snowbeast* is a good, albeit modest, example of how to construct a low-budget siege-mentality film (substituting a ravenous Sasquatch for a starving Grizzly Bear stalking a group of remote human settlers, for one example).

Clint Walker takes a brief but effective turn as a sheriff who meets his match when he steps into the line of fire of the Snowbeast. Likewise, Bo Svenson's Olympic gold medal–winner having to beg for a job is a sad dilemma for any heroic protagonist to have to face and overcome. After a series of professional disappointments that has left him virtually unemployable, Svenson's fallen hero gets a shot at redemption where he least expects it — as back-up lodge "ranger" tasked with capturing or killing a Sasquatch. What begins as a down-on-his-luck lark proves to be just the last-chance opportunity the aging skier needs, which is a nice, and underplayed, bit of character business.

Because of its generally well-realized mood and spooky tone, *Snowbeast* made a big impression during both its initial prime-time broadcast and subsequent reruns in the years to follow. While never considered more than an average Ciné du Sasquatch effort, *Snowbeast* has earned a growing, vocal minority of cult movie fans who adamantly defend the film's quiet intensity. The location photography that is both authentic and authentically gorgeous doesn't hurt either; until the action is practically buried under a blizzard during the last third of the picture, there is much Golden Hour sunset photography in effect which makes the splendid contrast of the wintery landscapes all the more spectacular. With its larger than average cast for a M.O.W., then-novel setting for the action (a ski lodge), and simple but effective use of largely off-screen monster techniques, *Snowbeast* achieves a kind of perfect balance of everything that once made such routine B-movie programmers so commonplace then and so long-vanished today: great casts given good dialogue; an interesting premise transformed with creativity into something that goes beyond watchable into involving; and, above all else, a sense of place and time.

A sense of "dig the magic while the magic is happening" sensibility is definitely at play with such 1970s TV fare as *Snowbeast*, wherein one senses the creative forces behind the decision-making are trying to push the envelope's edge at every turn, but always encountering the usual problems: network interference or censorship; reshoots and re-edits; and the firing and hiring of key personnel. That a result as diverting and non-patronizing as *Snowbeast* was the positive by-product of such a process is a testament to the pros involved. With its assured disco-flavored ski suits, 1970s blow-dried hairstyles, and groovy monster design, *Snowbeast* manages to rise above the average heights of Ciné du Sasquatch, wherein thin oxygen levels often suffocate even the best-intentioned efforts (usually owing to a certain feeling of narrative narcolepsy). It keeps the air intake pressure "on" by spinning the scenario in as many suspenseful directions as it can, and then, when it's in danger of becoming tedious, the movie decisively wraps up in an explosive fashion.

Snowbeast was a nasty little hominid shocker for its tamer era, featuring lots of uncomfortable (if mostly implied) violence and a definite sense of being willing to go for the viewer's throat if left unprotected. Until *Night of the Demon* a few years later, it would be hard to find a hominid so hell-bent on "attack and destroy" than the one depicted in *Snowbeast*. It still remains an extreme example of how vicious a movie Sasquatch can be in terms of unprovoked savagery.

Snowman (Doc) (2008)

Featuring Jimmy Wilson. Produced and Directed by Jimmy Wilson. USA. Color. Stereo. 30 Minutes.

Overview: Family filmmaker Wilson produces and distributes his own line of high-quality, violence-free family fare. In this direct-market DVD release, Wilson takes his show on the road to interview a host of wildlife biologists, law enforcement officers, medical doctors, and others who've had long-term knowledge about Yeti through their professional lives, and whether they believe such a hominid could still exist in today's world.

So Weird ("Sacrifice") (1999) (TV)

Starring Cara DeLizia, Alexz Johnson, Mackenzie Phillips, Patrick Levis, Erik von Detten, Eric Lively, Belinda Metz and Dave "Squatch" Ward.

Produced by Henry Winkler, Tom J. Astle, Michelle Davis, Alec Griffith, Ali Marie Matheson, Jon Cooksey, Larry Sugar, John Mandel and Bruce Zimmerman. Written by Bruce Zimmerman. Directed by Alan Simmonds. Canada/USA. Color. Stereo. 30 Minutes.

Overview: Teenager Fiona Phillips spends time on the road with her famous rock star mother Molly Phillips, acting as a daughter, bodyguard, and even semi-manager. Fiona creates a Fortean website to help ease her boredom on the tour bus and is surprised when it becomes an underground fave. As various folks post on Fiona's site and relate their own, never-before-told encounters with the unknown, Fiona and her equally bored mom Molly begin to visit the various website writers when Molly's tour brings them within the writers' respective areas. Both daughter and mom are oblivious as to where their newfound passion is leading them, irresistibly drawn to the inherent power of solving such profound mysteries in a modern world of prevailing skepticism.

In "Sacrifice" the story centers on a local Bigfoot that Fiona encounters while lost in the snowy woods. After having to help the cryptid survive by hiding its existence and protecting the beast from extinction at the hands of those who want it dead, Fiona learns that she is not the first human being to "sacrifice" to the hominid species shivering before her. Local legend has it that years earlier a brave soldier gave his life in order to keep the creatures' tiny population secret. She realizes that despite the fact many human beings have despicable attitudes about other life forms and environmentally betray the Earth hourly, there are also those who not only care, but will make the ultimate "sacrifice" (i.e. their own lives) when necessary to insure not just our own kind's survival, but the continuous shared co-existence *with* (instead of *in the place of*) other life forms on the globe.

It's a shame that Disney didn't apparently enjoy the darker tone of *So Weird* during its initial run on the network. Given the pre-teen and barely-teen Emo Girl audience the series so desperately sought to (and for the most part does) connect with, the corporate giant would have been far wiser to nurture *So Weird* rather than allow it to die through neglect, finally orphaning it to the NickToons cable channel for a brief run in syndication after the show was cancelled.

Sons of Butcher ("Huntin' the Legend") (2005) (TV)

Featuring the voices of Dave Dunham, Jay Ziebarth, Trevor Ziebarth, Ron Pardo, Jeff Lumby, Max Smith and Peter Cugno. Produced by Adrian Carter and Max Smith. Written by Max Smith, Jay Ziebarth, Trevor Ziebarth and Dave Dunham. Directed by Karl DiPelino. Canada. Color. Stereo. 30 Minutes.

Overview: The trifecta that runs the Sons of Butcher Quality Meats in their washed-out former steel mill home city are Sol Butcher, his brother Ricky, and their odd-man-out Doug Borski. They also front for a rock trio calling themselves the "Sons of Butcher" who play any clubs willing to book them for a modest rate.

In the second-ever episode, entitled "Huntin' the Legend," Sol enters himself into an annual competition to bag the most impressive hunting specimen of the day and also obtain all the necessary "$tew meat" he will need to feed himself and loved ones during the harsh winter months. Though Sol stalks and fails to kill a clever buck every bit his match on multiple occasions, the final challenge evolves into Sol versus an innocent Sasquatch who would otherwise prefer to be very much left alone. Sol's ferocious one-man-force-of-nature personality, however, all but makes a *humano a cryptido* showdown a foregone conclusion.

During all of this, the Sasquatch abducts Doug Borski and awakens the horrified human to the cryptid's real agenda — Sasquatch is a transvestite who wants them both to dress in women's lingerie before they make love to one another in the creature's hidden love den. Doug tries to accept it all in the name of survival, as every time he tries to dissuade the creature from any more attempts at inter-species indiscretions, Bigfoot grows more enraged and potentially violent. Doug finally forms an uneasy if chaste relationship with the tranny Bigfoot, and the two become fast friends.

Eventually, Doug and Sasquatch meet up with Sol and Ricky in the woods. Ricky, who is experiencing an LSD flashback due to being strung head-over-his-heels for hours on end in one of Sol's devious traps, argues that he is the Lord of the Woods and that the animals must obey his every command. Meantime, Sasquatch takes a bullet for his newfound human friends when Sol goes ballistic while encountering a group of local hunters, thereby causing a shooting match to erupt. As Sasquatch lies dying, having sacrificed himself, Sol realizes that he hasn't captured his winter meat supply. Realizing it is best to dispose of the Bigfoot carcass in an environmentally-friendly way, Sol decides to store some Sasquatch steaks for the long, hard winter ahead (as well as enjoying a few plates of shredded Yeti while the meat is curing). Doug is inconsolable at the loss of his cross-dressing cryptid buddy Bigfoot, but Sol is too busy telling the media about how he bagged and will be stewing genuine Sasquatch filets to really notice.

* * * * *

That the new techniques that immigrated from the Internet, such as Flash animation software (the driving engine behind most of the video and cartoon content you see made expressly for the web), have made an impact upon filmmaking and television production is obvious at this point. Flash, a vector-based animation program, allowed a whole generation of self-taught cartoonists to let loose with their own versions of *Scooby Doo*, *The Groovy Ghoulies*, and the like — occasionally with truly professional-looking results, even when only small teams of production personnel were involved. While these pieces are generally intended as little more than glorified sample reels for effects houses, filmmakers, animators, etc., some Flash-based web content develops serious followings and migrates into other media formats, with varying degrees of success.

Part of the intrigue of the new medium of Flash animation is that it removes the entry barriers that formerly existed for all but prodigies in terms of traditional, cel-drawn animation. The software largely makes the traditional layers of stacked animation elements so commonly used throughout cel animation endlessly repositionable, reusable, and resizable, and without the cost of cel paints, cels, and the overhead animation hardware, as well as film stock and processing. Because the software also allows for extensive previewing of wireframes and other non-completed shots, it saves animators many dead-end hours spent chasing angles down unusable alleys, which is very expensive when done by hand.

All of which is why series such as *Sons of Butcher* is all the more likely to be a preview of things to come in terms of eccentric, non-corporate adult animation, even if its tenure was short-lived. It was made relatively free from production constraints because of freelance, creator-owned computer systems allowing maximum creative decision-making up until the last possible moment of rendering and delivery, and because it enshrines a quirky, less-streamlined narrative and approach to characterization than the norm. The result is akin to the restless energies tapped by R. Crumb and his fellow underground cartoonists in the 1960s with their combined output of the myriad comic strips and characters in self-produced, limited-run comic books (then called "comix" as a play on the X-rating of the era) and radical-left publications. There is a promise of bubbling zeitgeist seemingly poised to overtake the events of the day with something new, however ill-defined.

Freed from commercial restrictions beyond the barest production costs, the animation houses behind such fare as *Sons of Butcher* often take maximum advantage of the "mixed media" collage that has recently been in vogue in commercial filmmaking and television. For example, *Sons of Butcher* has characters with realistic albeit photocopied human heads over smaller, less-realistically drawn body types. This gives the entire show a bizarre feeling, as if one is watching a shared infantile nightmare, with a constant cast of seemingly rational adults who are actually hysterical, tantrum-prone kids with Big Head Syndrome. But as *everything* is out of proportion to reality in most of *Sons of Butcher*, including the protagonists' huge heads, it actually works to increase the show's disturbing charm.

The characters are Grand Guignol with a Canadian accent. Just the physical act of running, walking, and other related "perils" of the real world prove to be a challenge for the trio. Sol is the Rambo wannabe of the lot, a stealth survivalist macho warrior who only thinks and communicates in the most manly of manly terms. Ricky, his rotund younger brother who is a New Age stoner mystic, is reminiscent of Fat Freddy from the old Gilbert Shelton–created *The Fabulous Furry Freak Brothers* comix (minus the cat). This prototype — the slacker doper who lives at peace in such Quantum-inspired ideas as multiple reality realms, owing to said character's "altered" point of view — has already become a staple in the Ciné du Sasquatch genre, most notably in *Tenacious D and the Pick of Destiny* and *The Sasquatch Gang*. Again, however, it has grown to ubiquitous proportions since its introduction into the Bigfoot genre during the late 1960s–1970s era of more liberal film standards.

The bizarre combination of art styles always present in any given shot is either amusing or a breaking point for some viewers. If one doesn't mind an endless bombardment of stylistic overkill via the technique, the fluidity of the Flash mixing (at the hands of skilled creators) so many different "looks" into one semi-cohesive whole is impressive. For example, Sasquatch is almost as crudely drawn and stereotypically-depicted as a late-era Jay Ward Studios background player; while the weird style that unites what appears to be digitally-snapped and then Photoshop-altered "talking heads" of the actors superimposed atop the smaller cartoon bodies is both creepily surreal and disturbingly grotesque (like a Goya). Other aspects of the production design are even more impressive and add charm to this low-budget Canadian variation on *The Mighty Boosh* (rendered in Saturday-morning-from-hell cartoon style). This despite the low-brow comedy of playing Sasquatch as a cross-dressing cryptid who is "into" grooving with humans, or the flashback nature of Ricky's chemically-induced mystical oneness with nature.

In a bizarre twist that actually plays into the current limits of Ciné du Sasquatch itself, the humans freely admit in the closing moments to having butchered Sasquatch to fill their winter larder with stew meat. Their last-second admission apparently costs them a Hunter of the Year Award for most outrageous game kill, but nevertheless provides some needed solace for the recent heartache of Yeti's loss. While there has always been a cryptid hominid as devourer of human flesh as an archetype of the Ciné du Sasquatch genre, here the mythic mask is removed to reveal the human as alpha hunter over *all* life forms, including the Bigfoot in question. "Huntin' the Legend" does all of this is a blackly comic manner, but the underlying tenets of the genre are firmly entrenched, including having the Carl Denham Syndrome personified as elder brother Sol. Sol is portrayed as being at perpetual war with himself and others over the least bit of decorum being violated, however unwittingly. His testosterone-filled state of semi-rage, combined with a hair-trigger mental state that seeks to shoot first and *maybe* ask questions later, makes Sol the perfect heir apparent to the exploitation maniac Carl Denham himself, as both seek to exploit the exterior world's Last Great Mysteries in order to rid themselves of enormous personal debts or world-weary ennui, or both. The fact Sol later degenerates into a semi-cannibalistic state (if one argues that Sasquatch is a closely-related offshoot of our own *Homo sapiens* branch, that is) without even being bothered by the thought speaks volumes. Sol readily devours Bigfoot not only because Sol can justify it with his "as long as it is game" philosophy, but also because it lets Sol direct the "ultimate at'cha!" at his macho rivals — how many of *you* Sons of Butchers have eaten Sasquatch meat, eh?

The boast is as fittingly wild as this series, which mixes crude laughs with a knowing sense of pop culture — especially the essence of Ciné du Sasquatch.

South Park ("ManBearPig") (2006) (TV)

Featuring the voices of Trey Parker, Matt Stone, Gracie Lazar, Mona Marshall and April Stewart. Produced by Kyle McCulloch, Trey Parker and Matt Stone. Written by Jane Bussmann. Directed by Trey Parker. USA. Color. Stereo. 30 Minutes.

Overview: Ex–vice president Al Gore visits the kids of tiny South Park, Colorado, to lecture them on the stark peril living in their small hamlet. He refers to none other than ManBearPig, a strange Bigfoot variant with cloven hooves. Convinced the creature is real, Gore conducts a one-man jihad against the monster, determined to destroy it before it destroys the Earth. He enlists Kyle, Kenny, Cartman and Stan to help him track down the murderous ManBearPig in the dark caverns of the popular Colorado tourist attraction, Cave of the Winds.

Alas, Gore mistakenly believes he's found ManBearPig's home and fires off a shotgun with manic intensity to celebrate, unwittingly causing an avalanche. Gore escapes but the four childhood friends are left for dead, buried beneath the rubble. A frantic rescue operation is mounted by the South Park residents and police to free the children. Meanwhile, Cartman discovers a hidden treasure and greedily swallows it all, piece by piece, rather than have his friends also share in the wealth. His plan: hold onto the loot until after they're rescued and then "recapture" it all for himself.

Gore tries to convince the police authorities that ManBearPig is the real culprit behind the cave in, but no one will believe him. Determined to kill the creature, Gore steals a bulldozer and uses it to create a river flood that pours directly into the Cave of the Winds, thus drowning anything that once lived in the subterranean caverns. Saddened by the loss of the children, Gore paints them as loving martyrs to the cause at a town memorial service for the young victims. Just then the kids emerge from a nearby culvert and lay blame on Gore. They claim everything that has gone wrong was Gore's fault and that he should "stay the hell away" from them from now on. Self-delusionally believing he's stopped ManBearPig, and ignoring the slack-jawed looks of disbelief from the South Park citizens who are eyewitness to the former vice president's mental instability, Gore dons a superhero cloak and "flies" around the startled witnesses, pretending to be a caped crusader.

* * * * *

Given its constant skewering of all things Middle American, it was only a matter of time before *South Park* dealt with Bigfoot. While technically called "ManBearPig" rather than Sasquatch, there is no doubt from the moment Gore unfurls his crude drawing of the cryptid that it represents Bigfoot (save for the cloven hooves). Everyone in the town of South Park reacts with the same degree of shocked disbelief when Gore first announces his obsession, clearly placing ManBearPig as a nominal substitute for a Sasquatch in terms of popular perception.

Of course, ManBearPig never actually appears as a living cryptid in the show. In fact, it is suggested that ManBearPig is but a figment of the former VP's lonely imagination — a walking windmill monster of his mind with which he may endlessly joust à la Don Quixote. Sadly, no one has the guts to call him on his improbable quest, worried that his "lack of friends" makes him pathetic beyond repair. So the populace humor and patronize Gore, instead.

This is very funny satire, however, given Gore's well-known climate change scenario as outlined in his Academy Award–winning documentary *An Inconvenient Truth*. The single-minded determination with which Gore sets forth to destroy ManBearPig is entertaining parody because it so aptly mirrors his global warming warning persona — all business-styled stiff upper lip, with little humor or personal warmth ever seeping through the straight-laced veneer. The creators have Gore sputtering every few lines, "I'm *cereal!*" (as opposed to "I'm serious!") in response to others' doubting ManBearPig's existence. The verbal joke grows tired far before the end credits roll, but does capture the innate comic silliness of having a man such as the Nobel Peace Prize–winning Gore obsessed with Sasquatch, à la Ahab with his white whale.

In fact, "ManBearPig" works perfectly well within the Ciné du Sasquatch genre as a prime example of how its existing clichés can be tweaked to produce new takes on the old ideas. By switching the titular monster from Sasquatch to ManBearPig, the *South Park* creators gain considerable freshness, as instead of having everyone in the fictitious township realize Gore is simply a Bigfoot hunter, they are forced to first process the very concept of a weird combination of a man, a bear, and a pig. When pressed about what percentage of the creature is which species (is it more man than pig, or...?), even Gore cannot answer the question. He hides behind his ridiculous drawing of the monster instead, as if producing a sketch based solely on his own eyewitness testimony were conclusive proof.

Parker and Stone satirically portray Gore as a one-sided, self-obsessed egotist whose goal is to bag Bigfoot no matter the cost. This darker, Carl Denham-esque vision of the hominid hunter is completely within genre character, which makes it all the more amusing that it arrives so blatantly intact within the oblivious Gore, who sees no contradiction between his quest to save the world from climate change and his persecuting a lonely, last-of-its-kind creature. Fusing Gore's good guy persona with an unworthy goal may seem juvenile (and everything that appears between the opening and closing titles of *South Park* usually is), but it brings a tragic dimension to his perpetual gloom and doom persona that is hilariously unexpected. For once, Gore has gotten it wrong, and boy, when the man is wrong, *South Park* suggests, he is spectacularly so. Silly but not without redeeming, gutter-level laughs, "ManBearPig" is a look at the quirky nature of America and its insistence on believing and perpetuating its mythic lore beyond any probability the tales are true. Like sightings of Elvis at time share condos, with Jim Morrison and Michael Jackson as the King's roommates, the legend of the ManBearPig itself is larger than life and designed to remain forever so. Folklore is not meant to be taken apart by intellectuals or studied for deeper meanings by analysts. It is primarily designed to render for younger generations the way the past often felt as *lived* by the humans who suffered through it, not necessarily to be a recorded transcription of actual history. By this standard, "ManBearPig" definitely feels like folklore from its era, encapsulating both a prevailing cynicism towards any figure of authority, and a longing for a time when denizens such as ManBearPig were the worst threats we faced as a species, instead of real world examples such as nuclear terrorism, the latest animal pox outbreaks, and other apocalyptic scenarios.

Southern Fried Bigfoot (2007) (Doc)

Featuring Calvin Anderson, Barry Bagert, John Bindernagel, John Blanton, Russell Scott Boyd, Zane Boy, Vaughn Bryant, Sallie Ann Clarke, Loren Coleman, Graham Criglow, Matthew J. Fazio, Carl Finch, Ron Gardner, Bing Graffunder, Richie Kay, Randy King, Thomas Lynch, Dan Maloney, Gary Matthews, Chester Moore Jr., Lee Murphy, Bill Rebsamen, Rob Riggs, Christopher Sabat, Hope Stedman, Dexter Sumpter, Patrick Trumble, Mitchel Whitington, Cynthia Whitley, Shane Whitley and Craig Woolheater. Produced by Sean Whitley and Mike Zeitzmann. Written and Directed by Sean Whitley. USA. Color. Stereo. 60 Minutes.

Overview: This look at the fetid swamp apes of the South — known individually as the Fouke Monster (Arkansas), the Skunk Ape (Florida), the Honey Island Swamp Monster (Louisiana), and the Lake Worth Monster (Texas), but herein collectively dubbed "Southern Fried Bigfoot" — is a well-produced independent documentary with strong regional interest. Featuring a variety of experts and recreated encounters, it echoes the documentary realism of *The Legend of Boggy Creek* but keeps its head above swampy waters to stake its own claim to fame. It includes interviews with Loren Coleman, the renowned author and curator of the International Cryptozoology Museum in Portland, Maine, and Craig Woolheater of Texas Bigfoot research circles. For those with a love of Southern culture and its accompanying folklore, *Southern Fried Bigfoot* is a guaranteed Ciné du Sasquatch crowd pleaser.

Poster art for the DVD release of *Southern Fried Bigfoot*, featuring artwork by Bill Rebsamen.

Spaced Out Bunny (1980) (TV)

Featuring Mel Blanc. Produced and Written by Chuck Jones. Directed by Chuck Jones and Phil Monroe. USA. Color. Stereo. 6 Minutes.

Overview: Bugs Bunny is kidnapped by Marvin the Martian, a tiny alien with a large single orb, in order to keep his lonely pet Abominable Snowman named Hugo company. Though he's minus his feathered friend Daffy Duck during this second encounter with the Snowman (the first being *The Abominable Snow Rabbit*), Bugs nonetheless quickly sets about creating enough off-world mayhem that it seems a fine ending indeed for Marvin when Mars has seen the last of the Earthling rabbit, who is blasted back to his home planet. The Abominable "adopts" the startled Marvin as his new friend to hug and cuddle.

* * * * *

Chuck Jones returns to Ciné du Sasquatch but changes the setting from the Himalayas to the red planet Mars! Bugs seems right at home on the arid planet of war after all the wrong turns he has made prior when traveling to Albuquerque — seen one desert, seen them all throughout the galaxy is Bug's blasé response to interplanetary abduction by Marvin. The rascally rabbit is only slightly more surprised to see Hugo yet again, proving Bugs always worked deadpan to good effect — not much fazes a talking, dancing, glove-wearing rabbit, after all.

Though it works hard to recapture the same comic energy of Hugo's debut in *The Abominable Snow Rabbit*, adding Marvin the mumbling Martian to the mixture doesn't really make much in the way of either narrative impact or logical sense. In no uncertain terms, Marvin acts as the surrogate for Daffy Duck when Bugs and Daffy first met in the 1960 short film. The tiny alien swaps roles with Bugs constantly during the short's highlight sequence, each trying to convince the dimwitted Hugo that the other is the *real* pet the desperate Yeti truly wants to keep as its permanent plaything. Again, this echoes the same comic triangle between Bugs, Daffy, and Hugo in the first Yeti outing.

The animation is fine, although lacking the imaginative sense of stylistic playfulness that characterized Jones' best work decades earlier. But if it is rougher around the edges and less a full-on laugh-getter, *Spaced Out Bugs* does demonstrate that the loveable Hugo was an audience favorite even after a 20-year absence from the Chuck Jones *oeuvre*. Given that Hugo has little more to do in this outing than virtually repeat his role from his 1960s premiere, the towering hominid acquits himself well, determined to have a pet of his own no matter the cost to the living being involved. The latter is a novel twist on the common Carl Denham Syndrome, with the human exploiter Denham archetype not reflected in the human (or Martian!) leads, but in the cryptid itself. In this case, Hugo wants to cage a life form he deems inferior to himself in order to alleviate boredom. The motives between them are different — Denham wants money for his enslavement of a wild hominid, while Hugo wants to fill his own emotional needs at the expense of the possessed "pet" he grasps — but the outcome is the same: One life form is made subservient to another.

Of course, it's all played for laughs in *Spaced Out Bugs*, but there is a reason both Marvin and Bugs are so frantic to convince the cryptid that the other is more worthy of being kept as Hugo's pet, and that is this: underlying his dopey nature of innocence, there is a level of implicit violence within Hugo that is frightening to all smaller creatures around him. Like a spoiled child who may suddenly point a loaded gun at his horrified parents, Hugo is an infantile force of unbridled passions. What sways Hugo from moment to moment will soon become both the object of his affection and concurrent obsession to own and possess. Hugo cannot help himself, Jones seems to suggest. Hugo is a child locked in a hominid's hulking physique, complete with all the issues of mood lability that entails.

Though probably unintentional, Jones has captured the perfect comedic representation of how humans tend to view the situation when it is in reverse — that is, when *we* are the hunters and Bigfoot is *our* prey. Only by picturing Hugo as the humongous hunter coming after *us* do we understand the powerful threat we represent to the Sasquatch in most other movies and TV shows. This illustrates why Bigfoot typically opts for violent self-defense in a majority of screen and TV visualizations rather than opting to establish a truce between species. We are too dangerous to approach on any presumed equal footing, the wary Yeti seem to realize; we will use our advantage against any opposing species, as the hominids learn first-hand (if they did not already hold this opinion of our kind) as the story progresses. In this situation the rules of engagement are clear from the outset: It's every living being for himself, genetic encoding be damned. What better ambassador of comic chaos to illustrate this natural conflict than Bugs Bunny, the proverbial provocateur, in order to heighten the laughs as the two opposing species wage all-out war?

Der Spiegel (1990s) (TV) (Doc)

Featuring Richard Greenwell and Peter Byrne.

Overview: This German television magazine format show featured an in-depth examination of the American Bigfoot phenomena, including various point-of-view recreations of infamous Sasquatch encounters. The producers sent a production crew to the Pacific Northwest to shoot original footage of many real-life cryptozoologists and witnesses. Even though the English-speaking interviewees in *Der Spiegel* aren't subtitled, the voices are still clearly audible under the German-language voiceovers. The program also includes clips from the Patterson-Gimlin footage.

Spotlight on the Patterson/Gimlin Film (2007) (Doc)

Featuring M.K. Davis. Produced by John L. Johnsen and M.K. Davis. Directed by John L. Johnsen. USA. Color. Stereo.

Overview: Cryptozoologist M.K. Davis gives an in-depth, thoughtful, and controversial overview of his novel theories in regards to the Patterson-Gimlin film, which is given frame-by-frame analysis by narrator Davis. Indeed, even the world famous 16mm film's aesthetic and technical qualities are considered, with shutter speed, film stock emulsion, and other characteristics receiving scrutiny in relationship to how the images of Sasquatch were recorded, and how such analysis helps determine the authenticity (or not) of the depicted hominid. Also included is an interview with a witness to the excavation of giant hominid bones found buried deep beneath the western Nevada desert in remote Lovelock Cave. The same filmmaker also made the cryptid docs *Keeping the Watch* and *Hunt the Dogman*.

Squatching (2002) (Doc)

Featuring Loren Coleman, Scott Herriott, Ed Marques and Jonathan Winters. Produced, Written and Directed by Scott Herriott. USA. Color. Stereo. 43 Minutes.

Overview: Television host and documentary filmmaker Scott Herriott has a life-long obsession with Sasquatch. From an early age,

when he was exposed to the Patterson-Gimlin film, until his own encounters with the beast himself as an adult on two occasions, Herriott details the personal thrill and anguish over experiencing a life-changing event that no one believes. Herriott camps the Northern California area with a buddy and his older parents, no less, which gives rise to conversations about Herriott's monomania regarding Bigfoot and first-hand stories from Herriott's own upbringing.

Often bittersweet, *Squatching* proves how the blessing of the encounter is most often accompanied by the curse of the disbelievers and the realization that one is alone in one's newfound perspective. Making cameos are Loren Coleman, noted cryptozoologist, author, and museum curator, and none other than Jonathan Winters, who — though in his senior years — demonstrates an uncanny ability to summon the mirth and twinkle in his eyes so key to the success of a documentary such as *Squatching*, which relies more on human interaction than any exciting Bigfoot encounter recreations to make its points. Also accompanying the DVD release of *Squatching* is a shorter film by the same filmmaker called "Journey Toward Squatchdom," which features on-camera host Herriott skewering some of the more ridiculous Bigfoot sighting claims. Both films make for offbeat takes on Ciné du Sasquatch in one man's personal terms who has claimed an encounter with the cryptid in question.

Star Trek (1966) (Multiple Episodes) (TV)

Starring William Shatner, Leonard Nimoy, DeForest Kelley, Nichelle Nichols, James Doohan, George Takei, Walter Koenig, Majel Barrett and Grace Lee Whitney. Produced by Gene Roddenberry, Robert H. Justman, Herbert F. Solow, Gene L. Coon and Fred Freiberger. Written by Gene Roddenberry, George Clayton Johnson, Don Ingalls, Oliver Crawford and Shimon Wincelberg. Directed by Marc Daniels, Robert Gist and Robert Butler. USA. Color. Mono. Approximately 50 Minutes.

* * * * *

Overview: Space cryptids are by no means an anomaly in science fiction, whether it is literature, television or movies. Conversely, they rarely name their hominid creatures as Bigfoot, Sasquatch or Yeti (except in advertising campaigns) for one obvious reason: However much the producers, writers and directors may be drawing upon cryptid legends and sightings in the crafting of their hominids, they tailor their creatures' names to fit the genre itself. To wit, most science fiction employs futuristic or alien-sounding names, such as Gort (the robot from *The Day the Earth Stood Still*) or Chewbacca (from the *Star Wars* film series). This, of course, is preferable in most instances to "Space Robot" or "Space Bigfoot" because it creates a more exotic tone and establishes viewer suspension of disbelief. The giving of names, in essence, establishes individual identification over generic species grouping, the latter of which tends to dehumanize the cryptid character and leave the viewer feeling cold towards potential personification.

Star Trek employed several remarkable space cryptids throughout its initial three-year run. In fact, the first pilot episode, "The Cage," that was shot for the series (and later abandoned by NBC because they wanted adjustments in the series' tone and content) included a brief cameo by a space cryptid. As the original U.S.S. Enterprise leader, actor Jeffrey Hunter played Captain Pike. He is taken prisoner by a trio of hostile, psychic aliens when the Enterprise crew lands on Talos IV in search of survivors from a wrecked survey ship, the S.S. Columbia. Pike is held below the surface for the potential pleasure of human female Vina, the only survivor of the Columbia's crew. Pike notices a hallway lined with partitioned, force field–enclosed rooms that hold other life forms just as he is imprisoned. Among the enslaved specimens is an irate space cryptid clearly raging against its confinement. Resembling Bigfoot, the unidentified hominid later re-appears in the re-edited, two-part version of "The Cage" that series creator Gene Roddenberry cleverly utilized as the basis for a new storyline called "The Menagerie," in which Spock is put on trial for treason by aiding a dying, disfigured Captain Pike. Interestingly, "The Menagerie" actually aired *before* "The Cage" because NBC executives ordered changes to "The Cage" prior to the series' debut. "The Cage" only saw the light of day in 1988 because of a writers' strike and the need by the broadcaster to show only Writers' Guild–compensated work.

There are two other notable space cryptid appearances in the series. In "The Galileo Seven" Mr. Spock and six crew members are forced to land on an uncharted planet and attempt to repair the damaged shuttlecraft Galileo in order to return to the Enterprise before it leaves their quadrant. Alas, the crew is not alone, as the planet is home to a savage group of hominids towering a dozen feet tall. The cryptids begin picking off the human crew members one by one, creating tension between the Vulcan and the surviving Earthlings. Spock insists on using logic to solve the problems at hand, even while the Galileo's human crew begins to believe a mutiny will be necessary because of the Vulcan's inability to relate to their terrified emotions and offer any form of psychological comfort to them. Eventually the shuttle is repaired and the handful of survivors makes it back to the Enterprise, but not before they leave several of their colleagues dead on the harsh world they've escaped.

The cryptids presented in "The Galileo Seven" are perhaps borderline–Sasquatch at first glance. For example, they do employ a crude form of technology — the making of spears, which they hurl with lethal accuracy — and therefore initially appear more like giant cavemen than a tribe of hominids. However, the fact that they're never fully shown in the episode, only briefly glimpsed from behind when they attack in the planet's perpetual fog banks, combined with their savage assault upon the Galileo itself (wherein they hurl huge boulders atop it from the canyons above), leaves little doubt as to their hominid status. The latter incident is almost an exact recreation of the famous Ape Canyon attack as reported by miner Fred Beck in 1924. According to Beck, he and several miner friends shot and possibly killed a Bigfoot near Mount St. Helens in the state of Washington late one afternoon. Later that night their flimsy cabin structure was allegedly attacked by the towering cryptids, whose primary form of assault was the launching of boulders and rocks onto the miners' cabin roof from high above in the canyon. This true-life episode is so eerily mirrored in "The Galileo Seven" that one might speculate writers Oliver Crawford and Shimon Wincelberg were influenced by the Ape Canyon tale. For example, the creatures in "The Galileo Seven" use a form of guttural howling which drives the shuttlecraft members nearly insane with dread; this is precisely what Beck reported was the modus operandi of the Bigfoot tribe that assaulted him.

Another interesting though unrelated tidbit is the report from Lt. Commander Kelowitz, a search party member returned from the planet the lost Galileo is stranded upon, which is viewed by Captain Kirk on the bridge. Uniform ripped to pieces and face bloodied, the traumatized Kelowitz reports having encountered similar cryptids on another world, Hanson's Planet, "only [the latest ones are] much, much bigger ... maybe ten, twelve feet in height." Evidently the galaxy may be full of such space cryptids, though one hopes the others are not as savage as the ones portrayed here.

In terms of graphic realization, the makeup initially created for the creatures by William Ware Theiss and John Chambers was definitely hominid in design, but rather than weaken the suspenseful set-up by showing the monsters full-on, the intended facial shots were rejected in favor of only showing the cryptids' immense height and bulk as they ruthlessly exterminate several of the unfortunate Galileo crew. One attack in particular is horrifically rendered, showing a defenseless astronaut battered about in the mist like a human rag doll. Keeping the visage of the planet's inhabitants hidden ultimately makes these attacks all the scarier. Indeed, all the fearful crew can do is listen to the monsters' mournful shrieks and the eerie scratchy sounds the space cryptids make by rubbing their spearheads against stones in a nerve-wracking ritual signifying their imminent attack.

A final noteworthy space cryptid appearance in Star Trek came in the episode "A Private Little War," which features the oft-ridiculed but equally popular Mugato. Best described as an alien hominid crossbreed of part-simian and part-reptilian origin, the Mugato is a fierce alpha predator with a poisonous bite that inflicts a slow, painful death on all who suffer the misfortune to be ravaged by it. Aggressive and willing to attack without provocation, the Mugato is feared by all of the human-like inhabitants of the primitive planet, as only the race of mystical witch women who live on the wayward world have a cure for its lethal bite, and such a cure is never surefire. Because the humanoids are without any advanced technology beyond spears, the most they can hope for is to avoid an attack, and then defend themselves as best as their crude weapons allow during an encounter.

Kirk, Spock and McCoy beam down to the planet on a surveillance mission. Thirteen years prior to the episode's opening, Kirk had lived among a group of the peaceful inhabitants and reported favorably to Star Fleet Command of their high intelligence and benign, accepting nature. Because the Prime Directive Kirk and company must act within forbids any interference in any intelligent species' development, Kirk left the humanoid tribe as he found them, abiding in a relative paradise untouched by the horrors of warfare. But soon Kirk learns, to his dismay, that the tribesmen have developed crude versions of flintlock guns during his absence and are engaged in a small-scale but growing war between intercine factions. Deeper investigation reveals the culprits behind the sudden and unexpected introduction of weaponry to the planet: The Klingons, the Federation's arch enemies and a warlike civilization, have been covertly arming some of the tribes and deliberately leaving others unarmed so that the armed humanoids will quickly dominate the others, thus establishing secret control of the planet as a mining resource for the Klingon Empire. Kirk is faced with a terrible choice: Intervene and teach the friendly tribal people how to counter the Klingon influence for self-protection, or allow them to perish because they lack the necessary weapons of warfare to defend themselves.

The episode is variously characterized as both juvenile and bold by *Star Trek* fans. Some see it as a thinly-disguised, badly-written diatribe about the horrors of the Cold War and the Vietnam conflict. Others defend "A Private Little War" as a kind of spiritual forerunner to *Avatar*'s storyline, showing the effects an advanced civilization's technology can suddenly and dramatically have on a less-advanced one, and the unexpectedly tragic consequences such rapid innovations can wreak, especially where warfare is concerned. Neither observation is particularly relevant, however, to the success of the episode in terms of its placement in Ciné du Sasquatch. Suffice it to say that the Mugato — while not a "pure" species of bipedal hominid in the classical Earthbound sense — shares enough similarity with the Yeti (minus the reptilian additions, which are minor, and the poisonous bite) to warrant inclusion herein. Of particular relevance in terms of the Bigfoot genre's thematic core is the manner in which the humans on the planet relate to the Mugato as a species: They recognize it is the dominant two-legged predator and react accordingly, allowing an uneasy but respectful coexistence whenever possible. In this regard they are not unlike the Sherpas of the Abominable Snowman legends, who both fear and respect the Yeti as an equal if not superior life form to themselves. In both "A Private Little War" and Himalayan folklore, neither human nor hominid can eliminate one another and must therefore to some degree share the same geographical resources to survive. As such, they have formed an uneasy détente, which has evolved over the eons to maintain a necessary if fine-line balance between predation and avoidance.

This becomes a subtle echoing in the main plot of "A Private Little War." The introduction of weaponry, such as the flintlocks, threatens to not only destabilize the human populations into a dominant versus slave society (where all were formerly free people), but reduces the Mugato to a species that may soon be hunted into extinction. The moral conflicts are thus portrayed both on a human level (the conflict of technology versus progress) and an ecological one (the conflict of technology versus the environment). For despite its awesome powers, the Mugato is limited in its abilities and thus—with the coming of lethal human technology—unable to guarantee its own species' survival without human intervention. We see such a reality-based struggle happening in today's world, of course, in the increased disappearance of such once-plentiful animals as polar bears and great apes. This is true whether the reduction in species is purposeful—as in the hunting of the prairie buffalo in the Old West—or indirect, due to global climate changes which destroy the native habitats of endangered species.

It is this latter observation of technology's boon to mankind at the expense of other life forms that is so relevant to Ciné du Sasquatch. From the very first cryptid movie, *Conquest of the Pole* in 1912, to the present day Bigfoot entry, environmental conflict between man and hominid is always a central motif in all but a rare handful of titles. In this regard, Bigfoot, Sasquatch and Yeti movies and TV shows can be seen as emblematic illustrations of the last vestige of mankind's "primitive self" being threatened with extinction, even as we, as *Homo sapiens*, supposedly advance beyond the pull of our ancestral forerunners. The question these films and shows ask in regards to technology and its unforeseen outcomes is this: At what cost to both our environment and ourselves do we rely on a spirit of hopeful progress and ignore the mounting evidence that we employ it only to accelerate our own demise? The vanishing population of bipedal cryptids thus becomes shadowy reflections of ourselves in a possible, not-too-distant dystopian future, where we are but a mere vestige of our former selves as a species, too.

Chewbacca (Peter Mayhew) towers over his human companions in George Lucas' *Star Wars*. Some fans believed the Wookie was supposed to represent an interstellar Bigfoot.

Star Wars (1977)

AKA: *Star Wars: Episode IV—A New Hope*. Starring Mark Hamil, Harrison Ford, Carrie Fisher, Alec Guinness, Peter Cushing, Peter Mayhew, Anthony Daniels, David Prowess, James Earl Jones and Kenny Baker. Produced by Gary Kurtz, Rick McCullum and George Lucas. Written and Directed by George Lucas. USA. Color. Stereo. 121 Minutes.

Overview: Chewbacca the Wookie from the *Star Wars* films is a source of debate both for fans of the George Lucas series and cryptozoology cinema enthusiasts. In fact, when the *Star Wars* movie buzz first surfaced at science fiction and comic book conventions in 1976

prior to the film's release in May of 1977, more than a few who saw the early pre-release stills and slide shows assumed the towering cryptid was Sasquatch transposed into outer space.

Of course, since Lucas' morality play by definition takes place "a long, long time ago in a galaxy far, far away," it seems unlikely in the extreme that Chewbacca is the predecessor to the Earth-based Bigfoot lineage. But consider: Wookies are intelligent, bipedal hominids who cannot vocalize in human languages but utilize a series of guttural barks, wails and groans to convey their emotions; they're very tall compared to the average human; on their home world they prefer forest and jungle dwellings; and they are typically shy and reclusive when dealing with outsiders.

It is true the Wookies are technologically much more adept than most Ciné du Sasquatch cryptids, but consider the possibility that as space travelers who possess the ability to utilize hyper-jumps between star systems, they could conceivably have visited our Earth in eons past and left behind crew members and/or become stranded without the ability to return to their own galaxy. Not unlike with

Erich Von Daniken's theory, à la *Chariots of the Gods* (only with Wookies instead of E.T.-styled aliens), Bigfoot's ancestral family tree may be *speculatively* said to be of extraterrestrial origin. This is fanciful, granted, but only a rogue space pilot on the order of Han Solo would dismiss the possibility out of hand; after all, more than one report of UFO and human encounters also includes sightings of Sasquatch concurrent with or shortly after the event. And as *Invasion of the Animal People*, with its giant Yeti arriving via a crashed UFO, demonstrates, the idea of a cryptid from outer space is hardly a new one.

So whether this is a cinematic example of *Star Wars* being influenced by Bigfoot sightings or vice versa, there exists an intriguing if unspecified connection between Earthly cryptids and cosmic Wookies.

Strange but True? ("Bigfoot") (1993) (TV) (Doc)

Featuring Michael Aspel and John Rackham. Produced and Written by David Alpin. Directed by Tracy Jeune, Cameron McAllister, Nigel Miller, John Morgan and Mark Redhead. UK. Color. Stereo. 30 Minutes.

Overview: Though well-produced, *Strange but True?* definitely suffers from a case of "overly-familiaritis." The typical Fortean focus falls on UFOs, vampires, faith healers, past memory regression, psychic pets, and the like. Only one episode, called "Bigfoot," was specifically devoted to Sasquatch, and it split the show's brief half-hour running length with another segment, called "Ouija Boards," devoted to spirit communication using a popular, occult-themed children's game board. Even for Warhol, 15 minutes was necessary to consume one's quota of pop fame; given that *Strange but True?* was actually only 22 to 24 minutes of content, it's hard to fault the show for its less than conclusive handling of the hominids.

The Strange Case of Captain Ramper (1927)

AKA: *Ramper, der Tiermensch*; *Ramper, the Beastman*. Starring Paul Wegener, Mary Johnson, Hugo Döblin, Georg Guertler, Camillo Kossuth, Max Schreck and Hermann Vallentin. Written by Curt J. Braun, Max Mohr and Paul Wegener. Directed by Max Reichmann. Germany. Black & White. Silent.

Overview: Eager young airplane navigator Captain Remper embarks upon his latest attempt to make aviation history—a pioneering flight across the Arctic Circle! But mechanical troubles force Ramper to make an emergency landing in the frozen wastelands. Ippling, Ramper's ever-faithful mechanic and sidekick, is killed in the landing, but Ramper survives. As good luck would have it, a previous expedition has left supplies in an emergency survival hut that Ramper stumbles upon. Though well-stocked, it is a tiny, claustrophobic shelter, and a hellish place in which to survive. As bad luck would have it, it takes 15 *years* for the world to find Ramper again.

Ramper has "let himself go native" and not shaved, groomed, or even worn clothing in over a decade, as his garments eventually were worn into non-existence. To fight against the bitter cold, Ramper has grown thick, wooly fur from head to toe and fallen into select mutism. He has had no communication with mankind during this 15-year time period; his wild facial hair literally blocks all but his eyes behind a hirsute mask.

Enter Captain Balhaus and his Arctic expedition, who find Ramper and reasonably assume he is a living Yeti. Though nominally grateful to be "rescued" by Balhaus, Ramper finds himself in worse straits than before when the bored Balhaus and crew sell Ramper into slavery to a carnival sideshow as a mute "beast man" freak. Toured throughout Europe but never in his home land of Germany, Ramper begins to see the darkest sides of humanity as he's exhibited as a carnival attraction.

During one such exhibition of himself as a monster, Ramper is touched when a lovely young woman clearly feels his pain at being so shamelessly held up to mockery and ridicule simply because he is different. Alas, despite his hopes rising that at long last love may have found him, Ramper is forced to realize that the young woman is actually happily engaged to marry her poor fiancé; the two simply lack the financial resources to wed, but work to save for such a day. Concurrently, a semi-recovered Ramper is given a financial settlement by the government to compensate for his pain and suffering as an explorer for king and country. Ramper faces a decision: use the money to try and break up the young woman's romance so that he might take her for himself, or face the fact that money alone is no longer enough to insure his happiness in society (if it ever was). He decides upon a novel variation, giving his new fortune to the struggling young couple so they may immediately marry. The destitute Ramper staggers back towards the lonely Arctic exile he now prefers as home, a man reduced by the elements of nature to a simple, unassuming hominid who willingly abandons his last vestiges of humanity and therefore is completely without need of mankind's civilization.

* * * * *

In *The Strange Case of Captain Ramper* the human observers are the ones projecting *their* belief that Captain Ramper himself is the Abominable Snowman. How else to explain the tall, fur-covered "wild man" the curious crew lead by Captain Balhaus recover in the Arctic wastelands? Appropriate to the title, this is a strange inversion of the usual "man in an ape suit" motif in which a supposedly legit Sasquatch is revealed as a hoax by the conclusion; Ramper in *The Strange Case of Captain Ramper* is the "ape in a man suit" reversal, with the Yeti being a case of mistaken identity.

Ironically, in considering Ramper's designation as a de facto member of his own species, humanity itself becomes a questionable commodity which is arbitrarily given and taken away by fellow human beings. This doesn't occur among any other known animal,

The explorers search a desolate polar icescape for any signs of a reported Yeti in *The Strange Case of Captain Ramper*.

insect, or plant society on Earth. The genteel European society of *The Strange Case of Captain Ramper* (it is set 15 years in the future from its actual 1927 release date, or a fictionalized 1942) has no use for a once famous explorer who is already forgotten by them, let alone a mute "Ice Man" who seemingly lacks even rudimentary intelligence or the proper esteem for such truly important skills as pinkie extension during high tea.

As *The Strange Case of Captain Ramper* shows, even a genuine specimen of *Homo sapiens* can be reduced to less than human *if* the perception by the masses around him exists that said subject is somehow inferior or lacking in the "good genes" of the human DNA genome. In this sense, we glimpse the underlying roots of racism, class divisions, uber-nationalism, and many other inherent social ills; our own biased nature works to insure that these moral failings will be a steady by-product of our largely chaotic creation of a civilized society. That the decision to reduce Ramper from exploration demigod to sub-humanoid status is largely arbitrary and outside Ramper's control, without any critical debate at all by the human participants, is grotesque in the same vein as *The Elephant Man* or Tod Browning's *Freaks*. It suggests the cruelty humanity is capable of invoking to exclude its own kind for the most superficial of reasons, even as it creates societal structures to reward those who already have plenty. Indeed, it is as if we are witness to a pagan ritual in which the crowd is chanting for more sacrifice at whatever cost, offering up burnt embers of self-destruction and never once seeing that their actions are ultimately short-sighted, with tragic consequences soon to follow. Into this scenario Ramper offers up the perfect wrecked psyche for the ever-fascinated public to consume. Ironically, Ramper has become trapped like Prometheus in a series of soul-stealing tableaux (first the living icon of explorer and aviator; later as the frozen man unable to muster an emotional response in the modern world). Beyond these two "identities," it is as if Ramper the man never existed, nor ever will.

This would surely provide much comfort to most modern men — i.e., societal respect; an unrequested monetary settlement from the government; a thoroughly-obsessed public who hang on your every action and word. But for Ramper, these are mere distractions, the trappings of artificiality one must endure in polite society if one is to extract monies to finance world-challenging expeditions of

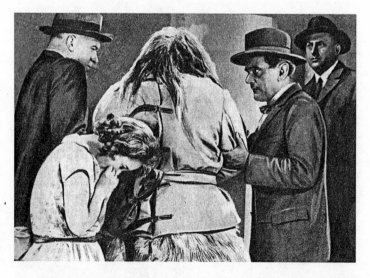

As Ramper (Paul Wegener) is lead away, his heartbroken fiancée (Mary Johnson) grieves for her loss and his lonely fate. From a serialized newspaper insert promoting *The Strange Case of Captain Ramper.*

conquest and discovery. Ramper is not a preview of the ruthless egomaniac Carl Denham in *King Kong*; rather, he is Denham if Denham were suddenly crushed beyond repair, as if Carl Denham finally gave up on even his own narcissistic facade of manliness and collapsed inward into a smoldering ruin of stewing, psychic regret.

The cast and crew are excellent. Known mainly as an actor from his series of German films featuring the Golem character, Paul Wegener was a key player in the expressionist tendency in German filmmaking circa the 1920s, also writing, directing, and producing movies. Max Schreck, the memorable Count Orlock from the original *Nosferatu*, here has a dual role, one minor and one major: As a sailor in the Captain Balhaus rescue party, Schreck blends into the crowd directed; as the embodiment of a series of horrors that befall Ramper during his 15-year-long ordeal of estrangement, Schreck plays a series of representative woes (such as Cold, Loneliness, etc.). The latter sequence is the most expressionistic of the entire film, using near-operatic intensity to suggest states of mental being (and non-being), with Schreck tormenting Ramper, year after desolate year, like some kind of demonic ice harpy placed there by some truly angry Teutonic gods.

The film loses much viewer interest after the melodramatic return to the social worlds of Europe. This is mostly because the hero is never fully "awakened" from his frozen state, either physically or emotionally, and it's difficult for such a physical actor as Wegener to play such a constrained, depressed protagonist. It hardly matters as far as this Ciné du Sasquatch guide is concerned; as *The Strange Case of Captain Ramper* is never truly a story about a Yeti but a shaggy dog tale of a Yeti who suddenly vanishes after a good haircut and grooming, revealing the human lurking beneath.

Still, it is an undeniably interesting entry in the genre. The fact two of the greatest pioneers of German filmmaking for an entire generation — Wegener and Schreck — share rare screen time together in a virtually unheard-of picture (even to many devotees of Ciné du Sasquatch) renders *The Strange Case of Captain Ramper* as a curiosity item for film lovers. But with its examinations of what it means to be a human versus what it means to be able to live as a human in human society, *The Strange Case of Captain Ramper* is also very much a genuine Bigfoot entry, even if the cryptid in question is a human being, not a creature. Movies in which a ravaging Sasquatch attacks a group of bickering, formerly-disunited humans in the woods and causes them to unite under their common umbrella as a shared species (if only temporarily) in order to survive are so basic to the Bigfoot film canon as to be deemed primordial in narrative construction. Here the opposite side of the xenophobia comes through: The Yeti is just a convenient marker for "non-human" in polite society more concerned with learning how to socially engineer the exclusion of "undesirables" who threaten the status quo and its sense of well-being. In this one eerie sense, *The Strange Case of Captain Ramper* was dead-on accurate, as by 1942 in the real world, Germany was deeply into enacting its monstrous legacy as social engineers-turned-genocidal maniacs.

Strange Nation ("Searching for Bigfoot") (2008) (TV) (Doc)

Featuring Shane "Shooter" Nelson and Tom Biscardi. USA. Color. Stereo. 24 Minutes.

Overview: This television pilot for a never-produced series centers on the quest by Tom Biscardi's Bigfoot, Inc., to explore a sighting outside of Paris, Texas, where Bigfoot encounters are frequently reported. Locals interviewed in the street by youthful host Shane "Shooter" Nelson range from believers in Bigfoot to skeptics who react with comic disbelief. Much of the Biscardi moments revolve around the use of night vision goggles and other high-tech equipment used by Bigfoot, Inc., to distinguish the for-profit group from so-called "amateurs" who cannot afford such gadgetry.

The timing for the production at first seemed foolproof, with Biscardi garnering much coincidental attention shortly after *Strange Nation*'s completion when he went public with his support for the Georgia Bigfoot discovery, in which it was reported two amateur cryptozoologists and law officers had recovered a relatively fresh Bigfoot corpse. As Internet photos released by "unknown sources" of the creature's body (stuffed into an old, rusty freezer) circulated the globe, the *Strange Nation* producers must have believed they'd hit the jackpot. But though the 2008 Georgia Bigfoot find would become one of the hottest media stories of the year, that lasted only until the bubble was finally burst by the admission of the men involved that it was all a hoax. Only later, and after appearing on major news stations across the planet, did Biscardi recant his story and admit he had been "fooled" by the Georgia hoaxsters; but for the Ivan Marx protégé Biscardi, with a long series of hoaxes associated with his name, it forever rendered his legacy tarnished by multiple "mistakes" on his behalf in regards to hyped media events (which he is especially good at orchestrating). It perhaps doomed any chance *Strange Nation* had of achieving legitimate distribution and/or pick-up as a television series, as the fallout from the revelation of the hoax was predictably harsh on those associated with Biscardi and the Georgia tricksters.

Strange Universe (Multiple Episodes) (1996) (TV) (Doc)

Hosted by Emmitt Miller and Dana Adams. Featuring Clint Catalyst, Donald G. Jackson, Rich Knight, Robert Wesley Knight, Cassandra Peterson, Franklin Ruehl, Scott Shaw, Julie Strain, Loren Coleman and Adam Zuvich. Produced by Paul Barrosse, Yasmin Brennan, Brian Peter Falk, Craig D. Forrest, Drew S. Levin, Mark Marabella, Joe Marotta, Margaret Roberts, Jordan Silver and Adam Zuvich. Written by Paul Barrosse, Yasmin Brennan and Matthew Malach. USA. Color. Stereo. 24 Minutes.

Overview: Hosts Emmitt Miller and Dana Adams take a peek at strange phenomena such as Bigfoot, the Loch Ness Monster, and the Chupacabra. Most segments feature recreations of encounters, which add to the show's effectiveness. Loren Coleman, noted cryptozoologist, acted as a consultant for some of the show's research, giving it an authenticity many series in the genre lack. Episodes of interest to Ciné du Sasquatch fans include: "Monkey Man," "Texas Bigfoot and Lake Monster," "Himalayan Snow Creature," and "Bigfoot from Space."

Strange Wilderness (2009)

Starring Steve Zahn, Allen Covert, Jonah Hill, Joe Don Baker, Harry Hamlin, Robert Patrick, Justin Long, Jeff Garlin, Kevin Heffernan, Ashley Scott, Seth Rogen and Ernest Borgnine. Produced by Adam Sandler, Jack Giarraputo, Allen Covert and Peter Gaulke. Written by Peter Gaulke and Fred Wolf. Directed by Fred Wolf. USA. Color. Stereo. 87 Minutes.

Overview: A college-aged man named Peter Gaulke inherits a terrible animal nature TV series as producer when his father, the show's creator, passes away. Gaulke, a dope-smoking slacker, takes what little dignity the stodgy show possesses and squanders it within weeks as its new producer. The cable access quality aftermath show—basically nothing but stoner jokes and animal hi-jinks footage badly edited into MTV-styled montages—has only two weeks to live be-

cause the itchy execs want to axe the ratings bomb. Realizing he must somehow rise to the occasion and save his father's dying legacy, Gaulke concentrates on revitalizing the show in the allotted two week time frame. Gaulke's plan: use the news his father's old survivalist buddy has brought forward of a map to a Sasquatch lair in Costa Rica as a "special investigation" episode to awaken audience interest. The entire on-the-fly documentary will be a thrilling, "you are there" type of adventure as Gaulke and his documentary unfurls, unscripted, as they go in search of Sasquatch.

Setting out in a small group, the TV producer and crew of demented dopers drive Gaulke's Winnebago—now loaded with video production gear—to the Ecuadorian jungles. There they plan to stake out the territory and prove once and for all the existence of Bigfoot. But along the way they encounter a crazy survivalist and a better-funded, better-equipped rival, among other obstacles. Will Guile fold under the mounting pressures, or will he uncharacteristically rise to the occasion?

* * * * *

Strange Wilderness is a notable failure in the Ciné du Sasquatch genre, at least in terms of commercial expectations versus box office realities. While no one expected it to be *Ghostbusters* in terms of box-office appeal, its lackluster $4 million theatrical opening (where it ranked an ominous 13th for overall gross versus its competitors in release), and subsequent less than stellar DVD and cable performance, proved it to be a severe underperformer, even by *Saturday Night Live* movie factory standards (the filmmakers were graduates of the series as weekly writers).

Promotional artwork for the theatrical release of *Strange Wilderness*.

Partly it is because the film is an admittedly off-the-track piece of goofball unreality even on a stoner movie level, lacking a believable, cohesive plot to sustain even its economic 87 minutes of running time. The film also often feels improvised and padded, though this may actually be more a case of using out-takes to bolster the film's scant length. Though it's cut down to the bone, *Strange Wilderness* is a hodgepodge of various "baked" doper film motifs mixed with a smidgen of Bigfoot to enliven interest.

A film like *Strange Wilderness*, as a broad comedy, all comes down to taste (or lack thereof). As far as "shocking vulgarity at the cineplex" movies go, it falls short (which may be to its credit) of the non-stop crudity necessary for this kind of youth satire to work, à la *There's Something About Mary*. But as a bona fide entry into Ciné du Sasquatch, it offers the customary viewpoint so often taken post–*Harry and the Hendersons* re: hominids — that Sasquatch is basically just a misunderstood Ewok on Earth, huggable and loveable, provided you first bond with him. This comedic starting point of "humanizing" Bigfoot at the expense of the icon's darker, beastlier side has numerous pitfalls, however, as precedents such as *Little Bigfoot*, *Cry Wilderness*, and others demonstrate. By pandering to the audience's expectations that the creature will only act within a range of conduct considered "family friendly," these movies often sacrifice the complexity of a fully-rounded cryptid character in favor of something less subtle but supposedly more commercial — a funny Bigfoot or a wizened Sasquatch. While it's true *Strange Wilderness* treats its Bigfoot subject matter with less than G-rated reverence, it still places Sasquatch within the satiric rather than scary range.

The cast is uniformly (and surprisingly) good for such a low-budget studio offering. And while none are offering their best performances, neither is the material requiring much. The elderly Ernest Borgnine was 91 years of age when he was shooting his cameo and seems as much amazed to still be working as caring much about

whether or not he's still being directed by the likes of Sam Peckinpah. Likewise, Joe Don Baker makes one pine for his earnest earlier work, such as in Phil Karlson's epic Southern actioner *Walking Tall*, where he played the charismatic Sheriff Buford Pusser with smoldering conviction; here he's almost like a Dickensian "ghost from Christmas past" paying a sudden, frantic visit to Gaulke's confused young TV producer. But it's the odd but likeable casting of Justin Long as a stoner tagalong to the documentary crew that shines through the latter half of the film. Particularly amusing is when Long's character has his eyelids tattooed as if they're still open so that he can sleep without anyone knowing. The hangdog look Long projects while asleep, with the creepy, non-blinking eyes staring like a saddened Christ image, is genuinely comical and reminds one of his equally satisfying performance in another (more successful, if less cynical) Bigfoot movie — *The Sasquatch Gang*.

Strip Mall ("Burbank Bigfoot") (2000) (TV)

Starring Julie Brown, Jim O'Heir, Tim Bagley, Eliza Coyle, Allison Dunbar, Loretta Fox, Amy Hill, Gregory Itzin, Bob Koherr, Jonathan Mangum, Maxwell Caulfield, Tasha Taylor, Chris Wylde and Victoria Jackson. Produced by Julie Brown, Charlie Coffey, Alan Cohn, Noa James Krauss, Gregg McBride and Emily Wolfe. Written by Judi Diamond and Ken Rathjen. Directed by Alan Cohn, Bobcat Goldthwait, Sam Irvin and Bob Koherr. USA. Color. Stereo. 30 Minutes.

Overview: A former child star named Tammi (who insists on pronouncing it "Tah-MEE") struggles to make the post-career adjustment as an adult in Van Nuys, California. Broke and working as one of two skanky waitresses at a strip mall bar called the Funky Fox, Tammi marries an overweight dry cleaning store owner, mistakenly believing him to be a millionaire. Desperate, Tammi tries any number of schemes and manipulations to get back into the entertainment business, but nothing ever works, and quite often her petty attempts result in her shaky stock sinking even lower.

In "Burbank Bigfoot" Tammi learns that a number of non-celeb locals claimed to have seen Bigfoot and are receiving big-time TV coverage due to their fantastic stories. Thinking this a golden opportunity to reignite her career with a new by-line as "the former child star who has discovered Sasquatch," Tammi sets out to track and capture a cryptid species that has eluded even the world's greatest hunters, scientists, and cryptozoologists. But her actions cause a ripple effect throughout the tiny little strip mall community, making Tammi learn by show's end that despite her "nothing" status as a cocktail waitress in the tiny Plaza del Toro strip mall, her actions do have an impact on those around her, however oblivious she is to this reality most days and nights.

* * * * *

Strip Mall co-creator, co-producer, and co-star Julie Brown (best known for her role as Candy in *Earth Girls Are Easy*, for which she also co-wrote the screenplay) lead a talented ensemble cast for this short-lived Comedy Central sitcom. The set-up was actually quite good — the various shenanigans that occur behind the scenes at several small businesses located in a dismal Valley-based L-shaped mall known as "The Plaza del Toro" — and the execution

Peter (Steve Zahn) ponders the profound mysteries of nature while Bigfoot (David Mattey) ponders the endless variety of dumb humans. (From *Strange Wilderness*.)

was always professional and adroit. The scripts were fast-paced and well-written, and tended towards a Robert Altman–esque interweaving of divergent stories that unfolded simultaneously within a small, self-contained cadre of individuals.

As far as the Bigfoot genre goes, "Burbank Bigfoot" is quite typical of sitcom-styled Sasquatch cameos post–*Harry and the Hendersons*: It is played mostly for laughs, and even the absurdity of having a hominid stalking a major metropolitan area like Los Angeles is passed off as something the viewer should accept without question. Given that most of these shows feature Bigfoot onscreen for a scant few minutes by design (in that cryptid costumes on TV shows are never believable unless done by a thoroughly professional make-up and costuming team, which costs more money than the average sitcom's budget can handle), it's understandable most comedy shows go for a satirical approach to Bigfoot—a cheap laugh. Too, it's within the format of the "situational comedy" to exploit such ridiculousness for maximum effect over any inherent tone of respect for its subject matter.

If anything, "Burbank Bigfoot" may be of more interest for its show's title than the content of the episode itself. Most assuredly without intent, *Strip Mall* makes reference to John Chamber's infamous "Burbank Bigfoot"—in which the make-up artist created a full-size monster suit under mysterious circumstances never quite made public—and which many have served as the suit utilized in the Patterson-Gimlin film of 1967 (though this remains conjectural). Though again this is surely coincidental, it nonetheless shows how intertwined Ciné du Sasquatch's fictional and non-fictional histories have co-evolved, influencing one another and each revitalizing the other medium by always raising the cinematic and televised stakes. Bigfoot is just another way into showbiz, as "Burbank Bigfoot" would have the viewer believe—as necessary as knowing someone who knows someone or having a relative who works at a talent agency. As *King Kong* demonstrates (but even *The Conquest of the Pole* hints at), anyone attempting to capture a hominid is, de facto, involving oneself in the area of entertainment, as the public interest and news outlet hunger is such that *any* announcement of Bigfoot—whether fictional or reality-based—causes an immediate frenzy of speculation and interest. Julie Brown as Tammi makes the logical intellectual leap that discovering an urban Bigfoot will again make her famous, her only real goal in life.

Suburban Sasquatch (2004)

Starring Sue Lynn Sanchez, Bill Ushler, Dave Bonavita, Juan Fernandez, Wes Miller, Loretta Wascavage, Troy Stephen Sanders, Dallas Quinn, Hunter Quimby, Edward Wascavage Sr., David Weldon, Linda Jamison, Ryan Miller and Alisha Irwin. Produced, Written and Directed by Dave Wascavage. USA. Color. Stereo. 97 Minutes.

Overview: A planned suburban development of upscale homes is invaded by a savage Sasquatch intent on preventing further encroachment into its once rural domain. Unable to deal with the unexpected ferocity of the murders, the local two-man police force elects to show up after each slaughter and shake their heads in bewilderment. Meanwhile, a reporter with ambitions to escape the small-town newspaper he works for decides the killings are his ticket to the big-city media world—if only he can get the scoop before someone else beats him to it.

Also tracking the marauding monster is a vision-questing young Native American woman whose grandfather has tasked her with thwarting the beast. She teams up with the reporter, telling him that only magical weapons, such as the crossbow she possesses, can destroy a spiritual cryptid entity. Together the two hunt the Bigfoot, intent on stopping its unabated killing spree. They have to face not only

the beast itself, but local hunters intent on mounting the monster's head on their wall. Who will prevail—men, woman or monster?

* * * * *

Suburban Sasquatch may well be the epitome of bad "Bigfootage" (to coin a term), shot as it is on a home camcorder, featuring as it does a Bigfoot suit that not only is unconvincing as a cryptid but unconvincing as a "man in a gorilla" costume, and sporting as it does equally non-professional acting. This is not to say *Suburban Sasquatch* lacks entertainment value; quite the contrary. But like *Robot Monster*, *The Alien Factor*, and other examples of the amateur-released-as-professional ilk, it strains credulity with every passing moment of screen time.

Suburban Sasquatch begins like so many films in this genre—with drivers encountering the monster on a remote roadway. In this instance, a young couple intent on making it to an outdoor party meet their doom for having the audacity to brake after the shaggy beast runs across their path. It smashes the driver's side window and yanks the helpless young man outside. Seconds later it claws him to shreds before killing his screaming date. With obvious, home-computer-generated CGI blood spurts and rubbery, fake limbs flying, the tone of unintentional camp is immediately set. The inadvertent hilarity of this opening sequence, however, is quickly matched by the arrival of the two Abbott & Costello cops. The head cop inserts his own hand into the Bigfoot track left behind at the murder scene—so much for preserving the evidence untainted!

The next slaughter tops even the opening, however, for Benny Hill–styled rubber dummy shenanigans. Two drunken buddies fish near a highway, lamenting how few trout remain as a result of the recent construction efforts. Moments later Bigfoot appears, walking straight to the first angler with an almost slow-motion gait. Without further ado, the beast rips the man's heart out of his chest and then stuffs the gooey, beating organ into the dead-on-his-feet victim's open mouth. Convinced the "heart tartar" entree is not sufficient punishment, Sasquatch yanks an arm from the dead fisherman. As more crudely-matted CGI blood spurts from the crimson stump (why are the victims in these low-budget affairs *always* conveniently wearing white tee shirts?—a rhetorical question, of course, given that dark-colored tees wouldn't show the blood stains), the growling Bigfoot hurls the detached arm into the second fisherman's chest, knocking the stunned friend unconscious.

This may read as gruesome stuff; but it's difficult to convey the astonished laughter these scenes induce in all but the most squeamish of viewers (i.e., the kind of person who objects to Bugs Bunny blowing Elmer's face off with a shotgun, only to have Elmer perfectly fine the next moment). *Suburban Sasquatch* features some of the most ineptly staged attack sequences ever produced in the genre. There is an unintentional ferocity of manic pacing and mismatched jump cuts that reminds more of a Three Stooges short (minus their verisimilitude for making the comical violence effective). It's as if the filmmakers sensed the ludicrous nature of the footage, but rather than discard the failed sequences, they decided to cut them into MTV fast-cut snippets. The rapid-fire cutting adds to the bizarrely comic effect. Think Bela Lugosi wrapping himself into the unresponsive tentacles of the rubbery octopus in Ed Wood's *Bride of the Monster*, then substitute drunken buddies, home video technique, and a vaudeville-styled man in a gorilla suit with green ping pong ball eyes. It's truly one of those "must be seen to be *dis*believed" movies; and even after several viewings, *Suburban Sasquatch* has the ability to induce guffaws.

One feels especially uncharitable in attempting to ridicule *Suburban Sasquatch*. Clearly, the one-man wonder behind it all, David Wascavage, was overextended from the outset. Not only did Mr. Wascavage have the unenviable tasks of writing, directing, editing, producing, scoring, *and* designing the creature costume, but he was also laboring under a budget even Sid and Marty Krofft would have found challenging. But with that duly noted, the sheer audacity of the film's unrelenting improbability and lack of any discernible directorial control really do place it in the pantheon of all-time worst Bigfoot films. More often than not it leaves the viewer reaching for the remote to rewind the footage, gasping aloud, "Did I *really* just see what I thought I saw?"

Among the more outrageous scenes are: Bigfoot lifting a green-screen-matted patrol car above his head and — chromakey lines horrendously visible throughout — tossing it (somewhat) off-screen; Bigfoot throwing "boulders" that look less convincing than the video game equivalent of what Donkey Kong might have hurled in the Atari game; and Bigfoot utilizing a fallen CGI log to block two magic arrows intended to destroy him and break his evil curse. Again, these not-so-special effects are the modern equivalent of the carpet monster of *The Creeping Terror*, the cult classic that featured struggling victims who had to pull themselves into the carpet monster's mouth.

Should it seem uncharitable that Bigfoot takes the "bulk" of the blame, it can also be said with some critical certainty that the cast are entirely non-professionals. In this kind of movie, the worse the better, at least for jaded viewers (presumably the only ones willing to watch until the end credit crawl) looking for laughs in all the wrong places (as the Urban — or is that Suburban? — Sasquatch once crooned).

It must be said that *Suburban Sasquatch* delights in particular with the "lawman with a past" stereotype; in this version the poor sheriff's ex-wife was abducted by a killer Bigfoot, no less! The flashback in which the cursed cop tells his Barney Fife–like second (and only) in command about the incident is another milestone in bad Bigfoot cinema. As his wife semi-dozes on the front porch of their remote country home, Bigfoot materializes on the horizon. In a shot like something out of David Lean's *Lawrence of Arabia*, Sasquatch slowly walks across an open field in broad daylight. As seconds pass like minutes, it makes its way towards its intended victim. Incredibly, rather than react, the woman merely squints, staring without moving, until the monster slings her over his shoulder. Actually, slinging is a misnomer; she magically appears on the monster's shoulder after a cutaway to the husband grabbing his gun. Given the woman's ample size, the viewer can readily believe Sasquatch is strong enough to have hoisted the police car earlier in the movie.

If it seems too easy (and uncharitable) to point out *Suburban Sasquatch*'s shortcomings, at least it can be said that the filmmaker incorporated many of the classic hallmarks of the genre. For example, there is a gorilla suit passing as hominid; a spiritually-inclined Native American elder who guides his offspring in the task of slaying Bigfoot (*Sasquatch, the Legend of Bigfoot*); a reporter anxious to convince his disbelieving editor (*Kolchak the Night Stalker* and *The Legend of McCullough's Mountain*); myriad encounters with the beast in which it attacks without the slightest provocation (*Bigfoot* with John Carradine); frequent and gory bodily dismemberment (*Shriek of the Mutilated*); the idea of placing the cryptid in a suburban environment (*Harry and the Hendersons*); mystical abilities of the Bigfoot to dematerialize and vanish; and the unfortunate overuse of daylight attack sequences. Given that any one of these clichés turns up repeatedly in a myriad of entries in Ciné du Sasquatch, *Suburban Sasquatch* at least has the distinction of using one and all.

In regards to the plethora of daytime attacks, one is tempted to rationalize the influence of the Patterson/Gimlin footage, which was taken in the late afternoon. However, much more likely is the fact it's simply cheaper and faster to shoot in the daylight without expensive and time-consuming lighting. As the best of the Savage Sasquatch movies (such as Hammer's *The Abominable Snowman*,

Creature from Black Lake, *The Legend of Boggy Creek*, and *Abominable*) demonstrate time and again, there's something primordially more frightening in these cryptids creating mayhem by night than in the more comforting glare of day. This might be as simple as the fact the darkness hides the obvious costume deficiencies in most of these low-budget efforts. However, there is also the truism that such tales are best told around the proverbial campfire in the woods (a scene which almost all such films that feature night photography in the genre inevitably contain). Such sequences usually focus on the characters spouting expository history about the various legends of Bigfoot in the woods around them while the crackling fire eerily lights their listeners' frightened faces. It's simple and expected, of course; but setting is everything to our psyches in terms of the ability to suspend disbelief.

Swamp Apes (2006) (Doc)

Produced, Written and Directed by Jay Michael. USA. Color. Stereo. 40 Minutes.

Overview: Southern states throughout America have a long history of folklore and sightings of a hairy bipedal being with such colorful monikers as Haints, Hoodoos or Wild Men, depending upon the region. This documentary focuses on the swamps, bayous, thickets and forests of the Southeastern United States, recounting various stories and published accounts of Sasquatch with a Southern accent. This comes from CryptoVideography, the same one-man company that produced *Bigfoot FAQ* and *Bigfooting in Oklahoma*.

Tanya's Island (1980)

Starring Vanity, Richard Sargent, Mariette Lévesque, Don McLeod and Donny Burns. Produced by Pierre Brousseau, Gary Mandell and Jean-Claude Lévesque. Written by Pierre Brousseau. Directed by Alfred Sole. Canada. Color. Mono. 82 Minutes.

Overview: Tanya is a young media professional in the proverbial Big City who is having a difficult time with the constant pressures of modern living, loving, and surviving. She is forever late to her TV production job where she works as a professional sound editor. Her artist loft-living boyfriend Lobo makes matters worse when he seeks to end their relationship. Feeling trapped and alone, Tanya dreams about escaping to a fantasy island away from the daily grind.

She returns to her apartment to find a door upstairs from which emanates growls and fog. Opening the door, Tanya discovers a secret passageway onto a deserted tropical island stocked with all the food and easy sources of natural shelter one could desire. She and Lobo explore the newfound frontier, dropping all clothing and other signs of outward civilization, and letting their wild sides shine forth.

After many idyllic interludes, the initial conflict between Tanya and Lobo reemerges, owing to Lobo's increasing boredom on the island. It turns out they are not alone, however. One day while riding horseback (à la Lady Godiva), a naked Tanya stumbles upon Blue, a blue-eyed Bigfoot. Tanya passes out in fright, but when she recovers atop a bed of crushed flowers inside Blue's cave, she realizes the man-ape means her no harm, and has instead made an offer of friendship. Tanya returns to Lobo, but Blue is never far from her thoughts. Soon she visits Blue, and the two begin to fall in love.

Tanya is attracted to Blue's sensitivity. Compared to the brutish Lobo, Blue is a rarified gent. Meanwhile, sensing a rival, Lobo dedicates himself to uncovering the truth about Tanya's prolonged disappearances. Outraged when he discovers Tanya is seeing a lover from another species no less, Lobo captures Blue and keeps the helpless beast imprisoned in a series of torture devices and cages. Disgusted by Lobo's animal behavior, Tanya frees Blue and flees with him to the other side of island, hoping to avoid any other contact with Lobo. But bloodthirsty Lobo has digressed to a primitive status, demanding retribution against the beast who has bested him in love, no matter the cost.

To effect the final confrontation, Lobo takes Tanya prisoner and awaits Blue. Blue arrives as anticipated and a death battle ensues. Tanya is not surprised to see Blue triumph, but she is stunned when instead of claiming her gently as he has done previously, Blue is without regard to her physical comfort and rapes her in the tall grass. Tanya awakens at this point, realizing it was all a dream, and chilled to her core to learn that such a violent emotional catharsis as nearly breaking up with Lobo could cause such phantasms in her dreams.

* * * * *

Alfred Sole, director of the cult favorite *Alice, Sweet Alice*, with Brooke Shields, never ventured into the mainstream of Hollywood filmmaking. This "take it or leave it" artistic approach so evident in his work (and this one in particular) will alienate many traditional

Tanya (Vanity) is wooed by Blue (Don McLeod) the hominid in *Tanya's Island*. The painstaking prosthetics, make-up and detailed hairline work by artists Rick Baker and Rob Bottin are superb.

studio-only viewers, who prefer the classic "invisible" director at work — as will *Tanya's Island* itself, which is a cinematically lethargic but nonetheless often intriguing cult film. Because one senses the filmmakers were seriously attempting to tinker with the genre's conventions even as they were hedging their bets by including as much onscreen nudity and violence as they could get, there is an interesting contradiction going on within the film itself. On the one hand, the sheer ridiculous nature of the narrative (which is more akin to a short story than a feature-length treatment) and its anemic sense of unfolding events lacking any discernible meaning stifle interest. On the other hand, there is the hallucinogenic nature of the performances and photography, which super-saturates color schemes and lighting patterns to make much of the film seem surreal, à la the jungle sequences in *Apocalypse Now*. While *Tanya's Island* is never more than an interesting failure in dramatic terms, it is also never less than a successful dream-like distillation of many Ciné du Sasquatch conceptual motifs and visual stratagems present throughout the genre's history. This is why it has held a very marginal but growing influence as a positive viewing experience for fans of Ciné du Sasquatch who can appreciate the many inherent influences the film self-acknowledges in typical postmodern fashion — it demonstrates that even as the genre was gaining a wider audience, there was beginning to stir a reaction against the traditional Benign Bigfoot vs. Savage Sasquatch paradigm. That is, in the hands of a skillful independent filmmaker like Sole, there existed the possibility of examining the genre's dramatic limitations without abandoning all hope at the box office. And indeed, if Sole's creepy if erotic exploration reflects *The Beast* by Walerian Borowczyk (an obvious influence), at least it can be said the director refused to make a Canadian clone of his inspiration. In actuality, the film's first half is like *Beauty and the Beast* if it were set on Brooke Shield's *Blue Lagoon* island; while in the second half it abruptly becomes more like Boorman's *Hell in the Pacific*, with its two fierce warriors dueling for survival on a remote island (with an added love interest!).

The entire spectrum of Ciné du Sasquatch is amply illustrated throughout *Tanya's Island*— bestial love attraction, the degeneration of mankind into primitive form when confronted by a hominid Other (the latter of which is often superior in many ways to humanity), and the embedded scenario that when and if *Homo sapiens* and hominid finally meet, one (if not occasionally both) genetic strain must be terminated in an unabashedly primordial struggle for survival. While *Tanya's Island* is a distillation of these themes, there is hardly much more than this as far as narrative depth goes. Like a series of nightmarish waves, Sole abandons narrative logic and instead opts for narcoleptic dreaminess. Long passages languidly elapse in *Tanya's Island* as if one were watching an extended music video, which, given the era of production, is probably not completely unintentional. Though the cinematography is often mesmerizing, these dead-end stretches have kept the film from gaining wider cult audience acceptance in the decades since its initial spotty theatrical release.

But there are also stunning sequences that erupt from the boredom, which shock the viewer with their audacity of violence and frank sensuality. Here is where *Tanya's Island* mirrors *The Beast*, dramatically using the implicit threat of the collapse of a "just moral order" as background to the Sasquatch action (in both films a repressive sexual atmosphere pervades — in *The Beast* it's Victorian-era prudishness, and on *Tanya's Island* it's Reagan-era puritanism). There is a "threat" implicit in taboo sexuality that is both socially and self-repressed, the films suggest, and the beastly Bigfoot is really nothing more than a form of Freudian revenge made manifest in the flesh — an incarnation in the physical realm representing the unleashing of heretofore hidden passions and urges beyond control. There is a fairy tale quality to these types of narratives, and indeed, *Tanya's Island* embodies them distinctly, as the entire island narrative is shown from the beginning to be but an extended dream sequence (as was much of *The Beast*'s sexual encounters rendered as a young lady's erotic dreams). If dreaming is the dissolution of conscious mind into a subconscious state, then note how this dissolution prevails as a dramatic device in unending portrayals of *Beauty and the Beast*'s prototypical set-up throughout human history, wherein only when humans enter into dreamlike worlds of co-existence with hominids does the possibility suddenly open of formerly verboten affairs of love and sexual desire. It is the meeting of opposites, in essence, that suspends the narrative engine — much like the descriptions of those falling in love who proclaim such maxims as "Time seemed to stand still!" In *Tanya's Island* and other Ciné du Sasquatch taboo variants, time *does* stand still as soon as hominid meets human mate, and sets the two lovers adrift in a strange, suspended world where love transcends all boundaries, especially between species.

Only with the primal reaction by mankind (typically in the form of a jealous human male lover, as in the case of *Tanya's Island*) who attempts to subdue and/or kill the cryptid can order be restored to the fragile world of human power affairs, wherein perception is everything and reality a myth to be formalized for the faceless followers. In human hierarchy, there is mankind and there is the rest of all life on Earth. Bigfoot threatens this long-established human conceit, toppling mankind from alpha predator to shared participant status. If there is one truism in all of Ciné du Sasquatch as a genre, it is this: No amount of human technological supremacy will guarantee dominance over Bigfoot's native cunning and superior stealth abilities, and thus, defeated by the very tools which have given him dominion over the Earth, man typically meets his match in the wily Sasquatch. But this defeat will never come without the resulting promise on mankind's part to "get even" with the rival cryptid species. In a strange inversion of Biblical mythology, humans are the fallen angels, bested by their own vanity and savagery, while Sasquatch is the preserved race, protected by the invisible hands (or is that paws?) of an unseen but omnipresent cryptid god. It is as if Bigfoot remained in the Garden of Eden even as Adam and Eve were resentfully glancing back over their shoulders at their hairy hominid cousin. There is bad blood between the species far worse than Cain and Abel, though akin in terms of envy and greed; and in most Ciné du Sasquatch films this ancient blood feud can only be met with more spilled crimson. Like cats and dogs, humans and hominids are doomed to eternal cycles of prey vs. predator roles (though in the case of Bigfoot, the roles of who is predator and who is prey often shift, even within the same film or TV show).

The make-up effects for Blue were a pressure-filled, time-constrained triumph of collaboration between Rick Baker and Rob Bottin (indeed, the two were nominated for a Canadian Genie Award for Best Costume Design for their contributions to the Canadian-made *Tanya's Island*). Baker started the design but had to bow out due to other contractual obligations when the assignment went past the initially agreed upon deadline; a young Bottin showed he was every bit up to the task by finishing the costume and performing the convincing role of Blue, which garners much empathy in large part because of the surprisingly tender nature of the hominid's portrayal. Though Blue looks fierce and (as the finale demonstrates) is more than capable of defending itself against violence, there is little doubt of Sole's intent. Contrasting the sadistic nature of Lobo (Tanya's hilariously-named male human lover) with Blue's own relaxed, loving nature (when not provoked), one sees why Tanya conjures an image of a hominid as she does: Blue is capable of the physical intimacy Tanya requires, but at the same time is able to act as a spiritual protector when Tanya only wants refuge from a competitive world. This creature is not a depiction of the worst in mankind, but rather the best of Blue's beastly nature. As Lobo deliberately degrades himself and takes on the worst aspects of the human condition in order to destroy Blue, so Blue digs deeper into himself to offer the wounded Tanya a deeper spiritual "island" where none but she and her primordial primate may dwell. The ordeal basically makes a man out of the hominid and a beast out of the man. Neither species is superior by design or default; each succumbs and rises to the specificity of the occasion.

Blue finally succumbs to the pressures of constant contact with a diseased human mind (and some might say becomes temporarily, if darkly, "human") when the creature bests Lobo only to turn on Tanya, raping her at the film's disturbing finale before she awakes to realize it

Tanya (Vanity) adores her hominid lover Blue (Don McLeod), while Blue symbolically mounts a tree trunk on the secluded *Tanya's Island*.

was "all only a dream." Is Sole implying that even a benevolent innocent like Blue will eventually become degraded by contact with humanity and ultimately develop into a cruel being as a result? Blue is shown overcoming every form of horrid human treatment, as represented by the endless contraptions of confinement and torture Lobo devises to inflict unwarranted pain upon his adversary. But each step also brings the beatific beast closer to a shocking truth: that it, as a species, shares more with humanity than a bipedal gait. What is shared, Blue learns (to his regret), is a capacity for unmitigated evil.

By surviving the assault by mankind on its own turf, Bigfoot maintains its sense of dignity; but unlike most Bigfoot films that end on such a note, *Tanya's Island* lingers a few beats longer to speculate on the cost to Sasquatch. For once, Bigfoot is as much the loser as mankind, and is left pondering a ruined soul in the wake of having had contact with human beings. In many ways it's the most sobering, adult viewpoint yet of what emotional price a complex psychological being like Sasquatch would actually pay for having mingled with humanity. Not unlike the empathy gained for the lost souls who are the Yeti holdovers in *The Abominable Snowman* from 1957, *Tanya's Island* features a lonely, nearly extinct hominid that pays the ultimate emotional price for daring to love a human woman, even as King Kong paid the maximum penalty for the same crime by forfeiting his life. Blue is spared death, but is left a humbled hominid thereafter suffering from post-traumatic stress because of its encounter with man, who has riddled Blue's soul with more doubt and regret than even an Earthly paradise like Tanya's dream island can heal.

Tenacious D ("Death of a Dream") (1999) (TV)

Starring Jack Black, Kyle Gass, John C. Reilly, Paul F. Tompkins and Ernest M. Garcia. Produced by Jack Black, Kyle Gass, Jerry Adams, David Cross, Tom Gianas, Bob Odenkirk and Mara B. Waldman. Written by Jack Black, Kyle Gass, David Cross, Bob Odenkirk, Bill Odenkirk and Tom Gianis. Directed by Tom Gianis. USA. Color. Stereo. 12 Minutes.

Overview: JB and KG, two lifelong stoners who desire to be rock 'n' roll gods more than getting high itself (or equally as much, at any rate), stage an unsanctioned "meet and greet" tee-shirt and photo autograph night at Captain Ed's head shop for their nonexistent fan base. Depressed that no one attends the show or the signing, they pour out their woes to the joint's owner, Captain Ed. The good captain explains he was once in a band that had *actual* talent and further discourages the duo—who bill themselves as Tenacious D—from pursuing their musical dream, telling them believing in their talent is akin to believing in Bigfoot: It just doesn't exist.

Humiliated, JB and KG go through several stages of grief. First, they use anger to slander Captain Ed. Next comes denial, as they rehearse for their nonexistent world tour and Grammy attendance. Soon they've worked their way to the inevitable conclusion, however: Captain Ed is right, the Tenacious D duo have no talent, and their dream to be rock stars is dead.

At a campfire the two friends incinerate their Tenacious D tee shirt stock and prepare to smash their guitars in a ceremony of self-release from their identities as rockers. However, right after JB demolishes his instrument, Sasquatch appears and befriends the two shocked buddies. JB and KG accompany Sasquatch back to the creature's cave

lair, whereupon he jams with them on the drums. Tenacious D politely decline Sasquatch's invitation to become a power trio, however, accustomed as they are to being a duo on stage. Sad but understanding, Sasquatch bids his new buds goodbye and wishes them well as they return to their city world, now fully reenergized and ready to take on the rock world.

The duo knocks out a small club with their mesmerizing rendition of a heavy metal Bigfoot tune which clearly draws upon their personal feelings of allegiance to the big guy. Unbeknownst to JB and KG, Sasquatch has journeyed to the metropolis to catch their act on stage. The melancholic monster asks the club manager to remember him to Tenacious D and then departs, howling, as he races back into the deep woods.

KG (Kyle Gass) and JB (Jack Black) form the inseparable duo of wannabe metal musicians known collectively as *Tenacious D.*

* * * * *

There's something especially entrancing about the manner in which Jack Black and company treat the myth of Sasquatch in *Tenacious D.* They walk a delicate divide between outright mockery of Bigfoot and an obvious love of the Ciné du Sasquatch genre, stating as they do in their delightful Bigfoot song how *In Search of Bigfoot* with Leonard Nimoy "was a great show" which spread the fame of Sasquatch worldwide. It's very unusual to see such a postmodern approach work so consistently; the genre tends to pander to those who know the references over those who are left in the dark. This episode of *Tenacious D* does neither. Instead, it tells a mini-story of belief, self-defeat, and emergence from the ashes, phoenix-like, all set to some perversely funny lyrics by the real-life talents of Kyle Gass and Jack Black. Black's blistering performance of the vocals is like watching a male Bette Midler meets Meatloaf circa *The Rocky Horror Picture Show*, given his sheer, well, tenacity.

John C. Reilly as Sasquatch is unrecognizable beneath the makeup but nonetheless empathetic and hilarious in the role. Reilly's comic timing is superbly droll, and his physical ease in the suit is equally hilarious. Even granted that he's a large-framed actor, he still inhabits the baggy costume with such charm and comic agility it's easy to see why the character was brought back for the equally entertaining "acid flashback" Bigfoot dream sequence in the feature-length *Tenacious D in the Pick of Destiny* that followed this popular cable series. Jack

Black and Kyle Gass likewise bring their Mutt and Jeff duo to life with natural charisma (or, in Gass' case, anti-charisma). They're especially effective in the early scene when they are first told by Captain Ed that Bigfoot belief is equivalent to believing in the Easter Bunny or (far worse, they are told) the Rock and Roll ethos. Even more so than hearing that their beloved heavy metal music is nothing but a showman's con, the two stalwarts seemed devastated beyond reasoning when they are told Sasquatch is a legend and not a scientific reality, as they had presupposed. The look on Jack Black's face in particular epitomizes in one frozen expression the hurt of such "not *really* real" discoveries that begins with Santa and the Tooth Fairy, and cascades thereafter (depending upon one's point of view) to unquestioned belief in church, state, or the notion of lasting peace on Earth. It's a sad but bravura moment, and showcases why the actor went on to much bigger acclaim.

It's therefore a true pleasure when the boys encounter Sasquatch and realize everything the cynical Captain Ed ("that joint sucker!" Jack Black has earlier called him) was untrue. The life-liberating energy that suddenly fills Tenacious D as they race through the woods with their childhood hominid hero is both hilariously well-executed and quasi-poignant. It is nothing less than the rebirth of the lost innocence of youthful self-belief, and it is as thoroughly predictable as it is emotionally moving. The satirical lyrics ("Couldn't be a man in gorilla suit/No fuckn' way!/Now, you know he's REAL!"), however, reminds the viewer of the show's overall desired effect and target audience. Bumbling, inept, but stalwart true believers in themselves and Sasquatch, Tenacious D truly rock the Ciné du Sasquatch genre to new heights of hominid hilarity. The montage in which JB and KG try to convince the skeptical Captain Ed with a plaster cast and an audio tape of its growls while they sing on the soundtrack about how "scientists have proven Sasquatch is real!" is laugh-inducing, but it ironically encapsulates the divide between believers and skeptics as adroitly as any documentary (and in only 30 seconds). No self-respecting Ciné du Sasquatch follower would miss this parody tribute to the wonders of Bigfoot belief.

Tenacious D in the Pick of Destiny (2006) (Cameo)

Starring Jack Black, Kyle Gass, Dave Grohl, Amy Poehler, Tim Robbins, Ben Stiller, Meat Loaf and John C. Reilly. Produced by Jack Black, Cale Boyter, Richard Brener, Stuart Cornfeld, Elaine Dysinger, Toby Emmerich, Kyle Gass, Georgia Kacandes, Steve Moramarco and Ben Stiller. Written by Jack Black, Kyle Gass and Liam Lynch. Directed by Liam Lynch. USA. Color. Stereo. 93 Minutes.

Overview: When wannabe rock stars JB (Jack Black) and KG (Kyle Gass) meet in Venice, California, they decide to become the greatest rock 'n' rollers in musical history. Lacking much in the way of talent and connections, however, they realize just how difficult their task may be. So they take the easy way out — or so they believe — and instead embark upon a quest to secure the so-called Pick of Destiny. The Pick is a legendarily secret guitar pick made from the chipped tooth of Satan used by all the greatest musicians in order to play inhumanly well and launch their megastar careers. Currently housed in a rock n' roll museum, it sits waiting to be freed by anyone smart and daring enough to "liberate" it.

Alas, their journey proves to be anything but simple. Along the way, JB accidentally ingests LSD and takes a hallucinogenic trip with an imaginary Sasquatch. The two fly high above a fantasy land of psychedelic colors and sing a heavy metal duet in which Sasquatch and JB reveal they're blood relatives. JB's trip comes to an abrupt end, however, when he falls out of the branches of a tree and painfully

crashes to the ground. He and KG eventually obtain the fabled Pick of Destiny but wind up in a showdown with none other than Satan himself for the final disposition of the fallen angel's chipped tooth/Pick of Destiny.

* * * * *

Though Sasquatch only features in an extended cameo sequence in *Tenacious D in the Pick of Destiny*, the clear love of cryptid subject matter both Jack Black and Kyle Gass display makes it feel more akin to a short film that has been grafted onto the feature. In fact, the entire sequence plays like an homage to the Brothers Krofft and their equally lurid, super-saturated use of colors and obviously fake sets circa *H.R. Puf'n'Stuf* and *Lidsville* (as well as their hominid outing *Bigfoot and Wildboy*). As Sasquatch reveals in lyrical form to JB that the hairy hominid is JB's father, and the joyous JB bellows in response how passionately alive such a revelation makes him feel, one has the feeling there is more than mere parody underlying the sequence. In essence, it plays like a glorious recreation of "wasted" youth (pun appropriate, given that JB and KG spend as much time as possible stoned). Likewise, director Liam Lynch's postmodern approach to utilizing cheesy matte lines and undisguised low-budget video techniques to recreate the 1970s Saturday morning kiddy programming

Theatrical poster for *Tenacious D in the Pick of Destiny*.

era adds just the right amount of self-referential satire without tipping over into outright camp. In a movie with many hilarious episodes, the Sasquatch/LSD sequence ranks near the top for sheer "high" lights.

Academy Award–winning actor John C. Reilly portrays Sasquatch in an uncredited cameo, though he's all but unrecognizable beneath the make-up and suit. Still, the talented actor brings the cryptid to life with such a playful sense of harmless fun and youthful vitality one can easily see his performance as a recreation of Cookie Monster from *Sesame Street* as played as an 8-foot-tall monster hominid. Not only does Reilly momentarily steal the show from the charismatic Black, but he maintains the unique position in Ciné du Sasquatch of having been the only Oscar-winning actor to ever play Bigfoot. His Sasquatch remains one of the more enjoyable in the modern era, and as a continuation of the same character he played on the *Tenacious D* television series, a big "leap" forward in cinema cryptid characterization. After all, it's not every movie in the genre that has a singing Sasquatch who can fly and talk!

The Terrible Giant of the Snow (1962)

AKA: *El terrible gigante de las nieves.* Starring Joaquin Cordero, Ana Bertha Lepe, Jose Chavez, Elizabeth Dupeyron, David Hayat, Jose Eduardo Perez, Antonio Raxel, Andrés Soler and Amado Zumaya. Written by Federico Curiel and Alfredo Ruanova. Directed by Jaime Salvador. Mexico. Black & White. Mono. 72 Minutes.

Overview: Years after the terror-stricken villagers of the small Mexican town of Popocatépetl have finally settled back into the routines of life, the terrible Yeti seemingly strikes again from the nearby mountain top. The same wealthy ranching family plagued by the first nightmare Yeti attack is once again targeted by the new Yeti, who utilizes a form of long-distance thought projection from high atop his mountain cave to communicate with this psychically-linked human slaves in the valleys below. The family is besieged by the worried villagers (some of whom work in the family's various business ventures, such as mining and ranching), who want them to deal with the monster's latest appearance once and for all. The distraught family must also battle the fiendish demands of the hidden Yeti as well.

Eventually the family realizes the beast is not invulnerable. They trap it outside its mountainous lair, and a fierce battle between humans and cryptid ensues. Finally the beast is revealed to be a human imposter who has perpetrated the hoax in an effort to extort the family into paying for the Yeti problem to go away.

At the end of the violent struggle, the imposter hominid lies bleeding in his costume, shot to death. The family, twice-terrorized by a Yeti (one a legitimate monster and the other a cruel extortionist's trick), retreats from the murderous mountains of the Abominable Snowman, whose appearances have always been met with abominable fortune for the cursed family.

* * * * *

The first Mexican Yeti film, *The Monster of the Volcano*, was such a success that this sequel was hastily concocted and rushed into theaters the same year as the first hit film. Basically a loose remake of the earlier picture, this movie is a bit slower to start and definitely disappointing in the finale, with its "it was just a guy in a Yeti suit" ending. The costume itself is less convincing than in the former film; in *The Monster of the Volcano*, the wide girth of the creature was compensated for by its commanding sense of menace, whereas in this sequel the hominid is portrayed from the beginning as what it turns out to be — a hoaxer attempting to pass himself off as the Abominable Snowman. It makes the final confrontation between hominid and humans particularly lame, especially when the Mexican hero uses some then-novel kung fu moves against the barely moving Yeti.

It's hard to blame the filmmakers for wanting to cash in on the success of *The Monster of the Volcano*. In technical terms, the cinematography is even better in this effort than in the previous Yeti opus, with richer contrasts between dark pools and key lighting that achieves a look reminiscent of the old Universal horror pictures from the 1940s. Alas, the storyline is a basic rehash, and was told much more effectively in the first film (with the added satisfaction of the hominid being real). Genre movies in which their titular monsters are revealed to be only imaginary are apt to be roundly dismissed by critics and fans alike; there's no denying the cop-out feeling is difficult to avoid in such obvious endings.

Still, though *The Terrible Giant of the Snow* is less exciting than *The Monster of the Volcano* (mainly because the narrative is so similar in construction and execution in both films), the two movies together in one profitable year does beg the question: Where is the continuing legacy of Yeti movies in the Mexican cinema after these two signature Ciné du Sasquatch entries? Considering these films can't be blamed for much worse than being routinely dull between monster attack sequences, and that they were both commercially successful in their era, it makes one wonder if there is perhaps a Yeti film rebirth coming in Mexican cinema in the near future. Given the wide range of fantasy monsters imaginatively treated by the Mexican film industry throughout its long history of producing horror fare featuring vampires, werewolves, witches, zombies, and beyond, there does seem to be an inexplicable absence of good hominid films on the production slate.

Terror in the Midnight Sun (1959)

AKA: *Invasion of the Animal People; Horror in the Midnight Sun; Space Invasion of Lapland.* Starring Barbara Wilson, Sten Gester, Robert Burton, Bengt Blomgren, John Carradine, Åke Grönberg, Gösta Prüzelius and Lars Åhrén. Produced by Bertil Jernberg and Gustaf Unger. Written by Arthur C. Pierce and Robert M. Fresco. Directed by Virgil W. Vogel. Sweden/USA. Black & White. Mono. 73 Minutes.

Overview: A meteor-shaped spaceship crash lands in the Swedish Lappland mountains. Aliens conduct experiments from inside their ship on the local Saami native population by releasing their gigantic Yeti, who follows their orders and explores the snowbound countryside.

Alerted to the crash, Dr. Frederick Wilson, an American geologist, and Erik Engström, a Swedish researcher from the Royal Academy of Sciences, journey to the icy Arctic area in search of the meteorite. They are joined by the elderly geologist's attractive daughter, Diane Wilson. Because this is the dead of winter and no roads exist that far north, the trio must make their way by skiing the great distance between civilization and the area in which the alien object landed.

Along the way they discover many half-eaten reindeer, which the Saami tribesmen explain cannot be the result of polar bears because of the sheer amount of deer devoured. Stories abound of missing skiers who have vanished without a trace, as well. After an extended search, the scientists locate the meteor-shaped alien spaceship hidden in an ice cave. Diane is terrified by the aliens, who confront her, but is rescued by Engström. The aliens retreat into the ship and summon their Abominable Snowman to protect themselves.

Engström takes Diane to a remote research cabin to help her recover her senses. After she calms down, he leaves her temporarily in order to seek help. Before he can ski far, however, the Yeti attacks, destroying the cabin. Engström helps Diane escape, but the Yeti gives chase, never abandoning the pursuit. Eventually the Yeti destroys an entire Saami village until it locates Diane and retreats with her. The angry Saamis and the scientists follow. When the Yeti is cornered by a cliffside, Engström throws a torch onto it. Frightened, the Abominable Snowman releases Diane and, engulfed in flames, falls to its death. The aliens fly away as the wide-eyed scientists watch, still not believing what they've witnessed.

* * * * *

Terror in the Midnight Sun is actually two different movies — or, rather, can be seen in two different though very similar versions. The first, known as *Rymdinvasion i Lappland* (*The Invasion of Lappland*), was a Swedish-American co-production, which is why actress Barbara Wilson and character actor Robert Burton are headliners along with Swedish leading man Stan Gester. This first version was made in 1959 to take advantage of the fading but still profitable "alien invasion"' series of B-movies that flooded American and foreign theaters, such as *Invasion of the Saucer Men* and *It Came from Outer Space*. In fact, the alien spaceship in *Terror in the Midnight Sun* is eerily similar to the geodesic-shaped UFO from *It Came from Outer Space*, right down to the glowing windows geometrically aligned as if designed by Buckminster Fuller. American writer (and later director) Arthur C. Pierce crafted the story and script, with (uncredited) help from Robert Fresco. Pierce would later become a low-budget SF filmmaker (sub)par excellence, writing and/or directing *The Navy vs. the Night Monsters*, *Cyborg 2087* and *The Human Duplicators*, among others. And American studio editor turned director Virgil Vogel brought a technical proficiency to *Terror in the Midnight Sun* far in excess of its obviously challenged budget. Vogel, whose editing credits include *Touch of Evil* and *This Island Earth*, is perhaps best remembered by SF film fans as the director of the cult favorites *The Mole People* and *The Land Unknown*; however, in a long career that followed this film, he directed literally hundreds of television episodes for shows such as *Honey West*, *The Six Million Dollar Man*, *The Streets of San Francisco*, *Knight Rider* and *Miami Vice*.

Then, in 1962, American exploitation film "remaker" Jerry Warren (who had earlier directed *Man Beast*, also a Yeti film) purchased the rights to the film and re-edited it. He spent what appears (given the results) to be a long weekend shooting John Carradine on a small set (weakly resembling a laboratory) narrating the film's proceedings, as well as inserting additional footage of a women being interrogated by police officers after she claims to have been stalked by a Yeti. The new material was haphazardly patched into the now-butchered *Terror in the Midnight Sun* and released to an unsuspecting viewing public as *Invasion of the Animal People*. Actually, Warren was master of such cinematic sleight-of-hand (as in *very* sleight), as his later output of other re-edited fare from foreign lands, such as *Face of the Screaming Werewolf*, *She Was a Hippy Vampire*, *Attack of the Mayan Mummy* and *Curse of the Stone Hand*, demonstrates. Warren was a true Ed Wood–styled one-man cinematic wrecking ball, often shooting the new material, directing, writing, producing and even scoring it himself! The results, alas, all too often speak for themselves in terms of quality, although *Man Beast* and earlier films for which he didn't rely as heavily on stock footage are far more entertaining.

Terror in the Midnight Sun is actually quite watchable if one allows for the slow pace; *Invasion of the Animal People*, on the other hand, is best viewed only by those wishing to punish themselves for any imagined or real sins. *Terror in the Midnight Sun* follows the typical erstwhile "men of science meet the aliens" formula so prevalent in the 1950s SF genre; and while Pierce's screenplay prevents director Vogel from stamping any sense of urgency on the film, Vogel at least offers convincing location photography and a sincere approach to the material. But the John Carradine–hosted *Invasion of the Animal People* is an altogether different matter. Even the amiable Carradine later confessed he believed this effort was the worst he ever appeared in (and given his later credits, this is quite a statement). The problem Warren faced — how to turn the film into a more incident-laden and plot-driven version — is readily apparent; alas, his solutions border on the incomprehensible. One begins to long for the comforting te-

Erik Engstrom (Sten Gester) and Dr. Frederick Wilson (Robert Burton) marvel at otherworldly spacecraft in this lobby card from in *Terror in the Midnight Sun* (under its alternative moniker *Invasion of the Animal People*).

dium of *Terror in the Midnight Sun* by comparison, as at least the first version offers travelogue footage of a country rarely seen in cinema in general, let alone Ciné du Sasquatch.

Much has been made by Bigfoot film fans of the novel approach the filmmakers took in creating their cryptid. In fact, replace the dark fur with white, and the depicted Yeti would look somewhat like the Wampa that later makes a cameo on the ice planet of Hoth in *The Empire Strikes Back*. Both have strange walrus-like tusks that curve up and offer a slightly novel look to the usual simian hominid approach favored by a vast majority of Sasquatch filmmakers. While it does make the Yeti in *Terror in the Midnight Sun* decidedly goofy-looking, it also gives the cryptid a strangely endearing quality. At the very least, most who see it rarely forget it and often remark favorably (if amusedly) on its unusual appearance. Vogel goes to great lengths to convince the viewer of the Yeti's height by cleverly shooting it tow-

The alien-lead Yeti from *Terror in the Midnight Sun* (aka *Invasion of the Animal People*) wreaks havoc. These scenes play like an icebound restaging of *King Kong*'s Skull Island village destruction sequence.

ering over miniatures of the Saami teepee-like tents and the researchers' log cabin, as well as shooting from low angles with a wide angle lens so that the creature seems truly gigantic.

Of course, why the aliens feel the need to land, release the cryptid and then suddenly flee without explanation is, well, never even vaguely explained. Suffice it to say that the action occurs, the scientists comment upon how unusual the incident was, and the end credits roll. Admittedly, this leaves the audience as bewildered as the research team members—why an Abominable Snowman versus any other particular form of life? While space cryptids are not unusual in Ciné du Sasquatch (other notable entries include *Horror Express, The Six Million Dollar Man* and Chewbacca in the *Star Wars* films), it is an unusual choice given that the aliens themselves appear as the more typical bald-headed humanoids with telepathic abilities. In fact, the majority of the shots of the invaders are actually just the same shot from inside the spaceship, done over-the-shoulder style, of a lone alien endlessly twisting the dials of a television monitor which displays various scenes and characters in the film. This one image is utilized in almost every instance to signify the aliens themselves, and were it not for a sequence in which a number of aliens appear outside the craft to harass Diane Wilson, most viewers would rightfully assume there is but one humanoid alien and one cryptid hominid!

While it never explores any new Ciné du Sasquatch territory, *Terror in the Midnight Sun* does offer a fun if campy final 20 minutes, reserving most of its action for the finale. See this version if you have a choice between it and *Invasion of the Animal People*, as *Invasion of the Animal People* only subtracts from the original film's strengths and adds its own weaknesses.

Terror in the Swamp (1985)

AKA: *Nutriaman: The Copasaw Creature.* Starring Keith Barker, Chuck Bush, Gerald Daigal, Albert Dyket, Billy Holliday, Chuck Long, Mark Peterson, Ray Saadie, Michael Tedesco, Mike Thomas and Claudia Wood. Produced by Martin Folse. Written by Henry Brien, Martin Folse, Terry Hebb and Billy Holliday. Directed by Joe Catalanotto and Martin Folse. USA. Color. Mono. 87 Minutes.

Overview: Deep in the bayou backwaters, a small research company is experimenting with the super-enrichment of nutria, a cousin of the swamp rat, which is valued for its hide. Alas, the company loses funding and dumps the remains of its experimental chemicals into the swamp, which soon gives rise to the dreaded Nutriaman, a man-sized hominid cousin to the Skunk Ape.

The monster soon develops a taste for crusty backwoods types. When these pickings run slim, the creature begins attacking closer to population centers, which rouses the sleepy bayou hamlet into action. Realizing government help is useless because the State and Fed personnel don't know the backwaters the way their own kind do, the emboldened rednecks take to the swamps loaded with shotguns, rifles, and semi-automatics, prepared to slaughter anything that remotely resembles a Skunk Ape. Every rusty boat and leaky skiff within 50 miles is commandeered by the rural avengers in an effort to search each nook and cranny of the swamp's many inlets and coves.

The overwhelmed good ol' boy Sheriff attempts to bring some semblance of order to the posse, but the blood-simple crowd is in no mood to be corralled. With the waterways dangerously choked beyond navigation by bounty-seeking hunters tossing lit sticks of dynamite at anything that moves, the government steps up their effort to disperse the mob and intervene. But can they stop Nutriaman, too?

* * * * *

Although it technically defines its monster as a nutria mutation, *Terror in the Swamp* is a Bigfoot movie by any other name. While

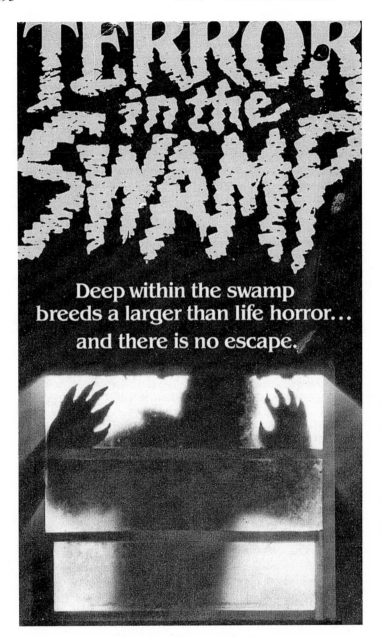

Cover art for the VHS release of *Terror in the Swamp.*

it's nowhere nearly as professionally accomplished as the previous decade's *The Creature from Black Lake, Terror in the Swamp* could easily play on a double bill with that earlier Skunk Ape horror feature without anyone noticing the latter film actually calls its cryptid something other than Bigfoot. This is because the formula presented by the filmmakers is so genre-tested that nothing new need be added. Indeed, the nutria aspect is forgotten by both audiences and creators of this film by its midway point, proving it a pointless distraction before the end credits roll.

Terror in the Swamp is often plodding in pacing but offers some plusses for less-discriminating viewers, such as the professional cinematography highlighting the shooting location's natural spookiness (the film was mostly shot in remote Houma, Louisiana). Alas, the screenplay is too meandering and slow-paced to generate much in the way of narrative tension between the occasional Nutriaman attack sequences. A local thespian by the name of Michael Tedesco plays a swampbilly to horrific perfection, right down to the overalls, Avery

Schreiber–styled frizzy hairdo, and ZZ Top droopy beard. Alas, the director must have sensed a good thing in front of the lens when he saw it and overuses Tedesco's modest charm as a would-be Skunk Ape poacher. But at least the authenticity of both accents and location photography work to *Terror in the Swamp*'s advantage, as not since Charles Pierce's landmark *The Legend of Boggy Creek* has a Ciné du Sasquatch feature so heavily relied on local non-professional actors and backwater locales.

None of these qualities really rescue *Terror in the Swamp* from being much more than what it obviously is: a typical 1980s direct-to-video B movie (with the usual good and bad in terms of production quality, writing, directing, and related departments). It lacks a central character strong enough to involve audience interest, and the cryptid creature lacks the empathy that Pierce's prototypical effort engendered as the last lonely one of its kind. The creature is portrayed as a Bigfoot monster with modest alterations to invoke the nutria influence (for example, the monster has nutria-like claws instead of the simian-styled or human hands typical of most hominids). Since the dark photography often causes the creature to disappear into the shadowy recesses of the swamp or become silhouetted behind screen doors, the nutria influence is negligible, as the creature photographs as simian in furry outline and its bipedal locomotion. There's nothing inherently special about *Terror in the Swamp* to distinguish it from lesser entries in Ciné du Sasquatch, but neither is it entirely so inept nor unwatchable that it rates as sub-par in the genre either. Like quicksand, it holds onto the viewer, slowly pulling him or her under, but it lacks much beyond a sense of inevitability.

There's Something Out There: A Bigfoot Encounter (2007) (TV) (Doc)

Featuring Darcy Fehr, Chris Charney, Cheryl Costen, Tracy McMahon, Kyle Sanderson, Kelly Wolfman and Leigh Enns. Produced by John Barnard, Kyle Bornais and Caelum Vatnsdal. Written by John Barnard and Caelum Vatnsdal. Directed by Caelum Vatnsdal. Canada. Color. Stereo. 60 Minutes.

Overview: Documentary filmmaker and Bigfoot fan Caelum Vatnsdal experiences a dream come true when he stumbles upon a story worthy of a deeper look—that of ferry boat operator Bobby Clarke. Clarke, a life-long resident of Manitoba, has experienced a life-changing Bigfoot encounter when he captures a 40-second video of a supposed bipedal cryptid. The rub is that the Canadian media machine that descends on the tiny town of Norway House, Manitoba, stirs up a lot of resentment and anger. Clarke soon learns that many in his community wish he'd kept his mouth shut about the supposed Sasquatch footage. They are embarrassed and humiliated to be associated with anything Bigfoot related, especially as the media predictably exploits the topic for ratings. An interesting tale of tabloid sensationalism fueling small-town resentments and igniting a firestorm that has nothing to do with less than a minute's worth of blurry Bigfoot video footage ensues in this quirky, off-beat look at how real-world Sasquatch sightings have unforeseen ramifications.

They Call Him Sasquatch (2003)

Starring Neal McDonough, Tom Bresnahan, Warren Berlinger, Garry Marshall, Vene L. Arcoraci, Chuck McCann, Jeffrey Phelps, E. Sean Griffin, Jordan Black, Peter Fluet, Randy McPherson, Rebecca Brand, Trever O'Brien and Meghan Pool. Produced by Tom Bresnahan, Michael Dieveney, Mike Dieveney, Edward Hunt and David H. Venghaus Jr. Written by Juan Ros and David H. Venghaus Jr. Directed by David H. Venghaus Jr. USA. Color. Stereo. 100 Minutes.

Overview: When Stu, an Emmy-winning television producer, sends his young newshound Ned Dwyer, a metrosexual narcissist, into the wilds to follow a group of diverse Bigfoot hunters, all hell breaks loose in the woods. Ned hates the assignment at first, thinking it nothing more than pointless fodder. But Stu insists it could be Emmy material (mainly to get the rambling Dwyer off his telephone), which convinces the vain Ned Dwyer the story indeed deserves his grandiose attention.

Throughout his reporting, Ned documents a wide variety of amateur and professional cryptozoologists and cryptid hunters. The motives and personalities of these individuals are wildly divergent. Two hunters merely aim to be the first to bag a Bigfoot, regardless of any moral concerns, intent on the riches such a specimen would produce for them. Two senior cryptozoologists are self-styled experts who spend more time bickering between themselves than contributing much in the way of valuable expertise. The suburban Stuckling

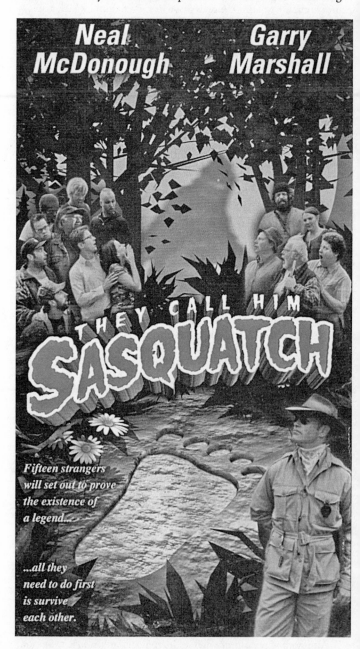

Cover art for the VHS release of *They Call Him Sasquatch*.

Family claims the mother has a psychic connection to Sasquatch, which she unexpectedly channels without warning. Professor Neil Ingraham, a respected zoologist, aims to find conclusive proof of the cryptid's existence, even while his nymphomaniac wife Bella would rather divert his attention to more pleasurable (for her) activities. By the time the group encounters Sasquatch in the concluding scenes, Ned Dwyer is convinced of one salient fact: No matter how strange Bigfoot may turn out to be, the creature cannot exceed the bizarre depth of variance among humanity.

* * * * *

Playing almost like a low-budget riff on *It's a Mad Mad Mad Mad World*, but with Bigfoot as the ultimate prize instead of stolen money, *They Call Him Sasquatch* is a well-intended, generally inoffensive comic parody that's easy to watch but not inventive in terms of the genre itself (even though entirely self-aware in this regard, set as it is in a milieu that all but accepts Sasquatch as a barely-hidden "sure fire" discovery for some lucky explorer). Though it meanders and feels very much like an improvisational comedy sketch that was video-taped on location, *They Call Him Sasquatch* at least remains true to its generally lighthearted nature, never really "playing blue" for obvious R-rated raunchy humor nor taking the ridiculousness on display too seriously. Both are wise directorial decisions, given how difficult such affairs as *They Call Him Sasquatch* are to successfully produce on barely adequate funding. Though it is technically a bit dodgy at times, the overall level of achievement is still professional in quality, especially when the production relocates to the sunny woods.

Helping matters along is the wide variety of characters and sub-plots that complicate things throughout the movie's length. This comedic tapestry is skillfully interwoven at a relaxed pace, so *They Call Him Sasquatch* favors viewers who are willing to forgo immediate payoffs. Chuck McCann (fondly remembered for his thankless Alan Hale, Jr., homage in the kiddy cult favorite Saturday morning TV series *Far Out Space Nuts*) plays Bob Mabely, an octogenarian cryptid tracker who is feeling the pressure to see his life's work amount to more than just speculation. Real-life producer Gary Marshall has a brief cameo as Stu, the Emmy-obsessed TV producer who is so insecure he leaves all of his vast collection of statuettes forever on display as expensive paper weights atop his modest work desk. Neal McDonough plays Ned Dwyer, a modern reincarnation of *The Mary Tyler Moore Show*'s Ted Knight meets Fox Network's news commentator Shepard Smith, with an eye on getting one of the desk weights securing Stu's important printed paperwork for himself. These veteran actors, as well as the lesser known cast members add immeasurably to the production's modest charms. The amusing cameos and seasoned acting vets give *They Call Him Sasquatch* a much-needed jolt when it occasionally strays narratively; it is disjointed by design, even if it follows the conventional Ciné du Sasquatch arc of having the protagonists stumble into the hidden horrors willingly and then flee for their lives after realizing the foolish error of their ways.

Like many other Bigfoot comedies (a legitimate branch of Ciné du Sasquatch, as the popularity of the *Messin' with Sasquatch* TV commercials proves), *They Call Him Sasquatch* is more focused on producing laughs than expanding the genre's boundaries. In this regard it amply fulfills all of the Bigfoot film genre conventions (and is particularly rich in well-cast minor characters, each of whom is fleshed out far beyond the norms of the *oeuvre*) while remaining safely ensconced within them. As a kind of *Airplane*-styled satire on the entire Ciné du Sasquatch genre, *They Call Him Sasquatch* accurately if gently skewers the often seemingly contradictory, self-serious personalities on display in the crypto communities around the world. Fans of both fictional and documentary Bigfoot movies and TV specials will find the humor more compelling than non-cryptid believers

or the merely disinterested; still, those willing to allow the cast's genuine commitment to the material to wash over them will find much to smile about while watching the mildly subversive *They Call Him Sasquatch*.

To Catch a Yeti (1995) (TV)

Starring Meat Loaf, Chantellese Kent, Richard Howland, Jim Gordon, Leigh Lewis, Jeff Moser, Michael Panton, Mona Matteo, Ria Franchuk, Reginald Doresa, Andreas M. Haralampides, David Walberg, Rob Rutter, Audrey Barraclouth, Neil Verburg, Stacey Simon, Dave Goguen, Carolyn Tweedle, Ron Donovan, Terry Logan, Jayme Hutchinson, Sam Stragies, Zebulon Reid, Benjamin Cooch, Erinn Thompson, Alexis Aitken and Kevin Robbin. Produced by Noel Cronin, Peter Reid, Beverley Shenken and Lionel Shenken. Written by Paul Adam and Lionel Shenken. Directed by Bob Keen. Canada. Color. Stereo. 95 Minutes.

Overview: Big Jake Grizzly and his partner are professional game hunters. Their latest paying gig: capture a Yeti. The client: a wealthy man who will spare no expense to purchase for his spoiled brat of a son anything and everything the boy desires, including a hominid for a pet! But the trip to the Himalayas to abduct a Yeti goes awry, with the tiny creature escaping the clutches of the bumbling hunters and instead boarding a plane to New York City undetected as a stowaway in an unsuspecting passenger's backpack.

The passenger's daughter discovers the backpack's contents when her father returns. She quickly names the cute cryptid Hank. They bond as she serves the hungry hominid Oreo cookies and hot dogs. Meanwhile, Big Jake Grizzly and his sidekick deduce the creature is living with the daughter and father in their apartment. They attempt to steal the tiny Hank, but the daughter saves the day. Eventually she flies the Yeti back to Tibet and allows him to return to the wild.

* * * * *

As far as insipid Benign Bigfoot films go, *To Catch a Yeti* is just as unwatchable as most examples of harmless hominid films in the Ciné du Sasquatch genre. It has all the faults inherent in, say, *Return to Boggy Creek* (the "friend" versus "fiend" portrayal of Bigfoot) but taken to excessive extremes. Whereas *Return to Boggy Creek* has among its modest merits a sense of authenticity due to the rugged location photography and an earnest approach, *To Catch a Yeti* abandons all pretense as to being anything other than an amalgamated by-product of the postmodern mentality which spawned it. The starring animatronic Yeti puppet is clearly based on the titular creatures from *Gremlins*. With mews and coos, the emphasis on "cute" in Benign Bigfoot films reaches its nadir here, reducing the already half-sized threat level of the *Little Bigfoot* movies to less than a foot tall (as embodied by Hank the Abominable Snowman). It is difficult to overemphasize the inanity of having a hominid so small as to be backpack-friendly. It begs the question of whether the creature isn't actually some new type of cryptid along the lines of a pygmy hominid.

From its endless riffs on such Hollywood kid films as *E.T.*, *Home Alone*, and *Harry and the Hendersons*, *To Catch a Yeti* suffers from a poor script and clinically detached direction. Special effects artist turned one-time director (for this effort only) Bob Keen has credits in makeup effects that stretch from the *Hellraiser* series to the much-admired *Hardware*, but he cannot wear the additional hat without apparently sacrificing both quality of direction and the puppetry on display, which is so bad it becomes annoying.

Meat Loaf is wildly unpredictable and equally incomprehensible in his role as Big Jake Grizzly (surely taken as a character name from an existing adult film star's non de plume?). Sadly, the vital rock and roll star of *The Rocky Horror Picture Show* is reduced to near Alan Hale Jr.–styled antics in *To Catch a Yeti*. He goes over-the-top from frame one but still only manages to top the hammy Yeti puppet Hank by the merest of inches.

As bad as the proceedings are in *To Catch a Yeti*, it should be remembered it was a modest effort made primarily as kiddy fodder by the Canadian television system. Far worse is watched with avid interest by children and 'tweens every day in the cable universe. But lacking any insight into Ciné du Sasquatch, and unaware of its own profoundly sappy tone, *To Catch a Yeti* is not worth the effort unless you're a true die-hard fan of the genre.

To the Ends of the Earth: Bigfoot Monster Mystery (1997) (TV) (Doc)

Featuring Henry Franzoni, John Waters, Larry Lund, Dr. Henner Fahrenbach, Ron Morehead and Todd Neiss. Produced by Marcus Sulley. Directed by Norman Hull. UK. Color. Stereo. 60 Minutes.

Overview: This Channel Four–produced documentary series attempts to examine the Bigfoot case from a more critical but objective viewpoint, with British nature photographer John Waters hosting and narrating. Several eyewitnesses are interviewed, including Ron Morehead, who plays audio recordings he and fellow camper Alan Berry made of a reported Sasquatch vocalizing in the woods. Henry Franzoni plays bongos in the woods in an attempt to draw the curious if shy creatures into his realm, believing that humans never encounter Bigfoot unless the creature wills it. Dr. Henner Fahrenbach discusses genetic evidence in regards to Sasquatch hair samples and his opinion as to the hominid's existence. Hoaxes are given considerable coverage with Larry Lund comparing various faked videos made in the days since the Patterson-Gimlin footage set the gold standard for cryptozoology moviemaking. The most entertaining sequence is dedicated to the crew hiring a professional special effects team to design and inhabit a Bigfoot costume, with the idea of recreating the Patterson-Gimlin film. Even though they are handsomely-paid professionals given time to plan and execute their costume, their design is amateurish compared to the infamous 1967 effort in terms of believability; they nearly trip every time they attempt to replicate the unusual gait of Roger Patterson's photographed hominid in the inhospitable undergrowth of the Bluff Creek location in Northern California.

Tom and Jerry Tales ("Sasquashed") (2009) (TV)

Featuring the voices of Don Brown, Sam Vincent, Nicole Oliver, Michael Donovan, Chantal Strand, Richard Cox, Gary Chalk, Kelly Sheridan, Brian Drummond and Trevor Devall. Produced by Bobbie Page. Written and Directed by Spike Brandt and Tony Cervone. USA. Color. Stereo. 7 Minutes.

Overview: While on a camping trip, Tom and Jerry are startled to hear a local radio station announce that Bigfoot has been sighted. Worse still, the hominid was seen in the very campgrounds they're set to sleep in. That night Tom pulls a prank on Jerry and convinces the frightened mouse that Bigfoot is on the prowl. Jerry races out of his tent, terrified, only to come face-to-face with Sasquatch. The Bigfoot turns out to be as advertised in terms of feet size but only stands as tall as Tom the cat. He is also a vegan, as he tells a stunned Jerry, and basically doesn't want any attention for fear of being exploited by the media.

At this point Tom arrives, video camera in paws, determined to capture the best footage of Bigfoot ever recorded. Jerry helps the scared Sasquatch elude Tom's determined paparazzi tactics until Tom falls prey to a tar trap set by Jerry that leaves Tom coated and looking like a monster himself. Upon his humiliated return to camp, Tom is mistaken for a monster by his owner and beaten as she screams, "Bigfoot!" Jerry and Bigfoot, hiding nearby, enjoy a private laugh.

* * * * *

The mighty Hanna/Barbera's historic animation dominance in Ciné du Sasquatch (for both volume and the influential nature of many of the episodes themselves) continues unabated for four decades and counting with this playful entry. While it doesn't rival the Chuck Jones appearances of Hugo the Abominable Snowman for sheer laugh-getting buffoonery, "Sasquashed" has a few moments of mirth to make it recommendable to fans of the Benign Bigfoot camp. From the nasally, Paul Lynde–ish voice of the Bigfoot, the creature's shortened height, his orange pompadour (piled high and designed to make him seem taller), and his stated preference to live as a vegan, this is one hominid that will never inspire terror in any eyewitnesses who happen upon it.

It's amazing to see that the post–Hanna/Barbera creative teams who handle the original artists' creations still include a Sasquatch appearance as part of the studio's ongoing legacy. Clearly the impact of Bigfoot as a popular figure of the imagination has not been lost on the company.

The Tonight Show with Jay Leno ("Anna Marie Goddard") (TV)

Featuring Jay Leno and Anna Marie Goddard. Directed by Ellen Brown. USA. Color. Stereo. 10 Minutes.

Overview: While appearing on *The Tonight Show*, *Playboy* Playmate Anna Marie Goddard (whose biggest claim to fame besides dozens of adult titles for *Playboy* is listed on her résumé as "Henchwoman" in *Austin Powers: Goldmember*) was asked about the infamous "Redwoods Video" in which she and a small traveling video crew saw and videotaped Bigfoot outside a production RV's window while shooting on location in the Northern California redwoods. Goddard never appears on the videotape with the cryptid, but is among those who are stunned to see the creature and whose reactions are captured on the tape after the sighting, which shows the shaken cast and crew trying to regain their wits.

Perhaps not unexpectedly, given her credentials, the "Redwoods Video" has been derisively called the "Playmate Bigfoot Video" by some who wish to build the connection between beauty and the beast that really only exists tangentially to the actual encounter (which was witnessed by others, not just Goddard herself), and by others who wished to exploit the subject matter in the media. As a probable result of the salacious nature of the Playmate and Bigfoot juxtaposition, speculation arose that the video analysis reveals, among other dubious suppositions, the depicted cryptid's penis length. To her credit, Goddard maintained to Leno that what she saw that night was real as far as she was concerned, and that the possibility it had been a hoax was very remote given that no one else was in the deep woods proximity (as far as she knew) before, during, or after the incident.

Trailer Park Geocachers Meet Bigfoot (2005)

Starring Zartimus, Tripper and Grizzly G. Produced, Written and Directed by David Carriere. USA. Color. Stereo. 29 Minutes.

Overview: Three buddies go geocaching for fun in the deep wilderness. To their surprise, a carnivorous Sasquatch is lurking in the very woods they use for recreation. The trio make a casting of a

Bigfoot print with Rice Krispies cereal they have on hand and collect a specimen of Sasquatch scat (one on the bottom of his hiking shoes). They set a trap for the creature but it backfires, leaving one of the geocachers swinging from a tree.

Eventually the geocachers bullwhip the Sasquatch, and one of the humans takes a ride, dragged along by the fleeing hominid. The beast's arm is pulled free by the ordeal, revealing Bigfoot to actually be a robot. The resourceful geocachers rig a radio-controlled toy truck with a video camera and send it after Bigfoot, startling the cryptid into fleeing for its life. Eventually Bigfoot realizes the pursuing toy cannot harm him and tries to stomp it to pieces with its large feet. The truck hits a log and flies into the monster's derrière, stunning it. The geocachers decide they'll rope the carcass to their truck and return to the city, prepared to sell the remains for big-time money.

Alas, the same UFO that dropped off the cybernetic Sasquatch returns, zapping the trio of geocachers with a ray gun and beaming up the bionic Bigfoot in the process. Only one geocacher, who was smart enough to prepare for the eventuality of an alien assault by wisely wearing an aluminum foil cap to deflect the invaders' thought rays, remembers the ordeal afterwards. His two geocaching friends laugh him off, convinced he's a nutcase for believing they've encountered Sasquatch, let alone that they've been mind-assaulted by an alien spacecraft.

Behind the scenes on the soon-to-be-released follow-up *Trailer Park Geocachers Meet Bigfoot 2*. A third installment has also been announced in the series.

* * * * *

This funny home-brewed short video found exposure via Internet distribution and quickly gained a small but fierce following of like-minded Bigfoot fans, geocache geeks, and related techno nerds who appreciated the goofball sense of possibility and Three Stooges style of physical humor. While it is very crudely produced, using only the most basic of PC video gear, *Trailer Park Geocachers Meet Bigfoot* (what a great title!) still manages to pack in more laughs in its brief half-hour running time than many recent Hollywood attempts to tell the same story (more or less) on multi-million-dollar budgets. Flaws and all, *Trailer Park Geocachers Meet Bigfoot* is the modern day equivalent of Ray Dennis Steckler's *Lemon Grove Kids Meet the Monsters*—that is, an amateur effort that transcends its limitations to offer genuine entertainment value.

Nothing is taken seriously, least of all the sport of geocaching. Geocachers use the global positioning hardware readily available to pinpoint hidden caches in wilderness (and even urban) areas. They hide the loot, tag the coordinates, and then upload them onto an Internet website where others can download the coordinates and then track down the caches for themselves. In no uncertain terms, the irony of *Trailer Park Geocachers Meet Bigfoot* is that it was "discovered" by the talented filmmakers using geocache-friendly techniques — the completed movie was uploaded onto a web server, and the coordinates to the file were downloaded by a growing number of the curious, drawn by word-of-mouth/link/email. So successful has the response been that the filmmakers are working on not one but two feature-length follow-ups, in which the geocachers return to the forest with no less than bazookas, assault weapons, and even a Sherman tank, intent on taking down the bionic Bigfoot once and for all.

Production values are low but inventive, given the non-professional status of the video. The filmmakers never err on the side of pretentiousness, instead opting to parody the idiotic nature of their own inane effort even as it unfolds. It's a winning strategy that helps paper over the slow spots when the editing is a bit off or the acting

This promotional still from *Trailer Park Geocachers Meet Bigfoot* captures the often satirical nature of the Internet-launched cult favorite.

breaks down; these moments are thankfully brief, and the video's charm overcomes most of these dead zones. The Bigfoot costume is ridiculous, but again, the filmmakers play this up rather than down. The quota of fart and poop jokes is about on par for a similar-toned gross-out comedy, but thankfully the typical mean-spirited quality that goes along with such juvenile humor is absent from *Trailer Park Geocachers Meet Bigfoot*. In its place is a clearly loving sense of "retro-stalgia" on the part of the director, dedicated to a time when the very idea of a bionic Bigfoot was so cool that no one cared if the actual execution of the premise was on par with an average Charles Gemora gorilla suit flick from the 1940s. Cheesy, but deliberately so, *Trailer Park Geocachers Meet Bigfoot* is a half-hour of easy laughs, as painless as it is pointless.

Trog (1970)

Starring Joan Crawford, Michael Gough, Bernard Kay, Kim Braden, David Griffin, John Hamill, Thorley Walters, Jack May, Geoffrey Case, Robert Hutton, Simon Lack, David Warbeck, Chloe Franks, Maurice Good and Joe Cornelius. Produced by Herman Cohen and Harry Woolveridge. Written by Peter Bryan, John Gilling and Aben Kandel. Directed by Freddie Francis. USA. Color. Mono. 93 Minutes.

Overview: When a prehistoric hominid is discovered by spelunkers in the English countryside, female anthropologist Dr. Brockton mounts a trip to tranquilize the "missing link" and return it to her research facility in the English countryside for scientific study. This despite the fact that the creature killed one of the cavers when it was discovered by them. Unafraid, Dr. Brockton manages to tranquilize the creature deep in the recesses of its cavernous home. She names it Trog (short for Troglodyte).

Alas, the locals do not cotton to the idea of having a murdering hominid in their midst. They are egged on in their protestations by a greedy realtor who senses an opportunity to snap up Dr. Brockton's desirable property on the cheap should anything go wrong with her harboring of Trog. To this end the greedy developer deliberately frees Trog from confinement to wreak havoc in the village. After doing just that, Trog abducts a school girl and retreats to a nearby cave for shelter. Dr. Brockton arrives and attempts to intervene. But only the girl is saved, as Trog pays the ultimate price for his rampage.

* * * * *

So much camp journalism enthusiastically extolling the wondrously "so-bad-it's-good" quality present throughout *Trog* crowds the field that it is often overlooked as a minor "foot"-note in the Bigfoot film pantheon. And indeed, in sheerest technical terms it is not a full entry in Ciné du Sasquatch, since the species at hand is named *Homo troglodytes* by Dr. Brockton and therefore excluded from being a bipedal cryptid hominid. Or, rather, *not*. Just as most traditional Caveman films depict pre-humans as looking like *Homo sapiens* in their physical features (a far-fetched concept at best, given the extreme anatomical changes between modern humans and our prehistoric predecessors), *Trog* insists on blurring the lines between scientific realities and filmic rubbish will alarming alacrity. This applies to its insistence on portraying Trog as a hominid on the one hand and a "caveman," with the emphasis on its human aspects, on the other. Like other entries such as *Missing Link*, *Altered States*, and *Skullduggery*, *Trog*

begs for genre exclusion because it deals with a "labeled" species rather than unknown one, or one in which the hominid is called "Bigfoot" or "Yeti" by name by the film's title or characters.

This is especially true when dealing with mature hominids that are depicted as smaller than human in stature. Even though actual sightings document encounters between humans eyewitnesses and smaller-sized hominids (see Orang Pendek), one is tempted to exclude the fictitious small-sized cryptids from being listed under the Ciné du Sasquatch genre moniker. This is both understandable and somewhat accurate for these films as they relate to the genre. Like *King Kong* has an undeniable influence upon the Bigfoot genre and yet, ironically, stands apart from it by definition, so, too, do most "small hominid" movies serve as partial, incomplete examples inhabiting the Bigfoot film realm, thus making them fascinating "almost" entries that run parallel to Ciné du Sasquatch. At the same time, they curiously do not influence the Bigfoot film genre nor negate its growth, even as they share many of the same themes, plot dynamics, etc.

In truth, when the first movie Yeti appeared — in *The Conquest of the Pole* back in 1912 — the audience thereafter seemed to prefer giant-sized hominids over everyday-sized ones. Perhaps the psychological "threat level" is raised by simply increasing the monster's size; there's no denying that gigantism connotes menace in most fairy tales, heroic myths, and campfire stories. But just as Willis O'Brien's genre-defining work *The Dinosaur and the Missing Link: A Prehistoric Tragedy* from 1916 demonstrates with its depiction of a hominid barely as tall as the *Homo sapiens*, the Bigfoot genre by definition allows for a wildly varying physical "look" or "size" for the depicted cryptid. Granted, most tend towards the modified gorilla style; but there are huge variants, such as the portly Yeti in the *Dr. Who* series, which easily fit inside the Ciné du Sasquatch parameters. The key aspects tend to be how the plot is constructed around the encounter with the creature by the human protagonists, and the resulting aftermath of any sudden but prolonged human and hominid cohabitation. In most entries the humans stumble into a territorial dispute with a cryptid(s) at some point, resulting in a battle for survival. In

The captive *Trog* (Joe Cornelius) snarls at his human gawkers. Whenever a hominid is caged, rampant *Homo sapiens* slaughter soon follows.

variations, humans encounter Bigfoot and learn he is a misunderstood Noble Savage and that we, as humans, have much to learn from the green-loving Sasquatch. In the latter mutations of the myth, Sasquatch is to be protected, most often from a human in the form of a hunter or obsessed expert who wishes to exploit the cryptid for profit.

And then, in variations that go one step beyond, there are the films like *Trog*, which sit uncomfortably between genres. Earlier in the picture, *Trog* plays as a suspense film. Later it plays as a laughable remake of the first version of *My Friend Flicka*, with a troglodyte substituting for the mustang, and an aged Joan Crawford for the youthful Roddy McDowell. This is especially true during their endless bonding scenes wherein Crawford teaches her pet hominid to fetch a ball, wind up dolls, etc. And in its concluding third, *Trog* becomes a more conventional, gore-spiked horror film, complete with a butcher being impaled on his own meat hook by the angry Trog in a bit of over-the-top violence that belies the movie's more innocuous stature as a child-friendly film.

Crawford's portrayal draws both ire and admiration. It's perhaps the softest of her later appearances, most of which tended to be overly arch even by Joan Crawford's wide-ranging standards. Still, whether one admires Crawford's turn or not, it is without a doubt the kind of otherworldly acting most resembling the style embodied by Faye Dunaway in the equally campy *Mommie Dearest* via her manic-tinged performance as Crawford. For example, there is the unforgettable moment wherein Dr. Brockton confronts the errant hominid, who has just snatched a school girl for unexplained reasons and holed up with her in a cave. "Put the child *down*, Trog!" Crawford intones in a combination of earnest begging and fatalistic despair that is every bit the "No wire hangers, Christina!" mantra of *Mommie Dearest*. In such fleeting moments of campiness, *Trog* is worthy of John Waters' admiration.

Supposedly the costume was a leftover from the Stanley Kubrick production of *2001* and was recycled for use as the star cryptid. It is easy to see this in the facial structure and primitive animatronics on display. Likewise, the way in which Trog's fur appears like a mane on his head and shoulders is also reminiscent of the Kubrick hominids at the beginning of his space epic. But the manner in which the costume suddenly ends at the actor's chest feels cheap and ill-advised. It renders the effect darkly comic, as Trog is clearly 100 percent human beneath those areas of his upper body concealed by a pretty obvious latex mask and fur shawl. Casting Paul Cornelius and showing his smaller physique in order to make Trog seem more childlike until the monster goes berserk both lessens the threat of Trog as monster and simultaneously adds a level of maudlin pathos, which is where the film works best. With Crawford on hand to evoke the great heyday of melodrama itself, the inevitable violent ending for the beast, and the kidnapping of the girl and retreat to his lair (so deliberately reminiscent of *King Kong*), *Trog* is a misfire as a horror or science fiction movie, but completely serviceable as campy melodrama of the type Douglas Sirk would have appreciated in his more tolerant moods. It is corny and slow-paced, filled with unexpected moments of high humor and, above all, "properly distanciated" (sic), as Douglas Sirk himself used to call the perfect summation of triangulation between audience, actor, and the heightened sense of melodrama created when the director manipulates this space and time in filmic terms. *Trog* is distanciated all right — almost all the way out of Ciné du Sasquatch and into a genre all its own.

2 Shocking 4 TV (2003) (Doc) (TV)

Starring Tori A. Artz, Clay Chappell, Curtis Cowart, Mark DiCarlo, Don Dowes, Paul Kimmel, Jesse Flanagan, and James Ford. Produced by Gary Auerbach, Rick Austin, Paul Harrison, Chad Horning, Audrey Morrissey and Monica Stock. Written by Paul Harrison and Dave Polsky. Directed by Paul Harrison. USA. Color. Stereo. 30 Minutes.

Overview: Reality television (two concepts that generally do not appear consecutively together in the English language) featuring supposedly real video footage taken by various amateurs and then commented upon by host John O'Hurley. A majority of the segments are oriented towards a *Weekly World News* mentality. Bigfoot is highlighted in one segment. From the producer of such other mentally-challenging (or is that simply challenged?) reality television series as *Paranormal State*, *Ghost Lab*, and *Karaoke Superstars*.

2001: A Space Odyssey ("The Dawn of Man") (1968) (Influence)

Starring Keir Dullea, Gary Lockwood, William Sylvester, Daniel Richter, Leonard Rossiter and Douglas Rain. Written by Arthur C. Clarke and Stanley Kubrick. Produced and Directed by Stanley Kubrick. USA. Color. Stereo. 141 Minutes.

Overview: Moon Watcher, the leader of a tribe of starving pre-human hominids, is enlightened to the possibilities of technology when an alien intelligence visits the Earth and implants psychic visions into Moon Watcher via an enigmatic black monolith. The next day at the watering hole Moon Watcher and his tribe shares with a competing hominid group, Moon Watcher uses his newfound technological know-how to create a weapon from a bone and kill the rival group's leader. Asserting territorial dominance over the bleak dawn of man landscape and a pathetically small source of water, Moon Watcher triumphantly throws his bone weapon skyward, whereupon it is seamlessly intercut with a shot of a nuclear payload satellite orbiting the Earth hundreds of thousands of years in the future.

* * * * *

Though many would rightly reject classing the extended "The Dawn of Man" sequence as an example of Ciné du Sasquatch, *2001: A Space Odyssey*'s famous simian opening scenes remain a formidable distillation of the evolutionary arc of our species by depicting a hominid predecessor to our own DNA which is much like us prior to our human obsession with manufacturing technology, even technology which in retrospect threatens our ever-tenuous existence because of environmental degradation and climate change created in large part by old technology run amok. The vicious circle poised on the moral question of justifiability in hindsight is perfectly illustrated by "The Dawn of Man" with Moon Watcher's slaying of his nemesis in a competing tribe. Rather than use his new power to try to unite the tribes and forge alliances among his own kind, the primitive man is shown to prefer the shortcut provided by the treacherous use of technology instead. Ironically, it is only because Moon Watcher employs technology and the convenience (if moral ambiguity) of murder as a means to an end that his tribe survives and thrives over the weaker-minded, weaker-willed tribe whose leader is slain. The Darwinian logic is thus visually expressed in brutal but naturally efficient images of great imagination: Moon Watcher and his band who are willing to slay their own kind for advantage will pass along their dominant genes, whereas the lesser tribes will perish in the eons of evolutionary time because they were unwilling to assert themselves and triumph by natural selection.

There has never been a more succinct distillation of anthropological and zoological theory crystallized into better cinematic clarity. Even more impressive is that Kubrick's opening is wordless, as the depicted hominid tribe does not use a spoken language. So strong is *2001*'s opening that "The Dawn of Man" sequence alone survives even to this day as one of the great film achievements in narrative Hollywood cinema. The final use of the murdering bone weapon created by Moon Watcher intercut back and forth momentarily with the orbiting nuclear payload ready to destroy entire nations back on Earth is a coda of devastatingly accurate insight, and a moment rarely matched in all of cinema history for sheer bravado.

2001: A Space Odyssey's influence on Ciné du Sasquatch derives from "The Dawn of Man" and its symbolic echoing of what are also themes heavily present in Bigfoot cinema: survival, competition among similar species, and the bitterly-won cultural transcendence that often occurs when two such groups meet in conflict, and one or the other lives long enough to see the typically bloody conclusion. These are the basic tenets of Ciné du Sasquatch transplanted back in time to a setting wherein modern mankind cannot be the culprit, but the hominids themselves are to "blame" for their actions and re-actions to their environment. Instead of humans transgressing upon the terrain of a hominid, however, the field is leveled to pit hominid against like-minded hominid. Otherwise, much of the tone and mood of "The Dawn of Man" plays like a Bigfoot movie, but with diminutive hominids instead of the usual 7-foot-tall variety. In essence, one tribe of hominids invades another's sense of territory, and violence ensues when the threatened clan unleashes holy hell upon the intruders. The intruders are forced to flee under the assault of the superior hominid tribe, thus re-establishing the natural order that existed prior to the movie's beginning, wherein Sasquatch is dominant in his prescribed zone.

There is a more mundane but no less profound influence here upon the genre, as well. The intense Kubrick's endless experimentation with the hominid make-up resulted in bold steps forward in the design and mechanics of existing effects technology. One big winner from the technical achievements in this regard was the use of early animatronic cables embedded in latex make-up masks that would enable invisible wire manipulation of various, smaller portions of a mask's pliable features (i.e., lowering the eyebrows, opening the mouth, flaring the nostrils, etc.).

As successful in their era as these seamless advances were, it is surprising that *2001* did not receive a special award for make-up effects. But as Arthur C. Clarke speculated numerous times in the years afterward, it was entirely possible the Academy voting members did not understand that they were watching actors and not trained simians in the lead roles of Moon Watcher and his tribe. While this seems preposterous in today's photo-real world of filmmaking, it shows how the technical bar was raised by *2001*'s release, and how it affected subsequent Bigfoot movies.

Increasingly because of the commercial success of pictures like *2001* and *Planet of the Apes*, filmmakers were finding it untenable to simply rent a bargain basement gorilla costume for their newest Sasquatch exploitation film. Instead, there would be an overall rising of technical standards for the pictures in subsequent Ciné du Sasquatch efforts as a result of *2001*'s profound if indirect influences on hominid costume design and portrayal.

2002 Texas Bigfoot Conference (2002) (Doc)

Featuring Robert W. Morgan, D.L. Tanner, William Dranginis, Chester Moore, M.K. Davis and Dr. John Bindernagel. USA. Color. Video. Stereo. 2-Disc DVD Set.

Overview: Coverage of the annual Texas Bigfoot Conference, which is an ongoing event and considered one of the premiere cryptozoologist conferences held in the United States. The video features highlights of guest speakers, footage of attendees and some of the mem-

orabilia on display in the dealers' room. The 2002 event was held in Tyler, Texas, with Craig Woolheater, creator of the popular website *Cryptomundo*, organizing the event.

2004 East Coast Bigfoot Conference (2004) (Doc)

Featuring Eric Altman, Bill Dranginis, Rick Fisher, Mike Frizzell, Rosemary Ellen Guiley, Travis McHenry and Daniel Perez. Produced and Directed by Craig Hines. USA. Color. Stereo. 3-Disc DVD Set. 330 Minutes.

Overview: Coverage of the 2004 East Coast Bigfoot Conference, with interviews of the featured speakers, photo gallery, sighting maps, trailer, and video footage. Topics addressed include Bigfoot on the East Coast, ghosts and hauntings. Sponsored by the Pennsylvania Bigfoot Society, a not-for-profit "Non-Kill" Sasquatch research group.

2005 Sasquatch Research Conference (2005) (Doc)

Featuring Loren Coleman, Dr. Jeff Meldrum, Lloyd Pye, Autumn Williams, Owen Caddy, Jimmy Chilcutt, Thom Powell, Rick Noll, Dr. Robert Alley, Thomas Steenburg, Al Berry, Ron Morehead, John Andrews, Todd Neiss and John Kirk. Hosted by Autumn Williams. USA. Color. Stereo. 2-Disc DVD Set.

Overview: Coverage of the 2005 Sasquatch Research Conference held in Bellingham, Washington. Various guest speakers are highlighted. Conference producer Autumn Williams is a founder of the website *OregonBigfoot.com*, and hosted as well as helped organize the event.

2008 Jeep Liberty Bigfoot Commercial (2008) (TV)

USA. Color. Stereo. 30 Seconds.

Overview: Sasquatch is slowly poking his way through the woods when he comes across a fully-loaded 2008 Jeep Liberty vehicle. Fully-loaded, that is, save for its human owners, who are out somewhere in the forest enjoying their outing. Realizing he's alone, the friendly cryptid avails himself of the spacious interior. Bigfoot noticeably appreciates the reclining bucket leather seats and spacious leg room, large enough even for his massive limbs. Also meeting Bigfoot's approval is the sun roof, which he towers over while standing in the Jeep and stretching in the lazy afternoon sun. Finally bored of his exploration, Sasquatch sighs and grabs a fallen tree branch, stumbling away with a dispirited cry that sounds suspiciously like Chewbacca the Wookie's from the *Star Wars* series.

The spot is well-produced, but the actual Bigfoot suit is a bit of a step down, as the facial features are not as expressive as the clear model for the construction, Rick Baker's Academy Award–winning *Harry and the Hendersons* design.

Ugly Americans (2010) (TV) (Cameo)

Featuring the voices of Matt Oberg, Kurt Metzger, Natasha Leggero, Randy Pearlstein, Michael-Leon Wooley and Larry Murphy. Produced by Aaron Augenblick, Devin Clark, Craig DiGregorio, Colin A.B.V. Lewis and Jeffrey Poliquin. Written by David M. Stern. Directed by Devin Clark, Lucy Snyder and Aaron Augenblick. USA. Color. Stereo. 30 Minutes.

Overview: In an alternative reality version of New York City, a miserable desk jockey named Mark Lilly works in the Office of Integration helping various mutants, monsters, and freaks of nature find meaningful employment, housing, and related socially-necessary support. It's a tough job, and he's not particularly passionate about it, but there's no denying that monsters are helped by the system, however slowly and minutely the progress.

* * * * *

Ugly Americans takes an adult-themed look at monster and human relationships as if the two coexisted in a bustling metropolis and inverts many of them, portraying the various beasts and nightmare creatures as lonely, misunderstood, or confused by human behavior. The pilot episode featured characters complaining about the traffic snarls caused by a Yeti convention. As they mention the con, we are shown the teeming convention center overrun with briefcase-carrying, blandly middle-class looking, white-furred Abominable Snow(business)men as they scurry from one conference room to the next, wait in line to pick up their credentials at the admittance kiosks, and engage in other related *Death of a Salesman*–type behaviors. It's a fast, cheap laugh, but it captures the surreal tone of the series in one short shot. The poor hominids seem about as noteworthy as color television, with the hustling city dwellers around them paying no real attention, thus distilling perhaps the ultimate sad destiny for any self-respecting Sasquatch — to wind up the equivalent of a cryptid Fuller Brush salesman at a "Yetis Only" business convention.

Ultraman ("The Phantom Snow Mountain") (1966) (TV)

Starring Susumu Kurobe, Akiji Kobayashi and Hiroko Sakuraij. Produced by Eiji Tsuburaya. Japan. Color. Mono. 30 Minutes.

Overview: Science Patrol is an investigative agency of the Japanese government designed to intercept all alien and monster threats and terminate said threats before they reach critical mass. When reports from the remote Niigata Prefecture of a giant snow monster named Woo reach Science Patrol, the stalwart team of crack scientists decides to pay a visit. There they encounter a little girl named Yuki who has a psychic connection to the towering snow monster. She implores the hominid to avoid contact with humans and acts as Woo's benefactor whenever any human attempts to fire a weapon at the beast or otherwise harm it.

Formerly tolerated as an eccentric orphan, Yuki finds herself ostracized when Woo's actions accidentally lead to the death of a tourist. Yuki tries to defend Woo, explaining it meant no harm, but a vicious mob forms and decides to take matters into their own hands. They chase Yuki and capture her, attracting the attention of Woo. Seeing Yuki in harm's way, Woo reacts to defend her, destroying a village in the process as the monster is overcome with rage at the puny humans' attempt to harm Yuki. Alas, the stereotype of Yeti as a monster is reinforced by Woo's actions in the eyes of the irate mountain dwellers.

Science Patrol member Hayata exercises his secret ability to transform into Ultraman, a giant-sized defender of humanity from deep space. After a long battle in which the local ski lodge is leveled (thus ironically punishing the villagers for their premature wrath against Yuki), Ultraman convinces Woo that his presence is endangering not only the local environment but Yuki as well. Saddened, but realizing Ultraman has spoken truly, Woo spontaneously fades from existence, seeking his destiny in a higher dimension beyond this one. Yuki watches her spiritual guide vanish, realizing she is finally prepared to make her own way in life.

* * * * *

The international success of the legendary *Ultraman* TV show was a huge influence on *tokusatsu* ("special effects") series in Japan and beyond. The ridiculous nature of the premise and non-stop action proved a potent combination, unleashing an entire generation of spin-offs, rip-offs, and remakes of the concept.

The huge Yeti in "The Phantom Snow Mountain" is known as Woo, and is subtitled as the "Legend Monster" (*Densetsu Kaijū*). This indicates right away the important mythological nature and reverence for Woo that is demonstrated throughout the episode. Unlike the usual Bug-Eyed Monster wreaking indiscriminate havoc, or the latest Giant Robot running amok, Woo is regarded with a tenderness that is remarkable for *Ultraman*. Even the battle between Woo and Ultraman is kept pro forma as an apparent nod to the respectful attitude towards the venerable Abominable Snowman's stature as a beloved figure worldwide.

The Yeti suit is not the best costume ever featured on the show, but even with its stiff facial expressions and limited movement, Woo is a formidable screen presence. It helps that the creators shoot the monster in fog or snow storms, so that the lack of details in Woo's costume are not as apparent beneath the barrage of bad weather effects. Woo basically hasn't much to do between limited calls for his appearance in the fast-paced script until the action-packed finale, which further helps obscure the obvious Yeti suit's seams until such delicacies no longer matter, as the two giants slug it out to see who will stay and who will go.

Woo would appear later in an *Ultra*-based spin-off series called *Ultra Fight*, as well as in the series *Ultraman Ace*. Never to keep a popular supporting monster down, Woo was also resurrected for both the *Redman* and *Ultraman 80* TV off-shoots as well.

Unsolved Mysteries (1987) (Multiple Episodes) (TV) (Doc)

Featuring Robert Stack. Produced by John Cosgrove, Terry Dunn Meurer, Stuart Schwartz and Jeannie O'Neill. Written by John McLaughlin, Jim Lindsay, Christopher Meindl and Mitch Rosa. Directed by Kabir Akhtar, Gerald Massimei and Michael Scott. USA. Color. Stereo. 60 Minutes.

Overview: Character actor Robert Stack wound down his storied career with this long-running exposé show which attempted to offer enough "viewer information" by recreating unsolved mysteries that the TV audience would flood its call center, where the producers' operators dutifully fielded the incoming barrage for each and every case. Many real-life homicides and missing persons cases were solved because of the show's spotlight (some might argue exploitation). Whatever one's judgment as to the show's merits, it was an enormous cultural influence during the years it was shown on network television. Of particular interest to Ciné du Sasquatch fans will be three episodes that deal with hominids and humans when they encounter one another. These are "Yeti," "Bigfoot," and "Skunk Ape." No episode of *Unsolved Mysteries* ever involved any Bigfoot harming or murdering humans to cash in on life insurance policies, settle any personal vendettas, or the like. Indeed, in terms of dredging up the darkness of the world and its subsequent rankings in the light of day, the trio of Bigfoot-related episodes of *Unsolved Mysteries* seems lighthearted compared to the real-world horrors of serial killers, child abductors, and related atrocities most often profiled on the "based on a true case" series.

Valley of Flowers (2006)

AKA: *La Vallée des fleurs*. Starring Milind Soman, Mylène Jampanoï, Naseeruddin Shah, Eri, Jampa Kalsang Tamang and Anil Yadav. Produced by Jean-Baptiste Babin, Karl Baumgartner, Denis Carot, Christoph Friedel, Kenzô Horikoshi, Marie Masmonteil, Atsuko Ôno, Dilip Shankar, Claudia Steffen and Mihir Upadhyay. Written by Pan Nalin, Anurag Kashyap and Sarah Besan Shennib. Directed by Pan Nalin. India, Japan, France, Germany. Color. Stereo. 155 Minutes.

Overview: Jalan and his gang of freelance outlaws plunder wealthy travelers along the Silk Road circa the 1800s. They have a Robin Hood–styled code of ethics wherein they take only from those who can afford to lose, do not harm their victims (when possible, of course, and within reason), and generally stay wary of outsiders. When a lovely young woman is left behind after a caravan robbery, Jalan is forced to choose between sending Ushna, the newcomer, away on her own — with a dubious chance for survival (or so it would seem) — or risk alienating his loyal men by taking her under his wing.

When Ushna proves valuable to all concerned, however, by displaying an uncanny ability to pick and choose which opportunities to exploit for criminal gain, the resentful men slowly begin to accept Ushna as one of their own. Jalan, secretly pleased, falls in love with her and they make love. Emboldened by their newfound passion, the couple takes greater and greater risks in each new theft. Ushna's supernatural streak of good fortune continues until soon the fearless lovers literally steal into the realms of the gods. A fearsome but wizened balance of Nature herself, Yeti, becomes intrigued by Jalan and Ushna's audacity — never before have humans shown such disrespect and simultaneous cunning. Yeti uses his supernatural powers to alter the outcome of their escapades, eventually reducing them to friendless, penniless, and even temporarily estranged from one another in an awesome display of Karma personified. Despite their ordeals, the couple soon reunites and vows to remain together no matter what comes their way.

* * * * *

The epic sweep of *Valley of Flowers* is remarkable in the genre of Ciné du Sasquatch. Very few productions ever attempt such boldness of vision as shooting on location at 20,000 feet elevation in the actual Himalayan Mountains (no mean feat for even experienced mountain climbers, let alone professional actors and crew members). It has the kind of rich, visual density of production design and sweep of narrative that reminds one of romantic epics from the Hollywood factory's best decades. Indeed, while echoing visual motifs from any number of Eastern and Western martial arts films and sword and sandal adventure sagas, *Valley of Flowers* is able to add much production value to its U.S. $9 million budget and give the film the international feel of world cinema. While CGI work is used to enhance compositions and add luster, most of the production relies on classical compositions and a sense of big-scale action and adventure to make such alterations and additions largely unnecessary. It is an impressive example of four different countries cooperating to produce one very unified film experience; this is rarer in international co-financed productions than one might think.

Of course, the use of the Yeti here is more metaphorical than literal. The supernatural Yeti is actually personified as a human being with long, white dreadlocks and frosty beard, which — when combined with his white garments — give him the requisite stature to be both a human *and* the repository of viewer-supplied projections of Yeti in the more traditional cryptid incarnation. And incarnation, Karma, and other Eastern mythologies are very much at play in the film's narrative. *Valley of Flowers* lifts the typical Western elements out of the genre tale — the quest for a single god's triumph; the lone individual as superior or at least equal to his society; and the idea of material gain as something desirable rather than necessary — and inserts more Eastern notions, such as spiritual destinies fulfilled, a pantheon of gods and goddesses, and a sense of inevitable fate as determinant of one's destiny rather than a vengeful deity asserting dominance over a humbled mankind. While much of the action and acting remains very Western, the heart of the matter has been beautifully, if at times boringly, transplanted, alive and well, with a Buddhist philosophy and Eastern viewpoint that gives the film the power to entrance (at least for Western viewers willing to suspend their own cultural bias and see beyond, of course).

The approach is not flawless. The narrative leaps in fitful starts and stops, sometimes rushing headlong with dizzying intensity and other times slowing down to artfully explore visuals the director finds entrancing or illuminating. This is always a matter of balance. And *Valley of Flowers* will be a challenge for many viewers who don't wish to suspend their disbelief for a pace and storyline that doesn't conform to the typical three-act Hollywood movie plot. Given that the film is, in essence, a love story told across the ages, it is never meant to be anything more than deftly romantic; and here its lush cinematography and multiple settings work well to add a sense of lush production value to the film's overall dreaminess, which is its defining characteristic. Finally, many Ciné du Sasquatch viewers will object to the personification of Yeti as a human being rather than a hominid. This is, of course, a matter of taste rather than absolutes. If one is in a speculative mood and open to cross-cultural experiences, then *Valley of Flowers* is a mixed blessing, but one never less than visually sumptuous.

Venture Brothers ("Home Insecurity") (2004) (TV) (Cameo)

Featuring the voices of James Urbaniak, Patrick Warburton, Michael Sinterniklaas, Christopher McCulloch, Doc Hammer and T. Ryder Smith. Produced by Keith Crofford, Mike Lazzo and Rachel Simon. Written and Directed by Jackson Publick. USA. Color. Stereo. 30 Minutes.

Overview: The Venture Brothers are the second generation heirs to a once-fabulous security corporation built by their scientific genius grandfather. Alas, hard times have befallen the Ventures financially, which sees their formerly vast holdings reduced to a mere secret island headquarters or two. The earnest brothers try to live up to the incredible feats of their deceased grandpappy, but find the world a much more complicated place within which to operate than did their ancestor, who relied on fat government contracts and international demand for his services to amass his empire.

In "Home Insecurity," the Venture Brothers' stalwart personal bodyguard, Brock, takes a much deserved wilderness camping vacation. Alas, he soon finds himself face-to-face with Sasquatch one night and is forced to engage the enraged hominid in hand-to-hand combat. To Brock's stunned amazement, a human in a red jumpsuit intervenes on behalf of Sasquatch just as Brock has gotten the upper hand in their fight. It is none other than Steve Summers, a former astronaut turned bionic man who has desperately fallen in love with Sasquatch. So true is Summers to his feelings for his short-term companion that he drops out of his covert service working for the U.S. government without warning, intending to stay awol with Bigfoot at his side.

After hearing Summers' tale of interbreeding gone awry, Brock agrees to help the love-stricken duo of man and monster escape from a pursuing squad of soldiers intent on arresting the errant spy for his desertion. He disguises the two as Vietnam veterans and bypasses a crucial check point, thereby assisting the two to freedom. Brock is glad he helped in retrospect, but offended that when he shaved Sasquatch to help with the beast's disguise, Brock discovered that Sasquatch was male, not female, as he had initially assumed. Hilariously, Brock has no problems with a man and a hominid having sex — so long as it is heterosexual in orientation and not homosexual.

* * * * *

The Venture Brothers was based on a simple comic "what if" scenario: What if after Dr. Quest from *Jonny Quest* died and left his fortune to a grown-up Jonny and his siblings, things just didn't quite work out for the second generation of Quest family members as they did for the founding patriarch? This funny look at the resulting dysfunction between the Venture family members as they struggle to maintain the crumbling family empire is the sardonic result.

The Sasquatch referenced herein is clearly the Bionic Bigfoot from the original *The Six Million Dollar Man* TV series, complete with Steve "Summers" (the Bionic Woman's surname inserted in place of Austin, the Bionic Man's original last name), who even explains that it cost the United States government six million dollars to rebuild him as better, stronger, and faster than before! The comedic conceit that the two are in love is funny when contrasted against Brock's stiff, Republican mantle — he's anything but a liberal tree hugger, after all. Especially funny is the idea that the homophobic Brock has to wrestle with the inner angst that discovering Sasquatch is a Hesquatch unleashes in Brock's tortured soul. It's a fresh, funny take on the entire "Beauty and the Beast" standard but flipped for homoerotic laughs. Given the similarity, this episode may have been an inspiration for the producers of *Yeti: A Love Story*, which also includes a gay Sasquatch love affair as part of its central narrative.

Washington State Sasquatch Research Group (Assorted Titles) (Doc)

Produced by the Washington State Sasquatch Research Group. USA. Color. Stereo. 60 Minutes.

Overview: The Washington State Sasquatch Research Group has produced a series of five direct-to-video, one-hour titles documenting their field exploration of the Pacific Northwest Bigfoot phenomena over the past decade. The documentaries are: *On the Track of the Pacific N.W. Sasquatch* (2001), which includes first-hand evidence, such as recorded vocalizations, scat droppings, and hair samples, which are analyzed by Dr. Dr. Henner Ferenbach of the Oregon State Primate Research Center for his expert reaction; *In Pursuit of the Olympic Rain Forest Sasquatch* (2006), documenting newly-found hand and footprints from Sasquatch, recorded Bigfoot tree knockings, and the so-called Wedekind Creek Footage (unedited and in its entirety); *Sasquatch of the Olympic Mountains: Evidence Revealed* (2009), which records the research team meticulously investigating the Quinault, Queets, and the Hoh Rainforest Valleys for living hominid evidence; *Operation In-Depth: High Altitude Bigfoot Research* (2009), which chronicles the team's ascent to the peaks of the Olympic Mountains with professional trackers in tow to help them capture imagery and collect evidence in regards to Sasquatch; and their newest release, *Sasquatch of Canada* (2010), wherein the hardy researchers venture into the remote British Colombian mountain range of Canada, bringing along their high-definition video gear as they track an elusive cryptid through the dense snow fields and nearly corner it at one point. This last documentary breaks the 60-minute barrier of the other docs in the series with a length of 90 minutes, which is used to highlight more night-recorded Sasquatch vocalizations, topographical maps of areas surveyed, etc. Given that these five documentaries are entirely self-financed and modestly produced, the

success of the series has been remarkable, selling mostly via the Internet by the organization itself, which recently changed its moniker to the Washington State Bigfoot Research Center, dropping "Sasquatch" from the group's official title.

Watchers (1988)

Starring Michael Ironside, Christopher Cary, Graeme Campbell, Dan O'Dowd, Lala Sloatman, Corey Haim, Dale Wilson, Blu Mankuma, Colleen Winton, Duncan Fraser, Barbara Williams, Lou Bollo, Jason Priestley, Matt Hill, Andrew Morkey, Norman Browning, Ghislaine Crawford, Justine Crawford, Tong Lung, Keith Wardlow, Don S. Davis and Freda Perry. Produced by Roger Corman, Mary Eilts, Damian Lee and David Mitchell. Written by Paul Haggis (uncredited), Bill Freed and Damian Lee. Directed by Jon Hess. Canada. Color. Mono. 91 Minutes.

Overview: When a protester detonates a small bomb at a top-secret government research facility to oppose the cruel treatment of test animals, two covert government experiments are unintentionally unleashed on the unsuspecting Canadian public. One is Furface, a golden retriever which has been genetically altered to have the intelligence of a human being. The other is OXCOM, a hominid monster which is telepathically linked to Furface. Their designed purpose: Furface hunts down enemy combatants and keeps them distracted until the monstrous OXCOM shows up and rips them to pieces before they know what hit them. Furface and OXCOM are separated during the explosion. Furface is adopted by a teenage boy named Travis and taken into a modest domestic scene comprised of Travis and his divorced mother Nora. Soon OXCOM begins reading Furface's mind from afar and hones in on the mental signal the dog is projecting, killing its way across the Canadian countryside as it makes it way towards Furface to complete its murderous mission.

Eventually Travis is able to convince his mother that Furface is not a normal canine in any sense of the word, and that OXCOM is after them. A special agent named Johnson shows up and warns them to run for their lives. Nora and Travis hide in a remote cabin, hoping to avoid their seemingly grisly fate, but Johnson turns out to be the third experimental subject himself, activated and sent to retrieve OXCOM and do whatever is necessary to clean up any evidence that would implicate the government. In a stand against OXCOM and Johnson, Travis and Nora battle for their lives in a long dark night of non-stop siege.

* * * * *

To many, *Watchers* is not a legitimate Ciné du Sasquatch effort because the beast is revealed to be a genetic slave to the government's desires for a more effective killing machine, thereby making it anything but a hominid. But as the Bionic Bigfoot from *The Six Million Dollar Man* demonstrates, the cryptid in question in a Bigfoot entry need not necessarily be described as such, nor even necessarily look like real-world descriptions of the hominid itself. So as far as purity of genre is concerned, *Watchers* arguably falls within the Ciné du Sasquatch parameters based on the presentation of the monster and storytelling techniques, which are closely aligned with the genre overall.

A great deal of lingering resentment surrounds *Watchers* from diehard Dean Koontz fans, a vocal majority of whom believe the book by Koontz was maligned during the cinematic adaptation, which took great liberties with central characters, plot threads, etc. But like the successful novelist back in the studio days of Hollywood said when an interviewer asked how it felt to have his latest novel ruined by the filmic adaptation, "My novel is not ruined. It's just fine. It's sitting right there behind me like it always has been, perfectly the same." Though probably apocryphal, the story does illustrate a larger truth: A movie cannot "ruin" a book any more than a book can ruin a movie. They are independent art forms, each translatable to some extent into the other, but never completely dependent upon one another for success or failure.

Still, the confusion because of the changes does beg the question: Is OXCOM, the genetically-altered simian, actually a Bigfoot specimen, or is it merely a modified simian with distinct differences from the *Homo sapiens*/hominid branch of evolution? Because the script avoids self-analysis as to the "why" of its many changes, some — such as the cryptid monster itself— seem poorly chosen and underdeveloped. It feels as if the producers decided early on to incorporate the relentless pursuit formula so critical to the (then) recent success of *The Terminator* by Jim Cameron and transform OXCOM into a psychic Savage Sasquatch which will stalk the protagonists no matter where they go. The problem with this conceit is that we're never really shown nor told why the government decided upon Bigfoot, or if the film is implying that they somehow altered the genes of an existing simian species and therefore "grew" the creature into a Bigfoot-sized, human-maiming hominid. Both the dog and the covert agent are revealed as part of the same experiment, and yet both are shown in their "correct" genetic forms. The monster, however, when finally shown briefly at the climax, appears far closer to a Charles Gemora killer gorilla suit mixed with a Sasquatch's ability to walk in a bipedal fashion. Again this begs the basic question: Just what *is* this creature to begin with, anyway? Simian? Hominid? Neither? *Both*? Simply using a Bigfoot and then pretending it is not so (or, rather, leaving obscure the rationale behind the visualization of such an important part of the storyline) with a clever "altered DNA" explanation is a murky cop-out.

Most of the sequences involving the monster are relatively well-shot, with plenty of shadows, off-screen attacks, a hairy arm smashing through a cabin ceiling, etc. The final shots revealing its gorilla-like appearance are disappointing, as noted, so unlike the special effects–packed termination of *The Terminator*, the creature reveal feels anticlimactic and dissipates any marginal suspense that preceded the conclusion. Given the lack of impact the suit makes in terms of believability, the director makes a wise choice in deliberately keeping the monster off-screen for most of *Watchers'* running time; the problem, of course, is that when finally presented in all its glory, there is no glory present to make the sleight-of-hand of the creature's previous non-appearances significant. In fact, revealing the less-than-scary appearance of the monster reduces it to little more than a marginal threat, guaranteeing the audience will be let down by such a poorly-wrought conclusion. This is a problem throughout the history of Ciné du Sasquatch: How does one envision the creature in a consistent manner that both maintains audience believability and at the same time satiates a visual medium's insistence on "showing the monster" for the audience's final satisfaction? Filmmakers have tried everything — from building a better suit to keeping the creature mostly off-screen — but no surefire method exists, save good story-telling, believable acting, and a clever ability to misdirect the audience without landing the whole film in the ditch. It is no easy task, which is why such breakout films in the genre like *The Legend of Boggy Creek* and *Harry and the Hendersons* (two extremes and yet both successful as motion pictures in and of themselves) are the notable exceptions rather than the rule in a genre heavily populated by misfires.

Watchers was followed by several sequels, each of which continues the basic formula. Ciné du Sasquatch students will find it an atypical genre effort and may wonder if it truly is worthy of being labeled a "Bigfoot movie" because of its many contrivances and avoidance of such a label. But in the end, the simpler logic for inclusion prevails: If it acts like a hominid, walks in a bipedal fashion like a *Homo sapiens*, and is shown to resemble Sasquatch more than a mountain gorilla, then it's a Bigfoot by any other name, OXCOM included.

Weird Travels ("Investigations of the Unexplained" and "Bigfoot") (2003) (TV) (Doc)

Featuring Loren Coleman and Don Wildman. Produced by Kathleen Cromley, Kari Anne Olson, Dana Langford, Audrey George and Amy Woods. Written by Naomi Yasuda, Helga Eike, Gayle Gawlowski, Gabriel Lewis and Sarah Wetherbee. Directed by Emre Sahin. USA. Color. Stereo. 60 Minutes.

Overview: This short-lived but well-regarded cryptozoology-oriented series produced by the Travel Channel highlights various areas of the world that have experienced unusual sightings and encounters with UFOs, Bigfoot, the Jersey Devil, and other phenomena. Noted cryptozoologist Loren Coleman appears on camera, and acted as a research source for the show's producers and writers. In "Investigations of the Unexplained," Bigfoot is examined, along with segments on demonic possession, paranormal activity as related to ghost manifestations, and the infamous Myrtle Plantation in Louisiana, which has always been a reported "hot spot" of ghostly activity. The episode simply titled "Bigfoot" is an hour-long showcase dedicated to America's favorite hominid. The series ran from 2003 to 2006 on the cable network.

The Werewolf and the Yeti (1975)

AKA: *Night of the Howling Beast*; *Horror of the Werewolf*; *Hall of the Mountain King*; *The Curse of the Beast*. Starring Paul Naschy, Grace Mills, Silvia Solar, Gil Vidal, Luis Induni, Josep Castillo Escalona and Verónica Miriel. Produced by Modesto Pérez Redondo. Written by Paul Naschy. Directed by Miguel Iglesias. Spain. Color. Mono. 87 Minutes.

Overview: While exploring the Himalayan Mountains for evidence of the elusive Yeti, a small team of scientists are attacked and killed by the very cryptid they seek. Back in Spain, Count Waldemar Daninsky, a refined gentleman of means, is urged to put together a second party and search for clues as to why the first expedition met

Lurid artwork from a Spanish release poster designed to highlight local horror actor Paul Naschy as El Hombre Lobo. Note the Lon Chaney, Jr., influence.

with death (their bodies having been recovered). There is talk that the Abominable Snowman was the culprit behind the scientists' deaths, but the only evidence recovered besides a Yeti scalp the scientists themselves were carrying when attacked is a camera. The developed photographs, however, show the blurry images of what may or may not be a Yeti attacking the men. Intrigued but apprehensive, the Count—who is an armchair cryptozoologist of sorts—undertakes the secondary expedition at his friends' behest, an invaluable member of their team because he speaks the Sherpa language.

In the desolate mountains of the Himalayas the expedition encounters immediate difficulty when the roads prove to be infested with bandits intent on murdering anyone they encounter. In order to protect themselves, Daninsky and his party split into two groups, hoping this will at least insure one group makes it through the dangerous passages should the other fall prey to the bandits. When the Count and his Sherpa guide become separated from his group, he takes shelter in a remote cave. To his surprise, the cave is inhabited by two voluptuous women. They tend to the exhausted men, nursing them back to health. Daninsky falls prey to the attractive sirens' charms and has sex with both. Eventually, the two seductresses reveal their true nature: they transform into wolf women and devour the poor guide. The Count awakens from his sexually-depleted state to witness their frenzied feeding on the entrails of his former guide. Realizing he has seen them in their true form, the wolf women attack Daninsky, intent on making him dessert. But Daninsky overpowers them, impaling them to death, but not before one of them bites him on the chest.

Meanwhile, the other group of explorers is captured by the bandits after a shoot-out leaves the remainder of Daninsky's original team dead. The Count's girlfriend escapes enslavement, but the others are taken by the evil Genghis Khan, who has used sorcery to remain alive for countless centuries. Khan imprisons the helpless explorers in his secret mountain lair, allowing the sorceress he keeps as part of his dark empire to torture them at will. Tracking them down, the Count transforms into a werewolf and mauls to death Khan's guards. Eventually Daninsky locates the cell containing his girlfriend while in human form, but Khan's men take the Count prisoner, too. Khan's evil mistress uses her black arts to cure the lesions that have appeared on Khan's back by slicing the skin off a live captive women in a sacrificial gesture. Each treatment restores the powerful warlord, but only temporarily—hence his need to forever capture new women victims.

Daninsky and his girlfriend escape before she can be sacrificed, destroying Khan and his sick mistress in the process. But as they flee into the snow-covered mountains, the Yeti appears. Daninsky transforms into the werewolf and, as his girlfriend looks on in horror, the titular battle royale between lycanthrope and bipedal hominid rages. Daninsky triumphs but is mortally wounded in the process, reverting to human form as he lies dying in his girlfriend's arms.

* * * * *

The Werewolf and the Yeti is a distinctly minor entry in the Bigfoot genre, but nonetheless possesses all the classic ingredients of the typical Paul Naschy werewolf pictures: many gory onscreen deaths; unflinching, sadomasochistic sex and violence; and the unique "leaping *lobo hombre*" himself, Count Daninsky, who, in lycanthrope form, propels himself during attack scenes with airborne agility not unlike a masked *lucha libre* wrestler or human-sized flying squirrel. The star of many such werewolf movies based on his admitted idol Lon Chaney Jr., Naschy forged an entire career out of recreating the Universal monster series in his native Spain, though his most successful screen appearances were inevitably as the aristocratic wolf man. While many of Naschy's films were handsomely photographed, the majority are slow-paced, melodramatic affairs of the crank-em-out variety, of which *The Werewolf and the Yeti* is a familiar example.

A lurid photograph montage from the American pressbook hyping the Spanish-produced entry *The Werewolf and the Yeti*. Paul Naschy stars as the Wolfman, but the Yeti's appearance is only a cameo.

Not that fans of such lugubrious filmmaking will be completely disappointed. *The Werewolf and the Yeti* does offer a lot of European shock value so typical of the era, including female nudity, gory effects, and fighting sequences to satisfy the less demanding viewer. But any Ciné du Sasquatch watcher will be sorely disappointed, as the Abominable Snowman is relegated solely to the opening attack sequence and—after much unrelated storytelling—to the end fight between wolf man and Yeti. The latter, however, is decidedly anti-climactic, given the film's title. Naschy transforms into the werewolf, jumps atop the unconvincing Yeti a few times, and is flung off by the annoyed cryptid. Finally, the werewolf tears at the Yeti's throat and leaves the hominid bleeding to death in the crimson-soaked snow.

There are many of the usual cinematic Snowman trappings herein—the Himalayan setting, the fearful Sherpa guides, the warnings from monks who respect the Yeti as a force of nature, etc. But none of it amounts to much in terms of narrative impact; it's just window dressing for what is, in essence, an umpteenth retelling of the tired *loup-garou* formula. It begs credulity when the Count's girlfriend must be told that only her love for the afflicted werewolf himself, or a pure silver bullet, can stop her beloved's rampage. What cloistered environment has the poor woman inhabited that she doesn't know such common European folklore? This kind of mythology dates back to antiquity in her character's native land, so the portrayal of being shocked by this revelation plays unwittingly like Claude Rains' famous "I'm shocked, *shocked* to find that gambling is going on in here!" line from *Casablanca*, even as the croupier hands Rains his nightly winnings. Alas, this is why *The Werewolf and the Yeti* is so banal—the viewer is always a few paw steps ahead of this "shaggy wolf" story.

Cryptid fans who desire to see every entry in the genre may wish to secure a copy for viewing; otherwise, all but the most die-hard Ciné du Sasquatch completists should skip this entry. It is a better fit with its *Night of the Howling Beast* moniker than *The Werewolf and the Yeti*, which—despite the brief appearances by the Snowman—feels altered for box office considerations rather than actual hominid screen time.

The Wild Man of the Navidad (2008)

AKA: *The Wild Man of Navidad*; *The Wildman of Navidad*; *The Wildman of the Navidad*. Starring Justin Meeks, Stacy Meeks, Patrick Hewlett, Alex Garcia, James Bargsley, Jacob Bargsley, Edmond Geyer, Shasta Gaydos, William Booth, Shannon Biggers, Duane Graves, Kevin Graves, Tim Harden, Kim Henkel, Gary Houser, William McBride, John Sholtis and Tony Wolford. Produced by Justin Meeks, Kim Henkel, Duane Graves, Roxanne Robertson, Dale S. Rogers, Lauren Stett and Tony Wolford. Written by Justin Meeks, Duane Graves and Dale S. Rogers. Directed by Duane Graves and Justin Meeks. USA. Color. Stereo. 86 Minutes.

Overview: In the deep-thicket country along the Navidad River outside Sublime, Texas, a local legend persists across generations of townspeople. According to them, a hairy monster known as the Wild Man lurks in the 600 acres owned by shy, retiring Dale S. Rogers. Along with his wheelchair-bound wife Jean and live-in caretaker Mario, Dale ekes out a marginal living, unable to maintain the costs of his drooling spouse's medications due to his chronic underemployment. Dale could easily rent out the vast acreage which has been bequeathed to him and charge fees for local hunters to prowl the bottoms filled with game, but he refuses to do so, knowing the legends are factual: The beast is real. So real that Dale makes a peace offering in exchange for a Bigfoot detente. Each night Dale slides a tray of food onto his porch and waits for the Sasquatch to noisily devour the meal. In exchange, the beast leaves him and his family alone.

Circumstances take a turn for the worse when Dale loses his welding job and he's forced to begin allowing hunters to pay him to venture into the pristine backwoods, which have not been invaded by humans in over three decades. Dale attempts to steer the interlopers into what he hopes are the safest areas so that their lives

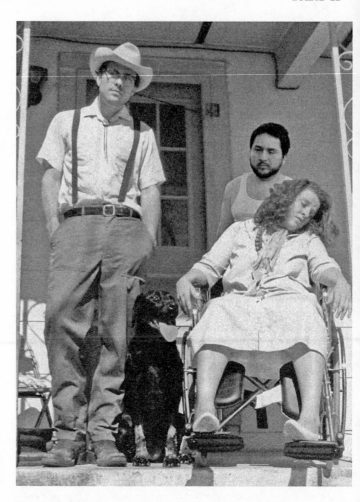

Shy Dales S. Rogers (Justin Meeks), his invalid wife Jean (Stacy Meeks), and their hired helper Mario Jalisco (Alex Garcia) fearfully anticipate sundown and the coming of *The Wild Man of the Navidad*. (Photograph courtesy Greeks Prods.)

will hopefully be spared by the territorial monster. Alas, the Wild Man tolerates no encroachments, inflicting a series of gut-ripping attacks on the human intruders.

Finally riled to action after the grisly attacks, an enraged mob of Sublime citizens take to the restricted woods, screaming "Lynch that son of a bitch!" and other cat-calls uncomfortably reminiscent of past troubled times in the Deep South. In a bullet-riddled showdown, it's all out warfare — rednecks versus the monster — until the beast is finally slaughtered (but not before taking down a handful of hunters with it). When the carcass is displayed for the surviving townspeople to see, the folks of Sublime realize, to their shock and horror, that their own fury and greed to exploit the bottom lands may have caused them to commit homicide, so human-like is the creature. Afraid of the repercussions of their vigilante act, they decide to keep quiet about the incident. Alas, Dale S. Rogers, guilt-ridden over his own contribution to the massacre, keeps a secret journal which will later expose the truth, to their undying humiliation.

* * * * *

A remarkably self-assured debut feature film made on a minuscule budget, *The Wild Man of the Navidad* is a loving homage to prior Ciné du Sasquatch films, most notably Charles Pierce's *The Legend of Boggy Creek* (Pierce receives a special thanks in the film's credits), even extending to naming characters "Pierce" and "Crabtree" (the latter the name of a lead character in *The Legend of Boggy Creek*).

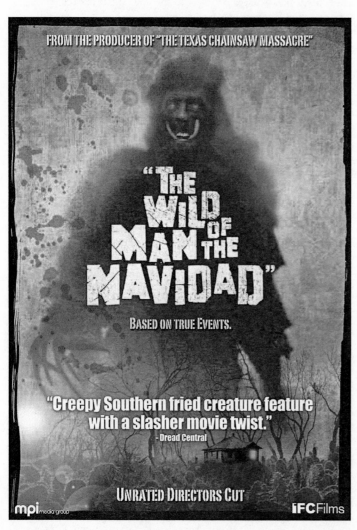

Cover art for the DVD release of *The Wild Man of the Navidad*.

With its insistence that it is based on the true-life journal of Dale S. Rogers (à la the Smokey Crabtree tales that inspired *The Legend of Boggy Creek*), the intertwining of locals playing themselves with the more polished results of the lead actors (such as Justin Meeks and Alex Garcia), and even the soggy bottomlands of the creature's domain, *The Wild Man of the Navidad* revels in its references to Pierce's defining Ciné du Sasquatch effort.

This is not to imply, however, that *The Wild Man of the Navidad* lacks its own unique brand of originality, as it stands on its own shaggy two legs and works as a quirky regional viewing experience whether one has seen Pierce's seminal film or not. By concentrating not on the Wild Man from its own perspective but on the residents' terrified viewpoint, the filmmakers emphasize tension over outright terror, and psychological suspense over visceral horror. The underlying horror of under-educated, gap-toothed local yokels idly trying to maintain their dying town, à la *The Last Picture Show*, combined with the largely sympathetic treatment of the Wild Man's lonely plight, actually renders the human characters far more sinister by light of day (and even night, at least until the Bigfoot goes on its nocturnal prowls). Only the introspective Dale Rogers seems sympathetic in such a hateful town without pity.

Not that *The Wild Man of the Navidad* is violence free; far from it. Though the brutal attacks are mostly suggested rather than overtly shown in lingering, gore-filled close-ups (though, again, it has its share of onscreen mayhem), the film nevertheless refuses to allow the viewer to forget the demonic strength of the Wild Man and its willingness to butcher all interlopers. As a result, the Sublime residents have no PETA-styled love for it. If anything, the humans and the cryptid are in a perpetual stalemate, with intrusions frequently resulting in bloodshed on both sides of the species spectrum. This is, of course, one of the central tenets of the Ciné du Sasquatch genre as a whole, and *The Wild Man of the Navidad* does an excellent job of illustrating just how effective the theme remains when cinematically well-crafted.

By using authentic locales and a mostly non-professional cast of real-life residents, *The Wild Man of the Navidad* never feels like a studio version of the same story one might encounter coming from Hollywood, complete with bad Southern accents and palm trees clearly swaying in the background. Instead, co-directors Meeks and Graves wisely cast with an eye and ear towards believability within their limited budget. In fact, the cloistered, often cruel nature of the Sublime residents, mixed with the melodramatic story of Rogers and his invalid wife, is every bit as Southern Gothic as anything concocted by Faulkner or Flannery O'Connor. As they spend their days monotonously swilling moonshine and passing silent judgment on one another, the Sublime citizenry seem more subconsciously hell-bent on *self*-destruction than destroying any legendary cryptid. After all, the beast poses no threat to them as long as they keep out of its domain; whereas they constantly undercut one another and humiliate anyone who doesn't toe the small-town line — that is, ironically, killing the community slowly but surely.

Only reclusive Dale Rogers manages to see through the heartless culture engulfing him and from which he withdraws with his book collection, an act of defiance which has already earned him the town kook moniker. His sense of longing to escape is palpable, but with his invalid wife and no financial resources save selling his inherited acres (which would mean the Bigfoot coming into contact with and killing humans), Rogers' guilt and inability to act seems very adroit in terms of psychological realism. This sympathetic touch is heightened by Justin Meeks' performance, which is the cornerstone of the film and its only truly resonant center of emotion. It's this foreboding sense of utter futility which elevates *The Wild Man of the Navidad* above so many efforts in the genre. By shooting on location in the nearly impenetrable, desolate brush lands, and acutely rendering the locals' dead-end lives of failed dreams (they seem almost wearily grateful to succumb to death at the hands of the Wild Man, as if unable to shoulder the oppressive weight of their own miserable existences any longer), the film has an often elegiac tone rarely found in horror films, let alone those within Ciné du Sasquatch.

Given the filmmakers' use of actual locales, particularly the claustrophobic backwoods, one is not surprised to find the guiding hand of producer Kim Henkel involved in the production. Best known for his role as producer of the original *The Texas Chain Saw Massacre* and subsequent remakes, Henkel met the pair of moviemakers while teaching them screenwriting in a University of Texas film program classroom. Recognizing their talent, he acted in a mostly advisory capacity on the production; but given his native roots, Henkel surely was a positive influence, at least in terms of using authentic location photography and crafting a sense of menace through bizarre set dressings — two qualities found in abundance in both *The Texas Chain Saw Massacre* and *The Wild Man of the Navidad*.

Too, the portrayal of rednecks as inbred savages awaiting the slightest provocation to go shotgun ballistic hasn't been this dire since H. G. Lewis' *Two-Thousand Maniacs*. Whereas recent efforts in the comedy and dramatic genres have sought to soften this admittedly stereotypical image of so-called Good Ol' Boys with such notable figures as Larry the Cable Guy and Jeff Foxworthy, *The Wild Man of the Navidad* abandons all pretense of political correctness and viscerally captures the sinister, often unexamined sadism so prevalent in so much of male bonding culture: the womanizing, the hunting, and the non-stop drinking of oneself into oblivion. Few if any of the supporting characters are less than outright drunkards; the town sheriff transports the local moonshiner's "product" to willing customers without a trace of irony. There is no hint of progressive values displayed by the token female characters either, who go along with the dysfunctional patriarchy without question.

By focusing on the seamier side of such aberrant group behavior, in contrast to the creature's needs to forage for survival, the film explores territory similar to John Boorman's *Deliverance*. An uneasy re-

Much like its admitted influence, *The Legend of Boggy Creek*, *The Wild Man of the Navidad* uses lots of locals in key supporting roles to add regional authenticity. (Photograph courtesy Greeks Prods.)

alization presents itself from the opening moments of *The Wild Man of the Navidad*: Man's inhumanity to man far outweighs any act carried out by the monster itself. As the human population goes about their daily lives passively taking their pleasure at each new unfortunate mishap experienced by their fellow citizens (because it alleviates their boredom), it takes an innocent "monster" to make them briefly reflect on their own truly monstrous inner natures. Think of it as a Bigfoot movie in the mold of *Twin Peaks* or Clouzot's *Le Corbeau*, in which long-held, simmering grudges are silently avenged with smirks of satisfaction by the survivors.

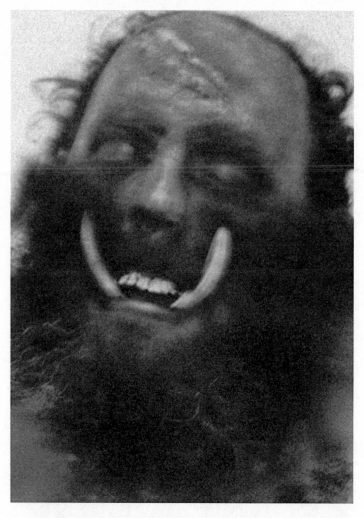

The Wild Man (Tony Wolford) is decidedly more human than simian, portrayed as a Skunk Ape derivative. Tusks on film hominids are rare but do occur in the genre. From *The Wild Man of the Navidad*. (Photograph courtesy Greeks Prods.)

While it is never slick in any Hollywood sense, and the performances are an acquired taste, *The Wild Man of the Navidad* is both a faithful throwback to the halcyon days of the Disco Bigfoot era of the 1970s and a somber, subdued critique of all that can be, and too often is, wrong with rural America. As such, it entertainingly demonstrates that dabblers in Ciné du Sasquatch can genuinely contribute to and remold the inherent limitations of the genre, provided they approach the material with imagination and introspection, as well as an acute knowledge of the genre's pitfalls (so as to avoid them).

The Wild Thornberrys ("You Ain't Seen Nothin' Yeti") (TV) (1999)

Featuring the voices of Arlene Klasky, Gabor Csupo, Steve Peppon, David Silverman and Stephen Sustaric. Directed by Mark Risley. Color. USA. 22 Minutes.

Overview: Eliza considers herself the luckiest kid in the world. Not only is she the daughter of a couple who travel around the globe in search of rare animals to document as professional photographers, but she has been blessed by a tribal shaman with the special power to communicate with animals in their own hidden tongues. In "You Ain't Seen Nothin' Yeti," Eliza becomes alarmed that no one will take her claims about the Yeti's existence seriously, and so she sets out, when her jet-set family is on assignment in Nepal, to prove the creature is real, once and for all.

The Wild Thornberrys was a successful Nickelodeon TV series that aimed to both educate children about the vast array of animal species outside their normal range of exposure and entertain with a quirky line style of animation that set it apart visually from the usual *Pokemon* clones. Eliza's ability to speak with the animals is straight out of *Dr. DooLittle*, of course, but the upbeat show never takes itself too seriously. The use of the Yeti is pretty typical in the genre post–*Harry and the Hendersons*, right down to the initially scary image quickly dissolving to the Benign Bigfoot incarnation shortly thereafter. Never groundbreaking, "You Ain't Seen Nothin' Yeti" is nevertheless a younger crypto cinema fan's idea of heaven, featuring an intelligent, resourceful heroine who not only believes, but actually encounters the legendary Abominable Snowman.

The Wildman of Kentucky (2008) (Doc)

AKA: *The Wildman of Kentucky, the Mystery of Panther Rock*. Featuring Krill, Gardiner and Clark Spencer. Produced by Reality Entertainment. USA. Color. Stereo. 60 Minutes.

Overview: This documentary details the mysterious happenings one night in Panther Rock, Kentucky, where two hovering lights are photographed on the horizon by a documentary crew which is there searching for the Wildman, a local Bigfoot variation. Music by Freakhouse, a speed metal band, and the non-stop use of video process filters very much makes this a generational divide in terms of approach and content. The speculation and grinding metal both run high, while hard data and relevant proof remain tone deaf. To enliven the visuals, *The Wildman of Kentucky* uses plenty of home-styled CGI to demonstrate Sasquatch striding across farm yards, crouching to eat in the fields, peering into barns, etc.

WLR — Bigfoot Sighting Commercial (2009) (TV)

Starring Kevin Gross. USA. Color. Stereo. 30 Seconds.

Overview: Kevin Gross, star of TV's *Hunting with the Pros*, tracks down Bigfoot to demonstrate the effectiveness of Scent Killer, a spray product designed to mask the smell of hunters from their prey. Gross sprays himself with the product but finds himself pursued by the bipedal cryptid when the creature catches sight of him anyway. Bigfoot then stomps on the spray bottle of Scent Killer that Gross leaves behind, squashing it. The Bigfoot suit was rented from a company located in North Hollywood.

The World's Greatest Hoaxes (1999) (TV)

AKA: *The World's Greatest Hoaxes: Secrets Finally Revealed*. Featuring Nacho Cerdà, Dean Cundey, Lance Henriksen, Jerry Romney, Jeff Meldrum and Stan Winston. Produced by David E. Ballard, Robert Kiviat and David Roehrig. Written by Robert Kiviat. USA. Color. Stereo. 60 Minutes.

Overview: The same network that sensationalized the first-ever airing of an authentic alien autopsy (later revealed to be a hoax) self-righteously turned agents of exposé for this tawdry one-hour debunking of the best current evidence for Bigfoot, UFO, Loch Ness Monster and related phenomena. The Patterson-Gimlin footage is given rough treatment, as is Jerry Romney, who acted in a movie made by the same company — American National Enterprises, Inc.— that later released *Sasquatch, the Legend of Bigfoot* to box office success. Romney denies being the costume wearer in the Patterson-Gimlin film, and clearly resents the implication he's lying. The producers doubt his veracity, however, showing Romney strolling parallel to the camera in a composition similar to the depicted creature in the Patterson-Gimlin film. They insist the gait preferred by both actor and hominid is too similar to ignore; in reality, the resemblance is passing at best and speculative at worst, in that the footage is only shown once and briefly so that no serious analysis is possible. The narrator concludes that Romney must be keeping mum about something that would clear the deck, essentially admitting in the final moments that everything that preceded the conclusion was rank speculation. Featuring lots of talking head cameos by recognizable names in cryptozoology circles and the Hollywood special effects make-up fields, *The World's Greatest Hoaxes* is never less than slickly produced, but its sense of tabloid television and rush to judgment on the flimsy evidence it presents on its own behalf is so over-the-top it is difficult to separate this entry from the alien autopsy footage in terms of believability. But since the same producer of *The World's Greatest Hoaxes* also wrote and produced *Alien Autopsy: Fact or Fiction?* for the Fox Network a few years previously, this is entirely to be expected.

The X Creatures (1999) (TV) (Doc)

Featuring Chris Packham and John Green. UK. Color. Stereo. 30 Minutes.

Overview: BBC-funded television series *The X Creatures* was short-lived but well-produced. Two episodes of this modern-day *In Search Of* redo are noteworthy for Ciné du Sasquatch: "Yetis, Myths and 'Men'" and "Shooting the Bigfoot." The first chronicles the history of mankind's encounters with Yeti. Shot in the Himalayas and featuring some well-staged recreations of famous sightings, "Yetis, Myths and 'Men'" benefits tremendously from the sense of adventure achieved by showing Packham walking the streets of Tibet as a bewildered arrival, stunned by the modern crowding juxtaposed with the ancient way of living. Watching him trek on foot into the Sherpa hinterlands of the Himalayan Mountains and nearly collapsing from exhaustion — still thousands of feet from the heights he will need to scale — while his Sherpa guides all but vanish ahead of him, adds a potent sense of isolation and the unforgiving toll on the human body such a task takes. "Shooting the Bigfoot" features an elderly John Green inviting Packham into his home to watch a high-quality print of the original Patterson-Gimlin 16mm film footage, which Green actually projects for Packham's benefit (rather than simply showing the visiting host a DVD transfer). The resulting quality of the Patterson-Gimlin footage on display is remarkably good, even though it appears the *X Creatures* crew videotaped the projected film from Green's wall. Location photography in the rugged Pacific Northwest is also superb, adding much in the way of production value.

Youthful host Chris Packham adds a pleasant sense of renewed vigor, a young man's keen interest in the material, and a much-needed sense of fresh eyes in terms of objectivity. By limiting both shows to

investigations into the biological possibility of such hominids (versus a focus on the stories surrounding said creatures), he also helps bring a refreshing sense of scientific inquiry to the documentary side of Bigfoot TV programming. Sadly, such clear thinking is absent from too many Sasquatch documentaries. Sadder still, the limited series has not as yet been released on VHS or DVD.

X-Men (1993) ("Repo Man") (TV) (Cameo)

Featuring the voices of Cedric Smith, Cathal J. Dodd, Norm Spencer, Chris Potter, Lenore Zann, Catherine Disher, Harvey Aitken, Melissa Sue Anderson, Barry Flatman, Don Francks, Rebecca Jenkins and Rene Lemieux. Produced by Stan Lee and Scott Thomas. Written by Len Wein. USA. Color. Stereo. 30 Minutes.

Overview: X-Men mutant hero Wolverine is captured by Vindicator and his Alpha Flight team members, the latter of which includes Sasquatch. Vindicator has convinced the otherwise peace-loving Alpha Flight that Wolverine poses a threat to law and order, what with the side-burned hero's recalcitrant ways and rogue nature. But when Vindicator subjects Wolverine to excruciating torture while attempting to discover the secret of Wolverine's Adamantium skeletal powers, Alpha Flight breaks from Vindicator, freeing Wolverine. Sasquatch, actually gifted scientist Dr. Walter Langowski when in human form, and the rest of Alpha Flight systematically defeat the robot guardians who try to prevent their escape from Vindicator's lair. Wolverine takes on Vindicator mano a mano and defeats his nemesis. Properly chastened, the Alpha Flight team vows to allow Wolverine to go in peace and never again seek his assistance nor whereabouts.

* * * * *

The popular Canadian-based super hero group Alpha Flight was a Marvel Comics attempt to create some Great Northern heroes in the tights-and-cape genre. As a former member of the group now gone renegade, Wolverine achieved a sort of mythic status within the ranks of the Alpha Flight members, including Sasquatch. His departure left a massive hole that Alpha Flight has subsequently been pressed to fill, creating an intriguing and tension-filled back story for the loner and his former friends.

As a scientific genius trapped in a Bigfoot's body, Sasquatch is a tragic figure, but one with nobility and self-respect. His calm manner and intellectual distance from matters at hand can and does give way to beastly savagery if and when Sasquatch is aroused. It's no wonder, then, that this popular Alpha Flight character has appeared opposite the Hulk in *The Incredible Hulk* animated series made a few years after this effort. Both offer the classic "man trapped within the beast of his own nature" theme as embodied most famously by Stevenson's *The Strange Case of Dr. Jekyll and Mr. Hyde*. Sasquatch has a smaller, more group-centric role in this *X-Men* adaptation, however; so his appearance here ranks as more cameo than full-fledged star.

The X's (2005) (TV) (Cameo)

Featuring the voices of Patrick Warburton, Wendie Malick, Lynsey Bartilson, Jansen Panettiere, Chris Hardwick, Tom Kane, Stephen Root and Randy Savage. Produced by Monique Beatty, Dave Marshall and Carlos Ramos. Written by Carlos Ramos, Tracy Berna, Dwayne Colbert, Steven Darancette, Evan Gore and Shahrzad Warkentin. Directed by Dave Marshall. USA. Color. Stereo. 30 Minutes.

Overview: Seemingly a model nuclear suburban family, the X family is actually a group of top secret spies that work for S.U.P.E.R.I.O.R., a covert intelligence apparatus of the American government. Their task is to smash and thwart the evil plans of S.N.A.F.U., a loose affiliation of bad guys and monsters hell-bent on wreaking havoc on civilization worldwide. Though the family struggles with all the usual suburban dramas a family of four might encounter, they are also subject to the stresses and comic strains of their day jobs as elite agents.

One of S.N.A.F.U.'s worst terrors is Sasquatch, a half-man, half-beast monstrosity who suffers from a clear sense of inferiority when it comes to humankind. Sasquatch has super powers, such as the ability to send hypnotic signals that induce all animal life he encounters to do his bidding. A hater of *Homo sapiens* for philosophical reasons, Sasquatch desires to lead an uprising against mankind by all the other animal life forms on Earth and banish humans from the planet. The X's fight and defeat Sasquatch, along with other scary members of S.N.A.F.U., always with an eye on the clock so the kids don't miss a soccer practice or band rehearsal.

* * * * *

Clearly inspired by *The Incredibles* and probably designed to capitalize upon it, *The X's* attempts to bring the same sense of 1960s-era James Bond coolness to a similar set-up. Instead of the suburban incognito family being super heroes, however, now they're super spies, complete with all the high-tech gadgets any self-respecting action sleuth would ever need. While it has the graphic look of *The Incredibles* down pat — a sort of Jack Kirby graphic style put into motion — *The X's* misses its inspiration's sense of wonder and excellent storytelling, and fails to offer much in the way of entertainment value.

Sasquatch is voiced by professional wrestler "Macho Man" Randy Savage, which does give the character a certain over-the-top charm. Sasquatch is not unlike some weary World Federation Wrestling reject, offering frequent boasts and promises of pain for his accursed adversaries. It's noteworthy that by this point in the genre, Sasquatch can be easily incorporated into even the most outlandish scenarios — in this case, as a super villain who can speak English and plot world domination — and still maintain the Ciné du Sasquatch rules. For example, Sasquatch is still obsessed with his domain having been despoiled by mankind, the same as he was when first seen in 1912 in *Conquest of the Pole*. Sasquatch is now plotting revenge for his ruined paradise lost. Although played strictly for laughs, Sasquatch maintains that he has been "treated unfairly" by the human species, and therefore longs to lead his animal brethren back to the top of the food chain, with mankind extinct or dying off.

That's a significant reversal of the normal "humans invade the Sasquatch's domain and then flee for their lives as the Bigfoot kills them off" scenario that typifies many Bigfoot movie entries. It helps establish compassion for Bigfoot in *The X's*, as his species has nearly been wiped off the planet because of mankind; it's therefore understandable that the hominid would desire revenge against his oppressors and near annihilators. It seems vengeance is sought not only by humans, but by hominids as well. While this is necessarily buried in the sub-text, it nevertheless is a novel way of inverting an old cliché of the genre and revitalizing it in the process.

El Yeti (1970)

Written by Francisco Ibáñez. Directed by Rafael Vara. Spain. Color. Mono. 10 Minutes.

Overview: Spanish comic book writer Francisco Ibáñez tries his hand at animation collaboration by adapting his own popular *El Yeti* comic book series into a short film. A beloved superstar of the comic format in Spain, he is best known for his *Mortadelo y Filemón* series (known in Germany as *Clever & Smart*), which details the bumbling exploits of two loveable dimwits stumbling into one misadventure after another. While *El Yeti* was a popular creation, this short

animated effort went undistributed beyond its native Spanish television airings and unseen outside of a handful of international film festivals. It remains unavailable for viewing.

Yeti: A Love Story (2006)

Starring Rachel Berliner, Laura Glascott, Adam Malamut, Joe Mande, Jim Martin, Loren Mash, David Paige, Noah Wolf, Adam Balivet, Konrad Brattke, Adam Deyoe, Eric Kench, Tim Faucher, Eric Gosselin, Sol Cattus Prifto and James Lesage. Produced by Adam Deyoe and Eric Gosselin. Written by Adam Deyoe, Eric Gosselin, Jim Martin and Moses Roth. Directed by Adam Deyoe and Eric Gosselin. USA. Color. Stereo. 80 Minutes.

Overview: Five bored and extremely cynical college students decide to take a trek into the wilderness for some recreation. Along the way they meet several bizarre locals in the small town in which they stop for provisions — beer, rolling papers and gas. When one of the students goes into the woods at night to get firewood after setting up camp, he is shot to death by an overeager Bigfoot hunter. His four remaining friends notice the next morning that their friend has gone missing, but decide to go fishing rather than bothering to look for him.

One of the students meets an eccentric punk girl who brings him back to her crash pad for rough sex. Her home turns out to be the

Cover art for the DVD release by Troma Studios for *Yeti: A Love Story*.

headquarters of a secretive Yeti-worshipping cult who sacrifice males to be sodomized by a gay Abominable Snowman as part of their dark festival of cryptid celebration. Realizing he is the next intended victim, the sex-depleted student attempts to flee but is held prisoner by the Yeti cult.

During this time, another of the male college students is abducted by the sexually ravenous Yeti. Held in the woods and forced to give the Yeti oral sex, the young man realizes that he's been gay all along and comes out of his self-repressed closet of both homosexuality and bestiality. He willingly fellates his new bipedal lover and gratefully encourages the Yeti to mount him, experiencing an ecstasy he has never before known. He vows to stay with his new Abominable Snowlover no matter how different their worlds.

Meanwhile, one of the female students learns, after visiting a church, that she has been chosen to be the divine huntress who must slay the Yeti and disband the debased cult of hominid-worshipping sodomites. After the priest gives her a magic crossbow and arrows, he dismisses her, informing her she must complete her task if she wishes to see her friends remain unharmed. Reluctant, but realizing she has been called to perform a true "mission from God," she seeks out the Yeti cult to destroy them.

A massive confrontation occurs the night the captive college student is bound to an altar in preparation for sexual sacrifice to the Yeti. As all hell breaks loose, cult members fight the college students for all-out survival. The cultists, as well as the Yeti, perish in the flames, and the mighty female slayer of the creature limps away, no longer afraid of her destiny as a crypto-huntress.

* * * * *

Perhaps the single most bizarre entry in the entire genre of Ciné du Sasquatch, *Yeti: A Love Story* is nearly beyond words in terms of critique and deranged, off-kilter comic sensibility. Fans of so-called Queer Cinema will definitely be more apt to find the blackly funny atrocities cataloged throughout its brief running time more to their liking than the average fan of straightlaced Bigfoot film fare. That's because the creators of this film clearly see the mythos underlying the Savage Sasquatch screen incarnation through such a sexually-skewed lens it's difficult to separate where fantasy, fetish and the merely fantastic begin or end.

This is not to say *Yeti: A Love Story* is without merit. In fact, besides being one of the most outré examples of Bigfoot filmmaking ever, it is also genuinely entertaining for the more liberal-minded viewer. Picture early John Waters circa *Pink Flamingos* as if he were directing a Sasquatch movie and you'll be at least in the same white trash trailer park as the filmmakers' scatologically-obsessed effort. And though it doesn't graphically depict any of its actors consuming canine feces, it still leaves nothing to the imagination in showing one of the male leads going down on the groaning Yeti, among other debauchery. Though it's comically rendered, complete with massive cryptid penis (an obvious rubbery dildo), there are definitely many Ciné du Sasquatch purists who will take offense at the non-stop satire of such subjects as small-town hypocrisy, religiously-obsessed types, sexual deviants, redneck hunters and the like. If you voted Republican the last time you cast your ballot, odds are you will find *Yeti: A Love Story* impossibly depraved.

Of course, it's clear that's precisely the audience the directors intend to offend. But while they save their best barbs for the conservative crowd, they also skewer the wacky cult members, the free-loving

Adam (Adam Malamut) has a gay bestial love affair in *Yeti: A Love Story*.

women who inhabit it, and modern life in America in general. In short, the film is an equal opportunity offender, which gives it a unique power to cause more tolerant audiences to appreciate its strange sensibility. Never played as anything more than a self-parodying camp effort, *Yeti: A Love Story* nevertheless achieves a genuine sense of style and consistent laughs. Rather than try to hide its deficiencies (it was shot in only five days, which is remarkable given the amount of camera set-ups and action), it gloriously holds them up for self-mockery. It's as if the filmmakers realized they had no possible chance of making a genuinely professional movie from the start and so decided to let the viewer in on the joke from the opening moments.

In most cases this results in unwatchably tedious moviemaking. And *Yeti: A Love Story* does have its stretches of dullness and jokes which simply fall flat. But the directors seem intent on simply tossing so much at the viewer that even if a joke doesn't work here and there, a formula is established wherein a few jokes down the line one *will* work, to unexpectedly comic effect. This proves to be an effective strategy and is why the film has garnered such a cult following in the brief years since its release. Considering the Yeti costume is flagrant in its badness (not unlike much of the rest of the film's non-production values), complete with gaping eye-holes in the mask, with the actor's face plainly visible beneath, surely *Yeti: A Love Story* must have *something* working beneath the obvious drawbacks to engender such a favorable cult reaction (at least, that is, among some fans).

The acting is demonstrably amateurish. Again, however, this doesn't matter; the script and deadpan delivery are reminiscent of Paul Morrissey directing amateurs to equal effect circa Warhol's *Bad* and *Trash*. Outlandish and over-the-top — and deliberately so — the thespians range from stilted to stupefying; but this works in the context of the larger picture as a whole. It is clear that the directors have at least orchestrated the non-talent on display to shoot for and largely achieve a shared consistent level of "badness" in their acting styles. This is again like John Waters and Paul Morrissey — deliberately campy direction rather than merely misdirected.

There is a playfulness on display that redeems the film at nearly every turn. From the hilarious sequence in which an exhibitionist serial killer confronts the two female campers (in the bathroom of the Sheriff's office no less!) and refuses to die even as the women fight back, stabbing, slashing and even pulling his intestines out, *Yeti: A Love Story* knows itself and its audience. To its credit, it delivers the laughs. Scathingly and scatologically satirical, this is one funny Bigfoot film.

Yeti! A Tale of the Brothers Krong (2005)

Starring Mike Weatherford, Aaron Weatherford and Steve Weatherford. Produced and Written by Mike Weatherford and W. Dave Keith. Directed by W. Dave Keith. USA. Color. Video. Stereo. 55 Minutes.

Overview: As infants, the Brothers Krong—Caspian and Brian— were given to a childless couple in the United States by a mysterious hooded Sherpa monk from the Himalayas. Left only with the message to instruct the two boys in the art of swordplay, and two ancient swords with which to practice their craft, the pair grew up never knowing any details of their true background.

As young adults, the Brothers Krong open a paranormal investigation agency called U.P.O.—the Unexplainable Paranormality Office. Funded by a secretive millionaire with an unconvincing British accent, the pair takes whatever strange paying case crosses their desktops. Their latest mission: find a famous cryptozoologist who has disappeared while attempting to locate the legendary Abominable Snowman of the Himalayas. The brothers are soon on the job in the mountains, only to encounter the very same Sherpa monk who dropped them off as babies. He is the last person to have seen the missing cryptozoologist. Mystery upon mystery unfolds as the Brothers Krong encounter the roaring Yeti themselves, with only their mighty swords to protect them from the voracious monster. Can they remove the medallion it wears around its white furry neck before the cryptid destroys the duo?

* * * * *

For every well-meaning no-budget Yeti feature there are the earnest if misguided talents behind the camera who strive to do the proverbial "best job they can" within limitations that even Roger Corman would find challenging. *Yeti! A Tale of the Brothers Krong* is no exception. On the one hand, the filmmakers are clearly in love with Ciné du Sasquatch, to the extent they previously dabbled in a Bigfoot short video prior to making this, their magnum non-opus. And yet(i) on the other hand, the viewer is left to sort through the failed good intentions and substandard results of the effort itself, eager to see the young filmmakers succeed while desperately trying to withhold too critical a judgment because, after all, everyone starts somewhere in their careers. Such is the case with *Yeti! A Tale of the Brothers Krong*, which features leaden, deliberately campy performances mixed with amateurish production values and a meandering, often pointless storyline.

Yeti! A Tale of the Brothers Krong is not without a handful of laughs. The basic premise is so ridiculous and unpretentiously developed— a sort of mutant hybrid of *The Adventures of Bob and Doug McKenzie* and *Dude, Where's My Cryptid?*— the movie does have intermittent charm. Between the lackluster, rotund Caspian, who talks in a monotone dribble, and his more well-adjusted but equally braindead brother Brian, there is a comic energy that occasionally rewards the patient viewer with low-range laughs. But one must get through a lot of cheese to taste the payoffs, and all too often the creators of *Yeti! A Tale of the Brothers Krong* stretch their 55 minutes into something every bit as padded as their hilariously and deliberately inept Yeti costume (which the director has admitted in interviews was merely an Easter bunny rental costume with store-bought Yeti mask added). Such is the lot of such hit-and-miss fare; and in this instance, the misses are far more common.

The effort was shot in Lawrence, Kansas, which in itself is telling. Rather than try to fake any Himalayan locations, the director and cast wisely decided to use existing Kansas locales "as is" and let the viewer in on the joke. Likewise, some roles are portrayed by actors far too young for their parts without explanation or rationale (for example, the hooded monk who left the Brothers Krong as infants Stateside and then reappears 20 years later in the plot looks 5 years younger than the two protagonists!) with the filmmakers playing the obvious age discrepancy for laughs. This only works occasionally, however, as more often than not one is simply reminded that one is watching an expanded home video that feels more like a junior college Monty Python skit than an actual feature film. Unless the viewer enjoys impoverished filmmaking on a Top Ramen noodles budget, *Yeti! A Tale of the Brothers Krong* is a tale for Ciné du Sasquatch completists only.

Yeti: Curse of the Snow Demon (2008) (TV)

Starring Carly Pope, Marc Menard, Adam O'Byrne, Ed Marinaro, Ona Grauer, Crystal Lowe, Brandon Jay McLaren, Elfina Luk, Kris Pope, Christian Tessier, Peter DeLuise, Taras Kostyuk, Josh Emerson and Aaron Pearl. Produced by Martin J. Barab, Aaron Barnett, Dana Dubovsky, Eric Gozlan, Michael Greenfield, Daniel Grodnik, Richard Iott, Mark L. Lester and Wendy Kay Moore. Written by Rafael Jordan. Directed by Paul Ziller. USA. Color. Stereo. 87 Minutes.

Overview: When an American college football team on its way to an international exhibition good will game aboard a jet crashes in the Himalayan Mountains, the handful of survivors must regroup and try to make the best of their situation. The dead bodies from the fuselage are hauled outside and a makeshift shelter is created from the plane's hull. Using blankets, the survivors keep the snowstorm raging outside at bay, but their chances of being rescued in a blizzard are nonexistent unless they can make direct radio contact.

Two of the survivors trek into the mountain to find the whereabouts of the jet's emergency radio transponder. They successfully locate the radio but accidentally stumble into a Yeti's cavernous home on their return to the other survivors. One escapes but the other athlete is devoured alive by the ravenous Abominable Snowman. Meanwhile, a conflict erupts between those who believe that a Yeti is stealing the dead bodies lining the perimeter of their camp (which go missing during the night) and those (the majority) who believe that the witnesses are merely hysterical.

However, a worse problem arises: After several days in the wilderness with nothing to eat, starvation has become a real issue for survival. The group further splinters over the moral choice clearly before them: devour the dead bodies or perish from hunger. They vote to wait another day and then eat the bodies if no sign of rescue is apparent. The day passes and the group indulges. One of the women present who cannot eat of her own kind's flesh sabotages the scheme before another feeding can take place by burning the bodies before anyone can stop her. Alas, the smell of human barbeque lures the hungry Yeti to attack and take living victims from the jet fuselage shelter when there are no more convenient human bodies for it to feast upon.

The surviving humans make a stand and then race for the bottom of the mountain, realizing that if they stay and weaken further, the Yeti will feed upon them, one by one, until all succumb. They face a grueling ordeal, however, as the Yeti sets upon them and picks them off at blind passes and snowy egresses that litter the frozen icescape. Eventually the survivors are forced to make a hand-to-claw stand against the attacking creature, which results in the Yeti and its mate being buried alive in their own shared lair. Though barely alive, the scattered survivors are rescued.

* * * * *

The Syfy Channel (or Sci Fi Channel as it was still known when this effort was first shown) has aired some regrettably lame efforts in the years since its inception, but *Yeti: Curse of the Snow Demon* ranks right alongside *Giant Shark vs. Mega Octopus* for sheer banality of premise, execution, and incompetence. Whatever hopes it has of achieving anything worthwhile in its own genre are obliterated within moments by the banality of the crash itself. While turbulence on the order of Hurricane Katrina devastates the outside of the obviously CGI jet airplane and causes its wings and nose to dip with gut-wrenching force, inside we are shown a few nervous passengers watching a cup of coffee slowly slide off a serving cart! This lack of apparent concern for consistency, internal logic, or basic continuity on the part of the creative team buries *Yeti: Curse of the Snow Demon* so deeply beneath the Tibetan snows that it may take eons for it to be rediscovered even by students of the Bigfoot film genre.

There are moments of Ed Wood–worthy hilarity throughout *Yeti: Curse of the Snow Demon* that may cause the astute viewer to ponder if this is unintentionally bad, or being exaggerated in its badness for camp effect. It is a distinct possibility, given how often the movie misfires, that the team responsible for it decided to play it more for laughs than gasps; but if so, there is no clear-cut dividing line between the absurd and the merely boring to help confirm such speculation. In fact, it tends to become luridly bad without warning, and then veer back onto the straight and narrow path of mediocrity between these hysterical breakdowns of veracity. This jagged feel makes the ensuing badness that much more laughable, as the audience is left wondering how much less intelligent the creators can deem them to be before the next ridiculous set piece unfolds.

The Yetis are particularly egregious and deserving of much of the wrath reviewers have heaped upon them. It is not the costume design per se, but the manner in which the director has resorted to visualizing the hominid's locomotion. For built into the premise behind *Yeti: Curse of the Snow Demon* is the notion that these beasts are fantastic leapers, super-human in their ability to scamper and bound faster than the eye can detect as they leap upon the unsuspecting human crash survivors. This could have been quite menacing if the director had devised a frightening off-screen approach in which the survivors are suddenly snatched away into the darkness from above; instead, the creative team behind this opus resorts to staggeringly bad CGI special effect shots of the creature leaping high as a three-story building and covering half a football field with each mighty pounce. These shots are so depressingly bad that they make one seriously question the impact of the entire digital special effects revolution. The mania for including special effects that are badly deployed but are retained because they suggest money was spent on the production runs rampant through *Yeti: Curse of the Snow Devil*. It would have been much more to the film's benefit had the producers demonstrated the courage to eliminate these completely unnecessary shots and allow the audience to imagine the process, even if this meant asking the audience to take a "leap of faith" with them.

Alas, it appears as if the actor wearing the costume often had difficulty merely walking in the snow drifts where the film was shot (to its credit, the movie is quite convincing in terms of location photography). In many shots it is clear the editors were cutting around the costumed cryptid, who is struggling to lift one hairy leg after another as he lumbers from one tree to the next. This lack of any convincing footage of the Yeti walking may have been a rationale for the producers to have computer technicians generate additional shots of the creatures leaping through the sky. This speculation is borne out by the drastic difference between the costumed Yeti and the CGI-visualized Yeti. The latter tends to resemble a video game avatar that has been layered atop a background plate shot on location. But to place undue emphasis upon the bad digital effects when so much else goes awry with *Yeti: Curse of the Snow Demon* misses the point; the entirety of the production itself shares blame across a multitude of cast, crew, and creators.

The plane crash that leads to the survivor's dilemma has been used before in the Ciné du Sasquatch genre (in *Sasquatch*, aka *The Untold*). Granted, it is expanded here to encompass a majority of the film rather than *Sasquatch*'s brief establishment of the premise, in which it was but a small portion of the set-up. *Sasquatch*, however, reveals the value of restraint by only showing glimpses of the ordeal of a Yeti versus human siege. While sieges have been a venerable staple in the genre, *Yeti: Curse of the Snow Demon* manages to reduce the hominid to second banana, so to speak. It misfires by centering the conflict of the second act on whether or not the surviving humans should enact a Donner Party feast and feed on the frozen corpses. While this might have made for an interesting if disquieting conflict in a scene or two, the filmmakers' insistence on shifting the narrative energy onto this sub-plot for long stretches of precious running time dooms *Yeti: Curse of the Snow Demon* from the second act forward.

The main protagonist's laugh-inducing dilemma — to win the Big Game of Life for his dying coach, à la the Gipper, by leading the remaining football team to safety — is about as ludicrous as the leaping snow monsters, the latter of which may or may not be an allusion to the Bionic Bigfoot of *The Six Million Dollar Man* (although it more accurately resembles the super-leaping, jaw-dropping ability of the Bigfoot from the Brothers Krofft's *Bigfoot and Wildboy*). The level of self-parody is so elevated during most of *Yeti: Curse of the Snow Demon*'s three acts that it's difficult to tell when the filmmakers genuinely wish to play off a moment for humor and when they simply didn't realize they were playing it so straight-faced that inevitable guffaws were sure to follow. In time, a minor camp following for lovers of bad movies is sure to develop for this film.

Yeti: Giant of the 20th Century (1977)

AKA: *Big Foot*; *Giant of the 20th Century*; *Ice Man*; *Yeti — il gigante del 20 secolo*. Starring Antonella Interlenghi, Mimmo Craig, Jim Sullivan, Tony Kendall and John Stacy. Produced by Wolfranco Coccia, Mario di Nardo, Gianfranco Parolini and Nicolò Pomilia. Written and Directed by Gianfranco Parolini. Italy. Color. Mono.118 Minutes.

Overview: Hunnicutt, a shopping mall tycoon, finances an expedition to secure a gigantic Yeti found frozen in a huge chunk of glacial ice. Under the watchful eyes of his hired scientist, Professor Wasserman, the towering cryptid is defrosted, loaded onto a huge support structure, and hoisted into the clouds via helicopter. Wasserman believes that lifting the Yeti airborne will revive the creature. As the helicopter takes it high into the skies, the Yeti awakens. But it panics, forcing the Professor and his pilot to land amid a crowd of spectators.

Enraged, the Yeti bursts free of its confines and scoops up Wasserman's two grandchildren — beautiful maiden Jane and her mute brother Herbie. Fleeing into the forest, the Yeti quickly falls in love with the enchanting Jane, offering the hungry siblings a meal of fish it catches for them from a nearby river. Jane and Herbie realize that although this hominid towers hundreds of feet above them, it is nonetheless not a monster but a fellow sentient being.

Alas, Hunnicutt will have nothing less than the Yeti at the grand opening of his latest supermall in Toronto, Canada; he ruthlessly hunts the roaming cryptid until it is once again captured. This time Hunnicutt flies the Yeti to Canada and lands it amidst a huge throng of screaming shoppers eager to see the media-hyped creature first-hand. Unwise photographers flash their cameras at the stunned Yeti until it breaks free of its cage, enraged. This time the creature refuses to spare human lives, rampaging through the streets of Toronto until it accidentally rips the cables suspending the elevator in which Jane hides. This causes Jane to plunge to her apparent death; but at the last second the Yeti grabs her in his massive paw and strolls through the skyscraper-lined boulevards, roaring at the puny humans who scatter in terror at its oversized feet.

Jane helps the Yeti escape certain death at the hands of the city's police force by guiding him into an enclosed baseball stadium. Alas, unbeknownst to Jane, her boyfriend Cliff is actually a double agent for one of Hunnicutt's business rivals. Cliff arranges for the murder of Professor Wasserman and frames the Yeti as the culprit. Worse, Cliff orders his hit men to destroy the creature so that Hunnicutt cannot re-capture it and profit from it. The Yeti falls into a semi-comatose state, his energies depleted from his recent efforts. Unable to find the cryptid, despite their best efforts, the hired hands abduct Herbie

The influence of *King Kong* via an oversized, mechanical ape hand is evident in *Yeti: Giant of the 20th Century.*

as a hostage, only to awaken the slumbering Yeti, who gives chase. After cornering Cliff and his henchmen, the Yeti crushes them to death in a fit of fury and frees Cliff.

The police surround Jane, Herbie and the Yeti, intent on destroying the bewildered Abominable Snowman. Jane convinces them the Yeti saved the life of her and her brother and deserves a chance to live free in the wilds. Touched, the police lower their weapons and allow the Giant of the 20th Century to wander into the forests, hopefully to live out the remainder of its life in peace.

* * * * *

Relentlessly cheesy, utterly predictable and mesmerizingly awful, *Yeti: Giant of the 20th Century* (which was designed to capitalize upon Dino De Laurentiis' *King Kong* remake of 1976) is truly one of the oddest entries in the already bizarre canon of Abominable Snowman

The Yeti (Mimmo Craig) strides through the streets of Toronto during *Yeti: Giant of the 20th Century*. This lobby card faithfully captures the film's atrocious matte work.

movies. While earlier, successful entries on the Yeti side of Ciné du Sasquatch have emphasized the cryptid's enormous stature (which actually goes against a majority of the actual reported sightings, wherein the Yeti is usually described as no taller than an average human), *Yeti: Giant of the 20th Century* goes so far as to suggest it is entirely logical to suppose there once roamed in prehistoric times a hominid as tall as a Saturn 5 rocket on its launch pad!

Yeti: Giant of the 20th Century as Ciné du Sasquatch actually demonstrates many of the genre's influences and, in turn, its influence on non-genre but closely related efforts, such as *King Kong*. For example, the earliest known cryptid film, *The Conquest of the Pole*, directed by Georges Méliès in 1912, features a towering Abominable Snowman almost the same size as the Yeti depicted in this Italian production. And not unlike in the original *King Kong*, the storyline has a gigantic cryptid falling for a beautiful woman. Interestingly, *Yeti: Giant of the 20th Century* goes even further in revealing a major literary influence upon Ciné du Sasquatch as well, as the woman Yeti falls in love with is named Jane. This harkens back to Edgar Rice Burrough's *Tarzan*, which, of course, had the simian-raised Lord Greystoke enamored of the aristocratic Jane Porter. Further revealing its precedents, *Yeti: Giant of the 20th Century* offers a backstory for the mute brother Herbie in which he was rescued from a plane wreck that killed his parents, which is the same set-up that saw Tarzan raised by the apes. Between being influenced by *King Kong* and *Tarzan* both, and reflecting the influence Ciné du Sasquatch has had upon Killer Gorilla and Giant Ape movies, *Yeti: Giant of the 20th Century* is a mutant entry of truly colossal proportions.

Much scorn greeted this film upon its initial release, and for deserved reasons: The story is an obvious rip-off of *King Kong*; the acting and directing are Ed Wood–ian in terms of insipidness; and the special effects are so variable that the creature's true scale is never fully established nor maintained — skyscraper-sized at one point, then much much smaller in another sequence. Still, in the years since its release many have come to see *Yeti: Giant of the 20th Century* in the same light as the Quentin Tarantino re-released *The Mighty Peking Man* (aka *Goliathon*) — that is, a campfest of the "tallest" order. In this light, of course, there is not much further need of commentary as an entry in Ciné du Sasquatch, save to note it fulfills expectations as both a "monstrous" parody of the genre and a distillation of every cliché in the genre in one unexpectedly (though not always) amusing effort.

The titular Yeti (played by Mimmo Craig, who also appeared in films such as Zeffirelli's *Jesus of Nazareth* and the Rod Steiger–starring Mussolini biopic *The Last 4 Days*) is often ridiculed by Sasquatch film fans for the creature make-up, which features (as at least one unkind reviewer has noted) "the largest mullet in film history"— an apt description of the ill-fitting wig worn by Craig in lieu of a prosthetic mask. Given the ridiculousness of the costume (which includes a fur thong!), and that he's reduced to screaming at the camera in close-up for most of his screen time, one is left feeling the need to spare Craig from further critical humiliation. Writer and director "Frank Kramer" (an Anglo pseudonym for Italian filmmaker Gianfranco Parolini) was a proficient director of Spaghetti Westerns, including well-regarded entries such as *Sabata, Adios Sabata,* and *Return of Sabata,* as well as *A Bullet from God* (aka *God's Gun*) and *The Three Fantastic Supermen.* The influence is obvious in *Yeti: Giant of the 20th Century* in terms of pacing and musical score. Never successful throughout and yet occasionally oddly enchanting as bad filmmaking worthy of at least one jaundiced viewing, *Yeti: Giant of the 20th Century* is an interesting mess that endears it to those who appreciate its bad taste qualities. Antonella Interlenghi, as Jane, is truly a beautiful if limited actress, which adds a dimension of easy watchability to the proceedings. She also acquitted herself well in the cult favorite *City*

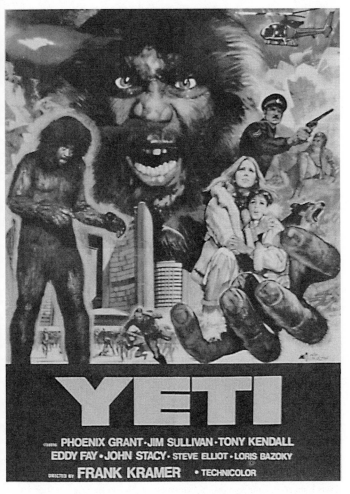

Yeti: Giant of the 20th Century was a blatant attempt to capitalize on the success of *King Kong* (1976) and the Bigfoot movie trend of that era. This is the Turkish theatrical release poster.

of the Walking Dead, directed by Lucio Fulci, but *Yeti: Giant of the 20th Century* affords her the most screen time of her career, and Parolini and cinematographer Sandro Mancori light her with Garbo-like attention to detail, clearly recognizing her superior photogenic quality. And one would be remiss if the Yetians, who sing a disco-tinged theme song, weren't mentioned for the unintentional laughs they provide. Not since the theme song for Toho's *The Green Slime* has a "rockin' poppin'" soundtrack for a science fiction movie featured such a ludicrously catchy ballad.

Still, there are long stretches of tedium and ridiculousness which even the most tolerant viewer will find excruciating to endure. As a "so bad it's good" rental, *Yeti: Giant of the 20th Century* is a time capsule look at how such paella-styled (as in every available ingredient tossed into one simmering stew) concoctions once ruled the low-budget end of internationally-produced efforts. As a bona fide example of Ciné du Sasquatch, however, it merely "apes" the themes and situations of countless efforts both before and after its production.

Yeti in the City (2007)

Starring Matt Bearden, Ishaq Clayton, Courtney Davis, Lee Eddy, Dan Eggleston, Chris Fairbanks, Beth Gosnell, John Merriman, Ray Prewitt, Jimmie Roulette and Alisa Sikelianos. Produced by Courtney Davis and T'Chaka Sikelianos. Written and Directed by T'Chaka Sikelianos. USA. Color. Stereo. 90 Minutes.

Overview: After being lost to his Yeti parents during a migration by the cryptid family higher into the Himalayan Mountains to avoid human encroachment, a baby Yeti grows up and decides, upon reaching maturity, to venture into the heart of the city to see what he can see of the wide wicked world. He winds up in a fantastic cityscape that is hellishly urban and at the same time surrealistically populated by both humans and talking animals. As he wanders about, the Yeti experiences a kaleidoscope of sights and sounds beyond his imagination. Street poets speak beatifically of their alienation and desperation from being caught in a steel rat trap of mirror-shiny towers. Lowlife humans and animals mix in off-color joints to play high-stakes poker. Wherever the Yeti roams he sees freedom, and how those experiencing it must pay a price for their enlightenment. Likewise, he sees all forms of self-enslavement caused by a willing ignorance of their deeper spiritual natures which they debase with easy worldly distractions. But can an innocent Yeti mix with the dregs of human and animal society and remain untainted by association?

* * * * *

Some folks who watch *Yeti in the City* will be put off by what they would doubtless label the filmmakers' "pretentiousness" of filtering this often charming, definitely unique Ciné du Sasquatch entry through a very egocentric, first-person point of view and an Eastern philosophical prism. Critics in this camp will cite the extended opening in which the director focuses solely on himself showering naked, meditating (clothed), and his living arrangement in a van behind a dive bar mostly frequented by blacks (the director admits he is the child of a mixed race marriage, which offers him the ability to blend in to various cultures without causing much notice). This rather mundane if embarrassing information, delivered as it is (without warning and out of context to the rest of what follows) feels like an afterthought on the part of the filmmaker to somehow put the disjointed narrative of *Yeti in the City* into some coherent pattern if thought Eastern of mystical. It doesn't work intellectually, but there's no doubt it does succeed in invoking a kind of playful "anything goes" sensibility.

The film is continuously deconstructing itself, threatening to derail the impatient viewer with so many false starts and stops before it kick-starts into gear. Eventually, however, the story settles down and is doled out in narrative heaps by a wizened sock puppet who speaks directly to the camera. The surrealistic impact of the sudden introduction of a sock puppet does little to prepare one for the coming shock of the metropolis into which the wandering Yeti stumbles. The actors who portray the animal characters wear normal human business suits and related attire, but their heads are oversized felt puppet masks with life-like animal fur and moveable mouth appendages for when they speak dialogue. Shot almost entirely against green screen, and matted atop moving video backgrounds, these segments actually stand out as some of the most inspired moments of the nonsensical allegory. The *H.R. Puf'n'Stuf* sensibility is rampant, even if Jim Henson's Muppets are not far around the bend either. The quality of the puppetry is rank amateur at times, but there is a consistency about the puppet head designs and low-budget execution that works quite well. It creates the schizophrenic feel that one finds in Henson's Hollywood fare, such as *Labyrinth* and *The Dark Crystal*, in which puppets and humans are intermixed without remark or special accent. It's never that successful, of course, but it is audacious.

Equally wild in the Bigfoot genre is *Yeti in the City*'s ability to shift from first-person narrative to animated cartoon to spoken word polemic to animal cops on the prowl to.... Even the film's harshest critics will have to concede that *Yeti in the City* is anything but predictable. Lacking the usual Bigfoot genre dynamics (an isolated group of humans fighting to survive, a bloodthirsty Bigfoot on the rampage, etc.), the film is certainly atypical of the recent trend in Ciné du Sasquatch to vilify the beast and reduce it to a simplistic attack machine.

It does require a Zen-like ability to allow long passages to pass that lack coherent meaning, and accept the subsequent sucker-punch from an amusing line of dialogue or preposterous set-up that reminds the viewer he or she is watching a genuine Bigfoot movie after all, however abstract and atypical. For such patient viewers, *Yeti in the City* is not without its gentle rewards. It is unconventional for sure, but like *The Long Journey Home: A Bigfoot Story*, it attempts to remold the clichéd genre scenario by infusing its own sensibility with an almost painful personal awareness on the part of the filmmaker. It is not a Ciné du Sasquatch trendsetter, to be sure; rather, it is like a Bigfoot version of *El Topo*, to be made of what you will.

Yeti, the Cry of the Snow Man (2000) (TV)

AKA: *Yeti, le cri de l'homme des neiges*. Starring Nar Banhadur, Pasang Chilime and Charles Maquignon. Written by Nathalie Auffret and Silvan Boris Schmid. Directed by Jérôme-Cecil Auffret. France. Color. Stereo. 63 Minutes.

Overview: This little-seen French TV movie was partially filmed in Nepal for added authenticity. It apparently aired in France and was quickly shelved thereafter. The film has not been released in America in any format and was unavailable for review.

Yeti Vengeance (2004)

Starring Suzanne Wallace Whayne, Barry G. Thomas, Dr. Frank Bettag, Todd Fjelsted, Anthony Giangrande, Damon Packard and John Sanderford. Produced by Ben Daughtrey and Suzanne Wallace Whayne. Written by Ben Daughtrey and George Maranville. Directed by George Maranville. USA. Color. Stereo. 20 Minutes.

Overview: Sleaze film producer Artie Novak finds himself in a pickle when his leading lady Casey (on and off-screen) quits his latest schlock effort, *Yeti Vengeance*, on the final day of shooting. The entire production grinds to a halt as Casey auditions for other projects while

Artie alienates his young college film school student directing protégé by forcing the director to wear the Bigfoot suit for the movie's final scenes. Allergic to the creature costume and fed up with Artie's indifference, the director quits, storming off the set in his underwear. Later, after a series of rejections in the tough world of Hollywood, Casey returns to the folds of Artie Novak Productions in order to finish the terror-filled finale of *Yeti Vengeance*, which involves her having to outwit a pursuing cryptid menace one dark night outside a desolate country shack. The film wraps on time and on budget as Artie and Casey kiss and make up.

* * * * *

As a mood piece and comedic example of film-within-a-film moviemaking, *Yeti Vengeance* is a well-crafted if occasionally cloying attempt at making an exploitation Bigfoot film actually watchable while at the same time allowing the audience to laugh off the ridiculous nature of the enterprise itself. As loving homage to all things Roger Corman by way of Harry Hovak, *Yeti Vengeance* is a successful combination of the type of behind-the-scenes trials and tribulations one endures on a low-budget production, and (less successfully) a romance between a man who loves to make money by making movies and his leading lady and lover who has grown comfortable (too comfortable?) as his starlet wife. As a directorial example, it's a good showcase, showing a love for the exploitation filmmaking world which it so cleverly captures.

Casting helps tremendously. The leads are a convincing age for their roles, which requires the two to understand that their sunset years will soon be upon them, and so had best enjoy what they have right now in front of them. Also noteworthy is cult filmmaker and actor Damon Packard, who plays the seedy cameraman who quickly takes over directing the picture when the first director (a spitting image of Peter Bogdonavich during his Corman days as director, editor, and actor) walks off the picture with a day's footage still needed to wrap the flick. Packard's "Fred" the cameraman is a hilarious take on the sleeping-on-the-job employee who only awakens during the rushes to see the close-up footage of the stand-in's breasts being fondled by the monster's claws. Given how effortlessly it all unfolds, and the high quality of production on display, *Yeti Vengeance* is a fun ode to the rapidly vanishing days of the lingering indie studios who once could afford to churn 'em out with regularity. Because such entities are a dying breed, it gives the proceedings a tone of elegy that is unexpectedly good.

Though nearly impossible to see, *Yeti Vengeance* is definitely worthwhile viewing for fans of the Bigfoot genre, especially because the film-within-a-film being created by the hardworking crew — *Yeti Vengeance*, the fictitious B-movie itself — so deftly skewers all that is so dreadful about so many entries in Ciné du Sasquatch. From the deliberately-evoked bad acting to the ludicrous Bigfoot costume, the movie they are all struggling to finish is as accurate a satire of bad Bigfoot filmmaking as you're likely to encounter. The short *Yeti Vengeance* is well-paced, has good production values, many good laughs, and plays like a Sasquatch version of Truffaut's *Day for Night*. Quite a oddity in the genre, all in all.

Yolanda (1981)

Starring Michelle Joyce. Produced, Written and Directed by George Kuchar. USA. Color. Stereo. 22 Minutes.

Overview: Experimental filmmaker George Kuchar's vast output of work is truly staggering in its complexity and wide range of themes and characters. In *Yolanda* he explores the mental breakdown of a reclusive woman named Yolanda, mostly from within the dark, depressing confines of her domestic abode. Yolanda's growing detachment from reality is reflected in her obsession with a 12-foot-tall hominid with amazingly huge feet that will swoop down and rescue her from her coming mental collapse. But based upon the disintegration we witness in just over 20 minutes, it is doubtful Yolanda could ever be rescued mentally, even by a Bigfoot in shining armor.

* * * * *

Told in a distracted, visually adrift manner that favors formalism over narrative content, "Yolanda" is about the most outré example in Ciné du Sasquatch filmic history in terms of mystifying intent on the part of the filmmaker versus his artistic stature and recognition. Kuchar is still regarded by such disciples as John Waters as an independent artiste without compromise, and indeed, as Kuchar states in the biopic documentary about him and his brother, *It Came from Kuchar*, they consider the very act of seeking profit from their passion unholy. Little wonder then that *Yolanda* plays as a quasi-real documentary look at the last moments of sanity for an already questionable mind. Apart from film clips playing on the television set in Yolanda's dreary home that show older simian films (perhaps offering the hallucinating Yolanda a well-spring source for her demented Bigfoot fantasies), there is no hominid depiction on the part of Kuchar, who is evidently not interested in exploring the concept of Bigfoot beyond its metaphysical (and in this case, metasexual) content. Not for most viewers, *Yolanda* may be enjoyed by a hardcore few dedicated to independent film, Warhol devotees, and punk cinema lovers. It's very strangeness is it's curse and redemption — *if* the viewer is in a forgiving mood.

Zoo Robbery (1973)

Starring Paul Gyngell, Denise Gyngell, Karen Lucas, Ronald Adam, Luke Batchelor, Walter McKone and Eileen Helsby. Produced by John Black, Edward Dorian and Matt McCarthy. Written and Directed by John Black and Matt McCarthy. UK. Color. Mono. 64 Minutes.

Overview: A group of childhood friends play cops and robbers daily on a barge that routinely makes it way up and down the Thames River under the tolerant eye of the Skipper. But when the children (Mike, Carol, Penny, Jimmy and Joe) discover that Yen Yen the Yeti, a popular attraction formerly housed at the London Zoo, has been kidnapped by a gang of thieves and is being held for ransom in the bowels of the barge itself, they realize they must act to help out their new friend the Yeti.

While the children try to figure out a way to free the cryptid, the zoo's caretaker is suspected of having stolen the Yeti, being the only logical suspect since there appears to be no sign of any outside inter-

ference. Afraid the cryptid will be harmed by the criminals should they call the police, the kids hatch a plot to free the confined Yen Yen and restore him to his home at the Zoo. But even as the tykes put their plan into action, the gang realizes they've been tricked and vow to do whatever is necessary to recapture their bounty, even if it means harming Yen Yen or the children in the process.

* * * * *

In an effort to bolster the quality of children's programming in the United Kingdom in the 1970s, the government funded the Children's Film and Television Foundation. The British equivalent of The Children's Television Workshop in America, which produced such fare as *Sesame Street*, *The Electric Company* and countless other PBS productions, the CFTVF amassed quite a catalog of telefilms aimed at younger audiences that featured uplifting storylines and child protagonists.

One such effort was the well-received (at least by younger viewers) *The Zoo Robbery*. *The Zoo Robbery*'s plot in some ways actually anticipates a similar set-up used in the later Spielberg-produced hit film *Harry and the Hendersons*. Though Yen Yen is abducted by a gang and hidden away to set up the children having to rescue and restore the hominid, this is much like the "Bigfoot removed from its forest home" set-up of *Harry and the Hendersons*. And while the Yen Yen the Yeti costume pales in comparison to the Academy Award–winning suit designed by Rick Baker for the later American film, it nevertheless has a lot of charm for its era. In its design and padding (probably to make the creature seem less threatening to youthful audiences), Yen Yen is actually a distant relative to the Yetis seen in the BBC SF favorite *Dr. Who*. Complete with a silly tongue and playful manner, Yen Yen (as it name suggests) was definitely an early forerunner of the Benign Bigfoot sub-genre of Ciné du Sasquatch that would (after *Harry and the Hendersons'* international success at the box office) become the norm for family films starring a cryptid. This trend continues to this very day, with little variation save complexity of cryptid costume design.

Because it was a low-budget effort, many of *The Zoo Robbery*'s scenes were filmed on location to reduce costs. Scenes were shot in actual locales, such as the London Zoo (which must have made for at least a few disappointed youthful zoo visitors who saw this telefilm only to discover there was no actual Yen Yen on display). Though the cast are largely unknown, Welsh-born Denise Gyngell (who played Carol, one of the children who help Yen Yen out of his predicament) went on to appear on such shows as *The Benny Hill Show* before touring with the popular rock band Tight Fit.

PART III
Interviews with Bigfoot Filmmakers

Ryan Schifrin (Director of *Abominable*)

Filmmaker Ryan Schifrin has directed several short films, such as *The Tiffany Problem* and *Evil Hill*, in addition to the feature film *Abominable* (2006). He is currently developing new projects to direct. He is the son of Hollywood film composer Lalo Schifrin, who contributed the musical score to *Abominable*. Ryan generously agreed to discuss his approach and intent in terms of Ciné du Sasquatch with me via email.

Q: In terms of Bigfoot films, did you do much research prior to crafting the script? I'm specifically interested in any films you may have seen that influenced your thinking towards the genre, such as The Legend of Boggy Creek.

A: I actually didn't want to watch too many Bigfoot films before writing *Abominable*, because the concept was to do *Rear Window* as a monster movie first. Then the question became: What monster should it be?

I've really been into cryptozoology since I was a kid. I've read tons of books about Bigfoot, and I figured that would be a good subject. I watched *Sasquatch* because it was recent, and *Harry and the Hendersons* because it was big budget. I wanted our Squatch to be really massive, with a lot of girth, so I was interested to see what the other suit designs were like. During Halloween, Quentin Tarantino appeared on a talk show, and he walked out wearing this big, hairy suit. I think it was from the movie *Little Nicky*. I showed that to our effects guy and said, "That's the kind of suit I want!" We ended up having the woman who made the *Little Nicky* suit make ours, which was really cool. The scene in *Harry and the Hendersons* where John Lithgow is confronted in the kitchen by Harry is actually really scary. If you watch that one scene you could really imagine how terrifying it would be if Harry was homicidal. That certainly got my wheels spinning.

Q: Despite a few graphic sequences, the gore quotient in Abominable *is actually quite restrained, as is your directorial style. It seems most of the other recent Bigfoot efforts use lots of hand-held camerawork, MTV-style editing, and frankly seem to attempt to obscure the creature costume as a strategy. Can you talk a bit about how you approached this in terms of pre-production?*

A: I sat down with Neal Fredericks, our director of photog-

raphy, for about two weeks straight and we made an elaborate shot list for each and every scene. I deliberately wanted to try and do a style in which you cut only when necessary. So you try and do these long takes where you move the camera or the actors and keep the shot going for a bit. M. Night Shyamalan does a lot of that. If you watch his films they are the opposite of the Michael Bay style of editing. Spielberg, of course, has always put together some incredible shots. They really help build a mood and a feel you can't otherwise get. There were a couple of sections later in the film where we went for some of that hand-held or fast-cutting style, but only in small doses. We also have a lot of close-ups in the movie to try and make the whole thing

Director Ryan Schifrin on the set of *Abominable* during one of its many night photography schedules. (Photograph courtesy Theresa Schifrin and Red Circle Productions.)

feel claustrophobic. The big challenge when doing a movie that takes place largely in one room, á la *Rear Window*, is to keep it visually interesting. The same angle over and over would become really boring, so we wanted to be sure we had a nice variety of angles and subtle camera moves.

Q: Abominable fuses genres and is playful about its sense of violence and horror. Was this a conscious decision? Or were you just "going with it" in terms of having such an original approach to what could have become a clichéd genre piece?

A: Here is my theory about directors: Their personality somehow comes through the film whether they want it to or not. My intention was never to make something that makes the viewer feel horrible like a torture porn film might. I always intended for it to be a fun ride, and there is definitely a playful attitude about the whole thing. It's a delicate balance because you still want it to be suspenseful and scary but also thrilling and exciting and fun without going too far into camp. There are Nazis in *Schindler's List* and there are Nazis in *Raiders of the Lost Ark*, but those two films couldn't be any more different in tone. The *Texas Chain Saw Massacre* remake was brutal in the *Schindler's List* sort of way. I wasn't interested in pursuing that kind of stark tone. I preferred more of the fun factor approach.

Q: Many of the films I've reviewed for this guide feature Bigfoot attacks that occur in daytime. Whereas you only shot the creature at night, which was very effective. But I'm guessing this must have been difficult in terms of lighting, staging and sheer exhaustion for the cast and crew?

A: You pretty much hit the nail on the head. The first company we almost made the film with wanted us to move the whole thing to daytime to save money. Night time *is* scarier. People are afraid of the dark and what's in the dark. We wanted to also have that foggy atmosphere, and to do it effectively it has to be at night. It definitely made it harder to shoot on a night schedule, outdoors in the freezing cold and occasionally in the snow! But pain is temporary and film is forever, right? At least that's what they tell me.

Q: Your Savage Sasquatch is both convincing and terrifying. Were actual sightings factored in, or was your primary motivation in terms of rendering the Sasquatch mostly cinematic impact?

A: It was a combination of research and taking references from real-life sightings, and then adding made-up stuff that would be cool onscreen. The big eyes were something I kept reading about in many Bigfoot sightings. I kept picturing these giant, almost curious, luminescent orbs — like owl eyes almost — peering at you from out of the tree line. We didn't really pull that off, but what I'm picturing in my head would have been very creepy. Our concept artist drew something totally different. His design was really freaky with those jagged teeth, and we went with that. We tried to put the big eyes in with that design, but I actually think we should have kept them small and beady. The dislocating jaw was just something we made up. I thought it would be neat to think, you know, what this beast is and what it can do, and then suddenly have it open really wide like that and catch you off guard.

Q: Matt McCoy reminded me of James Stewart in Rear Window, *for perhaps obvious reasons, and Jeffrey Combs' performance had a kind of goofball approach reminiscent of Dennis Weaver's in* Touch of Evil. *Was this a case of influences we all draw from playing into your vision and/or theirs as actors?*

A: Matt's favorite actor in the world is Jimmy Stewart. They even have the same birthday. I definitely told Matt that we needed his character to be likable like Jimmy Stewart. It was a challenge because at the start of the film Matt's character is depressed and morose over the death of his wife. He gradually comes out of his shell as the movie goes on. In *Rear Window*, Jimmy Stewart is charming and gregarious from the get-go. Jeff Combs actually came up with the entire oxygen tank, chain-smoking, goggle glasses shtick. He based it on a relative of his!

Q: Lance Henriksen holds a triple crown for Bigfoot movies roles. Did his appearances in Sasquatch *and* Sasquatch Mountain *influence your casting decision, or did you just feel, "Hey, here's a terrific actor, who cares about his prior screen roles?"*

A: Did you know that Matt McCoy is tied with Lance for a Bigfoot movie crown? Matt was also in *Bigfoot: The Unforgettable Encounter* and *Little Bigfoot!* Matt neglected to mention this to me before we started shooting! Lance had done *Sasquatch* but hadn't yet shot *Sasquatch Mountain* before he did ours, so it didn't even really occur to me. I figured that it's a different character, and any chance you have to work with Lance Henriksen, you take it! We shot Lance's scene months after we finished the rest of the movie. It was a chance to look at the pacing and realize we needed one more action scene to open it up a bit. The tone of that sequence is a lot different than the rest of the film, actually. That was a conscious decision on my part. It's actually my favorite scene in the whole movie.

Q: In the Sasquatch's cave sequence with Henriksen there is a shot of a Gigantopithecus skull. I liked the way this was simply "tossed in" and not pontificated upon. In fact, the entire movie avoids the usual, stereotypical "education" of the audience in all things cryptid.

A: I have a lot of faith in the intelligence of the audience. I knew there would be crypto fans watching it who would get a kick out of seeing the *Gigantopithecus* skull, and I thought it would be intriguing for people who have no idea what that is. Bigfoot is so well known and studied and talked about. I don't think Hollywood fully realizes or appreciates what an enormous fan base there is for the big guy! That *Gigantopithecus* skull, by the way, is sitting on my desk.

Q: All Bigfoot films seem to feature a scene wherein a character is assaulted while in a restroom. Abominable *follows this tradition, albeit with an effectively nightmarish "twist" (pun intended!). It also makes great use of windows as visual metaphors for vulnerability. There's a sense that anyone who approaches a window at any time will fall prey to Bigfoot. It's not unlike the way the water prevents visibility in* Jaws *and allows for off-screen space to suddenly, horrifically intrude.*

A: We definitely discussed *Jaws* a lot in planning this film. For example, in keeping the monster hidden for the first three-quarters of the movie, and making you feel that vulnerability and fear of the unknown. The bathroom death was more of a nod to Joe Bob Briggs' "three B's rule" of horror movies — blood, breasts and beasts. We had to have a girl taking a shower. If she's going to be grabbed through the window and pulled out, why not make it a tiny window and fold her in half? The other thing you have to consider is that when characters in horror movies do stupid things — i.e. go investigate that scary noise in the basement — you sort of lose identification with them because they are being idiots. For me, the scariest thing is to have the characters do what you would do... and then kill them anyway! So if these people realize it is dangerous outside, they are going to stay indoors. The only way to kill them is to snatch them when they get too close to a window.

Q: Last but not least: The sound design and music score are well-done and add a tremendous psychological punch. Can you comment?

A: I really do believe that fifty percent of the experience is the sound design and music. That's why it's best to see a movie in the theater, where the volume is cranked up and in surround sound. Watching it on a computer or iPod, you lose a lot of impact. With a horror movie, it's probably more like sixty-five percent of the experience. None of the jump scares work unless it's really loud, for example. As for building up atmosphere and a sense of dread, it just takes layers and layers of different sounds. It's a lot like painting. Ambient sound is really important in a horror movie. You make the crickets louder than you would in a romantic comedy. Eerie droning wind in the background, creaks — all that stuff subliminally puts you in a heightened state of fear and makes you more receptive to having the crap scared out of you! We spent more time on the sound design than anything else. There are just so many details and layers. It is very time consuming to do, but extremely important...and fun!

Kevin Tenney (Director of *Bigfoot*)

Filmmaker Kevin Tenney grew up in Hawaii dreaming of the day his Super 8mm childhood-directed epics would one day grace the 35mm screens as professionally-directed efforts. As the writer, producer, and director of numerous films, including the cult favorites *Witchboard* (1986), *Night of the Demons* (1988) and *Brain Dead* (2007), he has achieved his life-

The grotesque monstrosity from *Abominable* is truly one of the most viscerally terrifying of all movie Sasquatch visualizations, particularly with its massive, hinge-extending jaws. (Photograph courtesy Theresa Schifrin and Red Circle Productions.)

Ziegler Dane (Lance Herinksen, front) prepares to battle Sasquatch, while a nervous local Store Clerk (Jeffrey Combs) wishes he had stayed home. From *Abominable*. (Photograph courtesy Theresa Schifrin and Red Circle Productions.)

long dream and then some. The filmmaker was kind enough to discuss the direction of *Bigfoot* (2008), a film on which he was hired to replace a departing director, with me via email.

Q: *You grew up in Hawaii the son of a military officer. Were you familiar with the legendary stories of the so-called "Hawaiian Bigfoot" as told by Rob Carlson? The natives call this Sasquatch, who supposedly resides in the pineapple fields, "Aikanaka." I was just wondering what effect, if any, these "true life" Bigfoot tales and others had on you growing up?*

A: Get ready to be disappointed by my answer. Until you asked me right now, I'd never heard of the Hawaiian Bigfoot. And my father wasn't an officer; he worked for a living. He was a Chief Master Sergeant, the guys who actually run everything for the officers. He fought in the Pacific during World War II, and he was stationed in Viet Nam during the Tet Offensive. And even though I was born in Hawaii, I don't really remember it as well as Bermuda, where I went to grade school. And if they have some form of Sasquatch there, I've never heard of it either. How's that for an answer?

Q: *Were any of the early Sasquatch and Yeti films influential on you? For example, did you see* The Abominable Snowman, The Legend of Boggy Creek *or* Sasquatch, the Legend of Bigfoot *as a youngster?*

A: Okay, here comes disappointing answer number two. I've never seen *any* Bigfoot or Sasquatch movies, not even *Harry and the Hendersons.* I saw pieces of a Sasquatch-type film on the SyFy Channel, back when it was the Sci-Fi Channel, but I don't remember the title. I think Tiffany Shepis was in it, which was probably why I saw it. [Note: Tenney is most likely referring to *Abominable*, directed by Ryan Schifrin —*Author*]

Q: *You started by directing Super 8mm films as a child before attending U.S.C. I'm curious what kinds of films you made before film school cast its inevitable influence (both good and bad) on your movie imagination? Were any "hairy monster" type efforts?*

A: Actually, no. I wasn't into monster movies or horror films

as a kid. Almost all of my high school projects were action films. My friends and I would dream up stunts we wanted to perform (jumping from a roof, falling from a moving car, crashing through a glass door, etc.), and then I would write a script incorporating those particular stunts. Many of my friends and I were training in martial arts at the time, so we would choreograph elaborate fight sequences as well. One of my friends had a mom who was a cop, and she would lend us all of her guns with blanks, and we figured out a way to make our own blood squibs using red food coloring, baggies, and fire crackers. We'd also shoot car chases by going downtown early on a Sunday morning, when there was little to no traffic, and just speeding around like maniacs. Looking back now, I'm amazed none of us got killed or arrested. But even before that, I always knew I wanted to make films. Walking home from grade school I would see an alley and think, "That would be a cool location for a movie." When I was in fifth or sixth grade, Bell & Howell came out with a Super-8 camera that could be plugged into a cassette tape recorder; the camera would send a sync pulse to the recorder every time you turned the camera on and off. Then you could plug the recorder into the projector, and the cassette would play sync sound with the projected image. The down side was that everything had to be shot in sequence, you had to get each shot in the first take, and you couldn't do any editing afterward, other than to splice the different fifty-foot, three-minute rolls of film together. I begged my parents to get me the camera, projector, and tape recorder for Christmas, and although they were pretty expensive, my parents agreed. If they hadn't, I'd probably be a used car salesman now. My first production was a 20-minute gangster/detective film with all of my grade school classmates playing adult roles. It was pretty awful, but I was hooked on filmmaking from then on. After graduating high school and getting Associative Arts Degrees in Drama and Telecommunications at my local community college, I applied to the University Of Southern California. I got turned down by the Film Department three times, but I kept applying and pestering the faculty and department heads until I finally got in. The next year I wrote and directed a very sober and dramatic undergraduate film, *War Games*, which ended up winning an Emmy Award and a Rod Serling Writing Award. Two years after that, my graduate film, *The Book of Joe*, was screened for the Hollywood community, to rave reviews. It was a comedy. I ended up getting an agent at ICM, my own office on the Columbia Studios lot, and a three-picture deal with producer/director Ivan Reitman (*Ghostbusters*, *Stripes*), all while I was still a student at U.S.C. I'd written a full-length script in my Screenwriting Class entitled *Ouija*, which was not only the first feature screenplay I'd ever written, but my first horror screenplay as well. One of my classmates knew a commodities broker who was looking to break into the film business. He showed my screenplay to the broker, and he loved it. He started raising

Director Kevin Tenney (right) discusses a shot with an unidentified crew member on the set of *Bigfoot* (2008). (Photograph courtesy Alecia Ashby.)

money for *Ouija* while I was still in film school. I was four units away from my Masters Degree when he called to say he'd raised all the money, so I left school to make *Ouija*, which was later re-titled *Witchboard*, my first professional feature. I'm still four units short of my MS Degree, but directing my first feature, and having it open as the fifth highest grossing film of the week on 1,100 screens here in the U.S., was a dream come true, the culmination of everything I'd worked for. All these years later I can still remember what a thrill it was to drive onto the set that first day of production.

Q: Having directed 13 low-budget/medium budget feature films (many in the horror and SF genres), did you find it novel and/or disconcerting to find yourself directing a family film? Was it a case of keeping your more visceral instincts under control, or were you able to use certain techniques from your earlier cult films, such as Night of the Demons, *to shade certain suspense sequences in* Bigfoot*?*

A: Even though I'm best known as a horror director, I've made films in other genres, either professionally or in college. Plus, I was a teaching assistant in a Screenwriting/Production Class while at U.S.C. Also, most of my favorite films, like *The Ninth Configuration*, *The Stunt Man*, *Forrest Gump*, *To Kill a Mockingbird*, or *Ben Hur*, are not horror films. And the fact that I'm the father of two means I've seen every animated film that's come out in the last twenty years, like *Toy Story*, *Coraline*, *The Lion King*, and *The Nightmare Before Christmas*. Besides, like I told my wife when I was hired to direct *Bigfoot*, "I finally get the chance to make a family film, and I'm still dealing with an elaborate, animatronic monster." So I never really felt like I was out of my element.

Q: You once said that no matter the budget or even technical limitations, the audience will only be unforgiving if your story is weak. Given that Bigfoot *is one of the rare projects you've directed that you also didn't write, I was wondering how it felt to be working from Sanford Schklair's screenplay? Was it liberating to be able to concentrate on the execution with "fresh eyes" as opposed to bringing a movie to fruition conceptually, writing it and directing it to its conclusion?*

A: It is sometimes easier to bring fresh eyes to the screenplay, since you are not burdened with the baggage of previous drafts or half-realized ideas. You can just see that certain story elements either work or they don't. You mentioned *Night of the Demons* earlier, which is one of my most popular horror films. Like *Bigfoot*, this was a screenplay originally written for another director before I was brought aboard, so I was able to easily spot plot problems or character problems or dialogue problems that the producers and even the authors themselves were no longer able to see.

Q: Your films often feature elaborate special make-up effects for relatively modest budgets. How much contribution do you make in terms of writer/director in approaching your projects to insure that maximum impact is maintained when so many films in the genre fail to achieve the consistent results your films have in this regard? Is your approach hands on?

A: My approach is very hands on. I worked closely with Gabe Bartalos on *Pinocchio's Revenge* and *Brain Dead*, figuring out far in advance how I was going to shoot each specific effect, so that Gabe would know what part of each gag would be on camera, and which part could be open for tubes, wires, or puppeteers. This was especially important on *Brain Dead*, because every film Gabe or I'd ever made in the past was shot on 35mm film. To get the effect of a shotgun blast to a character's head, you fill the molded head with explosives and then film the explosion at high speed, i.e., slow motion. You have to shoot it this way, because the explosion is so violent it instantly vaporizes the head. Shot at real-time speed, the head would seem to just disappear. You need to slow the explosion down so that it can be seen on film. But *Brain Dead* was our first digital feature, and digital cameras can't shoot the kind of slow motion necessary to photograph a head explosion. So Gabe had to score the molded heads and blow them apart with compressed air. This enabled the explosions to be slowed down enough to be captured by the digital cameras. On *Night of the Demons*, Steve Johnson and I actually had a couple of very heated discussions about his make-up effects. I won some of them, and he won some of them. I came up with the idea of the infamous lipstick scene and told Steve how I wanted him to design it. He thought I was crazy, but I stuck to my guns. He argued with the cinematographer and me about how to light the rapid-aging effect on Linnea Quigley in the bathroom, and I finally agreed to do it his way. In both cases I believe the effects turned out better because of the collaborations. I was not as up-to-date with the visual effects or the make-up effects on *Witchboard*, and I was never fully happy with a lot of them. I'm much happier with the effects in *Witchboard 2*, because I was more involved. All collaboration is important. I would never have chosen to spend such a large part of my limited budget on the animated title sequence for *Night of the Demons*, but the writer/producer, Joe Agustyn, convinced me. I'm just glad I was smart enough to listen.

Q: Following up on the above question: did you have much interaction with the designer of the Bigfoot costume for Bigfoot*? If so, can you detail a bit of the process and how you went about deciding how to create the cryptid depicted in your film? Was it a case of playing upon reported sightings, using film references, or...?*

A: The original director of *Bigfoot* became ill three weeks before the beginning of principal photography. I was hired to take over in the eleventh hour. Because of this, the creature had already been designed and built. As I understand it, the designer, Kevin Brennan, was asked by ACI, the production company, to create something that resembled the creature from *Harry and the Hendersons*, but he fought to do something original, based on so-called sightings. Because this business is all about compromise and collaboration, they came up with something in the middle, with which they could all be happy. I personally think the finished creature looks great; his face is extremely articulated and capable of mimicking any and all emotions. And although he does resemble the *Harry* creature, our Bigfoot is much more animalistic, with canine teeth and a snout, rather than a more human-looking nose and teeth.

Q: Most of your cast members in Bigfoot *are quite young, and yet they achieve very professional results. Despite your background and experience, did you find it any more or less challenging to work with such youthful players? Was your directorial approach any different?*

A: This wasn't my first time working with youngsters. *Pinocchio's Revenge* had a nine-year-old girl as the main protagonist, along with an entire playground of grade school–aged extras; and *The Cellar* had a twelve-year-old boy as the lead, along with every kind of animal imaginable. In a weird coincidence that proves fact is stranger than fiction, I was hired to take the helm of *The Cellar* a week into production, after the original director left. The story was about a monster in the cellar of this young boy's house, and the monster had already been designed and built before I was hired. The designer was none other than Kevin Brennan, the creature designer who years later would be the designer on *Bigfoot.* Young actors like the ones we had on *Bigfoot* are no less talented or professional than their grown-up counterparts. What they *are* lacking, though, is the experience of the more seasoned adults. On a bigger budgeted film with a longer production schedule, the director can take the time to coax the performance he wants from his neophytes. This is a luxury you cannot afford on smaller budget films. So I asked George Shamiah, the producer, to hire the kids an acting coach who could work with them between takes, and he agreed. This enabled us to give the young actors the time and help they needed without impeding our schedule. I think the final results speak for themselves; the kids all give fantastic performances in the finished film.

Q: Finally, there seems to be a very distinct split in the Ciné du Sasquatch genre between Benign Bigfoot and Savage Sasquatch.

Note how the special effects artists who created *Bigfoot* (2008) blended in long, gray facial hairs to denote wisdom, despite the cryptid's overall youthful appearance. (Photograph courtesy Alecia Ashby.)

While some films use both, the divergence is remarkably consistent (for example, Little Bigfoot *is a friendly version, and* The Legend of Boggy Creek *a horror version). Did you consciously reflect on this when you directed* Bigfoot, *or was it mostly a case of following the screenplay and bringing it as faithfully to life as possible?*

A: I have children of my own, as well as nephews and nieces, who have never been able to see any of my films because I usually work in the horror, thriller, science-fiction, or action genres. I was excited to get the chance to make something for all of them. I read the screenplay, talked to George about what he wanted and what I envisioned, and then set out to make the finished film as funny, heart-warming, exciting, and entertaining for family viewing as I possibly could. I used everything I'd learned from my previous experiences as a filmmaker, so hopefully I managed to pull it off.

Michael Worth (Writer, Actor and Producer of *Sasquatch Mountain*)

Actor, writer, and producer Michael Worth is a veteran character actor who has appeared on such successful TV series as *Acapulco H.E.A.T.* and *The Unit.* He filled all three roles as the co-producer, author, and lead actor on the SyFy Channel offering *Sasquatch Mountain* (2006). During the film's initial promotion, Worth discussed the joys and limitations of working within Ciné du Sasquatch with cryptozoologist and author Loren Coleman. This interview initially appeared on the *Cryptomundo* website and is reprinted courtesy of both Coleman and Worth.

Q: Would you mind sharing (without giving away any spoilers to the film) your concept of Bigfoot?

A: Well, I had originally wanted to write about a story I had heard about someone who was apparently kidnapped by Sasquatch in the early 1900s and thought this would make a great idea for a film. True story, period piece and Sasquatch! But, before I could follow it through and research it, the producers were anxious for a bit more contemporary script. I love fish out of water stories and knew they wanted action so came up with an idea of a group of urban bank thieves (Craig Wasson, Karen Kim and myself) that go for an "easy" bank in a small rural town and during the getaway, crash into a young woman (Cerina Vincent) that forces them into the woods with the local law close behind. It is there, of course, where the new dilemma takes over. The original title was *Devil on the Mountain,* as I had heard of the term Mountain Devil for Sasquatch and liked the metaphor of all the characters confronting their own "devils" on the mountain during the process. The term survives still in one of the character's conversations, but for the TV release the title was changed for ease of understanding I suppose.

Q: How did you make the film's script fit with the literature?

A: Well, what was most important to me was keeping with the legend of Sasquatch and not just taking the idea of a big hairy ape and sending him on a rampage. That was why I was so attracted to the idea of the kidnapping story (be it true or not) as it could lead to a more interesting approach than the usual stalking storyline. Your books have so many great stories through history, including the Minnesota Iceman and the "discovery" of Bigfoot in Bluff Creek, that I felt were just ripe for making a film about. But since I had to cater to a certain audience, using your data bank of similarities in the sightings and patterns of the creature helped me formulate what we had in our film. But both Steven [Monroe, the film's director] and I felt if we kept Sasquatch along the lines of how we all really perceive him, not getting too close, slightly more mysterious, it would play better. Of course, my dilemma as a writer was trying to give the money people their "monster" but not turn Sasquatch into what I personally didn't like seeing him reduced to in other films. They wanted blood and death where I wanted more or less an eerie mystery, the kind of feeling you get in the pit of your stomach when you watch the Patterson film. It is not that you are horrified or petrified by that image, but you are held in a sort of awe, and the sight can be quite eerie. If I could translate that to a film, I would be doing my job. Reading your book *Bigfoot! The True Story of Apes in America*, the stories, sightings and folklore of Sasquatch hit my gut harder than any "scary monster" Bigfoot film. I wanted to capture that tone more in the story. So, to try and balance that out with the commercial fare of the film was both Steven and my job as filmmakers. That and budget restraints, of course. One of the ways I did that was to take Lance Henriksen's character (Chase Jackson) and model him loosely after Patterson in the sense that his wife and he see and shoot a quick video clip of Sasquatch in the film's opening. The footage itself, like with Patterson, turns the town into a Bigfoot tourist trap. I wanted to shoot it in Willow Creek, California, but the logistics were too tough financially. So we shot in Williams, Arizona. The major thing I had to justify was why Sasquatch would actually kill human beings. I didn't want to do it because he was hungry or just some angry animal. In fact, I at first handed in a draft where he didn't kill anyone, where the film relied on the eerie anticipation of "what's out there?" and how the humans turn on themselves as a result of the pressure. More *Blair Witch*–like. This, of course, didn't go over too well. So had to go back to the ol' "blood and guts" routine. But even so, this film avoids that trap a lot. I was able to give them enough of their body count and still in the end of the film make any Bigfoot fan walk away feeling the Big Guy's reputation is still intact. I think if you are a big horror/gore fan, it will probably not ring your bell as much. No heads get torn off, I'm sorry to say. As an actor, I tend to be more story and character-oriented in my scripts, using drama as the core. So, if you enjoy something that relies more on the characters, the lurking mystery and hopefully some good ol' movie humor, this will be right up your alley.

Q: So you used my book Bigfoot! *as a reference as you were writing the movie and then later during the filming? How did that work?*

A: Yes, your book was with me during the shoot of the film. In fact, I gave the cover photo to our director and the FX crew as a reference to what Sasquatch may look like.

Q: How did you extend your film's Sasquatch beyond the old classic stories about it?

A: Well, I have seen just about every Sasquatch film there is. A few just use him to fill the creature role of the film; others try to dip into his possible benevolent nature. I was really interested in the course of the story — using the creature as a means to unnerve you, but in the end, without giving too much away, show how sometimes it's the people that can be the scariest. I actually included a few lines that I researched through your book with regard to Sasquatch and Yeti. I didn't want to get too into a technical thing where someone sits down and tells the history and folklore of the creature (as that is best left to authors such as yourself), but at the same time use enough of what we know about them and include it in the structure of the story. Again, we are an independent film company with limited resources, so there are many things I would have like to have done here but could not afford to. But, even with any shortcomings, the film I think should resonate at least with the people that have been following Sasquatch over the years.

Q: Did you have fun with this film?

Writer, producer, and star Michael Worth awaits a set cue while Bigfoot actor "Tiny" Ron reveals that Sasquatch prefers to wear Birkenstocks. From **Sasquatch Mountain.** (Photograph courtesy Michael Worth.)

A: Filmmaking is usually a lot of work coupled with a lot of fun. This was no different. We shot in Flagstaff and Williams, Arizona, the pine tree capitol of the world, I believe. The clean area and nice people were wonderful to work with. We had such a great cast of actors, too. Lance Henriksen is probably the nicest guy in film history. Just a really cool and professional actor with no ego. Just steps on set and does his thing. Lance's character is the reluctant Bigfoot guru in the town who comes to the aide of the helpless group in the forest. We had Craig Wasson, of *Body Double* and *Ghost Story,* as well. Rance Howard (Ron's father) plays the sheriff, and then Cerina Vincent of *Cabin Fever* and a host of other charismatic actors, such as Karen Kim, Raffello Degratolla and Candace Raquel. Many of the cast members are people I have used in other films I have done, like *Ghost Rock* and *Killing Cupid.* They are a good ensemble group of people, and when you find those kinds of professionals that can work under at times less than perfect conditions (remember, we are shooting in the middle of nowhere with no red carpet and green M&Ms), I like to stick with it. Steven Monroe, our director, is another one that I work really well with, and he did a great job here. Actually, both Lance and Rance have been featured in past

This behind-the-scenes photograph demonstrates the painstaking hours cryptid actor "Tiny" Ron had to undergo each day for the making of *Sasquatch Mountain.* (Photograph courtesy Michael Worth.)

Bigfoot films before. A little tidbit: Our actor "Tiny" Ron, who plays Sasquatch, had to wear a yellow vest between takes, as it was hunting season and we had to make sure we didn't lose our main actor to a bullet! If the film does well and they call for another, I'll make sure to try my best to get in what we missed on the first one. But if they want something else, I think those Thunderbirds could be pretty cool.

Timothy Skousen (Director of *The Sasquatch Gang*)

Director Timothy Skousen was first assistant director on the acclaimed *Napoleon Dynamite* prior to directing *The Sasquatch Gang* (2006), his first feature-length credit. He was also the writer/director of the acclaimed short film "Leon," as well as producer and editor of *Awful Normal.* We emailed back and forth about his directorial experience making his entertaining entry into Ciné du Sasquatch filmmaking.

Q: The Sasquatch Gang has one of the most unusual plot structures of any in the genre. What were your cinematic inspirations for such a "fractured fairy tale"–type construction? I mean, Rashomon seems an obvious example, but were there others?

A: It's basically just *Rashomon.* I mean, I suppose you could say something like *Pulp Fiction* or *Go,* but all those films are sort of derivative of *Rashomon* in my mind. *Rashomon* was one of only a couple of films that my DP and I watched in preparation for the film (along with some classic Spielberg stuff). I'm a huge Japanese film fan. Five of my seven or so favorite directors are from Japan (Fukasaku, Kurosawa, Ozu, Miyazaki, and Satoshi Kon). In fact, the slow-motion shot of the whole group walking out to the site to have Dr. Snodgrass verify the find is a nod to Fukasaku Kinji's camerawork in his "Battles without Honor and Humanity" series. What I like about *Rashomon* is that the retelling of the story through different characters' eyes tells you more about the characters than the story itself. I like the characters from *The Sasquatch Gang* and wanted to tell parts of the story through their eyes to give the viewer greater insight into who they are. So certain chapters are mostly about a single character or characters. Chapter One is Gavin, Chapters Two and Four are Zerk and Shirts, Three is Sophie, Six is Hobie. In an early draft of the script, Chapter Five was about Maynard playing a bunch of pranks and then witnessing when Zerk tries to walk on water from the shore and thinking that he had seen a murder and someone dumping a body and calling Officer Chilcutt about it. But Chilcutt dredges the lake and finds no body, and so Maynard gets in big trouble, and that was why he couldn't come to laser tag, thus making Hobie the third wheel. But, alas, the script was too long at that point, so I cut it out.

Q: The portrayal of both Justin Long as Zerk and Joey Kern as Shirts are as good as any buddy duo in comedic films I've seen in years. Their codependent relationship is equal parts hilarious and yet also touchingly pathetic. Can you talk about how you approached writing these two loveable dimwits? Are they based on real-life folks you knew, or...?

A: I've always loved the comic pairing of what I call "the Mastermind and the Minion." One isn't necessarily smarter than the other, they just have a relationship where one likes to call the shots and the other is a humble guy who frequently shows that he is smarter than the mastermind. Penn and Teller run this gag like crazy. It's different from the straight man-funny guy combo of a team like Abbott and Costello. It's more the Laurel and Hardy routine. They can be found all over the place, but these two are based on several real people, starting with Mark Borchardt and Mike Schank from *American Movie*. Kern's character was highly inspired by Schank, and that is the reason that he holds a Coke cup for the whole movie. *American Movie* is one of my favorite docs. Parts of Zerk's character also came partly from Borchardt and partly from a friend in high school who was extremely jingoistic during the first Gulf War and would frequently talk about how

Harlan Knowles (Lance Henriksen, left) and Vin Stewart (Michael Worth) realize they are not alone in the woods. From *Sasquatch Mountain*. (Photograph courtesy Michael Worth.)

America "kicks ass" and how we had the best military in the world. Shirts' shirtlessness and shirtless family comes from a friend of my brother. The scene with Shirts' family eating dinner was an experience my brother had when eating at this friend's house. His dad came home from work (a white collar job at a bank no less) and removed his nice collared shirt for dinner. Then the younger brother came in shirtless, and the mother was cooking in a bikini top. Needless to say, my brother's friend was shirtless after a session of wakeboarding. My brother looked around and asked, "Hey guys, do I need to take my shirt off to eat with you guys or what?" Anyway, I wanted Zerk to be like an Oliver Hardy or a Moe character from the Three Stooges. Bossy but really not all that bright. Justin came in and just nailed it in the audition. He was the only one to get the blind bravado. I got Justin and Joey together for a call-back and their chemistry was just what I was looking for. At that point I knew I had the right guys to make that comedy pairing work. Working with a pair like this wasn't new to me. I did a pretty successful short film back in film school named "Leon" where the title character was played by Hubbel Palmer (Hobie from *The Sasquatch Gang*) and he had a minion character named Jimmy. Their chemistry was great as well, so I knew what I was looking for when meeting with Justin and Joey to make sure the comedy would play out.

Q: Joey Kerns' physical mannerisms and comic timing are so perfect, I was left wondering: Was this something the two of you worked out prior to shooting, or was this developed as shooting went along? It seems to arrive completely "pre-formed" onscreen, which is—ironically enough—often a sign of seamless but diligent rehearsal periods.

A: Like I mentioned about Joey's character, it came mostly from Mike Schank. Without even mentioning Schank to Joey, he came in doing Mike's distinctive voice but a little louder than

normal. He also chose to not blink if he could. We looked over his audition and he goes like seven minutes without blinking, which was amazing. When I had him come in for call-backs we discussed why he chose to audition the way he auditioned and he started by saying, "After reading the script..." Then he paused and said, "Have you ever heard of this documentary *American Movie*?" Right then I knew that he totally understood the character 'cause he had heard the dialogue in his mind the way I intended it when I wrote it. I had him tone down the loudness, which he said had come from a girl he knew in college who wouldn't blink and talked in a similar way to Mike Schank, but much louder. We did work together some before shooting, but if I can say one thing about Joey, he was the most prepared actor I've ever worked with. He was so prepared that sometimes it was tough to get him to change a read because he had practiced it so many times before stepping on set. But with a little work, he would always get me what I wanted. So I would say it wasn't so much diligent rehearsal periods, since on a low-budget film that is frequently difficult to do, but it was that immediate understanding about the character between us that allowed him to really prepare for inhabiting that role.

Q: Were you influenced by any Ciné du Sasquatch efforts growing up, such as The Legend of Boggy Creek, Harry and the Hendersons *or* Bigfoot and Wildboy? *If so, can you elaborate on any key pictures or shows that influenced your love of the cryptid genre and why?*

A: I love *Harry and the Hendersons*. Not just for the Sasquatch in it, but because it was such a great family adventure. And that final moment of the other hidden Sasquatches stepping out into plain sight really drove home the idea of Bigfoot living among us without being seen. I just remember being like 13 and leaving that movie and feeling satisfied in the way you often felt leaving a movie theater in the '80s. We just don't get good storytelling like that anymore. Maybe we're all jaded. Maybe we're too self-deprecating. Whatever it is, we just don't get those same feelings leaving movies today as we did then when Spielberg was in his golden age and you could still leave a *Rocky* film pretending you were him knocking out a Russian dude. But what really got me thinking more about Sasquatch for this film were two other places. The music video "Triple Trouble" by the Beastie Boys, and then the short film *Broadcast 23* (which wasn't exactly a great film dealing with Sasquatch, but nonetheless contributed to having the hominid on my mind about the time I was starting to write the script). Both of those short films reminded me of that exciting place that mystical beasts have in growing up. It's why Perseus and Pegasus are referenced in the film. There's an innocent time in people's lives where Bigfoot is as real as Santa Claus was before you found out the truth. And much of the film deals with kids who are still in that innocent time in their lives. So after those reminders of Bigfoot in a pop culture setting, it set me in motion to write the script. In fact, many of the characters in the film, including Zerk, Shirts, Gavin, Maynard, and Hobie, were all part of different scripts I was developing. Gavin, Maynard, and Hobie were in one script I was writing that was like 15 pages long. And Zerk and Shirts were in another script that was like 20 pages. Gavin was always interested in mythical beasts, and it wasn't until I thought of Bigfoot that I suddenly merged the two scripts together and made Zerk and Shirts neighbors of Gavin. Then everything just clicked and the script really wrote very quickly.

Tim Skousen, left, with Scott Walters as Sasquatch and Carl Weathers as Dr. Artimus Snodgrass, in a behind-the-scenes shot from *The Sasquatch Gang*. (Photograph courtesy Tim Skousen.)

Q: Does your interest in Bigfoot extend beyond the film's subject matter? Were you enthralled as a youngster by the "true life" tales reported in the media?

A: I wouldn't say it goes beyond the normal fascination that any youngster has in the Sasquatch or the Yeti. I read a lot of *Tintin* comics growing up, and the Yeti is prominent in *Tintin in Tibet*. So I think he was always there in the adventure stories that I liked to read, but it's not like I was overly engrossed in the mystery of whether he was real or not. I had seen the Patterson film back then, but didn't feel like it was absolute proof, so maybe I was just a skeptic at heart even back then.

Q: The original title of the film was shortened from The Sasquatch Dumpling Gang *to simply* The Sasquatch Gang. *Was this because Disney pressured you re:* The Apple Dumpling Gang, *or did you feel it would perhaps confuse the audience into thinking there was an association with that film, or...?*

A: It's still *The Sasquatch Dumpling Gang* everywhere else in the world but here. I could write a whole book on the tragedy of what happened with our film before and after it was purchased for distribution... then returned when the first distributor was shut down by its parent company and given back to us and resold a second time. But I won't get into it here. Basically, the original title is the proper title, but Screen Media were scared to death of getting sued by Disney, although they wouldn't cop to it, and changed the title (without my blessing, I assure you). They claimed that they had done some market testing and that's why they were changing it, but I know that's b.s., and why would the title make any difference when they weren't going to advertise the film anyway? I never had a title in mind when I wrote it, and the producer, Jeremy Coon, actually came up with *The Sasquatch Dumpling Gang*. We had both always loved *The Apple Dumpling Gang* and had watched it together when we were filming the title sequence to *Napoleon Dynamite*. When he mentioned it, I thought about both stories and saw some similarities if you generalized enough. In a way, they are both stories about some kids who find a treasure and two bad guys trying to make money off the discovery. Of course, one is a nugget of gold and the other is, well, I guess you could call it a nugget of another kind [Author's Note: The "dumpling" refers to a Sasquatch turd in *The Sasquatch Dumpling Gang*]. But that's really where the similarities end. It was a happy accident that really worked with that title, although I don't think it would have confused audience members. We got tons of positive comments during the film's festival run about our title, and some people came to see the film just because of the title. But, alas, now it's *The Sasquatch Gang* in my home country.

Q: Carl Weathers portrays Dr. Artimus Snodgrass, a famed cryptozoologist. As a vain, self-promoting glory seeker, he seems to embody the epitome of a sleazy con artist. Do you have any opinions about real-world crypto researchers in contrast to the admittedly parodic nature of Dr. Snodgrass?

A: I don't think I know enough about the real cryptozoologists to know if some of them are con artists like Artimus Snodgrass. I was fully aware that these people exist and attend seminars and conference to discuss the varying stories and evidence of Bigfoot's existence, and even went so far as to reference some of their names. Artimus Snodgrass is a nod to Artimus Bindernagle, author and expert on Bigfoot. Ed Chilcutt is a nod to Jimmy Chilcutt, a forensic police officer specializing in fingerprints who began to try and apply fingerprinting techniques to plaster molds to verify if the feet of the casts had real or realistic prints on the sole of Bigfoot's big foot. But the whole idea of Dr. Snodgrass relishing his role as the "be all, end all" of Sasquatch researchers came from discussions that Carl Weathers and I had before shooting. We decided that Snodgrass would be a believer, but would have doubts about Bigfoot's existence deep down. In the deepest part of his soul he wasn't sure. It was this idea that lead to that moment for Snodgrass when he first hears what he believes to be Bigfoot's voice, and he appears surprised. But then he immediately claims, "My theories were correct, he *can* talk!" We talked about him being like [the lead character in] *The Music Man*. He has mostly convinced himself that he's not really a shyster. But basically he is. I mean, he eats what he believes to be feces from a Sasquatch, and then claims that it is indeed a Sasquatch dumpling. It's not like it would be in his character to say it was something else. On a side note, there are a lot of strange people out there who believe in things like orbs as Sasquatches transporting themselves without being seen. We had a number of people who heard about us making the film and drop by to talk to us about evidence. One guy even gave us a manila envelope with an enlarged picture on it. It was a picture of some grass with a small circle of refracted light in the middle of the picture. Now, as a filmmaker and photographer, I'm pretty aware of what it looks like when light hits some dust on the lens of a camera, so I know what this glowing orb is. It's just light hitting dust on the lens. But to a believer, it's a Sasquatch traveling incognito. So having Artimus be the way he is isn't too big of a stretch.

Q: *When the two redneck buddies decide to sell fake plaster Sasquatch footprints on eBay, were such casts really being offered at the time by "real" sellers? Because while researching your film after seeing it, I noticed several "legitimate" casts were listed, and I couldn't help but think of Zerk and Shirts smirking at home as the bids rolled in.*

A: No doubt. People have been selling those things for a long time. I did some research myself when I first had this idea. I figured that in today's world, if there was one place that Bigfoot

The perennially shirtless Shirts Jokum (Joey Kern) hangs tough with his best bro and front man Zerk Wilder (Justin Long). Photograph from *The Sasquatch Gang* (courtesy Tim Skousen).

casts would be sold, it would be eBay. I checked during the writing phase and indeed there were several Bigfoot casts being sold at the time, which really sealed the deal on using the casts as a money-making scheme. We would regularly check up on bids on eBay during the shoot.

Q: *Though only briefly glimpsed, the Sasquatch suit is very well-designed. Can you talk a bit about how you approached visualizing the cryptid? After so many films, such as* Harry and the Hendersons *and others, have done such a great job, was it difficult to see this pivotal character in a different way?*

A: We definitely weren't trying to rewrite the book on what Sasquatch looks like in this film. His appearance is so brief that we were trying to stay in that world of instant familiarity. Our gaffer was a true believer and had a Sasquatch suit that was his own personal suit that he used occasionally at birthday parties or during Halloween. We did the makeup, but basically that's Scott in a Bigfoot suit that sits in his closet at home. He was pretty excited to get to use it, and the suit was actually very well made.

Adam Muto (Animator/Creator of Samsquatch)

Professional animator and animation writer Adam Muto has numerous credits for the TV series *Adventure Time* on his resume, but his short film contribution *Samsquatch* (2007) is the one credit that will forever endear him to Ciné du Sasquatch fans. Muto discusses the influences on his own cryptid belief system in this interview conducted via email.

Q: You seem a keen observer of Ciné du Sasquatch. You commented on your blog: "Sasquatch movies are usually cloying family fare or SyFy Channel 'Killer Bigfoot' fodder." Have you been a long-time fan of the genre, or was your interest sparked when you decided to create Samsquatch *and you subsequently researched the titles?*

A: Definitely the latter. Once I settled on the idea of using a young Sasquatch as the main character, I wanted to research what had been done before. That's also when I learned that animation studios are constantly being pitched Bigfoot shows, apparently.

Q: You state that you were very careful to keep your visualization of Samsquatch *as mostly accurate to real-world sightings. Are you a fan of the cryptozoological side of the phenomena as much, if not more so, as the cinematic incarnations to date?*

A: One of the first things I did when developing *Samsquatch* was to read *Bigfoot!* by Loren Coleman. There are just a lot more details to work with in eyewitness accounts, forensic evidence and observations based on the Patterson-Gimlin film. They all directly influenced the animation. For instance, Sam's posture

Artwork from a promotional postcard for Adam Muto's *Samsquatch*.

is always slightly hunched forward. When he turns to look at something he twists his whole torso, not just his head. It was much easier to draw inspiration from recorded observations than to look to men in fur suits baring their fangs at a camera. That being said, a Thunderbird and a Sea Monster also appear in the short.

Q: What are some of your choices for the better examples of Bigfoot and Yeti movies, if any, and why? And conversely, what and why for the worst for you personally?

A: I avoided watching too many fictional depictions during production. While I was working on the storyboards, though, I had *The Mysterious Monsters* running in the background a lot. I liked how much the word "probably" showed up in that one. Since one of the characters in the short was a monster hunter, I also watched *Sasquatch Odyssey* to learn more about the real people who had made Sasquatch their life's work. The MST3K version of *Boggy Creek II: And the Legend Continues* is the worst Bigfootsploitation I think I've seen so far.

Q: The evolution, so to speak, of Samsquatch *underwent quite a change. The final version is both enchanting and reminiscent of older drawing styles—such as the blank eyes. Likewise, he wears the boxer shorts with the trees emblazoned on them, which make him seem child-like. Can you discuss this constant process of change a bit, and how you worked with your creative collaborators, such as Larry Leichliter, Saelee Oh and Ed Juan, in this regard?*

A: That was mostly a design choice, but his eyes looked much more mysterious without pupils. They also suggest the reflective nature of an animal's eyes and give him a slightly glazed expression; he doesn't fully comprehend the modern world around him. Larry was responsible for all the timing direction in the short. We agreed that Sam should always have an extra sense of weight about him — the exception being a scene where he does a *Bigfoot and Wildboy* leap. He also helped me develop a good heavy-footed walk cycle for Sam. Originally I imagined the backgrounds being more of an assemblage of paper cutouts and crayon, with bare wood to represent the sky. Seonna Hong came up with a more subdued "paint-by-numbers" look, which worked well with Ed Juan's graphic backgrounds. She also used a dry brush technique to achieve a wood grain texture for the skies. Saelee used photographs of actual wood grain for the Sasquatch body textures to suggest a natural camouflage. Her personal work often has a "woodsy" palette, so it was a natural fit.

Q: When you first screened Samsquatch *in front of an audience, you remarked how surprised you were by their reactions. While they found him comedic, there was a concurrent reaction of how adorably cute he struck them, as well. Do you think there is an inherent "cuddly" quality to Bigfoot as a "youngster" which accounts for the plethora of child-friendly Bigfoot fare versus the larger, "mature" version which seems to strike fear in viewers?*

A: To be honest, the final character design was cute, and we cast a cute kid's voice to go along with it. I'm not sure why I thought the effect would be otherwise. The idea of a baby Bigfoot is probably unavoidably cuddly. A smelly full-grown

Bigfoot is inherently menacing. In the short, I exaggerated that menace (partially inspired by the ridiculous *Yeti: Giant of the 20th Century*) by having the Momsquatch be 50 feet tall. It seems to be just a matter of scale.

Q: Were you fascinated by the Patterson/Gimlin film as a kid, or, for example, Harry and the Hendersons *or* The Six Million Dollar Man *appearances of Bigfoot?*

A: I'm originally from Seattle, so growing up in the Pacific Northwest, I remember being aware of Bigfoot from an early age. I don't recall whether it was presented as real or as a fictional character. *Harry and the Hendersons* is definitely the movie that shaped what I thought Bigfoot would act like. For *Samsquatch*, though, the blasé Bigfoot in the game *Sam & Max Hit the Road* are closer media relatives. Samsquatch is played as a hairy little kid whose extraordinary existence is treated matter-of-factly.

Index

Numbers in ***bold italics*** indicate pages with photographs.

Abominable 36, **39**, 40–41, ***319***, 320–***321***
"The Abominable Snow Rabbit" 22, 41, 125, 141
The Abominable Snowman (1957) 2, 23, ***24***, ***25***, ***41***, 42–43, 46, 139, 167
The Abominable Snowman (1996) 43
The Abominable Snowman (2008) 43–44
Abraham, F. Murray 156
Adams, Dana 283
Adlum, Ed 264
Adventure 43–44
The Adventures of Sam & Max: Freelance Police 44–45
The Adventures of Sass Parilla, the Singing Gorilla 45
The Adventures of Tintin 45–46
Agar, Ivan ***264***
Agustyn, Joe 323
Aikanaka 322
Ajouba Kudat Kaa 46–47
The Al Hodgson Interview 47
Alcock, Dr. James 103
Alley, Dr. Robert 300
Alma 153, 158, 170, 186
Almost Live! 47–48
Alpine Affairs 48
Alston, Emmett 109
Altered States 48–49, 64, 116, 191, 298
Altman, Eric 3, 300
American Dragon Jake Long 49–50
American National Enterprises 74, 309
Among Us 50, ***51***, 52, 68
Amora, Queen 130
Ancient Mysteries 52
Anderson, Richard Dean ***182***–183
Andre the Giant 31, 63, ***266–267***, 268
Andrews, John 300
Andrews, Roy Chapman 1
Angela Anaconda 52
Animal X 52–53
Animal X: Natural Mystery Unit 52
Animus 61–62
Ankrum, Morris 138, 140
Answers About Creation 53
Ape Canyon 53, 259
Ape Canyon siege 246, 279
The Ape Man ***16***, ***18***
Archer, Michael 147
Argosy magazine ***8***, 126, 133, 136, 246, 270
Arledge, R.G. 258
Arthur C. Clarke's Mysterious World 53–54

Astroboy 54, 57–58, 114, 235
Attack of the Yeti Hand 54
Auberjonois, Rene 92
Aykroyd, Dan 223–224
Aykroyd, Peter 222–224

Baack, James 84
Backwoods Bloodbath 55
The Backyardigans 55
Bailey, Shara 153
Baker, Joe Don 284
Baker, Rick 28, 34, 42, 68, 76, 132, 142, 155, 171, 191, 199, 252, 261, 268, 287–288, 300, 317
Baker, Tom 114
Baltic Bigfoot 153
The Barbaric Beast of Boggy Creek 30, ***56***–57
Barbeau, Adrienne 102–103
Battle of the Planets 57
Bauer, Michelle 109
Baum, Jim 105
"Bauman Incident" 215
The Beachcombers 58
Bear, Cindy 81
The Beast 58–59, 287
Beast of the Land Between the Lakes 147
The Beauties and the Beast 20, 60–***61***, 62
Beauty and the Beast 18, 19, 206, 288
Beck, Fred 246, 279
Becker, Tony 249
Behind the Cameras: The Unauthorized Story of Charlie's Angels 62–63
Benson, Dr. Robert 238
The Berenstain Bears Meet Bigpaw 63
Bergmann, Charlie ***200***
Beringe, Captain Robert von 15
Bernard, Stan 132
Berry, Al 300
Bertges, Jim 109
Best Evidence 64
Beuchler, John 108–109
Big and Hairy ***64***–65
Big Foot: The Giant Snow Monster Game 7
Bigfoot (1970) 20, ***29***, ***65***, ***66***, 67
Bigfoot (1987) ***67***–68
Bigfoot (2006) 68, ***69***, ***70***
Bigfoot (2008) 70, ***71***, 72, ***322***, 323–***324***
Bigfoot: A Beast on the Run ***72***–73
Bigfoot: Alive and Well in 82 73
Bigfoot: America's Abominable Snowman 27, 73–74

Bigfoot and Wildboy 31, 76–***77***, 313
Bigfoot at Holler Creek Canyon 77–***78***
Bigfoot FAQ 79
Bigfoot Field Research Organization 53
Bigfoot Lives! 79–80
Bigfoot: Man or Beast? 74–75
Bigfoot Meets the Thing 80
Bigfoot Research Project 52
Bigfoot: The Making of a Documentary 75
Bigfoot! The True Story of Apes in America 325, 330
Bigfoot: The Unforgettable Encounter 35, 75–76
Bigfooting in Oklahoma 81
Bigfoot's Reflection 81
Bigfootville 81
Bindernagel, John A. 237, 245, 277, 300
The Bionic Woman 31, 60, 81–82, 266–267, 303
Birdman & the Galaxy Trio 82
Biscardi, Tom 72–73, 79–80, 136, 149–150, 165, 211–213, 282–283
Bixby, Bill ***150***–151
Black, Jack ***289–290***, 291
Blanc, Mel 41, 85
Bloodstalkers 75, 83–84, 91
Bloody Rage of Bigfoot 84
Blue Creek Mountain film 47
Bomba 21
Borchardt, Mark 327
Borgnine, Ernest 284
Borowczyk, Walerian 59
Bosley, Tom 176
Boston Pizza Sasquatch commercials 84
Bottin, Rob 186, 287–288
Bova, Ben 163
Boyle, Terry 103
Boys, Beastie 60, 328
Brandy, Mycle 130
Brennan, Kevin 324
Bridgforth, Anna 265
Brothers, Ramsay 47
Brothers, Shaw 189
Brown, Julie 284–285
Buettner, Justin 250
Bugs Bunny's Bustin' Out All Over 85
Building a Thrill Ride: Expedition Everest 85–86
Bumble ***233***–234
Bunny, Bugs 22, 41, 85, 110, 125, 148, 156, 204, 277–278, 285
Burbank Bigfoot 161, 178, 285

Burman, Tom 202, 222
Burns, Bob 131–132
Burroughs, Edgar Rice 15
Burton, Dallas 211, *212*, 213
Burton, Robert *292*
Burtsev, Igor 153
Butcher, Joseph 77
Buzzkill 86
Byrne, Peter 52, 126, 149, 164, 197, 202, 245, 262, 278

Caddy, Owen 300
Calhoun, Rory 229
Callahan, Shane 249
Camacho, Art 176
Cameron, JoAnna *154*
Campbell, Bruce 144–145
Campbell, Joseph 20, 43, 198
Cannom, Greg 183
Capps, Al 247
Captain Ed's Head Shop 289
Captain Planet and the Planeteers 86
The Capture of Bigfoot 30, *87*–88, 122, 273
Carl Denham Syndrome 22, 67, 72, 98, 192, 195, 200, 239, 249, 276–277
Carr, John Dickson 96
Carradine, John 2, 20, 21, 23, 61, 65, *66*, 67, 138, 140, 166, 184, 286, 292
Carroll, Leo G. 185
Carson, John David *101*
Cassidy, B. Arthur 184
Caveman 89
Celebrity Deathmatch 89–90
Chambers, John 26–27, 64, 161, 178–179, 202, 279
Chaney, Lon, Jr. 21
Chang 17
Charmed 89–90
Chase, David 161
Chayefsky, Paddy 49
Chewbacca 65, 85, 278, *280*–281, 293, 300
Chilcutt, Jimmy 238, 300, 329
Chill Out, Scooby Doo 91–92
Chilly Beach 92–93
Chissel, Noble "Kid" 66
Choose Your Own Adventure: The Abominable Snowman *93*–94
Ciné du Sasquatch, definition 11
Ciochon, Dr. Russell 238
The Clan of the Cave Bear 190
Clarke, Arthur C. 53–54, 300
Clarke, Bobby 294
Clawed: The Legend of Sasquatch 94–95
Clutch Cargo *95*
Coast-to-Coast 73, 80, 213
Colbert, Stephen 105
Coleman, Loren vi, 1–*3*, 52, 98, 139, 142, 179, 195, 196–197, 199, 277, 278, 283, 300, 304, 324–326, 330
Colonel March of Scotland Yard 96
Collins, Murray 262
Colvin, Andy 198
Combs, Jeffrey 40, 320–*321*
Conan Doyle, Arthur 181
The Conquest of the Pole 12, *13*, 14, 19, 21, 22, 23, 37, *97*–98, 207, 224, 268, 314
Conway, James 91
Coon, Jeremy 328
Cooper, Merian C. 17–18
Corman, Roger 7

Cornelius, Joe *298*–299
Corolla, Adam 100
Corwin, Jeff 98
Corwin's Quest 98
Courage the Cowardly Dog 98–99
Craig, Mimmo *314*, *315*
Crane, Kenneth 140
Crank Yankers 99
Crawford, Joan 299
The Creature 23, 27, 42, 114
Creature from Black Lake 30, 100, *101*, 102
Creature from the Black Lagoon 20
Creepshow *102*–103
Creepy Canada 103
"Cripplefoot" hoax 164–165
Criscoulo, Jason *239*
Criswell, Dick 213
Cromer, James "Bubba" 177–178
Crosby, Linda 66
Crowe, Ray 105
Crowley, Lawrence 75
Crumb, R. 7, 136, 275
Cry Wilderness *103*–104
Cryptomundo 80, 98, 142, 324
cryptozoology, definition 1
Cundey, Dean 101, 308
The Curse of Bigfoot 104–105
Cushing, Peter 23–24, *25*, 42–43, 46, 139, 142, *145*–146, 173, 196

Daegling, Dr. David 152
Dahinden, Rene 47, 74, 126, 150, 159, 194, 245
The Daily Show 105
Danger Mouse 105–106
Dante, Joe 37, 120
Dark Star 252
Dark Stalkers 106–107
Darwin's Theory of Evolution 112
Davies, Adam 153
Davis, M.K. 72, 147, 158, 172, 278, 300
Davison, Donn 126–127, 169–171
"The Dawn of Man" 129, 299–300
Dawson, Anthony M. 272
Dear, William 33, 141, 157
DeAtley, Al 74
Degratolla, Raffello 326
Demarbre, Lee 144
Demonwarp *107*, 108, 109
De Palma, Brian 40, 175, 245
Destination Truth 109–110
Dewhurst, Colleen 68
Dexter's Laboratory 110
DCA Pictures 23
Dino Boy in the Lost Valley 111
The Dinosaur and the Missing Link: A Prehistoric Tragedy 111–112, 181, 229, 298
Disotel, Todd 153
Ditmars, Raymond 1
Dr. Pepper commercials 112
Dr. Who 27, 31, 54, 112, *113*, 114, 115–116, 299
Dods, John 127–128
Dogman of Kentucky 147
The Don McCune Library 115
Downes, Jonathan 218
Downtime 115
Dranginis, William 147–148, 300
Drawing Flies *116*, *117*, 118
Duck, Daffy 41, 110, 118, 148, 277
Duck Dodgers 118
Duncan, Sandy 81–82

d'Usseau, Arnaud 146
Dyer, Rick 73, 80

Ed Wood 8
Eddie Murphy Delirious 119
The Edge of Reality 119–120
Eerie, Indiana 37, 120
Elam, Jack 100–101
Ellis, George 170–171
Ellis, Tawm 264
The Empire Strikes Back 120, *121*
Encounters: The Hidden Truth 121
Encounters with the Unexplained 121
Enger, Anna *249*
Eubanks, Corey Michael 76

Fahrenbach, Dr. Henner 296
The Fairly Odd Parents 121–122
Family Guy 123
Fear Runs Silent *123*, 124–125
Felix the Cat 126
Ferrigno, Lou *150*–151
Film noir, characteristics 11–12
Fimple, Dennis *101*
Findlay, Mike 263–264
Fisher, Rick 300
Five Million Years to Earth 23
Flaherty, Wally 88
Flocker, Dave 105
Flocker, James 105
Flower, George "Buck" 88
Focus on the Family 168
Fontana, D.C. 163
Foot: Phantom of the Forest *126*
The Force Beyond *126*, 127
Ford, Harlan E. 172–173
Ford, Yvonne 173
Forest Story 127–*128*
Fouke Monster 6, 7, 29, 57, 63, 141, 148, *166*, 180, 197, 213, *227*, 251
four-wall technique 74, 247
Frankenheimer, John 36, 143, 222
Fredericks, Neal 40, 319–320
Freeman, Paul 238
Freeman, Richard 218
Friedman, Alvin 161
Friedman, David 258
Friends 128–129
Frizzell, Mike 300
Fromkin, Victoria 162
Frostbiter: Wrath of the Wendigo 129
Furst, Stephen 176
Futurama 129

"The Galileo Seven" 27, 279
Galligan, Zach 207–209
Garcia, Alex *306*
Gass, Kyle *289–290*, 291
Gates, Josh 109–110
The Geek 130–131
Gemora, Charles 17, 131–132, 298, 304
Georgia Bigfoot freezer hoax 73, 80, 149, 211, 283
Gerhard, Ken 163–164
Gerrold, David 162–163
Gester, Sten *292*
The Ghost Busters 131–132
ghost-squatch 50
Ghosts: True Hauntings in Montana 132
Giganto: The Real King Kong 132

Gilbert, Wayne 211, *212*, 213
Gimlin, Bob 26, 47, 74, 152–153
Girdler, William 36, 127
Goddard, Anna Marie 296
Godfrey, Linda 147
Godzilla 2, 20, 23, 35, 73, 132–133, 138–139
Godzilla and the Super 90 132–133
The Good, the Bad & the Ugly 7, 9
A Goofy Movie 133
Gordon, Bernard 104, 146
Gore, Al 276
Gorilla at Large 17
Gorilla Woman *21*
Grant, Arthur 23, 42
Grant, Jonathan 210
Grass 17
Grassman 6, 105, 168–169, 197, 246, 265
Graves, Duane 307
Graves, Peter 198, 202–203
Gray, Bob *69*, 70
Green, John 47, 74, 81, 115, 126, 150, 194, 202, 218, 245, 309
Greenwell, Richard 278
Gregory, Shawn 164
Griffo, Joseph 175, 177
The Grim Adventures of Billy & Mandy 134–135
Grizzly 36
Groves, John 68
Guenette, Robert 202–203
Guest, Val 23, 42, 139
Guiley, Rosemary Ellen 300
Gulager, Clu 146–147

Haas, Clark 95
Haijcek, Doug 237–238
Hair of the Sasquatch 135–137, 160
The Hairy Horror 137
Half Human 1–3, 22–25, 29, 66–67, 108, 125, *137–138*, 139, *140*, 142, 167, 229, 271
Hall, Kevin Peter 34, *141*, 142
Hallenbeck, Bruce G. 120
Hanabari 140–141
Hanna-Barbera studio 80, 82, 96, 111, 133, 188, 254–255, 259, 296
Harris, Jack 252–253
Harrison, Jack *248*
Harry and the Hendersons 3, 8, 31, 33–*34*, 47, 65, 68, 71, *141*, 229, 317, 319, 327, 331; *t.v. series* 34, 142, *143*, 144
Harry Knuckles and the Pearl Necklace 144
Harryhausen, Ray 112
Hart, Melissa Joan 236
Hastings, Jim 245
Heart of Dorkness: Behind the Scenes of "My Name Is Bruce" 144–145
Heironimus, Bob 153, 198–199
Henkel, Kim 307
Henriksen, Lance 40, 237, 244–245, 308, 320, *321*, 325–*327*
Herbig, Michael 174
Herge 46
Hero of 1,000 Faces 20, 43
Herriott, Scott 52, 278
Herrmann, Bernard 40, 137
Herrmann, Edward 132
Hessler, Gordon 161
Heuvelman, Bernard 1
Hickson, Charles 6, 126
Higgins, Carolyn 195

Hillary, Sir Edmund 1, 22, 44, 52, 97, 114, 197, 225
Hitchcock, Alfred 7, 15, 40, 48, 75, 103, 137, 161, 184, 185, 215, 217, 236, 261
Hodag, Black 55
Hodgson, Al 47, 52
Holbrook, Hal 102
Holbrook, Seth 195
Holden, Jeremy 262
Holmes, Lynn 130
Holyfield, Dana 172–173
Honda, Ishiro 2, 138–140, 206
Honey, I Shrunk the Kids: The TV Show 145
Hong, James 92
Horror Express *145–146*
House of Frankenstein 21
Hovind, Dr. Kent 53
Howard, Clint 76, 177
Howard, Rance 76, 245, 326
H.R. PufnStuf 31
Hugo the Abominable Snowman 85, 277–278
Hunt for Bigfoot 146
Hunt the Dogman 147
Hunters of Unknown Animals 147–148
Hurt, William 171
Huston, Danny 68
Hyde & Sneak 148

Ibáñez, Francisco 310
In Search Of 30–31, 52, 105, 121, 148–149, 169, 172, 179–180, 186, 196, 260, 309
In Search of Bigfoot 75
In Search of Yeti *149*
In the Shadow of Bigfoot 149–150
The Incredible Hulk (1978) *150–151*
The Incredible Hulk (1996) 151–152
Interlenghi, Antonella 315
Into the Unknown 152
Is It Real? 152–153
Isis 153–*154*

Jack Link's Beef Jerky 154–156
Jackson, Dan 158
Jacob's Creature 199
Jaws 36, 40
Jeremy, Ron 79
Jim, Jungle 21
Johnsen, John L. 147, 158
Johnson, Lynn 164
Johnson, Stan 213
Johnson, Steve 323
Jones, Chuck 41, 85, 118, 277–278
Jonny Quest 82, 95, 110, 133, 135, 188, 255, 259, 303
Journey to the Center of the Earth 156–157
Juan, Ed 330
Julius and Friends 157
Jung, Carl 14, 24, 110

KaBlam! 157
kaiju film 81, 301
Karloff, Boris 21, 97
Kassem, Casey 92
Kaufmann, Lloyd 207
Keach, Stacy 124
Keating, Don 105, 203, 243, 245–246
Keel, John 198
Keen, Bob 295
Keeping the Watch 158
Kennedy, George *107*, 109

Kennedy, Richard 88
Kennedy, Tara 109
Kern, Joey 326–*329*
The Kids in the Hall 158
Kiel, Richard *161*, 192, 197, 226
Killer Gorilla genre 13; definition 16
Kim, Karen 324, 326
Kimmel, Jimmy 100
King, Stephen 102
King Kong 17, *18*, *19*, 20, 21, 28, 42, 50, 59, 65, 112, 158–*159*, 181, 189, 271, 314
Kipp, Shawn *69*, *70*
Kirk, John 147, 300
Kiviat, Bob 198–199
Kloepfer, Ken 105
Kneale, Nigel 23, 42
Kokanee beer commercials *159–160*
Kolchak: The Night Stalker 160–*161*, 183, 192
Konga 17
Koontz, Dean 303–304
Kostyuk, Taras *237*
Kove, Martin 249
Kraft, Evelyne 189
Krantz, Grover 52, 74, 179, 194, 197, 202, 230, 245
Kricfalusi, John 157
Krofft, Marty 7, 31, 76–77, 153, 162, 286
Krofft, Sid 7, 31, 76–77, 153, 162, 286
The Krofft Supershow 77
Kubrick, Stanley 59, 155, 214, 299
Kuchar, George 137, 316–317

LaBeef, Sleepy 192
Land of the Lost 31, 76, 161, *162*, 163
Landis, John 27, *252*–253
LandSAR commercial 163
Landsberg, Alan 148–149, 186
Langton, Paul 271
Lansdale, Jim 164
Lansing, Joi 66
Lapseritis, Jack "Kewaunee" 245
The Last of the Mohicans 20, 23, 89, 247
Leakey, Phil 25, 42
Lee, Christopher *145*–146
Lee, Jason *116–117*
Legend Hunters 163–164
The Legend of Bigfoot 30, 164–165
The Legend of Boggy Creek 2–3, *6*, 8, 29, 34–35, 57, 88, 148, 165, *166*, 167, 229, 251, 306–308
The Legend of Desert Bigfoot 167–168
The Legend of Grassman 168–169
The Legend of McCullough's Mountain 126, 169–171
The Legend of Sasquatch *171*–172
The Legend of the Honey Island Swamp Monster *172*–173
Legend of the Sandsquatch 173–174
Leichliter, Larry 330
Leone, Sergio 7
Lidsville 31
Lissi and the Wild Emperor 174
Lithgow, John 34, 141
Little Bigfoot 35, 174–175, 177, 201, 320, 324
Little Bigfoot 2: The Journey Home 35, 175–176, 201
The Little Documentary That Couldn't 176
Little Nicky 176–177, 319
Loaf, Meat 295
Lockhart, June *179*

Long, Greg 74
Long, Justin 240, 284, 326–*329*
The Long Way Home: A Bigfoot Story 36, 167, *177*–178, 232–233
Lost in Space 27, 114, 178–*179*, 202, 268
Lost Tapes 179–180
The Lost World 19, 180–181
Lovitz, Jon 204
Lucas, George 121, 280–281
Lugosi, Bela *18*, 21
The Lumberjack of All Trades 181–182
Lund, Larry 296
Lyman, Will 152

MacGyver *182*–183
Macy, William H. 93
Maher, Joseph 68
Majors, Lee 31, 62–63, 81, *266*–267
The Making of Bigfoot 74
Making Wolvy 183–184
Malamut, Adam *311*
Malinger, Ross 175
Man Beast 2, 20, 22–25, 59, 66, 119, 125, 136, 139, *184*–*185*, 188, 219, 261, 271, 292
The Man from U.N.C.L.E. 185–186
Manbeast! Myth or Monster 186
Marle, Arnold *24*
Marshall, Gary 295
Martin, Eugenio 146
Martin, Lock 271
Martyr, Debbie 262
Marvel Comics 80, 151, 309
Marx, Ivan 30, 72–73, 79, 136, 149–150, 164–165
Mattey, David *284*
Mayhew, Peter *280*
Maynard, Ken 66
McBride, Jon 51–52
McCallum, David 185–186
McCann, Chuck 295
McCoy, Matt 75, 175, 320
McCullough, Jim, Jr. *101*
McCune, Don 115
McDonough, Neal *294*–295
McGavin, Darren *161*
McHenry, Travis 300
McLeod, Don *287*
Meeks, Justin *306*–308
Meeks, Stacy *306*
Meet the Vancouver 2010 Mascot commercial 186–187
Meldrum, Dr. Jeffrey 52, 64, 73, 109, 152, 196, 199, 230, 238, 245, 300, 308
Méliès, Georges 12, *13*, 97–98
Messin' with Sasquatch *37*, 154–156
Messmer, Otto 125
Metty, Russell 214
Michael, Jay 172
The Mighty Boosh *187*–188
Mighty Joe Young 21
Mighty Mightor 188
The Mighty Peking Man 188, *189*, 190
Miller, Emmitt 283
Mills, Billy 172
Mimieux, Yvette 273
Mindrum, Neal 198
Minnesota Iceman hoax 74, 149, 325
Missing Link *190*–191
Mitchum, Chris 66
Mitchum, John 66

Mobius, Hans 79–80
Molina, Alfred 92
Monroe, Don 73, 79
Monroe, Steven R. 244, 325–326
The Monster and the Stripper *191*–192
Monster Auditions *192*–193
Monster Beach Party 193–194
Monster Central 163–164
Monster from Green Hell 23
Monster Hunters: Ordinary People on an Extraordinary Mission 194
Monster in the Woods 194–195
The Monster of the Volcano 195–196
MonsterQuest 37, 196–197
Monsters, Inc. 198
Monsters! Mysteries or Myths? 197–198, 202
Montana, Rick 258
Montgomery, Elizabeth 235
Montoro, Edward 127, 170
Moore, Chester, Jr. 3, 164, 300
Morehead, Ron 300
Morgan, Robert W. 74–75, 83–84, 91, 197, 202, 241, 300
Moriarity, Pat 216
The Most Dangerous Game 18, *19*
The Mothman's Photographer 198
Mount Saint Helens eruption 75
MSNBC's Countdown with Keith Olbermann 198–199
Mugato 27, 279
Mulhare, Edward 260
The Mummy 3: The Tomb of the Dragon Emperor 38, *199*
"Murders in the Rue Morgue" 15–16, 140
Murders in the Rue Morgue 21
Muto, Adam 329–331
My Friend the Yeti 199–*200*
My Pet Monster 200–201
Mysterious Encounters 201–202
The Mysterious Monsters 198, *202*–*203*, 330
The Mystery of the Sasquatch Triangle 203
mythobiologist 50

Nadel, Arthur 154
The Naked Prey 251
Naschy, Paul *304*–*305*
Nelvana 46, 201
The New 3 Stooges 203–204
Newland, John 214
NewsRadio 204
Newton, Dr. Craig 238
Night of the Demon 20, 32–33, 35–36, 59, 61, 94, 119, 136, 173, 188, 204–206, 217, 219, 222, 251, 265, 274
Night of the Sassy 206–207
Nightbeasts *207*–209
Nimoy, Leonard 30, 52, 75, 148–149, 172, 196, 260, 278, 289
Niven, Larry 163
No Burgers for Bigfoot 209–210
Noble Savage, Rousseau's 24
Noll, Rick 300
Noory, George 80
Norman, Scott 218
Northern Exposure 37, 210
Not Your Typical Bigfoot Movie *211*–*212*, 213
Nunnelly, Bart 147

O'Brien, Willis 19, 111–112, 132, 181, 298
Oh, Saelee 330

O'Hurley, John 299
Olsen, Jon 53
On Bigfoot's Mountain 213
On the Fringe 213
One Step Beyond 213–214
O'Neil, Shaquille 60
Opsasnick, Mark 3
Orang Pendek 57, 110, 152–153, 158, 262, 298
Orbach, Jerry 121
Oregon Bigfoot: Search for a Living Legend 214–215
Ormond, June 191–192
Ormond, Ron 191–192
Osment, Haley Joel 219
Ostman, Albert 136
Ostroznie, Yeti! 215
The Other Side 215

Packard, Damon 226, 316
Packham, Chris 309
Pal, George 26, 261, 273
Pál, Péter *261*
Pampalini Łowca Zwierzat 215
Paper Dolls 36, *216*–217, 242
Parker, Calvin 6
Parker, Trey 276
Parolini, Gianfranco 315
Pascagoula Abduction 6
Patterson, Roger 26, 47, 64, 66, 74, 114, 152–153, 165, 178, 245, 247, 296
Patterson-Gimlin film 26, 30, 52, 62, 64, 98, 114, 126, 135, 140, 152–153, 158, 196–197, 204, 238, 247, 278, 309, 325, 330
Peake, Don 165
Penn & Teller: Bullshit! 217–*218*
Pennsylvania Bigfoot Society 3
Perez, Daniel 3, 243, 300
Perverted Stories #35 218–219
Petrified Beast of the Frozen Zone 219
Phillips, Shawn C. 239
Picket Fences 219
Pierce, Arthur C. 292
Pierce, Charles B. 6–7, 29–30, 34, *56*, 88, 101, 165, *166*, 167, 173, 178, 180, 206, 228, 230, 294, 306
Pizza Hut Bigfoot commercials 219
Plan 9 from Outer Space 8
Planet Cook 219–220
Planet of the Apes 26–27, 179
Plato, Dana *228*–229
PM Entertainment 175
Poague, John 79
Polanski, Roman 215
Polonia, John 52
Polonia, Mark 52
Pop-Tarts Yeti commercials 219
Powell, Thom 73, 300
Power Rangers: Operation Overdrive 220–221
Primal *221*–222
Primal Man from *Altered States* 49
"A Private Little War" 27, 279
Project Bluebook 223–224
Prophecy 36, 143, *222*
Pryce, Jonathan 152
PSI Factor: Chronicles of the Paranormal 222–224
Psycho 15, 273
Pye, Lloyd 158, 173, 300

Quantum Leap 224–225
Quatermass, Professor 23
The Quatermass Xperiment 23
Quest for the Yeti 225
Quigley, Linnea 323

Radford, Benjamin 152
Ragozzino, Ed 246–247
Randall, Tony 261
Rango 17
Raquel, Candace 326
Rasche, David 75
Ray, Nick 109
Rear Window 40, 319–320
Rebane, Bill 87–88, 169, 273
Rebsamen, Bill 3
The Red Files 225
The Red Green Show 225–226
Redwoods video 296
Reeves, Michael 154
Reflections of Evil 225
Regan, Jana 195
Reilly, John C. 289–291
Reitman, Ivan 322
Remi, George 46
Remote Jockey Digest **8**–9
Return of the Forest Monster 226–**227**
Return to Boggy Creek 30, 34, 57, 141, 160,
   227-**228**, 229, 330
Revenge of Bigfoot 30, 229–230
Reynolds, Burt 268
Rhys-Davies, John 171
Rocky Mountain Bigfoot 230
Rodnunsky, Serge 124
Romero, George 102
Romney, Jerry 309
Ron, "Tiny" **244**–245
Roosevelt, Teddy 52, 119, 170, 215, 246
Roswell Conspiracies: Aliens, Myths & Legends
   230–231, 235
Roth, Andrea 237
Route 30 **231**, 232–233
Rudolph, the Red-Nosed Reindeer **233**–234
Rugrats 234
Russell, Ken 49
Ryūsei no Rokkuman Toraibu 234–235

Saami 292–293
Sabrina, the Teenage Witch 235–236
Saenz, Andrea **239**
Salvador, Jaime 196
Samsquatch **330**–331
Sanctuary 37
Sanderson, Andrew 153
Sanderson, Ivan T. 1
Sarmiento, Dr. Esteban 237
Sasquatch 236–**237**
Sasquatch Assault **238**–**239**, 240
The Sasquatch Gang 117, 177, 213, 217, 232,
   240–241, 275, 284, 326–329
The Sasquatch Hunters (1997) 241
Sasquatch Hunters (2005) 241–243
Sasquatch Lake... The White Bigfoot Video 243
Sasquatch: Legend Meets Science 237–238
Sasquatch Mountain **243**–**244**, 245
Sasquatch Odyssey: The Hunt for Bigfoot 245,
   330
Sasquatch Science: Searching for Bigfoot 245
Sasquatch... the Evidence Mounts 245
Sasquatch, the Legend of Bigfoot 30, **246**–247

Savage 247, **248**–**249**, 250
Savalas, Telly 146
Savini, Tom 102
Sawtooth 250–251
Saxon, John 81, 266
Scare Tactics 251
Schank, Mike 327
Schick Sunn Classics International 246
Schifrin, Ryan 40, 177, **319**–321
Schlock! 191, 251–**252**, 253
Schlossberg-Cohen, Jay 104
Schoedsack, Ernest B. 17–18
Schreck, Max 282
Schritter, Esther 81
Schwartzman, Jason 157
Scooby Doo Meets Laurel and Hardy 253–254
Scooby Doo, Where Are You? 254–255
Scopes Monkey Trial 269
Scream of the Sasquatch **255**–256
Screams of a Winter's Night 256–257
Search for the Beast 20, 48, 61, 120, 176, 221,
   257–259
"The Secret of Bigfoot" 31
The Secret Saturdays 259–260
Secrets and Mysteries 260
Secrets of the Unknown 260
Sell, Mike 79
Selznick, David O. 18
Serling, Rod 120, 148, 197–198, 202, 214, 223,
   260, 268, 322
Sesquac: The Story of Sasquatch 260
The 7 Faces of Dr. Lao 26, 141, **261**–262, 273
The Seven Year Itch 20
Shaawanoki 262
The Shabbos Bigfoot 262
shadow self 14, 18, 24, 49, 110
Shea, Kevin 239
Shealy, Dave 105, 158
Shealy, Jack 105, 158
Shermer, Michael 230
Sherpa guides 22, 232, 271
Sherpa monks 24, 43, 279
Short Man of the Forest 262
Shriek of the Mutilated 83, 94, 122, 166, 173,
   263–**264**, 286
The Shrieking 265
Sightings 265
The Simpsons 265–266
Sirk, Douglas 299
The Six Million Dollar Man 27, 30–31, 54, 81–
   82, 114, 119, 144, 250, **266**–**267**, 268, 303,
   313
Skaff, George 184
Skousen, Timothy 326–**328**, 329
Skullduggery 268–**269**
Skunkape 270
Slick, Tom 52, 98, 245
Smith, Dick 64
Smith, Kevin 117–118
Snell, Derek "Bamm Bamm" 163–164
The Snow Creature 2, 22–25, 160, 184, 261,
   270–271
Snow Devils 271–273
Snow Walker footage 52
Snowbeast 88, 122, 273–274
Snowman 274
So Weird 274
Sole, Alfred 287–289
Soles, P.J. 175
Solomon, Carol 158

Son of Kong 21, 50
Song of the South 23, 139
Sons of Butcher 274–276
South Park 276
Southern Fried Bigfoot **277**
Spaced Out Bunny 277–278
Spelling, Aaron 63, 74, 91
Der Spiegel 278
Spielberg, Steven 33, 37, 46, 328
Spinrod, Norman 163
Spotlight on the Patterson/Gimlin Film 278
Spottsville Monster 147
Squatching 278
Stack, Robert 301
Star Trek 27, 30, 114, 125, 131, 148, 153, 161,
   202, 249, 254, 268, 278–280
Star Wars 7, 51, 65, 87, 114, 121, 203, 228, 278,
   280–281, 293, 300
Starr, Ringo 89
states' rights distributors 88
Steenburg, Thomas 300
Stefano, Joe 273
Stewart, Jimmy 40, 245, 320
Stone, Matt 276
Stooges, Three **204**
Storch, Larry 131
Strange but True? 281
The Strange Case of Captain Ramper **281**–**282**
Strange Nation 282–283
Strange Universe 283
Strange Wilderness **283**–**284**
Strasenburgh, Gordon 245
Strip Mall 284–285
Sturgeon, Theodore 163
Suburban Sasquatch 285
Sullivan, Pat 125
Swamp Apes 286
Swett, Wallace 153
Swindler, Dr. Daris 237
Sword of Doom 33
Syncro-Vox 96

Tanner, D.L. 300
Tanya's Island 186, 199, 206, 286, **287**–**288**,
   289
Tarantino, Quentin 144, 177, 189, 257, 314, 319
Tarzan 14–16, 20–21, 28, 31, 77, 80, 153, 156,
   162, 181, 189, 268, 314
Tarzan and His Mate **14**
Tarzan, Lord of the Apes 16
Tarzan the Ape Man **15**
Taylor, Dub 100, **101**
Tedesco, Michael 293–294
Tenacious D **289**–290
Tenacious D in the Pick of Destiny **290**–291
Tenney, Kevin 32, 72, 321, **322**, 323–324
The Terrible Giant of the Snow 196, 291
Terror in the Midnight Sun **291**–**292**, 293
Terror in the Swamp 293–294
Thayer, David 72–73
*There's Something Out There: A Bigfoot En-
   counter* 294
They Call Him Sasquatch **294**–295
Thomas, Richard **64**–65
Thomason, Harry 229–230
Thomerson, Tim **243**, 245
Thurman, Bill 101
Tillman, Peggy 243
"Tintin in Tibet" 45–46, 56, 328
To Catch a Yeti 295–296

To the Ends of the Earth: Bigfoot Monster Mystery 296
Tom and Jerry Tales 296
The Tonight Show with Jay Leno 296
Toth, Alex 82, 188, 259
Trailer Park Geocachers Meet Bigfoot 296–298, *297*
Trinklein, Mike 230
Trog! *298*–299
Troma Studios 32, 69, 87, 144, 181, 207, 239, 310
Tropi tribe *269*
Tse, Dr. Peter 153
Tsuburaya, Eiji 23, 138–139, 301
Tucker, Forrest *41*, 42–43, 131
Tucker, Todd 183
Turner, Ted 86
Tuttle, William 186, 261
2 Shocking 4 TV 299
2001: A Space Odyssey 299–300
2002 Texas Bigfoot Conference 300
2004 East Coast Bigfoot Conferences 300
2005 Sasquatch Research Conference 300
2008 Jeep Liberty Bigfoot commercial 300

Ugly Americans 300–301
Ultimatte 76
Ultraman 301
University of Southern California 322
Unsolved Mysteries 301

Valley of Flowers 302
Vanity *287–288*
Vatnsdal, Caelum 294
Vaughn, Robert 185
The Venture Brothers 302–303
Vercors 268
Verne, Jules 12
Video Nasty 33, 205
Viet, Tran Hong 147
Vincent, Cerina 324, 326
Vogel, Virgil 292

Von Puttkamer, Peter 194, 245
Von Puttkamer, Sheera 194, 245

Wagner, Lindsay 81–82, 267
Walas, Chris 89
Walker, Clint 273–274
Wallace, Edgar *18*
Walters, Scott *328*–329
Wampa 120, *121*
Warren, Jerry 22, 184–185, 292
Wascavage, David 285–286
Washington State Sasquatch Research Group 303
Wasson, Craig 245, 324, 326
Wasson, James C. 32
Watchers 303–304
Waters, John 178, 264, 311
Weathers, Carl 177, 240, *328*–329
"The Web of Fear" 27
Webb, Jack 223–224
Webster, Nicholas 186
Wegener, Paul *282*–283
Weird Travels 304
Welker, Fred 134
Welles, Orson 6, 126
Wells, Dawn *228*
Wendigo *90*–91, 109, 129, 154
The Werewolf and the Yeti 206, *304–305*
The White Gorilla 17
White Pongo 17
"Whiteman Meets Bigfoot" 136
Whitton, Matthew 73, 80
Wilcox, Lisa 249
The Wild Thornberrys 307
Wilder, Billy 22
Wilder, Myles 271
Wilder, W. Lee 22, 271
The Wilderness Hunter 52
The Wildman of Kentucky 308
The Wildman of the Navidad 62, 167, 305, *306–307*, *308*
Williams, Autumn 201–202, 214–215, 300

Williams, Billy Dee 124
Wilson, Jimmy 274
Winer, Harry 165
Winston, Stan 309
Winters, Jonathan 278
Withnail & I 187
WLR — Bigfoot Sighting commercial 308
The Wolfman 21
Wolford, Tony *308*
Wood, Ed, Jr. 51
Woolheater, Craig vi, 3, 52, 277, 300
The World's Greatest Hoaxes 308
Worth, Michael 245, 324–*325*, 326–*327*
Wray, Fay *18*, *19*
Wynn, Keenan 161

The X Creatures 309
X-Men 309
The X's 309–310

El Yeti 310
Yeti: A Love Story 20, *310–311*, 312
Yeti! A Tale of the Brothers Krong 312
Yeti: Curse of the Snow Demon 312–313
Yeti: Giant of the 20th Century 146, 189–190, 204, 313, *314–315*, 331
Yeti in the City 315–316
Yeti skull cap *22*
Yeti, the Cry of the Snow Man 316
Yetians 315
Yolanda 316–317
Yordan, Philip 104, 146
Young, Ray *77*
Yowie 5, 52–53, 110, *192*, 194

Zahn, Steve *284*
Zapuncic, William 105
Zimet, Julian 146
Zoo Robbery 317
Zwigoff, Terry 136